A

NEW ENGLAND
UPLAND

ADIRONDACK PROVINCE

COASTAL
LOWLANDS

GREAT VALLEY
OF THE
APPALACHIANS

CENTRAL

LOWLANDS

LAKE
PLAINS

APPALACHIAN PLATEAU

APPALACHIAN MOUNTAINS

BLUE RIDGE

PIEDMONT

TIDEWATER

ATLANTIC OCEAN

OZARK PLATEAU

SOUTHERN

LOWLANDS

FLOOD PLAINS

GULF
PLAINS

GULF OF MEXICO

# WESTWARD
★ EXPANSION ★

## *A History of the American Frontier*

This important work traces the impact of the frontier on American life, from the first Spanish and French outposts to the close of the 19th century. Several notable features make this a splendid book, not only for the historian, student and scholar, but for the history-lover who desires an unusually stimulating approach to unusual material.

*Westward Expansion* is the first history of the frontier to be based on Professor Turner's epoch-making theory of the significance of the frontier in shaping the American genius.

For the first time the role of the land speculator as an important frontier type is fully explored, and the effect of speculation on the settlement process considered in detail.

The non-English frontiersman is adequately treated. Several chapters show the role of the Spanish and French in the Southeast and Southwest. One unique chapter traces the northward movement of the Mexican frontier as a necessary prelude to the Spanish occupation of Texas, New Mexico, Arizona and California.

Much space is devoted to the impact of the frontier on American life. Four chapters are devoted to the sectional controversies of the 1830-1860 era; another to the agrarian unrest of the post-Civil War era.

Two final chapters analyze the effect of the closing of the frontier on agriculture and society in general. In addition, the frontier movement is considered in its relations to diplomacy, politics, and sectionalism.

The book is illustrated by nearly a hundred specially drawn maps, which locate every geographic term used in the text. A full critical bibliography of more than a hundred pages will be found particularly valuable.

# RAY ALLEN BILLINGTON

Ray Allen Billington received his Ph.B. degree
at the University of Wisconsin, his M.A. degree at
the University of Michigan, and his Ph.D. degree
at Harvard. From 1937-44 he was associated with
the history department of Smith College; and
from 1944 has been Professor of History at Northwestern University. He has been visiting Professor of History in summer sessions at Western Reserve, The Ohio State, and Harvard universities.
In 1943 he received a Guggenheim Fellowship
grant to write this book. Professor Billington is
author of *The Protestant Crusade, 1800-1860*, and
co-author of *The United States: American Democracy in World Perspective*.

THE MACMILLAN COMPANY
NEW YORK · CHICAGO
DALLAS · ATLANTA · SAN FRANCISCO

THE MACMILLAN COMPANY
OF CANADA, LIMITED
TORONTO

# Westward Expansion

## A HISTORY OF THE
### *American Frontier*

By RAY ALLEN BILLINGTON
PROFESSOR OF HISTORY, NORTHWESTERN UNIVERSITY

WITH THE COLLABORATION OF JAMES BLAINE HEDGES
PROFESSOR OF HISTORY, BROWN UNIVERSITY

THE MACMILLAN COMPANY : NEW YORK

*To Frederick Merk*

Whose inspirational teaching and meticulous scholarship

perpetuate the traditions of Frederick Jackson Turner

# PREFACE

This book attempts to follow the pattern that Frederick Jackson Turner might have used had he ever compressed his voluminous researches on the American frontier within one volume. In his teaching Professor Turner stressed the geographic continuity in the settlement process rather than the chronological; he viewed American expansion as a series of conquests in which physiographic province after physiographic province was overrun by westward-moving pioneers. Each successive conquest, he believed, differed from the ones preceding, as the unique environment of the new area placed its stamp upon the conquerors. The differing civilizations resulting from this interaction of men and nature accounted for the sectional conflicts that plagued the nation long after the frontier passed by. Professor Turner saw that these important controversies, which were essential to the interpretation of early American history, could be understood only by emphasizing the close connection between the pioneers and the environment in which they lived. The stage, in his eyes, was as important as the players.

In seeking to use that point of view as the basis for an entire volume on American expansion, I have been bold enough to follow not only Professor Turner's basic premise but such specific suggestions as he left behind in his writings. The outline used to give order to the following pages is roughly that prepared by Professor Turner for his course on the history of the frontier at Harvard University. Several of the chapters follow closely the parallel essays in his *Frontier in American History* or in his other works. I have, however, modified both the concepts and the organization in the light of more recent studies. While making no pretense of original scholarship except in isolated instances, I have attempted to present a synthesis of the thousands of pages of writings—in texts, monographs, and learned journals—inspired by Professor Turner's original essays.

The task of preparing this volume was originally a joint enterprise in which Professor James Blaine Hedges of Brown University was the leader. Unforeseen circumstances forced him to abandon his original plan of writing all the portions dealing with the trans-Mississippi West, and he was able to prepare only chapters XXIV, XXV, and XXVII. In addition he and his wife, Nina Hedges, have read and helpfully criticised the entire manuscript.

I am especially indebted to three great teachers who made frontier history live for me and who inspired me to work in the field. The late Frederic L. Paxson introduced me to the subject while I was an undergraduate at the University of Wisconsin; Frederick Merk and James Blaine Hedges guided me as a graduate student at Harvard University. I have a special obligation to Professor Merk of Harvard University, whose course on the History of the Westward Movement I attended as a graduate student. Professor Merk was a student and colleague of Professor Turner, and a coauthor with him of the revised *List of References on the History of the West*. His course has served me specifically with contributions of analysis and interpretation, and generally as a guide in the preparation of many chapters in this volume.

I am grateful to numerous others whose unselfish co-operation has vastly improved my own efforts. A fellowship from the John Simon Guggenheim Memorial Foundation allowed the writing to be accomplished with a minimum of interruptions. A grant from the Committee on Research of the Graduate School of Northwestern University made the final preparation of the manuscript less arduous. Numerous friends have also contributed generously of their time and wisdom by reading portions of the manuscript. Dr. Fulmer Mood of the University of California, whose recent studies have done so much to illuminate Professor Turner's ideas, has read the first chapter as well as those dealing with the seventeenth century. Professor-emeritus James Alton James of Northwestern University has kindly criticised the chapters dealing with the Revolutionary period that he knows so well. My colleagues in the history department at Northwestern University, Professor Philip W. Powell and Mr. Alfred Rockefeller, Jr., have given me the benefit of their extensive knowledge in the fields of their special interest: Latin American history and the history of the American Indian. To my wife, Mabel Crotty Billington, I am indebted not only for helpful criticism but for that freedom from responsibility that is essential to uninterrupted research. For the errors that must inevitably creep into such a work I am alone responsible.

*Evanston, Illinois*                                                        R.A.B.

# Contents

## SECTION III

# THE TRANS-MISSISSIPPI FRONTIER

# Maps

# CHAPTER I

# The Frontier Hypothesis

✳ Suggest the term "frontier" to the average movie-addicted, pulp-devouring American of today and you will conjure up in his mind happy visions of painted Indians, gaudily-dressed hurdy-gurdy girls, straight-shooting cowboys, and villainous badmen, all besporting themselves beneath sun-bathed western skies. The frontier was truly a land of romance, but it also helped shape the distinctive civilization of the United States. America's unique characteristics stemmed from no single source; the European heritage, the continuing impact of ideas from abroad, the mingling of peoples, the spread of the industrial revolution, and the growth of class consciousness all contributed. Yet no one force did more to "Americanize" the nation's people and institutions than the repeated rebirth of civilization along the western edge of settlement during the three centuries required to occupy the continent.

This was first realized during the 1890's by Frederick Jackson Turner, a young history instructor at the University of Wisconsin. Trained in the seminars of Johns Hopkins University, where he was taught that institutions evolved from earlier "germ cells" without reference to environmental factors, Turner rebelled against a concept which was at variance with observable phenomena in his own Middle West. His historical declaration of independence was a paper, "The Significance of the Frontier in American History," which he read at the Chicago meeting of the American Historical Association in 1893. The European heritage, he insisted, accounted only for the similarities between European and American society; to explain the hitherto-neglected differences historians must look to the distinctive environment of the United States.

The most unique characteristic of that environment, Turner felt, was the presence of an area of free land on the western edge of the advancing settlements. Into that unoccupied region poured a stream of settlers from

1

Europe or the East, attracted by the hope of economic betterment or the chance for adventure. They came as easterners, bringing with them the complex political, economic, and social customs required in the stratified societies they left behind. In their new homes on the "hither edge" of the wilderness these imported institutions were out of place; hence the "cake of custom" was broken as new customs better adapted to a primitive society were substituted. Highly developed political forms gave way to simple associations of settlers or rudimentary representative bodies. Specialized trades were forgotten in a land where tasks could best be accomplished by individuals or groups without a division of labor. Complex social activities were abandoned in favor of simpler pastoral pursuits: husking bees, cabin raisings, log rollings, and play parties. "Cultural" developments lagged as emphasis shifted to the primal tasks of providing food, clothing, and shelter. In thought and habit men reverted toward a state of nature; they altered their ways of life, invented new means for using natural resources, or adapted older practices to the new environment. Innovation, adaptation, and invention—in economics, social organization, and government—were characteristics of frontier life.

As newcomers drifted into each pioneer settlement, increasing the ratio between man and nature, the social organization steadily climbed back toward complexity. Governmental forms grew more rigid. Economic specialization set in as eastern capital was imported to begin roads, mills, and primitive industries. Social activities expanded and grew more complex. Eventually, as man conquered the wilderness, a fully developed society evolved, complete with manufacturing establishments, accumulated capital, cities, co-operative institutions, mature governmental practices, and cultural outpourings. The resulting civilization, however, differed from that of the East, modified by the accident of separate evolution and by the unique physical environment. As the matured area assimilated itself with the region just to the east, the frontier passed on westward to begin the transformation of a more advanced area.

This was the process that was repeated for three centuries as Americans colonized the continent. The story of westward expansion was one of the continuous rebirth of society, a repeated "beginning over again" in the West, with the results the same on every frontier, although with essential differences due to time, place, and the manner of men who peopled each area. This continuous throwing of men into contact with the simplicity of primitive society left traditions, memories, and characteristics which persisted long after the frontier passed. Those pioneer traits were strongest in the newer regions, but they greatly influenced the adjacent transitional zone and to a lesser degree the matured social order still farther east. The result was the "Americanization" of both men and institutions. The unique character of American civilization, Turner believed, could be ascribed to the continuous "evolution and adaptation of organs in response to changed environment." "The existence of an area of free land," he wrote, "its continuous recession, and the advance of American settlement westward, explain American development."

Since Turner first advanced the "frontier hypothesis," scholars have subjected his concept to a minute examination. Their careful study modified, but did not refute, his basic doctrine. Few would agree today that the westward-moving "area of free land" alone explains "American development;" indeed Turner himself was less guilty of such overstatement than some of his too-enthusiastic disciples. The persistence of inherited European traits, the continuous impact of changing world conditions, and the influence of varying racial groups were equally important forces in shaping the nation's distinctive civilization. Yet the most carping critic will agree that the unusual environment, and the continuous rebirth of society in the western wilderness, endowed the American people and their institutions with characteristics not shared by the rest of the world.

The moulding effect of this unique environment can best be understood by picturing the Anglo-American frontier as a migrating geographic area which moved westward from Atlantic to Pacific over the course of three centuries. Here was the outer edge of advancing settlement, the meeting point of savagery and civilization, the zone where civilization entered the wilderness, the "region whose social conditions resulted from the application of older institutions and ideas to the transforming influences of free land." In this geographic sense, the frontier has been usually defined as an area containing not less than two nor more than six inhabitants to the square mile. Census Bureau statisticians have adopted this definition in tracing the frontier's advance from the records of each population poll since the first tabulation of 1790. Decade by decade they have drawn narrow bands across the map of the United States, each farther west than the last, as virgin territory was engulfed by migrating pioneers.

This strict definition, although satisfactory to statisticians, fails to reflect the evolutionary nature of the frontier process. The frontier can be pictured more accurately as a series of contiguous westward-migrating zones, each representing a different stage in the development of society from elemental to complex forms. As the westward movement gained momentum, a standardized zonal pattern developed which, although varying slightly with time and place, remained largely consistent until the continent was occupied.

The initial zone was the domain of the fur traders. These restless nomads led the way westward virtually from the time Europeans first set foot on American soil. They blazed the trails across the Piedmont and through the Appalachian Mountain barrier, pioneered on the "Dark and Bloody Ground" of Kentucky, crossed the Mississippi far in advance of the first farmers, traced the eastward-flowing streams to their sources in the Rockies, scaled the Sierras, and descended the Pacific slope to run their trap lines through California's interior valleys or along the beaver streams of the far Northwest. Always far in advance of civilization, the fur traders crossed the continent with such speed that they made little permanent impression on the wilderness. Usually they were psychological types who found forest solitudes more acceptable than the company of their fellow men. So they adapted themselves to the ways of the natives, borrowing their clothes, their living habits, their forest lore, and often their wives. Yet traders did much to prepare the way for later comers. They broke down Indian self-sufficiency, accustoming red men to the guns, knives, and firewater of the white men's higher civilization. They weakened the natives by spreading diseases and vices among them, or by providing some tribes with the guns that led to the slaughter of their wilderness enemies. They explored every nook and cranny of the West, seeking out passes through mountain barriers, investigating river routes to the interior, and discovering favored agricultural sites. Traders' posts served as nucleuses for hamlets and cities; traders' "traces" were widened into roads over which came later pioneers. Theirs was the role of advertising the West and introducing the disintegrating forces of civilization into the primitive Indian society of the forest.

Behind the fur traders came the second group on each frontier—the cattlemen. They, too, were ever-present in the continent's conquest. Early Boston had its "cattle frontier" in the Charles River Valley; early Virginia boasted "cowpens" among the canebrakes and peavine marshes that fringed the farming regions a few miles from the coast. As farms advanced westward the cattlemen steadily retreated, into the Piedmont and Great Valley of the Appalachians, across the mountains to the rich valleys of Ohio or the grass-blanketed prairies of Illinois, southward to the piney woods of Mississippi where, mounted on "low built, shaggy, but muscular and hardy horses of that region, and armed with rawhide whips . . . and sometimes with a catching rope or lasso . . . they scour the woods . . . sometimes driving a herd of a thousand heads to the pen." Cattlemen led farmers into the trans-Mississippi West, there to build their cattle kingdom on the gargantuan grassland of the Great Plains before succumbing once more to pressure from farmers, and retiring to the fenced pastures of today. Like the fur traders, the cowmen contributed little to the conquest of the wilderness; instead they reverted to the primitive themselves before the stronger force of nature.

Wherever conditions were favorable a third zone preceded the advancing farmers—that of the miners. The mining frontier, which depended on the exploitation of rare pockets of mineral wealth, advanced in less orderly fashion than that of the traders or cattlemen; at times it leaped far in advance of settlement, at others it lagged behind while previously discovered riches were developed. Yet miners played a persistent role in the frontier advance. They were present in colonial Virginia and Massachusetts, seeking deposits of "bog iron" in the forest beyond the settlements. During the early nineteenth century they led the way into western Georgia and Alabama where gold discoveries were responsible for "wild west" boom towns, grizzled prospectors, and a moral level considered by easterners to be "deplorably bad." At the same time the discovery of lead outcroppings in northwestern Illinois transformed the hamlet of Galena into the leading Gomorrah of the West as well as the territory's most populous city. During the next generation the mining frontier engulfed the trans-Mississippi country in the wake of exciting "strikes" in California, Nevada, Colorado, and the northern Rockies. Many who participated in these "rushes" were from older mining areas; Georgia's mines contributed heavily to the Colorado gold fields, lead miners from Illinois were prominent among the San Francisco '49ers, and "yonder siders" from California pioneered in the Rocky Mountain country. The miner was a distinct frontier type, ready to rush wherever opportunity beckoned. He, like the traders and cattlemen, was content with surface exploitation; after skimming off the visible wealth he moved on, leaving the still rich land to actual settlers.

They were the pioneer farmers, who made up the fourth frontier zone. Unlike those who preceded them, the farmers made no compromise with nature; their task was not to adapt but to conquer. They viewed the forests or grasslands of the continent as obstacles to be subdued; millions of acres of virgin timber were stripped away by their axes, millions of acres of prairie sod were turned under by their plows. They hated Indians with a fervor born of experience in savage massacres, cursed traders for supplying red men with firewater or firearms, and wanted only to see the natives exterminated. They professed, some of them, to prefer wilderness solitudes to the fellowship of other humans, but all were anxious for new settlers to join them, knowing that numbers meant safety and an increase in land values. Although many pioneer farmers were perennial movers who shifted with the frontier until they became shiftless themselves, their objective was to transform the western wilds into replicas of eastern communities, with no trace of the natural environment remaining.

Theirs was a romantic, if arduous, existence. They were first into each new area, alone or with a handful of kindred spirits. They made the first rude clearings, built the first rough dwellings, laid out the first passable trails through the underbrush or across the plains. Often they made no attempt to buy land, simply squatting on the public domain. As year after year of backbreaking labor passed, more and more land was cleared. In time enough was under cultivation to support the pioneer and his family; then still more timber was cut away to produce agricultural surpluses for export. As this went on other frontiersmen moved in, roads reaching back to the eastern settlements were improved, and open country began to vie with forested regions for supremacy. When this occurred the pioneer farmer was often infected with the wanderlust. Sometimes he was driven onward by dislike of civilization and its ways, sometimes by the prospect of better lands ahead, but more often by the hope of gain. His cleared fields mounted steadily in value as population increased; if he was a squatter he could sell his "improvements" at a profit; if he owned his farm he could dispose of his excess holdings, then the farm itself, for a handsome sum, while he moved on westward to begin the process anew. Many pioneer farmers shifted their homes six times or more in their lifetimes.

When they sold it was usually to the "equipped farmers" who made up the fifth frontier zone. These were men of some capital who were drawn from adjacent farming regions, the East, or Europe. They came intending to stay and develop their newly acquired acres; hence they continued the clearing process with greater thoroughness, grubbed out the stumps, built frame houses, fenced their lands, and improved the roads. Each year, as the cleared areas increased, the amount of exportable surplus mounted; and each year, in return, more wealth flowed into the community. As this mounted the prospering farmers were able to pay for services they formerly performed for themselves. Their demands not only led to a division of labor which marked a maturing civilization, but called into being the final frontier zone.

This was the urban frontier. The specialists drawn to the West by the magnet of opportunity—millers, merchants, grain dealers, slaughterers, distillers, speculators, schoolmasters, dancing teachers, lawyers, and editors —chose their homesites at strategically located points in the center of agricultural communities, usually selecting a crossroads, a point at the head of navigation on some stream, or an advantageous spot on a canal or railroad. As more and more concentrated there, a hamlet, then a village, then a town, gradually took shape. To a casual observer these pioneer villages varied little from the towns of the East, but actually they differed in economic activity, institutions, and attitudes. Their unique characteristics stemmed largely from the manner in which urban pioneers made their living. Their task was threefold. Some gathered agricultural surpluses from the neighborhood for processing and shipment; they erected sawmills to produce lumber, grist mills or distilleries to transform bulky grain into exportable commodities, slaughter houses to prepare hogs and cattle for market. Others served as importers to supply farmers with the machinery, furniture, food, and luxuries that were no longer produced on the farms. Still others catered to the newly awakened taste for culture which developed in each area as wealth increased; they set up schools for the neighborhood children, offered dancing instruction to the elder daughters, legal service to those in need, and news of the world to those who subscribed to their primitive newspapers. Processers, merchants, and sellers of culture made up the bulk of the inhabitants in every frontier town.

The attitudes of urban pioneers differed from those of eastern city dwellers as markedly as did their economic activities. Most were restless seekers after wealth who, driven onward by failure at home or the hope of greater profits in a new country, deliberately selected a promising frontier community as the site of their next experiment in fortune making. There they built a mill, opened a general store, set up a portable printing press, or hung out a shingle as lawyer or dancing teacher, confident that the town's rapid growth would bring them affluence and social prominence. When they guessed right and the village did evolve into a city they usually stayed on as prosperous businessmen or community leaders. When, more often, the site proved ill advised, they moved on again to a still newer town. Urban pioneers advanced westward just as did pioneer farmers; one might live in Rochester, Buffalo, Cleveland, Detroit, Chicago, and Milwaukee before fortune nodded. Their mobility and restlessness distinguished them from the more stable souls who filled the eastern cities.

Institutions also marked the frontier towns as distinct from their counterparts in the East. Most rooted their political systems in eighteenth-century liberalism, with emphasis on legislative power, frequent public meetings for charter changes, and provisions for constant civic improvement. Yearly elections to the town councils were the rule; in one an ordinance allowing councilmen to hold office three years was defeated as "placing them beyond the reach of public opinion for a time almost equal to an age in older communities." Yet, with typical frontier inconsistency, all regulated services touching upon the public welfare with a stern hand. Ordinances in every pioneer town provided for a strict control of markets, fuel distributers, and food handlers, and for careful provisions respecting health and cleanliness. The most striking characteristic of the frontier cities was the similarity of their institutions. Cleveland copied its charter from Buffalo, Chicago from

Cleveland. Practices found suitable to the western environment were first tested, then generally applied along the advancing urban frontier.

The town frontier was the last zone in the migrating geographic area where the frontier process operated; along its eastern borderland lay a fully settled region. Those parallel, ever-moving belts—of traders, cattle-men, miners, pioneer farmers, equipped farmers, and townsmen—persisted through the three centuries required to people the continent. Frederick Jackson Turner described part of the process in classic terms: "Stand at Cumberland Gap and watch the procession of civilization, marching single file—the buffalo following the trail to the salt springs, the Indian, the fur-trader and hunter, the cattle-raiser, the pioneer farmer—and the frontier has passed by. Stand at South Pass in the Rockies a century later and see the same procession with wider intervals between." Only when that march-ing procession reached the Pacific was the westward expansion of the Ameri-can people brought to a close.

During the three centuries that the movement went on the rate of advance varied greatly with time and place. Three factors contributed to every man's decision to move to the frontier: conditions at home, the ease with which he could reach the West, and the attractiveness of the region ahead. If lands in the East were worn out by repeated cultivation, if over-crowding had reached the point where men were unable to adapt themselves to the diminished area, if overcompetition lessened economic opportunity, the dissatisfied were inclined to look to the frontier for rehabilitation. "Our lands being thus worn out," wrote a Connecticut farmer in the eighteenth century, "I suppose to be one Reason why so many are inclined to Remove to new Places that they may raise Wheat: As also that they may have more Room, thinking that we live too thick." Yet no amount of dissatis-faction could set the westward-moving tide flowing unless the road to the frontier was open. Whenever natural obstacles stood in the way—whether an Appalachian Mountain barrier, a phalanx of hostile Indians, or an un-familiar environment such as the Great Plains—the frontier advance slowed or even halted momentarily. Then the dammed-up population increased to the point where the sheer force of numbers pushed the barrier aside. Always progress was most rapid when adequate transportation routes led westward; highways—whether forest trails, roads, or railroads—were the arteries that fed each new frontier. Equally essential in accounting for the ebb and flow of the westward movement was the desirability of the area just ahead, for the promise of better soil or more favorable climate was a magnet that few frontiersmen could resist. Whenever a particularly attrac-tive spot beckoned, the advance was rapid; the rush into the bluegrass country of Kentucky, the cotton lands of the Gulf Plains, and the fertile prairies just west of the Mississippi illustrated the effect of unusual soils on migration. Economic opportunity, however, was not the West's only lure. The challenge of a new country, the call of the primitive, were important psychological attractions to men "with the west in their eyes." Many a pioneer left the East in search of the adventure and romance that waited on the hither edge of the wilderness.

An eighteenth-century traveler wrote in universal language when he described the migrations from his native New England: "Those, who are first inclined to emigrate, are usually such, as have met with difficulties at home. These are commonly joined by persons, who, having large families and small farms, are induced, for the sake of settling their children comfortably, to seek for new and cheaper lands. To both are always added the discontented, the enterprising, the ambitious, and the covetous. . . . Others, still, are allured by the prospect of gain, presented in every new country to the sagacious, from the purchase and sale of new lands: while not a small number are influenced by the brilliant stories, which everywhere are told concerning most tracts during the early progress of their settlement."

The lure of the West did not affect all easterners in the same way. Perhaps many desired to take advantage of frontier opportunity, but few were able to do so; every individual's migration depended on three ingredients: proximity, skill in pioneering techniques, and capital. Certainly the history of westward expansion demonstrated that proximity was of primary importance; unless nature's obstacles intervened each new region was settled from neighboring areas rather than distant points. New Englanders peopled western New York, their sons moved on to the Old Northwest, their grandsons to the upper Mississippi Valley. This was a universal rule; even in the 1850's when abolitionists and southern fire-eaters urged partisans in the slavery controversy to occupy disputed Kansas, few responded; instead that territory was settled by hard-headed realists from Missouri, Illinois, Indiana, Kentucky, and Tennessee. "In thirty States out of thirty-four," wrote the Superintendent of the Census in 1860, "it will be perceived that the native emigrants have chiefly preferred to locate in a State immediately adjacent to that of their birth."

Distance and inadequate training in agricultural pursuits closed the frontier to eastern workingmen; instead America was settled by successive waves of farmers who were already skilled in wresting a living from the soil. Farming, even before the day of mechanization, was a highly technical profession; frontiering required a knowledge of even more specialized techniques. Clearing the land, building a home, fencing fields, solving the problem of defense, and planting crops on virgin soil all demanded experience few easterners could boast. During the colonial period, when the distance between the East and West was small, numerous workers made the transition to farming, not because the prospect pleased them, but because industrial opportunities were so few that mechanics were forced to turn to agriculture. After the industrial revolution of the early nineteenth century, however, the frontier seldom served as a "safety valve" for working men, although a few skilled workers from the East and a larger number from Europe did succeed in making the change.

The cost of moving to the West was also a barrier that few easterners could overcome. If a prospective pioneer wanted to begin life anew cheaply, he must move to the extreme edge of the frontier, appropriate government land, clear his own fields, and personally conquer the wilderness; this required technical knowledge acquired by generations of pioneering. When such skills were lacking, his only choice was to settle in a community already undergoing development. This was expensive. In the middle-nineteenth century he would be forced to pay between $1.25 and $10 an acre for land, $5 to $20 an acre to have it cleared, $112 for a split-rail fence, from $100 to $375 for tools, $150 for draft animals, $50 for a log cabin, $25 for transportation, and $100 for food to support his family until his own farm came into production. Few eighty-acre farms were established that did not cost their owners at least $1,500—a sum far beyond the reach of the average eastern working man whose wages seldom rose above $1 a day. Moreover when the pressure to escape to the frontier was greatest—in periods of depression—laborers were particularly unable to make the transition, for each panic was preceded by a boom period of high prices which swept away their savings. Even those who sought to become independent farmers by working first as hired hands in the West found the path difficult; they learned the needed skills but found it impossible to save the money to buy a farm from their wages of $150 a year and keep.

Little wonder that most new areas were occupied by trained farmers from nearby regions who had either the frontier skills to begin life anew cheaply or the capital necessary to put land into production. Yet the constant drain of farm workers from eastern to western lands was not without its effect on the East. Many who drifted westward might otherwise have gone into the cities in quest of factory jobs. The frontier served as a "safety valve" during the first half of the nineteenth century by draining off potential laborers; in the post-Civil War years even that influence declined as the gap between the pioneer zone and industrial areas widened. The trans-Mississippi frontier recruited its settlers from adjacent agricultural regions rather than from the industrialized East. Through the history of America's westward expansion the farmer, blessed with wealth, skills, and proximity, was the average frontiersman.

As he moved westward he found awaiting him in the American wilderness a variety of geographic conditions destined to exert a modifying influence on his ways of life and thought. For the North American continent was not uniform; instead a series of differing physiographic provinces lay before the migrating peoples, each with a distinct soil structure, topography, and climate. In this checkerboard of unique environments occurred an interplay of migrating stocks and geographic forces, to produce in each a distinctive type of economic enterprise best suited to the natural conditions and imported habits of the settlers. In many ways these "sections" resembled the countries of Europe; each had its own history of occupation and development, and each was so conscious of its differences that it possessed a sense of distinction from other parts of the country. This stemmed largely from the economic habits of the people; in one, staple agriculture might be best suited to natural conditions, in another diversified farming, in another cattle raising, in another industry. As specialization developed, each section demanded from the national government laws beneficial to its own interests; hence the sectional concept implied a degree of rivalry comparable to the ill-feeling that has marked Europe's national history.

This was the heritage of the frontier's advance. As the successive Wests became Easts a mosaic of sections was left behind, each bent on shaping national legislation to its own ends. At times sectional antagonism led to civil war; more often the federal government reconciled antagonisms by compromise or allowed the sections themselves to effect workable combinations for legislative purposes. These conflicts were not solely responsible for the pattern of American history. Sectional lines were often blurred by the influence of national parties, the growth of class divisions, the intellectual traits and ideals of the people, and the presence within each section of smaller regions differing from the majority point of view. Yet no understanding of American development in the eighteenth and nineteenth centuries is possible without a proper recognition of sectional influences.

The following pages tell the story of the successive occupation of America's physiographic provinces by advancing waves of frontiersmen. Romantic characters took part: coon-skinned trappers and leatherclad "Mountain Men," starry-eyed prospectors and hard-riding cowboys, badmen and vigilantes. But the true hero of the tale was the hard-working farmer who, ax in hand, marched ever westward until the boundaries of his nation touched the Pacific. The history of the American frontier is not only one of the conquest of a continent and of expanding opportunity for the downtrodden; it is the history of the birth of a nation, endowed with characteristics which persisted through its adolescence and influenced its people long after the West itself was gone.

# SECTION I

# The Colonial Frontier

# CHAPTER II

# Europe's First Frontier

## 1492-1615

The settlement of the American continent was the last stage in a mighty movement of peoples that began in the twelfth century when feudal Europe began pushing back the barbarian hordes that had pressed in from east, north, and south to threaten the Holy City of Rome itself. The first step in this expansion was taken by zealous crusaders who in the twelfth and thirteenth centuries battered back the Moslems upon their eastern borders in a vain effort to wrest Jerusalem from infidel hands. They failed, but the plundered wealth with which they returned sent new life coursing through Europe's stagnant economic system, and their tales of the riches of the Near East conjured up dreams of splendors all but forgotten by peoples accustomed to frugal feudalism. Venetian traders followed close on their heels to establish trade routes with Constantinople and other Levantine cities which sent unaccustomed luxuries of the Levant flooding over Europe: spices to relieve the monotony of coarse food, "notemuge to putte in ale," rich tapestries, gems, and precious stones.

Quickening economic life stimulated the kings of the shadowy realms that survived the Middle Ages to reassert themselves; from the thirteenth to the sixteenth centuries they waged bitter war on their feudal lords to build on the ruins of the seignorial system the nations of modern Europe: Portugal, Spain, France, England, and the Netherlands. In each country this conquest was aided by the rising merchant class, thus placing the monarchs in the debt of the monied interests. Royal efforts to repay these obligations hurried the commercial exploitation of the New World. Business leaders knew that the exotic goods of the Levant were brought by caravan from distant eastern lands. Travelers—such as Marco Polo—told them that in those mysterious realms of Cathay (China) and Cipango

15

(Japan) the cities had "walles of silver and bulwarkes or towers of golde" and were filled with palaces "entirely roofed with fine gold," and with lakes of pearls. "Whoever won-teth golde," Europeans read, "diggeth till he hath found some quantitie." Their own wealth was steadily draining eastward to purchase the exotic goods that Europe now demanded, while the end of crusading had stopped the flow of plundered Near Eastern gold into their coffers. What magnificent profits would be theirs if they could establish direct trade with the Orient!

This was the incentive that sent the nations of western Europe along the path to new frontiers. Portugal, a compact, well-governed little country, took the lead by sending her explorers southward during the fifteenth century in search of a route around Africa. When Bartholomew Diaz rounded the Cape of Good Hope in 1486 the goal was in sight, and a suddenly alarmed Europe awakened to the possibility that the Portuguese might monopolize the rich Oriental trade. Spain was especially fearful, but Ferdinand and Isabella, the joint rulers, were busy driving Moorish invaders back to Africa and could do nothing until the last enemy stronghold at Granada fell in 1492. Six months later they sent a Genoese navigator named Christopher Columbus on his memorable voyage across the Atlantic, realizing, as did all intelligent people of the day, that the world was round and that ships could reach the East by sailing west. Seventy days after his three tiny vessels left the Azores, Columbus made his landfall in the West Indian islands. He found no crowded city of Quinsay, no rich realms of Cipango or Cathay, no empire of the Grand Khan. But he returned to Europe convinced that he had hit on some outlying portion of Asia and that further exploration would reveal the fabled riches of that fabulous land.

Within ten years after Columbus' first voyage the Spanish explorers who followed in his wake showed that he had discovered not the Orient but a great mid-Atlantic barrier between Europe and the Far East. The disappointment caused by this revelation was only momentary; might not this mysterious new world hold wealth to rival that of Asia? Columbus had found a few gold trinkets among the natives on his first voyage, and on his second in 1493 carried 1,500 colonists who built the first permanent European settlement in America on the island of Hispaniola (Haiti) and turned at once to the search for the precious metal. They soon found that enslaved Indians could be forced to work the primitive gold mines which existed on many of the islands. Here at last was the wealth Spain sought; excitement swept the nation as eager colonists fought for the privilege of going to America. These adventurers, wrote one chronicler of that day, "dreamed of nothing but gold, . . . it was gold that they there sought for, gold that they extracted from the Indians, gold that was given to satisfy them, gold that clinked in their letters to give them standing at Court, and gold that the Court demanded and coveted."

Under this stimulus, plus royal zeal for conversion of a vast new heathendom, the settlement on Hispaniola expanded rapidly until by 1513, when Spain made her first assault on the North American coast, seventeen towns dotted the island, and colonies were established on Puerto Rico, Jamaica, and Cuba. Life in these villages followed a pattern that was to be often duplicated as America's mining frontier moved westward across the continent. Lavish spending and utter profligacy were the rule. Officials strutted about in rich silks, brocades, and embroideries, lived with Indian mistresses, and gambled for preposterous stakes; they taught their horses to dance and curvet, and their principal sport was hunting Indians with hounds. Banquets were given where gold dust was served instead of salt and musicians were imported "to make the people merry." Only lynch law was needed to transform these boisterous towns into the typical American mining camps of a later period.

For a few years the island settlements provided Spain with sufficient wealth, but the mother country's insatiable appetite for gold and souls soon turned attention to the mainland. With this move there rose to prominence a new type of Spanish frontiersman, the *conquistadors*. These hardy adventurers were minor noblemen who, having lived by their swords during the long Moorish wars, were left at loose ends when peace settled on Spain in 1492. Their adventurous past made industry or commerce seem prosaic and their independent spirits rebelled against servile adherence to royal absolutism. Many drifted to America, lured by the promise of excitement and wealth. Cruel, devout, hard-fighting men, they blazed a trail of conquest and salvation westward as they planted the flag of their king and the cross of their church across the face of the continent. Pity and fear were unknown to these robust swashbucklers who led Spain's assault on North America; they slew their enemies as boldly as they faced death themselves.

Juan Ponce de Léon was the first. Unable to settle down to court intrigues after the Moorish wars, he turned to the New World, going with Columbus on his second voyage and later "pacifying" Puerto Rico by the usual process of killing or enslaving the natives. There he heard of the island of Bimini lying to the north, where gold was plentiful and a magic spring spouted waters that brought perpetual youth to all who drank. Armed with a patent to discover and people this island, Ponce de León sailed from Puerto Rico in March, 1513. Sighting a strip of coast which he named Florida, he landed near the mouth of the St. John's River, then journeyed around the peninsula as far as Pensacola Bay. Hostile Indians thwarted him at every stop and he returned to the islands without gold and without having drunk of the fabulous fountain. Two other explorers took up the task of determining whether Florida was really the magic isle of Bimini. In 1519 an expedition under Alonso Álvarez de Pineda skirted the northern coast of the Gulf of Mexico, stopping to trade with the natives, investigate bays, and take possession of the land. Álvarez returned to Jamaica with lying tales of plentiful gold and giant natives, but he did establish the fact that Florida was part of a larger mainland. A year later a second party equipped by Lucas Vásquez de Ayllón added proof by exploring the eastern shore as far north as Cape Fear, where 150 natives were captured and taken back to the West Indies as slaves.

Ponce de León was sufficiently alarmed by these encroachments on a domain that he considered his own to obtain a new patent authorizing him to settle "the Island of Bimini and the Island of Florida," and in 1521 he landed two ship loads of men near Charlotte Bay. Again hostile Indians drove off the colonists, wounding Ponce de León so severely that he died a short time after returning to Cuba. Vásquez de Ayllón immediately set out for Spain to secure the patent vacated by Ponce's death, taking with him an Indian named Francisco Chicora who delighted Charles V and his Spanish court with marvelous tales of his homeland. The people there, he told his credulous listeners, were white with long tails which were "not movable like those of quadrupeds, but formed one mass, as in the case with fish and crocodiles, and was as hard as bone. When these men wanted to sit down they had consequently to have a seat with an open bottom; and if there were none, they had to dig a hole more than a cubit deep to hold their tails and allow them to rest." Gold and precious stones, of course, abounded among these natives. The king was charmed by this gifted liar into granting Ayllón the charter needed to settle that fantastic country.

After preliminary explorations, Ayllón set out from Spain in 1526 with six vessels and five hundred settlers. Failing to find the country described by Chicora in the Cape Fear region, he moved his elaborate force southward, to the banks of a river—probably the Pedee—where he built a few flimsy huts that were glorified as the settlement of San Miguel de Guadalupe. Cold, starvation, and disease took a frightful toll during the winter of 1526-27, and in the spring the 150 survivors struggled back to Hispaniola, leaving behind them the body of their leader who had fallen prey to the wilderness he tried to conquer. Thus ended Spain's first serious effort to found a colony in what is now the eastern United States. Insufficient knowledge of frontier technique proved so disastrous that for twenty years the Spaniards made no further attempt to settle that forbidding coast.

Instead new prospects lured them into the interior of the continent.
Their interest was turned in this direction by the conquests of Hernán
Cortés in Mexico (1519-21) and Francisco Pizarro in Peru (1528), for
these two *conquistadors* found in the central cities of the Aztecs and Incas
the fabulous wealth that Spaniards had long been seeking. If Central and
South America held such riches, the unknown interior of North America
might conceal even greater fortunes! The search for loot, land, and souls,

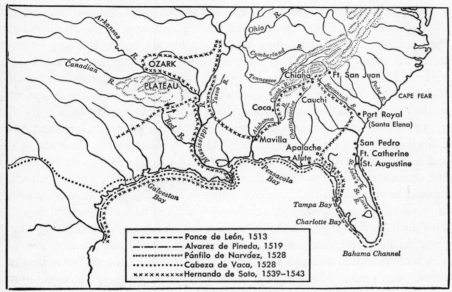

The Spanish in Eastern North America, 1513–1590

rather than the settlement of swampy coastlands, became the objective of
Spanish adventurers.

First to take up the quest was Pánfilo de Narváez, who landed at Tampa
Bay with four hundred followers in April, 1528. His ambitious plans
called for the founding of several cities along the Gulf coast to serve as
bases for raids on the interior Indian tribes, but these were forgotten when
natives showed him a few gold trinkets which, they said, came from the
village of Apalache where the white men would find all the yellow metal
they could carry. Why wait to establish towns when a second Mexico City
lay just ahead? For two months Narváez led his men northward through
swamps and thickets and hostile savages, until finally they burst upon
Apalache. Instead of a great city they found forty thatched huts, instead
of gold and silver a few half-starved natives, instead of rich mines a countryside of "great lakes, dense mountains, immense deserts and solitudes."

The disappointed Spaniards did not stay long, for the Indians were anxious to be rid of the ravenous invaders and sent them on by telling them that a town to the southward held the yellow metal they sought. Again the tiresome march was resumed, and again the hoped-for city proved to be a miserable Indian village. Thoroughly discouraged, the Spaniards pressed on to the sea at Apalachee Bay.

The hope of the 242 survivors was to reach Mexico. Five crude boats were built of boards hacked out with swords and held together by nails melted down from armor. In these overloaded craft they set out to sea in September, 1528, sailing westward along the coast until they reached the mouth of the Mississippi where raging waters and strong winds swamped three of the boats. The remaining two, with eighty survivors, kept on until they were wrecked on an island near Galveston Bay. Friendly Indians, "howling like brutes over our misfortunes," took the Spaniards to their villages and tried to nurse them back to health, but by the spring of 1529 only fifteen remained alive. Six years later this number had dwindled to two, one of whom was Álvar Núñez Cabeza de Vaca, who had established a reputation as a healer and medicine man. Resolving at last to escape, Núñez set out alone along the Texas coast, where he found three other Spaniards held in slavery by the Indians. With them he started the overland journey to Mexico. In each village he used his healing arts with such success that marvelous cures followed his prayers and mystical rites. As he progressed his fame spread; tribes welcomed him, showered him with presents, and escorted him to the next Indian town after he had cured their sick. His journey became a triumphant procession—four tattered Spaniards marching at the head of as many as four thousand painted natives—until he arrived in Mexico City in April, 1536.

Cabeza de Vaca's straightforward account of what he had seen should have ended Spanish interest in North America, for he had found no permanent cities, no gold or silver, and only poor savage Indians who lived on roots, spiders, and an occasional deer that was exhausted by an all-day chase. Instead Spaniards preferred to listen to the fanciful imaginings of Indians who were always ready to conjure up tales that would please the white men—of wealthy interior tribes and especially of "seven very large towns which had streets of silver workers" and gold in plenty. Could these be the cities of the seven bishops who, according to hoary Spanish legend, had fled west in the eighth century to set up seven episcopates on fabulously rich lands across the Atlantic? Even Cabeza de Vaca, succumbing to popular pressure, decided to tell his countrymen what they wanted to hear rather than the truth. When he visited Spain a year after his return he found such eager listeners among the noblemen that he let his imagination run wild and in great secrecy "gave them to understand that it was the richest country in the world."

One man listened with particular interest. Hernando de Soto, a wealthy noble with considerable colonial experience who had just secured Narváez's grant to eastern North America, realized that Cabeza de Vaca's ramblings promised him not only great wealth but plentiful recruits for the expedition he was organizing. All Spain caught the excitement; noblemen sold their estates to buy places on de Soto's ships or fought for the privilege of going, and when he sailed in 1538 so great a company assembled on the docks that many "who had sold their goods, remained behind for want of shipping." After wintering in Cuba, the elaborate force of six hundred soldiers, great herds of horses and swine, packs of hounds, and mountains of equipment, landed on the east shore of Tampa Bay in May, 1539. There began four years of fruitless wandering over 350,000 square miles of wilderness, guided only by Indians who discovered that they could best rid themselves of the plundering Spaniards by telling them that the next village was richer than their own.

De Soto spent the first winter at Apalache, where he learned of a northern province governed by a woman, "the town she lived in being of an astonishing size, and many neighboring lords her tributaries, some of whom gave her clothing, others gold in quantity." They found this lady on the Savannah River, but her "astonishing" village held only a few flimsy huts, and her wealth consisted of a handful of spoiled fresh-water pearls. The country about the upper Savannah proved so uninviting that the Spaniards headed south again as far as Mavilla where a disastrous fire destroyed even the meagre plunder they had gathered, then turned to the northwest and spent the winter of 1540-41 near the Yazoo River. With spring they wended their weary way onward until they came upon the Mississippi a few miles south of present Memphis. De Soto was annoyed rather than pleased at his discovery, for the expedition had to pause while barges were built before the men could cross. Again the northern country proved unattractive, but the Indians told of large towns to the south and the summer was spent searching the Ozark region for the fabled seven cities. After wintering on the Arkansas River near its junction with the Canadian, de Soto started his tattered followers back toward the Gulf to renew their equipment. To his great disappointment the Arkansas River led them again to the broad Mississippi rather than to the sea. There, while his men were building boats and fighting off hostile natives, de Soto "took to his pallet" and died.

The remnants of the expedition first tried to march west to Mexico, but after a year of wandering turned back to the Mississippi, built seven boats, and floated down to the Gulf on the spring floods of 1543. Alternately praying and rowing, they made their way along the coast until September 10, 1543, when they turned into the Río De Pánuco. There they learned that a Spanish town was only fifteen leagues away. "Many, leaping on shore, kissed the ground;" wrote their chronicler, "and all, on bended knees, with hands raised above them, and their eyes to heaven, remained untiring in giving thanks to God." Of the six hundred men who started with de Soto four years before, 311 survived the incredible hardships with sufficient spirit to criticise the poverty of the Spanish town where fate had cast them! Here was proof of the prowess of the *conquistadors*.

De Soto's disastrous failure, by ending hope of rich finds in the interior of eastern North America, ushered in a phase of the Spanish conquest in which colonization rather than exploitation became the ambition of the nation's rulers. This decision was forced upon them by the need of occupying the Florida coast, a step deemed necessary to protect Spain's thriving possessions in Central and South America. By this time Mexico City was the principal city of New Spain, its treasure houses bulging with wealth from native mines. This gold and silver was carried to Spain in great galleons which sailed across the Gulf, through the Bahama Channel, and northward along the coast of Florida before spreading their sails to the easterly blowing Atlantic trade winds. If enemy vessels were allowed to lurk in the many inlets along the Florida coast they could pounce on Spanish shipping almost at will. As France, England, and Holland, the other maritime powers of the Atlantic seaboard, were casting covetous eyes at Spain's New World wealth, the Spanish authorities realized that they must act. Only by winning over the coastal natives and making eastern Florida so thoroughly loyal that no enemy vessel dared touch there could they protect their treasure route.

Philip II, ruler of Spain, planned two settlements, one at Santa Elena and the other on the Gulf of Mexico. In June, 1559, his expedition sailed, with 1,500 colonists under the command of Don Tristán De Luna y Arellano. They landed at the port of Ichuse, on Pensacola Bay, where De Luna ordered the first settlement built. The usual Indian gossip of plentiful gold in the neighboring province of Coca upset these plans, when three hundred badly needed soldiers were sent on a futile search that ended at a miserable little village of thirty huts on the Coosa River. On their return they found the colony torn by dissension, with its leaders bickering among themselves and most of the settlers anxious to return home. News of this sorry state of affairs finally reached Mexico. De Luna was sent packing, and a new leader, Ángel de Villafañe, took over the ill-fated expedition.

He fared no better, for when he tried to move the colonists to Santa Elena in the spring of 1561 his ships were buffeted by storms that finally drove him back to Hispaniola. Thoroughly discouraged, Philip II decreed in September, 1561, that no further attempts should be made to settle Florida.

The ink on this proclamation was scarcely dry before a French threat forced a reversal of Spanish policy. The ambitions of Gaspard de Coligny, Admiral of the Realm, were responsible. Staunch patriot and zealous Huguenot, he had long dreamed of establishing the colonial prestige of his beloved France by founding a Protestant settlement on the northern Florida coast. An opportunity arose in the spring of 1562. His five ship-loads of volunteers under Jean Ribaut selected a site for their colony at Santa Elena, which they renamed Port Royal, and there began construct-ing crude mud huts surrounded by log fortifications. While work was going on, Ribaut sailed back to France for more supplies, but civil wars in the homeland delayed his return until his colonists were reduced to near-starvation. In desperation they finally set out for France in a tiny vessel built with their own hands, only to lie becalmed in mid-Atlantic until their food gave out and they were reduced to cannibalism before being rescued by a passing British ship. A Spanish expedition that sailed from Cuba in the spring of 1564 to drive out the hated Frenchmen found only the decaying remains of their abandoned fort.

Coligny was not ready to give up. Even as the Spaniards were returning triumphantly to Cuba a second French expedition under René de Laudon-nière was on its way to Florida. This time the Frenchmen built their settlement, which they called Ft. Catherine, on the St. John's River. The hardships of the first winter almost forced them to give up the attempt, but when Jean Ribaut arrived to take command in the spring of 1565 with seven shiploads of supplies, new colonists, and abundant food, the outpost's future seemed secure. The Spaniards were horrified. "They put the Indies in a crucible," one wrote frantically from Mexico, "for we are compelled to pass in front of their port, and with the greatest ease they can sally out with their armadas to seek us, and easily return home when it suits them." Philip II acted with all possible speed. A noted soldier, Don Pedro Menéndez de Avilés, was selected as Spain's avenger with orders to drive out the French "by what means you see fit" and found a colony in Florida that would forestall future intrusions.

The first task proved easier than the second. Menéndez, with a strong fleet and 2,648 followers, dropped anchor on August 28, 1565, at the mouth of a small river which he called the St. Augustine. After seven days preparation he sailed north, only to have the French cut their cables and drift to sea before he could attack. When an all-night pursuit of the fleeing enemy proved fruitless he returned to Ft. Catherine, which was now well guarded by three warships that had been lurking in the river. Menéndez, afraid to risk an open attack, retraced his steps to the St. Augustine where his men began constructing the first enduring white settlement in what was to become the United States. While this went on both commanders decided to take the offensive, Ribaut by sea and Menéndez by land. Fate played against the Frenchmen. Violent storms scattered their fleet on its way to St. Augustine and left Ft. Catherine's 240 defenders at the mercy of the Spaniards when they struck on September 30 after a quick overland march. Within an hour 132 had been put to the sword, even the sick being dragged from their beds and murdered. During the next weeks nearly 400 more Frenchmen who survived the wreck of their fleet, including Ribaut himself, were slaughtered along the Florida coast. "I put Jean Ribaut and all the rest of them to the knife," Menéndez wrote Philip, "judging it to be necessary to the service of the Lord Our God, and of Your Majesty."

The founding of outposts to hold Florida against future intruders proved more difficult. Menéndez set out from St. Augustine in 1566 with three ships and 150 men, going first to Santa Elena where, on the swampy shores of Parris Island, the willing ship's crew fell to building a fort or presidio which they called San Felipe. After leaving 110 men to guard that strategic spot he turned south to Cumberland Island where the presidio of San Pedro was built and garrisoned by eighty soldiers. The spot on the St. John's where the French had reared Ft. Catherine was selected for the final northern fort, which was called San Mateo. South of St. Augustine a presidio was located on the St. Lucie River and two more on the west coast at Tampa and Charlotte bays. With the coast secure Menéndez turned to the more difficult task of fortifying the back country. Captain Juan Pardo was sent west from Santa Elena with a small force, first to the upper reaches of the Broad River where he built Ft. San Juan, then on to the Indian villages of Chiaha and Cauchi near the headwaters of the Chattahoochee River where small presidios were constructed. A handful of men was left at each of these tiny outposts with instructions to convert the natives to Christianity and search for the fabled mines supposedly in that region.

From the first these frontier posts fared badly. Most of them were located on swampy ground where mosquitoes made life intolerable, diseases took a heavy toll, and the few farmers assigned to each presidio were unable to raise sufficient grain for the garrisons. Hostile Indians and delays in importing food from Spain increased the hazards of presidio life. Dissension soon developed among the idle troops, who had little to do but complain, and Menéndez spent his declining years in a losing struggle to hold his feeble domain together. His death in 1573 was the signal for an outbreak of Indian hostility that his nephew who succeeded him as governor of Florida, Pedro Menéndez de Márquez, was unable to check. The garrison at Tampa Bay was massacred, the post at Charlotte Bay was abandoned in the face of hostile demonstrations, and lurking savages surrounded each of the other presidios, ready to pounce on stragglers. This smouldering enmity burst into open rebellion in 1576 when the starving soldiers at San Felipe attempted to force corn from a neighboring tribe. Two thousand war-crazed Indians swept down on the feeble outpost, forced the tiny garrison to flee toward St. Augustine, and burned the fort. The interior posts suffered a similar fate, and even the presidio of San Mateo was dismantled under the pressure of native hostility.

Menéndez de Márquez tried to salvage what he could from the wreckage of his defenses. A new fort of logs and oyster shells, surrounded by sixty sturdy houses, was built at Santa Elena during the summer of 1577, but the task was hopeless. Even while he was at work on this outpost word reached Menéndez that Frenchmen had landed a few leagues to the north where they were erecting a fort. He had too few men to drive out the intruders, but the following spring he led the largest force he could muster along the coast, capturing nearly a hundred French interlopers and killing their leader, a piratical corsair named Nicolas Estrozi. This step only made the situation worse, for the Caribbean swarmed with English and French pirates and freebooters, many of whom now vowed to avenge their comrade's death. For the next two years these adventuresome outcasts kept the Florida coast in a constant state of turmoil, fomenting Indian rebellions and raiding Spanish supply ships on their way to aid the harassed garrisons. Not until the autumn of 1580, when additional troops arrived from Spain, was Menéndez able to punish the offending natives by a northward march that ended for the time being the danger of a joint French-Indian attack on St. Augustine.

This warfare along the borderlands showed that Spain's frontier technique, which depended on native labor to exploit a region's tangible wealth, was entirely unadapted to eastern North America. In Central and South America the labor of large numbers of relatively advanced and frequently docile Indians could be utilized for work in mines and fields, so that comparatively few Spaniards could control large areas. North of the Gulf of Mexico, however, the country was poor and the native population wild and thinly scattered. The disastrous experiences of the two Menéndez demonstrated that these uncivilized red men could not be forced to work, while the colonists, accustomed to living on the labor of submissive natives, were usually unwilling to perform the back-breaking tasks themselves. Nor could the mother country send out enough white settlers to hold the northern coast; all but the most loyal Catholics were forbidden to emigrate and most of these preferred the safety of their native land or the greater opportunities elsewhere.

Under these circumstances Spain was forced to devise a new frontier technique suitable to the peculiar conditions of North America. Her answer was the mission station. Earnest friars, clad in fibre sandals and sackcloth gowns worn scant and thin, painfully learning the native tongues when they found to their mild amazement that "the Indians did not understand Latin," succeeded where the armed might of Spain failed. They established their tiny chapels in the forbidding wilderness, gathered about them groups of Indians who were taught agriculture as well as Christianity, and gradually extended their influence through conversions until all northern Florida was pacified. Thus the holy fathers built up a loyal population, ready to defend for crown and church a great domain that might otherwise have fallen sooner into alien hands.

Jesuit and Franciscan missionaries visited North America with the earliest explorers but not until 1593, when a band of twelve Franciscans under Fray Juan de Silva reached Florida, did they play a major role in the Spanish conquest. A number of mission provinces were established at once: Apalache on the northern gulf coast, Timucua in the Florida peninsula, Guale in present Georgia, Orista extending northward through modern South Carolina, and Tama embracing the interior. The first arrivals were dispersed over Guale, where the Indians were so hostile that the presidio garrisons did not dare hunt or fish beyond the protection of their forts. Within three years the whole region was at peace, 1,500 natives had been baptized, and others were flocking from the interior to seek religious instruction. The friars used these willing neophytes to erect chapels at the principal Indian villages along the coast: San Pedro on Cumberland Island, Santiago De Ocone on Jekyl Island, Asao on St. Simon Island, Tolomato and Tupique on the mainland. Garrisons were still maintained near these mission stations at presidios on Amelia, Cumberland, Sapelo, and St. Catherine islands, but the soldiers had little to do. By 1596 the whole northern frontier was peaceful and loyal to Spain, and plans were being laid to extend the missionaries' activities into Tama.

This tranquil progress was rudely checked in 1597 by the Juanillo Revolt. Trouble began when Juanillo, a warlike Guale brave who was angered by the friars' refusal to let him become chief of his tribe, gathered other discontented spirits and murdered the missionary at Tolomato in the midst of morning devotions. This act, he told neighboring tribesmen, would result in general punishment unless they drove the white men from the land. The simple savages were so much impressed by this warning that they slaughtered the Franciscan friars on St. Catherine, St. Simon, and Jekyl islands in a series of sudden raids. Word of the revolt was hurried to St. Augustine, but a relief expedition that marched from that stronghold in October failed to capture more than a handful of the rebels, although several Indian villages were burned and crops destroyed. The mission station on Cumberland Island, which had survived one attack

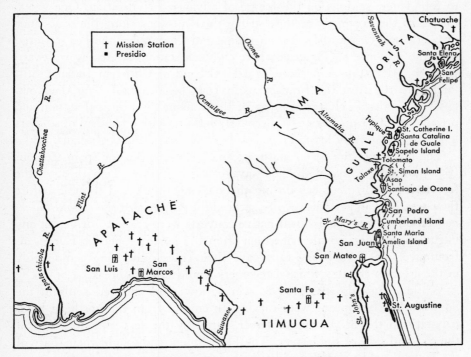

The Spanish Mission Station Frontier in the Southeast, 1590-1630

with the aid of friendly natives, was judged unsafe and abandoned before winter. In a few months the savages destroyed the patient labor of years, leaving the northern Florida frontier a wilderness, broken only by the isolated presidio at Santa Elena.

Starvation which swept through the native ranks following a punitive expedition in 1598 broke their rebellious spirit and by the spring of 1600 humiliated chiefs were flocking to St. Augustine to ask forgiveness. The task of restoring the missions was begun in 1603 and went on rapidly; within three years new stations were erected at San Juan, Santa María,

San Pedro Macoma, Talaxe, and Santa Catalina de Guale, all occupied by newly arrived Franciscans who administered to a growing group of docile Indians. This triumph was celebrated in 1606 when the Bishop of Cuba, with an elaborate retinue of civil and ecclesiastical followers, visited each station in turn to baptize 2,453 natives in impressive ceremonies.

This episcopal visitation launched the Spanish missions on a period of prosperity that lasted for half a century. During these years steady streams of Franciscan friars reached St. Augustine and plunged into the wilderness to found new stations on the fringe of advancing civilization. One group turned to the north where they strung their missions along the sea islands of Guale and Orista as far as San Felipe and Chatuache; another scattered over the province of Timucua where eighteen stations stretching westward from St. Augustine ministered to a loyal band of Christian Indians. Still farther to the west the Franciscans in 1633 began establishing their outposts in Apalache, clustering most of them about the principal station and presidio at San Luis. By 1650 these holy fathers, with a handful of soldiers in a few strategically located forts, controlled almost 26,000 Indians.

The mission stations won southeastern North America for Spain. Zealous friars, willing to live with their savage wards, follow them through the forests in search of acorns during the starving times, and tremble before their treachery in periodic revolts, secured the empire that the *conquistadors* had failed to win. Their loyal native converts were ready to drive out any intruders, be they hostile tribesmen from the north or heretic Europeans from overseas. The Franciscans gave their church and king a monopoly in the Florida country which latecomers would have to break.

While Spaniards struggled to win yellow gold and red souls in the South, other Europeans were carving an empire from the northern lands tributary to the St. Lawrence River, lured by the less romantic flesh of the cod and skin of the beaver. The Frenchmen who sought their share of the New World's wealth amidst the sparkling streams and deep forests of this north country entered the race for America late; until 1529 when the Peace of Cambrai ended a long period of war at home they had neither time nor energy for overseas conquest. With peace their monarch, Francis I, displayed an immediate interest, for he lived in extravagant splendor and coveted "diamonts" and "golde ore" as did few other men. To find them, and to seek the fabled Straits of Anian that would allow ships to sail through the North American continent to the riches of the Orient, he sent out Jacques Cartier in 1534 on the voyage that laid the basis of France's American empire.

Cartier, with two tiny vessels, touched first on Newfoundland, then sailed north and through the Straits of Belle Isle into the Great Bay, as he called the Gulf of St. Lawrence, which he explored thoroughly. He found no gold or precious stones, but the broad river that entered into the Great Bay might lead to the Pacific Ocean, and he returned a year later to venture as far inland as the present site of Montreal. That winter of 1535-36 he spent on the St. Charles River, near present Quebec, among Indians so friendly that they bribed the Frenchmen not to leave and even dressed as devils "with horns as long as one's arm and their faces coloured black as coal" to overawe the explorers into staying. Cartier returned to France in the spring, still without gold or silver, but with tales of a fertile and beautiful country that deserved further exploitation.

By this time France was at war again and not until 1541 could Cartier start on his third voyage. His backer now was Sieur de Roberval, a Norman knight and freebooter, who had glimpsed a vision of empire and wanted to plant a colony of his own. Cartier sailed first with five ships and wintered near present Quebec; his patron followed a year later with three more vessels laden with colonists recruited from Paris slums and jails. In a Newfoundland harbor he met Cartier heading back for France, wild with excitement over a few barrels of iron pyrites—mica and quartz that he had mistaken for gold. Roberval continued on, but one winter with his unruly convict crew was enough, and in 1543 he returned to France. This ended the first French attempt to found an outpost in the New World, for the mother country was so weakened by renewed religious dissension and civil war that her rulers lost interest in a barren wilderness promising no immediate returns.

For the next half-century France was too absorbed in her internal difficulties to concern herself with nebulous wealth beyond the seas. Yet during this interim her claim to northern North America was firmly established, not by haughty noblemen in tall ships, but by humble fishermen. The first explorers to cross the Atlantic brought back tales of seas off Newfoundland "full of fish, which are not only taken by a net, but also with a basket, a stone being fastened to it in order to keep it in the water." This was important news to Catholic Europe, and as word of these Newfoundland Banks spread through the docks of Bristol, Lisbon, Rouen, St. Malo, Dieppe, and other ports, hardy fishermen set out to exploit these fishing grounds. As early as 1527 an explorer who put into the harbor of St. Johns found "eleven sail of Normans and one Britaine and two Portugal Barques, and all a-fishing." Frenchmen were especially active on the Banks, particularly after 1539 when the discovery of the principle of tacking reduced the time required by the Atlantic crossing from months to weeks. By 1578, one hundred fifty French vessels were busily engaged in the trade, against fifty from England, Holland, Spain, and Portugal.

An unrecorded event that took place somewhere, sometime, on the bleak Newfoundland coast turned the attention of France from the sea to the land. Each year the fishing fleets, after casting their nets at the Banks, put in to the nearest harbor to split, salt, and dry the codfish before journeying back across the Atlantic. The Indians who gathered to watch these strange rites were fascinated by the knives of the Frenchmen, for their own stone-age implements seemed crude by comparison. One of them, watching with covetous eyes a gleaming knife of a fisherman as he split open a fat cod, managed to signal that he would give anything he possessed for that glittering blade. The sailor, noticing the fine cloak of beaver skins worn by the savage, indicated that he was willing to trade. Thus was born the fur trade on which the French occupation of North America rested.

At first the trade was haphazard, carried on by ships' crews and captains who stuffed their sea chests with knives, beads, metal mirrors, pots and pans, and other items that the natives seemed to want. But by the 1580's French merchants who entered the field were sending their vessels farther and farther up the St. Lawrence to intercept the interior furs on their way down to the coast. Through the next two decades a number of small companies plied the trade vigorously, making yearly trips to Tadoussac to meet the Indians who slipped down the Saguenay River with canoes brimful of shining peltry, then distributing the furs over Europe to be converted into beaver hats for aristocratic gentlemen or luxurious coats for fashionable ladies. As these activities increased and the value of the trade dawned on merchants of other nations the French king, Henry of Navarre, decided that rich Canada must be secured. France, although newly united after a century of religious wars, was so poverty stricken that he was forced to turn to his old military associates for financial aid, promising them a monopoly of the fur trade if they would establish a colony in Canada. Thus was brought together in 1603 the little group of adventurers who founded French Canada: Sieur de Chastes, Sieur du Pontgravé, Sieur de Monts, and Samuel de Champlain, with de Chastes as their leader and patron.

The company's first expedition linked the men who contributed most to Canada's early history, Champlain and Pontgravé. Pontgravé was the sailor, making dangerous journeys across the North Atlantic as regularly as clock work and minimizing by his skill the difficulties of navigation in that primitive day. Thirty-six-year-old Champlain was the explorer, driven always by a burning desire to see what lay beyond the next bend in the stream or over the next hill. Colonization and the fur trade interested him far less than the sight of a new mountain range or the discovery of a new lake or river. His wanderings, as he sought to satisfy that insatiable curiosity, gave France an empire in the New World.

Champlain began to pry into Canada's secrets in 1603 when Pontgravé's ship carried him to Tadoussac. There he had his first chance to talk with the Indians. He learned from them of a river and portage route along the Saguenay-Mistassini traverse to a great body of salt water lying to the north (Hudson Bay), of a passage through lakes and rivers south of the Richelieu River "which leads down to the coast of Florida" (Lake Champlain and the Hudson River), of a portage route to large

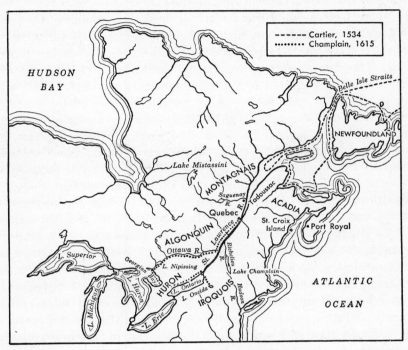

New France, 1534–1615

inland lakes (the Great Lakes) along the Ottawa River, across Lake Nipissing, and down the French River. The St. Lawrence intrigued him most, for the natives told him of Lake Superior and Lake Erie, and gave him a sketchy picture of Lake Huron. Here, he thought, might be the long-sought route to the Pacific. While Champlain was making these surprisingly correct deductions on American geography, Pontgravé loaded his ship with enough furs to show a handsome profit when they returned to France in the autumn of 1603.

This tidy sum allowed the company, now enlarged and headed by de Monts, who succeeded to the presidency on de Chastes' death, to attempt its first colony planting a year later. Two ships were sent out, one to trade at Tadoussac, the other to found a settlement on the Bay of Fundy. De

Monts, who accompanied the latter vessel, finally chose a site on St. Croix Island where, in June, 1604, Frenchmen began building their first homes in the New World. His selection was unfortunate; the tiny island offered neither shelter from the cold winds of the North Atlantic nor game to vary the monotonous diet of salt meat, and the little group under Champlain who wintered there suffered severely. In the spring of 1605 they showed that they had learned their first lesson in frontier technique by moving their colony to Port Royal, on the mainland of Nova Scotia, where they planted grain and erected a sturdy log fort containing comfortable living quarters, warehouses, magazines, and a forge, all surrounding a spacious central court. Here the colonists lived regally during the next winter. The fifteen officers, organized informally as "L'Ordre de Bon Temps," each day elected one of their members a Grand Master whose duty it was to provide the company with food obtained by hunting or barter. Every dish was served with elaborate ceremony; the table frequently groaned under the flesh of moose, caribou, deer, beaver, otter, hare, bear, ducks, geese, sturgeon, and trout. These merry times, which contrasted markedly with the suffering of the year before, attested to the ease with which the French adapted themselves to a forest environment.

For three years the tiny settlement prospered, while Indian friendship was won and Champlain spent happy days exploring the Acadian coast. But while de Monts' company triumphed over the wilderness, de Monts proved less successful with the intrigue of the French court. Jealous merchants finally persuaded the king to break the company's monopoly in 1607, leaving Champlain and his followers no choice but to return to France that fall. Neither he nor Pontgravé were willing to abandon their wilderness life, however, and their arguments finally convinced de Monts that a permanent post on the St. Lawrence would allow the company to prosper even without the advantages of a monopoly. By the summer of 1608 both were back in Canada, where Pontgravé fought off Basque intruders while Champlain searched for a favorable site for their colony. He finally chose a spot beneath a high promontory overlooking the St. Lawrence, and there in July, 1608, were built the first crude huts of the town of Quebec. A year later de Monts' company failed, but this tiny outpost continued to cling to existence amidst the Canadian wilderness.

Champlain was its guiding spirit. Neglected by king and countrymen and ignored by the royal favorites who held the fur monopoly during the next quarter-century, he clung tenaciously to his forest post, contented to rule over his handful of turbulent followers, seek the friendship of the neighboring tribes, and press the explorations that were his real love. Quebec was a colorful place under his rule. Here each summer the trading ships from

France dropped anchor and sent their men ashore to erect booths where they could display their knives and mirrors and bright colored cloths. Indians gathered from miles around, bearing the furs accumulated during the past winter. Never had the rich green forests of Quebec witnessed such sights as these—the painted savages decked in their barbaric finery, the Bretons gorgeous in blue and red and purple coats, the Basque and Norman fishermen in their colorful garb, all shrieking in a medley of a dozen tongues as they haggled over the price of a shining beaver skin. Over these wild scenes presided Champlain, ready always to settle disputes or soothe feelings ruffled by too enthusiastic bartering, and far more at home among the red men of America than his own countrymen.

His principal task was to maintain the Indian alliances which kept a steady stream of peltry flowing toward Quebec. This was difficult, for when the French settled in Canada they became unwilling participants in an ancient wilderness war being fought for the control of the St. Lawrence Valley. On one side in this struggle were three tribes living north of the waterway: the Montagnais who roamed the country about the headwaters of the Saguenay, the Algonquin of the Ottawa River Valley, and the Huron who lived between the Ottawa River and Lake Huron; on the other the loose confederation of five Iroquois tribes whose long houses dotted the region south of Lake Ontario. When Europeans first entered the valley the triumphant Iroquois, who controlled Lake Ontario and the upper St. Lawrence as far as Quebec, were steadily extending their conquests eastward. The French unwittingly took sides in this forest war when they opened trade with the Montagnais at the mouth of the Saguenay River. Within a few years the Algonquin and Huron were also making regular trading trips to Tadoussac over a difficult route that crossed the headwaters of streams tributary to the St. Lawrence.

This trade gave the Montagnais-Algonquin-Huron confederation both an immediate advantage over the Iroquois, and a new incentive to press the war against their ancient enemies. Their objective now was to drive their rivals from the St. Lawrence Valley. This would assure their continued monopoly over the French trade; an important consideration to primitive peoples who viewed knives and utensils with such awe that they sincerely believed the king of France made all the pots and pans himself— surely a man capable of such wonders deserved to rule his people. The expulsion of the Iroquois would moreover allow the Algonquin and Huron to reach Tadoussac over the Ottawa River or St. Lawrence routes, rather than along the difficult path to the Saguenay. Inspired by these prospects, the northern tribes waged a bitter war through the sixteenth century, so intense that peaceful bands of Indians seen by Cartier were gone when

Champlain reached Canada, crushed between the two powerful foes. By 1608 they had driven their enemies south of the St. Lawrence and controlled the prized valley.

The Iroquois menace still remained; warriors of that powerful confederation might push northward at any time, cut the trade routes between the Huron or Algonquin country and Quebec, and stop the eastward flow of furs. Champlain, who saw that this vital highway could be kept open only by crippling the Iroquois, was so concerned that he consented to join the northern Indians in their continuous warfare against the southern tribes, particularly because he saw that these raiding parties offered an excellent chance for exploration. His first journey was in 1609 when he and two other Frenchmen joined a band of Algonquin in a march up the Richelieu River, across Lake Champlain, and to the present site of Ticonderoga, where a group of Iroquois, terrified by their first sight of guns, were decisively defeated. In 1615 he set out again, this time to aid the Huron in their perpetual war against the Onondaga, one of the Iroquois tribes. With a few Norman musketeers he journeyed up the Ottawa River, across Lake Nipissing, and to Georgian Bay, blazing a trail that was to be the principal French route to the interior for many years. There he joined 2,000 Huron in a march to Lake Ontario, which they crossed in canoes, to surprise an enemy village near Lake Oneida. Champlain spent that winter of 1615-16 with his red-skinned allies on Georgian Bay, then returned to Quebec to pass the remaining nineteen years of his life while younger men braved the hardships of exploration.

This tiny outpost nestled against the banks of the St. Lawrence was the one tangible monument to the men and treasure that France poured into the New World. Far to the south the other minute settlement of St. Augustine with its surrounding ring of presidios and mission stations stood guard over a forest empire that bore but faint resemblance to the dream worlds of the *conquistadors*. Between the two lay a great unoccupied wilderness that seemingly contained none of the gold or furs so eagerly sought by the Spaniards and French. Into this area came a little group of English laborers and gentlemen, to begin that slow process of expansion which ended only when France and Spain and the wilderness were pushed aside, and the continent settled.

# CHAPTER III

# The Southern Frontier

## 1600-1700

During the first half of the sixteenth century—while Frenchmen and Spaniards greedily staked their claims to the New World—England's Tudor monarchs were too interested in separating their newly united realm from continental intrigue and papal power to concern themselves with colonies beyond the seas. Bold navigators occasionally searched the icy waters about Labrador and Hudson Bay for the fabled Northwest Passage to Cathay, and hardy fishermen regularly cast their nets off Newfoundland for the cod and mackerel that tradition, if not religion, demanded in England, but these voyages served only to give Englishmen a thorough knowledge of the North American coast. Not until the 1570's were they ready to make their first assault on that wilderness.

At that time Queen Elizabeth, sensing that her nation was strong enough to enter the race for colonial possessions, abruptly reversed her traditionally friendly policy toward Catholic Spain. Swashbuckling adventurers, led by Francis Drake, sallied out to plunder Spanish treasure ships or raid the rich towns of Central and South America. The success of these piratical ventures convinced Sir Walter Raleigh, a wealthy court favorite of great influence, that the time was ripe to plant a colony in America; such an outpost, he saw, would not only limit Spain's expansion but would serve as a base for further raids on that nation's possessions. With the queen's tacit consent, he sent three expeditions to Roanoke Island in 1584, 1585, and 1587, but the first two returned to England and the last—the famous "Lost Colony"—disappeared before a relief ship arrived. These futile efforts irked Spain as much as the plundering Sea Hawks and contributed to the outbreak of the open warfare which began in 1588 when the mammoth

Spanish Armada sailed north to suffer the defeat that established England as mistress of the seas.

The English learned two valuable lessons from Raleigh's disastrous experiments. One was that the type of colony traditionally used by Europeans—a trading post to collect goods already gathered by the native population—was not suited to the North American wilderness. The country was so poor and the Indians so primitive that colonies could prosper only by producing their own wealth. This would require the permanent establishment of settlers who could till the soil, set up a civil government, and develop agricultural surpluses for shipment to the homeland. Raleigh's ill-fated efforts also taught England that the wealth of any one man, no matter how great, was insufficient for colony planting; the resources of many individuals must be combined to support an overseas plantation until it attained self-sufficiency. This realization discouraged the efforts of the old individualistic feudal class to tap the New World's wealth, but the rising merchant class was unwilling to forsake any field that promised profits. Their solution was to apply joint stock company methods to colony planting. These companies, which had been used since the sixteenth century to finance trading ventures, were even better suited to establishing settlements; depending as they did for support on many investors they could collect the large sums needed to nurture a plantation to maturity.

These lessons could not be applied so long as the war with Spain gave Elizabethan Sea Dogs the chance to chase enemy treasure ships, but the peace arranged by James I shortly after he ascended the throne in 1603 closed this exciting source of profits and turned Englishmen to the more prosaic task of founding settlements. The time seemed ripe for overseas expansion. Times were bad in England, for the long war had closed old continental trading routes and the enclosure of fields for sheep growing had loosed "monstrous swarms of beggars" upon the countryside. Colonies, the people were told by Richard Hakluyt and a host of other propagandists, would restore prosperity by reviving commerce and draining away surplus population. Moreover religious fervor was high after the wars with Catholic Spain, and Englishmen were anxious to preach their version of the Gospel to the heathen. These forces—economic, social, and spiritual—which were to send men to new frontiers across the face of the American continent, were all operating in the England of James I.

Two groups of merchants and governmental officials in London and Plymouth responded first when, in 1605, they separately petitioned the crown for the right to establish colonies. James I brought both together as the Virginia Company. The Royal Charter of 1606 provided for a central governing board, meeting in England and appointed by the king, which would supervise the two plantations planned. The London group was authorized to plant its settlement between the 34th and 41st parallels, the Plymouth group was given the region between the 45th and 38th parallels, and the overlapping strip between 41° and 38° was opened to both. Each group was empowered to "make habitation, plantation, and to deduce a colony of sundry of our people into that part of America commonly called Virginia." The colonists were guaranteed the "liberties, franchises, and immunities" that they enjoyed as Englishmen, but they were expected to work for the companies, which would give them their support and a share of the profits. Each colony was to be governed by a council of thirteen, appointed by the central board, and authorized to name one of its members as president. Thus general administrative control was retained by the king but the actual business of settlement was left to the companies.

The London group, which succeeded in planting the first permanent English settlement in North America, was granted the physiographic region known as the Southern Tidewater. This low-lying area, laced by rivers and cut by swampy inlets, stretched along the coast from New Jersey to Georgia and extended inland from 50 to 150 miles. The northern portion was dotted with great bays and river estuaries that allowed the small ships of that day to sail far inland; farther south lay the Cape Fear region with its multitude of sea islands and its vast swamps where rice culture was to center. The many rivers that twisted their slow way through this flat countryside formed numerous peninsulas and promontories where the silt-laden soil was ideal for agriculture, even south of the Savannah River where the streams ran almost level with the land and inundated great areas during the spring floods. Near the western edge of this coastal plain a fifty-mile belt of sandy soil covered by twisted pine forests ran across the Carolinas and Georgia, serving as a barrier to the westward movement of the agricultural frontier.

The soil of the Southern Tidewater was rich but thin, particularly on the ridges between river valleys where erosion left only four or five inches of fertile land over a sterile subsoil. The river bottoms, where the land was deep and enduring, were the prized farming areas. The heavy rainfall, averaging between forty and seventy inches a year, and the warm climate which assured a long growing season, made the Tidewater ideal for the production of staple crops suited to semitropical conditions. Nor was the task of clearing the land so difficult here as on later frontiers, for while the coastal plain was covered with a dense growth of hardwoods, pine, palmettoes, and cypress, the underbrush which plagued most pioneers was lacking. For this blessing the settlers could thank the Indians, who regularly burned over the region to drive game into traps. The forests were teeming with wild life: deer, buffalo, bears, and other animals in profusion, turkeys that weighed seventy pounds or more, and ducks so numerous that flocks seven miles long shut out the sunlight as they passed overhead. Streams swarmed with fish so large that ordinary nets would not hold them and so plentiful that a horse could not wade across a river where they were running. Sturgeon twelve feet long were killed with axes, and oysters thirteen inches across were seen along the coast. Once the Englishmen learned to use these resources they were assured a bountiful living.

Yet the first settlers starved to death amidst this plenty. They came in the spring of 1607—three shiploads of laborers and gentlemen sent out by the London Company to transfer England's civilization to the New World. The James River was selected for their settlement because its broad estuary seemed to promise a giant river system that might lead to the fabled Northwest Passage. After exploring the stream's lower reaches for about thirty miles the colonists came upon a peninsula two or three miles long and a mile and a half wide, covered with marsh and woodland, where the water was so deep that ships could be tied to trees on shore. Here, on May 24, 1607, the 105 settlers began building the fort and clustered houses which they called James Fort, and later Jamestown. This was cruelly hard work for gentlemen who had hoped to stuff their pockets with the gold that was scattered over America, but grim necessity drove them on. As land was cleared for lumber they planted wheat, only to see it shoot upward into seven-foot stalks with no grain; not until two years later did they learn from the Indians that the excessive fertility of the soil must be drained by several plantings of corn before wheat could be grown. This disappointing crop, inadequate supplies from England, and the mosquitoes and diseases natural in that swampy country took a heavy toll that first winter; by spring only thirty-eight men remained alive.

The "Starving Time" had two beneficial results. It elevated to the presidency of the local council a robust braggart named Captain John Smith who stopped treasure hunting, forced all to work at useful tasks, and secured enough grain from the Indians to support the feeble colony. And it led the king to grant a new charter to the London Company in 1609 which substituted an autocratic governor for the bickering council, changed the boundaries by granting the company a strip of land running two hundred miles north and south of Point Comfort then "up into the land, throughout from sea to sea, west and northwest," and provided that the governing council in England be elected by the stockholders rather than appointed by the king.

The results of these changes began to show in 1611 when Sir Thomas

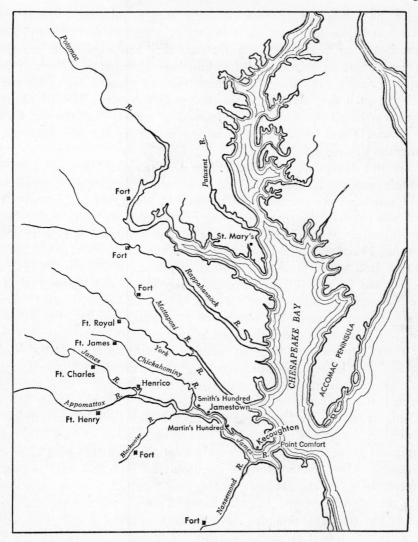

The Tidewater Frontier, 1607-1675

Dale began an eventful seven-year period as deputy governor. Settlers were sent out, fields planted, the forts and houses put in good condition, and a new settlement begun at Henrico, near the "Falls of the Farre West." The high ground of this site proved so much healthier than the swampy Jamestown peninsula that by 1616 Henrico was the colony's leading town, with substantial brick or frame houses, and a thriving agricultural population protected from Indian attack by a two-mile palisade between the James and Appomattox rivers. By this time the Virginia settlement was beginning to assume an aspect of permanence. The Englishmen were becoming "seasoned"—which meant they had acquired an immunity against American diseases and a rudimentary knowledge of frontier technique. Friendly Indians taught them how to plant corn, capture wild turkeys, catch fish, and clothe themselves in the warm skins of animals; from less hospitable natives they learned to venture into the forest only in groups. These lessons were to be applied during the whole history of American expansion.

Yet two things were needed before Virginia could prosper. One was a staple crop which could be sold in England, the other a more satisfactory land and labor system than that imposed by the London Company. The first was provided in 1612 when one of the colonists, John Rolfe, began experimenting with native tobacco. He soon produced a type that was "strong, sweet and pleasant as any under the sun." An acre of Virginia bottom land would produce five hundred pounds of the weed, which sold in England for five shillings a pound. Here was wealth undreamed of by the peasants who had come to America. The second proved more difficult. The company pictured the settlers as its servants, employed to labor on company lands and deposit their produce in company storehouses, in return for their keep and one share of stock which sold on the London market for £12 10s. In addition the governing council decided in 1612 to grant each planter one hundred acres of land after seven years, with additional grants if the first was used properly.

This system proved unworkable, largely because colonists refused to labor for absentee English stockholders even when driven by such a tyrannical governor as Dale. The only solution was a transition to private ownership. Two methods were employed to introduce this important reform. In 1616 Dale began granting one hundred acres to each settler with the incentive of an additional hundred acres if the first was well cultivated, the company retaining several large reserves which it hoped to develop with tenant farmers. By 1619 this transition was completed. The second means used was inaugurated in 1617 when the company granted large tracts of land, called "Hundreds" or "Particular Plantations," to groups willing to buy a sizeable block of stock in return for the privilege of sending out their own settlers. The first, a grant of 80,000 acres to the Society of Smith's Hundred, was followed by forty-three others between 1617 and 1623, although only a few of these were actually settled. Eventually most of this land was assigned to private individuals.

Tobacco planting and private ownership brought Virginia its first real prosperity. In vain did company and king rail against "this deceavable weede Tobacco, which served neither for necessity nor for ornament to the life of man." A man could earn £25 a year growing tobacco—five times as much as he could with grain—and by 1619 even the company bowed to the inevitable by sending out farmers to plant the "weed." At the same time, to make the colony more attractive and lure other settlers, it granted Virginia a legislative assembly to execute "those things as might best tend to their good." During the next three years the population increased from six hundred to more than 3,000, all eager seekers after good tobacco lands. At first the palisaded peninsulas held them in, but they soon burst these bonds and spread along the lower James from Kecoughton to Henrico. They felt secure against Indian attack even though far from the forts, for John Rolfe had married Pocahontas, daughter of the Indian chieftain Powhatan, and the two races seemed destined to perpetual peace.

Lulled by this false sense of security, the colonists were unprepared when the death of Powhatan elevated a hostile chief named Opechancanough to the leadership of his tribe. Thoroughly alarmed by the rapid extension of white settlements, he decided to make one great effort to drive the intruders into the sea. The blow that fell on March 22, 1622, took the Englishmen so completely by surprise that 357 were killed and every isolated plantation destroyed over night. Those still alive scampered for the safety of Henrico, Shirley Hundred, Jamestown, or Kecoughton, formed armies, and marched against the foe. For two years this warfare went on, with regular fall marches into the tribal villages to destroy crops, until the Indian power was broken. The two races lived in peace for the next twenty years.

The Massacre of 1622 did much to destroy the waning prestige of the London Company, already torn by factional disputes and engaged in a bitter controversy with the king over customs duties on tobacco. James I seized on the opportunity to appoint an investigating commission which reported that the company was ready for receivership. When its officers refused the offer of a new charter the king began legal proceedings that only ended in 1624 with the company overthrown and Virginia a royal colony, its governor and council appointed by the crown rather than by the stockholders. Charles I, who now ruled England, was an absolutist with no intention of re-establishing representative government in America, but in this he reckoned without the wishes of the Virginians. Like all Englishmen they treasured their liberties; like all frontiersmen they believed that no outsider understood their peculiar problems. Thus motivated by tradition and environment, they demanded authority to discuss specific subjects in 1628 and 1629, and after 1630 held regular assemblies that gradually assumed the law making power. The king, busy with his affairs at home, finally accepted the authority of this House of Burgesses, thus giving America the precedent on which its representative rule was to be based.

The new government was successful from the first. Its immediate task was an efficient defense system, for the Massacre of 1622 indicated that continued friendly relations were impossible. "Either," wrote a governor, "we must cleere them or they us out oft the country." Two methods were devised: marches and palisades. The former were regular expeditions into the Indian country, staged by militiamen whose heavy armor made them walking fortresses safe from the arrows of the enemy. They seldom caught an Indian, but their systematic destruction of crops after the harvest season drove the savages westward to safer regions. The use of a palisade was suggested shortly after the massacre when the assembly proposed erecting a six-mile-long wall, interspersed with blockhouses that could house garrisons, between Martin's Hundred and the York River. This, when completed in 1630, provided protection for 300,000 acres containing many of the settlements. Yet even by this time the palisade had outgrown its usefulness; it could not shift with the advancing frontier and was soon left behind by westward moving settlers. This was recognized when the legislature in 1630 tried to form a living wall against attack by offering large land grants to groups who would settle at dangerous spots. Although only one adventurous band took advantage of this offer, precedent was provided that was to be imitated often in the westward march of civilization. Thus did Englishmen, confronted with problems rising from a totally new environment, experiment until they found a solution.

The lessons learned by Virginia's pioneers made the establishment of the second Tidewater colony far easier. The region north of the Potomac was granted in 1632 to George Calvert, Lord Baltimore, a prominent English Catholic who wanted to found a New World haven for the persecuted members of his church. His first colonists reached Maryland in February, 1634, and after selecting a site for their town of St. Mary's on the St. George River, fell at once to building a fort, a storehouse, a chapel, and substantial houses. The high, fertile spot, and the generous price paid the Indians for the land, assured them freedom from the disease and warfare that had harried the Virginians. From their neighbors they learned to fell the timber, plant corn and tobacco, and live bountifully from the wilderness. From them, too, they caught the frontier spirit of independence; when Lord Baltimore tried to establish an archaic governmental system which restricted the legislature to advisory functions they resisted so lustily that within fifteen years the Maryland assembly virtually ruled the colony.

For the next half-century the two tobacco colonies expanded rapidly.

The Virginia settlements, which had been confined to the James Valley and the Accomac peninsula during the 1620's, pushed northward during the next decade to the banks of the York River. The bottom lands of that stream proved just as fertile as those of the James, and the deep-flowing river provided equally good transportation facilities for the shipment of tobacco. Encouraged by this, planters moved on to fill the valleys of the Rappahannock and Potomac rivers, advanced slowly westward until they reached the first waterfalls that stopped navigation, then spread out between the streams into the less-fertile uplands. Another group carved their homes from the country south of the James, occupying the valleys of the Nansemond and Blackwater rivers first, then the higher land between. The expanding tobacco frontier in Maryland also followed the waterways, moving first around Chesapeake Bay where ocean-going ships could come directly to the plantations for the heavy hogsheads of tobacco, then up the northern bank of the Potomac. By the 1670's the Tidewater in both colonies was comfortably settled by hard-working farmers.

The causes of this rapid expansion were those that led to the peopling of the entire American continent: expelling forces which drove people from their homes, and attracting forces which lured them westward. Most important was a large reserve population sufficiently dissatisfied with existing conditions to brave the wilderness. The troubled England of the late seventeenth century provided this; for a time the autocratic rule of Charles I drove a stream of Protestant dissenters beyond the seas, then the period of Puritan control between 1649 and 1660 sent thousands of Anglican yeoman farmers to Virginia and Maryland. With the restoration of Charles II in 1660 it was the turn of Roundheads and Puritans to flee once more. All of these swelled the population of the tobacco colonies. In America the newcomers were driven to the frontier by the agricultural methods employed, the ease with which they could secure land, and the distinctive labor system.

The primitive farming methods of the seventeenth century sent many pioneers westward. Tobacco was planted year after year, without any attempt to restore the soil's fertility by crop rotation or fertilization, until the mineral salts were exhausted. Usually three successive plantings were enough to cause the yield to decline, as tobacco was a heavy consumer of nitrogen and potash. Then the planter grew several crops of corn or wheat before abandoning the worn-out land and pushing farther into the wilderness, leaving behind a wake of "old fields" that rapidly reverted to forest. This process went on with increasing rapidity as the century advanced. By this time the river bottoms, with their deep silt deposits, were settled, turning pioneers to the thin surface soils of the uplands which disintegrated rapidly under intensive cultivation. In this hilly country, too, the primitive, surface-scratching plows encouraged rapid erosion during the heavy summer rains. Moreover the attempts of the colonial legislatures to prevent a glutting of the market by limiting the number of plants that each farmer could grow encouraged a rapid movement to virgin soils when the plants would be large and the crop, sold by weight, proportionately more valuable. Parliament also speeded the westward movement by the Navigation Act of 1660 which forbad the direct export of tobacco to Europe, for this discouraged the production of cheaper types that could be grown on poor land. All of these factors accounted for the rapidity with which the soil's fertility was exhausted, driving frontiersmen steadily onward in their search for wealth.

The evolution of a land system which allowed planters to secure their farms cheaply and easily also contributed to the rapid westward movement of the frontier. In neither Virginia nor Maryland could lands be purchased during the seventeenth century, for the rulers believed that the colonies would develop most rapidly if plots were given to individuals only in return for meritorious service. Both, however, awarded a "headright" of fifty acres to every person transporting a servant to America. As the demand for land increased with the rising population, these headrights were converted into convenient means for its sale. They were easily obtainable; accommodating officials granted them so freely that two hundred acres passed into private hands for each person crossing the Atlantic; the merchant sending him, the ship captain carrying him, the planter purchasing his services, and the servant himself all secured headrights at no expense. By the last of the century even planters crossing the ocean for business purposes, and the crews of ships engaged in colonial trade, regularly applied for fifty acres each time they landed. When government clerks began selling these warrants openly the authorities finally succumbed to popular pressure, and Maryland in 1683 and Virginia in 1705 legalized their sale. After this they were peddled legally at the rate of five shillings for fifty acres.

Some of the headrights issued to ships crews, servants, and travelers were sold directly to farmers who used them to secure certificates from county authorities entitling them to fifty acres of unoccupied land. More found their way into the hands of speculators. Ship captains and contractors who received large grants were always ready to sell their rights for a low cash price, and even those granted sailors were secured by jobbers who herded whole crews into the county offices, helped them to secure their headrights, and then purchased all the warrants immediately. In this way absentee owners engrossed much of the best land in advance of settlement, forcing newcomers to extend the settled areas by seeking less valuable spots in the interior. The activity of speculators was partially responsible for the 135 per cent increase in Maryland land prices between 1660 and the end of the century.

Almost as important as soil exhaustion and the land system in explaining the rapid settlement of the Tidewater was the type of labor employed. Much of the work was done by indentured servants who bound themselves to labor seven years for a planter in return for their passage across the Atlantic, their keep, and equipment to start a farm of their own when they earned their freedom. Although most of these servants were honest English cottagers who came to America because their only saleable asset, their labor, brought a higher price than in crowded England, their coming hurried the westward movement. Like all bond labor they encouraged soil exhaustion, having neither the knowledge nor the inclination to preserve the fertility of the fields they tilled. Moreover, when they completed their period of indenture, they usually sold the hundred acres granted them by the colony, then sought a cheaper home on the fringe of settlement. Through the seventeenth century a steady migration of these freed servants pushed the frontier westward.

The results of this expansion were as important as the forces that called it into being. From it stemmed two problems that plagued frontiersmen across the face of the continent: how could they protect themselves from the Indians who pressed upon them from the west? How could they guard themselves against easterners who tried to make them accept institutions ill suited to the wilderness environment?

The need for defense rose during the 1640's when the natives, alarmed by the steady encroachment of whites upon their lands, rose in revolt. Isolated raids by the Susquehannocks of the Susquehanna Valley on the Maryland back country began in the first years of the decade, but warfare was not serious until 1644 when the old Powhatan chief, Opechancanough, determined to strike while the English were torn by the Puritan Revolution. So helpless that he could not rise from a litter and so weak that attendants lifted his eyelids when he wished to see, his cunning mind could still plan an attack that took the colonists completely by surprise. This fell in the spring of 1644, so suddenly that before the whites could rally their forces nearly five hundred men, women, and children were killed. The English struck back with fierce marches that destroyed the Indians' crops, but not until Opechancanough was captured and treacherously put to death did the disheartened savages retreat into the wilderness. With the war over the victors turned belatedly to the problem of defense.

Their solution was twofold. Recognizing that friction between whites and red men was one cause of difficulty, they made separation a definite policy. A treaty in 1646 forced the Indians in the James-York peninsula to move into the country west of the Tidewater. Three years later Maryland attempted to remove another source of irritation by forbidding settlers to purchase land directly from the natives; Virginia imitated this excellent example in 1658, and in 1662 went so far as to declare all such transactions void. Maryland also in 1650 forbad Indians to enter certain settled areas under any pretext. In 1653 a more significant step was taken when the English began assigning some of the tribesmen to reservations, giving each warrior fifty acres of land and the privilege of hunting over other unoccupied territory. In groping after answers to an important frontier problem, the colonists established practices that were to be employed repeatedly in the next two centuries.

Yet separation might not keep peace, and even while working out this policy the authorities turned their attention to other means of protection. Palisades were unsatisfactory and marches more valuable in punishing Indian attacks than defending the settlements. Hence Virginia in 1645 decided to erect a chain of forts along the western edge of the Tidewater, manned by small garrisons which could beat back minor attacks or warn the colonists of threatening danger. Before these were built the legislature in 1646 hit on the happier scheme of offering land bounties to prominent citizens who would assume the burden of defense. Grants of 600-acre plots were sufficient to secure four forts: Ft. Royal on the York, Ft. Charles on the James, Ft. James on the high ridge overlooking the Chickahominy, and Ft. Henry on the Appomatox, each defended by a small garrison and governed by a frontier leader. As the threat of danger passed, most of these fell into decay, but they were re-established at public expense in the 1670's when a new Indian attack was rumored. By this time the more extended settlement required more forts, and the legislature in 1675 and 1676 provided for additional outposts on the Potomac, Rappahannock, and Mattaponi rivers in the north, and at the headwaters of the Blackwater and Nansemond rivers south of the James. Together they formed a ring of fortifications about forty miles apart around the colony.

Forts were expensive to maintain and as the threat of danger again passed the settlers cast about for other means of protection. In 1682 both Virginia and Maryland began employing patrols of mounted border rangers to ride constantly along the frontier, ready to fend off minor raids or give warning of major attacks. Clad in buckskin, carrying guns and long knives, mounted on spirited ponies, and steeped in the lore of the Indian and forest, these rangers were true frontiersmen whose wilderness skill testified to the amount learned by Englishmen since the first colonists starved to death amidst plenty at Jamestown. Yet the border patrols were so costly that Virginia cast about for a better system of defense. Her assemblymen made a final attempt to solve the problem in 1701 when they agreed on grants of from ten to thirty thousand acres to groups of frontiersmen who would settle at exposed spots. The statute decreed that each settler must be a "warlike christian man between sixteen and sixty years of age perfect of limb, able and fitt for service;" they were to erect a palisade to be used in case of attack, and each was to be assigned a half-acre house lot and a two-hundred-acre farm near the fort. The "warlike christian men" desired by the legislature never assembled—the Virginians were too individualistic to be confined within a narrow fort—but the measure provided a precedent for the Kentucky "Stations" of a later generation.

Dominating easterners always bothered frontiersmen as much as menacing Indians. Virginians discovered this as early as the 1620's when they demanded their own legislature to solve problems that a distant parliament could not understand, but not until half a century later did a serious East-West conflict develop within the colonies. The rapid advance of settlement made this struggle inevitable, for by the 1670's the westward movement of the frontier had created a series of distinct zones, each representing a transitional stage in the development of civilization, and each with peculiar problems that demanded home treatment. The attempt of the more thickly settled East, which controlled the colonial legislatures, to force its institutions on the western zones, bred the first of a series of bitter conflicts that marred the history of the American frontier.

The extreme westerly areas of settlement were most affected by the wilderness environment. Along the edge of the Tidewater and spilling over into the hilly country beyond was the fur trading frontier. Here, in the log forts erected at the falls of the rivers, lived leather-clad pioneers who felt more at home leading their pack trains along silent forest trails than in the cramped streets of Jamestown. Over them ruled a number of border barons who owned the forts—Colonel William Byrd, Captain Abraham Wood, Major Lawrence Smith, Henry Fleete—busily engaged in harvesting a fortune from their peltry traffic while they spied out the riches of the western country. Also near the western edge of the Tidewater and extending slightly beyond was the cattle frontier where cows and horses roamed wild, watched over by nomadic herdsmen who built crude huts near the peavine marshes where the animals grazed. Each fall the cattlemen staged a roundup to single out beeves for market and burn their identifying brands on the new-born calves. "They go in ganges," a traveler wrote, ". . . which move (like unto the ancient patriarchs or the modern Bodewins in Arabia) from forest to forest in a measure as the grass wears out or the planters approach them." In the wild lives of these cowmen and fur traders there was little of the civilization they had left behind.

East of the cattle and trading frontiers was the zone where pioneer farmers were busily transforming the wilderness into fertile tobacco fields. To this outpost came indentured servants who had worked out their terms of servitude, new immigrants from England, younger sons of established easterners, and planters from the East whose lands were exhausted by successive plantings of tobacco. Most were so poor that they could not pay the high prices demanded by speculators for good land near civilization; many were squatters. All were willing to pit their strength against nature in quest of the wealth that society denied them.

The manner in which the pioneer farmers lived showed how quickly Englishmen learned the frontier technique. They usually moved west in the autumn until they found a heavily timbered spot that pleased them, for large trees meant good soil. The first task was to girdle the trees by cutting a notch around the trunk a few feet from the ground; this allowed sunlight to penetrate their skeleton-like dead branches. Crude axes and mattocks were then used to fell enough timber to build a house, the great trees being trimmed on two sides and fitted together into solid walls. A heavy oak door facing a hand-dug well, windows with sliding wooden panels, holes bored at intervals to hold guns, and a plank roof completed the crude home. Nails were used as sparingly as possible for they were expensive; when a settler moved he frequently burned his house to retrieve the precious metal. With a shelter erected the pioneer farmer spent the winter cutting the giant trees and piling them for burning. In April he planted his first crop of corn among the standing dead timber and by August the ripe ears were ready for drying on tall wooden frames. This dried corn, with turnips and beets grown in a small garden and pork from acorn-fattened hogs, assured his family a plentiful diet of those foods already becoming staple in the southern diet: hog and hominy, bacon and greens, corn bread, hoe cake, and corn pone.

Sometimes during the first year, always in the second, the best portion of the cleared land was set aside for tobacco. A sheltered, sunny spot near the forest edge was planted to seed in March; two months later the fragrant green plants were moved to other fields where they were hoed regularly until September when the yellowing leaves warned that harvest time was near. Then they were cut, tied on strings to cure, and finally fastened in bundles which could be laid in huge hogsheads for shipment to England. The hogshead or two of tobacco sold each year paid for the gunpowder, sugar, tea, and iron implements that the farmer could not fashion with his own hands. Beyond this he was self-sufficient; he raised his own food, built his own crude furniture and primitive agricultural implements, and dressed in clothes sewn by his wife from the skins of animals or from wool produced in the neighborhood. He wanted little from society and expected to give little in return.

East of the pioneer-farmer zone was the fully matured social order of the seaboard. The planters who lived there dwelt on farms no larger than those of the frontiersmen, for the great plantations of the South did not develop until the eighteenth century when slave labor was introduced in large quantities. Seventy-five per cent of the Maryland farms contained less than 250 acres at the close of the century and in Virginia the proportion of large estates was even smaller except on the Accomac peninsula where some tendency toward combining holdings was noticeable. Despite this, the eastern planter differed from the western farmer in his social attitudes, largely because he was less self-sufficient. Tobacco was the region's staple crop—even food was imported from the up-river settlements—and the whole area was bound to England by close commercial ties. Looking always to the mother country, the average planter of the lower Tidewater consciously patterned his life on the model of the English aristocracy. He dressed in a peculiar assortment of homespun and imported fineries, lived in a small frame dwelling with a chimney at either end which he casually referred to as the "Manor House" or the "Great House," sat in the best pew of the parish church, sent his children to England for a polite education, and considered himself on a higher social plane than the farmers of the back country.

The development of these two antagonistic societies in the upper and lower Tidewater predestined trouble. One was aristocratic, conservative, and bound by close cultural ties to England; the other democratic, liberal, and dominated by free and easy frontier concepts. Both were bound together by artificial colonial boundary lines. Only a specific grievance was needed to precipitate a serious conflict.

This developed during the 1670's when the easterners, reflecting the mounting conservatism of the mother country during the Restoration period, attempted to sweep away the few political rights that the frontiersmen enjoyed. They were led by their governors, Sir William Berkeley in Virginia and Charles Calvert in Maryland, who reflected the reactionary trend of the times. Berkeley, a "peevish and brittle" old man who abhorred popular rule, refused to allow a new assembly to be elected after 1661, using his power of prorogation to maintain in office the loyal followers who had been chosen that year. This virtually ended self-government, for the governor previously had the right to appoint the council, or upper house of the legislature, and the justices of peace who controlled the counties.

Heavy poll taxes that fell equally on rich and poor were levied by the justices in secret sessions, "by which the poor people not knowing for what they paid their levy did allways admire how their taxes could be so high." Calvert did not go quite so far in Maryland, but he did follow Virginia's example by restricting the franchise to large property holders.

Popular dissatisfaction with the autocratic governmental system was accentuated by bad economic conditions during those years. Wars with Holland in 1664 and 1673, bad storms, a "Dreadful Hurry Cane," and a glutting of the world's tobacco markets all contributed to a serious depression which gave every evidence of permanence. Planters pleaded in vain with the colonial legislatures to limit production by law, but neither Maryland nor Virginia dared act without the co-operation of the other and this was not forthcoming. By the early 1670's tobacco went begging at a penny a pound while mobs roamed the countryside burning crops in a vain attempt to force prices up. Conditions were particularly bad in the back country, where small farmers lacked the reserves that allowed eastern planters to weather the worst years.

The smouldering resentment of the frontiersmen was fanned into flame by a new Indian disturbance. The Susquehannock tribe, driven south and east from its lands in the Susquehanna Valley by a losing war with the Iroquois, was pressing upon the outskirts of settlement in Virginia and Maryland by 1675. Intermittent warfare which began that year reached a climax when a Maryland-Virginia expedition slaughtered five innocent Indians who had approached with a flag of truce. The angry natives responded by falling on isolated settlements with increased violence, until by January, 1676, they were massacring as many as two score whites each day and the frontiersmen were loudly demanding aid from the Maryland and Virginia governments. Berkeley turned a deaf ear to these requests. Insisting that he had no authority to start an army west until the assembly met in March, he went doggedly ahead with plans for new forts along the back country. The westerners, knowing that they would all be scalped before these could be built, grumbled that Berkeley was sacrificing them to protect his own fur trading interests. By March several hundred whites were dead and the frontiersmen seething with rage. Neglect, tyranny, and depression they had endured, but now they drew the line.

Trouble started in Virginia when angry backwoodsmen gathered near Ft. Charles, at the falls of the James, during the spring of 1676 to plot a march on the Indians without the governor's consent. Colonel William Byrd and his wealthy friends, who dominated the fur trade from their large estates in the West, were secretly delighted, as Berkeley had recently restricted trade to five of his own favorites and they could hope to restore their profitable business only by unseating the tyrannical governor. None of them was willing to lead the rabble that assembled near Byrd's plantation, but their pressure helped persuade a high-spirited young Whig named Nathaniel Bacon to undertake the rebellious mission. After bolstering the spirits of the volunteer army with a liberal supply of rum he led three hundred of them to a decisive victory over the Indians.

Berkeley, horrified at this unauthorized expedition, set out to arrest the rebellious Bacon, but when he left Jamestown he found support for the frontiersmen so strong that he was forced to issue a call for a new election instead. Bacon, who was named delegate from Henrico, dominated the new assembly completely. One by one the old tyrannical laws were repealed, the franchise was again broadened, and an army of a thousand men was formed with Bacon as commander. This was going too far; Berkeley stoutly refused to deliver a military commission to a rebel. When Bacon learned of this he hurriedly departed westward, gathered a force of five hundred men, marched on the capital, and forced the reluctant governor to surrender the needed papers. Triumphantly bearing these he started against the Indians again while Berkeley retreated to the Accomac peninsula. The old tyrant was so popular in that stronghold of conservatism that he easily gathered a force of six hundred to march on Jamestown. His victory was shortlived, for when Bacon returned to besiege the city, Berkeley's defenses collapsed. While he fled once more to Accomac the rebels entered Jamestown and burned it to the ground.

In the hour of his triumph Bacon suddenly died, in October, 1676, abruptly ending the rebellion. Berkeley, assuming control once more, began such a bloody purge of his opponents, that even Charles II grew alarmed at the excesses of his deputy in Virginia. "That old fool," he wrote, "has hanged more men in that naked country than I have done for the murder of my father." Only a royal commission which sent Berkeley packing back to England in disgrace ended the period of reprisal, but not until thirty-seven rebels were executed. All along the back country, frontiersmen, convinced that the end of Bacon's Rebellion doomed them to continued control by the conservative East, slipped farther into the wilderness or away to other colonies.

Maryland's outburst was less violent than Virginia's. In September, 1676, a band of discontented backwoodsmen gathered at the plantation of Thomas Barbary on the Patuxent River to demand reform, but popular sympathy was lacking and the authorities easily captured and hanged the leaders. Hatred of the colony's aristocratic rulers continued strong along the frontier where several minor outbursts occurred during the early 1680's. This reached a climax in 1689 when the Maryland officials refused to support the Glorious Revolution or to recognize William III as their new monarch. "Two rank Baconists," Josias Fendall and John Coode, seized the excuse to gather an army of frontiersmen, march on St. Mary's, and seize control of the government. The popular assembly that they called asked the king to abolish proprietary control by making Maryland into a royal colony—a step taken in 1691. Frontier dissatisfaction temporarily cost the Calvert family a province.

One unforeseen result of these frontier uprisings was a steady exodus of dissatisfied backwoodsmen southward to bolster a new colony taking shape there. This was Carolina, stretching between Virginia's southern boundary and the 31st parallel, and granted by the crown in 1663 to a group of eight commercially minded proprietors, all of whom were already engaged in flinging back the borders of Britain's expanding empire in other parts of the world. By the 1670's two centers of settlement were developing. One was nestled in the forests and swamps about Albemarle Sound, where Virginia had planted a band of pioneers in 1653 to guard her southern border. Others filtered in during the next years, attracted by the prospect of living in an isolated region where they would be safe from tax collectors or reforming ministers, until by 1677 some 2,500 people lived there. The other center of population was established when the proprietors in 1670 sent colonists to lay out Charles Town on the Ashley River some twenty-five miles from its mouth. This site proved so unsatisfactory that ten years later the whole colony was moved to the junction of the Ashley and Cooper rivers. There a stout palisade inclosed government buildings and thirty houses, surrounded by settlers' fields.

The settlements about Charles Town grew slowly. Thirty years after the colony was founded the frontier line was nowhere more than fifty or seventy-five miles from the coast and extended from Port Royal to the valley of the Santee River. Two things prevented the rapid dispersal of population that had marked the westward advance in Virginia and Maryland. One was the failure of the colonists to find a suitable staple; tobacco did poorly in this swampy country and England's own crops were ill suited to the semitropical climate. Not until the 1690's did Carolinians begin the experiments with rice culture which brought them fortunes in the next century. The other was the need for defense. Southern Carolina was flung into the very teeth of the Spaniards and their Indian allies; Charles Town was only 250 miles from St. Augustine while to the north five hundred miles of lonely forests and dreary swamps separated it from the James River settlements. Almost at its doorstep were the outposts of the Florida mission frontier, which had been driven back beyond the Savannah River by Indian attacks in 1661 but still stretched northward as far as St.

Catherine's Island where the Franciscan station of Santa Catalina de Guale and its protecting presidio guarded a band of loyal Indians. Normal agricultural expansion was impossible where isolated settlements might fall prey to marauding Indians or Spanish troops.

Instead the Carolinians turned to the fur trade in their search for wealth.

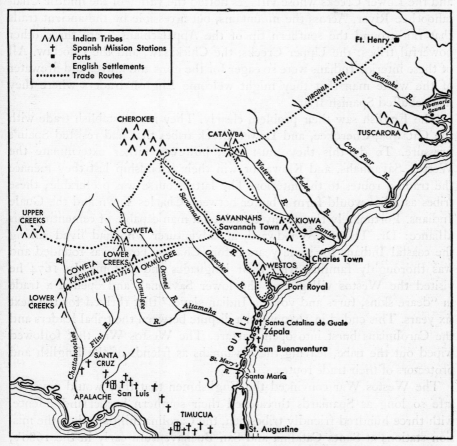

The Carolina Frontier, 1670-1700

This promised them not only an export staple but a chance to build up Indian alliances against the inevitable day of reckoning with Spain. The situation was ideal for their purposes. In Guale, Apalache, and Timucua lived some 26,000 natives whose loyalty to the Spanish mission fathers could probably not be broken. Just north of this enemy country was a borderland occupied by three small tribes only nominally under Spanish influence: the Westos about Port Royal, the Savannahs along the middle

Savannah River, and the Kiowa in the country west of Charles Town. Beyond these was a circling ring of powerful tribes over which the Spaniards had no control: the Tuscarora whose hunting parties ranged between the Roanoke and Cape Fear rivers, the Catawba along the upper waters of the Wateree River, the Cherokee about the headwaters of the Savannah River, and the Lower Creeks whose villages dotted the valley of the middle Chattahoochee River. Across the mountains, but accessible by the ancient trails that ran around the southern tip of the Appalachians, were three other powerful tribes: the Upper Creeks, the Chickasaw, and the Choctaw. All of these interior Indians were so eager for the guns and knives and firewater of the white man that they might welcome English traders where they had rebuffed Spanish friars.

The English saw their problem clearly. They must establish trade with the Catawba, Cherokee, and Lower Creek tribes that had resisted Spain's pressure. To do this they must first, however, either exterminate the Westos, Savannahs, and Kiowa, or win their friendship lest they menace the trading routes to the interior. The latter course was preferable; these tribes as allies would form a buffer between Charles Town and the Guale Indians. Fortunately the colony contained a man capable of cementing this alliance: Dr. Thomas Woodward, an adventurer who had lived among the coastal Indians for some years before Charles Town was founded and was thoroughly familiar with their languages and customs. In 1674 he visited the Westos villages on the lower Savannah and opened a trade in "deare skins, furrs and younge Indian slaves" that thrived for the next six years. This ended in 1680 when a dispute between the tribal leaders and the Carolinians burst into open warfare. The Westos War that followed wiped out the tribe, leaving the Savannahs as friends of the English and protectors of their trade routes.

The Westos War convinced the Englishmen that they would never be safe so long as Spaniards threatened their southern borderland. Hence, with three hundred friendly tribesmen, the Carolina militia fell on the mission stations at Santa Catalina and San Buenaventura early in the 1680's, driving the friars to the protection of the presidio of Zápala on Sapelo Island. Even this strong post was menaced by English raiding parties and marauding pirates, until the Spanish in 1684 gave up the struggle for Guale and retreated to Amelia Island where the Santa María station became their new northern outpost. Even more alarming to the Spaniards was the way in which their Indian allies deserted to the side of the victorious English rather than following the missions southward; the powerful Yamassee in particular went so far as to move their villages to the lands formerly occupied by the Westos on the lower Savannah. An attempt to regain prestige failed when an expedition sent to demolish Charles Town in 1686 was scattered by "a Hurricane wonderfully horrid and destructive," after wiping out a small settlement of Scotch covenanters at Stuart's Town on Port Royal.

The English traders, no longer fearing a flank attack from northern Guale, immediately extended their operations toward the interior. This was a move long dreaded by the Spaniards, for if the Carolinians won over the Lower Creeks they would be within striking distance of the important Apalache mission station and presidio of San Luis. Even while the war in Guale was going on, officials of New Spain vainly sought permission to found a mission in the Creek country, and when this was not forthcoming, set up the station of Santa Cruz de Sábacola at the junction of the Flint and Chattahoochee rivers in 1681 as a center for a few friendly Indians. These preparations were not wasted. Four years later Dr. Woodward with a handful of followers reached the Creek villages of Coweta and Kashita with a small pack train of trading goods. The horrified commander at San Luis marched north to drive him out, but Woodward only disappeared into the wilderness while the Spanish were near and continued trading until the fall of 1685 when he left for Charles Town with 150 natives laden with furs. Other traders who followed on his heels finally forced Spanish officials to agree to a fort in the Creek country, although the construction of this post—in 1689—had hardly the effect intended. Instead of welcoming the Spaniards the Indians were so angered by the attempt to end their trade that a year later the entire tribe moved east to the valleys of the Oconee and Ocmulgee rivers where they could be nearer the English.

From this time on the Carolina traders did a prosperous business. Every spring they gathered, three or four hundred strong, at Savannah Town, a frontier village established on the Savannah River about 1690, where each fitted out his twenty-horse pack train with blankets, ironware, guns, knives, rum, and trinkets. Forming into caravans of a hundred horses or more they set out along the well-marked trails into the Indian country. Some followed the Savannah River to the Cherokee villages, then on to the Catawba country where they usually met rivals from Virginia. Others continued along the trail to the ford over the Ogeechee River where they divided to take either the Upper Path that led to the Lower Creek village of Coweta or the Lower Path to Okmulgee. All during the fall and winter they wandered from tribe to tribe carrying on their trade. If they were honest they drove as hard a bargain as they could; if they were unscrupulous, which was far more likely, they treated the savages to liberal portions of rum before beginning negotiations. In the spring they turned their pack horses, laden now with bundles of deer skins and peltries, back to Charles Town for a few weeks of riotous living while they sold their catch and bought fresh goods. This tiny town was a colorful spot during their visits. Their caravans clattered through its quiet streets, their picturesque costumes lent variety to the dull garb of its citizens, and their inordinate thirst cheered the heart of many a tavern keeper. "Those sparkes," wrote one observer, "make little of drinking 15 or 16 £ in one Bout in Towne." Most important of all, they brought prosperity to southern Carolina, for during the 1690's Charles Town annually shipped some 54,000 deer skins to London markets.

By the end of the seventeenth century England's hold on the southern coast of North America was secure. Sturdy yeoman farmers and adventurous traders, building their empire on a firm foundation of tobacco and furs, were joyously engaged in the task of driving back the Spanish overlords who had monopolized that region. The conquest of the continent by the English was well under way.

# CHAPTER IV

# The Northern Frontier

## 1600-1700

While some Englishmen moved slowly across the southern Tidewater seeking fertile soil for their tobacco plants or friendly Indians along the Spanish borderlands, others carved out a new frontier in the region that became the northeastern United States. During the seventeenth century the coastal lowlands and river bottoms of this domain were filled by home-seekers who transformed the wilderness into a new civilization vastly different from that of the South.

The first assault on this northern frontier ended disastrously when colonists sent out by the Plymouth Company in May, 1607, returned to England a year later after an "extreme unseasonable and frosty" winter on the Kennebec, then called the Sagadahoc River. With this half-hearted effort the company lapsed into inactivity that only ended in 1620 when its more ambitious members effected a reorganization into the Council for New England. Although blessed with a royal grant to all lands between the 40th and 48th parallels the Council failed to secure enough financial support to plant its own colony and contented itself with granting lands to small groups of settlers. These hardy pioneers founded the New England colonies.

The first grant was to a little band of religious dissenters called Separatists whose dissatisfaction with the established Anglican Church drove them first to Holland early in the century, and then to America. Their objective, when they sailed on the *Mayflower* in 1620, was a Particular Plantation in Virginia which had been purchased from the London Company, but storms which blew them from their course cast them on the Massachusetts coast. Realizing that they were beyond the pale of the law and intruders on lands to which they had no title, the Pilgrims signed a brief agreement before they landed, binding themselves into a "civill body politick" to enact laws "unto which we promise all due submission and obedience." The famous Mayflower Compact, applying as it did the principles of church covenants to this unique civil problem, was the first of a series of squatters' agreements to which pioneers resorted as a basis for temporary self-government whenever their westward march carried them beyond the bounds of orderly society. With their immediate governmental needs provided for, the 102 colonists landed, and in December, 1620, began building their homes at Plymouth.

The land system insisted upon by the London capitalists who financed the voyage—they were to labor for seven years on a company plantation—worked so badly that in 1623 the division of lands among private owners began. This proved successful; within ten years the colony was completely self-sustaining, with its English backers paid in full and the people prosper-ous. The Pilgrims' ability to maintain themselves without aid from the mother country impressed contemporaries far more than the religious ex-periment they were conducting, and encouraged other groups to migrate to the New World. While realizing this state of happy self-sufficiency the Plymouth settlers constantly cast about for some exportable staple com-parable to Viriginia's tobacco. When experiment showed that the diversified agriculture suitable to the climate and soil of Massachusetts could produce no crop sufficiently prized in England to be profitable, they turned, like the Carolinians, to the fur trade. Here they were more fortunate. The neigh-boring Indians were skilled in producing wampum—the native currency made by stringing together tiny beads carved from the inner whorls of coast shells and bored with a flint drill—which was highly valued by the more primitive tribesmen of Maine. By 1628 the Pilgrims were buying up wam-pum in Massachusetts, carrying it northward in their shallops, and bartering there for beaver, marten, and otter skins. Within a year they were able to erect a trading post, or "trucking house," at Cushenoc on the Kennebec River to serve as a center for their traffic, and until 1640 when the near-extermination of the beaver ended trade, this was their principal source of wealth.

By that time the Plymouth colony was well established. New settlers who arrived during the 1620's moved first north along the low-lying coast to found Duxbury, Marshfield, and Scituate, then turned southward to lay out Taunton and build their homes about Buzzard's Bay and the lower reaches of Cape Cod. There they discovered coastal marshes where they could pasture their cattle and fertile fields to grow corn and other foodstuffs. This expansion gradually transformed Plymouth into a prosper-ous agricultural colony, with cattle raising as its principal industry. The whole process was carried on without serious Indian opposition, for Chief Massasoit of the Wampanoags, whose country the Pilgrims occupied, kept a pledge of peace made with the first settlers until his death in 1662.

While the Plymouth colony was taking root in Massachusetts soil other English outposts were planted to the northward. Fishermen and traders found that stern and rockbound coast such an attractive field for their operations that by the end of the 1620's their tiny settlements dotted the New England shoreline from Casco Bay to Boston Harbor. The most important of these trading posts was one at Salem operated by a small English corporation. The struggles of this company to maintain its precarious foothold attracted the attention of a group of wealthy Puritan clergy and business men who conceived the idea of taking over the colony as a joint commercial and missionary enterprise. With this in mind they formed the Massachusetts Bay Company and in 1628 secured a grant from the Council for New England to a strip of territory lying between a point three miles north of the Merrimac and another three miles south of the Charles, extending from sea to sea. A year later a royal charter confirmed this allotment and officially incorporated the company.

Among the stockholders of the Massachusetts Bay Company was a locally influential Puritan, John Winthrop, who was interested in founding a New World colony where members of his sect could follow the dictates of their consciences on religious matters. Noticing that the charter, probably through oversight, failed to state that meetings of the corporation must be held in England, Winthrop conceived a bold plan. Why not transfer the entire government to America, setting up there a Puritan commonwealth which would be virtually self-governing within its corporate rights? The rest of the stockholders readily agreed to his proposal and in 1630 Winthrop, newly elected governor, sailed away with a thousand colonists to plant his wilderness Zion. Destitute Salem proved little to the Puritans' liking so they continued south until they found a magnificent harbor into which jutted a broad peninsula. On this safe and healthy site they built the town of Boston. Englishmen were now so skilled in frontier techniques—planting corn, establishing friendly relations with the Indians, importing cattle to graze on the marshes—that the colony was firmly established within two years. By this time half a dozen small towns were clustered about the shores of Boston Harbor: Roxbury, Dorchester, Watertown, Medford, and Newtown or Cambridge.

During the next decade the Massachusetts Bay Colony expanded rapidly. Some 24,500 newcomers arrived at Boston during those ten years of the "Great Migration," driven overseas by bad conditions in the homeland. Many came from southeastern England where a succession of poor harvests and a declining textile trade brought hard times. Others fled to the colonies from the harsh absolutism of Charles I, who dissolved parliament in 1629 and entered upon a period of personal rule which only ended with revolution. Puritans suffered greatly during his reign, for he was an uncompromising believer in high-church Anglicanism and staunchly supported the campaign begun in 1633 by William Laud, Archbishop of Canterbury, to stamp out England's dissenters. Non-conformists' services were broken up, their churches dissolved, and their ministers deported. Thousands of believers, convinced that salvation was impossible in an England unaccountably delivered into the devil's hands, departed for homes beyond the seas between 1630 and 1640.

Few stayed in Boston where the system of government was nearly as autocratic as that from which they fled. John Winthrop and the Puritan clerics who guided his hand were no believers in democracy. They knew that they, as divinely appointed interpreters of the Holy Writ, alone understood God's will; popular rule would defeat His whole purpose in establishing this wilderness Zion. At first they tried to rule without the General Court, or legislature, authorized by the charter, but popular resentment forced them in 1634 to call an assembly made up of delegates from the various towns. Before doing so they carefully protected themselves by decreeing that only freemen could vote or hold office. As only church members could become freemen, and only men approved by the clergy become church members, the leaders were able to continue their autocratic rule behind this democratic facade, ruthlessly stamping out all dissent against the established order. Their harsh rule bred a whole stream of rebels, some famous but more unsung, who went forth into the wilderness to found villages where they could practice their own beliefs—and be intolerant of others.

The dispersal of population went on so rapidly in New England that the usual sequence of frontier types was less apparent than later when fur trader, cattle raiser, pioneer farmer, and equipped farmer passed in orderly procession. All were present, but they succeeded each other so rapidly that only the fur trader was distinguishable. He was in the van as usual, spying out the best lands, reducing the self-sufficiency of the Indians by giving them the tools and vices of the white man, and paving the way for later settlers.

Interest in an interior trading frontier was awakened in 1631 when the chief sachem of the Mohegan Indians—a Connecticut Valley tribe—visited the settlements. He brought tales not only of plentiful furs and natives eager for trade, but of a hated rival already in the field. The Dutch, he told the horrified Englishmen, had founded a settlement called New Amsterdam on Manhattan Island, and were sending their expeditions northward along the coast to barter for peltries. The Plymouth authorities were sufficiently aroused to send out an exploring party under Edward Winslow in 1632. His glowing reports, and news that the Dutch were establishing a post at the House of Good Hope on the lower Connecticut, sent both colonies into action in 1633. A Plymouth expedition under Captain William Holmes reached the valley first and sailing boldly past the Dutch, built a trucking house at the mouth of the Farmington River. This was followed a few months later by a small party from Massachusetts Bay led by John Oldham which investigated the Connecticut Valley during the autumn months. Oldham was back in the spring of 1634 to build a trading post at the present site of Wethersfield. A second Massachusetts trader, William Pynchon, explored the country in quest of a good spot for a trucking house during 1635. All of these men brought back enthusiastic accounts of rich soil, level fields, and friendly Indians.

These reports fell on the ears of men willing to listen, for by 1635 the people in the towns clustered about Boston felt the effects of overcrowding. Many, finding the sandy soil of their new homes unsuitable to agriculture, were anxious to turn to cattle raising, but the limited lands of Newtown, Dorchester, Roxbury, and Watertown gave them no room for pasturage. Others chafed under the autocratic rule of the Boston governors, especially as the clergymen in each of these towns quarreled with the ruling hierarchy and infected their congregations with dissatisfaction. Still others were moved, as they put it, by "a strong bent of their spirits for change," as they felt that restlessness which was becoming an American trait. They began drifting into the Connecticut Valley in small groups during the summer of 1635 when the General Court, after vainly trying to divert migration to the Merrimac River, finally authorized their departure. Crude huts were thrown up about the trucking houses at Windsor and Wethersfield and a settlement was begun on the site of present Hartford before an extreme winter drove most of the pioneers back to the comparative comfort of Boston. Only one settlement survived: a small outpost called Saybrook established during 1635 by a group of wealthy Puritans under the leadership of John Winthrop, Jr. The relatively milder climate of the Long Island Sound spared its settlers the rigors of that cold winter.

With the spring of 1636 the movement began again. In the lead were the inhabitants of Newtown who sold their homes to a newly arrived congregation from England and, led by their minister, the Reverend Thomas Hooker, started westward along the old Bay Path, driving their 160 cattle before them. This first mass migration in the history of the American frontier lasted two weeks before they began building their houses at Hartford. Other eastern groups were also on the move. From Dorchester went the settlers who had been driven back during the winter, taking their friends with them in another overland expedition to found Windsor. Most of the Watertown citizens joined in chartering a ship to carry them to Wethersfield where they gave that infant settlement its first permanent character. Another band from Roxbury followed William Pynchon, whose fur trading activities made him familiar with the entire valley, to Springfield where they signed a compact governing their civil and religious affairs and laid out their town. Through the remainder of 1636 and the summer of 1637 newcomers continued to arrive, until the Boston authorities grew alarmed lest their own population be seriously depleted.

For a time these river towns were claimed by both Massachusetts and the Saybrook colony until the settlers, distrustful as were all frontiersmen of outside authority, took matters into their own hands. Inspired by a sermon of Thomas Hooker's which defended the right of people to name their own rulers, they sent delegates to a Hartford convention in January, 1639, to draw up the famous Fundamental Orders of Connecticut. This compact vested the principal power to rule in a legislature made up of four delegates from each town; its members could call meetings or adjourn when they chose and its laws were not subject to veto by the governor. Although the provision that only religiously orthodox freemen could vote for delegates to the General Court excluded some two-thirds of the people from the franchise, the system was far more democratic than that of Massachusetts Bay where an autocratic governor and a small oligarchy of assistants and ministers reigned supreme.

While these Puritans carved their homes from the Connecticut wilderness another group of rebels against Massachusetts authority founded the first towns of Rhode Island. Roger Williams, a kindly humanitarian whose belief in religious toleration and Indian rights made him unpopular in both Salem and Boston, led the way when he was banished from the Bay Colony in 1635. After spending the winter with Massasoit he moved south with a few friends from Salem to found Providence. At his heels came others who had aroused the ire of Massachusetts' authorities by listening to the unorthodox teachings of Anne Hutchinson; they established Portsmouth in 1638. A year later this tiny settlement split in two, with one faction under the eccentric Samuel Gorton breaking away to found Newport and Warwick. Roger Williams erected such a liberal governmental structure for the Narragansett Bay communities that they served during the next years as a constant haven for discontented elements from Massachusetts.

Rebellion against harsh Bay Colony rule drove another stream of dissenters north to lay out the first New Hampshire towns. First to arrive was the Reverend John Wheelright, a victim of the Anne Hutchinson controversy, who established Exeter in 1638. In the same year a group that had seceded from the Lynn church laid out pastures for cattle raising at Hampton. Nearer the coast Rye, Portsmouth, and Dover were settled at about the same time by English Anglicans. When these towns found themselves the subject of a jurisdictional dispute between Massachusetts and the Council for New England they followed the usual frontier practice of drawing up a compact "to make and set up such government as shall be to our best discerning." This instrument, more democratic than the Mayflower Compact or the Fundamental Orders, provided the colony with an orderly government until it was absorbed by Massachusetts in 1641.

The first extension of the northern frontier into Connecticut, Rhode

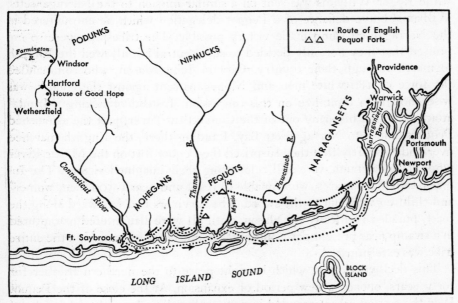

The Pequot War, 1637

Island, and New Hampshire, dictated as it was by a desire for fertile land, left great stretches of hilly wilderness still occupied by Indians. These natives, and particularly those between the Connecticut River and Narragansett Bay, viewed the advance with alarm, realizing that they were caught between two arms of settlement which threatened to squeeze them from their hunting grounds. Most fearful were the Pequots, who had only recently been pushed into the area between the Thames and Pawcatuck rivers by wars with the Iroquois, and could count on the friendship of none of the surrounding tribes: the Podunks and Mohegans of the Connecticut Valley and the Narragansetts who lived east of the Pawcatuck River. To make matters worse they had aroused English enmity by trading exclusively with the Dutch. Sensing the fate that awaited them if white encirclement continued, they decided to fight back.

The Pequot War was touched off in the summer of 1636 when the Boston trader, John Oldham, was murdered on Block Island. Instead of seeking a peaceful settlement, the Massachusetts authorities decided to punish the offenders by sending an expedition through the Indian country to destroy villages and burn crops. This harsh act stirred the tribe to such fury that by the spring of 1637 the war was in full swing. The river towns, knowing that they must bear the brunt of the fighting, hastened to localize the conflict by winning Uncas, the principal sachem of the Mohegans, to their side, while Roger Williams was sent on a similar mission to the Narragansetts. Williams' brave defiance of a Pequot delegation which he encountered in the Narragansett camp made victory possible. The tribesmen were so impressed that they not only decided to stay neutral but allowed the English to march through their country. Captain John Mason, who commanded the force of 180 white men and Mohegans sent against the enemy, was wise enough to capitalize on this concession. Instead of risking a frontal attack he sailed his army out of the Connecticut River, past the astonished Pequots, and into Narragansett Bay. Landing there, the English marched overland so swiftly that they surprised the Pequot fort on the Mystic River while its inhabitants were still celebrating their imagined victory. The Indians, caught unawares, were unable to resist and nearly 500 men, women, and children were put to the sword. The survivors fled westward along the coast, pursued ruthlessly by Mason, until all were slaughtered or captured in a swamp near present-day Southport. In one heartless campaign the entire tribe was exterminated.

This decisive victory, which brought peace to the northern frontier for forty years, opened a new period of expansion. At the close of the Pequot War the settled areas extended in a straggling line down the Maine coast, broadened to include the towns about Boston Harbor, hugged the coast again at Plymouth, and then swept inland to encompass the settlements along the Taunton River and about Narragansett Bay. West of the Connecticut River in the lands explored during the Pequot War lay another region that was developing rapidly; New Haven was founded there by a group of English Puritans in 1638 and Guilford, Branford, Milford, Fairfield, Stamford, and Greenwich followed within five years. All of these settlements bordered the coast; only the Connecticut Valley frontier—which stretched northward to Springfield—penetrated the interior. The task of the colonists in the forty years of peace between the Pequot War and King Philip's War was to fill the gaps between their coastal settlements and begin the conquest of the upcountry.

As usual the fur traders were in the van. The trail to a new northern frontier for Massachusetts was blazed by Simon Willard, who as early as 1635 established a post at Concord where he could intercept the furs coming down the Merrimac and Concord rivers on their way to trucking houses

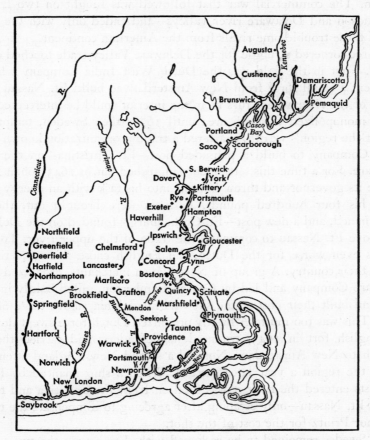

The New England Frontier in the Seventeenth Century

at Cambridge. His success not only inspired a rival outpost at Lancaster on the Nashua River, but finally led Willard to move nearer the Merrimac and found Chelmsford in 1655. There he did a profitable business for the next twelve years, buying out the Lancaster post, exploring much of lower New Hampshire, and amassing a fortune in the process. This same role in the Connecticut Valley was played by William Pynchon and his son, John, who dominated trade there after his father's retirement in 1652. Their agents established trucking houses at Northampton in 1654 and

Hadley in 1665, as well as exploring the northern country where Deerfield and Northfield were soon to be founded.

The rapid expansion of the fur trading frontier brought New England traders into conflict with two other colonizing powers, Holland and Sweden. The commercial war that followed was fought on two fronts—the Hudson and Delaware river valleys—and ended only with the expulsion of those troublesome rivals from the American continent.

A three-cornered struggle for the Delaware Valley trade touched off the rivalry. First in the field was the Dutch West India Company which in 1623 sent a small force from New Amsterdam to build Ft. Nassau at the mouth of the river where furs from the interior could be intercepted. The Dutch monopolized this rich area until 1638 when Sweden, tempted by tales of the region's wealth, chartered a trading organization known as the South Company to build a palisaded post—Ft. Christina—on the lower Delaware. For a time this settlement languished but in 1643 Johan Printz became its governor and threw himself into his task with an energy which belied his four hundred pounds. Farmers were brought out, the fort strengthened, and a new post—Ft. Gothenburg—founded on the Delaware just above Ft. Nassau to command the trade of the upper river. To make matters even worse for the Dutch, the English chose this same time to invade their country. A group of New Haven merchants, organized as the Delaware Company and led by George Lamberton, sailed boldly into the river and built their post at the site of Philadelphia, above those of both rivals. This was too much. A hastily organized Dutch force swept down on the English fort in 1643, trounced its defenders, and carried them in triumph to New Amsterdam. Nor did a second New England attempt to invade the region a year later succeed. When a ship financed by Boston capitalists entered the river it was fired on from Ft. Christina and turned back at Ft. Nassau—only escaping after agreeing to compensate the thrifty Governor Printz for the cost of the shot.

The Swedes remained to be reckoned with. For a time the two nations sparred by building new posts, each higher up the Delaware or Schuylkill rivers than the last, but by 1651 the Dutch were ready to act. With a fleet of eleven ships and an army of 120 men they appeared suddenly before Ft. Christina to demand its surrender. Governor Printz grumblingly turned over his command to the Dutch who insured their conquest by building Ft. Casimir at the entrance to the Delaware. Three years later a Swedish fleet that surprised Ft. Casimir when its defenders were inopportunely out of powder recaptured the region, but the intruders were driven out by a superior Dutch force in 1655 to end the days of New Sweden in America. On this Delaware River battleground Holland was completely victorious.

The commercial warfare between Dutch and New Englanders for the trade of the Hudson River Valley was more serious. This was the heart of New Netherland. The Dutch West India Company, failing to lure many farmers to its New World possessions, depended for its prosperity on trade with the powerful Iroquois Confederation of the Mohawk Valley. They found the Indians especially eager for guns that would allow them to regain superiority over their traditional Algonquin-Huron enemies who had been armed by the French, and a thriving trade that brought wealth to the Hollanders and power to the natives was soon in progress at the Dutch post of Ft. Orange. Boston and New Haven merchants, covetously watching this business grow, were soon plotting to establish posts in the Hudson Valley.

They tried first in 1646 when a group of New Haven business men established a small trucking house on the Naugatuck River near its junction with the Housatonic and only about sixty miles from Ft. Orange. This threat sent the Dutch governor, bluff old Peter Stuyvesant, storming into Hartford to protest, but the New England authorities remained firm; the Hudson River, they insisted, was theirs rather than Holland's. Although this venture languished, a Boston firm made another attempt to tap the Iroquois trade in 1659 when it sent William Hawthorne and John Pynchon to spy out the ground and secure permission to found a town near Ft. Orange, ostensibly to raise cattle for the Dutch traders. Wily Peter Stuyvesant was not deceived by this stratagem; his refusal forced the new company to cast off all pretence and obtain a Massachusetts charter authorizing a trading post near present Poughkeepsie. Colonial authorities supported the traders' claims so vigorously that war threatened for a time, before excitement attending the restoration of monarchy in England ended this second venture.

These squabbles over trade led directly to the annexation of New Netherland. Charles II, anxious to reward the commercial classes which had aided his restoration, in 1664 ordered the seizure of the Dutch possessions in America. New Netherland became New York, a proprietary province under the control of the Duke of York, who granted its southern portion to other court favorites as the colony of New Jersey. Clashing trading frontiers had helped to add another possession to the growing British empire.

The westward march of the traders paved the way for a rapid expansion of the agricultural frontier between the Pequot War and King Philip's War. As this movement went on, certain differences distinguishing the New England advance from that of the southern colonies became clear. In the South the wilderness was pushed back by individuals who sought out the best lands, purchased them with headrights or from speculators, cleared their own fields, and turned as rapidly as possible to the production of staples. In the Puritan colonies the people moved west in groups, judged their land by its adjacence to settled areas rather than fertility, secured their titles from the General Court without cost, subdued the forest by co-operative effort, and devoted themselves to diversified agriculture. The explanation for these radically different frontier techniques—developing simultaneously among settlers with approximately the same English background—can be found in the New England land system. This, in turn, was based on the section's peculiar geographic features and the religious concepts of the settlers.

To the Puritan fathers who shaped the method of land disposal, profits were less important than the erection of a commonwealth peopled by men of unquestioned faith who would rigorously obey God's ordinances. This belief led them to abandon the system of headrights and individual grants authorized in the colonial charters and vest in the legislature of each colony sole control over the "sitting down of men," with the understanding that the public domain be divided among the orthodox in any way that would advance the true religion. This could best be done by gifts of plantations or town sites to believers. Hence the New England legislatures made two types of grants: to individuals and to groups. The former were relatively unimportant, although magistrates and governors who controlled land disposal showed some tendency to allot themselves sizeable plots. Thus of 130,000 acres given individuals by the Massachusetts General Court between 1630 and 1675 about half went to favored officials and the remainder to ministers, military veterans, and schoolmasters. Far more important were grants to groups of men willing to plant a new town on the frontier.

The procedure for allotting town sites was simple. Several families wishing to move west would together petition the General Court for a "Plantation Right" authorizing settlement. The legislature, after deciding that the petitioners were of proper economic and religious orthodoxy, and that the proposed site was fertile, easily defended, and sufficiently near other habitations, named a committee to locate the town and extinguish the Indian title. Usually a plot about six miles square contiguous to other settlements was chosen, but all efforts to run boundaries "in a comely form" through the hilly countryside failed, and the towns were often irregularly shaped with ungranted lands lying between. This having been done, the original petitioners became the proprietors of the new town with sole authority to sell the land, give it away, or will it to their heirs. In return they were expected to divide the plot, build roads and a church, locate a minister, and bring in acceptable newcomers within a two or three year period.

The proprietors' first step was to select a committee to lay out the town. Near the center they set aside a plot for the village green, with a church, parish house, and usually a school nearby. Often they offered other lots to grist mill operators, blacksmiths, and even, in at least one case, a midwife "to answer the town's necessity, which at present is great." About the green they laid out house lots to be divided among the proprietors, varying in size from half an acre to ten acres but always large enough for a home, barns, a garden, and an orchard. These were assigned the settlers by lot, which was believed a just way of determining "the judgement of God." The marshy lands along the river or sea were then apportioned in the same way

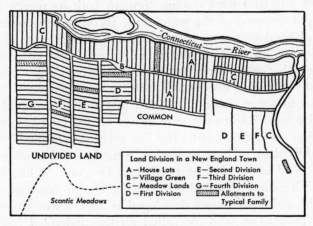

A Typical New England Town: Enfield,
Connecticut

for use as pasturage or as a source for hay. Finally a large upland field of several hundred acres was divided into rectangular strips which were again distributed among the proprietors according to the laws of chance, although those drawing particularly undesirable plots could "pitch" their land elsewhere. As soon as this field was cleared and under cultivation a second was laid out and similarly apportioned. After several of these divisions an inhabitant would own a number of strips scattered through the town fields as well as a home and meadow lot. The "undivided land" remaining belonged solely to the proprietors, who also controlled a "common field" that was usually used for pasture.

In all divisions of land the settlers were given not equal amounts but a share proportionate to their wealth. Thus when a new field was divided, a man worth £50 might be given one strip, another worth £100 two strips, and a third worth £200 four strips, although most towns decreed that the richest proprietor should own no more than from four to ten times as much as the poorest. This inequality was defended by the Puritans on two grounds; the wealthy, they said, contributed more to the cost of planting the town, and they had demonstrated their ability to use the land wisely by the mere fact of becoming rich. Actually these excuses only rationalized the artistocratic prejudices of the New England leaders who instinctively distrusted the leveling effects of an equal land division. Some feared, too, that liberal grants to the poor would lead, as John Winthrop put it, to "the neglect of trades" as mechanics and workers were drawn west by the magnet of free lands. Through the history of the frontier eastern employers opposed a liberal land policy on this ground.

The New England land system, through both its merits and defects, led to a rapid dispersal of the population. Its advantages were obvious: it induced a planned migration that spared the settlers most of the discomforts of pioneer life and assured them spiritual and economic security. Less apparent, but more important, were the system's deficiencies, for these sent a steady stream of disgruntled farmers westward.

Their dissatisfaction rested on the fact that a small group of proprietors or their heirs in each town not only owned all the land but exercised sole authority over its disposal until the last division was made. At first this caused no difficulty; so long as settlers were few and lands plentiful the proprietors lived up to their implied trust by granting lots freely to all families of adequate means and orthodox beliefs. As newcomers increased, however, three distinct classes developed in each town: the small group of original proprietors who controlled all the undivided land, the later arrivals, or "freemen," who owned the fields that had been granted them and enjoyed full political rights but had no voice in the disposal of the lands not yet divided, and the laborers, or "cottagers," who built their huts on unwanted land "onely at the towne's courtesie" and had no vote in the town meeting. Trouble began as soon as the freemen and cottagers outnumbered the proprietors and demanded a further division of the town's lands in which they would share.

The proprietors could meet these protests either by admitting the freemen to their closed corporation or by dividing the land more equitably among them. This they were reluctant to do, for as lands grew scarce in the older towns they felt a normal desire to retain their excessive holdings against the day when sale at high prices would be possible. This speculative spirit existed only in embryo form in seventeenth-century New England, but it was sufficiently strong to array the proprietors against the freemen as soon as the latter demanded a share of the undivided lands. Wherever this occurred a bitter conflict developed. Sometimes this was settled by a compromise that gave the freemen small concessions; sometimes by arbitors

called in from neighboring towns to decide how much territory the proprietors should relinquish. More often the struggle ended before the law
courts which inevitably ruled against the freemen. The proprietors then
usually formed separate corporations to control the undivided lands without
interference from the town meetings, a step that was legalized by the
colonial legislatures in the late seventeenth century.

These controversies, culminating in proprietory victory in each case, were
an important factor in propelling freemen and cottagers toward the frontier.
Probably few of the disgruntled individuals whose dreams of expanding
acres and greater prosperity were shattered by adverse court decisions became proprietors themselves; the aristocratic General Court hesitated to
assign the task of laying out new towns to men of such small property. Instead most of them moved as individuals to frontier communities where
proprietors had not yet caught the speculative fever and would be more
generous in their allotments.

The distinctive form of settlement induced by this land system—one of
advancing tiers of adjacent towns—was ideally suited to both the religious
ideas of the Puritans and the geographic conditions of New England. Isolated settlements by individuals were frowned upon by all-powerful ministers whose sole concern was to assure each pioneer proper church facilities
"for safety, Christian communion, schools, civility and other good ends."
Moreover many of the new towns were laid out by groups from older
towns who, having differed with their neighbors on matters of religious
opinion, moved west in a body to found a settlement where they could
enforce their own doctrines. Even these strong religious forces working
toward compact settlements might have broken down if New Englanders
were able to produce a staple, for then the temptation to leap ahead to
rich soil areas would have been irresistible. Instead the short growing
season, the hilly countryside, the sandy soil strewn with rocky glacial debris,
and the absence of navigable rivers condemned them to a self-sustaining
type of agriculture that emphasized cereal production and grazing. With
neither a staple nor a market, 85 per cent of the farmers were content to
care for themselves and grow the small surplus needed by the 15 per cent
engaged in nonagricultural pursuits.

The New Englanders, moving westward in groups, were forced to develop different frontier techniques than those employed by the Virginians.
They soon learned to girdle trees and plant their first corn crop among
standing dead timber as did the southerners, but here the similarity ended.
The land was always cleared by joint enterprise with the town authorities
deciding which trees should be removed and which preserved, for community spirit overbalanced the natural frontier tendency to squander

natural resources. As soon as the fields were laid out each farmer planted his strips to the crops best suited to the soil—usually corn, barley, or rye, although wheat was widely grown in such favored areas as the Connecticut Valley. New Englanders soon found that much time was wasted in going between their scattered plots and began to concentrate their holding by exchanging lots, despite official warnings against this "buying and purchasing Home Lotts and laying them together;" by the end of the seventeenth century most of them owned large fenced fields. They supplemented their income with cattle, which were as important as corn in the primitive life of the section. In every town large herds of tough, big-boned beasts pastured on the undivided land or the common, each marked with a brand that his owner registered with the authorities.

Few New England farmers grew wealthy, but they lived well. Their homes, clustered about the village green, were sturdy frame dwellings, with outbuildings and barns attached to make chores easier during the long winters. Each morning they left their houses to labor in their fields, using crude wooden hoes and mattocks fashioned by their own hands, or a clumsy plow pulled by four oxen. Each night they returned, to sit before the broad stone fireplace on fall or winter evenings and build the many necessities that their slender resources did not allow them to buy from England. Everything from plows to furniture was constructed at home; a task in which the wives joined with their spinning wheels, candle moulds, and churns. Yet this marginal existence had its compensations. Near at hand were neighbors for pleasant companionship, the church to assure salvation, and a school to dose the young with liberal potions of piety and knowledge. Such conservative easterners as Cotton Mather might bemoan the tendency of people to "*Go Out* from the Institutions of God, Swarming into New Settlements, where they and their Untaught Families are like to *Perish for Lack of Vision*," but the New England frontiersman enjoyed far more comfort than the isolated pioneer in the southern colonies.

The attractiveness of frontier life, the dispersing effects of the land system, and the constant religious disputes natural among a pious people, sent the New Englanders pouring westward between 1640 and 1675. In Maine and New Hampshire settlements still clung to the coastal lowlands where the many trading posts were converted into farming communities, but in Massachusetts, Rhode Island, and Connecticut the conquest of the interior proceeded rapidly. From Boston and Plymouth settlers pushed outward along the river bottoms to found Lancaster, Marlboro, Grafton, Mendon, and a host of other towns during the 1650's, while another advancing stream from Rhode Island moved up the Blackstone Valley to Woonsocket and Seekonk. West of this line the forest stretched unbroken—except for the tiny outpost at Brookfield where six or seven adventurous families built their homes in 1667—as far as the former Pequot country about the Thames River. Here New London, founded in 1646 by John Winthrop, Jr., served as a center for a steady expansion that scattered several towns along the upper Thames. Another arm of settlement extended northward along the Connecticut, filling in the lower reaches of that rich valley, pushing west along the Farmington River as far as Simsbury, and moving steadily north to plant Hatfield, Deerfield, Greenfield, and Northfield. In the New Haven country pioneers not only laid out new coastal towns between Guilford and Greenwich but during the 1660's advanced up the river valleys to establish Killingworth, Wallingford, Waterbury, and Woodbury. Some 50,000 men, women, and children lived in the settled regions guarded by this northern frontier in 1675, while other New Englanders had left their native soil to establish towns on the eastern tip of Long Island and in New Jersey.

The fruits of this rapid expansion were harvested between 1675 and 1677 when King Philip's war, one of the most devastating conflicts in the history of the frontier, ravaged the New England back country. To the Indians, hostilities appeared not only justified but necessary. Advancing tiers of towns were pressing upon their tribal lands, catching in a crushing vise the Wampanoags who occupied the territory east of Narragansett Bay, the Narragansetts and Nipmucks who were caught between the coastal and valley settlements, and the Mohegans, Podunks, and River Tribes of the Connecticut Valley. They must either fight to retain the large areas needed for their primitive economy or become vassals of the white men. The fate of Indians who had already submitted to English rule made this choice easy. Some had been pushed onto six Massachusetts reservations where they were compelled to obey Puritan laws that forbad them to hunt on the Sabbath, denied them firearms and firewater, ended their accustomed freedom, and condemned them to servile dependency. Others who lived near the settlements were mercilessly abused. Thus one Connecticut law forced any drunken Indian to work six days for the colony and six for the informer; any unscrupulous colonist could secure free labor by giving a brave a few drinks of rum. Still others who succumbed to the lures of well-meaning missionaries were gathered in villages of "Praying Indians." The restricted lives of these Christian warriors did not appeal to free-living red men who treasured their independence and ancient customs above all else. Even war against the whites was preferable to such a fate.

Their smouldering discontent was fanned to open rebellion in 1671 when the English attempted to disarm the Wampanoags. King Philip, the sachem of the tribe, knowing that his people would starve without their hunting

guns, resisted strenuously, but the Plymouth and Boston authorities remained firm. A humiliating treaty which warned Philip that "if he went
on in his refractory way he must expect to smart for it," left him so angry
that he spent the next three years trying to arrange alliances with the
Narragansetts and Nipmucks against the colonists. In this he failed, but the
young warriors of his tribe sensed their chief's resentment and decided to
act. Raiding parties fell on the Plymouth frontier in the spring of 1675; by
July the whole back country was aflame. Five hundred soldiers from
Plymouth and Boston were hurriedly gathered, and after a march through
the Mount Hope country, they drove Philip and his followers into Pocassett
Swamp.

English strategy at this point was obvious. They should have penned in
the few rebellious Indians by surrounding the swamp, while agents convinced the other New England tribes to remain neutral. These steps would
have nipped a minor insurrection in the bud. Instead the colonists committed two grievous errors. One was to leave the rear of the swamp unguarded; the other was to send the entire Massachusetts army into the
Narragansett country to overawe that powerful tribe. If the authorities had
consciously tried to prolong the war they could have taken no more effective steps than these, for Philip's forces promptly swam the Taunton River
and slipped northward to join the Nipmucks, while the Narragansetts took
to the warpath to protest the invasion of their tribal lands.

The Massachusetts officials responsible for this blunder probably wanted
to carry the war into the Narragansett country. Hatred of Rhode Island
and the ambitions of land speculators were responsible. Roger Williams'
colony had long been a sore spot in Puritan New England; the freedom
of conscience allowed dissenters, the tolerance extended to all creeds, and
the humanitarianism shown in dealings with the Indians constantly rankled
the stern Bostonians. They knew that war on the Narragansetts would hurt
the many Rhode Islanders who traded with that tribe. Extermination of the
Narragansetts would also benefit Massachusetts land speculators who found
Rhode Island a profitable field for exploitation. Their activities in the
Narragansett country had long annoyed colonial officials; now they seized
on the outbreak of warfare as a golden opportunity to settle their claims for
all time.

Massachusetts land jobbers began to operate in Rhode Island during
the late 1650's when two groups of merchants organized as the Petti-
quamscutt Company and the Misquamicutt Company illegally purchased
blocks of land from the Indians, but not until 1659 when the Atherton
Company was formed did their speculations arouse Williams' followers.
This corporation, which included in its ranks most of the leading capitalists

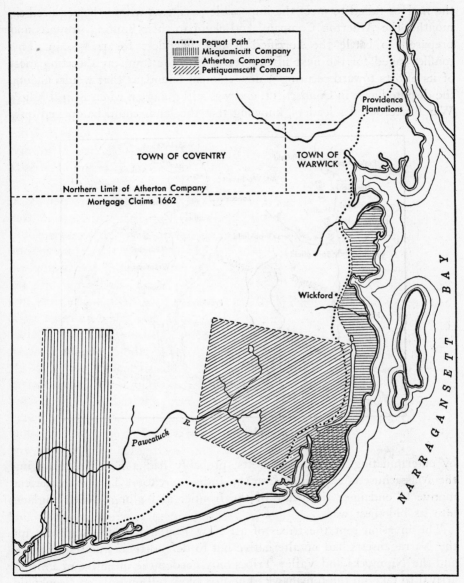

Land Speculation in the Narragansett Country

of Boston, Taunton, and Portsmouth as well as Governor John Winthrop, Jr., of Connecticut, began operating modestly by buying two tracts of Indian territory lying south of Warwick. A year later it extended its claims over the entire Narragansett country by assuming a heavy fine levied against the tribe, securing in return a mortgage on all their lands. When the natives failed to meet the impossible payments within the required six months, the Atherton Company laid claim to their hunting grounds and prepared to battle the horrified Rhode Islanders for possession. This conflict raged for the next fifteen years, with the company directing most of its efforts toward securing a new colonial boundary that would include the disputed area in Connecticut, and was still going on when King Philip's War broke out. Its leaders, knowing that the lands could be opened only

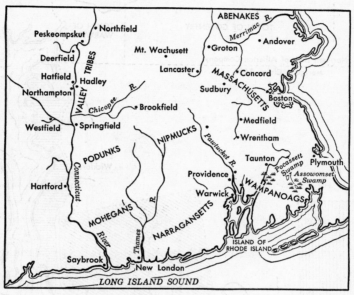

King Philip's War, 1675-1676

by exterminating the Narragansetts, probably had a hand in arranging the Massachusetts expedition into the Indian territory. This was sufficient motive to endanger the peace of the frontier and plunge New England into its bloodiest war.

The invasion sent the tribes of all New England on the warpath, for the Narragansetts had no alternative but to defend their hunting grounds and the Nipmucks and Valley Tribes only needed the incentive of Philip's arrival to take up the tomahawk. The first blow fell on isolated Brookfield whose few families watched the destruction of their homes from a strong garrison house, then scurried to the safety of fortified Hadley. There too the Indians threatened until an English force from the valley towns fell on them at Hopewell Swamp in August, 1675, administering a sound defeat. These early successes lulled the overconfident English into a sense of false security that was shattered only when another raiding party burned Deer-

field and swept northward to lay siege to the stockaded outpost of Northfield. A relief expedition from Hadley drove off the savages, but the
Massachusetts authorities, deciding the town was too dangerous to defend,
sent sixty men with wagons to bring in the crops from all the northern
Connecticut Valley. On their return they were ambushed a few miles south
of Deerfied while fording a small stream since known as Bloody Brook.
Only two white men escaped, and crops needed to feed the troops in the
lower valley were destroyed. Flushed with success, the Indians fell on
Northampton, Hadley, Hatfield, and even Springfield so long as the fall
foliage clung to the trees to give them ambush.

With the coming of winter the center of fighting shifted to the Narragansett country where that tribe, after a few forays against isolated settlements, had retreated to several islands in the great coastal swamps. There
they were found by an army of a thousand men sent south from Massachusetts. Marching over the frozen ground, the troops surprised the principal
Indian village on December 19, 1675, slaughtering some three hundred
women and children with merciless thoroughness. Most of the braves
escaped but for the next month the English tramped through the tribe's
lands on a famous "hungry march," burning towns, destroying crops, and
putting captives to death with such heartless cruelty that their purpose
seemed one of extermination. By the end of January most of the women,
children, and old men of the Narragansetts were killed while the warriors
had fled northward to join the Nipmucks. The Atherton Company lands
were freed of Indians.

The maneuver, however, created new difficulties on the northern frontier.
The Nipmucks' slender food supplies were soon exhausted by the new
arrivals, forcing the Indians to plunder towns or face starvation. All
through the winter of 1675-76 these raids went on, as the savages fell upon
Lancaster, Concord, Groton, and Medfield in turn. Their victory at Lancaster was most complete; they not only destroyed the town but captured
one of the garrisoned houses, killing the men and carrying the women into
captivity.

With the coming of spring Philip and his followers continued to attack
the eastern settlements, hoping to lure troops from the upper Connecticut
Valley so that squaws could grow food there. Using Mt. Wachusett as
their headquarters, they struck along the entire frontier with such devastating thoroughness that the skies from Warwick to Groton were lighted
with the flames of burning dwellings. Town after town was deserted before
this steady onslaught, until the line of settlement was driven back to Sud-
bury, Wrentham, and Providence. Even the seaboard cities trembled before
the savages as citizens fled Providence for the safety of the island of Rhode

Island, and Cambridge and Boston hurriedly threw up fortifications against the impending attack. For a time in that dread spring of 1676 victory seemed within the grasp of the red men, but the turning point was near. In April reluctant Massachusetts authorities finally consented to employ "Praying Indians" as scouts to protect their troops from the ambushes that had taken such a heavy toll in the past. For the first time the English armies were able to win some engagements. The most important success was enjoyed by a small force that marched north from Hadley in May, 1676, to take the Indian village of Peskeompskut by surprise, slaughter a large number of men, women, and children, and destroy vast quantities of crops.

Indian resistance suddenly collapsed after the Battle of Peskeompskut, much to the surprise of the English who did not know that they had accidentally hit on the one vulnerable spot in the red men's armor when they ravaged the grain fields of the upper valley. Realizing that starvation almost certainly faced them in the coming winter, the savages abruptly lost heart. A combined force of Connecticut troops and friendly Mohegan Indians that swept northward in June found resistance at an end and drove the weary enemy into the wilds of New Hampshire. Philip knew the day of reckoning was at hand. With a few faithful followers he fled back to his old hunting ground east of the Taunton River. There the English forces began the task of "exterminating the rabid animals, which, by a most unaccountable condition from heaven, had now neither strength or sense left them to do anything for their own defense." Philip managed to escape into Assowomset Swamp, but one of his followers betrayed him to the colonial troops, and on the night of August 12, 1676, he was captured and shot. Neither a great fighter nor a particularly gifted leader, Philip had little to do with the war to which he gave his name and his life. Yet to the thousands of New Englanders who had trembled before the tomahawk he was a symbol of all the cruelty of Indian warfare; for the next quarter century the sight of his mummied head perched on a pole in Plymouth gave them cheerful assurance that savage resistance was crushed.

There was good reason for their relief. King Philip's War was one of the bloodiest in the history of the frontier. More than six hundred men—one-sixth of the male population of New England—were killed, £90,000 expended, and twenty-five towns destroyed. In Maine where fighting went on until 1678, only six villages managed to withstand attack. Little wonder that the colonial authorities treated the remaining Indians with a cold brutality that belied their Christian principles. Those suspected of taking part in the war were slaughtered or sold into slavery, while the remainder were herded onto reservations or bound out to work for white men. In every colony their lands were awarded the soldiers as bounties. The Indian power was broken, assuring the English peace until they pushed into new frontiers.

For the remaining years of the seventeenth century the expansion of New England went on without serious difficulty, until by 1700 the lowland areas were filled. Fringing the settlements now to ward off savage blows was a ring of frontier towns, protected by palisades or garrisoned houses, each inhabited by thirty or forty families who were willing to risk their lives for the generous land grants offered settlers at these outposts. Massachusetts initiated this system in 1695 when the legislature designated eleven towns—York, Wells, Kittery, Amesbury, Haverhill, Dunstable, Chelmsford, Groton, Lancaster, Marlboro, and Deerfield—as frontier posts, and Connecticut completed the protective circle in 1704 when Symsbury, Waterbury, Danbury, Colchester, Windham, Mansfield, and Plainfield were added. Behind this living screen the older settlements grew rapidly. The New Englanders, like the Tidewater planters, were thoroughly adjusted to the strange environment of the New World and ready to begin that march upward into the western hills that only ended when they spread over the interior of the continent.

CHAPTER V

# The Old West

## 1700-1763

By the closing years of the seventeenth century the choicest lands of the coastal plains and tidal valleys were cleared and pioneers were ready to swarm over the physiographic province known as the Old West. Here, in the New England highlands, the broad river bottoms of New York and Pennsylvania, and the rugged uplands of the southern Piedmont, they created during the first half of the eighteenth century a new society with distinctive frontier institutions and social attitudes that retained few remnants of the Old World heritage.

Peculiar geographic features gave the Old West a unity which transcended artificial colonial boundary lines. In the south the province was separated from the Tidewater by the "Fall Line," where tumbling cataracts two hundred feet high ended navigation on the coastal rivers, and, south of the Roanoke, by a thirty-mile strip of forbidding pine barrens that towered six or seven hundred feet above the level countryside. Beyond these barriers the Piedmont sloped gradually upward toward the Appalachian Mountains. A land of rolling hills and swift-flowing streams, of abundant rainfall and temperate climate, of rich, red, residual soils, its forest-covered slopes offered tempting farm sites for land-hungry easterners. Along its western edge stretched the steep walls of the Blue Ridge Mountains, cut at intervals by flaring water gaps where the Delaware, Susquehanna, Potomac, and James rivers tumbled downward toward the sea. Pioneers passing through these emerged on the Great Valley of the Appalachians, a broad floor dotted with hills and interlaced with level plains where the limestone soil was deep and good. Seventy-five miles beyond rose the jagged peaks of the Allegheny Front, a jumbled mass of mountains three or four thousand feet high where passes were few and crossing difficult.

The Great Valley of the Appalachians linked the southern and northern portions of the Old West, for it extended across Pennsylvania and New York as far as Lake Champlain. The river bottoms of this region attracted settlers early in the eighteenth century—a restless stream that filled the valleys of the Delaware, Susquehanna, Hudson, Mohawk, and upper Connecticut and Merrimac before spilling over into the highlands and plateaus on either side. Here, as in the South, their westward march was checked

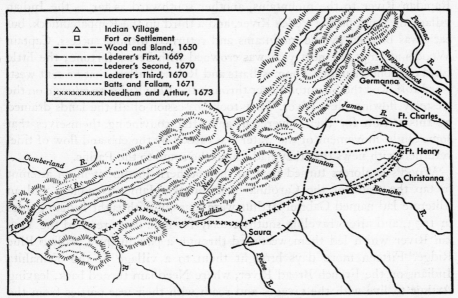

The Exploration of the Piedmont

by forbidding mountain ranges that stretched along the back country from the White Mountains of New Hampshire to the point where the Appalachian Ridges of Pennsylvania blended into the Allegheny Front. This barrier, the unifying influence of the Great Valley, and the impossibility of direct communication between the interior uplands and the seaboard bound the pioneers who settled the Old West together, whether they built their cabins along the sparkling Juniata or staked their "tomahawk claims" on the upper reaches of the Yadkin.

The southern Piedmont was settled first. The exploration of this hilly region was begun in mid-seventeenth century by the commanders of Virginia's "Fall Line" forts who were naturally interested in the trading or mineral wealth concealed in the unknown West. Captain Abraham Wood, who ruled over Ft. Henry at the falls of the Appomattox, led the way in 1650 when he and a companion, Edward Bland, made a five-day journey to the forks of the Roanoke in search of choice spots for a land-jobbing scheme they had in mind. They were highly pleased with the rolling countryside, but settlement was not ready to follow, and not until the late 1660's was exploration resumed by both Captain Wood and Governor Berkeley. Passes through the Blue Ridge to allow trade with the western Indians were now the objective. Berkeley sent out three expeditions under a German physician, John Lederer, in 1669 and 1670, one across the Rapidan River to the mountains, another southward as far as the Indian village of Saura on the Pedee River, and a third up the Rappahannock, but each was blocked by the mountains and returned without success. Captain Wood's attempt the next year was crowned with better fortune; the little band of pioneers under Thomas Batts and Robert Fallam that he sent westward followed the Staunton River through the Blue Ridge to emerge on the westerly flowing New River. They took possession of all the lands drained by this stream for their sovereign, and after convincing themselves that some slight movement of the water was caused by the ebb and flow of tide, returned with news that they had found the route to the Pacific.

Wood's explorers turned next to the southern Piedmont in an attempt to tap the trade of the Carolina back country. James Needham and an illiterate lad named Gabriel Arthur were sent out with eight Indian guides in 1673, and after traveling southwesterly for nine days, reached the Yadkin River which led them westward through a pass in the Carolina Blue Ridge. Fifteen more days brought them to a village of the Tamahita Indians on the French Broad River, where Needham turned back, leaving Arthur to live with the savages and roam with their war parties from the Ohio to the Floridas before returning safely to Ft. Henry in June, 1674.

Bacon's Rebellion ended further official exploration, but by this time the fur traders were ready to take over the task. From each of the Fall Line forts their hundred-horse pack trains, with harness bells tinkling a merry song, moved farther and farther into the wilderness. Some followed the trail blazed by Batts and Fallam along the New and Kanawha rivers until by the 1690's they were trading on the banks of the Ohio. Others who made the fort on the Rappahannock their headquarters crossed the Blue Ridge in the 1680's to drain peltry from the Shenandoah Valley. Still others made their way along Needham's route—known to woodsmen as the Occaneechi Path—to the Carolina Piedmont or the interlacing waters of the Savannah and Tennessee river systems where the Cherokee eagerly awaited them. The more adventurous pressed even farther south to round the tip of the mountain system and compete with the Carolina traders for the business of the Creek and Chickasaw Indians. Wherever they went they spied out the choice lands and broke down the self-sufficiency of the natives. The way was prepared for the first settlers.

The westward push of Virginia farmers began soon after Bacon's Rebellion and was in full swing by 1710. In the van as usual were the cattle ranchers who grazed their herds on the open meadows and canebrakes or built enclosed "cow-pens" surrounded by rude cabins and half-cleared fields where they grew corn for themselves and their animals. Each of these rude clearings became the nucleus for a small settlement as homeseekers from the Tidewater moved west. Some of these newcomers came directly from England, but more were from the East where large importations of Negro slaves at the turn of the century stimulated the rapid development of plantation agriculture. The expansion of these great estates crowded out thousands of small farmers who turned west to begin life anew. This whole process was stimulated between 1710 and 1722 by Governor Alexander Spotswood, who herded the Piedmont Indians onto a reservation at Christanna, founded a settlement of indentured German servants at Germanna on the Rapidan to protect the northern frontier from attack, and in 1716 led an elaborate exploring party through the James River watergap into the Shenandoah Valley where these Knights of the Golden Horseshoe, as they styled themselves, toasted each new discovery with the rum and wines provided for the occasion.

Governor Spotswood's solicitous interest in the West was not unselfish for he, with other governmental officials and influential easterners, had succumbed to the speculative fever which raged through the colonies during the eighteenth century. This was a day of bold enterprise on both sides of the Atlantic—of reckless commercial ventures, of sudden wealth, of the fantastic South Sea Bubble—when business leaders scrambled to pyramid fortunes amidst the limitless possibilities of an expanding empire. In America this spirit was expressed by a mad rush to engross the best lands against the day when they could be resold to settlers at fabulous profits. The speculator was suddenly catapulted into a position of importance; from New England to the Carolinas his agents were at work, hunting out choice spots, bribing legislatures and officials into favorable terms of sale, and reshaping the whole course of the westward movement by their shady dealings.

Governor Spotswood could no more remain aloof than any other wealthy man. He first tried to check speculative buying as his royal instructions ordered, then gave up the struggle and not only built up large estates for himself and his Tidewater friends but shaped Virginia's laws to increase the value of his holdings. Typical of his efforts was an act of 1720 which divided the Piedmont into the two counties of Brunswick and Spotsylvania, bound the colony to care for all their religious and educational needs, and exempted landholders there from taxes or quitrents for ten years. When the crown refused to approve this outrageous measure until land grants in the new counties were limited to a thousand acres, Spotswood and his fellow planters were not discouraged. They used dummy grantees for a time, then the law was simply ignored by speculators who secured grants of from ten to forty thousand acres from the governor by the simple expedient of winning his friendship and promising future payment.

In the Carolinas, where royal officials vainly tried to stop the assembly from making large speculative grants to Tidewater planters, the situation was even worse. The legislators were so determined to award themselves and their friends western estates that they sliced away most of the governor's salary to show their displeasure, then defied a royal agent who appeared in 1739 with orders to limit the size of holdings. This official not only recognized the force of public opinion by giving up the struggle, but stayed on to build up grants of a million acres for himself.

By the middle of the eighteenth century the entire Virginia and Carolina Piedmont was in private hands, and speculators were beginning to accumulate estates in the Great Valley. Most of the grants, which ranged from ten to forty thousand acres, were held by Tidewater planters, but two were awarded court favorites by the Restoration monarchs. One, controlled by Lord Fairfax, comprised the whole "Northern Neck" of Virginia between the Rappahannock and Potomac rivers including much of the Shenandoah Valley; the other was owned by the Earl of Granville and covered most of northern North Carolina. On both of these giant estates minor agents assigned lands, collected rents, and engaged in fraudulent practices that kept the tenant farmers in a turmoil of discontent.

The engrossment of western lands by speculators both encouraged and discouraged the movement to the frontier. Some owners tried to lure settlers to their holdings by making elementary improvements, bringing out immigrants from Europe, maintaining agents in eastern ports to steer new arrivals toward the Piedmont, and circulating promotional literature which described the West as "the best, richest, and most healthy part of our Country." More, however, simply held their lands while they waited for the price rise that would make them rich. Some refused to sell at all but insisted on renting, others encouraged settlement and then demanded an exorbitant fee for the improved land. Worst of all was the fact that hastily drawn boundaries between the grants were usually so inaccurate that a farmer who purchased from one speculator was often forced to repurchase at a higher price from another after ownership was finally settled. The total effect of speculation was to hinder, rather than hurry, the westward advance.

Yet settlements spread westward, moving up the river valleys of the Virginia and North Carolina Piedmont, then out over the highlands to form a compact agricultural frontier. In South Carolina, the advance was less rapid, for Indian troubles, the forbidding barrier of pine barrens, and the slow development of that colony combined to keep the frontier east of the Piedmont until after 1730. Not until another column of pioneers moved down the Great Valley from the Middle Colonies, pushed through the mountain gaps, and overflowed the Carolina back country from the west did the southern Piedmont receive its first sizable migration.

This stream of homeseekers was deflected southward from New York and Pennsylvania by conditions within those colonies which discouraged frontier settlements there. In New York the activities of fur traders and land speculators were responsible. Powerful trading interests, centered at Albany where they bartered with the Iroquois for peltry, blocked the only path that settlers could follow toward the interior: up the Hudson between the towering peaks of the Catskills and Berkshires and westward along the level Mohawk Valley. This gateway the traders guarded jealously, knowing that any advance of the farming frontier would drive away the Indian middlemen who supplied them with furs. Schenectady was settled in 1661 with their reluctant permission only after the fourteen families who founded that town agreed not to engage in trade. From that time on they resisted every invasion of their domain.

The expanding population east of Albany which might have brushed the traders aside failed to develop until late in the eighteenth century because of deficiencies in New York's land system. The colony's laws provided that to obtain a grant a colonial favorite had only to obtain authorization from the governor, purchase the plot he desired from the Indians, finance a survey, and then secure the final patent from the governor and his council. Every step in this process invited fraud. Influential colonists found that they could trade their political support for vast estates, or that greedy officials were willing to make large grants in return for a share of the proceeds. Moreover the taxes and quitrents were low; the legislature hesitated to relinquish its control over the purse strings by allowing royal governors to supplement their incomes by revenues from land, and ordinarily demanded only a raccoon skin, a bushel of wheat, or a few shillings a year from the largest holders.

The first large grant was made in 1684 and others followed rapidly, particularly between 1702 and 1708 when an avaricious governor, Lord Cornbury, rewarded his favorites with a free hand. By 1710, as a result, the entire Hudson River Valley was in the hands of speculators, whose holdings varied from the millions of acres of the giant Kayaderosseras and Hardenbergh patents to the smaller but still sizeable estates of the Cort-

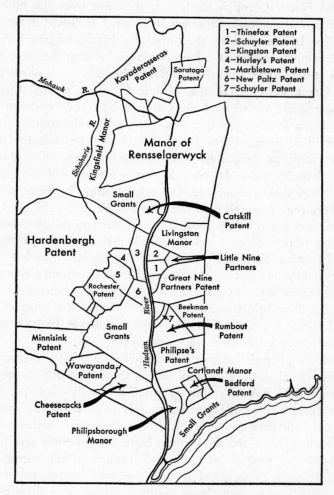

1—Thinefox Patent
2—Schuyler Patent
3—Kingston Patent
4—Hurley's Patent
5—Marbletown Patent
6—New Paltz Patent
7—Schuyler Patent

Land Grants in the Hudson River Valley

landt and Philipsborough manors. Few of these landlords were willing to sell; instead they tried to rent to tenant farmers as a means of holding their possessions until prices rose. Pioneers were unwilling to live in New York under these conditions when neighboring colonies offered full ownership at fairly low prices. Little wonder that most of the estates had only a few families scattered over their thousands of acres, or that virgin forest blanketed nearly all of this fertile valley at a time when other coastal river beds were under cultivation.

This state of affairs alarmed royal officials, and their concern started a new immigrant stream toward the Old West—the Palatine Germans. These sturdy aliens came from the Rhinish Palatinate, a fruitful area which was laid bare by marching armies during the Thirty Years' War, by plundering petty princes who wrung from starving serfs the money needed to transform their tiny courts into replicas of fashionable Versailles, and by French invaders who swept over the countryside with the outbreak of the War of the Spanish Succession in 1702. On the ears of suffering Palatines fell tales of America's riches; they read glowing letters sent by fortunate relatives who had reached the land of promise, or listened eagerly to *Neuländers*—men hired by immigration and shipping companies to loaf about villages in gaudy clothes boasting that their fortunes were made in the colonies. The rumor spread, too, that England would transport all Protestants who reached her shores to America.

This agitation bore its first fruit in 1708 when a little group of Palatines led by the Reverend Joshua Kocherthal loaded their scanty possessions on boats and drifted down the Rhine to Holland, where English ships carried them to London. That fall fifty-five of them were sent to New York where land along the Hudson was given them to lay out the town of Newburgh. News of their success drifted back to a Germany caught in a new disaster, for the winter of 1708-9 was one of such unseasonable cold that vines and fruit trees of countless peasants were killed. With spring the mass migration began, gathering momentum steadily until June when Palatines arrived in the Low Countries at the rate of a thousand a week. British agents welcomed them there and sent all Protestants to England; that nation was delighted to build up its colonies without depleting its home population. By the fall of 1709, some 13,500 Germans overflowed London, filling the taverns and public squares where the army erected tents to house them. Their dispersal through the empire began in the spring; some stayed in England, others were sent to Ireland or the Carolinas, but the largest group of 3,000 was dispatched to New York.

Here, officials planned, they would earn their keep by producing naval stores—tar, pitch, and tall masts—needed by the royal navy. Governor Robert Hunter selected a site for the experiment near the estate of a great landholder, Robert Livingston, who was authorized to feed the Germans at government expense. There, in October, 1710, two villages of East Camp and West Camp were laid out, the Palatines established, and the work of producing naval stores begun. The project fared badly from the first, largely because the local farmer hired to supervise production knew nothing about extracting pitch from virgin pine. After two years of blundering, Parliament ended the whole disastrous enterprise in 1712, leaving the Germans free to go where they wished.

Some scattered along the Hudson or over the neighboring colonies, but the largest group turned toward the Schoharie River Valley where, rumor had it, Governor Hunter had intended to plant them in the first place. Sending a few deputies ahead to buy land from the Indians, the Palatines wintered in Albany before pushing on to their new homes in the spring of 1713, dragging their humble belongings on sleds through waist-deep snow. Seven villages were laid out to hold the five hundred settlers who reached there that year. Their poverty was appalling; they borrowed one horse and one cow which were teamed to a crude plow, fashioned essential farm tools from wood and stone, carried their grain on their backs to Albany or Schenectady mills fifty miles away, and subsisted until the first harvest on roots and berries. Yet perseverance triumphed, and by 1714 the little community was firmly established. Their difficulties were not over, however. For the next seven years they fought a losing battle with Albany speculators who owned the land on which they had located; a struggle that only ended in 1721 when the governor offered all Palatines who would move free lands farther along the Mohawk. Some took advantage of this opportunity to establish the towns of Palatine and Stone Arabia, others went on to found Herkimer in 1723, while the remainder either moved to the Tulpechoken district of Pennsylvania or came to terms with the speculators.

The coming of the Germans signaled the end of the Albany traders' monopoly over the Mohawk Valley and opened a new period of feverish activity for land jobbers. Between 1713 and 1738 they scrambled for grants there, then turned their attention to the unexploited country south of the Mohawk. This region, cut off from the older New York settlements by mountains, seemed uninviting so long as land was available along the Hudson, Mohawk, and Schoharie rivers, but in 1740 a pioneering Scotchman, John Lindesay, laid out a village on Cherry Valley Creek and the rush began. Not of settlers—Cherry Valley grew slowly and no other towns were started for many years—but of speculators. Again they besieged the governors; again great manors were erected in this remote wilderness, until most of the best land was absorbed by individuals or small companies. New York, as a result of this overabundance of speculative activity, presented a sorry picture in the 1750's. Its prized river valleys and rolling hills were blanketed with land patents, but of settlers there were few. A scattering of tenant farmers on the great estates along the Hudson, a few

pioneers grouped around Albany and Schenectady, a cluster of settlements
built around Ft. Hunter after that blockhouse was erected in 1712, the
isolated outposts at Cherry Valley, a row of tidy German towns along the
Schoharie and upper Mohawk—those were the only monuments to a
generation of frontier activity. Those and the land warrants locked in the
trunks of a legion of speculators.

Conditions in New York deflected the immigrant tide that flowed from

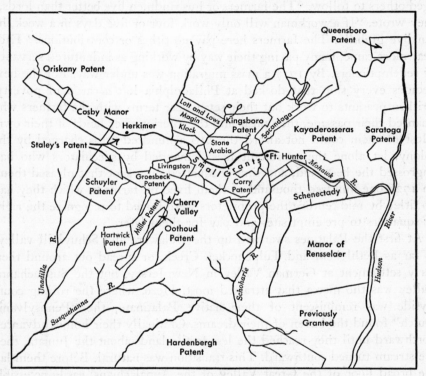

Speculation on the Mohawk Frontier, 1700–1763

Europe during the eighteenth century southward to the beckoning harbors
of Pennsylvania. There the tolerant Quakers who had built their homes
in Philadelphia and along the banks of the Delaware and Schuylkill rivers
made them welcome, knowing that William Penn viewed his colony as a
sanctuary for Europe's oppressed. News of this haven was carried to the
continent by Penn himself, who not only visited Germany to tell persecuted
minorities that land and understanding waited them in America, but used
printer's ink liberally to make Pennsylvania the best known of all the
colonies. While this invitation was spread among European peoples, fur
traders spied out the interior lands where they were soon to settle. Their

trading posts on Conestoga and Pequea creeks served as centers for the exploration of the Susquehanna Valley from the 1690's on, while their tendency to move steadily westward (the post at Shamokin monopolized trade after 1708) lured Indians away from the lower valley. That rich region was ready to receive settlers by 1710.

The tide began to flow that year when some of the Palatines shipped from London found their way to Pennsylvania. Their letters home encouraged others to follow. "The farmers or husbandmen live better than lords," they wrote. "If a workman will only work four or five days in a week, he can live grandly. The farmers here pay no tithes or contributions." Each year more came, many paying their way by working as indentured servants, or redemptioners. By 1717 a mass migration was under way. For the next decades every ship that docked at Philadelphia left a cargo of poverty-stricken peasants to work out their seven-year terms with the farmers who financed their passage, then push into the interior after lands of their own. Most of them could not afford the £10 a hundred acres charged by the colony, let alone the exorbitant fees demanded by speculators who had engrossed the best land, and simply squatted on a spot that pleased them. In 1726 one hundred thousand of them lived on farms to which they had no title; by mid-century the proprietors were forced to recognize the right of squatters to pre-empt sites and pay for them later.

At first the Palatines swarmed up the Delaware and Schuylkill valleys as far as Bethlehem and Tulpehocken Creek, or spread out around their early settlement at German Valley in New Jersey, but the Susquehanna Valley was the mecca that attracted most. Here, where the rolling countryside was reminiscent of their native Palatinate, the "Pennsylvania Dutch" found the haven of their dreams. Gradually their homes advanced northward until they reached the less fertile lands about the Juniata, then the stream turned southward. This transition was natural. Before them lay the broad floor of the Great Valley of the Appalachians, easily accessible in eastern Pennsylvania through gaps in the low South Mountains, where streams were plentiful and the limestone soil fertile. As they moved along this natural highway they found that land prices steadily declined; Pennsylvania charged £15 for each hundred acres after 1738, Maryland only £5, and Virginia speculators in the Shenandoah Valley even less. This was the magnet that drew the Palatines steadily southward.

The movement began in 1726 when German families crossed the South Mountains through Crampton's Gap and followed Monocacy Creek into the Potomac Valley where they built such towns as Monocacy and Frederick. Others went on across the Potomac at Old Packhorse Ford to lay out New Mecklenburg that same year. The first Palatine to make his way into the Great Valley of Virginia was Adam Müller who settled on Hawkswill Creek in 1727; within three years he had the satisfaction of luring half a dozen more German families to his clearing. More prominent was the town of Winchester, laid out in 1731 by a band of eleven families under Justus Hite. This became a center for the German migration that filled the Virginia back country during the next decade; by 1740 their settlements extended as far west as Patterson's Creek and south to the James River, while an overflow was already spilling eastward through the mountain

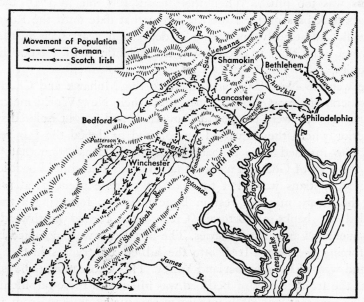

The Settlement of Pennsylvania and the Great Valley
of Virginia

gaps into the Piedmont. When a colony of German Moravians purchased 100,000 acres near the Yadkin River in 1751 the march southward began once more, ending a decade later when the North Carolina Great Valley and Piedmont were comfortably settled. A zone of German farmers fringed the colonies from the Mohawk Valley to the Carolinas.

The Palatines did not have the West long to themselves. Close on their heels came another European migratory stream, this one from northern Ireland. The bulk of these Scotch-Irish were lowland Scots and Englishmen who had been planted there early in the seventeenth century in a vain British effort to tame and convert the wild Irish tribesmen, but they included a liberal sprinkling of Scotch Highlanders and southern Irishmen. Most had learned the rudiments of frontier technique when they cleared their Ulster fields or battled the fierce Irish tribes; all hated England for the harsh laws that drove them to the New World. Parliament passed a series of these acts between 1665 and 1680 forbidding the importation into England of Irish livestock, meat, and grain; then, when Ulsterites built a new economic life based on wool growing, ended that in 1699 by prohibiting the export of woolen goods. While they still staggered under this blow a Penal Act of 1704 excluded Presbyterians from all civil and military offices and forbad their ministers to perform the marriage service. This was too much. When their leases fell due in 1717 and 1718 thousands took passage for America. From that date until the Revolution the tide flowed steadily, increasing in depression years such as 1740 and 1741 when more than 12,000 crossed the Atlantic, until 300,000 lived in the colonies.

Some went to New England, others to the Mohawk and Cherry Valley frontiers, but most made Pennsylvania their New World mecca. Like the Germans they were too poor to buy lands and sought isolated spots in the interior where they squatted unmolested or defied the few rent collectors who invaded their domains with the bold assertion that "it was against the laws of God and nature, that so much land should be idle while so many Christians wanted it to labor on to raise their bread." By the 1730's they were moving west in large numbers, following a trail that paralleled the banks of Octorara Creek, then turned northward along the Susquehanna and its tributaries. The best lands were occupied by Germans, forcing the Scotch-Irish into the hillier country beside the Juniata River and west of the Cumberland Valley. This whole mountainous region as far as the frontier post of Bedford was filled with these turbulent immigrants by mid-century, while others were only restrained from moving on to the lands about the Forks of the Ohio by the Pennsylvania proprietors.

As the lands of interior Pennsylvania filled, the stream turned southward, particularly after 1738 when Virginia and North Carolina promised freedom of worship to Presbyterians. By this time the northern-sloping half of the Great Valley of Virginia was occupied by Germans, forcing the Scotch-Irish to push on southwest of the James River. North Carolina doubled its population between 1732 and 1754, largely by their influx. Some overflowed into the Carolina Piedmont, but most of the migrating families sought homes in the linestone valleys that fringed the western edges of the Appalachian Mountains. There they were led onward by the western-flowing rivers of the upper Tennessee system, until their settlements dotted the banks of the Greenbrier, the Holston, the Watauga, and the Nolichucky. In these wilderness outposts the Scotch-Irish built their crude cabins, raised their large crops of children and their small crops of corn, and succumbed rapidly to the forest environment. "The clothes of the people," wrote a visitor to one of their villages, "consist of deer skins, their food of Johnycakes, deer and bear meat. A kind of white people are found here, who live like savages. Hunting is their chief occupation." Bold, devout, shrewd men, hating Indians and easterners with impartial vigor, and determined to "keep the Sabbath and everything else they could lay their hands on," the Scotch-Irish made ideal pioneers in the westward march of civilization.

While they and their fellows subdued the southern back country, other frontiersmen advanced into the upland plateaus and mountain valleys of New England. The settlers who made their homes in this rugged hill country came not from Germany or Ireland but from the coastal lowlands where Puritan fathers proved more productive than their shale-strewn fields. The large families which overcrowded the bottom lands, eager to be on the move at the close of the seventeenth century, proved a greater temptation for speculative enterprise than officials and business men could resist. Money overflowed the coin chests of eastern merchants, for fortunes were being made in commerce, and crown restrictions on manufacturing closed that form of investment to their capital. If they could buy up land in anticipation of the impending rush, the riches of Midas would be theirs! Under this pressure the New England land system was completely transformed as legislatures, succumbing to the speculative fever, made profits rather than the propagation of the Gospel their goal. This transition reshaped the whole course of settlement.

The spirit of speculation was first shown early in the eighteenth century when Boston and Salem business men began buying plots from proprietors of new towns or from old towns where undivided fields were still available. For a time the Massachusetts General Court resisted their demand and made grants as it had in the seventeenth century—to non-profit-seeking groups of religiously orthodox individuals—but by 1727 the pressure was too strong. In that year nine new towns were laid out along the northern border to satisfy land bounties issued during King Philip's War; in the next five years thirty-five more were created in Maine, Massachusetts, and New Hampshire, all for the benefit of speculators. From this time on all pretext of creating contiguous, church-dominated towns was abandoned as the legislature granted lands freely to any speculative group able to bring enough pressure. The next logical step, the sale of town sites by the colony, followed by the late 1740's and continued until 1762, when the last remaining land in Massachusetts was auctioned off.

The other New England colonies followed a similar course. Connecticut sold a large block at auction first in 1715, and by 1720 was committed to this policy of land disposal. These sales reached their height in the late 1720's when the vast area west of the Connecticut River was divided between the colony and the towns of Hartford and Windsor, carved into towns, and disposed of at a series of spectacular sales that attracted speculators from the entire seaboard. In Maine, which was an undisputed part of Massachusetts after 1677, land jobbers revived twenty-four "ancient patents" issued by the Council for New England a century before, formed themselves into such companies as the Masonian Proprietors, Lincolnshire Company Proprietors, and Pemaquid Proprietors, and set out to lure European immigrants to their shadowy domains. In their eagerness to sell they not only built forts, saw-mills, and other necessities, but introduced into America the device of free grants to enhance the value of sections retained. Even Vermont, which was claimed by both New York and New Hampshire, felt the impact of this speculative fever. Between 1749 and 1764 Governor Benning Wentworth of New Hampshire granted 129 townsites there to speculators, carefully reserving five hundred acres in each for himself. Most of the recipients of these infamous "New Hampshire Grants" had no intention of settling in their towns; instead many owned shares in several villages and one notorious speculator was a proprietor in at least eighteen towns at the same time.

This burst of activity changed the whole course of New England's westward movement. No longer was each town controlled by an interested group of resident proprietors who cared for its needs and freely divided its fields among acceptable newcomers. Now absentee proprietors, concerned only with allotting the lands among themselves and selling their portions profitably, governed each new settlement. Some made a conscious effort to lure immigrants by sending agents through the colonies or to England to sell lots, but far more were content to do nothing while waiting for prices to rise. Pioneers accustomed to the benevolent paternalism of the older system, which had provided them with mills, schools, churches, and defense, were quick to object. They complained that the Boston capitalists who owned the land not only did nothing to make pioneer life easier, but charged exorbitant prices, withheld the best land from sale in anticipation of price rises, and reaped an unearned profit without sharing the dangers and poverty of the frontier. Worse still, settlers insisted, was the tendency to create towns so rapidly under speculative pressure that settlers were not available to fill them, leaving a weak frontier line at the mercy of attacking Indians. Dissatisfaction bred of this eastern proprietary monopoly did much to foster the spirit of radicalism which flourished in western New England through the Revolutionary Era.

The rapid settlement of the back country in the face of these handicaps testified to the section's expansive power. All through the early eighteenth century advancing waves of settlers moved upward from the coastal lowland into the New England hill country, augmented now and then by a trickle of immigrants from Europe. One group, led by bands of Scotch-Irish, began the assault on the hilly plateau of central Massachusetts about 1718. Worcester, the principal town, became the center for westward-moving pioneers who founded villages as far west as Ware and Amherst, many of them Scotch-Irish driven from older settlements by the hostility of Puritan clergy who feared the corrupting effect of Presbyterianism on their charges. Other pioneers moved west from the Connecticut Valley into the Berkshires, where they met another stream advancing up the Housatonic River from Connecticut and joined with them in founding a string of picturesque hill towns between Sheffield and Williamstown. By mid-century the Berkshire regions of both Massachusetts and Connecticut were filling so rapidly that settlers spilled over into lands claimed by New York. Their coming aroused such dissatisfaction among the tenant farmers on the manorial Hudson Valley estates—who hoped that Massachusetts would allow them to trade their serf-like status for actual ownership of their farms by annexing the area—that they waged war on their landlords during the 1750's. Only a crown decree fixing the New York-Massachusetts boundary at a point twenty miles east of the Hudson ended this border fighting.

The establishment of this boundary turned the westward-marching New Englanders northward toward Vermont, New Hampshire, and Maine. These border regions had grown slowly to that time, despite a flurry of activity in New Hampshire when Londonderry, Concord, Amherst, Atkinson, Rochester, and a few other isolated towns were planted by Scotch-Irish and lowlanders in the 1720's. Now the boom began. Between 1760 and 1776 seventy-four new towns were settled in Vermont, one hundred in New Hampshire and ninety-four in Maine, many of them peopled by restless migrants making their second or third move toward the frontier. By the time of the Revolution this great northern country was being converted into a peaceful farming area. Yet so strong was the expansive spirit that even these provinces failed to satisfy the New Englanders. In 1754 a group of Connecticut speculators, organized as the Susquehanna Company, purchased from the Indians a two hundred mile tract in the beautiful Wyoming Valley of Pennsylvania, and with the blessing of their colony (which claimed that region under an ancient charter), began sending out settlers in 1762. Despite Indian troubles and indignant protests from Pennsylvania, the towns of Wilkes-Barre and Plymouth were laid out by 1768. Another Connecticut enterprise, the Delaware Company, enjoyed less success but did plant a handful of pioneers along the upper Delaware River in Pennsylvania.

The frontiersmen who hewed out their clearings beneath the long shadows of Vermont's Green Mountains or beside the rippling waters of the Susquehanna typified the changes wrought on New England's institutions by contact with the American wilderness. No longer were the Puritan fathers content to move slowly westward, taking their neighbors and ministers with them, in an orderly march of contiguous settlements. Instead the speculative fever was on them; they were more interested in saving dollars than souls, more concerned with good land than compact villages, more excited about individual wealth than group welfare. They still settled in communities, but good soil rather than adjacence to other towns and churches dictated their choice of sites. Some, indeed, were ready to leave the settled frontier far behind in their search for favored agricultural regions. "The newcomers do not fix near their neighbors and go on regularly," complained one observer in Vermont, "but take spots that please them best, though twenty or thirty miles beyond any others." Limitless opportunity, in the form of cheap land that could be farmed or resold, was the catalyst reshaping New England's social structure.

This transformation typified the changes taking place along the entire back country. In the Old West a new society was born in the eighteenth century, enriched by borrowings from European peoples and shaped by the frontier environment. Each of the migratory groups that sought homes there—the Yankees, Southerners, Scotch-Irish, Germans, Welchmen—contributed something to the social order as they adapted themselves, for the first time in the history of the frontier, to a life completely isolated from European influences. From this blending emerged distinctive characteristics that stamped these woodsmen as typical Americans: emphasis on the practical, intense optimism, impatience with the slow workings of the law, a compelling restlessness, love for oversimplification, mechanical ingenuity, versatility, respect for the individual, tolerance of different religious ideas. Neither the forest nor the European heritage alone shaped these points of view; both contributed.

Every pioneer who moved to the Old West, carrying his ax and gun and driving his livestock before him, felt the impact of the wilderness environment. He knew that he would be able to till only a few acres of land yet he always took out more than he needed, realizing that any excess could be sold at a profit to later comers. With this purchased, or acquired by the simpler expedient of squatting, he felled trees to build a log cabin, notching the ends to fit snugly together, and leaving a hole in the split-board roof to let some of the smoke out—a technique acquired from the Swedes who contributed this distinct architectural form to America. Neighbors usually assisted in this task, for settlements were always near enough together to encourage community co-operation. "They make it a point of hospitality to aid the new farmer," a traveler wrote. "A cask of cider drank in common, and with gaiety, or a gallon of rum, are the only recompense for these services." Only the methodical Germans scorned these methods. Their homes were built of square-hewn logs, with thatched roofs and a center chimney to conserve fuel, dominated by a great barn with stone basement, broad threshing floor, and ample lofts. The "Palatine Barns" proved so useful that they were generally adopted through the West.

With shelter assured, the frontiersman began clearing his land. If he lived in New England or was a German he followed the "Yankee Method" of cutting down the trees and calling in neighbors to roll the logs together for burning; if he was southern or Scotch-Irish he girdled the trunks and let them rot away. Four or five years of back-breaking labor was needed to clear the ten or fifteen acres necessary to support a family. During this period the pioneer lived on grain purchased from nearby farmers, but two good crops would pay for the farm and all improvements. Corn was the great staple of the Old West, although rye was often grown as a first crop in northern New England, and wheat in the Mohawk and Shenandoah valleys. The Germans especially found the latter profitable; they shunned the usual exploitive methods of frontiers agriculture, guarding their soil so carefully that they made fourteen successive plantings before allowing a field to renew its fertility by lying fallow. The grain was consumed at home, sold to newcomers, or transported to the nearest markets either on the backs of settlers or in the Conestoga wagons that the Palatine introduced into Pennsylvania and the Great Valley. These sturdy vehicles, painted blue and covered with tightly stretched cloth, were soon adopted generally along the frontier and as "covered wagons" carried thousands of migrating families westward.

Most of the frontiersmen, even in the primitive settlements that fringed the western edge of civilization, lived well. Self-sufficiency was a necessity here. Only two things the pioneer must have: his ax and his gun. The long handled ax was a universal tool; with it the farmer built his cabin, cleared his land, fashioned crude furniture and wooden dishes, hacked out his cumbersome farm instruments, and even "edged her up a bit and shaved with her" on rare state occasions. Often his skilled hands fashioned a spinning wheel and loom so that his overworked wife could make her own poke bonnet, jacket, and linsey petticoat. His own clothes he patterned after the Indians': a fur cap, leggings of buckskin or elk hide, and a fringed hunting skirt that hung loose from the shoulders to the knees and was drawn in at the waist by a broad belt. All these were made at home; only iron, salt, and a few luxuries had to be imported.

The rifle was just as essential. On it the frontiersman depended for game to supplement his meagre larder, protection against outlaws, and defense against the Indians. Everyone over twelve was expected to share these burdens and those who refused were either laughed out or "hated out" of the community. Because a straight-shooting gun spelled safety and comfort to the pioneer his pointed criticisms of European weapons—directed at the German gunsmiths of Lancaster or other western towns—brought magnificent results. These skilled craftsmen gradually modified the ponderous rifles used on the continent to meet American conditions. They lengthened the stubby barrels to six feet or more for accuracy, reduced the bore to a third of an inch to conserve heavy lead bullets, made the trigger guards smaller and more massive to withstand hard treatment, enlarged the sights for better aim amidst forest gloom, and most important of all invented the "grease patch." This was a small circle of tallow-soaked cloth that was placed under the bullet in loading. Instead of driving the ball down the barrel by hammering on an iron rod, as in the older guns, the frontiersman could now load quietly and quickly with a light hickory ramrod. The result of this experimenting was the deadly "Kentucky Rifle," a weapon that had much to do with the speedy conquest of the frontier.

One of these rifles, a well-poised ax, possibly a horse or two—these were the only tools needed to start life anew in the American wilderness. The men who used them, justly proud of their skill, pitied the helpless easterners, all unaware that they themselves were scorned in the coastal settlements for their crude manners, lack of education, emotional methods of worship, and unorthodox legal devices. This frontier arrogance bound the people of the Old West together, for whether they lived in the Berkshires or the Carolina Piedmont they were supremely aware that they were westerners, and hence superior to the rest of mankind. They were united, too, by their tendency to look to Pennsylvania for leadership. From this Quaker colony Lutheran and Moravian ministers went forth to preach at the tiny log chapels built by the Palatines or to plod along a thousand mile circuit through the southern back country. Presbyterian ministers who carried the word of God to the Scotch-Irish settlements of the Great Valley were trained there, most of them at the famous Log Cabin College established by the Reverend William Tennent in 1728 or, after his death in 1746, at Princeton. Pennsylvania was also the terminus of most of the trade routes of the Old West, as farmers living in the

Great Valley of Virginia or the Carolinas found that their best markets lay not across the impassable mountains but in Philadelphia or, after 1730, Baltimore. Common problems, common interests, and common grievances bound the people of the uplands together.

This unity was not without its dangers. By mid-eighteenth century the Old West stood apart as a distinct section, differing in racial composition, agricultural methods, and social attitudes from the Tidewater and coastal lowlands. Its democratic, poverty-stricken small farmers had little in common with the aristocratic plantation owners or merchant capitalists of the seaboard, yet the two were bound together by artificial boundary lines in each of the colonies. Neither could understand the other. Westerners looked on easterners as money-mad tyrants selfishly engaged in accumulating fortunes or aping English society while others performed the arduous task of subduing the wilderness. Easterners looked on westerners as illiterate, ungodly savages who were poorly equipped by their oversimplified life to handle complex problems of government. Unfortunately for the frontiersmen, the planters and merchants were in a position to carry their prejudices into practice. They dominated the colonial legislatures at the beginning of the eighteenth century, and as the West was settled perpetuated their control, either by erecting large western counties with the same number of representatives as the smaller eastern units, or by assigning interior counties fewer delegates than those along the coast. This thoroughly enraged the westerners. Not only were they deprived of an equal voice in government, but their counties were so large that local government broke down, inadequate defense was provided, and county courts were so distant that few could seek the protection of the law. Their discontent, and eastern misunderstanding, gave birth to the first sectional conflicts in the history of the frontier.

In most of the northern colonies and Virginia frontier dissatisfaction was kept below the surface until after the Revolution, although in New York tenant farmers rebelled against their landlords during the 1750's and in New Jersey a proprietary attempt to eject squatters aroused rioters who raged through the back country between 1745 and 1754. The outburst in Pennsylvania was more serious. There the westerners, already rankled by the fact that their five interior counties were allowed only ten representatives in the legislature to twenty-six from the three eastern districts, were goaded to rebellion by Indian attacks between 1754 and 1763. For nine years the savages ravaged the back country while frontiersmen pleaded for aid from the Quaker assembly, only to be turned away with pacific platitudes or the galling assurance that their own quarrelsome actions caused all the trouble. Rumors, natural in such a tense atmosphere, flew through the West: the easterners refused to fight because war would interfere with their fur trade; a group of peaceful Moravian Indians in Northampton County was harboring raiding parties; another village of christianized Conestoga Indians in Lancaster County was supplying the enemy with guns. The governor finally consented to move the Moravian Indians to Philadelphia, but before he could protect the Conestoga village the frontiersmen acted. A mob from Paxton and Donegal descended on the harmless red men on December 13, 1763, killing six and wounding several more, then attacked again on December 27 after the tribe had been hurriedly removed to Lancaster by the government.

The horrified assembly immediately issued warrants for the arrest of the "Paxton Boys," ordering them brought east to Philadelphia to stand trial for the cold-blooded murder of friendly Indians. This was the signal for a new outbreak. The frontiersmen, knowing they could never expect justice from an eastern court, formed a ragged army which marched toward Philadelphia. A government force was sent against them, but fortunately the persuasive Benjamin Franklin, who met the rebels first at Germantown, convinced them to substitute a moving "Declaration and Remonstrance" for battle. This heart-rending protest won them only a few minor concessions in the form of greater representation, and western antagonism continued into the Revolutionary Era.

In North Carolina the sectional struggle took its most violent form. Conditions in the back country were particularly bad; Tidewater planters not only controlled the legislature but dominated western local government through the governor who appointed both the law-making justices of county courts and the law-enforcing sheriffs. These ruling bodies levied only poll taxes which fell equally on rich and poor. This was bad enough, but corrupt tax collectors made life intolerable. Usually they called when least expected, demanded payment in specie, and when this was not forthcoming hurried off to sell the farm for tax arrears to one of their speculating friends. Sometimes the farmer was able to borrow money from neighbors to beat the collector in a race to the county seat; more often he could only recover his property in the law courts where fees from lawyers, clerks, and judges left him penniless. Pioneers who lived on the Granville estates in the northern half of the colony had, in addition to these grievances, to pay high quitrents to the proprietor's agents.

Resistance started there in 1759 when rioters who captured one of Lord Granville's collectors were jailed, then released by a mob that swept through the West until subdued by hastily summoned sheriffs from the East. Ten years of peace followed, but in 1768 the frontiersmen began forming an extralegal body which they called "The Regulation," binding themselves by compact to pay no taxes until they were satisfied that the money was legally used and collected. At first the Regulators asked only to meet with proper officials to air their grievances; only when Governor William Tryon unjustly branded them as insurrectionists and called out the militia to capture their leaders did they turn from protest to rebellion. Rioting about Hillsboro grew increasingly violent until 1770 when the governor issued warrants for the arrest of the Regulators and ordered out troops to enforce them.

An attempt to serve these warrants in the spring of 1771 brought matters to a climax. Tryon, at the head of one provincial army, marched into Hillsboro without resistance, but another body of troops under General Hugh Waddell was turned back at Salisbury by a band of Regulators. When Tryon attempted to join his confederate he was met by a tattered mob of some two thousand Regulators drawn up on the banks of the Alamance River. Thinking that they could overawe the governor by this show of force, they were taken completely by surprise when the militia fired on them. This Battle of the Alamance, fought on May 16, 1771, cost each side nine men killed and a number wounded, and broke the strength of the Regulator movement, for the rioters were not rebels and dispersed rapidly before this show of force. By midsummer most of the leaders who had not been caught and executed had fled the colony; resistance was at an end.

South Carolina had a Regulator movement of its own with results almost as serious. The grievances were the same—high taxes, corrupt officials, underrepresentation in the legislature, oversized counties—plus two others: a complete lack of courts in the interior which necessitated a two-hundred-mile journey to Charleston for every legal action, and the assembly's refusal to erect any new western counties until their inhabitants agreed to support the Anglican Church. Resistance first developed in 1767 when settlers on the upper Pedee and Congaree rivers organized groups of vigilantes to defend their property and punish criminals, calling themselves Regulators. Their motives were as thoroughly misunderstood as in North Carolina. They were denounced as traitors, the militia was called out against them, and scattered fighting went on between the summer of 1768 and March, 1769, when the two forces met in a pitched battle on the Saluda River. Civil war was only averted when the troops were withdrawn and the legislature hastily summoned to pass a circuit court bill which provided adequate protection for the interior. With this victory the Regulators dissolved, although lack of representation rankled for many years.

The back country gained little in a sectional struggle which only intensified eastern fear of western "radicalism," but the results were far reaching.

So bitter was the hatred engendered that for many years the two sections remained at swords points. This was shown during the Revolution when internal antagonism led them to take opposite sides whatever their personal convictions; thus in Pennsylvania the West supported independence when the seaboard remained loyal to England while in the South the back country became a center of loyalism because the Tidewater favored the patriot cause. A more important immediate result was to send a new stream of population westward as disgruntled pioneers, their hopes for reform dashed by eastern victories, turned to isolated lands beyond the mountains where they could rule themselves as they pleased. Before they could people the broad plains of the Ohio Valley, however, that region must be won by England. There the French were firmly established; only a series of imperial wars lasting over the course of a century expelled the intruders and opened the heart of the continent to Anglo-American frontiersmen.

# CHAPTER VI

# The French Barrier

## 1615-1763

While English farmers toiled methodically over the rolling hills of the Old West, the pioneers of New France swept their frontier westward with breath-taking speed. For a century and a half their spectacular conquest of the continent went on, until the whole interior, from the Great Lakes to the Gulf of Mexico, was in their hands. Before British frontiersmen could crowd through the mountain gaps to overrun the Mississippi Valley the French barrier must be pushed aside—by intrigue, Indian diplomacy, commercial conflicts, and four great wars.

France built her New World empire on the fur trade, and Samuel de Champlain was its architect. At Quebec, where he presided over a nondescript crew of traders until his death in 1635, Champlain laid down the broad principles on which French expansion rested: trade with the Huron Indians of the Georgian Bay region who could first serve as middlemen, then open the road to the tribes of the Great Lakes country. Too old to do more than plan wisely, Champlain sent out a number of reckless youths to cement the forest alliances necessary: Etienne Brulé who explored the northern shore of Lake Huron and probably ventured into Lake Superior; Jean Nicolet who followed the Ottawa River route to Georgian Bay, passed through the Straits of Mackinac to Lake Michigan and Green Bay, and ascended the Fox River to a point where the Mississippi was only three days travel away. There he found the Winnebago Indians so friendly that he was fired with ambition to extend the trade of New France to the Wisconsin country. "Champlain's Young Men" were aided in their explorations by Jesuit missionaries who first reached Quebec in 1632. During the next years hundreds of black-robed friars arrived, to master the Indian's tongues, eat their miserable food, live in their wretched hovels, minister to their ungrateful souls, and frequently earn the highest tribute that a savage could pay a foe: death by slow torture. By 1641 a dozen devout Jesuit fathers were laboring in as many Huron villages, while two were at Sault Ste. Marie where they said mass before a group of awe-struck Algonquin. Gradually French influence was reaching out toward the Great Lakes country.

Expansion was brought to a rude halt in the 1640's by the sudden rise to power of the Iroquois. Supplied with guns by Dutch traders and united in a loose confederation, the five tribes that had earlier lived peacefully between Lake Champlain and the eastern tip of Lake Erie—the Mohawk, Oneida, Onondaga, Cayuga, and Seneca—overnight blossomed into one of the continent's most powerful Indian nations, ready to spread devastation among weaker neighbors who still depended on primitive bows and arrows. Iroquois wrath would naturally have been directed against their traditional enemies, the Algonquin-Huron group, but warfare was made even more serious by the realization that this was no wilderness skirmish. The Five Nations were middlemen for the Albany Dutch, the Hurons for the Quebec French. Each wanted the trade of the Great Lakes Indians. Only the extermination of the Hurons and their French backers would open the continent to Iroquois traders.

The Iroquois Wars began in 1642 when raiding parties sliced northward through the Huron lands to close the Ottawa River route to the interior. This accomplished, the raiders turned with savage fury against their forest enemies, slaughtering Hurons and Jesuit missionaries indiscriminately, until all the country east of Lake Huron was in their hands. News of their victories spread panic among the Lakes Indians. Through Michigan and the Ohio country small tribes folded their wigwams and retreated westward, pursued by roving bands of Iroquois, who reached the shores of Lake Michigan in 1652. "They came like foxes," wrote a weary French chronicler, "attacked like lions, and fled like birds." Algonquin from northern Michigan, Sauk from the Saginaw Valley, Potawatomi, Ottawa, and Miami from southern Michigan and Ohio, all crowded into Wisconsin on the heels of the Huron in a headlong flight that only ended when they reached the upper Mississippi Valley lands of the powerful Sioux. Not until 1653 did the Iroquois, worn by the long struggle and with communication lines stretched dangerously thin, consent to accept the overtures of a French peace delegation and bring the war to a temporary close.

The end of hostilities did not solve the problems of the Quebec traders, for their former customers were now dispersed far beyond the forbidding waters of Lake Michigan. Fortunately the Indians were as anxious to resume trade as the white men. In 1654 a party of Algonquin from Green

Bay reached Three Rivers over the difficult St. Maurice River route with a few furs and such an insatiable appetite for trading goods that an adventurous *voyageur*, Médard Chouart, Sieur des Groseilliers, was dispatched to accompany them on their return journey. His report, when he reached Quebec again in 1656, was enthusiastic: Wisconsin teemed with natives who were starved for French goods and rich in furs. During the next few summers some thirty traders rushed west to tap this market,

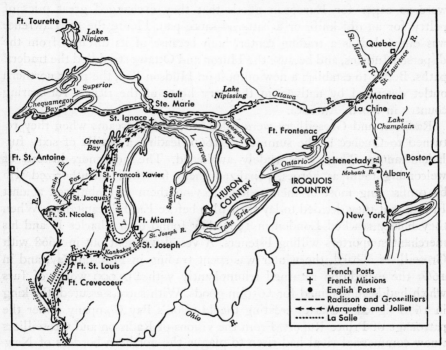

New France, 1615-1689

either traveling by canoe over the Ottawa River route or portaging across southern Michigan. Again New France prospered, and again expansion into new trading areas began.

The leaders in this period of activity were Groseilliers and his brother-in-law, Pierre Esprit Radisson. They made an ideal pair. Radisson was the impetuous adventurer, Groseilliers the shrewd business man; both were experienced Indian traders and both loved the lonely life of forest and stream. "We weare Cesars," wrote Radisson on one voyage, "being nobody to contradict us." They set out in August, 1659, with seven canoe loads of friendly natives, slipping quietly away without the official observer appointed by the governor to accompany them. Quickly traversing the Ottawa

River-Lake Nipissing route, they passed from Georgian Bay into Lake Superior, skirted the southern shore of that great body of water, and on the banks of Chequamegon Bay built a sturdy trading hut. A winter of bartering for the thick northern furs of that cold country convinced them they had found a solution to the trading problem of New France. Traders could profit most, they saw, by avoiding sophisticated Huron or Ottawa middlemen and dealing directly with the primitive interior tribesmen who were so eager for European goods that they exchanged great piles of peltry for an old knife or a battered sauce pan. Hence the St. Lawrence was outmoded as a trading center, both because of its distance from the dispersed Indians, and because the Huron and Ottawa straddled the traders' paths. Better to establish a new outpost on Hudson Bay, the great northern outlet described by natives, in the very heart of the richest fur-bearing country in North America.

Radisson and Groseilliers were filled with these dreams when they returned to Quebec in the summer of 1660, leading a flotilla of sixty fur-laden canoes. They were rudely awakened. The governor, instead of welcoming them as heroes, penalized them for their unauthorized trip by confiscating most of their peltry, leaving them so embittered against France that they decided to lay their plan before English capitalists. When they finally reached London in 1665 they found both Charles II and his merchant supporters willing listeners. A vessel was sent out in 1668 with Groseilliers aboard, the winter was spent trading in Hudson Bay, and in 1669 the expedition returned triumphantly with £19,000 worth of furs which had been obtained for £650 in goods. With success assured, the king in 1670 signed a charter creating the Hudson's Bay Company under the patronage of Prince Rupert. From the visions of Radisson and Groseilliers a new commercial rival had risen to plague the northern borders of New France.

In the meantime the settlements along the St. Lawrence were being strengthened. When Louis XIV assumed the reins of French government in 1661 a new day dawned for French colonial possessions. Prodded by his principal minister, Jean Baptiste Colbert, he decided in 1663 to convert New France into a royal province, governed by a royally appointed council of seven, a governor to carry out the council's orders, and an intendant to enforce the royal will. The intendant, as personal representative of the king, was the most important of these officials. To this vital post Colbert in 1665 named an experienced administrator, Jean Talon, the "Great Intendant," whose able rule elevated New France from a struggling outpost to a thriving colony. The next ten years witnessed the most remarkable expansion in the history of the New World.

When Talon took over his post he found trade disrupted by a renewal of the Iroquois Wars. Disdaining halfhearted measures, he marched an army of a thousand men into the country of the Five Nations, crushing resistance so thoroughly that the Indians sued for peace in 1666. With the Ottawa River-Lake Nipissing route again open, a trader, Nicolas Perrot, was hurried westward to recement trading alliances; through 1668 and 1669 Perrot traveled through the Wisconsin country making treaties with the principal tribes before returning to Quebec with nine hundred Indians and so many furs that the bottom dropped out of the market. The dispersed tribes, he reported, were drifting back to their old homes—the Huron, Algonquin, and Ottawa to the upper peninsula of Michigan where they could catch whitefish, the Sauk, Potawatomi, Fox, and Winnebago about Green Bay where they could feast on wild rice, the Ouiatanon around the lower tip of Lake Michigan. All were eager to trade.

Here, Talon saw, was a golden opportunity to win the whole interior for his king. His first step was to send an expedition to take formal possession, guided by Nicolas Perrot and headed by a young nobleman newly arrived from France, Francois Daumont, Sieur de St. Lusson. Their elaborate following reached Sault Ste. Marie in June, 1671. Before chiefs and delegates from fourteen tribes, St. Lusson broke off a piece of turf, raised it aloft, and officially proclaimed his monarch the ruler of this vast domain. The elaborate pageantry, the booming muskets, the shouts of "Vive le Roi" echoing through the wilderness silence, sent the natives back to their villages deeply impressed with the power of this master who proclaimed himself their ruler.

But Talon knew that permanent conquest must rest on trade rather than ceremony. Each year, he decreed, twenty-five licensed traders would make the journey westward to supply the Great Lakes Indians with needed goods. Jesuit missionaries, too, were urged to extend their operations into Wisconsin; between 1670 and 1672 two stations were built—St. Francois Xavier on Green Bay and St. Jacques on the Fox River—where ten earnest friars labored to win savage souls for their God and savage subjects for their sovereign. Even then Talon was not satisfied. Beyond the Wisconsin tribes, he knew, were other natives who might welcome French brandy and firearms. To open trade with them, and to explore a great interior river that the Indians described to traders, he sent out an important exploring expedition, ably commanded by two seasoned woodsmen, Father Jacques Marquette and Louis Jolliet. Starting from St. Ignace where Father Marquette had conducted a mission station since 1670, they traversed Green Bay and the Fox River, portaged to the Wisconsin River, and entered the Mississippi on June 17, 1673. Their journey down the Father of Waters was disappointing, for when they reached the mouth of the Arkansas River they learned that the Mississippi emptied into the Gulf of Mexico rather than the Pacific Ocean, and turned back. Returning by the Illinois portage to Lake Michigan, they reached Quebec early in 1674, excited by the prospect of an all-water route between the Great Lakes and the Gulf of Mexico.

Two men listened to their tales with special interest. One was Louis Count de Frontenac, who became governor of New France on Talon's recall in 1672. The other was Robert Cavelier, Sieur de La Salle, an energetic visionary whose trading expeditions had carried him into the Ohio Valley and given him a thorough knowledge of Indian ways. Why not, they reasoned, establish a chain of posts across the Lake country and down the Mississippi River, each controlled by a trader who would gather furs from neighboring tribes, and visited yearly by large vessels that would ply the Great Lakes and the interior river system. The furs, exported through either Quebec or the town they hoped to establish at the mouth of the Mississippi, would spell prosperity to New France, while the chain of posts hemming in the English colonies would secure the heart of the continent for their sovereign. Moreover they would reap fortunes for themselves through the trading monopoly they hoped to obtain in return for this service to the crown.

The scheme was launched auspiciously in 1675 when La Salle returned from Paris with official blessings and a five year monopoly over the fur trade. Four more years were needed for preparations, including the building of a stout stone fort, Ft. Frontenac, as a basis for operations on Lake Ontario, but in August, 1679, La Salle started west in a large sailing vessel, the *Griffon,* while his lieutenant, Henry de Tonti, pushed ahead with a small party to collect furs. At Green Bay the *Griffon* turned back with a full load of peltry while La Salle and fourteen men pressed on by canoe along the shore of Lake Michigan. At the mouth of the St. Joseph River, where they paused to build a palisaded post, Ft. Miami, they were joined by Tonti and seventeen more *voyageurs.* The enlarged party used the Kankakee portage to reach the Illinois River where a second post, Ft. Crevecoeur, was constructed. There they separated. Tonti was left in charge of the fort while a missionary member of the party, Father Louis Hennepin, started north to explore the upper Mississippi and La Salle returned to Ft. Frontenac. There disquieting news awaited him: the *Griffon* had been lost with its cargo of furs, and the garrison at Ft. Creve-coeur was in revolt against Tonti. Hurrying west once more, he found the whole country ravaged by a new Iroquois invasion which precluded further activity that year.

Not until the autumn of 1681 was the frontier sufficiently peaceful to begin the task of post-planting anew. Starting from Ft. Miami, La Salle and a little party of twenty-three Frenchmen followed the Kankakee portage to the Illinois River, then descended that stream and the Mississippi in an uneventful journey that brought them to the Gulf of Mexico on April 9, 1682. On the return journey a new fort, Ft. St. Louis, was built on an easily defended natural fortress called Starved Rock which overlooked the Illinois River. Around this La Salle gathered several thousand friendly Indians, all eager to trade. Apparently his dream of an interior empire was near realization; he had won over the Illinois natives, built a strong post as headquarters, and developed a year-around route for the export of furs. Only a post at the mouth of the Mississippi was needed to crown his enterprise, but this proved La Salle's undoing. Realizing that such a fort could best be established from the mother country, he returned to France, then set out in February, 1684 with four ships and four hundred men. After a stormy voyage, they missed the mouth of the Mississippi, landing instead at Matagorda Bay, where La Salle was murdered by his rebellious followers. Like many visionaries, La Salle failed because he was in advance of his times, but he did not sacrifice his life and fortune in vain. His explorations gave New France a claim to the continent's interior, and his dreams inspired a later generation of Frenchmen to build the chain of settlements along the St. Lawrence-Great Lakes-Mississippi waterways that he had planned.

La Salle's ill-fated venture turned French interests from the Illinois to the Lake Superior country where Daniel Greysolon, Sieur Duluth, a Frenchman of good family who had come to America to recuperate his fortunes, in 1684 built a trading post, Ft. Tourette. His dreams of a profitable trade in that rich northern country were soon dashed, however, for in that same year the outbreak of a new Indian war forced him to retire from the West. The French-Iroquois War that began in 1684 was apparently only another of the wilderness conflicts that had occurred intermittently since the days of Champlain. Actually it was far different. Ranged behind the warriors of the Five Nations now were a group of newly awakened British officials who, unlike the Dutch merchants of old, were well aware of the connection between trade and empire. The flag, they saw, would inevitably follow the paths blazed by traders. The nation that controlled the commerce of the Mississippi Valley would eventually win the continent's interior. This realization transformed the Iroquois Wars from forest skirmishes into a century-long conflict between England, France, and Spain, with North America as the prize for the victor.

The struggle began in 1684 when an imperial-minded governor of England's New York, Thomas Dongan, goaded the Iroquois into striking westward and northward against the French and their Indian allies. Once more tribesmen in the Great Lakes country trembled before the wrath of the dread raiders; once more *voyageurs* and missionaries fled eastward for their lives. Within two years the West was deserted, while bands of Iroquois carried the war to the gates of Montreal itself. An energetic governor, the Marquis de Denonville, who assumed control of New France in 1686, tried to rescue something from the debacle. Nicolas Perrot, the skilled forest diplomat, was hurried to Wisconsin to supervise the building of two forts—Ft. St. Antoine on Lake Pepin and Ft. St. Nicolas on the Wisconsin River—to impress the Indians with French power; the Jesuits were goaded into founding a new mission at St. Joseph; and Denonville himself led eight hundred troops in a destructive march through the Iroquois country during 1687. He killed so few Indians, however, that the infuriated warriors only struck back with new fury during the next two years. Their raids reached a climax on a stormy night in August, 1689, when 1,500 painted savages surprised the little village of La Chine, massacred two hundred of its settlers, and carried away ninety more as captives. Before this assault even Ft. Frontenac was abandoned while Denonville concentrated his defenses in the lower St. Lawrence Valley.

Yet worse was to come. In 1689 Louis XIV's refusal to recognize the ascension of William of Orange to the English throne plunged the two nations into the first of four wars for control of North America: the War of the Palatinate, or King William's War as it was known in the colonies. Fortunately for New France, royal officials recognized the gravity of the situation and returned Frontenac as governor. That grizzled old warrior threw himself into his task with an energy that belied his seventy years, perfecting defenses, whipping an army into shape, rebuilding decayed Indian alliances, and planning an invasion of the English colonies. Throughout Quebec hope displaced despair as the "Iron Governor" won over tribe after tribe in the Northwest; on one occasion Frontenac convinced a visiting party of chiefs to cast their lot with New France by interrupting a conference with a war whoop, seizing a tomahawk, and leading the excited natives in a furious war dance. Here were allies to carry the scalping knife against English settlements on the three fronts where the war was fought: the New England-New York borderland, the Great Lakes country, and about Hudson Bay.

The first blow fell on the New York frontier on the bitterly cold night of February 9, 1690, when a force of two hundred French and Indians surprised the outpost of Schenectady after its guards had retired to warm beds, leaving two dummy snow men to watch the gates. Sixty were massacred and twenty-seven more carried into captivity on that raid. From that time on the attacks fell with devastating regularity along the whole back country of New York and New England. Their savagery was shown by an incident that occurred after an assault on Haverhill, Massachusetts. One of the captives carried away was a housewife, Hannah Dustin, who was captured by a band of two braves, three squaws, and seven Indian children. During the march to Quebec she managed to escape. Instead of slipping quietly away, she recalled the high bounty paid by Massachusetts for native scalps and, seizing a tomahawk, killed ten of her sleeping captors, sparing only a young child and a wounded squaw. Despite such acts of brutality, the French held the upper hand in fighting on this borderland.

They were equally successful in the Great Lakes country, where the conflict was not of arms but of Indian alliances. Despite the tight cordon thrown around the Northwest by Iroquois warriors, despite the invasion of the Ohio Valley by English traders with low-priced trading goods, Frontenac managed to hold that vital region's loyalty. His most effective agents were sent there when hostilities began: Nicolas Perrot to Wisconsin, Henry de Tonti to Illinois, Pierre le Sueur to the Lake Superior country, the Sieur de Mantet to the St. Joseph region. By 1696 the earnest pleas of these mighty ones for Indian support were bearing fruit, but in that year Frontenac's plans were rudely interrupted. An order from the crown forced him to abandon all western posts and cancel all trading contracts there! This stunning reversal of policy was prompted partly by pressure from the Jesuits, who resented the corrupting influence of *voyageurs* on their converts, and partly by a glutted fur market at home. By 1698 only missionaries roamed the vast forests where a generation of Frenchmen had labored in vain.

On the third front, about the icy shores of Hudson Bay, French gains were more enduring. There the Hudson's Bay Company operated a number of posts commanding the interior rivers: York Factory on the Hayes River, Albany on the Albany River, Moose Factory on the Moose River, and Rupert's House on the Rupert River, all established during the 1670's. Skirmishing for these posts began even before war broke out in Europe, for in 1686 a French commander, Pierre Le Moyne d'Iberville, led a hundred men overland from Quebec to capture Moose Factory, Rupert's house, and Albany after a brisk fight. This started a seesaw battle which lasted more than ten years, with forts changing hands almost yearly. The climax came in 1697 when Iberville, in a single ship, routed four English vessels protecting York Factory, then captured the post. The war ended with York Factory in French hands, but with England in control of the three forts about James Bay.

King William's War came to a close in 1697 with neither side completely victorious. The indecisive results were reflected in the Treaty of
Ryswick which provided that each nation must return its conquests, with
the exception of York Factory which remained a French possession. Clearly
this was only a truce designed to give the warring factions a breathing
spell. Both nations, certain that war would soon be renewed, spent the next
five years jockeying for position in America's interior. England's moves were
made by traders and a few farseeing colonial governors; those of France
were part of a well-conceived scheme to secure control of the heart of the
continent. The effect of both was to shift the scene of conflict from the
Great Lakes to the lower Mississippi Valley.

Attention was focused on that region by the action of Charleston traders.
Those adventurous wanderers, extending their trails around the southern
Appalachians farther westward each year, reached the Mississippi as early
as 1698, to ply their trade with the Chickasaw and the smaller tribes about
the mouth of the Arkansas River. That was bad enough in the eyes of
New France, but even more alarming was the conduct of her own *voyageurs*. Many of these woodsmen, when deprived of a market for their
peltry at Quebec by the royal order of 1696, turned instead to the English
colonies. Here was a real danger! If those renegades, or *coureurs de bois*
as they were derisively labeled, should lead the English back through the
passes in the mountains, all the interior might fall into England's hands.
The danger was brought home to New France when a *coureur de bois*,
Jean Couture, a deserter who had served with La Salle and Tonti, reached
the Carolinas after an eastward journey along the Tennessee River, then
returned at the head of a trading party which descended the Tennessee,
Ohio, and Mississippi rivers to the Arkansas River. Unless the French
acted quickly British traders would overrun the whole western country!
Frantic pleas from Quebec officials finally bore fruit when Louis XIV, at
the close of the century, rescinded his order of 1696 and threw the interior
open to French trade once more.

*Voyageurs* swarmed into the Great Lakes country during the summer
of 1700, but wise Quebec leaders realized that trade might not be enough
to hold the wavering Indians in the face of cheaper English manufactured
goods. Occupation was the only answer. That year a stout warehouse, with
a garrison attached, was built on strategic Mackinac Island; a year later
the important post of Detroit was constructed on the narrow waterway
connecting Lake Erie and Lake Huron. Friendly Indians were encouraged
to settle nearby, partly to satisfy traders, partly to strengthen the feeble
garrisons left in control. The occupation of the Illinois country was entrusted to missionaries. First to arrive were a band of priests from the

Seminary of Foreign Missions; they reached the West under Tonti's guidance in 1699 and selected a site for their chapel at the Indian village of Cahokia. The Jesuits, resenting this intrusion of a rival order, promptly retaliated by founding their own mission station among the Kaskaskia Indians on the fertile bottom lands just south of the Kaskaskia River. Traders and farmers who drifted in during the next few years transformed Kaskaskia and Cahokia into thriving wilderness towns.

The French founded outposts in the Northwest without opposition, but when they tried to occupy the lower Mississippi Valley they became involved in a three-cornered conflict with England and Spain. Spain was naturally interested, for she considered the northern shore of the Gulf of Mexico her exclusive domain. England's ambitions were centered in an adventurer, Dr. Daniel Coxe, who had inherited an ancient royal patent to the province of Carolana which entitled him to all territory between the 31st and 36th parallels. His ambition was to found a colony at the mouth of the Mississippi, peopled by French Huguenots driven from their homeland by the revocation of the Edict of Nantes.

All three contestants moved into action in October, 1698, when a Spanish force sailed from Vera Cruz to secure both Pensacola Bay and the Mississippi outlet, Dr. Coxe left England with two shiploads of colonists, and Pierre Le Moyne d'Iberville set out from France in command of two hundred soldiers. The race was won by Iberville, who in March, 1699, built a small post on the lower Mississippi while the Spaniards were still at Pensacola Bay and Dr. Coxe's party lingered at Charles Town. Quickly he cemented his hold by building other posts: Ft. Maurepas at Biloxi Bay, Ft. Mobile at the mouth of the Tombigbee River, and a small outpost at the mouth of the Ohio River. His new colony of Louisiana fared badly during the next few years, largely because selfish Montreal merchants forced the crown to decree that all furs from the upper Mississippi Valley be exported through the St. Lawrence rather than down the river, but Iberville's new colony nevertheless strengthened New France. When the next colonial war began a string of French outposts hemmed in the English colonists.

The War of the Spanish Succession, or Queen Anne's War, broke out in 1702 when a vastly strengthened France challenged England's might by denying Anne's right to the throne. The American phase, which lasted until 1713, was fought on two fronts: the borderland between the Carolinas, Florida, and Louisiana, and the wilderness frontier separating New England from Canada.

England's campaigns in the southern theater were mapped by Governor James Moore of the Carolinas. Realizing that the road to Louisiana could only be opened by first defeating France's Spanish allies along the Gulf of Mexico, he sents his troops storming into Guale and Florida with such success that by the end of 1702 all that land was at his mercy except for a band of defenders besieged in the strong stone fortress outside the city of St. Augustine. A year later English troops overran Apalache, destroying the fort at Ayubale and thirteen mission stations, and assuring England's

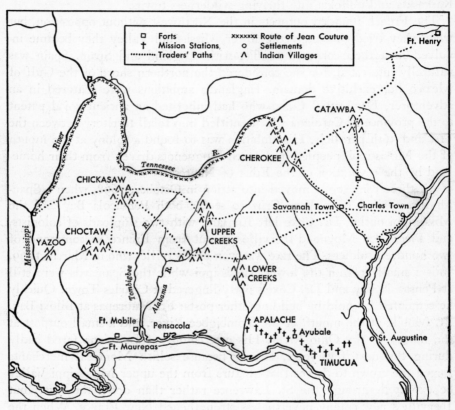

The Southern Theater of Conflict, 1697-1713

forces an unguarded path for the planned attack on Louisiana. To prepare for this decisive expedition, traders were sent westward between 1703 and 1707 with orders to win over the Indians by offering them fantastic bargains. One by one the tribes succumbed: the Alabama in 1703, the Chickasaw in 1704, the Creeks in 1705, and the Tallapoosa and Yazoo in 1706, until only the Choctaw remained loyal to France. Yet the English attack never materialized; inefficiency and the constant threat of a naval attack on Charles Town kept the Carolinians at home and deprived England of a golden opportunity to win the lower Mississippi borderland.

On the northern front fighting was confined to the New England borderland when the Iroquois, with bitter memories of their sacrifices in King
William's War, declared their neutrality. The conflict began in August,
1703, when a band of Frenchmen and Indians destroyed the town of
Wells, Maine, and grew in intensity during the next five years. By 1709
conditions along the frontier were so bad that the New Englanders decided
to take matters into their own hands. Forming an army of 1,400 men, they
sailed away for Port Royal, the powerful Acadian outpost of New France,

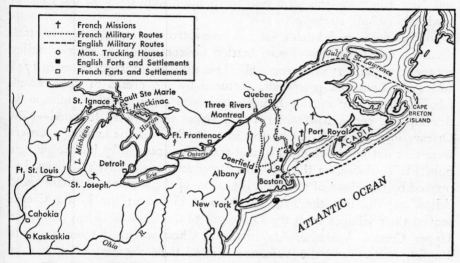

The French-English Theater of Conflict in the North, 1697-1713

whose three hundred defenders had no choice but surrender. This important
fort, which had long served as a nest for attacks on English shipping, passed
forever into the hands of Englishmen, who renamed it Annapolis. A year
later a giant naval expedition against Quebec ended in failure when its
inefficient leader, insisting on using his own meagre skill as a navigator in
the treacherous Gulf of St. Lawrence, sacrificed ten of his ships and nine
hundred of his men on the fog-hidden shoals of the lower bay.

This was the last expedition of the war, for preliminary peace terms were
accepted in 1711 and the Treaty of Utrecht signed two years later. Both
France and Spain were made to pay heavily for the success enjoyed by
British arms throughout the world. Spain gave up Gibraltar; France surrendered Newfoundland, Acadia, and all the territory draining into Hudson Bay, and recognized the British overlordship of the Iroquois. Yet the
Treaty of Utrecht, favorable as it was to the English cause, left many prob-

lems unsettled. The ownership of the interior of the continent, the division of the disputed territory about the Gulf of Mexico, and the exact limits of Acadia, or Nova Scotia as it was now called, were still to be determined. These differences made another war inevitable. That the two nations remained at peace between 1713 and 1744 was due only to the cautious policy of Sir Robert Walpole, Britain's prime minister; both used the period of truce to strengthen their positions for the final struggle. On five frontiers—the lower Mississippi Valley, the Hudson Bay region, about Lake Ontario, in the Lake Champlain country, and on the borderland between Nova Scotia and New England—this jockeying for position went on, with the English gradually gaining strength.

In the southern debatable land, where Carolina trappers, Spanish missionaries, and French *voyageurs* battled for control of the interior valley between 1713 and 1744, France gained the initial advantage. Between 1717 and 1731 Louisiana prospered, nurtured by the profits of John Law's fabulous Company of the Indies which was given royal permission to develop the entire Mississippi Valley. New towns were founded—New Orleans in 1718, Fort de Chartres in 1720, St. Philippe in 1726—settlers were sent out by the thousands, and trade was fostered by building a new post, Ft. Toulouse, on the Alabama River among the Creek Indians. Impressed by this show of strength, the tribes of the southern debatable land drifted rapidly into the French sphere of influence; the Lower Creeks moved their villages from the Ocmulgee to the Chattahoochee River, the Upper Creeks, Apalache, Alabama, and Choctaw closed their towns to English traders, and the Yamassee showed their changing allegiance by attacking the Carolina back country. The British, placed upon the defensive by this sudden shift, were forced to protect themselves by throwing up a ring of fortifications around their borders: Ft. King George on the Altamaha, Fts. Palachacola and Moore on the Savannah, and Ft. Congaree on the Santee.

If English prestige was to be restored, however, something more was needed. By the middle 1720's the South Carolina officials were busily at work among the wavering tribes, showering chiefs with presents, offering trading goods at low prices, and promising generous rewards for support. Their tactics succeeded. The Lower Creeks shifted allegiance first, followed by the Upper Creeks and portions of the Chickasaw. Only the Alabama, who lived under the shadow of Ft. Toulouse, and the Yamassee, who still smarted under their defeat at the hands of the Carolinians a few years before, remained friendly to France, and the latter were virtually exterminated in a new English-Yamassee War that flamed in 1728. To make matters even worse for Louisiana, the Yazoo and Natchez Indians of the Mississippi Valley, jealous of the superior goods that British traders offered eastern tribes, joined with the Chickasaw to fall suddenly on the French settlements in 1729. This blow launched the decade-long Natchez War, with the Louisianians and their Choctaw allies ranged against the rest of the lower Mississippi Valley natives. By the closing years of the 1730's the hard-pressed French were reduced to protecting their homes

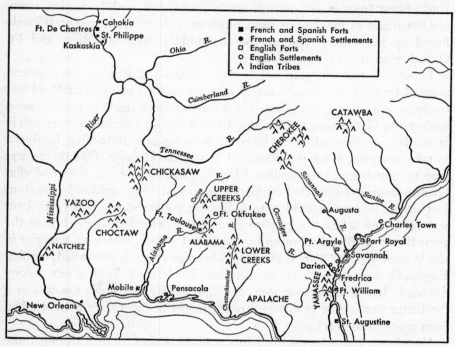

The Southern Borderland, 1713-1744

within Louisiana, with all hope of dominating the surrounding areas temporarily gone.

The Natchez War served as a protective screen behind which the English could continue their expansion in the southern debatable land. In 1732 James Edward Oglethorpe, a wealthy humanitarian, secured royal permission to found the colony of Georgia. From the day that his first settlers, recruited from the debtors' prisons of the mother country, began building their homes at Savannah, Oglethorpe devoted himself wholeheartedly to the problem of defense, realizing that Spanish or French retaliation was certain. He limited holdings to fifty acres to insure a compact village, banned Negro slaves, built a ring of forts to keep off raiding parties—Ft. Argyle on the Ogeechee, Ft. St. Andrews on Jekyl Island, and Ft. William on Cumberland Island—encouraged bands of immigrants to settle at such danger points as Darien and Fredrica, and regulated the Indian trade with an iron hand lest cheated natives take to the war path. Even liquor was outlawed in the colony rather than risk its falling into Indian hands, despite the settlers' complaint that they were ravaged with disease because "Water without any Qualification was the chief Drink." By 1735 England's latest frontier outpost was firmly established, with its traders roaming the forest as far west as the Chickasaw villages from two posts established by the colony: Augusta on the middle Savannah River and Ft. Okfuskee on the Tallapoosa River.

These preparations were not in vain. When the English government, aroused by tales of Spanish cruelty to her merchant seamen, declared war on Spain in October, 1739, only the Yamassee were ready to take up arms against the Georgians; the Creeks, Cherokee, and Chickasaw were safely in the British camp while the Choctaw were too busy defending Louisiana to take any part. With peace assured in western Georgia, Oglethorpe was free to march an army against Florida. One by one the towns of that Spanish domain capitulated during the spring of 1740, until only the stout fort at St. Augustine held out. A Spanish counterattack two years later was beaten off when the English successfully defended themselves at the gory Battle of Bloody Swamp on St. Simon Island. Georgia's victories in the War of Jenkins' Ear, as this Anglo-Spanish struggle was called, typified England's new strength on the southern borderland. With a new colony founded, Indian allegiance won, and Spanish rivals cowed, she was in a far better position to challenge French might in the 1740's than she had been a generation earlier.

French prestige also declined in the Great Lakes country during those years. The region was not officially in dispute—English traders were not yet ready to invade that distant country—but the officials of New France determined to use the period of peace after Queen Anne's War to prepare for the struggle that seemed inevitable. Between 1715 and 1718 half a dozen new forts were scattered through the area on strategic waterways and portages, ranging from Ft. Miami on the Maumee-Wabash portage to Ft. Kaministiquia at the entrance to the Grand Portage into the Rainy Lake country. These gains were offset when an attempt to force the Fox Indians to settle near Detroit started the decade-long Fox War. Until 1730 rebellious tribesmen roamed the forests with bands of Frenchmen in pursuit before the last was slaughtered. Even this did not bring peace, for other tribes of the Northwest took to the warpath to avenge their exterminated brethren. Never was French prestige in the Great Lakes country lower than in the early 1740's.

On two other friction points, New France gained steadily at English expense between 1715 and 1740. One was in the vast wilderness south of Hudson Bay where Quebec traders, led by the Sieur de la Vérendrye, made a valiant effort to divert the flow of peltry southward from the Hudson's Bay Company posts to the St. Lawrence Valley. By 1740 Vérendrye's strategically located trading factories dotted the country between the Grand Portage and the Assiniboine River, and the English company was express-

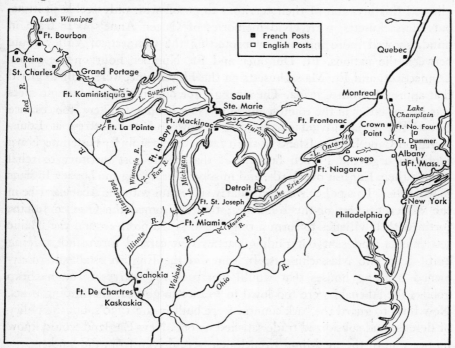

The Northern Borderland, 1713-1744

ing alarm at the diversion of peltry eastward. Even more concerned were royal officials who saw in the T-shaped string of forts thrown across the continent by France—from the St. Lawrence to the Rocky Mountains and extending southward along the Mississippi—a device to cut Britain's possessions in two. Even more serious, because nearer at hand, was French activity in the Lake Ontario country. This began in 1720 when a *voyageur*, Louis Joncaire, secured Seneca consent for a post on the Niagara River. The alarmed English officials, realizing that Iroquois furs—and allegiance —might swing to the French, retaliated by beating down opposition from the Albany traders and establishing Ft. Oswego on the Oswego River in 1725. From that time on agents from Ft. Niagara and Ft. Oswego roamed the Iroquois country, competing for peltry in every village. At this friction point the two nations were in direct commercial conflict by 1740.

Equally irritating to both was the contest for control of the Lake Champlain waterway and the New England-Nova Scotia borderland. The French, having learned the military value of Lake Champlain during the first two colonial wars, attempted to secure control of the lake in 1731 by building Ft. Crown Point at its lower end. Lethargic New York officials allowed this invasion of their territory to go on with only feeble protests, but Massachusetts, with vivid memories of Queen Anne's War fresh in mind, showed more initiative in protecting the Connecticut Valley route between the nations. Ft. Dummer and Ft. Number Four on the upper Connecticut, and Ft. Massachusetts on the Housatonic, were built to guard that approach from Canada. The struggle for domination of strategic spots was just as bitter in the country north of New England. There, too, France gained the initial advantage, building a powerful new fortress at Louisbourg on Cape Breton Island in the 1720's, then sending priests into Nova Scotia to urge the French farmers of that newly lost territory to rebel against their English overlords, and missionaries among the border Indians to win allies. This policy was particularly successful with the Abenaki tribe in the wilderness east of the Kennebec; they welcomed the Quebec Jesuits, fortified their villages to form a ring of palisaded posts around the Maine settlements, and sent out raiding parties that carried torch and scalping knife deep into Massachusetts. In vain did the English establish colony-owned trucking houses that would win back the natives through cheap goods; the Abenaki were too loyal to France to go near the trading posts. New forts to guard the back country were built in the 1730's, but the policy of defense and subsidized trade satisfied no one. New England would know no peace until the meddling Frenchmen were driven from the land.

On each of the French-English borderlands tension was high by 1744; in Georgia and Maine haphazard skirmishing had begun, in the regions about Lake Superior and Lake Ontario the two nations were locked in a bitter commercial war, and in the Lake Champlain country both were occupying military routes through which attacks must come. Yet friction had not reached the point that either welcomed the war that broke out in 1744. King George's War, or the War of the Austrian Succession as it was called in Europe, began when Frederick II of Prussia upset the balance of power by seizing Silesia, then found allies in France and Spain against England and Austria. Fighting was largely confined to the European theater; only on the New England-Nova Scotia frontier was any major engagement fought in America.

There the French struck first, sending an expedition to lay siege to

Annapolis during the summer of 1744. Although the attack was beaten off, the English realized that their Nova Scotian fortress would never be safe as long as the enemy controlled near-by Louisbourg. This was the objective of a force of 4,000 provincials who sailed from Massachusetts on a fleet of merchant vessels in the spring of 1745. Frenchmen watched the approach of the expedition with incredulous amazement; what could these untrained colonials hope to accomplish against a fort so impregnable that it was referred to as the Gibralter of America? They soon found that Yankee ingenuity could offset a lack of military training. The Americans landed under the stone walls of Louisbourg on April 30, 1745, captured a French battery, and turned the defenders' own guns against them with such devastating effect that after forty-nine days the fortress surrendered.

The wartime years were also notable for a shift in Indian diplomacy on the New York frontier. In the past England's relations with the Iroquois had been shaped by the Albany Commissioners, a small group of locally elected magistrates who reflected the traders' viewpoint in their concern for profits rather than expansion. Their insistence on keeping the Five Nations neutral at the start of King George's War so irked imperial authorities that their powers were stripped away and a single Indian commissioner named to formulate the colony's policy. William Johnson, who was to dominate frontier diplomacy for the next generation, was ideally suited for that post. As a trader on the New York borderland since 1738 he had won the respect of the Iroquois through his scrupulous honesty, lavish entertainment at his Mohawk Valley home, Ft. Johnson, and his sympathetic understanding of the native point of view. Under his prodding the tribe took to the warpath during the last years of the war, although their raids did little more than inspire retaliatory French attacks on Albany and Schenectady. Johnson's influence, however, insured Iroquois support in future struggles.

The halfhearted efforts of both French and English in King George's War indicated that neither expected the results to be decisive. The Treaty of Aix-la-Chapelle which ended the conflict in 1748 proved them right; it provided simply that each nation must restore its conquests in Asia, Europe, and America. Although New Englanders grumbled when hard-won Louisbourg was returned to France, they consoled themselves with the thought that peace was only temporary and an opportunity for revenge near.

During the next six years both nations girded themselves for the last of the eighteenth-century wars, fully aware that ownership of North America and of imperial possessions scattered over half the globe would be the prize of the victor. The French gained most during this breathing period, despite the neglect of the dissolute Louis XV who preferred to lavish wealth on mistresses rather than colonies, and despite the indifference of a succession of weak Quebec governors who showed more skill in plundering the royal treasury than the lands of their enemies. Minor officials—realizing as the English did not that any Indian tribe committing itself to either antagonist expected to be protected from the other—used the period of truce to construct a chain of forts that not only won New France invaluable allies but seriously threatened England's position in America.

This building program went on at each of the friction points where frontiers clashed. On the Lake Ontario borderland Ft. Toronto, at the foot of the Toronto portage, and Ft. Présentation on the upper St. Lawrence, served as headquarters for Joncaire and other French agents who worked effectively among the Iroquois. They found the tribesmen, disgusted by English inaction, ready to listen, especially after Johnson resigned his superintendency when the colony refused to reimburse him for presents given the natives. On the New England-Nova Scotia frontier England took the initiative by constructing a strong naval base at Halifax in 1749, and a new outpost, Ft. Lawrence, on the south side of the Missaguash River to guard the entrance to the peninsula. France responded by throwing up a strong fort, Ft. Beauséjour, on the opposite bank of that stream, and by urging the Acadians to rise against the English. In the southern debatable land English prestige also waned when the transfer of Georgia from proprietary to royal control in 1752 so absorbed colonial officials that they neglected their Indian allies. Alert Louisiana leaders seized the opportunity to make peace with the Chickasaw and to send such persuasive agents among the Cherokee and Creeks that by 1753 most of the latter were won over and the Cherokee so tempted that South Carolina built Ft. Prince George among them to prevent their defection.

Yet France, strong as it was on all these borderlands, would never have risked the final conflict if war had not been necessary to keep Englishmen from overrunning the Ohio Valley. Canadians first recognized the strategic importance of that waterway in the 1720's when the Fox Wars forced them to shift their trade routes from the Wisconsin and Illinois portages to the Maumee and Wabash rivers. The advantages of this path were obvious; not only did it shorten the distance between Montreal and the Illinois-Louisiana settlements, but won for France all territory west of the Wabash. Hence three garrisoned posts were erected to guard the portage route: Ft. Miami on the upper Maumee, and Fts. Ouiatanon and Vincennes on the Wabash, all completed before 1731. Frenchmen controlled the lower Ohio River Valley from that time on.

In the meantime English traders began entering the upper Ohio Valley. They came from Pennsylvania, lured west by migrating Shawnee and Delaware Indians who in the late 1720's were pushed from their Pennsylvania hunting lands to new homes at Kittanning and Logstown about the Forks of the Ohio. Traditionally friendly to the English, these tribes welcomed merchants from Lancaster who streamed westward over the West Branch and Juniata rivers, their packs bulging with rum, guns, and ironware. By the close of the 1730's, Englishmen dominated the trade

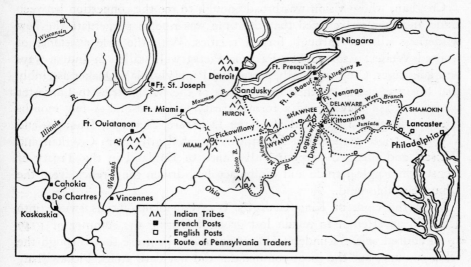

The Ohio Country, 1730-1754

of the upper Ohio Valley, just as the French controlled the lower reaches of that stream. Between the two was a wilderness occupied by tribes nominally friendly to France: the Wyandot, Miami, and Huron. Any expansion of either trading frontier would mean a clash, particularly if the English pushed far enough westward to threaten the Maumee-Wabash portage.

King George's War gave them a chance to do so, for Britain's mighty navy so disrupted French trade that Canadian merchants were unable to secure goods needed for the Ohio Valley tribes. Here was a golden opportunity for the Pennsylvania frontiersmen. That they rose to the occasion was largely due to the skill of a robust Irish trader, George Croghan, who owned a post on the Susquehanna frontier. By the close of 1744 he was operating trading centers at Pine Creek, Logstown, and Beaver Creek on the upper Ohio; from those bases trading expeditions were sent to the Miami and Huron villages and even to the Illinois Indians of the Mississippi Valley. Other traders who followed on the heels of this bold pioneer sent their pack trains along the Great Trail into the depths of the Ohio country, or threw up rough posts at Sandusky, on the Muskingum River, and at the mouth of the Scioto. Croghan climaxed this rapid expansion of the trading frontier in 1748 when he ordered the construction of a palisaded fort at the Miami village of Pickawillany in the very heart of French territory. By the close of King George's War Pennsylvania traders reigned supreme over the wilderness from the Alleghenies to the Wabash River.

Croghan, whose vision was broad enough to see the connection between trade and empire, realized that the time was ripe to perpetuate the new wilderness alliance through formal treaties. With the able assistance of Conrad Weiser, a soft-spoken Palatine Pietist well skilled in Indian ways and languages, Croghan finally persuaded Pennsylvania's Quaker assembly that this was necessary, then lured chiefs of the Miami tribe to Lancaster where in 1748 they signed a formal treaty of friendship. A few months later, in August, 1748, leaders of the Delaware, Shawnee, Iroquois, and Wyandot tribes gathered at Logstown, accepted gifts from Croghan and Weiser, and pledged perpetual allegiance to England in the Treaty of Logstown. English trade and diplomacy had driven the French from the Ohio debatable land.

With the close of King George's War Canadian officials swung into action in an attempt to regain lost ground. During the summer of 1749 two hundred soldiers under Céloron de Blainville were sent through the Ohio country, but the inept commander did not dare attack Pickawillany with his small force and retired in disgrace after burying a number of lead plates proclaiming French ownership of the land. This initial failure was more than overcome two years later when the able Marquis Duquesne became governor of New France. By this time the Ohio Indians were growing restless under English rule, some aroused by the corrupt practices of the Pennsylvania traders, others by the failure of the colony's Quaker legislature to build a fort that would protect their villages from French attacks. Sensing this dissatisfaction, Duquesne ordered a sudden attack on Pickawillany during the summer of 1752. The invaders—a band of French traders and Ottawa Indians under Charles le Langlade—struck so suddenly that Croghan's post was taken by surprise, its defenders killed, and £3,000 in trading goods carried triumphantly to Detroit. Awed by this show of force, the Miami, Huron, and most of the Shawnee deserted the English. The nation's prestige was as low at the end of 1752 as it had been high a year before.

Duquesne saw his opportunity. Why not secure the Ohio country for all time by building a chain of posts from Lake Erie to the Forks of the Ohio?

This would close the West to the hated Pennsylvania traders, guard interior tribes from Iroquois attacks, and give France control of the short French Creek-Allegheny River portage route between Montreal and the Mississippi River. Duquesne acted before the snow melted in the spring of 1753. A construction party that set out from Ft. Niagara in April stopped first at the Lake Erie entrance to the portage to throw up a strong post called Ft. Presqu'Isle, then moved inland to the head of navigation on French Creek where Ft. Le Boeuf was built. Leaving three hundred men to garrison those posts, the party moved on to the junction of French Creek and the Allegheny River where Ft. Venango was begun. An early winter forced the Frenchmen to return to Niagara before constructing a final fort at the Forks of the Ohio.

Alarm flared through the middle colonies. Particularly concerned was Virginia's vigorous Scotch governor, Robert Dinwiddie, who saw that the French move not only threatened his own trading and speculating activities, but promised to deprive his colony of a vast territory claimed under its 1609 charter. In this emergency, he shouldered the burdens of empire by sending a small party under twenty-one-year-old George Washington to warn the Frenchmen that they were on Virginia soil. Washington reached Ft. Venango late in December, 1753, and was well received by Joncaire. "The Wine, as they dosed themselves pretty plentifully with it, soon banished the Restraint," but the English accomplished nothing, for the French declared "that it was their absolute Design to take Possession of the *Ohio,* and by G— they would do it." After a similar reception at Ft. Le Boeuf Washington returned home to report that force alone would drive out the intruders.

Dinwiddie acted at once. In January, 1754, he ordered a construction crew westward to forestall the French by building an English fort at the Forks of the Ohio. The army of 150 men under Washington designated to occupy the fort did not start inland until April. At Wills Creek they met the work party, returning with the disquieting news that a large enemy force was already erecting a powerful fort, Ft. Duquesne, at the Forks. Washington, with more courage than good sense, decided to march against the French although his army was outnumbered ten to one. At Great Meadows, a treeless valley where traders pastured their pack animals, he stumbled on a small French scouting party which was decisively defeated. This foolish act placed Washington in difficulty, for if he advanced or retreated he would surely be surprised by an army from Ft. Duquesne bent on revenge. Hence he ordered his men to throw up earthworks, which they called Ft. Necessity, to wait the attack that was sure to come. There they were found by a French force on July 3, 1754, and after defending themselves valiantly in an all-day battle, accepted honorable terms of surrender. The English were driven from the Ohio country and the Seven Years' War had begun.

The next few years were dreary ones for England. General Edward Braddock, who arrived to take command with two regiments of regulars and a portfolio of very bad advice from the home government, devised a plan of campaign that courted disaster. Instead of concentrating his inadequate force in a drive northward that would cut New France in two, he split his meagre army into four parts, one to attack Ft. Duquesne, another to march on Ft. Niagara, a third to move against Ft. Crown Point, and the last to assault Ft. Beauséjour. This inept strategy brought disaster to three of the four expeditions.

He suffered the worst defeat himself. With three hundred axmen cutting the way, Braddock started for Ft. Duquesne in early June, leading 1,400 redcoats, 450 Virginia militiamen under Washington, and 50 Indian scouts. The large force moved slowly as streams were bridged and small hills leveled for the supply wagons. Sixteen days later, when word reached the English that French reinforcements were on the way, Braddock decided to press on more rapidly with 1,200 men, leaving the artillery and supply trains to advance more slowly. On July 8, 1755, this well-equipped army with flags flying and bagpipes shrilling emerged on an open plain seven miles from its objective. There 600 Frenchmen and 200 Indians, sent from Ft. Duquesne to delay rather than defeat the English awaited them. The two forces clashed at once, fighting in the open in the best European tradition of eighteenth-century warfare. With the first burst of fire Braddock's advance column fell back as it should, but the main body of troops failed to halt and the two surged together in a scene of incredible confusion. The French seized the chance to occupy a hill and ravine on either side of the British, and from this natural cover poured a deadly fire into the struggling mass of redcoats. The retreat finally ordered by the mortally wounded Braddock turned into a rout; of the 1,900 men who started west with Braddock, only 500 returned unharmed to Ft. Cumberland.

The other English campaigns of 1755 were almost as disastrous. The force sent against Ft. Niagara delayed so long that winter overtook the army while it was still at Oswego, while delays were also responsible for the failure of the attack on Ft. Crown Point, although the British did succeed in protecting the entrance to Lake Champlain by building two forts—Ft. Edward and Ft. William Henry—there. Only the third expedition enjoyed any success; Ft. Beauséjour surrendered to 2,000 New England militiamen in June. These inglorious defeats had their inevitable consequences; all along the back country Indians, impressed by French power,

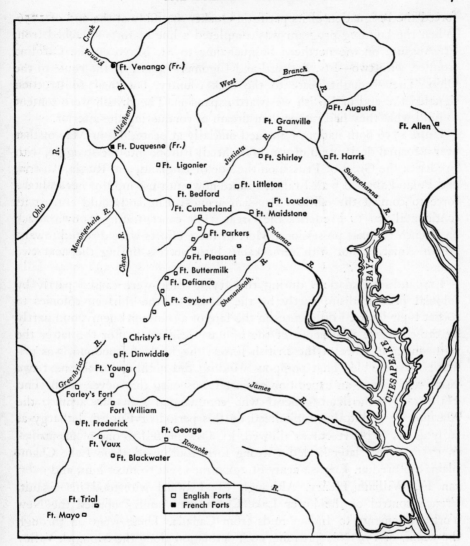

Defense of the Middle Colony Frontier, 1755-1757

flocked to the aid of New France. Their war parties, armed at Ft. Duquesne, harried the frontiers of Pennsylvania, Maryland, and Virginia during the winter and spring of 1756, until heart-rending petitions and grisly relics sent east by the suffering pioneers finally forced the legislatures of those colonies into action. Maryland and Virginia built two hundred posts and blockhouses to guard their western mountain passes during the next two years; Pennsylvania followed the same policy after outraged public opinion forced the resignation of its pacifistic Quaker assembly at the end of 1756. When the building program was completed a line of forts stretched from Ft. Augusta on the northern Susquehanna to Ft. Mayo on the Carolina frontier, with two—Fts. Bedford and Ligonier—guarding the route to the Ohio. They brought peace to the back country, but their construction signaled the end of British westward expansion. The British were content to hold what they had rather than dream of conquering the interior.

Until 1756 both nations remained officially at peace, but in May of that year a formal declaration of war brought all Europe into the struggle, with Frederick the Great of Prussia on the side of England, and Russia, Austria, and Poland aligned with France. France now must use most of her military force to combat the efficient Prussian armies; England could entrust its continental war to Frederick the Great while concentrating its own attack on French colonial possessions. Most of these efforts were directed toward North America, but with remarkably little success during the next two years.

England's tribulations during this trying time were caused partly by colonial provincialism, partly by the refusal of the thirteen colonies to forget their internal differences in the face of a common enemy, and partly by the complete inefficiency of the military leadership. For the latter the commander in chief of the British forces, the Earl of Loudoun, was primarily responsible. That pompous windbag did nothing for the next two years save launch an expedition against Louisbourg that never got beyond Halifax. The brilliant general who commanded Canada's armies, the Marquis de Montcalm, capitalized on this period of English lethargy as fully as his feeble resources allowed. Ft. Oswego fell to one of his armies in 1756; a year later he led a strong force southward along Lake Champlain, captured an English army of 2,000 men sent to meet him, and overran Ft. William Henry. Although Ft. Edward withstood his assault, French control of the lower Lake Champlain country opened the New York settlements to Indian raids from Canada. These went on through the winter of 1757-58, spreading such desolation along the Mohawk Valley that settlers scurried to the safety of Albany or Schenectady. There, as in the West, the victorious French and Indians pressed deep into the American colonies.

But the tide was about to turn. In the fall of 1757 a new ministry, dominated by the forty-eight-year-old William Pitt, was called upon to save the tottering empire. Pitt's imaginative enthusiasm, his reckless theatricalism, his bold energy, turned defeat into victory. Prussia, he saw, could handle the war on the Continent; England must furnish money, ships, and men to carry the attack against the enemy's far-flung world possessions. Parliament, catching his enthusiasm, voted unprecedented sums; "you would as soon hear 'No' from an old maid as from the House of Commons," wrote Walpole. Volunteers flocked to the colors, ships slid from the ways, and all England bustled with preparation, confident that victory was near. Most important of all was Pitt's selection of officers for the new offensive. Brushing aside the antiquated relics elevated to important positions in army and navy by age or social position, he raised brilliant young unknowns from the ranks to positions of power. Two of these dashing young commanders, Colonel Jeffrey Amherst and General James Wolfe, won North America for England.

Yet the first campaign of the spring offensive in 1758 was a failure, largely because its leader was General James Abercromby, an older general who had supplanted Loudoun as American commander the preceding autumn. Hoping to secure the water route that must some day be used for the assault on French Canada, Abercromby headed northward from Albany at the head of 15,000 troops, with a newly built French fort on Lake Champlain, Ft. Ticonderoga, as his objective. There Montcalm, with only 3,600 men prepared his defenses carefully. Electing to defend a low ridge just outside the fort, he threw up zigzag breastworks of earth and logs, reinforced with trees that had been felled to make their branches, trimmed and sharpened, comparable to a modern barbed wire entanglement. Instead of blasting this formidable barrier to pieces with his artillery, Abercromby led his closely packed redcoats in a direct frontal attack that began on the morning of July 8, 1758. Again and again brave troops hurled themselves onto the jagged timber barricade, only to melt away before the deadly fire of concealed Frenchmen. When Abercromby finally ordered a retreat he left 2,000 of England's best fighting men dead on the battlefield.

Montcalm's brilliant victory was in vain, for while he held the middle approach to Quebec the eastern and western gateways fell before the English assault. A formidable army of 12,000 men under Amherst and Wolfe captured the stronghold at Louisbourg on July 26, 1758, after battering breaches in its stout stone walls. At the same time another English force under Colonel John Bradstreet swept westward across the Mohawk Valley, built Ft. Stanwix to guard the Oneida Lake portage, and slipped northward to surprise Ft. Frontenac. When that outpost surrendered after a day's bombardment Canada was cut in two and the way opened for the conquest of the interior. This began in the fall of 1758 when 6,000 men, led by General John Forbes, cut their way slowly across Pennsylvania on the road to Ft. Duquesne. By the time they arrived the Indian allies of New France had deserted and the handful of defenders, realizing the futility of resistance, blew up their once proud stronghold on November 24. The fall of Ft. Duquesne and its reconstruction as Ft. Pitt so influenced the interior

Indians that they took over the task of driving the French from the Great
Lakes country. Through the winter of 1758-59 they carried the torch and
tomahawk against their former allies so effectively that within a year only
Ft. La Baye, Detroit, Mackinac, and the Illinois villages remained in the
hands of New France.

Little wonder, with the West won and the approaches to New France
secure, that England heralded the dawn of 1759 with elation. This was

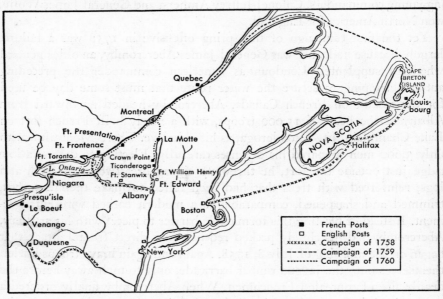

English Campaigns, 1758-1760

the year of the kill. Two expeditions were to close in on the St. Lawrence
Valley, one under Wolfe striking from the sea, the other under Amherst
by land over the Lake Champlain portage; while a minor force subdued
Ft. Niagara. These well-laid plans were carried out with only one hitch.
Niagara fell to a British army on July 25, but Amherst, after capturing
Fts. Crown Point and Ticonderoga, was unable to penetrate the French
defenses about Ft. Lamotte at the head of Lake Champlain. Winter found
him occupied in rebuilding the former French outposts into strong British
forts.

These successes were eclipsed by Wolfe's brilliant campaign against
Quebec. The thirty-two-year-old commander, with a giant fleet carrying
18,000 men, dropped anchor on June 26, 1759, below the towering cliffs
that guarded the formidable French fortress. Montcalm, who waited him
with 15,000 ill-trained provincials, spread his men between the Montmorency

and St. Charles rivers, for he realized that the English could never scale the three-hundred-foot rock walls that barred the northern approaches to the city. These defenses were so well planned that Wolfe spent the entire summer trying in vain to reach his objective. By the end of August, with winter at hand, he decided on a bold stratagem. On the night of September 12 he ordered his ships below the town to begin a heavy bombardment, then, with thirty boat loads of picked troops, started quietly up the river. Slipping past the sleepy French sentries, they landed at a small bay, Anse au Foulon, two miles above Quebec, where a path led upward through a rocky ravine. The twenty-four volunteers who ascended surprised the sentries at the top into surrendering without a shot. Sunrise found 4,500 British redcoats drawn up on the Plains of Abraham. Montcalm, hastily assembling his troops, marched out at 9:30 on that fateful morning of September 13 to give battle. His brave gesture was futile. The Canadian provincials were no match for the well-trained regulars; with the first volley and bayonet charge they broke and ran. Both Wolfe and Montcalm laid down their lives in that epic battle, but Wolfe's sacrifice was not in vain. Four days later the Union Jack floated over the supposedly impregnable French citadel. A year later Montreal surrendered to three giant armies that moved in from south, east, and west. The articles of capitulation signed on September 8, 1760, gave England Canada and all its dependencies.

Although the Seven Years' War was over in America, fighting continued in the rest of the world, with British armies sweeping all before them. Spain, in a futile effort to check the English juggernaught, entered the struggle in 1761, but this only gave England more territory to conquer. One by one the West Indian islands of that proud colonial power fell before the triumphant victors, until finally Cuba passed from Spanish hands in August, 1762. Two months later the Philippines surrendered, just as England's continental ally, Frederick the Great, trounced the last of his foes in Europe.

The Treaty of Paris, signed in 1763, reflected these triumphs. France ceded all territory east of the Mississippi excepting two tiny islands in the St. Lawrence Bay and the city of New Orleans, which was retained when gullible English ministers accepted a boundary drawn down the Iberville River rather than the main channel of the Mississippi. Spain gave up the Floridas in exchange for conquered Cuba and received from France, as an award for an immediate peace, the vast Louisiana Territory lying west of the Mississippi. The Seven Years' War drove the French from North America and opened the great valley of the Mississippi to eager Anglo-American frontiersmen.

# CHAPTER VII

# British Western Policy

## 1763-1776

England's triumphs in the Seven Years' War brought that nation face to face with a problem of unprecedented difficulty. What should be done with the western territories taken from France and Spain? Should they be opened to settlers or held for traders? Should they be governed by the crown or by the colonies? Should they be reserved for Indians or carved into new provinces? The blundering attempts of successive British ministries to answer these questions kept the West in a turmoil between the Treaty of Paris and the outbreak of the American Revolution.

The occupation of the western country began four days after Montreal fell when Major Robert Rogers was dispatched with two hundred Royal Rangers to force the interior French forts to surrender. As the English moved west along the shore of Lake Erie Indians hailed them as saviors, knowing that their coming foretold a day when trading goods would replenish stores exhausted by seven years of war. Rogers wisely encouraged this belief, promising that "all the Rivers would flow with Rum—that Presents from the Great King were to be unlimited—that all sorts of Goods were to be in the Utmost Plenty and so cheap." As overjoyed natives hastened to make peace with the advancing Englishmen, the French saw that resistance was useless, for without tribal aid their cause was lost. Many slipped down the Mississippi to New Orleans, leaving only a skeleton force to surrender Detroit to Rogers' Rangers in November, 1760. During the following summer the forts at Mackinac, St. Joseph, and La Baye were occupied and rebuilt, the latter as Ft. Edward Augustus. By the end of 1761 British arms were planted through the West, except in the Illinois country which was not molested until after the Treaty of Paris.

Traders and landseekers followed close on the heels of the army. From

Montreal and Albany and Lancaster they came, their pack trains and canoes heavily laden with trading goods, to swarm over the Michigan and Wisconsin country during the summers of 1760 and 1761. Some of them represented established Albany or Montreal firms, but more were dissolute wretches who took advantage of the ease with which licenses could be obtained—anyone could become a trader by paying a small fee to a colonial governor—to cheat and debauch the natives. "The most worthless and abandoned fellows in the Provinces," they were called, "being proficients in all sorts of vice and debauchery." They left in their wake a trail of Indian dissatisfaction which grew so intense by the fall of 1761 that Sir William Johnson was hurried to Detroit to quiet thirteen northwestern tribes threatening warfare. Homeseekers caused just as much trouble as they streamed west along the road cut by Forbes' army to the region about Ft. Pitt. By October, 1761, the neighboring tribes were so resentful of their encroachment that the commander, Colonel Henry Bouquet, issued a proclamation forbidding all settlement west of the mountains. Yet this was clearly a temporary expedient. On the shoulders of the home government fell the formidable task of developing a permanent policy for the trans-Appalachian regions.

Clashing interests, in England and America, made this difficult. Ministers, with no precedents to build upon, must devise a system that would satisfy jealous provincials, greedy traders, land-hungry speculators, English merchants, rabid imperialists, sentimental humanitarians, and individualistic frontiersmen. They had to weigh the claims of colonies whose boundaries extended to the Mississippi against the crown's own rights in the interior. They had to reconcile powerful interests that believed the West should be administered from England with equally outspoken provincials who wanted the colonies to control the trans-Appalachian country. Most discouraging of all was the fact that any western policy would certainly be opposed by one or the other of the two most powerful pressure groups in the eighteenth century—the fur traders and land speculators—for any system that would satisfy one was bound to arouse the ire of the other.

The traders wanted the West to become a permanent Indian reservation. They were supported by mercantile thinkers who insisted that colonies were valuable only for agricultural raw materials they supplied the mother country, and by humanitarians with the natives' interests at heart. These groups, and particularly the traders, were in a position to bring strong pressure on the government. Many of the woodsmen who roamed the American forest acted as agents for frontier firms which secured their goods from large merchant houses in Montreal or Philadelphia. These, in turn, purchased supplies from English companies—Robert Hunter Company, Watson and Rashleigh Company, Dyer, Allen and Company—which were influential in both Parliament and the Court. Moreover the large number of Scotch traders who settled in Montreal immediately after the English conquest enlisted the solid support of the Scottish parliamentary delegation so completely that any ministry attacking trade risked its opposition.

Even more influential were the land speculators who demanded that the West should be opened to settlers. They argued that the principal value of colonies lay in their ability to consume manufactured goods produced by the mother country. Expansion would encourage this, both by building up a large interior population and by checking local manufacturing which might develop if the Americans were confined to the seaboard provinces. These plausible rationalizations, however, concealed the speculators' real ambition: to expand their own fortunes rather than the empire. They realized that westward expansion, checked for a decade by war, would be resumed with peace; fabulous fortunes waited those fortunate enough to engross the interior lands before settlers reached there. These beliefs sent speculative fever surging to new heights between the Seven Years' War and the Revolution. Land was the magic lodestone to wealth, the panacea for all misfortune, the one word inevitably capitalized in all correspondence of the day. In England and in America humble commoners, merchant princes, and cabinet ministers scrambled to share the riches sure to be made; the people of all the empire, wrote George Croghan after a visit to London, were "land crazy."

Excitement was greatest in Pennsylvania and Virginia. In the former colony speculation was encouraged by the capital surpluses accumulating in the chests of thrifty Quaker and Jewish merchants and by the westward flow of migrating Scotch-Irish and Germans; prospective land jobbers received an exaggerated impression of the demand for interior lands. In the latter, poverty rather than wealth was responsible. When war and declining tobacco prices fastened a prolonged depression on the Tidewater during the 1760's, planters turned their eyes westward, hoping to recuperate their dwindling fortunes by speculation. In both colonies speculators were encouraged by the colonial governments; Virginia claimed much of the West under its 1609 charter, and Pennsylvania, with no such claims, was anxious to see the interior divided into new colonies by the crown. Yet jobbers realized that royal approval, as well as provincial support, was needed for any extensive grant. This could be obtained only by direct pressure on England's governing officials. For a dozen years speculators' agents swarmed over London, writing pamphlets, buttonholing ministers, and offering generous blocks of stock to governmental leaders in return for support. Bold indeed was the minister who dared defy them.

Several land-jobbing concerns were in existence by 1762 when the government began formulating its western policy, some of them dating back to the years before the Seven Years' War. First on the scene was the Ohio Company, formed by several prominent Virginians in 1747 as a trading and speculating enterprise. Its petition for a grant in the West reached the Board of Trade just as that royal bureau was seeking a means of strengthening England's position in trans-Appalachia. Hence in May, 1748, the

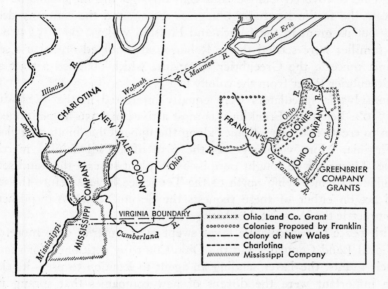

Land Speculation, 1748–1763

company was given 200,000 acres in the area bounded by the Ohio and Great Kanawha rivers and the Allegheny Mountains, with the provision that 300,000 more would be granted if one hundred families were settled within seven years. Although all efforts to secure immigrants failed, the Ohio Company engaged in extensive trading activities under the direction of a skilled woodsman, Christopher Gist, who established a storehouse at Wills Creek, laid out a crude trail to Redstone Creek, and explored much of the region. In 1752 the company petitioned for a revision of its charter, asking that it be given seven more years to plant three hundred settlers in the West, but an expected German migration failed to materialize and others hesitated to move to the frontier while war threatened between France and England.

The failure of the Ohio Company was due partly to Virginia's opposition; the Old Dominion never ceased insisting that the Board of Trade had no right to grant lands given the colony by the charter of 1609. Further crown raids on this territory, colonial officials believed, could be forestalled only if Virginia granted away its own lands. One man who felt this way, John Robinson, speaker of the House of Burgesses, gathered Colonel John Lewis, Dr. Thomas Walker, and other influential citizens together as the Loyal Land Company and obtained 800,000 acres of western territory from Virginia in July, 1748. Walker was sent to locate the lands, but although he discovered Cumberland Gap through the mountains he failed to locate the fertile Kentucky bluegrass region, and the company decided to lay out its grant in the Clinch and Holston valleys. By 1754 two hundred families were settled there. Robinson also helped organize a second Virginia concern, the Greenbrier Company, which obtained a tract along the Greenbrier River from the colony in 1751.

Pennsylvania speculators were equally interested in the West during the 1750's. Benjamin Franklin was most active; in 1756 he petitioned the crown to create two new colonies along the upper Ohio in an area claimed by Virginia. More visionary was the plan of a Philadelphia merchant, Samuel Hazard, who sought permission to plant several thousand settlers in a giant province lying north of the Tennessee River. Before the crown could act on either of these requests the Seven Years' War pushed all plans to settle the West into the background.

With peace the speculative fever swept over America once more. Both the Loyal Land Company and the Ohio Company petitioned for renewals of their grants, the latter sending an agent to London to press its claims. More important were the dozens of new companies that sprang up in England and the colonies. Many were abortive enterprises without capital or influence, but others enlisted the support of important financial and political leaders. Among the visionary schemes were the plans of a group of Scotch merchants to establish the colony of Charlotina west of the Wabash River, the ambitions of New York speculators to plant the province of New Wales on the lower Mississippi, and the efforts of a New Jersey company to convert the lands about the Forks of the Ohio into the colony of Pittsylvania. More practical was the effort of leading Virginians to capitalize on the land bounties granted soldiers in that colony's militia. Forming themselves into the Mississippi Company, with George Washington as its principal promoter, they purchased most of these small grants at a fraction of their value, then, in June, 1763, petitioned the crown for enough land at the junction of the Ohio and Mississippi rivers to satisfy the warrants. This company, in common with most of the others, kept an agent in London after 1763 to urge favorable action on its request.

It was amidst this atmosphere of conflicting demands from speculators and traders that the British government turned to the task of formulating a western policy. The principal burden fell on the shoulders of the Earl of Egremont, whose post as Secretary of State for the Southern Department gave him control of the colonies. He searched during 1762 for a satisfactory solution but before he could act a ministerial shift removed American affairs from his department and vested them in the president of the Board of Trade. The young man who held this post, the Earl of Shelburne, although inexperienced, had enough common sense to follow the advice of his more learned colleagues. Using the detailed outline already prepared by Egremont, and relying heavily on the help of Americans in London and sage advice from John Pownall, permanent secretary of the Board of Trade, Shelburne worked out a comprehensive plan which he submitted to the king on June 8, 1763.

This made no attempt to solve all American problems; such ticklish questions as the disposal of 10,000 troops then in the colonies, and the management of Indian affairs, were left for later study. Instead it sought to provide temporary protection for Indians by forbidding settlement west of a line drawn down the crest of the Appalachians—a line that veered to the east in New York and Georgia where natives still lived and to the west in Virginia to embrace white settlers there. Although the temporary nature of this boundary was stressed, Egremont and Shelburne realized that any restriction would be resented unless excess population was drained away to the north and south. This they hoped to accomplish by erecting three new colonies: Quebec, East Florida, and West Florida. Each was to be ruled by a royally appointed governor and council until the population was large enough, or well enough versed in English ways, to warrant a representative legislature.

This report was as intelligent as could be expected from ministers who knew little of American conditions. If adopted it would probably have satisfied both traders and speculators for the time being, or at least until a better plan could be evolved. Before the cabinet acted, however, disquieting news from America ended all hope of settling the western problem. The Indians were on the warpath once more, and England must push questions of administration aside until the Mississippi Valley was reconquered.

The causes that led to Pontiac's Rebellion were many. Most of the native leaders realized that the expulsion of the French from North America placed them at England's mercy, unable longer to play one nation off against the other. Fur traders and land speculators gave them a taste of their inevitable fate. Traders, left free by indifferent authorities to operate as they pleased, cheated and plundered Indians unmercifully; speculators, disguised as hunters to evade Bouquet's proclamation, spied out their lands and told them of the thousands of white men who would soon cross the mountains. Matters were made far worse by the attitude of Lord Jeffrey Amherst who, as commander of the military establishment, controlled Indian affairs. He despised red men as he did the beasts of the forest; "could it not be contrived," he wrote to Bouquet, "to send the Small Pox among those disatisfied tribes?" And Bouquet replied that he would try to distribute germ-laden blankets among them, adding, "as it is a pity to expose good men against them, I wish we could make use of the Spanish method, to hunt them with English dogs . . . who would, I think, effectually extirpate or remove that vermin." Officials with these views were hardly inclined to adopt the conciliatory attitude necessary to quiet native fears. In 1762 Amherst suddenly reduced the appropriation for the Indian department 40 per cent, at the same time writing Sir William Johnson: "Nor do I think it necessary to give them any presents by way of *Bribes,* for if they do not behave properly they are to be punished." The abrupt announcement that accustomed gifts would not be distributed during the winter of 1762-63 seemed to symbolize the fate awaiting Indians in English hands.

In this mood they listened eagerly to French traders—who told them their Great Father in France had been sleeping but was now ready to help them drive the "red-coated dogs" into the sea—and to a remarkable Ottawa chieftain named Pontiac. Working quietly through the winter of 1762-63, Pontiac carried his message of hate to the northwestern tribes, urging them to unite in a confederation that could push the English back across the mountains. The Indians struck on May 7, 1763, when a horde of savages led by Pontiac surprised Detroit; twenty days later Ft. Pitt was attacked by Shawnee and Delawares. Both garrisons managed to beat off the first assault, but other posts were less fortunate. Mackinac succumbed on June 2 when a band of Chippewa who were playing lacrosse beneath the walls of the fort rushed into the enclosure after a ball, then turned suddenly on the defending troops. One by one the other western forts followed, until the end of July only Detroit, Ft. Pitt, and Ft. Niagara still held out against the triumphant savages. In two months England lost all of the hard-won West.

Amherst struck back promptly. On June 12, 1763, he ordered two expeditions to the relief of besieged western posts. One, under Captain James Dalyell, reached Detroit with goods which allowed the defenders to hold their position; the other, led by Colonel Bouquet, defeated the Indians at the bloody Battle of Bushy Run on August 5 to lift the siege of Ft. Pitt. In October Pontiac, discouraged by these setbacks and heartbroken at the failure of the French to come to his aid, arranged a truce which allowed him to slip away to the Illinois country where he hoped to organize a new offensive. By that time, however, most of his followers had deserted him. Nearly all the western tribes accepted Sir William Johnson's invitation to a peace conference at Niagara in the early summer of 1764, and those that did not—notably the Shawnee and Delaware—were crushed by two expeditions that marched through the Ohio country in the next months, one under Bouquet which shattered Delaware resistance along the Muskingum River, the other under Colonel John Bradstreet that subdued the area below Lake Erie. Mackinac was rebuilt in September, 1764, as a powerful fortress on the south side of the straits, and the West was once more at peace.

Pontiac, however, still lurked in the Illinois country, and to General Thomas Gage, who succeeded Amherst as military commander, the time seemed ripe for an expedition to subdue that sullen chieftain and extend English authority over the neglected French villages. This delicate task was entrusted to the Pennsylvania trader, George Croghan, who started from Ft. Pitt in May, 1765, with a few companions and two boatloads of presents. Near the mouth of the Wabash the party was captured by Kickapoo and Moscoutin Indians and carried to the vicinity of Ft. Ouiatanon, but soon released when protests from all the neighboring tribes convinced the captors of their mistake. A short distance beyond they met Pontiac, on his way to confer with Croghan; arm in arm the two returned to the fort where they smoked the calumet in a grand council that arranged the final peace. "Pontiac and I are on extreme good terms," Croghan wrote, "and I am mistaken if I don't ruin his influence with his own people before I part with him." News of the treaty was hurried to Ft. Pitt, where a hundred troops set out to join Croghan for the final march to the Illinois villages. They reached Ft. de Chartres on October 9, 1765; a day later the commander raised the Union Jack over that venerable fortification and set up a military government to control the colorful crew of *habitants* and traders who lived in the wilderness outpost. Pontiac's Rebellion was ended, and the West secured for England once more.

The uprising, however, upset the plans of British ministers who were struggling to develop a satisfactory western policy. News of the Indian war reached them in August, 1763, just as a ministerial crisis drove Shelburne from the presidency of the Board of Trade. On September 28 his place was taken by the Earl of Hillsborough, a man of poor judgment and inadequate experience, who was nevertheless wise enough to see that the plan worked out by Egremont and Shelburne must be changed in one essential detail. No careful demarcation line could be run in the midst of an Indian rebellion; therefore he recommended that the western boundary for white settlers follow the Appalachian highlands, that Quebec, East

Florida, and West Florida be thrown open to settlement at once, that the trade of the Indian reservation be opened to all who obtained licenses from colonial governors or the military commander, and that all private land purchases from Indians be forbidden. In this form the proclamation was issued by the king on October 7, 1763.

Ignorance and indifference, combined with grim necessity, were responsible for several grievous errors in the Proclamation of 1763. Most glaring was the poorly run boundary which left several hundred whites in Indian territory. Pious phrases ordering frontiersmen who had "willfully or inadvertently seated themselves" on these lands "forthwith to remove themselves from such settlements" could not ease the suffering of those unfortunates. Almost as bad was the failure to provide any civil government for French settlers about Detroit and in the Illinois country; instead they were placed under military rule without access to courts or other bulwarks against tyranny. Even more tragic was the fate of the 80,000 inhabitants of Quebec, where, the Proclamation decreed, the laws of England were to be enforced. This thoughtless edict, which extended harsh antipapal statutes to a Catholic province, deprived the people of nearly all civil and political rights and left them at the mercy of unscrupulous Englishmen who during the next decade systematically stripped them of their property.

At least three men in America saw another fundamental defect in the Proclamation of 1763. Sir William Johnson, his deputy George Croghan, and Colonel John Stuart who became Indian Superintendent for the Southern Department in 1763, realized that trade with the natives must be carefully regulated to ward off another uprising. General Gage was impressed with their arguments, and during the winter of 1763-64 they planned with him a workable method of control. They retained the northern and southern districts, with the boundary line at the Ohio River and a superintendent over each. These were to be divided into two or three subdistricts under deputy superintendents, and into twenty-six smaller areas each embracing one tribe. A commissary, interpreter, and blacksmith were to be maintained at small posts in each tribal division. All trade was to be confined to these posts, where the commissary would set prices, supervise bartering, and protect the natives from unscrupulous traders. This was the plan that Croghan carried to England in February, 1764, seeking royal approval. For some time he cooled his heels in statesmen's offices; "Nothing has been Don Respecting North America," he wrote in March. "The people hear Spend thire time in Nothing butt abuseing one Another and Striveing who Shall be in power with a view to Serve themselves and Thire frends, and Neglect the Publick." Finally, on July 10, 1764, the Board of Trade tentatively adopted his proposals.

The measure, which called for a tax on trading goods to support the elaborate structure, required parliamentary approval, but the Board of Trade was so confident of favorable action that it ordered the two superintendents to put the system in force at once. Stuart was anxious to act, for his southern territory was so overrun with traders that competitive bidding forced fur prices down to a point where profits could only be made by cheating the Indians. This could be remedied, he knew, only by limiting the number of merchants entering the Indian country. Hence when he called natives and colonial officials together at a Pensacola conference to explain the new ruling he not only suggested that commissaries regulate trade in each village, but asked that governors grant licenses only to a few selected traders. Although the Indians hailed the plan with rejoicing, colonial authorities remained unmoved, knowing that traders' bribes and profits from license fees were two of their principal sources of income. The governors of Georgia and South Carolina flatly refused to limit the number of permits, while the governor of Virginia insisted that he had never heard of the Proclamation of 1763! All closed their courts to Stuart when he tried to punish offenders. With this the whole system broke down, leaving southern trade as chaotic as before.

Conditions in the Northwest were no better. Sir William Johnson ruled that all trade must be conducted at Detroit or Mackinac—Ft. Edward Augustus was never rebuilt after Pontiac's Rebellion—and forced all traders to post bonds that would be forfeited if they operated elsewhere. The results were disastrous. The Indians, long accustomed to regular visits from French traders, refused to make the trek from Wisconsin or Ohio to Detroit and Mackinac; honest traders who posted bonds and took out licenses waited in vain for natives who never came. Instead trade passed into the hands of two other groups: unlicensed traders from Montreal and Albany who slipped quietly into the wilderness to barter with the Indians, and illegal French *voyageurs* who swarmed over the northwest from the Spanish posts of St. Genevieve and, after 1765, St. Louis. Both sent their furs south to New Orleans and obtained trading goods from that port. By the close of 1766 the commandants at Detroit and Mackinac were complaining that the Plan of 1764 had diverted the trade of all the Northwest from England to Spain and demanding the right to send traders to the Indians once more. This was done during 1767 by the Mackinac commander, who paid for his folly with a court martial, but Johnson was finally convinced. That fall the region north of Lake Superior and the Ottawa River was opened to all licensed merchants; through the rest of the Northwest illegal traders gradually usurped most of the peltry traffic.

Only in the Illinois country did the Plan of 1764 operate with any suc-

cess. The riches concealed in that neglected region were first realized by
George Croghan, who returned from his western journey in 1765 fully
convinced that a fortune waited the firm that secured the right to supply the
Illinois Indians, *habitants,* and garrisons with supplies. With this in mind
he sought out friends in the prominent Philadelphia company of Baynton,
Wharton & Morgan, and, with a quarter of the profits as his own reward,
helped secure them a monopoly over the trade. Thus was launched the
"Grand Illinois Venture," the most elaborate trading scheme in colonial
America's history. All through the summer of 1766 pack trains plodded
between Philadelphia and the Ohio, fighting off hostile frontiersmen who
objected to the sale of guns and scalping knives to the Indians, while at
Ft. Pitt a crew of carpenters built boat after boat to carry goods westward.
In the autumn a fleet of sixty-five barges manned by 350 boatmen set out,
bound for stores that one of the partners, George Morgan, had built at
Vincennes, Kaskaskia, Cahokia, and Ft. de Chartres. When the vessels
reached their destination without mishap the Illinois venture seemed
launched on the road to success.

Almost from the first, however, the scheme was destined to failure.
Its magnitude was a drawback; not even the wealthy firm of Baynton,
Wharton & Morgan could stand the financial drain necessary before such
a giant enterprise paid profits. To make matters worse, the expected trade
did not develop. A rival concern secured the contract to supply the garrison
when Morgan refused to match its bribe, the French *habitants* preferred
to buy from their own countrymen across the Mississippi, and hoped-for
orders from the Indian commissary failed to materialize when General
Gage in 1768 forbad further presents to the tribes. Most serious of all
was the failure of the fur trade to show any profit. This was due partly to
the extermination of fur-bearing animals in that hunted-over region, but
more to the natives' refusal to come to Morgan's stores when they were
offered equally good prices by French traders from St. Louis and St.
Genevieve. By the end of 1768 the Grand Illinois Venture was an admitted
failure, and the firm of Baynton, Wharton & Morgan trembled on the verge
of bankruptcy.

The collapse of this trading structure demonstrated the failure of the
Plan of 1764. The need of reform was brought home to the British government by cold figures: peltry exports declined from £28,067 in 1764
to £18,923 in 1768. Officials at home and abroad conjured up schemes
to frustrate the French *voyageurs* who robbed England of her wealth:
to build forts at the mouths of the Ohio and Illinois rivers to turn back
their canoes and a canal along the Iberville River to give English traders
a direct outlet to the Gulf. Johnson, on the other hand, insisted that his

plan could never be properly tested until new posts were established at La Baye, Sault Ste. Marie, Sandusky, St. Joseph, Ouiatanon, and the Maumee River. He was answered by government agents who held that the cost of the system would then exceed its profits. These arguments gained strength after February, 1767, when a 25 per cent reduction in the English land tax made colonial economy imperative. Why, members of Parliament demanded, should they be taxed for the benefit of distant savages who paid back kindnesses with tomahawk and scalping knife? A less expensive Indian establishment was needed.

Dissatisfaction with the Plan of 1764 was only one factor underlying the demand for a revision of England's western policy. Even more insistent on reform were the land speculators. These avaricious individuals were not discouraged by the Proclamation of 1763. George Washington summed up their views when he wrote: "I can never look upon that proclamation in any other light . . . than as a temporary expedient to quiet the minds of of Indians. . . . Any person, therefore, who neglects the present opportunity of hunting out good lands, and in some measure marking and distinguishing them for his own (in order to keep others from settling them), will never regain it." In this mood, wealthy easterners listened eagerly to traders and hunters who returned from the West with tales of fertile lowlands in Kentucky and Ohio, of grassy plains in Illinois, of level timber lands about the Great Lakes—all waiting the magic touch of man to become prosperous farming communities. Fortune would surely smile on the landowner who was there when the teeming coastal settlers burst through the mountains! All along the seaboard influential colonists plotted means of engrossing western lands: George Washington kept a regular agent in the upper Ohio country staking out claims, George Croghan accumulated several hundred thousand acres about Ft. Pitt, Richard Henderson of North Carolina employed Daniel Boone to hunt out the choice Kentucky regions on his hunting trips, and hundreds of others scrambled to absorb the best regions before the Proclamation Line was moved west.

More important were the speculating companies that blossomed by the score between 1763 and 1767. Most of them were too small to influence the British government, but three made their weight felt. One was formed by General Phineas Lyman of Connecticut who in 1766 gathered some of the officers who had served together during the Seven Years' War into an organization known as the Military Associates. They petitioned the crown for a grant at the mouth of the Ohio. Another was originated by George Croghan, who saw that losses suffered by traders at the outbreak of Pontiac's Rebellion might be put to profitable use. During 1764 and 1765 he brought these "Suffering Traders"—who included the wealthy

Philadelphia firms of Baynton, Wharton & Morgan, and Simon, Trent, Levy & Franks—together into a compact organization, secured the blessing of Sir William Johnson and General Gage, and in March, 1766, launched the Illinois Company with the avowed purpose of securing 1,200,000 acres of land along the Mississippi as compensation for their losses. Benjamin Franklin was soon added to press its claims in England.

The third company formed between 1763 and 1767, the Indiana Com-

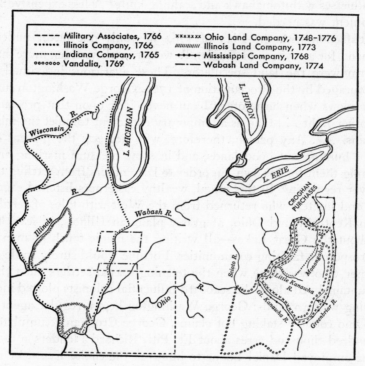

Land Speculation, 1763–1776

pany, illustrated the careful planning of the speculators. Its members were the same "Suffering Traders" who made up the Illinois Company: George Croghan, Joseph Galloway of Pennsylvania, Governor William Franklin of New Jersey, Benjamin Franklin, and the Philadelphia firms of Baynton, Wharton & Morgan, and Simon, Trent, Levy & Franks. Its objectives, however, were different. Instead of seeking a grant in the distant Mississippi Valley, the Indiana Company petitioned for a tract lying just west of the Proclamation Line between the Monongahela, Little Kanawha, and Ohio rivers. The astute jobbers who worked with Croghan were thus assured lands whatever the government's decision; if officials agreed to shift the

Proclamation Line westward the Indiana Company was on hand with its claims, if interior colonies were deemed wiser the Illinois Company could press for recognition. Both clamored constantly for a revision in western policy that would open the trans-Appalachian country to settlers.

Pressure from greedy speculators, dissatisfied traders, economy-minded parliamentarians, and idealistic Indian agents was so great by 1767 that the British government turned at last to revising its frontier policy. Once more the task of formulating a satisfactory system fell to the Earl of Shelburne who became Secretary of State for the Southern Department in a new ministry formed by William Pitt in July, 1766. His solution, embodied in a report that he laid before the cabinet on September 11, 1767, showed how completely he had succumbed to the wiles of the land speculators. He proposed to abolish the whole Indian department, return control over trade to the colonies, withdraw all troops from the West except for small garrisons at Niagara, Ft. Pitt, Ft. de Chartres, and Natchez, to build a new post on the Iberville River, and throw the whole Mississippi Valley open to settlement. Shelburne suggested three interior colonies: at Detroit, in Illinois, and on the upper Ohio,—two of them, strangely enough, on lands claimed by the Illinois and Wabash companies! Fortunately this scheme was never adopted, for it would have bred a new Indian war more serious than Pontiac's Rebellion. Before it could be acted upon a ministerial shake-up deprived Shelburne of his control over American affairs. These were centered in a new office, Secretary of State for the Colonies, which was assumed by Lord Hillsborough in January, 1768. Once more, as in 1763, policies developed by Shelburne were left to Hillsborough for application.

The new minister immediately recognized the glaring weakness of the proposals. His own recommendations, adopted by the cabinet in March, 1768, contained the first workable plan for the West yet devised. The Indian superintendents were retained, but with powers restricted to imperial functions: land purchases from the Indians, readjustments of the boundary line, and settling diplomatic questions. Local matters, such as the fur trade, were left in the hands of the colonies. This made western posts unnecessary and all were ordered abandoned except those at Detroit, Mackinac, and Niagara which were needed for protection or to offset French intrigue. Instead of setting up three western colonies, Hillsborough attempted to satisfy expansionists by ordering the Proclamation Line shifted westward. This pleased the fur traders, as well as assuring English merchants the interior trade which might have flowed south to New Orleans.

General Gage accepted the new regulations without comment and immediately began withdrawing the western garrisons; within a year only

Niagara, Detroit, Mackinac, Ft. Pitt, and Ft. de Chartres remained and in 1771 the latter two were abolished. At the same time the Indian superintendents dismantled their elaborate structure of commissaries, blacksmiths, and interpreters. The traders were delighted. Once more they swept into the West to establish their posts through the northern country as far as Lake Winnipeg and the Sioux lands beyond the Mississippi; in 1769 seventy-seven licenses were granted to small companies and the number steadily increased during the next years. Peltry again moved toward Montreal rather than New Orleans, but the change was not without its disadvantages, for Indians were soon grumbling their dissatisfaction at the conduct of the unregulated traders.

In the meantime orders to shift the Proclamation Line westward reached America. Both Stuart and Johnson welcomed the assignment. Stuart especially recognized the injustice of the older line; since 1765 he had sounded out the Creeks, Cherokee, and Chickasaw on a more acceptable boundary. By the close of 1767 he and the tribesmen agreed on a line running from Tryon Mountain in northern South Carolina across Georgia and around the coast of the Floridas to the Iberville River. The Creeks, who gained the portion of Georgia between the Ogeechee River and the original Proclamation Line, readily confirmed these earlier treaties at a conference in Pensacola in November, 1768. Although Stuart was unable to negotiate with the Choctaw and Chickasaw because of a Creek-Choctaw war then in progress, these tribes had agreed to a preliminary treaty in 1765 and for all practical purposes the boundary extended from North Carolina to the western limits of English territory.

These arrangements were made without difficulty because speculators had no interest in the Georgia and Carolina back country, but when Stuart attempted to extend the line northward across Virginia his troubles began. Dr. Thomas Walker and Colonel Andrew Lewis, who dominated the Loyal Land Company and the Greenbrier Company, were the principal architects of the colony's obstructionist tactics, for they knew that any properly negotiated treaty between Stuart and the Cherokee would place their lands beyond the white settlements. Under their prodding Virginia refused to recognize Stuart's authority to negotiate until royal orders arrived during the spring of 1768, then named Walker and Lewis to serve as the colony's representatives at the conferences. The superintendent recognized the folly of drawing up a treaty with these worthies present, especially as both openly declared their intention of pushing the demarcation line westward to the Tennessee River. Hence instead of struggling with two such uncompromising delegates he neglected Virginia entirely when he assembled the Cherokee at the Indian village of Hard Labor on

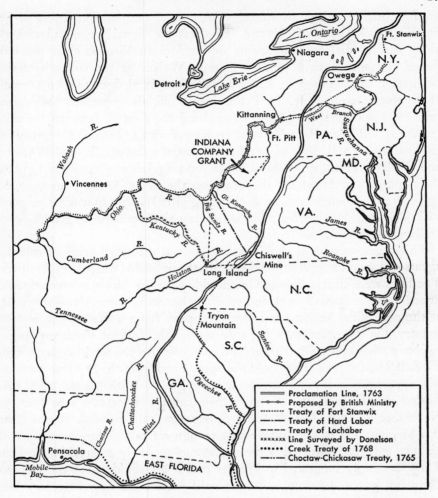

The Indian Demarcation Line

October 14 to draft the Treaty of Hard Labor. This extended the boundary northward from Tryon Mountain to Chiswell's Mine, then straight to the mouth of the Great Kanawha. Probably Stuart hoped that this line, which gave Virginia more territory than one originally plotted along the Great Kanawha, would so please the colony's officials that they would overlook his breach of diplomatic etiquette.

Sir William Johnson's task was to extend the boundary northward from the mouth of the Great Kanawha River across Pennsylvania to the Indian village of Owege in southern New York, leaving for subsequent negotiations the troublesome question of demarcation in the Iroquois country. To arrange this, he called a conference of most of the northern tribes at Ft. Stanwix in the autumn of 1768. This was the signal for speculators all along the colonial front to spring into action. In Virginia their pressure forced the appointment of Dr. Thomas Walker as the colony's official delegate to the meeting; he set out for Ft. Stanwix pledged to open as much of Kentucky as possible. In Pennsylvania officials impressed their commissioners with the importance of securing the country between the Susquehanna and West Branch rivers. In New York the Indiana Company set to work with a will. Two of its most influential members, Samuel Wharton and William Trent, spent the summer securing Johnson's promise to press their company's claims for the grant on the upper Ohio, then traveled through the Iroquois country distributing gifts lavishly to win native good will. The stage was set for a battle between rival speculating groups, with Indians the innocent sufferers.

This began as soon as the 3,400 natives and the small army of colonial agents and speculators assembled beneath the palisaded walls of Ft. Stanwix. The lines were clearly drawn. On one side were the Virginia interests, who hoped to upset Stuart's work and open the Kentucky country to settlement, at the same time keeping any other company from a share of their back country. On the other were the members of the Indiana Company, eager to obtain their upper Ohio grant, and conscious that the territory lay within Virginia's boundaries. They held the upper hand from the first, for Johnson was apparently a secret member of their group. With his aid, they persuaded the Iroquois to sell them their coveted 1,800,000 acre tract on November 3, 1768, but Walker's consent was still needed. It was clear this Virginia delegate would hesitate to sign a treaty ceding away part of his own colony. In this crisis the speculators probably arranged a bargain. They seemingly suggested to Walker that if he would accept the Indiana Company grant, Johnson in turn would extend the new boundary line past the mouth of the Great Kanawha to the Tennessee River. This would either force Stuart to redraw the southern demarcation line in such a way that lands of the Loyal and Greenbrier companies would be opened to settlers, or so confuse the whole boundary system that all Kentucky would be legitimate prey for speculators.

These were the provisions embodied in the treaty of Ft. Stanwix which was signed on November 5, 1768. The line began, not at Owege, but near Ft. Stanwix—thus securing much of southwestern New York for the English—cut west across Pennsylvania to open the Susquehanna Forks region to pioneers, and extended along the Allegheny and Ohio to the mouth of the Tennessee. In return the Indians were given gifts worth £10,460. Johnson explained the violation of his orders—which bound him to end the line at the Great Kanawha—by saying that the Iroquois insisted on ceding Kentucky to the English as proof of their ownership. There is no doubt that they were willing to sell their shadowy claims as a gesture of good will, but Johnson should certainly never have accepted. He was wise enough in frontier ways to know that his action not only upset the whole demarcation system, but angered the Cherokee, Shawnee, and Delaware tribes by depriving them of hunting ground they rightly considered their own, and left the whole West in a turmoil. Worst of all, his acceptance of the Tennessee boundary showed that the line could be shifted west by any speculators with enough influence over the superintendents.

The results of this ill-advised policy were foreordained. Dr. Walker returned to Virginia so determined to force a new treaty from Stuart that his pressure, combined with prodding from Colonel Lewis and colonial authorities, was irresistible. The superintendent, after delaying as long as possible, finally consented to extend the boundary west along the northern border of Tennessee to a point near the Long Island of the Holston River, then north to the mouth of the Great Kanawha. This was done at the Treaty of Lochaber, signed in October, 1770, with the Cherokee receiving compensation in the form of £2,500 worth of gifts provided by Virginia. Even now, with most of the lands claimed by the Loyal and Greenbrier companies opened at last, the process of grabbing Indian territory did not end. The party sent to survey the Lochaber treaty line in the spring of 1771, instead of turning north from Long Island toward the mouth of the Great Kanawha, started in a northwesterly direction—the fault either of poor instruments or of pressure from speculators on its leader, John Donelson. Reaching a river which they took to be the West Branch of the Big Sandy, Donelson persuaded the Cherokee accompanying him that it would be easier to run the line along the stream than directly through the wilderness. They agreed, for an additional £400, but unfortunately the river was the Kentucky rather than the Big Sandy, and their acceptance opened another large territory to the whites. Stuart accepted the Donelson line reluctantly, partly because the inaccurate maps of that day minimized the error, and partly because he recognized the futility of opposing the speculators.

The rapid westward shift of the boundary between 1768 and 1771 plunged Englishmen and Americans into a new period of speculation— with lands opened by the treaties of Hard Labor, Lochaber, and Ft. Stanwix as the prize. The older companies, many of them dormant for several years, led the scramble; the Ohio Company sent petitions and agents to London to urge a renewal of its grant, the Military Adventurers ambitiously requested the whole area between the Ohio and the Alleghenies, the Mississippi Company begged rights to the same vast region, and individual operators such as George Washington started west to stake out lands in the Great Kanawha country. More important were efforts of the Indiana Company to secure royal confirmation for its grant, for they launched the greatest speculative enterprise of America's colonial period.

These started modestly enough in December, 1768, when Samuel Wharton reached London with instructions to seek support from the Privy Council, rather than Lord Hillsborough, the Colonial Secretary, who was known to be unalterably opposed. Wharton saw at once that two steps were necessary: the Indiana Company must absorb rivals whose claims interfered with its own, and it must win enough political support by judicious stock distributions to override Hillsborough in the ministry. If all these groups were to be rewarded with land a larger territory was needed. Wharton worked through the summer of 1769, button-holing politicians and bargaining with agents of other companies, to shape a new organization that would make this possible. The Ohio Company and George Washington were persuaded to join in return for promises of sizeable grants. Thomas Walpole, a prominent banker and politician, was won over and helped to enlist a roster of distinguished men—George Grenville, Lord Hertford, Lord Camden, Thomas Pownall, and others from the Privy Council—all chosen carefully to give the company representation in the various political factions governing England. By December 1769, Wharton felt strong enough to lay his proposition before Lord Hillsborough. The Indiana Company, he announced, wished to buy the entire Ft. Stanwix cession, paying the crown £10,460, the exact amount spent at the conference.

Wharton, who expected immediate disapproval from Hillsborough, could scarcely contain his surprise when the Colonial Secretary not only seemed friendly but even suggested that the company's request was too modest. Why not, he proposed, petition for a grant large enough to form a new colony? The delighted speculators acted at once. On December 27, 1769, they met in London, drew up articles of agreement as the Grand Ohio Company, and petitioned the crown for a tract extending from the Forks of the Ohio south to the Greenbrier River and west to the mouth of the Scioto—some 20,000,000 acres in all. They would, they agreed, establish a proprietary colony known as Vandalia (in honor of the royal consort who was supposedly descended from the Vandals), bear all expenses of colonization, and pay the king a quitrent after twenty years.

When Hillsborough suggested the larger grant he did so only because he believed that the request would be too unreasonable to be considered by the government. He failed, however, to count on the enormous political power of the company. The petition was approved by the Lords of the Treasury in April, 1770, sent to the Privy Council in May, and referred favorably to the Board of Trade. Hillsborough's influence was strong enough in that body to delay action until April, 1772, when the board finally reported against the grant. This was the signal for the Colonial Secretary's political opponents, who were strongly represented in the company, to leap to the attack. They were so successful that Hillsborough was forced to resign from the ministry on August 1, 1772. The new Colonial Secretary was the Earl of Dartmouth, an enthusiastic supporter of the Vandalia claims, who ten days later issued a report endorsing the colony. This was accepted by the King and Privy Council on August 14, 1772. All seemed clear sailing for the jubilant Wharton who had apparently engineered the greatest speculative *coup* of the eighteenth century.

Only one thing more was needed: a charter authorizing the proprietors to set up a governmental system for Vandalia. This step, which seemed a simple formality, actually proved a fatal stumbling block, largely because interest in the colony declined steadily after August, 1772. This was partly due to the fact that many ministers who voted for the grant only to embarrass Hillsborough were no longer interested, and partly to the growing revolutionary agitation in America; the home government hesitated to establish a new province until excitement died down. Wharton stormed and pleaded in vain. Ministers turned a deaf ear to his entreaties until the Revolutionary War ended all hope for Vandalia's prompters.

The collapse of the Walpole Company, as it was known after its principal patron, opened the way for several minor speculating schemes that flourished briefly just before the colonies declared independence. One was hatched by General Phineas Lyman who obtained several thousand acres of West Florida land in 1773 and vainly petitioned the crown to recognize his holdings as the colony of Georgiana. Two others sprang from an ingenious interpretation of an English legal opinion by William Trent, a prominent speculator active in the Grand Ohio Company. In 1772 he stumbled across a statement issued in 1757 by the Earl of Camden, the Attorney General, and Charles Yorke, the Solicitor General, concerning land ownership in India: "In respect to such places, as have been or shall be acquired by treaty or grant from the Grand Mogul or any of the Indian princes or governments, your Majesties' letters patent are not necessary, the property of the soil vesting in the grantees of the Indian-grants." Trent carefully copied this sentence, leaving out "the Grand Mogul" to make the decision apply to America, and interested some of his Vandalia friends in the bold plan of purchasing western lands directly from the

Indians—despite the obvious fact that the justices intended their words to apply to the highly developed Indian princes rather than the primitive savages of the colonies.

Acting in great secrecy, they sent instructions ordering Croghan to buy Ohio lands from the Indians. Unfortunately these orders were entrusted to another speculator, William Murray, who opened the letter as soon as he was at sea and, realizing the possibilities, determined to beat Trent at his own game. As soon as Murray reached Philadelphia he interested several merchants in this promising gamble and together they formed the Illinois Land Company and the Wabash Land Company, in April, 1774. Lord Dunmore, governor of Virginia, was included in the latter to insure that colony's support. Four large tracts in the Illinois country and along the Wabash River were purchased from the natives, despite a firm warning from the Earl of Dartmouth that the Camden-Yorke decision did not apply to America. The speculators, hoping for a reversal of British policy, continued to claim their tracts until the outbreak of the Revolution. In the meantime Croghan accumulated nearly 6,000,000 acres between the forks of the Ohio and Big Beaver Creek for the Trent interests. Both Croghan and Trent also attempted to revive the Indiana Company, taking advantage of the strained relations between the colonies and the mother country to begin selling land at a Pittsburgh office opened in January, 1776.

The persistence of these speculating concerns demonstrated the failure of England's western policy. Instead of checking their greedy operations, the revised Proclamation Line of 1768 only inspired them to new efforts or sent them scurrying to buy land illegally from the Indians; so long as they believed the interior would someday be opened to settlers no imaginary boundary could keep them out. The only actual sufferers were the pioneer farmers and the Indians, for the former could not gamble as could the speculators on claims that might be declared void by the crown, and the latter were left at the mercy of avaricious land seekers and unregulated traders. American greed and British stupidity combined to produce an ill-conceived and poorly executed system that bred colonial discontent without settling any of the problems of the frontier.

Nor did the final step taken by the home government in its attempt to create a satisfactory western policy improve matters. The Quebec Act, passed by Parliament in 1774, was designed to right the wrongs suffered by French-Canadians under the Proclamation of 1763 and provide civil government for the inhabitants of Detroit, Mackinac, and the Illinois villages. It granted complete religious toleration to Quebec Catholics, gave them a greater degree of self-government, ordered the courts to administer French civil law, and extended the boundaries of the province west to the

Ohio and Mississippi rivers. This tolerant measure suffered a sorry fate in the hands of the intolerant colonists. Virginia vehemently denied the crown's right to award her western territories to another colony, speculators protested against an act which closed the Illinois country to their fraudulent schemes, and traders denounced a measure which promised to bring them under the closer regulation of Montreal officials. In the popular mind the Quebec Act was linked with the "Intolerable Acts" passed by Parliament at the same time and universally damned for its enlightened stand on "Popery." To most Americans it seemed to crown the edifice of British blunders that had been reared since 1763.

# CHAPTER VIII

# Settlement Crosses the Mountains

## 1763-1776

The speculators who argued for a western policy that would foster colonies in the Mississippi Valley realized that nothing could hold back the pioneers who in 1763 were poised on the crest of the Appalachians, ready to move into the interior of the continent. For a century and a half colonists had been hemmed in by towering mountains, hostile Indians, and warlike Frenchmen, while immigrants and natives vied for overcrowded coastal lands. Now the barriers were down—the French subdued, the Indians cowed, the mountains pierced by military roads—and even before the Seven Years' War ended pioneers cast covetous glances toward the rolling hill country that fringed the western edge of the Great Valley. During the next dozen years frontiersmen assaulted that wilderness so successfully that by the time of the Revolution their lonely cabins dotted the lowlands about the Forks of the Ohio, the bluegrass region of Kentucky, and the winding valleys of the upper Tennessee River.

That Pennsylvania, New Jersey, Virginia, and North Carolina contributed most heavily to this migration was due partly to the pressure of surplus population in these Middle Colonies, partly to the presence there of routes to the interior. The Scotch-Irish and German immigrants who made their homes in the western valleys of those provinces filled them to the saturation point. Before the cramped pioneers lay tempting highways westward. From Pennsylvania, Maryland, and Virginia they could follow the crude traces—Braddock's Road or Forbes' Road—cut by Britain's armies to the Forks of the Ohio. From western Virginia and Maryland they could make their way along the valleys of the Cheat or Youghiogheny rivers to that same spot. Farther south lay one of nature's grandest passageways, Cumberland Gap, which offered easy passage from back-country

Virginia and North Carolina into the hilly uplands of Kentucky. Other travelers could follow the Watauga, Holston, and Clinch rivers into eastern Tennessee. This combination of land-starved frontiersmen and easy transportation routes explains why the Appalachian frontier bulged first in the center.

The movement began long before the Seven Years' War. Thomas Cresap, a restless woodsman, spied out the country about the Forks of the Ohio as early as 1750. Three years later Christopher Gist blazed a trail from the Potomac River to Redstone Creek, a tributary of the Mononga-

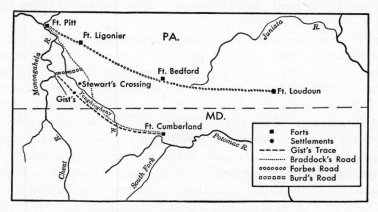

Western Pennsylvania, 1760–1776

hela, where he built a cabin and persuaded eleven other families to settle near by. Not far away William Stewart founded a small settlement at Stewart's Crossing during the same year; others followed until by the end of 1754 a sizable group peopled the middle Monongahela. The outbreak of the Seven Years' War drove them back, but Forbes' successful expedition against Ft. Pitt in 1758 set the tide flowing again. They came by the score now, some along Braddock's Road and an extension built by Colonel James Burd to Redstone Creek in 1759, others along the Ft. Pitt highway cut through the wilderness by Forbes. By 1760 a dozen cabins clustered about the mouth of Redstone Creek, while Ft. Pitt was surrounded by 146 hastily built houses.

This rush of settlers into a region guaranteed the Indians by treaty—the Treaty of Easton (1758)—alarmed British officials who realized that tribesmen would not sit idly by while pioneers turned hunting grounds into corn fields. Colonel Henry Bouquet, the commandant at Ft. Pitt, sought to check the movement in 1761 by forbidding all settlement west of the mountains, but still they came, disguised now as hunters to escape royal wrath. In vain the indignant colonel stormed through the countryside, burning cabins and herding inhabitants eastward. The wilderness was too large to patrol; craving for cheap lands was too strong to check. The people, wrote one official at the time, "will remove as their avidity and restlessness incite them. They acquire no attachment to Place: but wandering about Seems engrafted in their Nature; and it is a weakness incident to it that they Should forever imagine the Lands further off, are Still better than those upon which they are already Settled." The movement went on until 1763 when Ft. Pitt was surrounded by several hundred houses and a thin band of settlements bordered the upper Monongahela River.

Chief Pontiac succeeded where Colonel Bouquet failed. His savage Delaware and Shawnee warriors wiped out six hundred settlers and sent the rest scurrying for the safety of Ft. Pitt, Ft. Ligonier, or Ft. Bedford. For two years western Pennsylvania was deserted except for garrisons and triumphant Indians, until Colonel Bouquet's 1764 Ohio expedition allowed a new westward surge of the frontier. Then the Monongahela Valley filled rapidly with persistent pioneers who recrossed the mountains to bury their dead and build new cabins on the blackened ashes of the old. By 1768 2,000 Americans lived along the Youghiogheny, Monongahela, Redstone, and Cheat valleys and this time they were there to stay. Not even the frantic efforts of General Gage and George Croghan, who issued repeated proclamations against encroachment on lands guaranteed Indians, could dislodge them; nor were they frightened when the Pennsylvania legislature in 1768 decreed the death penalty for those who did not return to the white territory east of the Proclamation Line. A few timid souls obeyed, but more defied Pennsylvania and the Crown until the Treaty of Ft. Stanwix opened the whole region south and east of the Ohio River in 1768.

This treaty, which removed the last obstacle to expansion, sent a stream of settlers westward toward the Forks of the Ohio. Land was easily obtainable; both Virginia and Pennsylvania claimed the region and sold territory freely to homeseekers and small speculators. Most of the farmers bought directly from a Pennsylvania land office established at Pittsburgh (as the settlement at the Forks was now called) in April, 1769; on its first day of business, 2,790 purchasers stormed the office doors and within four months a million acres were sold. By this time nearly 5,000 families lived on the Pennsylvania frontier. "All this spring and summer," wrote Croghan in 1770, "The roads have been lined with waggons moving to the Ohio." In 1771 the population reached 10,000 families; two years later a traveler reported the country thickly settled for 150 miles south of the Forks. So rapid was the expansion that by 1774 General Gage was again warning pioneers not to cross the Ft. Stanwix boundary into the Indian reservation.

While the Pennsylvania frontier was filling, other immigrants moved down the Greenbrier and New rivers to the fertile valley of the Great Kanawha. Lewisburg and Peterstown were laid out in 1769 and 1770 by frontiersmen from Virginia, and three years later Thomas Bullitt, another adventurer from the South Fork frontier, built his cabin on the Great Kanawha. The few dozen families who followed him were joined by others who advanced along the south bank of the Ohio from Pittsburgh, until by 1776 the whole triangle between that river, the Great Kanawha, and the

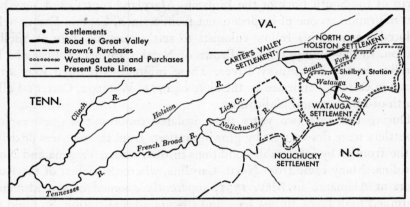

The Eastern Tennessee Frontier, 1760–1776

mountains was being settled. As the newcomers were well in advance of Virginia's surveyors, most of them simply blazed a few trees and constructed a cabin to establish a "tomahawk claim" to their lands. All were seasoned frontiersmen, who, having learned the ways of the wilderness in the mountainous valleys they left behind, were equipped to live well in their forest surroundings.

A third trans-Appalachian area settled during those years was in eastern Tennessee where the twisting tributaries of the Tennessee River promised homeseekers rich valley farms. The prospects of that region were made known by a few pioneers who settled there before the Seven Years' War—a hunter, Stephen Holston, built a cabin on the banks of the stream that bears his name as early as 1746 and a few others followed—but Indian raids drove them back and not until 1768 did immigration set in. In the van was William Bean, a trader and farmer from western Virginia, who selected the Watauga River Valley as a site for his cabin, hiding it well as protection against Cherokee attacks. His tales of the fertile soil and natural beauty of his new home attracted others during 1769 and 1770; by the autumn of

1770 their clearings dotted the banks of the Watauga for several miles. This tiny outpost was visited that fall by the man destined to become its leader: James Robertson, a young Scotch frontiersman from the Yadkin River settlements of North Carolina. He was so pleased with the country that he returned in the spring of 1771, accompanied by his family and sixteen friends. The cluster of cabins that they built near the mouth of the Doe River became the center of the Watauga settlements.

Other pioneers moved in around them. John Carter, a trader who established a post just west of the Holston in 1769, was followed to that outpost by a handful of settlers. More of them drifted toward the valley country north of the South Fork of the Holston. Maryland contributed heavily to that migration, as one of its prominent frontiersmen, Captain Evan Shelby, induced many of his fellow colonists to settle near his store at Shelby's Station. In the same year Jacob Brown of North Carolina established a few families on the Nolichucky River. These migrations planted four settlements in eastern Tennessee by the close of 1771: Watauga, Carter's Valley, North-of-Holston, and Nolichucky.

During the next two years those isolated communities grew rapidly, as settlers were drawn west by glowing reports from the pioneers or driven to the frontier by intolerable conditions in their native Virginia and North Carolina. Many came from North Carolina, where the defeat of the Regulators at Alamance in May, 1771, apparently doomed backwoodsmen to continued high taxes, unjust fees, and corrupt administration. So rapid was the emigration that the membership of one Baptist church in the Carolina upcountry declined from 606 to 14 during 1771. The movement continued during 1772 as discontented Regulators who delayed to sell their lands before migrating swelled the stream. Others moved west from Virginia and Maryland, lured by the promise of fertile farms and the speculative profits that awaited pioneers on any new frontier. By the close of 1772 several hundred families lived in eastern Tennessee.

Then, suddenly, the very existence of the Watauga settlements was threatened. The surveys of the Lochaber Treaty line, completed in 1772 along the southern boundary of Virginia, disclosed that while the North-of-Holston settlements lay within the area granted England by the Cherokee, the Watauga, Nolichucky, and Carter's Valley communities were in Indian territory. News of this disturbing decision, carried to the frontiersmen by Colonel Stuart's agents, threw them into a turmoil. Some who lived deep in the Indian country saw that resistance was useless—John Carter abandoned his outpost in Carter's Valley and Jacob Brown led his Nolichucky followers northward—but instead of retreating into the region opened by the Treaty of Lochaber, both groups settled in the Watauga settlement where they prepared to defy Stuart and all other royal officials who might try to drive them from their homes.

Their first need was an agreement with the Indians. Two commissioners, James Robertson and Robert Bean, were delegated to obtain a long-term lease from the Cherokee, for all purchases from natives were illegal under the Proclamation of 1763. Fortunately the Indians were in such a friendly mood that two large tracts were secured without difficulty, one embracing the region south and east of the South Fork of the Holston, the other the country where the Nolichucky settlers made their homes. Probably the money for this transaction was supplied by some eastern speculator, such as Judge Richard Henderson of North Carolina, who hoped eventually to transform the lease into a sale.

With land secured, the Wataugans turned to the related tasks of providing law and order for their isolated community and forming a united front against royal officials wishing to oust them from their illegally held homes. In this situation they resorted to a practice usual to frontiersmen whose westward advance temporarily carried them beyond the protection of the law: they called a convention of all arms-bearing men to draw up a compact. All signers of the Articles of Association agreed to obey five commissioners who were given both legislative and judicial powers; they were to keep order, enlist a militia, record deeds for land sales, issue marriage licenses, and try offenders. This Association was not, as some historians have stated, a landmark in the development of American democracy. Instead it was an ordinary squatters' agreement, stemming from necessity and rooted in Presbyterian religious beliefs which emphasized the original compact between God and man. The Wataugans viewed their Association just as the Pilgrims viewed their Mayflower Compact: as a temporary expedient to endure only until a regular government was established and as a means of protecting illegal land holdings.

Certainly the Watauga Association did not attract other liberty-seeking pioneers to that isolated valley, for while the westward movement continued unabated during 1773 it was directed now to the North-of-Holston settlements that were clearly within Virginia. These grew rapidly, fed by a steady stream of homeseekers from western Virginia and North Carolina. As early as 1773 they had reached such an advanced stage that two roads were begun to connect them with the Great Valley of Virginia, the "Island Road" to the Long Island of the Holston River, and the "Watauga Road" to the Doe River. Along these crude highways trundled the heavy wagons of the early settlers, carrying grain and tobacco to Baltimore or Philadelphia markets, and returning with the few manufactured goods that the pioneers could not produce themselves. By the time of the Revolution the eastern Tennessee communities were beginning to pass beyond the primitive stage.

Beyond them a new frontier took shape in 1774 and 1775 as pioneers pushed deep into the wilderness to plant England's most westerly outpost on the banks of the Kentucky River. There, in a land of forest-clad hills and fertile lowlands where lush bluegrass grew tall and thick, they reared the "Kentucky Stations" that held back the Indian tide during the war for independence and helped win the continent's interior for the newborn American republic.

The usual shock troops of civilization swept across the Kentucky country for some years before white men made their first permanent assault on that "Dark and Bloody Ground." First came the explorers, led by Dr. Thomas Walker, who started west in March, 1750, hunting a site for the 800,000 acres that Virginia had granted his Loyal Land Company. Leading his tiny party through the Blue Ridge, across the Holston Valley, and over Powell's Mountain, he emerged in April in Powell's Valley, where the flaring portals of Cumberland Gap led to the interior lands he sought. Whether Walker stumbled on this gateway or learned of its existence from Indians was less important than the fact that he had discovered the outlet which governed the course of western settlement until after the Revolution. Passing through the gap, the explorers followed a well-worn Indian trail, the Warriors' Path, northward, pausing only to build a cabin that would bolster their claims to the region. The hilly country discouraged Walker before he found the level fields along the Kentucky River, and he turned his followers eastward to explore the forks of the Big Sandy River. There too the rough, mountainous terrain was so uninviting that the disgusted woodsmen continued east across the Cumberland Mountains to Staunton, Virginia, having failed to find the garden spot which was to become the mecca of pioneers a generation later: the bluegrass country.

To a Pennsylvania trader fell credit for first confirming Indian stories of the richness of that prized spot. John Finley, on his way down the Ohio with several canoes of trading goods, was captured by a party of Shawnee near the Falls of the Ohio late in 1752 and carried to the Indians' village in the Kentucky lowlands. There he learned from visiting traders that the fertile country where he found himself was readily accessible from Cumberland Gap. Finley returned to Pennsylvania filled with the importance of his discovery, but before his news could do more than spread among his frontier acquaintances, the Seven Years' War ended further exploration. Not until the war was won and Pontiac's Rebellion crushed did interest in Kentucky revive along the back country.

First to reawaken to the possibilities of that new frontier were hunters, their appetites whetted by traders' tales of wild turkeys so thick they broke branches from trees where they settled, deer that crowded unafraid around salt licks, and buffalo so numerous that herds might trample an unwary wanderer to death. Small parties of riflemen invaded Kentucky during the summer of 1766. Captain James Smith of Pennsylvania was probably the first; with four companions he passed through Cumberland Gap and hunted along the Cumberland and Tennessee rivers. Another party of five hunters under Isaac Lindsey followed the same course but

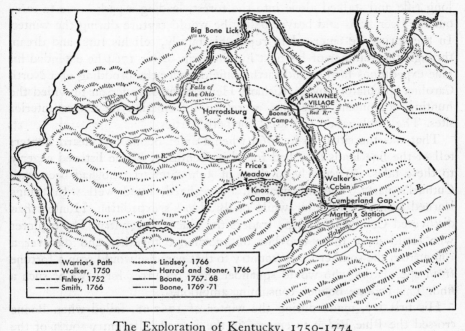

The Exploration of Kentucky, 1750-1774

continued down the Cumberland as far as Stone River where two other woodsmen, James Harrod and Michael Stoner, who had made their way along the Ohio and Cumberland rivers from Ft. Pitt, were encountered. Even more spectacular were the exploits of another expedition led by Benjamin Cutbird of North Carolina. Crossing the Appalachians by a little-known Indian trail, Cutbird hunted across southern Kentucky and northern Tennessee to the Mississippi, then descended that river to New Orleans where he sold his furs.

The principal importance of this bold journey was to interest Daniel Boone in Kentucky, for his brother-in-law, John Stewart, was a member of Cutbird's party. This remarkable woodsman, whose name is forever associated with the early history of the Southwest, had been reared in the primitive Yadkin Valley settlements where he learned to farm and hunt and to love the haunting solitude of the deep forest. He fought for a time during the Seven Years' War, serving as a wagoner in Braddock's expedition where he met John Finley, then returned to his beloved Yadkin Valley where he slipped back into the seminomadic life of the advanced frontier. His was a pleasant existence for one who enjoyed silent woodlands more than his fellow men. Each spring Boone planted a crop on his half-cleared fields; each fall when the harvest was in he shouldered his long rifle and stalked alone into the forest, leading a pack horse to carry out the deer skins and beaver peltry he would capture during the winter. In the spring he emerged to rejoin his family, sell his furs, and dream through the summer of his next hunting trip. After 1764 he extended his lone expeditions farther and farther afield under the prodding of a North Carolina speculator, Judge Richard Henderson; Henderson provided the hunting equipment, receiving in return information on choice interior sites. The combination was ideal for both parties.

That was the situation in 1766 when Daniel Boone first heard hunters tell of the fine lands they had found in Kentucky. Boone listened eagerly to these tales, particularly to those of John Stewart who had been with Cutbird's party. The information, he realized, fitted well with things learned from John Finley while on Braddock's expedition. Hunters had discovered Cumberland Gap; traders the bluegrass country. The explorer who could piece those two bits of knowledge together and discover a route from the southern back country to that paradise would reap a fortune from speculators who would squander their resources for news of such a find. This became Boone's consuming ambition.

His first try, made during the winter of 1767-68, failed when Boone crossed the Blue Ridge to emerge in the jagged hillcountry south of the Big Sandy River. This was not the Kentucky of Finley's descriptions, and he returned in the spring of 1768 with a harvest of furs but with his appetite for knowledge of the bluegrass region still unsatisfied. Before he could set out on his wanderings again his plans were upset by the unexpected arrival in the Yadkin Valley of John Finley, who had abandoned the adventurous life of the fur trader for a less hazardous career as peddler of pins, needles, linen, and other wares designed to catch the eye of frontier housewives. Finley was easily persuaded to spend the winter as a guest in the Boone cabin; all through the cold months the two men talked of Kentucky, and planned an elaborate assault on its mysteries. Finley, who was sure that he could find Cumberland Gap from descriptions given him by traders, was to serve as guide. Boone and four backwoods companions were to hunt, and Judge Henderson was to provide supplies. In May,

1769, the little party set out, each riding a wiry mount and leading a pack horse.

Finley located Cumberland Gap easily enough and the group followed the Warriors' Path across Kentucky as far as Station Camp Creek where they built a shelter to house the furs they captured. There the men separated into pairs to explore the countryside. All went well until December, 1769, when Boone and Finley were captured by a band of Shawnee who raided the main camp and carried away most of the stores and ammunition. The two seasoned woodsmen managed to escape by diving into a giant canebrake where thirty-foot-tall weeds hid them, but most of the party were so disheartened by the loss of their supplies that they wanted to return home. Only Boone and his brother-in-law, John Stewart, stayed on, moving their camp to the mouth of the Red River where they would be safe from war parties using the Warriors' Path. There they were joined by Daniel's brother, Squire Boone, who came out to meet them with fresh supplies and a lone companion.

Things went badly during that winter of 1769-70; Stewart failed to return from one of his solitary hunting trips and Squire Boone's comrade lost heart and returned east, leaving the two brothers alone in the wilderness. In the spring Squire Boone set out for North Carolina to replenish their dwindling supply of ammunition. Daniel, completely alone, spent the next few months roaming the forest, dodging Indian war parties, sleeping in canebrakes, and living from the country. His solitary wanderings took him as far north as the Ohio, along the Kentucky and Licking river valleys, and over most of the bluegrass region. By July 27, 1770, when he rejoined Squire Boone at their old camp on the Red River, he knew more of Kentucky than any other white man. That summer the brothers hunted along the banks of the Kentucky River, then in the fall shifted their operations to the Green and Cumberland valleys where they spent the winter of 1770-71. Finally, in March, they started east, their pack horses loaded with a modest fortune in furs. Fate, however, was unkind. Near Cumberland Gap they encountered a band of Indians who took their peltry, their horses, and their supplies, leaving the discouraged men to tramp homeward with nothing to show for two years of hunting.

Boone's disastrous experience typified the fate awaiting any individual who ventured alone into Kentucky, for there, as on all frontiers, the group was needed for protection. This was realized by Uriah Stone, a skilled hunter who had accompanied Captain James Smith's exploring party, even before Daniel Boone and his brother had returned empty handed from their journey. Stone saw that safety could be assured only if hunters ventured into Kentucky in large bands capable of beating off Indian war parties. With this in mind he sent word along the back country for all hunters interested in Kentucky to meet on the New River in June, 1769. The several dozen who responded followed the well-marked trail through Cumberland Gap, then separated to found camps at Price's Meadow on the Cumberland and Station Camp Creek. From these bases they roamed the country, shooting and trapping. Game was plentiful and easily captured; riflemen had only to wait along trails converging on the numerous salt licks to slaughter deer and buffalo crowding down to lap the briny fluid. They returned east in the fall with pack horses staggering beneath a wealth of furs.

The success of that expedition encouraged another the next year, this time under the leadership of James Knox and made up of forty hunters from upcountry Virginia. From a base near Price's Meadow they roamed over most of western Kentucky, operating especially in the hitherto neglected Green River Valley. There in the fall of 1770 they happened upon Daniel Boone, lying on his back and singing so loudly for the sheer joy of his wilderness life that they believed when they first heard him they had discovered some strange new animal. Boone spent the winter of 1770-71 with them, then left for the East in the early spring while the Knox party stayed on to hunt southward toward the Cumberland. When they returned to the Green Valley in the fall they found that Indians had carried away their carefully cached furs. After carving a lusty protest on a tree—"2300 deerskins lost. Ruination, by God"—they set out for home, still carrying a comfortable catch to pay for their two years of wandering.

These "Long Hunters," as they were dubbed because of their extended journeys, were living examples of the Americans' mastery of frontier techniques. Half civilized and half savage, they were as much at home in the towering Kentucky forests as in the cabins that dotted the agricultural settlements. To them the woods held no mysteries; they could read the message told by a broken twig or the cry of a distant animal as easily as their red-skinned foes. They saw the wilderness not as a forbidding obstacle but as a source of adventure and wealth. From it they took the necessities of life: game and wild vegetables and salt for food, hides to fashion their coonskin caps and leather hunting shirts and buckskin leggings, furs to trade for the few things the wilderness did not provide: a hatchet and hunting knife to thrust into their belt, a long rifle to carry in the crook of their arm, "traps, a large supply of powder and lead, a small hand vice and bellows, files and screw-plates for fixing the guns if any of them should get out of fix." That was all, for so long as their long rifles could shoot, the woods offered them safety and comfort. They loved their nomadic life, and their tales of the level fields, gently flowing streams, and majestic forests of "Kaintuck" did much to interest less adventurous frontiersmen in moving there as settlers.

After the explorers and hunters, in the succession of pioneers who subdued Kentucky, came the land speculators. These astute individuals, whose fingers were always on the pulse of the frontier, realized that Americans were ready to swarm across the mountains, regardless of royal proclamations or Indian treaties. Fortunes awaited the lucky land jobbers who could engross the best lands before they arrived. Speculators knew, moreover, that the land bounties issued to Virginia's soldiers during the Seven Years' War offered a means of securing title. Because these warrants antedated the Proclamation of 1763, Virginia maintained that none of the subsequent treaties affected them; their holders could locate claims anywhere in the Indian country. Although most of the bounties had been purchased by a group under George Washington there was scarcely a speculator in the Old Dominion who did not have at least one. Any land jobber could go west, ostensibly to locate his bounty claim, and while there survey a larger grant in anticipation of the rush of settlers to come.

The first surveying party was organized by a speculator, Captain Thomas Bullitt, who in October, 1772, advertised in Virginia and Pennsylvania newspapers that all interested in marking out bounty lands should gather at the mouth of the Great Kanawha the following spring. The large expedition that formed moved slowly down the Ohio, pausing to survey choice spots: the mouth of Limestone Creek, Big Bone Lick where the bones of thousands of animals whitened the ground about a salt spring, the Kentucky Valley, and the Falls of the Ohio. In the spring of 1774 the jobbers were back again, in three groups this time, headed by Colonel William Preston who was official surveyor for western Virginia, William Crawford who had long served as Washington's land agent, and a minor speculator named James Harrod. Once more they worked through the early summer staking out extensive claims for themselves and their backers along the Ohio, Kentucky, and Licking rivers. The Virginians under James Harrod were so impressed with the rich country near Dick's River that they built cabins and laid out the town of Harrodsburg.

That the conquest of Kentucky could go on without Indian retaliation was too much to expect. Although no tribe actually occupied the "Dark and Bloody Ground," both the Cherokee of Tennessee and the Shawnee of Ohio fought and hunted there. The Shawnee especially looked on the region as their own, remembering that before moving to the Scioto Valley as vassals of the Iroquois they had lived along the Cumberland River. For some years they watched the gradual encroachment of white men: hunters who ruthlessly slaughtered game, traders who carried compasses—"landstealers," the natives called them—to mark out choice sites, surveyors who told of settlers soon to come. Little wonder that by 1771 the Shawnee were seeking alliances with the Cherokee, Seneca, and other tribes to drive the intruders from Kentucky. Only Sir William Johnson's frantic efforts to keep the Six Nations neutral delayed the war until 1774.

The conflict that broke out then—Lord Dunmore's War—was a struggle for land between two antagonistic civilizations. The Indians wanted Kentucky for a hunting ground; the Americans wanted Kentucky for homes and farms. There was no reconciling these views; war was inevitable. Lawless frontiersmen who realized this began the conflict in 1773 with isolated attacks on the natives: one trapper killed an Indian and a squaw suspected of stealing his dog, another murdered a dozen friendly warriors after plying them with liquor until they were helplessly drunk. Until the spring of 1774 the Shawnee showed greater restraint than these outrages warranted, hoping that the Pennsylvania Quakers who controlled the Forks of the Ohio would find some peaceful solution. This last hope went glimmering early in 1774 when Virginia, which claimed all western Pennsylvania under its 1609 charter, forcibly seized the disputed area. Governor Dunmore's appointment of a wild Irishman, Dr. John Connolly, as commander at Pittsburgh was the last straw. Now the whole frontier was dominated by land-hungry Virginians.

Dr. Connolly, who claimed extensive tracts of Kentucky land himself, evidently decided to hurry the coming of the inevitable conflict. In April, 1774, he used a minor Shawnee attack on a surveying party as an excuse for a fiery proclamation which urged the frontiersmen to defend themselves. Such an order as this was as good as a declaration of war to Indian-hating pioneers; all along the back country they waylaid Shawnee hunting parties and raided native villages. Even this was not enough to goad the Indians into war. Only when messengers sent to Pittsburgh to plead for peace were first rebuffed, then attacked by Dr. Connolly's troops did Shawnee patience finally reach a breaking point. Then hot-headed young warriors fell on several outlying settlements, killing thirteen men to avenge the thirteen Indians who had died in the skirmishing. There was no turning back now; on June 10 Governor Dunmore sent word to the frontier settlements that war had begun.

A thrill of alarm swept through the West, for with the Shawnee on the warpath farmers and hunters from the upper Holston to the Ohio faced death. Dunmore's first thought was for the surveyors scattered over Kentucky. Daniel Boone and another woodsman, Michael Stoner, were hurried west to warn them of their danger. Traveling through the pathless forests on foot, those two skilled frontiersmen journeyed eight hundred miles in sixty days, stopping only at Harrodsburg where Boone's land hunger so overbalanced his caution that he paused to stake out a claim and build a cabin before issuing his warning. The Watauga settlers, living beyond the pale of civilization, could expect no such attention. Their only hope was to keep the Cherokee neutral. James Robertson was called on to use his considerable diplomatic skill in this emergency, and after a prolonged conference his persuasive eloquence won the day. This not only saved the Watauga settlements but cost the Shawnee their principal southern allies. At the same time Sir William Johnson and George Croghan worked feverishly to win the Iroquois and Delawares to the English side. In the end the Shawnee were left with only the Ottawa and Mingo to aid them.

With the safety of isolated settlers secured and the diplomatic battle won, Governor Dunmore turned to the conquest of his redskinned enemies. On July 24, 1774, he dispatched four hundred men under Major Angus McDonald to the newly built Ft. Fincastle with orders to march up the Muskingum Valley and destroy any Indians they found, thus throwing a screen between the Ohio tribes and the upper Ohio settlements. This done, Dunmore planned two expeditions into the Shawnee country, one from Pittsburgh, the other from upcountry Virginia, which would unite at the mouth of the Great Kanawha to march northward. Dunmore, who commanded the Pittsburgh army, changed his plans as his 1,100 militiamen drifted down the Ohio, and decided to strike directly at the Shawnee villages by way of the Hocking River. Pausing only to build an outpost, Ft. Gower, to guard his supply lines, he sent word to the thousand Virginians under Colonel Andrew Lewis who were moving down the Great Kanawha to cross the Ohio and ascend the Scioto, then headed northward into the wilderness.

The Shawnee commander, Chief Cornstalk, was overjoyed when scouts told him of this change. The Virginians were divided; he could fall first on one army and then the other! Gathering a thousand warriors, he slipped quietly southward, crossed the Ohio in the very teeth of Colonel Andrew Lewis' advancing troops, and prepared to fall on the upcountry militiamen who had descended the Great Kanawha to Point Pleasant, near the river's mouth. The attack came at daybreak on the morning of October 9, 1774. What might have been a complete surprise was averted when hunters who saw the Indians gave the alarm; the militiamen sprang to their guns and deployed through the woods for a typical frontier battle. All day long the fight raged, with neither side able to gain any advantage, until dusk when Chief Cornstalk mistook a Virginian flank attack for the arrival of reinforcements. Disheartened, he ordered a retreat. That night the Shawnee slipped across the Ohio as quietly as they had come. Colonel Lewis, who had expected fighting to continue, thankfully gathered his battle-scarred forces for the march northward along the Scioto War Trail to the Shawnee villages.

News of the Battle of Point Pleasant reached Dunmore while he was still moving slowly up the Hocking Valley. He was wise enough to realize that a sudden attack on the Indians now, while they were cowed by defeat, would probably end the war. Hence instead of waiting for Lewis he marched boldly into the Shawnee country. The red men, fearful lest their women and children suffer, sued for peace at once. Dunmore forced the leading chieftains to sign the Treaty of Camp Charlotte; they would, they agreed, consent to the occupation of Kentucky, cease hunting there, and stop molesting boats plying the Ohio River. Lord Dunmore's War was over, the last obstacle to the settlement of Kentucky removed.

The one man who above all others realized the importance of the Shawnee defeat was Judge Richard Henderson. That wealthy speculator, who had dabbled in western lands for a decade as Daniel Boone's employer, had just retired from the North Carolina bench to concentrate on land sales. He saw that two factors favored a bold bid for the interior. One was the presence of a vast population poised to push across the mountains, including many men who had learned something of Kentucky while serving with Colonel Lewis' army. The other was the undisputed ownership of that region by the Cherokee, for the Iroquois gave up their claims at the Treaty of Ft. Stanwix, and the Shawnee at the Treaty of Camp Charlotte. Direct purchase was impossible, but an alert speculator might obtain a long-term lease to Kentucky that would be just as profitable. Such a land jobber, moreover, would probably be able to turn possession into ownership should the Crown ever open the region to settlement.

With this in mind, Henderson called some of his well-to-do North Carolina friends together in August, 1774, to form the Louisa Company. They planned to lease a large tract south of the Ohio and west of the Great Kanawha, together with a right-of-way through Cumberland Gap. Henderson and one of his partners set out at once to open negotiations with the Cherokee, who assured the speculators they were willing to negotiate if a price could be agreed upon. So confident were the members of the Louisa Company that Kentucky was theirs that in December, 1774, they advertised for settlers in Virginia and North Carolina newspapers, offering five hundred acre plots at a price of twenty shillings for each hundred acres with an annual quitrent of two shillings.

During the next few weeks Henderson, suddenly changing his plans, decided to buy rather than lease Kentucky from the Indians. This reversal may have been due to word of the Camden-Yorke decision but was more probably a product of turbulent conditions in the colonies. The drift toward revolution during the winter of 1774-75 undoubtedly convinced Henderson that he could make good a purchase from the Indians in the troubled times ahead. Whatever the reason, in January, 1775, he reorganized the Louisa Company as the Transylvania Company and sent runners to summon the Cherokee chiefs to a conference at Sycamore Shoals on the Watauga River in March. Negotiations lasted from March 14 to March 17 when the Treaty of Sycamore Shoals was signed. In return for £10,000 worth of trading goods the Indians ceded all lands between the Kentucky River and the highlands south of the Cumberland, together with a strip between the Holston and the Cumberland Mountains. In addition the Watauga settlers took advantage of the natives' generous mood to turn their lease into a purchase, and Jacob Brown bought two large tracts along the Nolichucky River where his followers were established. Only when the last transaction was completed did Henderson wheel out the casks of rum which launched a wilderness celebration wild even for those half-savage peoples.

The Treaty of Sycamore Shoals had no more validity than any other purchase made under the Camden-Yorke decision. Every English precedent vested title to colonial lands in the Crown, not in the native population; Indian treaties were only devices to remove troublesome occupants from lands already owned by the king. Individuals who made such treaties actually usurped territory which legally belonged to their sovereign. Henderson, like most of the other speculators who used the Camden-Yorke decision, probably realized this. His object was to obtain possession of Kentucky, then hold the region during the confusion of the coming revolution.

Certainly he moved with unseemly rapidity to establish his company's claim. On March 10, 1775, when negotiations were just getting under way, he sent Daniel Boone with thirty axmen to cut a road to the Kentucky River where Henderson planned to plant his first settlement. That was the origin of the famous Wilderness Road, which began at the Long Island of the Holston, passed through Powell's Valley and Cumberland Gap, and emerged on the Kentucky River where Boone and his followers built their cabins. Henderson set out over this trail on March 20, with forty riflemen, a number of Negro slaves, and a train of wagons and pack horses loaded with provisions and ammunition. In Powell's Valley he found the first intruder on his domain, a trader, Joseph Martin, who was operating a newly built trading post. Henderson, recognizing the value of a station at that strategic point, gladly guaranteed Martin his land in return for aid given settlers on their way west. While still there he was joined by a small group of immigrants under Benjamin Logan who were bound for Kentucky, and on April 8 the combined party started westward over the Wilderness Road.

At Cumberland Gap they met forty pioneers fleeing toward the East with tales of a new Indian uprising, but Henderson only sent a runner

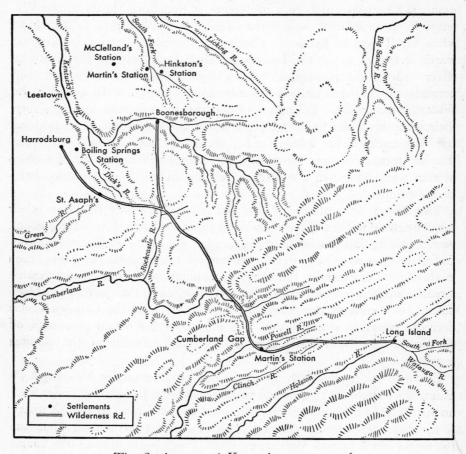

The Settlement of Kentucky, 1775-1776

ahead to warn Boone to hold his ground and pressed on more rapidly than before. A second setback occurred just beyond Rockcastle River when Logan, who refused to recognize the Transylvania Company's authority, broke away from the main party and led his followers off toward Harrodsburg to found their own settlement, St. Asaph's Station. The remainder pushed on to the Kentucky River where they were welcomed by a twenty-five gun salute from Boone's men. All were enchanted by the beauty and richness of the level country that lay before them. "Perhaps no Adventureor Since the days of donquicksotte or before," wrote one awe-struck pioneer, "ever felt So Cheerful & Ilated in prospect, every heart abounded with Joy & excitement." That sight of tossing white clover, level bluegrass, and the gently flowing river was to cheer many a weary traveler at the end of the Wilderness Road.

Boone's axmen had thrown up a few cabins but no stockade, for the men had suffered so severely from land fever that they had spent their time staking out sites for themselves rather than preparing for Henderson's settlers. Nor could Henderson dissuade them from this exciting task. He planned to erect a fort called Boonesborough on the model of Martin's Station, with a series of cabins connected by log stockades to house the pioneers. Instead his settlers spent the first week marking out lots, surveying fields, and prospecting for land despite all the pleas of their proprietor. Even after the first excitement passed they showed so little inclination to work that the fort was not completed until after the start of the Revolution. Only the friendliness of the natives saved Boonesborough from extinction during those months.

More annoying than this to Henderson was the steady intrusion of newcomers who had no respect for his authority. Benjamin Logan's followers at St. Asaph's Station had already defied him. James Harrod also returned in May, 1775, to rebuild Harrodsburg, while some of his fellow immigrants split away to found Boiling Springs Station in the Dick's River Valley. All of these men denied the Transylvania Company's right to Kentucky and stoutly maintained that Virginia was in control—largely because that distant colony would not bother them. Henderson was wise enough to see that he could establish his authority over these unruly settlers only by giving them such an orderly government that they would be willing to pay for their land in return. His opportunity came when thirty new arrivals from North Carolina established themselves near Harrodsburg over the protests of that town's inhabitants. This, he insisted, showed the need of some agency to settle disputes, and he invited the four stations to send delegates to Boonesborough on May 23, 1775, to enact laws for the colony of Transylvania.

On the appointed day eighteen frontiersmen selected by the towns met under a great elm tree at Boonesborough and listened to a resounding address in Henderson's worst eighteenth-century style. "You are," he told those rough-hewn woodsmen, "fixing the palladium, or placing the first corner-stone of an edifice, the height and magnificence of whose superstructure is now in the womb of futurity, and can only become great and glorious in proportion to the excellence of its foundation." Lulled by this oratory, the delegates passed laws setting up a court and militia system, and providing for the punishment of criminals, the preservation of game, and the proper breeding of horses. They also adopted something like a constitution which was carefully drawn by Henderson to vest governmental power in the Transylvania Company, despite a number of deft phrases seemingly promising democracy. He was, he sincerely believed, erecting a new proprietary colony in the heart of America, with himself at its head.

This constitution, and the land system that Henderson tried to introduce, were both monuments to his dreamy impracticability. Any sensible man would have known that the freeborn woodsmen of Kentucky, steeped in traditions of liberty and democracy, would never accept a proprietary government just as they were on the verge of rebelling against a distant king who had denied them the right to rule themselves. Common sense should also have told Henderson that his land system would never be accepted. His price was low enough—twenty shillings for each one hundred acres—but each purchaser was to pay an annual quitrent of two shillings for every hundred acres he held. Although this archaic system had long since failed in the East, Henderson had the audacity to believe that he could force unruly, individualistic frontiersmen to promise him regular payments through their lifetimes. He was completely out of touch with his times, a renegade from an earlier century.

Henderson's outmoded idealism doomed the Transylvania Company to many dreary months of conflict. New settlers crowded onto its lands during the summer of 1775, to fill the older towns and to lay out new stations: Leestown, McClellands's Station, Hinkston's Station, and Martin's Station. No one paid the slightest attention to the company; the immigrants reasoned that it had obtained possession illegally and they would do the same. The Transylvania proprietors were too busy to protest, for the Continental Congress was meeting and they were in the East vainly petitioning for recognition as the fourteenth colony. Realizing that this would never be forthcoming over the protests of Virginia and North Carolina, they finally determined to snatch what profits they could. Land prices were raised sharply on December 1, 1775—from twenty shillings to two pounds ten shillings a hundred acres. This unwise step only increased dissatisfaction, nor did Indian raids during the winter strengthen the company's position. By the spring of 1776 discontent was boiling through Kentucky.

This came to a head in June, 1776, when a leader arrived to shape the popular revolt. George Rogers Clark, a fiery twenty-four-year-old Virginian, well trained in wilderness ways, sensed the discontent of the people at once and issued a call for a convention to meet at Harrodsburg on June 6, 1776. The assembled delegates from all stations divided their time between denouncing the Transylvania Company and drawing up a petition to Virginia asking that Kentucky be made a county of that colony. On adjournment they named a revolutionary Committee of Twenty-One to govern the region until Virginia's authority was extended over them. Henderson hurried away to the colonial capital to protest this rebellion, but his efforts were in vain. Early in 1777 the House of Burgesses formally annexed the Transylvania Company domain as Kentucky County. Henderson was given 200,000 acres between the Ohio and Green rivers as compensation for his efforts, and in 1783 North Carolina awarded him the same amount in the Powell and Clinch river valleys. Thus ended the grandiose scheme of one of America's most visionary speculators.

But neither Henderson nor other pioneers who dreamed of trans-Appalachian colonies labored in vain. They had built a new frontier—one that stretched from the Monongahela Valley across western Virginia to Kentucky and eastern Tennessee by 1776. There lived thousands of men and women, all engaged in clearing away the age-old forests and planting civilization in a conquered wilderness. These were the pioneers who bore the full brunt of Indian raids during the Revolutionary War, and helped win the West for the new nation born of that struggle.

# CHAPTER IX

# The West in the American Revolution

## 1776-1783

The West played only a minor role in the epic events leading to the American Revolution. The provincialism, democracy, the distrust of external interference underlying that rebellion against established authority were all frontier characteristics, bred into the colonists by the New World environment, but the isolated backwoodsmen showed little concern with the issues that started Americans along the road to independence. Duties on molasses and tea aroused little interest among frontiersmen who had never seen those luxuries, nor could they grow wrathful about "taxation without representation" when their own delegates were denied seats in colonial legislatures. They resented bungling British attempts to limit their expansion, but even on this sore point they knew better than easterners that mythical boundary lines could be crossed at will. Yet the indifferent westerners were destined to play a major role in the War for Independence. For seven years they trembled in their lonely cabins with fear of the savage tomahawk and scalping knife heavy in their hearts or ventured forth to hurl back fierce attacks by redcoated or redskinned warriors. Thousands paid with their lives for the right to freedom and expansion.

From the beginning of the war it was clear that Indians would play a leading role in the West, and both English and Americans set out to win their support. The British enjoyed a marked advantage in this wilderness contest. They could offer the natives proven friends in the Indian Superintendents—John Stuart in the South and Sir John Johnson, who ascended to the northern superintendency on the death of his father in 1774, in the North—protection at Detroit, Mackinac, Oswego, Niagara, and other

English controlled posts, a well-established fur trade, and superior trading goods. The Americans, on the other hand, having no manufactured goods of their own, could give the Indians only high-flown speeches on liberty which sounded ironical to red men who knew the land-hungry colonists wanted their lands. Most natives believed they could win back their conquered hunting grounds only by casting their lot with England.

Hence British commanders had only to give the word to send most tribes storming against the settlements. They hesitated to do so for they shrank from the barbarism of Indian war. Their problem was to solicit enough native aid to protect their interior posts, while restraining the red men from shedding the blood of innocent victims. On the other hand the Americans, who would have welcomed active aid against their enemy's forts, were wise enough to see that this was unobtainable. Instead the three Indian Commissioners appointed by the Continental Congress in July, 1775, concentrated on keeping the tribes neutral. Conferences with the northern Indians at Pittsburgh during the summers of 1775 and 1776 showed the magnitude of their task; only two, the Shawnee and Delawares, responded favorably, and their action was due more to smarting memories of Lord Dunmore's War and fear of the fierce Virginia "Long-Knives" than to any sympathy with the American cause. The southern commissioners enjoyed even less success. Although the Creeks grudgingly agreed to refrain from attacks for a time, the Cherokee broke up a conference at Ft. Charlotte in April, 1776, by proclaiming their allegiance to George III. The colonists began their Revolutionary War hemmed in by a ring of hostile tribesmen, all poised to pounce on back-country settlements whenever British commanders gave the word.

This they were reluctant to do. Colonel John Stuart's task was most difficult, for the Cherokee, chafing under the presence of the Watauga and Nolichucky settlers, demanded the right to attack immediately. Colonel Stuart's brother, Henry Stuart, was assigned the impossible task of restraining them. When a visit to the Cherokee villages in April, 1776, convinced him there was no holding back the onslaught, he warned the Wataugans they must either defend themselves or move to safer quarters. Hence the Americans were ready when the blow fell, safe within two strong fortifications: Eaton's Station at the Long Island of the Holston and Ft. Watauga at Sycamore Shoals. There, on the morning of July 20, 1776, word reached them that seven hundred Cherokee under Chief Dragging Canoe were approaching. Instead of waiting, the 170 defenders of Eaton's Station sallied forth to meet the Indians, who were defeated after a fierce battle beneath the walls of the fort. A similar attack on Ft. Watauga the next day also failed, and the Cherokee retreated in disgrace to their villages.

This raid lighted the torch of war along the southern frontier; overnight the inflamed Cherokee, Creeks, and Choctaw swept down on outlying settlements.

The southern states struck back relentlessly in September and October, 1776. Twenty-five hundred regulars and militia from North Carolina fell first on the Middle Cherokee towns, then joined with a smaller force from South Carolina to lay waste the Lower Towns while a Virginia expedition

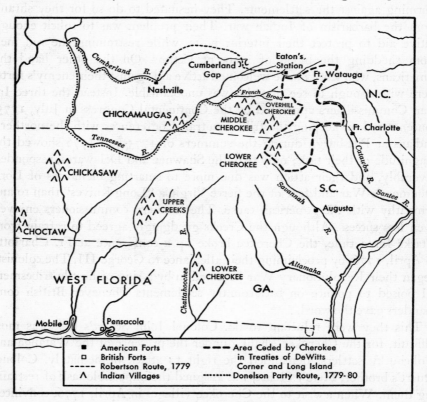

The Southern Frontier in the Revolution, 1776–1780

spread devastation among the Overhill tribe. By the end of October, when the victorious southerners returned to their homes, Cherokee power was broken, tribal villages smoking ruins, crops destroyed, and warriors scattered. A few months later the remnants of the once-powerful tribe were forced to sign two humiliating treaties: the Treaty of DeWitt's Corner (May 20, 1777) in which the Lower Cherokee surrendered their remaining territory in South Carolina, and the Treaty of Long Island (July 20, 1777) where the Overhill Cherokee gave up their lands east of the Blue

Ridge together with the region occupied by the Watauga and Nolichucky settlements. This decisive victory assured two years of peace for the southern frontier.

This was fortunate, not only for the pioneers of the Carolina back country, but for Kentuckians as well, as those harassed pioneers were left free to repel Indian and British raiders from across the Ohio. To the Indians of that country—the Delawares, Shawnee, Ottawa, and Miami—the Revolution was a golden opportunity to drive American intruders from their hunting ground, for on no other frontier were the British so willing to aid the red men. Captain Henry Hamilton, lieutenant-governor of England's northwestern territories, had only 120 men to protect his own post at Detroit and smaller garrisons at Mackinac, St. Joseph, Ouiatanon, Vincennes, and Kaskaskia. This skeleton force must guard thousands of miles of wilderness, a dozen Indian tribes, and a population of Frenchmen whose sympathy lay more with the Americans than with George III. Hamilton, who had no more liking for savage warfare than Colonel Stuart, did his best to keep his red-skinned allies in check, but circumstances compelled him to use them almost from the beginning of the war.

Raids began in the summer of 1776, when bands of Shawnee and Delaware warriors slipped across the Ohio to lurk about the Kentucky stations. As the attacks grew in intensity, station after station was abandoned, the inhabitants either trudging back east or moving into one of the stronger settlements, until by the beginning of 1777 the whole Kentucky population was concentrated in the three largest posts: Boonesborough, Harrodsburg, and St. Asaph's. These were feverishly transformed into strong forts. Each was a large rectangle—that at Boonesborough was 260 by 180 feet—formed by the backs of cabins and a ten-foot-high stockade of pointed oak logs set upright. At each corner a block house with a projecting second story allowed defenders to fire along the walls, while the stockades were also equipped with loopholes. Even the roofs of the cabins sloped inward so that protectors could extinguish flame arrows without showing themselves to the enemy. Within these hollow squares a large population could live safely, if not comfortably, through any siege that impatient Indians could conduct. The Kentucky Stations were to prove themselves, in the dark days of the Revolution, the most efficient means of defense devised on the frontier.

Their completion in the spring of 1777 came none too soon, for that "year of the three sevens" was long known as the "Bloody Year" in Kentucky's history. Raids began on March 7 when Chief Blackfish and three hundred Shawnee warriors fell on Boonesborough. The inhabitants managed to "fort up" safely, but throughout that summer Blackfish slipped from station to station, keeping all in what amounted to a state of siege. Outside aid was needed if Kentuckians were to be saved and crops planted. A plea to Virginia finally bore fruit in August when Colonel John Bowman with a hundred troops reached Harrodsburg from the East, to be followed in September by fifty more from the Yadkin district. Chief Blackfish retreated across the Ohio rather than face this new army, leaving a badly battered Kentucky behind him; no crops were planted, every larder was empty; in all the land, one soldier complained, there was "no bread, no

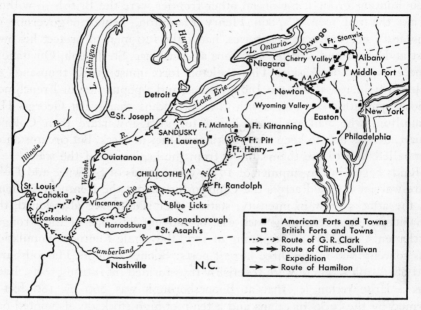

The Northern Frontier in the Revolution, 1776-1780

salt, no vegetables, no fruit of any kind, no ardent spirits, nothing but meat."

The Kentuckians could endure this meagre fare but complaints from eastern soldiers were so insistent during the winter that in January, 1778, Daniel Boone determined to silence them. With thirty men he set out for a salt spring at Blue Licks on the Licking River, where the whole party settled down to the tedious task of boiling down the briny water that gushed from the ground. While the men were still there, Boone, on a lone hunting trip, was captured by a large Indian war party bound for Boonesborough. Realizing that an attack on the unprepared settlement would mean the massacre of women and children, he led the raiders to Blue Licks where he persuaded the salt-makers to surrender, knowing that such a prize would satisfy the warriors. They were carried triumphantly to the Indian village of Chillicothe where their bravery so impressed the red men that sixteen were adopted into the Shawnee tribe, Boone becoming the foster-son of Chief Blackfish. That winter and spring the Kentuckians lived with the savages until early June when Boone learned that another attack on Boonesborough was planned. He must, he knew, warn the Kentuckians. Opportunity came while returning from a salt-boiling expedition; he fell behind his captors under pretext of adjusting his salt kettles, then dashed into the wilderness. Four days later, on June 20, 1778, Boone reached Boonesborough, having covered 160 miles of trackless forest.

His warning that four hundred raiders were on their way came none too soon, for the station's defenses had been allowed to rot away. The sixty men in the fort worked so furiously that by September 7, 1778, when Chief Blackfish and his party appeared, Boonesborough was again able to resist. For a time the two forces parleyed, as Blackfish reprimanded Boone for leaving the Shawnee and tried to persuade the settlers to surrender peacefully, but after two days the attack began. The Indians followed their usual tactics: they rushed the fort, were beaten back, noisily prepared to depart, and filed away into the forest. When this traditional ruse failed to deceive the Boonesborough woodsmen the Shawnee returned and settled down to a siege. This lasted for nine days, until a heavy rain renewed the fort's water supply and caved in a tunnel the Indians were digging beneath its walls. This time, when the attackers slipped away into the wilderness, they were gone for good. The cheering settlers, warmed by the thought they had withstood the longest siege in the history of Indian warfare, led their half-starved cattle out to pasture once more. Yet bands of Indians roamed Kentucky through the autumn of 1778, pouncing on unwary wanderers, seizing livestock, and for the second year preventing the harvest-ing of badly needed crops. The settler's defensive policy was an obvious failure.

This lack of aggressive tactics also spelled disaster on the rest of the northern frontier between 1776 and 1778. Along the upper Ohio River Virginia contented itself with throwing up four forts to guard its long border: Ft. Kittanning, Ft. Pitt, Ft. Henry at the site of Wheeling, and Ft. Randolph at the mouth of the Great Kanawha. These did little good; Ft. Henry was raided twice by Delaware and Shawnee war parties during 1777 and the whole back country between Pittsburgh and Kentucky ravaged by such savage attacks that no crops were planted. The Continental Congress made only one attempt to improve the situation. In February, 1778, it ordered Brigadier General Edward Hand, who commanded the few federal troops at Ft. Pitt, to invade the Indian country as far as Sandusky, destroying villages and crops as he went. Heavy rains, poor leadership, and inadequate supplies doomed the expedition from the start, and Hand returned in disgrace after killing a few friendly Delawares. On the Upper Ohio, as in Kentucky, the Americans were hard pressed by 1778.

The situation on the New York frontier was even worse during the first two years of the Revolution. There the British could rely not only on the powerful Iroquois under their able Mohawk chieftain, Joseph Brant, but on a number of Loyalists whose bloody deeds made even their savage allies shudder: Sir John Johnson and Guy Johnson, son and nephew of Sir William Johnson, Colonel John Butler and his band of renegades who called themselves the Tory Rangers, and Colonel Guy Carleton, all well equipped and strategically based at Niagara or Oswego. They swung into action during the summer of 1777 when the English high command sent General Barry St. Leger to Oswego with orders to march his army of Indians and Tories east along the Mohawk to join General John Burgoyne— who was descending Lake Champlain from Canada—on the Hudson River. St. Leger, with 1,700 followers, met his first obstacle at Ft. Stanwix where 750 well-armed Americans awaited him. Confident that the rebels would surrender, he began a siege that ended seventeen days later when the British gave up hope of routing the stubborn patriots and retreated to Oswego. Yet the American triumph was not complete; a relief expedition of eight hundred men and boys under General Nicholas Herkimer, bound for Ft. Stanwix from the East, marched into an ambush only eight miles from the fort on August 5. The Battle of Oriskany, which cost two hundred lives, was one of the most disastrous in the history of the frontier.

With the spring of 1778 the attacks began again. Joseph Brant led the assault on May 30 when his three hundred Iroquois stormed the little town of Cobleskill, then swept westward along the Mohawk, destroying as they went. While this force ravaged outlying New York settlements, another under Colonel John Butler moved quietly southward toward the Wyoming Valley of Pennsylvania. The 5,000 inhabitants of that fertile region, left virtually without protection by the exodus of men to serve in Washington's army, were crowded into the one defensible spot in the valley, a large palisade known as Forty Fort, when Butler's thousand Indians and Tories arrived on June 3. Instead of defending themselves three hundred American men and boys foolishly sallied out to meet the attackers. The result was the Wyoming Massacre; 360 were killed outright and countless others who escaped into the forest died of exposure or starvation. His bloody work done, Butler rejoined Brant to raid along the Mohawk and Schoharie valleys. By the end of June, 1778, no frontier settlement was safe; even the people of Albany and Schenectady trembled lest they feel the savage wrath.

Clearly the defensive policy followed in the West had failed; aggression alone would drive back the enemy hordes. Only a practical demonstration of the success of offensive action was needed to convince Congress. This was provided by George Rogers Clark, a fiery young Kentuckian, who, suffering with his fellow frontiersmen in their wilderness stations, decided that Indian attacks could best be ended by striking against the British posts north of the Ohio. During the winter of 1777-78 he persuaded the Virginia authorities to authorize an expedition against the Illinois villages, knowing that the French inhabitants would aid the invaders. Moreover the capture of that region would allow Americans to import supplies from New Orleans over the Mississippi route, as well as bolster Virginia's claim to the Northwest. Clark was made a lieutenant colonel with authority to raise a force of militiamen for his task.

He set out from Ft. Massac, ten miles below the Falls of the Ohio, on June 26, 1778, with 175 well-trained Indian fighters. Cutting across country rather than risk discovery along the river route, the little army reached Kaskaskia on July 4, approaching so stealthily that the English commander did not know of their presence until the Americans pushed open the gates of the palisade. The British had no choice but surrender, particularly when Clark won over the French inhabitants by telling them of the newly concluded alliance between the United States and France. Cahokia also capitulated without resistance; a little later Vincennes surrendered to a Kaskaskia priest who journeyed to that village with news of the Kentuckian's arrival. By mid-August Clark controlled the Illinois country. He capitalized on his success by summoning neighboring Indians to a conference at Cahokia, where his arrogant speeches, blustering manner, and judicious distribution of presents completely captivated the red men. Before the session adjourned most of the Wisconsin and upper Mississippi tribes, as well as a few from Ohio, swore allegiance to the United States.

Clark's convincing proof that an offense was the best defense forced Congress to imitate his example elsewhere on the frontier—with less satisfactory results. An expedition into the Ohio country, with Detroit as its final objective, was clearly called for. After the Delawares had been cajoled into permitting an army to cross their tribal lands, the force set out from Ft. Pitt in October—a thousand men under General Lachlan McIntosh. They paused to build Ft. McIntosh at Big Beaver Creek—the first American foothold on the right bank of the Ohio—then turned westward, driving fleeing savages before them, until cold weather turned them back. The expedition did little good; few Indians were killed and fewer villages destroyed, while garrisons left at Ft. McIntosh and Ft. Laurens, a more advanced outpost on the Tuscarawas River, irritated rather than overawed the red men. Nor did the aggressive program attempted in western New York during the autumn of 1778 fare better. A small army from the East which wiped out the two Indian villages of Unadilla and Oghwaga so infuriated Joseph Brant that he turned his raiders against the substantial town of Cherry Valley, one of the few remaining strongholds south of the Mohawk. Striking suddenly on November 11, 1778, his well-trained fighters cut down thirty of the defenders and wounded seventy-one more before they withdrew.

These disastrous autumn campaigns in New York and Ohio did much to offset the influence of Clark's success; tribes that manifested friendship toward Americans during the summer swung abruptly back into the British camp. To make matters worse, Captain Hamilton at Detroit threatened to undo all Clark accomplished. As soon as Hamilton heard that the Illinois villages were captured, he set out with an army of five hundred Indians and British to retake them. Vincennes was captured without difficulty in December, when the French garrison deserted rather than face the British, but constant rains that flooded the flat Indiana countryside forced Hamilton to settle down there for the winter.

Clark first heard this discouraging news from a trader who reached Kaskaskia on January 29, 1779. He realized that his own small force could never defeat the superior English army and that his only hope was a surprise attack. With 172 men he set out for Vincennes, 180 miles away, on February 6. The journey was one of unprecedented difficulties. Trails were ankle-deep in mud, game was scarce, and cold rain fell steadily. For the last twenty miles the men waded through water, sometimes up to their shoulders, breaking ice as they went. Yet on the afternoon of February 23 they reached their goal. The British, not anticipating Clark's bold move, were caught napping when the American marched quietly into Vincennes under cover of an early winter dusk. The garrison, which was comfortably housed in the fort in the town's center, did not even know Clark was near until the Americans opened fire at the palisade. All night the battle went on, but the British were so demoralized by the accurate fire of the Kentuckians—who picked off English gunners by firing through port holes of the fort—that they surrendered on the morning of February 24, 1779. Hamilton and his fellow officers were packed triumphantly off to Virginia, and again American prestige was high throughout the Northwest.

Clark, knowing that nothing impressed the Indians like success, laid plans to march on Detroit at once. Fresh troops were needed to replace the exhausted veterans of the Vincennes campaign. A hurried call to Virginia brought only 150 raw recruits rather than the five hundred requested, while the expected contingent from Kentucky never arrived. Its commander,

Colonel John Bowman, succumbing to the blandishments of his frontier followers, turned aside to burn the Shawnee village of Chillicothe. By that time the two-month enlistment term of his troops was up and they returned home, leaving Bowman only thirty men when he finally reached Vincennes. Clark did not dare proceed with that small force; "Detroit lost for want of a few men," he ruefully wrote.

He could find consolation in the fact that his brilliant triumphs inspired victories on other frontiers during 1779 when American military success in the West reached its high-water mark. General Washington planned two expeditions on the upper Ohio-New York borderland. One under Colonel Daniel Brodhead marched from Pittsburgh into the Seneca country, leaving behind a trail of ruined villages and crops. The other, made up of two strong armies under Generals James Clinton and John Sullivan, moved west from Albany and north from Easton, Pennsylvania, to join at Tioga Point. There the combined force, numbering 3,200 men, started west along the Chemung River into the heart of the Indian country. British and Indians, securely entrenched behind earthen embankments, awaited them at the native village of Newtown. The Battle of Newtown (August 29, 1779) was disastrous for the British. Sullivan's seasoned fighters battered down their defenses with cannon fire, then dashed upon the terrified red men. Only thirty-three of the enemy were killed, but the rest fled in disgrace with Sullivan at their heels, cutting a swath of destruction through the Iroquois country. For a time at least the Six Nations were so cowed that the New York frontier was safe from attack.

The Americans were just as successful in subduing a new flare-up in the South during the summer of 1779. This centered in the Chickamauga villages along the Tennessee River where a thousand disgruntled Cherokee warriors had lived since they fled west in 1776. Aroused by American victories, they took to the warpath in the spring of 1779. A Virginia-North Carolina expedition under Colonel Evan Shelby moved through the Chickamauga country in April, destroying eleven villages and 20,000 bushels of grain. Again in the fall when the Indians showed war-like tendencies a South Carolina force wiped out six more towns. This was enough; for the rest of the war the southern Indians remained neutral. There, as in New York and Ohio, the war seemed over by the autumn of 1779.

This was cheering news to harassed frontiersmen. Since the start of the war they had fled eastward before threatened Indian attacks; now, even though the frontiers were far from safe, population moved west once more. Land in Tennessee and Kentucky was easily obtainable under liberal laws enacted by North Carolina and Virginia; the North Carolina statute, passed in 1777, allowed purchasers as much as 640 acres at fifty shillings for each hundred acres, while a Virginia law of October, 1779, set a price of £40 for a hundred acre plot. Actually settlers paid far less than this, as both states accepted payment in their own depreciated paper currency. Pioneers bought Kentucky land for about ten shillings a hundred acres, while those living in the West before 1778 were given four hundred acres free of charge.

The settlers who took advantage of those bargains moved westward in a steady stream all through the summer and fall of 1779. By the end of the year their cabins dotted the Tennessee countryside along the Holston as far south as the French Broad River. The migration to Kentucky did not reach full tide until the spring of 1780. Then the Wilderness Road was crowded with new arrivals, while so many came down the Ohio that by mid-summer Louisville, founded at the Falls of that stream, boasted a thriving population, rectangular streets, and even a city park. Before snow fell Kentucky teemed with 20,000 inhabitants who filled the older stations, spilled over into new towns, and turned the war-scarred wilderness into a bustling frontier of civilization.

So strong was the expansive spirit that an entirely new settlement sprang up during the winter of 1779-80. This outpost, at Nashville on the Cumberland River, originated in the speculative ambitions of Judge Richard Henderson who turned his attention to the southern portions of his Cherokee purchase after Virginia in 1777 decided against the Transylvania Company's claim to Kentucky. As leader for his enterprise he selected James Robertson, already trained in frontier life by his long career at Watauga. Robertson started westward with a small advance party in February, 1779, to lay out a town and plant corn against the coming winter. Henderson sent the rest of his prospective settlers to Nashville in two parties, one overland through Cumberland Gap during the cold winter of 1779-80, the other by boat along the circuitous Tennessee-Cumberland River route. The latter arrived in April, 1780, just as Henderson returned from a corn-buying trip into Kentucky, and the work of planting the new settlement began. Eight small stations, centered about Bluff Fort at French Lick, were erected along the river bank to hold the three hundred inhabitants. Having launched his enterprise successfully, Henderson headed east to protest in vain while North Carolina followed Virginia's example by holding his claim invalid. Nashville, as a part of North Carolina, expanded slowly under Robertson's leadership during the next years.

The rapid advance of the frontier during 1779 and 1780 was based on the belief that war in the West was over. Unfortunately this was not the case, for the successes of 1779 were more apparent than real. Clark's victories were based on audacity rather than military power, Bowman's campaign antagonized rather than crushed the Shawnee, and Sullivan's devastating march through New York left the British in control of Niagara and Oswego. English goods still reached the Great Lakes Indians over Lake Ontario and Lake Erie, and the poverty-stricken Continental Congress could not afford the gifts needed to cement its newly won Indian alliances. By the end of 1780 most of the interior tribes were back in England's camp, and for the next three years Americans fought a losing battle to retain control of the West.

In New York the counterattack began in the early spring when a raiding party from Oswego swooped down on the little town of German Flats. Again in May Sir John Johnson led his savage charges in a sweep westward along the Mohawk from Lake Champlain to the site of his father's old home, while Brant cut a swath of destruction between Ft. Stanwix and Canajoharie. In August the two armies, after joining at Unadilla, marched eastward along the Charlotte River, laid waste the Schoharie Valley, burned Middle Fort, and killed more than a hundred people. A hastily summoned militia force from Albany chased the raiders to Stone Arabia, where they were defeated, but when the cautious American commander refused to pursue farther, the British returned to the attack. Even Albany and Schenectady feared an Indian raid during the dismal fall of 1780.

The plight of settlers along the upper Ohio and in Kentucky was almost as desperate, due largely to the failure of two American expeditions aimed at Detroit. General Washington planned one of these, with Colonel Daniel Brodhead of Ft. Pitt in charge, but the militia needed to guard the Ohio River forts while regulars marched against the enemy refused to leave their homes and the Continental Congress was unable to provide supplies. Instead of leading a triumphant army into Detroit, Brodhead spent the summer of 1780 fighting off Seneca raiding parties that operated as far south as the Monongahela River. The second expedition was authorized by Virginia, which instructed George Rogers Clark to raise a thousand men and subdue the enemy outpost. Clark began his enlistment campaign with high hopes of success, but the Kentuckians simply refused to serve. They were willing to fight the Shawnee whose troublesome raids began again in 1780, but could see no reason to attack a distant enemy post. Clark railed and ranted in vain, even closing the land office to turn the people from speculation to fighting. In the end he bowed to frontier provincialism, sullenly retiring to build a new fort, Ft. Jefferson, near the mouth of the Ohio.

These failures vastly strengthened England's hand as vacillating Indians, sensing the declining American power, hurriedly aligned themselves with the British. Two English expeditions were planned to capitalize on

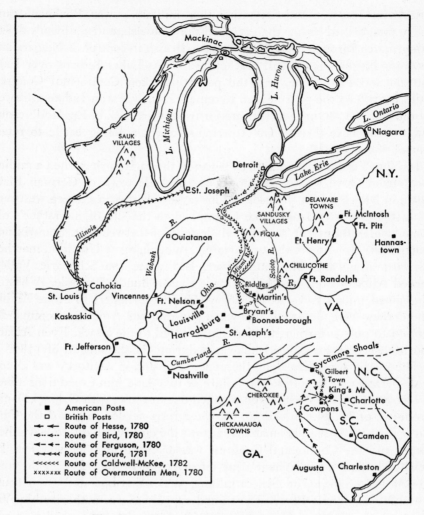

The Frontier in the Revolution, 1780–1783

this shift in the wilderness balance of power. A major force under Emanuel Hesse was to move south from Mackinac, overwhelm the Illinois villages, descend the Mississippi River, and help recapture West Florida from its Spanish conquerors. At the same time a smaller army, led by Captain Henry Bird, was to draw Clark's troops east by harrying Kentucky, thus opening the Mississippi to Hesse's force.

Fortunately for the Americans, these well-laid plans went astray. Hesse reached Cahokia in May, 1780, with a thousand British and Indian followers, but Clark had anticipated his coming and was waiting in that garrisoned post. His mere presence was enough to overawe Hesse's redskins who, after a few halfhearted sallies, forced their commander to move on to St. Louis. There too they were expected. Instead of surprising a handful of demoralized Spaniards, the English were met with cannon fire which sent them scurrying to safety. The expedition retired to Mackinac in disgrace after burning a few farmhouses. Hesse, fearful that Clark was at his heels, hastily moved his fort to an island in the Straits of Mackinac. The American commander, with too few troops to pursue the fleeing enemy, contented himself with sending a small force under Colonel John Montgomery to punish the Wisconsin Sauk for participating in the British raid.

Captain Bird enjoyed more success than Hesse. He left Detroit in April with 150 whites and a thousand Indians, crossed the Ohio, and ascended the Licking Valley which was dotted with small settlements. The pioneers in the first of these, Riddle's Station, prepared to resist, knowing that their palisaded fort could withstand a long siege, but when Bird's men produced two cannon they saw their cause was lost. On June 20, for the first time in history, a Kentucky Station surrendered. A week later Martin's Station fell before the battering of British artillery, and terror swept over the countryside. Bird, it appeared, could sweep all before him. But by this time the English commander, who deplored Indian warfare and feared his savage followers would get out of hand, had enough. With a hundred prisoners he started for Detroit.

When news of the "Bird Raid" reached George Rogers Clark at Kaskaskia on June 5, 1780, he immediately started east, disguised as an Indian to escape enemy raiders. This time recruits for the retaliatory expedition which he organized at Harrodsburg were plentiful. With a thousand men, Clark marched to Old Chillicothe, burned the town, then moved on to the Indian village of Piqua on the Big Miami River where several hundred savages under a Tory, Simon Girty, awaited him. This time it was the Americans' turn to produce cannon and batter down the enemy defenses. After several hours of fierce fighting the natives broke and fled. Again Clark's vigorous campaigning freed Kentucky from attack for the rest of the year.

Despite this victory the American position in the Northwest was far weaker at the close of 1780 than in 1779. Most of the savage tribes were still loyal to the British, for Bird was as successful as Clark, and England's trading goods far superior to those of the United States. More serious, however, was the drift of French Illinoisans away from their American alliance. By the autumn of 1780 they were on the point of revolt, angered by the strict military rule imposed on them by Virginia, the lack of trading goods, the corrupt speculators who appropriated their lands, and the flood of depreciated Continental currency which disrupted their business. Their discontent was fostered by a fiery French agitator, Colonel Mottin de la Balme, who began plotting against Virginia soon after he reached Kaskaskia in July, 1780. De la Balme was massacred that fall while leading a French force against Detroit, but dissatisfaction remained. Apparently the United States was on the verge of losing control of the whole region that Clark had won.

Only in the South did Americans in 1780 retain prestige won the previous year, and there the victories were gained at the expense of British regulars rather than Indians. By that time the center of the eastern war was in the southern states; Charleston fell to England in May, 1780, and a strong British army under Lord Cornwallis started north to crush the rebellious colonists between that city and New York. Cornwallis, to guard his left flank, dispatched a dashing young Scotch Highlander, Major Patrick Ferguson, to enlist Tories in the Carolina back country. Ferguson's appeal was so great that he soon commanded a thousand Loyalists who roamed the interior, destroying Whig property and lives. For a time a group of mountain men under Colonel Charles McDowell and Isaac Shelby offered some resistance, but when the American defeat at Camden in mid-August 1780, left them at the mercy of the British they fled westward with Ferguson's horsemen in hot pursuit.

There they might have stayed had not the arrogant Tory commander sent word that he planned to invade their hilly lair. Frontiersmen trained in the Indian tradition of aggressive fighting had only one answer to such a challenge; a call went through the back country for volunteers to assemble at Sycamore Shoals on September 25, 1780. As the leather-clad woodsmen who responded moved east from their rendezvous they were joined by others, until the force that crossed the Blue Ridge numbered 1,500 trained forest fighters. Ferguson, rather than risk open combat, started east from Gilbert Town to join Cornwallis' main British force at Charlotte.

News of this move reached the Americans while they were camped at Cowpens, feasting on cattle seized from a Tory owner. Nine hundred horsemen set out in pursuit, and after an all-night ride through a steady drizzle, caught their quarry at three o'clock in the afternoon of October 7, 1780. They found the British camped on a rocky spur that jutted from King's Mountain—a flat table of rock rising sixty feet above the level countryside—a spot chosen by Ferguson because he believed frontiersmen could not stand against bayonet charges. The Americans attacked at once, creeping upward through the trees and debris in Indian fashion. The advantage was theirs from the outset. When Tory troops charged down one side of the mountain, driving patriots before them, they exposed their backs to the withering fire of others. At last the Americans, reaching the summit, closed in among the trees, dropping Ferguson's men with their deadly long rifles. When the valiant commander fell the British gave up; 225 Loyalists were killed, 163 wounded, and 715 taken prisoner in the Battle of King's Mountain, while the Americans lost only 28 killed and 62 wounded.

This famous engagement ended Tory raids on the back country and allowed the over-mountain men to return home in peace. There, however, disturbing news awaited them: the Cherokee had seized on their absence to begin raiding again. They acted at once. A force was raised, commanded by Colonel Arthur Campbell of Virginia and Colonel John Sevier who became leader of the Watauga settlements on Robertson's departure. Through the autumn of 1780 they marched through the country of the Overhill Cherokee, destroying crops and towns, and leaving the Indians to face a winter of starvation. Again in the spring of 1780 Sevier took to the warpath, this time against the Middle Towns along the upper French Broad, striking swiftly and cruelly. When he led his raiders back to their Watauga homes the red men's power was broken. Sevier forced the subdued Cherokee chiefs to sign the second Treaty of Long Island (July 26, 1781) in which they surrendered another slice of territory to the land-hungry Americans. For the next two years the southern back country enjoyed a well-earned peace.

Vigorous action also ended the Revolution on the New York frontier during 1781. This only came after British and Indian raiding parties had reduced the Mohawk Valley to a virtual desert and carried their attacks to the doors of Schenectady and Kingston; by midsummer only eight hundred arms-bearing men remained in the whole valley and even they dared not venture beyond the blockhouses that offered the sole means of defense. The plight of these unfortunates finally forced New York to act. A strong army of seasoned soldiers, led by Colonel Marinus Willett, marched west in August, driving the intruders before them. In October the campaign reached its culmination when Willett caught the retreating British as they forded West Canada Creek, fell upon them, and slaughtered large numbers. Only a few isolated raids by Brant's declining forces broke the calm in western New York after that.

In the Northwest, on the other hand, Americans during 1781 and 1782 lost much they had won during the first years of the Revolution. Their cause appeared bright enough in the spring of 1781, particularly after a band of Spaniards and Indians from St. Louis, led by Captain Eugene Pourée, demonstrated British weakness by destroying the post at St. Joseph. But from that time on the list of disasters mounted. Clark spent the summer urging Kentuckians and Virginians to enlist for the often-planned attack on Detroit, but frontier provincialism, military jealousy, and the poverty of Congress proved obstacles that even this forceful leader could not overcome. By fall he had given up hope and fell to constructing a new fort, Ft. Nelson, at Louisville, while Indian raiders stormed about his ears. All through that dark winter attacks continued while Virginia, its economy strained to the breaking point by a depreciating currency, allowed the chain of forts along the Upper Ohio to moulder into decay. Yet worse was to come. In the spring of 1782 three hundred hot-headed Pennsylvanians, ousted from their homes by the settlement of the Virginia-Pennsylvania boundary dispute, crossed the Ohio to seize lands. They were entertained for three days at the Indian village of Gnadenhutten, where ninety friendly Delawares lived under the guidance of Moravian missionaries; on the fourth day the white men fell on their hymn-singing hosts in the Moravian church, slaughtering all of them—men, women, and children—"in a most cool and deliberate manner." This wanton brutality gave the Ohio Indians a new motive; the Delawares threw off all pretext of neutrality to join the Shawnee and Wyandot in a savage assault upon the northwestern borderland. By May the raids were so intense that the whole frontier was threatened. Again an expedition from Ft. Pitt marched into the Ohio country, this one under Colonel William Crawford, with the Sandusky villages as its objective. On the upper reaches of that river the Americans met a band of Shawnee and Delawares, fought a bitter one-day battle on June 4, and began a retreat that soon turned into a panic-stricken rout. Fifty were killed and nine carried away to the Delaware villages to be tortured to death. Crawford himself died by slow roasting—the sign of supreme Indian contempt.

The British were quick to take advantage of the aggressive spirit in their allies. During the summer of 1782 two expeditions left Detroit. One, led by Joseph Brant, attacked Ft. Henry and carried faggot and tomahawk as far as Hannastown, Pennsylvania. The other, under Captain William Caldwell and Alexander McKee, followed the usual path into Kentucky where Bryant's Station was stormed unsuccessfully, then headed east with a hastily formed army of Kentuckians at its heels. Canny old Daniel Boone warned his comrades that something was wrong; there was so much Indian "sign" left by the fleeing British that an ambush seemed likely. The reckless young men refused to heed his sound advice, even when Boone pointed out a likely spot for a surprise attack in a ravine just across the Licking River. Instead they rushed into the very trap the wise old frontiersman feared; sixty Americans died in that Battle of Blue Licks, the British escaping to Ohio. Not even a successful march against Chillicothe and

Piqua in November, led by George Rogers Clark, wiped out the sting of that defeat.

That was the last campaign of the Revolution; when Clark returned to the Ohio he learned that a preliminary peace treaty had been signed. Not since 1779 had American fortunes in the West been at lower ebb. Kentucky was still theirs, but the Indians were all in the enemy's ranks, Detroit and Mackinac were British-held, and even the Illinois country was lost when Virginia withdrew its troops from Kaskaskia in 1781. What Clark had won in his brilliant campaigns was lost through vacillating American policies, the poverty of Congress and Virginia, and the provincialism of frontiersmen who would defend their homes but refused to march against vital distant objectives. England had a far better claim to the Northwest at war's end than in 1780, but what the Americans lost on the battle field they gained at the peace table. The diplomats who met at Paris in 1782 to write the treaty giving the United States independence accomplished more for the West than all the bloody campaigns of the war.

Each negotiator had his own ambitions. Benjamin Franklin and John Jay, who represented the United States, wanted England to recognize their country's independence as a preliminary to further negotiations, then hoped to secure as favorable boundaries and concessions as possible. The Earl of Shelburne, who became British prime minister in July, 1782, and his agent, Richard Oswald, wished to separate the Americans from their French and Spanish allies. The Comte de Vergennes, French foreign minister, faced a more difficult problem. He had carried his country into war in 1778 by signing a treaty which bound France to continue fighting until American independence was won. He had lured Spain into the struggle a year later by promising continuous war until Gibraltar was restored to that nation. Now France was ready for peace, but the Mediterranean fortress was still in English hands. Vergennes' task was to secure independence for the Americans, then end the war by satisfying Spain with territorial concessions less difficult to obtain than Gibraltar. The fourth nation, Spain, was dominated by an able and aggressive foreign minister, the Count de Floridablanca. That hard-headed realist was determined to secure Gibraltar and to transform the Gulf of Mexico into a Spanish lake by acquiring the Floridas, exclusive navigation of the Mississippi River, and possibly a strip of territory east of that stream.

Vergennes saw his problem clearly. He knew that both France and the United States, although anxious for peace, were bound by treaty obligations to continue fighting until Spain was ready to lay down its arms— or until Gibraltar was restored. War might go on for years unless he could bribe Floridablanca into accepting peace. Why not, Vergennes

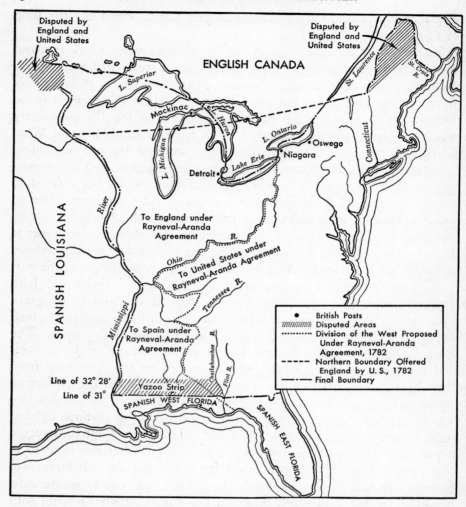

The West in the Peace Negotiations

reasoned, offer the Spaniards enough territory in the American West to compensate them for their failure to recapture that rocky fort. This seemed reasonable to the French foreign minister; he had made no boundary commitments to the United States and could with a clear conscience look on the trans-Appalachian country as conquered territory which could be assigned to any one of the allies. Hence he asked his secretary, Gérard de Rayneval, to work out a division of the West satisfactory to the Spanish ambassador to Versailles, the Count of Aranda. After several conferences Aranda agreed that the region north of the Ohio should be retained by England, Kentucky and eastern Tennessee should go to the United States, and the area south of the Cumberland and west of a line zigzagging to the Gulf at Apalachicola Bay should be assigned to Spain. This would give the Spaniards control of both banks of the Mississippi south of the Ohio and bar Americans from the river entirely. On September 6, 1782, Vergennes delivered this proposal to the American commissioners as his "personal ideal," keeping Spain's part in its formulation secret.

John Jay, who was acting alone due to Franklin's illness, was horrified. Vergennes, it seemed, was willing to carve up the new-born Republic for the benefit of greedy European neighbors even before independence was won. While Jay still pondered this unpleasant fact he received two other bits of information that apparently confirmed his worst fears. On September 10, 1782, Oswald handed him captured dispatches which proved the Chevalier de La Luzerne, French minister to the United States, guilty of trying to influence Congress to accept an Appalachian boundary. On the same day he learned that Rayneval had departed secretly for London to confer with Shelburne. Jay leaped to the conclusion that he had gone to persuade England to accept the Appalachian boundary or even offer that nation a separate peace. In the face of this seeming betrayal by an ally, why should the United States adhere to its outworn pledge of 1778? Better to protect the national interest by concluding an immediate treaty with Britain.

Jay acted at once. Oswald was told that the Americans were ready to negotiate, even without preliminary recognition of their independence, if his commission was altered to authorize dealings with agents of the United States—this being considered tacit recognition. At the same time Jay sent one of his own employees, Benjamin Vaughan, to assure Shelburne that the United States was ready to make an immediate peace if England would grant the Mississippi boundary and other concessions. The canny prime minister saw at once that this was a golden opportunity to split the allies. Oswald's new instructions were hurried to Paris by courier, reaching there on September 27, 1782. Negotiations began at once, and by October 5 Jay and Oswald agreed on a preliminary treaty which included the Mississippi line and a provision that both nations share navigation of that river. This draft proved unacceptable to England, for by the time it reached London on October 11 the government knew that a last allied assault on Gibraltar had failed. Hence Shelburne insisted on further concessions from the United States, particularly compensation for British merchants with outstanding loans in America and Loyalists who had abandoned property there.

John Adams, a third American delegate who arrived in Paris at that time, readily agreed to follow Jay's leadership. Together they persuaded

Franklin to proceed without consulting Vergennes. Negotiations went forward rapidly until November 3, 1782, when preliminary articles were signed. These gave the British their choice of two northern boundaries. Both began at the St. Croix River and followed the "highlands" between the Atlantic and St. Lawrence to the Connecticut—a provision that led to a prolonged controversy, as the location of both the St. Croix and the "highlands" was disputed. One possible boundary ran due west from the Connecticut along the 45th parallel to the Mississippi; the other followed that parallel to the St. Lawrence, then through the Great Lakes and across the Grand Portage to the northwest corner of the Lake of the Woods. From that point the line extended "due west to the Mississippi"—another source of dispute as that river terminated south of the Lake of the Woods—down the Mississippi to the 31st parallel, east to the Chattahoochee, south along that stream to its junction with the Flint, east once more to the St. Mary's, and down the center of that twisting river to the sea. Because the fate of the Floridas was unknown at that time, a secret provision in the preliminary treaty provided that should England secure those provinces the southern boundary of the United States was to begin at the mouth of the Yazoo River and run east to the Chattahoochee along the line of 32° 28' rather than along the 31st parallel. This too caused controversy, as Spain ultimately secured the Floridas and laid claim to the whole "Yazoo Strip" that Jay and Adams were willing to grant their enemy but not their ally.

These boundaries were as advantageous as could have been expected. By deserting France and playing on England's desire for an immediate peace, the American commissioners gave their country a vast western territory that might otherwise have gone to Spain. In its other provisions the preliminary treaty was almost as favorable. The United States and England shared the right to navigate the Mississippi, Americans were granted fishing rights off Canada, and agreed to put no obstacles in the way of merchants or Loyalists trying to recover their property. British garrisons in the Northwest Posts that lay south of the border were to evacuate them "with all convenient speed." Shelburne accepted those provisions at once, after choosing the Great Lakes boundary, and on November 30, 1782, the preliminary treaty was signed by both sets of commissioners. Vergennes, who was shown a copy the next day, was probably secretly pleased that the Americans had violated their pledge and made a separate peace, for the desertion of an ally helped him persuade Spain to give up the fight. Five days later the Spanish government agreed to accept the Floridas and Minorca instead of Gibraltar. Anglo-French and Anglo-Spanish treaties were concluded by January 20, 1783, automatically putting the Anglo-American agreement into effect. By September 3, 1783, both England and the United States had ratified and signed the final treaty.

American diplomats won a significant victory for their fellow country-men when they secured the West—even at the risk of angering their French allies and saviors—after military conquest failed. Yet even their repudiation of the Franco-American treaty would not have brought this triumph but for the generosity of Lord Shelburne. He, above all other statesmen, realized that frontier expansion was inevitable and that the American people would never be satisfied if their westward path was blocked. "The deed is done," he wrote later, "and a strong foundation laid for eternal amity between England and America." The vision of an enemy minister and the willingness of American negotiators to place national interest above international ethics secured the trans-Appalachian wilderness for the new republic.

# SECTION II
# The Trans-Appalachian Frontier

# CHAPTER X

# The Western Problem

## 1783-1790

The Treaty of 1783 brought the infant American government face to face with the same staggering problems that plagued England's ministers after the Seven Years' War: how could Indians be removed from the trans-Appalachian wilderness, lands disposed of, and settlers governed? Britain's best statesmen failed to find an answer; now an untried congress, torn by dissension and weakened by sectional jealousies, must succeed or witness the collapse of the entire democratic experiment. To make matters even worse, the solution was complicated by the presence of a welter of conflicting interests involving land companies, traders, foreign intrigue, and state claims. Little wonder that some observers who remembered England's groping efforts viewed the task as insurmountable.

Congress' first step was to secure undisputed control of the West, for at the start of the Revolution the over-mountain region was claimed by seven of the thirteen states on the basis of the crown-granted sea-to-sea charters to which they owed their origin. Massachusetts, Connecticut, North Carolina, and Georgia contended that their original grants, which provided each with a strip of coast and northern and southern boundaries running to the Pacific, extended their territories to the Mississippi. South Carolina, whose sea-to-sea charter was disputed by Georgia, laid claim to a fifty-mile strip between the 35th parallel and a line drawn west from the junction of the Tugaloo and Keowee rivers. Virginia insisted that her 1609 charter, extending the Old Dominion's boundaries "up into the land, throughout from sea to sea, west and northwest," gave her control of Kentucky and virtually all lands north and west of the Ohio River. New York claimed the same region, not on the basis of a colonial grant, but because her jurisdiction over the Iroquois applied to all lands conquered by that tribe.

From the beginning of the Revolution both national statesmen and representatives of the six landless states urged the cession of the western lands to the United States. The former argued that the trans-Appalachian domains were common property because they were "wrested from the common enemy by the blood and treasure of the thirteen states," that a nationally owned West would serve as a bond of unity during trying days when interstate rivalries threatened the Republic, that central control would satisfy frontiersmen who clamored through the war for a better form of government than individual states could provide, and that the lands were needed both for revenue and for satisfying bounties promised men who had enlisted in the Revolutionary armies. Spokesmen for the six states which did not claim western territories not only echoed these arguments but pointed out that cession was necessary to protect their own commonwealths. States with territories in the West, they argued, could care for most of their expenses by selling land. Those without would be forced to resort to higher taxes, driving their inhabitants to the landed states. The depopulation of stretches of the seaboard loomed as an unpleasant possibility.

Most of those who argued in this way were sincere, but the more vociferous were representatives of land companies who saw a chance to turn the conflict to their own advantage. Firmly against cession in each commonwealth were speculators who hoped to use their local influence to secure state-granted lands in the West. Arguing for cession were two organizations that antedated the Revolution, the Indiana Company and the Illinois-Wabash Land Company, both of which claimed lands in western Virginia on the basis of purchases made under the Camden-Yorke decision. Their leaders knew that Virginia would never recognize their claims, especially after 1776 when the legislature specifically voided all titles acquired directly from Indians. Congress, however, might be more lenient. With this in mind both companies were reorganized soon after independence to include leading politicians in the landless Middle States. These men, working together under the able leadership of Robert Morris of Pennsylvania, formed a solid congressional bloc in favor of immediate cession. They were a power to be reckoned with, for they could always count on the support of Maryland, Pennsylvania, New Jersey, and Delaware, and could usually capture additional votes from Rhode Island and New Hampshire.

The Middle State speculators showed their hand first by attempting to write a clause into an early draft of the Articles of Confederation authorizing Congress to define state boundaries and erect new western states, but the seven land-owning states defeated that proposal, substituting in the final draft a guarantee that "no state shall be deprived of territory for the benefit of the United States." When the Articles were submitted to the states for ratification, the speculators and nationalists had their revenge. On December 15, 1778, Maryland announced it would never ratify until the landed states surrendered their holdings to the central government. This resolution was couched in patriotic language and stressed Congress' need for territories to satisfy soldiers' bonuses, but the influence of jobbers became apparent two days later when Virginia offered to provide all lands required for this purpose free of charge. Now the Maryland speculators had no choice but to state their position openly. The formal declaration of the state's intentions, submitted to Congress on January 6, 1779, stressed only the common right of all the people to all parts of trans-Appalachia not granted to individuals before the war. The issue, as Virginia saw it, was clear: should she surrender her western lands to the Indiana and Illinois-Wabash Land Companies, or keep them to be exploited by her own speculators?

Others, however, did not realize this, and Virginia's position grew steadily weaker during the next two years. Her attempt to expose the companies by opening the West to settlement backfired when a congressional committee, dominated by representatives of the landless states, adopted a resolution in November, 1779, urging that no western territory be sold until after the war. To make matters worse, New York ceded its shadowy claims in February, 1780, setting a precedent dangerous to Virginia's interests. Many prominent men, even within the Old Dominion, were won to cession by the military reverses of that year. Better to strengthen the American cause by ceding the West and allowing the Articles of Confederation to go into effect, they argued, than risk defeat by England. This mounting pressure was too much to resist, but Virginia was not ready to surrender completely. In September, 1780, it agreed to turn over its western lands only if Congress guaranteed that no private purchases previously made there would be recognized.

This unlooked-for development sent the speculators into action. Petitions were signed, pamphlets circulated, and stock judiciously distributed among doubting congressmen. These efforts bore fruit in October when Congress accepted the Virginia cession only after striking out the provision respecting private purchases. Undaunted, the House of Burgesses on January 2, 1781, ceded the United States all lands north of the Ohio, but with restrictions on land companies intact. This maneuver placed the decision squarely up to Maryland; refusal to ratify now would prove it was acting in the interest of speculators rather with the nation's welfare at heart. On February 2, 1781, the state's legislature formally accepted the new frame of government.

The land companies were still not ready to surrender. Virginia had ceded, but Congress might be persuaded not to accept the cession until the obnoxious provision on private purchases was stricken out. For the next three years they worked frantically, but to no avail. Twice speculator-dominated committees insisted that the national government already owned the trans-Appalachian country and could grant it without respect to Virginia's wishes, one maintaining that Congress inherited the West from England, the other that the New York cession included all territory claimed by the Old Dominion. Fortunately neither report was adopted, for sentiment was swinging against the speculators as their role in the sordid controversy became clear. A few greedy individuals, Americans saw, were denying Congress a domain badly needed to ease the nation's financial burdens and satisfy bounty-holding Revolutionary heroes. The shift in popular opinion was shown in June, 1783, when a new committee, made up largely of representatives of landholding states, urged Congress to accept the Virginia cession with all restrictions attached. This report was adopted in September, and on March 1, 1784, jubilant Virginia officials, happy in their victory over the speculators, transferred their state's western holding to the United States.

In her cession Virginia set a pattern that other states later followed. All had issued land bounties to their Revolutionary militia and were now faced with the necessity of retaining enough western territory to satisfy those claims. Hence the Virginia assembly retained a "military reserve" between the Scioto and Little Miami rivers as well as a 150,000 acre plot opposite Louisville which was awarded George Rogers Clark and his men. Only the lands north of the Ohio River were included in the cession, as most of Kentucky was already sold and that region was kept as a county until ready for statehood.

The other northern states quickly followed the example of New York and Virginia. Massachusetts ceded all its lands west of New York in November, 1784, reserving a claim to the western portion of that state. Connecticut succumbed to popular pressure in May, 1786, when it surrendered all its interior territory save a "Western Reserve" of nearly 4,000,000 acres in northeastern Ohio. By the end of 1786 the United States controlled all of the Northwest, except the Virginia and Connecticut reserves.

The states south of Virginia proved less responsive to public opinion, for most of them had suffered heavily during the war and were anxious to profit from their western lands. The eagerness of the legislatures of North Carolina, South Carolina, and Georgia to reap large returns from their interior territories proved an irresistible lure to speculators and plunged those southern governments into a labyrinth of intrigue that lasted for a quarter-century.

The situation was particularly bad in North Carolina. As soon as popular interest in cession began to develop, the assembly, in 1783, hurriedly threw open the Tennessee country to settlers, setting aside only a military reserve

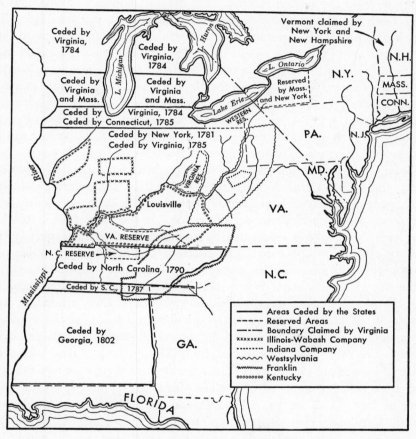

Western Land Cessions, 1780–1802

for bounty holders in the Cumberland Valley. The low price asked—about $5 for one hundred acres—sent Carolina land jobbers upon a speculative rampage; within seven months 4,000,000 acres were sold at the Hillsboro office. By that time sentiment for cession was developing rapidly, fomented by eastern planters who disliked paying taxes to protect distant frontiersmen, and by western speculators who looked to the national government for improvements that would increase the value of their holdings. Their influence resulted in an act in June, 1784, ceding the Tennessee country to the United States, and specifically stating that all previous grants there must be respected. The measure was passed over the protests of frontiersmen who hesitated to trade the assured protection of North Carolina for the nebulous advantages of national control.

The westerners determined not to accept the decision without protest. When news of the cession reached their overhill homes a spontaneous call went forth for a convention to meet at Jonesboro in August, 1784. The rough woodsmen who assembled in that wilderness town decided on their future course at once: they would set up a government and enter the Union as an independent state. This seemed legal and proper; Congress had just resolved to admit new states into the Republic, and only separate existence would assure protection for their homes and lives. Hence they drew up a petition to Congress, laid out boundaries that included much of southwestern Virginia as well as eastern Tennessee in their new commonwealth, and provided for a second convention to frame a constitution.

Before this convention met the situation had changed. In November, 1784, the North Carolina legislature, alarmed by the separate-statehood movement and swayed by a humanitarian desire to deal more fairly with the westerners, repealed the act of cession. At the same time it tried to win back the revolting woodsmen by giving them their own court system and an efficient militia force. The effect of this appeasement policy was shown when the frontiersmen assembled in December to draw up a constitution for their new state. Where the August meeting had been harmonious, the new gathering was divided into two groups. One, headed by John Sevier of the Holston settlements who had been a leader of the statehood movement from the first, insisted on separation despite North Carolina's action. The other, led by Colonel John Tipton, long a rival of Sevier, favored immediate capitulation. The separate-state men were in a majority and after riding roughshod over their opponents, agreed to create a new state of Frankland—or Franklin as it was soon called. After the laws of North Carolina were adopted as a temporary constitution, Sevier was chosen governor by acclamation. Frontier pride and provincialism had launched a wilderness experiment in self-government.

The State of Franklin fared badly from the first. Its survival depended on congressional recognition, yet Congress not only refused to consider admitting the new state but adopted a decidedly hostile attitude which was shown especially in dealing with the Indians. The Franklinites, with the usual frontier disregard for native rights, attempted to secure lands for expansion by forcing a handful of minor Cherokee chiefs to sign the so-called Treaty of Dumplin Creek in May, 1785. This illegal agreement, which extended the whites' territory as far as the watershed of the Little

River, was protested so vigorously by the rest of the tribe that national authorities felt called upon to intercede. The United States commissioners sent to meet the Indians in November, 1785, not only disavowed the Treaty of Dumplin Creek but drew up their own Treaty of Hopewell in open defiance of the Franklin government. The lines established by the Treaties of DeWitt's Corner and Long Island were recognized, a narrow strip in North Carolina purchased from the Cherokee, and a boundary run west-

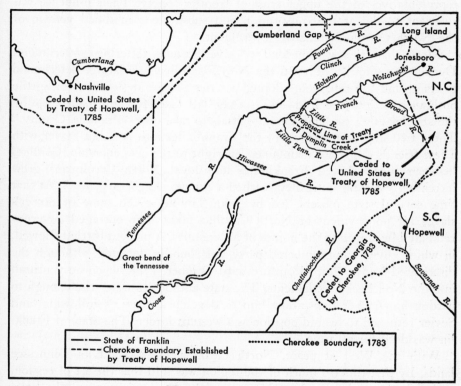

The State of Franklin

ward from Long Island through Cumberland Gap and along the Cumberland River to place the Nashville settlements in American territory. The disgruntled frontiersmen were forced to watch their hoped-for lands turned over to savages by a government whose support they had anticipated.

Neither congressional hostility nor internal dissension could discourage the optimistic westerners; instead they believed that the constant disputes between Franklinites, anti-Franklinites, and government men would "be found useful in forming the manners of the people; . . . the next generation in Frankland will vie with Athens itself." In this cheerful mood they met together in November, 1785, to draw up a constitution for their state. The document that emerged was surprisingly democratic; it swept away nearly all property qualifications for office holding, introduced manhood suffrage, a popularly elected one-house legislature, the registration of voters, election by ballot, and a crude form of referendum. These liberal features were little to the liking of Governor Sevier or his little clique of friends who had no more sympathy with true democracy than any other representatives of the upper crust of frontier society. Their influence was sufficient to defeat the constitution and substitute a modified version of the North Carolina frame of government.

More than this was needed to save Sevier's tottering government. During the summer of 1786 the North Carolina legislature, determined to stamp out the rebellion, adopted a series of laws designed to bring the outlaws back into the fold—one forgave all taxes for any man accepting the state's authority—and named officials to take over "Franklin County." These two steps swung most of the Franklinites into line, but Sevier with a few friends doggedly maintained his right to the governorship. Conflicts between the outlawed Franklinites and loyal North Carolinians grew increasingly serious until they reached a climax in February, 1788. At that time several state officers, led by John Tipton, seized some of Sevier's slaves for nonpayment of North Carolina taxes. The outraged governor retaliated by storming the homes of his enemies. A pitched battle followed, in which Sevier's outnumbered party was soundly defeated, although the discredited leader escaped capture until October, 1788, when he ventured into the Nolichucky settlements. The state authorities were wise enough to pardon him rather than allow him to develop a martyr's following, and Sevier returned to his old position as a western leader. The State of Franklin was dead for all time.

With the West at peace, North Carolina again ceded its Tennessee lands. By that time so much of the region was sold that the act of cession, passed in December, 1789, and accepted by Congress two months later, conveyed little more than jurisdiction. In the meantime South Carolina turned over its narrow strip in August, 1787, leaving Georgia the last state to surrender its western territories. There too the hope of financial returns delayed the final surrender; the legislature in 1789 and again in 1795 sold the whole tract to speculating companies, then rescinded the sales. Not until 1802 was the last cession completed and the United States assured possession of the vast wilderness between the Appalachians and the Mississippi.

Congress had begun to shape the United States' western policy long before this, for when Virginia ceded its holdings in 1784 the others were bound to follow. During the next few years, and with a systematic progression that resulted from chance rather than plan, the three most important problems were solved: how to sell the public domain, how to clear away the Indian inhabitants, and how to govern the federal territories. The monumental laws embodying these decisions set a pattern that was followed through the history of the frontier in determining relations between the government and the West.

The nation's first concern was a means of selling the newly acquired lands, for money was needed to reduce the Revolutionary debt and meet part of the government's expenses. The complexities of the problem immediately became clear. Congress must choose between two established systems: the New England practice of surveying lands before settlement and selling them in orderly blocks, or the southern custom of "indiscriminate location and subsequent survey" which allowed a settler to purchase a warrant, lay out his plot where he wished, and then have it surveyed. Both methods had elements of strength and weakness. The northern system did away with conflicting titles and assured pioneers protection as they advanced westward in compact tiers, but discouraged immigration by overemphasizing the social group and by forcing the purchase of bad land along with good. The southern system, although favored by frontiersmen, bred a welter of conflicting titles, for each homeseeker avoided poor soil by laying out irregularly shaped plots which could not be surveyed accurately. Somewhere between those two extremes—one sacrificing settlement for order and the other impossible to administer—Congress must find the answer to its problem.

Suggestions began pouring in as early as 1781 when a pamphleteer, Pelatiah Webster, urged the government to divide the West into square townships to be auctioned off at a minimum price of a $1 an acre. For the next three years the question was debated occasionally, but not until March, 1785, when a committee was set up to recommend a definite program, did Congress act. The report proposed that the public domain be divided into townships seven miles square, that these be sold at auction with a minimum price of $1 an acre, and that only whole townships be disposed of to united groups of frontiersmen. This proposal, which virtually adopted the New England system, aroused southern congressmen. They pointed out that individualistic pioneers from their states were unwilling to band together for township purchases, thus giving socially minded northerners an undue advantage. These valid criticisms led to a general modification of the proposal in the month of debate that followed. The result was the Ordinance of 1785, adopted on May 20 of that year—one of the most important legislative measures in American history.

All government-owned lands, it stated, would be divided into townships six miles square. These, in turn, would be subdivided into thirty-six numbered "sections," each containing one square mile or 640 acres. Alternate townships would be sold as a whole and in sections, thus satisfying both New Englanders who wanted large units and southerners who wished smaller plots. The auction method was adopted, with regular sales in each state, and a minimum price of $1 an acre. Congress reserved four sections in each township for subsequent disposal and set aside one—section sixteen —to maintain schools. The Ordinance stated that the first "base line,"

Proposed Survey of First Seven Ranges Under Ordinance of 1785

A Township as Numbered Under Ordinance of 1785

The Ordinance of 1785

as the east-west surveys were called, should run due west from the point where the Pennsylvania boundary crossed the Ohio River, and that north-south "range lines" should extend southward from this to the Ohio. As soon as the first "Seven Ranges" were surveyed the whole tract, in the southeast corner of present Ohio, would be opened to settlers.

When Congress adopted the Ordinance of 1785 it traded the immediate benefit of land sales for a well-ordered future. The measure did end the confusion prevalent under the southern warrant system; now a prospective settler purchased a definite, previously surveyed tract—section twenty in township number three, for example—rather than title to a plot that he could lay out himself. Yet months, or even years, would be needed to complete the laborious surveys necessary before sales could begin. More years might be required to convince independent frontiersmen to buy well-marked government tracts rather than to select choice lands that pleased them. The warrant system not only promised Congress better financial returns, but was better suited to the needs of the frontier. By limiting sales to auctions in eastern states, barring purchases of less than 640 acres, and decreeing that the minimum price for a plot should be $640, the Ordinance prevented pioneer farmers from buying government land, for no frontiersman needed such a large tract nor could he afford to buy on those terms. Instead the door was opened to speculators who could purchase sections

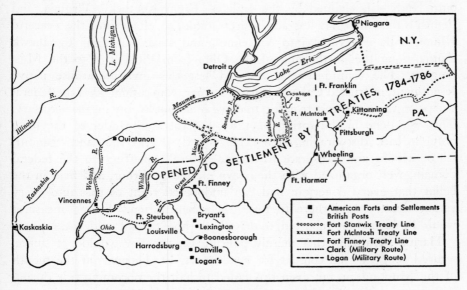

Indian Relations in the Northwest, 1783-1787

or townships at eastern auctions, then parcel them out to users in smaller tracts and on credit. This probably was in the minds of Congressmen, many of whom were land jobbers themselves.

While surveys were getting under way, Congress turned to the second step needed to open the West: removal of the Indians. The five commissioners already named to treat with the northwestern tribes were instructed to visit the Ohio country, meet the natives, and establish a boundary extending the area open to settlement west to the Falls of the Ohio. Three of them went at once to Ft. Stanwix where they badgered the Iroquois into surrendering all claims to the Northwest for a few paltry presents. A little later, on January 21, 1785, the Chippewa, Ottawa, Delaware, and Wyandot tribes were summoned to Ft. McIntosh and intimidated into giving up all their Ohio lands except a reservation between the Cuyahoga-Tuscarawas portage and the Maumee River. Even this region was not completely theirs; the United States retained several strategic spots on the Maumee, Sandusky, and Great Miami rivers for trading posts.

The Treaties of Ft. Stanwix and Ft. McIntosh complicated, rather than solved, the northwestern Indian problem. Neither satisfied the natives; the Iroquois cession only angered Ohio tribesmen who claimed the Six Nations had no right to cede their hunting grounds, and the Ft. McIntosh agreement was useless because the Shawnee refused to sign. To make matters worse they gave frontiersmen an excuse to swarm across the Ohio River onto lands still claimed by the Indians. From Kentucky, Virginia, and Pennsylvania these lawless adventurers came, to elbow into the peaceful Illinois villages, crowd into Vincennes, and stake out their tomahawk claims along the north bank of the Ohio from Pittsburgh to the Muskingum. The commissioners, alarmed lest this invasion arouse native resentment, instructed Colonel Josiah Harmar, who commanded the federal troops on the northwest frontier, to drive them out by any means necessary. This was done in the spring of 1785, but the commander of the force brought back discouraging news. He found several thousand "banditti whose actions are a disgrace to human nature" squatting on the federal domain, well organized with their own elected governor, and firm in the belief that every American had "an undoubted right to pass into every vacant country, and there to form their constitution." Strong measures would be needed, he reported, to drive back those defiant wilderness spirits.

Harmar, realizing that merely policing the frontier would not suffice, secured congressional consent for a new fort, Ft. Harmar, at the mouth of the Muskingum, but even this failed to halt the oncoming tide during the summer of 1785. Most embarrassed of all by the illegal migration were the Indian commissioners who were laboring to secure Shawnee consent for the northwestern land cessions. In an effort to placate their native charges, they sent out runners summoning the Ohio tribes to a new conference at the mouth of the Great Miami in October, 1785. After a month of waiting a few Wyandot and Delaware chiefs straggled in, although the Shawnee remained aloof until a threat of war brought 150 sullen warriors to the meeting ground early in January, 1786. Three weeks of negotiations, marked by threats from the officials and grudging concessions from the Indians, were climaxed by the signing of the Treaty of Ft. Finney—named after a blockhouse thrown up by the American troops while they were waiting—on January 31, 1786. The Shawnee reluctantly agreed to the Ft. McIntosh cession and to an extension of the boundary westward along the White River to the mouth of the Wabash, but they repudiated the agreement as soon as they returned to the safety of their villages.

That tribe's defiance of the United States brought Indian dissatisfaction to the boiling point in the spring of 1786. Through the Ohio country bands of natives fell on traders and raided settlements, while the Iroquois renounced the Ft. Stanwix treaty and threatened war if their lands were occupied. These attacks were climaxed on July 15 when five hundred Miami warriors surrounded Vincennes and demanded the right to slaughter all Americans there. When their cold-blooded request was refused they retreated grumblingly, letting it be known they would soon return. If the frontier was to be saved from war something more was needed than the feeble efforts of an impoverished Congress and the inadequate protection of the few soldiers at Ft. Harmar and Ft. Finney. As usual in such a situation westerners took matters into their own hands. Throughout Kentucky the demand rose for George Rogers Clark to save the Northwest.

Clark, despite advancing years and a growing tendency toward alcoholic overindulgence, rose to the emergency in his usual capable fashion. Two expeditions were planned; one under Clark to march north from Ft. Steuben, a new federal outpost across the river from Louisville, to destroy the Miami villages on the upper Wabash and Miami, the other to advance along the Great Miami River into the Shawnee country. The latter, led by Colonel Benjamin Logan, destroyed ten towns and 15,000 bushels of corn, but Clark's 1,200 militiamen mutinied at the mouth of Vermillion Creek and returned in disorder without sighting a single foe. The Indians, encouraged by this failure, held two conferences during the winter of 1786-87 to repudiate the treaties of Ft. Stanwix, Ft. McIntosh, and Ft. Finney and declare that "the line now cutting Pennsylvania shall bound them on the sun-rising, and the Ohio shall be the boundary between them and the Big Knives."

Congress was helpless in face of this native demand for the whole Ohio country. It attempted to better relations by passing the Ordinance of 1786 which set up an Indian Department patterned after the earlier English model, with superintendents for the regions north and south of the Ohio River authorized to bar unlicensed traders and guarantee the red men fair prices for furs. This halfhearted palliative meant nothing, as the United States had no manufacturing establishments to provide trading goods, even if the day for peaceful negotiation had not passed. When raids mounted in intensity during the spring of 1787 Congress, recognizing the need for force, strengthened the garrisons at Ft. Pitt, Ft. McIntosh, Ft. Harmar, Ft. Finney, Ft. Steuben, and Vincennes. A war was needed before the Northwest was safe for settlers.

Yet the government's financial needs required an immediate sale of western territory. Hence as soon as the treaties of Ft. Stanwix and Ft. McIntosh were signed, work began on the first base line, or "Geographer's Line" as it was called, of the "Seven Ranges." The task proved formidable —surveyors worked over rough, forested country under constant threat of Indian attack—but the little band of men stuck doggedly to their task between September 1785 and April 1787. By that time only four ranges were laid out and Congress, impatient under its financial burdens, decided to throw these open to settlement at once. The first sales, held at New York in September and October, 1787, were disappointing; buyers were few, bidding so listless that the price seldom rose above the minimum, purchases small, and the total profit only $176,090 in depreciated currency. This was not the fortune needed to retire the national debt. The land system must be revised to bring in larger returns.

Congress was moved to make this change by pressure from one of the most important land companies in history, the Ohio Company. This influential organization was the brain child of Brigadier General Rufus Putnam, a Revolutionary veteran from New England. Putnam knew that Washington's soldiers were mustered out with their pockets stuffed with "certificates of indebtedness"—depreciated government securities issued in lieu of back pay—which Congress would accept at par value in any land sales. Why not form a company, sell stock to veterans in return for those worthless certificates, and purchase a large tract in the Ohio country? With this in mind Putnam persuaded his close friend, Brigadier General Benjamin Tupper, to join the party surveying the Seven Ranges with an eye to spying out a suitable spot for a colony. Tupper's few months in the West had convinced him that the garden spot of the Ohio region was the Muskingum Valley, a fertile area guarded by Ft. Harmar and adjacent to the Seven Ranges.

His glowing report so fired Putnam's enthusiasm that the two men lost no time in inserting "A Piece called Information" in the Massachusetts papers, asking all former soldiers interested to meet at the Bunch of Grapes Tavern in Boston on March 1, 1786. The eleven delegates who gathered that day were easily persuaded to endorse the scheme. Then and there they formed the Ohio Company, pledged themselves to sell $1,000,000 worth of stock for Continental certificates, and agreed to migrate to the Ohio lands that would be purchased with this sum. When they met again a year later only 250 thousand-dollar shares had been sold, but they decided to buy as much as possible with the money on hand, hoping to expand their holdings when their successful colony brought a rush of new subscribers. The task of negotiating with Congress was entrusted to a shrewd Ipswich clergyman, the Reverend Manasseh Cutler, who reached New York, where the government was meeting, on July 5, 1787.

His proposal—that Congress overthrow the entire principle of small sales underlying the Ordinance of 1785 by selling his company a plot at less than a depreciated dollar an acre—aroused so little congressional enthusiasm that by July 20 Cutler was on the point of admitting defeat and returning to New England. At that point, he received a call from Colonel William Duer, secretary of the Board of Treasury which handled all land sales. A "number of the principal characters in the city," his visitor explained, were interested in the success of the Ohio Company sale, but only if they could share secretly in the proceeds. This was sufficient to interest Cutler, who was enough of a Yankee to know an opportunity when he saw one, and the two men set out for Brooklyn where, over an excellent oyster supper, they hatched one of the nation's most important speculations.

Duer's scheme was as simple as it was dishonest. He represented a number of congressmen, government leaders, and business men who were anxious to buy Ohio land but could not because of their official positions. They wished the Ohio Company to apply for 1,500,000 acres for itself, to be paid for in two $500,000 installments, one when the sale was made and the other on completion of the surveys. At the same time it was to purchase an additional 5,000,000 acres for Colonel Duer's associates, who were to organize as the Scioto Company and pay for their tract in six installments. In return for this service Colonel Duer agreed to loan the Ohio Company the money needed to complete its down payment and to take Cutler and one of his associates, Winthrop Sargent, into the Scioto Company. They would, Duer explained, be given thirteen shares between them, Duer and his friends would keep thirteen more, and six would be sold in Europe. The profits from those six would allow the company to meet the few payments necessary until its option was sold to some other speculating concern at a handsome profit. All parties would benefit: the Ohio Company would get 1,000,000 acres of choice land for about eight cents an acre, Duer and his associates would have an option on 2,000,000 more acres, and Cutler and Sargent would control an equal amount—all for the cost of one oyster supper and a loan of $200,000 in depreciated currency. Little wonder that the speculation promised to be one of the most profitable in history.

Colonel Duer, who agreed to push the sale through Congress, lived up to his bargain well. He and Cutler reached an agreement on July 21, 1787. Two days later Congress authorized Duer's Board of Treasury to sell large blocks of land to companies, and on July 24 Cutler laid down his terms, announcing with a great show of bluster that he would leave the city unless they were accepted. After three more days—to create an impression of proper deliberation—the board agreed to the sale. Two plots were turned over to the Ohio Company. One lay along the Ohio River between the seventh and seventeenth range lines and extended inward far enough to include 1,500,000 acres—although when the surveys were completed the company actually received 1,781,760 acres. The second embraced 5,000,000 acres between the first tract and the Scioto River. Cutler received only an option on those lands, requiring payment at the rate of 66⅔ cents an acre in four semiannual installments beginning six months after the

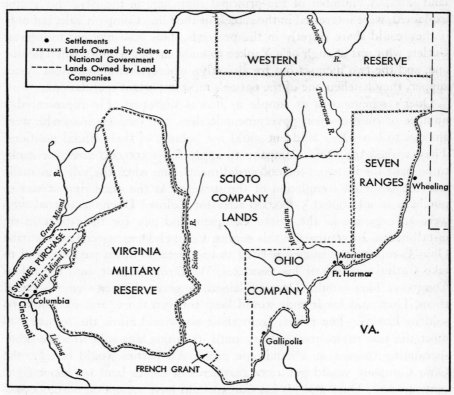

The Ohio Country, 1787–1790

external surveys were completed. This he turned over to the Scioto Company.

Cutler was still not satisfied, even with a bargain that gave his company 1,500,000 acres at eight cents an acre and himself a sizeable interest in a giant speculation. He pointed out to Congress that orderly government for the Ohio country must be provided before the Ohio and Scioto companies could hope for profitable sales. His prodding was responsible for the Ordinance of 1787, a measure that ranked with the Ordinance of 1785 in shaping the future of the West.

Congressmen had long wrangled over a governmental system for the western territories before the energetic Cutler whipped them into action. On one point they agreed unanimously: they must not repeat the mistakes that had been responsible for the Revolution. Their problem, they knew, was the same that faced Parliament before 1776, for the public domain was really a vast colony owned jointly by the thirteen states. England's empire collapsed because it failed to grant sufficient autonomy to the component parts; American Revolutionists had insisted on a system of co-ordinacy which would have placed colonies and mother country on an equal footing, bound together only through the allegiance both paid the king. When Parliament failed to recognize this and tried to rule the king's American subjects, war followed. Hence Congressmen realized they must grant autonomy to their own colonies to escape a second revolution. The Union could exist only so long as no one of its parts was subservient to any other.

This was made clear by the rebellious attitude of westerners during and just after the Revolution. Frontiersmen who lived beyond the mountains were men of a different world—the "Western World" they called it—who demanded the right to shape their own destiny. What did self-satisfied easterners know of life on the frontier, of the need for protection, easy land laws, and less burdensome taxes? Petitions sent over the mountains to protest rulings of a distant legislature were strangely reminiscent of protests that colonists of an earlier generation showered on Parliament. Moreover, when demands were ignored, these colonists of the West showed a dangerous tendency to take matters into their own hands. Separate statehood movements flourished and died in the West all through the Revolutionary Era. Pennsylvania was so plagued by demands of its over-mountain citizens for independence that in 1783 it threatened all agitators with the death penalty. North Carolina lost control of its frontiersmen entirely for a time when they formed their own state of Franklin. Kentucky nourished a similar separatist movement for some years after 1780. North of the Ohio squatters fought eviction by petitioning for admission as a new state. Even the handful of settlers on Clark's grant opposite Louisville in 1785 proclaimed the right to make their own laws in the absence of adequate government. Surveying this turbulent scene, Congressmen realized that the West would be satisfied only with the same rights and privileges under the central government that the East enjoyed. Those could be granted only by erecting the trans-Appalachian territories into states, to be admitted into the Union on terms of full equality with the original states.

This principle was clearly stated in October, 1780, when Congress tried to persuade the landed states to cede their western holdings by promising that all cessions would be "formed into separate republican states, which shall become members of the federal union, and have the same rights and sovereignty, freedom and independence as the other states." From that time debate hinged only about the size and method of admission of new states. Numerous plans were suggested. An "Army Plan" submitted by a group of officers in 1783 proposed statehood for present Ohio as a means of caring for soldiers' land bounties; a "Financiers' Plan" offered by several business leaders two months later would have divided the West into territories embracing two degrees of latitude and three of longitude which would become states as soon as their population reached 20,000. More important was a plan submitted to Congress in March, 1784, by one of its own committees. Thomas Jefferson, who as chairman was largely responsible for the report, suggested that the Mississippi Valley be divided into fourteen districts, each with an impressive classical name. The first settlers would set up a temporary government with a legislature, elective officials, and delegate to Congress, which would control the district until its population reached 20,000 when it would be admitted "into the Congress of the United States, on an equal footing with the said original states."

Jefferson's Ordinance of 1784 never went into effect, for Congress ruled that it should operate only after all landed states ceded their western territories and long before that time several of its features were attacked. Westerners disliked its emphasis on rectangular state boundaries rather than divisions provided by nature. Easterners had two more important complaints. One was levelled against the large number of states planned for the Mississippi Valley. These would, alarmed Congressmen pointed out, eventually outnumber the older dominions, wrest control of the government from the East, and rule the nation in the interests of frontier agriculture. Fewer and larger western states would alone protect the seaboard's economy. Equally alarming to conservative eastern representatives was the complete democracy provided by Jefferson's ordinance. They insisted that frontiersmen were incapable of ruling themselves and that external control, at least in the early stages of each new territorial government, was needed to assure an orderly administration.

Congress was still debating these controversial points in July, 1787, when the Reverend Manasseh Cutler appeared with his petition. His prodding forced the appointment of a new committee on July 9; two days later its report, modified by many of Cutler's own suggestions, was presented and on July 13 the Ordinance of 1787 was adopted by the unanimous vote of the eight states present. The first of its three sections erected the "Territory North West of the Ohio" into one temporary district with the provision that it eventually be carved into not less than three or more than five territories. If Congress decided on three, one north-south boundary was to run through the mouth of the Great Miami River, the other through Vincennes to the Wabash and down that stream to the Ohio. If five territories were agreed upon an east-west line touching the southern tip of Lake Michigan was to be added.

The second section of the Ordinance established three stages in the evolutionary process by which each territory was to become a state. In the first the people were to be controlled by a governor, secretary, and three judges named by Congress, authorized to enforce laws and control the militia. When the adult male population reached 5,000 the territory would enter the second stage, with an elected legislature to share its power with a council of five selected by the governor and Congress. The assembly was to name a delegate to Congress who could speak but not vote. The final stage would be attained when the territory's inhabitants numbered 60,000. It then could frame a constitution and apply for admission into the Union on equal terms with the older states. The third section of the Ordinance contained a noteworthy bill of rights which guaranteed the people of the Northwest Territory freedom of worship, proportional representation, jury trial, privileges of the common law, the writ of habeas corpus, and security for private contracts. Slavery was prohibited and aristocratic inheritance laws designed to perpetuate great estates were forbidden.

The Ordinance of 1787, a conservative document written by jealous easterners who wanted to guard their own political and economic supremacy, failed to satisfy the West. Frontiersmen objected to the oversized states, the complete lack of self-rule during the early territorial stage, and the absolute veto power of the governor during the second. They resented property qualifications which required all voters to own fifty acres of land and all legislators two hundred, not because these restricted the franchise, but because such checks were out of keeping with the democratic spirit of the frontier. Despite these faults the Ordinance of 1787 did more to perpetuate the Union than any document save the Constitution. Men could now leave the older states assured they were not surrendering their political privileges. Congress had not only saved the Republic, but had removed one great obstacle to the westward movement.

This was shown by the immediate burst of activity in lands opened by the Ordinance. The Ohio Company moved first. Its advance parties, setting out from Massachusetts and Connecticut during the winter of 1787-88, beached their boats on the sloping shores below Ft. Harmar on April 7 and fell at once to building a town they called Marietta. The whole process was carefully supervised by the company which donated land for the village, paid for the first buildings, laid out lots and farms, awarded free "Donation Lands" to "Warlike Christian Men" who would settle at dangerous spots in the interior, offered waterpower sites to gristmill and sawmill operators, and divided the lands among the settlers: a town lot, an eight-acre field near the village, and a 116 acre pasture along the Ohio going to each. Here, in other words, was a New England village transplanted bodily to the Ohio wilderness, with a paternalistic colonizing company playing the same valuable role that town proprietors played in seventeenth-century Massachusetts. Their concern was the welfare of their people, not profits, and they looked after their charges with solicitous attention, even planting shade trees along the Marietta streets and issuing each settler half a pint of whiskey to assure a proper celebration of the first Fourth of July spent in their new homes. Seldom have a people migrated with less hardship than the New Englanders who moved west with the Ohio Company.

This was in marked contrast to the suffering of immigrants lured to Ohio by less scrupulous speculators between 1787 and 1789. First to arrive were a group under John Cleves Symmes, a New Jersey politician who in October, 1787, petitioned Congress for 1,000,000 acres of the rich, rolling country between the Great Miami and Little Miami rivers. Without waiting for final action on his request he started west in the spring of 1788 with a few followers who purchased sites along the Ohio. Scarcely had Symmes reached his projected colony when he learned that Congress had sold him only a twenty-mile-wide strip on the east bank of the Great Miami rather than the lands requested. Many of the plots already sold lay beyond his purchase and Symmes, hoping to persuade the government to give him the tract he first requested, continued to make grants in that region. One was to a group of pioneers who laid out the town of Columbia a short distance below the mouth of the Little Miami in November, 1788. More important was the sale of a plot opposite the mouth of the Licking to a small company of Kentucky speculators. These frontiersmen—who demonstrated their classical knowledge by naming their settlement Losantiville (L for Licking, os for mouth, anti for opposite, ville for city)—hit upon one of the garden spots of the Ohio Valley. Their village was destined to expand into the West's principal metropolis under the slightly less burdensome name of Cincinnati. Yet neither of these outposts prospered as did Marietta, for Symmes contributed nothing but oppressive prices and conflicting titles which discouraged settlement. He, like most speculators, hindered rather than aided the frontier advance.

This was even more true of the Scioto Company. Colonel Duer and his associates, all of whom were involved in a score of bold speculations, had no intention of developing their 5,000,000 acres. Instead they hoped to sell six of the company's thirty-two shares in Europe, use the returns from these to make payments needed to keep their option, and finally unload the whole tract on other speculators to parcel out among individuals. This scheme depended on selling the six shares in Europe at a price high enough to meet at least the first installment due the government. That task was intrusted, strangely enough, to Joel Barlow, a dreamy young lawyer who was famed for his authorship of a bombastic poem called *The Vision of Columbus* rather than for his business acumen. His success in selling Ohio Company shares endeared him to Cutler, however, and Colonel Duer reluctantly consented to his appointment, perhaps thinking that a poet was well-suited to sell lands that the company did not own.

Barlow never understood the scheme in which he was involved. Instead of disposing of the option or shares in the Scioto Company he tramped the streets of Paris for ten months trying unsuccessfully to peddle small tracts of territory. At this point, in the summer of 1789, he had the bad fortune to fall into the hands of a corrupt Englishman, William Playfair, who made a most sensible suggestion. The French, he said, would never purchase land from an unknown foreigner, but would buy anything from a seemingly respectable company. Barlow was so impressed that he agreed to help form a new corporation, the Compagnie de Scioto, and to sell it 3,000,000 acres of Scioto land, to be paid for in regular installments as the territory was sold. Playfair, as the concern's agent, launched an intensive selling campaign at once. Maps and pamphlets were strewn over Paris, showing the Seven Ranges and Ohio Company tracts as settled, describing a gleaming white city of Gallipolis (City of the French) at the mouth of the Great Kanawha, hinting that the capital of the United States would soon be moved there, and urging Frenchmen to seize the opportunity to live in comfort supported by a bountiful nature. Hundreds rose to the bait; by the end of 1789 150,000 acres were "sold," to innocent victims who never suspected that the Compagnie de Scioto owned no land and that the elaborate certificates they purchased conveyed no title whatsoever. Proudly Joel Barlow gathered those unfortunates together, sending word to Duer in January, 1790, that he was sailing with six hundred immigrants who had been promised transportation and homes in Gallipolis.

Duer was thunderstruck. Settlers would mean expense—for the journey to Ohio, homes, and surveys—but worse was the fact that the Scioto Company owned no land on which to plant them. The first payment to Congress had not been made, and even the site of Gallipolis was shown by surveys to be on the Ohio Company grant. Something must be done. Frantically Duer arranged to purchase the tract opposite the Great Kanawha for his unwanted colonists, then send a crew of axmen west to build huts for the newcomers. In the meantime the six hundred Frenchmen arrived at Alexandria, Virginia, where agents met them with the sad news that they had been duped. Some drifted to New York or Philadelphia, others returned to Paris, but most insisted on being moved to the promised lands. Finally, in June, 1790, they were started west, and by mid-October all reached Gallipolis. What disappointments waited the weary travelers! No gleaming white city, no fertile countryside, no luxurious homes, no golden fields ripe for the harvest—only an unbroken forest, a half-cleared village, a few rows of ugly log cabins met their eyes. If they had only known they could have found consolation in the fact that William Playfair vanished with all funds collected by the Compagnie de Scioto, leaving Colonel Duer the unpleasant task of meeting all their expenses himself. But even this cheering news did not reach them as they settled down to the backbreaking task of clearing a frontier and planting vineyards. Some eventually moved to a 24,000 acre "French Grant" given them by a pitying Congress in 1795, but most stayed at Gallipolis to live out their lives in squalor and poverty—a fitting monument to the Scioto Company's unethical manipulations.

Yet darker years lay ahead for those suffering Frenchmen and for the sturdy Kentuckians and New Englanders who were hewing out the first clearings on the north bank of the Ohio. Congress had solved two western problems; it had set up a land system and installed a form of government which promised better times for the future. But all attempts to cope with the third task—removal of the Indians—failed. Once more, during the 1790's, the frontier was destined to ring with the war whoops of savage warriors and the agonized shrieks of their victims. Diplomatic skill and military valor had to be called into play before the pioneers at Marietta and Gallipolis and Losantiville could rest peacefully in their wilderness homes.

# CHAPTER XI

# The West in American Diplomacy

## 1783-1803

Of the three western problems facing Congress during the Critical Period—erecting a satisfactory land system, devising a form of government, and pacifying the Indians—the last proved hardest to solve. For the tribes that harassed the borderland were only pawns in the hands of intriguing European nations that hoped to fatten their empires at the expense of the dissension-torn American Republic. Both its former allies, France and Spain, and its erstwhile enemy, England, were only too glad to use the loosely worded Treaty of 1783 as an excuse to devise plots that were to keep the West in a turmoil for twenty years and at times to threaten the nation's existence.

The conflict with England involved the string of Northwest Posts that controlled waterways along the Canadian-American border: Dutchman's Point and Point-au-Fer on Lake Champlain, Oswegatchie and Oswego near the eastern tip of Lake Ontario, and Niagara, Detroit, and Mackinac at the Great Lakes passageways. All were south of the border and were, according to the treaty of peace, to be "evacuated with all convenient speed," but Canada's officials found at least two good reasons to retain them when the war was over. One was the desire to keep control of the fur trade in the Great Lakes country, the other the fear that removal of British troops would incite the Indians to rebellion, for the interior tribes were already on the verge of revolt against their new overlords. Economic good sense and humanitarian idealism both determined General Haldimand, the Governor General of Canada, to stand firm. Having made up his mind, he three times refused to surrender the posts to congressional emissaries from the United States, at the same time besieging his home government for authorization for his stand.

This was not long in arriving. British ministers at London were just as anxious to hold the Northwest Posts as Canada's officialdom, partly because they, too, were subjected to pressure from fur traders, partly because England's control of the back country would be advantageous should the quarreling American states give up their attempt to live peacefully together, as appeared likely at the time. But some justification must be found to occupy another nation's territory! The ministers wrote their answer into instructions sent to Haldimand on April 8, 1784. The United States, they said, had failed to live up to the sections of the Treaty of 1783 which forbad the states to put obstacles in the way of merchants or Loyalists seeking to recover lawful debts. Hence England would keep the Northwest Posts "at least until" her traders could remove their goods. This stand placed Congress in a hopeless situation. It had no power to coerce the states under the Articles of Confederation, and although it urged them to open their courts to British creditors, they turned a deaf ear.

With this official backing, Haldimand moved into action in the Ohio country, for he realized that more than the Northwest Posts were at stake. If he could unite the tribes there in a strong confederation, they could not only keep out American settlers but perhaps bludgeon the United States into relinquishing the whole region to the red men as a buffer state under English protection. With this as their objective, Haldimand's aides—Sir John Johnson, Joseph Butler, and especially Joseph Brant—worked steadily among the tribes between 1785 and 1787, gradually shaping the needed confederation. By the beginning of 1788 the Iroquois, Wyandot, Shawnee, Delaware, Miami, Ottawa, Chippewa, and Potawatomi had joined; all had pledged themselves to cede no more land to the United States without the consent of the confederacy, to repudiate the treaties of Ft. Stanwix, Ft. McIntosh, and Ft. Finney, and to insist on the creation of an Indian buffer state with its borders at the Ohio River. Yet Haldimand's efforts were to no avail, for two insurmountable obstacles precluded the peaceful establishment of the red man's nation that he invisaged.

One was the refusal of individualistic Indians to co-operate. This became apparent in 1788 when some of the more aggressive chiefs, spurred on by British agents, decided to press for a treaty with the United States recognizing their right to the entire Ohio country. Preliminary conversations showed the natives hopelessly divided; the Shawnee, Kickapoo, and Miami insisted on the Ohio River boundary at all costs, the Wyandot, Delaware, and Seneca refused to endorse a plan that would surely lead to war. In vain did Joseph Brant suggest a compromise line giving Americans the region east of the Muskingum. When the sought-for conference with agents of the United States was finally held at Ft. Harmar in January, 1789, the In-

dians were so torn by dissension that Arthur St. Clair, who represented the
United States as governor of the newly created Northwest Territory, was
able to dictate a treaty as obnoxious as the old. By the treaty of Ft. Harmar the red men accepted the lines drawn at Ft. McIntosh and Ft. Finney,
then drifted back into the wilderness, sick at heart that their union had
failed them. Equally destructive of any peaceful solution was the attitude
of the Kentucky frontiersmen. Fearful lest the proposed confederation en-

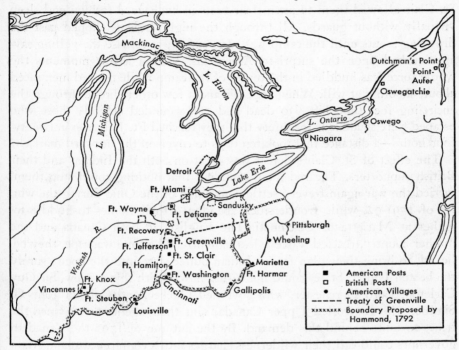

The Northwestern Indian Problem, 1789–1795

gender a new war, these bold spirits began sending small raiding parties
against the Indians as early as the summer of 1788. When the natives struck
back the United States found itself involved in a new Indian war by the
autumn of 1789.

The first two expeditions formed to crush the rebellious red men fared
badly. General Josiah Harmar, commander of the western army, led the
first northward from Ft. Washington in the autumn of 1790, but he moved
so slowly that the Indians were amply warned and disappeared into the
forest about the Maumee River. After searching vainly for the foe, Harmar
started south again in late October, then paused while a detachment of several hundred militiamen slipped back toward the Maumee in the hope of

surprising the returning Indians. Instead the tables were turned; the poorly trained militia walked straight into an ambush that cost 183 lives. The second expedition was made up of an elaborate force of 3,000 men under Arthur St. Clair. That inept commander fussed the summer of 1791 away at Ft. Washington, then led his men toward the Maumee country, pausing to build three log forts—Ft. Hamilton, Ft. St. Clair, and Ft. Jefferson—on the way. When the tired troops reached the Maumee on November 3, St. Clair allowed them to pitch their tents in haphazard fashion and sleep virtually without guards. All through the night Indians slipped past the drowsing scouts until the camp was surrounded; at sunrise the yelling savages rushed upon the surprised Americans. Within a few moments the whole force was huddled in the center of the camp while the red men raced about, shooting at will. When St. Clair and a few others broke through the encircling foes they left 630 dead and 283 wounded behind; those who escaped were so anxious for safety that they reached Ft. Jefferson in twenty-four hours—a distance that took ten days to cover on the outward march.

The effect of St. Clair's defeat was great on both the Indians and their British supporters. The red men, confident that nothing could stop them, carried the war against every settlement north of the Ohio during the winter of 1791-92, while frontiersmen abandoned their homes to huddle together at Marietta or Cincinnati. The English, in both Canada and the mother country, reacted scarcely less violently. The time was ripe, they believed, to bring their plan for an Indian buffer state into the open; surely the beaten United States could not refuse now! With this in view, Sir Guy Carleton, Lord Dorchester, who governed Quebec, and Colonel John G. Simcoe, who controlled Upper Canada, sent their agents to convince the tribes to unite behind this demand. By the autumn of 1792 the Canadian governors could call their wilderness charges into a conference at the Maumee River rapids, assured that all were represented. There the Indians agreed to demand the Ohio River boundary when they met with American commissioners in a scheduled conference at Sandusky the next spring. If the United States refused, they decided, the war would go on until the Ohio country was won.

While Simcoe and Dorchester carried on their forest intrigue, British statesmen worked steadily to secure the barrier state through diplomatic channels. Negotiations began when the new American government under President Washington, with power now to force the states to deal fairly with British merchants and Loyalists, began hinting commercial retaliation unless England consented to discuss the differences between the two nations. The young minister named to carry on these conversations, George Hammond, bore rigid instructions concerning the Northwest: he was to press for a neutral state bounded by the Ohio or, if that was impossible, a line following the Cuyahoga-Tuscarawas portage and the Muskingum River; offering in return British mediation with the Indians and surrender of the Northwest Posts. These demands made little impression on Thomas Jefferson, the American secretary of state. When conversations opened in March, 1792, Hammond's earnest argument for retention of the posts was speedily demolished by the skillful American secretary, his offer of mediation was summarily dismissed on the ground that there was no call for external interference between a government and its subjects, and his request for a new boundary was answered by the indisputable phrases of the Treaty of 1783. By December both he and his home government recognized that negotiations were futile; only further victories by their Indian allies would force the United States to back down on a buffer state.

This realization focused the attention of both nations on the American-Indian conference scheduled to meet at Sandusky in the spring of 1793; perhaps the natives could use the threat of renewed war to secure the settlement desired by England. The three commissioners named by Washington to attend this meeting expected to make radical concessions, even to surrendering all Ohio lands not actually occupied by the Ohio Company and Symmes Associates, but fortunately for them the conference never assembled. The American agents, learning on their way west that the Indians would insist on the Ohio River boundary, retraced their steps to warn President Washington that continued war was inevitable. The President, having anticipated such a report, sent word at once to his new military commander in the West, General Anthony Wayne, to begin the attack. Wayne, too wise to risk a fall campaign, advanced instead to a point six miles beyond Ft. Jefferson where he built a new outpost, Ft. Greenville. There he spent the winter of 1793-94, drilling his thousand seasoned troops, subjecting them to rigid discipline, and preparing for a spring offensive that would forever settle the troublesome northwestern problem.

His preparations were necessary, for during the winter the situation changed radically. England, plunging into war against the French Revolutionists, was again interfering with American shipping so drastically that the United States threatened to enter the conflict on the side of France. The tense atmosphere created by this possibility led Lord Dorchester to commit two colossal errors. In February, 1794, he told a visiting delegation of western chiefs that war was inevitable; when it came, he said, British and Indians would fight side by side to restore the red men's hunting grounds. A week later he ordered Simcoe to build a new post, Ft. Miami, on the Maumee River to protect Detroit from an attack by Wayne's army. These two moves convinced the overjoyed Indians that they could count on British aid against the Americans; war belts were hurried through the forest to summon warriors, until by mid-June some 2,000 of them waited under the walls of Ft. Miami, all confident of ultimate victory.

Meanwhile Wayne moved his army slowly northward, stopping at the site of St. Clair's defeat to build Ft. Recovery where, in late June he beat off a sizable Indian attack. With the natives weakened by that defeat, he pushed on along the Au Glaize River until the Maumee was reached on August 8, 1794. From a rough fortification thrown up there by his seasoned campaigners Wayne sent word through the forest that on August 17 he would march against the position selected by the Indians for their defense— a spot near Ft. Miami where a tangle of fallen trees afforded excellent protection. This misinformation was broadcast intentionally, because the American commander knew the Indian habit of fasting before a battle. On the appointed day he started forward, but instead of attacking, camped ten miles away. For three days he stayed there, while his starving enemies waited impatiently. Finally, on August 20, five hundred warriors wandered away to gorge on food provided by the garrison at Ft. Miami. This was the moment chosen for the American attack. The well-trained troops moved forward in two columns, one for a frontal attack, the other to pour a withering fire into the left flank of the eight hundred red men who crouched behind their jagged barrier. For a few minutes the Indians stood their ground, then broke and fled. The Battle of Fallen Timbers, which had required months of preparation, was over in less than two hours.

Wayne's victory was decisive not because he crushed his enemies—only fifty Indians were killed—but because their spirit was broken when the British refused to aid them. For in the supreme test the commander at Ft. Miami dared not risk war with a neutral nation by sending his men to fight at Fallen Timbers. Disheartened by the realization that they must fight alone, the natives crept back to their villages with word that they must move west once more, to lands not wanted by the white men. Wayne took advantage of their broken spirit. After destroying a few villages and building a new fort to guard his conquest—Ft. Wayne at the head of the Maumee—he gathered the scattered chiefs together at Ft. Greenville early in 1795 to dictate the terms of the Treaty of Greenville. The Indians surrendered all Ohio except a strip along Lake Erie, a triangle of land in Indiana, and sixteen small spots for trading posts on strategic waterways. Wayne had broken the power of the northwestern Indians, severed their alliance with the British, and cleared a new stretch of territory for American expansion.

There remained only the task of driving the English from the Northwest Posts. Negotiations which settled that thorny issue began during the summer of 1794 when President Washington, in a last effort to dissolve the difficulties between the two nations by any means short of war, sent John Jay to London with full authority to make any concessions necessary. The times were auspicious for such a move. Britain's European position was weakening rapidly; the First Coalition built up to fight the French Revolutionists was crumbling as Spain talked of a separate peace and Prussia showed a declining interest; the countries of northern Europe were uniting in a League of Armed Neutrality to protest England's high-handed interference with their shipping. Rumors were rife that the United States would join the League, and this the British could not allow, depending as they did on American trade to finance the war. Better to back down on the Northwest Posts than lose everything, especially as those forts were no longer deemed as important as in the past. Reports from Montreal showed the fur trade south of the Great Lakes declining. In this case, why waste the £5,000 needed to repair the posts and the 4,000 men necessary to garrison them? Better to give them up in a munificent gesture that might keep the United States out of the League of Armed Neutrality.

England's decision to surrender the Northwest Posts was reflected in the first conversations between Jay and Baron Grenville, Secretary of State for Foreign Affairs, but in September, 1794, Grenville's attitude suddenly stiffened. Dispatches from George Hammond, his minister to the United States, were responsible. Alexander Hamilton, Hammond reported, had asured him that the United States would not enter the League and that all talk of war against England was mere bluff. Supported by this guarantee, Grenville made no more concessions; from that time on he dictated terms while Jay humbly acquiesced. Jay's Treaty, signed on November 14, 1794, was a monument to Hamilton's colossal blunder. England agreed to surrender the Northwest Posts by June 1, 1796, but in return the United States guaranteed Canadian traders perpetual passage over portages along the border, allowed them to operate south of the boundary, promised not to tax the furs they carried back to Montreal, and agreed to levy the same tax on their trading goods as on those of its own nationals. Yet Jay's Treaty, and the Treaty of Greenville that followed a few months later, freed one important borderland from intrigue and brought peace to the Northwest for a generation.

On the southwestern frontier the post-Revolutionary diplomatic conflicts were settled less easily. The antagonists there—Spain and the United States —were both well equipped for the struggle. Spain's North American colonies were governed efficiently under the able Charles III (1759-88); an army officer in each town, directly responsible to the governor of Louisiana, rigidly controlled the 25,000 French, Spanish, British, and Greek inhabi-

tants who occupied East Florida, West Florida, and Louisiana. In addition
Spain could count on the aid of some 14,000 warriors from the four principal tribes of the southern borderland: the Creeks, Cherokee, Chickasaw,
and Choctaw. This was sure to be needed, for pressing upon the Spanish
lands were the 120,000 Americans whose homes fringed the southwestern
frontier in 1783—in Kentucky, the Nashville and Holston settlements, and
the Georgia back country. All were aggressive expansionists, eager to overrun international boundaries in their search for wealth. Little wonder that
Spain feared she had created a Frankenstein monster by helping them win
independence, for now England's restraining hand no longer checked their
westward march. Instead they were poised to sweep over the debatable land
between Louisiana and Georgia like the "Goths and Vandals, with the
Treaty of 1783 in one hand and a carbine in the other." Spain's principal
task was to hold back that surging horde.

Her most effective weapon was control of the mouth of the Mississippi;
by closing the river to American trade she could strangle the West economically, as settlers could market their bulky agricultural products only
by sending them to New Orleans on flatboats. Spain realized she must use
the weapon carefully, lest western dissatisfaction lead to retaliation in the
form of filibustering expeditions against Louisiana, yet even that danger
was not serious. The distance from Kentucky or Tennessee was too great for
a sustained attack unless the frontiersmen were aided by some strong naval
power. Through the whole controversy Spain's principal fear was an Anglo-
American alliance which would give the westerners sea power; whenever
such a union seemed possible she adopted a conciliatory attitude.

The immediate cause of conflict was the disputed Yazoo Strip. That
territory was granted the United States in the Anglo-American Treaty of
1783, which established the 31st parallel as the southern boundary of the
new Republic, but was also claimed by Spain on the basis of the Anglo-
Spanish Treaty provision that she "retain" West Florida. Her ministers
rightly argued that this meant control of the region north to the line of
32° 28', as that was the boundary of the province under English rule. Neither nation was anxious to take the first move toward settling the conflict.
Spain, in actual possession of the Yazoo Strip, saw no reason to upset the
status quo; the United States was content to wait until time worked in its
favor, knowing that its population was increasing while Louisiana's remained static. Yet each was ready to take advantage of any shift in the international situation to press for a settlement.

Until the right moment arrived the struggle for the Southwest was carried on by those perennial shock troops of empire—speculators and traders.
They clashed first when land jobbers, anxious to exploit Georgia's western

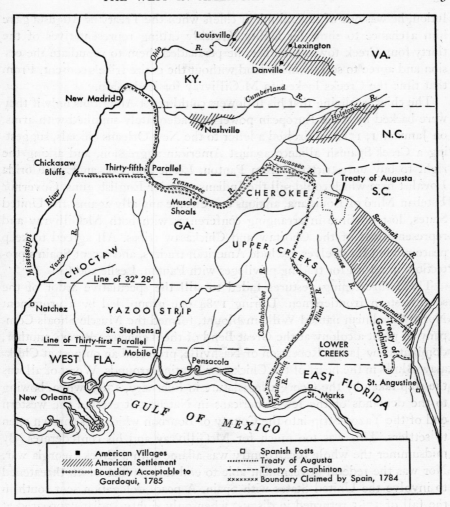

Spanish-American Relations in the Southwest, 1783-1788

lands before the state ceded its holdings to the United States, persuaded
authorities to negotiate the Treaty of Augusta (November 1, 1783), with
two weak Creek chiefs. The principal effect of this land-grabbing treaty,
which transferred a tract between the Oconee and Tugaloo rivers to the
state, was to elevate a young chief, Alexander McGillivray, to leadership of
the Creek tribe. That gifted half-breed inherited from his Scotch father a
frail body, a cowardly temperament, an undying hatred of Americans, and
an uncanny skill as a diplomat. Having fled westward to join his mother's
people when his Loyalist father was driven from Georgia during the Revo-

lution, he was one of several minor chiefs when the Treaty of Augusta gave him a chance to show his ability. Quickly calling representatives of the thirty-four Creek towns together, he persuaded them to repudiate the cession and agree to sell no more land without the entire tribe's consent. From that time the Creeks looked to McGillivray for leadership.

The chief, realizing that his followers could resist Americans only if they were backed by some European power and adequately supplied with arms, on January 1, 1784, addressed a letter to the New Orleans officials, suggesting a Creek-Spanish alliance against American aggression, and asking the right to buy unrestrictedly from Panton, Leslie and Co., an East Florida Loyalist firm which could sell the Indians superior English guns. Governor Esteban Miró of Louisiana, anxious to welcome any ally against the United States, lost no time in arranging conferences with both McGillivray and representatives of the Choctaw and Chickasaw tribes. All agreed to keep peace among themselves, exclude American traders, and accept Spain's protection, in return for trading privileges with Panton, Leslie and Co.

These threatening gestures failed to still the speculative ardor of the southwestern frontiersmen. During 1784 one group, led by a prominent North Carolinian named William Blount, formed the Muscle Shoals Company to plant a colony at the Great Bend of the Tennessee River; another, dominated by James Robertson of Nashville, projected an outpost at Chickasaw Bluffs in the heart of the Chickasaw hunting grounds. Worst of all was the step taken by the Georgia legislature in February, 1785, when, bowing to the demands of the few Americans in Natchez, it erected the western end of the Yazoo Strip into the County of Bourbon which was thrown open to settlers. This was too much for McGillivray and his confederates. By midsummer the whole back country was aflame with a Creek-Georgia war. Nor was the federal government able to end this conflict which threatened to involve the United States with Spain. A peace delegation sent south in the fall of 1785 returned in disgust when only eighty Indians appeared at the treaty grounds. In the end this futile effort did more harm than good, for a delegation of Georgians who had accompanied the American agents stayed on to negotiate the Treaty of Galphinton (November 12, 1785), which ceded additional Creek lands south of the Altamaha River. This was immediately repudiated by the rest of the Creeks, who now redoubled their attacks.

Nor did Congress fare any better in diplomatic negotiations going on at the same time. These were initiated by the Count of Floridablanca, Spain's able foreign minister, who on June 26, 1784, closed the Mississippi River to American navigation, then dispatched an agent to the United States in hopes of capitalizing on western discontent by wringing a favorable treaty from that dissension-torn nation. The diplomat selected for this post, Don Diego de Gardoqui, was ordered to press not only for the Yazoo Strip and American recognition of Spain's exclusive control of the Mississippi, but for all the western country south of the Tennessee and west of the Hiwassee and Flint rivers. This region, Floridablanca contended, was Spain's by right of conquest and occupation. In return Gardoqui was allowed to offer the United States trading concessions and a defensive alliance containing mutual territorial guarantees.

The first conversations between this shrewd bargainer and John Jay, secretary of foreign affairs, showed that they stood so far apart on boundaries that there could be no compromise; Gardoqui would offer nothing more than a line along the 35th parallel and the Hiwassee-Flint rivers, while Jay clung to the 31st parallel. On other questions the commercially minded American diplomat adopted a more conciliatory tone, for he was dazzled by the promise of Spanish trading privileges. By August, 1786, they had reached a tentative agreement, which Jay laid before Congress. American ships, the negotiators proposed, would be admitted to Spanish ports, each nation would guarantee the other's possessions against external attack, the United States would give up the right to navigate the Mississippi for twenty-five years, and the boundary dispute would be settled later. Was Congress willing, Jay asked, to grant him the right to close the Mississippi for that period? The seven northern states, tempted by the prospect of trade, voted "Yes," the five southern states "No," while Delaware's delegates refused to commit themselves. This victory for the commercial elements meant nothing, as the votes of nine states were required to ratify a treaty and the southern representatives announced they would never yield. Jay and Gardoqui, realizing that further conversations were useless, abandoned their meetings.

But the harm was done. News of the vote, reaching the West in December, 1786, spread like wildfire among the frontiersmen. Seven states were willing to inflict economic strangulation on the Mississippi Valley to further their selfish commercial ambitions! Why remain loyal to such a government—a government that gave them no right to rule themselves, no protection from Indians, no cheap lands, no manufactured goods? Why not set up a trans-Appalachian republic under Spanish protection? Spain might be willing, in return, to open the Mississippi to their goods. All during the summer of 1787 revolutionary documents were exchanged by committees of correspondence in Nashville, Holston, Franklin, Kentucky, and even western Pennsylvania. Never had separatist sentiment in the West been higher.

James Wilkinson, a colorful scoundrel fast rising to an important position in Kentucky, sensed the possibilities of the situation. Why not turn the dissatisfaction bred of congressional neglect and the anger engendered by the Jay-Gardoqui negotiations to his own benefit? If he could foment a revolution with Spain's aid a glittering future lay ahead: unrestricted trading privileges and land grants, leadership in a Mississippi Valley republic, the plaudits of a grateful people who would hail him as the Washington of the West. With this mirage leading him on, Wilkinson during the summer of 1787 enlisted the support of other Kentuckians who were dissatisfied with American rule: John Brown, Harry Innes, Benjamin Sebastian, and others. As soon as these separatists began to stir up discontent, Wilkinson set out for New Orleans, taking with him a fleet of flatboats laden with tobacco and flour. There he was well received by Governor Miró, who listened gullibly to Wilkinson's tales of a western republic and pressed the American for advice on how to proceed. He was then told that the desired objective could be secured if several prominent men in each settlement were allowed to ship goods down the Mississippi; they in return would forestall any attack on New Orleans and win converts for the proposed revolution. Wilkinson, of course, suggested himself as agent for Kentucky, and asked the privilege of sending $60,000 worth of goods south yearly.

Governor Miró was delighted. He promised to lay Wilkinson's plans before the king, authorized the Kentuckian to ship $30,000 worth of supplies to New Orleans annually, and had him swear allegiance to Spain—a ceremony which meant nothing to that gifted fabricator who would swear to anything if he could turn a dishonest dollar. Having completed arrangements, Wilkinson departed for Kentucky where he arrived early in 1788. His first opportunity to serve his Spanish masters came in July when a convention of Kentuckians assembled to protest Virginia's refusal to grant them separate statehood. Wilkinson, Sebastian, Brown, Innes, and other conspirators were much in evidence, but all their pleas for revolution fell on deaf ears. Much as westerners hated Congress, they realized that they lacked the wealth and numbers to erect an enduring new government; many, too, shrank from aligning themselves with autocratic Spain. In the end the convention, after defeating a proposal to draft a new constitution, adjourned to wait the outcome of the constitutional convention then meeting in the East, hoping the new Congress might give them statehood where the old one failed.

This was a sad blow for Wilkinson, but more were to come. During the autumn he learned that Spanish officials had granted George Morgan, of Indiana Company fame, the right to plant a colony on the west bank of the Mississippi not far below its junction with the Ohio. If this plan were carried out, Wilkinson knew, Kentuckians would be able to sell their produce at the proposed settlement, New Madrid, rather than through his own profitable monopoly in New Orleans. Hastening southward in the spring of 1789 to protest, he was met at New Orleans with still more disquieting news. The king, Miró informed Wilkinson, had not only refused to enter into any conspiracy with the Kentuckians, but had ordered a complete reversal of Spanish policy. From that time on all Americans willing to pay a 15 per cent duty were to be allowed to ship their goods through New Orleans. Those who wished to escape this fee were encouraged to move into Louisiana; to stimulate migration frontiersmen were to be granted easy conditions of entry, religious toleration, equal commercial privileges, free land, and the right of selling tobacco at high prices to the king's warehouses. Spain, wisely placing no hope in conspiracy, had determined to strengthen her feeble colonies by supplying them with the settlers needed to build up a strong population. Wilkinson's intrigue was nipped in the bud, for the time being at least. When he returned to Kentucky late in 1789 he found his countrymen busily engaged in drawing up the constitution under which the state entered the Union two years later.

In other parts of the West the Spanish Conspiracy never reached serious proportions, largely because the conspirators were more concerned with winning concessions for themselves than independence for their neighbors. The plot in eastern Tennessee was originated by James White, a former congressman, and John Sevier, the discredited leader of the defunct State of Franklin. Sensing frontier dissatisfaction with the Creek-Georgia War and the failure of Congress to agree to separate statehood for the region, they drew up several memorials to Gardoqui, promising to forge a western state under Spanish protection in return for commercial concessions and the right to plant a colony at Muscle Shoals—a speculation in which both men were interested. When the Spaniard refused to grant them any financial aid and suggested that they lay the subject of the Muscle Shoals settlement before Governor Miró the conspirators lost interest. The intrigue in the Nashville settlements was equally halfhearted. There James Robertson, anxious to end the Creek attacks that cost his followers so heavily, suggested to Miró that he might be willing to lead his people out of the United States and into the Spanish empire if the Indians were restrained. In all probability he, like Sevier, was simply pulling Spain by the nose; Robertson was willing to talk disunion if his words paid dividends, but his loyalty was unquestioned. When the Spanish governor showed no interest, plotting came to an end.

Although the collapse of the Spanish Conspiracy in 1789 temporarily ended the threat of secession in the West, the new government under George Washington which assumed office at the same time realized that the

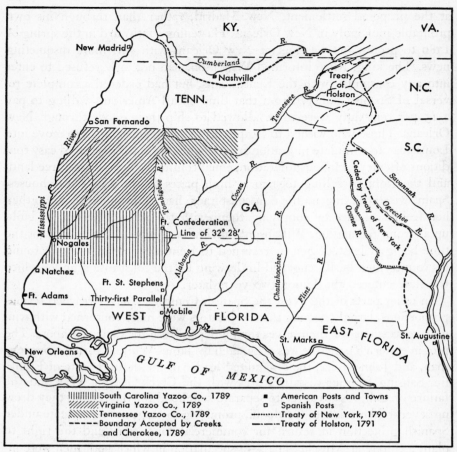

Spanish-American Relations in the Southwest, 1789-1803

problem was not settled. The bitter dregs remained: disgruntled leaders, dissatisfied frontiersmen, and above all the rankling causes of western discontent. Washington saw that the West could never know peace until the former plotters were pacified and the conditions that bred rebellion removed. The first task was easily accomplished, for most of the conspirators had embarked on their intrigue with Miró not because they were disloyal to the United States but because they thirsted for power or wealth. The President, wisely reasoning that they could be won back by suitable rewards from their own government, made William Blount governor of the Southwestern Territory that was created in 1790, appointed John Sevier and James Robertson brigadier-generals in the western army, and named James Wilkinson a lieutenant-colonel in the federal forces. Washington was so anxious to convince frontiersmen that his administration was friendly to them that he chose Thomas Jefferson rather than the hated John Jay secretary of state in his first cabinet.

Removing the causes of western discontent proved more difficult. The frontiersmen wanted two things: a diplomatic settlement with Spain that would open the Mississippi to free navigation, and peace with the Indians. The first would have to wait until the shifting sands of European diplomacy forced Spain into a position where she would have to back down, and even the second seemed impossible to achieve. The greed of the Georgia legislature was responsible. Knowing that all other states had ceded their western lands to the United States and that popular pressure would soon force them to follow, the members of that body determined to reap all possible profits first. On December 21, 1789, the assembly sold 25,400,000 acres in the Mississippi, Tombigbee, and Tennessee valleys to three speculating companies formed for the purpose: the South Carolina Yazoo Company, the Virginia Yazoo Company, and the Tennessee Yazoo Company. The presence in the concerns of such seasoned speculators as John Sevier, George Morgan, George Rogers Clark, James White, and Patrick Henry accounted for the fact that they purchased the vast tract for $207,580. With the sale completed, all three began selling lands and organizing colonists, with the lead taken by the South Carolina Yazoo Company under the colorful Irish rogue that acted as its general agent, Dr. James O'Fallon.

President Washington was horrified, knowing that continued invasion of the southern Mississippi Valley would not only antagonize Spain but prolong the Creek War. While he was still casting about for some means of stopping the companies, a fortunate incident, the Nootka Sound Controversy, provided him with the answer. This conflict centered in Nootka Sound, a relatively unimportant harbor in the Pacific Northwest where British ships stopped on fur-seeking expeditions. During the summer of 1789 the Spaniards, long resentful of England's invasion of their Pacific domain, confiscated several vessels that were anchored there. Britain, seizing the opportunity to challenge Spain's monopoly in the Pacific while that country's ally, France, was in the throes of revolution, first demanded immediate satisfaction, then began preparations for war. For several months a conflict seemed certain before Spain backed down. In October, 1790, her ministers signed the Nootka Sound Convention which yielded every disputed point to England.

The threat of an Anglo-Spanish war during the summer of 1790 played directly into Washington's hands in his dealings with both the Creeks and the Yazoo companies. Alexander McGillivray, realizing that war would leave him at the mercy of the Georgians by cutting off his supply of arms, was ready to receive the peace emissary sent south by the President in the spring of 1790. Together they journeyed northward in an elaborate procession—a few favored chiefs on horseback at its head, twenty-six others in three wagons next, and the American agent bringing up the rear in a sulky. At New York they were escorted to Federal Hall by the largest crowd to assemble since the inauguration of Washington, led by the Sons of St. Tammany in full regalia. McGillivray was too canny to be swept away by this display, and the Treaty of New York that was signed on August 7, 1790, was by no means a complete surrender. The Creeks ceded a large strip between the Ogeechee and Oconee rivers, receiving in return a perpetual guarantee to their remaining hunting grounds, including those claimed by the Yazoo companies. At the same time McGillivray was made a brigadier-general in the American army at a salary of $1,200 a year. These satisfactory arrangements, and the acknowledged bribe to the chief, brought peace to the southern frontier for the first time in a decade.

The Nootka Sound crisis also doomed the Yazoo companies. Dr. O'Fallon first heard of the threatened war between Spain and England while he was gathering colonists for the South Carolina Yazoo Company in Kentucky. To him, and to thousands of other westerners, this seemed the long-awaited chance to wrest New Orleans from the Spanish with England's aid. Hence in July, 1790, he addressed a bellicose letter to Governor Miró, threatening to lead an army against Louisiana unless his company was granted the right to plant its settlers peacefully. At the same time he recruited a warlike force, secured George Rogers Clark as its leader, and made plans for a joint military-colonizing expedition against New Orleans. Having displayed his hand, O'Fallon could not back down when the hope of war went glimmering in the fall of 1790. By winter not only his grandiose plan, but the Yazoo companies as well, had collapsed. An international crisis over which he had no control had helped Washington remove a serious threat to the peace of the southwestern frontier.

More important than the effect of the Nootka Sound crisis on either the Creeks or the Yazoo companies was its impact on Spain. That country's officials emerged from the controversy with the firm conviction that their frontier policy was a failure. They had relied on three devices to defend Louisiana against the United States: Indian alliance, intrigue, and immigration. The Treaty of New York indicated that Indian allies could not be depended upon, intrigue was dead with the collapse of the Spanish Conspiracy, and every dispatch from Louisiana testified to the failure of the immigration policy. American settlers simply were not responding to the bait of free lands, religious liberty, and commercial privileges promised them. The reasons for their reluctance were not hard to find. New Spain could not offer them the democratic institutions of their homeland, the promised religious freedom included only the right to practice Protestantism in private, and the hoped-for relief from Indian attacks failed to materialize. More important was the discovery that Spanish law made land grants nontransferable, thus removing the opportunity for speculation that every frontiersman sought, and a royal order of December, 1790, drastically reducing the price paid for tobacco at government warehouses, an act which demonstrated the insecurity of property under an absolute monarchy. Deterred by these handicaps, only a handful of Americans crossed the Mississippi. Spain's immigration system was an admitted failure by the close of 1791.

This realization resulted in a complete revision of Spanish policy which led first to a momentary flurry of expansion, then to a period of retreat as American frontiersmen pressed in from east and north, and finally to the diplomatic settlement that ended intrigue in the Southwest. The era of expansion was inaugurated by the Louisiana governor who replaced the disgraced Miró late in 1791, Hector, Baron de Carondelet. A man of poor judgment and furious action who lacked knowledge to move wisely and humility to accept the advice of others, Carondelet needed only three months to perfect his plans. He would build up a giant Indian confederation, shower arms upon the natives, and send them forth to drive Americans back across the mountains! Anyone familiar with the frontier could have told him that the Indians were so torn by dissension and such poor fighters that the scheme was predestined to failure. But Carondelet refused to listen. Instead he sent his emissaries through the forest during the summer of 1792, promising Creeks, Cherokee, Chickasaw, Choctaw, and Chickamauga guns, ammunition, land guarantees, and unrestricted trading rights with Panton, Leslie and Co. if they joined his confederation. The Indians were ready to listen—McGillivray even accepted a pension $800 larger than that being paid him by the United States—but when Carondelet tried to bring them together in the spring of 1793 to establish the confederacy, he realized the futility of his efforts. By that time the Creeks and Choctaw were engaged in a minor war, and the remainder wanted only protection from the Americans, not aggression. The discouraged governor agreed to build a new post, Ft. Confederation, in the Choctaw country, then skulked away to New Orleans, knowing his plan a failure.

The collapse of the Spanish offensive opened the way for new attacks on Louisiana from both the north and the east. The attack from the north materialized when the Kentuckians, wildly supporting the newly formed revolutionary government in France, suddenly realized that the international situation played into their own hands. Spain and France were at war; Louisiana was filled with liberty-loving Frenchmen who sympathized with the revolutionists across the Atlantic. Surely an expedition against New Orleans would succeed now. So reasoned excited frontiersmen as they gathered to talk of these prospects during the summer of 1793, or formed themselves into Democratic societies modeled on the Jacobin clubs of France. Only a leader was needed to send the westerners storming against the ramparts of Spain's Mississippi Valley colony.

That individual reached America during the summer of 1793 in the person of Citizen Edmond Genet, the fiery French minister to the United States. Inspired by his faith in the revolutionary cause and backed by the plentiful resources of his home government, Genet immediately laid plans for a large expedition against Louisiana. George Rogers Clark, who volunteered his services, was made major general of the "Independent and Revolutionary Legion of the Mississippi," agents with well-stuffed pockets were sent west to enlist recruits, and the secret approval of Secretary of State Jefferson was secured. During the summer and fall of 1793 Kentucky hummed with activity as Democratic societies carried on a furious correspondence, Clark supervised boat building, recruits drilled, and prominent citizens such as Governor Isaac Shelby issued proclamations urging support for the expedition. The doom of New Orleans seemed at hand. Yet the harassed Carondelet, watching these preparations with foreboding, had little to fear. When Genet's flagrant violations of American neutrality led to his recall in November, 1793, the whole movement collapsed.

Scarcely was that menace removed when another rose to plague New Spain. This time the "Goths and Vandals" threatened from the east, where Georgia speculators were again on the march. In January, 1795, the state legislature, still hoping for some profit before ceding its western holdings, sold most of Alabama and Mississippi to four large concerns: the Upper Mississippi Company, the Tennessee Company, the Georgia Company, and the Georgia Mississippi Company. The second Yazoo Sale was even more fraudulent than the first; the speculators secured the vast region for about one cent an acre, tax free until it was settled. Their dreams of vast profits were short-lived, for when Georgians learned that every legislator but one who voted for the grant was a member of the companies, an "Anti-Yazoo Ticket" swept the next election, rescinded the sale, and publicly burned the deeds by fire drawn from heaven—with the aid of a magnifying glass.

Yet the Yazoo sale, coming on the heels of the threatened attack by Genet's Legion of the Mississippi, convinced the terrified Carondelet that Louisiana could be saved only by falling back on two oft-used devices: forts and intrigue. During the spring of 1795 he strengthened the posts at St. Louis, Nogales, Natchez, and St. Stephens, improved newly built Ft. Confederation, and erected a new fort, Ft. San Fernando, at Chickasaw Bluffs.

At the same time he welcomed the intrigue that was suggested to him by that irrepressible scoundrel, James Wilkinson. The fact that he was now an officer in the American army did not deter that polished liar from conniving with foreign officials; in January, 1794, he wrote Carondelet a full account of the Genet expedition, hinted that he had been responsible for saving Louisiana from attack, and warned that other assaults might come unless Spain hired trusted agents to keep the frontiersmen peaceful and foment a separatist movement. Wilkinson, of course, suggested his willingness to serve and volunteered to find others. Carondelet, who knew little of Miró's fruitless plotting, was delighted. He dispatched urgent letters to Madrid asking for money and then, afraid aid might come too late, took matters into his own hands. Wilkinson was granted $16,000 in addition to his $2,000 pension and told to enlist leaders for the cause.

That proved easy. The time was ripe for a western uprising against Washington's government. In the five years the President had held office he had failed to open the Mississippi River, refused to aid France's struggle for liberty, enacted a whiskey tax that fell heavily on the frontier's principal export crop, and generally had governed the nation to please commercially minded Federalists rather than interior Jeffersonians—especially after December, 1793, when Thomas Jefferson, their last friend in the cabinet, resigned. Yet most of the prominent Kentuckians who joined with Wilkinson were probably loyal to the United States; the threat of rebellion was, in their eyes, only a device to force more equitable treatment from their own government. This was shown when Carondelet sent an agent to New Madrid in July, 1795, to arrange the delivery of twenty cannon and 10,000 rifles that Spain set aside for the conspirators' use; not even Wilkinson dared meet him to launch the revolution. By the end of 1795 Carondelet reluctantly concluded that he was only serving as a pawn for the Kentuckians, and the second Spanish Conspiracy came to an end.

All the events that had kept the southwestern borderland in a turmoil between 1789 and 1795—plots and counterplots, Indian wars and tribal confederations, infamous speculations and abortive military expeditions—apparently were of little significance, for the relative positions of the two quarreling powers remained unchanged over those years. Spain still held the mouth of the Mississippi, still exacted duties from American shippers, still clung to the Yazoo Strip, and still dominated most Indian tribes. Actually, however, the backwoods conflicts formed the backdrop against which the United States and Spain eventually settled their differences over the conference table. Had American frontiersmen not conspired and fought and speculated as they did, the treaty that ended the contest for the southern debatable land would not have been so favorable to their nation.

The chain of events leading to the diplomatic settlement began when Spanish alarm over the Nootka Sound Crisis forced that haughty nation to suggest it was willing to negotiate its differences with the United States. When this news reached the United States in December, 1791, Secretary of State Jefferson saw the occasion was not auspicious; by this time the Anglo-Spanish war threat had passed and Spain would never back down unless her position in Europe was so perilous that she was forced to court American friendship by making unusual concessions. Hence instead of accepting the invitation, he ordered two minor employees of the State Department, William Short and William Carmichael—neither sufficiently influential to inspire Spain's confidence—to proceed to Madrid as slowly as possible. When they arrived in February, 1793, they realized that the new Spanish chief of state, Manuel de Godoy—an impetuous young incompetent who had risen to power through the queen's influence—was no more anxious to reach a settlement than they. Half-hearted negotiations dragged on until the spring of 1794 with nothing accomplished. Both parties were waiting a more favorable European situation to press for a solution.

At that time the turn of fortune's wheel favored the United States. Things were going badly for Spain in the European war, her treasury was bankrupt, and her alliance with England crumbling. From America, too, came disquieting news: an army forming in Kentucky to attack Louisiana, an envoy named John Jay on his way to London to draft a treaty that might ally England with the United States against Spain. Better to secure American friendship than risk an Anglo-American attack on New Spain when conditions in Europe were so bad that colonies could not be defended. In May, 1794, Godoy told Short and Carmichael his nation might be willing to trade the Yazoo strip and navigation rights on the Mississippi for a defensive alliance if a properly authorized plenipotentiary could come to Madrid.

Thomas Pinckney, American minister to Great Britain, was selected for this important task. He had so little faith in his mission that he delayed until June 29, 1795, before reaching Spain, thus losing a chance to capitalize on Spanish fear of an Anglo-American alliance. By the time he arrived Godoy had seen a copy of Jay's Treaty and had assured himself that there was no danger of an accord which would send the navies of England and the armies of the United States against Louisiana. Yet conditions were far more favorable than Pinckney knew. As early as March, 1795, Godoy had decided to withdraw Spain from a war that meant only military defeats, popular resentment at home, and court intrigue aimed at his regime. This meant withdrawal from the alliance with England, and almost certain retaliation from that nation, probably in the form of a naval attack on Spanish colonies in the Gulf of Mexico. Should that come, American friendship was essential to save Louisiana. Surrender on the minor points in dispute was a cheap price to pay for aid against the English dogs of war.

Having reached his decision, Godoy first made separate peace with France through the Treaty of Basle (July 22, 1795), then called his Council of State together to disclose his intention of backing down before the American demands. Retreat was justified, he told the ministers, by the failure of Spain's frontier policy. Indian alliances built up by Miró and Carondelet were useless, the immigration policy a failure, and the intrigue between the Louisiana governor and Wilkinson futile. Spanish resources were too depleted by the European war to defend New Spain against a combination of wrathful frontiersmen and vengeful English men of war. Spain must surrender the Yazoo Strip and navigation of the Mississippi or lose all. His gloomy advice carried the day; the Council of State voted to seek a treaty that would cement ties of Spanish-American friendship.

With this decision made, negotiations between Pinckney and the Spanish spokesmen moved rapidly forward until October 27, 1795, when the Treaty of San Lorenzo was signed. Spain gave up the Yazoo Strip and agreed to move all garrisons from the territory north of the 31st parallel within six months. Americans were granted the right to navigate the Mississippi from its source to its mouth, and were extended the "privilege" of deposit at New Orleans for three years, with the understanding of probable renewal. This was an important concession, for now westerners could land their goods at designated warehouses and transship them to ocean-going vessels without paying custom duties. The agreement also gave the United States commercial privileges in Spain, but not in the Spanish colonies.

The Treaty of San Lorenzo—or Pinckney's Treaty—ended the troublesome conflicts that had kept the frontier in a turmoil for a dozen years. Carondelet, heartsick though he was at the surrender, undertook to carry out its provisions to the letter. The Mississippi was opened to American ships in December, 1796, and two months later the task of dismantling the forts at Natchez, Nogales, Confederation, San Fernando, and St. Stephens was begun. Scarcely had work started when new dispatches from Madrid caused an interruption. These orders, dated October 29, 1796, told of the outbreak of war between Spain and England, of the necessity of warding off an English attack on Louisiana from Canada, and of the dangerous manner in which the Federalist Presidents, George Washington and John Adams, were openly aligning themselves with Britain. Carondelet was ordered to delay executing the treaty until the situation changed. Joyfully the Louisiana governor hurried word to his followers, telling them to regarrison the forts once more. The American commissioner at Natchez, watching with grim satisfaction as Spanish soldiers carried guns and supplies from that fortification, was amazed on March 22 to see them suddenly retrace their steps, remount their cannon, and prepare to defend their outpost once more.

The result of this shift in policy was nothing Godoy could foresee: his hasty action set in motion a chain of events that led finally to Spain's loss of Louisiana. Had he been better versed in frontier affairs he would have known that the settlers in the southern borderland would never accept renewed Spanish rule, for most of them were British Loyalists or Americans, now united by the Anglo-Spanish war. They made their feelings known as soon as they learned of Spain's decision to retain the Yazoo Strip. In Natchez mobs that raged through the town held the Spanish deputy governor a prisoner until he resigned. In the border towns of West Florida dozens of conspirators—British, American, and Spanish—hatched revolutionary plots to free the Floridas and Louisiana from Spanish rule. In the southern United States William Blount, now senator from Tennessee but still an enthusiastic plotter, planned four military expeditions to wrest away Spain's North American colonies. Faced by this solid phalanx of opposition, Godoy was forced to reverse his policy once more and in March, 1798, directed Carondelet to surrender the disputed territory. But the harm was done. Having tasted action, the American frontiersmen were unwilling to accept a peaceful settlement.

Their objective now was nothing less than ownership of both West Florida and Louisiana. A successful attack on those Spanish colonies would not only insure the West against any future closing of the Mississippi but open new trading routes along the Alabama and Tombigbee rivers and allow the filibusterers to grab off speculative land claims in the conquered territory. The United States, drifting toward war with both France and Spain during 1797 and 1798, would probably welcome such a blow. Through those two years frontiersmen talked constantly of expeditions or laid elaborate plans. Alexander Hamilton suggested one scheme—a march to liberate not only Louisiana but Mexico and Latin America from Spanish rule—but frontiersmen refused to follow this arch-Federalist who was more interested in aiding England than helping them. More to their liking was a filibustering expedition launched in 1799 by a Loyalist, William Augustus Bowles. With three hundred Indians and renegade whites, that adventurer captured the fort at St. Marks in May, 1800, and seemed on the point of overrunning the Floridas when a larger Spanish force dispersed his followers and sent Bowles off to death in Spain.

These attacks were of more than local importance, for they strengthened a belief growing in the minds of Spanish rulers since the Treaty of San Lorenzo: Louisiana was an expensive luxury that must be sold before England or the United States took it by force. The colony cost Spain dearly—customs duties never paid more than one-fifth the sums needed for its administration—and gave the Spanish little in return, for Louisiana purchased its industrial goods from France and shipped its agriculture produce there in payment. Little wonder that Spain was willing to dispose of its American white elephant at almost any price after Pinckney's Treaty removed its value as a bargaining instrument in dealings with the United States.

France was anxious to buy, partly because its rulers envisaged future profits from the growing sugar and cotton production in Louisiana, partly because Napoleon's victories reawakened dreams of a vast new empire. Negotiations between the two powers, carried on since 1795, reached a climax in 1800 when Napoleon's European conquests gave France the territories needed to bargain with the Spanish monarch, Charles IV. In the Treaty of San Ildefonso, signed on October 1, 1800, Spain agreed to transfer Louisiana to France, in return for Napoleon's promise to carve out a Tuscan kingdom for Charles' indigent relatives of the House of Parma. The First Consul never lived up to his part of the agreement. Instead of continuing the continental war until he secured the promised Italian lands, he abruptly brought his war with England to a close through the Treaty of Amiens (1801), then demanded that Spain turn over Louisiana at once without compensation. The powerless Spaniards, unwilling to risk the enmity of both France and England, reluctantly complied. On October 15, 1802, orders reached New Orleans to surrender the colony to its new masters.

News of the cession sent a wave of terror through the West. Spain could be bullied into keeping the Mississippi open, but powerful France would be impossible to control. As westerners discussed their fate, an event occurred that seemed to confirm their worst fears. On October 18, 1802, New Orleans officials quietly posted a proclamation ending the right of deposit. Actually France had nothing to do with the order, which was a belated Spanish attempt to stop American abuses of the deposit privilege: contraband trade, evasion of duties, and smuggling of gold and silver. But frontiersmen did not know these circumstances. In their eyes this was an example of the treatment they could expect from the new masters of the lower Mississippi. As the news spread northward newspaper extras were published, people gathered in excited knots to discuss and condemn, and legislatures passed fiery resolutions urging France to retract. Nor did the half million people in the West stand alone. New York and Philadelphia merchants who supplied the interior with manufactured items, eastern ship owners who imported goods for the frontier, and New England wholesalers who shipped their produce across the mountains, all faced ruin if western buying power declined. A united nation demanded that the government meet this crisis, even if it were necessary to take New Orleans from France by force.

President Thomas Jefferson, the anti-Federalist now controlling national affairs, was particularly alarmed, not only because of his inherent sympathy for the West, but because the growing anti-French sentiment would react against his party in the elections of 1804. As usual he hit upon the correct strategy. The United States, he realized, must purchase New Orleans and enough of West Florida to give it control of the mouth of the Mississippi. This could be arranged only if a new Anglo-French war broke out, for then France might be willing to cede rather than risk a British naval attack on Louisiana. A waiting game was clearly called for, but in the meantime Jefferson subjected France to a barrage of propaganda designed to show that the United States was so hostile to the French and so friendly to the English that an attack on New Orleans was imminent. Letters proclaiming America's intention to "marry ourselves to the British fleet and nation" were allowed to fall into the hands of the First Consul's agents; hours were spent convincing French and Spanish ministers that the whole nation wanted war so ardently that only the President's desire for peace prevented an immediate invasion of Louisiana. Jefferson also persuaded Congress to authorize an army of 80,000 troops and a navy of fifteen Mississippi gunboats. Then, amidst this carefully created hostile atmosphere, he sent James Monroe to Paris to buy New Orleans.

The results of Jefferson's blustering policy were gratifying. Spain backed down first, hurrying word to New Orleans to reopen deposit at that port before the frontiersmen could attack. At the same time Napoleon decided that he would sell not only New Orleans but all Louisiana. The war with England, he knew, would soon be resumed, and he could no more risk an Anglo-American attack on his new colony than could Spain. Moreover the failure of his best troops to subdue a slave insurrection in Santo Domingo had lessened his enthusiasm for empire building. Having reached his decision in March, 1803, Napoleon instructed Talleyrand, his foreign minister, to broach the subject to the resident American minister, Robert Livingston. Talleyrand waited until April 11, then in the midst of an ordinary conversation suddenly asked, "What would you give for the whole of Louisiana?" Livingston, who was slightly deaf, could scarcely believe his ears but he had the presence of mind to indicate that he was interested. Negotiations went forward rapidly until April 30, 1803, when a treaty was signed transferring Louisiana to the United States for 80,000,000 francs—about $15,000,000.

There remained only the task of taking over control of New Orleans and its far-flung hinterland. Spain was still in possession when news of the purchase reached the city in August, 1803, but the French agent waiting to take over Louisiana insisted that he have the glory of surrendering the territory to the United States. Hence on November 30, 1803, the colony passed into French hands, just as James Wilkinson with 150 men set out from newly built Ft. Adams to receive jurisdiction. The second ceremony was held in the public square of New Orleans on December 20. Beneath a clear warm sun the French agent delivered the city's keys to Wilkinson and William C. Claiborne, the second American commissioner. Claiborne then addressed the small crowd, assuring the people protection for their property and religion, before the three-colored flag of France was hauled down and the Stars and Stripes hoisted in its place. Wilkinson, who had carried out the transaction in an efficient manner, characteristically wrung $12,000 from the retiring Spanish governor for his "Reflections" on Spain's policy—a hodge-podge of outworn revelations and obvious advice—then used the same information as the basis for a long report to President Jefferson. The man's duplicity was unequalled.

The Louisiana Purchase fittingly climaxed the diplomacy of the Revolutionary period. Gone from the Mississippi Valley were foreign agents who incited Indians to attack American settlers, commercial restrictions that throttled the economic life of the West, unpatriotic westerners willing to preach rebellion for a price. With the extension of American rule over the interior of the continent peace settled upon the frontier. Once more the westward march could be resumed, as homeseekers pushed inland to exploit the domain won by the blood and sweat of their nation's statesmen and soldiers.

CHAPTER XII

# Settling the Appalachian Plateau

## 1795-1812

For a generation before 1795 the westward march of the American people
was halted while independence was won, a workable government system
established, Indians subdued, and foreign intrigue swept from the borderlands. Now frontiersmen were ready to move again, as Jay's Treaty,
Wayne's victory, the Treaty of Greenville, and Pinckney's Treaty cleared
the way. From New England, the Middle States, and the South they came
—eager homeseekers with their families, young axmen hunting a homesite
for the expectant bride waiting patiently behind, starry-eyed speculators in
search of choice lands, shiftless ne'er-do-wells cast out by the older societies
of the East, zealous ministers in quest of souls, sharp-tongued young
lawyers seeking a more liberal atmosphere to nurture political ambitions,
journeymen printers carrying type for a frontier newspaper, merchants,
millers, blacksmiths, artisans, rogues, and saints—all rubbing elbows on
the trails that led to the mecca beyond the mountains. For seventeen years
the tide of population flowed west—the greatest movement of peoples
America had known—until 1812 when a new war closed the gates of the
frontier once more.

Unusually choice lands were not the magnets which drew these pioneers
toward the frontier, for the best spots had already been appropriated by
the bolder spirits who had ventured across the Appalachians just after
the Revolution: the valleys of eastern Tennessee, the Nashville Basin, the
limestone areas of Kentucky, and the Ohio River lowlands. For the newcomers there remained the hilly areas of the physiographic region known
as the Appalachian Plateau. There rolling foothills, sloping gradually
downward to merge with the level Lake Plains Province, and broad valleys
that marked the former course of glacial rivers, offered tempting prospects

to farmers grown weary of wresting a living from New England's stubborn soil or crowded from their southern homes by advancing plantations. The whole region, between New York and northern Alabama, was interlaced with swift-flowing streams and covered with a heavy growth of hardwood that testified to the soil's fertility. Yet settlers who went west during those years were less concerned with finding ideal conditions in their new homes than escaping bad conditions in the old. In each of the three sections contributing to the migration—New England, the Middle States, and the South—people were discontented and anxious to be on the move.

Overcrowding was the principal expelling force in New England. For more than a century the Yankees had been held back, their path westward across New York State blocked by the powerful Iroquois Confederation. A few bold spirits made the lengthy trek to the Wyoming Valley or the Ohio country, a few others moved northward to hilly Vermont, but the majority remained at home to compete for the few lands available. This sent prices soaring, until by the 1790's even moderately good farms sold for from $14 to $50 an acre. Younger sons—and they were plentiful in prolific New England families—refused to pay such prices for rock-strewn hillsides when they could buy fertile lands in the West for $2 or $3 an acre. That price discrepancy underlay the migration, but other New Englanders went west to escape the established Congregational church of Massachusetts and Connecticut, or to seek a more liberal social order than that rock-ribbed Federalist stronghold. High taxes, normal in well-established communities, drove others toward the frontier.

Those same conditions—overcrowding, high prices, exorbitant taxes, and conservatism—also existed in the Middle States and South, but other factors in both those sections helped speed the exodus. Many who left New York and Pennsylvania were frontiersmen who, living on the western fringe of civilization, drifted naturally with the moving tide. In Virginia, Maryland, and North Carolina soil exhaustion forced thousands to abandon their farms, particularly in the hilly Piedmont region where heavy rains had washed essential minerals from cultivated soil. More were driven from their homes by the expansion of plantation agriculture into the Piedmont and Great Valley during the post-Revolutionary years. Some of the democratic small farmers occupying the region went west to escape contact with slavery, others disliked the new class stratification which placed them on a lower level than the great planters, while still others were displaced when their lands were absorbed by plantations. Between 1790 and 1800 thirteen counties in Maryland and twenty-six in Virginia lost population, so rapid was the migration.

Important as these expelling factors were, the mass exodus of the post-

Revolutionary years owed its magnitude also to improved roads connecting East and West. These had been built during an internal improvement craze that swept over the new nation in the 1790's. Most of the highways scarcely deserved the name; they were made by chopping out underbrush and small trees in a swath ten to thirty feet wide, cutting off the larger timber eighteen inches from the ground, and leaving the largest trees

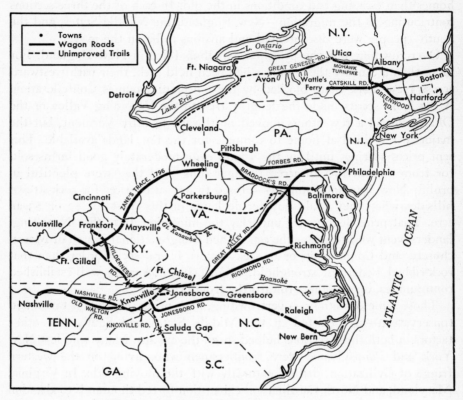

Principal Routes to the West, 1795-1812

standing even in the middle of the thoroughfare. Small streams were bridged with logs, but only fords or ferries on the main-traveled routes allowed passage over rivers. Although these roads were impassable quagmires in wet weather and unsatisfactory under the best conditions, they were still better than the trails used in the past. In winter especially, when deep-packed snow smoothed the rough surfaces, pioneers could quite easily move household goods westward by sled. Most settlers migrated just before the spring thaw for that reason.

The three road systems built westward from New England, the Middle

States, and South had much to do with the course of the westward movement, for all converged in the upper Ohio Valley. One led from Boston and
Hartford to the Hudson River where it connected with two highways across
New York State, the Mohawk Turnpike which was opened as far as Utica
by 1793, and the Catskill Turnpike, built between Catskill and Wattle's
Ferry on the Susquehanna in 1792. The Middle States were connected
with the West during the 1780's by two military highways constructed
during the Seven Years' War, Forbes' Road and Braddock's Road, which
were improved by Pennsylvania and Maryland until they were passable for
wagons as far as Pittsburgh. Migrating Virginians could travel over those
Middle State routes, or follow the Great Valley Road or the Richmond
Road, both built before the Revolution, to Ft. Chissel. From that post a
single wagon road led to Cumberland Gap, two hundred miles away,
where it joined the Wilderness Road across Kentucky to Louisville and
Frankfort. That highway was opened to wagon traffic in 1795, while a
branch built a few years before allowed settlers to reach either Maysville
on the Ohio or Ft. Gillad on the Green River. Tennessee was equally
accessible over the Knoxville Road, built between the Wilderness Road and
the mouth of the French Broad River between 1791 and 1795, the Nashville Road constructed by North Carolina in 1788, and the Old Walton
Road that was opened in 1795 as an alternate route to the Cumberland
settlements. In addition to the wagon roads, several unimproved trails
were widely used, especially the twisting paths across western Virginia to
Parkersburg and the mouth of the Great Kanawha, and the trace that
used Saluda Gap, in the eastern mountain wall, to connect Georgia with
the Holston frontier.

Over those roads went the pioneers. Between 1790, when the Southwest
Territory was erected with William Blount as governor, and 1795, the
migratory stream moved toward eastern Tennessee. The Holston settlements could not hold the thousands who sought homes there; instead the
frontier surged westward so rapidly that when Blount chose a central
site for the territorial capital in 1792 he laid out the new town of Knoxville at the mouth of the French Broad. As soon as Pinckney's Treaty ended
the threat of Indian attacks and Spanish intrigue the tide set in toward
Nashville. Immigrants were so thick on the Old Walton Road during
the summer of 1795 that they crowded each other from the highway;
26,000 crossed the Cumberland in two months. Through the cold winter
that followed the exodus continued—thousands of ragged men and women
tramping barefooted through the snow because "every body says it's good
land." By 1796, when 77,000 people lived in Tennessee, the territory was
ready to enter the Union as a state. Others sought homes in Kentucky

after Wayne's victory ended fear of Indian raids, filling the Blue Grass country, pushing into the hills about the Big Sandy, and spreading westward along the valley of the Green River. More than 220,000 people occupied Kentucky by 1800.

Both Tennessee and Kentucky filled so rapidly that the transition from frontier to civilized community was accomplished almost overnight. Pioneers in each new settlement bore the typical backcountry stamp; they built crude log cabins, cleared thirty or forty acres from their larger speculative holdings, lived on corn meal, pork, and game, and dressed in the fringed hunting shirt, leggings, and moccasins that were standard garb in the West. As their fields extended year after year their wealth steadily increased, for the rich bottom lands produced from seventy-five to a hundred bushels of corn an acre and the price was steady at twenty-five cents a bushel. Four years of such harvests allowed a farmer to build a frame house, buy a suit of clothes, subscribe to the weekly newspaper just started by a journeyman printer in the nearby town, send his children to the classical academy opened there by an itinerant schoolmaster, and perhaps buy a carriage to carry his proud family to church on Sundays. Most made this transition; the misfits who could not moved farther west after selling their improvements to newer settlers.

Despite the rapid evolution, society remained predominately rural. Lexington, the largest city in the West, had only 1,795 inhabitants in 1800, while the population of Louisville, Frankfort, Nashville, Knoxville, and the other towns was less than five hundred. Farming was the principal occupation, corn the leading crop. Transportation difficulties discouraged the production of tobacco, cotton, and wheat except in the Cumberland and bluegrass settlements where flatboats were used to carry those bulky goods to the New Orleans market. Corn, on the other hand, was ground into meal for local consumption, concentrated into whiskey for export, or fed to cattle and hogs who could carry themselves to market. By 1800 whiskey from the many small distilleries that dotted Kentucky and Tennessee was displacing rum as America's national drink, while large herds of cattle and hogs, driven north along the Great Valley Road or south through Saluda Gap, were bringing prosperity to the frontier. Yet money remained scarce, for profits went to buy manufactured goods in Baltimore and Philadelphia, or to pay the $6 or $7 per hundred pounds demanded by wagoners who carried freight between the seaboard and the West. Only the Nashville settlements and the bluegrass country, where cotton and tobacco were grown, rose above the primitive economy usual in frontier communities. There, in the first years of the nineteenth century, thrifty farmers expanded their holdings at the expense of less fortunate neighbors, elaborate frame houses testified to a new affluence, and young lawyers such as Andrew Jackson dominated political affairs rather than the Indian fighters who had captured the imagination of an earlier generation.

The transition from frontier to civilized community was particularly rapid in Tennessee and Kentucky because land could be purchased cheaply from either the states or the army of small speculators operating there. In the northern portions of the Appalachian Plateau—New York, western Pennsylvania, and the Northwest Territory—the course of settlement was different, largely because neither the states concerned nor the national government had developed a satisfactory method of selling the public domain to pioneer farmers. Failure to do so plunged the United States into a period of speculative activity unrivaled in its history. Everywhere land jobbing companies sprang up, financed by European or American capitalists who saw in the combination of a westward-moving population, a stable new government, and greedy states eager to sell their western holdings, a formula almost certain to spell handsome returns. Land companies played a larger role in the westward movement during those years than at any time before or since.

Western New York felt their influence first. Settlers from the eastern part of the state and New England drifted into that war-torn region after 1783, to lay out a few scattered towns along the upper Mohawk and Unadilla rivers, but no mass migration could begin until Indians were removed and ownership of the area—which was claimed by both Massachusetts and New York—finally established. The first proved easy, for the ravages of the Revolution and an exodus to Canada left only about 6,000 of the once-proud tribesmen in the coveted territory. A commission named by the state legislature set to work in the spring of 1785; by 1789 the Oneida, Tuscarora, and Cayuga tribes, had surrendered their former hunting grounds in return for cash settlements, annuities, and small reservations. New York then possessed all lands west to Lake Seneca except those north of the Mohawk River claimed by the departed Mohawk Indians, and these were secured in 1797 for a payment of $1,600. Thus were the mighty warriors who had held the English at bay for a century reduced to a servile life on the scattered reservations allotted them.

While that was going on, the New York legislature opened negotiations with Massachusetts to determine which state really owned the ceded lands, for Massachusetts had specifically retained its colonial claims to a strip across New York when turning its western territory over to Congress. Commissioners from the two states met at Hartford during the summer of 1786 and after the usual amount of wrangling settled the problem by drawing a Pre-emption Line south from Sodus Bay to the Pennsylvania border. New York retained all territory east of the line, together with a mile-wide strip along the Niagara River and sovereignty over the whole region on both sides of the boundary. Massachusetts was given the lands west of the Pre-emption Line, and 230,400 acres on the Susquehanna River.

Both states were ready to dispose of their holdings immediately; moreover their empty coffers suggested rapid sales in wholesale quantities

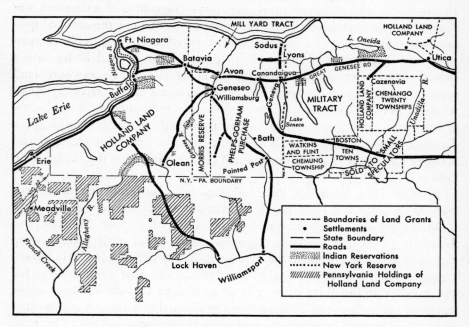

The New York-Pennsylvania Frontier, 1790–1812

rather than the slower process of parceling out the land to individual farmers. Massachusetts, in 1787, sold its entire Susquehanna Tract, known as the Boston Ten Towns, to a group of speculators for 12½ cents an acre. New York, which began selling its lands in 1789, auctioned off the whole region between the Unadilla River and the Pre-emption Line during the next few years. Nearly all went to speculators, some organized into companies to purchase such large tracts as Chemung Township, the Watkins and Flint Purchase, or the Chenango Triangle. Other areas, such as the Chenango Twenty Townships, went to a number of small buyers. This was also the fate of the Military Tract that New York set aside to satisfy bounties issued Revolutionary soldiers. Distribution of those lands began in 1791 and as the military warrants were transferable, most were absorbed by land jobbers. Speculators sold their purchases to settlers so readily that by 1795 the region east of the Pre-emption Line was thinly settled.

In the meantime Massachusetts turned to the disposal of its 6,000,000 acres west of the line. For a time individual sales to farmers were considered, but the need for quick profits and pressure from speculators who hoped to divide the land among themselves finally proved decisive. On April 1, 1788, the whole tract was sold to Oliver Phelps and Nathaniel Gorham, two wealthy land jobbers with excellent political influence. They agreed to pay the state £300,000 within three years—in Massachusetts currency which was so depreciated the actual purchase price was only $175,000 in gold, or about three cents an acre. Even that sum was more than Phelps and Gorham could raise and for the next year they struggled frantically to secure help from other capitalists of New England, New York, and Pennsylvania.

While Gorham sought out fellow speculators in the quest for additional capital, Phelps went west to supervise surveys and sales. His first task was to extinguish Indian title to the tract, as the New York treaties secured only the region east of the Pre-emption Line. Hence he went immediately to Buffalo Creek where, in July, 1789, he persuaded the Seneca to give up 2,500,000 acres east of the Genesee River, plus the Mill Yard Tract on the west bank of that stream, for $5,000 and an annuity of $500. That done, Phelps set surveyors to work, built a storehouse and land office at the foot of Canandaigua Lake, and began public sales. Within a year a thousand settlers were scattered over the rolling hill country of the Phelps-Gorham Purchase, Canandaigua was a bustling little town of thirty cabins, and a rival village called Geneva was taking shape at the foot of Lake Seneca. Most of the newcomers were from New England, although New Yorkers and Pennsylvanians who had followed the Susquehanna north were in evidence.

Sales were encouraging, but the credit system used brought in little actual cash and left Phelps and Gorham with the task of raising money needed for their three annual payments to Massachusetts. That proved difficult. Many New York and Pennsylvania speculators who had promised aid backed out, while the hope of selling Pennsylvania the so-called "Erie Triangle" vanished when the federal government decided that area was not a part of New York. Worse still was the rapid rise in the price of Massachusetts securities. Phelps and Gorham planned to buy depreciated state notes at a low figure, then turn them over to Massachusetts at par. During 1789 those seemingly worthless notes skyrocketed in value as rumors spread that the national government planned to assume the state debts. Dozens of speculators, including Phelps and Gorham, who counted on making payments in a depreciated medium were faced with the dismal prospect of cash prices, particularly after 1790 when Secretary of the Treasury Alexander Hamilton carried his funding plan through Congress. To make matters even worse an opposition party within the Massachusetts legislature, led by the ever-popular Samuel Adams, threatened to revoke the contract on the slightest excuse.

Phelps and Gorham managed to pay their first installment, but hopes of meeting the next two were slim. Rather than risk losing all, they agreed in March, 1790, to turn back the western two-thirds in return for full title to the eastern third. The exploitation of even that smaller plot so strained their resources that they leaped at the first opportunity to sell. On November 18, 1790, Robert Morris of New York bought the Phelps-Gorham Purchase for £30,000—about eight cents an acre. A few months later Morris purchased from Massachusetts the whole western portion of New York for an additional £45,000. This wealthy speculator, whose two spectacular bargains made him the largest landholder in America, was already well known in the money markets of the United States and Europe. He was wise enough to know that even his vast resources were insufficient to develop the tract he had contracted to buy; instead he made the purchase to test a shrewd theory of his own. The speculative spirit, he knew, was running high among European bankers who commanded far more capital than any jobber in poverty-stricken America. He realized, too, that his own name was known and trusted abroad, for he had served successfully as secretary of finance during the latter years of the Revolution. Therefore he would market his New York lands in Amsterdam, London, and Paris, hoping to find there the profitable resale that was every speculator's dream.

For that purpose Morris divided his holdings into three tracts. The middle section along the Genesee River was the best; this he kept himself. The eastern portion, consisting of the Phelps-Gorham Purchase, he sold for £75,000 early in 1791 to a syndicate of English capitalists headed by Sir William Pulteney—a sum that gave him a tidy profit of £45,000. In casting about for a purchaser for the western half of his property, Morris hit on four prominent Amsterdam business concerns then speculating in American securities. Their agent in the United States, Theopile Cazenove, proved interested, partly because Hamilton's funding program was reducing profits from financial ventures, and partly because he had already made two minor purchases from New York—one just east of the Military Tract and the other north of the Mohawk—and was sufficiently infected with land fever to want more. Cazenove's enthusiasm proved so contagious that his Dutch backers decided to enter the speculative field on a wholesale scale. They added two more banking houses to their number, organized themselves as the Holland Land Company, and instructed Cazenove to buy widely for them. By December, 1792, the ambitious agent completed arrangements with Morris to take over 2,500,000 acres in western New York, and in the next few months he secured another 1,500,000 acres in Pennsylvania.

The series of purchases which delivered most of western New York and Pennsylvania into the hands of European speculators greatly affected the development of that region. The English and Dutch business men now in control had capital to develop their holdings—something completely lacking among American jobbers who usually operated on a shoestring and counted on a quick turnover for profits. This advantage was first realized by Charles Williamson, the agent sent to the United States by the Pulteney Estates. He reached western New York in the spring of 1792 filled with ambitious plans; he would build roads, improve rivers, erect stores, taverns, gristmills, and sawmills, provide centers for amusement, and turn his wilderness estate into the garden spot of the West. His backers, he knew, were wealthy enough to afford the expense, and he reasoned that grateful Americans would repay them by purchasing lands at unusually high prices. Thus originated the "hothouse" method of developing the frontier.

A rapid survey of the Pulteney Estates convinced Williamson that export centers should be established on Lake Ontario, the Genesee River, the Seneca River, and the Cohocton River. Hence he set crews to work on carefully planned cities controlling those routes. At Bath, at the head of navigation on the Cohocton, he built houses, farm buildings, a gristmill, two sawmills, a tavern, a theater, and a race track. Williamsburg on the Genesee and Lyons on the Seneca were also provided with homes, storehouses, distilleries, and mills. The Sodus development on Lake Erie was even more ambitious; in addition to constructing dwellings, stores, and mills, Williamson improved the harbor and erected a large wharf. Settlements already begun at Canandaigua and Geneva were similarly improved. Over the whole area he scattered gristmills, distilleries, farmhouses, and cleared fields to lure homeseekers. Equal care was spent on a road system connecting the cities with rural regions. One long highway was built from Williamsport, on the Susquehanna River in Pennsylvania, to Williamsburg, another from Sodus to Geneva. At the same time Williamson in 1794 persuaded New York to extend the Mohawk Turnpike through Geneva and Canandaigua to the future site of Avon on the Genesee. The Great Genesee Road, as it was called, gave the Pulteney Estates direct access to Albany and New York markets, while the southern road to Williamsport allowed shipments to Philadelphia and Baltimore.

In the ten years that Williamson pushed this building program he spent $1,000,000 and took in just $146,000 from land sales, although more was due under the six-year credit system allowed. By that time his wealthy supporters were so alarmed that he was displaced in 1801 by an agent who emphasized returns rather than expenditures. Although the Pulteney interests did little more than break even on their investment, they took solace in the fact that Williamson's efforts hurried the advance of settlement. By 1800 population was well established over the whole region, with most of the settlers scattered along the Great Genesee Road and about Bath. The frontier was ready to pass beyond the Genesee River, where the lands of the Morris Reserve were filling rapidly, into the domain of the Holland Land Company.

During the 1790's that wealthy European concern was experimenting with the "hothouse" method of settlement on its two tracts in eastern New York. Within five years $128,000 was squandered on the plot south of Lake Oneida, much of it on the city of Cazenovia where a brewery, a distillery, sawmills and gristmills, a potash works, two stores, and a tavern were built. Even more was spent on the region north of the Mohawk River, where a disastrous experiment in maple sugar production cost the company $15,000 even before the usual developments began. These included model farms, two well-equipped towns, and purchase of a tract along the Mohawk for a new village, Utica, to provide a market and export center. Between 1794 and 1798 $15,000 a year was poured into the small area. By that time the directors of the Holland Land Company, disturbed by the large expenditures, ordered an end to developments in both tracts. Theopile Cazenove was replaced by a more conservative agent, and the company prepared to reap some return on its investments.

Those expensive experiments convinced the thrifty Dutch bankers there should be no "hastening of civilization" west of the Genesee. Settlers were paying the high prices asked for improved lands, but just as many were going to nearby regions on which the owners spent nothing. The American frontiersman, they saw, did not want cleared fields and trim frame houses; he was enough of a speculator to want cheap land that he could improve with his own labor. The "hothouse" method transferred the profits gained from the initial risk to the company. Nor were gristmills, sawmills, and distilleries necessary; they sprang up in each frontier community as soon as the demand was great enough. The company's decision to leave all but necessary improvements to private initiative was a wise one.

The first step in opening the Holland Land Company's territory was to extinguish Indian title. That was accomplished in the Big Tree Treaty, signed by the Seneca on September 15, 1797, after chiefs, interpreters, and watching government officials were bribed into accepting terms distasteful to the majority of the tribe. With the way cleared for settlement, Joseph Ellicott, an experienced American woodsman who had no sympathy with "hothouse" methods, was appointed agent. By the spring of 1800 the region was divided into townships six miles square, while those marked for immediate sale were subdivided into 360 acre plots. Sales started in 1802, at a land office in the new town of Batavia. When the paucity of purchasers convinced Ellicott that the $2.75 an acre asked by the company was too high, he lowered the price to between $1.50 and $2, eliminated down payments, and allowed ten years credit. Such a rush of customers followed that he was obliged to open the whole Genesee country to settlers. The price was gradually increased over the next years, until by 1811 the average sum received for an acre was $2.30 and in 1817 $5. Although collections were slow and payment often in goods rather than cash the Holland Land Company eventually retired from its venture with a comfortable profit.

This was partly due to the manner in which the economy-minded Ellicott confined himself to the most essential improvements. Some roads were built to supplement the Great Genesee Road after the state extended that highway to Buffalo between 1798 and 1803: one from Niagara through Batavia to Geneseo where it connected with the transportation system of the Pulteney Estates, another from Geneseo to Olean at the head of navigation on the Allegheny River, and a third from Buffalo along the shore of Lake Erie to Erie, with a branch running southeast to the Pennsylvania border. Although these highways were well built—underbrush and small trees were cleared away in a forty-foot path and a sixteen foot swath level with the ground cut down the middle—they cost little as Ellicott allowed farmers to pay for land by road work. Those were virtually the only improvements, aside from two unsuccessful mills at Batavia and a grant of two hundred acres in each township for schools and churches. Individual artisans soon appeared to supply the sawmills, gristmills, and distilleries needed.

The Holland Land Company and other European speculative concerns vastly stimulated the peopling of western New York. Their improvements, whether confined to road building or on a needlessly grandiose scale, made settlement easier; their advertising in eastern states lured thousands of homeseekers westward. Much of this was concentrated in New England, where, speculators realized, the people were ready to move. As hard-working farmers in that section read gaudy circulars distributed by the companies or listened to enthusiastic letters from the first arrivals in western New York, their dissatisfaction with their rock-strewn soil increased. Why dedicate yourself to a lifetime of backbreaking toil when the western country beckoned? As more and more reasoned in that way a "Genesee Fever" swept through the eastern states. Everywhere, from Massachusetts to New Jersey, men sold their farms and began the long trek to the frontier.

All through the 1790's the numbers moving west increased year by year until by 1800 a mass exodus was under way. A traveler in 1797 counted five hundred wagons a day on the roads through Albany, and a few years later the Catskill Road, now extended to Canandaigua, was just as crowded. By 1800 immigrants overran the Military Tract and Pulteney Estates; five years later they were moving across the Genesee lands of the Holland Company where Batavia, Buffalo, Stafford, and other towns blossomed into tiny cities overnight. "The woods are full of new settlers," wrote an observer near Batavia in 1805. "Axes are resounding, and the trees literally falling about us as we passed. In one instance we were obliged to pass in a field through the smoke and flame of the trees which had lately been felled and were just fired." In 1812 200,000 people lived in western New York, 25,000 of them in the Holland Land Company purchase, and the region was passing beyond the frontier stage.

More than two-thirds of the pioneers were New Englanders, most of whom came from Massachusetts, Connecticut, or Rhode Island. The wholesale departure of these thousands spread alarm through the ranks of those who stayed behind. Their own states, they noted, were lagging significantly behind the rest of the nation in population increase, their best and youngest citizens were moving away, and both land values and the social structure were suffering. These good fathers could not know they were witnessing the first stages of that century-long process known as the rural decay of New England. Instead they sought vainly to offset the advertising of the land companies by propaganda of their own. Newspapers in the early 1800's bristled with lurid descriptions of dangers of frontier life or with such verses as:

> Let the idle complain
> And ramble in vain,
> An Eden to find in the West,
> They're grossly deceiv'd,
> Their hearts sorely griev'd,
> They'll sigh to return to the East.

"Actual calculation has evinced," wrote the Reverend Jedidiah Morse in the 1796 edition of his famous *Geography*, "that any quantity of the best mowing land in Connecticut produces about twice as much clear profit as the same quantity of the best wheat land in the State of New York." These calamitous voices cried in a wilderness of indifference. More than words were needed to keep an American at home when good soil lay ahead.

Or even, in that restless day, poor soil. For while the main stream of westward-moving population inundated the Genesee country, two subsidiary rivulets branched off to engulf the mountainous wastes of Pennsylvania and northern New York. Pennsylvania threw open its last unsettled portions, the northwestern region obtained from the Iroquois in the second Treaty of Ft. Stanwix, in 1792. The land law passed at the time was so loosely worded that untold confusion had resulted; farms could be obtained for twenty cents an acre either by squatting or buying a warrant, all plots were to be settled within two years unless Indian disturbances intervened, and surveys were to follow rather than precede purchase. Those vague phrases, intentionally inserted by speculators, made Pennsylvania a happy hunting ground for land jobbers. Within a few years the whole area was engrossed by their agents, most of it by two large companies: the Holland Land Company, and the Pennsylvania Population Company. Neither had any hope of settling its domains within the prescribed two year period. When the state finally tried to force them to do so in 1797 they began a long legal battle that only ended in 1805 when the United States Supreme Court ruled that the 1792 law was too poorly worded to be binding. This litigation discouraged settlement, although a large number of squatters—some hired by companies organized for the purpose—planted themselves on speculators' lands in hopes of securing title through possession. After 1805, with ownerhip clear and a state road opened from Lock Haven to the border, sales began at the Holland Land Company's offices in Meadville and Kittanning. By 1812 the region was sparsely settled with Erie and Meadville its principal towns, but the mountainous terrain failed to attract a large population. Certainly speculators discouraged rather than aided the westward movement there.

They played a more valuable role in peopling the two habitable portions of northern New York: the hill country between the Black River and Lake Ontario, and the woodlands bordering the St. Lawrence River. A commission created by the legislature began selling plots in the first area during the late 1780's; by 1795 nearly all was in the hands of small speculators who spent the next years developing their tracts. The most ambitious of those jobbers was a New York merchant, George Scriba, who secured the region north of Lake Oneida, laid out two towns, built a connecting road, and made the usual improvements designed to lure settlers. It was in this territory, and just south of a grant made to Baron Steuben for his part in the Revolution, that Cazenove bought the tract the Holland Land Company placed on the market in 1794.

Speculation in the St. Lawrence country was on a more spectacular scale. The first region to be surveyed, a fertile area known as the St. Lawrence

Ten Towns, was auctioned off in 1787 to a syndicate of jobbers led by Alexander Macomb, a bold plunger with large resources. Macomb's appetite for land was only whetted; he began negotiating at once to secure the millions of acres surrounding his tract. Arrangements were completed in 1791 when he bought all of the unpatented lands remaining in northern New York—4,000,000 acres in all—for eight cents an acre. Macomb, who

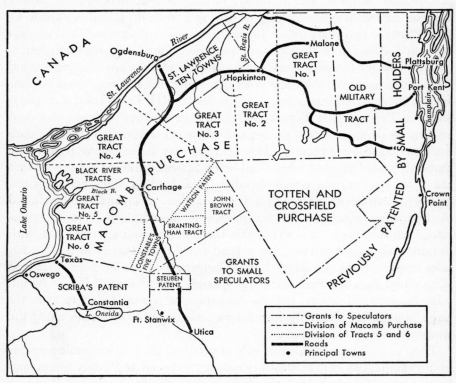

Northern New York, 1790-1812

realized he could meet the first of five annual payments only by immediate resale, divided his purchase into six tracts which were assigned to lesser speculators for development and sale. Most prominent among these was William Constable, who received Tracts Four, Five, and Six. Those were disposed of during the next few years, Tract Four to a group of Belgium capitalists organized as the Antwerp Company, part of Tract Five to a group of refugees from Revolutionary France, and the remainder to smaller American operators such as William Inman and John Brown, the wealthy Providence merchant. The land Constable was unable to sell he developed himself as Constable's Five Towns. In this way most of the

Black River region was parceled out between 1793 and 1812, but the distance from markets and the rough country kept the population small.

The northern portions of the Macomb purchase went through a similar evolution, for these too were assigned to smaller speculators for improvement and sale. One, Samuel Ogden, laid out the town of Ogdensburg in 1801, built the usual mills, and constructed a passable road to the Black River where it connected with a highway just completed to Utica. Some settlers drifted in over this, but more came from Vermont, attracted by Ogden's advertising and the cheap lands of the wild St. Lawrence country. Some were pioneers from southern New England who drifted on now with the advancing frontier; others were established farmers weaned from rugged Vermont by promises of "lands not lying edgewise." The crude "winter road" from Lake Champlain to the mouth of the St. Regis River was crowded each year with hundreds of moving families, dragging their household goods on sleds over the hard-packed snow. The region around Ogdensburg and the valley of the Oswegatchie River filled up first, but three toll roads built by turnpike companies between 1810 and 1812— the St. Lawrence Turnpike between Carthage and Malone, and two highways connecting Hopkinton with Lake Champlain—turned the tide of settlement toward the interior. Although northern New York did not pass beyond the primitive stage of frontier development before the War of 1812, great timber rafts drifting down the St. Lawrence to Montreal and barges deep laden with flour and potash bound for that Canadian port testified to an advancing civilization.

Northern New York and western Pennsylvania developed slowly because they were only eddies in the main frontier stream sweeping westward from New England and the Middle States. Settlement was more rapid at the terminus of that swift-flowing current in the Northwest Territory. The peopling of that region began in 1795 when Wayne's Treaty of Greenville removed Indians from much of the Ohio country. In the van were the pioneers who had crowded together in the river towns during the wars; all through the summer of 1795 they poured out of Marietta, Massie's Station, Columbia, Cincinnati, and North Bend on their way to the back country. Before autumn set in they were joined by a horde of land-seekers from Pennsylvania, Virginia, and Kentucky, who started west as soon as news reached them that the frontier was safe. Some followed the Wilderness Road to Maysville; more reached Redstone or Pittsburgh over Forbes' or Braddock's Roads, bought flatboats, and drifted down the Ohio to a site that pleased them. For the next dozen years a regular procession of those ungainly craft floated westward with a perspiring landsman at the sweeps, a horse and a few cows munching at the haystack in the

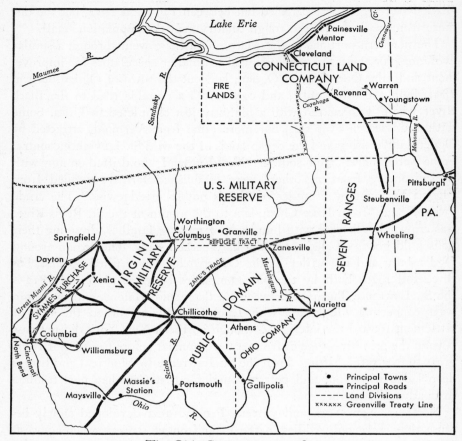

The Ohio Country, 1790-1812

prow, a handful of ragged children playing on the roofed portion of the stern, and a busy housewife hanging out her washing or churning her butter as she would on shore. Seldom had the frontier developed a more convenient form of transportation than flatboats. They cost only $30 or $40, allowed normal life to continue during the journey, and were broken up for lumber to build the settler's home.

Some pioneers purchased land from the small speculators operating in the Seven Ranges or about Steubenville. Others bought from the Ohio Company in such quantities that the villages there—Marietta and newly established Athens—began to lose their New England character. Still more made their homes on the lands east of the Scioto which the government took back from the defunct Scioto Company, or in the federal Military Reserve that was laid out in 1796 to satisfy the bounties promised Revolutionary veterans. There, as in the Virginia Military Reserve, nearly all purchases were made through speculators, for the transferable warrants issued soldiers usually found their way into their hands. Symmes Purchase also filled rapidly during the late 1790's. By the end of the century squatters in the unsurveyed region west of the Great Miami River had extended the frontier as far as the boundary established at Greenville only five years before.

Speculators in the Ohio country not only provided pioneers with needed credit but helped establish interior towns. Speculation in village sites, which absorbed more and more of the energy of land jobbers, promised even greater profits than farm lands. Most "paper towns" never passed beyond the planning stage, but some expanded into Ohio's leading cities. Hamilton was founded by a prominent speculator, Israel Ludlow, in 1795; in the same year a syndicate that he headed laid out the streets of Dayton. Nathaniel Massie played a similar role. The station he established on the north bank of the Ohio in 1790 grew into the city of Manchester, and the site he selected for another town, Chillicothe, proved so advantageous that the village soon rivaled Cincinnati. Most of the other towns founded between 1796 and 1803—Portsmouth, Columbus, Williamsburg, Deerfield, Caesarville, Xenia, and a dozen more—owed their existence to the vision and luck of some land jobber. Pressure from speculators was also partially responsible for the congressional grant that made possible the first road across Ohio, Zane's Trace, in 1796.

They were even more influential in peopling the Western Reserve, that northeast corner of Ohio retained when Connecticut ceded its lands to Congress. The first step toward disposing of the area was taken in 1792 when the legislature granted 500,000 acres on the western edge of the Reserve to 1,870 inhabitants of coastal towns whose property was destroyed by British raids during the Revolution. When it became clear that these "Fire Lands" could never be disposed of until the region east of them was thrown on the market, the whole tract was sold in 1795 to a group of thirty-five speculators under Oliver Phelps, organized as the Connecticut Land Company, for $1,200,000. Moses Cleaveland, an able young Yale graduate who was named general agent, started west in the spring of 1796 with a party of surveyors and instructions to begin sales at once. Stopping first at Buffalo, where he purchased the region east of the Cuyahoga from Indians for £500, two beef cattle, and a hundred gallons of whiskey, Cleaveland reached the mouth of Conneaut Creek on July 4, 1796, and there established his headquarters. Surveys went on rapidly, a village bearing the agent's name—later shortened to Cleveland—was laid out at the mouth of the Cuyahoga River, and settlers began flocking in. Nearly all came from New England, over the Great Genesee Road and an extension built by the company from Erie to Cleveland, attracted by good land which sold for only $1 an acre with five years credit. By 1800, thirteen hundred people lived in the Western Reserve, most of them clustered about villages that sprang up in the Mahoning and Cuyahoga valleys or along the lake shore.

The influx of settlers, in the Western Reserve and the river bottoms north of the Ohio, fostered a growing demand for a greater degree of self-government. The frontiersmen were not only familiar with the provisions of the Ordinance of 1787 but thoroughly dissatisfied with the administration of Governor Arthur St. Clair. That crotchety old ruler, who was disliked for his military failures, his autocratic leanings, and his staunch Federalism, was finally goaded into ordering a census in 1798. When this showed that many more than the needed 5,000 adult males lived in the territory he was forced to call a general election to select a legislature. The twenty-two men named to that body in December, 1798, were not completely representative, for property qualifications kept many people from voting, yet nearly all were anti-Federalists and a contest between them and the governor was inevitable. The clash came over the election of a delegate to represent the Northwest Territory in Congress. St. Clair and his small following of aristocratic Federalists backed the governor's son, Arthur St. Clair, Jr., while the Republicans chose as their candidate a twenty-six-year-old stripling already distinguished as a military leader in the Indian wars, William Henry Harrison. After a spirited campaign the legislature selected Harrison by a vote of eleven to ten. Despite all of St. Clair's ranting that able young Jeffersonian set out for the nation's capital during the winter of 1799-1800.

The Republican revolt against Federalist control of the frontier had two important results: it forced Congress to recognize the growing influence of the West in its legislative program, and led to a redivision of the Northwest Territory and to statehood for Ohio. Harrison was responsible for the first. He reached Washington aflame with zeal for one great cause: he would remake the land laws to allow direct individual purchases of small plots on extended credit at offices conveniently located along the frontier. Fortunately the time was ripe for such a change, for when Harrison laid his proposals before Congress in February, 1800, the political revolution that led to the overthrow of the Federalists a few months later was already taking shape. Most congressmen were sympathetic, and some—notably those from Kentucky, Tennessee, western Pennsylvania, Virginia, and the Carolinas—were as enthusiastic as their frontier constituents. Harrison's ready tongue made him an admirable spokesman for this western pressure group. The result was the first workable land law in American history.

The East did not bow completely before frontier demands when it accepted the measure that passed Congress on May 10, 1800; while the law was more liberal than the Ordinance of 1785 or the modifying act of 1796 which raised the price to $2 an acre but allowed a year's credit on half the amount, it still reflected eastern conservatism. The minimum price of $2 an acre was retained, with the additional provision that lands not sold after three weeks on the auction block could be purchased for that sum at land offices in Cincinnati, Chillicothe, Marietta, and Steubenville. The smallest amount purchasable was lowered from 640 acres to 320 acres. More important was a provision in the Act of 1800 which allowed a buyer to pay only one-quarter of the purchase price down and the remainder within four years. This credit feature, which made it possible to buy a 320 acre farm for only $160 in cash, did much to satisfy western demands. Speculators, other than those dealing in town sites, were virtually eliminated as settlers flocked to buy directly from the government in such large numbers that the phrase, "doing a land office business," was added to the American vocabulary. Congress was so impressed by the financial returns that in 1804 it further liberalized the land system by lowering the minimum amount purchasable to 160 acres.

Just as influential in speeding the advance of settlement were the governmental changes that followed Harrison's election to Congress, for that manifestation of Republication discontent with Federalist rule set in motion the chain of events leading to statehood for Ohio. St. Clair, seeing the way the wind blew, acted first, hoping to ward off the admission of a new state that would almost certainly support Jefferson. In February, 1800, he asked Harrison to introduce a bill dividing the Northwest into three territories, with boundaries running north from the mouths of the Scioto and Kentucky rivers. This, St. Clair reasoned, would not only split the Republican strength, which was concentrated in the Scioto Valley, but allow the strong Federalist organization in Marietta to dominate the region east of the river and his own Cincinnati machine to control the West. Moreover no one of the three territories would have the 60,000 inhabitants needed for statehood. No sooner had St. Clair shown his hand, however, than the Republicans leaped into action. The scheme they laid before Harrison called for two territories, divided by a line running north from the mouth of the great Miami River. This plan was as clever as that of the Federalists; it would keep the Scioto Valley Jeffersonians united, assure immediate statehood for the eastern territory they dominated, and probably shift the capital from Cincinnati to the centrally located Republican city of Chillicothe.

Harrison, when confronted with the two proposals, decided to support the second, although he realized the difficulty of pushing a Republican-sponsored bill through a Federalist Congress. His strenuous efforts were rewarded on May 7, 1800, when an act setting up two territories, separated by a line running from the mouth of the Kentucky to Ft. Recovery and then north to the Canadian boundary, finally passed. Harrison was rewarded by the governorship of the new Indiana Territory created in the West.

From that time on the movement for Ohio statehood was rapid, for St. Clair's obstructionist efforts made more enemies than friends. A relentless Republican campaign, inspired partly by a desire to oust the ill-tempered governor, reached a climax on April 30, 1802, when Congress passed an enabling act authorizing a convention to decide whether statehood was desirable. This met at Chillicothe in November, and after listening to an anti-Republican tirade from St. Clair, the delegates voted with only one dissenting voice for immediate admission into the Union. The constitution as adopted reflected both the southern background of most of the delegates and the liberal influence of the frontier. It was modeled after Tennessee's frame of government, but swept away all property qualifications for voting, vested more power in the legislature, and made the governor a figurehead who could hold office only two years and had no veto power. Even the state judges were to be elected by the legislature. The convention also agreed the new state would not tax public lands until five years after they were sold, if the United States in return would set aside one section in each township to support schools and donate 3 per cent of all land sales for road building. Congress accepted both the constitution and these provisions, and Ohio, the first state to be formed from the public domain, entered the Union.

Both the governmental changes and the liberal Land Act of 1800 stimulated the settlement of the Northwest. From New England, the Middle States and the South the immigrants came in ever-increasing numbers: southern Quakers fleeing before the advancing slave frontier; upcountry farmers from the Virginia or Carolina Piedmont driven westward by worn-out soils; pioneers from Kentucky and Pennsylvania drifting onward with the advancing settlements; New Englanders who moved as individuals or in whole villages, intact with pastors and school masters and deacons, to found at Granville and Worthington and other Ohio towns exact replicas of the quiet villages they left behind. Some bought from speculators who offered land in the United States and Virginia military reserves, or in the Refugee Tract set aside by Congress for Canadians who aided the American Revolution. More patronized the government land offices; 3,374,843 acres were sold in the Northwest in the first eleven years after the passage of the Act of 1800. Still others purchased from the Connecticut Land

Company or from the Firelands Company which was formed by the share-holders in the Fire Lands of the Western Reserve. By 1812 more than 250,000 people lived in Ohio, and the whole region north and west to the Greenville Treaty line was beginning to resemble an eastern state with passable roads, bustling cities, and a spreading blanket of cultivated fields.

So rapid was the influx into Ohio that some newcomers moved over into Indiana Territory, which increased its population under Harrison's able leadership until a legislature could be called in 1805. At the same time the northern portion was set aside as Michigan Territory, although that isolated region did not feel the impact of any considerable migration until after the War of 1812. More new settlers sought homes in the country west of the Wabash, where they clustered about the French villages of Kaskaskia and Cahokia, laid out primitive new outposts at Ft. Massac and Shawnee-town, or cleared the fertile lands of the American Bottom opposite St. Louis. The difficulty of administering those distant settlements from the Indiana territorial seat at Vincennes led Congress in 1809 to set up the separate Territory of Illinois, governed by Ninian Edwards of Kentucky. By 1812, when Illinois entered its second territorial stage with the election of a legislature, 13,000 persons were scattered through the region, while Indiana's population was 25,000. Both were in a primitive frontier stage when the outbreak of a new wilderness war brought the westward move-ment to a temporary close.

# CHAPTER XIII

# The West in the War of 1812

## 1812-1815

The issues that plunged the United States into its second war with England seemingly were of little interest to frontiersmen. Why should they grow wrathful about a distant death struggle between Britain and the newly risen colossus of the Continent, Napoleon? What matter to them that both warring powers confiscated American cargoes or that England's navy impressed British deserters from American ships? The Appalachian barrier protected them from Europe's raging storms and their self-sufficient economy made them immune to the Atlantic's trade rivalries. As loyal Jeffersonians, westerners could be expected to applaud their president's efforts to keep peace and to support his application of economic sanctions to both belligerents. As ardent nationalists they would certainly boil with indignation at each new attack on their country's shipping. But neither partisanship nor patriotism seemed sufficient to send the West along the road to war.

Yet frontier demands forced the War of 1812 on a reluctant East, frontier arms accounted for the few American victories, and frontier ambitions dictated the peace. The answer to this apparent paradox can be found in the practical problems facing the West in 1812. A serious depression engulfed the back country, an expansionist fever raged along the Canadian and Florida borders, fur traders were engaged in a losing struggle with intruding rivals, and an Indian war ravaged outlying settlements. The average westerner believed that England was responsible for all these troubles and that only a war with that power would bring security to the frontier.

An economic depression that shackled the West between 1808 and 1812 was the basic grievance. This was due to the unsound economy forced on

268

the Ohio Valley by its inadequate transportation system. The bulky farm goods produced there could be marketed only in New Orleans. Western farmers had to select their cargoes for export in the light of price information a month old, spend another month and a large sum of money reaching the market, and compete with dozens of other sellers who arrived at the same time. Often backwoodsmen who had braved snags and pirates in the tortuous journey down the Mississippi were so overawed by the bustling strangeness of teeming New Orleans or so afraid of contracting tropical fevers that they sold their cargoes hurriedly at ridiculously low prices. Only the fortunate few were able to sell at a profit under those conditions.

The West did not feel the full impact of its economic maladjustment until 1808, for until that time the influx of new immigrants not only absorbed agricultural surpluses but kept the frontier supplied with ready cash. Thus the depression coincided with England's blockade, and to frontiersmen the two events were intimately connected. So long as American ships reached Europe the Ohio Valley enjoyed prosperity; when Britain closed that market hard times followed. Prosperity would only return when the English fleet allowed the United States to trade with the Continent once more. Westerners, reasoning in that fashion, solidly supported the Embargo of 1807, objected strenuously when eastern pressure forced Congress to adopt the less stringent Non-Intercourse Act in 1809, and adopted a belligerent I-told-you-so attitude when hard times grew more acute in the next three years. By 1812 frontiersmen agreed that war was necessary to restore prosperity. "The true question," said one of their congressional representatives, ". . . is the right of exporting the productions of our soil and industry to foreign markets."

The impact of the depression on western belligerency was demonstrated by the correlation between the warlike demands and marketing facilities of different areas. The farmers of Vermont and northern New York, who carried their grain and potash to Montreal on rafts, not only opposed war but persisted in their trade after the Embargo made exports illegal. In western Pennsylvania and Virginia easy communication with the East kept the peace party in control until hostilities began. Only in the lower Ohio Valley, Kentucky, Tennessee, and portions of Mississippi Territory was sentiment solidly for war. There poverty-stricken frontiersmen, goaded into action by hard times and their inability to meet payments on government lands which they had contracted to buy, believed hostilities necessary to protect their homes as well as their country's honor.

Scarcely less important than the depression in developing a war-like spirit was the westerners' desire for expansion into Canada and Florida. That would not only provide frontiersmen with new opportunities for speculation and agriculture, but promised to help solve other distressing problems. The conquest of Spanish Florida would open new trade routes along the Alabama, Pearl, and Apalachicola rivers, thus easing hard times in the area south of the Ohio River. Expansion southward would also end chaotic conditions along the southern border, where renegades, runaway slaves, and lawless Indians took advantage of Spain's preoccupation at home to roam about unmolested. Western expansionists were equally anxious to add Canada to the United States. This would not only protect fur traders from unwanted competition and end a threatening Indian war, but would offer one possibility of forcing England to abandon her commercial decrees. The British, pioneers reasoned, would be glad to allow

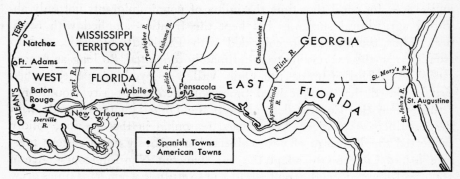

Expansion in Florida, 1803-1812

American ships to trade with Europe if the United States would return a portion of its conquered province.

The appetites of land-hungry frontiersmen who lived along the southern borderland were whetted by a series of events which had taken place in the decade preceding 1812. Chief among these were the gradual infiltration of Americans into West Florida and growing official interest in the region. Settlers, lured southward by Spain's liberal land policy, drifted into the region west of the Pearl River in such large numbers that by 1809 nine-tenths of the district's inhabitants were loyal to the United States. Their presence encouraged President James Madison to make a bold bid for the whole region. Taking advantage of Spain's absorption in the Napoleonic Wars, Madison suddenly advanced the theory that West Florida was part of the Louisiana Purchase. The Treaty of 1803, he pointed out, gave the United States Louisiana "with the same extent that it now has in the hands of Spain, and that it had when France possessed it." Actually those two provisions were irreconcilable; the eastern boundary of Louisiana under Spain was the Iberville River, while under France in 1763 the province extended on to the Perdido. Madison's determination to secure West Florida by claiming the latter boundary was an invitation to Americans there to take matters into their own hands.

They acted in September, 1810, when a group of revolutionists formed an army, seized the Spanish fort at Baton Rouge, and captured the governor. Three days later a convention of insurrectionists formally requested annexation by the United States. President Madison responded on October 27, 1810, when he issued a proclamation annexing the region between the Iberville and Perdido rivers. This order was carried into West Florida by Governor David Holmes of Mississippi Territory with a detachment of regular troops; no resistance was encountered and on December 10 the American flag was raised over Baton Rouge. Mobile, however, remained in Spanish hands, nor did the President dare use force to oust its strong garrison so long as the United States remained at peace. The promise of that rich prize, which controlled the trade of the Alabama Valley, helped to create a western demand for war with Spain and her English ally.

The war spirit was fanned in the Southeast by demands for East Florida, although there the situation was slightly different. The many Americans living in that province were not only well satisfied with Spanish rule but realized that annexation would stop the importation of slaves and end the smuggling of foreign imports across St. Mary's River—a trade that brought prosperity to northern Florida after passage of the Embargo Act. North of the border, however, desire for East Florida was strong, inspired partly by land hunger, partly by a desire to end turbulent border conditions, partly by the success of the West Florida revolution, and partly by the enthusiasm of an ardent expansionist, George Mathews, a former governor of Georgia who began building up a revolutionary party in the autumn of 1810. That winter Mathews laid his plans before President Madison with such success that when he returned to Georgia in the spring of 1811 he carried an official proclamation authorizing him to secure East Florida for the United States either by negotiation or, if any foreign power threatened to take possession, by force. With him too, in all probability, went the President's assurance of aid should Mathews succeed in stirring up a rebellion. Certainly the troops and warships that Madison dispatched to the Georgia border indicated a plan for armed intervention on the slightest excuse.

Mathews spent the rest of 1811 building up a revolutionary party among Americans in East Florida. By March, 1812, he was ready to act. With a following of two hundred volunteers he fell first on the Spanish town of Fernandina on Amelia Island, then started a march on St. Augustine, followed closely by American troops who refused to take part in actual fighting but occupied each conquered town. By mid-April the Florida capital was under siege and Mathews was dispatching urgent messages to Madison asking authority to use the regular army for its reduction. The President dared not go that far in face of Spain's vigorous protests and the criticism from the antiwar faction in Washington. Instead he dismissed Mathews, ordered the army back to the St. Mary's River, and placed control of border relations in the hands of the Georgia governor. News of this step aroused resentment throughout the southern borderland from Savannah to Nashville. Expansionists, with East Florida snatched from their grasp, believed war with England and Spain necessary before they could complete a conquest they considered rightfully theirs.

In the Northwest expansionist sentiment was stimulated by a desire for Canada. Neither land hunger nor hope for new trade routes was responsible; plentiful lands still awaited the westward marching pioneers while the St. Lawrence route to the sea, although closed to Americans, was too roundabout to be coveted. Instead conquered Canada promised two important benefits: it would end an irritating dispute over the fur trade, and check a serious Indian outbreak then well underway.

The trading dispute was more imagined than real. Since the drafting of Jay's Treaty Canadians roamed the country south of the border, operating from posts at Green Bay, Prairie du Chien, and other strategic spots. Zebulon M. Pike, an army officer sent to explore the Mississippi headwaters in 1805, found them everywhere in the northern woods, entirely unaware that they were on American soil. Their presence alarmed westerners who not only resented the drain of peltry northward, but believed Canadian trappers armed and incited the Indians. Those fears were not shared by the men most affected—the American traders. United States trade was dominated by John Jacob Astor's American Fur Company which, after a period of cutthroat competition with the Canadian North West Company, agreed in 1811 to divide the trade of the West with its rival. The American Fur Company, operating through a subsidiary corporation known as the South West Company, was given exclusive trading rights east of the Rockies, while the Canadian concern was awarded the far-western area. Astor was well satisfied with that arrangement and shied from a war that would upset his carefully worked out plans. Frontiersmen, however, knowing nothing of those international agreements, believed a conflict with England desirable if only to wipe out the clauses of Jay's Treaty that allowed Canadian traders to operate south of the border.

Far more important in sending the West along the road to war was the Indian unrest that boiled through the back country by 1812. Responsible for this were land-grabbing treaties, forced upon the natives by avaricious frontier officials. Thomas Jefferson, whose frontier background transcended

his well-known humanitarianism, was to blame for these. Under his administration Indian agents were instructed either to convert western tribesmen to
agriculture or move them to unwanted lands beyond the Mississippi. Those
harsh orders invited trouble in both South and North. The principal southern agent, a sincere friend of the red men named Benjamin Hawkins, made
an honest attempt to transform his charges into farmers, but when this
failed he had no choice but to begin absorbing their lands. Between 1802,
when the Creeks ceded territories east of the Oconee and north of the St.
Mary's rivers, and 1806, millions of acres in central Georgia, southern
Tennessee, and Mississippi Territory were taken from the Cherokee, Choctaw, and Chickasaw, leaving the Indians dissatisfied within their restricted
hunting grounds.

Conditions in the Northwest were even worse. Jefferson's agent there
was Governor William Henry Harrison of Indiana Territory whose avaricious desire for Indian lands was tempered by neither sympathy nor
humanitarianism. He showed his colors first in 1802 when he called representatives of the Kickapoo, Wea, and Delaware tribes together at Vincennes
to adjust disputes growing out of the Greenville Treaty line surveys across
Indiana. To their amazement Harrison not only proposed to define that
boundary, but demanded they cede the territory supposedly purchased
by the Wabash Land Company a quarter of a century before. When the
chiefs indignantly refused, the governor assured them the lands already
belonged to the United States and would be occupied by force unless they
backed down. This threat, together with bribes and cajolery, proved effective, although the cession was smaller than Harrison wished.

The Treaty of Vincennes set a pattern that was duplicated time and time
again over the next seven years. Conferences were called almost yearly,
some at the insistence of the Indians to protest illegal cessions, others by
Harrison to correct an alleged wrong done the red men. In each the result
was the same, for the natives were powerless before the governor's bribes and
threats of force. In 1803 he persuaded the weakened Kaskaskia to surrender
their flimsy title to the Illinois country by promising them aid in a
threatened war with the Potawatomi. A year later the Sauk and Foxes gave
up 15,000,000 acres south of the Wisconsin River in return for annuities
and the surrender of a tribesman accused of murdering a white man. When
native objections to these tactics reached Harrison's ears he called a conference at Grouseland, his newly completed mansion at Vincennes, then pitted
the assembled tribes against each other to extract another 2,000,000 acres
from them. Those treaties, together with smaller cessions from the Delawares and Piankashaw and a giant grant arranged by Governor William
Hull of Michigan territory, gave the United States control of eastern

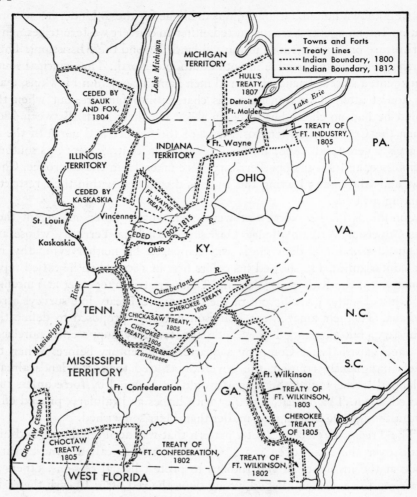

Indian Land Cessions, 1800–1812

Michigan, southern Indiana, and most of Illinois by the close of 1807.

Indian resentment at Harrison's land-grabbing activities would probably have subsided eventually had not two unforeseen events altered the situation. One was the advance of the powerful upper-Mississippi tribes—the Sioux and Chippewa—into the Wisconsin country in search of peltry. There they formed an impenetrable barrier; Great Lakes Indians, no longer able to move westward to new hunting grounds, must fight to maintain their homes. The other was the rise of two leaders for the red men: a Shawnee chieftain, Tecumseh, and his brother, The Prophet. Tecumseh saw that his people suffered because small tribes bowed to Harrison's pressure. If all natives were united in a confederation, with members pledged to make no land cessions without the consent of all, they could resist American demands. That was the message Tecumseh began spreading through the Northwest in 1805, aided by The Prophet, a one-eyed, epileptic medicine man believed by the natives to possess supernatural powers. Together they traveled among the tribes, preaching the need of unity and urging Indians to give up the foibles and firewater of the white man that they might gain strength to win back their lands.

Harrison first heard of their spreading influence in 1806, and although not greatly alarmed, decided to warn the natives against their newly risen prophet. "If he is really a prophet," the governor wrote the Delawares, "ask him to cause the sun to stand still, the moon to alter its course, the rivers to cease to flow." Unfortunately his letter fell into the hands of Canadian traders, who told The Prophet an eclipse of the sun would take place on June 16, 1806, and that he had only to forecast this to establish his reputation. From that time on the word of both Tecumseh and his brother was accepted as law by the Indians; had they not accepted Harrison's challenge to blot out the sun? As tribe after tribe aligned itself with their confederation, the two conspirators were encouraged to take two significant steps during 1808. One was to found the village of Prophetstown at the junction of the Wabash River and Tippecanoe Creek where they could extend their influence over Illinois and Wisconsin tribes. The other was to visit the British post, Ft. Malden, established on the Canadian shore of the Detroit River after Jay's Treaty had forced the evacuation of Detroit. Tecumseh was warmly received by the skilled agent in charge, Captain Mathew Elliott, for the English expected war to follow the controversy over impressment and welcomed a chance to build Indian alliances. At a great council Elliott urged the red men to unite and expressed concern over their loss of lands, but cautioned them not to strike the first blow. Tecumseh, however, was convinced that he could count on British aid.

In the meantime, Harrison, blissfully unaware of this forest intrigue, went ahead with plans for another land-grabbing treaty. The occasion was the creation of Illinois Territory in 1809; many of the earlier cessions were in what was now Illinois and the inhabitants of Vincennes professed alarm at a demarcation line only twenty miles from their doors. Runners spread word of the conference so widely that 1,100 natives were assembled at Fort Wayne when the governor lighted the council fire in September, 1809. Again one tribe was played off against another, particularly after Harrison found the Delawares and Potawatomi anxious to increase their annuities by selling some of their territories; again bribes and presents were dangled before wavering chiefs. In the end the Treaty of Fort Wayne transferred

3,000,000 acres of Indiana land to the United States, in return for $7,000 in cash and an annuity of $1,750.

That was the final blow. Since the turn of the century nearly 110,000,000 acres of choice hunting land had been wrung from natives by bribery, threats, and treaties with tribal fragments. Tecumseh, hurrying to Vincennes with a small group of followers, recited his people's grievances in the great council hall at Grouseland. The land, he told Harrison, was the common property of all the red men; no one tribe had a right to sell. Hence the Treaty of Fort Wayne was invalid, and any attempt to occupy the territory would be resisted. Harrison replied that the lands were acquired legally and would be settled by force if need be. The issue was now clear and war certain.

Attacks on outlying settlements began in the spring of 1810. By autumn, when 6,000 Indians visited Ft. Malden to plead for arms, a border war was in full swing. Major General Isaac Brock, governor general of Upper Canada, was thoroughly alarmed by these developments, fearing England would be blamed for inciting the natives, but his pleas for peace came too late. Young warriors, their fear of the dreaded "Long Knives" forgotten, passed war belts through the forests during the winter of 1810–11 or boasted about council fires that their new unity would drive the whites back to the sea. Tecumseh, however, worked frantically to restrain his over eager braves so long as Harrison made no attempt to occupy the Fort Wayne Treaty lands. In July, 1811, he visited Vincennes with news that he was on his way to enlist southern tribes in his confederacy, and to assure the governor that war could still be avoided if the disputed territory were left alone. When Harrison reiterated his determination to carry on surveys, the two men parted in an atmosphere of mutual distrust.

Tecumseh, with twenty-four Shawnee followers, continued south to meet the Creeks, Cherokee, and Choctaw in a conference on the bank of the Tallapoosa River. There, with his face painted the black war color, he urged his 5,000 listeners to attack. "Burn their dwellings," he shouted. "Destroy their stock. Slay their wives and children. The red people own the country. . . . War now. War forever. War upon the living. War upon the dead; dig their very corpses from the grave; our country must give no rest to a white man's bones." His savage plea won over the Creeks, but the Choctaw and Cherokee preferred to accept the humility of further land cessions rather than risk annihilation.

In the meantime hostilities began in the North. When Tecumseh left Vincennes on August 5, 1811, Harrison recognized a golden opportunity. A march on Prophetstown would goad young warriors, freed from their chief's restraining influence, into an attack that would allow him to ad-

minister a crushing defeat. With a thousand troops from Washington and
Kentucky he started northward along the Wabash on September 26, 1811.
Pausing on the way to erect two strong fortifications, Ft. Harrison at the
site of Terre Haute, and a log blockhouse at the mouth of the Vermillion
River, the army reached Prophetstown on November 6 and camped three-
quarters of a mile from the town, choosing a ten-acre triangle of level land

The Northwest in the War of 1812

bounded by a thick marsh, a creek, and heavy woods. That night the men
slept on their arms, while in the neighboring village The Prophet performed magic rites to render the enemy impotent and his own warriors invincible.

Just before daylight on the morning of November 7 the Indians moved
forward through a cold, slow-falling rain to surround the sleeping Ameri-

cans. Before they attacked, however, one of Harrison's guards detected a movement in the bushes and fired. With this the red men rushed pell-mell into the camp, sweeping past the outposts and into tents where soldiers were still asleep. No surprise could overawe the seasoned fighters Harrison had assembled. Within a few minutes they beat off the first attack, formed solid lines, and began pouring a murderous fire into the savages. The Indians, disheartened by resistance from soldiers supposedly made helpless by The Prophet's magic, first fell back, then broke completely when Harrison's cavalry charged upon them from two directions. The commander, unable to believe victory was his, kept his men erecting breastworks until November 8 when scouts brought back word that Prophetstown was deserted. The village was destroyed before the American army started back to Vincennes.

The Battle of Tippecanoe was no decisive victory. Harrison's men, who outnumbered the enemy by almost three hundred, held their ground, but their losses were as large as those of the Indians, each side counting thirty-eight killed and 150 wounded. Nor did the victory end the Indian menace in the West. Instead Tecumseh, on his return, sent his followers storming against American outposts with fire and tomahawk. Tippecanoe only scattered Prophetstown fanatics along the frontier to launch the Northwest on a serious Indian war. By the spring of 1812 settlers were fleeing from outlying cabins and fear was sweeping even the thickly settled regions of Ohio and Kentucky.

Hostilities, every westerner believed, could be laid directly at England's door. British agents lured the savages to Ft. Malden, supplied them with guns and ammunition, and drove them forth to murder American backwoodsmen! Harrison reflected the popular view when he wrote: "The whole of the Indians on this frontier have been completely armed and equipped from the British King's stores at Malden." The solution seemed equally simple. The United States must conquer Canada, wipe out Ft. Malden, and end forever the unholy alliance between redcoats and red men. The conquest of Canada in their eyes was no expansionist's dream, but a practical means of protecting their homes. Little wonder that western banquets drank toasts to the "starry flag of 1812" which would soon "float triumphant over the ramparts of Quebec," or that western congressmen echoed their section's belligerent attitude. "The conquest of Canada is in your power," Henry Clay, brilliant young representative from Kentucky, told his fellow legislators. "I trust I shall not be deemed presumptuous when I state that I verily believe that the militia of Kentucky are alone competent to place Montreal and Upper Canada at your feet." Others took up the cry; again and again Congress rang with their demands for war until one eastern representative declared in disgust: "We have heard but

one word—like the whip-poor-will, but an eternal montonous tone—Canada!
Canada! Canada!"

Those westerners—threatened by Indians, eager for Canada and Florida,
plagued by depression—were by 1810 thoroughly disgusted with Madison's
half-hearted efforts to force England's hand with economic pressure. In
the congressional elections of that year they chose a group of vigorous
young men who openly favored aggression. The "War Hawks" descended
on Washington when Congress met in November, 1811, seized on the even
division between North and South to wrest control of the House from conservatives, chose one of their number, Henry Clay, speaker, and raised
their voices in a resounding chorus for war. Clay used his position to pack
congressional committees with War Hawks, who flooded Congress with
reports favoring a larger army and navy and other warlike measures. While
delegates from commercial states protested in vain, western pressure wrung
a war message from the reluctant President. Congress responded on June 18,
1812, by declaring a state of war to exist between the United States and
England.

Seldom had a nation been so poorly prepared for a major conflict. Half a
dozen warships, an ill-trained army of 6,700 men led by two inept major
generals, Henry Dearborn and Thomas Pinckney, an overly cautious President, a people generally indifferent or, in the case of the New Englanders,
openly hostile to war—those were the assets on which the United States
relied to win victory from the world's foremost military power. Nor did
popular apathy dissolve when fighting began; an appeal for an $11,000,000
loan brought in only $6,000,000, while a call for volunteers to raise the
regular army to 35,000 men was so disappointing that from then on principal reliance was placed on state militia. Yet the optimistic westerners were
not discouraged. Canada was defended by only 4,500 troops and Florida
poorly guarded; both would surely fall to American arms before the year
was out.

Those dreams were rudely shattered. Within a few months after fighting
began even the cocksure Ohio frontiersmen found themselves on the defensive rather than engaged in a spectacular conquest of Canada. The first
blow fell when one of their own outposts, Ft. Mackinac, was surprised by
a superior British force from nearby St. Joseph Island on July 17, 1812,
and forced to surrender without a shot being fired. This disappointment was
forgotten amidst plans for an invasion of Canada which would not only
recapture Ft. Mackinac but reduce Ft. Malden as well. Westerners could
not know that their very enthusiasm for the war ruined their nation's
chance for victory. Proper American strategy called for a drive against
Montreal through the Champlain Valley, cutting Canada in two, stopping

the flow of British supplies to western Indians, and forcing Upper Canada to surrender. Such a campaign was impossible. Only the West would provide men and materials needed for a Canadian invasion, and the West demanded the immediate capture of Ft. Malden. Hence American strategists decided to direct their principal attack against that distant fortification.

General William Hull, the sixty-year-old governor of Michigan Territory named commander of the western army, realized the hopelessness of his task. His force, he pointed out, must be supplied from Ohio. Food, ammunition, and other essentials could be shipped to Detroit either across Lake Erie or along the banks of the Detroit River. Neither route could be used; English gunboats controlling the lake menaced shore roads, while land transportation was made additionally difficult by the Black Swamp, a tangled morass along the Maumee River lying squarely across the American path. Ft. Malden could never be taken, Hull insisted, until the United States controlled Lake Erie, but like every good soldier he obeyed his orders. Raising 2,000 men, he marched rapidly to Detroit which was reached on July 7, 1812. After a brief pause, the army crossed the Detroit River to Canadian soil where the overly cautious Hull hesitated before launching his attack. General Isaac Brock, British commander in Upper Canada, seized on this opportunity. A small British force was dispatched by water to capture the little village of Brownstown which lay squarely athwart American supply lines on the lower Detroit River. Hull was terrified. When an attempt to dislodge the Brownstown captors failed, he fell back to Detroit, then, as his supplies dwindled, sent one-quarter of his men southward to by-pass his troublesome enemies and reopen communication lines.

That was the moment chosen by General Brock for his attack. On August 16 the entire English army crossed the Detroit River to storm the town's defenses. Hull, his supplies dwindling and his force weakened, had no choice but surrender. The first Canadian invasion resulted not only in defeat but the loss of Detroit to the enemy! Nor did disasters end there, for just as Hull surrendered, another western outpost, Ft. Dearborn, fell. The garrison of that fort, marching to join the defenders of Detroit, was ambushed by Indians amidst the sand dunes of lower Lake Michigan; twenty-six men were killed outright and nine others tortured to death in the "Dearborn Massacre."

Even now the West was not discouraged. The energetic William Henry Harrison, who succeeded Hull in command, had no difficulty raising troops for a fall attack on Canada. Before the Americans could march, they found themselves, to their surprise, on the defensive as British and Indian raiding parties swept down from Detroit against the Ohio forts. Harrison was forced to spend the summer beating off attacks on Ft. Wayne and Ft. Harrison rather than leading a triumphant army northward. When he was finally ready to march in October, 1812, the Black Swamp was impassable and he set his men building military roads across its treacherous surface. Thus ended the glorious dreams of the expansionists in that winter of 1812-13, with their army grubbing its way through the mud of an Ohio swamp and both Canada and three of their own forts in British hands.

Nor did the 1812 campaigns on the New York frontier succeed any better. Two invasions of Canada were planned for that autumn, one across the Niagara River, the other along Lake Champlain. The former was launched on October 18, 1812, when the commander of the state militia at Ft. Niagara threw 6,000 men across the river to capture the heights surrounding the strong British fort of Queenston. Reinforcements needed to turn this initial triumph into a victory never arrived, for Brigadier General Alexander Smyth, commander of the regular army at Niagara, refused to let his men cross the river, insisting that a militia action was no concern of his. As more British troops were rushed into action the outnumbered militiamen fell back slowly until they reached the rushing waters of the Niagara where they surrendered. Petty jealousies and weak discipline cost the United States an army. Equally disheartening was the American failure at Lake Champlain. There General Henry Dearborn drilled 5,000 troops until mid-November, then marched northward. At the Canadian boundary the militia refused to go on, insisting they were to fight only in their own state. Dearborn, who was old and weak, bowed to the mutineers and led his men back to winter quarters at Plattsburg. He alone among the American commanders saved his army, but only by keeping it well away from the enemy.

Events in the southern theater during the first year of war were slightly more favorable. When hostilities began only Mobile and Pensacola remained in Spanish hands in West Florida, while in East Florida the American army of occupation, commanded by Governor D. B. Mitchell of Georgia, controlled the country west of the St. John's River and held St. Augustine in a state of siege. Every expansionist was certain that a formal declaration of war would be followed by a rapid conquest of the whole region by the regular army. Spain, however, refused to play into their hands, for her officials, recognizing their country's weakness, steadfastly refused to abandon their neutrality. President Madison, sorely disappointed, was forced to leave the situation to Governor Mitchell and his small army of "patriots." Even they fared badly after St. Augustine officials encouraged the Florida Indians to take to the war path. So many American soldiers scurried off to protect their homes that the remainder, fearing an attack on their thin supply lines, gave up the siege of St. Augustine and fell back to Georgia soil. In November, 1813, disappointed expansionists in that state's legislature grumblingly informed Congress that unless troops were sent against East Florida they would take matters into their own hands.

President Madison, certain that this show of feeling would persuade Congress to authorize an attack on Spanish possessions, hurried word to Andrew Jackson, commander of the Tennessee militia, to raise 1,500 men for a march on Mobile, Pensacola, and St. Augustine as soon as congressional approval was secured. With preparations made, the President in January, 1813, asked Congress for authority to annex both Floridas, charging that negotiations with Spain had broken down and that England or France would occupy the strategic territories if the United States did not. His proposal was decisively defeated on February 2, 1813, by a combination of northern and Federalist votes, leaving Madison no choice but to dismiss Jackson's army. Southern expansionists were only partly placated when Congress did authorize the occupation of Mobile and West Florida, a move carried out by General James Wilkinson during the next months.

Disheartening as were these events, the Americans were destined to still more trying days before they tasted the sweets of victory. The winter of 1812-13 in the Northwest was spent preparing for a march across the ice to Ft. Malden. That expedition was abandoned when a thousand of Harrison's men, disregarding his orders, struck out on their own to capture Frenchtown, a little settlement on the Raisin River. There they were surprised by a war party of British and Indians on the morning of January 22, 1813. The River Raisin Massacre not only cost the Americans 250 dead and 500 prisoners, but ended all hope of a Canadian invasion. Instead Harrison devoted himself to strengthening Ohio's defenses, knowing the jubilant British could now count on aid from most of the western Indians. Nor was he mistaken. While his men labored on the stout walls and blockhouses of a well-located new fort, Ft. Meigs, skilled English agents scoured the forests between Georgian Bay and the Mississippi for native recruits. By spring a thousand warriors were camped about Ft. Malden, waiting the signal to attack from Colonel Henry Proctor, who succeeded to the western command when General Isaac Brock was killed at the Battle of Queenston.

This came in mid-April, 1813, when Proctor led his thousand regulars and an equal number of Indians southward to lay siege to Ft. Meigs. From April 28 to May 7 British batteries hammered at the American works, but Harrison's defenses were so well planned that the cannon balls buried themselves harmlessly in earthen barricades protecting the fort's wooden walls. When 350 frontiersmen braved enemy fire on May 6 to spike the English guns, the attackers lost heart; the next day they silently dismantled their cannon and vanished into the forest. Three months later they were back again, this time with 1,400 Indians recently arrived from the Wisconsin country. Harrison, sure that Ft. Meigs could care for itself, left its defense to subordinates while he moved his main force to the Sandusky River country. Two forts commanded that valley: Ft. Stephenson on the lower river and Ft. Seneca several miles to the south. Deciding the former was too weak to withstand a serious attack, Harrison concentrated his men at Ft. Seneca, leaving only 150 militia under a twenty-one-year-old stripling, Major George Croghan, at Ft. Stephenson. The American commander diagnosed the situation correctly; on July 29, 1813, the British abandoned their siege of Ft. Meigs to descend on the Sandusky Valley, marching first against the poorly defended lower fort. Major Croghan, instead of burning the palisade and retreating, decided to make a stand. Loading his one cannon with grapeshot and arranging his handful of followers carefully about it, he waited until the enemy rushed through a breach in the walls, then raked them with a deadly fire from pointblank range. Those not killed broke for the woods where they encountered a strong force under Harrison that had started north at the sound of gunfire. Within a few hours the thoroughly beaten attackers were slinking back toward Ft. Malden, their spirits broken by two failures to penetrate American defenses.

The victory gave Harrison a chance to turn to a task more to his liking: a new attack on Detroit and Ft. Malden. Preparations were already under way. Washington officials, finally realizing that control of Lake Erie was essential to a successful western campaign, had entrusted twenty-seven-year-old Oliver Hazard Perry with the task of building a fleet strong enough to defeat the British gunboats. Perry's sturdy vessels, painstakingly built at Erie of materials transported from the East by wagon train, sailed westward on August 12, 1813, in search of the British force, which was anchored under the guns of Ft. Malden. Not daring to engage the enemy amidst the treacherous currents of the lower Detroit River, the Americans waited at Put-in-Bay Harbor on South Bass Island, knowing the enemy would have to attack or lose control of Lake Erie by default. On September 10, 1813, the two fleets met in a furious three-hour engagement that ended in complete victory for the superior American force. Harrison heard the good news a day later when a small boat rowed furiously up the Sandusky River bearing an officer who delivered Perry's famous message scribbled on the back of an old envelope: "We have met the enemy and they are ours."

The imposing task of ferrying the whole United States army—recently augmented by the arrival of 3,500 Kentucky militia—to the Canadian shore began at once, and on the afternoon of September 27 a landing was made three miles below Ft. Malden. There word reached Harrison that the British, acting on the sound assumption that it was better to lose a province than an army, had started east along the Thames River. The pursuit began at once, with 3,000 picked men leading the way and supplies following on river boats—an advantage that allowed the Americans to gain rapidly on the slow-moving enemy. On October 5, when only a few miles separated the two armies, General Proctor decided to make a stand. The battle ground selected was a level plain between the Thames River and a dense swamp. There Proctor posted his scanty force: four hundred regulars spread between the swamp and river in two thin lines, six hundred Indians under Tecumseh scattered through the swamp to pour fire upon the attackers.

These elaborate preparations were in vain. At 2:30 on that quiet afternoon Harrison ordered a charge. His Kentucky cavalrymen, yelling like demons, swept through the flimsy British lines, slaughtering as they went, while the infantry plunged into the swamp after the outnumbered Indians. A few minutes of furious fighting and all was over; the entire English force was either killed or captured, Tecumseh dead, and Proctor fleeing toward the neighboring village of Moravian Town. The Battle of the Thames was one of the decisive victories of the War of 1812, for it broke Indian power in the Ohio and Wabash country, scattered Tecumseh's confederation, and convinced the red men they could not depend on their English allies. To make matters even worse from the Indian point of view a second American army, made up of 1400 Illinois and Missouri militia and commanded by General Benjamin Howard, at the same time spread a path of destruction through Illinois. By the winter of 1813 all the Northwest was in American hands, with the exception of a few British-held posts.

On other fronts the United States enjoyed less success during 1813. Minor skirmishing along the New York frontier accomplished nothing. In the Southwest a new British ally, the Creek tribe, took to the warpath during the spring, and by midsummer frontiersmen in the whole southern borderland were scurrying into hastily built blockhouses for protection. One rude fortification, built by Samuel Mims on the lower Alabama River, held 553 persons on August 30, 1813, when a horde of yelling savages swarmed through the gates before the surprised defenders could protect themselves. The Ft. Mims Massacre not only brought home the seriousness of the Creek War, but forced the southern states into action.

Although the two small armies that marched west from Georgia accomplished little, a third column from Tennessee was more successful. This was commanded by Andrew Jackson and composed of 5,000 militiamen who assembled at Fayetteville on October 4, 1813. Marching rapidly south to save Huntsville from a rumored attack, the Tennesseans moved into the heart of the Creek country, pausing only to construct a well-

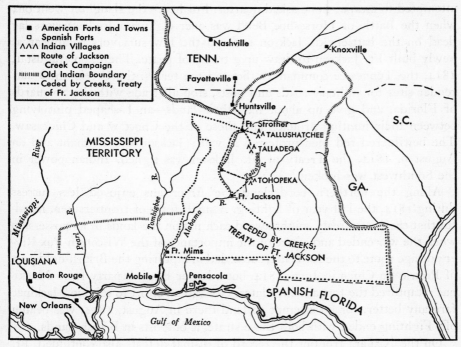

The Southwest in the War of 1812

guarded supply road between the Tennessee and Coosa rivers. From the fort at the southern end of that portage route, Ft. Strother, Jackson sent a series of raiding parties to destroy Creek villages; Tallushatchee was wiped out with its two hundred defenders and Talladega subdued with three hundred more. By that time winter ended operations except for one unsuccessful January raid on the Creek town of Tohopeka at Horse Shoe Bend on the Tallapoosa River. Even that defeat reacted in Jackson's favor, as the Indians, convinced this village was impregnable, flocked there in large numbers during the next months. The Americans had only to wait until spring to strike a decisive blow at the whole Creek tribe.

By March 27, 1814, 3,000 troops were camped before Tohopeka where a thousand braves waited them behind a zigzag log barricade that protected a hundred-acre peninsula. Jackson turned his cannon against the fortification at once, but before his six-pounders opened a breach, a number of friendly Indians swam the Tallapoosa River to attack the defenders from the rear. Instantly all was confusion within the village. Jackson seized the opportunity to order a charge which sent his shouting infantry swarming over the barricade and into the midst of the outnumbered Indians. None attempted to escape; none asked quarter. For hours the slaughter went on; when the Battle of Horseshoe Bend was over eight hundred warriors lay dead on the battlefield. Jackson ordered the few survivors to appear at newly built Ft. Jackson to draw up a treaty of peace. There, on August 1, 1814, the Tennessee commander dictated the terms: the Creeks must surrender sites for military roads and posts, stop all trade with the Spaniards of Florida, and give up about half their lands—an L-shaped plot lying between their hunting grounds and those of the Choctaw and Chickasaw. The bewildered red men protested in vain; Jackson was adamant and on August 9, 1814, the Treaty of Ft. Jackson was signed. Indian power in the Southwest was broken.

Along the northern borderland the Americans enjoyed less success during 1814, the last year of fighting. A small force of frontiersmen, mindful that the peace treaty might award each nation the lands in its possession when the war ended and aware of the importance of the Wisconsin-Fox River portage route to the fur trade, succeeded in capturing the British-held post of Prairie du Chien in June, 1814, but a larger English party from Mackinac recaptured the fort a month later. Nor did an effort to subdue Mackinac fare any better, for an attempt to land there in August, 1814, was beaten off. Fighting ended with both those strategic outposts in British hands.

On the Niagara frontier the record of dismal defeats also continued. Ft. George, a Canadian outpost captured by a United States naval force early in 1813, was recaptured by the English in December of that year. From that time on they harried Americans constantly; expeditions that crossed on the Niagara River during the winter of 1813-14 destroyed Ft. Niagara, burned Buffalo, and ravaged the countryside. Not until March, 1814, when two able generals, George Izard and Jacob Brown, replaced inefficient commanders did the tide turn. After whipping an army into shape, Brown led his men across the river in July to best British defenders at the Battles of Chippewa and Lundy's Lane before returning to American soil. The summer of skirmishing accomplished little but did prevent an invasion of New York at that point.

Fighting on the Lake Champlain frontier was more serious, as that was the route chosen by British authorities for the final attack on the United States that would end the war. There they concentrated the seasoned veterans released for American service by Napoleon's defeat; by September 18,000 trained troops stood poised at the northern end of Lake Champlain, waiting the signal to advance. Opposing them at Plattsburg were 3,300 American regulars and militiamen commanded by General George Izard. In this apparently hopeless situation only one factor favored the United States. The British must gain naval control of Lake Champlain before they could attack, and a sufficiently powerful American fleet might turn the scales toward victory. All that summer of 1814 skilled shipbuilders labored at the southern lake ports, while in the north English workers fashioned vessels for their commanders. By September 3 the Canadian general, Sir George Prevost, was ready. His fleet of sixteen vessels and his army, reduced to 11,000 men when no more appeared necessary, started south.

At Plattsburg fourteen American gunboats waited them. Their brilliant young commander, Captain Thomas Macdonough, knowing he was outnumbered and must make every shot tell, prepared for the onslaught by providing his anchored vessels with devices that allowed them to swing about quickly. This proved the deciding factor. When the English fleet sailed into Plattsburg Harbor Macdonough's gunboats were able to exchange broadside for broadside, then as British fire weakened, warp about to bring freshly loaded cannon to bear. A few hours of this crippled the strongest enemy ships and forced the remainder to surrender. The Battle of Lake Champlain was decisive, for when Prevost heard of the defeat he turned his army back toward Canada. New York, and perhaps the whole nation, was saved by a young commander's strategy.

Only one more battle remained to be fought, and that in the Southwest. There the English, hoping to secure control of strategic ports against a possible peace treaty that would award spoils to the victors, began an offensive in August, 1814, by landing at Pensacola as a prelude to attacking Mobile. Andrew Jackson, whose triumph at Horse Shoe Bend had been rewarded by a generalship in the regular army, managed to beat off the assault on Mobile but the worst was yet to come. While those maneuvers absorbed American attention a British expedition of fifty ships bearing 10,000 troops set out from Jamaica for New Orleans. News of this new threat sent Jackson west at the head of 12,000 Tennessee volunteers. On December 1, 1814, he began preparing the city for attack, building forts along the lower river and at the entrance to Lake Ponchartrain, throwing up earthworks along the Chef Menteur Road that offered the one land approach, and clogging the bayous along Lake Borgne with fallen trees.

Unfortunately the English hit upon the one flaw in those defenses. On December 22 a landing party found the Bayou Bienvenue was not yet blocked; by noon of the next day several thousand redcoats were drawn up below the city. Jackson, although caught napping, threw the enemy into confusion by an immediate attack, then used the time gained to build earthworks between the British and New Orleans. That delay cost the English leader, Sir Edward Pakenham, the battle, for by the time he turned to the assault the Americans were too well entrenched to be dislodged. A frontal attack failed first, then a heavy bombardment that scarcely marred Jackson's stout defenses. Finally on January 7, 1815, Pakenham adopted the one device that might have succeeded: he sent part of his army across the Mississippi to turn captured American batteries against Jackson's earthworks while his own infantry stormed forward. A sudden fall in the river that night delayed the troops assigned the task of crossing the Mississippi; at the time agreed on for attack on the morning of January 8 they were still far below the American batteries. Pakenham, unaware of this, ordered his men to charge. Wave after wave swept forward, to be met with the steady fire of the frontiersmen. By nightfall Pakenham and 2,000 of his men lay dead on the battlefield, while Jackson had lost only six men. A few days later the British force straggled back to its ships. The War of 1812 was over, Jackson the new hero of the West.

The Battle of New Orleans did not affect the outcome, for two weeks before Jackson's victory the peace treaty had been signed. Negotiations were begun at Ghent in August, 1814, just as American fortunes were at their lowest ebb; Mackinac, Niagara, and eastern Maine were in British hands, the capitol and White House recently burned, and two powerful English armies preparing to invade the United States through Lake Champlain and New Orleans. From this debacle of wrecked hopes the able American commissioners—John Quincy Adams, Albert Gallatin, Henry Clay, James A. Bayard and Jonathan Russell—must gain what concessions they could. Little wonder that few informed men on either side of the Atlantic expected them to emerge with one, let alone both, of their avowed objectives: a specific English agreement to respect American maritime rights in the future, and the abrogation of the sections of Jay's Treaty which gave Canadian traders the right to operate south of the border. The victorious British would scarcely back down on those two points.

Preliminary negotiations convinced the American agents they had no hope of securing both their demands and that peace could only be secured if they gave ground on one. This one, they saw, must concern neutral rights, partly because the English would never compromise on that issue, partly because frontiersmen would rebel against a treaty unfavorable to their section. Hence they informed the British negotiators that the United States would accept a treaty that did not mention neutral rights—a tacit admission that England's stand was accepted—if the British would agree to their contentions on the West. For a time negotiations hung in the balance as commissioners deliberated this offer, but time was on the side of the Americans. Word that Prevost's Lake Champlain expedition had failed helped convince the English; so did mounting pressure for peace from taxpayers tired of twenty years of war, and the realization that the United States could never be conquered until Lake Erie and Lake Champlain were controlled. England did not dare begin that slow and expensive task when her crumbling European alliances made a new continental war seem possible. Hence her agents agreed to back down in their western demands for a barrier state, a renewal of Jay's Treaty, and a boundary revision giving Mackinac, Prairie du Chien, and the head of the Mississippi River to Canada. With those mutual concessions, the Treaty of Ghent was signed on December 24, 1814.

Its provisions were far from happy for the United States: a restoration of all territorial conquests by both nations, and a tacit recognition, by omission, that the United States accepted England's provisions concerning neutral rights, while Britain gave up all claims to trade south of the Canadian border. Only one section referred to the Indians and this, although promising them all rights enjoyed in 1811, was so vaguely worded that it meant little. Technically the United States lost the war, as none of the objectives for which it fought was attained. Actually the peace spelled victory, particularly for the West. By signing a treaty of *status quo ante bellum* the British signified their intention of abandoning the Indians to land-hungry frontiersmen. No longer could the red men count on aid from Canadian trappers, or rally behind a prophet who promised them English aid. The way was cleared for a new era of westward expansion that would carry the frontier to the Mississippi.

# CHAPTER XIV

# Settling the Lake Plains

## 1815-1850

When the Treaty of Ghent rang down the curtain on the War of 1812 the settled portions of the United States comprised a giant triangle, its base the Atlantic seaboard and its apex the junction of the Ohio and Mississippi rivers. To the north and south lay two physiographic provinces, the Lake Plains and Gulf Plains, whose towering forests and rolling prairies were unsullied by the cabin homes of pioneers. In the next quarter century those two areas were inundated by a surging tide of westward-moving frontiersmen who swept forward in the greatest population movement the nation had known. By 1850 the peopling of the eastern half of the continent was completed.

Scarcely was the last shot fired when western pressure forced the federal government to open the Lake Plains to pioneers. The first step was to pacify the Indians who, sullen and restless after a war that cost them dearly, seemed ready to take to the warpath at any moment. Three peace commissioners named by President Madison met 2,000 tribesmen at the little village of Portage des Sioux in July, 1815. One by one the grievances of various tribes were settled until by September, when the last warrior departed satisfied, the frontier was technically at peace once more. Yet the Treaties of Portage des Sioux did not completely end the threat of war, for delegates from the Fox and Sauk tribes had stalked angrily from the conference grounds after refusing the terms offered them, and the Kickapoo and Winnebago were left discontented. Clearly something more than presents, promises, and honeyed words were needed to protect the advancing settlements.

This realization led the national government to launch a fort-building program designed to throw a protecting screen between Indians and pioneers. Work went on rapidly through 1816 and 1817; older outposts at Ft. Wayne and Ft. Harrison in Indiana were rebuilt, Ft. Shelby in Detroit and Fts. Gratiot and Mackinac along the eastern edge of Michigan were garrisoned, and Fts. Dearborn and Clark were re-established to protect the Illinois settlements. More important were new fortifications in the Mississippi and Wisconsin country. Ft. Edward in western Illinois, Ft. Armstrong on Rock Island, Ft. Crawford at Prairie du Chien, and Ft. Howard near the mouth of the Fox River, all built in 1816, together guarded a four-hundred-mile strip of back country between Lake Michigan and the warlike northwestern tribes. Each fort consisted of a stoutly built stone or timber palisade, with blockhouses at each corner and barracks within to house a hundred or more troops. For the next years these outposts stood guard over the Indians, ready to quell rebellious warriors or nip incipient uprisings in the bud. As their garrisons restored order to the hinterland the federal government extended its control over more and more tribes; Ft. Snelling on the upper Mississippi, Ft. Saginaw in Michigan, and Ft. Brady at Sault Ste. Marie, all erected between 1819 and 1822, testified to the expanding sphere of American influence.

While establishing those garrisoned outposts, the United States sought to break the traditional British-Indian alliance by expelling Canadian traders from native villages. The need for action was demonstrated in 1817 when a military expedition under Major Stephen Long reported the upper Mississippi country swarming with Montreal *voyageurs* and the tribes completely loyal to England. Authorities at Washington were wise enough to see that the intruders could never be driven out, despite the provisions of the Treaty of Ghent, and that their influence could best be nullified by persuading the natives to trade with American agents. With this in mind government trading factories, which offered goods at cost, were established throughout the Northwest in the years after the war. They proved effective, but the very success of the factories spelled their doom. Private trading companies objected so strenuously to government competition that Congress abandoned the system in 1822. By that time, however, British influence in the West was dead, and the natives at the mercy of the American government.

The postwar Indian policy had only one objective: to bring the tribes so completely under American control that they could be pushed from their ancestral lands. This ambition was as old as English settlement in the New World, but the methods were new. Instead of bribing a few weak chiefs into signing a land-grabbing treaty, the commissioners named to deal with the northwestern Indians acted with brutal directness. The pattern was set in September, 1817, when representatives of the half-dozen tribes still owning lands in Ohio were called together, informed they must cede their claims in return for annuities and presents, and forced to sign a treaty of cession. For the next four years that ruthless process went on, with tribe after tribe surrendering its territories and agreeing to live within the confines of a reservation or move to the un-

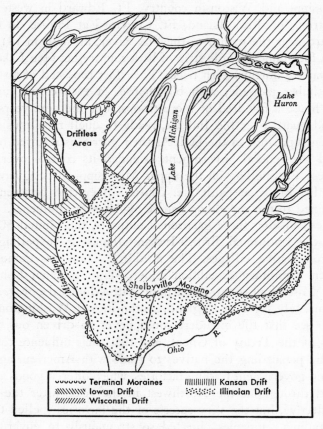

Glaciation in the Northwest

wanted wilderness beyond the Mississippi. Powerless without the help of their British allies, the natives had no choice but to give way. By the end of 1821 nearly all of Indiana, Illinois, and Michigan were in American hands, ready to receive westward-moving pioneers.

Nor were the settlers long in coming. Both the attractiveness of the Lake Plains country and disturbed conditions in the East combined to drive the frontier rapidly westward. Certainly the Northwest seemed an agricultural haven to farmers from the hilly East. The whole region had at one period in geological history lain beneath the ocean, gradually lifting to form a level lowland, comparable to the coastal plains of Virginia and the Carolinas. Over this, in the later Pleistocene period, moved the great glaciers that pushed slowly downward from the polar ice cap, grinding rocks into fertile soil, leveling the land, and leaving rugged moraines to mark their temporary or permanent stopping places. Two of those ice sheets played a particularly prominent role in shaping the surface features of the Lake Plains. One, the Illinoian Drift, covered the area north of the Ohio River with a deep layer of rock waste and glacial debris. The other, the Wisconsin Drift, moved southward over that barren mass at a later time, smoothing off hills and laying down a deep layer of soil rich in the elements needed for agriculture. This beneficial glacier did not cover the whole Northwest; its extreme southern advance was marked by the Shelbyville Moraine which ran through central Illinois and across Indiana and Ohio. North of that line the gently rolling countryside was rich and good, with loam soils enriched by humus and lightened by sand; to the south jagged hills and a stubborn clay soil discouraged farming. Early settlers were quick to notice the difference; they referred to the rough southern country as "Egypt" and to the bountiful northern lands as "God's Country," where the yield was a third more and the price of land almost twice as high as in the south.

Important as were these soil differences in shaping the course of settlement, the first pioneers were influenced even more by the region's natural vegetation. This, in their minds, divided the countryside into three areas of varying desirability. One was the densely wooded section of southern Illinois and Indiana where a thick forest of hardwoods covered the land. Particularly prized were the silt-filled river bottoms, but even the hilly portions were eagerly sought after, for the plentiful timber promised profitable farming to westerners who judged the richness of land by the density of its forests. The American Bottom, a seven-mile-wide plain stretching for forty miles along the Mississippi just north of the Kaskaskia River, was an especially choice spot that early attracted settlers.

Beyond the wilderness area lay a broad belt in central Indiana, Illinois, and southern Michigan where forests alternated with treeless prairies. In Michigan the open stretches resembled islands in a timbered sea. Some, known as Oak Openings, were sprinkled with tall oaks growing so far apart that a wagon could drive between them and were as free of underbrush as an English park. Others, the Prairie Rondes, were tiny prairies formed on beds of extinct glacial lakes where rich soil fostered such a luxurious growth of grass that trees could not take root. In western Indiana and central Illinois grasslands predominated, formed in some forgotten day by Indians who destroyed the forest with underbrush fires designed to drive game to a central point. The rolling prairies stretched for miles, broken only by occasional clumps of trees on some humid spot, or by sentinel-like rows of scrub growth along a meandering stream. Particularly impressive was the Grand Prairie of central Illinois. No traveler failed to be impressed by the magnitude of that vast plain, stretching away as far as eye could see, and covered with a six-foot growth of grass that billowed gently in the wind or, in the spring, dazzled onlookers with its color-splashed carpet of wildflowers. Yet the prairie country was shunned by the first settlers, whose frontier technique was adjusted to a wooded country. The grasslands were avoided until the pressure of increasing population forced pioneers to adapt to this newer environment. Even less hospitable was the third vegetation area of the Lake Plains, the belt of pine forests and conifers that grew in the sandy soil of northern Michigan and Wisconsin.

The wooded stretches of southern Indiana and Illinois, however, offered both adequate soil and familiar vegetation, and it was toward that area homeseekers turned just after the War of 1812. During this first period of Lake Plains settlement, between 1815 and 1830, immigrants came largely from the southern uplands. Disturbed social conditions there hurried them westward. Many were seasoned pioneers from Kentucky and Tennessee who, having been held back by a generation of Indian warfare, now resumed their advance. More were small farmers driven from their southern homes by the rapid extension of the plantation system, which engulfed the western Carolinas, Georgia, and eastern Tennessee during the postwar years. Some from those regions sought homes in the Northwest because their dislike of slavery made life amidst bonded labor unpleasant, others because the aristocratic social distinctions inherent in the plantation system were distasteful to their democratic instincts, and still more simply because their lands were absorbed by richer plantation owners. All these forces, operating in the fifteen years after the war, drove thousands of southerners across the Ohio.

They came in swarms. Some, from the back country of Virginia and Maryland, trekked westward along the National Road, a broad paved highway built across the mountains by the federal government. By 1818 this important route was opened as far as Wheeling where water transportation on the Ohio River was available; in 1833 its extension reached Columbus, Ohio. Others crowded along the crude roads built by southern states: the trail from Richmond to the Kanawha River, the pathways that utilized Ward's and Saluda gaps through the Blue Ridge to reach the western waterways, and especially the old Wilderness Road across Kentucky to

Louisville, Cincinnati, and Maysville. From the embarkation points on the
Ohio—Louisville and Shawneetown—they made their way northward
along a network of territorial roads built between 1817 and 1822: to
Lafayette and Vincennes in Indiana, to the Mississippi towns of Kaskaskia,
Cahokia, St. Louis, and Alton, or to the farming lands bordering those
forest trails. The roads were only crudely cut slashes through dense wilderness, dotted with stumps and interspersed with bottomless mudholes, but

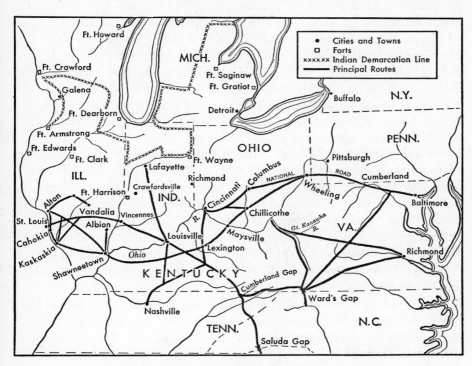

Settlement of the Lake Plains, 1815-1830

they did guide immigrants to their chosen destinations while tavern keepers
along the way offered conveniences that helped speed the westward
advance.

Over those rough trails came the settlers, bringing their few household
belongings in Conestoga wagons or hand carts, and driving their hogs and
cattle before them. Year after year the migration went on. "Old America
seems to be breaking up and moving westward," wrote one traveler on the
National Road in 1817. "We are seldom out of sight, as we travel on this
grand track, towards the Ohio, of family groups before and behind us."
Another, watching the steady procession of immigrant-laden flatboats down

the Ohio, observed: "The numerous companies of immigrants who flock to this country, might appear, to those who have not witnessed them, almost incredible. But there is scarcely a day . . . but that there is a greater or less number of boats to be seen floating down its gentle current, to some place of destination."

The mecca of the first comers was the American Bottom and other river lowlands of Indiana and Illinois; after 1818 when these spots were filled, settlement spilled over into the uplands lying between the valleys. By that time land sales, at Vincennes and Brockville, which had handled most of the public domain sold in Indiana, were declining as business shifted to the Crawfordsville office where interior lands were obtained. In Illinois half a million acres yearly passed into private hands. Not until 1830 did migration from the South diminish, and by that time the wooded hill-country of southern Indiana and Illinois was filled. Most newcomers found homes below a line—soon followed by the National Road—from Richmond, Indiana, through Indianapolis and Vandalia to St. Louis, although towns along the upper Wabash between Lafayette and Ft. Wayne testified to the attractiveness of the river lands. In Illinois the strip of lowlands bordering the Mississippi to a point well beyond the Illinois River was occupied, largely by veterans of the War of 1812 who were given bounty lands there. Nearly all pioneers avoided the prairies, although a group of several hundred English immigrants under a wealthy farmer, Morris Birkbeck, who arrived in 1818 without the prejudices of forest-trained American frontiersmen made their homes in the grasslands about Albion and Wanborough.

Most who came before 1830 purchased directly from government land offices, for the credit system used until 1820 and the low price of $1.25 an acre charged after that time discouraged speculators. A few companies did deal in farm lands, particularly in the Military Tract of western Illinois where 160-acre land warrants could be secured from the 18,000 veterans of the War of 1812, but their holding seldom exceeded 10,000 acres. Two of the most important, the American Land Company and the Boston and Indiana Land Company, owned at the height of their activity 8,000 and 29,000 acres each. More speculative activity was concentrated on prospective town sites. Hundreds of favorable spots were snapped up by individual jobbers or small companies, converted into "paper towns," and sold to gullible easterners while the town itself was still an unbroken wilderness. Although a few—such as Terre Haute in Indiana—attracted settlers and paid their promoters dividends, more eventually were sold as farms for little more than their purchase price. Despite these activities, speculators played a less important role than on earlier frontiers.

**While** farmers spread over the timbered lands of the southern Lake Plains other pioneers from the South moved northward in search of a new source of wealth. Their goal was the Driftless Area of northwestern Illinois and southwestern Wisconsin, a region of rugged hills and deeply eroded streams by-passed by the glaciers which smoothed the surrounding country. That rough area offered few agricultural possibilities, but lying beneath thin layers of eroded shale were outcroppings of rock containing rich veins of lead and other minerals. Both Indians and French traders had tapped this mineral wealth, but systematic exploitation did not begin until 1822 when a Kentucky promoter, Colonel James A. Johnson, arrived with supplies, miners, and 150 slaves. His success inspired a mining rush; by 1830 10,000 frontiersmen had staked out claims, built the bustling town of Galena at the head of navigation of the Fever River, and were shipping 15,000,000 pounds of lead yearly to New Orleans. The lawlessness of the Fever River district—the saloons, gambling halls, bowie-knife fights, and vigilance committees that made violent mayhem a daily occurrence—was typical of all mining communities where the lure of sudden wealth drew frontiersmen beyond the restraining forces of the law.

The rapid peopling of the Driftless Area and the rush of settlers to the southern Lake Plains country convinced the federal government that more Indian lands must be opened to the swarming pioneers. From that belief stemmed an important change in Indian policy. In the immediate past American agents persuaded tribes to trade their hunting grounds for reservations where natives could subsist by farming. Now the rush of population indicated that even those tiny areas would soon be absorbed. The only solution was to transfer the red men to unwanted lands beyond the Mississippi. By 1825 the federal government decided upon removal as a definite policy.

The first step was taken in August of that year when a thousand representatives of all the northwestern tribes gathered at Prairie du Chien in response to an invitation from two agents of the War Department, Governor Lewis Cass of Michigan Territory and General William Clark. They had been called together, they were told, to agree on specific tribal boundaries as a means of maintaining peace; actually the United States wanted those divisions to facilitate land cessions. Some inkling of this made the red men wary, but presents and annuities won most of them over and the Treaties of Prairie du Chien divided the Northwest among existing tribes. With that accomplished, agents turned at once to wresting land from the natives. In 1826 the Potawatomi ceded an enormous territory in Indiana, while the Miami turned over their remaining reservations in that state for $55,000 and an annuity of $25,000. For the next four years treaty making went grimly on, with tribes surrendering either their ancestral lands or their newly acquired reservations in Ohio, Indiana, and Illinois. Should the process go on unchecked, chieftains saw, every red man in the Northwest would be forced to move beyond the Mississippi.

That realization, and the rise to tribal power of younger warriors who had forgotten the horrors of the War of 1812, was responsible for the last two native uprisings in the history of the Old Northwest. The first began in the spring of 1827 when the Winnebago chief, Red Bird, alarmed by the treaty making and the steady encroachment of Fever River settlers on his lands, led his tribe against the farmers around Prairie du Chien. Red Bird hoped his attack would lead to a general native uprising, but this failed to develop, largely because more farseeing Indians realized the hopelessness of resistance without British aid. The Winnebago, their hope of allies gone, retreated eastward along the Wisconsin River, pursued by a hastily gathered army of frontiersmen and regulars under General Henry Atkinson. At the Fox-Wisconsin portage another force from Ft. Howard awaited them. Caught between two armies, Red Bird surrendered at once. The outbreak, although not serious, convinced the United States a new fort was needed to guard the frontier. Ft. Winnebago, erected near the spot where Red Bird gave himself up, played a prominent role in the second Indian uprising.

This involved the Sauk and Fox tribes whose villages dotted the fertile river bottom just below the junction of the Rock and Mississippi rivers. The richness of those lands proved the Indians' undoing, for lawless miners from the Fever River District soon decided no red men should be allowed to hold such a choice spot. Acting on that frontier-like premise, the settlers formed a mob in the spring of 1829, descended on the principal Sauk town, and drove the peaceful natives from their own corn fields. The principal chieftain, a wise old leader named Keokuk, counseled his people to follow him to the safety of lands across the Mississippi, but one minor chief refused. Black Hawk, a haughty warrior of sixty summers whose hatred of Americans transcended his good judgement, announced that he and his followers would continue to occupy the lands of their fathers despite white pressure. They did so until the spring of 1831, when Illinois authorities finally convinced themselves that the presence of the peaceful natives endangered the frontier. In June a force of 1,500 militia gathered, warned Black Hawk to leave, and then marched against his villages. The Indians, seeing that resistance would be suicidal, slipped across the Mississippi before the army reached them.

Black Hawk and his followers spent a miserable winter, having reached the Iowa country too late to plant corn or arrange shelter. As they shivered

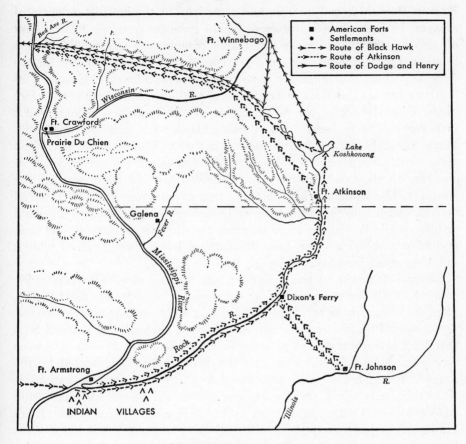

The Black Hawk War

in icy blasts and wasted away with starvation, a vision rose in their minds—a vision of the peace and plenty of their homeland. If they could only return they would know contentment again! By spring Black Hawk had charted his course. He would lead his people back across the Mississippi, explain to Americans that they only wished to plant their crops, and settle quietly on the fields of their ancestors. Certainly white men would not object if he moved openly and disavowed any warlike intentions. With that alluring prospect before him, he gathered nearly a thousand fellow tribesmen and on April 6, 1832, returned to the Rock River Valley, crossing the Mississippi in full view of the garrison at Ft. Armstrong. His peaceful purpose was attested by the fact that six hundred of his party were women and children who would never accompany a war party.

Black Hawk's return sent a wave of panic sweeping over the frontier.

Rumors flew thick and fast: he had come back at the head of an army of savages, he had secured promises of help from other tribes, he was bent on driving the whites from the Illinois country. A call for volunteers brought 1,300 frontiersmen to Ft. Armstrong within a few weeks. On May 10, 1832, the imposing force with General Henry Atkinson at its head started up the Rock River, driving the bewildered red men before them. Four days later the advance unit of 340 horsemen encountered a little party of forty Indians led by Black Hawk a few miles above Dixon's Ferry. Black Hawk tried to surrender, but when his emissaries were fired upon by the inexperienced militiamen, decided to sell his life as dearly as possible. In the brief skirmish that followed his tiny band beat off the attackers. The saddened chief, knowing that war was now inevitable, moved his headquarters to the swamps about Lake Koshkonong where women and children could be hidden while warriors roamed the countryside. Between mid-May and the end of July the Indians killed two hundred whites, suffering equal losses themselves.

General Atkinson, in the meantime, was training new volunteers at Ft. Johnson, built for the purpose on the upper Illinois River. By June 19, 1832, he was ready to take up the chase once more, with an army of almost 4,500 men. His raw recruits moved so slowly through the tangled bogs that long before they reached Lake Koshkonong Black Hawk was on his way west, bound for the safety of the Iowa shore. Discouraged by the rough country, the white army paused to throw up new fortifications at Ft. Atkinson, while a small party under General James D. Henry and Major Henry Dodge pushed on to Ft. Winnebago for supplies. Black Hawk might have escaped entirely had not this party happened to cross his trail on its return trip. Henry and Dodge, realizing that the Indians were near, decided to take up the pursuit, at the same time sending word to Atkinson's main force to join them.

Black Hawk's doom was sealed. He managed to hold off his pursuers at the Wisconsin River while the main Indian party crossed the stream but that was only a temporary reprieve. His warriors were so weakened with hunger that they dropped dead along the way as they stumbled doggedly westward. In that pitiful state they were set upon by Atkinson's army just as they reached the Mississippi. Black Hawk saw the hopelessness of the situation. Behind him were well-supplied Americans, ahead a gunboat floated on the broad surface of the Mississippi. Once more he tried to surrender but his flag of truce was answered by a burst of fire from the vessel. For the next three hours a merciless slaughter went on as red men were driven into the river at bayonet point, then shot as they struggled in the water. By nightfall only 150 of the thousand Indians who set out for the Rock River Valley three months before remained alive and they were prisoners, including Black Hawk himself. The Bad Axe Massacre, as it was called, was one of the bloodiest tragedies in the sad history of American-Indian relations.

American ruthlessness in the Black Hawk War had its desired effect on other tribes of the Northwest. Resistance, they saw, meant only extermination; better to move west than be annihilated. Their cowed spirit was recognized by American agents, who went rapidly ahead with treaty making. Starting in 1832 when the Winnebago traded most of their Wisconsin lands for hunting grounds in the Far West, tribe after tribe succumbed to white pressure until by 1837 nearly all the Northwest was held by the United States. In those five years 190,879,937 acres were secured at a cost of $70,059,505 in gifts and annuities. Indians still remaining after 1840 despite those cessions were "escorted" to their trans-Mississippi lands by troops. By 1846 the last saddened tribe had departed for its unwanted new home; the few scattered warriors remaining were too weak to interfere with the advancing frontier.

The peopling of northern Indiana, northern and central Illinois, and southern Michigan began while Black Hawk's war still raged on the western borders of the Lake Plains. For twenty years—from 1830 to 1850—population moved steadily into the region, until the whole Northwest was filled. The source of this migratory stream was New England and the Middle States. Thrifty Yankees, driven westward by unsettled economic conditions at home and lured onward by improved transportation routes to the West, in those years filled the northern portion of the Lake Plains as solidly as their southern compatriots had the bottom lands of the Ohio Valley.

Better facilities for reaching the West shaped the course of the new migration. Some pioneers from the Middle States continued to use the old routes—the National Road, Forbes' Road, or the Catskill Turnpike—to reach the Ohio, then made their way down the river and northward to central Indiana or Illinois. More took advantage of a newly completed all-water route between East and West. The Erie Canal, opened to traffic in 1825 from the Hudson River to Lake Erie, offered the first really satisfactory means of reaching the Lakes country from New England. Travelers might complain of overcrowded canal boats, poor food, and swarming mosquitoes, but they were nevertheless able to travel cheaply, take their household goods with them, and be sure of reaching their destination without losing a wagon in a mudhole. Little wonder that the Erie Canal overnight became the most important route to the West, or that thousands of homeseekers made their way westward on its horse-drawn barges.

The principal effect of this waterway was to deflect the immigrant stream from the Ohio Valley to the Great Lakes. Passengers from the East, on reaching Buffalo, sought passage on lake steamers, particularly after 1833 when a packet line opened regular service between Buffalo and Detroit. Deck passage cost only about $3, allowing a traveler to secure fairly comfortable transportation from Massachusetts to Michigan for less than $10. Little wonder that few immigrants made the hazardous voyage down the Ohio; instead they followed this all-water route to the country about Lake Erie and Lake Michigan.

These new highways could not have played their role had not unsettled conditions in New England turned thousands of easterners toward the Northwest. An economic revolution was taking place there. Through the first two centuries of its existence New England was a region of small farms and self-sufficient agriculture, largely because the lack of markets discouraged the production of staples. By the 1830's, for the first time in the section's history, markets developed as non-food-producing communities sprang up around the factories that America's industrial revolution concentrated there. Between 1810, when the factory system was introduced, and 1860 urban dwellers increased from 7 to 37 per cent of the population. This potential market tempted farmers to abandon their old self-sufficient economy and specialize in the crops for which their soil was best suited. Some, in the Connecticut River Valley, turned to tobacco growing, others to market gardening, and still more to the production of wool. This last crop caused the trouble, as the demand for wool remained steady at spawning textile mills and the breed of Saxony Merino sheep introduced into New England in 1824 proved ideally adapted to local conditions. A "sheep craze" swept over Massachusetts, Connecticut, and Vermont between 1825 and 1840 as farmer after farmer turned his cultivated fields into pasture lands.

The effect was momentous. Sheep grazing required little manual labor but much land. Hence farms increased rapidly in size as the fortunates who switched to wool growing early bought out their neighbors. Dispossessed farmers could move into the valley towns seeking jobs in mills, or go west to the fertile Lake country. During the years of the "sheep craze" the rural population of New England steadily declined as immigrants trekked westward to begin life anew.

The end was not yet. After 1840 eastern agriculture staggered under a new blow: ruinous competition with cheaply produced farm goods from the West. Grain growers suffered first as Ohio Valley wheat and corn, moved eastward over the Erie Canal, invaded coastal markets. By 1845, when the cost of shipping a bushel of wheat from Chicago to New York was only twenty-five cents, nearly 1,500,000 bushels yearly passed through Buffalo, in addition to 700,000 barrels of flour. The flood of cereals from virgin western soils lowered prices so radically that thousands of New England farmers gave up the struggle, most of them moving west themselves. Others, who turned to wool growing, found their reprieve only temporary, for during the 1840's a "sheep craze" swept across Ohio. Again the eastern farmer was faced with importations of cheaply produced western goods, and again had no choice but surrender, as sheep could be fed more economically on the fertile fields of the Old Northwest than on the rock-strewn New England pastures. Thousands admitted defeat and, having

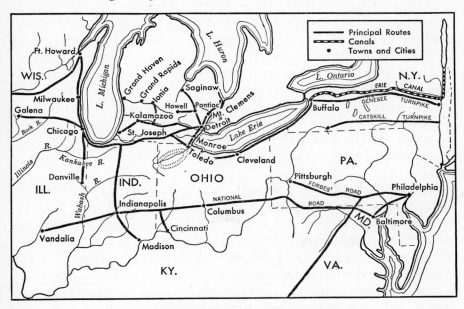

Settlement of the Lake Plains, 1830-1850

no alternative now, turned their footsteps west, sometimes driving their herds before them. Between 1840 and 1850 wool production in the Northeast declined 50 per cent; abandoned farms dotted the countryside in mute testimony to the rural decay of that once-prosperous section.

In the Middle States the same expelling forces were at work, although in somewhat modified form. The worn-out soils of New York and Pennsylvania proved incapable of competing with the virgin lands of the West in cereal production, forcing farmer after farmer into market gardening, cattle raising, or the dairy industry. This agricultural upheaval released thousands of men for the westward migration, just as had the "sheep craze" in New England. From both sections a stream of excess workers made their way to the Lakes Plains, there to produce more and more grain, ship greater quantities eastward, drive prices still lower, and encourage others to follow in their footsteps. So rapid was the influx that the usual frontier lines were blurred; settlers transformed Michigan, Indiana, and Illinois from wilderness wastes to settled regions almost overnight.

Michigan, lying at the opposite end of Lake Erie from the terminus of the Erie Canal, felt the impact first. In 1830, when the movement began, the territory's settlements were confined to a ring of towns circling Detroit—Mt. Clemens, Pontiac, and Rochester in the Clinton River Valley, Ann Arbor and Ypsilanti on the Huron River, and Monroe, Tecumseh, and Adrian along the Raisin River—all established by pioneers or speculators between 1817 and 1826. Beyond stretched the unbroken forest, for until the Erie Canal directed pioneers to the Lakes country, Michigan lay far from immigrant routes. Moreover the territory was poorly advertised; a hurried official survey made in 1815 branded Michigan as a "poor, barren, sandy land, on which scarcely any vegetation grows, except very small scrubby oaks." That false picture discouraged homeseekers until new explorations in the 1820's proved the soil as rich and the forests as luxurious as any in the Northwest. By the 1830's, when eastern papers and guide books accepted this corrected account, the time was ripe for a rush of settlers.

Detroit felt their impact in 1831, as lake steamers deposited the first immigrants at its docks. "Almost every building that can be made to answer for a shelter is occupied and filled," the local newspaper reported that summer. More were hastily thrown together, and the sleepy little frontier village rapidly emerged as a new metropolis. By 1836 it boasted 10,000 inhabitants, a theater, a museum, a public garden, schools, churches, a library, a lyceum, a historical society, a ladies' seminary, a water and sewage system, and street lights of such remarkable inefficiency that—if the city's newspaper can be believed—only a few more were needed to produce total darkness.

Despite these improvements most newcomers did not stay in Detroit; instead they fanned out to people southern Michigan. Many went west along the two roads then available: the Chicago Road which was completed in 1832, and the Territorial Road that was authorized by the territorial legislature in 1829 and opened to St. Joseph in 1834. Those highways traversed a region of rolling hills, level plains, and fertile soils that held infinite promise to land-hungry easterners. By 1837 25,000 people lived along the Chicago Road and almost as many more in the Kalamazoo River Valley. The latter, a particularly prized spot, was dotted with Prairie Rondes—some as large as eleven miles across—the deep black soil of which was ready for the plow without the backbreaking task of clearing. These, and the Oak Openings, were sought out first, then immigrants turned to the conquest of surrounding forests and to the building of towns at favorable sites along roads and rivers.

Other settlers moved north from Detroit to the valley of the Saginaw River where numerous Oak Openings offered tempting homesites. Although the town of Saginaw was laid out in 1832, mass migration did not set in until three years later when a highway was completed to Detroit. At the same time pioneers made their way to the forested lands along the Grand River, traveling northward first along Indian trails that crossed the Territorial Road, then following a highway opened between Marshall and Ionia in 1836. After 1838 they utilized the Grand River Road from Pontiac to Howell. By that time a sizeable town existed at Grand Rapids where an eighteen-foot fall in the river provided abundant water power. Another settlement was being nursed to maturity by speculators at Grand Haven. Most of the pioneers in the Grand River Valley, as in the rest of southern Michigan, were transplanted New Englanders who had come westward with a song of hope upon their lips:

> Come all ye Yankee farmers who wish to change your lot,
> Who've spunk enough to travel beyond your native spot,
> And leave behind the village where Ma and Pa do stay,
> Come follow me and settle in Michigania,—
> Yea, Yea, Yea, in Michigania.

Another northwestern state, Indiana, fared less well during the 1830-50 migrations. While its northern counties were settled by the overflow from the Chicago Road, its central portions were largely neglected until the 1850's. Two false impressions were responsible for this lag: the belief held by most immigrants that lands in the northeastern portion of the state were too wet to be attractive, and the hope of a handful of speculators that Indiana's prairies were so superior they would command a fabulous price.

The former illusion was fostered by travelers who journeyed westward through the tangled morass of the Black Swamp or picked their way among sluggish streams north of the Wabash. Their exaggerated tales of a whole countryside under water spread to editors of eastern newspapers and guide books who customarily referred to the "swamps and bogs of Indiana," while failing to mention the equally swampy regions of Illinois. That tradition, which persisted well into the 1830's, discouraged some settlers, but a more important deterrent was the engrossment of land by eastern speculators. This began in 1832 when a Connecticut business man, Henry L. Ellsworth, visited Indiana as Indian commissioner. Struck by the beauty of the prairie country between the Wabash and Kankakee valleys, Ellsworth began buying land there in 1835, moving west a year later to settle on his 18,000 acres. His large scale agricultural methods and specially devised machinery proved so successful that he not only made additional purchases, but became a rabid advocate of prairie farming.

Ellsworth's enthusiasm was responsible for a speculative boom in Indiana land. His eastern friends began buying on his advice in 1836, but wholesale purchases did not begin until 1838 when he described the beauties and opportunities of the countryside in a widely circulated book, *Valley of the Upper Wabash*. He would, Ellsworth stated in that publication, gladly purchase prairie lands for any investor, manage estates for absentee owners, and guarantee a profit of 8 or 10 per cent, with anything above that figure divided between owner and operator. That attractive offer, coming just as the Panic of 1837 reduced investment opportunities in the East, led to a rush of speculative buying, with purchases ranging from a few hundred to many thousand acres. Within a few years most of northwestern Indiana was held by absentee owners, whose glorified conception of the value of their holdings led them to set prices of $5 or $10 an acre. Few buyers were willing to pay that much when good lands elsewhere were obtainable for $1.25 an acre. Northern Indiana remained largely without settlers until the 1850's when popular pressure and mounting taxes forced speculators to unload at more reasonable prices. Most of the purchasers at that time were from southern Indiana, a fact explaining the predominantly southern character of that state's population.

Illinois, suffering no handicaps such as these, gained population rapidly between 1830 and 1850. The rush to Chicago began in 1835, sending that tiny town, incorporated only two years before, into a transformation similar to that which rocketed Detroit to a position of importance four years before. "Almost all vessels from the lower lakes are full of passengers," one editor wrote, "and our streets are thronged with wagons loaded with household furniture and the implements necessary to farming. Foot-passengers, too, with well-filled sacks on their shoulders come in large numbers." A year later 450 vessels disgorged their human cargoes, while the air rang with the sound of hammers as carpenters worked feverishly to keep pace with the growing demand for houses. For the next decade migration steadily mounted until observers wondered whether the whole East would not be left depopulated.

From Chicago settlers fanned out over northern Illinois, first seeking such choice spots as the Rock and Illinois river valleys, then filling in the forested uplands between. When these were occupied, later comers were brought face to face with an important problem. How could they make the transition from accustomed timber lands to the prairies of Illinois where cheap land alone remained? The task was formidable; to conquer the grass-lands pioneers must discard their prejudices, shatter past traditions, and develop an entirely new frontier technique. They had, for generations, judged the richness of land by the density of its forest growth, used wood for everything from homes to fences, and obtained fuel, game, and water from the wilderness. Now they must settle on a barren waste apparently incapable of supporting forests, unprotected from winter blasts or summer heat, without logs for their cabins, rails for their fences, or fuel for their fires. They must dig wells rather than depend on rippling forest streams, and provide drainage to carry spring rains from level lands. Worst of all, they must devise some means of breaking the tough prairie sod which shattered the fragile wooden plows to which they were accustomed.

Little wonder that settlers hesitated at the edge of the prairies before making the transition. Eventually, however, as each grassland was sur-rounded by homes, the conquest began. The shift was usually gradual; a farmer living near a prairie broke a little of the sod, using the rest for pasture. As others imitated his example a ring of fields spread around the edge of the grassy plot. Later comers pushed beyond to make their homes on the prairie itself, until eventually the whole area was under cultivation. This process was repeated again and again in northern Illinois, until by the end of the 1840's the entire state was settled. Only the central portions of the Grand Prairie were avoided until the 1850's when railroads brought them near enough to markets to make their cultivation profitable.

The development of new techniques made the conquest possible. Capital, prairie pioneers soon learned, was necessary, so they customarily worked for some other farmer for a year or so. Their carefully hoarded cash was then used to purchase a farm and pay for the initial sod breaking. This was done by a neighbor with the special equipment necessary: a garantuan plow built for the task and from three to six yokes of oxen. Two dollars an acre was the usual price charged—more than the cost of the land—but then the principal expense was over. The first "sod crop" was planted by hacking the upturned furrows with an ax and dropping in a few kernels of corn; this usually produced about fifty bushels to the acre even without cultiva-tion—enough to pay back part of the initial investment and finance more sod breaking the next year. In the meantime lumber for a home was either cut from a neighboring wood lot or hauled in, a well was dug, and fences constructed. This last proved most difficult, as the split-rail fences that were alone available cost from $150 to $300 for a forty-acre farm. The heavy expenses, running as high as $1,000, did not alarm frontiersmen who knew two or three good crops would pay off the entire investment.

So attractive were the prospects that by the end of the 1830's enough of northern Illinois was filled to send an overflow spilling into Wisconsin. Some 30,000 pioneers lived in that pleasant land of rolling hills and small prairies in 1840, most of them in the farming communities around the Fever River District or along the federal road opened in 1837 between Chicago and Ft. Howard. In the next decade population increased to 305,000 as New Englanders flocked to the lake front counties or marched northward along the Rock River Valley. There they met other migrants, largely from the Middle States, advancing north and east along the Mississippi and Wisconsin rivers. To that region, too came the vanguards of the European population streams that flooded the Old Northwest during the next decades. Some were Norwegians who built their Old World colonies about Lake Koshkonong, others were Irish laborers who turned to farming after completing the roads on which they had labored, but most were thrifty and hard-working Germans. Driven from their homes by a potato famine and the disrupting effects of the unsuccessful uprisings of 1848, these poverty-stricken refugees took passage on the cotton ships plying between European ports and New Orleans, then ascended the Mississippi until they found cheap, slave-free lands. In 1850 640,000 foreign born lived in the Lake Plains area, forming about one-eighth of the population.

By that time the whole section was passing beyond the frontier stage, except in northern Michigan and Wisconsin where less hospitable soils and dense pine forests discouraged settlement until the coming of the railroads. The 4,500,000 people whose homes dotted the Old Northwest in 1850 were drawn from a variety of older societies, as the following table of origins shows:

|  | NEW ENGLAND | MIDDLE STATES | SOUTH | NORTHWEST | NATIVE BORN | EUROPE |
|---|---|---|---|---|---|---|
| Ohio | 66,000 | 300,000 | 150,000 | ——— | 1,284,000 | 200,000 |
| Indiana | 11,000 | 76,000 | 175,000 | 130,000 | 500,000 | 55,000 |
| Illinois | 37,000 | 112,000 | 138,000 | 110,000 | 344,000 | 110,000 |
| Michigan | 31,000 | 150,000 | 4,000 | 18,000 | 140,000 | 55,000 |
| Wisconsin | 27,000 | 80,000 | 5,000 | 23,000 | 63,000 | 107,000 |

In the Lake Plains they met and mingled, blending the social manner-isms and economic habits of their homelands to create a unique society, distinct from those contributing to it and modified by the impact of the frontier. In Ohio, Michigan, and Wisconsin, where northerners predominated, the institutions of the Northeast held sway, in Indiana the social order was patterned on that of the South, while in Illinois the even balance between northerners and southerners forced a compromise between disciples of the two sections.

These divisions became apparent when the people of the Lake Plains turned to erecting their governmental systems. Indiana in 1816 and Illinois in 1818 entered the Union with constitutions that reflected both the preponderantly southern nature of their populations and the liberalizing influence of the frontier; property qualifications for voting were swept away, popularly elected legislatures were made supreme, and the franchise was awarded all adult males who had lived within the state for six months or a year—yet in Illinois slavery was allowed to continue under the guise of indentured servitude. Michigan's frame of government was equally liberal when it applied for statehood in 1837, and Wisconsin's outdid them all in guaranteeing unrestrained popular control: governor, legislators, and even judges were elected for short terms, all native born males were given the right to vote after one year's residence and all foreign born when agreeing to a simple oath of allegiance, small homesteads were exempted from seizure for debt, and married women were allowed to control their own property. Wisconsin became a state under this liberal document in 1848.

Those institutions were typical of the land that gave them birth. Timothy Flint, an acute observer of the West, summed up the section's social metamorphosis when he wrote: "The society thus newly organized and constituted, is more liberal, enlarged, unprejudiced, and, of course, more affectionate and pleasant, than a society of people of *unique* birth and character, who bring all their early prejudices, as a common stock, to be transmitted as an inheritance in perpetuity."

# CHAPTER XV

# Settling the Gulf Plains

## 1815-1850

While Yankees, southerners, and Germans transformed the Northwest into a land of fertile farms and bustling villages, another immigrant torrent inundated the Gulf Plains of the Southwest. That bountiful countryside of gentle hills and colorful red soils attracted, in the quarter-century after the War of 1812, the hordes of small farmers, lordly plantation owners, and docile slaves needed to erect a unique social order, built on black labor and white cotton.

The Southwest was opened to settlement in 1798 when Mississippi Territory was created, but only a handful of pioneers made their homes there in the next dozen years. Cheap and readily available lands in Georgia and Tennessee, Spanish control of the West Florida ports through which the region's produce must be exported, and the presence of the powerful Creek and Cherokee tribes in western Georgia, all discouraged any mass movement to the territory. Equally important was the lack of direct communication with the settled areas of the Southeast. The two federally built roads opened before 1812 from Nashville to Natchez and from the Ocmulgee River to St. Stephens on the Tombigbee River were only crude trails utterly impassable during much of the year. Those obstacles kept migration at a minimum; in 1812 the white population of the territory consisted of 20,000 Spaniards, Loyalists, and Americans grouped about Natchez or spread along the lower Tombigbee River.

The metamorphosis of this backward frontier region into a prosperous land of farms and plantations can be explained in one word: cotton. Southern interest in that important crop began to develop in the late eighteenth century when English inventors perfected the machinery needed to produce cotton cloth mechanically. Those epoch-making machines—James Hargreaves' "spinning jenny," Richard Arkwright's automatic carder,

Samuel Crompton's "mule," and Edmund Cartwright's power loom—launched England on its industrial revolution. Before the turn of the century British mills produced cotton cloth more cheaply than the underpaid workers of India who had long enjoyed a virtual monopoly in world production. The market was limitless; the whole world waited to be reclothed in cheaper fabrics than the expensive woolens traditional to Europe and America. Machines, workers, and power could be supplied in Britain; only raw cotton was needed.

News of these developments caused a flurry of excitement along the Atlantic seaboard during the 1790's. Plantation owners, struggling to make a profit by producing tobacco for an overcrowded world market, saw that fortunes awaited those switching to the promising new crop. They knew that two types of cotton could be grown in the South. One, Sea Island Cotton, had long silken fibres that could easily be separated from the glossy black seeds either by hand or by a simple machine known as a gin—two closely placed rollers which drew the lint through while the seeds popped out behind. Cultivation of this variety began in Georgia in 1786, but its commercial importance was limited by the fact that it could be grown only on the coastal islands and swampy lowlands between the St. John's and Santee rivers. The other, Upland Cotton, did not require the warm, moist climate of the Sea Island type and could be grown over most of the South. Its commercial production was impossible, however, because of the difficulty of separating its short fibres from their fuzzy green seeds. They clung so tenaciously that a slave could clean only a pound or two a day. Large scale cultivation would only be practicable if some mechanical means of cleaning Upland Cotton was devised.

There was much talk of such an invention among plantation owners during the early 1790's. Word of this fell on the ears of a young Yale graduate, Eli Whitney, when he arrived at a plantation near Savannah in the fall of 1792 seeking a post as tutor. Whitney was interested enough to begin experimenting, and within a few weeks produced the first workable cotton gin. His invention consisted of a wooden cylinder bristling with stiff wires which revolved against the slatted sides of a box of cotton. The wires tore away bits of fibre while the slats held back the seeds, then the lint was brushed from the wire points by a second revolving cylinder set with brushes. This simple device, when harnessed to water power, cleaned a thousand pounds of Upland Cotton a day; when saw-toothed iron disks were substituted for the wires the amount was doubled. Within a few years gins, located everywhere in the seaboard South, were ginning cotton for $1.50 a hundredweight.

Wherever soil and climate were suitable planters turned excitedly to the new crop. The price was high—forty cents a pound when production started —and profits fantastic. The Tidewater, where the plantation system was well established, made the transition first, but in 1800 the cotton plant started its march westward over the Virginia and Carolina Piedmont. During the next decade the economy of that section was revolutionized; small farms were engulfed by great estates, grains gave way before the new staple, and democratic free labor was displaced by the expanding slave system. Between 1800 and 1810 the number of bonded servants in the lower Piedmont increased 70 per cent. By 1812, when war temporarily halted expansion, the cotton frontier was ready to advance across the Gulf Plains.

The War of 1812 paved the way, both by opening trade routes between the Southwest and the Gulf, and by preparing the Indians for removal. The routes were opened when Mobile and other Spanish Gulf cities fell to American forces during the fighting, thus assuring interior planters unmolested river shipments directly to the sea. At the same time Andrew Jackson's victory over the Creeks at the Battle of Horse Shoe Bend taught the United States that the southern tribes were so weak and torn by dissension they would be unable to resist forceful removal. The time was ripe to push them from their ancestral lands: the Creeks from the country between the Ocmulgee and Tombigbee rivers, the Cherokee from their mountain homes in northern Georgia and eastern Tennessee, the Choctaw from the wooded lands separating the Tombigbee and Natchez settlements, and the Chickasaw from northern Mississippi and western Tennessee.

That realization, and pressure from cotton planters anxious to invade the Gulf Plains, turned the government's attention to land cessions as soon as the war was over. A series of treaties forced on cowed tribes between 1816 and 1821 opened several tracts in central Georgia, western Alabama, and western Tennessee, but the rapidity with which these were overrun convinced the United States that something more was necessary. Nothing would satisfy land-hungry cotton growers but the removal of all Indians to lands beyond the Mississippi. Andrew Jackson, acting as agent for the War Department, first attempted that solution when he gathered a handful of reluctant Cherokee together in July, 1817, and by threats and bribery forced them to exchange their tribal lands for an equal number of acres in the Far West. Every Cherokee had the choice, according to the treaty, of settling down in the East on 640 acres of land, or of moving to the West; those who chose the latter course were given free transportation, a gun, a blanket, a kettle, and a year's supplies. To Jackson's disgust virtually the entire tribe remained in the East, the natives settling down to a peaceful agricultural existence. Nor did a similar treaty with the Choctaw arranged by Jackson in October, 1820, convince that tribe to move beyond the Mississippi. A more aggressive policy was needed to open the Southwest.

This began in 1825 when President James Monroe publicly endorsed removal as a means of protecting red men from the evils of white civilization. Although Monroe did not openly suggest the use of force, his agents were convinced he would condone more vigorous methods than the peaceful persuasion attempted in the past. Their first victims were the Creeks, whose presence in western Georgia long rankled officials of that frontier state. The farseeing Creek chieftains, anticipating the American policy, in 1824 decreed the death penalty for any chief selling or exchanging tribal lands. Undeterred by that threat, Monroe's agents determined to follow the usual practice of dealing with a bribed faction of the tribe. A meeting with a few greedy chiefs headed by Chief William McIntosh on February 12, 1825, resulted in the Treaty of Indian Springs, a scandalous document ceding all the Creek land and promising the tribe would leave for the Far West by September 1, 1826.

The majority of the Creeks, whose leader was the able Chief Big Warrior, met in council to decide on a policy suited to the emergency. Without hesitation, they pronounced the death penalty for the traitorous Chief McIntosh; a few weeks later his house was surrounded and he and two of his followers shot down. At the same time the Creeks refused to recognize the Treaty of Indian Springs or admit that any of their lands were sold. Their resistance bore some fruit. John Quincy Adams, who had replaced Monroe in the White House, was as sympathetic to the removal policy as his predecessor, but he was convinced that an injustice had been done and ordered a thorough investigation. When this not only disclosed the fraud used at Indian Springs but demonstrated that forty-nine out of every fifty Creeks opposed the treaty, President Adams did not hesitate. Authorized leaders of the tribe were requested to send a truly representative delegation to Washington where, in January, 1826, the Indians signed a new treaty slightly more to their liking. Unyielding government pressure forced them to agree to removal, but they were given until January 1, 1827, to begin their migration, and the rewards for those agreeing to go were substantially increased.

Georgia's governor, a hotheaded backwoodsman named George M. Troup, flew into a tower of rage when he learned of the Treaty of Washington. His state, he loudly proclaimed, refused to recognize the new agreement and would begin occupying the Creek lands on September 2, 1826. President Adams was helpless before this determined resistance; even the United States marshal resigned when ordered to arrest intruders on Indian lands. The President had no choice but to urge the red men to move as speedily as possible. The migration began in November, 1827, when the first large party made its way down the Tennessee and Mississippi rivers, then ascended the Arkansas River to the assigned territory. For the next two years the movement went on, as natives were rudely uprooted by Georgians who overran their villages or appropriated their fields. By the end of 1829 only a handful of Creeks remained in the state. The hurried departures and the failure of the United States to provide promised supplies, meant untold suffering for the mistreated tribesmen, many of whom failed to survive the journey.

The removal of the Creeks left only the Cherokee in possession of Georgia lands. The leaders of that powerful tribe, realizing their turn must come soon, decided to use their advanced civilization as a cloak to guard their ancestral territories. They were, they knew, well adjusted to the white man's way of life; the 15,000 members of the tribe owned 22,000 cattle, 1,300 slaves, 2,000 spinning wheels, 700 looms, 31 grist mills, 10 saw mills, 8 cotton gins, and 18 schools. Their written language, invented by Chief Sequoya, was employed in a newspaper, *The Cherokee Phoenix*. Obviously they were no nomadic barbarians who could be easily pushed aside. Why not convince the Georgians of their stability, and at the same time solidify the tribe, by forming their own government? With this in mind delegates gathered at New Echota, Georgia, on July 4, 1827, to draft a constitution for a Cherokee Republic. Within a month the frame of government was ratified, Chief John Ross elected president, and a solid front formed against white aggression.

Georgia's reaction was one of mingled fury and delight. The anger was aroused by the Cherokee's determination to retain lands coveted by frontiersmen; the delight by the realization that the Indians had taken a step which would lead to the tribe's undoing. The Constitution of the United States forbad the erection of any new state within an existing state without the latter's consent. The New Echota constitution violated that provision. Therefore, Georgians reasoned, the federal government must punish the Cherokee by removing them from Georgia. This demand was voiced by the state legislature in December, 1827, when resolutions were adopted demanding national help in expelling the Indians. Congress responded by appropriating $50,000 for Cherokee removal. Armed with that sum, War Department agents attempted to persuade the Indians to move peacefully, promising each lands in the West, transportation, a blanket, a rifle, a kettle, five pounds of tobacco, a year's supplies, and $50 in cash. During the summer of 1828 these inducements were dangled before the natives by skillful diplomats, but to little avail. The Indians were determined to cling to their lands at all costs.

The election of Andrew Jackson in 1828 ended the brief period of peaceful persuasion. That outspoken frontiersman, whose lack of sympathy for the Indians was well known, used his inaugural address to advocate their removal as the only means of preserving the sovereignty of the state. Georgia, sure now of presidential support and spurred on by the discovery of gold in the Cherokee country, acted immediately. Resolutions hurried through the legislature provided that after January 1, 1830, all state laws applied to Indians, who were also denied the right to be a witness or party in a legal suit where a white man was involved. Those two brutal measures not only broke down the tribal organization on which the red men depended, but placed them at the mercy of unscrupulous whites who appropriated their lands without fear of legal redress. Little wonder that the Cherokee appealed to Washington for the protection due them as wards of the government. Their answer came in May, 1830, when Congress passed a Removal Bill authorizing the president to move any eastern tribe to trans-Mississippi lands—by force if need be. In desperation they fell back upon their last hope; the Supreme Court was asked to issue an injunction restraining Georgia from carrying out its cruel laws. That body, in the case of *The Cherokee Nation vs. Georgia,* reluctantly decided the Indians did not constitute a foreign nation within the meaning of the Constitution and therefore had no right to bring suit before the Court.

The helpless Indians were now at the mercy of an unsympathetic president and ruthless state officers who vied with each other in making life unpleasant for the red men. Payment of annuities was stopped, debts owed them were declared cancelled, their lands were seized, and their homes appropriated. Agents were sent among them to pit clan against clan and family against family in the hopes of breaking down tribal unity. When heartsick Christian missionaries among them protested these criminal acts they were sentenced to four years at hard labor as a reward for their pains. The clergymen's appeal to the higher authority of the Supreme Court gave the red men a brief flurry of hope, for Chief Justice John Marshall held in the famous case of *Worcester vs. Georgia* that the Cherokee possessed the status of a "domestic dependent nation" under the protection of the federal government, and that Georgia had no right to molest them. This decision meant nothing, however, when Jackson held Marshall's opinion was too preposterous to be enforced. The stage was set for the final act in the sordid drama.

That was not long in coming. While the Cherokee appealed vainly for aid, federal agents worked quietly among them in hope of finding a minor faction which could be bribed into deeding over all the tribe's lands. Such an unscrupulous minority, led by Chief Major Ridge, was unearthed during 1834, and after two unsuccessful attempts, persuaded to sign the Treaty of New Echota in December, 1835. That infamous document ceded all Cherokee lands to the United States in return for $5,600,000, guaranteed the Indians reimbursement for their improvements, and promised them free transportation to their new western homes. The majority renounced the agreement but realized it sealed their doom; now the United States could drive them from their homelands by force. For the next three years little bands straggled across the Mississippi, although the last did not depart until December, 1838, when troops were used to drive them west. About a quarter of the Indians perished in the cruel winter migration.

Georgia's ruthless example was imitated throughout the Southwest. Mississippi in 1830 and Alabama in 1832 extended their laws over all Indians within their borders, forbad meetings of tribes or councils, and threatened to punish chiefs who tried to carry out the functions of their offices. The red men, their tribal organization disrupted by these measures, fell easy prey to wily agents sent among them by President Jackson. Those experienced land grabbers operated in the usual way: they sought out a few selfish chiefs, bribed them into ceding all the tribe's lands, then forced the majority to accept and move beyond the Mississippi. The Choctaw succumbed in September, 1830, when a minority faction signed the Treaty of Dancing Rabbit Creek, giving up all eastern lands for a similar acreage in the West, annuities, moving expenses, and supplies. The remnant of the Creek tribe remaining in eastern Alabama accepted a similar agreement in March, 1832, and the Chickasaw followed with the Treaty of Pontotoc Creek in October of that year.

During the next five years the members of the latter tribe drifted to their new homes, but the Choctaw and Creeks made more trouble. A provision in the Choctaw treaty allowing heads of families wishing to remain in the East 640 acres each caused the difficulty with that tribe. By 1834 the 540 natives signifying their intention of staying held warrants entitling them to lands. Those "floating claims" attracted the attention of speculators, who descended upon the innocent red men, bribed them into making false claims for more territory, and began a wholesale campaign designed to defraud the Indians. Within a few months one company amassed 1,280,000 acres; another land jobber secured 250 claims. A congressional commission which uncovered the whole sordid story soon sent the innocent Indian victims of white greed scurrying westward with nothing to show for their pains but an unpleasant experience.

The removal of the Creeks was even more disgraceful. Their treaty allowed each head of family to retain a half section which could either be sold or reserved for occupancy should the Indian decide to remain in the East. Surveys completed in December, 1833, showed the natives entitled to 2,000,000 acres; the remaining 5,000,000 acres formerly occupied by the tribe were thrown open to sale. This was an opportunity no speculator could resist—millions of acres of rich land in the hands of helpless red men who could count on no protection from their wrecked tribal organization or an unsympathetic government. They swarmed from all over the South, those greedy land grabbers. The more honest cheated the natives of their lands by paying them in worthless bank notes, whipping them until they consented to sell, or buying when the red men were hopelessly drunk. The less scrupulous hired gangs of Indians to swear they owned lands that were not theirs, or set up stores selling only tobacco and whiskey where Indian landowners were encouraged to spend freely, then turn over their estates in payment. For months wholesale cheating went on until by 1835 the pitiful survivors were reduced to raiding settlements for food. That gave President Jackson his excuse; troops drove the last Alabama Creeks west at bayonet point.

Only one tribe remained in the South: the Seminole of Florida. When the United States took over that Spanish territory in 1821 the tribe accepted a large reservation north of Lake Okeechobee, but that was soon coveted by the whites. In 1833 a tribal fragment was persuaded to sign a treaty of cession and removal. The Seminole, refusing to accept that fraudulent agreement, found a leader in Chief Osceola and took to the warpath. The Seminole War dragged on until 1842 when the last defeated band was driven across the Mississippi, or into the inpenetrable depths of the Everglades. All the East was open to settlement; all the natives were in the distant lands of the Far West which were to be theirs "as long as trees grow and the waters run."

Long before the last embittered red man began his weary trek westward white settlers swarmed over the Southwest. The migration differed markedly from that to the Northwest; instead of being drawn from all parts of the United States and much of Europe the pioneers came from only one section: the seaboard states of the South Atlantic. That region sent its excess inhabitants to the frontier in such large numbers between 1815 and 1850 that its own population remained almost stationary. By 1850 40 per cent of all native-born South Carolinians then alive lived beyond the borders of their home state, 30 per cent of the North Carolinians, and 25 per cent of the Georgians. The remarkable exodus, which gave the Gulf Plains a strangely homogeneous population for a frontier area, was caused partly by unsatisfactory conditions in the Southeast, partly by the development of easily traveled routes between the two sections, and partly by the attractiveness of the western country toward which the pioneers turned their footsteps.

The principal expelling force was the wornout soil of the seaboard. Successive plantings of tobacco for more than a century, primitive agricultural methods, and the temptation normal in staple producing areas to "butcher" or "mine" the soil, left a monument of exhausted fields, gullied hillsides, and declining crops. Nor did the spread of cotton planting relieve the situation. While the older South momentarily benefited from a new plant that consumed still-present minerals, the worn soils could not stand the abuse of repeated croppings long. That was especially the case as the cotton frontier spread over the hilly Piedmont, for high prices after the War of 1812 encouraged successive plantings, and the shallow humus soils were quickly washed away by the heavy southern rains once they were loosened by the plow. The whole country, one traveler complained, "is a scene of desolation that baffles description . . . farm after farm . . . worn out, washed and gullied; so that scarcely an acre could be found in a place fit for cultivation." Another commented upon the "dreary and uncultivated wastes, a barren and exhausted soil, half-clothed negroes, lean and hungry stock, houses falling to decay, and fences wind shaken and dilapidated."

For a time, during the 1820's, southeastern planters tried to improve their farms by adopting scientific methods; agricultural societies and farm journals blossomed everywhere to tell farmers of improved plows, horizontal furrowing, crop diversification, and fertilizers. The new hope was short-lived, as most of the advice was based on inadequate information and failed to improve fields worn beyond repair. At the end of the 1820's, when the failure of science became apparent, a wave of despair swept over the Southeast. One farm journal poet complained:

> No smiling pastures spread inviting here,
> But dry hot fields on ev'ry side appear.
> A sultry scene, a dismal waste, alas!
> Where man's great object is to kill the grass.

There was only one solution: trade the butchered lands of the East for the virgin fields of the West. Thousands of farmers who reached that conclusion swelled the population of the Gulf Plains.

Migration was made easier by the network of highways built by the state and national governments in the years after 1815. Three roads led to the Gulf Plains from the older South. Two, the Fall Line Road and the Upper Road, converged at Columbus on the Chattahoochee River to form the Federal Road to St. Stephens, Mobile, and Natchez. The third ran along the Great Valley of the Appalachians to Knoxville where it divided, one branch leading to Nashville and eventually on to Memphis, the other turning southwest to Huntsville in the Tennessee Valley. From that junction a highway led settlers southward to the Black Warrior River Valley while another carried them west to Florence and the old Nashville-Natchez Road. An even better route to southern Mississippi was provided in 1820 when Andrew Jackson, as commander of the western army, opened the Military Road between Florence and Lake Pontchartrain. The federal gov-

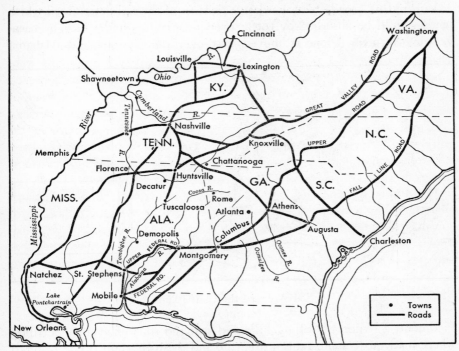

Settlement of the Gulf Plains, 1815-1850

ernment was responsible for another improvement, the Upper Federal Road across Alabama, which was authorized in 1833. Although all were only crude mud tracks through the forest—bottomless quagmires in wet weather and rutted horrors in dry—they provided sure if comfortless routes to important parts of the Gulf Plains. Steamboats were also used by immigrants, for by 1820 they were ascending the Oconee to Milledgeville, the Tombigbee to Demopolis, and the Tennessee to Florence.

The magnet that drew men westward over those wilderness trails was cotton land. This was rigidly defined by the natural conditions under which cotton plants would thrive. One necessity, a long growing season with at least two hundred days between frosts, fixed the northern limit of the cotton belt at a line extending from the northeast corner of North Carolina across northern Georgia and Alabama, then sweeping northward to include western Tennesse. Beyond that point cotton could not be profitably produced except in unusually favorable years, although the lowlands of the Tennessee River Valley were an exception. On the south the boundary of the cotton belt was set by the autumn rainfall, for more than ten inches of precipitation during the fall interfered with picking.

Within that broad area the relative richness of the soil determined which lands should be absorbed by cotton-growing planters and which by corn-growing farmers. Pioneers moved first over the Georgia and Alabama

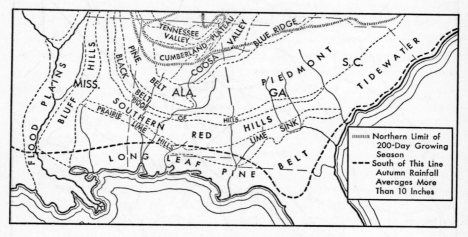

Soil Areas of the Gulf Plains

Piedmont, a region of rolling hills and stiff red soils of average fertility, where inadequate subterranean drainage and the hilly countryside fostered rapid soil exhaustion. As gullied fields drove them on, frontiersmen found even less hospitable lands ahead. In northwestern Georgia and northern Alabama the Piedmont hills gave way to the rugged peaks of the Blue Ridge Mountains, the level reaches of the Coosa River Valley, the ridges and narrow valleys of the mountainous Cumberland Plateau, and the gravelly wastes of the short-leaf pine belt. Only the Coosa Valley had the warm climate and deep limestone soil suitable to cotton growing, and there transportation difficulties stopped production. This upland region along the northern fringe of the cotton belt became a land of small farms occupied by yeoman farmers and poor whites who produced cereals for the larger plantations.

On either side of this unattractive area lay rich regions where plantations centered. One was the broad valley of the Tennessee River, a level plain fifteen miles wide where the calcareous limestone soil was fertile and deep. The other was the treeless Black Belt, which ran three hundred miles across central Alabama and Mississippi. Its rotted-limestone earth, as productive as any in the South, supported magnificent plantations after pioneers overcame their prejudice against prairies. The southern edge of the Black Belt was bounded by a row of low hills, called the Pontotoc Ridge in Mississippi and the Chunnennuggee Ridge in Alabama, where the sandy loams were also extremely fertile and highly prized for cotton growing. Below this was a rugged red-soil belt of Red Hills, a country of varying soil richness that attracted both plantations and small farms. The Lime Sink area of Georgia, the Lime Hills of Alabama, and the Central Prairie of Mississippi were also suitable for plantations, especially the Central Prairie which resembled the Black Belt. The long leaf pine country bordering the Gulf was less desirable; its gravelly soil, wire grass, and excessive rainfall combined to discourage most agricultural pursuits. That desolate region became the home of poor whites, small farmers, and cattle grazers.

Along the western edge of the Gulf Plains were two other regions that played an important role in the history of the Southwest. One was the forty-mile strip of Bluff Hills that ran through central Mississippi, an area so fertile that cotton planters sought land there despite the rugged character of the countryside. The other was the Mississippi Flood Plain, which stretched between the Gulf of Mexico and southern Missouri. That broad valley, formed by successive deposits of silt as the river flooded and receded, was among the richest areas in the United States. Although generally level except for the hills about Vicksburg and Natchez, the delta was avoided by early settlers who feared floods. Not until the 1840's when levees made life there reasonably safe was the region transformed into one of the South's prize agricultural areas. There, in the Tennessee Valley, and in the Black Belt the large plantation system was most securely entrenched.

The prospect of finding such lands as these was one of the strongest forces driving men west in the years after 1815. In the vanguard, there as in the North, was the small farmer, driven from his eastern home by soil exhaustion. After selling his worn fields to a nearby planter whose large-scale methods allowed greater profits, he loaded his family and belongings on a wagon or two, and driving his livestock before him, began the trek westward. He timed his arrival for the early spring so he could girdle the trees and plant his first corn crop in April. By the time roasting ears were ready three months later he had built two square log cabins ten feet apart, connected by a covered passage where cooking was done during the hot months. Then, while his corn ripened, he cleared enough land to plant cotton the second year. If his farm was good neighbors drifted in around him; within three or four years clearings dotted the wilderness and cotton exports were steadily increasing.

While the community was still in a primitive stage it was usually visited by a wealthy eastern planter seeking a favorable spot for settlement. That lofty individual probably owned a large plantation and many slaves in the East but he had decided to move, either because he was alert to the first signs of soil exhaustion in his old fields or because he recognized the chance for greater profits on the West's virgin land. His investment was too great, however, to risk any haphazard step; hence he was interested only in areas where pioneer farmers were testing the earth's fertility. When he found a likely site he either bought out several small frontiersmen or purchased adjacent land from the government, returned east to sell his old estate, and started to his new home with the elaborate retinue needed to move an entire plantation: several wagons filled with household goods, herds of livestock, a band of slaves marching together, and the planter's family in a horse and buggy. Travelers along the Federal Road reported a constant stream of those migrating parties, moving westward by day and camping by the roadside at night.

On arriving at his newly purchased estate the planter directed his slaves into the many tasks needed to lay out a plantation; some were set to building log cabins that would serve the owner's family until a lordly frame house was constructed, others to clearing land and planting the first crop of cotton. As the remaining lands were cleared during the next few years the planter's profits steadily mounted, for his slave labor allowed him to extend his cultivated areas more rapidly than the small farmers around him, and his large-scale methods brought him a larger return on his investment. Profits were used to absorb his smaller competitors, one after the other, and to purchase slaves needed to operate their lands. Plantation expansion went on constantly, but most rapidly in periods of great prosperity or acute depression; in good times high cotton prices favored the planter who specialized in that crop, in bad small farmers were less able to survive than their wealthier neighbors.

That process, repeated time and time again across the face of the Gulf Plains, explained the rapid expansion of the frontier. The plantation was a dynamic institution, constantly crowding out adjacent small farmers. As pioneers were displaced they moved west again, only to have planters reappear, buy out their lands, and send them on to new frontiers. An Alabama politician summed up the whole process when he complained: "Our small planters, after taking the cream off their lands, unable to restore them by rest, manures or otherwise, are going further west and south, in search of other virgin lands, which they may and will despoil and impoverish in like manner. Our wealthier planters, with greater means and no more skill, are buying out their poorer neighbors, extending their plantations, and adding to their slave force. The wealthy few, who are able to live on smaller profits, and to give their blasted fields some rest, are thus pushing off the many, who are merely independent." Slavery and the plantation system permitted wealth to perpetuate itself and combined to drive the less fortunate westward.

Expansion began as soon as the War of 1812 was over, spurred on by a combination of thirty-cent cotton, eastern lands worn thin by a generation of cotton planting, western territories newly cleared of Indians, and postwar prosperity, which sent a rush of farmers across western Georgia and Alabama in a "Great Migration" lasting until 1819. The Georgia Piedmont was engulfed first as population, dammed up behind the Ocmulgee River line for a generation, swept into each new block of Indian lands opened by cession, encouraged by the state's practice of granting 202 ½ acre plots free to those drawing lucky numbers at lotteries. The rapid growth of plantations there was illustrated by the increase in the number of slaves: from 14,064 in 1810 to 39,601 in 1820, 93,186 in 1830, 156,799 in 1840, and 232,193 in 1850.

Others rushed into Alabama, to besiege the land offices at Huntsville, St. Stephens, and Catawba with dollars in hand; government sales skyrocketed from 600,000 acres in 1816 to 2,278,045 three years later. Bidding between speculators and settlers was so spirited that prices soared to $30 or even $50 for good bottom lands and promising town sites. Those fantastic sales brought an influx of speculators from all over the United States, bent on sharing the harvest. Their presence at Huntsville, where the prized Tennessee Valley lands were sold, accounted for sales that reached the amazing figure of $7,000,000 in 1818, the peak year. Even the wholesale engrossment of cotton land by jobbers failed to check migration; instead the nationwide excitement caused by the Alabama boom attracted even more settlers. One North Carolina planter wrote in 1817: "*The Alabama Fever* rages here with great violence and has carried off vast numbers of our citizens. I am apprehensive, if it continues to spread as it has done, it will almost depopulate the country."

By the close of 1819, when a serious panic slowed the westward march, 200,000 people lived in the Gulf Plains and one-half the nation's cotton was produced there. Western Georgia was comfortably filled, except for lands still occupied by Creeks and Cherokee. In Alabama one arm of settlement extended up the Tombigbee River as far as Demopolis, the head of steamboat navigation; another followed the Alabama River to Montgomery, a village laid out by speculators a short time before. From towns along those streams cotton was floated to Mobile in flat-bottomed barges or on primitive steamboats, to transform that sleepy Spanish port into a thriving American metropolis of 3,000 souls. Central Alabama gained less by the rush, partly because its water outlets were not satisfactory and partly because pioneers avoided the prairie lands of the Black Belt. A sprinkling of settlers who made their way west over the Great Valley Road from the Virginia and Carolina back country were clustered about Tuscaloosa. Northern Alabama, where tempting lands of the Tennessee Valley beckoned settlers from Tennessee and Georgia, profited more. By 1820 most of the area's cotton country was under cultivation and a bustling commercial life developing at Tuscumbia and Decatur where cotton bales were stored until they could be floated over the Muscle Shoals rapids in periods of high water. In Mississippi the principal growth was about Natchez and along the Nashville-Natchez Road. Seventy-five thousand people, of whom 32,000 were slaves, lived there in 1820.

The "Great Migration" into the Gulf Plains made statehood possible for both Mississippi and Alabama. Mississippi acted first, for its concentrated population was able to apply greater pressure, and in 1817 entered the Union; Alabama followed two years later. Both adopted constitutions reflecting the leveling influence of the frontier. Neither required property for voting; both granted the franchise to all male whites residing there one year. Each made the legislature supreme over the governor—whose veto of any act could be overridden by a simple majority vote—and vested in that elective body power to appoint most state officials including judges. Representation in the assemblies was apportioned on the basis of free white population, thus giving the planter no advantage over the small farmer in government matters. The liberalism of the constitutions served as an additional inducement to settlers.

The migratory stream continued to flow through the 1820's, although in diminished volume. The few Indian cessions during the decade meant that most immigrants would direct their footsteps to the already settled areas of northern and southern Alabama and southwestern Mississippi, where population increased from 200,000 to 445,000. That many new-comers were planters was indicated by the mounting number of slaves: from 31 to 38 per cent of the Alabama population. Many small farmers displaced by growing plantations sought homes in two new regions opened during the 1820's. Those moving to Florida when that area was secured from Spain in 1821 were destined to disappointment; sandy soil and the Seminole War soon dashed their hopes of bountiful crops of cotton, sugar, coffee, oranges, almonds, olives, silk, and other semitropical products. Those entering western Tennessee were more fortunate, for rich alluvial soils produced large cotton crops. Settlement began in 1819 when speculators under Andrew Jackson laid out Memphis. During the rest of the decade the back country around that well-placed commercial town filled in rapidly.

The trickle of immigrants moving west during the 1820's swelled to flood proportions again in the prosperous 1830's. Prices and profits were fantastic during those boom years; returns of 35 per cent yearly were common, while one planter who equipped a plantation at a cost of $15,000 marketed a $50,000 crop two years later. Such fortunes proved an irresistible magnet, drawing settlers westward to the Indian lands obtained during Jackson's presidency. Some swept over the Creek and Cherokee lands of northern Georgia and eastern Tennessee to lay out farms and commercial towns: Atlanta, Rome, and Chattanooga. Others showed tardy appreciation for Alabama's Black Belt, bidding so enthusiastically for its lands that prices rose to $35 an acre. Still more carried the cotton frontier across central Mississippi, filling the Back Belt and northern Bluff Hills, and pushing on to unsettled portions of western Tennessee. A Huntsville newspaper correspondent, watching the migration, wrote in 1833: "It would seem as if North and South Carolina were pouring forth their population by swarms. Perhaps I have gone by in the Creek nation, over 3,000 persons, all emigrating, including negroes, of course. The fires of their encampments made the woods blaze in all directions." During the decade cotton exports from New Orleans doubled, while those from Mobile increased three fold.

By 1840 the boundaries of the cotton kingdom were marked out; only the fringes and a few by-passed wilderness islands remained to be settled. They were filled during the next twenty years as transportation improvements opened isolated areas. One was the Coosa Valley of western Georgia where small farmers were gradually replaced by cotton planters after railroads penetrated that region. Another was in east-central Mississippi, a rich-soil country formerly given over to cattle grazing due to the distance from water transportation. More important was the rush of planters to the Mississippi Flood Plains after 1842 when devastating floods brought home the need of co-operative efforts to protect the region. County supervisors were named to collect contributions, levees built, flooded areas drained, and the delta converted into a tempting agricultural country. The excellent silt soil soon attracted large planters, until by 1850 the Flood Plains rivaled the Black Belt in the size of holdings and concentration of slaves. By that time the fully settled Southwest produced nearly three-quarters of the nation's cotton.

The social order created by this rapid expansion differed markedly from that developing in the Northwest at the same time. The Lake Plains by

1850 was a land of democratic small farmers producing a diversified list of cereal crops and livestock. The Gulf Plains was a region where rigidly drawn class lines stratified the social order, where concepts of democracy and equality were in bad repute, and where a few fortunate individuals controlled the best land, most of the slaves, and a disproportionate share of the wealth.

At the top of the social pyramid were the few great planters—never numbering more than 46,000—who owned one or more plantations, fifty or more slaves, and collectively three-quarters of the wealth of the south. Those "cotton snobs" lived pleasure-packed lives; they wintered in great white-pillared houses at Montgomery or Mobile or Natchez, summered at popular watering places, read the best English literature or such polite native journals as *The Southern Literary Messenger*, dabbled in law and politics, and indulged in a constant round of gay balls, fox hunts, and horse racing. Those who sought a serious end in life served as justices of the peace, members of their state legislature, congressmen, or military leaders; those were the respectable professions alone acceptable in that highly stratified society. The majority were content to manage their estates or pursue pleasure with an avidity that suggested boredom.

They were supported by the several plantations that each owned in the Black Belt or Flood Plains. These estates contained a thousand acres and a hundred slaves—that being an efficient size which combined the economies of large-scale production with the compactness needed to keep workers from wasting too much time going to and from the fields—and were operated by a hired overseer. Dominating each plantation was the owner's great frame house with its spacious porches and classical colonnades. Around it were clustered the outbuildings, storage sheds, and log slave cabins. Near at hand was the cotton gin, a board structure set on pillars with a central hub reaching through to the ground level. Horses driven in a circle transmitted power to the gin on its raised platform, while the elevation allowed raw cotton to be fed directly into the machine from wagons. The cleaned lint was blown into another bin that reached to the ground in the rear. Close by was a bailing press, also operated by horsepower, where fibres were pressed into bales of standardized size and weight for shipping.

Most plantation overseers divided their crop about equally between cotton and corn, largely because slaves could plant and care for twice as much cotton as they could pick. Hence cotton acreage was determined by the picking capacity of the field hands and enough land was put into other crops to keep them employed the rest of the year. That was especially necessary as most of the planter's capital investment was in his workers; his return depended on the efficiency with which they were employed. For that reason he often divided them into gangs under minor overseers, with one doing nothing but hoeing, another plowing, and the like. In that form the plantation system was one of the most efficient devised in the history of agriculture. Yet it depended for its success on exploitive methods, as neither the slaves nor overseers were interested in preserving the soil's fertility. Large scale methods allowed plantation owners to buy out less fortunate neighbors, but doomed them to hard times once the initial fertility of their fields declined.

Influential as the great planters were, they were far outbalanced numerically by the social group next below them, the "one-horse" planters who operated their own estates with the help of from one to twenty bonded servants. About 20 per cent of the southern whites were in this class. Most of them lived squalid lives on the less fruitful lands, either supervising their own Negroes or working beside the slaves in the fields. Their homes were log cabins or unkempt frame dwellings, their pleasures few, and their cultural interests confined to the bombastic outpourings of local newspaper editors whose concern was the moral and mental delinquency of rival publishers rather than conveying news. This miserable existence was forced upon the small planters by their all-consuming ambition: their one object was to multiply acres and slaves until they crossed the gulf into the planter class. A few saw their dream come true, but far more spent their lives in the hopeless pursuit of an unattainable ideal.

The middle-class group did much to popularize slavery among the non-slave-owners who made up the bulk of the South's population. Small planters might spend their days in blue jeans and boots, sweating at the plow beside their Negro servants while their homespun-garbed wives tended to the dairying or labored over a spinning wheel, but on Sunday or election day they were transformed into the envied upper class in each southern town. Clad in the distinctive broadcloth coat and high hat of the aristocracy, they voiced their opinions with an assurance becoming their exalted station. They naturally defended slavery, for only the perpetuation of the institution would allow them to become great planters, and their views helped win the masses of the people to support the system.

The small and large planters together, with their families, constituted about 23 per cent of the southern white population. The remaining 77 per cent were non-slave-holders. Most were hard-working yeomen farmers whose tiny holdings dotted poor-soil areas not suitable to plantation agriculture: the mountainous country, the pine barrens, and the northern and southern fringes of the cotton belt. There they lived in ramshackle log cabins, dressed in dejected woolen hats, tow shirts, and blue jean breeches held up by a single "gallus," and spent their days in the backbreaking task of trying to scratch a living from a stubborn soil. Their appearance was deceiving, for most were earnest, hard-working men. Pleasure and culture were equally unknown in their squalid lives, but only because they chose to work endlessly toward the day when they could buy a slave and begin the slow climb upward toward a position in the great planter class. Although they were the principal victims of the slave system, they were among the institution's most violent defenders, believing its perpetuation would make their dreams of a planter's life come true.

Far below the yeoman farmers in the South's social scale were the poor whites who, as "crackers," "hillbillies," or "sandhillers," were scattered in small communities through the poorest southern lands: the Georgia pine barrens, the sandy-woods section of southern Mississippi, the piney forests of Alabama, and the worn-out soils abandoned by cotton planters. Most of them made a pretence of planting a crop but lethargy overcame them once the seed was in the ground. They depended for food less on their weed-choked fields than on omnipresent hogs who cared for themselves and on game they brought down with their long rifles. Unkempt, illiterate, shiftless, and lazy, these miserable by-products of the plantation system were condemned to their squalid existence by more fortunate neighbors who pushed them onto unproductive lands, then kept there by the ravages of the parasitical hook worm which left them lethargic and listless. Yet they too defended slavery, largely because they subconsciously realized that this artificial barrier alone kept them from the very bottom of the social scale.

That place was reserved for the slaves, who in 1850 numbered 1,841,000 for the lower South as a whole, as compared to 2,137,000 whites. Most were taken to the Gulf Plains by their masters, although a slave trade between the older seaboard states, where an excess supply existed, and the newer states of the Southwest developed as early as the 1820's. The majority worked as field hands on cotton plantations where they were fairly well treated, for owners soon found that workers declined in efficiency when discontented. Yet this modicum of security hardly compensated for the low living standard, lack of educational opportunity, and complete absence of individual freedom that slavery forced upon them.

The southern social structure, built upon a mudsill of bonded labor, was fully developed by 1850. Differing radically from that of the Northwest in basic crops, agricultural methods, form of labor, and social philosophy, the unique society reared in the South helped create the sectional conflicts which plagued the nation through the first half of the nineteenth century and eventually found expression in civil war.

# CHAPTER XVI

# The Economics of Sectionalism

## 1815-1837

The settlement of the trans-Appalachian frontier brought the United States face to face with a terrifying problem: how could an industrialized Northeast, a cotton-growing South, and a small-farming West live side by side in peace? In each of these sections the people were wedded to a distinctive type of economic enterprise and demanded national legislation beneficial to them, regardless of its effects on their countrymen. They soon realized that no one section could triumph in a three-cornered battle for federal favor; rather two must unite to bludgeon Congress into passing favorable laws. That realization launched the nation upon a generation of controversy as Northeast and South, recognizing the complete incompatibility of their own systems, struggled to win the support of the West. False promises, legislative favors, emotionalism, vote-swapping—those were the weapons employed by both sides in their frantic wooing of the West—yet final victory was determined by forces over which neither antagonist had any control. Roads and canals and railroads, built by humble men whose concern was profits rather than political dominance, eventually settled the battle of the sections by welding Northeast and West so firmly together that no amount of legislative manipulation could separate them.

The object of those builders, whether they lived in the Northeast or the South, was to tap the surplus-producing areas developing in the trans-Appalachian country as the self-sufficient economy of the frontier gave way to crop specialization during the 1820's. The cotton belt, stretching across the Gulf states from Georgia to Louisiana, was one potential exporting region eyed covetously by eastern commercial interests. North of this, in Kentucky, Tennessee, and southern Ohio, Indiana, and Illinois, lay a zone where tobacco and corn vied for supremacy. By 1840 only Virginia

329

surpassed Kentucky and Tennessee in tobacco production, while Tennessee was also the leading corn-growing state of the Union with Kentucky close behind. Together those two commonwealths were responsible for one-quarter of the nation's corn, and enough more was grown in the valleys of the Scioto, Miami, and Wabash rivers to bring the section's production to 56 per cent of the national total.

Much of the crop was fed to livestock. Some went to the pigs that roamed everywhere until, fattened by a winter's feeding in a field of standing corn, they were sold to wandering drovers for the trip to market. During the 1820's herds of several thousand grunting porkers were driven southward through Saluda or Cumberland gaps to the cotton plantations, but the difficulty of driving unruly hogs such distances encouraged the development of local slaughtering centers in the West. Cincinnati, favorably situated at a spot where drovers' trails and water transportation met, won acclaim as the "Porkopolis of the West" by 1840 when it boasted sixty-two slaughtering houses. Cattle raisers were also attracted to the Ohio Valley by the abundance of corn for fattening purposes. Herds of rangy steers from the prairies of Indiana and Illinois were driven eastward to the Scioto Valley, gorged on unhusked ears of corn for a year and a half, then started on their journey again in time to reach New York or Philadelphia between April 15 and August 1. Travelers who complained of slow-moving herds that blocked the Pennsylvania roads were justified; by 1825 15,000 cattle from the Scioto country reached the East each year and the number continued to increase until 1840.

North of the zone where corn and livestock ruled was the wheat belt, stretching across northern Ohio and Indiana, southern Michigan, and the Rock River country of Illinois to the limits of settlement in southeastern Wisconsin. Everywhere within this domain, where winter frosts loosened the soil and summer sun assured bountiful harvests, wheat was the staple crop, but much of the production was centered in Ohio. By 1840 that state, with a yield of 17,000,000 bushels, wrested from New York and Pennsylvania the position as the nation's leading wheat producer, while the remaining states of the Northwest accounted for almost one-third of the national supply. Most of the grain was ground into flour at local mills to escape the heavy export costs.

The presence of the surpluses produced in the trans-Appalachian zones presented a problem to the West and a challenge to the Northeast and South. From the western point of view there were only two possible solutions: the surpluses must be consumed at home or shipped to distant markets in non-food-producing areas. For a time during the 1820's, when agricultural specialization was just beginning, westerners flirted with the possibility of developing a local outlet by fostering industry in the Ohio Valley. The idea was attractive; home industries would not only consume the produce of western farms but remove the double transportation costs which frontiersmen paid when they shipped grain east and manufactured goods west. Yet inducements offered industrialists to lure them to the Ohio Valley brought few results. While a few firms engaged in processing agricultural goods took root at Pittsburgh, Cincinnati, and the Miami River Valley, the bulk of the industries attracted by the region's promoters soon languished. By the mid-1820's even the most optimistic westerner admitted that manufacturing could never keep pace with farming in a section where land rather than jobs was the principal loadstone attracting immigrants.

Nor did the second solution to the West's marketing problem—developing markets in other parts of the nation—offer greater possibilities, as neither of the two outlets available in the 1820's could be used profitably. Export southward on the Mississippi River highway was unsatisfactory, partly because of heavy losses inevitable on the slow-moving barges universally used, and partly because low water during much of the year forced the West to dump its accumulated surpluses on the New Orleans market during the spring and fall floods, with a depressing effect on prices. Moreover grain spoiled rapidly in the humid heat of the lower Mississippi. Nor was the eastern outlet more satisfactory, for the towering peaks of the Appalachian mountain barrier were crossed only by a few roads where wagon freighters charged exorbitant rates. To send a hundred pounds of goods from Ohio to Philadelphia cost $10 and took a month; charges that excluded all produce but whiskey, hemp, and a few other expensive items. Westerners believed inadequate transportation not only doomed their section to continued poverty but threatened the structure of society. Insufficient markets, they insisted, bred indolence and laziness by stifling incentive to produce.

The West's problem spelled opportunity for the other two sections. No seer was needed to convince northeastern or southern commercial leaders that a fortune waited the lucky individuals who devised some way of tapping the trading areas beyond the mountains. Nor was a political sage required to demonstrate that more than riches would reward the victor. The section winning the trade of the West would win that region's allegiance as well. As Northeast and South squared away for the conflict that would determine which would dominate the nation's legislature both dimly realized that the one establishing economic ties with the West would emerge triumphant.

The accident of technological advance gave the South an initial advantage in the struggle for western trade. The development of the steamboat in the early years of the nineteenth century converted the Mississippi River into a giant artery binding the two sections together. The conquest of the western waterways began in 1811 when an eastern syndicate launched a 371 ton steamship, the *New Orleans,* at Pittsburgh, then sent it bravely off to New Orleans with instructions to demonstrate its ability to stem the swift current at each town. Four years later, when another vessel, the *Enterprise,* shattered the arguments of scoffers by ascending the river from New Orleans to Louisville in twenty-five days, the rush to capitalize on the new invention was on. By 1819, thirty-one boats plied the Mississippi and Ohio waterways; by 1825 the number was 75 and by 1840 187. All were operated by individual owners or small syndicates. An attempt by an eastern corporation to monopolize western commerce collapsed before hostile frontier pressure, while combinations were so abhorred that the first one—the Ohio and Mississippi Mail Line to carry freight between Louisville and New Orleans —dissolved in 1833 after a year of combating freedom-loving western opinion. The highly competitive system of individual ownership forced freight rates down until the hundred pounds of produce that cost $5 for the New Orleans-Louisville trip in keelboat days was carried for $2 in 1820, and for 25 cents in 1840.

The lowered rates were made possible by technical contributions of western engineers. Two problems faced them when the first cumbersome eastern boats invaded the Mississippi River system: they must build vessels with enough power to stem swift-flowing currents, and with light enough draft to navigate the shallow streams of the West. The first was solved by developing the high-pressure engine, which was light yet so powerful that its coughing exhaust could be heard for miles and its rhythmic strokes set the whole ship trembling. The second was more difficult, but over the course of years designers gradually lengthened their vessels, lightened the draft, and added two or three upper decks to offset the loss of cargo space below the waterline. The giant Mississippi steamboats that evolved by 1840 were ridiculed by humorists as "engines on a raft with $11,000 worth of jig-saw work," yet they were thoroughly practical. Three decks high, 250 feet long, with pilothouse perched fifty feet in the air and the whole superstructure splendid with rococo ornaments, they carried two tons of freight for every ton of boat while drawing from two to four feet of water. Some captains even boasted their ships could navigate on a heavy dew.

These improvements allowed steamboats to extend their trading areas until they conquered all but the shallowest of the Mississippi's tributaries. Louisville yielded its place as head of navigation on the Ohio in 1820 when a vessel ran the rapids there and reached Pittsburgh; ten years later ships plied the upper reaches of that stream as far as Olean on the Allegheny

River. The conquest of the Cumberland River began in 1818 when the first steamship reached Nashville, and of the Tennessee three years later when Florence, at the foot of Muscle Shoals, was visited by a light-draft vessel. Not until 1828 did a steamboat succeed in running those dangerous rapids and inaugurating service on the upper Tennessee as far as Knoxville. Each year thereafter adventurous river captains pushed farther and farther up the shallow streams that drained the Mississippi Valley; Indianapolis on the White River was reached in 1831, Lafayette on the Wabash in 1832, South Bend on the St. Joseph in 1834, Peoria on the Illinois in 1830.

By that time every hamlet on a creek large enough to wade in dreamed of becoming a "river port" and vied in offering lavish rewards to the first steamships reaching its wharves. Typical was Delphi, on the upper Wabash, which finally persuaded the captain of a light-draft vessel to make the attempt during spring high water in June, 1834. When the ship ran aground a few miles below the village the whole citizenry turned out, drafted twenty yoke of oxen into use, and literally dragged the tiny steamboat through mud to its destination. Even though the boat sank on its return trip, Delphi boasted from then on of its direct water communication with New Orleans. More practical men formed interstate associations to dredge out streams, remove snags, and construct canals around obstacles to navigation; the most successful was the Louisville and Portland Canal Company which in 1825 completed locks around the Falls of the Ohio at Louisville.

These herculean efforts seemed worth while when the reward was economic independence for the West. No longer would hard-earned dollars be drained eastward by exorbitant freight rates and high-priced eastern goods; now the Ohio Valley could sell in the South and import needed manufactured items from New Orleans. Yet by the 1830's the dreams of that prosperous millennium were fading as westerners realized the steamboat only intensified their dependence on the East. The more the West sold, the more the section must buy from beyond the Appalachians. Manufactured goods did not reach the Ohio Valley by steamboat, as the roundabout water trip via New Orleans proved too expensive for all but the bulkiest items; they continued to cross the mountains in costly wagon trains. Even worse was the realization that the steamboat did not solve all the section's marketing problems. Despite all the efforts of inventors, the bulk of navigation on the Mississippi's tributaries was still confined to the high-water periods accompanying spring and fall floods. That meant glutted markets, low prices, and heavy spoilage for grain reaching the South on the crest of the spring floods when shipping was easiest. The hazards of nature, and the failure of southerners to develop industries, destined the river trade to failure as a solution for the West's economic problem.

This was the East's opportunity. If the mountain barrier could be pierced, western trade would swing to the Atlantic states, giving easterners cheap food and westerners inexpensive manufactured goods. But how could the Appalachians be crossed? Roads were not the answer; the total traffic on the Old National Road and the Pennsylvania turnpike system in 1825 amounted to only 40,000 tons against 1,500,000 bushels of wheat and corn shipped southward that year. Some other transportation system must be devised, and fortunate indeed would be the eastern city or state that happened upon the solution. That was the incentive which plunged the seaboard commercial cities—New York, Boston, Philadelphia, Baltimore, Charleston, and Savannah—into a quarter-century of competition and experimentation that ended with the mountains conquered and Northeast and West bound firmly together.

New York gained the first advantage. Stretching westward behind the city was the broad Mohawk Valley, a natural pass through the mountains that rose no more than 578 feet above sea level. Why not utilize that splendid highway for a canal tying Lake Erie and the Atlantic together? New York flirted with the intriguing plan for a decade, while popular pressure mounted and petitions showered upon the legislature, before the decision was reached in April, 1817. The law passed then authorized the use of state funds for two canals, one from Lake Erie to the Hudson River, the other from the Hudson to Lake Champlain. Work began at once and progressed rapidly, despite inexperienced engineers and sickness which ravaged the workers as they dug their way through germ-infested swamps. By 1823 the canal was completed from the Hudson to the Genesee rivers. The most difficult stretches lay ahead; a stone aqueduct eight hundred feet long must be built across the Genesee River and five large locks constructed at Lockport to surmount the steep Niagara escarpment. One by one the obstacles were overcome until, in October, 1825, the whole 363-mile length of the canal was thrown open to traffic with elaborate ceremonies.

The Erie Canal cost New York State $7,000,000 but seldom had an American commonwealth made a sounder investment. Within nine years toll collections amounted to $8,500,000—enough to pay for all construction and interest charges—but more important was the stimulus given the state's economic development. By lowering freight rates between Buffalo and New York from 100 to 15 dollars a ton, and the time from twenty to eight days, the Erie attracted a volume of western trade which invigorated commercial activity along its entire length. Farms bordering the route doubled and quadrupled in value, underdeveloped areas on either side blossomed as feeder canals were built during the next years, and New

York City spurted into a period of unparalleled growth that established its supremacy over its traditional commercial competitors—Boston, Philadelphia, and Baltimore. Overnight the city was converted into the nation's leading metropolis as its less fortunate rivals watched with ill-concealed envy.

Their jealousy played an important role in strengthening the commercial ties between Northeast and West. No sooner was the Erie Canal completed than Boston, Philadelphia, and Baltimore began clamoring for canals which would allow them to share the western trade. Boston acted first in February, 1825, when pressure from its representatives forced the

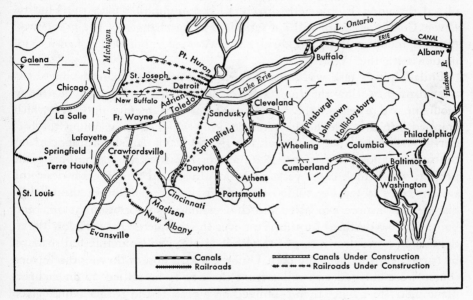

Western Transportation Routes in 1840

Massachusetts legislature to order surveys of possible routes across the state. When those were completed a year later they discouraged all but the most optimistic; four hundred locks were needed between Boston and the Connecticut River, while the Berkshires could be crossed by either a long tunnel through Hoosac Mountain or a devious route across Vermont where 220 locks were required within eighteen miles. Although an enthusiastic legislative committee estimated the system could be built for $6,000,000 and urged immediate action, wiser counsel prevailed.

Boston's merchants, although disappointed, were not ready to give up hope of tapping western trade. Their pressure forced the Massachusetts legislature to back an equally impossible scheme: a railroad across the

Berkshires to Albany. The charter for the first of several small lines designed to span the state, the Boston and Worcester Railroad, was granted in
1830 to Boston capitalists willing to risk their fortunes on what appeared to
be a fantastic venture. All went well, however, and five years later the first
steam cars entered Worcester. In the meantime a second company, the
Western Railroad Corporation, was formed in 1833 to undertake the more
difficult task of extending the line across the mountains to Albany. Money
came in slowly—even the promoters believed no profits could ever be
made by such an expensive road and appealed for funds only on patriotic
grounds—but in 1835 work began. Seven years later the road was completed, bringing Boston into direct rail communication with the Hudson
River. Conditions were still not satisfactory, for changes of gauge required
transshipments at West Stockbridge and Worcester, but Boston had its connection with the West.

Philadelphia's task was somewhat easier. Preliminary surveys indicated
a canal might follow the Juniata River to its source, where only a narrow
mountain ridge barred the way to the roaring Conemaugh River which
emptied into the Allegheny. After debating whether to surmount the barrier by inclined planes or tunnel, the Pennsylvania legislature decided on
the former and in February, 1826, authorized work to begin. This giant
project, which took eight years to build, illustrated the feverish desire of
eastern cities to tap the trade of the Ohio Valley; seldom in the world's
history had a more expensive and cumbersome transportation system been
built. Cargoes destined for the West over the completed network left Philadelphia on horse-drawn cars of the Philadelphia and Columbia Railroad, or
by barge over the privately built Union Canal. Those following the former
course were stopped two miles from the city to be pulled up an inclined
plane 2,805 feet long, then continued on by rail to the Susquehanna River
at Columbia where they were transshipped to canal boats. Following the
principal canal of the system through 108 locks they eventually reached
Hollidaysburg where the Allegheny Portage Railway began. There the
goods were loaded on cars and hauled ten miles up a series of five inclined
planes by stationary engines placed at the top, then coasted down to Johns-
town where canal boats waited them for the last 104-mile stretch of the
journey into Pittsburgh. The unwieldy Pennsylvania Portage and Canal
System was 320 miles long and cost $10,000,000, yet hardly a Pennsyl-
vanian doubted the wisdom of investing so much if a share of the western
trade was secured.

Baltimore's problem was still more difficult, for any canal reaching the
Ohio Valley must surmount a mountainous elevation of 2,754 feet. Undaunted by that formidable obstacle, the city's merchants held a series of

enthusiastic mass meetings, then in 1827 organized a private company, the Chesapeake and Ohio Canal Company, to undertake the task with government support. So anxious were citizens of the Potomac Valley for western trade that financing the project offered no problem; Baltimore pledged $1,500,000, the city of Washington a similar amount, and Congress agreed to purchase $1,000,000 worth of the company's stock. Yet from the first things went badly. Lawsuits over the right of way plagued the company, construction in the narrow Potomac River gorge proved difficult, financial support dwindled as backers failed to live up to their pledges. When the Panic of 1837 halted work temporarily the Chesapeake and Ohio Canal reached only a hundred miles westward, and although construction was carried on halfheartedly until 1850 the waterway never passed beyond Cumberland at the base of the mountains. The ill-fated venture cost its supporters $11,000,000 and was important only in showing the absurd lengths to which eastern cities would go in their quest for the West's trade.

Even more fantastic was a second project stemming from Baltimore's desire to tap the Ohio Valley markets. While plans for the canal were still in the discussion stage rumors reached America of a newfangled English contraption called a locomotive which ran on rails at breathtaking speeds of fifteen miles an hour. A few enterprising Baltimore business men were interested enough to investigate, raise money, and petition the Maryland legislature for the right to build a railroad westward to the Ohio country. Their charter, granted on February 28, 1827, to the Baltimore and Ohio Railroad, launched the first successful American experiment with this new means of locomotion. Work began on July 4, 1828, and though none of the engineers had ever seen a railroad, let alone built one, construction proceeded rapidly. By 1831, when the tracks were at Frederick, profits from local traffic were so great that three locomotives were purchased to replace the horse-drawn cars used at first. Litigation with the canal company and the effects of the Panic of 1837 slowed the line's advance during the next years but Cumberland was reached in 1842. During the next decade the Baltimore and Ohio crossed the Appalachians to become a major link in the East-West transportation network.

The strenuous efforts of northern cities to reach the interior spurred the commercial cities of the Southeast into action, although there the initial objectives were somewhat different. The merchants of Richmond, Charleston, and Savannah had no thought of tapping Mississippi Valley markets when they first turned to internal improvement projects; they simply wanted to extend their trading areas to offset the economic stagnation settling over the seaboard as the center of cotton production moved westward. This could be done, they reasoned, by pushing railroads farther and farther into the interior, as freighting over highways was too expensive and canals were ruled out by the steep Blue Ridge. Their ambition launched the South on its first railway-building projects and prepared the way for later intersectional lines.

Charleston, its commercial supremacy threatened by steamboats which drained the trade of its own back country southward to Savannah, took the lead in promoting railroads. In 1833 its merchants completed the Charleston and Hamburg Railroad to the central Savannah Valley where goods

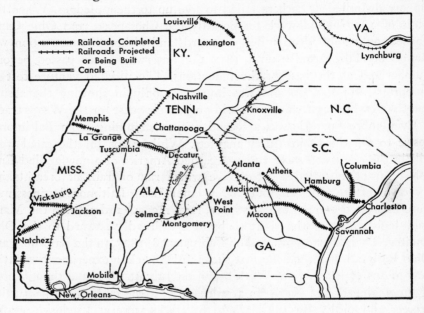

Principal Southern Railroads in 1840

bound down the river could be diverted eastward. A year later they financed the Georgia Railroad, designed to build two lines westward toward Athens and Atlanta. The tracks of this road extended as far as Athens and Madison before hard times halted construction in 1841. In the meantime Charleston's activity stirred its commercial rivals into action. Richmond, which was already connected with Lynchburg by canal, brought pressure on the Virginia legislature in 1831 to charter the Lynchburg and New River Railroad in the vague hope of reaching the Ohio Valley. Savannah, alarmed by the threat of the Charleston and Hamburg Railroad to its trade, in 1833 prodded Georgia's lawmakers into organizing the Central of Georgia Railroad to build across the state toward Macon. The city's business men also backed the Monroe Railroad, formed at the same time to connect Macon with Atlanta. Work on both lines progressed slowly during the next years; the Central of Georgia did not reach its terminus until 1843.

Those roads, fanning out into the interior from the seaboard, would have been only locally important had they not attracted the attention of business leaders in two ambitious western cities—Cincinnati and Memphis. Why not, they reasoned, build lines to meet the advancing eastern railroads? Such connections would give them something always coveted by the West: a choice of markets. If they established rail outlets through Charleston or Savannah they could sell either there, at New Orleans, or in the East over the New York and Pennsylvania canals, wherever the price was highest. No longer would they be at the mercy of shrewd buyers at the mouth of the Mississippi.

The first of these projects was touched off by a giant mass meeting at Cincinnati during the summer of 1835. Bombastic resolutions urging railroad connections with Charleston were passed and a committee under William Henry Harrison named to secure the co-operation of states along the way. That proved easy. South Carolina was already eager, eastern Tennessee favored railroads to end its economic isolation, and Kentucky succumbed when the promoters promised a branch line to Louisville. One by one their legislatures during the winter of 1835-36 issued charters to the Louisville, Cincinnati and Charleston Railroad, until by spring the organizers could turn to raising funds. That too was easy at first, especially in the South where the sectional implications of the project were apparent. Robert Y. Hayne, South Carolina's brilliant statesman, summed up the southern case when he told a meeting of Charleston business men that a railroad connection with the Northwest would not only open more lands for cotton growing by guaranteeing a plentiful food supply, but encourage westerners to found textile mills. These, he said, would join the two sections in perpetual economic union, assuring the continuance of slavery despite the hostility of the Northeast. Both prosperity and sectional peace, Hayne believed, hinged on the road's success.

Although the South united on such broad issues, the route of the proposed railroad caused more difficulty. South Carolina's representatives in the company insisted the line should run through Columbia to Knoxville, then utilize Cumberland Gap to enter Kentucky; Georgia's delegates were just as firm in demanding an extension of their state's railroad network from Atlanta to Knoxville. When the road's directors finally voted to build through Columbia the irate Georgians refused to continue support; with other disgruntled members from eastern Tennessee they withdrew from the company and laid plans to build a separate road along their favored route. The result was the chartering of two lines in 1836, the Hiwassee

Railroad from Knoxville to the state line, and the Western and Atlantic Railroad from Atlanta to the Tennessee border. This schism proved disastrous to both the Georgia interests and the Louisville, Cincinnati and Charleston Railroad, for the none too plentiful funds raised by private subscription and state aid were divided between the rival projects. All three lines struggled along until 1839 when hard times and languishing interest stopped construction. Thus ended the South's most ambitious scheme to tie itself to the West economically.

Nor did the plans of a second western city to connect with the southeastern seaboard prove more fruitful. Memphis shared with its sister cities on the banks of the Mississippi a growing alarm as New Orleans doubled its population decade after decade while they lagged behind. A railroad to Charleston or Savannah would divert some river traffic eastward through Memphis, as well as expand the back country tributary to that port. In the Southeast Charleston was just as interested. Its merchants envisaged handsome profits from handling the foodstuffs and cotton that would flow eastward over such a line, while its politicians realized the sectional importance of a direct connection with the West. John C. Calhoun was particularly concerned, partly because his rival in South Carolina politics, Robert Y. Hayne, would enjoy a great advantage should the Cincinnati-Charleston road materialize, partly because he foresaw the day when slavery would split the Union in twain. A railroad to Memphis would promote southern nationalism by tying Southwest and Southeast together.

Agitation for the line began in Memphis in 1833 when a local business leader, Edmund Pendleton Gaines, stirred up sentiment with mass meetings, newspaper articles, and speeches. His efforts aroused such interest that within a year surveys were completed for three possible routes, terminating in the East at Baltimore, Charleston, and Savannah. Gaines and his supporters agreed the Charleston terminus was best, partly because South Carolina promised greater financial support, partly because such a road could incorporate a small line around Muscle Shoals—the Tuscumbia and Decatur Railroad. Practical as their plans seemed, the promoters were doomed to failure. They first tried to form one company to build along the entire route. When support was not forthcoming they settled on several smaller lines designed to connect key cities between Memphis and Atlanta. The failure of South Carolina, already deeply involved in the Cincinnati venture, to pay more than lip service to the companies, and economic chaos following the Panic of 1837, ended all hope for success. When work halted in 1839 only eight miles of track on one of the connecting roads, the Memphis and LaGrange Railroad, were in operation.

Ill fated as the Memphis projects were, they set another Mississippi

Valley city to dreaming of eastern rail connections. Merchants of Vicksburg, anxious to extend their trading sphere and challenge the supremacy of New Orleans, began in the mid-1830's planning a through road from their city to Macon where it would meet the advancing tracks of the Central of Georgia Railroad. No great statesmen such as Hayne or Calhoun were ready to back their scheme, nor did their ranks include a promoter of Edmund Pendleton Gaines' stature. Hence no attempt was made to give unity to the plan. Instead the few short lines—later welded into the road connecting Vicksburg with Savannah—were projected by local groups who failed to realize their sectional importance. One, the Vicksburg and Jackson Railroad, was completed across central Mississippi by 1840; another, the Montgomery Railroad between Montgomery, Alabama, and West Point, Georgia, succumbed to hard times in the late 1830's after only a few miles of track were laid.

Ineffectual as were the efforts of river cities to secure eastern connections, they alarmed business men of New Orleans and Mobile, who knew a railroad between the Mississippi and the seaboard would divert traffic eastward. Their solution was to augment their own river routes with railroads. Mobile talked much of the lines it must build—to Jackson in Mississippi, to the Tennessee Valley, to the new town of Chattanooga—but financial support was lacking, and when hard times ended construction in 1840 only two railroads were under construction, the Selma and Tennessee Railroad and the Wetumpka and Coosa Railroad. New Orleans fared slightly better in its plan for a railroad to Nashville as a bid for the trade of the Cumberland and Tennessee valleys. Mass meetings in both cities led to the chartering of the New Orleans and Nashville Railroad early in 1837 but before construction more than began the Panic of 1837 ended financial support. Twenty-three miles of rickety track in Louisiana were the sole monument to the promoters' dreams.

A decade of grandiose planning brought the South few tangible benefits. Its hopes for a connection with the Ohio Valley vanished when local jealousies doomed the Louisville, Cincinnati and Charleston Railroad; its dreams of uniting the Mississippi Valley with the seaboard were dissipated by indifference, poverty, and regional conflicts. When hard times ended railroad building the section was neither a compact economic unit nor united commercially with the West. Yet the few roads completed served as a framework for the southern rail system that emerged with the financial recovery of the 1840's and 1850's.

Like most southerners, westerners during the period of road and canal building preceding the Panic of 1837 thought of internal improvements in local rather than national terms. Canals, in their eyes, were needed to carry bulky crops to nearby river ports. Every list of commodity prices in the local papers argued for waterways; corn which sold for 20 cents a bushel in Indianapolis or Columbus brought 50 cents along the Ohio River. The differential of 30 cents a bushel allowed farmers to compute astronomical figures on the savings canals would effect; on every acre producing 60 bushels of corn canals would save the owner $18 yearly, on every 160 acre farm the increased profit would be $2,840, on every township $408,960. Lead-pencil engineers only needed enough ciphering paper to prove that internal improvements would pay for themselves a thousand times over simply by local savings. Moreover canals between the Great Lakes and the Mississippi River system would give westerners a choice of markets, allowing them to choose between eastern and southern buyers. Little wonder that pressure for internal improvements, to be built at state expense, reached a higher point in the West than in any other section.

Ohio, located near the terminus of the Erie Canal, caught the fever first. Popular enthusiasm forced the legislature to order surveys of possible routes in 1822, and when those proved favorable a monumental act passed in February, 1825, committed the state to a giant building program. Two canals were authorized; one, the Ohio Canal, would use the Scioto, Muskingum, and Cuyahoga river valleys to cross the state from Portsmouth to Cleveland, the other, the Miami and Erie Canal, would follow the Miami River between Cincinnati and Toledo. Work was begun, with the usual orations and ceremonies, on July 4 of that year. Despite labor scarcities, the ravages of malaria, and periodic shortages of cash, 2,000 workers dug away steadily during the next years, living in crude shantytowns and braving long hours in unhealthy swamps for the magnificent pay of $15 a month. The Ohio Canal was opened in 1833; a year later the last lock was completed on the portion of the Miami and Erie Canal connecting Cincinnati with Dayton. The state's reluctance to continue the Miami and Erie northward into the thinly settled areas of northwestern Ohio vanished in 1828 when the federal government voted a sizeable land grant for the purpose, although a boundary dispute with Michigan delayed completion of the canal until 1845. By that time small feeder canals connected much of the back country with the two main waterways, while two privately built waterways, the Pennsylvania and Ohio and the Sandy and Beaver, united the Ohio Canal with the Pennsylvania internal improvement system.

Ohio's canals gave farmers market outlets but the cost was heavy. The sound financial system set up by the legislature authorized the commissioners entrusted with building the canals to raise needed money by selling state-backed stock certificates paying 6 per cent interest. A sinking fund to retire the indebtedness by 1850 was also provided. Unfortunately the

$4,433,000 raised in that way and the $2,000,000 realized from the sale of federal land grants proved insufficient. The commissioners, unwilling to let the people know how expensive the canals were, resorted to borrowing from the sinking fund to pay building costs. The state might have weathered even that threat to its economy if popular enthusiasm for internal improvements had not plagued the legislature into a last disastrous step.

That was taken in 1837. The possibility of railroads was dawning on the western horizon as work progressed on the first two privately built lines in Ohio, the Mad River and Lake Erie Railroad from Sandusky to Springfield, and the Little Miami Railroad from Springfield to Cincinnati. Caught up in enthusiasm for this new means of transportation, Ohio in 1837 offered to buy one-third of any railroad company's stock as soon as the other two-thirds was subscribed. The fraudulent possibility of the "Plunder Law" occurred to a number of unscrupulous promoters; they could form a company, sign their names as "subscribers" to two-thirds of the stock, and receive a handsome gift from the state! Railroad corporations mushroomed in the next few years; by 1840 when a sadder and wiser legislature repealed the "Plunder Law" forty companies had absconded with $3,000,000 in state funds. Ohio wakened from its internal improvement spree with a debt of $15,573,000, a depleted sinking fund, and a shaky financial structure.

Yet Ohio's record was conservative when compared to the giddy speculative course followed by the other northwestern states. Indiana's record was typical. Its program was launched in comparatively modest fashion when the legislature, after listening to the governor's assurance that a canal would "increase the value of the soil, lead to culture and refinement, induce immigration, broaden the horizon of the people, and prevent feuds and political brawls," in 1826 passed a resolution urging the state's congressional representatives to secure a federal land grant for a waterway between the Wabash and Maumee rivers. This grant, of alternate sections ten sections wide along the right of way, was forthcoming in 1827, but construction was delayed until 1832 by lack of funds and a dispute with Ohio over the portion of the canal crossing that state. Difficulties were finally resolved when Indiana pledged its credit to repay the construction bonds and Ohio agreed to build the section of the waterway within its borders in return for a share of the federal land grant. Work on the Wabash and Erie Canal began near Ft. Wayne and progressed slowly southward toward Lafayette, the head of steamboat navigation on the Wabash River. By 1835 thirty miles were opened to traffic.

That progress, and the heady prosperity of the 1830's, combined to send

Indiana into an internal improvement splurge rarely equalled in history. Everywhere people clamored for canals or railroads between their communities and the main canal, everywhere mass meetings drafted petitions to the legislature. When that body caught the fever in 1835 the only necessity was a measure broad enough to benefit every hamlet in the state. For a year lawmakers struggled with that problem, before emerging with a fantastic solution. The Internal Improvement Act of 1836 authorized a canal along the Whitewater River, another from Evansville to the Wabash and Erie Canal, a third from Lafayette through Terre Haute to the Central Canal. It provided for two railroads—from Madison to Lafayette and from New Albany to Crawfordsville—and a host of highways, river-improvement schemes, and other catchalls dear to the hearts of politicians. The improvements would cost $13,000,000—one-sixth of the total wealth of the state—but no one doubted the wisdom of borrowing that huge sum when tolls would pay off the whole debt in a few years.

The awakening was not long in coming. The commissioners in charge of the program insisted on starting all their projects at once, with the result that neither workers nor money were sufficient to push any one rapidly. A bad situation was made worse by their flagrant mismanagement of funds; millions were squandered on worthless experiments, lost, or allowed to drift into pockets of unscrupulous politicians. When a bewildered legislature finally awakened to the situation in 1840 some $15,000,000 was spent, the state's finances in a chaotic condition, and the citizens burdened with a debt that would take years to repay. In return Indiana had a few miles of badly graded railroad bed, some half-completed highways, and less than two hundred miles of canals. Little wonder that disgusted officials ordered all work halted or leaped at the opportunity to sell the partially built railroads and the Whitewater Canal to private companies. Only the Wabash and Erie Canal remained in state hands; that was completed between Toledo and Lafayette in 1843, then gradually extended southward through Terre Haute to Evansville which was reached in 1854. The 458-mile-long waterway, which never paid for itself, was eventually abandoned.

Illinois' disastrous attempt to create an internal improvement system almost paralleled that of Indiana. The craze in that state began modestly with plans for a canal between Lake Michigan and the Illinois River, apparently a feasible undertaking as in high water boats passed between the two without difficulty. A federal land grant launched the project in 1827, but funds were not forthcoming until 1836 when the legislature authorized the issue of bonds backed by the credit of the state. On July 4 of that year work began. The start of the Illinois and Michigan Canal sent a wave of excitement through Illinois; overnight every backwoods settlement discovered that only a canal was needed to transform it into a thriving metropolis, every speculator found that transportation would turn his paper city into a densely populated community, every river town awakened to the need of a railroad to extend its trading area. Throughout the state newspapers bristled with arguments for railroads or waterways, while in the capitol legislators fought for pet schemes that meant prosperity for their constitutents and votes for themselves. Amidst that atmosphere the legislature turned to formulating a measure that would please the whole state. The result was the fabulous Internal Improvement Act of January, 1837, a law that dwarfed even the Indiana Bill in its utter impracticability.

The act called not only for completing the Michigan and Illinois Canal, but for 1,300 miles of railroad crisscrossing the state in every direction: the Central Railroad from Galena to Cairo, the Northern Cross Railroad from Quincy to Danville, the Southern Cross Railroad from Alton to Mt. Carmel, and a host of lesser lines to every obscure village. In addition the measure provided for roads and river improvement, and divided $200,000 in cash among the few counties not benefiting from the building program. In one stroke the legislature committed the 400,000 inhabitants of rural Illinois to an expenditure of $10,250,000 in addition to the large sums needed to complete the Illinois and Michigan Canal.

The result was inevitable. The commissioners named to supervise the work were forced by local jealousies to start all projects at once, spreading labor and money so thinly that little progress was made. For three years they poured funds loaned by gullible English creditors into the program or wasted them in foolish expenditures, while the people waited in vain for promised railroads and canals. When the legislature belatedly investigated in December, 1839, $15,000,000 was spent and only one railroad, the Northern Cross, beyond the grading stage. The lawmakers lost no time in halting work on the rest. Only the Northern Cross Railroad and the Illinois and Michigan Canal held any promise of future returns. The former was completed between Quincy and Springfield in 1842 while the canal, after being taken over by the state's creditors, was opened to traffic in 1848. The additional funds they raised for the work proved a wise investment, for the waterway enjoyed prosperity from the day it was opened and eventually paid off its backers in full. Illinois, however, emerged from its internal improvements spree with a debt of $15,000,000.

Even the new state of Michigan was swept along by the transportation fever into an experiment in railroad building that burdened its taxpayers with debts for the next forty years. This began during Michigan's territorial stage when charters were granted nineteen railroad corporations—one the Erie and Kalamazoo Railroad which opened the first line in the West between Toledo and Adrian in 1836—but not until 1837 when statehood removed external restraints on the region's finances was the program inflated dangerously. An act passed that year authorized a Board of Internal Improvements to borrow $5,000,000 for three railroads—the Michigan Southern from Monroe to New Buffalo, the Michigan Central from Detroit to St. Joseph, and the Michigan Northern from Port Huron to Grand Rapids—as well as canals between the Saginaw and Grand rivers and the Detroit and Kalamazoo rivers. For a time work went on; by 1840 the three railroads were surveyed and graded, track was laid as far as Hillsdale on the Michigan Southern and to Ann Arbor on the Michigan Central, and a canal was open between Mt. Clemens and Utica. Yet the end was already in sight. The two eastern banks contracting to buy the state's internal improvement bonds collapsed in 1840 and 1841, leaving Michigan with a network of half-finished projects and neither money nor credit to complete them. Sadly the legislature disposed of the canal, turned the roadbed of the Michigan Northern Railroad into a highway, and carried on a halfhearted effort to raise funds for a continuation of the two remaining railways.

The collapse of grandiose transportation "Systems" in Michigan, Illinois, Indiana, and Ohio left the Northwest in a sorry state by 1840. Half-finished public works, skyrocketing debts, mounting tax rates, declining immigration, shattered hopes—those were the surface results of a speculative splurge which should have brought prosperity and plenty in its wake. Yet wise observers knew that the effects of the internal improvements actually constructed could not be measured solely in terms of debts and taxes. More significant was their impact on the economy of the regions through which they passed. Wherever canals touched they raised the prices of grain, boosted real estate values, lowered the cost of imports, and stimulated settlement. Wheat that sold for 20 cents a bushel in central Ohio or Indiana in 1823 brought 50 cents ten years later when canal transportation was available, while in the same years the price of such imports as coffee, salt, tea, and sugar was cut in half. Declining prices attracted immigrants; the population of counties adjoining the Indiana canal system increased five-fold between 1835 and 1840, those along the Illinois and Michigan Canal nearly forty-fold in the decade of the 1830's. That this was not due entirely to the prosperity of the times was shown when regions bordering the Wabash and Erie Canal gained at the rate of 400 per cent in the decade after that waterway was opened, while the rest of the state showed gains of less than 200 per cent. Westerners might grumble about debts and taxes, but their internal improvements were far more valuable than they imagined.

More important was the effect of the new transportation routes on national trade, although there results were less startling than the promoters hoped. Both Northeast and South planned to capture western commerce in their nework of canals, railroads, and steamboats; the West in turn dreamed of competitive prices drawing its produce to South or Northeast wherever the highest returns waited. The improvements made this physically possible. By 1835 Ohio farmers had a choice of three markets: south by canal and steamboat to New Orleans, east over the Pennsylvania system of canals and portages, or northeast by lake steamer to Buffalo where produce followed the Erie Canal to New York City or the Welland Canal—built by Canada in 1833 to by-pass Niagara Falls—to Montreal and Quebec. The latter outlet was particularly important after 1831 when Canada opened her ports to American wheat duty free, as flour ground in Quebec could enter English markets still closed to the United States.

Actually, however, the wide range of markets for the West was more apparent than real, as differences in shipping cost over various routes tended to offset price differences paid at the terminal points. To carry a ton of goods a mile by canal boat cost 1½ cents exclusive of tolls, by railroad 2½ cents, by lake steamer from 2 to 4 cents, and by river steamer from ½ to 1½ cents. That variation, which tended to turn bulkier western goods to the southern outlet, was accentuated by higher handling costs on produce moving to the East or Northeast. The frequent transshipments between canal barges and lake or river boats required on both these routes also raised costs.

The result was hardly that foreseen by westerners: a division of the West into two trading areas, each shipping to the nearest markets. One lay in the Ohio River Valley south of the Old National Road where corn and its by-products were the principal staples; that region continued to send its marketable produce southward by steamer to New Orleans. The other was the portion of the Northwest draining into the Great Lakes; the prohibitive cost of canal and river transportation to the South turned that area's trade to the Northeast, and to a lesser extent eastward over the Pennsylvania system. The results were shown in the percentage of exports from the West to the South, Northeast, and East:

| | | VOLUME SHIPPED | | PER-CENTAGE SOUTH | PER-CENTAGE NORTHEAST | PER-CENTAGE EAST |
|---|---|---|---|---|---|---|
| WHEAT | 1835 | 150,000 | bushels | 17 | 83 | — |
| | 1840 | 2,000,000 | bushels | 2 | 97 | 1 |
| FLOUR | 1835 | 400,000 | barrels | 70 | 20 | 5 |
| | 1840 | 800,000 | barrels | 53 | 40 | 7 |
| CORN | 1835 | 1,000,000 | bushels | 98 | 2 | — |
| | 1840 | 1,000,000 | bushels | 98 | 2 | — |
| PORK | 1835 | 200,000 | barrels | 100 | — | — |
| | 1840 | 300,000 | barrels | 69 | 12 | 19 |

Internal improvements wrought no transformation in western trade routes; rather they fostered the rapid development of the northern portion of the Northwest, allowed the Northeast to make a few inroads on the monopoly formerly enjoyed by the South, and accentuated the interdependence of all three sections.

Nor did the growth of intersectional transportation facilities change the buying habits of westerners, who continued to buy from East, Northeast, and South just as before. The table below shows the effect of trade routes on imports into the West:

|      | TOTAL VOLUME OF IMPORTS | FROM THE SOUTH | FROM THE NORTHEAST | FROM THE EAST |
|------|-------------------------|----------------|--------------------|---------------|
| 1835 | 150,000 tons            | 65,000 tons    | 50,000 tons        | 35,000 tons   |
| 1840 | 170,000 tons            | 60,000 tons    | 60,000 tons        | 50,000 tons   |

The actual amount entering the Northwest from the South decreased only 5,000 tons, but the relative amount declined from 44 to 30 per cent. The West still divided its purchases among other sections as it did its sales, but eastern merchants were gaining over southerners as their communications improved.

The first phase of internal improvement building wrought no revolution in sectional relations. All three were still bound together by strengthening commercial ties, with neither the South nor the Northeast enjoying any distinct advantage in their efforts to capture the trade of the West. Yet a discerning observer could recognize danger signals as canals and railroads encouraged each section to specialize more and more. Southerners turned increasingly to cotton growing as western food released their land, easterners concentrated on manufacturing for the same reason, westerners on the agriculture that would satisfy those customers. As specialization increased each section demanded legislation beneficial to its own type of economic enterprise. The basis was laid for a sectional conflict destined to absorb national attention during the trying years ahead.

# CHAPTER XVII

# The Emergence of a Sectional Pattern

## 1815-1837

The sectional conflicts that racked the nation in the second quarter of the nineteenth century were basically economic; Northeast, South, and West, with their specialized economies, clashed as they sought to mould the national will to their own interest. Yet underlying their herculean struggles was something deeper than mere hope of gain. Each, during those years, developed what amounted to a sectional consciousness. By the close of the 1830's every one-horse planter in the cotton belt, every coonskin-clad farmer along the western waters, every shopkeeper in the smoky mill towns of New England, was blindly loyal to the region where he lived. This spirit of sectional patriotism alone allowed Americans to place regional interests above those of the nation.

The West was the first section to become aware of its unique position. The realization was born partly of the arrogant sense of superiority long basic in frontier thought, but more of the need for united action in the grim years following the Panic of 1819. That catastrophe, which pricked the postwar inflationary bubble, brought incredible hardship to the trans-Appalachian country. It began when conservative eastern bankers, alarmed by the upward spiral of prices and credit, sought to check the trend by presenting large quantities of banknotes to the weak state banks issuing them, with the demand that they be repaid in specie. In the West especially many state-chartered institutions were unable to comply, for speculation in frontier lands after 1815 led them to issue paper money without adequate gold backing. Helpless before this pressure, they called in their loans, suspended specie payment or, if all else failed, closed their doors. Merchants, unable to meet their obligations, had no choice but bankruptcy. As their purchases of farm produce declined prices fell rapidly; cotton, which sold at 32 cents a pound in 1818, touched 17 cents in 1820. With southern planters unable to buy food the price of western grains tobogganed until by 1821 corn at Cincinnati sold at 10 cents a bushel, wheat at 25 cents, and whiskey at 15 cents a gallon. Throughout the West crops rotted in the field, trade stood still, and helpless farmers watched miserably as a numbing paralysis settled upon the section.

That was bad enough, but worse was the fate waiting at least one-third of the frontiersmen. They were buying land on credit, taking advantage of the liberal Land Law of 1800 which allowed a small down payment and spread the cost over the next years. Now, unable to pay, they faced the terrifying possibility of losing their farms, their improvements, and their homes; perhaps even a term in debtors' prison. Their cries of anguish forced Congress to revise the land laws. A system of cash purchases was restored in 1820, despite western support for credit sales, but the legislators bowed to frontier pressure by lowering the price from $2 to $1.25 an acre and the minimum amount purchasable from 160 to 80 acres. A year later the Relief Act of 1821 helped farmers still more by allowing purchasers unable to meet their payments three alternatives: they could relinquish a portion of their lands and apply payments already made on the remainder, continue their payments at the reduced rate of $1.25 an acre, or spread installments still due over a long period. Frontiersmen thankfully took advantage of the measure, but memories of the panic years before the relief act was passed plagued them the rest of their lives.

The thoroughly shaken West that emerged from the depression was convinced such a debacle must never happen again. Moreover, westerners knew what caused their suffering and how to assure prosperity for the future! The Panic of 1819, they believed, stemmed from the collapse of European markets. Recent history seemingly indicated this; the frontier prospered during the early Napoleonic wars, suffered hard times when the Embargo shut off exports, and basked in luxury again when peace allowed the hungry Continent to buy American foodstuffs. In 1819, when a fully recovered Europe was feeding itself, hard times returned. Such an unstable market was untrustworthy, but worse was the realization that western agricultural production was outstripping Europe's consuming power; flour exports in 1819 were about those of 1790 while the grain-producing capacity of the United States increased sixfold in the period. Moreover foreign markets were unsatisfactory because good prices tempted Americans to spend money on imported luxuries, thus draining away specie needed at home. The West would never know enduring prosperity, the people believed, until a means was found "to prevent our money travelling over the mountains for English clothes."

If the problem was clear, the solution was obvious. Henry Clay, brilliant young representative from Kentucky, put the answer that was on every westerner's lips in classic form when he told Congress in 1824: "We must speedily adopt a genuine American policy. Still cherishing the foreign market, let us create a home market, to give further scope to the consumption of the produce of American industry." Here was the panacea that would lift the West to eternal prosperity. Home markets for farm goods must be created by fostering the industrial development of the Northeast. From New England's factories manufactured goods would pour over the nation, ending the drain of specie abroad. To them would go the cotton of the South to be transformed into textiles, the grains and livestock of the frontier to feed workers clustered beneath their smoking chimneys. Industrial establishments, westerners saw, could only be reared with federal aid. Protective tariffs must be passed to shield them from foreign competition, internal improvements built to facilitate the marketing of their products, easy credit provided to finance their development. From that day on those were the basic planks in the West's legislative program, almost as important in the eyes of frontiersmen as liberal land laws. This platform united the West and instilled into the people a sectional consciousness that shaped their attitude toward public questions for a generation.

— The years that brought unity to the West developed an even stronger sense of regional nationalism in the southern states. The event that made southerners aware of their unique position was the struggle over Missouri's admission to the Union. Debate on that issue, which began in routine fashion when the usual Enabling Act was laid before Congress in February, 1819, was lifted from the ordinary when Representative James Tallmadge of New York moved an amendment prohibiting the introduction of slaves into the proposed state and freeing all slave children there when they reached the age of twenty-five. The "Tallmadge Amendment" touched off the first national debate over slavery; northerners rose to denounce the South's institution while southerners flocked to defend their labor system. The controversy still raged when Congress adjourned in March, but when members assembled again in December a solution was at hand. Maine was also ready for statehood; perhaps the two new states could be linked together in some compromise measure. The successful formula was devised by Senator Jesse D. Thomas of Illinois who on February 3, 1820, proposed that Maine be admitted as a free state, Missouri as a slave state, and the remainder of the Louisiana Purchase north of the line of 36° 30′ be free territory. Moderates on both sides of Mason and Dixon's line rallied to the support of Thomas' bill, which became a law on March 2, 1820.

The brief struggle culminating in the Missouri Compromise profoundly affected southern thought. Few southerners were immediately concerned; most owned no slaves and almost none of those who did contemplated moving to Missouri. Nor were they alarmed lest the even balance between slave and free states be upset in favor of the North; sectional views on such public issues as the tariff and internal improvements were not sufficiently crystalized to make the South fearful of northern domination in Congress. Instead the southern defense was based on emotionalism. The logic of those who championed the southland was crystal clear: slavery was attacked, slavery was essential to their economy, therefore slavery must be defended. From 1819 until the Civil War that was the South's primary concern. Protection of an unpopular labor system was the basis of southern nationalism.

Those who mounted the rostrum to parry assaults on slavery from north of the Mason and Dixon line soon fell to weighing all questions in terms of their effect on the South's labor system. Any successful attack on slavery, they reasoned, must come from a strong central government; hence a weak Congress and strong state governments were desirable. Protective tariffs were frowned upon, partly because the use of implied powers necessary for their passage strengthened congressional power, partly because the South, as an exporting region, wished to trade its cotton for tax-free English manufactured goods. Similarly federally supported internal improvements were resented both because they would strengthen the national government and because they promised to drain so much money from the treasury that Congress might seek additional revenue by raising tariffs. Southerners also swung to a conservative position on the land question in the years after 1820, holding the public domain should be sold at high prices to increase federal revenues and decrease the need for high customs duties. On every important issue of the day the South, struggling to defend an unpopular institution and an unsound economy, took an uncompromising stand.

The Northeast developed its sectional consciousness more slowly than the South or the West, for conflicting economic interests made unity on any legislative program impossible. The shipping and commercial classes, strongly entrenched in New England, wanted low tariffs to stimulate foreign trade. Hence they looked with disfavor on federal expenditures for internal improvements just as did southerners. On the other hand manufacturers, whose principal strength was in the Middle States, saw protection as a panacea. Realizing that nationally built roads and canals would expand their markets and open the way for higher customs duties, they worked constantly for federal improvements. Those antagonistic points of view meant that northeastern opinion was divided in the early years of sectional controversy. Time, however, favored the position of the industrialists, for as mills and factories multiplied in both the Middle States and New England their political strength increased until their views became the views of the whole Northeast. From the beginning both commercial and millowning classes opposed any liberalization of the land laws which would drain needed workers westward.

By the middle 1820's the people of each of the three sections were committed to legislative programs which, they believed, were essential to their economic well-being. Their ambitions can be summarized in this way:

WEST: low-priced public lands, protective tariffs, federally built internal improvements.

SOUTH: low tariffs, no nationally supported internal improvements, high-priced public lands.

NORTHEAST: high protective tariffs, high-priced public lands, federally built internal improvements.

An observer viewing that hodgepodge of conflicting desires could draw several conclusions. One was the weak position of the South. While West and Northeast agreed on tariff and internal improvements, the slaveholders' legislative platform had nothing in common with either. Equally apparent was the fact that no single section could hope to carry out its program without aid from one of the others. That might be achieved by happenstance; thus Northeast and West could unite behind a protective tariff bill beneficial to both. Or an alliance might be formed if one section consciously tried to win the support of another; conceivably the South might work for cheaper lands in return for western help in securing a lower tariff. Those bargains would necessarily involve agreements on secondary issues, for no one of the three antagonists would back down on its major demands; the Northeast and South would never compromise on the tariff, nor the West on land policy. This was the basis for the legislative conflicts that kept the nation in a turmoil for the next generation.

The South, still smarting under northern abuse during the Missouri debate, first awakened to the need of seeking a sectional ally in 1824. Behind its decision lay both the growing spirit of southern nationalism and the realization that delay might be fatal. Two occurrences that year convinced planters that Northeast and West, if left to themselves, would drift into a union fatal to southern ambitions. One was the election that ended the Era of Good Feeling. That contest, waged between five Jeffersonian

Republicans who sought James Monroe's mantle, ended in the House of Representatives after the electoral college vote failed to give one candidate a majority. The decision rested in the hands of Speaker Henry Clay, a defeated aspirant himself, whose influence could award the prize to any one of the three candidates remaining: John Quincy Adams of Massachusetts, William H. Crawford of Georgia, or Andrew Jackson of Tennessee. Sectional differences forced Clay to eliminate Crawford, whose states' rights views conflicted with Clay's western belief in government aid to business and transportation, while personal rivalry turned him against Jackson. Adams seemed a logical choice; that granite-cold New Englander was no outspoken champion of the "American System" but he leaned toward high tariffs and federally built internal improvements. Clay's pressure placed Adams in the White House where the new president reciprocated by making the westerner his secretary of state. Southerners believed they saw a Northeast-West alliance forming that might be translated into legislative action against their own section.

Just as alarming was the drift of those two regions into the same camp on the all-important tariff question. Friends of protection were dissatisfied with the Tariff of 1816 then on the statute books, especially after the Panic of 1819 when its mild 20 per cent duties seemed inadequate to guard the iron and textile industries from foreign competition. Their first bid for reform failed in 1820 when a slightly higher measure was defeated by a single vote in the Senate, but in 1824 they were back again with new hope for success. The bill introduced that year boosted textile duties to a stiff 33⅓ per cent, raised the level substantially on iron, lead, and hemp, and taxed raw wool 30 per cent in a bid for support from New England sheep growers. The vote on that protective measure reflected the growing sectionalism:

| | FOR | AGAINST |
|---|---|---|
| NEW ENGLAND | 15 | 23 |
| MIDDLE STATES | 57 | 9 |
| SOUTH | 6 | 70 |
| WEST | 29 | 0 |
| | 107 | 102 |

The South and the vacillating commercial regions of New England stood alone; Northeast and West were united. Southerners could never secure low tariffs until that union was broken.

The South's only hope was an alliance with the West, for the Northeast was hopelessly wedded to protection and so firmly committed to an antislavery stand that co-operation was unthinkable. Southern statesmen realized the strong western support for protective tariffs, but knew frontiersmen wanted cheap lands even more. If the South supported liberal land laws, perhaps the grateful West would reverse its stand on the tariff. That seemed worth trying in view of confused opinion on the question within Adams' administration. The President's eastern supporters, led by Daniel Webster of Massachusetts, favored expensive lands to stop the drain of laborers westward, but feared returns from the public domain would give free traders an argument for lowered duties. Their solution, placed before Congress in 1824 and frequently thereafter, was to distribute proceeds from land sales among the states in proportion to population. Westerners within the administration, under the banner of Thomas Hart Benton of Missouri, refused to follow a course which denied them cheaper lands. Benton's counter-scheme, presented to Congress in 1824, proposed a graduated reduction in the price of lands remaining unsold at $1.25 an acre; after a set period they would be lowered to $1 an acre, then to 75 cents and finally to 50 cents, when if no takers appeared they would be given away to settlers. The division between Northeast and West within the administration—one wanting Distribution, the other Graduation and Donation—suggested that the South could use the land question to break the Northeast-West alliance.

That was the dream of Andrew Jackson, still rankled by his defeat in 1824, and John C. Calhoun of South Carolina, his vice-presidential candidate. Representing the South and West personally, they thought in terms of an alliance between their two sections which would give them strength to win the election of 1828. Conditions seemed favorable for such a union, as both southerners and westerners disliked Adams; the former because he spent money lavishly on internal improvements and supported protection, the latter because he advocated high-priced lands. As indignation over these policies mounted, the old Tennessee warrior's prospect brightened with each passing month. His tide was running so strong when the election year dawned that success seemed certain on no stronger platform than promises of democratic reforms, ridicule of Adams' aristocratic leanings, and denunciation of the "corrupt bargain" that made Clay secretary of state as a "reward" for placing the President in the White House.

Jackson's managers, however, were unwilling to trust to fate. They knew their candidate's success hinged on his ability to carry such northeastern states as Pennsylvania where protectionist sentiment was strong. Name-calling and shibboleths were not enough to win a region where Adams' high tariff stand was immensely popular; the manufacturers must be shown that Jackson also favored protection. How could that be done without offending the South? The solution was as ingenious as it was unethical. On January 31, 1828, the Jackson-packed Committee on Manufactures of the House reported out an amazing new tariff. Duties on raw materials—pig iron, bar iron, hemp, flax, raw wool, and molasses—were raised sky high, the tax on ordinary woolen cloth radically advanced, and the tariff on other items left at the 1824 level or slightly increased. Jackson's friends planned to push the measure to a final vote without amendments, then defeat it by a combination of southern and New England votes. They could then pose as friends of protection in the Middle States, appeal to Pennsylvania iron manufacturers and western wool growers by showing they tried to secure higher duties on those materials, discredit Adams by pointing out that his own New England defeated the measure, and pacify the South with the assertion that no higher tariff was passed.

The plans went through without a hitch until the last moment. Then, when the final vote was taken in March, 1828, the bill passed Congress! Jackson's plotters failed to take into account growing sentiment for protection in New England; enough representatives from that region were favorable to carry the day:

|  | FOR | AGAINST |
|---|---|---|
| NEW ENGLAND | 16 | 23 |
| MIDDLE STATES | 57 | 11 |
| WEST | 29 | 1 |
| SOUTH | 3 | 59 |
|  | 105 | 94 |

Daniel Webster, who gave the principal speech against the Tariff of 1824, spoke so feelingly for the Tariff of 1828 that the measure passed the Senate, twenty-six to twenty-one.

The South was horrified. Southerners opposed the 1824 bill largely on constitutional grounds; by admitting Congress' right to levy protective duties they strengthened the hand of a central government which might someday interfere with slavery. Now their opposition was based on something stronger: the realization that protection and cotton growing were economically incompatible. Two-thirds of the South's crop was marketed abroad, largely in England. Britain bought cotton only where it could pay in manufactured goods. Tariffs, by preventing English produce from invading the United States, not only forced southerners to accept lower prices for the materials they sold, but doomed them to pay higher prices for the industrial products they purchased. Why, they asked themselves, should one section pay perpetual tribute to another? Why accept the "Tariff of Abominations" without protest?

South Carolina, whose worn soils produced less bountiful crops than virgin western lands, led the chorus of dissent that swelled from below Mason and Dixon's line. Yet even representatives of that suffering state dared not go too far, lest they open the way for the re-election of Adams. For a time they hesitated, then decided on a course that would lay the basis for future action without upsetting the political applecart. John C. Calhoun, their able leader, was commissioned to prepare a written protest making the South's position clear. His famous South Carolina Exposition was a classic statement of the nullification doctrine. The federal government, Calhoun asserted, was created by the states to care for their common needs. They remained the final judges of all its acts; should Congress deliberately exercise powers any one state decided were not delegated to it, that state could annul the unconstitutional law by refusing to obey. Such an annulled law would then not be binding on any of the states. The Tariff of 1828 was of that sort; South Carolina granted Congress the right to levy duties for revenue only, not for protection. Hence the state could legally nullify the obnoxious bill. That was Calhoun's answer to northern protectionists, but his state hesitated to translate his theories into practice. The South Carolina legislature refused to nullify the "Tariff of Abominations" although it did print 5,000 copies of the Exposition.

The South failed to act in 1828 because its leaders believed Jackson's election would cement their alliance with the West on the land question, giving them enough western votes to sweep away the protective system. Hence southerners hailed Old Hickory's victory with joy, watched hopefully as he set up his government, then waited patiently for a chance to win western gratitude by supporting the section's land policy. That was not long in coming. In December, 1829, when one of Henry Clay's Distribution bills reached a vote in the House, West and South united against the measure; the West fearing continued high land prices, the South disliking a bill which bolstered the arguments of protectionists by draining funds from the treasury.

More significant was the reaction of both sections to an ill-tempered resolution introduced in December, 1829, by Senator Samuel A. Foote of Connecticut. That spokesman for northeastern industrialists proposed that the Senate Committee on Public Lands inquire into the expediency of limiting land sales to those already on the market and ending for some time further surveys. Senator Benton protested for the West; he branded the measure a flagrant manufacturers' attempt to force low wages on workers which "taxes the South to injure the West to pauperize the poor

of the North." More significant was the attack launched by Senator Robert
Y. Hayne. That vigorous South Carolinian spoke not as a southerner but
as a champion of the West; the Northeast, he maintained, sought to rob
frontier states of their manpower just as it robbed southern states of their
wealth through tariffs. Only by uniting against their common enemy could
they save themselves. Daniel Webster, who rose to the defense of his
section, was wise enough to divert attention from the main question by
turning from specific issues to the general nature of the Union. The magnificent Webster-Hayne debate that followed did not obscure the fact that
the South was bidding for western support against eastern industrialists.

Even more significant was the willingness of southern congressmen to
practice what they preached. When one of Benton's perennial Graduation
and Donation bills reached a House vote in May, 1830, they lined up
with the West:

|           | FOR | AGAINST |
|-----------|-----|---------|
| NORTHEAST | 14  | 59      |
| SOUTH     | 37  | 15      |
| WEST      | 17  | 8       |
|           | 68  | 82      |

The sectional alliance was even more marked in the Senate, where all
but one western and two southern delegates were in favor and all but
one northeastern senator opposed. The South was courting the West; would
the West respond by supporting the South's low tariffs?

The answer to that question was not long in coming, for by 1832 the
tariff issue was again squarely before Congress. The enemies of protection were the aggressors now. They pointed out that national prosperity
and the high duties of the Tariff of 1828 brought so much money into
the treasury that the total United States debt would soon be paid off.
Why, they asked, should exorbitant taxation continue when money was
not needed? That telling argument sent protectionists into a flurry of
activity lest their system be swept away on the tide of public opinion;
better to back down slightly, they reasoned, than lose all. The tariff they
introduced in the spring of 1832 was designed to continue protection while
correcting some defects in the hated Tariff of 1828. Duties on woolen
textiles and iron, although still high, were lowered to the 1824 level, flax
was placed on the free list, the duty on hemp reduced one-third, and the
tax on raw wool left unchanged. The House vote was not strongly sectional
—New Englanders voted against the lowered duties on woolen goods and

some southerners were so delighted to escape the burdens of the 1828 measure they reacted favorably—but the pattern was still clear:

|           | FOR | AGAINST |
|-----------|-----|---------|
| NORTHEAST | 69  | 35      |
| SOUTH     | 45  | 30      |
| WEST      | 18  | 0       |
|           | 132 | 65      |

The West, obviously, was so firmly committed to protection that no amount of southern pleading could change its mind. A break in the sectional alliance was at hand.

Events stemming from the passage of the Tariff of 1832 vastly widened the gulf between West and South. Moderate as the measure was, it still horrified southern extremists who hoped for free trade under President Jackson. South Carolina, where the tradition of rebellion was strongest, led the protest. A call went out at once for a popularly elected convention to decide the state's course. When that body met in November, 1832, it unhesitatingly nullified the Tariffs of 1828 and 1832, outlawed appeals to the Supreme Court in cases arising under the Nullification Ordinance, and threatened secession if the United States tried to enforce the laws. Jackson met the challenge to national authority with his usual vigor. On December 10, 1832, he issued a Nullification Proclamation, denying the legal validity of nullification and called on the state to obey the nation's laws, at the same time asking Congress for authority to use force against the rebellious southerners. When this was granted after the South's representatives withdrew, the President talked boldly of leading an army into South Carolina.

Jackson's forceful action proved effective. When the other southern states refused their support, the South Carolinians, rather than risk presidential wrath alone, took no steps to nullify the tariff on February 1, 1833, as they threatened. The state's hesitation gave compromisers a chance to avoid a serious conflict; if Congress could agree on a lower tariff at once bloodshed might be avoided. Even Henry Clay, staunch protectionist that he was, saw this was necessary. Acting hurriedly, he framed a bill providing for a gradual reduction of all customs duties to July 1, 1842, when none would remain over 20 per cent. The passage of the Compromise Tariff of 1833 by thumping majorities ended the Nullification Controversy, for South Carolina, recognizing a chance to save its face, hurriedly repealed its

Nullification Ordinance. Yet the harm was done. The West, most national-istic of all sections, was horrified by southern defiance of the Union. The tariff controversy showed that South and West had neither a material nor idealistic basis for union; the hoped-for alliance between the two was forever severed.

Equally important was the impact of the violent sectional struggle on the nation's politics. The South Carolina controversy crystallized differences between the two new political parties that dominated the national scene until the Civil War. Since the collapse of the old Federalist Party the United States had been governed by Jeffersonian Republicans whose prin-ciples represented a strange blend of Jefferson's democracy and Federalist nationalism. The harmonious era of one-party rule was threatened during the 1828 campaign, when mounting sectional and class antagonisms split the Jeffersonian Republicans into two antagonistic camps. On one side were the supporters of Jackson, made up of western small farmers led by the candidate himself, eastern working men and liberals under the leadership of Martin Van Buren of New York, and southerners who fol-lowed John C. Calhoun. On the other were commercial and business leaders of the West with Henry Clay as their leader, and manufacturers and con-servatives of the Northeast under John Quincy Adams, Daniel Webster, and other spokesmen for the industrialists. Two new parties were apparently beginning their evolution.

The nullification controversy forced a reshuffling. John C. Calhoun, one of Jackson's staunchest supporters, was leader of the South Carolina nullifiers, and his violent states' rights views thoroughly shocked the nationalistic President. Until that time Jackson planned on making Calhoun his political heir; now he cast the southerner aside, selecting Van Buren as his vice-presidential running mate for the election of 1832. Calhoun led his followers into the fold of the rival faction, where he was heartily welcomed despite any lack of unity between his states' rights principles and the American System of Clay and Adams. Strengthened by this addition, the Adams-Clay-Calhoun faction, with nothing in common save hatred of the President, prepared to challenge Jackson in the election of 1832. By autumn of the campaign year they called themselves National Republicans and were developing the cohesion necessary for a political party.

The issue that led to the final break between the parties was provided by the effort of the Second Bank of the United States to secure recharter. Since its founding in 1816 that venerable institution had steered the nation's finances along a middle path which aroused resentment from both liberals and conservatives. The liberals—those who wanted greater infla-tion of the currency—were bankers, speculators, and business leaders in

West and South who rebelled against the control of state-chartered banks by the financial "monster." They knew that in the past state banks provided the large amounts of currency needed for speculation; all were authorized to print banknotes—or paper currency—on the basis of a specie reserve varying from one-third to the full amount of notes in circulation. In 1823 the Bank of the United States, with Nicholas Biddle as its new president, assumed the role of watchdog over state banks; if it believed one was issuing more currency than reserves justified it set a high discount rate on that institution's notes, granting only 60 or 70 cents in specie or United States Bank Notes for each dollar of the state bank's notes. That was bad enough, but worse were the methods used against banks suspected of being weak; at times the national bank refused to accept their notes for taxes or other government dues, at others it collected large quantities of currency issued by a state bank and suddenly presented the whole amount for payment in specie. The effect was to keep the state banks rigidly in line and prevent them from circulating the inflated dollars wanted by speculators or business men.

The financial conservatives who lifted their voices against the policies of the Bank of the United States were western agrarians, eastern working men, and southern small farmers under the banner of Andrew Jackson. In their eyes the evils that beset the nation's poor—high prices, low wages, and mounting debts—were caused by an inflated currency, especially when this could be manipulated by the upper classes for their own speculations. The solution, they agreed, was to abolish paper money, except in large denominations needed for commercial transactions, and return the United States to a specie basis, with all debts and wages paid in gold or silver. That was impossible so long as the Bank of the United States ruled the country's finances; the institution's sin, Jacksonians believed, was not its curbing of state banks but the overissue of its own bank notes. These increased from $4,500,000 in 1823 to $21,000,000 nine years later, flooding the country with a cheap money that bore down heavily on the overburdened shoulders of the poor. Jackson's decision to curb the "financial octopus" was bolstered by the bank's open hostility to his administration, for he knew its funds went to elect his party's opponents and smear his own name.

That was the situation when friends of the Bank of the United States, aware its charter expired in 1836, turned to the task of winning a new grant of life from the hostile Jackson forces. Henry Clay, a staunch friend of both the bank and Nicholas Biddle, brought the issue into the limelight. Knowing Congress was strongly in favor of recharter, he convinced Biddle to send in his application on the eve of the election of 1832. That astute move, Clay believed, would force Jackson either to veto a popular measure and face defeat at the polls, or accept the new charter. The plans went through without a hitch. The recharter bill was introduced in January and, despite frantic efforts by Thomas Hart Benton and others among the President's supporters, passed Congress in July, 1832. Jackson, whose principles always transcended political ambitions, did not hesitate; he returned the measure with a resounding veto message which branded the national bank as a giant credit monopoly operated for the benefit of a few eastern and foreign stockholders. Should so much power be left in the hands of a privileged few, he asked, "will there not be cause to tremble for the purity of our elections in peace, and for the independence of our country in war?"

The issue was clear now, and the voters must decide. Both sides were confident; Biddle and the National Republicans were so scornful of the half-truths and nationalistic bravado in the veto message that they printed 30,000 copies for circulation as campaign propaganda. Those aristocrats knew little of the true temper of the American people. For every person who agreed with them that the President's economic arguments were faulty, a dozen thought "Old Hickory" gave "The Monster" just what it deserved. Jackson would probably have been re-elected despite the bank controversy, but his impressive majorities certainly reflected popular support for his program. That, at least, was his own interpretation. He emerged from the election firmly convinced there must be "a complete divorce of the government from all banks." From that day the Bank of the United States was doomed.

The charter, however, did not expire until 1836. Should the bank be allowed to handle government money until that time, or should some new method of caring for the nation's finances be put into operation at once? Nicholas Biddle unwittingly supplied the answer during the winter of 1832-33. By that time continued prosperity had piled up such a surplus of government funds that Jackson saw the way clear to realizing one of his great ambitions: retiring the last of the United States debt. Hence he informed Biddle that on January 3, 1833, money for this must be returned to the treasury. Unfortunately for the Bank of the United States, the government deposits were on loan to investors; its harried officials were forced to tell the President funds could not be provided immediately. Jackson, his favorite dream shattered, leaped to the conclusion the bank was no longer a safe place for government money. In a towering rage he accepted the advice of his attorney general, Roger B. Taney of Maryland, to remove the government deposits at once, distributing them among a few selected state banks where they would be secure. After long debate in the cabinet and the ousting of one secretary of the treasury unwilling to take this step, removal began on October 1, 1833.

Jackson was wise enough not to ruffle the nation's financial structure by suddenly withdrawing all funds from the Bank of the United States; money already there was drained away slowly to meet current expenses. All new revenue, however, was deposited in eighteen carefully selected state banks which were required to give adequate security, provide weekly reports to the government, and stand ready to redeem the funds at any moment. On the whole the system worked well and was popular with the people. Only in Congress, where the National Republicans controlled the Senate, were objections raised. There Clay and Biddle shaped a careful campaign of debate, petition, and abuse that continued until the elections of 1834 returned Jacksonians to control of both houses.

The Bank War, coming on the heels of the nullification controversy, drove the final wedge between the two parties. By the spring of 1834 the President's followers among eastern workingmen, western farmers, and southern small planters called themselves Democrats, taking their name from the happy phrase—Jacksonian Democracy—used to characterize their idol's administration. Personal loyalty to their leader and a common interest in legislation beneficial to the nation's masses bound the party together. Their rivals were less well knit. The bankers, business men, and wealthier farmers from Northeast and West, the planters and commercial leaders of the South who deserted the Democrats during the nullification controversy, and the southern small farmers under Calhoun's leadership, had little in common save their hatred of Jackson. On no other platform than opposition to "executive usurpation" they began in 1834 calling themselves Whigs, a name symbolizing their rebellion against "King Andrew's" iron rule. Yet basically the two parties did differ; the Democrats were oppressed common people, the Whigs conservative upper classes who saw in popular rule a threat to their swollen property holdings. A class division was developing to plague a nation already torn by economic sectionalism.

The results became apparent when a new sectional controversy developed during Jackson's second administration. The issues were different now, the tariff question having been settled for a decade by the Compromise Tariff of 1833. In its place rose an equally troublesome problem: what to do with surplus government funds piling up in deposit banks. By January, 1835, the public debt was extinguished and $9,000,000 rolling into the treasury yearly above current expenses. Everyone recognized the evils of a situation which removed cash from the channels of trade, but few suggested a workable solution. No one dared tamper with the Tariff of 1833, the principal source of revenue. Spending the money was equally impossible, since Jackson's veto of the Maysville Turnpike Bill in 1830 placed his administration on record against using public funds for internal improvements. There remained only two possible solutions. The surplus could be distributed among the states for canal building and education; that was the Whigs' answer, even though they recognized western and southern opposition. Or unneeded funds could be reduced by slashing land prices; that was the remedy proposed by Democrats despite the certainty of eastern objections. The basis was laid for a new political and sectional conflict.

Actually the outcome was never in doubt, for despite personal loyalty to Jackson, both the West and South viewed Distribution—which now meant distribution of all surplus funds rather than simply those derived from land sales—with far less jaundiced eyes than in the past. Southerners were formerly opposed because money drained from the treasury strengthened protectionists arguing for higher duties; now the tariff question was settled until 1842. Westerners had feared a division of government surpluses would serve as a bribe which would keep eastern states from lowering land prices; now soaring prosperity made the $1.25 an acre charged for public lands more acceptable. Most important of all in accounting for the shift of opinion was the pressing need for funds to continue internal improvement programs. Southerners who dreamed of railroad lines between the Atlantic and the Mississippi, or frontiersmen who talked of networks of canals between their states and seaboard markets could hardly remain hostile when a beneficent federal government asked them to accept millions of dollars without obligation. As the craze for public works mounted, the fear of Distribution melted away.

Mounting popular clamour swept even the staunchest Jacksonians into the Distribution camp by the spring of 1836, when the treasury surplus amounted to $36,000,000. Knowing some bill was certain to pass Congress, they framed a measure designed to meet the President's constitutional objections. The Deposit Act provided that after January 1, 1837, all surplus funds in the treasury over $5,000,000 be parcelled out among the states in four quarterly installments. Technically the money was only "deposited with" the states, although everyone understood it would never be recalled. "It is," wrote Benton of the bill, "in name a deposit; in form a loan; in essential design a distribution." Yet Jackson dared not face the popular wrath his veto would arouse, and on June 3, 1836, affixed his signature.

The promise of forthcoming federal funds was the final stimulus for a giddy speculative spree that swept the nation during the next eighteen months. States with giant canal or railroad building programs wondered why they had been so modest and set engineers to work on plans that would double or triple expenditures. Those with none blossomed with fantastic schemes which somehow seemed perfectly logical amidst the feverish atmosphere; when Michigan's 200,000 poverty-ridden frontiersmen embarked on an $8,000,000 program and pledged another $6,000,000 to aid private construction no one in the state was alarmed. All over the nation the story was the same: reckless expenditure against the day when completed highways and waterways brought new prosperity. The situation would have been bad enough if the states had been spending their own, or even the federal government's funds. Instead they resorted to borrowing on an unprecedented scale. Easy credit caused both the boom of the middle 1830's and the Panic of 1837.

Money was ridiculously simple to obtain. Much came from abroad; any state wanting to embark on an internal improvement program had only to issue bonds and turn them over to an eastern bank, which would deliver them to an English banking house—Baring Brothers was the most prominent—for resale. In England the securities were snapped up by country gentlemen, business leaders, and small investors who, failing to distinguish between state and federal bonds of the United States, believed they were making the safest of investments. Little did they know the unsound finances of American states, nor understand state immunity from suit in case of default. Money poured across the Atlantic, $66,000,000 in British capital was invested by 1835, another $108,000,000 by the close of 1837. Much of this flowed back again as foreign funds allowed states to bid against each other for laborers, wages skyrocketed, luxury buying increased, and imports of English goods mounted to satisfy the demand. By 1836 United States imports from England exceeded by $20,000,000 its exports to that country. This buying stimulated business in Britain, brought prosperity to business men and landlords, and encouraged them to buy more American bonds. So long as borrowing continued prices were bound to spiral upward on both sides of the Atlantic, but a day of reckoning was sure to come.

Funds for internal improvements were also obtained by recklessly inflating the currency. The state-chartered banks that sprang up by the score in the booming 1830's were responsible. In the West nearly all states succumbed to the temptation to finance their public works in that way; any state needing money founded a number of banks, capitalized them with bonds that were exchanged for a share of the bank stock, then borrowed back the bank notes issued on the basis of the state's own securities. Officials honestly believed this method would not only supply money needed for construction but eventually pay for the improvements, as the bank stock was expected to pay dividends of 8 to 10 per cent for all time. Those returns, plus tolls from canals and roads, would eventually pay off the entire investment and provide so much income taxes could be abolished! That was the talk, not of wild dreamers, but of sober business men. Little wonder that thirty-two banks were chartered in Ohio during the decade, fifty in Michigan, and smaller numbers in other western states.

The South succumbed to the mania as thoroughly as the West. Credit was needed there not only for public works but for loans to planters anxious to expand their land and labor supply in a day of high cotton prices. The Land Banks founded between Florida and Louisiana to meet the demand were financed by state bonds sold in Europe; the money obtained was loaned to planters in return for mortgages on their plantations, and the mortgages were then used as security for bank notes. Between 1830 and 1837 the number of unsound institutions in the South increased from fifty-one to eighty-two, financed by $50,000,000 borrowed from trusting English investors on the security of state bonds. The long-term mortgage loans of the southern banks left them unable to obtain specie needed for a sudden run or prolonged depression.

The willingness of wildcat banks in both West and South to loan bank notes on flimsy security not only encouraged the states to spend recklessly but sent the whole nation into a speculative rampage. Everywhere men borrowed money hand over fist to expand their businesses, buy land, or embark on any speculation that offered itself. Matters were made worse by the government's financial policy which, laudable as were the motives behind it, still fostered the inflationary trend. The deposit system was particularly vicious in that respect; by the end of 1836 $49,378,000 was parcelled out among eighty-nine state banks. There was little truth in the charges of Jackson's enemies that the "Pet Banks" were selected for political purposes—every effort was made to check their soundness regularly— yet the federal funds in their vaults were more of a temptation than most bankers could resist. Nearly all loaned government money recklessly, increased their note issues beyond reason, and acted as though the vast sums were their own. Millions of federal dollars were turned into over-swollen trade channels; between 1830 and 1837 bank loans increased nearly five-fold, from $137,000,000 to $525,000,000.

Speculation was spurred on by the increase in the money supply as state banks poured their bank notes into the nation's markets. Between 1832 and 1836 the country's circulating currency mounted from $59,000,000 to

$140,000,000 with the usual inflationary effect on prices. Even worse was the fact that many notes issued by western and southern institutions were without adequate specie backing, for lax laws and improper inspection in most states left bankers free to follow unscrupulous ways. By 1836 most banks had a specie relationship of ten or twelve to one—ten or twelve paper dollars in circulation for every gold dollar in their vaults—although some ran as high as thirty to one. Suspicious merchants, refusing to accept notes from suspected banks at face value, often demanded a discount of 10 to 40 per cent. With bills from hundreds of banks in circulation, all varying in value, the financial situation was chaotic. One traveler pictured the inconveniences of the system when he wrote:

> At Wheeling exchanged $5.00 note, Kentucky money, for notes of the Northwest Bank of Virginia; reached Fredericktown; there neither Virginia nor Kentucky money current; paid a $5.00 Wheeling note for breakfast and dinner; received in change two $1.00 notes on some Pennsylvania bank, $1.00 Baltimore and Ohio Railroad, and balance in Good Intent shinplasters; 100 yards from the tavern door all notes refused except the Baltimore and Ohio Railroad. . . .

Little wonder speculation was rampant amidst this flood of cheap money.

Seldom had the United States enjoyed such a buying orgy as in 1836 and early 1837. Prosperity was everywhere, prices were high and going higher, bank vaults were bulging and bankers eager to loan. That was too much of a temptation for such optimists as the Americans who rushed to purchase everything possible that promised to rise in value. The principal speculation was in land; sales which averaged three or four million acres a decade in the past skyrocketed to 38,000,000 acres between 1835 and 1837. Of this speculators secured at least 29,000,000 acres, nearly all with money borrowed from state banks. Often the currency was used again and again; money loaned by a state bank went to a government land office, then was returned to the state bank with other deposits of government funds, to be loaned to a speculator once more. So active were jobbers in laying out "paper towns" that one westerner proposed a law setting aside two sections in each township for agriculture; more serious observers were genuinely alarmed lest the best lands of the West be removed from production by speculative holders.

By 1836 the inflationary hurricane reaching such alarming proportions that Jackson felt called upon to act. His Specie Circular, issued on July 11, 1836, decreed that after August 15 only gold and silver would be accepted for government land, although actual settlers buying less than 320 acres could use banknotes for four more months. Neither this nor any other gesture could halt the speculative tide. The old general stepped down from office that year, pleased that he had placed his appointed heir, Martin Van Buren, in the presidency, but saddened by the spectacle of a people gone mad. He knew good times could not continue in a nation whose economy was expanding so rapidly that supplies of capital and labor were both exhausted. That was shown by rising interest rates and mounting wages as producers bid against each other for money and workers. Increased costs reduced profits so radically that only a continued flow of capital from Europe kept the boom alive until 1837. The time was ripe for a panic that would shake the nation's economy to its foundations and revive in a new atmosphere the sectional problems of old.

# CHAPTER XVIII

# The Shifting Sectional Pattern

## 1837-1850

During the early stages of the sectional struggle both South and Northeast failed to achieve their goal: an economic and political alliance with the West. In the dozen years after 1837 the situation changed radically as Northeast and West drifted together into a loose Union that excluded the South. The reshuffled sectional pattern was far from complete in 1850, yet the basis was laid for the emergence of the two new sections—North and South—which made the Civil War possible. Underlying the change was a growing sense of sectional consciousness stemming partly from the depression which gripped the nation during the early 1840's and partly from mounting tension over the institution of slavery.

Few issues in American history have stirred emotional convictions as deeply as the fate of slaves. The question was not new when it reached a boiling point in the middle 1830's; from the days of the Revolution enlightened humanitarians in both North and South freely confessed the evils of a system which held human beings in bondage. The northern states, swept along by the liberalism of the Declaration of Independence, freed their slaves in the half century after independence, until by 1820 bonded servitude was abolished in both Northeast and Northwest. Southerners, equally certain that slavery was wrong but hesitant to face the social problems that would arise should millions of freed Negroes be released in their midst, resorted to "colonization." The American Colonization Society, formed in 1816 to send emancipated blacks to Africa as fast as their masters were persuaded to grant them freedom, was a southern institution. So were the other antislavery societies that blossomed before 1830; as late as 1827 106 of the 130 organizations working to free slaves were below Mason and Dixon's line.

Emancipation could never become a sectional issue so long as northerners and southerners agreed on one basic concept: that Negroes were biologically inferior to white men. That false premise was universally accepted in the North until 1830; states closed their schools to men of color, prohibited them from voting or bearing arms or serving in militia companies, and punished them as slaves rather than equals. The shift in northern opinion that elevated the antislavery cause to a position of national importance began in the late 1820's when a few reformers, caught up in a wave of religious revivalism engulfing the United States, voiced the radical doctrines of abolitionism. Slavery, they said, was not merely a social evil; an institution which kept fellow-Christians in bondage only because of the color of their skins was a sin against the laws of God and mankind. The slaves must be freed, educated, and equipped to take their place in society on terms of full equality with their whiter-skinned brethren.

The standard of abolitionism was raised by the zealous William Lloyd Garrison when in January, 1831, he published the first issue of *The Liberator*, an ill-natured Boston weekly demanding immediate emancipation and full recognition of Negroes' rights. Two years later a western leader appeared in the person of James G. Birney, a wealthy Kentuckian whose conviction that slavery was wrong had earlier found expression in the colonization movement. With a handful of followers, he boldly proclaimed his faith in racial equality. Birney's plan for freeing the slaves was more practical than Garrison's. Recognizing the impossibility of immediate emancipation through congressional action, he urged a program of gradual emancipation which would win state after state to freedom. This would be accomplished, he planned, by an educational program blending humanitarianism with religious revivalism. Birney's ideas proved acceptable to the delegates from Northeast and Northwest who gathered at New York in December, 1833, to form an abolitionist society. The American Anti-Slavery Society, although enlisting the support of Garrison and his disciples, was pledged to a program of gradual emancipation and racial equality.

There remained the stupendous task of winning over the northern people. Less zealous men might have faltered in face of the obstacles that faced them. Most northerners resented any agitation which would offend the South; still more were unwilling to admit Negroes were their equals. The crusader best equipped to brave this hornet's nest of opposition was a fanatical young westerner, Theodore Dwight Weld, who was a divinity student at Lane Theological Seminary in Cincinnati when the American Anti-Slavery Society was formed. Already converted to abolitionism by Birney, Weld persuaded his fellow students to endorse the new society, a step that led to their mass expulsion by a faculty sympathetic to colonization.

The "Lane Rebels" transferred in a body to a newly established Oberlin College in northern Ohio. From there they traveled over the state, conducting protracted abolition meetings with the fervor of evangelists, until opposition broke down, and town after town was converted. By the end of 1835 Weld and his disciples extended their influence westward over Indiana and Illinois, eastward across New York and Pennsylvania. Behind them sprang up branches of the American Anti-Slavery Society; three hundred were founded by 1835, five hundred by 1836, a thousand by 1837. A rolling tide of abolitionism was engulfing the northern states, convincing hundreds of thousands that slavery was a sin which must be abolished.

The South watched the spreading contagion with horror. Southerners realized the issue was not simply one of preserving a labor supply which was becoming increasingly valuable as cotton plantations spread westward, but involved the far more touchy question of racial superiority. This was something on which they would not compromise. Their irate legislatures during 1836 passed resolutions threatening to boycott northern states that did not suppress antislavery societies, their governors urged laws decreeing the death penalty for abolitionists caught within their borders, and their postmasters openly burned abolition literature which arrived in the mails. Most outspoken of all were the South's representatives in Congress. Goaded beyond endurance by repeated denunciations of slavery from northern spokesmen, they united with Democratic congressmen from the North in May, 1836, to adopt a resolution laying all petitions concerning slavery on the table without debate. The "Gag Rule" thoroughly aroused the North. The issue was not slavery or freedom, but the sacred right of every American to freedom of speech and the right of petition. "The contest," wrote one abolitionist, "is becoming—has become—one, not alone of freedom for the *black*, but of freedom for the *white*. It has now become absolutely necessary that slavery should cease in order that freedom may be preserved in any portion of our land." Thousands who hesitated to affiliate with antislavery societies before now rushed to join.

By the close of 1837 the northern attack and southern defense left nerves taut and tempers raw on both sides of Mason and Dixon's line. Not all northerners were abolitionists; perhaps one in twenty supported the antislavery societies while more resented the South's interference with their civil liberties. Yet every southerner was certain every northerner was a "black abolitionist" bent on subjecting the Southland to Negro rule; thousands of northerners believed every southerner was a bestial slave beater who took sadistic joy in breaking the laws of God and man. Amidst such an atmosphere of hate and distrust, the settlement of sectional conflicts became increasingly difficult. The slavery issue, which brought Northeast and

West nearer together, created a fathomless gulf between the South and the other two sections. The South through the 1840's still hoped its native sons who had settled beyond the Ohio River would save the northwestern states from abolitionists, but that was grasping at straws. The shifting sectional pattern which eventually united the two northern sections was already taking shape.

Just as important in increasing tension between the sections was the depression gripping the nation between 1837 and 1842, for compromise on economic legislation was impossible when laws might spell the difference between starvation and survival. The crash that ended the prosperity of the early 1830's came with sickening suddenness in the spring of 1837. The chain of events leading to the collapse began in England the preceding fall when the Bank of England, alarmed by heavy American borrowing which reduced its specie reserves from £11,000,000 in 1833 to £4,300,000 three years later, raised its interest rate from 4 to 5 per cent in August, 1836. A few months later New Orleans cotton brokers, who had counted on British loans to finance their purchases from planters, began closing their doors. Their collapse carried down the New York firms that handled their cotton; ninety-eight business houses with liabilities of $60,000,000 went into bankruptcy during April. Because all owed large sums to New York banks, the rumor spread that those institutions were too hard hit to meet their obligations. Overnight runs began, as worried investors rushed to convert bank notes into specie. By early May, 1837, every bank along the eastern seaboard faced a stream of depositors demanding repayment in gold or silver.

This pressure came at an unfortunate time. The Specie Circular caused a movement of bullion westward to finance land purchases, while specie reserves of eastern banks were depleted by the recent payment of $9,000,000 to the states as the second installment under the Distribution Act. With most of the nation's gold drained West, New York banks were unable to stand the strain and on May 10, 1837, suspended specie payments. Others caught the alarm; throughout the nation bank after bank closed its doors during the next few days. When even the Bank of the United States, operating under a Pennsylvania charter, refused to redeem its notes the panic spread to business of all sorts. Factories stopped work, stores were boarded up, commerce declined. By the end of 1837 half of the Northeast's business concerns were closed, beggars roamed the streets of every city, unemployed workers fought for meagre fare doled out by soup kitchens, and Horace Greeley's New York *Tribune* urged the poor to "Fly, scatter through the country, go to the Great West, anything rather than remain here." In the South conditions were just as bad, as tumbling cotton prices forced planters to unload their lands and slaves so rapidly the price of a good field hand dropped from $1,200 to $200 within a few months. Only the West survived the early stages of the panic. Agricultural prices remained fairly high while a bountiful crop in 1837 postponed the full impact of the depression.

How could order be restored amidst financial chaos? That was the problem facing the special session of Congress called by President Van Buren for September, 1837. The first debate showed the solution would not be easy, for the members were divided into three hostile camps, each bent on following its own road to recovery. The Whigs, led by Henry Clay, insisted Jackson's financial policies underlay the panic, which would only end when the United States restored a national bank and an adequate currency supply. A second group, made up of conservative Democratic planters and business men under William C. Rives of Virginia and Nathaniel D. Tallmadge of New York, agreed that paper money issues should go on, but wanted the deposit system continued in twenty-five carefully regulated state banks. Opposed to both were Van Buren's regular Democrats, strengthened now by the return of Calhoun and his small-farmer disciples of the South who seized on Jackson's retirement to end their uncomfortable alliance with the Whigs. This faction reflected the advanced ideas of the Locofocos, a liberal group of New York working men who had labored within the party since 1835 in behalf of hard money and abolition of monopolies. Holding the depression was caused by fluctuations of paper currency, they demanded the complete separation of government and banking, and the return of gold or silver coins as the ordinary circulating medium.

Van Buren embodied the principal points of the Locofoco platform in the measure he laid before Congress in September, 1837. The United States, he said, should set up an Independent Treasury System, storing its specie in vaults of mints, post offices, and customs houses throughout the country. Money from tariffs and land sales would be paid into the depositories in gold or silver coins; government expenses would be met by delegating proper officials to pay out public money on a cash basis. That would stop speculation, insure safety for the nation's funds, and do away with the necessity for any such credit monopoly as a national bank. Congress, the President insisted, should set up the system at once to restore confidence in the government's finances.

The first debate on the bill revealed the rocky road ahead, for while Whigs and conservative Democrats agreed on no scheme of their own, they could unite against the Independent Treasury. Spokesmen from both factions charged Van Buren's plan would dangerously increase the national government's power, reduce property values by two-thirds, depress wages, and fasten a permanent depression on the country. Their arguments failed to win the administration-dominated Senate but in the House they carried the day. The President's bill was tabled by a vote of 120 to 107, with 93 Whigs and 27 conservative Democrats in opposition. The most significant feature of the vote was the 41 ballots cast against the Independent Treasury by western Whigs and Democrats. Van Buren saw he could never hope to triumph without more support from that section, and was wise enough to know any appeal for the West's votes must recognize the region's desire for cheap lands. His realization linked land policy and public finance once more; for three years the struggle over those issues absorbed the nation's legislature.

The President made his bid for western support in a message to the regular session of Congress which assembled on December 5, 1837. Immediately after recommending the Independent Treasury plan, he declared his administration favored a land policy that would encourage the early settlement of the West. This could be accomplished, he said, by lowering the price of lands remaining unsold after a set period, turning over unsalable areas to the states for disposal, and allowing actual settlers on the public domain to purchase lands they occupied at the minimum price. Van Buren, in asking Congress to erect his program into law, pledged his support for three measures long coveted by the West: Graduation, Cession, and Pre-emption.

His inspiration was a happy one. Frontiersmen welcomed the prospect of Graduation and Cession, but in their eyes Pre-emption was absolutely necessary. Squatting on the public domain was not new—from one-half to two-thirds of the settlers in any new region normally squatted on government land—but the problem of buying land when it was finally placed on the auction block was growing more serious daily. Before the Panic the money needed could be borrowed from local banks; now purchase must be in gold or silver which was obtainable only from eastern "loan sharks." Those scoundrels were not content with the 10 or 12 per cent interest allowed by law but made a practice of buying squatters' improved farms themselves, then reselling on credit at a price which gave them a 30 or 40 per cent return. Pre-emption would end that scandalous procedure, giving frontiersmen a chance to buy at a reasonable price. Little wonder the newer states of the West were solidly behind Van Buren's proposal.

The Graduation and Pre-emption bills introduced into Congress on the heels of the President's message were soundly denounced by Whigs—Clay branded squatters as "lawless rabble" and warned the laws meant wholesale raids on government lands—but administration machinery worked smoothly with solid western support. By June, 1838, a Pre-emption Bill entitling any squatter then on the public domain to buy his farm at the minimum price passed both houses and received the President's signature. The Graduation Bill enjoyed less success when House Whigs buried the measure in committee, but that made little difference. Van Buren gave the West an important concession; would the West reciprocate by supporting his Independent Treasury Plan?

The answer was not forthcoming at once. Before the issue could be decided the administration's plans were upset by the machinations of Nicholas Biddle. That unreformed worthy was still striving to restore the Bank of the United States and nationalize the monetary system on the basis of paper currency. To do so, he realized, he must not only defeat the Independent Treasury Bill, but demonstrate his own bank's soundness, even under a Pennsylvania charter. If he could, in addition, help end the depression he would be in a position to dictate his own terms to the government. The canny financier spent many a day after the crash searching for the right solution, but not until the winter of 1837-38 did he find the answer. The giant speculation which he launched at that time blocked Van Buren's legislative program, lifted the nation from depression, and restored world-wide prosperity, only to collapse a few months later in the worst financial debacle yet known in the United States.

Biddle's plan was as simple as it was daring. During the winter of 1837-38 his Bank of the United States and two or three co-operating eastern banks issued several million dollars worth of 6 per cent short term notes. The reliability of the institutions was such that British firms eagerly purchased all placed in circulation for use instead of bullion in international exchange. Money obtained in that way was used to buy cotton until Biddle controlled the American supply. This he planned to hold until British textile mills, starved for raw materials, bid the price upward until he emerged with a profit. By the spring of 1838 the effect of the bold speculation was felt throughout the United States. Cotton prices spurted upward, business revived, closed banks reopened their doors or resumed specie payments, work was resumed on bogged-down internal improvements, land sales increased, employment mounted. English investors, their fears forgotten, once more poured an invigorating stream of gold into the nation's channels of trade. Biddle had apparently lifted the country out of a depression by his own efforts. Throughout Congress probank sentiment was so high the Independent Treasury Bill seemed doomed.

Administration forces, however, did not have to wait long for revenge. Biddle's speculation depended on a rapid rise in cotton prices that would allow him to sell his cornered supply before the short-term notes fell due during the summer of 1839. Instead of rising, British prices slumped sharply, due partly to a depression that closed textile mills in Belgium, Prussia, and Saxony with a corresponding decline in the demand for English yarn, and partly to grain failures at home which forced large expenditures of capital abroad for food rather than cotton. At the same time the Bank of England, alarmed by the renewed flow of money abroad, again raised its interest rate from 5 to 5½ per cent. Those two blows were more than Biddle and his fellow conspirators could stand. Unable either to sell their hoarded cotton or borrow money to meet the interest due on their notes, they had no choice but bankruptcy. The Bank of the United States closed its doors in September, 1839, with $5,000,000 in unpaid obligations. In the flurry of panic that followed hundreds of banks followed its example or suspended specie payments. Business houses followed, unemployment mounted, month by month conditions grew worse until the late autumn of 1839 when the United States was in the grip of a worse depression than two year before.

President Van Buren watched the collapse with mingled feelings. His political good sense told him the renewed panic ruined his chances of re-election in 1840, yet he could not help gloating over the discomfort of his opponents. There was no question that his Independent Treasury plan would be accepted now; the whole nation was convinced that public funds would never be safe in private banks run by Biddle or his fellow manipulators. The bill was laid before Congress in January, 1840, adopted by the Senate a week later, and passed the House of Representatives in June by a vote of 124 to 107. Western ballots were responsible for the President's success. Instead of voting heavily against the measure, the section divided its support evenly with thirty-two in favor and thirty-three opposed. When Van Buren signed the bill on July 4, 1840, he ended for a time the struggle between the government and the banks.

In the end, however, the administration lost more than it gained. The collapse of Biddle's speculation plunged the nation into a grueling depression that lasted until 1842. This time the eastern states escaped the full effects of deflation while the burden of suffering was shifted to South and West. Conditions there were appalling. Prices plummeted; by 1841 cotton sold at 6 cents a pound, flour at $2.50 a barrel, wheat at 40 cents a bushel, corn at 25 cents. Those ruinous prices, which scarcely paid for production, left farmers and planters with no funds to meet their obligations. One after the other banks closed their doors until not one remained open in the South or West. That was bad enough for business but worse for states that purchased bank stock during the internal improvement boom of the 1830's. Now the securities were worthless, except as dismal reminders of the debt burden fastened on the people by the collapsed banking structure. Alabama owed $10,000,000, Ohio and Illinois a like amount, Indiana $12,000,000, Louisiana $23,000,000—and all were without a cent in their treasuries. For the next generation the political thinking of southerners and westerners was shaped by one great question: how could they lift the burden of debt from their shoulders?

The immediate impulse in both sections was to lock the barn now the horse was stolen. Banks and paper money caused hard times, therefore banks and paper money must go! So reasoned the people as "No-Bank" sentiment swept across the Mississippi Valley. "A bank of Earth is the best bank," one farmer declared, "and a plough share the best share." Illinois was without any banking facilities until 1851, Wisconsin until 1853. Iowa and Wisconsin wrote into early drafts of their constitutions clauses outlawing banks. Other western states, although unwilling to go that far, passed laws limiting the note issues of institutions still in operation, provided for their regular inspection, and made the directors liable for any losses incurred by depositors or note holders. No section of the country was as rigidly conservative as the West during the "Hungry 'Forties."

The harassed debtor states still faced the problem of meeting their staggering obligations. Taxes would never do; in Louisiana an annual levy of $3 on every man, woman, and child would only meet interest charges. Why burden Americans with such a load when the debts, due hated foreigners or easterners, might be repudiated? Nine of the states showed the way the wind blew when they refused to pay interest on their bonds during 1841 and 1842, at the same time debating whether to pay at all. In each case the argument was bitter, but in the end Mississippi repudiated two bond issues totalling $7,000,000 after a popular referendum, Florida cancelled $4,000,000 in debts when a similar sampling of popular sentiment showed overwhelming support, Arkansas and Michigan declined to pay a portion of their obligations, and Indiana and Pennsylvania refused payment on most of their internal improvement securities. In all English investors lost $100,000,000 by the states' unethical action.

Bad as the situation was for western debtors and British bondholders, there were some who viewed the plight of the newer states with ill-concealed delight. Whig politicians saw that opportunity knocked on their party's door. Of the states in the worst financial difficulty—Ohio, Indiana, Illinois, Michigan, Arkansas, and Louisiana—all but Indiana were normally Democratic. If the Whigs could find a formula to ease their debt burdens, grateful voters would support the party's candidate in the election of 1840. The obvious solution was national assumption of state debts, and during the winter of 1839–40 most Whig papers blossomed with such proposals. One, the New York *Courier and Enquirer,* put the matter in concrete form by suggesting that a national bond issue of $3,000,000 be apportioned among the states, then gradually retired with proceeds from land sales. The effectiveness of the appeal was unquestioned, despite Democratic counter-blasts charging the scheme was hatched by British bankers anxious to salvage something from worthless loans.

Whig politicians were afraid to go as far as their newspapers in favoring assumption, but the reception accorded the *Courier and Enquirer's* proposal convinced them the depression could be used politically. They made their stand clear in January, 1840, by introducing a new Distribution Bill into the Senate. Although the measure was defeated by the Democratic majority, the nation now knew a Whig victory in 1840 would assure the distribution of funds from land sales among the states. The Democrats, recognizing the effectiveness of their opponents' plan, saw they could retain support in the West only by advocating a program even more pleasing to frontiersmen. They turned again to liberal land laws. A Graduation Bill failed to pass the House in early 1840, but another retrospective Pre-emption Act similar to the law passed two years before was adopted in June with solid Demo-cratic support. The issue was now clear. If the voters wanted Distribution they could elect a Whig president, if they favored Graduation and Pre-emption they could back the Democratic candidate.

Political juggling probably had little to do with the outcome of the election of 1840. In the popular mind the Democratic candidate, Martin Van Buren, was so linked with the depression that any change was for the better. To make matters worse the Whig nominee, William Henry Harri-son, proved a surprisingly popular choice. The famed frontiersman wisely said little, but his managers staged an effective campaign. Taking their cue from a rival editor's ill-natured remark that Harrison would be happy for life if given a pension, a log cabin, and a barrel of hard cider, they painted their Indian fighter as a rough-and-ready man of the people, in contrast with the snobbish Van Buren who scented his whiskers with cologne water, played billiards, and ate imported delicacies from gold plate. The idea took hold at once; log cabins were dragged through the streets by singing mobs of coon-skinned Whigs, or set up in village squares to dispense free hard cider to thirsty voters. In vain the Democrats pointed out that they were the party of the common people and the Whigs representatives of the upper classes; amidst a campaign of emotion and unreason Harrison was swept into office by an electoral vote of 234 to 60.

Van Buren's followers saw only one ray of light through the haze of gloom surrounding them when returns were announced. The Whigs were not the friends of frontiersmen they represented themselves to be; if that could be demonstrated while Democrats still controlled Congress the West would return to its political senses. Thomas Hart Benton sought to expose Whig duplicity with the famous "Log Cabin Bill" which he introduced in December, 1840. This provided for permanent Pre-emption; any adult male could pre-empt a quarter section of the public domain by building a cabin and making certain improvements, then buy the land at the minimum price when it went on sale. Let the Whigs support a truly western measure, Benton told his fellow senators, or admit they won frontier votes fraudulently. The Democrat's strategic move threw Clay and his followers, who were the last men in the world to want liberal land laws, into a turmoil. Every effort was made to obscure the issue by amendments, but when those were shouted down by the Democratic majority, the Whigs were forced into the open. On February 2, 1841, the Log Cabin Bill passed the Senate by a vote of thirty-one to nineteen, with seventeen Whigs and two eastern Democrats in opposition. That the measure was adopted too late to be considered by the House made no difference to the Democrats. "The log cabin Federalists," wrote one jubilant editor, "are now uncabined."

Henry Clay, however, was far from discouraged, for he counted on his legislative program to regain any prestige his party lost in the skirmish. His prospects were encouraging; the Whigs controlled both houses of Congress, the President was old and politically inept, and the depression-burdened nation in a mood to welcome vigorous leadership. Clay would provide this, sitting behind the throne while disciples pushed his legislative panaceas through Congress. So eager was he that he persuaded Harrison to call a special session for May 31, 1841, then set out to fill important government posts with his own supporters. His well-laid plans were upset when the aged President, plagued beyond endurance by office seekers, suddenly died only a month after the inauguration. Harrison's death brought to the presidency the vice-president, John Tyler of Virginia, a conservative states' right representative of the planter class who had been added to the Whig ticket to win Democratic votes. Tyler's inaugural address indicated his willingness to support Distribution as a means of aiding debtor states, but he was lukewarm toward a national bank and openly hostile to a higher tariff. Clay, although disappointed, was not ready to give up hope; with Congress behind him he might still force the President to accept his program.

The platform he laid before Congress on June 7, 1841, contained most of the "fundamental" Whig measures: Distribution, repeal of the Independent Treasury, a national bank, and customs duties high enough to yield adequate revenues. Clay's suggestion that fiscal issues be dealt with first was welcomed by the Whig majority as a means of sweeping away the hated

Independent Treasury system. This was accomplished by mid-August, but substituting a national bank proved more difficult. Administration forces, sensitive to Tyler's opposition, proposed a Fiscal Bank of the United States, incorporated in the District of Columbia to avoid constitutional objections, and with no power to establish branches in any state without the state's consent. Although Clay was far from satisfied with the half-hearted measure, he threw his weight behind the act which passed in late July. Ten days later the President plunged the Whigs into confusion by returning the bill with his veto. When Democratic and administration votes sustained Tyler, the Whig cause was lost. The party was split in two and Clay's program destined to failure.

That became clear when Congress turned to the next point in the platform: a Distribution Bill. Even the effervescent Clay saw the measure had little chance; southerners were solidly opposed to a treasury-draining scheme that would provide high-tariff advocates with ammunition, and westerners to anything interfering with Graduation and Pre-emption. The South, he knew, could never be budged, but the West might support his plan if he promised the section something in return. Hence, on June 24, 1841, Clay introduced a combined Distribution-Pre-emption Bill. One section provided that proceeds from land sales be distributed among the states in proportion to their population after 10 per cent was deducted for states in which the lands lay; the other gave every adult male the right to pre-empt 160 acres of surveyed land by erecting a dwelling and making certain improvements. The measure was an open bid for the western support needed to pass any essential Whig bill.

Debate in the House was bitter, especially during a heated ten-hour session when thunder and lightning provided a fitting background for the sulphurous oratory, but Whig lines held and after more than a hundred amendments offered by Democrats were shouted down, the measure was passed by a party vote of 116 to 108. For a time Clay's forces anticipated equal success in the Senate; then debate turned to the effect of Distribution on the tariff which must be framed in 1842, and discipline collapsed. Southern Whigs joined with Democrats to denounce the bill so vigorously that some compromise was obviously necessary. The suggestion of a Georgia senator, that Distribution not go into effect while duties were above 20 per cent, provided a solution; Clay resisted for a time then gave the amendment his support. In this mangled form the measure received President Tyler's signature on September 4, 1841.

Like most compromises, the Distribution-Pre-emption Law of 1841 pleased almost no one. The West was delighted with Pre-emption, but frowned upon a Distribution measure which promised to influence the older states against admitting new territories to share federal funds. The Northeast heartily disliked Pre-emption and was far from satisfied with the Distribution Bill, for so long as the 20 per cent clause was attached western states would oppose higher tariffs rather than lose their share of government money. Only the South gained from the legislative hodge-podge. Southerners were little concerned with Pre-emption, but were delighted with the clause of the Distribution Act which served as a perpetual bribe to keep tariffs below 20 per cent. Such were the necessities of political juggling that the one section least favored by Clay won the lion's share of the benefits.

There remained one step before the Whig platform was completed: a new protective tariff to replace the Compromise Tariff of 1833 due to expire in 1842. Even the most ardent antiprotectionist admitted some revision was needed, for the 20 per cent level reached on July 1 would not provide enough revenue to relieve the government of the $14,000,000 deficit facing it in 1842. Yet any change would be difficult now that the tariff and Distribution were linked together. The Northeast wanted protection, the bankrupt West Distribution, the South neither. Henry Clay, master strategist that he was, saw he could probably push a combined high tariff-Distribution bill through Congress with northern and western votes. The question remained: would President Tyler accept a measure that violated the Pre-emption-Distribution Act of 1841 by distributing funds while duties were over 20 per cent? There was only one way to find out. Clay's forces launched a trial balloon in June, 1842, by introducing a bill postponing the cut in duties to 20 per cent from July 1 to August 1, yet providing distribution begin at once. This was squeezed through both houses, but on June 30 it was vetoed by Tyler as repugnant to both the Compromise Tariff of 1833 and the Distribution-Pre-emption Bill of 1841. A day later customs duties dropped to 20 per cent amidst the outraged cries of northern manufacturers.

Clay had his answer. Tyler would veto any bill combining Distribution and high duties. There remained four possibilities, all unpleasant: a low tariff and Distribution which would displease the Northeast, a high tariff without Distribution that would anger the West, a high tariff and Distribution which would be vetoed by Tyler, or separate high tariff and Distribution bills, thus placing on the President's shoulders the delicate task of deciding which to accept. Of these alternatives Clay dismissed the first two as politically inexpedient. The third was also distasteful, for if the Whigs gave the nation neither protection nor Distribution both Northeast and West would be dissatisfied. On the other hand, much could be said for separate bills. If the President accepted both, Clay's program was triumphant; if he vetoed either he offended one of the sections so seriously that his wing would be read from the party, leaving Clay in control.

Having decided, the antiadministration Whigs moved into action. A tariff bill raising duties to the 1832 levels, with special high rates on coarse cotton cloth, iron, sugar, and salt, was railroaded through Congress over southern opposition. A Distribution Act followed at once. On August 30, 1842, Tyler signed the tariff measure which he felt necessary to bolster the nation's revenue, at the same time vetoing the Distribution Bill. That was the signal for open warfare among Whigs; the President's faction was ousted from the party amidst a chorus of name calling that continued as long as Tyler remained in the White House.

The full effect of the internal warfare was not realized until two years later when the Whigs entered the presidential contest so badly divided their defeat was certain. Clay, who captured the party's nomination, staged a dismally ineffective campaign, stressing domestic issues in a day when the nation's imagination was caught by the vision of expansion. His Democratic opponent, James K. Polk of Tennessee, judged the popular temper better; realizing the people were more concerned with the annexation of Texas and the occupation of Oregon than with the moth-worn questions of tariff or public finance, he pledged himself to secure the transcontinental boundaries needed to make the United States a world power. To make matters worse for the Whigs, abolitionists entered the election under the banner of the Liberty Party. Their candidate, James G. Birney, polled only 62,300 votes, but most of those would have been Whig and many were from crucial northern states. The result was far from decisive— the combined Clay-Birney vote was greater than Polk's—but the Democrats triumphed.

The victors emerged from their four-year period of eclipse with high hopes of solving the domestic problems that baffled the Whigs. Two objectives were uppermost in the minds of Polk's followers: to re-establish the Independent Treasury and return the lower tariff levels desired by southern farmers who wielded such influence within Democratic ranks. The first proved easy. In August, 1846, a bill setting up a treasury closely modeled on Van Buren's original plan was carried through Congress and signed by the President. A tariff acceptable to the congressional majority was harder to frame, yet Polk's persistent efforts not only secured a satisfactory revenue law but disclosed an important shift in the sectional alignment.

Both the President and his secretary of the treasury, Robert J. Walker of Mississippi, realized that no drastic reduction in duties would be possible without votes from the West. Party loyalty would furnish some but not enough; more must be obtained by convincing the traditionally protectionist region that free trade was to its advantage. Westerners must be shown that their principal future markets lay not in the Northeast but in the mill towns of England! Even before he received the nomination in 1844 Polk sent a close friend to London to sound out leaders of the Tory government and Whig opposition on the possibility of reducing duties on American grain in return for similar reduction on British manufactured goods. While no commitments were made, Democrats were sure any concessions by the United States would be matched by England. The movement for reciprocal tariff reductions gained momentum late in 1845 when Walker, as secretary of the treasury, submitted a thorough analysis of the whole customs structure to Congress. Pointing out that western farmers already produced more than could be consumed at home, he suggested England as the best future customer, prophesying that any reduction in American rates would inspire that nation to admit grain from the United States duty free by repealing its Corn Laws.

Walker's report had a profound effect on both sides of the Atlantic. In England it was read at free-trade meetings and incorporated bodily in the speeches of Sir Robert Peel, the Tory prime minister, which led to the repeal of the Corn Laws in June, 1846. In the United States its suggestions were reflected from every line of a tariff bill laid before Congress on July 30, 1846. This intelligent measure levied duties of 40 to 100 per cent on such luxuries as spirituous liquors, spices, and snuff, taxed iron, raw wool, woolen textiles, and manufactured goods 30 per cent, charged cotton cloth 25 per cent, and admitted coffee, tea, and other necessities duty free. All duties were *ad valorem*. The average on all items ranged from 23 to 26 per cent—enough to provide adequate revenue without allowing manufacturers an undue profit.

The vote on the Walker Tariff illustrated the effect of Polk's propaganda campaign on the West, which strongly supported the low-tariff measure:

| | FOR | AGAINST |
|---|---|---|
| NORTHEAST | 26 | 63 |
| SOUTH | 58 | 22 |
| WEST | 30 | 10 |
| | 114 | 95 |

Western votes carried the day; if the section had continued to side with the protectionist Northeast the bill would never have passed. The shift was caused partly by a continued desire to win southern support for liberal land laws, partly by party loyalty, and partly by the growing realization that the home market would never absorb the agricultural surpluses of the Mississippi Valley. Walker's arguments helped convince westerners they must cultivate markets abroad, but more effective was a practical demonstration still fresh in their minds. Between 1831 and 1842 they sold large quantities of wheat and livestock to Canada, for England allowed flour and meat from that dominion to enter the British West Indies duty free, and England itself at appreciably lower rates than goods from the United States. In 1842 and 1843 the Canadian government laid heavy duties on American grain in retaliation, westerners believed, against the high tariff of 1842. Their profitable trade could be restored only by convincing England the United States would accept its manufactured goods. The West, like the South, was becoming an exporting region and shaping its policies accordingly.

Instead of drawing the two sections together, the shift in western opinion drove them even farther apart. As both directed their trade abroad their mutual interdependence lessened; they were bound increasingly to England rather than to each other. The Tariff of 1846 ushered the nation into an era of prosperity but it did not symbolize any new alliance between South and West. Instead observers realized the Mississippi Valley was still an independent section, going its own way without regard to the wishes of the other two.

The differences between South and West were deepened by a change in the sectional attitude toward land policy during the late 1840's. In the past those two sections usually acted as one on this vital issue, partly because southerners welcomed a practical means of winning western support for low tariffs. During the years between 1845 and 1850 the alliance was displaced by a new union between West and Northeast which further emphasized the growing isolation of the South.

The cleavage was brought about by an abrupt reversal of both northeastern and southern opinion on the land question. Southerners, in those trying days of conflict over slavery, took to judging all matters in relation to their own peculiar institution. As they did so they realized a liberal land policy did them harm. Low priced lands meant a rapid advance of the northern frontier into trans-Mississippi regions made free by the Missouri Compromise. On the other hand the South, its westward path blocked by the inhospitable wilds of the Ozark Plateau and the arid reaches of the Indian country, gained no new slave lands by expansion. Southerners realized that continued migration would carve the whole Far West into free states, thus bolstering the North's legislative strength. In desperation the section swung to advocate Distribution and other devices designed to keep land prices high—much to the disgust of the West.

More important was the evolution of northeastern opinion to the point where two important segments of the population advocated cheap lands for the West. One was the influential employer class, which had steadfastly opposed liberal land laws lest laborers needed for eastern industries be drained away. As wealthy industrialists gained security in their new position they realized every westerner was a potential customer for the products of their factories, every western enterprise a possible field for the investment of surplus capital. The money flowing westward after the economic recovery of the early 1840's—into canals and railroads, copper mines and lumber preserves, town sites and farming lands—convinced thousands of easterners their interests would best be served by building up the West through attractive land laws. Their conversion was hastened by the flood of cheap labor inundating the Northeast in the wake of hard times in Ireland between 1845 and 1850. Irish immigrants drifted into the mill towns in such numbers that employers no longer feared labor shortages as they had in the past.

Even more important was the development of working-class sentiment in favor of liberalized land laws. This gained strength during the depression years of the early 1840's, when farseeing labor leaders, realizing their miserable lot would never improve so long as overcrowding in the Northeast gave mill owners a chance to inflict starvation wages on workers, turned to the land system as a means of draining away excess labor. Most influential among them was George Henry Evans, a humanitarian long associated with the working class movement, who in 1844 founded the National Reform Association to unite eastern laborers behind the cause of land reform. Within two years the association had branches in eight states, numbered such influential publicisits as Horace Greeley of the New York *Tribune* among its converts, and was attracting the attention of politicians. So effective was its propaganda that by 1846 workers of the Northeast were ready to unite with industrialists behind any land system promising to people the frontier territories with the greatest speed.

The policy which gave those strange bedfellows a chance to ally with the farmers of the West was Homestead. Agitation for free land developed in the West when the passing years showed Pre-emption to be no panacea. Speculators still operated along the back country after 1841, hiring armies of squatters to pre-empt lands for them. Loan sharks still exacted a heavy tribute from poverty-ridden westerners who borrowed at ruinous interest rates to purchase pre-empted farms. All those evils frontiersmen believed would vanish if the government gave every actual settler a quarter section of free land. The Northeast was just as enthusiastic. Industrialists warmed to a system that promised to build new markets for their gimcracks; workers

pictured free lands as a magnet drawing surplus laborers westward. Moreover abolitionists backed Homestead, realizing that any measure which
disposed of the public domain in small units would block the extension of
the plantation system.

When the Homestead issue first emerged into the limelight in the middle
1840's the West was enthusiastic, the Northeast interested, and the South
divided in opinion, with the seaboard states opposed and the lower Mississippi Valley in favor. The first Homestead Bill considered by Congress
was introduced by Felix Grundy McConnell of Alabama in January,
1846, while others that followed during the next years were sponsored
largely by Andrew Johnson of Tennessee. None of these early measures
attracted much attention in a legislature absorbed in debating the broader
issues of slavery. Not until 1850 was the subject publicly discussed by Congressmen and not until 1852 was one of Johnson's bills brought to a vote.
This passed the House 107 to 56 with opposition centered in the Southeast, but was never considered by the Senate. The Homestead question,
although destined to bulk large during the next decade, even in 1850 provided the basis for a new sectional alignment on land, with Northeast and
West united against the South.

The dozen years following the Panic of 1837 wrought no revolution
in the relationship of the sections. The Northeast and the South in 1850
were openly antagonistic, just as they had been in 1837, with the West
hanging in the balance between them. Yet a careful observer could notice
certain significant trends threatening national harmony. One by one the
ties that bound South and West together were severing, as those two sections
developed antagonistic economic interests. Step by step the Northeast and
West were brought closer together as their views on public finance, slavery,
and land gradually merged. Civil war was still far away in 1850, but the
changing sectional patterns which produced the irrepressible conflict were
taking shape. Only the stimulus of new controversies—already developing
beyond the Mississippi—was needed to translate sectional misunderstanding
into a national catastrophe.

# CHAPTER XIX

# Railroads and Sectionalism

## 1837-1850

The legislative record of the 1840's—the congressional battles which brought Northeast and West gradually together and left the South alone —only mirrored the nation's shifting economic pattern. Almost imperceptibly during that decade western farmers came to see that their dream of competitive markets could never be realized, and that the wage earners of the Atlantic mill towns must absorb most of their surpluses rather than the slaves who labored in southern cotton fields. They would willingly have sold to both South and Northeast, and did so as long as steamboats and canal barges carried their produce. But by 1850 a lusty young rival challenged water transportation. The railroad, rapidly passing beyond its experimental stage, brought North and West together commercially just as their common ideology united them emotionally.

Work on the few railroad lines projected before 1837 came to a standstill during the depression. When construction was resumed in the 1840's the lessons learned during the years of hard times reshaped building practices. The most important change was in ownership. Before the Panic most roads were either state owned or subsidized; afterward construction was entrusted to private corporations financed by eastern stockholders. The shift was partly due to necessity—the European capitalists who supplied the states with money in the past were now so angered at debt repudiation they applied a financial boycott—but more to the burnt-child attitude of American taxpayers. They did not realize that the brief period of public ownership carried railroad construction through its costly experimental stage, or that the collapse of state building programs was due to a national depression rather than local inefficiency. Aware only that they must assume heavy tax burdens to pay for apparently useless internal improvements, Americans were glad to let private enterprise assume the risks.

The withdrawal of states from railroad building allowed some sections to forge ahead of others, as not all could produce sufficient capital to meet construction costs. The South failed to do so, committed as it was to a plantation economy which diverted all available funds into land and slaves; hence that section lagged behind. Nor could the frontier West raise enough money now that European credit was cut off. Only the Northeast contained wealthy capitalists ready to invest the swollen fortunes cascading from the counting rooms of their mills and factories in any enterprise which promised profits. Railroads were a tempting bait; they had been nursed through the experimental stage at state expense and were now ready to yield up returns. Eastern investors who rose to this lure were interested both in roads close to home and those that would stimulate the trade of their factories. Those answering these qualifications were the lines between Northeast and West, for each new connection with the Ohio Valley meant not only cheaper food for eastern workers but expanded markets for eastern manufacturers. This prospect attracted money into railroads that extended the trading areas of the Northeast, as well as the main roads across the mountains. The rapid development of transportation in those two sections was due primarily to available capital.

Businessmen in eastern cities which emerged from the depression with poor western connections awakened to the possibilities first. Merchants of Baltimore, long covetous of the trade enjoyed by Philadelphia and New York, began agitating in 1842 to continue the Baltimore and Ohio Railroad beyond Cumberland where work ended with the panic. Six years were needed to raise the necessary capital, but construction was resumed in 1848, and by 1853 the road was completed to Wheeling on the Ohio River. This activity alarmed Philadelphia merchants who recognized the unsatisfactory nature of the Pennsylvania Canal System. When in 1843 promoters in the western part of the state chartered the Pittsburgh and Connellsville Railroad to connect Pittsburgh with the Baltimore and Ohio, Philadelphians realized that they must keep pace with the times or lose the trade of their own back country to Baltimore. Their answer was the Pennsylvania Railroad, formed in 1846 to build westward along the route of the canal. Although the state protected its own interests by forcing the new road to pay the canal authorities three cents for each ton-mile of freight carried, stock was quickly oversubscribed and work began in 1847. By the end of September, 1850, the eastern division was completed to Hollidaysburg; the conquest of the Alleghenies over the rugged Juniata-Conemaugh Pass proved more difficult, but the whole line between Philadelphia and Pittsburgh was opened in December, 1852.

New York's western connections developed in a haphazard fashion, for the success of the state-owned Erie Canal doomed any railroad to a period of bitter competition. That was demonstrated in the building of the first cross-state route. Just after the completion of the canal, a group of Schenectady and Albany business men conceived the idea of an intercity road to divert trade southward from the Erie to Albany. The Mohawk and Hudson Railroad, which was opened in the late summer of 1831, proved so profitable that other promoters became interested in extending the line

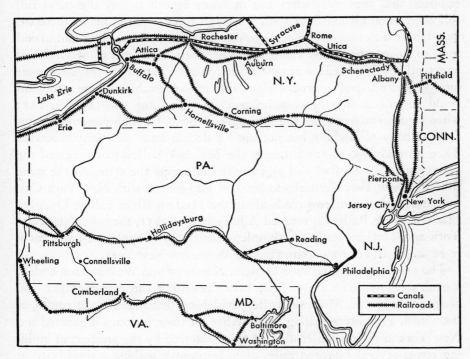

Principal East-West Trade Routes, 1840-1855

on westward from Schenectady. The next link, the Utica and Schenectady Railroad, was completed in 1836 and also returned large profits, despite a clause in its charter forbidding it to carry the freight that formed the bulk of the canal's business. Agitation developed at once to extend the line to Syracuse. The Syracuse and Utica Railroad, completed in 1839, only whetted the appetite of the road builders for more. So great was the interest that two routes were used to reach Rochester: the Direct Road along the canal, and the Auburn and Syracuse Railroad and Auburn and Rochester Railroad southward through Auburn, Geneva, and Canandaigua. The latter was completed in 1841, the Direct Road not until ten years later. In the meantime Rochester capitalists, interested in extending their trade westward, began work on the Tonawanda Railroad which connected their city with Attica in 1842. There it joined with the last link in the chain, the Attica and Buffalo Railroad. By 1842 an all-rail route stretched across New York from Albany to Buffalo.

Transportation conditions were still far from satisfactory. All the roads were forbidden by law to carry freight; not until 1848 was the restriction removed and then only after the railroads agreed to pay the canal full toll charges on all goods carried. The high rates required under these circumstances discouraged shippers; so did the failure of the eight end-to-end lines to co-operate. Transshipment was necessary at several points, trains of one road seldom made connection with those of another, travelers were inconvenienced, and journeys slow and uncomfortable. These problems could be solved only by consolidation. The first step was taken in 1843 when representatives of all the lines agreed to run through passenger trains from Albany to Buffalo, but not until a decade later was unity achieved. Then an exchange of stock among the Mohawk Valley roads created the New York Central Railroad as a single line across the state. At the same time the New York Central was brought into contact with New York City by the completion of two roads along the Hudson River valley. One, the Hudson River Railroad, reached Albany late in 1851, the other, the New York and Harlem Railroad, completed its tracks to the same point early in 1852. An all-rail route connected the West with New York.

The process of forging links between Northeast and West was not ended. Farmers of southern New York State, resenting the transportation improvements in the Mohawk Valley, had long demanded trade routes of their own. Promoters willing to capitalize on their jealousy organized the New York and Erie Railroad in 1832, undeterred by the prospect of building across several hundred miles of hilly country without a single city of more than 3,000 inhabitants. Money was raised, but construction came to a halt when the Erie went into bankruptcy during the depression. Not until 1847 was the company reorganized; this time building forged ahead until the 460 miles of track between Piermont on the Hudson and Dunkirk on Lake Erie were opened in 1851. During the next few years better terminal points were secured at both ends of the line; on the east an extension to Jersey City opened the New York market to the Erie, and on the west two locally-built roads—the Buffalo and Cochecton Railroad and the Attica and Hornellsville Railroad—brought it in touch with Buffalo.

As the through rail routes between the seaboard and the interior waterways neared completion, eastern capitalists turned their attention to the western states. They realized they could never capture the West's trade without further effort; so long as the section depended on its canal and river system to carry produce to shipping points along the Ohio River many valuable commodities would be diverted southward to New Orleans. Nor could eastern manufacturers hope to broaden their markets while paying the high transportation charges exacted by the canals of Ohio, Indiana, and Illinois. Goods reaching their final destination by rail, they knew, would sell more widely than those moved westward to the Ohio River over the Pennsylvania Railroad, transshipped to steamboats for the journey

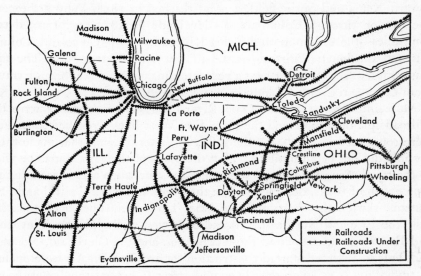

Principal Western Railroads in 1855

to Portsmouth or Cincinnati, then sent northward by canal barge to the interior. Western extensions of the East-West railroads—the Pennsylvania, Baltimore and Ohio, Erie, and New York Central—would not only attract food from the West and open wider markets for the East, but return sizable profits on investments. Money must come from seaboard capitalists, as frontier states either lacked sufficient funds or were struggling to complete their out-of-date canals. This was the East's opportunity. By 1847 capital was flowing across the mountains from Boston, New York, and Philadelphia to launch the West on its bonanza era of railroad building.

Ohio felt the effect first. By 1846 interest revived in some of the railroads that collapsed during the panic; a step made easier when the legislature authorized counties to help finance lines within their borders. Promoters, spurred on by the promise of support, reorganized the Mad River and Lake Erie Railroad in 1846, secured enough capital to resume work stopped eight years before, and by 1848 completed the road between Springfield and Sandusky. At the same time another North-South line, the Mansfield and Sandusky Railroad, began laying the tracks which by 1848 reached Newark on the Ohio Canal. This construction, which threatened to make Sandusky the state's most important Lake Erie port, stirred Cleveland businessmen into action. Their ambition was an all-rail route to Cincinnati which would attract the produce of central Ohio northward. One link, the Little Miami Railroad, was already building northward toward Xenia and Springfield, a point reached in 1848. Why not extend the line on through Columbus to Cleveland? In 1847 they formed two companies—the Columbus and Xenia Railroad and the Cleveland, Columbus and Cincinnati Railroad—raised money, and started work. The first was completed in 1850, the next a year later, making possible through travel from Cincinnati to either Sandusky or Cleveland.

More important than the Ohio River-Lake Erie connections were the railroads planned to extend the main East-West lines across the state. Few were completed by 1850, for the influx of eastern capital that made them possible did not begin until 1847, but the plans of their promoters testified to the revolution in western trade bound to occur when they were finished. One group of roads, designed to lengthen the New York Central and Erie systems, skirted the shore of Lake Erie. Three companies undertook the task, the Erie and Northeast Railroad built west of Buffalo, the Cleveland and Erie Railroad connected those two cities, and the Cleveland, Norwalk and Toledo Railroad started construction toward Toledo. All were opened to traffic in 1853. Two other lines undertook to extend the Pennsylvania Railroad by building westward from Pittsburgh: the Cleveland and Pittsburgh Railroad, built between 1849 and 1853, and the Pittsburgh, Ft. Wayne and Chicago Railroad which started bravely across Ohio toward Chicago. The latter reached Crestline, on the Cleveland, Columbus and Cincinnati Railroad, in 1853 to complete the first rail route between Cincinnati and Pittsburgh. A year later Indianapolis was added to the East's trading sphere when the Bellefontaine and Indiana Railroad reached Crestline.

Indiana's railroad network was still in the planning stage in 1850, but enough was accomplished to show the developing East-West routes that were soon to break the trading alliance between the South and the Ohio Valley. One minor road, the Madison and Indianapolis Railroad, chartered in 1843 to take over the right of way of a line projected before the panic, was completed seven years later. By that time eastern money was entering the state and promoters joyfully laying out a network of lines radiating out of Indianapolis toward Cincinnati, Jeffersonville, Peru, and Lafayette.

More important were the two roads designed to connect with the East-West lines of Ohio. One, the Bellefontaine and Indiana Railroad, was completed in 1853; the other, consisting of the Indiana Central Railroad and the Terre Haute and Richmond Railroad, was opened across the state in the same year. By that time goods from Philadelphia could be sent by rail as far as the western border of Indiana either through Crestline, Springfield, Dayton, and Richmond, or via Crestline and Indianapolis to Terre Haute.

Michigan, developing rapidly under the stimulus of wholesale immigration, also played a prominent role in forging the railroad network between Northeast and West. The two roads started by the state before the depression—the Michigan Central Railroad and the Michigan Southern Railroad—were partially completed and operating profitably in 1845 when the legislature, frightened by the prospect of raising additional millions for their completion, decided to place them on sale. News of this fell on the ears of a group of Boston and New York capitalists led by John Murray Forbes. Knowing the tremendous profits to be realized from Michigan's fear of public ownership, Forbes and his cohorts hurried representatives west, made their offer, and early in 1846 acquired both roads at a cost of less than $2,500,000. The new owners pushed construction rapidly; by 1849 the Michigan Central's tracks reached New Buffalo where water connection across Lake Michigan was established with Chicago. Two years later they extended across Indiana to the Illinois line. In the meantime the Michigan Southern built steadily westward to LaPorte, Indiana, in 1851. From that time on both roads raced towards Chicago in a bitter contest that ended the next year when their parallel tracks brought the two leading cities of the Great Lakes into direct rail communication.

While the states along the eastern fringes of the Old Northwest forged steadily ahead in railroad building, Illinois lagged behind. Memories of the disastrous Internal Improvement Scheme of 1837, the lack of an important city to press for trade outlets, and the distance from eastern lines all kept interest in transportation at a low ebb through most of the 1840's. By 1848, however, the situation was changing. Towns and counties, forgetting their previous losses, again offered to help railroads, Chicago demanded better outlets, and eastern capital moved into Illinois as the expanding eastern network approached the state's line. The renewed interest was reflected in a burst of local activity during the last two years of the decade; the Galena and Chicago Union Railroad began building westward from Chicago to the lead mining districts, the Chicago, Burlington and Quincy Railroad and the Rock Island Railroad were chartered to connect Lake Michigan with the Mississippi River, and the Chicago, Alton and St. Louis Railroad started laying its tracks toward St. Louis. Two of those

lines were welded to the East-West lines in the early 1850's when the
Michigan Central Railroad arranged to use the Galena and Chicago Union
Railroad in reaching the Mississippi and the Michigan Southern Railroad
reached a similar understanding with the Rock Island Railroad.

More ambitious than the cross-state lines was a project to connect Chicago with Mobile, Alabama. The promoters were less conscious of the sectional importance of their road than of the local benefits to be derived from
trading along the Mississippi Valley. The plan for a railroad along the
length of Illinois was hatched in the little village of Cairo. Businessmen
there saw that a direct line northward to Galena would divert the traffic
of that prosperous mining center from the Mississippi to their own portals.
Their first efforts came to naught when a central railroad attempted in the
Internal Improvement Scheme of 1837 collapsed with the panic, but by the
middle 1840's Cairo promoters were pressing both the state and Congress
for aid. Their insistence attracted the attention of Stephen A. Douglas,
representative and senator from Illinois, who saw the road would harm
his native Chicago by diverting the trade of northern Illinois southward. To
defeat the efforts of the Cairo group Douglas drew up an ambitious plan
for a central railroad with two branches, one to Galena and the other to
Chicago. Because such a line required federal aid, he proposed seeking a
land grant similar to those awarded the western states for canal building.
Knowing the impossibility of winning congressional support without southern backing, Douglas linked the Illinois road with another line already
started from Mobile to Cairo and suggested that both be given lands.

The result was the monumental land grant bill which passed Congress
in May, 1850. Under its terms the federal government granted the states
of Illinois, Mississippi, and Alabama the right-of-way for a railroad from
Chicago and Galena to Mobile, together with alternate sections on either
side to a distance of six miles. Thus was established the important principle
of railroad land grants which cost the public domain 132,000,000 acres of
land in the next twenty years. There remained the task of chartering a company to build the Illinois section of the road. The Cairo group expected
to secure the privilege, but when they appeared before the state legislature
in 1851 they found themselves opposed by a rival concern backed by New
York and Boston capitalists and headed by such influential railroad builders
as John Murray Forbes. For a time the two rivals battled, using bribery
and public opinion as their principal weapons, although the outcome was
never in doubt. On February 10, 1851, the eastern syndicate secured the
right to build the Illinois Central Railroad from Cairo to Galena and Chicago. Construction went on rapidly until the main line to Galena was completed in 1855 and the branch to Chicago a year later.

The burst of railroad building during the late 1840's settled few sectional problems; the West at the close of the decade was still as firmly connected economically with the South as with the Northeast. Yet the revolution in trade routes destined to occur during the 1850's was already forecast. Each mile of road built in the western states or across the mountains shifted a portion of the West's commerce to the Atlantic seaboard and diminished the flow of goods down the Mississippi. That meant prosperity for Ohio Valley farmers as lowered carrying costs increased profits on goods sold and lower prices on commodities purchased, but it meant also that a new alliance with the Northeast was being forged with dangerous implications for the future.

The shifting sectional pattern that brought the two northern regions nearer together was emphasized by developments in the South during the 1840's. Railroad building there increased the section's isolation. During the decade few southerners dreamed of uniting the cotton belt with the West; they devoted their energy instead to East-West trunk lines, hoping to tie the lower Mississippi Valley and the South Atlantic states together in a compact economic unit. Poverty prevented them from realizing their ideal before 1850, but the roads projected showed that the South was committed to a policy of commercial nationalism which widened the gulf forming along Mason and Dixon's line.

When the pall of depression lifted, railroad building began first in the trading areas of southeastern seaports. Merchants of Charleston and Savannah, long rivals for the commerce of the South Atlantic states, already had railroad connections with central Georgia but were still not satisfied. Each group threw its support behind a pet project in a race to reach Atlanta and the trade of the Chattahoochee Valley; Charleston promoters backed the Georgia Railroad while those of Savannah financed the Macon and Western Railroad, formed in the postdrepression years to connect Atlanta with Macon. Tracks of both reached the terminus only a month apart in 1845. Their completion stimulated the state of Georgia to resume work on the stagnant Western and Atlantic Railroad which finally entered Chattanooga in 1849. Now all western Georgia and eastern Tennessee was tributary to the two seacoast cities.

The building of the Georgia roads revived the ancient southern dream of East-West lines between the Mississippi Valley and seacoast. The time seemed ripe; rising cotton prices promised to provide the wealth necessary. All the South buzzed with the exciting possibility when a group of business and political leaders, sensing popular interest, issued a call for a great commercial convention at Memphis on July 4, 1845. This was a chance to organize railroads that would bind the section into a firm economic unit against the hated Northeast. Some, with deeper insight, thought the convention might even forge commercial ties with the West. "Now is the time," wrote one South Carolina delegate, "to meet our Western friends at Memphis—to set the ball in motion that must bring the Valley to the South." That was the hope of the five hundred enthusiastic representatives of southern and western states who gathered in the Tennessee town on the

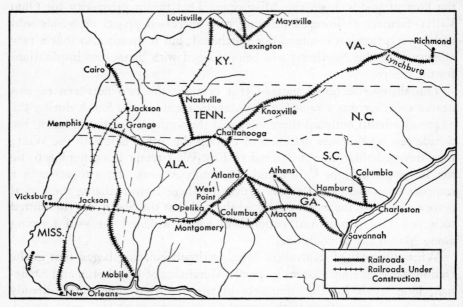

Principal Southern Railroads in 1855

nation's birthday. They chose John C. Calhoun their presiding officer, listened to innumerable optimistic speeches, passed grandiose resolutions urging railroads, factories, and public improvements in both West and South, and then adjourned to wait developments.

These were not long in coming, for the Memphis Convention set four giant railroad schemes in motion. None, significantly enough, was designed to lure western trade southward; all were East-West lines that would link the principal cities of the seaboard and interior: Nashville and Charleston, Memphis and Charleston, Memphis and Richmond, and Vicksburg and Savannah. Southerners were no longer as interested in winning allies against the Northeast as in solidifying their own economic strength. For the next decade their energies were absorbed in translating the dream of four southern trunk lines into reality.

The first project, a railroad between Nashville and Chattanooga where rail connections with Charleston or Savannah waited, was launched by delegates freshly returned from the Memphis Convention. Calling a convention of their own at Nashville in November, 1845, they adopted resolutions urging the legislature to authorize immediate construction. That body responded in early December with a charter for the Nashville and Chattanooga Railroad; surveys were begun the following May, and in the spring of 1848 construction started. Work went on slowly for six years before the road was completed. In the meantime a northern extension was undertaken in 1850 when Kentucky chartered the Louisville and Nashville Railroad between the Ohio and Cumberland rivers. That support came largely from Louisville rather than its commercial rival, Cincinnati, illustrated the change in sectional opinion during the past decade. The Ohio metropolis, which had been so eager for a Charleston connection a few years before, was now so absorbed in establishing contacts with the Pennsylvania and Baltimore and Ohio Railroads that it paid little attention to developments in Kentucky or Tennessee.

The two proposed roads between Memphis and the seaboard fared less well. Delegates who formulated their plans during the 1845 Memphis convention secured a charter for the Memphis and Charleston Railroad in February, 1846, but money was so scarce in the western country that construction did not begin until 1850. In the same year work started on three end-to-end railroads to bridge the gap between Chattanooga and Richmond, thus bringing the Virginia city into rail communication with Memphis. Those lines—the East Tennessee and Georgia Railroad, the East Tennessee and Virginia Railroad, and the Virginia and East Tennessee Railroad— were completed during the 1850's.

The last southern trunk line—between Vicksburg and Macon—began taking shape in 1845 when the Central of Georgia Railroad set up a subsidiary concern, the Southwestern Railroad Company, to build westward toward Columbus, Georgia. This inspired the Alabama promoters of the defunct Montgomery and West Point Railroad to reorganize their company, raise capital, and lay track between Montgomery and West Point on the Chattahoochee River. Two smaller companies—the Atlanta and LaGrange Railroad and the Columbia and Opelika Railroad—were formed soon afterward to fill the gaps between Columbus, Atlanta, and the Montgomery line. In the meantime work on the western portions of the road was started. Rails laid before the panic already spanned the distance between Vicksburg and Jackson, Mississippi; there remained the task of connecting Jackson with Montgomery, Alabama. The Southern Railroad Company, formed for that purpose in 1846, raised only enough capital to build a few miles east of Jackson during the decade. The Vicksburg-Savannah line, like its competitors building east from Memphis and Nashville, illustrated the South's growing emphasis on economic nationalism. The section was withdrawing into its own shell to escape the storms of controversy raging along Mason and Dixon's line.

That southerners did not entirely forget their dream of rail connecting with the West was due less to farseeing statesmen than to greedy Mobile and New Orleans merchants. Alarmed by the prospect of East-West railroads robbing them of their river trade, they sought to neutralize competition by sponsoring their own North-South lines. Mobile's businessmen moved first. Committees were formed, surveys made, mass meetings held, and in 1847 the Mobile and Ohio Railroad was chartered to build from the Gulf of Mexico to St. Louis. No sooner was construction begun in 1849, however, than word from Washington forced them to change their plans. Stephen A. Douglas, they learned, while casting about for a southern road to link with his proposed Illinois Central, had selected their line. The prospect of a bountiful land grant convinced the Mobile interests to make Cairo rather than St. Louis the northern terminus for the Mobile and Ohio. During the next decade construction went steadily ahead but the road was not completed until just before the Civil War. New Orleans's bid for the trade of the Mississippi Valley was not made until 1852 when the New Orleans, Jackson and Great Northern Railroad was chartered.

The local profit seekers who planned the southern railroad network did their section immeasurable harm. Totally unconcerned with the broader implications of the communication system, they laid out East-West roads which promised to be profitable but failed to weld the South to either of the other sections. That was suicidal. The slave states could hold their own in the sectional struggle only by winning the support of the West. Nature laid the basis for a commercial union by placing a formidable mountain barrier between Northeast and West while connecting South and West with a natural river highway. Southerners had only to prevent any interference with natural trade routes to perpetuate their alliance with the Ohio Valley. This they failed to do. While easterners built railroads and canals across the Appalachians, southerners blindly committed themselves to a program which only increased their section's isolation. One editor with more vision than his fellows, surveying this scene at the end of the 1840's, wrote: "Trade has been diverted from its natural channel. The East by internal improvements has overcome the natural advantages of the South."

The pessimist who voiced those sentiments spoke wisely but too soon. Changing transportation routes wrought no revolution in western trade by 1850. Goods still followed the Mississippi, where 740 luxurious river queens plied between South and West. Flatboats were also used increasingly in the down-river trade; nearly 3,000 of those cumbersome craft reached New Orleans in 1847, all brimful of grain, pork, and whiskey from Ohio Valley ports. Yet each year the portion of the West's exports moving southward declined as shippers realized that eastern railroads offered safer and more dependable transportation. Steamboats might be cheaper, but they followed roundabout routes which were closed in winter or during low water, and they were always in danger of knocking their bottoms out on a snag or sending their cargoes sky-high if a boiler blew up. Insurance underwriters, impressed with the fact that the average life of a Mississippi steamboat was only nine years, soon learned to charge higher rates on goods entrusted to the unreliable craft than to railroads. Those charges, which absorbed most of the money saved on shipping costs, shifted more and more traffic to the railroads yearly, until by 1850 most passengers and light produce moved by rail, leaving river boats only heavy freight. Each western shipper who turned from water to rail transportation strengthened the commercial bonds between Northeast and West.

Just as important in explaining the transition was the realization that the Northeast offered a better market for the West's produce than the South. The relative ability of the two sections to consume the grain and meat exports of the Ohio Valley determined which would provide a better outlet. The situation was graphically illustrated by the per capita production of wheat, corn, and a combination of the most important six cereals in the various sections in 1850:

|  | WHEAT | CORN | SIX CEREALS |
|---|---|---|---|
| NEW ENGLAND | 0.4 bushels | 3.70 bushels | 7.99 bushels |
| MIDDLE STATES | 5.75 bushels | 9.11 bushels | 26.15 bushels |
| SOUTH | 2.47 bushels | 30.83 bushels | 37.92 bushels |
| WEST | 7.52 bushels | 44.14 bushels | 59.62 bushels |

Most of the grain was consumed at home; the average American used four bushels of wheat and twenty-five bushels of corn yearly. Hence New England had to import 3.6 bushels of wheat and 21.30 bushels of corn per capita, the Middle States had a surplus of 1.75 bushels of wheat but had to bring in 14.89 bushels of corn, and the South needed only 1.53 bushels of wheat and had an excess of 5.83 bushels of corn. The West, on the other hand, must sell 3.25 bushels of wheat and 19.14 bushels of corn for each of its inhabitants. Obviously its best market was not in the South, where yeoman farmers produced most needed food, but in the Northeast where the demand far exceeded the supply.

Nor did domestic consumption tell the whole story. During those years the center of the nation's agricultural export trade gradually shifted from

Gulf ports to cities of the North Atlantic seaboard. The transition occurred during the 1840's; at the beginning of the decade New Orleans was the nation's leading exporting center with shipments valued at $50,000,000; at the end it was surpassed by New York, Philadelphia, and other ports in the Northeast. No single factor wrought the change, although the rise of eastern ports could not occur until transportation costs between Northeast and West were lowered by competing canal and railroad lines. Once those were built, westerners learned, their grain reached foreign markets through New York more cheaply than through New Orleans. The first shipments eastward demonstrated the superiority of the Atlantic outlet. Wheat that spoiled in the humid warmth of the lower Mississippi kept perfectly in the East's temperate climate. Money to finance the export trade was also available in the Northeast; New York wholesalers could advance cash that allowed western commission merchants to hold grain purchased during the winter until canals opened in the spring, thus doing away with the necessity of shipping southward immediately. Most important of all was the development of new markets for American cereals in regions best reached through New York rather than New Orleans.

Until the early 1840's most of the country's farm surplus was sold in the West Indies or South America where corn meal and wheat flour were in great demand. So long as trade routes ran in that direction New Orleans, lying squarely across the shortest path to the markets, enjoyed an advantage over other ports. That situation, so advantageous to the South-West alliance, was upset in 1846 when England repealed the Corn Laws that had closed Britain to American grain since 1828. By doing so that heavily industrialized nation announced its willingness to be fed by the rest of the world —news of particular importance to farmers of the West. The new market promised greater profits than Brazil or Cuba; overnight the center of the export trade shifted to the Atlantic ports closest to Britain's consumers. High prices which followed crop failures in England and Europe during 1846 and 1847 offered an additional incentive. In the decade after the repeal of the Corn Laws exports of grain from the United States increased 170 per cent, nearly all due to the demand from England. As cereals, flour, and meat moved eastward toward the new market, the commercial ties between Northeast and West were steadily tightened while those between West and South suffered in proportion.

The effect of the fortuitous combination of circumstances—improved East-West transportation facilities, adequate credit, and expanding domestic and foreign markets—meant that more of the West's trade would move toward the Northeast with each passing year. The result is illustrated in the following table which shows the percentage of western exports reaching the other sections in typical years:

| | | AMOUNT EXPORTED | | PERCENTAGE SHIPPED TO: | | |
| --- | --- | --- | --- | --- | --- | --- |
| | | | | NORTHEAST | EAST | SOUTH |
| WHEAT | 1839 | 2,000,000 | bushels | 97 | — | 3 |
| | 1844 | 4,000,000 | bushels | 96 | — | 4 |
| | 1849 | 5,500,000 | bushels | 92 | — | 8 |
| | 1853 | 11,000,000 | bushels | 99 | — | 1 |
| FLOUR | 1839 | 800,000 | barrels | 40 | 7 | 53 |
| | 1844 | 1,500,000 | barrels | 63 | 6 | 31 |
| | 1849 | 3,000,000 | barrels | 63 | 6 | 31 |
| | 1853 | 3,000,000 | barrels | 62 | 10 | 28 |
| CORN | 1839 | 1,000,000 | bushels | 2 | — | 98 |
| | 1844 | 1,500,000 | bushels | 10 | — | 90 |
| | 1849 | 6,000,000 | bushels | 60 | — | 40 |
| | 1853 | 8,000,000 | bushels | 63 | — | 37 |
| PORK | 1839 | 300,000 | barrels | 12 | 19 | 69 |
| | 1844 | 800,000 | barrels | 7 | 12 | 81 |
| | 1849 | 1,500,000 | barrels | 9 | 11 | 80 |
| | 1853 | 1,500,000 | barrels | 18 | 24 | 58 |
| WHISKEY | 1839 | 10,000 | barrels | — | 4 | 96 |
| | 1844 | 100,000 | barrels | 1 | 4 | 95 |
| | 1849 | 200,000 | barrels | 8 | 25 | 67 |
| | 1853 | 250,000 | barrels | 11 | 33 | 56 |

Those columns of figures spelled out the South's coming doom for those few who could read. The West's wheat exports, which doubled between 1839 and 1844 and increased another three fold by 1853, consistently sought an eastern outlet, but shipments of flour swung steadily away from the South until only 28 per cent of that important commodity reached New Orleans in 1853. The transformation in the shipment of corn and its by-products—pork and whiskey—was even more startling. While the South absorbed nearly all those commodities in 1839, by 1853 only 37 per cent of the corn, 58 per cent of the pork, and 56 per cent of the whiskey moved in that direction. The East was rapidly absorbing most of the West's exportable surplus.

That did not mean the whole West abruptly shifted its commercial allegiance from one section to another. In the early 1850's the Old National Road was still the dividing line between areas shipping most of their produce southward and those selling primarily to the Northeast; the remarkable increase in shipments to the Atlantic seaboard indicated a growth in the productive capacities of the Great Lakes country rather than a change in the trading outlets of the Ohio Valley. Yet important changes in the traditional pattern were becoming apparent. Much of the pork exported through Cleveland came from south of Columbus over the Cleveland, Columbus and Cincinnati Railroad. Other produce formerly moving southward was drained to the East by the opening of the Pennsylvania Railroad and the Baltimore and Ohio; the marked decline in flour and pork receipts at New Orleans by 1853 was due primarily to that shift.

Not only did the South lose favor as a market for western produce during the 1840's; its shipments to the Ohio Valley also declined in relative importance:

| | TONS OF GOODS IMPORTED FROM: | | |
| | NORTHEAST | EAST | SOUTH |
| 1839 | 60,000 | 50,000 | 60,000 |
| 1844 | 77,000 | 52,000 | 86,000 |
| 1849 | 170,000 | 65,000 | 125,000 |
| 1853 | 470,000 | 90,000 | 225,000 |

Westerners, who at the beginning of the decade bought 35 per cent of their imports from the lower Mississippi Valley, at its close purchased only 28 per cent there. More and more they were dependent on the Northeast for merchandise, salt, railroad iron, furniture, and hardware. Improved East-West transportation routes not only allowed eastern merchants to offset any advantages the South gained from improvements in steamboat navigation but to advance steadily at the expense of that section.

The statistics for both the export and import trade of the West showed that railroads and canals had effected no revolution in internal trade by 1850, but that a significant new pattern was taking shape. New transportation routes were weaning westerners from their traditional southern customers and building a commercial alliance between West and Northeast. That was of immense advantage to farmers of the Ohio Valley who could choose between markets at Boston, New York, Philadelphia, and New Orleans to sell where the price was highest and buy where the cost was lowest. During the next decade they found that continued improvements in East-West transportation made the Atlantic seaboard constantly more attractive both as a market and source of manufactured goods, until eventually the two sections were bound by such firm economic ties that they merged into one section, the North. The new alignment, which arrayed two giant sections against each other, made civil war inevitable; only the emotional excitement bred of the efforts of each to control new frontiers beyond the Mississippi was needed to touch off the irrepressible conflict.

# SECTION III
# The Trans-Mississippi Frontier

# CHAPTER XX

# The Natural Setting

During the first half of the nineteenth century, while ax-swinging pio-neers stripped away the virgin forests of the Lake Plains and transformed piny woodlands along the Gulf into fields of snowy cotton, more adventur-ous Americans pressed beyond the Mississippi to begin the conquest of a new frontier. There, in a garagantuan land of rolling prairies, grass-blanketed plains, towering mountains, and parched deserts, they found what they sought: fertile farming country, lush green pastures, glittering pockets of precious metals, and a king's fortune in shining beaver peltry. News of this wealth set other frontiersmen marching westward in an ever-growing migra-tion that continued until the director of the census could announce, in 1890, that the unbroken frontier line was a thing of the past.

The rapid conquest of an area greater than that peopled during the two preceding centuries was evidence enough of the remarkable expansive power of Americans, but even more amazing was the fact that the advance into the Far West required a continuous adaptation to new and strange environments. No longer could the pioneer employ techniques learned by generations of his forebears. He knew how to subdue the wilderness—by girdling trees, planting his crop of corn, building his cabin, clearing the land year by year—but in most of the trans-Mississippi West forests were absent. He knew how to conquer the prairie—by breaking the sod, planting an "ax-crop" of corn, and hauling in lumber needed for his home—but in the interminable plains the lessons of the past no longer applied. He knew how to manage a small farm, but beyond the Father of Waters he dis-covered that subhumid climates required extensive rather than intensive agriculture. Those obstacles, placed in the path of westward-marching pio-neers by nature, must be surmounted before the continent was settled.

Frontiersmen did not come face-to-face with those barriers until they passed beyond the first tier of states bordering the Mississippi. Southerners advancing into Louisiana or moving northward into Arkansas and Missouri found a familiar environment waiting them, where the verdant forests, good soils, and abundant rainfall of the Southern Lowlands encouraged the production of cotton or other semitropical crops. Only in northwestern Arkansas and southern Missouri did they encounter the first obstacle: the Ozark Plateau. That rugged upland of eroded hills and pine-covered highlands, guarded on the north by the dome-shaped St. Francis Mountains and on the south by the steep ridges of the Ouachita range, served as an effective barrier to frontier advance, for its rough topography and sterile soils discouraged settlement until better lands were exhausted. No such obstacle faced northern pioneers as they moved into the trans-Mississippi portions of the Central Lowlands. Instead they found a gently rolling prairie, covered with a luxurious growth of tall grass which stretched unbroken to the horizon except where belts of trees marked some river bed. To frontiersmen skilled in prairie farming the tall grass country of Iowa, northern Missouri, southern Minnesota, and eastern Kansas and Nebraska offered no difficulties. There, as in the southern Mississippi Valley, good soil and adequate rainfall promised profits to farmers.

Once frontiersmen passed beyond the western border of Missouri they entered the first of the unfamiliar regions which made pioneering in the trans-Mississippi West difficult. Stretching away before them was the giant physiographic province known as the Great Plains. That tilted plateau was formed over the course of centuries by streams flowing eastward from the Rocky Mountains into the Mississippi River. As rivers rushed down steep mountain slopes they picked up dirt and debris which was gradually deposited until a platform higher than the surrounding countryside was formed. Then the stream swung to right or left, seeking lower ground, which was in turn slowly elevated by continuous silt deposits. As this went on through geological age after geological age a great upland gradually took shape, sloping gently downward from its elevation of 5,000 feet at the foot of the Rockies to a point three or four hundred miles away where a sharp eastward-facing escarpment marked the junction of the Great Plains and the Central Lowlands.

Within the province the continued operation of natural forces created several regions which affected the course of American settlement. North of the Platte River the many streams which formed the Missouri River system cut deeply into the gravelly soil, leaving a maze of eroded river beds and extensive badlands which made travel difficult and farming or grazing impossible. Dotting the Missouri Plateau were several groups of domed mountains such as the Black Hills of South Dakota, survivors of the erosive process that cut down the rest of the countryside to a lower level.

Although mineral wealth buried beneath the forest-clad hills soon attracted settlers, most pioneers shunned the inhospitable region. "The country," wrote one early traveler, "is here spread into wide and level plains, swelling like the ocean, in which the view is uninterrupted by a single tree or shrub, and is diversified only by the moving herds of buffalo. The soil consists of a light-colored earth, intermixed with a large proportion of coarse gravel without sand, and is by no means as fertile as the plains . . . lower down the Missouri."

South of the Platte River the erosive action of wind and water shaped the Great Plains into three distinguishable regions. Along the eastern edge —in eastern Nebraska, central Kansas, and much of central Texas—was the Low Plains country, where rainfall wore away the light soils to leave a low-lying grassland, similar in some respects to the Central Lowlands. Just to the west, and separated from the Low Plains by a steep scarp known as the Break of the Plains, were the High Plains of western Kansas and the Texan Panhandle. Protected by a heavy grass matting from wind erosion and watered so infrequently that little soil washed away, the High Plains looked down upon the lower areas to either side. Beyond them, nestling beneath the foothills of the Rockies, a long Upland Trough stretched from New Mexico to Wyoming. There the scanty vegetation was insufficient to protect the light soil from blustery winds which carried away enough of the surface over the centuries to leave a chain of connected valleys—the Pecos Valley, the Colorado Piedmont, and Goshen Hole— which together separated the High Plains from the Rocky Mountains. Each region presented frontiersmen with a different environmental problem which must be solved before settlement could go on.

Despite local variations the Great Plains province was distinguished by certain natural characteristics: a level or rolling surface, a complete lack of forest growth, and in most areas a subhumid climate. Of these the lack of adequate rainfall was most important. The phenomenon was explained by the mountain ranges lying to the west; easterly blowing winds from the Pacific were drained of moisture as they crossed the California ranges, picked up some water from the parched country between the coastal mountains and the Rockies, and were wrung dry again as they passed over that high range. Hence they blew, hot and dry, across the Great Plains, soaking up life-giving moisture as they passed, until they reached central Kansas or Nebraska where they deposited their burden in the form of rainfall. East of this "Line of Semiaridity" annual precipitation was normally the twenty inches or more needed for ordinary farming; to the west less than that amount fell each year. For the Great Plains as a whole the average was only fifteen inches—not enough to support agriculture. To make matters worse most rain fell between April and November when the glaring sun and hot summer winds quickly drained the water from the soil. The southern portions suffered most from evaporation, losing forty-six inches of moisture during the growing season while in the north the loss was only thirty inches.

The subhumid climate accounted for the types of vegetation that strug-

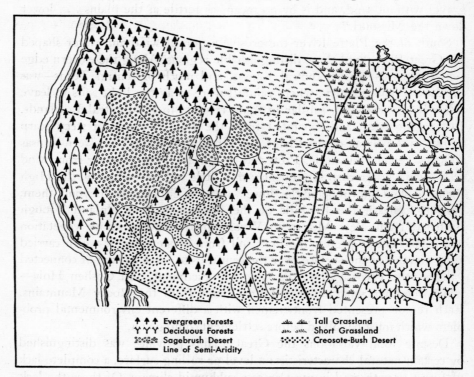

Natural Vegetation of the Trans-Mississippi West

gled for existence on the Great Plains. Forest growth was absent except along the streams or on such isolated elevations as the Black Hills. Instead the province was carpeted with the varieties of grass that could survive its semiarid climate. Along the eastern border was a "tall grass" country where waving stands of luxurious foliage three to six feet high testified to the rich soil and adequate rainfall. In two places arms of prairie vegetation thrust well beyond the Line of Semiaridity; one in North Dakota where cold weather kept the earth moist by retarding surface evaporation, the other along the Platte River in central Nebraska. West of the "tall grass" grew a matting of short grass that, in the southern portions where rapid evaporation occurred, extended some distance east of the Line of Semiaridity. Still farther south on the plains of Texas, where precipitation was too scant to support a solid earth covering, the short grass gave way to desert grass or mesquite, growing in clumps, with bare patches of sun-baked soil between.

The Great Plains supported a wide variety of animal life which early lured trappers and hunters to the Far West. Beavers were plentiful in the many streams that coursed through the Missouri Plateau. Throughout the Plains lived other species whose remarkable speed enabled them to thrive in an open country where safety depended on ability to detect and escape enemies: keen-sighted and swift-legged antelope, donkey-eared jack rabbits whose powerfully developed hind legs could put an amazing distance between them and hunters in a short space of time, slinking wolf-like coyotes with an ability to scatter miles behind them that always amazed travelers. Those miserable, carrion-snatching creatures were everywhere present, ready to steal anything living or dead which could possibly be eaten. "The coyote," wrote Mark Twain after a trip across the Plains, "is a living, breathing allegory of want. He is *always* hungry. He is always poor, out of luck, and friendless. The meanest creatures despise him, and even the fleas would desert him for a velocipede." More abundant than the coyotes were the buffaloes, who reproduced so rapidly amidst the favorable environment that millions existed, wandering in great herds covering as much as fifty square miles of prairie. The shaggy beasts were poorly equipped to defend themselves, for their poor eyesight, clumsy gait, and awkward movements made them easy prey for Indians or hunters. From them the nomads —red or white—who roamed the Plains secured all of the necessities of life: fresh or "jerked" (dried) meat, clothing, bedding, tents, skin boats, and even fuel in the form of dried dung or "chips."

The presence of buffalo accounted for the character of the Indian civilizations frontiersmen encountered when they entered the Great Plains. With plentiful food assured them, the grassland tribes lived nomadic lives rather than following the sedentary agricultural pursuits of natives east of the Mississippi. Their natural roving tendency was accentuated during the seventeenth century when Spanish traders supplied them with horses. By 1800 the animals were in general use among Plains Indians, who developed a remarkable skill on horseback which encouraged them to roam widely in pursuit of game or on warlike expeditions against enemy tribes. The natives' absolute dependence on the buffalo for food, shelter, and clothing, and their use of horses, not only marked them as a distinctive culture group but made them formidable foes. No longer could white men strike at red men by destroying their crops; now the tribes must be fought on equal terms, with the Indians equipped to do battle or run away as circumstances dictated. The long period of nineteenth century warfare before the last tribesmen accepted defeat attested to their remarkable ability as warriors.

Within the Great Plains the many tribes developed differences in living habits that reflected the varying environments. The warlike red men who occupied the High Plains were completely nomadic, with no permanent villages or gardens to bind them to any one locality, and with a culture dependent on the horse and buffalo. Of these the Blackfeet, Crows, Grosventres, and Teton-Dakota were most important on the northern High Plains, while to the south the Arapaho, Cheyenne, Comanche, and Kiowa were dominant. To the east and west of the central group of tribes were others whose living habits showed characteristics of both a plains and forestland culture. Occupying the Low Plains east of the Line of Semiaridity were a number of "prairie Indians"—the Mandan, Iowa, Kansa, Missouri, Omaha, Osage, Pawnee, Eastern Dakota, and Wichita—who planted maize and erected permanent villages of earth or bark lodges to which they returned each fall after summer excursions in pursuit of buffalo. West of the High Plains, in the foothills and valleys of the Rockies, lived the Bannock, Nez Percé, Ute, and Shoshoni Indians who also hunted the buffalo during the summer, then returned to semipermanent winter camps. Unlike the eastern village groups they seldom grew corn, relying instead on wild roots and berries to supplement their diet of bison meat.

Despite differences in living habits, the material culture of the Plains Indians was much the same. All used stone knives, scrapers, and bone awls, all depended upon the bow and arrow in hunting and warfare, and all warriors carried into battle a long buffalo lance tipped with stone. Their remarkable skill with those weapons, particularly their short bows of wood or sinew-backed strips of mountain sheep horn, made them dangerous enemies. Until the introduction of the Colt revolver and repeating rifle, Plains Indians enjoyed a marked advantage over white men; a mounted warrior could send half a dozen arrows against his opponent while a frontiersman was cramming one bullet into his muzzle-loading gun. Their mobility also gave them strength in warfare. Their villages consisted of buffalo-hide tepees which could be folded quickly when an enemy approached, loaded on an A-shaped travois or carrying frame made from the tepee poles, and spirited away behind fast ponies before an attack was possible.

The Plains Indians were especially dangerous because physically they were among the finest types in all America. Their skin was a reddish chocolate, their hair black and straight, their eyes brown. Those who lived in the north were above average in height, with many six-footers among them, while the southern tribesmen were slightly smaller. The men dressed in a breechcloth, usually supplemented with long leggings which extended from hips to ankles, a buffalo robe thrown around the shoulders in winter, and among the northern Indians a "scalp shirt" of leather when on the war path. Women wore sleeveless dresses of deer or elk skin, and both sexes used moccasins with a double rawhide sole for protection against hard ground.

The social organization of the Plains Indians was based on "bands" of three to five hundred people, under a "chief," who was usually the most influential and respected warrior of the group. Each was governed by a council of elder men meeting with the chief to decide all questions. Their decisions were enforced by small societies of warriors known as "soldier bands" which not only kept order, settled disputes, and punished offenders, but regulated hunts and ceremonies during peacetime and guarded against surprise attack when on the warpath. All plains tribes had several "soldier societies," and a young brave normally advanced from one to another as his age and deeds justified promotion in the hierarchy they represented. Usually the societies had such names as Foxes, Crows, Bulls, or Dogs, which were adopted by the warriors as part of their names; the "Dog Soldiers," thus, might include braves called Crazy Dog, Mad Dog, Foolish Dog, Young Dog, and Big Dog. Despite division into these "soldier societies," the bands maintained a high degree of autonomy and acted as individual units in both war and peace.

The only restriction upon the independence of the bands were loose tribal organizations which united various groups of Plains Indians on the basis of similarity of language or customs, or through the happenstance of geographical distribution. Thus the Dakota Indians, the great Siouan-speaking group of the northeastern Plains, were divided into seven tribes, each containing several bands. Ordinarily the bands making up a tribe had little to do with each other, since the tribal unit was too large to obtain sufficient subsistence when hunting together, and the quest for food, as usual among primitive peoples, was all-important. Occasionally, however, bands making up a tribe assembled for ceremonies or to agree upon some action. Thus the four bands of the Cheyenne tribe—the Aorta Band, the Hairy Band, the Scabby Band, and the Dogmen band—met regularly at an appointed spot, camping about a central tepee where chiefs and elders of each band conferred. More often tribal unions failed to function; frequently several bands within a tribe were on the war path while others remained at peace. This haphazard type of confederation complicated relations between the Indians and the United States government when the frontier advanced into the Plains region.

Less important to the Great Plains Indians than tribal organizations— but nevertheless essential to understanding their civilization—were the linguistic groups into which they were divided. Seven languages were spoken: *Siouan* by the Crows, Dakota, Iowa, Kansa, Mandan, Missouri, Omaha, Osage, and Oto; *Algonkian* by the Arapaho, Blackfeet, Cheyenne, and Grosventre; *Caddoan* by the Pawnee and Wichita; *Kiowan* by the Kiowa; *Shoshonean* by the Bannock, Comanche, and Shoshoni, and *Athapascan* and *Shahaptian* by smaller tribal units. Local dialects varied, but most tribes within a group were able to make themselves understood. In addition the Plains Indians developed a universal sign language which allowed natives of different stocks to communicate with each other, often at a distance.

Despite the complex hierarchy of tribes and linguistic stocks, the band was the all-important social and economic unit among Plains Indians. Within those tight-knit groups each warrior strove to gain social prominence and superiority over his fellow braves. That could be done by two means. He could secure a large number of horses which were the universal measure of wealth; stealing horses from other tribes or from whites was a practice which touched off many localized Plains wars. Or he could demonstrate his bravery in battle, for war deeds carried great weight in determining social rank. "Counting coup"—touching an enemy or capturing his weapons—was considered the greatest form of bravery and was far more widely practiced than killing and scalping. Those distinctions were widely sought not only to gain recognition but also because only the bravest and wealthiest warriors were allowed to enter into polygamous marriages. Numerous wives were an economic asset since the job of preparing hides or making clothes and tepees was a tedious one.

The principal economic function of the band was to engage in buffalo hunts. This important task required the co-operation of everyone. The usual method was the "surround," in which the herd was nearly encircled by warriors, then allowed to run while mounted men cut down the animals on flank and rear with bow and lance. Women, children, and older men followed to skin the slain beasts and cut up the meat. Unlike later white hunters, the Indians used nearly every part of the buffalo. The hide, after being fleshed and scraped, was treated with mixtures of fat and brains until cured and ready to use in clothing. The fresh meat was eaten raw, roasted, or boiled in a rawhide-lined earthen pit by dropping heated stones into the water. That not consumed on the spot was preserved; some by drying or "jerking" in the arid Plains air; some by cooking, shredding, and mixing with wild berries and fat to be stored in the rawhide bags as "pemmican," a lightweight emergency food highly prized by hunters for its nutritive value.

The religious ceremonies of the Great Plains Indians also focused on the band. Like most natives of North America, the western tribesmen believed in no single God but in a series of controlling powers which shaped the events of the universe. Of those the sun was paramount, but the earth, sky, moon, rocks, wind, and water were also felt to exert a continuous influence upon man and nature. Indians with special concessions from those powers were called "medicine men" or shamans, and were consulted in time of sickness, stress, or when members of the band were about to embark on the warpath. Hence the shamans were powerful men in each band, often able to decide between war and peace. They were not alone in possessing occult powers; the Plains Indians believed every young warrior, by fasting, prayer, and self-torture, could insure for himself a portion of divine wisdom. The lonely "vision quests" of youthful braves usually ended in semidelirious dreams which, when interpreted by the shaman, guided each man through his lifetime. Moreover every Indian constantly carried a "medicine bundle"—made by the shaman from bits of hair, stones, and animal teeth—supposed to give great power. The bundles were jealously guarded, for if one were lost doom inevitably followed.

The most important religious ceremony of the Plains natives was the Sun Dance, an eight-day-long ceremony held by united tribal bands during the summer months. Gathering around a central tree or "sunpole," the warriors of an entire tribe danced, sang, and performed ceremonial rites, gazing steadily at the sun as they moved through traditional patterns. The messiah enthusiasm induced by these rituals often inspired self-torture among the dancers, who dragged buffalo skulls attached to their flesh with leather thongs, ran skewers or ropes through the fleshy portions of their breasts or backs, and even sliced layers from their arms. Indians under the influence of religious excitement were particularly warlike, nor was the problem of handling them made easier by the fact that Sun Dance rituals allowed bands to unite for tribal action against their enemies.

Wandering bands of warlike red men, drifting herds of bellowing buffalos, a seldom-veiled sun beating down upon parched earth from blue skies, endless vistas of grey-green grasslands stretching unbroken to the horizon—those were the impressions of the Great Plains carried away by Anglo-American frontiersmen who ventured upon their broad surface. On the whole, pioneers found little there to their liking. The cloudless heavens, the baked soil, the absence of timber, all created an impression of a desert unsuited for human habitation. Tales of a Great American Desert brought back by trappers and explorers were readily accepted by geographers. Across their maps they lettered in those discouraging words; until after the Civil War the impression persisted that the farming frontier could never invade that inhospitable region. For a generation the Great Plains were looked upon as a barrier standing between the Mississippi Valley and the fertile areas beyond, to be passed over as quickly as possible.

Nor did the next physiographic province to the westward prove more attractive. Along the rim of the Plains rose the towering peaks and rugged rock masses of the Rocky Mountains. That giant mountain chain, which stretched along the backbone of the continent from Alaska to central New Mexico, was divided into two distinguishable systems. In Idaho, western Montana, and northern Wyoming was a sprawling, ill-defined maze of north-south ranges and valleys which together comprised the Northern Rocky Mountain Province. The eastern edge of the mass was formed by the Lewis Range, the steep, glacier-cut walls of which marked the continental divide, and by the Big Horn Mountains which thrust an arm eastward into the Great Plains to enclose the fertile basin of the Big Horn River. Beyond those two ranges lay a valley, the Rocky Mountain Trench, where the level surface and forest-covered soil attracted farmers drifting westward to raise food for prospectors and miners. West of this lowland the Bitterroot Mountains rose precipitously. Although steep and high, the range was easy to cross along the many streams that drained westward into the Columbia River. Of these the Snake River was most important. Its level plain, extending eastward around the southern spur of the Bitterroots, served as a highway for Oregon pioneers making their way toward the Pacific. Just south of the Snake River plain lay the Wasatch Mountains on the eastern border of the Great Salt Lake. The mineral wealth hidden in the Northern Rockies made the region an early center in the advance of the mining frontier.

Below the Northern Rocky Mountain Province, in western Wyoming, was a broad plateau known as the Wyoming Basin. More truly a westward extension of the Great Plains than a part of the Rockies, that 250-mile-wide upland played a leading role in the American conquest of the Far West. Its level floor provided the single uninterrupted route through the mountains from the Plains to the intermontane lowlands beyond. Dotted with hills and covered with a sagebrush growth that offered no handicaps to travelers, the highway was discovered early in the nineteenth century by fur traders who gave it the name of South Pass. Through it passed the overland trails leading to the Pacific coast, and through it in a later day were laid the tracks of the nation's first transcontinental railroad, the Union Pacific.

South of the Wyoming Basin were the Southern Rockies, a wild and rugged mass of snow-clad peaks and high grassy valleys or "parks." Two ranges fringed the eastern border of the system, the Colorado Front Range which rose 6,000 feet above the Plains and was crowned by towering

Pike's Peak, and the Sangre de Christo Range which extended from the Arkansas River into central New Mexico. West of these interlacing systems and separated from them by a series of intermontane parks, were the Sawatch Range of Western Colorado and the San Juan Range of Colorado and northern New Mexico. The Southern Rocky Mountain system was important in frontier history largely as a barrier to expansion, as its maze of majestic mountains and rock-strewn valleys contained few passes such as those penetrating the Northern Rockies. In one section—the region about Pike's Peak—gold discoveries attracted miners at an early date.

The vegetation and wild life of the Rocky Mountain Province was as much a product of the unique environment as that of the Great Plains. Precipitation was abundant, wrung from passing winds by the high peaks. Most fell during the late winter and early spring months in the form of snow which accumulated to a depth of twenty-five feet or more. The life-giving moisture encouraged a heavy growth of pine, fir, and spruce trees which grew so thickly that passage through them was difficult. Wild life abounded amidst those favorable conditions. Beaver were plentiful along the lower courses of the snow-streams, while bear were abundant in the higher altitudes, and mountain goats inhabited the rocky crags beyond the timberline. Although savage grizzlies and bloodthirsty mountain lions made life hazardous in the Rockies, trappers and traders were early lured there by the hope of obtaining beaver peltry and black bear skins. Indians also ventured into the forested valleys in search of game, but no tribe made its permanent home there.

Unattractive as the Rockies were, they were no more inhospitable than the physiographic region lying to their west, the Intermontane Province. That giant area, which comprised the whole country between the Rocky Mountains and the Pacific Ranges, was made up of three sections. To the north lay the Columbia Plateau, a high-lying upland of lava soil laid down in fairly recent geological times by the eruption of now extinct volcanoes. The weathering of the hardened mass left the country level except where rivers, cutting down through soft lava, gouged out deep gorges; the Snake River ran through a canyon 4,000 feet deep. Even those offered few obstacles to travelers, as routes followed by pioneers ran east and west along the stream's banks, making crossing unnecessary. Nor did the vegetation that covered the Columbia Plateau hinder migrations westward; most of the semiarid region was carpeted with sparse forest growth or with the plant indigenous to the northern deserts, the sagebrush. That dwarfed, drab-green shrub, which ranged in height from a few inches to four feet, offered poor fodder for horses, but its gnarled branches lighted many a cheery campfire for weary overland travelers. Only a lack of precipitation kept other types of vegetation from flourishing. Settlers found the rich lava soil produced abundantly on the few spots where rainfall was sufficient.

South of the Columbia Plateau was a depression known as the Great Basin, where scattered ranges of low-lying mountains were interlaced with level, desert-like valleys and plains. The distinguishing feature of the Great Basin Province was its lack of rainfall; over it swept westerly winds wrung so dry by the lofty Sierra Nevada Mountains they actually picked up moisture from the already parched earth. The lack of rainfall and the high mountains which rimmed the region made it a basin in fact as in name; streams originating along its edges lost themselves in the sandy soil without ever reaching the sea. Of those the most important were the Humboldt, a river that meandered across northern Utah before disappearing in a swampy lake bed known as Humboldt Sink, and the Carson, which flowed eastward from the Sierras to vanish in the great depression of Carson Sink. Along those two waterways marched the California pioneers on their way west. Sagebrush covered the northern half of the Great Basin; in the south where rainfall averaged only two inches a year arid deserts predominated: Death Valley and the Mojave Desert of California, the Gila Desert of Arizona. Even the hardy sagebrush could not survive there; the only vegetation was cacti and ugly creosote bushes, their dark leaves covered with an oily substance as protection against the beating rays of the sun.

In that harsh environment the life of the widely scattered Indian tribes— the Bannock, Shoshoni, Ute, Paiute, Gosiute, and Snake—was dominated by the food quest. A few, located on the richer Columbia Plateau or on the eastern fringes of the Great Basin, lived above the subsistence level on fish, bear, elk, and jack rabbits, but in the semi-desert country of Nevada where game was scarce and vegetation scanty the miserable savages were reduced to eating anything that could run, crawl, wriggle, or squirm— "anything," as Mark Twain remarked, "they can bite." Grasshoppers, snakes, reptiles, vermin, rodents, and such small game as they could capture formed a regular part of their meagre diet, usually supplemented with roots and tubers painfully dug from the dry ground, grass seed, and berries; their constant digging after food won them the contemptuous name of "Digger Indians" from the whites.

Occupied fully in getting a living, their culture was simple in structure and content. Their homes were brush huts, lean-tos, or holes scooped in the earth; their clothing either a breechcloth or nothing at all; their implements such primitive devices as digging sticks and coiled baskets; their weapons the bow, club, and wooden lance. The basic social unit was the immediate family, for no larger group could be supported; only in rare periods of plenty did they gather in bands under the leadership of a chief. Ceremonies and religious activities were few in a land where food was insufficient to support extensive gatherings, nor could the "Diggers" take time from their perpetual food quest to war on each other or on the whites. An early explorer left a vivid picture of their barren lives:

> In the Great Basin, where nearly naked he traveled on foot and lived in the sagebrush, I found him in the most elementary form; the men living alone, the women living alone, but all after food. Sometimes one man cooked by his home, his bows and arrows and bunch of squirrels by his side; sometimes on the shore of a lake or river where food was more abundant a little band of men might be found occupied in fishing; miles away a few women would be met gathering seeds and insects, or huddled up in a shelter of sagebrush to keep off snow.

Little wonder that Mark Twain called the "Goshoots" the "wretchedest type of mankind I have ever seen."

Between the Great Basin and the Southern Rockies was the broad plateau of the Colorado River, an extensive upland where the elevation ranged between 5,000 and 11,000 feet. Much of the province was so arid that only sagebrush existed on the gravelly soil, although greater rainfall at higher levels supported yellow pine, piñon, cedar, and juniper. Explorers who crossed the desolate highland were more impressed, however, with the hundreds of river gorges—such as the Grand Canyon of the Colorado—which cut the rough surface into an impassable maze. Most ranged from 500 to 5,000 feet deep and were impossible to cross; even today the Colorado Plateau is by-passed by all but two railroads which skirt its northern and southern edges. This unattractive region was avoided by all early pioneers except trappers who sought beaver along its streams, and miners who prospected for gold amidst its rocky hills.

Uninviting as the Colorado Plateau and southern Great Basin Provinces were, they supported a numerous Indian population when the invasion by American frontiersmen began. Three types of native societies flourished in the southwestern culture area, each fully adjusted to local variations in environment. The central portion—western New Mexico and eastern Arizona—was the home of the Pueblo dwellers, a highly civilized group of tribes of which the Hopi, Zuñi, and Rio Grande Pueblos were most important. Living on a subdesert plateau which was bitterly cold in winter, and harassed constantly by powerful Ute Indians from the north and war-like Comanche from the east, these sedentary natives survived by building communal houses of adobe brick or dressed stone on inaccessible mesas or cavelike cracks in cliffs. Their elaborate dwellings could be entered only by ladders which reached a terraced second floor; access to the solidly walled first floor was gained by descending through holes left in the wooden ceiling. Within these fortlike homes the Pueblo lived their quiet lives, each family having two rooms for sleeping, eating, and grinding grain. Although they occasionally hunted antelope and deer with bows or throwing sticks, their principal food came from their own corn fields which, in that arid country, were sometimes as much as twenty miles from their homes. Their constant struggle to stave off starvation made the Pueblo a highly cultured people, well versed in weaving cotton or yucca fibres into cloth and fashioning baskets or pottery. They were also a peaceful people, content to leave their neighbors alone so long as they were not molested. Seldom did the Pueblo take to the war path against the whites, and then only to protect their homes.

Equally sedentary were the second group of Indians in the Southwest, the Village Dwellers who occupied the Gila and lower Colorado River valleys. Differing from the Pueblo in their dwellings—circular thatched huts covered with mud or straw—and emphasis on family living rather than communal groups, they nevertheless resembled their neighbors in their dependence on agriculture and in their remarkably developed civilization. The Village Dwellers were sufficiently advanced to combat the arid climate by flood plain farming and by irrigation, while their woven baskets and mats were as skillfully made as those of any tribe in North America. They were, like the Pueblo, a friendly people who did not interfere with the advance of the Spanish or American frontiers, although among themselves they practiced a highly institutionalized warfare in which losses were slight. A few cracked skulls and bruises settled the most serious encounters to the satisfaction of all concerned, while no war was too serious to prevent frequent truces for meals or festivals. Most prominent among the several tribes making up the Village Dwellers were the Pima and Papago.

The third group of Indians in the Southwest were the Camp Dwellers, composed largely of Navaho and Apache who during the thirteenth or fourteenth century migrated from the Great Plains to homes in eastern New Mexico and western Texas. Their culture blended institutions adapted to both the Plains and Plateau environments; they lived in tepees, mud huts, or brush shelters, engaged in agriculture to supplement their principal food supply of game and wild berries or fruits, dressed in either the buckskin of the grasslands or the colorful two-piece cotton suits of the Navaho, and spent most of their lives in nomadic wanderings, although maintaining fields and storing food whenever possible. The Navaho especially showed tendencies to adopt the sedentary existence of the Pueblo;

they herded sheep, produced intricate silver ornaments, wove color-splashed Navaho blankets, and turned out beautifully designed baskets.

The Apache, on the other hand, were among the most warlike of all tribes. Excellent horsemen, skilled plains travelers, adept in the use of the short bow and lance, they raided whites and fellow Indians alike whenever possible. Like the red men of the Plains their basic organization centered about the band, although constant losses through fighting prevented the groups from developing any stability; instead bands joined or broke apart according to the needs of the time. In the main, however, there were six tribal divisions—Jicarilla Apache, Mescalera Apache, Mimbreños, Chiricahua, San Carlos, and Coyotero—each subdivided into bands. Social organization reflected their seminomadic life; the highly developed controls usual among sedentary peoples were not needed. Tribal and band affairs were regulated by a chief, often elected by the elders for life. Separate chiefs were usually chosen for warfare and several bands sometimes joined under one leader when on the warpath. The warlike Apache made life in the Southwest even more unattractive to frontiersmen than the obstacles strewn by Nature across that wasteland.

More to the liking of pioneers than the Intermontane Province were the majestic peaks and fertile valleys of the Pacific Coast Province. Dominating that area was a formidable mountain range which stretched like a giant letter H across the western border of the continent. To the northeast were the Cascades, a chain of noble mountains sixty to eighty miles wide. Along their edges steep-walled valleys 3,000 feet deep provided well-watered farming land, while abundant passes allowed early travelers to reach the coastal lands beyond. In northern California the Cascades merged into the Sierra Nevadas, a towering mountainous wall from 12,000 to 14,000 feet high. They were difficult to cross, as their eastern slope was steep and their western cut by glacial gorges. The few passes were found only on the flanks of mountains 5,000 to 9,000 feet above sea level. Both the Cascades and Sierra Nevadas were heavily forested and deluged by heavy rainfall averaging more than seventy inches yearly, in contrast to the five or ten inches falling on the Great Basin a few miles east.

The Klamath Mountains of northern California, a rugged mass of wooded hills, joined the two interior chains with the coastal ranges which stretched northward and southward along the banks of the Pacific. These interlacing parallel ridges, broken by river gorges and plentifully watered with ocean rains, encased a number of small valleys where good soil and adequate precipitation offered excellent farming opportunities. The Coastal Mountains descended precipitously to the very edge of the Pacific, forming a wall of forbidding cliffs broken by only a few good harbors—one at San

Diego, a shallow inlet at Monterey Bay, a magnificent landlocked bay at San Francisco, and a well-protected harbor at Puget Sound. The paucity of good ports concentrated commercial activity along the Pacific coast in a few favored spots.

Embraced within the mountain ranges were four valleys destined to play a prominent role in the history of the frontier. North of the Columbia River, and nestled between the Cascades and the northern coastal ranges, was the 350-mile-long Puget Sound Trough—level, fertile, and well watered, with the nearby harbor at Puget Sound providing a convenient outlet. Even more tempting was the Willamette Valley south of the lower Columbia River. That broad alluvial plain, drained by the Willamette River and plentifully moistened by rain-bearing winds from the Pacific, proved extremely attractive to American pioneers; most of the immigrants who trekked westward along the Oregon Trail in the 1840's and 1850's sought farms on its fertile surface. The remaining two valleys were in California—the Sacramento Valley to the north, the San Joaquin Valley to the south—both taking their names from rivers emptying into San Francisco Bay. Inadequate rainfall, evidenced in the sagebrush and bunch grass dotting their level floors, handicapped normal agriculture, although the lower Sacramento Valley could be farmed profitably. That region, where good soil and grasslands already shorn of trees made pioneering easy, was the mecca of the frontiersmen whose covered wagons cut the deep ruts of the California Trail during the 1840's.

When white men entered the Pacific Coast Province they found perhaps 150,000 Indians in possession, a prodigious number for a California that was not the land of milk and honey modern imagination and irrigation have made it. The natives were notable for their linguistic and tribal diversity; they were broken into countless small bands or tribes that not only lived in semi-isolation but spoke their own local dialects of the linguistic stocks represented there: Athapascan, Shoahonean, and Yuman. Division was made necessary by the environment, for along the coast, as in the Great Basin, the paucity of natural foods forced Indians into small bands in their perpetual quest for subsistence. Their material culture was correspondingly low; they lived in brush shelters or lean-tos, wore only breechcloths, used simple weapons, and either dug roots from the ground or ate anything, living or dead, they could lay their hands on. Only in basketry did they show any degree of advancing civilization; their coiled and twined baskets were as skillfully constructed as those of any other North American Indians. In common with all nomadic peoples who roamed constantly in search of food, the social organization developed by the "Diggers" of California was at a low level. Controls were based largely on the family; on the rare occasions when they united in bands their leaders were little more than "talking chiefs" with no real power over the group. Unlike the Plains Indians, the California natives were short, stout, and dark skinned, with prominent Mongoloid features.

Variants of this culture were evident in northern California, Oregon, and Washington, where more abundant food supplies in the form of forest animals and salmon allowed the tribes to develop a richer life. Plank houses, canoes, and extensive wood working, as well as a highly structured social and political organization, evidenced a degree of civilization shared to some extent by the northern California Karok, Yurok, Shasta, and Hupa tribes. More warlike than the pitiful natives of the lower Pacific coast, who were virtually exterminated by the failure of Spain's mission system and cruel treatment at the hands of gold-rushing '49ers, the northern Indians gave up their lands to the whites only after a bitter struggle.

This was the panorama which lay before American frontiersmen as they crossed the Mississippi to begin the conquest of the Far West. A land of magnificent vistas, grass-tufted plains, soaring mountain peaks, parched deserts, subhumid climate, and savage Indian bands awaited the pioneers. But in that land were fortunes in buried mineral wealth, riches in beaver peltry waiting in every stream, green grasslands that offered ideal pasturage, and fertile valleys where good soil needed only the magic touch of man to yield up its rich bounty. Those garden spots lured adventurers westward during the nineteenth century until the conquest of the continent was completed.

# CHAPTER XXI

# The Spanish Barrier

## 1540-1776

The westward advance of the Anglo-American frontier was accomplished only by absorbing or pushing aside prior occupants of the continent. Some were natives; they were driven slowly backward, then crowded into reservations. Others were fellow Europeans. During the seventeenth century the Dutch of New York and the Spaniards of the Carolinas were thrust aside. In the eighteenth century the eastern Mississippi Valley was wrested from its French overlords. Now, in the nineteenth century, the same fate waited the Spanish-Americans whose ranches, mission stations, pueblos, and presidios dotted the trans-Mississippi West from Texas to California. Before American frontiersmen could reach the shores of the Pacific the Spanish barrier must be overrun.

Spain's advance toward the Southwest began in 1519 when Hernán Cortés led a band of stout-hearted followers into the heart of Mexico, convinced some of the Indians that he had come to deliver them from oppressive rulers, and with their help marched into lake-encircled Tenochtitlán, capital of the Aztec "empire." There Cortés found the wealth long sought by *conquistadors*, and there the delighted Spaniards established headquarters for their New World domains. From this Mexican city conquerors went forth to subdue neighboring provinces and press natives into service as laborers on ranch and in mine, or to fan out over the neighboring countryside in quest of new sources of wealth. By 1522 these adventurers were at Zacatula, on the Pacific, where a shipyard was built, vessels constructed, and the task of exploring the northern coast begun. Eleven years later a skilled navigator, Fortún Jiménez, discovered what he took to be a beautiful island far to the westward; California, he called it, after a mythical land which story tellers placed "at the right hand of the Indies . . . very close to the Terrestrial Paradise." Not until 1539 did another follower of Cortés, Francisco de Ulloa, demonstrate that this landfall was a peninsula rather than an island. Sailing northward along the Lower California coast, he reached the head of the Gulf of California, ascended the Colorado River for a short distance, and returned after taking possession in the name of his ruler.

The barren wastes and arid deserts which greeted explorers should have convinced them that the northern country concealed no fortunes in precious metals, but more was needed to quench the ambitions of Cortés' rival and successor, Antonio de Mendoza, who arrived as first viceroy of New Spain in 1535. The coast might be inhospitable, but from the interior exciting tales poured into Mexico City. An Indian slave told of journeying forty days northward, where he saw "seven very large towns which had streets of silver workers." A Franciscan friar, Fray Marcos de Niza, confirmed those tales when he returned from a solitary expedition to that unknown land; he had seen one of the villages from across a valley and swore it was larger and richer than Mexico City. Surely, Mendoza reasoned, these must be the fabled Seven Cities of Cibola, founded, according to hoary Spanish legend, by seven bishops who fled westward in the eighth century to a fabulously rich land beyond the Atlantic. Perhaps wealth would be found there to rival that of Mexico or Peru! Little wonder the viceroy burned with ambition to conquer the Seven Cities, or that *conquistadors* vied for the privilege of leading the expedition against them.

Francisco Vásquez de Coronado, a loyal follower of Mendoza, won the coveted post. He fitted out an elaborate retinue—225 mounted cavaliers, 62 foot soldiers, 800 Indians, 1,000 Negro and native slaves, herds of horses, oxen, cows, sheep, and swine, droves of laden mules—sent three supply ships up the coast with more equipment, enlisted Fray Marcos as his guide, and on February 23, 1540, set out from the Spanish town of Compostela into the unknown northland. From the first bad luck dogged his footsteps. The supply ships entered the Colorado River safely but failed to locate the main party, which was struggling northward across the dry plateaus of northern Mexico amidst curses voiced by blue-blooded cavaliers as they painfully learned the difficulties of packing a mule or wringing subsistence from poverty-stricken Indians. In July the Spaniards reached their objective, the first of the Seven Cities, but they found no streets of silversmiths, no olive-skinned countrymen, no civilized domain. Instead a mud-walled pueblo of the Zuñi Indians, perched on the high plateau between the Little Colorado and Rio Grande rivers in New Mexico, awaited them. "Such were the curses that some hurled at Friar Marcos," wrote the awed chronicler, "that I pray God may protect him from them."

The heartbroken Coronado moved on to the banks of the Rio Grande to establish a winter camp. Small expeditions that roamed between the Grand Canyon of the Colorado and the southern Rockies brought back enough

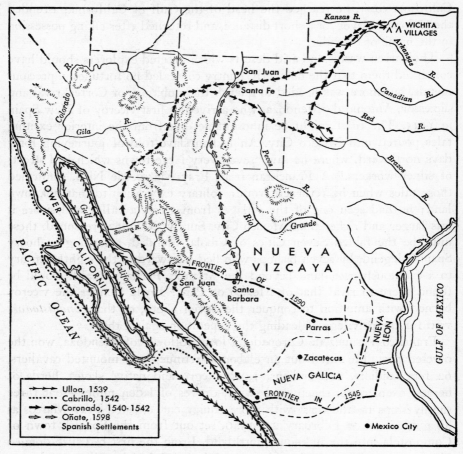

The Northern Mexican Frontier in the Sixteenth Century

plundered food to keep the men alive, but of gold and silver they found none in all that plateau country. Nor did Coronado care. During the winter he stumbled upon a plains Indian, held as a Pueblo slave, who told marvelous lies of a city of Quivira, far to the north and east, where a noble lord "took his afternoon nap under a great tree on which were hung a great number of little gold bells, which put him to sleep as they swung in the air. . . . Everyone had their ordinary dishes made of wrought plate, and the jugs and bowls were of gold." With the first hint of spring the excited Spaniards were off once more, taking with them the slave, whom they called The Turk "because he looked like one." The vast expanse of the High Plains and the roving herds of buffalo amazed them; "the country is like a bowl, so that when a man sits down, the horizon surrounds him all around at the distance of a musket shot," wrote one, and another complained that for many leagues "they had seen nothing but cows and the sky." Across to the Pecos and the Brazos rivers they went, then northward for forty-two days until they reached Quivira—a collection of grass huts of the Wichita Indians on the Kansas River, where the chief wore a copper plate about his neck but there was no gold. Thoroughly discouraged, Coronado turned back to Mexico City which was reached early in 1542.

Mendoza was still not convinced that all the northland was barren. In June, 1542, he ordered two tiny ships and a nondescript crew under Juan Rodríquez Cabrillo to sail northward along the unexplored west coast of Lower California. Stopping frequently to take possession of the soil "in the name of His Majesty and of the most illustrious Señor Don Antonio Mendoza," Cabrillo pressed on until January, 1543, when an infected leg caused his death. His lieutenant, Bartolomé Ferrelo, continued until storms near the 42nd parallel turned him back. He sailed too far from land to discover the harbors at San Francisco and Monterey, but he located the bay at San Diego, later to become an important Spanish stronghold on the California coast. The explorations of Ferrelo, Cabrillo, Coronado, and Ulloa vastly enlarged man's geographical knowledge and gave Spaniards a firm claim to the Southwest.

When Mendoza left the viceregal office in 1550 exploration beyond the northern fringes of New Spain was temporarily halted. His successors, realizing that no great wealth lay hidden in the heart of the continent, turned to developing resources nearer at hand. During the next half-century the Mexican frontier moved slowly northward, with miners, ranchers, and mission fathers as its trail-blazers. The advance began when discoveries of silver at Zacatecas in 1546 precipitated such a mining rush that the region north of Mexico City, the province of Nueva Galicia, was rapidly populated after 1548. During the next decade a number of mining sites still farther north were settled by adventuresome Spaniards and their Indian allies, who encountered great difficulties in subduing the nomadic natives and putting them to work in the mines. Bloody wars handicapped the extension of the new mining frontier; most labor was provided by sedentary southern tribes that were brought northward. By the early 1560's the country beyond Nueva Galicia was organized as the province of Nueva Vizcaya, with the energetic explorer and town-builder, Francisco de Ibarra, as governor. Mining towns and ranches grew rapidly there, while Ibarra himself led or inspired exploring expeditions which searched for new mining sites in such distant regions as the Sonora River Valley. His untiring efforts extended Mexico's northern frontier as far as southern Chihuahua before 1590.

If left to themselves, New Spain's miners and ranchers would have continued the slow movement northward until they engulfed all Mexico and the southwestern United States. Instead the threat of foreign intruders sent the frontiers forward in a series of spectacular thrusts which planted Spaniards in the American Southwest while great portions of northern Mexico remained unsettled. In Spanish eyes, rapid advance was necessary. By 1580 precious metals from Zacatecas, Nueva Vizcaya, Peru, and the mines of South America poured eastward through Panama or Mexico City to Spanish-bound ships waiting in the Caribbean. Through the same channel flowed wealth from the recently conquered Philippines, brought to Mexico in Manila galleons which regularly plied the Pacific with cargoes of spices, silk, chinaware, and gold. Officials realized the zone between Mexico City and southern Panama was a vulnerable spot in the empire's trade routes; should any foreign intruder reach that highway the wealth of New Spain would be his for the taking.

The first such intruder was Francis Drake, a bold son of England's Devonshire, who had learned to hate the Spaniards while an Elizabethan Sea Hawk and an audacious raider along the Spanish Main. During the gloomy September of 1578 Drake's stout ship, the *Golden Hind*, beat its way through the Straits of Magellan "with its hell darke nights and the mercyles fury of tempestuous storms," to emerge on the broad Pacific where Spaniards gathered their treasure without thought of danger. From port to port he sailed, loading his vessel with gold, silver, and "goodly great emeralds" as long as one's finger. Off the coast of Peru he fell upon a treasure galleon, subdued its amazed crew (who no more expected to see an Englishman in the Pacific than in Heaven), and transferred to his own ship "great riches, as jewels and precious stones, thirteen chests full of reals of plate, fourscore pound weight of gold, and six and twenty tons of silver." The *Golden Hind* was loaded to the gunwales now; hence Drake sailed northward as far as the California bay bearing his name, nailed to "a faire great poste" a brass plate proclaiming England's owner-ship of "New Albion," and on July 23, 1579, turned his vessel's prow west-ward to complete the circumnavigation of the globe.

He left a horrified New Spain behind him. If one Englishman could invade the Pacific, others might follow; the New World's wealth would never be safe until the approaches to Mexico were guarded. Colonies must be planted throughout the northern hinterland; the expense would be insignificant compared to the losses of another Drake's raid. Moreover still-hidden mines might be found there, or Indian workers to replace the worn-out natives of Mexico, or native souls for conversion. Those were the prospects that set Spain's officials to colony planning even before the *Golden Hind* reached England. For a time they could only plan—while the war with England that culminated in defeat for the Spanish Armada (1588) absorbed Spanish wealth and energy—but by 1595 they were ready to launch their projects.

One was the occupation of the California coast, both to guard the northern approach to Mexico and provide a haven for Manila galleons on their way back from the Philippines. The first necessity was a favorable harbor. A search for a site undertaken by the captain of a treasure ship in 1595 ended disastrously when the vessel was wrecked in Drake's Bay, but a second expedition in 1602 enjoyed more success. This was led by Sebastián Vizcaíno, a navigator of considerable experience but little skill, who commanded three ships and two hundred men. Sailing northward from Mexico around the stormy tip of Lower California, he reached a good harbor previously noted by explorers, giving it the name of "the glorious San Diego." The Santa Catalina Islands were discovered as he continued on to Monterey Bay, which Vizcaíno believed was the harbor sought by Spain. He carried on his search, however, as far as Drake's Bay, missing San Francisco Harbor once more. His enthusiastic reports convinced Spanish officials Monterey Bay was an ideal site for a colony, but before the settlement materialized the end of the English war made an outpost seem unnecessary.

The second colony planned to frustrate English intrusions in the Pacific fared better. This was in the interior, for Drake's raid convinced Spaniards that the Elizabethan seaman had discovered the fabled Northwest Passage. The fate of New Spain depended on forestalling England's occupation of that waterway. Selected to lay out the settlement was Juan de Oñate, a rich mine owner of Zacatecas, in whose veins flowed the blood of the *conquistadors*. By offering generous land bounties, he recruited a little force of 130 soldier-settlers; with them, an equal number of slaves, and eight Franciscan missionaries, he set out for his unpromising domain in February, 1598, driving 7,000 cattle and eighty-three loaded wagons. Marching northward from Santa Bárbara, the party crossed the Rio Grande below present-day El Paso, then followed the river northward to the mountain-rimmed valley of the Chama River. There Oñate called on friendly Indians to help build his town, which he called San Juan, and to construct a dam, an irrigation ditch, and a church. For a time things went badly; Oñate wanted to search for gold mines while his men preferred ranching or farming, but other settlers drifted in to lay out new towns such as Santa Fe (c. 1609). By 1630 the province of New Mexico was firmly established, with a population of 250 Spanish pioneers and 500 loyal Indians.

The burst of expansion that pushed New Spain's frontier northward into New Mexico ended in 1605 with the close of the Anglo-Spanish war. With England no longer feared, expenditures on profitless outposts did not seem justified. Neither were private adventurers attracted to a region whose meagre resources and wild Indians promised neither wealth nor an adequate labor supply. Spain's frontier advance might have halted in southern Nueva Vizcaya had not one type of pioneer been undeterred by unhospitable conditions. That was the missionary. For the next seventy-five years Dominican, Franciscan, and Jesuit priests moved steadily northward, until all northern Mexico was occupied and settlement ready to push on into Texas, Arizona, and California.

The mission as a frontier institution was not new; on every Spanish borderland cross and sword moved forward together. In the past, however, missionaries aided *conquistadors* and settlers by pacifying previously conquered natives. Now the role was reversed. Friars, advancing into the wilderness in their endless quest for souls, were followed by soldiers or ranchers who came to guard the mission stations or capitalize on wealth uncovered by mission fathers. The pattern became standardized. A lone friar with a few friendly natives set out from the mission frontier to seek a location for a new station. He chose an Indian village in some fertile valley, returned to his own mission, and led back a party of three to ten missionaries, as many families of Christianized Indians, and a handful of soldiers. Once on the chosen spot they urged tribesmen to help build crude habitations, then began the task of religious instruction. Within a year or two the faithful were set to work on a permanent church, often an elaborate structure of plastered adobe, richly ornamented to please the primitive natives. Nearby were scattered a home for the missionaries, a blacksmith shop, flour mill, weaving rooms, carpentry shops, and the homes of Indians who had been persuaded to abandon their nomadic lives for Christianity and the ways of the white man.

There the friars labored mightily. Their task was not only to win souls, but to teach the agriculture and industries which would convert Indians into useful citizens. Hence each missionary was not only a religious instructor but a manager of a co-operative farm, a skilled rancher, and an expert teacher of carpentry, weaving, and countless other trades. The skill with which they executed these tasks attested to their considerable executive talents, just as the ease with which they pacified the most rebellious red men demonstrated their kindly personalities and diplomacy. Only rarely was the calm of a mission station marred by a native uprising; most Indians found the security of life in a station, the salvation promised them, and the religious pageantry ample compensation for the restrictions imposed on their freedom. Usually ten or more years were required to win over a tribe; then the station was converted into a parish church, the neophytes released from discipline and given a share of the mission property, and the friars moved on to begin the process anew. The mission station was a dynamic institution, forever intruding into new wildernesses, and leaving behind a civilized region.

When the mission frontier began its northern march at the opening of the seventeenth century the isolated New Mexican colony was separated from the Nueva Vizcaya settlements by six hundred miles of arid wastes and rugged mountains. The physiographic features of northern Mexico determined the nature of the mission station advance by dividing the region into three areas. Along the west coast ran a coastal lowland separated from the rest of Mexico by the lofty Sierra Madre Mountains, a formidable barrier of towering peaks and deeply etched canyons almost impossible to cross. The advanced coastal tribes and primitive Indians who occupied the mountain valleys were selected by the Jesuits for salvation. East of the Sierra Madres was the central plateau of Mexico, rising 7,000 feet above the coastal plain and sloping gradually downward to join the table-lands of Arizona and New Mexico. That was the domain marked out for the Franciscan conquest. The Dominican stronghold lay along the east coast where mountain ranges not only cut them off from their fellow religionists but barred their path northward. They played little part in the settlement of the American Southwest.

The Jesuits were the first to begin the advance. Their pioneer on the northern frontier, Fray Gonzalo de Tapia, established the station of San Felipe on the Sinaloa River in 1591, and within a year reaped a harvest of 2,000 native souls. Success encouraged Fray Gonzalo to move on to the Fuerte River, where an Indian uprising not only won him the crown of martyrdom but led New Spain's officials to send a detachment of troops to protect the missionaries. For the next three decades the hard-bitten, bandy-legged commander of these soldiers, Captain Diego Martínez de Hurdaide, worked hand in hand with Jesuits to push the frontier north-ward. One by one the tribes of the Sinaloa frontier were subdued and Christianized. The Fuerte Valley was entered and the station of Ahome founded, then the Mayo River Valley where the Tesin mission was estab-lished and the Yaqui Valley where in 1617 the Jesuits built an imposing church at Tórin. Ahead lay the peaceful tribes of the upper Yaqui River;

in 1620 the fathers founded the station of Batuco for their benefit. Ahead, too, lay the friendly Indians of the Sonora Valley who encouraged the Black Robes to found a group of stations about Pitic between 1638 and 1646. By that time the Jesuits maintained thirty-five missions along the coast, each caring for from one to four Indian towns. Although the advance slowed down as they entered the fringes of the hostile Apache country,

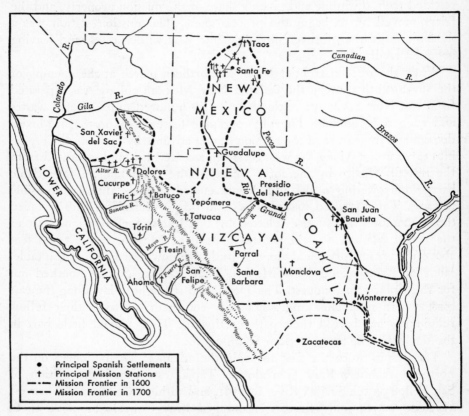

The Northern Mexican Frontier in the Seventeenth Century

they established the station of Cucurpe in the upper San Miguel Valley in 1687.

In the meantime other Jesuits moved northward along the eastern flank of the Sierra Madre Mountains. Saving the primitive tribes of that rugged upland proved difficult, for they were a wild, fleet-footed people, who did not take kindly to restraint. Obstacles only stirred the missionaries to greater efforts. Using the town of Parral as their headquarters, they extended their influence as far northward as the Tutuaca station by 1650. An Indian revolt that year wiped out these gains and discouraged Jesuit efforts for two decades, but in 1673 the northward march was resumed. Within five years stations at Tutuaca and Yepómera were established where eight Jesuits guarded the souls of Indians in thirty-two pueblos. By that time the Black Robes reigned over all the coastal plain and Sierra Madre country from central Mexico to a point near the present United States border.

While the Jesuits moved northward on lowlands and mountains, the Franciscans made spectacular gains on the central plateau. By 1645 their mission frontier reached the upper Conchos River and began to advance down that stream toward the Rio Grande. The most important gain was made in 1659 when a leading Franciscan, Fray García de San Francisco, led two companions overland to the Rio Grande ford near present-day El Paso to establish the station of Nuestra Señora de Guadalupe. The site proved so advantageous that within three years permanent buildings were completed, farmers drifted in, and the El Paso district assumed aspects of permanence. Its growth was hurried in 1680 when a revolt of the Pueblo Indians of New Mexico drove hundreds of settlers southward to the comparative safety of El Paso. The influx led Spanish officials to establish a presidio there in 1683; at the same time a mission was founded where the Conchos joined the Rio Grande.

A third arm of the Mexican mission frontier reached out toward the Northeast. Its center was the province of Nuevo León, established in the late sixteenth century with its capital at Monterrey, and its pioneers Franciscan fathers seeking a harvest of souls in the country below the Rio Grande. Best known was Fray Lários, an earnest friar, who in the years just after 1670 founded the station of Monclova as a center for a group of four missions along the Salado River Valley in the region later erected into the province of Coahuila. The fruits of these efforts were apparent by 1680. At that time the mission frontier stretched from Monterrey to the Conchos River, swept northward to include the numerous Franciscan stations in New Mexico, and reached the Pacific at the Sonora River. Behind lay a land of civilized and Christianized natives, ahead a land of unsaved souls that soon lured missionaries into the present United States. To the northeast the road was blocked by hostile Apache, but to the north and northwest lay an unexplored domain known to the Spaniards as Pimería Alta. There the missionaries first entered the American Southwest.

In the van was an Italian-born priest who almost single handed won a new domain for Spain. Fray Eusebio Francisco Kino, a man "merciful to others but cruel to himself," reached the Sonora borderland in 1687, built the mission station of Dolores high on the San Miguel River, and threw himself into the task of winning heathen souls. For a time he was busy founding a chain of missions along the Altar and Magdalena rivers, but Fray Eusebio was never content as long as unsaved humans or unexplored lands lay ahead. In 1691 his religious wanderlust carried him into Arizona where, along the Santa Cruz and San Pedro valleys, he found natives eager for word of the Gospel. Nothing would do but to build a station among them; after cattle ranches were established to assure a food supply Father Kino in 1700 led a party northward to lay out the mission of San Xavier del Sac. The venture thrived from the first. Other stations were established in the vicinity; cattle ranches and farms followed as settlers moved in. Over them all the padre ruled with benevolent skill, although his real interest was that of the explorer. In all he made fourteen journeys of from several hundred to a thousand miles each, either alone or with a few companions, and on his death in 1711 left a series of excellent maps which added immeasurably to Spain's knowledge of the northern frontier.

If left to themselves the Franciscans would have occupied Texas just as Kino and his Jesuit companions settled Arizona. By the middle seventeenth century their stations were advancing steadily in that direction, some northward in the Nuevo León province, others eastward to the El Paso district or from New Mexico. By that time, too, Franciscan explorers searching for unsaved souls were investigating the possibilities of Texas. One group from New Mexico reached the upper waters of the Colorado River as early as 1632, another visited the Tejas Indians of the Trinity River Valley in 1650, and a third from the mission station of Monclova baptized a number of Texan natives in 1675. Activities reached a near climax in 1683 when a delegation of Jumano Indians visited the El Paso district to ask the friars for spiritual guidance and the civil authorities for troops to protect them from threatening Apaches. The invitation sent the tiny Spanish outpost into a bustle of activity. Troops were raised, a delegation of missionaries selected, and a party formed to march northward as far as the junction of the Concho and Colorado rivers where a temporary altar was erected. The crop of souls and buffalo hides during a six weeks stay proved so satisfactory that both church and civil authorities determined to seek permission for a permanent station in Texas. Before they could do so alarming news shocked the northern frontier. A new invader threatened that poorly guarded borderland.

France was the villain now, and its agent was Robert Cavelier, Sieur de La Salle. That visionary empire builder, hoping to connect the St. Lawrence and Mississippi river systems with a chain of trading posts, set sail from France in 1684, bound for the mouth of the Mississippi where he planned to build a stronghold. Missing the mouth of the river, he landed at Matagorda Bay on the Texas coast in January, 1685. After throwing up a rough fort, Ft. St. Louis, La Salle spent the next two years searching for the elusive Mississippi. On the last expedition, early in 1687, his overwrought followers rebelled, murdered their leader, and set out on foot for the French settlements in distant Canada. The few who remained at Ft. St. Louis were either slaughtered or enslaved by Texas Indians.

Word of these events, reaching New Spain in the form of exaggerated tales from the red men, sent Spanish officialdom into a panic, for their fevered imaginations translated La Salle's venture into a threat against Mexico itself. Nine expeditions were hurriedly sent out to repel the invaders; one under Governor Alonso de León of Coahuila finally located the ruins of Ft. St. Louis and the charred bones of its murdered defenders in the spring of 1689. The welcome news of La Salle's failure, heard from the lips of two of his enslaved companions, did not quiet Spanish fears. The dread Frenchmen might try again; Mexico would never be safe until Texas was guarded. That warning, stated in emphatic language by de León, was echoed by the Franciscan missionary who accompanied him, Fray Damián Massanet. The Indians of Texas, the good friar reported to Mexico City, were ripe for conversion. Little wonder that the viceroy promptly consented to occupy Texas.

The expedition that set out from Monclova in the spring of 1690 under the joint command of de León and Father Massanet consisted of 110 soldiers and four Franciscan missionaries. They moved eastward to the headquarters of the Tejas tribe in the fertile Neches River Valley where they labored the summer through building the station of San Francisco de los Tejas. That fall three missionaries and as many soldiers were left to guard the tiny outpost. A year later the garrison was increased to nine, for by that time the Indians were so warlike that even the stout-hearted Massanet admitted the need of a presidio to guard the missionaries. Before one could be built a native uprising in the autumn of 1693 forced the friars to retreat sadly to the Rio Grande. For the next two decades Texas remained unoccupied. During those years the Mexican frontier advanced to its southern edge when in 1699 the presidio of San Juan Bautista and three Franciscan missions were established at Eagle Pass on the west bank of the Rio Grande.

While New Spain slept, New France acted. La Salle's dreams came true in 1699 when the French built their colony of Louisiana at the mouth of the Mississippi. In vain Mexico's officials protested to Madrid; Spain's throne was occupied by Philip V, grandson of Louis XIV, who stood docilely by while his grandfather's legions overran a land that might have been his. One among the patriots of New Spain refused to be discouraged by official indifference. Fray Francisco Hidalgo, who served for a time among the Tejas Indians, was so anxious to return to his former charges that he conceived a bold plan to stir his superiors into action. Early in 1713 he penned a veiled letter to the governor of Louisiana, hinting that French traders would be kindly received south of the Rio Grande. The

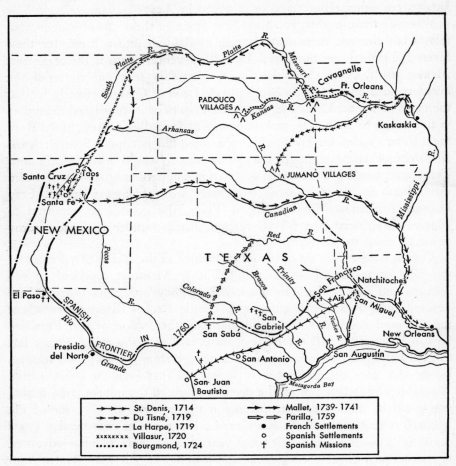

The Texas-New Mexico Frontier, 1700-1763

delighted governor responded as Hidalgo hoped; an experienced trader, Louis de St. Denis, was dispatched westward with a supply of trading goods. Proceeding at a leisurely pace, St. Denis paused to found a post at the Indian village of Natchitoches on the Red River, then journeyed across Texas to emerge at the presidio of San Juan Bautista in July, 1714.

The effect on Mexican officials was that foreseen by Hidalgo. St. Denis and his followers were clapped into jail. While they languished there

plans were formulated to forestall similar invasions. The reoccupation of
Texas was the only answer. An expedition set out in June, 1716, with a
soldier, Captain Domingo Ramón, in command, twenty-five soldiers, nine
missionaries, and St. Denis as guide, for that glib-tongued Frenchman not
only talked himself out of jail but into marriage with the presidio commandant's granddaughter. Reaching the Neches River in July, 1716, they
fell to building the mission station of Nuestro Padre San Francisco de los
Tejas and three minor stations, all east of the river. The presence of French
trading goods among the Tejas Indians warned Captain Ramón that this
outpost could be protected only by planting additional missions across the
path used by natives in reaching St. Denis' post at Nachitoches. Before the
year was out he built the Mission San Miguel only fifteen miles from the
Red River, and the Mission Ais between the Neches and Sabine rivers.
Six stations, all well equipped and guarded by a small presidio, then
challenged French intruders. Two years later the *villa* of San Antonio was
established in western Texas to guard the route between the frontier
outposts and Mexico.

Spain established its northern frontier none too soon, for enemies began
pressing upon its weakly guarded bulwarks even before the last outpost
was completed. They came as French traders, moving out of Louisiana
in quest of furs, hides, and gold. Their highways were the rivers that
fringed Texas and New Mexico—the Red, Canadian, and Arkansas; their
objective was the trade of the Plains tribes. For half a century they pressed
upon New Spain's northern hinterland while Spaniards fought back with
gun and Gospel to retain control of territories painfully won.

Skirmishing began in 1719 when three French expeditions used the outbreak of a European war between France and Spain as an excuse to test the
Texas defenses. The first, a tiny force of seven soldiers from Natchitoches,
captured the unguarded San Miguel mission in June, 1719, so alarming
the friars at the Neches missions that all fled toward San Antonio. The
second, a band of traders commanded by the bold Clause Du Tisné,
advanced overland from the Missouri River to the Jumano Indian villages
on the Arkansas River where they audaciously plied their trade on New
Spain's doorstep. The third struck even nearer. A trading party led by
Bernard de la Harpe explored the middle Red River, crossed to the
Arkansas and Canadian valleys, and attempted to open trade with the
nomads of that open country. Neither Du Tisné nor de la Harpe won over
the Indians they encountered, but the threat to Texas was nonetheless real.
Clearly the fortifications must be strengthened or the borderland might
fall to the French and their native allies.

The task was entrusted to two seasoned frontiersmen. The wealthy soldier-governor of Coahuila, the Marquis of Aguayo, raised five hundred mounted troops and in November, 1720, led them out of Monclova along the road to San Antonio. One by one the forsaken missions of eastern Texas were restored, then strengthened by the addition of a well-garrisoned presidio at Mission San Miguel. When Aguayo returned home during the winter of 1721-22 he paused to build a station and fort at Matagorda Bay. Although Texas was well guarded, the frontier would never be safe so long as Indians to the northward were open to French meddling; they must be won to Spain's side by a show of force. That was the objective of the forty-five soldiers and sixty friendly natives under Pedro de Villasur who set out from Santa Fe during the summer of 1720. They moved northward beneath the shadows of the Rockies without sighting a single Indian until they reached the Pawnee country near the junction of the North and South Platte rivers where they camped on August 12, 1720. All that night hostile Pawnee crept toward them under the protection of the tall grass, and at daybreak rushed pell-mell into the camp. The surprised Spaniards were unable to defend themselves against the sudden assault; Villasur was killed and only thirteen soldiers managed to escape. Seldom had a defeat cost so dearly. Spain's prestige was so low that every Plains tribe deserted to the French or sent its war parties to molest the enfeebled Spanish defenders.

The French were quick to take advantage of this golden opportunity. A skilled frontiersman, Étienne Veniard de Bourgmond, whose Indian wife and long career as a Missouri trader equipped him for the delicate task of tribal diplomacy, was hurried westward from Kaskaskia in the fall of 1723 with forty traders and a large store of trading goods. Moving swiftly up the Missouri, Bourgmond built a fortification, Ft. Orleans, in western Missouri, then pressed on along the Kansas River to the Padouca village on the upper reaches of that stream. There the skilled pioneer spread bale after bale of presents before the eager-eyed natives; all those and more, he said, would be theirs if they promised to trade only with Frenchmen. The Padouca chief readily agreed, assuring Bourgmond that although the Spaniards "bring us horses and bring us a few knives and a few awls and a few axes . . . they are not like you, who give us great quantities of merchandise, such as we have never seen before." Bourgmond's success seriously threatened New Spain's defenses; apparently the French were destined to make alliance after alliance until their native allies dominated the debatable land north of Texas. Yet the threat failed to develop when the outbreak of the Natchez and Fox wars east of the Mississippi during the 1720's forced New France to abandon its plans for a trading empire on the Plains country.

Not until the close of the 1730's could traders turn to molesting the Spanish borderlands once more. The leaders were two brothers, Pierre and Paul Mallet, who gained the idea that brought them fame while trading along the Mississippi. Why not, they reasoned, establish direct trade with the Spanish town of Santa Fe? Surely the Spaniards there, joined to Mexico by only a tortuous mountain trail, would pay well in peltry and silver for French goods; surely Indians along the way would welcome well-equipped traders. To test the idea the Mallets set out from Illinois in 1739, taking with them half a dozen companions and a plentiful supply of trading goods. Up the Missouri they went, until some Pawnee Indians corrected their hazy geographic notions, then out along the Platte and southward until they burst into Santa Fe on July 22, 1739. The reception waiting them reflected the eagerness of Spanish frontiersmen for manufactured goods; mission bells rang in welcome, splendid clothes were provided to replace their travel-stained garments, and comfortable homes were placed at their disposal. For nine months they lived luxuriously as guests of the New Mexican governor while a messenger hurried to Mexico City seeking permission for trade between Santa Fe and Louisiana. The answer, although not unexpected, was nonetheless disappointing; the Spanish empire, the New Mexicans were sternly reminded, was closed to all outside traders. The Mallets must be summarily deported.

This harsh decree meant little more to the inhabitants of Santa Fe than to the French traders themselves. Like all frontiersmen they were more concerned with getting what they wanted than with abstract theories of empire. One thing they coveted was cheap manufactured goods. Hence they let the Mallets know they would violate the orders of their distant viceroy and welcome merchants from Louisiana. Bearing that welcome news, the jubilant brothers began their return journey on May 1, 1740, blazing a new trail along a river since known as the Canadian. During the next decade a number of traders journeyed regularly between the Mississippi Valley and New Mexico, bringing out implements, cloth, and other manufactured goods which were bartered for gold, silver, and furs. At first expeditions originated in New Orleans but by the middle 1740's French diplomats won over the Comanche and Jumano Indians and planted Ft. Cavagnolle in the midst of the Kansa tribe, thus opening a route to Santa Fe from the Illinois villages. The Santa Fe trade not only drained wealth from New Spain's northern province but gave the French a chance to establish friendly relations with the Plains Indians whose hunting grounds fringed the Texas-New Mexico frontier.

There, as on other American borderlands where Spanish, French, and English civilizations clashed, Spaniards failed to win the friendship of native tribes because their frontier institutions were little to the liking of the red men. They offered the Indians salvation and civilization; the French promised brandy, guns, and knives. The Spanish urged natives to abandon nomadic ways for sedentary lives in mission villages; the Frenchmen followed the wandering Plains tribes across the vastness of the western prairies. Spaniards tried to recast natives in a Spanish mold and failed; Frenchmen learned to live as the natives did and succeeded. Only the French government's failure to exploit its advantage saved Spain's northern provinces during those years. But for royal indifference and the outbreak of King George's War, which cast the two nations as allies, both Texas and New Mexico would probably have fallen into the hands of French pioneers and their Indian allies.

By contrast, the efforts of Spaniards to defend their threatened domain were often inefficient and ineffective. On only one Texan frontier did they strengthen their position between 1740 and 1763 when the French made their spectacular gains. The southeastern coast of Texas, a neglected wilderness cut off from the rest of Mexico by the steep Sierra Gorda Mountains, was occupied by fragments of Indian tribes, renegades both white and red, and the outcasts found in any region beyond the law's pale. In 1746 that coastal lowland—between the Pánuco and San Antonio rivers—was set aside as the province of Nuevo Santander under the governorship of an experienced Indian fighter, José de Escandón. After several exploring trips into his domain, Escandón set out in December, 1748, from the neighboring state of Querétaro, leading five hundred colony planters secured by generous cash subsidies and promises of tax-free lands. At each favorable site he left a small garrison, missionaries, and a handful of farmers or ranchers until twenty settlements were scattered over the province. Most were south of the Rio Grande but two, Laredo and Dolores, were in Texas. An attempt to found a colony at the mouth of the Nueces failed when warlike Indians attacked Escandón's party, but during the next years settlers from lower Nuevo Santander drifted there, attracted by the ranching possibilities in that land of thick prairie grass, sparkling streams, and rolling countryside. By 1750 6,000 ranchers and miners in Nuevo Santander held southeastern Texas firmly for New Spain.

Less successful were Spanish efforts to expand the Texan frontier northward by winning over French-dominated tribes along the upper reaches of the Brazos and Colorado rivers. In 1746 several mission stations were established on the San Gabriel River, a tributary of the Brazos, at the request of minor tribes. Disease and raids by the fearsome Apache Indians forced the abandonment of the outposts nine years later. More enduring was the San Agustín mission, planted at the mouth of the Trinity in 1756 to hold back threatening French intruders. A final attempt to win the northern country was made that year when a delegation of Apache Indians visited Texas to ask for religious instruction and a presidio. The amazed Spaniards, who had battled those warlike tribesmen for a generation, seized the opportunity to found a mission on the San Sabá River a year later. Only after the station was established did the friars learn the reason for the Apache about-face; they wanted the Spanish to protect them from the dread Comanche. By 1758 bands of Comanche warriors were molesting the missionaries who sent out a call for aid. A punitive expedition of three hundred soldiers under Captain Parilla failed to ease the situation when it was decisively defeated by a Comanche war party on the Red River. Before the year was out the stations were withdrawn to the upper Nueces River and northern Texas abandoned to the savages.

That was the last attempt to push the Texan frontier northward, as the transfer of Louisiana to Spain in 1763 removed the French menace. For the next generation Texas remained a neglected province, peopled by 2,000 Spaniards and a handful of Christianized Indians. Over it swept the Plains nomads on their buffalo hunts, scarcely aware of the scattered missions, presidios, and villages which symbolized Spain's half-hearted efforts to hold that isolated frontier.

In the meantime the attention of New Spain was directed to the Pacific coast where a new foreign menace threatened the borderlands of Mexico. Russia was the villain. After 1741, when a Danish navigator, Vitus Bering, sailing in the service of the czars, discovered Alaska and the Aleutian Islands, Cossack traders pushed steadily southward along the North American coast in search of seal and sea otter peltry. By 1763 their vessels were cruising as far south as the Oregon country; near enough to threaten the California gateway to Mexico. So thought José de Gálvez, visitor-general of New Spain, a zealous administrator whose determination to revive the glories of New Spain amounted almost to fanaticism. Why not, he reasoned, forestall the Russians by seizing California at once? From the time that thought entered his mind he pursued the plan with remarkable singleness of purpose; every letter to the court of Charles III was filled with pleas for permission to extend Spain's empire northward. Such enthusiasm was infectious, and in 1767 consent came from across the sea. Gálvez, thoroughly delighted, hurried to Lower California to organize the colonizing party which would translate his dream into reality.

The time was ripe for such an enterprise. The Jesuits, who missionized Lower California, had recently been replaced by fourteen brown-robed Franciscans under Fray Junípero Serra, all inflamed with religious zeal and anxious to aid any enterprise promising a crop of souls. Their help allowed Gálvez to form two colonizing parties with unusual dispatch. One, composed of settlers under the skilled frontiersman Don Gaspar de Portolá and missionaries led by Father Serra, he planned to send overland. The other, made up of three vessels carrying additional colonists and supplies, would sail northward. They would meet at San Diego Bay, move on to Monterey Harbor, and there plant the flag and cross of Spain in the California wilderness.

By the early spring of 1769 all was ready. The ships set sail first and although one was lost at sea the other two reached San Diego Bay after

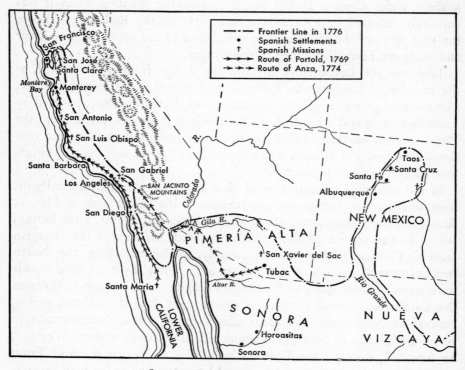

Spanish California, 1763-1776

a storm-plagued voyage which left the crews so weakened by scurvy they could scarcely launch the landing boats. The overland party fared better, despite the formidable task of crossing four hundred miles of unexplored desert with laden pack animals and several hundred head of cattle. An advanced group of twenty-five frontier-seasoned soldiers moved ahead to break trail; behind them came the rest of the immigrants with Portolá and Serra in command. At times water was scarce, at others the road lay deep in sand or twisted across mountain heights, but more often the path lay "level, straight and happy" through flower-decked meadows where "willows, tule and a glad sky" greeted the travelers. Six weeks of journeying brought the 126 survivors to San Diego on July 1, 1769. After Father Serra sang the *Te Deum*, they watched Portolá take formal possession of Spain's newest outpost in the name of his king.

Two weeks of rest was all Portolá allowed his tired followers and those were devoted to building the mission station of San Diego Alcalá for Father Serra. On July 14 the hardy commander set out again, with twenty-seven soldiers, bound for Monterey. Their path lay through fertile valleys "so green that it seemed to us it had been planted" and over low-lying coastal mountains where curious Indians, "as naked as Adam in paradise before he sinned," offered them tributes of friendship. For a time the formidable Santa Luciá Mountains held them back, but on October 1, 1769, the party stood on the shores of Monterey Bay. The sight that met their eyes was disheartening. Instead of the broad, land-locked harbor described by early explorers, they saw a shallow, shelterless bay. The disappointed Portolá, convinced Monterey must lie somewhere ahead, led his men on for another month before they reached Drake's Bay, the landmarks of which they recognized. They started back, but their greatest discovery lay just ahead. On November 1 a scouting party stumbled upon a harbor so large that "not only all the navy of our most Catholic Majesty but those of all Europe could take shelter." San Francisco Bay, after eluding Spain's navigators for a century, yielded up its secret to an overland party! Portolá's men were too exhausted to take advantage of their find; instead they headed back to San Diego where they arrived on January 24, 1770, "smelling frightfully of mules."

No relief awaited them there. Fifty of the little band left behind with Father Serra were dead of scurvy, the rest sick, and supplies exhausted. For a time despair reigned, even in Portolá's stout heart, but the timely arrival of a supply ship from Mexico, just at the end of a nine-day vigil of prayer, rekindled hope. After waiting a short time for weakened bodies and crushed spirits to be restored, the courageous leader started northward again, reaching Monterey Bay in March, 1770. There he set his men to building the presidio of Monterey and the mission of San Carlos. During the next two years three more outposts were established: San Antonio mission at the southern tip of the Santa Luciá mountains, San Gabriel mission north of San Diego, and San Luis Obispo mission on the central coast of California. By 1773 California was guarded by five stations and two presidios, manned by a pitifully small force of sixty-one soldiers and eleven friars.

The feeble settlements could be strengthened in only one way: an overland route to the Mexican province of Sonora must be opened. Such a road would lure settlers northward and, even more important, allow food to reach California from the farms of northern Mexico. Part of the trail was already blazed by a wandering Arizona priest, Fray Francisco Garcés, who in 1771, with "no other escort than his guardian angel," explored the deserts of southern California to the foot of the San Jacinto Mountains. The possibility of extending Garcés' explorations northward occurred to Juan Bautista de Anza, captain of the Pimería Alta fortress of Tubac, a desert-toughened frontiersman who had spent an adventurous lifetime battling the Indians of northern Sonora. His request for permission to lead an overland expedition into California having been granted, he set out on January 8, 1774, followed by twenty leather-jacketed soldiers, a handful of servants and muleteers, Father Garcés, and herds of cattle and pack animals. The party reached the Yuma Indian villages at the junction of the Colorado and Gila rivers without difficulty, but then their trials multiplied. For eleven days they struggled across shifting dunes and parched deserts, only to be turned back when supplies ran out. Again they made the assault, and this time stumbled upon the Cocopa Mountains, a range of sparsely grassed hills that led them to the foot of the San Jacinto Mountains. After those were surmounted, on March 22, 1774, Anza and his party burst upon the surprised missionaries at the San Gabriel mission amidst a chorus of ringing bells, booming muskets, and shouted greetings. By May 26 the explorers were back in Tubac again, having covered more than 2,000 miles of inhospitable country.

The way was clear for the last step in the Spanish occupation of California: the establishment of an outpost on San Francisco Bay. The task was entrusted to Anza, who was placed in command of a motley crew of 240 colonists scraped from the slums and villages of Mexico. They set out from the Sonora village of Horoasitas on October 23, 1775, and by early January were at the San Gabriel mission where Anza allowed his followers a month's rest before pressing onward. When they reached the San Francisco harbor he set them to work, some on the presidio of San Francisco at the tip of the jutting Fort Point peninsula, others on the nearby mission stations of Arroyo de los Dolores and Santa Clara. When those were completed, Anza returned to his beloved desert fortress in northern Mexico, leaving the task of expanding the California settlements to other men. That went on slowly over the next years; San José mission was built in 1777, the town of Los Angeles laid out in 1781, and the presidio and mission of Santa Barbara a year later. As settlers drifted in, growing herds of cattle and orderly irrigated fields testified to the permanence of the new colony.

By the close of the 1770's New Spain's frontier stretched across the back country from eastern Texas to the shores of San Francisco Bay; a vast bulwark against intruders who threatened rich Mexico. Yet more than a thin line of presidios and mission stations was needed to repulse the enemies who soon hammered at the gates of Spain's fortress. Even as Anza's weary colonists fashioned the log walls of their tiny fort, a new and more aggressive nation was born in the East. The Philadelphia bells which proclaimed the independence of the United States in 1776 tolled the death knell of Spain's North American empire. Over the next decades the lusty young nation sent a stream of pioneers westward, to wrest away the lands won by two centuries of Spanish toil, until the boundaries of the infant Republic reached the Pacific.

# CHAPTER XXII

# The Traders' Frontier

## 1776-1840

For half a century after New Spain flung its protective wall across the northern approaches to Mexico, the feeble barrier underwent a constant assault. Pressing from the northwest were Cossack fur hunters from Russia's Siberia, New England ship captains seeking native trade, and wilderness-wise agents of England's powerful Hudson's Bay Company. From the northeast came Canadian traders and their Indian allies, bent on winning the allegiance and trade of the Plains tribes. Advancing from the east were arrogant American frontiersmen—explorers, trappers, pioneer farmers, ranchers, and missionaries—all determined to exploit the wealth of Spain's forbidden empire. Before those invincible forces the Spanish first fell back, then surrendered chunk after chunk of hard-won territory until all the Southwest was in alien hands. Of the aggressors the most dangerous were Anglo-American frontiersmen, and their shock troops were the fur traders.

The attack began in the 1780's when agents of England's great trading companies—the Hudson's Bay Company and the North West Company—swarmed out of Mackinac and Prairie du Chien to barter with tribesmen as far west as the Mandan Villages of the central Missouri River. In 1791 the seriousness of Britain's threat was demonstrated when Spanish traders along the Missouri were forcibly turned back by Indians who insisted that Englishmen supplied all the goods they needed; in the same year citizens of isolated Ste. Genevieve demanded protection from British-armed Osage tribesmen. Spain was in danger of losing all northern Louisiana unless it acted. Nor could mission stations tame the primitive natives of the northern Plains country. In that emergency Spanish officials at New Orleans, turning instinctively to methods used effectively in the French frontier advance,

444

determined to use the fur trade to guard their hinterland. They would, they decided, win over the tribes along the Missouri with trading goods, establishing that river as the northern border of their domain.

The agents selected for the task were experienced French woodsmen acquired by Spain with Louisiana. Auguste Chouteau, a seasoned frontiersman who as a lad of fourteen helped found St. Louis, was dispatched in 1794 to build Ft. Carondelet among the Osage villages, partly to hold those hostile red men in check, partly to win their allegiance by supplying them with goods. At the same time French traders at St. Louis were authorized to form a trading company, The Commercial Company for the Discovery of the Nations of the Upper Missouri, to win the friendship of tribes along the Big Muddy. As an additional incentive officials offered $3,000 to the first Spanish subject following the Missouri to the Pacific. Three expeditions sent out by the Commercial Company during 1794 and 1795 failed to accomplish much; one was led by a schoolmaster who proved a better teacher than explorer, another was turned back by unfriendly natives, and the third never went beyond the Mandan villages. The leader of the last, a Spanish subject named James Mackay, found the Dakota country teeming with British traders who were summarily ordered to leave the "Catholic Majesty's Dominions," but more than bluster was needed. For the next years the trading frontiers of the two nations clashed in the Plains country, with the British making steady gains. By 1802 they dominated the region as far south as the Omaha villages and west to the Yellowstone and Big Horn rivers.

That was bad enough in Spanish eyes, but worse was the assault on their eastern borderland which began in 1803 when the United States acquired Louisiana. For the first time the two countries destined to battle for the trans-Mississippi West stood face to face. One was old, decadent, and weakened by European wars. The other was young, self-confident, and arrogantly determined to expand. Both sought to control as much of the Southwest as possible; a decision fostered by the Louisiana Treaty which gave the United States title to "the colony or province of Louisiana, with the same extent that it now has in the hands of Spain and that it had when France possessed it." With no boundaries established, rambunctious American frontiersmen felt free to enter any part of the West. For half a century they battered against Spain's outposts before they overran the defenses to sweep triumphantly to the Pacific.

Thomas Jefferson, president when Louisiana was purchased, mapped the strategy that opened the attack. For some time he had been interested in the unknown lands beyond the Mississippi. As a loyal patriot he felt the United States must locate unrevealed riches before any European power was tempted to settle uncomfortably close to the American borders. As a scientist he wanted to know what plants and animals abounded in the un- explored West, whether the fur trade could be developed there, and how the Missouri River might be used as a route across the continent. He had made a number of attempts to answer those questions before Louisiana was acquired. In 1786 he encouraged a colorful Connecticut wanderer, John Ledyard, to undertake a romantic foot journey that carried him almost across Siberia before Cossack police ended his hopes of crossing Bering Straits and exploring the North American interior. Again in 1792 Jeffer- son prodded the American Philosophical Society into financing the journey of a French scientist, André Michaux, who planned to "ascend the Missouri River, cross the Stony Mountains, and descend down the nearest river to the Pacific." That venture collapsed when the leader became involved with Citizen Genet in revolutionary intrigue. Jefferson's curiosity was still un- sated when he became President in 1801.

Two years later, and before Napoleon even offered Louisiana to the United States, Jefferson tried again. This time he secured a secret appropria- tion from Congress for an exploring expedition westward "even to the Western Ocean, having conferences with the natives on the subject of com- mercial intercourse." His object was different now, for his program of push- ing eastern Indians into small reservations necessitated the discovery of new trading areas for American trappers. That was the primary purpose in the President's mind when he selected as leaders for the expedition thirty- two-year-old Meriwether Lewis, whose skill in wilderness ways dated from a boyhood spent beneath the shadows of the Blue Ridge, and William Clark—younger brother of George Rogers Clark—a twenty-eight-year-old frontiersman and Indian fighter. Before they set out news of the Louisiana Purchase reached America. Exploration of the newly acquired domain was then an additional objective; the leaders were told to follow the Missouri River to its source, seek a water route to the Pacific, and make careful records of the soils, animal and vegetable life, minerals, and geography of the region which they traversed.

They set out from the East on July 5, 1803, gathered a crew of forty- eight strapping young frontiersmen along the way, and in late fall estab- lished winter quarters near St. Louis. Lewis and Clark spent the cold months drilling their men in frontier techniques. With the spring of 1804 the expedition started up the Missouri, traveling in an iron-reinforced keel- boat and two pirogues. All summer they worried their way up the Big Muddy, stopping frequently to talk with Indians or make scientific obser- vations, until the blasts of autumn found them at the Mandan villages. A blockhouse—Ft. Mandan—was built; there the explorers labored through

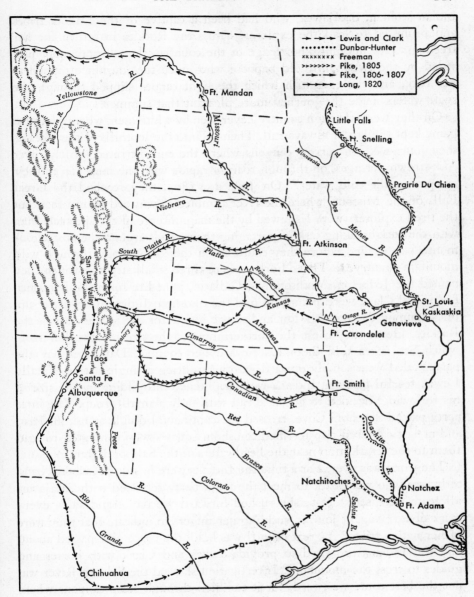

The Explorers' Frontier, 1776-1820

the cold Dakota winter on six dugouts to replace the cumbersome keelboat they had used. By April, 1805, they were ready to start once more. The keelboat with a crew of sixteen men was sent back to St. Louis; the rest of the party turned their faces westward, guided by a talented Shoshoni

Indian woman, Sacájawea, who had been a captive of the Dakota tribes and promised to lead the explorers across the Rockies in return for her freedom. Her uncanny knowledge of the country, the entertainment provided by the two-months-old papoose who made the journey strapped to her back, and the ease with which the light canoes slipped through the swift waters made the journey more pleasant that summer.

On they went, through country never seen by white men, where plentiful game kept the larder always full. Then up into the foothills of the Rockies they journeyed, in narrow canyons where the current raced swiftly, over rock-strewn portages, on through roaring rapids with the men "up to their armpits in the cold water." On June 13, 1805, they reached the Great Falls of the Missouri where the river tumbled downward eighty feet, but the tired explorers were less awed by the magnificence of the spectacle than with the back-breaking task of portaging their goods around the obstacle. A month was needed before they could be on their way again, through wild mountain country, to Three Forks, where three small streams, which they named the Jefferson, Madison, and Gallatin, joined to form the Missouri. Lewis and Clark were anxious to find the Shoshoni Indians to replace supplies running dangerously low and secure horses for the journey across the Rockies. Hence they chose the northernmost of the streams, the Jefferson, which Sacájawea told them led toward her country. Day after day the party toiled wearisomely onward without sighting a single native. Finally Lewis, fearful that the Indians were frightened into hiding by the size of his following, decided to go on ahead with only a small group. The little party passed Shoshoni Cove, crossed the continental divide at Lemhi Pass, and at last captured two terrified Shoshoni squaws who consented to lead them to the tribal camp near the headwaters of the Salmon River.

The worst was over. For a time the Indians were hostile but when a band of braves who went back to meet the main party returned with Sacájawea all fears were set at rest; she rushed forward "to dance and show every mark of extravagant joy . . . suckling her fingers to indicate that they were of her native tribe." A great council was held, the peace pipe passed about, and the Indians promised to provide Lewis and Clark with horses and guides to cross the mountains. Investigation showed the Salmon River was not the best route westward, for it tumbled through steep canyons where boats would surely be wrecked. Instead the travelers turned northward for a five day march into the Bitterroot Valley, then west again for ten days of weary plodding through snow flurries and drenching rain. On September 20, 1805, they finally emerged from the treacherous Lolo Pass into the open valley of the Clearwater River, where friendly Flathead Indians gave them food and shelter. A week of rest and the tired travelers

were on their way once more, using canoes obtained from the natives to
run the rapids of the Clearwater and Columbia, until finally in mid-
November they stood on the banks of "that ocean, the object of all our
labours, the reward of all our anxieties."

Winter camp was estabished on the banks of the Columbia a short distance
from the sea. There the explorers camped for four months of drizzle, rain,
and fog which left bodies weak and nerves frayed. The return trip was
begun in late March, 1806. Although forced to wait several weeks for the
snows to melt from Lolo Pass, they were safely in the Bitterroot Valley by

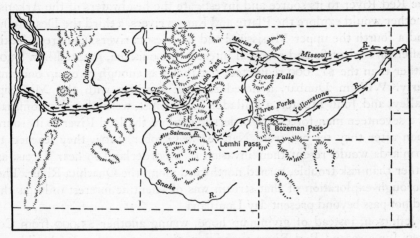

Lewis and Clark in the Northwest

the end of June. There the expedition split in two. One party, led by Clark,
retraced the outward trail to Three Forks where, under Sacájawea's guidance, it passed through mountainous Bozeman Pass to the upper Yellowstone River. On July 24, 1806, the group started downstream, taking careful note of the country traversed. In the meantime Lewis with nine followers crossed the continental divide through Lewis and Clark Pass, reached
the Great Falls of the Missouri, then turned northward to explore the
valley of the Marias River. That was dangerous country, roamed by hostile
Blackfoot and Grosventre Indians, but all went well until July 27 when
Lewis' men clashed with eight Grosventre warriors, killing two of them.
Realizing that the enraged tribe would be out in force for revenge, the
explorers immediately started east, galloping their horses at full speed for
more than a hundred miles before they dared rest. They reached the
Missouri safely, rejoining Clark's group a short distance below the mouth
of the Yellowstone. On September 23, 1806, the Lewis and Clark expedition emerged at St. Louis to end one of the epic journeys in the history of

exploration. They investigated thousands of miles of unknown country, found several usable passes through the Rockies, made important scientific discoveries, and established friendly relations with half a dozen Indian tribes.

Thomas Jefferson saw to it, however, that they did not monopolize the plaudits of the grateful nation. Even as they battled their way across the continent other explorers were on their way westward to unlock other secrets of the Louisiana Territory. The President began planning expeditions as soon as America secured the trans-Mississippi West; one would ascend the Red River to its source and investigate the headwaters of the Arkansas, another would explore the Platte and Kansas rivers, a third the Des Moines, and a fourth the upper Mississippi and Minnesota rivers. Congress, lacking Jefferson's scientific and practical interest in Louisiana, granted him $3,000 rather than the $12,000 requested, but that was enough to equip one small party. William Dunbar, a noted scientist familiar with the Mississippi Valley, and John Hunter, a Philadelphia chemist, were placed in command of a seventeen-man force with orders to explore the Red River to its source. Soon after they set out from Natchez in October, 1804, they learned the Spaniards would resent their invasion of a borderland so near Texas, and rather than risk trouble, turned northward along the Ouachita River. Their thorough exploration of that stream was of scientific interest only, as they did not pass beyond present-day Louisiana.

Jefferson, instead of giving up hope, wrung another $5,000 from Congress for a second Red River expedition, this one commanded by Thomas Freeman, surveyor and astronomer. Starting from Ft. Adams in mid-April, 1806, the party of thirty-seven men made its way slowly up the log-choked stream in two flat-bottomed barges, stopping occasionally to hold councils with Indians along the way. The arduous labors came to naught; after six hundred miles of effort they encountered a Spanish army from Texas whose commander ordered them to turn back. Freeman considered resistance for a time, but when common sense triumphed reluctantly retraced his steps. His expedition was hardly a success, as he traversed no ground not already explored by Spanish and French traders and brought back no word of the Red River's source.

With two failures in the South, Jefferson turned his attention to the less hazardous task of discovering the source of the Mississippi. His decision brought into prominence the explorer whose name has been forever associated with the conquest of the Far West, Lieutenant Zebulon Montgomery Pike. The twenty-six-year-old stripling began his discoveries in the fall of 1805 when he started northward from St. Louis with a well-stocked keelboat and twenty men. Stopping at the Falls of St. Anthony to purchase land for a government post and build a light barge, the party moved on to Little Falls where several log cabins were constructed for winter quarters. While most of the men settled down in cozy comfort, Pike and two companions pressed forward on sledges through the snow-blanketed Minnesota countryside. Here and there they found posts of the North West Company proudly flaunting the Union Jack, all occupied by cheerful Canadian traders who entertained the Americans royally and swore solemnly to display the Stars and Stripes in the future, knowing full well no one could punish them if they did not. At Leech Lake, which Pike falsely took to be the source of the Mississippi, the explorers started southward, reaching Little Falls on March 5. By the end of April, 1806, they were back in St. Louis.

That both the nation and Jefferson agreed with Pike's far-from-modest estimate of his accomplishments was shown when he was immediately sent out again, this time on the more difficult task of exploring the country between the Arkansas and Red rivers, winning the friendship of Indians there, and driving out unlicensed traders. By July, 1806, he was ready to take to the trail, leading twenty-three men up the Missouri and Osage rivers to the Osage villages, then across country to the Pawnee villages on the Republican River. He found the Indians ready to resist, having been recently visited by a Spanish army sent out to intercept the Americans, but Pike angrily told them the "warriors of his Great American Father were not women to be turned back by words," and pressed on. His trail led south now, to the Great Bend of the Arkansas River, then along that stream to the Rockies were a stout fortification was built as winter headquarters. For the next two months Pike explored the Colorado country, unsuccessfully tried to climb the peak bearing his name, and hunted in vain for the headwaters of the Red River.

Before snow left the mountain passes in the spring of 1807 he was on his way again, through the Royal Gorge of the Arkansas River, over the Sangre de Cristo Mountains, and across the San Luis Valley, to emerge on the upper Rio Grande where he ordered his men to throw up a stockade. Pike either believed or pretended to believe he was still on American soil but an army of a hundred mounted Spaniards from Santa Fe soon cured him of his illusion. He and his men were escorted into the New Mexican capital, questioned endlessly, hustled on to Chihuahua for more questioning, then marched across northern Mexico to Natchitoches where they were rudely deposited on the American side of the border. Although his maps and papers were taken from him, Pike managed to remember enough of conditions along the southwestern border to prepare a report which brought him wide acclaim.

For a decade after the return of Pike's expedition, interest in western exploration waned as the United States fought the War of 1812 or grappled with the problems of reconstruction. When government attention was turned to the West once more in 1817 its objectives were different; parties went into the Plains country to found military posts that would hold the Indians in check, open the way for fur traders, and clear a path for settlers. John C. Calhoun, the secretary of war, estimated that three forts on strategic waterways were needed first. Two, Ft. Smith on the Arkansas River, and Ft. Snelling at the junction of the Mississippi and Minnesota rivers, were built between 1817 and 1819 by expeditions under Major Stephen H. Long—both log blockhouses destined to play a prominent role in the advance of the frontier. Establishing the third proved more difficult. An elaborate expedition under Major Long and Colonel David Atkinson set out from St. Louis on July 4, 1819, bound for the Mandan villages, but the newfangled steamboats used broke down so regularly the party got no farther than Council Bluffs that year. There they built a log fort, Ft. Atkinson. Reports of mismanagement which reached the East during the winter so annoyed Congress that plans for an outpost at Mandan were abandoned.

Instead army officials decided on a last effort to seek the source of the Red River. Major Long, who was placed in charge of the nineteen soldiers assembled for the purpose, led the party out of Ft. Atkinson on June 6, 1820. Up the Platte and the South Platte they went, southward beneath the shadows of the Rockies where one of the men succeeded in climbing Pike's Peak, southward still to the Arkansas where the impressive Royal Gorge was re-explored. There they divided, one group to descend the Arkansas, the other under Major Long to press on in search of the Red River. The latter crossed the Purgatory and Cimarron rivers, then emerged on a large river which the leader took to be the Red. Thankfully he turned his men eastward along its banks, only to find he had hit upon the Canadian River which, to his great disgust, took him back to the Arkansas again. By mid-September, 1820, both branches of the expedition were safe at Ft. Smith, having accomplished almost nothing. The harmful effects of Long's fiasco were multiplied by the widely circulated report of his travels. "In regard to this extensive section of country between the Missouri River and the Rocky Mountains," he wrote, "we do not hesitate in giving the opinion that it is almost wholly unfit for cultivation, and of course uninhabitable by a people depending upon agriculture for their subsistence." The official map of his expedition labeled the whole Plains region as the "Great American Desert," a false designation destined to be copied by map makers for half a century. Major Long not only failed to unlock the secrets of the

Far West; he set up a psychological barrier that kept others from disproving his falsehoods.

Two decades of official exploration accomplished little. The fringes of the Louisiana Purchase were explored, a few important rivers—the Missouri, Arkansas, and Canadian—traced to their sources, and a minute portion of the vast territory investigated. But the routes of such important streams as the Red, Platte, Osage, Republican, and Kansas rivers were still unknown, no usable pass through the Rockies was discovered, and the central portion of the Great Plains between the Missouri and Arkansas rivers still waited investigation. Jefferson's dream of a series of thorough explorations revealing every secret of the Louisiana country failed to materialize.

Fur traders succeeded where official explorers failed. Unsung and unheralded, too busy—or too uneducated—to seek fame by recording their wanderings, driven onward by the quest for prosaic profits rather than scientific curiosity, adventurous frontiersmen penetrated into every nook and corner of the Far West between 1807 and 1840. Spurring them on was the realization that peltry was cheapest among unsophisticated Indians who would barter bales of furs for a handful of trinkets. That commonsense point of view gave the trading frontier its remarkable mobility; the constant object of every trapper was to break through the fringe of sophisticated tribes to the richer regions beyond. Those unofficial explorers spied out the secrets of all the West, plotted the course of its rivers, discovered the passes through its mountains, and prepared the way for settlers by breaking down Indian self-sufficiency. No single group contributed more to the conquest of the trans-Mississippi region than those little-known adventurers.

Their interest in the western country was aroused by the exciting news brought back by Lewis and Clark: tales of mountains teeming with beaver, of friendly Indians, and an all-water route along the Missouri River to the rich hunting ground. Through the winter of 1806-07 traders flocked into St. Louis, ready to start west as soon as ice broke in the Big Muddy, in a procession of barges, pirogues, and canoes, laden with knives, guns, whiskey, and knicknacks. The most important party was headed by a Spanish trader, Manuel Lisa, and made up of forty-two unruly trappers. They worked their heavy keelboat up the Missouri and Yellowstone rivers to the mouth of the Big Horn where Lisa set the men to building a timbered blockhouse which, with typical frontier modesty, he named Ft. Manuel. There they spent the winter of 1807-08, trapping, hunting, trading, and roaming widely among tribes of the Northern Rockies. The most ambitious trip was made by John Colter who, with only a gun and a thirty-pound pack, tramped through the Yellowstone country, reached the Green River, and explored the valley of the Big Horn—five hundred miles of lonely mountain travel amidst icy winter blasts.

Lisa's party returned to St. Louis in the summer of 1808 with a wealth in furs and a store of sound advice. This boiled down to one salient fact: only large companies could trade successfully in the Northern Rockies, partly because hostile Indians along the Missouri would turn back small parties, partly because the time consumed reaching the heart of the fur country required more capital than individual traders commanded. That message, preached throughout St. Louis by Lisa, led to the formation of

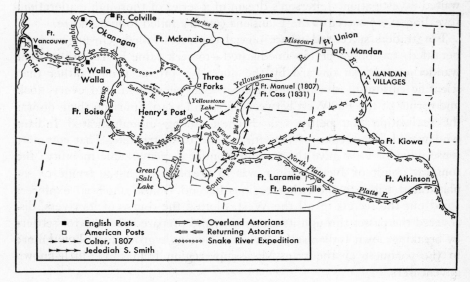

The Northern Traders' Frontier

the Missouri Fur Company. Organized in February, 1809, to pool the resources of most of the city's leading traders, the company included in its ranks Manuel Lisa, William Clark, Auguste and Pierre Chouteau, Major Andrew Henry and a host of others equally well known. For the next half-dozen years it dominated trade in the Northern Rockies.

The company's first expedition, which set out in the spring of 1809, included all the partners, 172 men, a score of Indians to be returned to the Mandan villages at government request, nine large barges, and enough trading goods to stock five or six posts. The traders stopped at the mouth of the Knife River to build a stockade, Ft. Mandan, where some men were left to obtain beaver from the Plains Indians, then moved on to Ft. Manuel where a brisk trade with the Crow Indians was plied through the winter of 1809-10. Although profits were good, some of the partners believed better furs could be obtained from the less sophisticated Blackfeet, whose villages lay just to the west. That would be dangerous—the tribe hated all whites since two warriors had been killed by Meriwether Lewis on his return journey—but a large enough expedition could probably care for itself. That reasoning led one of the partners, Major Andrew Henry, to start for Three Forks in the spring of 1810 with a sizable following. A log post was built first, then the traders moved cautiously into the forest in search of beaver peltry. The expected Blackfoot attack came on April 12 when a powerful war party swept down on the company fort, killed five men, and destroyed a large store of goods. Other raids cost three more lives before the traders rebelled and in July, 1810, returned to Ft. Manuel.

Major Henry was unwilling to give up. With a party of volunteers he started south along the Madison River, crossed the continental divide, and on the upper Snake River built a few log cabins to serve as a trading post. The cold winter of 1810-11 brought few rewards; game was so scarce they returned to St. Louis in the spring of 1811 with only forty packs of beaver. That costly enterprise proved the undoing of the company; resources were so depleted Ft. Manuel was abandoned in 1811 and Ft. Mandan a year later. The Missouri Fur Company continued to operate on the lower Missouri but made no further effort to penetrate the Northern Rockies. Poor management and undercapitalization ended the first attempt to exploit the West's wealth.

Interest in the region did not die. As one company passed from the scene, another rose to take its place: the American Fur Company, organized in 1808 by the German-born financial genius, John Jacob Astor, whose grandiose schemes were breath-taking. He would, he planned, plant a chain of posts across the Far West from the Great Lakes to the Pacific. His headquarters would be at the mouth of the Columbia where furs from all the Rocky Mountain country could be shipped to the Orient. The trade promised not only fantastic profits (as New England ship captains already plying the China sea lanes demonstrated daily), but would strike a fatal blow at his hated Canadian rivals, the Hudson's Bay Company and the North West Company. Neither could send furs to the Far East, an area monopolized by the East India Company; hence his greater returns would eventually allow Astor to drive both into bankruptcy. So Astor hoped as he set about translating his dream into reality.

He first created a subsidiary company, the Pacific Fur Company, to take charge of the Columbia River post. That done, two expeditions set out for the Pacific. One group of thirty-three traders left New York by sailing vessel in September, 1810, and after an uneventful voyage entered the Columbia River in March, 1812, where work was begun on a blockhouse, named Astoria. The second party, known as the Overland Astorians, started from St. Louis in March, 1811, with an inexperienced New Jerseyan, Wilson Price Hunt, in charge. News of the Blackfoot attack on the Missouri Fur Company post at Three Forks convinced Hunt the route blazed by Lewis and Clark was unsafe, hence he struck out across the plains with his party of sixty-three men and women. Weeks of plodding across the interminable grassland followed, then the struggle upward into the Rockies, the discovery of a route across the continental divide along the Wind River, and the pleasure of emerging on the headwaters of the westward-flowing Snake River. Traveling was no easier along the rocky banks of that canyoned stream, but the travelers struggled on until they burst upon half-completed Astoria early in 1812.

All was well in the post, for the loss of one supply ship to hostile natives was forgotten when a second landed in May, deeply laden with food and trading goods. By June stacks of shining pelts were accumulating in the warehouses and barter was both brisk and profitable. That was the welcome news carried east by a party of "Returning Astorians" who set out on June 29, 1812, crossed the Rockies through South Pass, and followed the Platte River into St. Louis—approximating the route later made famous as the Oregon Trail, and discovering the most important pass through the mountains. The promising start was deceptive. In January, 1813, news of the War of 1812 reached Astoria, together with the unpleasant information that a British warship was already on its way to capture the post. Astor's partners, knowing they could offer no resistance, sold the whole enterprise to the North West Company for the trifling sum of $58,000. The unfortunate accident of war ended American activity in the Northwest for a generation.

The withdrawal of the American Fur Company left the Pacific coast in the hands of England's North West Company. For a time this firm was too engrossed in a bitter trade war with the Hudson's Bay Company to develop the region, but in 1821 the crown forced the two rivals to merge into one company—the Hudson's Bay Company—which was given a twenty-one year monopoly in the Oregon country. The task of wringing a profit from the Columbia Department was entrusted to an able administrator, George Simpson, who was given control in 1822 and four years later made Governor-in-Chief of the company's American domain. No better man could have been found. Simpson combined within his own small person boundless energy, rare diplomatic skill, limitless vision, administrative efficiency, and a love of empire which elevated him to a position of pre-eminence in the fur trade.

All those qualities were needed. The Columbia Department was so unprofitable the Hudson's Bay Company was on the verge of abandoning the region when Simpson reached there in 1824 after a grueling trip across the continent. Realizing a strong base was needed first of all, he set his men to building a large stockade, enclosing hundreds of yards, in which were clustered cabins, storehouses, and offices. About Ft. Vancouver he laid out fields where traders, idle during the summer, planted grain and potatoes, or pastured herds of sheep and hogs imported from California. Most important of all was the selection of a superintendent. Simpson's fortunate choice was Dr. John McLoughlin, a great hulk of a man who had learned the fur trade in eastern Canada. "He was," wrote Governor Simpson, "such a figure as I should not like to meet in a dark Night in one of the bye lanes in the neighbourhood of London, dressed in Clothes that had once been fashionable, but now covered with a thousand patches of different Colors, his beard would do honor to the chin of a Grizzly Bear, his face and hands evidently Shewing that he had not lost much time at his Toilette, loaded with arms and his own herculean dimensions forming a tout ensemble that would convey a good idea of the high way men of former days." That was the man whose abilities won the fond title of "White Eagle" from the Indians and the respectable salute of "King of the Oregon" from his comrades.

Dr. McLoughlin's chief concern was new trading areas. In quick succession abandoned forts were rebuilt at Walla Walla and Okanagan, and a new post opened at Ft. Colville to command the commerce of the Columbia River. More important was the extension of the Hudson's Bay Company into the Snake River country, for there Dr. McLoughlin acted with imperialistic wisdom. The Oregon country, he knew, was in dispute between England and the United States. Ultimate ownership would go to the most securely entrenched nation; hence his duty was to keep Americans out. That could be done by stripping a zone east and south of the Columbia bare of all furs, creating a desert barrier to turn back traders from beyond the Rockies. Ruthless trapping there would not only help win Oregon but bolster the company's profits.

Exploitation of the Snake River country was entrusted to thirty-year-old Peter Skene Ogden. Gathering seventy-five trappers and four hundred pack animals, the skilled trader set out in December, 1824, pushing his way through the snow-choked passes to emerge at the Three Forks of the Missouri. The enmity of the Blackfeet turned him west along the Jefferson River, over the continental divide to the Salmon, and southward to the Snake, the men trapping and trading as they went. Exploration of the upper Snake and its tributaries led them along the Bear River to the point where it "discharged into a large Lake of 100 miles in length." Thus did Ogden record the discovery of Great Salt Lake. The expedition, retracing its steps to Three Forks, followed the Missouri almost to the Marias River before fear of the Blackfeet turned Ogden back to Ft. Vancouver which was reached after a year of wandering. The Snake Country Expedition opened a trading empire that was exploited by band after band of Hudson's Bay Company adventurers during the next dozen years. The Canadians, firmly entrenched, were truly lords of the Northwest.

Their secure foothold turned American traders from the Northern Rockies, as penetration there would touch off a trade war requiring greater resources than St. Louis business men could muster. The result was the first invasion of the central Rocky Mountain country where plentiful beaver and friendly Indians offered a more fruitful field for conquest. The pioneers were Major Andrew Henry who tasted the thrill of mountain life with the Missouri Fur Company, and William Henry Ashley, a Virginian whose skill as a merchant won him a fortune on the Missouri frontier. Together they organized the Rocky Mountain Fur Company in 1822 to trade along the upper Missouri, but two attempts to reach that distant region convinced them they must seek wealth elsewhere. Someone in the company had heard the Green River Valley teemed with beaver. Ashley decided to test the story by sending a small party westward.

The expedition brought into prominence two men destined to gain lasting fame in the Far West: Jedediah Strong Smith, a trail-blazing New Yorker whose explorations opened thousands of square miles of virgin territory, and Thomas Fitzpatrick, an Irish youth whose woodland skill won him a nationwide reputation under the Indian-bestowed title of "Broken Hand." With a few mounted followers they set out from Ft. Kiowa, a new post on the lower Missouri, in September, 1823. Winter found them in the Wind River Valley where friendly Crow Indians not only gave them shelter but told them of a nearby pass through the mountains. Smith was so anxious to confirm the news that he led his men out of camp amidst the bitter cold of a mountain February, reached the Sweetwater River, and turned west through the flaring South Pass gap described by the natives. By March, 1824, the party was on the Green River where the trappers turned to capturing the plentiful beaver of the over-mountain country. By June their pack horses were so loaded Fitzpatrick started back to St. Louis, leaving Smith and a few companions to continue trapping.

News of those events so excited Ashley that he decided to visit the spot himself. He started west from Ft. Atkinson in November, 1824, ignoring the warnings of friendly Pawnee who told him mountain travel at that season was suicidal. Ashley failed to discover the North Platte route to South Pass; his choice of the South Platte forced him to tramp through the rough Colorado country before he and his half-frozen followers finally stumbled on the gap. In April, 1825, they joined Smith in the Green River Valley. There an important decision faced the head of the Rocky Mountain Fur Company. Should he found trading posts, or devise some new method of securing furs? The disadvantages of posts were clear: Indians must bring their captured furs to the traders. This was something the Rocky Mountain natives showed little inclination to do, as most deserted the icy uplands for the Plains during the winter when pelts were prime while those who stayed were too haughty to search for beaver "in the bowels of the earth, to satisfy the avarice of the Whites." Moreover permanent forts aroused Indian resentment by symbolizing American occupation.

Swayed by those arguments, Ashley devised a revolutionary new trading method. Instead of depending on natives, he sent his own trappers along the mountain trails. Each spring they gathered at a central point to obtain trading goods sent by a caravan from the East, sell their winter's catch of peltry, and enjoy brief contact with their fellows before returning to the wilderness. That was the origin of the "rendezvous system." The first rendezvous was held in June, 1825, at a designated spot on Henry's Fork of the Green River. A colorful gathering assembled in that mountain-fringed valley. Eight hundred warriors with their women and children, a hundred Rocky Mountain Fur Company trappers, deserters from the Hudson's Bay Company, Spanish traders from Taos or Santa Fe—all clad in fringed hunting shirts, leggings, and fur caps. Pleasure first: whiskey in abundance, shooting matches, foot races, games, and general debauchery on a scale seldom rivaled. Then trading under Ashley's supervision went briskly on until goods brought from the East were exhausted. The leader of the Rocky Mountain Fur Company returned to St. Louis that summer with beaver skins worth $75,000.

The rendezvous system, used regularly in the Central Rockies for the next fifteen years, developed a colorful new brand of frontiersmen: the trappers who called themselves "Mountain Men." Bold, carefree, and restless; more at home amidst silent mountain forests than in the haunts of men; those heroes of the wilderness were never thoroughly happy unless wending their solitary way down some rippling stream beneath the shadows of snow-clad peaks. Each summer after the rendezvous was over, they vanished into the forest, taking only the few supplies not provided by nature—traps, tea, sugar, salt, a little pork, and flour—strapped beneath a skin tepee and buffalo robe on the back of a pack pony. Their long rifles and hunting knives supplied everything else their simple tastes required. All winter they roamed freely, trapping as they went. In the spring they drifted toward the agreed-upon rendezvous, to dissipate their season's earnings in a few days of riotous living. Then, loaded with whiskey and more supplies, they trekked back into the mountains again. Mountain Men explored every nook and cranny of the Rockies, and blazed the trails that made possible the settlement of the Far West.

They brought a fortune to the Rocky Mountain Fur Company, but by the early 1830's its palmiest days were ending as continued trapping depleted the fur supply, and fierce competition forced peltry prices down. The first competitors appeared at the 1832 rendezvous: Nathaniel J. Wyeth who came west from New England with twenty-seven followers, Captain Benjamin L. E. Bonneville with New York capital behind him and 110 traders at his beck and call, representatives of the newly formed St. Louis firm of Gantt and Blackwell, and dozens of small independents anxious to share the rich profits. None had the experience or backing needed to oust the Rocky Mountain Fur Company from its dominant position, but another intruder did.

That was John Jacob Astor's American Fur Company, which had operated in the Great Lakes country since the War of 1812. The giant organization began its westward advance in 1828 when Ft. Union was established at the mouth of the Yellowstone. Three years later, when a Hudson's Bay Company deserter with influence over the Blackfeet persuaded that traditionally hostile tribe to receive Astor's traders, Ft. McKenzie was built on the upper Missouri. In the same year its hold on the Indians was strengthened by the arrival of a steamboat at Ft. Union; the natives were so impressed by the sight of the "Fire Boat that walked on the waters" they shifted allegiance to the company responsible for the marvel. Gradually the Northern Rockies were transformed into a hunting ground for Astor's agents.

At the same time the American Fur Company moved southward into the Central Rockies. Ft. Cass, built at the mouth of the Big Horn in 1831, paved the way; a year later company traders were at Pierre's Hole in the Yellowstone country. Vainly the Rocky Mountain Fur Company offered to divide the territory; the haughty Astorites refused. For the next three years the two firms battled in the wilderness, using price cutting, free liquor, and open warfare as their weapons, with the outcome never in doubt. In 1835 the Rocky Mountain Fur Company gave up the unequal struggle, leaving the Rocky Mountain country to its powerful rival. From that time on the American Fur Company controlled the trade of the northern and central Rockies, sending out its caravans, arranging the annual rendezvous, and transporting bales of furs to its eastern headquarters. American trade was confined to the Plains region where trading posts such as Ft. Laramie and Ft. Bonneville sprang up as centers for a thriving commerce in buffalo hides.

While trappers explored the northern and central Rockies, another group of adventurers invaded the forbidden Spanish domain of the Southwest to snatch wealth from under the noses of its jealous defenders. Some who braved Spanish wrath sought furs from the tribesmen of the southern Plains and Rockies. They began moving out along the Arkansas and Canadian rivers just before the War of 1812, with Manuel Lisa and Auguste Chouteau in the van, but not until the postwar years did trade assume sizable proportions. Its principal organizer was Jules de Mun, a St. Louis merchant, who led parties of trappers into the upper Rio Grande Valley of

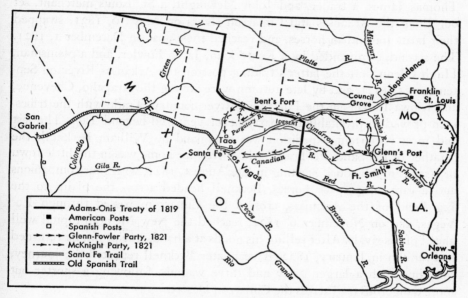

The Southern Traders' Frontier

New Mexico in 1816 and 1817, before Spain's aroused officials rallied to protect their borderland. De Mun paid $30,000 in confiscated furs to learn that Spaniards did not welcome traders from their northern neighbor.

More influential were the Santa Fe traders. Santa Fe in the opening years of the nineteenth century was a sleepy little town whose 2,000 inhabitants produced quantities of silver, furs, and mules. Its distance from Mexico—a tortuous mountain trail 1,500 miles long led to Mexico City—hampered the disposal of surpluses and doomed the New Mexicans to a perpetual shortage of manufactured goods. Direct trade between the Mississippi Valley and Santa Fe would benefit all concerned; Americans wanted furs and silver, Spaniards needed textiles, cutlery, and utensils. Why not use the short route between St. Louis and New Mexico to satisfy both? That was the ambition of the first bold traders who ventured into

Santa Fe, all unmindful of the fact that Spain's laws rigidly excluded foreign merchants. They were sternly reminded of their oversight; party after party between 1804 and 1812 was hurried off to Chihuahua jails where the members were given ample time to lament their errors. Not until the Mexican Revolution of 1820 cast off the shackles of Spanish mercantilism was the Santa Fe trade opened to frontiersmen from the United States.

News of that event was carried to the Mississippi Valley early in 1821 by traders recently released from the Chihuahua lockup by revolutionists. Three parties started west at once to test the information. One, headed by Thomas James, a trader, and John McKnight, a St. Louis merchant, set out along the Arkansas and Cimarron rivers on May 10, 1821, swapped their boats for Indian horses, and reached their goal on December 1, 1821. The second, commanded by a Kentuckian, Jacob Fowler, and a plainsman, Hugh Glenn, left the latter's trading post on the Arkansas River on September 25, 1821, and by late autumn were among the Arapaho, Cheyenne, and Kiowa Indians in the Purgatory River country. Trade with the tribesmen proved so profitable the party never ventured beyond Taos. The last and most important expedition was organized by William Becknell, the "Father of the Santa Fe Trail," whose frontier home was in the little town of Franklin, Missouri. Starting in late August, 1821, with four companions and a caravan of pack horses, Becknell headed across the plains to the Big Bend of the Arkansas, crossed the Cimarron, passed through Los Vegas, and on November 6, 1821, reached the New Mexican capital well ahead of his rivals. After selling his goods at a handsome profit, he returned to Franklin in January, 1822. A year later Becknell repeated the journey, this time with a larger party and three wagons, following a shorter but more dangerous trail across the Cimarron Desert.

The first successful expeditions encouraged so many imitators that by 1824 the Santa Fe trade was well established. Eighty men, with 25 wagons, 150 pack horses, and $30,000 worth of goods, made the journey that year, returning safely with silver and furs worth $190,000. Such profits encouraged imitation; each year thereafter the number of traders and the volume of trade rose steadily. At the same time a demand for government protection resulted in a commission to mark out the trail and arrange treaties with the Osage and Kansa Indians guaranteeing caravans immunity from attack. When the Comanche and Kiowa, who refused to sign, raided a trading party in 1828, troops were sent to accompany the caravans across the plains. Until 1830, when congressional economy ended military escorts, the road to Santa Fe was comparatively safe. After that the traders were forced to protect themselves.

Turning to the task with typical frontier ingenuity, they soon developed the methods which elevated the Santa Fe trade into a thriving business. Each spring traders gathered at Independence, Missouri, a town founded in 1827 after Franklin was washed away by a shift in the Missouri's channel. For a month all was bustle in the tiny community—steamboats unloading, wagons rumbling through the dirt streets, traders haggling with local merchants over the price of goods. As soon as the grass turned green heavy Conestoga wagons began pulling out of Independence, each carrying some two tons of merchandise and pulled by five or six span of oxen under a colorful crew of mule skinners and bullwhackers clad in the leather jackets, flannel shirts, and blue jeans affected by plainsmen. The 150 mile journey to the Neosho River was made haphazardly. Beneath the towering hickory trees of Council Grove they prepared for the dangerous Indian country ahead. One seasoned trader was chosen captain by popular vote. He divided the wagons into four groups, each under a lieutenant familiar with the procedure the caravan must follow. All traders were sworn to obey the elected leaders unquestioningly.

The organization completed, the expedition set out about May 1 in a mile-long column that wound slowly south and west toward the Big Bend of the Arkansas. Ahead rode scouts, ready to signal the captain at the first hint of Indian "sign." If this indicated marauding bands were near, the leader ordered the wagons into four parallel columns, with lieutenants in charge of each. Then they were safe from any attack; if raiders approached the vehicles quickly formed a hollow square that no Indian war party could penetrate. Thus they marched at the rate of fifteen miles a day; across the Arkansas, over the desolate sixty-mile stretch of Cimarron Desert where Comanche and Kiowa lurked, through northern New Mexico, until the adobe houses of Santa Fe were sighted. Immediately all order was forgotten as each wagoner whipped up his mules for a mad race to the town's gates. Within the New Mexican capital there was equal excitement, for the coming of *los Americanos* was the one event that broke the slumbering village's placid calm. Tavern keepers rushed to prepare beverages for parched wagoners, senoritas arrayed themselves in attractive garments, and every citizen who could walk or crawl crowded into the crooked streets to welcome the arrivals. All was bedlam during the next few days, as dress goods, shawls, cutlery, guns, pans, beaver skins, mules, Spanish dollars, and silver bullion changed hands. Then the traders started back along the nine-hundred-mile trail to Independence and peace descended once more. Each year, from 1830 until 1844 when Mexico closed Santa Fe to Americans, those scenes were repeated.

The Santa Fe trade was never particularly important to the American economy; the value of merchandize carried to New Mexico rarely exceeded

$130,000 and the number of persons involved was seldom more than eighty. Nevertheless the trade played a vital role in the advance of the frontier. The traders taught immigrants a safe and practical means of crossing the plains in wagon trains, provided the Mississippi Valley with needed specie, and brought back word of Mexico's feeble hold on her northern provinces. The pioneers who moved into Texas, New Mexico, and California risked conflict with the Mexicans because they were convinced little effort was needed to add the Southwest to the United States. Moreover the Santa Fe traders called attention to the possibility of trade with Indians whose villages bordered New Mexico. As early as 1828 three frontiersmen—Ceran St. Vrain, Charles Bent, and William Bent—built an adobe fortress, equipped with homes, warehouses, and an icehouse, on the upper Arkansas River. For the next fifteen years Bent's Fort dominated the trade of the Colorado country.

In the 1840's, when Santa Fe was closed to Americans and beaver diminishing in the central and northern Rockies, the day of the trader drew to a close. By that time Mountain Men and sun-darkened plainsmen had played their role. They deprived the red men of self-sufficiency by accustoming them to white men's goods. They found South Pass, and discovered such important highways as the Snake River route to Oregon, the Humboldt River trail to California and the Gila River road to the Southwest. They brought back word of fertile valleys hidden beyond the mountains, of distant grasslands where cattle could be fattened, of tempting lands weakly held by inefficient neighbors. The traders opened the gates of the West to settlers who soon followed their trails across the continent.

# CHAPTER XXIII

# The Mississippi Valley Frontier

## 1803-1840

The pioneer farmers who followed the traders into the Far West came largely from the Mississippi Valley frontier. There, in the tier of states bordering the Father of Waters, lived a hardier crew of frontiersmen than could be found elsewhere in the United States. Rich in experience but poor in cash, toughened by a rough-and-tumble environment where each man's revolver or bowie knife made the law, indoctrinated with a restlessness inherited from generations of pioneering forefathers, they made ideal colonizers. Between 1825 and 1845 they elbowed their way into Texas, peopled the lush valleys of Oregon, settled the forbidding wastes of the Great Basin, and muscled into Spanish California in such numbers the Mexican War only climaxed an annexation movement well under way. Their life in the Mississippi Valley endowed them with the bumptious arrogance, the perpetual wanderlust, the awe-inspiring strength which allowed them to play a leading role in the history of American expansion.

Adventurous pioneers drifted into the area just west of the Father of Waters as soon as the Louisiana Purchase opened the way. The southern portion, set aside as the Territory of Orleans in 1804, filled first, for there the nucleus of French settlement about New Orleans promised attractive economic opportunities. Ten thousand immigrants arrived during the next two years, 4,000 more between 1807 and 1809, many of them French refugees from the war-torn West Indies. When the census of 1810 showed that the population justified statehood, Congress gave its blessing over New England's protests and in April, 1812, Louisiana entered the Union.

The 75,000 planters and merchants whose homes dotted the new commonwealth lived lives unlike those of other frontiersmen. Louisiana's so-

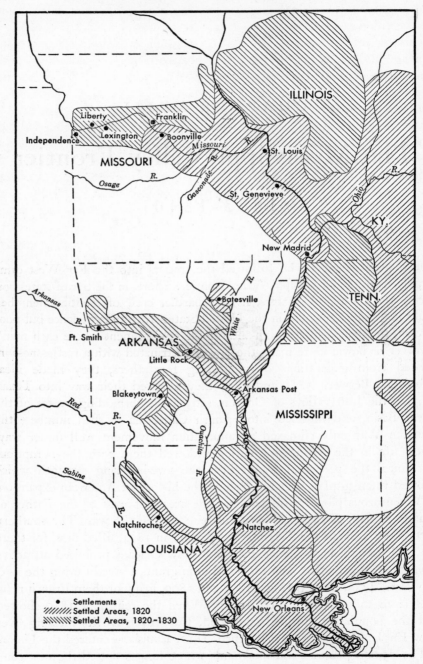

The Southern Mississippi Valley Frontier, 1815-1830

cial traditions were deeply rooted in the region's French and Spanish heritage. New Orleans, growing rapidly as trade down the Mississippi increased, set the pattern for all the state. There devout Catholics paid homage in imposing cathedrals which towered above iron-balconied homes, clumsy two-wheeled carts rumbled through dusty streets, hucksters shouted their wares from the public square in a medley of tongues, merchants in Parisian styles rubbed elbows with leather-clad traders, and riotous festivals enlivened existence in a way unknown to inhibited Americans. Beyond New Orleans were the plantations where slave laborers produced cotton, sugar, and other semitropical produce. By 1812 cleared fields extended along the Mississippi to the northern boundary, up the Red River as far as Natchitoches, and northward on either side of the Ouachita River. Eight years later 153,000 people lived in the state, which was thoroughly settled except for a few northern and western areas.

Outside of Louisiana progress was slower. The region was set aside in 1812 as the Territory of Missouri, but aside from the cluster of French towns about St. Louis and St. Genevieve few settlers lived there. The lag was partly due to the isolation of Missouri; the agricultural frontier was so far east of the Mississippi that only the boldest pioneers would hurdle a pathless wilderness to seek such distant lands. Partly responsible also was the ownership of Arkansas and Missouri by Indians until just before the War of 1812. Their removal proved easy, as most natives had followed the buffalo herds westward to the Great Plains. The Osage surrendered their claims to Missouri and the northern half of Arkansas in 1808, while in 1817 the Quapaw Indians ceded the remainder of Arkansas together with a strip between the Arkansas and Red rivers in Oklahoma. All of Arkansas and Missouri were open to settlement.

Missouri felt the impact of immigration first in the period of prosperity following the War of 1812. By that time the eastern agriculture frontier touched the Mississippi in Kentucky and Illinois, the Indians were cowed into submission, and tales of rich Missouri Valley lands were reaching the older settlements. Farmers came with a rush between 1815 and 1819; every day from thirty to fifty wagons loaded with homeseekers waited to cross the Mississippi at St. Louis. Most sought farms along the Missouri River where Boonville and Franklin were laid out in 1817, each with nearly a thousand settlers. Others ascended the tributaries of the Big Muddy—the Gasconade and Osage rivers—to stake claims on the lower reaches of those streams. By 1820 an eighty-mile-wide strip along the Mississippi was settled and an arm of advancing population followed the Missouri half way across the territory.

The influx aroused the usual demands for statehood. Congress responded as soon as the census of 1820 showed sufficient population and the Missouri Compromise settled the troublesome slavery issue. Missouri entered the Union in August, 1821, with its golden era just ahead. Each year the tide of immigration grew larger, attracted by the rising prosperity of the frontier state. The trade of all the Far West centered in Missouri; there caravans of covered wagons or river barges were formed to make their way to Three Forks, South Pass, and Santa Fe. Merchants were needed to supply traders with merchandise, farmers to feed both merchants and traders. The expanding market for agricultural produce attracted settlers whose westward advance along the Missouri Valley was marked by the founding of new towns: Lexington and Liberty in 1822, Independence in 1827. By 1830 all eastern Missouri was filled and settlements reached along the Big Muddy to the border.

The second state carved from the territory, Arkansas, grew more slowly. Until the War of 1812 only 1,500 people lived in the region, most of them around the ancient French town of Arkansas Post on the lower Arkansas River. During the next decade population increased steadily, as pioneers laid out farms on the rich silt beds bordering the Mississippi, or pushed up the White River as far as Batesville, the Ouachita to Blakeytown, and the Arkansas to Little Rock. The frontiersmen's insistence on self-rule led Congress to set Arkansas aside as a separate territory in 1819 when population numbered almost 14,000, an increase of 1,200 per cent in the decade. New settlers continued to trickle in. By the middle 1830's a thin line of farms extended westward as far as Ft. Smith on the territory's border and the people were thinking seriously of statehood. When an optimistic estimate in 1835 placed the population at 70,000, the territorial legislature called a constitutional convention to meet at Little Rock the following January. The resulting document fortunately reached Washington just as Michigan applied for admission, allowing Congress to dodge the slavery issue by admitting one free and one slave state. Under those terms Arkansas entered the Union in 1836.

While Missouri and Arkansas were filling with land-hungry easterners, other migrants from across the Mississippi moved into the area just west of those two states. The newcomers were driven to the frontier not by the hope of economic gain but by the bayonets of federal troops. They were the eastern Indians who, uprooted from their tribal lands, were forced to settle on unwanted reservations far from the haunts of white men. Between 1825 and 1840 they were driven westward by the national government, to establish a "permanent" Indian frontier beyond the 95th meridian. There the displaced tribesmen played a prominent part in the subsequent history of the trans-Mississippi frontier.

The concept of a "Permanent Indian Frontier," where red men would be forever removed from the path of the advancing white settlements, dawned on officials as soon as government explorers made them aware of western geography. The region west of the 95th meridian, pathfinders agreed, was an arid waste unsuited to habitation. Zebulon Pike spread the false impression first when he returned from his trek through the Southwest in 1806. "I saw in my route in various places," he reported, "tracts of many leagues where the wind had thrown up the sand in all the fanciful forms of the ocean's rolling waves and on which not a speck of vegetable matter existed." Farmers, he believed, would "be constrained to limit their extent in the west to the borders of the Missouri and Mississippi, while they leave the prairies incapable of cultivation to the wandering and uncivilized aborigines of the country." The legend of a barren wasteland grew as other explorers returned; Stephen H. Long in particular contributed to the belief with his widely circulated reports. By 1825 every literate American believed the region west of the 95th meridian to be a great, unusable desert.

Federal officials saw a possible solution to the vexing race problem in the explorers' tales. If all Indians east of the Mississippi were moved to the Great American Desert their valuable lands would be opened to settlement, friction between the two races removed, and natives protected from the sins and diseases of white men. The plan was first formulated in 1823 by John C. Calhoun, Monroe's secretary of war. He proposed to the President that the Indians of the Old Northwest, who were supposed to number about 14,000, be shifted to northern Wisconsin, the headwaters of the Mississippi, or the Plains region west of the Missouri River. The southern tribes, estimated by Calhoun to include 79,000 natives, he suggested moving to the Great American Desert west of the 95th meridian and south of the Missouri River. Gifts and annuities totaling no more than $30,000, he thought, would induce the red men to migrate, thus solving the Indian problem for all time. President Monroe laid the report before Congress in January, 1825; five weeks later it received legislative blessing.

The first step was to open the proposed reservation by clearing Plains Indians from west of the 95th meridian. That was accomplished in June, 1825, when the Osage and Kansa tribes surrendered all of Kansas and northern Oklahoma with the exception of two reserves: one for the Kansa along the Kansas River, one for the Osage on the northern boundary of Oklahoma. At the same time negotiations were begun with Choctaw and Cherokee who had been moved to Arkansas Territory between 1817 and 1820. That forested region was now considered too valuable for Indians; hence the usual pressures were applied to force the tribes to exchange their reservations for others farther west. The Choctaw succumbed in 1825, surrendering their Arkansas territories for a larger tract between the Canadian and Red rivers just beyond the 95th meridian. Three years later the Cherokee accepted a 7,000,000 acre reservation north of that assigned the Choctaw, together with a fifty-eight-mile-wide "Outlet" to the 100th

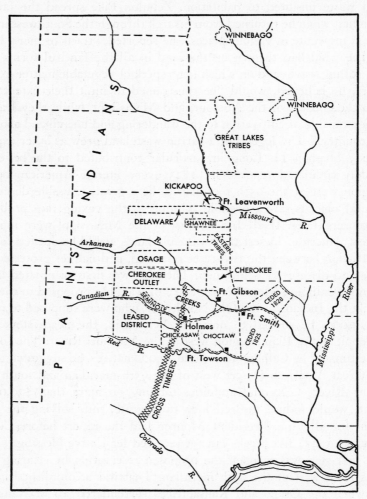

The "Permanent" Indian Frontier, 1820-1840

meridian through which they could reach the buffalo country.

For the next fifteen years the work of "persuading" eastern tribes to accept homes along the Indian frontier went grimly on. Usually agents bribed some corrupt chief into signing a removal treaty, then forced the entire clan to move west. The Shawnee of Ohio came first, to a twenty-five-mile-wide strip south of the Kansas River, where they were joined in 1829 by their old neighbors, the Delawares, who accepted a reservation on the north bank of the stream together with an outlet to the buffalo country. In quick succession other tribes of the Old Northwest—the Kickapoo, Sauk, Fox, Chippewa, Iowa, Potawatomi, Ottawa, Peoria, and Miami —were crowded into small reserves just west of the 95th meridian or, in a few instances, onto lands in western Iowa. The Five Civilized tribes of the South proved harder to uproot. The Choctaw came first in 1830 to lands just west of Arkansas; two years later the Chickasaw left Mississippi for a reservation adjoining that of the Choctaw. Both shared a Leased District through which they could reach the buffalo plains. The Cherokee followed in 1834 to occupy the territory north of the Canadian River already granted the tribe, while their neighbors, the Creeks, were assigned a large area still farther westward. They were compelled to share their holdings with the Seminole when those Florida Indians were finally driven to a strip of territory adjoining the Canadian River.

By 1840 the Permanent Indian Frontier was planted along the 95th meridian from the Red River to the Great Bend of the Missouri. In their reservations and on the Great Plains just beyond the red men were, in theory, to spend the rest of time, free from molestation by whites. Basic to the removal policy was the belief that the natives would obtain food and clothing from buffalo hunts or farming without aid from the government. Congress sought to secure them economic isolation by two laws; one in 1832 created the Bureau of Indian Affairs entrusted with the task of establishing schools and superintendencies where the red men could learn farming, the other—the Indian Intercourse Act of 1834—forbad all white men except properly licensed traders to enter the reservations. Those measures signified official determination to let the Indians shift for themselves.

Two things doomed the policy to failure from the outset. One was the inability of eastern natives to adapt to the strange environment of the Plains. Accustomed as they were to a sedentary agricultural existence in the humid East, they were unable to learn the horsemanship, nomadic practices, and hunting skills essential in the arid grassland. Just as fatal was the failure of the two groups of red men living in the West—the intruded Indians and the Plains Indians—to live together peacefully. Easterners scorned their wandering brethren of the prairies as primitive barbarians; westerners looked upon the newcomers as interlopers on lands rightfully theirs. Feeling was particularly strong in the Southwest, where the Osage blamed the intruders for the unpopular treaty that cost them their hunting grounds, and the Comanche, Kiowa, and Wichita tribes insisted that fully half the territory granted the Five Civilized Tribes was still their own. The United States, instead of being freed from Indian affairs, was not only forced to continue aiding the red men but was called upon to settle a series of near-wars which threatened to spread to the frontier settlements.

Conflicts began in 1823 when skirmishing between the Osage and the newly arrived Choctaw, Creek, and Shawnee tribes showed the stern hand of the Great White Father was needed to keep peace in the West. New forts, located strategically in the midst of the warring factions, seemed the answer. Two were established the next year—Ft. Towson on the Red River and Ft. Gibson on the Arkansas—and in 1827 a third, Ft. Leavenworth, was built on the Missouri River to control the intruded northern tribes. For the next half-dozen years those log and mud outposts stood guard over a thousand miles of Indian country, where constant efforts were needed to keep jealous tribesmen from flying at each others' scalp locks. Fear of federal troops rather than acceptance of the situation kept the hostile forces apart for a time.

In 1834 war began again, with Comanche and Kiowa as aggressors and traders and eastern Indians the victims. The secretary of war resorted first to diplomacy; commissioners were hurried west, presents gathered, and eight companies of dragoons marched out of Ft. Gibson to invite the hostile chiefs to a conference. The officer commanding the force, Colonel Henry Dodge, found the main Kiowa camp near the Washita Mountains in western Oklahoma. Skillful talk and good will engendered by the return of a Kiowa warrior who had been enslaved by the Osage convinced a delegation of fifteen chiefs to accompany him eastward. The Comanche, fearful of being left to fight alone, hurriedly delegated eight leaders to join the party. All went well until they reached the Cross Timbers, a thirty-mile-wide belt of hardwoods running across the Plains between the Arkansas and Colorado rivers. The Comanche, whose grassland habits made them wary of all forested regions, refused to go any farther. Colonel Dodge was wise enough to accept their ultimatum. The party established a headquarters, Camp Holmes, on the Arkansas River while runners were dispatched to summon the federal commissioners and agents of the Creek, Cherokee, Choctaw, and Osage tribes.

Unfortunately the American negotiators took so long reaching the treaty grounds that the Comanche scattered for their usual spring buffalo hunt before they arrived. The early summer of 1835 was spent cutting a wagon road to Ft. Gibson so that supplies could be hauled in; then the delegates settled down to await the Indians who straggled into camp during July. In all, some 7,000 natives gathered, representing the Plains Indians of the Southwest, the Osage, and the Five Civilized tribes. Negotiations duplicated those in dozens of similar meetings between the two races. In return for "a considerable supply of old flour and pork which," as one of the commissioners frankly stated, "if not consumed in this way, will be nearly a total loss," and an assortment of ornaments, knives, and gaudy gimcracks, the Comanche and Wichita accepted the eastern tribes as friends and allowed them to hunt the Plains east of Cross Timbers. Scanty as were the presents awarded the Indians, they were sufficiently alluring to bring the Kiowa, whose representatives failed to attend the conference, into line. A delegation from the tribe visited Ft. Gibson to ask similar treatment, which was accorded them in a separate agreement in May, 1837. If signed covenants meant anything, the southwestern frontier could expect a period of peace.

Yet the ink was scarcely dry on the four pages of marks made by chiefs on the Treaty of Camp Holmes before the Plains Indians grumbled they had not understood its meaning, that the presents given them were inferior, and that their hunting grounds must remain their own. Renewed skirmishing between eastern and western tribes followed, despite reminders from federal agents that the treaty was being violated; reprimands were shrugged away with the excuse that some other tribe was responsible or that younger warriors could not be restrained. Only the good sense of the intruded eastern Indians kept a major war from developing. A few battles with the brutal Comanche and Kiowa convinced the easterners that safety depended on staying east of the Cross Timbers where Plains Indians dared not intrude. The peace that reigned in the Southwest for the next dozen years was due to that practical realization rather than the success of the United States.

Despite the failure of the American government to satisfy either the intruded or Plains Indians, the creation of the Permanent Indian Frontier greatly affected the course of white settlement. All unwittingly, the government had thrown a barrier across the path of advancing southern pioneers. As Louisiana, Arkansas, and Missouri filled, the adventurers who continually sought homes on the fringes of civilization found they could no longer drift ahead to adjacent lands as their fathers and forefathers had done. Instead they must either hurdle the Indians reservation and the Great American Desert to seek farms in the fertile valleys of the Pacific coast, or forsake their native land for the alien soil of Texas. That the pioneers who invaded Oregon, California, and Texas were predominantly from the lower Mississippi Valley was due largely to this situation.

That was the case especially as no similar land shortage developed in the upper half of the valley. The American invasion of Iowa's lush prairies and Minnesota's deep forests began so late there was no overcrowding there

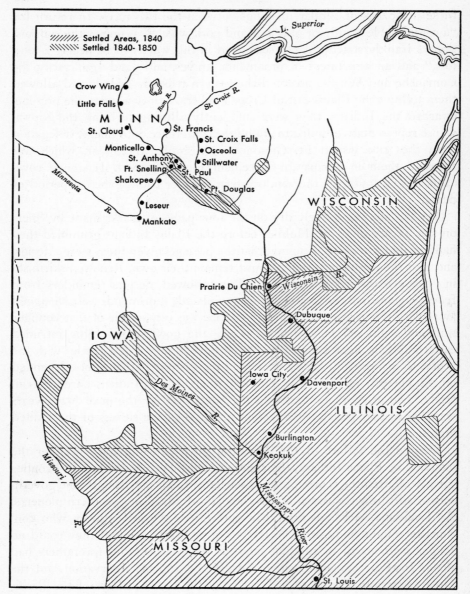

The Northern Mississippi Valley Frontier, 1830-1850

until after the Civil War. Before 1830 the whole region was controlled by native inhabitants—Sauk and Foxes along the Mississippi, Iowa on the banks of the Des Moines River, Oto, Missouri, and Omaha in the Missouri Valley, and Sioux and Chippewa in the northern wilds of Minnesota. Only whites able to win permission from the Indians could enter. Most prominent among the few who did was an ingratiating Frenchman, Julian Dubuque, who for twenty-two years before his death in 1810 commanded a colony of farmers and lead miners at the site of the Iowa city bearing his name. During the next twenty years only a handful of squatters managed to slip into the forbidden territory. Any mass invasion was impossible; miners who tried to exploit Dubuque's old lead mines in 1830 were rudely driven out by federal troops.

By that time the half-million people living in the adjacent states of Illinois, Missouri, and Indiana were demanding that the United States open Iowa to settlement. That their pleas did not fall on deaf ears was demonstrated in 1832 when the defeat of Chief Black Hawk and his Sauk followers gave the federal government a chance to act. Representatives of the beaten Sauk and Fox tribes were assembled at Ft. Crawford in August to learn the price they must pay for Black Hawk's audacity. The United States took a strip of Iowa land running along the west bank of the Mississippi from Missouri's northern boundary to the vicinity of Prairie du Chien. In return the Indians were granted a $20,000 annuity for thirty years, $40,000 more in the form of debt settlements, forty kegs of tobacco, and forty barrels of salt. On June 1, 1833, the "Black Hawk Purchase" was thrown open to settlement.

The rush began at once; all that summer land-hungry pioneers from Illinois, Indiana, Ohio, and Kentucky jammed the trails or waited days to cross the Mississippi on hand-rowed ferries. "The roads were literally lined with the long blue waggons of the emigrants wending their way over the broad prairies," wrote one who was moving west himself. Those arriving first staked out farms in the river bottoms where trees offered fuel, shelter, and a familiar environment; those coming later spilled out upon the rolling prairies where green grass grew shoulder high. Others made their homes in towns that sprang up at the terminal points of the Mississippi ferries: Dubuque, Davenport, Burlington, and Keokuk. No one worried that the migration began too late for extensive planting that summer; a little starvation was worth enduring for such good land. There was suffering in Iowa during the winter of 1833–34 when heavy snows drove away game counted on for food, but with the spring of 1834 hard times were forgotten as cheerful pioneers broke the sod, planted their corn, and joined in the "play parties" that signaled the raising of each new cabin.

For the next few years the migration went on, drawn from an ever widening area as news of Iowa's good land spread eastward into New England and New York. One typical estimate of the frontier's possibilities appeared in a Buffalo newspaper:

Taking into consideration the soil, the timber, the water and the climate, Iowa territory may be considered the best part of the Mississippi Valley. The Indians so considered it, as appears from the name which they gave it. For it is said that the Sioux (Sac) and Fox Indians, on beholding the exceeding beauties of this region, held up their hands, and exclaimed in an ecstasy of delight and amazement, "I-O-W-A," which in the Fox language means, "this is the land."

Little wonder, when such paeans of praise attracted immigrants, that population was estimated at 10,000 in 1836, that a new strip of territory had to be purchased from the Indians in 1837, or that by 1840 43,000 people lived in Iowa. By that time the southern half of the Black Hawk Purchase was filled and the frontier advancing northward daily.

The growth was especially remarkable in a region with neither a land system nor a government. The lack of the former did not embarrass the pioneers; they were too accustomed to the dilatory habits of Washington's officialdom to be surprised when no land office was established in Iowa until 1838. Instead of bewailing the neglect, they fell back on standardized frontier methods of acquiring land. Virtually all settlers simply marked out farms they wanted, then "squatted" upon them until the government was ready to sell. To protect themselves from speculators who might take away their improvements by higher bidding at government auctions, squatters formed "Claims Associations" in Iowa as they did east of the Mississippi. By 1840 about a hundred of those extralegal organizations existed in the territory, their members ready to eject from land sales any bidder who offered more than the minimum price for a farm occupied by a member. Those rough-and-ready methods allowed settlement to go on peacefully until the Pre-emption Law in 1841 ended the difficulty.

The problem of a satisfactory local government was less easily solved. Most settlers were law-abiding farmers, but the rough elements attracted to the Dubuque lead mining district and the "coarse and ferocious watermen" congregated about Keokuk made some law-enforcement machinery necessary. At first farmers took matters into their own hands in typical frontier fashion, forming vigilance committees, setting up people's courts, and administering harsh but effective punishment to criminals. The rude system was properly looked upon as a temporary expedient to be supplanted whenever Congress provided legal machinery. For a time congressmen refused to meet the responsibility, largely because southerners hesitated to take steps leading to the admission of another free state. In 1834 the area was attached to the territory of Michigan, then in 1836 added to Wisconsin Territory. Not until 1838 did local protests rise to such heights that the territory of Iowa was formed.

The first legislature, meeting in the fall of 1838, reflected the southern bias of its members by passing laws excluding Negroes and mulattoes from the territory, but more time was devoted to a furious debate over a site for the territorial capital. When legislators finally realized the intense local jealousies among existing villages would allow no compromise, they hit upon the device of a completely new town, which they called Iowa City. A commission selected the site in the spring of 1839, hired a farmer to plow a straight furrow a hundred miles across the prairies to the Mississippi as a guide to immigrants, and in August marketed the first lots. When the cornerstone of the capital building was laid a year later Iowa City boasted a population of twenty families.

Iowa was even more attractive with its self-governing legislature and territorial courts. So the rush went on. Little towns along the Mississippi blossomed overnight into proud cities, each boasting (in the words of a Burlington editor) of being "the largest, wealthiest, most business-doing and most fashionable city on, or in the neighborhood of the Upper Mississippi. . . . We have three or four churches, a theater, and a dancing school in full blast." Urban prosperity reflected the rapid settlement of the interior. By 1842 lands already obtained from the Indians were so well filled the government's treaty-making agencies were called into action once more, to wrest central and southern Iowa from the Sauk and Fox tribes. When the new purchase was officially opened at midnight of April 30, 1843, several thousand excited homeseekers were gathered for the first of the West's many rushes. At the deadline troops stationed along the border fired their guns into the air and the pioneers dashed pellmell forward to choice spots selected during earlier explorations. By daybreak of May 1 more than a thousand farms were staked out and half a dozen towns established along the Des Moines River. So rapidly did the new area fill that four years later the rest of western Iowa was secured from the Potawatomi to make room for advancing frontiersmen.

The migration gave weight to a growing demand for statehood. When a referendum during the spring of 1844 showed a majority in favor, a constitution was drawn up for submission to Congress. Opposition there was strong, partly from Whigs who rebelled against its democratic provisions, partly from western congressmen who insisted Iowa's boundaries were too extensive. Continued admission of giant states, they pointed out, would diminish the political influence of the West at a time when that nationalistic region was needed to hold the warring North and South together. The result was a two-year delay, while Congress insisted on contracting Iowa's size, and the frontiersmen stubbornly refused. In the end a compromise was necessary. A new constitutional convention in 1846 drafted a document which made slight concessions; Congress reduced the boundaries slightly to their present form and in December, 1846, welcomed Iowa into the Union. As a state its rapid growth continued until by 1850 its inhabitants numbered 192,212 and its corn production touched 8,600,000 bushels. Already "I-o-way" was becoming famous as "the land where the tall corn grows."

While Iowa filled, the frontier moved northward into the wilderness of Minnesota's lakes and forests. The first pioneers in that clear-aired north-land were traders whose cabins were built beneath the walls of Ft. Snelling after that outpost was established in 1819. Gradually others drifted into the primitive village of Mendota: agents of the American Fur Company, several hundred Swiss immigrants from the Hudson's Bay Company's Red River colony of Pembina, a few retired soldiers and trappers. Growth was necessarily slow, for all settlers were illegal squatters on either Indian lands or the federal military reservation about the fort. A new Indian cession was needed before the Minnesota country was ready to welcome a sizable migration. That came in 1837 when treaties with the Sioux and Chippewa gave the United States the triangle between the Mississippi and St. Croix rivers as well as a chunk of northern Wisconsin. The rush to the new frontier could begin.

The first arrivals were lumbermen, attracted by the towering stands of virgin pine and hardwood that covered all the wild country west of Lake Superior. Within a few years sawmills operated at favored waterpower sites along the St. Croix River—Point Douglas, Stillwater, Osceola, and St. Croix Falls—while gangs of Irish woodsmen cut away the forests. Another arm of the lumbering frontier advanced along the upper Mississippi River. The prize spot there, the beautiful Falls of St. Anthony, was appropriated by a fortunate speculator in 1837; within a year his mill was in operation. Others established lumbering towns higher up the river: at Monticello, St. Cloud, and Little Falls, or in the Rum River Valley where St. Francis was the leading community. Many were temporary settlements, representing a brief halting place in the northern advance of the timber frontier.

Like trappers of an earlier day, lumbermen looked with horror on farmers—prosaic individuals who appropriated lands better used for logging, or clogged streams with barges that hindered timber rafts bearing lumber to markets in the treeless prairies of Illinois or Iowa. Yet the logging camps themselves lured pioneer farmers into Minnesota by creating a demand for foodstuffs. At first supplies were brought in by keelboat, until news of high prices reached the ears of small farmers in Wisconsin, Illinois, and Iowa. They drifted in them, to till the acres cleared by foresters and sell their grain or pork to hungry loggers. Each lumbering town became the nucleus for a small agricultural settlement, with St. Anthony, St. Paul, and Still-water soon outstripping the others in size.

As growth went on, year after year, the thoughts of pioneers turned to self-government. They had reason to complain; for a time their isolated triangle of settlements was a neglected part of Wisconsin Territory then, after 1848 when Wisconsin became a state, was without any government whatsoever. A memorial praying for territorial status was prepared by a convention assembled at Stillwater in August, 1848, carried to Washington by an eloquent spokesman, and pushed through Congress in the spring of 1849. The new territory, although comprising all of Minnesota and most of the Dakotas, contained only 4,000 inhabitants, nor could more be expected so long as settlement was confined to the narrow area between the Mississippi and St. Croix rivers. The territorial government's first act was to press upon Congress the need for additional lands.

The response was gratifying. In 1851 the leading Sioux chieftains were brought together by the Indian Department, lavished with presents, and persuaded to sign away their claims to most of western Minnesota. News of the treaty, spreading like wildfire along the frontier, attracted settlers from the whole north country to the new mecca. In vain federal troops at Ft. Snelling tried to hold them back until Congress ratified the agreement; as well try to stop an irresistible force as an American frontiersman when good lands lay ahead. They surged across the Mississippi, cut roads through the forest, staked out farms, and formed Claims Clubs for protection until government surveyors caught up with their fast-moving frontier. By the end of 1852, twenty thousand pioneers lived in the new cession, and the air rang with the sound of axes or the crash of falling trees as loggers cut off the virgin timber and farmers grubbed out their clearings.

Expansion continued at an ever-increasing pace during the next few years. Some newcomers strengthened the existing settlements along the St. Croix or pushed the frontier along the upper Mississippi Valley as far as Crow Wing. Others congregated in the cities taking shape on the site of a few well-situated lumber camps; St. Paul's population skyrocketed from a few hundred to 8,000 in five years while a nearby rival, Minneapolis, laid out in 1852 on lands of the Ft. Snelling military reservation, gained even more rapidly. The mecca attracting most immigrants was the Minnesota River Valley—in the words of one pioneer "the prettiest country lying wild that the world can boast of, got up with greatest care and effort by old Dame Nature ten thousand years or more ago, and which she has been improving ever since." The fertile lands bordering the stream were rapidly engulfed by farms or towns—Shakopee, Leseur, Mankato—all little hamlets with a few log cabins and "enough imaginary public buildings, squares and streets for a moderately sized empire." In 1858 Minnesota became a state with a population that, according to the census of 1860, totalled 172,023.

Long before the last Mississippi Valley commonwealth joined its sister states in the Union, a new frontier was forming far to the westward. Its pioneers were the small farmers of Missouri, Kentucky, Mississippi, Arkansas, and Louisiana, with a sprinkling from the upper river country. Many restless drifters were ready to seek new homes by the close of the 1830's. A depression was upon them: the grim panic which paralyzed business and agriculture in the West from 1837 until the middle of 1840's. In the Southwest especially the economic picture was dark. Most of the states there, with typical frontier optimism, had backed wildcat banks or plunged recklessly into internal improvement schemes. With the collapse of 1837 they were left with staggering debts and half-finished railroads which might take years to complete. As Mississippi Valley farmers surveyed the debacle, they asked themselves why they should linger amidst such desolation. State debts meant years of burdensome taxes. The unfinished transportation facilities doomed them to another decade of low produce prices. Why not escape to better lands?

For pioneers of the upper Mississippi Valley this meant only a shift to the virgin soil of Iowa or Minnesota, but southerners faced a more difficult problem. The good lands of the lower valley were already absorbed; only the hilly Ozark Plateau and a few isolated poor-soil regions remained unsettled. Ahead lay the Permanent Indian Frontier, beyond that the Great American Desert. Their only solution was to reach the far-western country described to them by traders and explorers. Discontent, overcrowding at home, and lack of opportunity for contiguous settlements accounted for the fact that most of the immigrants who peopled Texas, Oregon, and California were from the lower Mississippi Valley frontier.

They were ideal colonizers, those bold frontiersmen who blustered their way into the lands of Spain and England during the 1830's and 1840's. Life along the Father of Waters attracted a higher percentage of arrogant, foolhardy, cocksure, lionhearted, muscle-proud, bragging egotists than could be found on any other frontier. The work they did—manning keelboats, digging lead from the Fever River mines, clearing away forests, tilling the heavy soil—was a sort that placed a premium on brawn rather than brain. The one boast of westerners was that they daily performed tasks which would have broken lesser men. So they developed a boastful pride in their strength. Throughout the Mississippi Valley every man was as good as the next and considered himself a whole lot better.

When such arrogance was injected into an already turbulent frontier society where law enforcement agencies were few the result was turmoil. All went about heavily armed, the lower classes with bowie knives or revolvers tucked in their boot tops, the upper with more dignified instruments for mayhem such as dirks and sword canes. The fights occurring daily in every community were rough and tumble affairs where the sole object was to incapacitate the opponent and no holds were barred. "When two men quarrel," wrote one shocked traveler, "they never have an idea of striking, but immediately seize upon each other, and fall and twist each other's thumbs or fingers into the eye and push it from the socket until it falls on the cheeks, as one of those men experienced today, and was obliged to acknowledge himself beat, although he was on top of the other—but he, in his turn had bit his adversary most abominably." Those who survived such eye-gouging, nose-chewing, ear-clawing battles had reason to feel proud of themselves.

They did. They were insufferable braggarts, the Mississippi Valley frontiermen. Their talk was of their skill with the rifle, their prowess in battle, their feats of inhuman strength. "I'm the darling branch of old Kentuck that can eat a painter, hold a buffalo out to drink and put a rifle-ball through the moon," one would shout, and another would reply: "I can wade the brown Mississippi, jump the Ohio, step across the Nolachucky, ride a streak of lightning, slip without a scratch down a honey locust tree, whip my weight in wildcats, and strike a blow like a falling tree." Those were the "ring-tailed roarers, half-horse and half alligator," who boasted they lived on "churnbrain whiskey and bear's meat salted in a hailstorm, peppered with buckshot, and broiled in a flash of forked lightning." They could outshoot, outride, outdrink, and outfight any man in all creation, and they could bluster their way into any man's nation with such bumptious assurance that no one dared stop them.

They made excellent colonizers, those ripsnorting, star-spangled frontiersmen from the Mississippi Valley. Respecting neither God nor man, proud of their country and disdainful of all other nations, as strong as the whiskey they drank and as brave as they pretended to be, they feared neither the redskinned "varmints" nor the white-skinned Europeans who blocked their path westward. Brushing aside obstacles as casually as they gouged out eyes or bit off ears, they carried the frontier westward in a series of dramatic moves that added Texas, Oregon, the Great Basin, and California to the United States.

# CHAPTER XXIV

# The Annexation of Texas

## 1820-1845

The quarter-century following 1825 witnessed the most remarkable burst of expansion in the history of the United States. At the beginning of the period the nation's boundaries were apparently firmly established. The southwestern border, agreed upon in the Adams-Onís Treaty with Spain in 1819, began at the Sabine River, crossed to the Red River, zigzagged westward along the Red and the Arkansas, followed the crest of the Rockies to the 42nd parallel, then turned west to the Pacific. Ownership of the Oregon country was in dispute between England and the United States, but the Hudson's Bay Company's firm hold there indicated the final settlement would be in Britain's favor. For all practical purposes, the Rocky Mountains in 1825 marked the extreme western limit of American influence. Yet twenty-five years later not only Texas and Oregon but the vast territory between the mountains and Pacific was occupied by Americans. The amazing advance was accomplished by a series of thrusts westward from the Missisippi Valley frontier. The first was into Texas.

No aspect of the American settlement of the Trans-Mississippi country has been more persistently misunderstood and misrepresented than the push of pioneers into that Mexican province. In the middle and later nineteenth century men, writing under the spell of the slavery controversy, were wont to view the penetration of Americans into Texas as part of a monstrous conspiracy on the part of the slave power to strengthen its hold upon the government of the United States by extending the area dedicated to slavery. Yet the extension of cotton culture into Texas was as natural a process as the creation of a wheat-growing empire in Minnesota and Dakota. The same inner urge which drove Missourians to Oregon in the 1840's

482

impelled them to migrate to Texas in the 1820's. In short, Texas lay athwart the westward path from Tennessee as did Iowa and Nebraska from Ohio. The American colonization of Texas was a normal and natural feature of the age-old American tradition of pushing on toward the Pacific.

That the heat engendered by the slavery issue was not necessary to attract American attention to Texas was shown by activities there long before the question of slavery became acute. By 1803 Americans were settled on the Ayish Bayou west of the Sabine; probably a few lived there long before that date. Traders and filibusters were also interested. Philip Nolan, the well-known friend and associate of General James Wilkinson, apparently traded with San Antonio as early as 1785. He was certainly engaged there prior to 1797, when Wilkinson forwarded to Jefferson "specimens" discovered by Nolan during his travels in Texas. In 1800 he led a party of adventurers as far west as the Brazos where he rounded up three hundred wild horses. On the return trip Nolan lost his life in an attack by a Spanish force.

During the next decade ill-feeling between Americans and Spaniards along the border grew apace. Adventurers of all sorts were eager to participate in forays into Spanish territory. In 1812 Bernardo Guttierez, a Mexican refugee, and Augustus Magee, a onetime officer in the army of the United States, inspired by an abortive Mexican revolution to believe Texas might welcome freedom, led a force of several hundred men deep into the province. Possessing all the characteristics of a filibustering expedition to free Texas from the Spanish yoke, the invading force attracted to it many disaffected Spanish residents and won some fleeting successes before suffering almost complete butchery at the hands of vengeful loyalists. Only a handful of the Americans returned to tell the story.

Dissatisfaction on the lower Mississippi with the Adams-Onis Treaty of 1819, relinquishing Texas to Spain, was the signal for the last filibustering venture across the Sabine. At a public meeting held at Natchez that year a force was formed for an invasion, and James Long was placed in command. Forming a provisional government at Nacogdoches, the invaders proclaimed the independent Republic of Texas, prepared to use the land to attract immigrants, and unsuccessfully sought the support of Jean Lafitte, the pirate chieftain of the Gulf coast. Upon the outbreak of the Mexican revolution in 1821, Long, in alliance with liberal leaders of Mexico, marched far into Texas, where he captured the town of Goliad. His success was of brief duration. He was soon killed and Long's Republic of Texas vanished.

Frontier disappointment at the surrender of Texas in 1819 was shared by men in high places. Senator Thomas Hart Benton, who strongly opposed the treaty giving away the region west of the Sabine, "wished to get it back whenever it could be done with peace and honor." Could he have foreseen coming events, his disappointment would have been tempered with the knowledge that even then a force was in motion which was speedily to make amends for the failure of American diplomacy. The fate of Texas, as of the entire Far West, was decided not by government officials in Washington, but by the expansive forces of the American frontier which were soon to bring the vanguard of American settlement into the northernmost province of Mexico.

The systematic colonization of Texas by Americans was first conceived by Moses Austin, whose career epitomized much of the westward movement in national life. Born in Durham, Connecticut, in 1761, Austin engaged in mercantile business, first in Philadelphia, then in Richmond. Hearing favorable reports of the lead mines of southeastern Missouri he set out in 1796 for the Spanish province, where he at first prospered in the manufacture of shot and sheet lead, only to suffer financial disaster within a few years. As early as 1813 Austin entertained a vague idea of trading with Texas, a prospect which grew more pleasing as his business reverses became more acute. In 1820 he visited the province to investigate possibilities. Upon arrival at Bexar he announced that he desired to settle on Spanish soil, that he spoke for three hundred families who wished to do likewise, that he was a Catholic and a one-time subject to the Spanish monarch. His petition for a grant of land on which to locate his proposed colony was granted largely because of his proof of earlier Spanish citizenship in Louisiana.

Overcome by exposure and exhaustion on the return trip from Texas, Moses Austin died in June, 1821, his last request being that his son, Stephen Fuller Austin, should complete his unfinished task. The son, to a much greater degree than the father, possessed the qualities necessary to carry the plan to a successful conclusion. The requisite traits, says Stephen Austin's biographer, were "deliberateness, patience, tact, ability to make allowances, diplomacy of a high order," if the settlement was to be piloted "through the labyrinth of Mexican suspicion and jealousy." A native of Virginia, Stephen Austin had been a member of the territorial legislature of Missouri and a circuit judge in Arkansas Territory. Then twenty-seven years of age, he was "well-educated for his day; experienced in public service and in business; patient; methodical; energetic; and fair-spoken; and acquainted from childhood with the characteristic social types that mingled on the southwestern border."

Taking with him from New Orleans "eight or ten" men, he set out for Texas on a tour of inspection with a view to selecting a location for the contemplated colony. He was well received by the governor at San Antonio, who recognized him as heir and successor to his father's plan of colonization.

In the course of his reconnaissance he covered the area now included in twenty-three Texas counties. Although he planned to locate his settlement in the Colorado and Brazos valleys, he requested the reservation of a substantially larger area. Returning to New Orleans, Austin bought a small ship, the *Lively*, which he fitted out with a party of settlers who were to sound the coast, land at the mouth of the Colorado, build a fort, and plant a crop of corn. Austin himself was to lead a party overland to the colony. Mistaking the mouth of the Brazos for the Colorado, the *Lively* failed to keep the rendezvous. There was, therefore, no crop awaiting the overland party on its arrival in December, 1821, with the resulting hunger and hardship which usually attended first settlements on all frontiers. Despite the difficulties, the little band that accompanied Austin to the banks of the Brazos established the first organized Anglo-American settlement in Texas.

Thus far a letter from the Texan governor was the only authorization for Austin's plan of colonization, and he apparently assumed that no further confirmation was necessary. Great was his surprise, therefore, when he learned in March, 1822, that approval by the Congress of Mexico was necessary. Although he could ill afford the trip financially, and feared for the embarrassment which his settlers would suffer through delay, there was nothing for Austin to do but to proceed at once to Mexico City to seek official approval.

However hopeful he may have been of prompt action, the political situation in Mexico, as well as customary Mexican procrastination, doomed him to disappointment. To his further surprise, instead of dealing with his request on an individual basis, the government lumped it with schemes of other American promoters then in Mexico seeking grants, and withheld action pending consideration of a proposed general colonization law for Texas and California. Displaying the inexhaustible fund of patience necessary in such a situation, Austin waited for nine months, when the colonization law was finally proclaimed in January, 1823. Thinking his mission completed, he was preparing to return to Texas when another overturn in the government occasioned further delay. In April, 1823, one year after Austin's arrival at the capital city, the general colonization law was suspended and Austin's petition was taken up for individual disposition. Soon thereafter confirmation was finally given.

Each of the three hundred families Austin planned to settle was entitled to one *labor* (177 acres) for farming, with an additional seventy-four labors for stock-raising, the whole constituting a *sitio* or square league. The provisions were sufficiently flexible to meet the needs of men with very large families and of others who merited special consideration. Austin was to found a town conveniently located with respect to the settlements. All settlers must be of the Roman Catholic faith and of good character.

During the absence of Austin in Mexico, immigrants arrived steadily in the colony, coming in response to the announcement of his plan which was published widely in the press of western and southwestern states and territories. By September, 1824, land titles had been issued to 272 men, some of whose families had not yet arrived. A census of the colony taken in 1825 showed a total of 1,800 persons, 443 of whom were slaves. Meanwhile, Austin applied for a new contract authorizing him to settle an additional three hundred families. "The conquest of the wilderness was well begun; the Indians were becoming respectful; food crops were abundant; comfortable cabins were building."

Upon Austin devolved the duty of dispensing justice and maintaining order, a task which, in view of the loose definition of his powers, occasioned considerable difficulty. Especially annoying was the problem of distributing land, which affected every family in the colony. Some settlers were disgruntled when they found they were denied the particular location they desired, suspecting that Austin was holding it for himself or a friend. Others objected to what seemed excessive grants to certain individuals, forgetting the special equipment of men with numerous slaves or the compensations earned by building gins, sawmills, and gristmills. There was especial dissatisfaction with Austin's charge of 12½ cents per acre, a purely nominal sum designed to cover the expense which the administration and settlement of the land entailed. Realizing he could not please all, Austin pleased himself by administering justice impartially.

The drafting of a state constitution for the province of Texas-Coahuila in 1827 allowed Austin to divest himself of his political powers and relieved him of the painful duty of governing his band of "North American frontier republicans." In the autumn of that year an election was authorized for an *ayuntamiento*, whose jurisdiction was to extend from the Lavaca to the watershed east of the Trinity, and from the Gulf to the San Antonio road. On February 3rd and 4th, 1828, the first legally ordained balloting in Anglo-American Texas took place, an event of little novelty to Austin's colonists with their background of political experience in the United States. "The jurisdiction of the ayuntamiento covered a wide range of subjects, including most of the functions of a modern city commission and some of those belonging to the county commissioners." The institution of the new government merely made Austin less responsible rather than less influential in the affairs of the colony. There was the "closest harmony and co-operation between Austin and the ayuntamiento, which always consulted him on matters of state or federal relations."

Meanwhile colonies and plans for colonies in Texas were being launched under other auspices. The colonization law of Mexico, an essential preliminary to any comprehensive scheme for settlement, was finally promulgated in August, 1824. It authorized the individual states, subject to certain stipulations, to dispose of the public lands within their confines and to supervise immigration thereto. The state laws must not, except with federal consent,

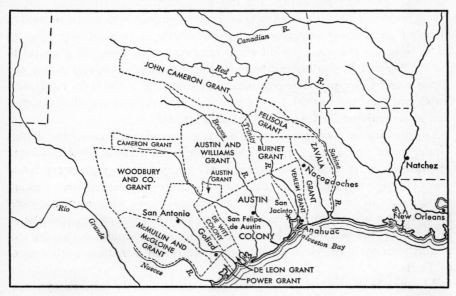

Texas in 1836

allow the settlement of foreigners within ten leagues of the coast or twenty leagues of the international boundary. Not more than eleven square leagues could be held by any one person, nor were nonresidents of the Republic to hold land.

In accordance with the provisions of the federal act, the law of Texas-Coahuila was enacted in March, 1825. It invited to the state immigrants who met the requirements of the federal law and provided for the needs of individual families and for colonies to be brought in by *empresarios*. An *empresario* must agree to establish one hundred families on the land, receiving in return a bonus of five leagues of grazing land and five *labors* of farming land. Contracts with *empresarios* were to run for six years and were void, without claim to compensation, if the required one hundred families were not settled within that period. Families brought in by the *empresario* were to receive one *labor* of farming land and twenty-four *labors* of grazing land, a total of a league, or 4,428 acres, for which a nominal payment of $30 a league was required in three installments.

Business with *empresarios* prospered from the first. Within six weeks after the enactment of the colonization law, four contracts were signed for the settlement of 2,400 families in Texas. A total of fifteen contracts were entered into by 1829, calling for the settlement of 5,450 families. Included in those was one with David G. Burnet, for 300 families, two with Joseph Vehlein, a German living in Mexico City, for 400 families, and one with Lorenzo de Zavala for the settlement of 500 families east of Nacogdoches. Those four contracts covered a compact area which seemed to offer an exceptional opportunity for large-scale settlement activities. In 1830 those *empresarios* pooled their resources with those of a group of New York and Boston capitalists under the name of the Galveston Bay and Texas Land Company. The organization planned to colonize its lands with Swiss and German settlers but its principal achievement was the introduction of several hundred American families into the area.

Of the fifteen contracts signed, not one was carried out to the letter. Under some not a single family was brought into Texas. Probably most *empresarios* entered into their agreements in good faith, with every intention of complying with the terms, but some were mere speculators seeking some means of turning the contract to financial profit without undue exertion. At least one of the contracts proved not only to be entirely speculative in character, but became the basis of a venture so fraudulent in character as to add materially to Mexican distrust of American intentions with respect to Texas.

Meanwhile Austin, whose original grant came directly from the national government rather than from the state, expanded the scope of his colonizing activities through additional contracts with Texas-Coahuila. Foreseeing the growth of an important cotton trade from Texas, he asked in February, 1825, for permission to settle another three hundred families. In support of his request he pointed out that numerous families of good character lived in the eastern part of Texas, where there was no local government and where they were unable to secure either title to the land or security against evil characters who preyed upon them. He proposed to settle those people on the Colorado and Brazos, above his original colony, where they would contribute their labor to the development of the country and serve as a buffer against Indian attacks. He also asked for a port on Galveston Bay, which he deemed essential to the successful development of cotton culture in the country. His request to settle three hundred families was granted, a figure shortly increased to five hundred. That was the first of Austin's three contracts with the state. One in 1827 called for one hundred families; another in 1828 authorized him to bring in three hundred more, a total of nine hundred families for the three contracts. Then, in 1831 he and his secretary contracted to introduce eight hundred Mexican and European families.

Strong as was the tide of American settlement moving into Texas in 1825, it would have been even stronger but for the uncertainty of prospective immigrants regarding Mexico's attitude toward slavery and religious toleration. Despite Mexican opposition to slavery, Austin obtained a Texas-Coahuila law in 1828 recognizing labor contracts in which the immigrant, after liberating his slaves, promptly made them indentured servants for life. The question of toleration was one which Austin dared not take up in any formal way with Mexican officials. Nevertheless, a satisfactory arrangement was worked out. While Protestants were denied the privilege of worshipping in their own churches, they were not required to attend the Catholic church. Hence the problem of religion bulked larger in the mind of the would-be than the actual settler.

It was not surprising that pioneers going to Texas should turn to Austin's colony rather than those promoted by other *empresarios*. His settlement was well established. He had demonstrated his ability to get along with Mexican officialdom. His settlers had received title to the land and were conquering the wilderness. They had solved the problem of maintaining security from Indian attack, and advanced beyond the primitive stage of pioneering to that where at least a rude comfort was to be had. Controversies with other *empresarios* over contracts merely stressed to potential emigrants the comparative tranquility prevailing in Austin's zone of settlement. Furthermore "Austin's boundaries included the fairest part of the Province then known—land of exhaustless fertility, abundantly watered and accessible to the sea, timber and prairie interspersed in convenient proportions, and a well-nigh perfect climate for eight months of the year, with the unpleasant heat of the remaining four tempered by the steady breeze from the Gulf. All who visited Texas and returned to the United States advertised its superior natural advantages, and men who had themselves no intentions of emigrating wrote Austin for reliable information which they might detail to others."

The steady growth of Austin's colonies was indicated by the increase in population from 2,021 in March, 1828, to 4,248 in June, 1831, and to 5,660 in June of the following year. By the close of 1833 he had issued land titles to 1,065 families, including 755 in grants from the state and 310 in his original grant from the national government. The majority of Austin's settlers came to Texas from the region west of the Alleghenies and south of the Ohio, with a large number from Missouri, whose contribution to his original colony was proportionately greater than to the later ones. It was the nonslaveholder or small slaveholder from the southwest that colonized Texas during the first decade. There were perhaps a thousand slaves in Texas in 1830 out of a total population of possibly 20,000. While one man was said to hold a hundred slaves, a very large part of the American families owned no slaves at that time.

While immigrants flocked to Texas under the auspices of *empresarios*, others arrived on their own initiative and expense. This was particularly true of the Nacogdoches area in the eastern part of the province. Many law-abiding pioneers, originally destined for Austin's colony, had settled in East Texas, built cabins, and raised crops without acquiring title to the land. Along with peaceful and respectful folk of this sort were "criminals of the old Neutral Ground, Spanish and French creoles, rough American frontiersmen—and fragments of a dozen Indian tribes in varying degrees of civilization." "Such a motley mixture of races, social classes and good and bad characters has never since jostled elbows on the stage of American history except in the mining camps of California and Arizona." It was in that area and among those people that was heard the early rumbling of trouble, which gave Mexican authorities their first feeling of concern for the future of Texas.

Among the *empresarios* active in Texas in the 1820's was one Haden Edwards, who in 1825 was authorized to settle 800 families in the area around Nacogdoches. His grant touched Austin's colony on the west at the San Jacinto, and extended eastward to the "twilight zone" where lived squatters who acknowledged no superior authority. His contract required that he protect the prior rights of earlier settlers against claims of his own colonists, that he organize and command a militia to maintain order, and that after he introduced one hundred families into his colony he must apply for the appointment of a commissioner to grant titles and lay out towns. Edwards proceeded in a peremptory manner with respect to the claims of earlier settlers, placing them on the defensive by calling upon them to show evidence of title to their land. The old inhabitants replied by a petition to the legislature asking that they be secured in their titles to the coast and border reservations, and to an additional twenty-five leagues around Nacogdoches. The uproar caused by the various indiscretions on the part of Edwards forced the Mexican officials to annul his contract and order him expelled from the country. The formal charges brought against him were "falsely styling himself military commander," compelling settlers to show title to their land under penalty of having it "sold to the highest bidder," depriving certain men of lands for the benefit of others, and pocketing the proceeds from land sales in the manner of an "absolute Lord and Master of those lands."

Despite the intercession of Austin in an effort to secure an inquiry into the merits of the controversy, the affair quickly got out of hand. Smarting under what he believed to be the unfair treatment accorded his brother, Benjamin Edwards on December 16, 1826, with less than a score of men, rode into Nacogdoches, unfurled a red and white banner inscribed with the words "Independence, Liberty and Justice," seized the old stone fort, and proclaimed the Republic of Fredonia. Although the border settlers were unsympathetic, exaggerated reports concerning the rebels' strength filled them with alarm. Believing they were forced to choose between strict neutrality and flight, many fled across the Sabine into American territory.

Edwards' one hope of success lay in the possibility of assistance from Austin's colony and the United States. Austin strove earnestly to persuade the rebels to ask for leniency at the hands of the government, to restrain men in his own colony from any radical move, and to induce officials to show moderation in dealing with the insurgents. The reply of the Edwards brothers was that they would accept nothing except complete "independence from the Sabine to the Rio Grande." Austin, however, not only succeeded in preventing his own men from casting their lot with the Fredonians but raised troops who marched with the Mexican forces against the insurrectionists. The rebellion collapsed with scarcely the firing of a shot, although Edwards made further unsuccessful attempts to enlist the support of American frontiersmen east of the Sabine.

This abortive Fredonian Uprising of 1826 should have been reassuring to the authorities in Mexico. It showed beyond possibility of doubt that the great mass of Anglo-American settlers in Texas, whether within or without Austin's colony, were loyal to the government and sincere in their resolve to be law-abiding Mexican subjects. Even the turbulent elements in the "twilight zone" along the eastern frontier had frowned upon the rebels. But the real significance of the affair was lost to Mexican officialdom. Instead of taking heart and regarding the experiment in American colonization of Texas as a success, they interpreted the insignificant incident as an indication of the aggressive designs of many Americans, in and out of Texas, upon the integrity of the Mexican Republic. The affair, affording additional proof that all-too-many Americans knew "no law but the sword," was one of numerous incidents which by 1830 convinced authorities in Mexico City of the need for a more cautious policy with respect to American settlement in Texas.

Among other factors arousing Mexican fears with respect to the security of Texas was the long-standing dissatisfaction in the United States with the boundary settlement of 1819. Not only had Thomas Hart Benton and other prominent individuals expressed disapproval of American relinquishment of claims to Texas, but the Adams administration, while admitting the legality of the Red River-Sabine boundary, in 1825 and again in 1827 sought to obtain modifications which would be to America's advantage. Because of the Mexican desire to push the frontier farther to the east, the efforts were unavailing. In 1828, in order to facilitate negotiation of a commercial treaty with Mexico, Joel Poinsett, American representative in Mexico, signed a new agreement confirming the boundary of 1819. That was approved by the Mexican Congress and the United States Senate, but because of Mexican tardiness in exchanging ratifications, was not put in force. Meanwhile, Mexican representatives in Washington, exaggerating the popular interest in Texas, reported alleged American plots for the acquisition of the province and stressed an imaginary connection between American settlements and Adams' efforts to rectify the boundary.

Typical of the reports reaching Mexico from Washington was a suggestion supposedly made by Jackson in 1824 that the United States should occupy Texas and then negotiate. Regardless of the truth of the report, Mexican fears were soon confirmed when the Tennessean became President in 1829. He promptly sent Colonel Anthony Butler to Mexico with instructions authorizing Poinsett to offer $5,000,000 for a boundary west of the Nueces; when justly outraged Mexicans asked for Poinsett's recall, Jackson named Butler American minister. Butler thereupon began six years of devious and questionable intrigue which convinced the Mexican government of Jackson's determination to acquire Texas.

Contemporaneously with Butler's departure for Mexico, there began in the administration press of the United States a campaign for the annexation of Texas. Equally alarming were advertisements of a fraudulent land company which used the columns of *The National Intelligencer* to offer for sale 48,000,000 acres of land in Texas-Coahuila. Making use of an *empresario* contract authorizing the settlement of only two hundred families, the company's advertising campaign gave the impression it could convey title to all Texas to American investors. Although such activities increased American interest in Texas and augmented the tide of immigration, they helped convince Mexico its northern provinces were unsafe.

By 1830 alarmed government officials had decided to canvass the whole question of the continued colonization of Texas. The immediate occasion for the formulation of a new policy was the report which General Terán made to his government. Terán, in charge of a Mexican scientific commission, had spent considerable time in Nacogdoches in 1828, where his observations of the "mixture of strange and incoherent parts" which made up the population of the area filled him with concern. In 1829 he was appointed commandant-general of the Eastern Interior Provinces of Mexico, a position which carried with it responsibility for the defense of Texas. He submitted to his government a plan for the preservation of Texas, together with a penetrating analysis of the American method of absorbing the territory of neighboring countries.

Terán's plan for saving Texas from the Americans called for the occupation of the province by Mexican troops, the settlement of Mexicans and Europeans as a counterweight to Americans already there, and the strengthening of economic ties between Texas and Mexico through the promotion of the coasting trade. On February 8, 1830, the Mexican Minister of Relations submitted to the Mexican Congress his suggestions for a law embodying Terán's proposals. He denounced the continued introduction of slaves into Texas in contravention of the federal law of 1824, and the systematic disregard of the requirement that settlers embrace the Catholic faith. He recommended that Congress deprive the state of Texas-Coahuila of all authority over colonization, that existing contracts be suspended, and that the federal government assume complete control of all further settlement in Texas. The great objective, he asserted, should be to offset the dominance of the American element through colonies of Europeans whose language, religion, and traditions would form a barrier to their co-operation with the restless Yankees. The result was the enactment of the famous Colonization Law of April 6, 1830.

The measure was designed to prevent further colonization from the United States. "Citizens of foreign countries lying adjacent to the Mexican territory" were forbidden to settle in Texas. The further introduction of slaves was prohibited and all foreigners crossing the frontier must be provided with passports issued by Mexican officials. The precise degree of hardship which the law would inflict upon American settlers and *empresarios* already in Texas depended upon the interpretation to be given to Articles X and XI. Article X provided that "no change shall be made with respect to the colonies already established," while Article XI said that "those contracts of colonization, the terms of which are opposed to the present article, and which are not yet complied with, shall consequently be suspended." Which of the American colonies in Texas were "established" and in which cases were the terms of the contract "not yet complied with" and, therefore, subject to suspension? Under a literal interpretation all contracts, including Austin's, could be regarded as incomplete and liable to suspension. Fortunately, a rule of reason was applied under which the word "established" was construed to mean a colony in which settlement was "well advanced." In practice, the introduction of one hundred families validated an *empresario's* contract and entitled it to the protection of Article X. That interpretation saved the contracts of Austin and also that of one Green De Witt, who had already settled some 150 families. In those colonies the settlement of Americans could continue until the stipulated number of families was introduced.

Of the four major objectives embodied in the law of 1830 only one was realized: the military occupation of Texas. The plan to foster the coastwise trade with Mexico was largely unsuccessful, while the scheme for the colonization of Mexicans and Europeans never materialized. The idea of damming up the tide of American immigration worked out in a manner not contemplated by Terán. Aside from the limited movement of respectable people who moved to Austin's and De Witt's colonies after 1830, the law merely served to exclude "substantial immigrants who could not afford to violate the law, while irresponsible and undesirable squatters drifted in at will." Among those who came uninvited was one Sam Houston, who first appeared on the unsettled frontier of east Texas in 1832.

Meanwhile Terán's military policy was giving rise to popular disaffection in east Texas. Even with the most tactful commanders the appearance of garrisons at various points was likely to occasion difficulty. When authorities appointed a hopelessly incompetent autocrat to the command of the garrison at the head of Galveston Bay, at the gateway to the unauthorized settlements in the "twilight zone," they were unconsciously inviting trouble. This was an American, Colonel John Bradburn, who, in spite of sound advice by Terán, soon antagonized many of the settlers. He employed the colonists' slaves without compensation in building fortifications, incited Negroes to rebellion, and arrested for military trial several of the Americans. The latter action prompted a small force from Brazoria to march against Bradburn's garrison in June, 1832. Despite the commander's resignation under pressure and the release of the arrested settlers, a skirmish ensued between insurgents and troops, in which the latter were defeated.

The uprising was directed against Bradburn personally and was in no sense a repudiation of Mexican authority. Nor were the great majority of American settlers involved; instead they desired to prevent the spread of the disturbance to other parts of Texas. Yet the handful of insurgents who participated in the revolt must rationalize their conduct. This they did by espousing the cause of Antonio Lopez de Santa Anna, a rebellious Mexican leader then championing the constitution and laws of Mexico against the autocratic regime in control of the nation. In the famous Turtle Bayou resolutions they pledged their lives and fortunes in support of this "distinguished leader" who was "so gallantly fighting in defense of civil liberty."

Once the civil war engineered by Santa Anna reached Texas, it became necessary for the American element to take sides. The decision of the conservative group would obviously be influenced by Austin's course. He entertained a favorable opinion of the "sincerity and patriotism of the Liberal party" in Mexico and he declared that "the happiness and peace of the nation demanded adherence to the plan of Santa Anna." He emphasized that there was "no secession sentiment in Texas, no disloyalty, no hostility" to Mexico's officers except Bradburn; but there was a strong desire for separation from Coahuila.

Having identified themselves with the successful revolutionary cause of Santa Anna, the Texans were in a strategic position to state their grievances and ask for a redress of the abuses which occasioned the recent difficulty. On August 22, 1832, therefore, they issued a call requesting each of the settlements to send five delegates to a convention at San Felipe on October 1, 1832. Although Austin doubted the wisdom of the convention, the wording of the invitation was no doubt his, and it was designed to give Mexican authorities a favorable view of the movement. It observed that with the spread of the civil war to Texas, the sporadic resistance in the province had been misinterpreted. Hence the convention was necessary to enable the Texans to affirm their support of the liberal movement led by Santa Anna.

The convention petitioned for a reform of the tariff which would allow the free importation of farm machinery, furniture, and clothing for another three years. The request for the repeal of the law excluding Americans from further settlement in Texas tactfully pointed out that it merely kept out law-abiding people, without restricting the more aggressive and turbulent elements. The convention asked for a more adequate Indian policy and for the appointment of a commissioner to adjust the land claims of the settlers in east Texas. Although Austin's proposal for a memorial against abuses in local government received scant consideration, approval was given to a petition requesting separation from Coahuila. It stressed the inequality of representation as well as the dissimilar soil, climate, and production in the two areas. William H. Wharton, leader of the more aggressive faction in Texas, was chosen to present the various petitions and memorials of the convention to the federal and state governments.

Because of continued civil strife in Mexico the demands of the convention of 1832 were never laid before the government. A second convention assembled, therefore, on April 1, 1833. Among the new men in attendance was Sam Houston, representing Nacogdoches where he had arrived the previous year. The assembly drew up a provisional constitution which, curiously enough, was patterned after the Massachusetts Constitution of

1780, with little effort to adapt it to the needs of a Mexican state. A memorial was then prepared asking the Mexican Congress to approve the document. Other requests were repeal of the American exclusion clause of the law of 1830, continued freedom from tariff duties, and better mail service.

In arguing for separation from Coahuila, the convention asserted the union was intended to be only temporary, and that separation did not necessitate the assent of three-fourths of the states, which was merely Mexico's requirement for the admission of new states. Fearing the Mexican government might propose territorial organization as an alternative to separate statehood, the members agreed in advance that such an expedient would not meet their needs. Although Austin believed the convention a mistake and thought the organization of Texas as a federal territory was the logical solution of its problem, he was given the task of placing the Texans' views before the government in Mexico City.

Austin's mission was foredoomed to failure. On the most important demand of the Texans—separate statehood—the Mexican authorities were unyielding and unsympathetic. While separation seemed a natural step to the American pioneers, Mexico regarded independence from Coahuila as a preliminary to secession from the Republic of Mexico. The government was equally adamant on slavery and the tariff laws, and would give no guarantee regarding further immunity from military control. Austin's one success came when Congress agreed to repeal the portion of the law of April 6, 1830, excluding American settlement in Texas. Believing further effort useless, he started on the return trip. At Saltillo he was arrested, apparently because of letters he had written advising the Texans to form a state government without Mexican approval. After lingering several months in prison without being confronted with charges, he once more set foot on Texas soil on September 1, 1835.

During Austin's absence, the conservative element in Texas was strengthened by a number of reforms which the legislature of Texas-Coahuila instituted for the benefit of Texans. A ban on foreigners engaged in retail trade was lifted, local self-government appreciably extended, added representation in the legislature granted, the use of the English language in public documents allowed, religious toleration guaranteed, and a judiciary act passed.

The adoption of those measures could not arrest the spread of uneasiness among many in Texas, nor could it prevent the growth of a war party recruited from Americans who had least to lose in the event of bloodshed. New developments played into the hands of the extremists. Santa Anna was strangling federalism in Mexico and gradually extending a firmer hand over the states. The initial step in that direction was the appointment of a military commandant for Texas, followed in January, 1835 by the dispatch of soldiers and a collector to reopen the custom house at Anahuac. The presence of troops led to an altercation in which Andrew Briscoe, a prominent merchant of Anahuac, was arrested. News of this arrived at San Felipe just as word reached there that Santa Anna had suspended all civil government in Texas-Coahuila. Moreover the Mexican leader was marching an army northward, crushing rebellious states on the way, and would soon reach Texas! Hurriedly assembling, the Texans adopted resolutions favoring the expulsion of Mexican troops from Anahuac. On June 29, W. B. Travis, with twenty-five men and a cannon, appeared before Anahuac to demand the surrender of the garrison. The following day the commander promised to lead his troops from Texas.

Upon his return to San Felipe, Travis found strong disapproval of his actions. A meeting at Columbia condemned his course and affirmed the loyalty of the people to Mexico. Other communities emulated the example of Columbia and declared their desire for peace. But again Mexican officials played into the hands of the radical group. The military commandant ordered the arrest of Travis and others, making it clear at the same time that, with heavy reinforcements, he planned to take charge in person at San Antonio. That, the extremists averred, could mean only one thing—military rule in Texas.

A meeting at Columbia on August 15, 1835, issued a call for a consultation to meet on October 15. Meanwhile revolution began. A Mexican colonel's demand for the surrender of a cannon held by Texans at Gonzales was followed by a skirmish on October 2, 1835, which marked the beginning of hostilities. The following day a decree issued in Mexico City destroyed federalism in the nation, root and branch, thereby confirming Austin's charge of Mexican intentions. State legislatures were abolished and all state officers became responsible to the central government.

When the consultation called for October 15 convened at San Felipe, adjournment until November 1 was quickly decided upon. Austin was absent with the army when the body finally settled down to work on November 3, but, fearing the group might go "too fast and too far" he forwarded a statement of what he thought they should attempt. Thanks to a sensible presiding officer, this plan became the agenda of the meeting. Austin's first suggestion was that the consultation should issue a formal declaration of the reasons which impelled the Texans to take up arms. This, of course, raised the basic question whether they were seeking independence or merely the preservation of the federal system. Following several days of debate, it was voted, thirty-four to fourteen, to form a provisional government based "upon the principles of the Constitution of 1824." Although the somewhat ambiguously worded declaration adopted the next day avowed the Texans were fighting for constitutionalism, it could also be interpreted as a move toward independence. The convention then formed a provisional government in the American tradition, drew up a scheme for the creation of a regular army, appointed three commissioners, including Austin, to visit the United States with a view to soliciting aid, and adjourned to meet again on March 1, 1836.

Before the arrival of that date events moved far and fast. Santa Anna, with his army, entered Texas. On February 24 came a heroic message from W. B. Travis, "To the People of Texas and all Americans in the world," calling for help for his group of Texans besieged in the Alamo—the mission station at San Antonio—by the Mexican leader with a thousand men. As the realization dawned that there was no hope of saving the beleaguered defenders of the Alamo from butchery, men of all shades of opinion hurriedly concluded that independence was the only recourse. Even Austin publicly declared for separation from Mexico. As soon as the convention met a committee was appointed to draft a declaration of independence. On March 2 the committee's report, declaring the political connection between Texas and Mexico forever at an end, was unanimously adopted. On March 4 Sam Houston was made commander-in-chief of the army. The convention drafted a constitution patterned closely upon the federal and state constitutions of the United States. As about nine-tenths of the delegates were natives of slave-holding states, it was not surprising that the constitution recognized slavery. Article IX not only forbade Congress to prevent Americans from bringing their slaves into the Republic but denied Congress the power to emancipate slaves in Texas. Free Negroes could not reside permanently in the country without the consent of Congress. After providing for a provisional administration of affairs pending ratification of the constitution and election of the officers of the new republic, the convention adjourned on March 17.

Meanwhile, hostilities were progressing. On April 21 Sam Houston's Texan force defeated and captured Santa Anna at the battle of San Jacinto. Two months later the Mexican leader was released on condition that he withdraw troops from Texas and use his influence to secure recognition of Texan independence. Independence became effective with that agreement, for despite rejection of the arrangement by the Mexican Congress, Mexico was never able again to impose her authority on the Texans.

Notwithstanding his undoubted interest in Texas and his earlier efforts to acquire it by purchase, President Jackson adopted a scrupulously proper attitude once there were forebodings of trouble in the province. As early as March, 1833, his secretary of state, Edward Livingston, wrote the

American agent in Mexico, who was trying to purchase Texas, that the critical situation of affairs there made "it important that . . . negotiation on that subject should be brought to a speedy conclusion." In short, a revolt in Texas was the last thing Jackson desired, since it would interfere with his plans for peaceful acquisition. Once the revolution broke out the administration pursued a policy of strict neutrality, which, of course, was at variance with the sympathies of a large segment of the American public. That the neutrality laws were violated, and that extensive aid in American men and materials was supplied to Texas was in spite of, rather than because of, the federal government's course. On such a far-flung frontier nothing less than a substantial army could have enforced the neutrality laws.

After the defeat and capture of Santa Anna, Jackson's course was one of "watchful waiting" to see whether the Texans could maintain their independence and establish a stable government. The President's official conduct was the more notable because it was not in harmony with his private views. As an individual he favored recognition and probably desired annexation. He believed, however, that Congress should first express a view favorable to recognition and he desired to save his successor, Martin Van Buren, the inconvenience which might follow should the executive arm of the government be pledged to a course disapproved by the legislature. Jackson also privately pointed out to Texan officials that opposition of the commercial interests of the East to annexation might be allayed by Texan acquisition of California with its fine harbor of San Francisco Bay. On December 21, 1836, exactly eight months after San Jacinto, Jackson advised Congress that recognition at that time "could scarcely be regarded as consistent with that prudent reserve with which we have heretofore held ourselves bound to treat all similar questions."

By March 3, 1837, Jackson had changed his mind. Several events occasioned his reversal. Both houses of Congress, in response to a wide-spread popular desire, had voted funds for a diplomatic representative in Texas whenever the executive deemed it expedient to name one. The American minister to Mexico had arrived in Washington bringing word that another invasion of Texas was impossible. Santa Anna himself had confessed his country's inability to hold the rebellious province. Finally, if Texans were coldly disregarded by the United States, they might, by commercial concessions injurious to American business, purchase the assistance of England, which was much interested in the young republic. In view of those circumstances, Jackson, on the last day of his term, appointed a chargé d'affaires to the Republic of Texas. American recognition of Texas, coming more than ten months after San Jacinto, was considerably less precipitate than recognition of Mexico's independence from Spain.

Even before recognition was disposed of, the question of annexation arose. In November, 1836, following a Texan vote in favor of accession to the United States, the Texan representative in Washington was instructed to raise the issue. On August 4, 1837, the Texan minister submitted to the secretary of state a formal proposal for annexation of his country. Although employing both cogent argument and the threat that rejection of the proposition might impel Texas to throw herself into the arms of Britain and make commercial concessions injurious to American trade, the offer was politely but firmly rejected. The reasons, the minister explained to his government, were "party trammels," treaty obligations with Mexico, opposition of the free states, fear of involvement in a war which would be unpopular at home, and the danger of disruption of the union resulting from the raising of such an explosive issue. In the face of the avalanche of petitions against Texas which poured in from northern and eastern states, the Van Buren administration dared not waver from its earlier decision, with the result that in October, 1838, the Texan offer was withdrawn.

For the next three or four years the question of annexation was in abeyance, both in Texas and the United States. During that time the views of the administration in Washington gradually changed. John Tyler had scarcely succeeded to the presidency when his close political friend, Henry A. Wise of Virginia, suggested that he acquire Texas at the earliest possible moment. The idea was favorably received; Tyler reasoned that annexation would bring fame to him and advantage to the United States. However, because of his fear of hostility in the Senate and preoccupation with the Webster-Ashburton negotiations, he withheld public announcement of his interest, giving rise to the impression beyond the Sabine that the American attitude toward Texas was what Sam Houston described as one of "habitual apathy."

Houston, the president of the Texan republic, countered by adopting a policy of studied indifference to annexation, ordering his representative in Washington to give the impression to American officials of a growing friendship between his country and England. In view of the fact that American expansion was always considerably motivated by suspicion of English designs, Houston was playing a clever game. Nor did he need to exaggerate the extent of British interest. Britain in the early 1840's was desirous of maintaining an independent Texas as a potential market for British goods, free from the annoying restrictions of the American protective tariff. She also wished, if possible, to see Texas develop as a cotton-producing rival of the southern states of the United States. But obviously Texas could compete with the South in cotton production only with the aid of slave labor, to which England was strongly opposed. Britain had withheld recognition of Texan independence until 1840 in the hope that Texas would abolish slavery as the price of recognition. She still hoped to bring about emancipation and would use a free Texas as a base to undermine slavery in the United States.

In March, 1843, England's design to injure American slavery by freeing the Texan slaves became known to Tyler. This intelligence produced such a reaction in Washington that the Texan minister thought if the government were aroused only a little more against the British it would move toward annexation. American opinion was further alarmed when in May the New York *Journal of Commerce* reported the existence in Texas of an abolition movement, believed to be backed and financed by England. In June at a World's Anti-Slavery Convention in London further talk of a free Texas as "an asylum for runaways and a perpetual incitement to murder, insurrection and outrage by the slaves of the Southern States" was not without its effect on the administration.

The impression of British designs on Texas was strengthened by a ruse of Houston, in which he made it appear that the truce between his country and Mexico had been entirely due to the good offices of England. Both official and unofficial circles, convinced of the seriousness of British purpose, reacted as the wily Texan president planned. On September 12, 1843, Andrew Jackson, living in retirement but still the most influential Democrat in the country, put aside his earlier caution to come out squarely for annexation. Now that the independence of Texas had been recognized by England and France, he said, the United States could negotiate with her as an independent nation. He declared the nation must acquire Texas, "peaceably if we can, forcibly if we must," as a means of checkmating English plans for an offensive and defensive treaty with that country.

The administration's reaction was made known to Texas on October 16, 1843, when Abel Upshur, Tyler's secretary of state, advised Isaac Van Zandt, the Texan representative in Washington, that recent developments in Europe had presented the question of annexation in "new and important aspects," and that he was prepared to make a proposition whenever he was assured Van Zandt had authorization to receive it. On the same day Van Zandt wrote the Texan secretary of state. He enclosed Upshur's note and expressed the belief that remarks of English officials had aroused the southern states, while fear that Britain might monopolize the carrying trade of Texas "seems to have touched the secret springs of interest" among manufacturers of the North. He believed that Texas and Oregon could be combined in a way to command widespread support in the United States, and added his opinion that if this opportunity were rejected by Texas she was not likely to have another so good.

After three months of waiting Van Zandt received a reply, dated December 13, 1843, which indicated that Houston was still playing the European powers against the United States. Texas, he stated, could not afford to compromise her good relations with Britain and France by staking all on an annexation proposal which Congress might reject. If, however, Congress would adopt a resolution authorizing the President to offer annexation, the proposition would receive the immediate consideration of the Texan government. In short, Houston would accept statehood in the Union but he could not afford to gamble. He must have assurance in advance.

In January, 1844, one of Tyler's aides asked Jackson to use his well-known influence with Houston to overcome the latter's opposition to annexation. This Jackson promptly did and his letters, combined with the undoubted eagerness in both Texas and Washington for incorporation, did much to overcome whatever opposition Houston still entertained. Nevertheless, Houston continued to be cautious and, before committing himself, submitted the proposition to the Texan Congress for consideration. His message to that body contained no specific recommendation. Although admitting that union was desirable, he stressed the threat of an unsuccessful effort to the good relations of his country with England and France. In any event, he thought, the attitude of the United States should be known in advance and Texas should avoid any appearance of eagerness.

In February, 1844, Upshur sent the Texas government a communication which forced Houston to take a more positive attitude. He argued at length the advantages to Texas of joining the United States and the disadvantages of continued independence. Texas might enjoy an alliance with Great Britain but, Upshur added, "the lamb can make no contract with the wolf, which will protect him from being devoured." How much better for Texas to join a rapidly growing nation such as the United States. Such an opportunity Texas now had, for, Upshur stated, "there is not in my opinion, the slightest doubt of the ratification of the treaty of annexation, should Texas agree to make one." In the Senate "a clear constitutional majority of two-thirds are in favor of the measure." Houston, convinced by this straightforward statement, appointed a special representative to aid Van Zandt at Washington in negotiating a treaty. In March, 1844, because of unsatisfactory relations with Mexico and the resulting fear of invasion, the Texan representatives were given even greater discretion in their negotiations; they were directed to conclude a treaty at once and on the best terms obtainable. As Upshur died before the conclusion of the treaty, the negotiations were continued by his successor, John C. Calhoun.

Tyler had consistently justified annexation on grounds of broad national interest, as a measure designed to benefit all sections of the country, and a move to aid the commercial interests of the North. But Calhoun, by injecting the slavery issue squarely into the discussion, made the question a bitterly sectional one. When he became secretary of state, he found on his desk a dispatch setting forth British policy with respect to Texas. In the communication was a frank statement of the already well-known fact that England was "constantly exerting herself to procure the general abolition of slavery throughout the world." Calhoun immediately seized upon that section. In a wholly disingenuous manner he sought to make it appear that for the first time the United States had learned of England's interest in universal emancipation, and that annexation was necessary for the protection of slavery in the United States against British designs.

Calhoun's ill-mannered remarks guaranteed defeat for the treaty by confirming northern suspicion that the movement for the acquisition of Texas was a slaveholders' "conspiracy." In his message transmitting the treaty to the Senate, Tyler tried hard to smooth the troubled waters. He emphasized the benefits annexation would confer on American settlers already in Texas, on the commercial interests of North and East, on the western states by creating a market for their products, and on the South by giving it security and protection. His efforts were in vain. Added to the opposition of the antislavery elements was that of Henry Clay and Martin Van Buren, the expected nominees of their parties for the presidency. Clay's famous "Raleigh letter," appearing in the *National Intelligencer* on April 27th, opposed annexation because it would lead to war with Mexico, was not desired by public opinion, involved danger to the Union, and was not even in the interest of the South, since much of Texas was not suited to slavery. Van Buren's letter, published the same day in the Washington *Globe*, minimized the foreign danger in Texas and declared annexation was likely to involve the United States in war with Mexico. On June 8th the treaty came to a vote in the Senate. Its supporters could muster but sixteen votes as compared with thirty-five against. Seven Democratic Senators voted against it, while only one Whig was in favor.

Meanwhile the question of annexation invaded the campaign of 1844. When Van Buren's letter opposing the treaty appeared, Jackson, notwithstanding his friendship for the New Yorker, suggested that James K. Polk of Tennessee seek the Democratic nomination as a compromise candidate. Others within the party had the same idea and Polk was nominated on a platform calling for "re-annexation of Texas at the earliest practicable period." A united Democratic party was assured when Tyler, who had been nominated by a convention of his supporters, withdrew following the declaration for annexation. Although Clay was defeated because his conflicting statements on Texas proved unsatisfactory to a small antislavery minority in the North, Polk's victory was not due to support of the slave interest, but to the rampant expansionist sentiment in the West. Except for Ohio, he carried every state beyond the Appalachians.

Tyler was so determined to receive credit for acquiring Texas that, even before the defeat of the treaty, he decided his objective could be achieved by an act of Congress, which required merely a majority vote of the two Houses. Hence he promised the Texan negotiators that, should the treaty fail of ratification, he would recommend admission of Texas as a state. Naturally, Tyler interpreted the outcome of the election as a mandate to proceed with his plan. In his annual message to Congress in December, 1844, he recommended that the terms of annexation contained in the defeated treaty be incorporated in a joint resolution to be "binding on the two countries when adopted, in like manner, by the government of Texas."

In pursuance of this recommendation a joint resolution was introduced in the House of Representatives. Although it was evident that a majority favored annexation, there was such difference of opinion over details as to threaten defeat. Despite this difficulty and the strong opposition of antislavery leaders, the resolution was adopted by the House on January 25, 1845, by a vote of 120 to 98. On February 27 the Senate accepted it in slightly amended form, 27 to 25. On the following day the House concurred in the Senate amendments by a vote of 132 to 76. The resolution was signed by Tyler on March 1.

The measure provided for the admission of Texas on condition that a popularly adopted state constitution be transmitted to the President of the United States by January 1, 1846. Texas was to retain title to the lands within her borders but was to assume responsibility for the payment of her debts. With her consent, not more than four additional states might be carved from her territory. The Missouri Compromise line was applied to the new state.

Although unable to re-establish authority in Texas, Mexico had never recognized the province's independence. Too late now the Mexican government made a move designed to terminate the long-standing difficulties with the rebellious Texans. Through the good offices of the British and French governments Mexico agreed in May, 1845, to recognize their independence, provided they would not annex themselves to another country. Thus Texas was free to choose between incorporation in the American Union and recognition by Mexico in a form which would preclude admission to the United States. Texas had no difficulty in deciding in favor of annexation. When Congress convened in December, 1845, President Polk reported the province had accepted the conditions of annexation and submitted her state constitution. On December 10th a joint resolution was reported, declaring Texas a state, on a plane of equality with other states. The resolution passed the House by a vote of 141 to 56. The Senate accepted it 31 to 14. When the President signed the resolution on December 29, 1845, Texas became a state.

One of the interesting questions relating to the independence and annexation of Texas is the degree of influence exerted by holders of Texas scrip and bonds in overcoming northern opposition to the acquisition of more slave territory. During the colonization period various speculative land companies, with dubious Mexican titles to land in Texas, sold their stock to an eager investing public. From the beginning it was extremely doubtful that the Mexican government would ever confirm these claims. As the years passed realization dawned that only through the creation of an independent Texas could the titles be validated and the stock rendered valuable. Here was one source of the widespread popular support which the Texan War for Independence received in the United States.

The independent republic of Texas was conceived in debt and nourished on depreciated paper, issuing bonds and then more bonds to sustain the original ones in their sagging state. By 1845, when the debt was estimated to be from $7,000,000 to $12,000,000, bonds bearing 8 per cent interest sold for three cents on the dollar. This depreciated paper was widely disseminated in the United States, and its holders realized it would never appreciate in value until the Republic's finances were stabilized by annexation. This was an influence toward union the precise significance of which cannot be determined. Jay Cooke, the later financier of the Civil War, was during the Texas difficulties associated with a Philadelphia banking house which was heavily involved. His biographer states that "Mr. Cooke always believed that the northern opposition in Congress to the addition of this large slave territory to the national domain was overcome through the selfish exertions in their own interest of the holders of the Texas debt certificates, many of whom were influential northern men." Observers such as the New York correspondent of the London *Times* expressed astonishment that holders of Texas bonds accepted the provision of the resolution of annexation requiring Texas to assume the burden of her debt. Although the state retained control of public lands, it was believed by "intelligent, well-informed people" that not for fifty years would the proceeds of land sales more than pay interest on the indebtedness.

The holders of Texas bonds had their day in court when the Compromise of 1850 was before Congress. This measure provided for the payment of $10,000,000 to Texas in consideration of her relinquishment of territory in dispute with New Mexico. Since the indemnity could be applied by

Texas to the extinguishment of her debt, the mere introduction of the bill produced a strong upsurge in Texas bonds. During the debate lobbyists fairly swarmed about the floor. Joshua R. Giddings, who possessed the stern New England conscience of the Connecticut Western Reserve, asserted that individual members were offered $50,000 for their votes. The speculative factor doubtless played an important part in the fortunes of Texas from 1830 to 1850.

During the period of her independence Texas grew steadily in population, despite an uncertain future and the constant threat of further difficulties with Mexico. Immigration from the United States continued without interruption; in 1844 alone not less than 5,000 souls passed through the frontier town of Van Buren, Arkansas, en route to the Republic. A new German colony of from 6,000 to 10,000 members was forming, while a French colony was underway. Immigrants from Holland came steadily. By 1850 Texas had a population of 212,000 of whom 58,000 were slaves. As in 1830 the natives of Missouri, Kentucky, and Tennessee were more numerous than those from the deep South. The proportion of slave to white population was greater than in Kentucky or Tennessee, reflecting the migration of substantial slaveholders into Texas after the Panic of 1837 in an effort to recoup their fortunes. Yet of the less than 8,000 slaveholders in the state in 1850, more than one-half owned fewer than five slaves each. Texas was still in its small-farming, frontier stage, but rapidly donning the garments of civilization.

# CHAPTER XXV

# The Occupation of Oregon

## 1825-1846

While one group of Mississippi Valley pioneers advanced into the South-west to wrest Texas from its Mexican owners, another moved toward the Northwest to battle England's fur traders for possession of the Oregon country. That domain of snow-capped mountains, deserts, and forested valleys had long been an object of contention among the colonizing powers of the Old and New Worlds. Four nations—Spain, Russia, England, and the United States—claimed ownership at the dawn of the nineteenth century. During the next years the field was narrowed to two. Spain withdrew in 1819 when the Adams-Onis Treaty established the 42nd parallel as the northern boundary of California. Russia followed in 1824 and 1825 when English pressure forced the Czar to sign treaties with Britain and the United States ceding all claims south of latitude 54° 40'. Now the issues and contestants were clearly defined; English and American pioneers must decide which nation should win the region between the 42nd parallel and the line of 54°40'.

Actually the whole area was never in dispute. The United States was always ready to accept an extension of the 49th parallel Canadian boundary to the Pacific, and on several occasions offered to settle on those terms. Nor did England aspire to the whole region as far south as the 42nd parallel. Its ambition was to make the Columbia River the southern border of northwestern Canada, for ownership of the river was believed essential to control of the interior fur trade. Thus the region actually in dispute was the triangle between the 49th parallel and Columbia River. That was the "core" of the Oregon boundary controversy. Neither nation was ready to press for a settlement when the dispute first arose. Instead they signed a treaty of joint occupation in 1818. The agreement, which was to continue for ten years, was renewed in 1827 with the understanding that either country might withdraw upon one year's notice. Each was content to let the future decide Oregon's fate.

Both England and the United States rested their claims to ownership on discovery and occupation. Britain justly said her explorers were first upon the scene. As early as 1778 Captain James Cook, a famous navigator, explored the North American coast between the 44th parallel and northern Alaska, seeking the fabled Northwest Passage. Captain Cook failed to find the legendary strait, but his men made another discovery equally important: sea otter furs secured from primitive Oregon natives for a few pence sold readily in China for $100 each. That exciting news sent a swarm of British merchants into the Pacific during the next two decades, some of them independent traders, others agents of King George's Company which was formed in 1785 to exploit Oregon's wealth. The traders aroused such interest in the region that England sent another official expedition there in 1792. Captain George Vancouver, its commander, mapped the coast from San Diego to Alaska and was the first to circumnavigate the island bearing his name. Each expedition, whether seeking trade or scientific knowledge, bolstered England's claims to Oregon.

Other explorers carried Britain's flag into the Northwest by arduous overland journeys. Foremost among them was a daring agent of the North West Company, Alexander Mackenzie, whose perpetual search for new trading areas brought him to the shores of the Pacific long before Lewis and Clark crossed the continent. His first effort ended in failure when the river he followed west from Great Slave Lake veered northward to the Arctic Ocean. "River Disappointment" he christened the stream, a name changed by others with less painful memories to Mackenzie River. Three years later Mackenzie was back again, this time to ascend the Peace River, winter in the Canadian Rockies, and emerge in the spring of 1793 on the upper reaches of a river which he took to be the Columbia. Not until 1807 did a later explorer of the North West Company, Simon Fraser, prove that Mackenzie had discovered the Fraser River rather than the Columbia. This did not detract from his glory; he and his fellow adventurers who came by sea firmly established England's title to the Northwest.

The American claims were scarcely less impressive. The glory of planting the infant nation's flag on the Oregon coast belonged to two ship captains, Robert Gray and Benjamin Kendrick, sent out by a group of Boston merchants who learned of the possibilities of the China trade from the published journal of Captain Cook's voyage. They sailed from Boston in 1787, spent the winter of 1788–89 loading with sea otter skins, journeyed on to Canton, and finally completed the voyage around the world with a cargo of oriental luxuries which rewarded their backers handsomely. News of any new trade was important to seafaring New Englanders whose commerce had suffered greatly as a result of independence. A number of expeditions were immediately planned, the most important a second voyage undertaken by Captain Gray. By the spring of 1791 he was off the Oregon coast once more, searching as usual for unsophisticated Indians willing to barter bales of peltry for handfuls of gimcracks. One spot investigated appeared to be a harbor guarded by a long sand bar over which breakers rolled continuously. For eleven days Captain Gray sought a pass through this barrier; when he finally succeeded he found himself not in a bay but on the bosom of a broad river to which he gave the name of his ship, the *Columbia*.

Those pioneering efforts brought an influx of American traders to Oregon. Profits were high in the China trade; one shipowner bought 560 sea otter pelts worth $20,000 for $2 worth of trinkets, another traded a rusty chisel for furs valued at $8,000. Rewards such as those brought a stream of Yankee ships to the Pacific during the 1790's, just as England's merchants were forced to give up trade when their nation became involved in the Napoleonic wars. By 1800 New Englanders controlled the Oregon coast so completely that all white men were called "Bostons" by the natives.

American success on the sea was more than matched by British victories in the preliminary contest to occupy the interior. The vanguard was composed of fur traders. The initial advantage gained by the United States when John Jacob Astor's Pacific Fur Company founded Astoria was short-lived; after 1813 the forced sale of the post to the North West Company allowed Canadian trappers to roam freely over the whole Northwest, and from that time on Britain dominated the interior just as thoroughly as the United States controlled the coast. The advantage was increased in 1825 when the Hudson's Bay Company, strengthened by its merger with the North West Company four years before, established Ft. Vancouver on the north bank of the Columbia with Dr. John McLoughlin in charge. The English were so firmly planted in Oregon that the task of dislodging them seemed hopeless.

Still worse from the point of view of American hopes, were the agricultural establishments reared by Dr. McLoughlin about his wilderness outpost. Necessity dictated his efforts, for the cost of transporting food to Oregon was so great Ft. Vancouver could never show a profit until made self-supporting. With that incentive, Dr. McLoughlin imported herds of cattle from California, pigs from Hawaii, and sheep from Canada; built a sawmill and a gristmill; and sent idle trappers out each summer to clear fields for wheat, corn, and oats. So successful were his efforts that by 1828 Hudson's Bay Company traders not only fed themselves but produced a surplus which was exported to Alaska and California by a subsidiary corporation, the Puget Sound Agricultural Company. Those activities not only helped the British maintain their strong position but directly influenced the controversy over the region. By the time Americans arrived a thousand Englishmen were firmly entrenched on farms dotting the Puget Sound Valley—the only area actually in dispute. If possession was nine points of the law, England's position was secure and the American cause hopeless.

The United States was first made aware of the imminent loss of Oregon by the valiant efforts of a few visionary expansionists who deliberately set out to warn their countrymen. The first of these was Dr. John Floyd, a Virginia congressman. Through his friendship with William Clark, the explorer, through his cousin, Charles Floyd, a member of the Lewis and Clark expedition, and through his acquaintance with several prominent Astorians, Dr. Floyd developed an enthusiasm for Oregon which made him "The Father of the Oregon Country." On December 19, 1820, Dr. Floyd moved in Congress the appointment of a select committee to "inquire into the situation of the settlements upon the Pacific Ocean and the expediency of occupying the Columbia River." With the adoption of the motion, Floyd was made chairman of the committee, whose report has been compared, in Oregon annals, with Hakluyt's *Discourse on Western Planting* in the colonization of the New World. In the words of Thomas Hart Benton, with this report "the first blow was struck; public attention was awakened, and the geographical, historical and statistical facts [concerning Oregon] set forth in the report, made a lodgment in the public mind which promised eventual favorable consideration."

The committee's bill urging annexation received scant consideration, despite a speech by Floyd stressing the importance of the fur trade and venturing the opinion that Americans could establish lines of communication between the Columbia and the Mississippi more easily than the British across Canada. Undismayed, Floyd in 1822 introduced a substitute measure notable partly because it provided that when the settlement on the shores of the Pacific had a population of 2,000 it should become a territory of the United States, partly because the name of the territory was to be "Origon," marking the first American application of the name to that region.[1]

---

[1] William Cullen Bryant had applied the name to the Columbia River in the first edition of "Thanatopsis." He doubtless acquired the term in the writings of Jonathan Carver who in turn borrowed it from Major Robert Rogers. As early as 1765 Rogers used the spellings "Ouragon" and "Ourigon" in petitions asking authorization of the British government for explorations west of the Mississippi.

In debate upon his bill, Floyd reviewed the persistent westward push of population from colonial days by way of refuting the charge that it was fantastic to suppose the tide would continue to the western ocean. Even at the moment wagon trains were crossing the desert plains in the newly opened trade with Santa Fe, foreshadowing a new chapter in the epic of American expansion. To those who asserted that distance and the mountain barrier made certain a separate republic on the Pacific slope, Floyd replied that in 1775 Kentucky was considered "too far away even to be a part of the Union." But, if separation must prevail, it was far better that the settlers in the rival republic should be American emigrants, speaking the language and cherishing the ideals of liberty and democracy. Floyd found capable supporters from Maryland and Massachusetts, who observed that Russian activity in the Pacific afforded convincing evidence of the valuable trade of the region. They not only stressed the importance of New England whaling in the North Pacific but showed an appreciation of Oregon's forest resources then quite unusual. On the basis of intelligence received from a New England ship captain, they predicted Oregon would supply South America with lumber.

Viewed in retrospect the arguments of the bill's opponents are of greater interest than those of its champions. Floyd's fellow Virginian, George Tucker, agreed that the westward-flowing tide of population could not be stemmed. Within less than half a century "Christian churches and temples of justice" would rear themselves in the wilderness along the Columbia. But, he contended, the people on the east and west side of the Rocky Mountains would have "a permanent separation of interests." East of the continental divide the country was held together by "the strongest and most indissoluble ties." It was "Atlantic country," and its commerce must forever remain tributary to that ocean. Not so with the population which would occupy the Pacific slope, whose trade would be drawn within the orbit of Japan, China, and the Philippines. Tucker therefore opposed governmental encouragement to a settlement which must inevitably be lost to the nation. Equally discouraging were New York congressmen who painted a dark picture of the obstacles to navigation at the mouth of the Columbia, and of the "bleak and inhospitable" climate which precluded the successful cultivation of cereal crops. The "impenetrable forests of hemlock, spruce and white cedar, of prodigious size" offered a further discouragement to the settler. Passage of the bill, they said, would result in the creation either of a colony or an independent state, neither of which would benefit the United States. Colonies were valuable only to manufacturing nations; moreover the possession of colonies was abhorrent to "the principles of our political institutions."

In January, 1823, the prolonged debate on Floyd's bill came to an end in the House and a vote was taken. The proposal was lost by a vote of 100 to 61. The idea of an American commonwealth on the Pacific was still too visionary for the average member of Congress to grasp. But Floyd's failure to achieve his immediate objective should not obscure his significant role in relation to the Oregon country. It was he who first stressed the possibilities of the region from the point of view of the immigrant. And it was the pioneer farmer, drawn to the attractive Willamette Valley, who ultimately made good the American claim to the far Northwest.

If American interest and activity in Oregon were to be kept alive, it must be through the exertions of private citizens actuated by any one of several different motives. Through accounts of official explorers and journals of fur traders there was available a substantial body of information regarding the region and its resources. All that was needed was a prophet, a champion of Oregon, endowed with sufficient imagination to extract from those works pertinent facts to arrest the attention of the people.

Such a promoter arose in the person of Hall Jackson Kelley, a Charlestown, Massachusetts, teacher, who soon usurped the place of John Floyd as the nation's leading Oregon enthusiast. Kelley became interested in the Northwest as early as 1818, and probably began advocating its settlement in 1824. By 1826 he was actively urging migration through correspondence with members of Congress. In February, 1828, John Floyd presented to Congress a "Memorial of Citizens of the United States," asking for government support in establishing a settlement in the country. The memorial was from the pen of Kelley. Assuming, as did most men of the time, the legal rights of the United States to the region, Kelley evolved a plan of colonization the success of which, he thought, was assured by the varied products of Oregon's soil and waters. Hampered by no great regard for accuracy of statement, he worked assiduously through speeches, broadsides, pamphlets, circulars, and letters in Boston newspapers to make Oregon known to the people of New England.

In 1828 Kelley organized an emigration society which by 1831 enjoyed a large enough membership to be incorporated. Its purpose was to transplant to Oregon a New England town, which he hoped would become the nucleus of a new state. He would "repeat with appropriate variations the history of the Puritan Colony of Massachusetts Bay." That Kelley could easily communicate his enthusiasm and idealism to others was shown by the rapid growth of his Colonization Society. But the successful execution of the plan called for organizing ability and practical skill, which he completely lacked. His significance in the history of Oregon lies in his influence upon others less visionary than himself.

Among those influenced by Kelley's propaganda was Nathaniel J. Wyeth, a successful Cambridge business man, who saw in Oregon one of the few remaining opportunities to bring a portion of the wilderness under control, a task for which he believed himself qualified. Wyeth originally planned to unite a company of his own followers with Kelley's society, believing the greater strength secured would be an added guarantee of success. When it became evident that Kelley's group would not get beyond the discussion stage, he abandoned the idea of co-operation. To use Wyeth's own words, his plan called for the "formation of a Joint Stock Trading Company of about 50 men to proceed to the Country, without positively settling the particular business in which they will engage but to be dictated by circumstances when there (probably the fur business will be selected)." The contract binding the company together was to endure for five years. Each member was required to furnish his own equipment and pay his own passage to Franklin, Missouri. He desired "especially coopers, blacksmiths, founders, and ingenious persons of any trade" and would have "nothing to do with any persons who are not industrious and temperate men, and of good constitutions and peacible [sic] dispositions."

By December, 1831, thirty-one men had enlisted under Wyeth's banner. For weeks members of the company met at Wyeth's house on Saturday nights, to perfect plans and become acquainted. On March 1, 1832, the group assembled on an island in Boston harbor where they spent ten days inuring themselves to frontier hardships and displaying their "showy and attractive uniform suits, a feature of which was a broad belt from which dangled bayonet, knife and ax." Rounding out their equipment was an "amphibious machine" which was alternately a wagon and a boat, depending upon the side which happened to be up at the moment. This was the butt of many jokes by the students of Harvard College, who christened it a "Nat-Wyethium."

Meanwhile, Wyeth had dispatched a vessel from Boston around the Horn to the mouth of the Columbia, where his overland party expected to meet the ship. He and his followers departed from Boston, in March, 1832, travelling by ship to Baltimore, whence they proceeded by way of Pittsburgh and Cincinnati to St. Louis, where the boat-wagon was abandoned. At Independence, Missouri, Wyeth was glad to attach his party to the yearly caravan of the Rocky Mountain Fur Company, under the experienced leadership of William L. Sublette.

Wyeth's *Journal* of the expedition across the continent constitutes one of the genuinely significant documents in the history of the Far West, recording as it does the experiences of the first Americans to make their way to the west coast by the historic route later christened the Oregon

Trail. When the group arrived at Pierre's Hole, the rendezvous of the fur company, disaffection broke out among Wyeth's men, largely because they learned that Sublette would be unable to accompany them farther. Calling a meeting, at which he forbad discussion, Wyeth put the question of going on. Nine men voted to return, reducing the already depleted party to eleven. Milton G. Sublette, a mountain man, piloted them through the Blackfoot country, where Wyeth engaged in trapping with considerable success. After receiving kind treatment at Ft. Walla Walla, the Hudson's Bay Company post, he pushed on to Ft. Vancouver, where he arrived in October, only to learn that his ship and cargo had been lost. Unable to pursue his trading plans because of the misadventure of the ship, Wyeth began his return in February, 1833.

Upon reaching Boston, Wyeth organized the Columbia River Fishing and Trading Company, with a view to exploiting the salmon fisheries of the northwest coast. After persuading his Boston backers to fit out another ship, the *May Dacre,* he set out in 1834 on his second overland trip to Oregon, accompanied by Jason and Daniel Lee, leaders of the first missionary band to the Columbia River country. As the Rocky Mountain Fur Company refused to purchase the goods he had brought, he was forced to build Ft. Hall, at the confluence of the Pontneuf and Snake rivers, to store his merchandise. He reached Ft. Vancouver a day in advance of his ship. As the latter was to have arrived early to take advantage of the fishing season, Wyeth postponed salmon packing for the year. Instead he built Ft. William at the mouth of the Willamette, in the very shadow of the Hudson's Bay Company headquarters. Although Wyeth possessed undoubted business capacity, his plan was doomed to failure. The Great Company treated him kindly but checkmated his every move. As a contemporary remarked: "They preceded him, followed him, surrounded him everywhere and cut the throat of his prosperity with such kindness and politeness that Wyeth was induced to sell his whole interest, existent and prospective, in Oregon, to his generous, but too indefatigable, skillful and powerful antagonist." The company also purchased Ft. Hall, which long remained a landmark on the Oregon Trail. The activities of Kelley and Wyeth made the Columbia country comparatively well known to a substantial number of Americans, yet no permanent results of a tangible nature flowed directly from their efforts.

Far more important were the efforts of pious men interested in saving souls in Oregon. The attention of missionaries was first directed to the region early in the century. In 1821 the Hawaiian station of the American Board of Commissioners for Foreign Missions had considered Oregon as a possible missionary field. Again in 1829 an agent of the American Board visited Oregon, by way of Hawaii, and recommended the founding of missions there. Because of the distance, expense, and preoccupation elsewhere the Board failed to act upon the suggestion. The actual beginnings of missionary activity in the Oregon country resulted from a chance journey made by some Northwest Indians out of sheer curiosity. In October, 1831, four red men accompanied a group of fur traders on their return trip from the Rocky Mountains to St. Louis, where they visited at the home of General William Clark, Superintendent for Indian Affairs. There they were seen by William Walker, an Indian trader who happened to be passing through St. Louis. Walker then wrote a letter to G. P. Disosway, agent among the Wyandot in Ohio, telling him of the four Flathead Indians who had been delegated by their nation to make the long journey to inquire of negligent white men about the Bible. Walker not only described their flat heads but told in detail how members of the tribe deformed the skulls in infancy.

Actually, the Indians had not flat heads, were not all of the Flathead tribe, and had not come to inquire about the Bible. This was less important than that a wide circle of readers believed Walker's statements. On March 1, 1833, the Methodist *Christian Advocate* published a letter from Disosway in which the story of "The Wise Men from the West" was vividly told, with a drawing illustrating the method of skull-flattening allegedly employed by the Flathead nation. The publication of the letter immediately galvanized Methodists into action. Disosway had succeeded where others had failed. Where ten years of discussion by the American Board had availed nothing, where Kelley's passionate pleas had been greeted in silence, where an eloquent address of the Methodist Conference and its Committee on Missions in 1832 had produced no response, Disosway, by a single letter, had set events in motion. His letter was important not for its revelation of an alleged desire for the Gospel by the Indians of the Far West, nor for the idea that the children of the forest came a long distance in search of the Bible, neither of which was true. Its compelling appeal was contained in the story of skull-crushing. To most people the Indians' need for the Bible was an academic question, but the heathenish practice of bruising babies' heads was one which called for action.

Contributions ranging from $10 to $2,000 began pouring into the *Christian Advocate*. The influential Wilbur Fisk, president of Wesleyan University, sprang to action and called for two men with the spirit of martyrs. The Reverend Jason Lee, a Canadian-born stripling of promise, earlier befriended by President Fisk, was clearly indicated as the leader of the mission. In November, 1833, Jason Lee, with his nephew Daniel Lee and Cyrus Shepard, was about to leave New York for St. Louis when he heard that Nathaniel Wyeth had just returned to Cambridge from his first expedition. He thereupon changed his plans and proceeded to Cambridge with a view to obtaining all possible information regarding the Northwest. He not only arranged with Wyeth for the shipment of mission goods on the latter's ship, the *May Dacre*, but agreed to cross the mountains with Wyeth and his company. Writing from the Missouri frontier on April 29, 1834, Lee announced that his party had been increased to five through the employment of P. L. Edwards and Courtney M. Walker,

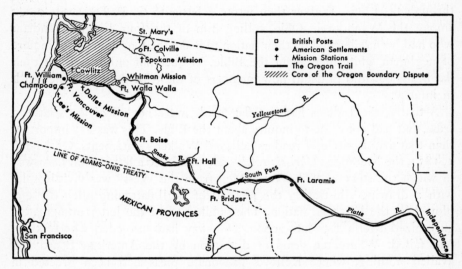

The Oregon Country

the latter not "a professor of religion," but a valuable addition because of his knowledge of Indian life.

After a not-too-difficult journey, in which they enjoyed the unfailing kindness and assistance of Wyeth's traders, they arrived at Ft. Vancouver, on September 15, where the usual hearty welcome was extended them by Dr. McLoughlin of the Hudson's Bay Company. On the 18th Jason and Daniel Lee, accompanied by men furnished by McLoughlin, departed on a tour of exploration of the Willamette Valley. They returned on the 27th, having been fifty miles up the river. Two days later they decided it was too late in the season to ascend the Columbia, and on the following day departed for a point about sixty miles up the Willamette Valley. Thus with comparatively little mental anguish was the choice made between the Flathead country and the Willamette. There was no further talk of a "Flathead Mission."

With the aid of Dr. McLoughlin, who lent them horses, oxen, cows, and calves, they built a log house near a settlement of some twenty families on the Willamette, the majority of them French Canadians with Indian wives, and most of them onetime servants of the Hudson's Bay Company who had established themselves as farmers on the fertile and attractive valley lands. The Indians in the vicinity were so decimated by fever and ague, so sickly and degraded, as to offer no very attractive opportunity for missionary effort. The mission, therefore, was dedicated primarily to the improvement of social conditions within the agricultural settlement on the banks of the river. The missionaries maintained a school, conducted religious services only imperfectly understood by the French, and formed a temperance society with which many of the men, through McLoughlin's encouragement, eventually affiliated.

This first agricultural community in the Oregon country was destined to provide the nucleus for further American settlement in the region. Although Jason Lee established a branch mission at The Dalles which became a religious station of importance, he was largely concerned with encouraging American migration to the Willamette Valley. His request for additional helpers was granted when in 1837 the Methodist Board of Missions sent out two parties with a total of twenty persons, including Dr. Elijah White, who was to become a conspicuous champion of American migration to the northwest coast. The following year Lee crossed the Rockies to the States. Accompanied by three half-breed children and two Indians, he lectured in the towns through which he passed. Although his primary purpose was to obtain funds to further his work, he succeeded in arousing a lively interest in Oregon on the part of potential emigrants. Lee also carried with him a petition, bearing the signatures of missionaries and settlers, asking Congress for legislation securing title to the lands they occupied, and for the extension of the laws of the United States over the region. The signers strongly asserted their belief that Oregon was to become a state of the Union.

Lee's tour of the East resulted in the appointment of twenty-one additional persons to the staff of the mission, of whom only five were ministers. The others included mechanics, farmers, teachers, an accountant, and a physician. Supplemented by their families, the party numbered about fifty persons and became known as "the great re-enforcement." Endowed with a grant of $42,000 for the purchase of machinery and equipment, they arrived in 1840. With a well-rounded and trained personnel, and with so much to be done by way of improving the economic life of the community, the religious activity of the mission was pushed into the background. This gave rise to complaints which led to the replacement of Lee by George

Gary in 1844, a move which was well advised. The community was sufficiently well-established to warrant the mission in concentrating upon religious work.

Meanwhile, the American Board's interest in Oregon revived. When in
April, 1833, the Reverend Samuel Parker, a resident of Ithaca, New York,
offered himself to the Board for service among the Flatheads or other
Indians, an old question was merely presented in new form. Parker's offer
met with a polite refusal, ostensibly because the Board's settled policy was
to avoid a field occupied by another organization. It seems probable, however, that this was an excuse rather than a reason, for the Board recognized
that Oregon contained many fields. Parker's age and lack of experience
were more important reasons. Moreover the Board was planning the
gradual extension of its activities, first to the Indians between the Mississippi
and the Rockies, later to the Pacific slope. Finally there was the ever-present
problem of finance.

But Parker was not to be discouraged. In January, 1834, he not only
renewed his offer, but interested the people of Ithaca in financing his
proposed trip across the mountains. This time the Board accepted, and
agreed to appropriate money to maintain his family during his absence.
Parker then enlisted Samuel Allis, a minister, and John Dunbar, a divinity
student, as associates. Due to faulty planning, his party arrived on the
Missouri too late to accompany the fur traders on their annual trip. Allis
and Dunbar occupied themselves with missionary work among the Indians
of the Council Bluffs area, while Parker, in the face of the disapproval of
his associates, returned to Ithaca, where the Board authorized him to
spend the winter arousing missionary sentiment among the people of New
York State. In the course of his winter's effort, Parker discovered the man
who was to become the most noted of all Oregon missionaries, Dr. Marcus
Whitman, of Wheeler, New York. On December 2, 1834, Whitman wrote
the American Board offering himself as a companion to Parker. Then
thirty-two years old, he had practiced medicine in Canada, but at the
moment of his enlistment was associated with his brother in operating a
sawmill at Rushville, New York.

Whitman and Parker arrived at St. Louis early in April, 1835. Proceeding up the Missouri River with the American Fur Company party to a
point near the present Omaha, an overland caravan was formed at the
trading ranch of Lucien Fontenelle. On June 22nd the trek began. Besides
Fontenelle and the two missionaries, there were some fifty other men, six
wagons, three yoke of oxen, and a large number of horses and mules. They
arrived at Ft. Laramie on July 26th, crossed South Pass on August 10th,

and reached the rendezvous on Green River on the 12th. There Whitman showed his medical skill by extracting an arrowpoint from the back of Jim Bridger. There, too, were assembled groups of Snake, Flathead, Nez Percé, and Ute Indians, who indicated their readiness to co-operate with a mission settlement in their country.

At this point it was decided that Whitman should return overland to New York for additional helpers, while Parker went on to the West with the Indians, gained their confidence, and spied out suitable locations for mission settlements. Although the latter made contacts at Ft. Walla Walla and Ft. Vancouver which ensured a friendly reception for the Whitman party when it came out the following year, he failed to return to the rendezvous with the information. Instead, he sailed for the States by way of Honolulu.

Upon his return to his native state, Whitman acquired a wife and obtained authorization from the American Board to return to Oregon on a mission to the Flathead Indians. The Whitmans were authorized to take with them another married couple and two single men. Whitman's selection of his associates was not an altogether happy one. The Reverend Henry H. Spalding was not well balanced mentally and was unable to work easily with other people. In addition, he had been a schoolmate and disappointed suitor of Whitman's wife. To make matters worse, Mrs. Spalding was an invalid, although strong of spirit. The farmer-mechanic of the party was W. H. Gray.

The Whitman-Spalding party started from St. Louis on March 31, 1836, accompanied as far as the Green River rendezvous by the American Fur Company caravan. From this point they enjoyed the protection of Hudson's Bay Company traders. Their wagon was taken as far as Ft. Boise, being the first to travel west of Ft. Hall. The expedition claimed the added distinction of being the first in which women crossed the continental divide. After recuperating at Ft. Walla Walla for a few days the party continued down the Columbia to Ft. Vancouver, where the accustomed hospitality of Dr. McLoughlin was shown them. Two mission stations were chosen in the interior of the Oregon country. One was at Waiilatpu, about twenty-five miles from Ft. Walla Walla, the other at Lapwai, Whitman going to the former, the Spaldings and Gray to the latter. Dr. McLoughlin provided the missions with bedding and clothing, allowed them to draw on Ft. Colville for grain and flour for two years, and permitted Mrs. Whitman to live as a guest at Ft. Walla Walla while her husband was preparing the mission building.

In the spring of 1837 Gray returned to the East for reinforcements, against the will of his associates. Despite misrepresentation and questionable practices on his part, of which Whitman advised the Board, the authorities in Boston decided to send additional helpers. Gray married while in the East and in 1838 returned to Oregon with his bride, three ministers and their wives, and a teacher. Of the three ministers—Cushing Eells, Elkanah Walker and A. B. Smith—the first two became important figures in the annals of early Oregon. Smith was sent to a post on the Clearwater, where he failed, while Eells and Walker established a mission among the Spokane, near Ft. Colville.

While the Methodist Church and the American Board were inaugurating the missionary movement in Oregon, the Catholics were not idle. Insofar as the Indians visiting St. Louis in 1831 were inspired by a desire for the Gospel rather than mere curiosity, it was "black robes" and not Methodist parsons they were looking for, since they had gained some knowledge of the Catholic faith from fur traders, explorers, and Iroquois Indians who intermarried with the Flatheads. The first Catholic missionaries to the northwest coast, however, came by way of British North America and in response to an appeal from French Canadian settlers in the Willamette Valley. The Bishop of Quebec appointed the Abbe Francois Norbet Blanchet as Vicar General in Oregon and the Abbe Modeste Demers as his assistant.

Arriving at Ft. Vancouver in November, 1838, they received the usual assistance from Dr. McLoughlin, who himself became a Catholic a few years later. A mission was established at Cowlitz, while services were held from time to time in the Willamette Valley in a church built by the French settlers. Their work among the Indians was successful from the first, thanks largely to the "Catholic ladder" devised by Father Blanchet. This was a graphic presentation of world and Christian history, capable of being readily grasped by the primitive mind of the Indian. Its use explains the marked success of Catholics, in contrast to their Protestant contemporaries, among the red men of the Northwest.

In 1840 Jesuits entered the Oregon missionary field when Father Pierre De Smet was sent in response to an appeal of the Flatheads to the Jesuit novitiate at St. Louis. De Smet founded the pioneer Jesuit Mission of St. Mary's in the Bitterroot Valley in 1841. Within a short time his missions had increased to six and largely covered the interior portions of the Oregon country.

In contrast with the success of Catholics, the missions of the American Board proved a grave disappointment to their sponsors. By 1841 Walker and Eells in the Spokane country had found the natives largely indifferent to their efforts. Indian interest in the schools declined and the natives lapsed back into accustomed vices and tribal religious incantations. The red men admitted a lack of concern with their souls and expressed the opinion that a good supply of tobacco would bring greater success to the missionaries. In 1847 Mrs. Eells wrote: "we have been here almost nine years and have not yet been permitted to hear the cries of one penitent or the songs of one redeemed soul." The missions at Waiilatpu and Lapwai were equally discouraging, due largely to internal dissension resulting from the incompatibility of the staff members. Gray disliked Spalding, the latter was envious of the Whitmans, no one approved of Gray, and Smith recommended the recall of Spalding. In 1842 the Board members decided the Spokane mission was the only one worth saving. They accordingly ordered the closing of Waiilatpu and Lapwai, assigned Whitman and Rogers to the northern mission, and recalled Spalding, Gray, and Smith.

Whitman, angered by this act, started overland for Boston, which he reached on March 30, 1843. There he persuaded the Board to continue the two southern stations. While in the States he also visited Washington and conferred with the secretary of war regarding the establishment of supply stations along the Oregon route for the benefit of emigrants. This was Whitman's famous trip to the East that formed the basis of the legend that he saved Oregon for the United States. Whitman returned to Oregon with the overland emigrants of 1843.

Still the missions failed to prosper. In May, 1845, Whitman expressed to the Board his doubts concerning the future of the venture. Indian apathy toward the missionaries was being transformed into outright hostility. Whitman cited his experiences as a physician ministering to the needs of emigrants and aborigines. When his treatment of measles was followed by the recovery of white children and the death of Indians, due to the latter's mode of life, the natives were convinced he used poison rather than medicine, and that this was part of a settled policy. This was the immediate background of the massacre of Whitman, his wife, and twelve other persons at the hands of the Cayuse Indians in 1847.

Had the Oregon missions of the American Board been located in the area of American occupation, as was the Methodist mission of Jason Lee, their history might have been far different. They, too, might have become the nucleuses of American settlement and influence, which would have guaranteed them success among the pioneers regardless of the outcome of their labors among the Indians. Irrespective of success or failure, however, the missionaries, almost single-handed, kept alive a degree of American interest in the region. The first American settlement in the region, Jason Lee's station in the Willamette Valley, demonstrated the agricultural potentialities of the area and turned the tide of emigration in that direction. And the propaganda of the missionaries, carried on through various channels, helped swell the tide.

Not until 1836, when the American establishment in Oregon consisted of two areas of missionary activity and a handful of settlers in the Willamette Valley, did the government take its first official cognizance of the country since the renewal of the treaty with Great Britain in 1827. In that year President Jackson sent W. A. Slacum to the Pacific coast to gather information about the area. Slacum made a careful survey of the region, mapped it, located Indian villages, studied the fur trade, visited Jason Lee's mission, and called upon most of the settlers in the Willamette Valley. His impressions were entirely favorable, while his enthusiasm for the country's grazing possibilities was especially pronounced. The settlers, however, were but meagerly provided with cattle, since the Hudson's Bay Company, although generous in lending oxen for work purposes, could not afford to deplete its own herds by selling breeding stock to the pioneers. With Slacum's encouragement, the pioneers organized the Willamette Cattle Company to import cattle from California, where Spanish breeds were plentiful. The Hudson's Bay Company, the Methodist Mission, individual settlers, and Slacum himself subscribed to the stock of the company. A delegation of settlers, headed by Ewing Young, who was thoroughly familiar with California, took passage on Slacum's ship in 1837, and brought back some six hundred head of stock. Not only did this move give impetus to stock raising, for which the valley was especially suited, but the news of it, carried eastward, helped plant the Oregon fever in the blood of many Mississippi Valley farmers.

In December, 1837, Slacum's report, the first detailed account of the Willamette Valley settlement, was laid before Congress, where it attracted much attention. Slacum strongly urged that the United States should insist upon the 49th parallel as the northern boundary, which would insure possession of Puget Sound. Thus the Oregon question was once more before Congress where it remained a subject of discussion until the ultimate settlement of the controversy.

Among those greatly interested in Slacum's report was Senator Lewis F. Linn of Missouri, who in 1838 introduced a bill providing for the military occupation of the Columbia and the creation of a territorial government for Oregon. Accompanying the bill was a report reviewing the history of American claims to the region and including interesting data, such as the crossing of the mountains by the two women of the Whitman-Spalding party. Scattered broadcast over the country at government expense, the report did much to spread knowledge of the northwest coast.

Equally effective was the petition of Willamette Valley settlers brought east by Jason Lee in 1838, which Linn laid before the Senate a year later. On the same tour Lee spoke at Peoria, Illinois, where he fired Thomas J. Farnham with the resolve to raise the American flag in Oregon. Although Farnham's westward journey accomplished little, he brought back a memorial signed by seventy settlers, praying for government protection. He also published his *Travels* which were widely read and did much to increase popular interest in the Oregon country.

Further publicity was given Oregon through the report of Lieutenant Charles Wilkes. Wilkes had been sent as commander of the government's Pacific exploring expedition in 1838. In 1841 he visited the northwest coast. One of the land parties sent out by him crossed the Cascades to Ft. Colville, Spokane Falls, and Coeur d'Alêne Lake, while Wilkes himself examined the Willamette Valley and the Methodist Mission. The latter, he was convinced, was much more interested in developing and settling the country than in saving the souls of Indians.

Although proponents of Oregon were deeply disappointed at the failure of the Webster-Ashburton Treaty of 1842 to secure a settlement of the boundary question, that year witnessed an occurrence of great significance in relation to American occupation of the area. Among the helpers sent to Jason Lee in 1837 was the Reverend Elijah White, who, because of a disagreement, returned east in 1840. Shortly thereafter the government decided to send an Indian agent to Oregon, a post for which White, with three years of experience in the field, was well qualified. He received the appointment and was instructed to take with him the largest possible party of emigrants. Through an enthusiastic speaking tour, through interviews with prospective emigrants, and in other ways, White assembled a group of 120 men whom he led successfully across the mountains in 1842. That was the first large party of emigrants to follow the overland route to Oregon.

With the benefit of hindsight it is clear that the failure of the Webster-Ashburton Treaty to solve the boundary problem offered no occasion for concern to earnest advocates of American claims in the region. For there was preparing at the close of that year an American migration to Oregon which would clinch American claims. Better, therefore, to let sleeping dogs lie than press for a settlement at that time. The correct American policy was to do nothing or, as Calhoun put it, a "policy of wise and masterly inactivity." President Tyler also foresaw that "a few years would see an American settlement on the Columbia sufficiently strong to defend itself and to protect the rights" of the United States in the territory.

A combination of factors conspired to bring about the great migration. A favorable report sent back by Elijah White from the mountains while en route in 1842, a prolonged period of hard times in the Mississippi Valley following the Panic of 1837, inadequate transportation facilities in many parts of the Middle West, and depressed prices for farm products all tended to drive farmers from the interior valley. The undoubted attractions of the Willamette Valley, made more alluring by the vivid imaginations of Oregon champions, transportation facilities afforded by the river itself, favorable markets for Oregon products in the Orient and the Pacific, and high prices in Oregon, all tended to draw men in that direction. Another factor was the pioneer instinct, the "strong bent" of men's spirits, the desire to blaze trails, to accept a difficult challenge, the thrill of opening a new country, as the long hunters had done in the Kentucky wilderness. And, finally, the Oregon fever was spread by a flood of propaganda literature: journals of traders and trappers, accounts of missionaries, descriptions of travelers, reports printed and circulated at government expense, and letters of earlier emigrants to friends back home describing their satisfaction with their new situation.

As a result there converged at Independence, Missouri, in the spring of 1843, a concourse of people who united for the overland trek. The leader of the party was Peter H. Burnett, who, in the autumn of the previous year had settled in Platte County, Missouri. He spent the fall and winter lecturing in neighboring counties of western Missouri, where hundreds of persons responded to his call. Small bands assembled also from Ohio, Indiana, Illinois, Kentucky, and Tennessee. Altogether the party consisted of about 1,000 men, women, and children, of all ages, and more than 5,000 oxen and cattle.

The march began on May 22nd. A military organization was adopted, with Burnett as captain and J. W. Nesmith as orderly sergeant. The expedition was divided into two columns, each consisting of sixty wagons. The first, or "light column," consisted of those who had few or no loose cattle; the second, or "cow column," comprised those with herds who must proceed at a more leisurely pace. Captain of the "cow column" was Jesse Applegate, one of the finest of the Oregon pioneers, who years later penned the classic account of this overland migration under the title "A Day with the Cow-Column."

For a two days' journey from Independence the Oregon and Santa Fe trails were one. Forty miles out a signboard pointed the way to the "Road to Oregon." At Ft. Laramie, where the trail left the plains for the mountain country, the emigrant had an opportunity to rest and redistribute his burden. On Independence Rock, 838 miles out, was the "register of the desert" on which family names were carefully inscribed. At South Pass, 947 miles, the pioneers crossed the continental divide through a broad valley of gentle slopes, at an elevation of 7,500 feet. Rest and repairs were to be had at Ft. Bridger, 1,070 miles from the starting point, which Jim Bridger, the famous Mountain Man, built that year to accommodate the immigrants to come. After a journey of 1,288 miles the caravan reached Ft. Hall on the Snake River, beyond which the California Trail branched off. Other milestones were Ft. Boise, a Hudson's Bay Company post on the Snake, and the Grand Ronde, a beautiful camping ground just east of the difficult Blue Mountains. After crossing the latter, the emigrants followed the Umatilla River to the Columbia, which in turn led them to Ft. Vancouver, 2,020 miles distant from the starting point.

As far as Ft. Hall the route was well marked but beyond that point it became a mere pack trail, unused by loaded wagons except the light vehicles of the Whitman-Spalding party. Finding the number of pack horses insufficient to carry families and goods to the Columbia, the emigrants had no choice but to continue by wagon. Being a large party, the men could be their own road makers, as the small parties preceding them could not. Furthermore, the 1843 caravan was accompanied by Marcus Whitman who, drawing upon his experience of 1836, was a skilled guide. Leaving Ft. Hall on August 30, they arrived at Ft. Boise twenty days later. On the last day of the month their eyes first rested upon the Grand Ronde whose tranquil beauty, after their desert experiences, elicited tears of joy. At Whitman's mission, Waiilatpu, they rested and obtained provisions for use at their destination. In late November they arrived in the Willamette Valley.

The caravan of 1843 employed the bivouac, familiar to plainsmen since wagons were first introduced on the Plains at the beginning of the Santa Fe trade. At night they drew the wagons up in a stockade or corral. In the words of Jesse Applegate the corral was "a circle one hundred yards deep, formed with wagons connected strongly with each other; the wagon in the rear being connected with the wagon in front by its tongue and ox chains. It is a strong barrier that the most vicious ox cannot break, and in case of attack from the Sioux would be no contemptible intrenchment." Bitter experience taught the members of the 1843 migration other lessons from which subsequent emigrants profited. They learned that baggage should be reduced to a minimum. The eastern portion of the trail was strewn with heavy and sometimes valuable furniture and equipment discarded because too burdensome. They discovered that wagons must be rugged and durable, and that oxen were preferable to horses as draft animals and less attractive to the Indians. Cattle from Illinois and Missouri were best because accustomed to feeding upon prairie grass. Too few tools, and the wrong type of clothes embarrassed many, especially the women.

The result was bare and bruised feet, and fine fabrics ruined by the dust and alkali of the desert. The older women adapted themselves to the requirements of the trek more readily than the younger ones, shortening their skirts to the danger point, while young ladies clung to eastern fashions. At the Snake River much of the finery went to the Indians in exchange for salmon, and the red men in their new raiment, "worn without regard to age or sex, were a costume picture only a trifle more fantastic than the emigrants themselves."

The great migration of 1843 proved a turning point in the history of Oregon. Skeptics had openly scoffed before the departure; no less a person than Horace Greeley thought "this migration of more than a thousand persons in one body to Oregon wears an aspect of insanity." Their doubts were dispelled by the news that even loaded wagons had successfully traversed the entire route. Enthusiastic letters from emigrants to the folks back home, printed in local papers, and widely copied by the city press, soon made Oregon a household word and helped swell the tide. The substantial emigration of 1844, delayed by an unduly wet season, arrived at the Willamette very late, with provisions depleted and spirits dampened by the onset of the rainy season. Their gloom, however, was easily removed in the spring by "the kindling rays of a bright Oregon Sun." In 1845 a migration of some 3,000 almost doubled the population of the country. This time there were not one, but many caravans, comprising from fifty to two hundred wagons. The journey was comparatively uneventful, except for the 150 wagons which abandoned the main trail beyond Ft. Boise in favor of a cutoff which a trader told them would save valuable time. Narrowly averting complete extinction in the most forbidding part of Oregon, the severely depleted party finally reached the Columbia after great suffering and the loss of forty days. With the accession of 1845, the population of Oregon was increased to 6,000. The vast majority of the pioneers were located in the Willamette Valley, not only because of its natural attractions but also because Dr. McLoughlin, believing that Great Britain would ultimately acquire the region north of the Columbia, had been at pains to direct the Americans south of the river. In this effort he was not entirely successful, for a few of the immigrants, not to be discouraged, settled near the later Olympia in the Puget Sound country.

Once more American pioneers on a far distant frontier found themselves in a wilderness beyond the pale of law and organized society. In view of their remoteness from the States it was unlikely they would calmly await the extension of American sovereignty over them. In such a situation frontiersmen always showed themselves capable of dealing with the situation in their own way, and the Oregon settlers were to be no exception.

Under the provisions of the joint occupation agreement, neither country could legally extend its jurisdiction over the Oregon settlers prior to a solution of the boundary difficulty. Great Britain authorized the Hudson's Bay Company to deal with minor infractions, but more serious cases were transferred to Canada for trial. American settlers were left to their own devices by the United States. Notwithstanding the uniform kindness and assistance which the American pioneers, whether missionaries or laymen, received at the hands of the Hudson's Bay Company, their feelings toward the Great Company were not sympathetic. The earliest American settlers were constantly aware of the company's hold, not only upon its retired employees settling in the country, but upon the Indians through its well-organized system of trade. This would give the company an advantage in the event of a clash between nationals of the two countries. It was only natural, therefore, that Americans should seek some counterweight to Hudson's Bay influence. This explains the memorial of Methodist missionaries to Congress in 1838, seeking recognition of land titles and the extension of American jurisdiction over Oregon. The next year proponents of the American viewpoint numbered seventy, a figure which was doubled by 1840 when a stronger petition warned against the Hudson's Bay Company. But still Congress remained indifferent.

In 1841 occurred an event which occasioned the first governmental action. Ewing Young, probably the most affluent of the pioneers, died intestate, leaving an estate which included some six hundred head of cattle. The disposition of his estate was a matter of concern to his neighbors, who met at the Methodist Mission on the day following his funeral. An *ad hoc* probate court was created with a judge authorized to administer the estate according to the laws of the state of New York. As no copy of the statutes of the Empire State existed in the settlement, the judge had to recreate the laws from his imagination. At the same time a committee was appointed to frame a constitution and code of law. With a view to gaining the support of French Canadian settlers, Father Blanchet was made chairman. The Father being unsympathetic and Dr. McLoughlin openly opposed to the idea, nothing was done.

The drive toward the creation of a frame of government was strengthened by the arrival of Elijah White's party of 120 immigrants in 1842. Further incentive resulted from the necessity of dealing with the menace of wild animals to the livestock of the settlers. This led to the so-called "Wolf Meetings," the first of which assembled in February, 1843, when a committee was appointed to consider the problem. At a second meeting on March 4, the committee's recommendation of a fund for bounties on the dead animals was approved, whereupon, W. H. Gray, one-time associate of Whitman but now residing in the valley, moved the appointment of a new committee to consider "the propriety of taking steps for the civil and military protection of the colony." The motion was carried, the committee appointed, and another meeting called for May 2 at Champoeg.

Pending this gathering a lively discussion revealed that not even all Americans were in agreement. Jason Lee, having petitioned for the extension of governmental authority over the settlement, approved action by the settlers themselves, but Elijah White counseled delay because he seemed to think he, as Indian agent, was authorized to govern the community. Americans generally, regardless of shades of opinion, sought to unite all nationalities against the Hudson's Bay Company. In this they were unsuccessful. When the meeting convened on May 2nd there was a full attendance of Canadians, who almost defeated a motion to organize a provisional government for Oregon. At that point most of the British faction withdrew. A legislative committee was allowed sixty days to frame a constitution and legal code, which were presented to the general meeting on July 5, 1843. On that day the assemblage adopted the "First Organic Law," based on the scanty legal lore to be found within the frontier community. The preamble, in the name of the people of "Oregon Territory," declared the laws were adopted "until such time as the United States of America extend their jurisdiction over us." Significant provisions were a plural executive, a legislative committee, voluntary subscription in lieu of taxation, and a prohibition upon slavery. Aversion to taxation seems to have been shared by the Oregon pioneers, in common with residents on other frontiers. Thus was a time-honored practice of the American frontier revived; another "compact" entered into by individualistic pioneers in a new homeland. The Oregon settlers were reacting to their wilderness setting as had the Watauga, the Transylvania, the Cumberland, and other frontier communities of an earlier day.

The great migration of 1843 was both an advantage and a disadvantage to the provisional government. It brought such able men as Burnett, Applegate, and Nesmith, whose talents were sorely needed by the new body politic. It also, by sheer weight of numbers, removed all doubt as to American preponderance in Oregon. On the other hand, many of the newcomers were rough frontiersmen, with no religious leaning or preference, who resented the evident resolve of the Methodist mission crowd to retain control. Orderly Americans came to favor reconciliation with their British neighbors, and a government satisfactory to all concerned. The Canadians, on their part, now felt the need for protection against the turbulent and unruly elements among the new American immigrants.

In 1844 the more responsible leaders among the newcomers took matters into their own hands. They reformed the land laws, provided for a governor in lieu of the executive committee, and created a unicameral legislature to replace the legislative committee. Voluntary contributions for raising revenue gave way to optional taxation; if one refused to pay his taxes he had no vote and no recourse to the law for any purpose. He thus became an outcast. In July, 1845, the amended laws were accepted by the electorate.

The extent to which the interests of British and American elements in the population were reconciled was indicated by the election of a high official of the Hudson's Bay Company as treasurer of the territory, and by an oath of office which merely required that the individual support the provisional government only so far as its laws were consistent with his "duties as a citizen of the United States or a subject of Great Britain." In August, 1845, McLoughlin, in behalf of the company, recognized the provisional government. He wrote: "we decided upon joining the association both for the security of the Company's property and the protection of its rights."

While the Oregon pioneers temporarily solved their governmental problems, England and the United States wrangled over the boundary question. On three different occasions the United States had offered to accept the 49th parallel as the demarcation line and as often Great Britain had countered with the proposal that the Columbia should delimit the spheres of the two countries. From this position neither party had retreated a single step between 1824 and 1842. The area really in dispute, therefore, was that between the Columbia and the 49th parallel.

In 1843 there was considerable stiffening of the popular attitude in the United States with respect to Oregon. Disappointment at the failure of Linn's second Oregon bill in the Senate, and the belief that the United States had been ready to cede the area north of the Columbia in return for British aid in securing northern California, aroused indignation in various parts of the Mississippi Valley. Local meetings were followed by an Oregon Convention at Cincinnati in July, 1843, attended by about one hundred delegates. The extreme American claim to the entire region between the 42nd parallel and 54°40′ advanced there became, under western influence, the Democratic rallying cry in the campaign of 1844. President Polk, apparently adopted the frontier viewpoint when, in his inaugural address, he declared American title to "the whole of Oregon is clear and unquestionable."

Actually, however, the supreme object of the United States was still the 49th parallel boundary. The heavy migrations seemed to bring the goal nearer. Calhoun, secretary of state in 1844, told the British minister that 1,000 Americans had located in Oregon in 1843, estimated that the migration of 1844 would add another 1,500 to the American colony, and added that the forces which had driven the tide of population across the Alleghenies to the Mississippi would drive it on with increasing power across the Rockies to the banks of the Columbia, which were "destined to be peopled by us." The English government was sufficiently alarmed to send two military officers westward to inquire into the requirements for British defense of the country. In the same year the frigate *America* visited Puget Sound under command of Sir John Gordon, brother of Lord Aberdeen, who sent an officer to Ft. Vancouver, seeking full information from Dr. McLoughlin regarding the relative strength of the American and British elements.

Yet, the American settlements were confined almost entirely to the Willamette Valley, south of the Columbia. Only a handful of settlers from the States were located north of the river. The American argument of actual occupation, therefore, had validity only for the area which Britain was *always* prepared to concede—the area south of the Columbia. Why, then, did Britain accept the 49th parallel as the boundary, thereby relinquishing the region north of the Columbia, which its own nationals held securely? The answer is that the Hudson's Bay Company, alarmed at the aggressive and turbulent character of many American settlers in the Willamette Valley, feared for the safety of stores and other property at Ft. Vancouver, on the north bank of the Columbia. So real was the danger that Governor Simpson in 1845 directed that the headquarters of the company be moved to Ft. Victoria, on Vancouver's Island. Furthermore, the fur trade was declining along the Columbia, causing the company to prize the region less highly than of yore. These facts were well known to the British government. They meant that since the Hudson's Bay Company was evacuating the area actually in dispute, British diplomacy could now yield gracefully and without the sacrifice of any important economic interest. Lord Aberdeen, the foreign secretary, therefore, in the spring of 1846 offered the 49th parallel to the channel separating the continent from Vancouver's Island, leaving the island in British possession. The Senate of the United States recommended that President Polk accept the offer, despite all the recent talk about "54°40' or fight." The treaty embodying those terms was concluded June 15, 1846.

There were other contributing factors to the amicable adjustment of the longstanding difficulty. One was the inherent desire on both sides to avoid hostilities. While both countries were prepared to fight rather than sacrifice any important national interest, both were equally glad to have peace with honor. The moderate tariff policy of the Polk administration as embodied in the Walker Tariff of 1846, also probably played a part. It mollified

English opinion, long opposed to American high protection, and aided the government in its policy of compromise.

With the boundary settled, there seemed to Americans in the Willamette Valley no reason why Congress should not create Oregon Territory at once. The slavery issue doomed them to disappointment. The provisional government had banned slavery from the Territory. A similar provision was now incorporated in the Oregon bill presented to Congress. This was sufficient to arouse such opposition from the proslavery forces that despite the friendly interest of President Polk and Senator Benton, the measure made no progress in 1846 and 1847. Not until the Whitman massacre in the latter year was it possible to secure action. This atrocity prompted the Oregon settlers to prepare a last memorial to Congress, earnestly praying that it take them under its protection. When this reached the East popular sympathy, already stirred by the butchery of the missionaries, forced the legislature to act. On August 13th, 1848, after a continuous session of twenty-one hours, the bill creating Oregon Territory was finally passed.

# CHAPTER XXVI

# The Great Basin Frontier

## 1830-1846

For two centuries the frontier advance followed a well-defined pattern: whenever conditions at home were bad enough and regions ahead sufficiently attractive a rapid westward movement took place. The migrations into Texas and Oregon ran true to that form. In each case overcrowding or depression in the Mississippi Valley uprooted pioneers; in each case they risked the uncertainties of wilderness travel to settle on rich lands which promised them the prosperity they had failed to find in the East. No such desires motivated the third company of immigrants who moved toward the Far West during those years. Their mecca was no black-soiled prairie or well-watered valley, but the arid desert of the Great Basin where sunbaked alkaline soils discouraged settlement by less hardy souls. Those newest pioneers were members of the Church of Jesus Christ of Latter-Day Saints, and they sought the most isolated, inhospitable spot on all the continent where they could worship God as they chose. They found their haven beneath the shadows of Utah's Wasatch Mountains.

The wanderings that brought the Mormons to this desert Zion began many years before they made their last great trek across the Plains. Persecution drove them onward, a persecution directed first against their prophet, Joseph Smith. Smith was the child of Vermont parents who shifted with New England's frontier until they became shiftless themselves; his father moved the family nineteen times in the ten years before 1816 when he finally appropriated unoccupied lands near the upstate New York village of Palmyra. There they were surrounded by other New Englanders, all steeped in the mystical, soul-searching traditions of predestinarian Calvinism, and all ready to rush headlong into every new religious experience which promised an exciting means of salvation. This was the spiritual atmosphere that nurtured young Joseph Smith's interest in the hereafter and gave birth to Mormonism.

His first concern over religious matters was manifested in 1820 when his family was hotly debating the merits of the Methodist, Baptist, and Presbyterian revivalists then exhorting the local camp meeting. Joseph, who was fifteen years old at the time, sought the answer in prayer, going alone into the forest near Palmyra to ask divine guidance. As he prayed a dazzling light revealed God and the Savior standing before him. He should, they told him, concern himself no more with the existing churches; the true faith had not yet been revealed to man. Joseph's mother, a mystical neurotic whose life was governed by visions, believed her son's story without question. From that day the family forsook other sects to await the revelation promised by the Almighty.

That came in 1827 when God again appeared before Joseph, to tell him that beneath a hill near Palmyra he would find a stone casket containing golden plates on which the story of the true belief was recorded. According to Smith's own account, the precious documents were removed from their hiding place and the work of translation begun. For the next two years the task went on, with Smith sitting in a curtained alcove in a neighbor's farmhouse (the Lord had warned that anyone but himself who looked upon the golden plates would be struck dead) reading aloud to a series of assistants in an outer room who wrote as he dictated. By 1830 the transcription was completed and the Book of Mormon published. In the same year the Church of Jesus Christ of Latter-Day Saints was organized.

This remarkable document, which was destined to be accepted as the Gospel by thousands of the faithful, was a lethally dull volume of 588 pages which recounted the story of America's settlement. First to arrive, according to the Book of Mormon, were a group of dispersed peoples from the Tower of Babel who quarreled so violently that nearly all were killed, although a few remained as ancestors of the Indians. The second comers were God's chosen people, a band of Israelites led by Lehi who found in the promised land of America "all manner of useful cattle and sheep and swine." For a time they prospered, but with the death of Lehi they fell into two factions, one headed by Nephi, the son of Lehi, the other by his brother, Laman. The Nephites, a peaceful people, spread over Mexico and Central America where they left behind evidences of their high civilization in ruins of ancient cities and temples. The Lamanites, on the other hand, moved northward to the present United States where they forgot the God of their fathers and fell upon such evil ways that the Lord darkened their skins to the color of their hearts. For years the two peoples warred, until finally they met in a decisive battle fought near Palmyra in 400 A.D. All the Nephites save Mormon and his son Moroni were slain; the two survivors spent the rest of their lives recording the story of their people upon the golden plates which Joseph Smith found.

Dull as this hodgepodge might appear to later critics, it appealed to emotion-starved frontiersmen of the 1830's. At first converts were few; Joseph Smith found almost no purchasers for the Book of Mormon even after a special revelation allowed him to lower the price from $1.75 to $1.25 a copy. Taking to heart the adage that a prophet is always without honor in his own country, he decided to move to a less-prejudiced region where his reputation as a shiftless dreamer could not plague his footsteps. The little town of Kirtland in northeastern Ohio was chosen as the new Zion on the advice of two Campbellite converts familiar with the region, and there Smith with his handful of followers moved in 1831. The Mormons experienced their first success in Kirtland; converts flocked in, fields were cleared, homes built, and a great temple begun. The prophet was in his glory. More and more he thought of himself as a messiah; he tried his hand at miracles, attempted to walk on water, sought to raise the dead, and was in almost continual communication with God. From his revelations a body of church dogma emerged, one feature of which was a communal organization for the Mormon community. The economic system proved so efficient that the Saints prospered mightily and seemed destined to a future of continuous prosperity.

The Panic of 1837 punctured their dreams. Joseph Smith had been tempted by the speculative fever of the 1830's to launch a flimsy banking enterprise which collapsed with most of the other banks of the nation, leaving the Mormons heavily in debt and surrounded by angry creditors. Most of the Saints turned furiously against their prophet, who responded by reading them out of the church in a language as inflammatory as their own, then fleeing westward with a few followers to join a small Mormon community recently established at the town of Far West on the Missouri frontier. These experiences, which would have humbled a less-confident man, only embittered Joseph Smith. He arrived in Missouri convinced that Gentile persecution was the cause of all his troubles and that the future could be secured only by meeting force with force. "Our rights," one of his disciples told the people of Far West at a 4th of July celebration in 1838, "shall no more be trampled on with impunity. The man, or set of men, who attempt it, does it at the expense of their lives. And that mob that comes on to us to disturb us, it shall be between us and them a war of extermination, for we will follow them till the last drop of their blood is spilled, or else they will have to exterminate us."

Fighting words such as these were only a challenge to the Missouri frontiersmen. They already disliked the Mormons—as New Englanders, as suspected abolitionists, as prosperous landholders, as unorthodox believers. They suspected that Joseph Smith's prophecies of the day when his people would inherit the earth cloaked a Mormon plot to take over the community by force; when they saw bands of young Saints drilling their suspicions seemed confirmed. Little wonder that anti-Mormon mobs began forming about Far West during the summer of 1838 or that guerilla warfare broke out in the fall. In vain Smith appealed to state officials for protection. "The Mormons must be treated as enemies," the governor of Missouri announced, "and must be exterminated or driven from the state, if necessary, for the public peace." Through the winter gangs of inflamed Missourians struck again and again at the harassed Mormons of Far West, driving them from their homes into fields and forests where suffering was intense.

They could no longer stay in Missouri, Smith saw, nor could they move farther west where the Permanent Indian Frontier blocked their path. Hence he turned his steps eastward, followed by faithful Saints whose loyalty mounted with each setback. The site selected by the Prophet for their new homes was a swampy lowland near Quincy, Illinois, which had been avoided by earlier settlers. Reaching this unpromising spot in the spring of 1839, Smith sized up the situation shrewdly. Illinois, he saw, was ready to welcome newcomers who would help share the debt burden inherited from the state's collapsed internal improvement program. Moreover the two political parties, Whigs and Democrats, were so evenly matched that either would make concessions in return for a block of votes. This was a chance to secure everything the Mormons needed. Seizing on the opportunity, Smith drew up a charter for a proposed city of Nauvoo which gave almost unlimited power to the local officials; they could pass any laws not repugnant to the national constitution, decide cases arising under the statutes in their own courts, and set up their own militia. The unorthodox document was then dangled before both parties, with promise of support in the election of 1840 for the one pushing it through the state legislature. The Whigs rose to the bait, thus giving Joseph Smith the thing he wanted: a private commonwealth within the borders of Illinois where he could rule as he pleased.

Prosperity smiled on the Saints now. Ardent missionaries roamed the United States and Europe, winning converts who flocked to Nauvoo in such numbers that the city's population skyrocketed to 15,000 in 1844 when it became the metropolis of Illinois. Farms were laid out, small industries started, a quarry and brick yard opened, a sawmill set up in distant

Wisconsin to provide lumber for homes and factories. Everyone was bustling, everyone happy. Each day religious pageants, athletic events, dances, song fests, or parades of the local militia company, the Nauvoo Legion, were staged to entertain the inhabitants. "I do not believe," one traveler wrote, "that there is another people in existence who could have made such improvements in the same length of time, under the same circumstances."

Joseph Smith was in his glory. His word was law in the Holy City, where he was mayor, commander of the Legion, and president of the church. Unfortunately the overdose of power was more than the Prophet could stand; as his strength increased his native shrewdness declined. Forgetting that anti-Mormon feeling persisted about Nauvoo, he went doggedly about the task of protecting his people. He issued an ordinance providing for the punishment of anyone using language disrespectful of the church, insisted that no Illinois law became valid in Nauvoo until it bore his signature, bargained overzealously with both parties before each election, and asked Congress to erect his city into a federal territory free of state control. Gentile grumbling that followed each dictatorial step rose to a crescendo when Smith announced himself a candidate for the presidency of the United States in 1844, on a platform that called for the freeing of all slaves and prisoners, a reduction in the number of congressmen, and the annexation of Mexico and Canada. The Whigs, who had supported the Mormons before, turned violently on Smith's followers, leaving them surrounded by a solid ring of enemies.

A united Nauvoo might still have held back the onslaught, but Smith's last revelation in July, 1843, sanctioning polygamy for a few church leaders, ended all hope. The furor caused by his pronouncement rocked the nation. Among Gentiles the reaction varied from outraged horror to stern indignation; newspapers everywhere attacked plural marriage as immoral, corrupting, irreligious, and dangerous to the sanctity of the home. The Mormons were scarcely less affected. Many, refusing to accept the pronouncement, banded together against the Prophet. To attract supporters, they founded a newspaper, the Nauvoo *Expositor*, which in its first issue of June 7, 1844, castigated both Joseph Smith's polygamy and his economic ideas, demanding "the unconditional repeal of the city charter—to correct the abuses of the unit power."

Smith acted at once against the dissenters. A hurriedly called meeting of the city council declared the newspaper a nuisance which should be destroyed, an order carried out three days later when the marshal broke into the *Expositor's* printing plant, smashed the press, and disposed of all available copies of the first issue. The editors fled to nearby Carthage, scattering flames of discontent along the way. There they swore out a warrant for Smith's arrest, listing the grievances which were rapidly arousing the countryside: suppression of the press, polygamy, and political dictatorship. As news of the dissension spread, mass meetings met to call for a "war of extermination" on the Mormons, mobs formed, feelings ran high. The state governor hurried from Springfield, but when he found the militia as rabidly anti-Mormon as the people he realized peace could be preserved in only one way. Joseph Smith and his brother were persuaded to surrender, then lodged for their own protection in the Carthage jail. Even that proved futile. On June 27, 1844, a mob stormed into Carthage, battered its way into the prison, and brutally slaughtered the two Mormon leaders.

The handwriting on the wall was clear to the Saints now: they would never be safe within the United States. Despairingly, they prepared to begin their wanderings once more. Their first need was a modern Moses to lead them to a promised land. The choice was a happy one. Brigham Young, an early convert and head of the Council of Twelve Apostles, was a hardheaded realist whose organizational talents equipped him for the difficult tasks ahead. Those were many. All about Nauvoo angry Gentiles threatened mob action unless the Mormons left Illinois at once. Young managed to keep the peace for a year, but during the winter of 1845-46 he held the enemies in check only by promising that his people would be on their way "as soon as the grass grew and the water ran." Within the city broken-hearted Saints prepared to move, selling their property at ruinous prices to buy wagons, supplies, and live stock. In February, 1846, 1,600 Mormons crossed the frozen Mississippi to the little hamlet of Sugar Grove, Iowa, where temporary headquarters were established. During the next few months the rest of the Nauvoo population followed.

When the exodus began, Brigham Young planned to lead his people to some isolated spot beyond the Rocky Mountains, although his geographic knowledge was so hazy he had no exact location in mind. Hence he determined to make the journey in stages, sounding out each step in advance. The first stopping place selected was on the west bank of the Missouri opposite Council Bluffs. While the Saints waited at Sugar Grove, an advance party rode ahead to mark the trail, build bridges, lay out roads, establish permanent camp sites, erect cabins, and plant crops that the immigrants could harvest. By the time the vanguard reached Council Bluffs in June, 1846, the main party was ready to start. Young planned so efficiently that the migration was accomplished easily. All summer bands of Mormons trekked westward, stopping to eat bountifully of crops planted for them and sleep comfortably in well-equipped cabins. "We are happy and contented," one Saint wrote, "and the songs of Zion resounded from wagon to wagon, reverberating through the woods, while the echo was returned from the distant hills." By fall 12,000 were camped on the banks of the Missouri at a spot called Winter Quarters.

The winter was one of suffering and hard work. Disease and icy blasts from the Plains took a toll of six hundred lives, but the survivors spent no time mourning their dead. Brigham Young was teaching them the secrets of Plains travel. He divided them into parties of a hundred with a captain over each, taught them how to drive their wagons in four parallel columns when danger threatened, showed them how to form their wagons into a solid corral at night, warned them never to forget their daily prayers, and cautioned them to obey orders blindly lest they fall prey to Indians. By spring the Mormons were as thoroughly disciplined as an army and as well versed in Plains lore as any one could be who had not actually traveled in the West.

The first party set out in mid-April, 1847—a well-organized Pioneer Band led by Brigham Young and made up of 146 young men and women riding in 73 wagons and driving a large herd of live stock. Instead of following the Oregon Trail along the south bank of the Platte, Young blazed a new route just north of the stream, partly because the higher ground there was better suited to wagon travel, more because he wished to avoid rowdy Missourians who frequented the regular trail. From the first he enforced rigid discipline—prayers at five each morning, on the road two hours later, a twenty mile march, a halt to form the nightly wagon corral with livestock within and sleeping tents without, evening prayers, bed at nine o'clock—that was the schedule followed day after day as the Pioneer Band plodded westward. Ft. Laramie was reached in early June. There the party halted to dry meat, fatten horses, and build ferry boats which were turned over to eight men left behind to carry later immigrants across the North Platte.

Then the difficult journey up into the mountains and through South Pass began. At Ft. Bridger, the trading post maintained by Jim Bridger, they heard discouraging advice. That seasoned old pioneer warned them only barren deserts lay ahead, so dry that neither animal nor vegetable life could possibly exist. He urged the Mormons to turn to the Willamette, Bear, or Cache valleys where white men and Indians produced crops as good as any grown in Kentucky. As for the Great Basin wasteland—he offered Brigham Young $1,000 for the first ear of corn raised there. The Mormons, seeking isolation as well as prosperity, refused to listen. They pressed on, over the rugged Uinta Range, across a sun-dried desert, into the eastern spurs of the Wasatch Mountains. There Brigham Young, struck down with mountain fever, took to a pallet in one of the wagons as they wended their way through steep passes and over breath-taking heights. Their days of anguish came to an end when they reached Emigration Canyon, a narrow defile opening upon the broad panorama of table lands surrounding Great Salt Lake. As they halted to observe the magnificent view Young rose from his bed and said, "This is the Place."

With joy in their hearts, the Mormons hurried on to their promised land, arriving on July 24, 1847, a day since celebrated as "Pioneer Day." The prospect would have brought despair to men of lesser faith. Above them towered the snow-capped peaks of the Wasatch Range, to the north and west was the glimmering surface of Great Salt Lake, but at their feet was a barren plain, cracked by the searing sun, dotted with a few straggling sagebrush plants, and inhabited by no living thing save a multitude of black crickets, lizards, and rattlesnakes. Members of the Pioneer Band, after shattering their plows in the dry soil, successfully dammed one of the two streams that gushed from the mountains, flooded a few acres until the ground was softened, then planted their first crops. Having supervised this experiment in irrigation and sent a party into California to buy cattle, Brigham Young started east with a few followers to organize the 1848 migration. Not far from Great Salt Lake his heart was gladdened by the sight of a great Mormon company plodding westward: 1,553 people, 2,313 cattle, 887 cows, 358 sheep, 124 horses, 35 hogs, 716 chickens. All along the trail he encountered similar bands; by the fall of 1847, 4,000 Saints were established about the southern tip of Great Salt Lake.

There was suffering that first winter among the ill-fed, ill-clad, ill-housed Mormons. Food was so scarce they were reduced to meagre flour rations and to grubbing out the roots of the sego lily. Lumber—which had to be hauled in from distant forest slopes—was so hard to obtain many braved winter's blasts in covered wagons. Yet there was no despair among the shivering, hungry Saints; they knew Brigham Young would lead them to prosperity as surely as he had guided them to their Zion. Fortunately their childish faith was justified. Young worked frantically in the East that winter, gathering immigrants for the spring migration. "Come immediately and prepare to go West," he urged his people, "bringing with you all kinds of choice seeds, grains, vegetables, fruits, shrubbery, trees, and vines— anything that will please the eye, gladden the heart or cheer the soul of man." Forty-five hundred settlers responded during the summer of 1848 but their coming did not ease suffering, for the 5,000 acres cultivated that year were insufficient to provide all with food. Even the meagre harvest was threatened when myriads of black crickets descended on the growing grain; only a visitation by sea gulls who gobbled up the offenders saved the food supply. The pious Saints, unaware that gulls flew in each year to feast on the crickets, laid their salvation to divine intervention; to this day a statue of a sea gull in Salt Lake City testifies to their gratitude. Despite this aid the extremely cold winter of 1848-49 was the Mormon starving time.

Amidst those hardships the work of rearing a permanent settlement went forward. In carrying out this task the Mormon church first exerted its great power to create a social order unique in the annals of the nineteenth-century frontier. Brigham Young prophesied the nature of society when he welcomed the Pioneer Band to Great Salt Lake:

> No man can ever buy land here, for no one has any land to sell. But every man shall have his land measured out to him, which he must cultivate in order to keep it.
> Besides, there shall be no private ownership of the streams that come out of the canyons, nor the timber that grows on the hills.
> These belong to the people: all the people.

In those words Young laid down the principles that governed the planting of settlements, the development of irrigation, and the expansion of the Great Basin frontier.

The disciples' first need was a city to harbor immigrants soon to come. A site was chosen southeast of Great Salt Lake yet near enough mountain streams for irrigation. Church committees under Young's direction divided the area into square ten-acre plots separated by streets 130 feet wide. Each block was subdivided into eight lots of 1¼ acres which were assigned families, with the understanding that houses be built twenty feet from the front line and the intervening space planted to trees and shrubs. Irrigation ditches along each side of the streets provided water for vegetable gardens and fruit trees. In the center of the spacious city a large square was reserved for public buildings and a temple. On the outskirts the land was divided into five-acre plots for the use of artisans or other townsmen who wished to supplement their larders by raising small quantities of produce. Beyond were larger lots, ranging up to forty acres, assigned to farmers. All plots were granted free of charge, with the understanding that they might be sold or exchanged, but with all speculation forbidden.

The theory underlying the land system—that the welfare of the social group transcended the welfare of the individual—was equally well expressed in the agricultural methods devised by the Mormons. Holding to the concept that "land belongs to the Lord, and his Saints are to use so much as they can work profitably," church leaders assigned free farms to families in direct proportion to need. Thus a man with plural wives, numerous children, and some wealth might receive from forty to eighty acres, while a husband with one mate and less property would be given only ten or twenty acres. All fields adjoined an irrigation ditch connected with a stream from the Wasatch Mountains. The main ditches were planned by a committee and built jointly by all who used them, each providing labor in proportion to the amount of land he tilled. Each farmer then dug smaller trenches from the central trough to his own plot.

Rigid controls governed the use of water. Each main irrigation ditch was supervised by a church committee which saw to it that farmers received just enough precious fluid for efficient agriculture. Thus a farmer with forty acres might be given the right to use water from two to five o'clock on Monday, Wednesday, and Friday; one with only ten acres would be assigned the period from nine to ten o'clock on Tuesday, Thursday, and Saturday. Within two years after the Saints reached the Great Basin the system was functioning smoothly.

The methods devised by the Mormons for allotting both land and water represented a degree of co-operation rarely found among individualistic American frontiersmen. Only once before in the history of the nation's expansion had a similar co-operative social order developed: among the Puritans of seventeenth-century Massachusetts. The similarity of the two groups of pioneers, although separated by two centuries and half a continent, explains their distinctive societies. Both Puritans and Mormons were an intensely religious people, governed by a closely knit hierarchy whose slightest whim was unquestioningly obeyed, and seeking isolation to worship as they please. The power of the church was one factor needed to assure social controls. Equally necessary were the inhospitable geographic environments in which both lived. The Saints were, in one sense, typical of all frontiersmen, who were less individualistic than opportunistic. The American pioneer wanted wealth and security. If those ends were obtainable by speculation and exploitation, as in the humid East, he adopted a system of individual competition; if harsh natural conditions made joint effort more satisfactory, as in rocky Massachusetts or barren Utah, he tried co-operation. The Mormons were simply wise enough to adopt an economic system suited to their unique environment. Thus a combination of religious and geographic forces weakened the centrifugal force of the frontier and made possible a Desert Zion which matched the Wilderness Zion of Massachusetts Bay.

Nevertheless, Brigham Young's wisdom in recognizing the need for joint effort cannot be overemphasized. Unity was needed especially for successful irrigation, and on that subject the Saints were completely without experience. Until they arrived at Great Salt Lake extensive irrigation was unknown anywhere in the Anglo-Saxon world. Yet within a brief period they not only devised a workable means of allotting water but developed a completely new legal concept to govern their enterprise. Rejecting the older common law system of "riparian rights" which forced every property owner who used water from a stream for power to return the same amount before the river reached his neighbor's lands, the Mormons adopted the Spanish "Doctrine of Appropriation." Brigham Young enunciated the revolutionary concept when he first reached Great Salt Lake, but not until 1852 was it given classic form by the territorial legislature: "The county court shall have control of all timber, water privileges, or any water course or creek, to grant mill sites, and exercise such powers as in their judgment shall best preserve the timber and subserve the interest of the settlement in the distribution of water for irrigation or other purposes." Young laid the basis for all subsequent irrigation law by evolving a doctrine which placed the good of the community above the interests of the individual.

The remarkable achievements in land distribution and desert agriculture assured permanence for the Mormon settlements, but their first prosperity was due to a happy accident. The California Gold Rush of 1849 sent a stream of miners pouring through Salt Lake City on their way west. Many inexperienced gold seekers who overloaded their wagons with clothes, tools, and machinery were anxious to sell before crossing the sandy deserts of the Great Basin and the precipitous trails of the Sierra Nevadas. They also needed fresh food and draft animals. The Saints found themselves in the fortunate position of being able to buy precious manufactured goods at prices lower than those of the New York wholesale houses, while selling mules at $200 apiece and flour at $25 a hundred pounds. Those not equipped to take advantage of this legalized robbery repaired broken wagons in return for unheard-of wages of $3 a day. Money, usually hard to get on the frontier, circulated freely in Salt Lake City by the close of 1849.

Continued prosperity was assured by a steady influx of new settlers over the next years. The Mormons were a zealous people; their missionaries roamed widely over the East, England, and the Baltic countries, preaching a message of hope to oppressed lower classes in industrial centers. Conversion, they promised, meant not only salvation but a chance to begin life anew in the church's desert utopia. Converts were won by the thousands, all of whom were urged to make their way to the Great Salt Lake. Those unable to pay their own expenses were aided by a Perpetual Emigration Fund established in 1849; money obtained from the faithful was loaned to immigrants with the understanding that it be returned as soon as they were financially secure. A program of public works was set up in Salt Lake City to help others earn enough to defray travel costs.

Still more were helped by a system which Brigham Young devised in

1856 to cut down the expenses of wagon travel across the plains. Immigrants arriving at Iowa City, the jumping-off place for the Mormon Trail, were met by a crew of carpenters sent by the church to build two-wheeled hand carts large enough to carry a settler's belongings. The first "Hand Cart Brigade"—five hundred men, women, and children—arrived in Salt Lake City during the summer of 1856, after pushing a hundred carts across the 1,200 miles of trail in about the same time taken by prairie schooners. A second party of a thousand migrants fared less well when caught by an early snowfall in mid-Wyoming. Two hundred perished before a relief expedition rescued the remainder.

Despite that setback settlers continued to stream toward the Mormon Zion, many using hand carts until the method was abandoned in 1861. The steady influx brought the church leaders face-to-face with three major problems. How could they provide homes for the incoming thousands in that desert region? How could they continue their complete isolation from the Gentile world? How could they govern themselves? The skill shown by Brigham Young and his fellow churchmen in answering those perplexing questions not only testified to their ability but assured the Mormons a prosperous future.

The problem of providing newcomers with farms allowed the Mormons to demonstrate the remarkable efficiency of their co-operative social order. From the first they realized that colony planting in the Great Basin would differ from settlement in the humid East; each townsite must be selected with an eye to irrigation possibilities and the limited water supplies must be controlled in the interest of community welfare. Hence every step was carefully planned. A committee was sent out first to select a likely spot where a stream gushed from the Wasatch Mountains. Then the pioneers were selected—a bishop or elder as leader, a few experienced farmers and herdsmen, a blacksmith, a carpenter, a flour miller, a schoolmaster, a religious teacher, a number of inexperienced immigrants who could learn from the seasoned planters. The "Call" to join a colonizing expedition was looked upon as an honored opportunity to "build the Kingdom of God on earth," and never refused. All selected sold their goods, secured the implements and tools needed, and set out for their new homes. The combination of skilled leadership and selected personnel allowed the Mormons to plant new towns with none of the suffering usual on the frontier.

Equally important in explaining the rapid expansion of the Great Basin frontier was the unquenchable ambition of Brigham Young. He looked upon new settlements as one important means of achieving isolation for the desert nation that was his dream. Such a state could survive only with an outlet to the sea; hence he planned a string of towns across Utah, Nevada, and southern California to the Pacific. These would be connected with roads over which immigrants and supplies, brought in by ship, could reach Salt Lake City. In that way a strong, independent Mormon country would be built up, cut off from the United States by the Great American Desert.

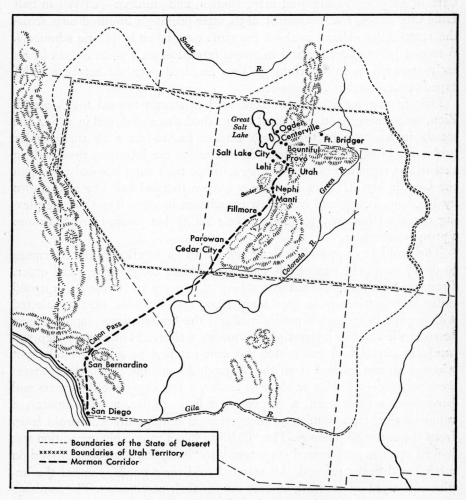

The Great Basin Frontier, 1846-1857

The "Mormon Corridor" from Great Salt Lake to San Diego was one of Young's great ambitions.

The Mormons directed most of their colonizing energies to the region south of Salt Lake City although three northern towns—Bountiful, Centerville, and Ogden—were planted between 1847 and 1850 on streams flowing into Great Salt Lake. Expansion southward along the "Mormon Corridor" began in 1849 when thirty families reached the shores of Utah Lake to lay out the town of Ft. Utah. Provo and Lehi were established on the edges of that large body of fresh water during the next year. Meanwhile other exploring parties, ranging farther afield, discovered the plentiful mountain streams that lost themselves in the arid San Pete Valley; there the villages of Nephi and Manti were settled in 1850. Still farther south in the valley of the Sevier River Fillmore was founded in 1851, while in southern Utah Parowan and Cedar City were colonized during the next few years. Both were established with an eye to industrial developments, for they were located near beds of iron and coal. At Cedar City mines were opened, a wood-burning smelter capable of producing a ton of metal a day set up, and five hundred acres irrigated to provide food for workers. Still not content, Brigham Young in 1852 sent a company of colonizers into southern California with instructions to found a settlement near Cajon Pass where they could "cultivate the olive, grape, sugar-cane, and cotton, gather round them the saints, and select locations on the line of the proposed mail route." The three hundred Mormons entrusted with the task of founding this key town on the "Mormon Corridor" reached Cajon Pass in the spring of 1852, chose a favorable site, purchased land, and laid out a city called San Bernardino. Two years later other small outposts were established along the corridor in the Nevada country. Into all moved new settlers as they came from the East or Europe; by 1856, 22,000 Saints lived about Great Salt Lake or in towns along the "Mormon Corridor." Their neat villages, well-irrigated fields, and prosperous industries were fitting tribute to Brigham Young's skill as a colonizer.

Closely allied with the program of expansion was the Mormons' attempt to achieve independence by diversifying their economy. Brigham Young believed this essential to the self-governing nation he hoped to create; "seek diligently," he told his missionaries in Europe, "in every branch for wise, skillful and ingenious mechanics, manufacturers, potters, etc." When craftsmen arrived they were set to work at their trades. A sawmill and gristmill were erected at once, a salt works opened on the shores of Great Salt Lake, and a soda spring nearby turned to the use of the Saints. During the next half-dozen years small factories were constructed, usually with church funds, to produce pottery, leather goods, textiles, nails, cutlery, wooden bowls, soap, paper, guns, and glass. Typical was one enterprise devoted to finding a substitute for sugar, which could not be grown in the arid climate. Some of the disciples knew from Old World experience that beets and corn produced a saccharine product. They directed the construction of a small beet-crushing plant in 1855, fashioning the machinery from old wagon hubs, rims, and scrap iron. Those expedients, together with goods brought by immigrants along the California Trail, allowed the Mormons to approach that economic isolation which seemed necessary to political independence.

Effective as were the Mormon colonizing and economic activities, their dream of a free desert nation was doomed from the outset. No expanse of Great American Desert could protect them from the wrath of their fellow-Americans; that they were left to their own devices for a few years was due only to American preoccupation with the Mexican War. When fighting ended in 1848 the alarming news reached Salt Lake City that the Mexican lands on which they lived were part of the United States. Brigham Young saw his Saints could be protected in only one way: immediate statehood alone would allow them to govern themselves, continue their religious practices unmolested, and guard their unpopular doctrine of polygamy. Hurrying into action, he issued a call for a convention which met at Salt Lake City in March, 1849, and adopted a typical frontier constitution, modeled after the frames of government in eastern states, but vesting complete power in popularly elected officials. Fear of outside aggression was reflected in a clause forcing all men between eighteen and forty-five to serve in the militia. The convention proposed the new state be called Deseret (a term taken from the Book of Mormon and meaning Honey Bee), and that it include all of present-day Utah, all of Arizona, most of Nevada, part of southern California, and portions of Idaho, Wyoming, and Colorado, with an outlet to the sea at San Diego.

While messengers carried the document east, the Mormons turned to creating a government which could function until statehood was granted. The election held that spring disclosed the close connection between church and state; Brigham Young was chosen governor, the lieutenant governor and secretary were his close associates, and the justices of the peace were all Mormon bishops. The State of Deseret was still a theocracy, although garbed in the regalia of civil government. The result was an extremely efficient rule which operated equitably for Mormons and Gentiles alike. Laws passed by the legislature which convened in July, 1849, provided for a system of courts and law enforcement officials that made Deseret a haven for overland immigrants seeking justice; non-Mormons stopping to smooth over differences or settle disputes universally praised the justices for their "fairness and impartiality." One grateful traveler wrote: "Appeals for protection from oppression, by those passing through their midst, were not made in vain; and I know of at least one instance in which the marshal of the State was dispatched, with an adequate force, nearly two hundred miles into the western desert in pursuit of some miscreants who had stolen off with nearly the whole outfit of a party of emigrants. He pursued and brought them back to the city, and the plundered property was restored to its rightful owners."

The efficiency of the courts failed to influence congressmen called upon to create the State of Deseret. Even Mormon leaders saw the cause was hopeless as soon as Congress began debating their petition in the spring of 1850; from every corner came a chorus of attack and vituperation: population was insufficient to warrant statehood, territorial claims were over-ambitious, the Mormon church was anti-Christian, the practice of polygamy must be forbidden. Amidst clamor from the opposition the Mormon committee changed its request to one for territorial organization. Congress responded on September 9, 1850, when the Territory of Utah was established, with a name derived from the Ute Indians, and boundaries that included all Utah and Nevada, the western third of Colorado, and part of Wyoming.

Mormon fears of unsympathetic federal control were set at rest when President Millard Fillmore named Brigham Young territorial governor and appointed three Saints and three Gentiles to the other administrative posts. The division of authority was potentially dangerous. The Mormons, in numerical control, used their power to continue a theocratic government; property disputes were settled in church courts, justice administered under ecclesiastical law, and affairs of state conducted with little regard to the statutes of the distant United States. Watching this unusual process, the three non-Mormon officials grew steadily more disgruntled. Outvoted at every point and virtually stripped of authority, two of them finally resigned in a huff, then carried eastward the inflammatory warning that the Saints sought to establish an independent nation within the United States. "The Mormons look to Brigham Young and to him alone for the law by which they are governed," the irate judges reported. "Federal officials of the Territory are constantly insulted, harassed and annoyed by the Mormons, and for these insults there is no redress."

The charges touched off a storm of protest against the Saints. Overland immigrants involved in the inevitable disputes over lost property or strayed cattle besieged Congress with complaints. The surveyor general of the United States charged that Mormons refused to let him operate in their territory. Indian agents claimed that "rude and lawless" young men from Utah were settling on Indian lands. Freighters and expressmen reported that "indiscriminate bloodshed" in the region about Great Salt Lake interfered with their business. No one in Washington bothered to determine that those reports were grossly exaggerated, for underlying the growing wave of antipathy for the Mormons was national contempt for polygamy. By the middle 1850's a score of books were in circulation branding plural marriage as lewd and immoral, newspapers filled their columns with vituperation, and ministers thundered from pulpits that the sinful practice must be stamped out. Amidst such an atmosphere every minor charge against the Mormons was magnified into a major error; justice and principles of religious freedom were forgotten.

Goaded on by the nationwide clamor, the federal government in 1857 named a non-Mormon governor of Utah Territory, ordered a strict enforcement of federal laws there, and dispatched 1,500 troops to escort the new officials into Salt Lake City and see to it their orders were obeyed. News that this force was approaching sent Mormons into a panic. Knowing nothing of its purpose, sure that their enemies in Washington were determined to kill their leaders and stamp out their faith, they rallied behind Brigham Young when he called upon the Saints to repel the invaders. A thousand militiamen were hurried east to barricade Echo Canyon, a narrow pass through which the army must pass, while others were sent ahead to harass the attackers. These guerrilla-like bands performed their part successfully; two wagon trains of supplies were destroyed, several hundred cattle captured, and the troops so delayed that their commander, giving up hopes of reaching Salt Lake City during 1857, went into winter camp on the Green River.

In the meantime all was feverish activity within Utah. Of one thing the Saints were sure: they would never stand aside while their leaders were slaughtered and their churches destroyed. Better to perish on the ramparts, better to burn their settlements and flee westward into the desert, than accept such treatment. Little wonder that, while preparing for such sacrifices, tension mounted until the Mormons were guilty of several unfortunate acts. Most brutal was the Mountain Meadows Massacre of September, 1857. The victims were 140 immigrants passing through Utah on their way to California. Coming as they did from the bitterly anti-Mormon regions of Missouri and Arkansas, their presence was greatly resented and their path across the territory marked by a series of irritating disputes. Matters came to a head when the travelers were attacked by a detachment of Mormon troops at Mountain Meadows in southern Utah. After a brief skirmish, they surrendered under a flag of truce. Then the whole helpless party, save seventeen children, was deliberately slaughtered. Although the crime was inexcusable, the tension on both sides during the "Mormon War" made the massacre understandable.

Events such as the Mountain Meadows Massacre, forecasting bloodshed should Mormon legions and federal armies ever clash, convinced federal officials that they must seek a peaceful settlement of the Mormon War.

The mediator selected for the delicate task was Colonel T. L. Kane, an old friend of the Saints, who was rushed overland to Salt Lake City during the winter of 1857-58. Only a few conversations with Brigham Young were needed for Kane to convince the harassed Disciples that the United States intended no interference with their religion and that they should admit the federal troops. Having paved the way, Kane crossed the Wasatch Mountains to the headquarters of the besieging army, where he persuaded the newly appointed territorial governor to accompany him into Utah without military protection. The peaceful gesture so allayed Mormon fears that they consented to accept American officials without further resistance. From that time a non-Mormon sat in the governor's edifice at Salt Lake City, but for all practical purposes Brigham Young continued to rule the territory. Gentile governors soon discovered that they were, in the pained phrase of one of them, "sent out to do nothing;" Utah remained a Mormon territory during its frontier period, founded, governed, and developed by Saints.

The peopling of the Great Basin was well under way by the close of the 1850's. Laboring side by side in unique co-operative ventures, spurred on by bishops who praised industrious husbandmen from their pulpits or publicly blacklisted shirkers, skillfully guided by able leaders along a path toward economic and political independence, the Mormons succeeded where others might well have failed. Their indomitable energy and all-prevailing faith brought a desert Zion into bloom.

# CHAPTER XXVII

# The Conquest of California

## 1830-1846

From the founding of the mission and the presidio at San Francisco in 1776 to the end of Spanish dominion in 1822 events in California were relatively unspectacular. In the Spanish American Wars of Independence which raged for a dozen years after 1808, the province played largely the part of an interested spectator. When word came of the success of the Mexican revolutionists under Iturbide the Californians readily acquiesced in the new order. In September, 1822, the Spanish flag was lowered at Monterey and the imperial banner of Mexico unfurled. The final break with the old regime came in 1825 when the Mexican Constitution of 1824, providing for a federated republic, was proclaimed and ratified in California.

Politically, the Mexican period of California's history was characterized by unrest and a growing conviction on the part of the people that they should enjoy a greater measure of autonomy and self government. In social and economic affairs Mexican policy was confined chiefly to the secularization of the missions and the parceling out of the land in large tracts. Secularization had been long considered. The process was actually begun in 1834 when ten missions were transferred to temporal use. Six additional missions were accorded similar treatment in 1835, while in the following year the remaining five were secularized. Contemporaneously with the crumbling of the missions there occurred the carving of large ranchos from the countryside. Although a few large grants had been made prior to Mexican independence, a great majority of the "Spanish grants" date from the Mexican era. Some twenty odd were made in the twenties; between 1830 and 1846 more than eight million acres passed into the hands of eight hundred persons. In this way was laid the basis for the most character-istic feature of life in California during the Mexican period.

Meanwhile the remarkable burst of expansion that carried American pioneers into Texas, Oregon, and the Great Basin during the 1830's and 1840's, led also to the peopling of Mexican California. There, as elsewhere in the Far West, the trader and settler were several jumps ahead of the government and its diplomacy. For more than half a century before the fortunes of war brought that Mexican province under the jurisdiction of the United States, there had developed a Yankee interest and influence in California which, soon or late, must have made it American territory.

The first American contact with California came through the sea otter traders, who had originally sought their peltry along the northwest coast. Soon the trade ceased to be restricted to the Northwest, as fur-bearing animals were hunted from South America to Alaska, but especially in Cali-fornia where they were particularly plentiful. New England ships of 100 to 250 tons usually consumed from two to three years on a voyage, during which one or two trips were made from the coast to China before returning to the home port. The number of skins taken to China was staggering. One of the New England traders believed 18,000 were carried in the year 1801 alone.

By 1820 the day of the sea otter trade was at an end. It had brought wealth to New England merchants and what was more important, allowed Americans to obtain their first glimpse of the wealth of natural resources which was California. Furthermore, the trade was responsible for the first known American account of the area. In 1808 there appeared in the *American Register* Robert Shaler's *Journal of a voyage from China to the northwestern coast of America made in 1804*, the California portions of which contain an enthusiastic description of the fine harbors and other attractive features of the province.

While California remained under Spanish authority foreign ships were theoretically excluded from its trade. But, as in other Spanish possessions, the law was honored more in the breach than in observance. Wholesale eva-sion resulted partly from the cleverness of Yankee ship captains, partly from the situation in which Californians found themselves. Remoteness from Spanish officials in Mexico made enforcement of the ban upon foreign-ers impossible, while the need for manufactured goods, which could come only from without, placed a premium upon law breaking. Moreover the most respectable elements in the population prized the foreign wares most highly. A multitude of products from China, Europe, and New England came to them in ships of fur traders, for which they bartered supplies of various sorts, especially grains and meat products. California fresh vegetables were also welcomed on ship board as insurance against scurvy. Few were the instances in which Spanish officials seriously attempted to interfere with the mutually advantageous trade.

The initial American acquaintance with California gained by sea otter and China traders was strengthened through the appearance of another group of enterprising New England mariners. After independence whalers from Nantucket and New Bedford resumed activity which the Revolution interrupted, rounded Cape Horn, and pushed their search into the North Pacific. Operating at such a distance from New England shores, a satisfactory voyage consumed three or four years, during which supplies must be acquired, rest for the crews obtained, and repairs made. For those purposes the harbors of Hawaii and California were ideally suited. A whaling ship normally carried a small supply of manufactured goods to exchange for necessary produce. Monterey and San Francisco were favorite ports of the whalers; as many as thirty ships frequently lay at anchor in the latter at one time. Their presence on California shores enlarged American acquaintance with the province's potentialities and whetted Yankees' appetites for the fine harbors there.

New England traders engaged in yet a third form of maritime activity in California—the hide and tallow trade. The beginnings of the cattle industry in California go back to the eighteenth century Spanish expeditions from Mexico to the province. All brought cattle, some of which survived and laid the foundations of subsequent great herds. Aided by a salubrious climate, abundant forage, and the natural aptitude of the Californians for pastoral farming, cattle raising became the predominant form of economic activity in the province and its principal source of wealth, while the *vaquero* and the annual roundup provided a picturesque and romantic touch to California life. Although steak from the lean, long-horned Spanish cattle was almost as well known for its flavor as for its toughness, the Californians, lacking a market for beef, utilized chiefly the hides and tallow. Only a small amount of those sufficed for the needs of the local market; the balance awaited an outlet. Although there was some traffic in hide and tallow with Mexican and South American ports, the trade remained of slight importance while restrictive Spanish commercial regulations continued in effect. Not until 1822 when Mexico won its independence did foreigners enter the trade, and the hide and tallow era in California history begin.

In one respect these traders had a significance not possessed by either sea otter traders or whalers. Their business required dealings in the interior with mission authorities and ranchers. They, therefore, either established a resident agent in California or sent with their ship a supercargo who traveled about on a horse, purchasing hides from missions and ranches. In this way the traders acquired a better knowledge of California and its people than their commercial predecessors.

With the achievement of Mexican independence, Bryant and Sturgis, an important Boston mercantile house, appointed W. H. Gale, a one-time sea otter trader, as their resident agent and began gathering hides for the market back home. In the same year the Brothertons, a Liverpool and Edinburgh firm, joined with John Begg and Company of Lima to establish William Hartnell and Hugh McCulloch as their agents. Within a year nine ships from various nations were competing with those pioneering firms, while the trade was developing the characteristics to be followed for the next quarter-century.

So largely did New England vessels predominate among American craft participating that all bottoms from the States were referred to as "Boston ships." Prior to the secularization of the missions in 1834 the hides were obtained largely from that source. Subsequently the ranches, of which there were ninety-two in 1842, were the principal source. The first port of call for a hide and tallow trader was Monterey, location of the one custom house in the province and its civil, military, and social capital as well. Every ship received a trading license and paid a duty on its cargo ranging as high as $25,000. Payment entitled the ship to distribute its cargo along the entire California coast, a process which consumed from one to three years. The effects of the heavy duty were somewhat alleviated by taking on additional goods from unlicensed traders lurking along the shore. That practice, combined with bribery of customs officials and actual smuggling, rendered the duty less onerous. Even if duties were paid in full the trader shifted much of the burden to the California consumer, who obtained the goods at a profit of 300% to the ship owner. Payment was either in silver or in hides, better known as "California bank-notes," at an average of $1.50 to $2.00 apiece. Such returns attracted more and more traders until on at least two occasions more than fifty ships were in California harbors at one time, the majority flying the American flag. Under such conditions two or three years were necessary to secure a cargo of 20,000 to 40,000 hides.

The hide and tallow business was mutually advantageous to Californians and to the traders. To the former it afforded virtually the one way of obtaining foreign goods, while customs duties defrayed the cost of the governmental establishment in California. To the New Englander it brought pecuniary rewards, an abundant supply of leather for the boot and shoe industry at home, and a market for countless articles of New England manufacture. But the trade had a larger and more lasting importance. From it New Englanders learned of California's resources and became interested in the province's destiny.

While New England ship captains established commercial contacts in California, American fur traders blazed the overland trails to the Pacific which the emigrant would some day follow. The pioneers in that bold enterprise were members of the Rocky Mountain Fur Company, and their agent was Jedediah Strong Smith—the "Knight of the Buckskin" his companions called him—whose discoveries rivaled those of Lewis and Clark. With his Bible and rifle as constant companions (and he never allowed his belief in one to interfere with the use of the other) he traversed thousands of miles of mountains and deserts, opened countless trails, and marked the path across the Great Basin to the interior valleys of California: the Sacramento and the San Joaquin. The quest for new beaver country drove him on, but his discoveries far transcended commercial importance.

His first journey began in 1826 when he reached the company rendezvous at Great Salt Lake with a supply of trading goods from the East. Leaving Salt Lake on August 22, Smith and his party travelled southwest to Utah Lake, then by the Sevier River, across a mountain range to the Virgin River. Following that stream they came to the Colorado, which they descended for four days until they came to a valley occupied by Mohave Indians. After resting and obtaining food, fresh horses, and two Indian guides, the explorers proceeded on their way, probably by much the same route as that of the Santa Fe Railroad of today. By November 27 they were in camp a short distance from the San Gabriel Mission. Thus they completed the overland journey to California, the first Americans to accomplish the feat.

Despite Mexican law, which forbad their presence in California, Smith and his men were hospitably received by the padres, fed and clothed, and allowed to rest. While his party remained at the mission, Smith visited San Diego to secure the governor's permission to journey through the province, a concession arranged by the gift of some fine beaver skins and the good offices of a hide and tallow trader. To Smith's disappointment, however, the most the governor would grant was the right to leave California over the route by which he had entered. Disregarding instructions, he led his men north into the San Joaquin Valley, down the valley to the Stanislaus or the Merced River, where he left all but two of his men, and up the middle fork of the Stanislaus to the crest of the Sierras. Once on the eastern slope of the latter Smith probably travelled along Walker River to Walker Lake. Then, following a northeasterly course, he arrived at the Great Salt Lake in June, 1827, after days of almost indescribable suffering and hardship.

On July 13, 1827, Smith set out again with nineteen men to join the hunters left in California. Travelling by the route of the previous year he arrived at the Mohave Indian settlement, where ten of his party were killed by natives. With considerable difficulty, Smith and the remainder arrived at Mission San Gabriel, whence he proceeded to the San Joaquin where he found the hunters left the previous spring. On this visit Smith was less hospitably received than the year before. At the Mission of San José he was arrested, thrown in jail, and for weeks denied the opportunity of seeing the governor. When he did, only the intervention of several American ship captains, who chanced to be in port, prevented Smith from being sent to Mexico as a prisoner. Instead, he was forced to post a $30,000 bond as

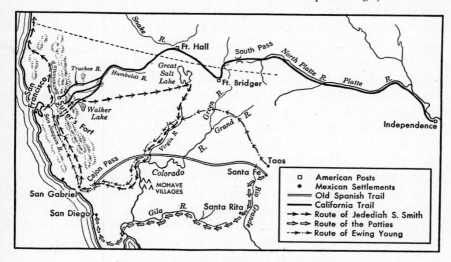

The American Occupation of California

a guarantee of his departure from California within two months. Travelling up the Sacramento Valley, Smith and his men failed to find a feasible pass through the Sierras. They then crossed the Coast Range Mountains and followed the coast to the Umpqua River in Oregon, from which they hoped to find the Willamette, which would lead them to the Columbia. While encamped on the Umpqua the party was surprised by previously friendly Indians who killed all except Smith and two of his men. The three survivors ultimately arrived at the Hudson's Bay post, Ft. Van-couver, where Dr. McLoughlin gave them his customary friendly greeting. He further sent a party to rescue the furs Smith had left on the Umpqua, which he agreed to purchase for $20,000. The latter action was the more notable since otherwise the furs would have been a total loss to Smith who had no means of transporting them to Salt Lake. In the spring of 1828 Smith made his way to Pierre's Hole. He had discovered two overland routes between California and the Great Salt Lake, revealed the matchless fertility of the inland valleys of California, travelled from the Mojave Desert to the Columbia, and made known to Hudson's Bay Company traders the route to the treasures of northern California. He, rather than Fremont, was the original California "Pathfinder."

If it was Jedediah S. Smith, the Puritan from New England, who first discovered an overland route to California, the southern uplander was not far behind. Among the Kentuckians who participated in the winning of the Far West, none was more genuinely a son of the frontier than Sylvester Pattie, who, finding life in his native state too tranquil, had sought adventure on the Missouri frontier as early as 1812. After a ten years' residence there he found the congestion so great he was again seized with an irresistible impulse to move on. In June, 1824, Sylvester Pattie, his twenty-year-old son James Ohio, and three other men set out on a trapping expedition to the Rocky Mountains. Foiled at Council Bluffs in their original plan to trade on the upper Missouri, they turned toward the Southwest, where they fell in with a party of Santa Fe traders on their way to New Mexico. Of the combined party of more than a hundred men Sylvester Pattie became the leader. Although they arrived at Santa Fe in November, 1824, without incidents unusual to the Santa Fe trade, this was but the beginning of the Patties' career in the Southwest. One searches the annals of the frontier in vain for a parallel with their varied experiences, their miraculous escapes, their repeated misfortunes during the next six years. Nor has the literature of western travel and exploration produced a work more notable than James Ohio Pattie's *Personal Narrative* of his experiences in the Southwest and California.

During 1825 and 1826 the Patties, despite repeated disaster, trapped on the Gila and operated copper mines at Santa Rita. The younger Pattie discovered a route from New Mexico to the eastern boundary of California, explored much of the Colorado River (including the Grand Canyon) traversed the central Rocky Mountain region as far north as the Yellowstone and the Platte, and followed the Arkansas to the south, whence he crossed to the Rio Grande which brought him back to Santa Fe. Then, obtaining permission to trap in Chihuahua and Sonora, the Patties left Santa Fe on September 23, 1827, for the Gila, which they followed to the Colorado. They trapped along the lower stretches of the river until deterred by the strong tide. Turning upstream they found the swift current an equally great obstacle. Unable to proceed in either direction, they cached their furs and started across the Lower California desert for the settlements on the coast. In March, 1828, they arrived at Santa Catalina Mission in Lower California, where they were received with scant hospitality. They were then sent under guard to San Diego where they arrived on March 27.

The Patties were placed in prison where the father died within a month. All efforts to secure the release of the son, including the intercession of Yankee ship captains at San Diego, failed until the outbreak of a severe epidemic of smallpox in the northern part of the province. As the disease spread southward, showing no distinction between Mexican and Indian, the authorities were powerless. Pattie fortunately had a quantity of vaccine which his father had brought from the Santa Rita copper mines. In return for his freedom, plus a monetary consideration, Pattie agreed to vaccinate the people of California. From San Diego to San Francisco he treated a total of 22,000 persons, a unique role for one who had illegally entered the province as an obscure trader and trapper. James Ohio Pattie returned to the States by way of Mexico, arriving at his Kentucky birthplace in August, 1830. In the words of Reuben Gold Thwaites, "brave, honest, God-fearing, vigorous in mind and body, dependent on their own resources, the Patties belonged to that class of Americans who conquered the wilderness and pushed the frontier westward." In the 1830's other fur traders followed in the steps of Smith and the Patties, entering California by the clearly defined routes blazed by those pioneers.

Meanwhile a regular intercourse was established between Santa Fe and southern California. The New Mexican capital was not merely the destination of the yearly caravans which went overland from Missouri, but the equipping center for trappers on the Arkansas, Green, Platte, and Rio Grande rivers. There, too, venturesome Americans obtained authorization for expeditions into Sonora and Chihuahua, whence they brought back precious metals and mules. Santa Fe was also the point of departure for those who ventured west to California.

Southern uplanders with a long frontier tradition behind them dominated the Santa Fe-California trade. A Tennessean, Ewing Young, was the one upon whom descended the mantle of the Patties. Departing from Taos in 1829, Young and his party travelled in a northwesterly direction to the Grand River, crossed to the Green, and followed Smith's route to California. Returning to Taos in the summer of 1830, Young became a business partner of William Wolfskill, a Kentuckian who for several years had engaged in the trade to Santa Fe and Chihuahua. Their plan was to trap in the interior valleys of California. Following the San Juan, Grand, and Green rivers, to the Colorado, they journeyed west to the Sevier River and southwest through the Mohave villages and Cajon Pass to Los Angeles. The Young-Wolfskill party blazed the "Old Spanish Trail" which became the regular caravan route for the Missouri-Santa Fe-Los Angeles trade.

The following year Young entered into another partnership under the name of Jackson, Waldo, and Young. The two companies sent by the new firm to California opened another route for the Los Angeles-Santa Fe trade. The first was designed to buy mules. Travelling by Pattie's trail through Albuquerque, Santa Rita, and the Gila to the Colorado, the party crossed the Imperial Valley and continued to San Diego and ultimately to San Francisco. The second, led by Young, trapped along the Gila and Colorado, before journeying on to Los Angeles where they met the first party in the spring of 1832. The two commanders merged their groups for the return to the Colorado. There they separated, one party continuing on with the seven hundred horses and mules acquired, while Young returned to California to trap. Young trapped in the San Joaquin and Sacramento valleys during the next two years, drove horses to Oregon in 1834, settled there, and became a regular dealer in mules between the Columbia and California.

Still another route to California opened in the 1830's was to become especially important in connection with later overland migrations. Joseph Reddeford Walker, a Tennessee native, after frontier experience as sheriff of a Missouri county, became a Santa Fe trader. When Captain Bonneville planned his expedition, made memorable by the pen of Washington Irving, he chose Walker as one of his assistants. On July 24, 1833, Walker and his party departed from the Grand River to explore the vast desert area west of the Great Salt Lake. Finding the headwaters of the Humboldt River, they followed it "until they ascertained that it lost itself in a great swampy lake," then crossed the Sierras by either Truckee Pass or the Walker River Valley. Walker's party was the first to cross the Sierras from east to west. Going up the San Joaquin Valley, they found Walker's Pass, through which they journeyed on their return to Bonneville on the Bear River in Utah.

Those were but a few of the many fur traders who found their way to California. One of the principal results of the expeditions was the inauguration of regular commercial intercourse between the western States and California—the well-known St. Louis-Santa Fe-California trade. Westbound, this traffic, which followed the "Old Spanish Trail" west of Santa Fe, carried American goods from St. Louis: blankets, woolen goods, and silver. In return there came silks from China—brought to the coast by trading ships—and horses and mules for the markets of western and southern states.

Strongly impressed by what they saw in California, some of the fur traders decided to become permanent residents. With those who had come by sea, they made a substantial American element in the population of the province. As they controlled in large measure the commerce and industry of the region, they exercised an influence out of all proportion to their number. Eventually the presence of the Americans in the territory made

Mexican officials uneasy. All sorts of rumors floated about as to the designs of the new arrivals, among them that of a plan to seize San Francisco. The fears of Mexican authorities were increased by the growing restlessness of the Californians themselves, who desired a larger measure of autonomy and the appointment of native sons to office. Certain American adventurers, for selfish reasons, fanned the flames of native discontent and certain ambitious Californians, for equally selfish reasons, were willing to make use of the services of these foreigners.

Out of this situation there developed the revolution of 1836 which elevated Juan Bautista Alvarado, a native son, to the governorship. An important figure in the uprising, and a tower of strength to Alvarado, was Isaac Graham, a native of Tennessee, who arrived in California in 1833 by way of Santa Fe. One of the more turbulent frontiersmen, he had established a still near San Juan which became headquarters for the foreign element of the community. Graham promised aid to Alvarado and recruited a force, composed partly of sailors of different nationalities and partly of American hunters, which was largely responsible for the success of the revolution. Alvarado admitted as much when he promised an appropriate reward in land to Graham and his associates.

Perhaps mindful of what Americans had done in Texas, Alvarado, once in power, lost much of his enthusiasm for his American accomplices. Crimination and recrimination resulted, in which Graham asserted that Alvarado owed his elevation to the governorship to him. In such an atmosphere Alvarado was particularly sensitive to reports that Americans were plotting a revolution. When rumors continued, in April, 1840, about a hundred British and American residents who lacked passports were arrested on the charge of participating in a plot to overthrow the government. Graham was alleged to be the leader. After rough treatment and a hurried trial at Santa Barbara, he and fifty conspirators were sent to Mexico, where the intercession of British officials secured pardon or acquittal for them. The so-called Graham affair of 1840 was symptomatic of trouble to come.

One other foreigner who arrived in the 1830's was cast for a prominent role. Johann August Sutter was a native of Baden who had sojourned in Switzerland. Arriving at Monterey in July, 1839, well armed with letters of recommendation and possessed of a winning personality, he had no difficulty winning the confidence of Alvarado who not only invited him to become a Mexican citizen but offered him attractive grants of land. Spurning various locations suggested, ostensibly because he wanted to settle on a navigable river but really because he desired to be a safe distance from California officials, he chose a site on the south bank of the American River near the Sacramento. He christened the spot New Helvetia, built a fort, established a ranch, and in 1840 became a Mexican citizen. Gradually Sutter's activities expanded as he indulged in trading and trapping, built an irrigation system, a distillery, a mill and a tannery, and engaged in weaving blankets. He was authorized to dispense justice in his district in the course of which he maintained harmonious relations with Indians and fur traders alike. His hospitality and kindness to wayfarers was reminiscent of that of Dr. McLoughlin at Ft. Vancouver. Sutter was for years a veritable frontier feudal baron in the Sacramento Valley.

The decade of the 1840's marked the opening of a new era in the history of American influence in California. This period was characterized by a migration to the province, the significance of which has been obscured by two more spectacular events—the Mexican War and the gold rush. Actually the settlers who moved to California during those years would have eventually added the province to the United States without war or the discovery of gold, just as a similar migration won Oregon and Texas. The same expansive forces which drove the pioneer across the Alleghenies or on to the Mississippi were pushing him to the shores of the Pacific; it mattered not to him that Oregon was in dispute between the United States and Great Britain or that Texas and California belonged to Mexico.

The pioneers' attention was directed toward California by the efforts of numerous "boosters"—disinterested and unselfish men who were so thrilled by what they saw there that they were seized with an irresistible urge to describe it. Those early California propagandists stressed the climate and potential agricultural wealth, the varied resources, and the abundance of game. By coupling with their glowing accounts of nature's lavish gifts a description of the province's defenseless state and the slothfulness of its population, they extended to the American settler an invitation to come and take possession.

The earliest American publicity material was written by Captain William Shaler, a sea otter trader, in 1808. Shaler wrote that "the climate of California generally is dry and temperate, and remarkabley healthy. . . . Most of the animals of Europe have been naturalized in California, where they have increased to a great degree; it is said that more than 80,000 cattle run wild in the mountains in the south part of the peninsula. This climate seems to be particularly favorable to horses and mules, as they retain their strength and vigor till past thirty years. . . . Most of the fruits and vegetables of Europe have been naturalized in California, where they come to great perfection." He added that "at great expense and considerable industry the Spaniards have removed every obstacle out of the way of an invading enemy. . . . The conquest of this country would be absolutely nothing; it would fall without an effort to the most inconsiderable force."

James Ohio Pattie, whose *Personal Narrative* appeared in 1831, wrote that California "is no less remarkable for uniting the advantages of healthfulness, a good soil, temperate climate and yet one of exceeding mildness, a happy mixture of level and elevated ground and vicinity to the sea."

Hall Jackson Kelley of Oregon fame was also an enthusiastic advocate of American settlement in California. Much of his report on Oregon, presented to Congress in 1839, was devoted to California and expressed the belief that "at no very distant day a swarming multitude of human beings will again people the solitude, and that monuments of civilization will throng along those streams whose waters now murmur to the desert." Thomas Jefferson Farnham, another Oregon booster, was a California visitor whose *Life and Adventures in California* outdid all competitors in its fulsome praise of the province. After asserting that "no country in the world possesses so fine a climate coupled with so productive a soil" he referred contemptuously to the "miserable people who sleep, and smoke and hum some tune of Castilian laziness, while surrounding nature is thus inviting them to the noblest and richest rewards of honorable toil."

Probably the most influential single bit of California propaganda was Richard H. Dana's *Two Years before the Mast*, first published in 1840. Dana, a Harvard student, came to California in January, 1835, on board the *Pilgrim*, a hide and tallow trader, and remained until May, 1836. He repeatedly visited every California port and spent four months at the hidehouses of San Diego. Of Dana's work a critic has said: "Notwithstanding its truth, Dana's narrative had all the fascination of Cooper's and Marryat's sea-stories, and it was doubtless this charm mainly that caused its immense popularity." After describing in lyrical vein the remarkable attractions of the land, Dana remarked: "In the hands of an enterprising people, what a country this might be!" Then added, "Yet how long would a people remain so in such a country? If the 'California fever,' laziness, spares the first generation, it is likely to attack the second."

These early California popularizers were merely visitors to the province. But permanent residents also aided materially in advertising the territory. Prominent among them was Alfred Robinson, whose *Life in California*, was published in 1846. Robinson had been for many years the representative of Bryant and Sturgis in California, and while his work was first published anonymously, it was obviously written by one thoroughly conversant with the situation in California. Other Americans desirous of diverting the tide of westward migration in their direction wrote no books about their adopted land, but corresponded regularly with friends in the East, writing in a manner to ensure publication of their letters in local papers. At least one wrote directly for newspaper publication. Thomas O. Larkin had arrived in California in 1832, built up a successful mercantile business at Monterey, and in 1843 became the United States consul. So well known was he that when interest in California began to evince itself in the States, prominent newspapers made him their correspondent, among them the *Sun, Herald,* and *Journal of Commerce* in New York, and the *Advertiser* in Boston. So eminently practical were Larkin's letters that they constituted a sort of settlers' guide, with advice on the equipment required by the prospective emigrant, descriptions of California crops, and counsel as to the procedure "on arriving on the banks of the Sacramento."

American settlers attracted to California by "boosters" and propagandists after 1841 differed markedly from those who arrived earlier. While the majority coming before 1840 had arrived by sea, those in the 1840's followed the overland route. They came chiefly from the Mississippi Valley, were attracted to the interior valleys rather than the coastal areas, were interested in agriculture rather than commerce, and avoided the native Californians. Few married native women, so they constituted a group apart. They were less welcome than their predecessors, since their agricultural economy competed with that of the natives instead of supplementing it as did the services of foreign merchants.

The point of origin of the first organized overland migration to California was Platte County, on the extreme western frontier of Missouri. Enthusiasm had developed there largely because of reports of a returned California trapper, Antoine Robidoux, "a calm, considerate man" whose "stories had all the appearance of truth." Robidoux's description of California as "a perfect paradise, a perpetual spring" prompted people of Platte County to form the Western Emigration Society, which sponsored a meeting of interested settlers addressed by the trapper. When a skeptical soul asked about the chills and fever, Robidoux replied that "there never was but one man in California who had the chills. He was from Missouri and carried the disease in his system. It was such a curiosity to see a man shake with the chills that the people of Monterey went eighteen miles into the country to see him." Robidoux's efforts were reinforced by letters of Dr. John Marsh, of Mt. Diablo, a onetime resident of western Missouri, which appeared in many of the local newspapers of the state. The California fever was further disseminated by the Western Emigration Society which spread propaganda throughout the Mississippi Valley. As a result members of the society signed a pledge late in 1840, binding themselves to meet at Sapling Grove in eastern Kansas in May, 1841, prepared for the great trek. Five hundred signatures were obtained within one month.

Alarmed by the prospective removal of so many people, merchants and landed proprietors of Platte County launched a campaign of slander upon California designed to discourage the migration. This was so effective that when the appointed day came in May, 1841, only sixty-nine persons appeared at Sapling Grove, and of those only one had signed the pledge the previous fall. This was John Bidwell, whose sterling qualities, manifest then and later, earned for him the title of "Prince of California Pioneers."

No Mountain Men or experienced western travelers were present to serve as an antidote to the geographical ignorance of the group. Nor was the prospect of a successful journey increased by the choice, for reasons of expediency, of John Bartleson of Jackson County, Missouri, rather than Bidwell, as commander of the company. A further complication resulted from the presence of a number of women and children. Fortunately, for the earlier stages of the trip, they fell in with two very helpful men, Thomas Fitzpatrick, the well-known trapper, and Father De Smet, who was en route to the Flathead Indians. From the great bend of the Missouri the party followed the route of the Oregon migrations to the Platte, Ft. Laramie, Independence Rock, and the Sweetwater to the Rockies, through South Pass, and the Green River Valley to Soda Springs near the present Pocatello, Idaho. There Fitzpatrick and De Smet took the trail toward Oregon with thirty-two emigrants, who preferred the known route to the Columbia to the virtually unknown trail to California. The remainder, including one woman and her young daughter, continued into the desert which Jedediah Smith and Walker had crossed.

With nothing to guide them save the admonition to bear due west from Salt Lake they plunged into the unknown, abandoning their wagons in favor of pack animals to gain time. On September 23 they came to the Humboldt which they followed to the Sink. Bearing southwest, they probably passed Humboldt and Carson lakes and came to the Walker River where they arrived on October 16. When a short reconnaissance revealed that "the mountains were barely passable" some members advised a return to Ft. Hall before winter's snow set in, but when the question was put to a vote the majority favored continuing. With their supply of beef exhausted and surrounded by "naked mountains whose summits still retained the snows of perhaps a thousand years" they struggled until October 29, when they despaired of reaching California. But the following day they discovered a westward-flowing river, the Stanislaus, which they followed to the site of Sonora. So exhausted were they when they arrived in the San Joaquin Valley that they could not believe they were in the promised land itself. California, some thought, must be five hundred miles away. Soon they found antelope in abundance, along with "ripe and luscious wild grapes." With the assistance of an Indian guide they arrived at the ranch of Dr. John Marsh, near Mt. Diablo, on November 4, 1841. Thus ended the first overland migration to California after a journey of six months.

Other parties followed. Within a few weeks the Workman-Rowland Company of twenty-five Americans and New Mexicans arrived from Santa Fe. In 1843 Lansford W. Hastings brought a group of forty pioneers by way of Oregon. The same year Joseph B. Chiles, one of the Bidwell-Bartleson party of 1841, led a large company from Missouri. Dividing at Ft. Hall, one group, proceeding by way of Oregon, arrived in the Sacramento Valley in November; the other, following the trail blazed by Joseph Walker a decade before, entered the San Joaquin Valley by way of Walker Pass. In 1844 Andrew Kelsey led thirty-six immigrants to California, while in the same year the larger Stevens-Murphy party earned the distinction of being the first group to bring wagons over the entire route from Missouri to California. Rumor had it that the immigrants of 1845 would be numbered in the thousands, but actually the total for the year was about 250, a large part of whom were included in the Grigsby-Ide party, who followed the Humboldt-Truckee route.

The outbreak of the war with Mexico in April, 1846, reduced, but failed to stop, the immigrant tide to California. That year was notable in the history of the overland migrations for the tragic fate which befell the Donner party. Organized largely in Illinois by George and Jacob Donner, this group left Independence in the spring of 1846 almost one hundred strong. As other parties joined them along the way, their number was increased to two hundred. All went well as far as Ft. Bridger. There they divided, the larger group following the usual route by Ft. Hall, the remaining eighty-seven taking the little-known Hastings' Cutoff on the south side of Salt Lake. The larger company arrived in California without undue suffering. The smaller was not so fortunate. They reached the south side of Salt Lake at the cost of a month's time and much of the strength of men and animals. Autumn was already upon them when they started across the desert. Late in the fall they arrived at the foot of the Sierra-Nevada Mountains in a completely disorganized condition. Torn by factional discord, they began climbing upward, only to have an abnormally early winter break upon them. Snowbound near the shores of Donner Lake, they suffered acutely from cold and famine. Of the seventy-nine persons who entered the mountains, only forty-five survived. Along with the sordidness, inefficiency, jealousy, and vacillation which brought tragedy to the party, there were bravery and heroism of a high order, without which the disaster would have been even more appalling.

While settlers were finding their way to California, officials in Washington were not indifferent to the fate of the province. Official interest dated from the time Andrew Jackson was made aware of the region's wealth by Anthony Butler, the American representative in Mexico City. In the course of his devious intrigues, Butler submitted a plan to acquire California, along with Texas and New Mexico, by placing $500,000 at the disposal of a Mexican priest, who would purchase Santa Anna's consent to the cession. Although Jackson rejected Butler's scheme of bribery, his desire to obtain California was strengthened by the glowing account of the country which he received from William A. Slacum, a purser in the United States navy. He accordingly instructed Butler to negotiate with Mexico for the cession of California north of the 37th parallel. As this area was north of the Missouri Compromise line, Jackson's objective was the acquisition of San Francisco Bay rather than the extension of slave territory. Nothing came of the plan; and Jackson, now convinced of Butler's dubious character, replaced him with another man.

When, after the battle of San Jacinto, Santa Anna sought American mediation between Mexico and Texas, Jackson formulated a plan to offer Mexico $3,500,000 for that part of California north of the 38th parallel. At the same time he suggested to W. H. Wharton, the Texan minister at Washington, that Texas should include California within its boundaries. By acquiring the great harbor of San Francisco Bay, Jackson thought the infant Republic would disarm the hostility of northern commercial interests to annexation.

After the failure of Jackson's various plans, Van Buren found himself too engrossed with financial problems to direct his attention to California. The Tyler administration, however, was quick to reaffirm American interest in the region. With Waddy Thompson, minister to Mexico, the acquisition of California amounted to an obsession. Profoundly impressed by the climatic, commercial, forest, and agricultural resources of the province, he hoped North and South would join hands to gain possession before France or England stepped in. Tyler, as well as Daniel Webster, the secretary of state, shared Thompson's views and authorized him to negotiate for the purchase of San Francisco and adjacent areas. It was hoped that Mexico might be induced to cede the region on condition of American assumption of claims against the country which the Mexican government was unable to satisfy.

Meanwhile Webster and Tyler formulated a more elaborate plan, the Tripartite Agreement, to which Great Britain, Mexico, and the United States were to be parties. Mexico was to cede Upper California to the United States for a sum not precisely stipulated. A portion of the money would be used to satisfy American claimants against Mexico, while the balance would liquidate claims of British creditors. The Oregon boundary was to be at the Columbia River. Webster and Tyler believed the acquisition of California would disarm northern hostility to the annexation of Texas, while the line of the Columbia would mollify more rabid western expansionists. For a time the Tyler administration pursued the plan with vigor. But with Webster's resignation as secretary of state, and the growing realization that no Mexican administration would dare sell California, lest it be immediately overturned, the plan lapsed.

The situation within California greatly affected the next stage in the negotiations. The passing years demonstrated repeatedly that the authorities in Mexico City lacked both the military and naval power necessary to defend the province. Communication between the colony and the mother country, whether by land or by sea, was far from satisfactory. Government was almost nonexistent. The administration of justice had broken down, finances were in a chaotic state, life and property were utterly insecure. As this anarchical state of affairs became progressively worse in the early 1840's California residents, whether native or foreign, realized that a change was necessary. Some natives favored annexation to the United States; some a protectorate under Britain or France; some independence. Of the foreigners, the majority wished to join the United States, a minority favored independence, and English residents desired British control.

Such was the situation when James K. Polk entered the White House in 1845. Polk was an ardent expansionist. Manifest Destiny "was as deeprooted in his convictions as the rigid Calvinistic theology to which he subscribed." As to the imminent separation of California from Mexico, Polk had no doubt. Nor was he any less certain as to its ultimate fate. It must be annexed to the United States.

Among the considerations influencing Polk in his resolve to acquire California was the fear of British designs. That the government in London was never sufficiently interested in California to support any of the schemes for annexation in no way diminished the influence such reports exercised upon officials in Washington. Most of them had sufficient foundation in truth to warrant acceptance by the government and public in this country. One of the first manifestations of British interest in California was the publication in 1839 of Alexander Forbes' *History of California*. Although Forbes, a British consul in Mexico, had never set foot on California soil, he obviously had reliable sources of information regarding conditions in the province. As he freely admitted, the purpose of his book was to foster British settlement in California. He suggested cession to liquidate the debt of $50,000,000 held by British bondholders in Mexico, and proposed that the creditors, organized as a company, play the role in California of a second East India Company. Forbes' words were interpreted by the Baltimore *American* as indicating a British plot to acquire California as a base for commerce with China and the East Indies. In the early 1840's newspapers in all sections of the country voiced similar opinions with respect to British designs. Britain's plans were believed by the press to be so inimical to the United States as to call for frustration at any cost.

Public concern over British schemes in California were shared by American officials. Waddy Thompson, the American minister in Mexico, constantly stressed the British menace in 1842 and 1843. Duff Green, whom Calhoun sent to Mexico as his confidential agent, wrote in similar fashion in 1844. Wilson Shannon, Thompson's successor in Mexico, reported negotiations for the sale of California to Britain. Reports from California were no more reassuring than those from Mexico. The Hudson's Bay Company was invading the province. Its trappers were active in the region, it had established a regular trading post at San Francisco, and it was asking for substantial grants of land from Mexican officials. In numerous ways the employees of the company showed a disposition to settle permanently there. The friendly attitude of some native leaders toward the company did not serve to quiet American fears.

The fund of information respecting British plans and activities in California available to Polk when he took office was soon amplified. In May, 1845, the President's agent in Mexico, William S. Parrott, reported the strengthening of British naval forces in the Pacific, with a view of taking over California in the event of war between the United States and Mexico. A short time later Parrott advised Polk of the plan of a youthful Irish priest, Eugene McNamara, to colonize California with settlers from his own country. McNamara, Polk was told, had received a grant of 3,000 leagues for this purpose, which constituted "a new feature in English policy and a new method of obtaining California." Polk's most pointed warning came from Thomas O. Larkin, the American consul in Monterey. On July 10, 1845, Larkin called the State Department's attention to the activities of the Hudson's Bay Company in California, the financial assistance of two British firms in Mexico to a plan for suppressing any revolution Americans might instigate in the province, and the appointment of a British agent, in the guise of a consul, to work secretly against American plans in California. The degree to which Polk's moves to acquire California were influenced by his concern over British designs there cannot, of course, be precisely determined. A judicious scholar, however, has expressed the matured judgment that "nearly every movement Polk made with regard to California was, in some measure, based upon the English situation."

Polk's plan for the peaceful acquisition of California was a dual one. On the one hand, he would offer to purchase it outright from Mexico. Late in the autumn of 1845, he selected John Slidell of New Orleans to conduct this important negotiation. Slidell's acquaintance with Mexican conditions and his knowledge of the Spanish language seemed to qualify him for the mission. Polk instructed him to purchase both New Mexico and California. He supposed the two provinces might be had for $15,000,000 or $20,000,000 but was prepared to pay $40,000,000 if necessary.

Confronted with this offer, the Mexican government was torn between two emotions. The chronic need for money, the precarious nature of Mexican control in California, and a desire to appease the government in Washington made it favorably disposed toward the sale. National pride, the opposition of Britain, traditional hostility to the United States, and the knowledge that any territorial cession would be the signal for a revolutionary overturn in Mexico made compliance hazardous. When Slidell embarked upon his errand, a revolution had only recently occurred in Mexico, in which General José Maria Herrera was elevated to the presidency as successor to the deposed Santa Anna. Herrera in turn was being carefully watched by aspirants to his high office. In this situation Slidell's mission was kept secret, as a means of protecting the Herrera regime. News of his coming, however, preceded Slidell to Mexico, together with the ugly rumor that he carried a handsome bribe for President Herrera. Herrera had two alternatives. He could receive Slidell, at the almost certain cost of a revolution; or he could refuse him, at great financial loss and at the risk of offending the United States.

Faced with this difficult decision, Herrera declined to receive Slidell, assigning technical reasons for his action. Actually his refusal was dictated by fear of being overthrown. Before Slidell departed from Mexico City, however, a bloodless revolution removed Herrera from office. When his efforts to open negotiations with the new regime were curtly rebuffed, he asked for his passport and returned to Washington, convinced of the utter futility of attempting to deal with a country whose government was so lacking in stability. Thus ended Polk's plan for the purchase of California.

Meanwhile the President placed another scheme in operation. In October, 1845, James Buchanan, secretary of state, appointed Thomas O. Larkin, since 1843 United States consul in California, the confidential agent of the state department. Larkin was to inform himself on the affairs of California, to "exert the greatest vigilance" to prevent a European country from obtaining control of it, and to encourage Californians to turn to the United States for aid and counsel. While the United States would not incite the Californians to rebel, Larkin might let them understand his country would play the part of protector if they should seek separation from Mexico. To promote the plans of the administration, to gain the good will of Californians, and to foil the designs of European powers, Larkin was to rely largely upon his own discretion.

As Larkin interpreted his instructions, he was to pave the way for the peaceful acquisition of California. With characteristic energy and thoroughness, he addressed himself to the task assigned him. To prominent Americans in the province, who had married California women and accepted Mexican citizenship, he wrote soliciting aid in winning the support of native Californians. Included in this number was Abel Stearns, whom he made his assistant in the Los Angeles area. Among Californians he found little love for Mexico, but some were predisposed to depend upon Britain for aid. Those known to be sympathetic to the American program he encouraged to affiliate with various juntos, which carried on active propaganda in support of his cause.

Larkin's campaign showed distinct indications of success. Some of the leading Californians rallied to his support, including General José Castro, who drew up a plan for "declaring California independent in 1847 or 48 as soon as a sufficient number of foreigners should arrive." No less hopeful were reports from the Los Angeles region. In the spring of 1846 it appeared to be but a short time before California would go the way of Texas—declare her independence and join the United States. Two events, however, intervened to spoil Larkin's plan of peaceful acquisition. One was the Bear Flag Revolt; the other the outbreak of war with Mexico.

The genesis of the Bear Flag Revolt is to be found in the restlessness of a handful of American landowners, traders, and trappers in the Sacramento Valley. Associated with them in some way not altogether clear was the enigmatic John C. Frémont. In the spring of 1845 Frémont, an official explorer for the United States, left St. Louis with a picked group which included some of the most notable of the Mountain Men, among them Kit Carson and Joseph Walker. They ascended the Arkansas River, penetrated the Colorado Rockies, crossed the Nevada desert to the Humboldt River, and explored the region between the river and Walker Lake. Then the party divided. Frémont, with fifteen men, advanced by the Truckee River to the summit of the Sierra Nevada Range, then descended the American River into the Sacramento Valley. Walker, with the remainder of the party, followed his old trail into the San Joaquin Valley. Failing to meet the Walker group at the appointed rendezvous, Frémont visited Thomas O. Larkin at Monterey, where he met General José Castro, then in command of the post. Although suspicious of the entrance of Frémont's armed band into the province without permission, Castro's fears were somewhat allayed by Frémont's assurance that his interest in California was entirely of a scientific nature. It was agreed the Americans might winter in California on condition they keep away from the coast settlements.

In February, 1846, Frémont was joined by the Walker party and went into winter quarters near San José. Shortly, however, he moved across the Santa Cruz Mountains into the Salinas Valley, in violation of his pledge to keep away from the coast. When General Castro ordered him to leave the province, he denounced the order as a breach of faith and an insult to himself and his country. He thereupon moved his quarters to Hawk's Peak, an eminence overlooking the surrounding plain, where he defied Castro. For three days the forces of Castro and Frémont faced each other without shedding blood. Frémont then quietly abandoned his camp and advanced slowly up the Sacramento Valley to Oregon. The incident at Hawk's Peak doomed Larkin's plan for peaceful acquisition of California. It outraged the Californians and encouraged the restless immigrants in the Valley in their contempt for provincial authorities.

Within a few weeks Lieutenant Archibald Gillespie of the United States Marine Corps arrived at Monterey, as an agent of the government in Washington. He was the bearer of various papers, including a packet of letters to Frémont from Senator Thomas H. Benton. Gillespie overtook Frémont near Klamath Lake, handed him the Benton letters, and informed him of the nature of Larkin's appointment and the objectives of Polk with respect to California. To this day, the exact contents of the communications are not known. In the words of a competent authority, however, "it is clear either that Frémont considered himself bound, explicitly or by implication, to return to California and take such part in forthcoming events as circumstances required, or else he saw in the situation an opportunity to make John Charles Frémont the Sam Houston of California."

Frémont made his way south to the Sacramento where the wildest rumors were rife as to the cruel fate American settlers were about to suffer at the hands of the California authorities. The settlers naturally turned to Frémont and his Mountain Men for protection. Regardless of whether Frémont instigated the revolt which followed, as Larkin and others alleged, his presence gave the insurgents the fortitude necessary for action. On June 10, 1846, a group of settlers led by Ezekiel Merritt, one of the more reckless frontiersmen in the valley, seized some horses intended for use by General Castro. A few days later a larger band invaded the village of Sonoma and carried Mariano G. Vallejo, California's wealthiest and most conspicuous citizen, a prisoner to Sutter's Fort, despite his well-known support of Larkin's plan of peaceful acquisition.

During the next few days the revolt in the Sacramento Valley became general. Disturbing news fanned the flames: General Castro was marching north from San Francisco to retake Sonoma and punish the rebels. Frémont threw off all pretense of neutrality now. Sending twenty of his riflemen south to meet the Mexican force, he called the settlers together at Sonoma and on July 4, 1846 (a great day for revolutions), urged them to declare their independence and drive Castro from the country. Inspired by his fighting words the Americans ran up an unbleached cotton flag bearing the crude likeness of a grizzly bear and proclaimed independence for the Republic of California. That done, Frémont headed south on General Castro's trail, followed by a makeshift army of 150 Mountain Men and pioneers.

Yet neither Larkin's policy of peaceful annexation nor Frémont's hope of revolutionary conquest was ever realized. Scarcely was the Bear Flag Revolt launched than news from the East changed the whole picture. The United States and Mexico were at war! The glory of winning California was to fall upon unnamed soldiers who a year later battered their way into Mexico City and dictated a peace adding all the Southwest to the United States.

# CHAPTER XXVIII

# The War with Mexico

# 1846-1850

That the frontier surge which carried American pioneers across Texas and into the valleys of California could go on without protest was unthinkable. Those were Mexican territories. Won by the blood and sweat of early conquerors, they had been viewed for generations as essential barriers against aggressive frontiersmen from the United States. Public opinion in Mexico solidly insisted the northern provinces never be surrendered; public opinion north of the border was almost as united in support of annexing California. This was the basis for the conflict which began in 1846 and ended only when a triumphant United States wrested from its beaten opponent not only California but the whole region north of the Gila and Rio Grande rivers.

The causes which impelled both nations to welcome the Mexican War were far from simple. Historians a generation ago who maintained the United States was goaded into an imperialistic war by greedy slaveholders seeking more territory for their peculiar institution ignored both the psychology of the American people and the attitude of their government. Every patriot who clamored for Mexico's provinces would have indignantly denied any desire to exploit a neighbor's territory. The righteous but ill-informed people of that day sincerely believed their democratic institutions were of such magnificent perfection that no boundaries could contain them. Surely a benevolent Creator did not intend such blessings for the few; expansion was a divinely ordered means of extending enlightenment to despot-ridden masses in nearby countries! This was not imperialism, but enforced salvation. So the average American reasoned in the 1840's when the spirit of manifest destiny was in the air.

The impact of those intellectual currents on the American government was demonstrated repeatedly in the attitude of presidents from Jackson to Polk. All wanted the northern Mexican provinces, and Polk at least was determined to secure them, but he looked upon war as a last resort. He and his predecessors tried bribery, purchase, and intrigue before reluctantly deciding the stubborn Mexicans could be convinced only by force. No one could condone the greedy determination to appropriate a neighbor's territory, yet Polk's most hostile critics were forced to concede that he tried every peaceful method before taking up arms, and that his reasons for coveting California were more humanitarian than mercenary.

Nor could anyone deny that the United States had grievances against Mexico which in the eyes of both American and European statesmen fully justified war. Those grew out of Mexico's turbulent governmental system. Its people, newly emerged from centuries of despotic rule, were ill-prepared to shoulder the burdens of democracy; its elected leaders, inexperienced in the republican tradition, were ill-equipped to guide a nation along the path to security and order. The inevitable result was a post-revolutionary era of periodic uprisings, chronic bankruptcy, property destruction, and utter failure to meet either national or international obligations. Neither the United States nor the European powers could see that the confusion was the product of immaturity rather than design. They viewed the frequent Mexican revolutions as signs of anarchy rather than as necessary steps in the evolution of a workable government, the failure of Mexico to pay its debts as an indication of fraud rather than a normal breakdown of the credit structure, the destruction of foreign life and property as a sign of international lawnessness rather than an example of chaos usual in periods of change. The Mexicans were guilty of being poor neighbors; the Americans were equally at fault for failing to excuse the sins of their inexperienced friends below the border.

Differences between the two powers began to develop as soon as Mexico's independence was won. The United States faced the problem of Mexican inefficiency first when it asked the new nation to reaffirm the Spanish Treaty of 1819 establishing western boundaries for the Louisiana Purchase. For seven years American ministers battled official indifference before an agreement was reached, and four more years were needed before that was ratified by the Mexican legislature in 1832. The treaty provided for a joint commission to survey the line, but despite American pleading, Mexico failed to name its representatives until the understanding lapsed and had to be renegotiated. Not until pressure was brought on the Mexican president did the laggard nation finally co-operate. Equally annoying was Mexico's failure to agree on a treaty of commerce and amity. Two treaties drawn up during the 1820's were rejected by the Mexican Congress, and no settlement reached until 1831. For that whole time American business men clamored in vain for the right to trade in their neighbor's ports.

Still worse in American eyes was Mexico's failure to protect life and property during the frequent revolutions which racked the infant republic. One shocking example occurred in 1835 when twenty-two American citizens accused of plotting with a revolutionary were executed without proper trial. More lost property during the periodic uprisings, and their strenuous efforts to recover created one of the most troublesome differences between the two nations. Their claims, as was usual in such circumstances, were directed first against Mexican officials who gave them no satisfaction, then the American government was called upon for aid. President Jackson responded to the creditors' pressure in 1829 when he asked the United States minister in Mexico City to intercede in their behalf. For the next seven years every request for payment was met with "cold neglect," until the fiery Jackson was convinced that Mexico's attitude "would justify in the eyes of all nations immediate war." He might, he wrathfully told Congress, make the next demand for settlement from the deck of a warship.

Jackson retired from office before making good his threat, but his successors were just as aroused by continued Mexican delays. Not until 1839 did they goad that nation into accepting a mixed arbitration commission with power to determine the justice of all claims and the amount due each creditor. That body, made up of two representatives from each country and an impartial commissioner named by the King of Prussia, met in August, 1840, and after several months of deliberation awarded American claimants $2,026,000 to be paid in five yearly installments. Three payments were made before Mexico announced her inability to continue. Little wonder that both disappointed creditors and government agents operating in their behalf became convinced Mexico was an irresponsible menace in the congress of nations. That their sentiment was shared elsewhere was shown by the attitude of England and France, whose nationals also lost heavily during the Mexican outbreaks. Both adopted a more belligerent tone than the United States, France going so far in 1838 as to fight the so-called "Pastry War" to collect defaulted debts. President Polk was not alone in believing Mexico's behavior left no room for peaceful settlement.

The grievances, however, were not all on one side. Viewed through Mexican eyes, the relations between the two powers during the twenty years before 1845 constituted one continuous aggression on the part of the powerful northern neighbor, directed toward dismembering Mexico and annexing its northern provinces. The history of Texas seemingly provided perfect proof. First the United States had disclosed its intentions by trying to buy, then when Mexico refused to sell, disguised troops were sent to wrest the province away by force! Everyone remembered the aid given Texan revolutionists by Americans who crossed the border to fight at San Jacinto, the half-hearted gestures of federal troops to stop those illegal excursions, and the joking manner in which newspapers condoned the invasion of a neighboring power. The United States, all Mexico believed, stooped to such unneutral conduct only because it engineered the revolution which made Texas free.

Additional proof was apparently provided by the "Gaines Affair" which occurred while Texan independence was being won. Major-General Edmund P. Gaines was sent to the Louisiana-Texas border in 1836 to protect American settlements from marauding Indians. Although ordered to maintain strict neutrality, he violated his instructions when a band of fleeing raiders took refuge in Texas, pursuing them across the international boundary as far as Nacogdoches. There he stayed through the summer, while irate Mexican officials bombarded Washington with complaints that he was aiding the revolutionists and must be withdrawn. For a time war threatened before Gaines returned to his own soil in the autumn and the differences were patched up. From that time on every Mexican was sure that an official American military expedition openly aided the Texan rebels.

America's imagined role in Texas was bad enough, but even worse from the Mexican standpoint was its identical activity in California. To their horror they saw the whole process repeated there: the early efforts to purchase the region, the infiltration of armed frontiersmen, growing differences between the invaders and the Mexican officials, the first clashes, and finally open rebellion and the proclamation of independence. The parallels between the Texan and Californian revolutions were too clear to be ignored; this was design rather than coincidence! Piece by piece Mexico was being dismembered. Better to resist than wait until the whole nation was gobbled up by the colossus of the north. There was no basis for alarm, of course, but every Mexican believed unquestioningly the lesson learned from the sequence of events.

An episode in 1842 capped the climax. In the fall of that year an American naval commander, Commodore Thomas Ap Catesby Jones, heard while cruising off the Peru coast that a Mexican war had begun and that California was to be surrendered to England to keep it from his own nation. Without pausing to test the truth of the rumor, Jones sailed northward to Monterey which he reached on October 18, 1842. Although the port was "quiet, peaceful, and normally dilapidated," he sent a landing party ashore, seized the surprised Mexican defenders, ran up the Stars and Stripes, and proclaimed California annexed to the United States. Not until two days later did he make the embarrassing discovery he had captured a city belonging to a friendly power. Commodore Jones made the best of a bad situation by withdrawing after elaborate apologies. The Mexican governor, not to be outdone in courtesy, tendered the Americans a "well and brilliantly attended" ball before they sailed away. Those pleasantries could not hide the fact that the United States expected war and had instructed its officers in the strategy to follow when hostilities began. Tension was high from that time on.

The breaking point came when Texas entered the Union. No longer could the role of the United States in the Texas Revolution be ignored; Mexicans were convinced the whole revolutionary process was aimed toward annexation. On March 6, 1845, only a few days after Congress voted to welcome the new state, the Mexican minister asked for his passport, leaving the two nations with no means of diplomatic communication. That was particularly unfortunate as the Texan Republic bequeathed the United States a series of ancient disputes which must be settled. Most dangerous was a controversy over the southern boundary. As a republic Texas insisted its southern border extended to the Rio Grande, a claim Mexico justly refuted by proving the old province of Texas-Coahuila never extended south of the Nueces and that the region between the two rivers was part of the neighboring state of Tamaulipas. Although Texans could support their right to the Rio Grande boundary only by such questionable evidence as an agreement wrung from General Santa Anna under duress, President Polk felt obliged to back their claim. His noisy insistence that the Nueces-Rio Grande strip belonged to the United States widened the breach between the two countries.

Polk was still unwilling to abandon hope for a peaceful settlement. When inquiries convinced him that Mexico would receive a commissioner authorized to "settle the present dispute in a peaceful, reasonable and honorable manner" he sent John Slidell packing off to Mexico City, with authority not only to purchase California but to end the troublesome Texan boundary problem by assuming all claims against Mexico in return for the Rio Grande line. When the Mexican officials refused to receive him, Slidell wrote Polk: "Be assure that nothing is to be done with these people until they shall have been chastised."

When that message reached the President on January 12, 1846, he saw that war was certain. There remained only the task of maneuvering Mexico into striking the first blow. With that in mind Polk, on January 13, 1846, ordered a detachment of troops under General Zachary Taylor into the disputed area between the Nueces and the Rio Grande. For the next three months they waited there, hoping to goad the Mexicans into an attack, while tension mounted steadily. Polk succumbed to the pressure first. When Slidell reached Washington on May 8, 1846, with tales of his inhospitable treatment at the hands of the Mexicans, of war fever among the populace, and of the government's determination to fight, the President decided the time for action had come. The next day he called his cabinet together and announced his decision to recommend war to Congress, basing the demand on Mexico's refusal to meet its financial obligations, receive Slidell, or settle disputes by peaceful means. All agreed the step justified save George Bancroft, secretary of the navy, who advised delay until the Mexicans committed an act of aggression. When this suggestion was overruled, Polk left the meeting to begin work on a war message.

The message was never written, for electrifying news reached the capital that very night (May 9, 1846). A Mexican force under General Mariano Arista had crossed the Rio Grande from Matamoros on April 25, ambushed an American patrol, and killed or wounded sixteen men. This was the excuse Polk was waiting for. Hurriedly he drafted a new message which was read to Congress on May 11. The long-standing grievances between the two powers were scarcely mentioned in that amazing document. "Now, after reiterated menaces," Polk told Congress, "Mexico has passed the boundary of the United States, has invaded our territory and shed American blood upon the American soil. She has proclaimed that hostilities have commenced, and that the two nations are now at war. As war exists, and, notwithstanding all our efforts to avoid it, exists by the act of Mexico herself, we are called upon by every consideration of duty and patriotism to vindicate with decision the honor, the rights, and the interests of our country." Two days later Congress declared that "by the Act of the Republic of Mexico a state of war exists," authorized the President to raise an army of 50,000 men, and appropriated $10,000,000 for military purposes.

False as was Polk's summary of the situation, there was no doubt that Mexico welcomed the outbreak of hostilities more enthusiastically than the United States. The majority of literate Mexicans recognized that their army, on paper at least, was five times as large as the American force. They knew their people were eager to avenge past wrongs and confident of victory; one officer boasted that his cavalry, equipped only with lassos, could beat the American infantry easily. They believed that Indians and slaves would rise to join them as they marched triumphantly northward. Intoxicated by those heady dreams, Mexicans refused to listen to English and French warnings of the superior latent power of the United States. If the nation was strong, they asked, why had it failed to take Canada in the War of 1812? Why had Polk tried to buy California rather than using force? The Americans, they agreed, were so torn by sectional conflicts that no united resistance was possible. Mexico did not need to divide and conquer; the enemy was so divided only conquest was necessary.

The American people, on the other hand, were of two minds on the desirability of war. A majority in the northeastern states were opposed, some because they looked upon the struggle as a southern aggression to win more "slave pens," others because they feared the creation of agricultural states from conquered Mexican lands when their own interests were increasingly industrial. The Massachusetts legislature reflected the section's attitude when it branded the war as "hateful in its objects . . . wanton, unjust and unconstitutional." Those sentiments were also expressed in the South and West, although there opposition came principally from Whig politicians anxious to smear the Democratic Polk. One told Congress the Mexicans should greet American troops with "bloody hands," and welcome them to "hospitable graves," while Abraham Lincoln gained momentary fame through his "Spot Resolutions" asking Polk to show the spot where American blood was spilled on "American soil." Wealthy southern planters were also inclined to distrust a war which might precipitate a controversy over slavery. For the most part, however, those two sections were the principal supporters of the United States' cause. The extent of sectional feeling was illustrated by the fact that the densely populated Northeast furnished only 7,930 volunteers, the expansionist West almost 40,000 and the South 21,000. The Northeast, the nation's richest region, also refused to aid the war financially.

Whether the American people liked it or not, they were at war. The first blow was struck by the Mexican commander, General Mariano Arista, who on May 8, 1846—five days before war was officially declared—threw his army across the Rio Grande in the hope of opening the road to Louisiana by defeating Taylor. The American commander, too canny to be caught napping, met the invaders in two desperately fought battles at Palo Alto and Resaca de la Palma, defeating them in both and driving them back across the river. What Polk chose to define as American soil was freed of the enemy. The President could turn to a long-range plan for the defeat of Mexico.

Two objectives underlay the strategy mapped by Polk and his military advisers. One was to win the northern Mexican provinces. On the day war was declared he told his cabinet: "In making peace with our adversary, we shall acquire California, New Mexico, and other further territory, as an indemnity for this war, if we can." He planned to secure the territories by a joint operation; an army—large enough to conquer but small enough not to alarm the conquered—would march westward through Santa Fe into southern California where it would join a second sea-borne force in the conquest of that province. The second objective was to end the struggle quickly. For this another army would move south against Mexico City where, Polk hoped, the terms of surrender would be dictated. He believed the joint campaign would bring the war to a speedy close, an object greatly desired partly because a lengthy contest would prey on his conscience and lessen his popularity, partly because any prolonged war would play into the hands of the Whigs. Both ranking generals—General Zachary Taylor and General Winfield Scott—were members of that party, and Polk was determined to keep either from entering the White House as a military hero. "A peace," said his secretary of war, "must be conquered in the shortest space possible."

The "Army of the West," which was assigned the task of winning New Mexico and southern California, was placed in the capable hands of Colonel Stephen W. Kearny who assembled his force at Ft. Leavenworth on the Missouri River in the spring of 1846. His was a strange assortment of soldiers: three hundred regular dragoons, a thousand Missouri frontiersmen, five hundred Mormon youths recruited from the camp at Council Bluffs where Brigham Young was preparing to lead his people westward, enough miscellaneous recruits to bring the total to 2,700 men. They set out from Ft. Leavenworth on June 30, 1846, across the eight hundred miles of plains and deserts that led to Santa Fe. For days they were without adequate water or food, but the hardened plainsmen were so accustomed to hardships they frequently outdistanced the cavalry. By August 13, when almost within sight of Santa Fe disquieting news reached Kearny: 3,000 Mexicans lay in wait along the rim of a narrow canyon through which they must pass.

Rather than risk a frontal attack, Kearny resorted to diplomacy. James Magoffin, a wealthy Santa Fe trader taken along for just such an emergency, was sent ahead to plead with his good friends, the New Mexican officials, not to risk disaster by opposing the Americans. The governor of New Mexico, Manuel Armijo, a mountain of a man whose tastes ran to food and commerce rather than fighting, had no stomach for his task at best; when Magoffin appeared he was easily persuaded to flee southward with the bulk of his defenders. Five days later Kearny's army marched unmolested into Santa Fe. There he issued a proclamation which openly avowed the American intention to annex New Mexico, promised the citizens a democratic form of government as a prelude to territorial organization, and named a governor to administer the province. The liberal pronouncements won over most New Mexicans so completely that a detachment of troops which marched through southern New Mexico found the people generally loyal to the United States.

Kearny could turn to the next step in his program. He divided his army into three parts. One was left to administer New Mexico. That task proved difficult when a rebellion broke out in January, 1847, under the leadership of a disgruntled Mexican official who had failed to receive the extensive estates promised him for helping surrender the province. Not until scaling ladders were used to drive the rebels out of the adobe church at Taos was the uprising put down. A second small army of three hundred Missouri volunteers under Colonel A. W. Doniphan started south to take the Mexican city of Chihuahua. The undisciplined, tumultuous, profane crew of frontiersmen stormed into El Paso after defeating a Mexican force four times its size, crossed the deserts of northern Mexico, overwhelmed the 4,000 defenders of Chihuahua, and on March 2, 1847, took formal possession of that city of 14,000 inhabitants. Doniphan then turned his column of self-styled "ring-tailed roarers" eastward to Parras where they waited the army moving against Mexico City.

In the meantime the third segment of the force that took New Mexico, three hundred dragoons under Kearny, left Santa Fe on September 25, 1846, for California. Moving swiftly down the Rio Grande and westward toward the Gila River, they soon met a small party of scouts led by the famous Mountain Man, Kit Carson, bearing the welcome news that California was already won. Kearny, delighted at the prospect of a peaceful journey, sent most of his men back to Santa Fe and, pressing Kit Carson into service as a guide, started west with only a hundred companions.

California had fallen before the assault of the United States navy and the Bear Flaggers. The Pacific squadron which helped win victory was cruising off the coast of Mexico when word arrived on June 7, 1846, of the declaration of war. Its commander, Commodore John D. Sloat, acting under instructions dated a year earlier, sailed at once to Monterey which was occupied without much resistance on July 7. A few days later San Francisco was taken and California formally annexed to the United States. Word was hurried north to the Bear Flaggers who were only too glad to join in the conquest. Captain Frémont, with 150 mounted men, started south at once to join Commodore Robert F. Stockton, who had replaced the less-aggressive Commodore Sloat, at San Francisco. During the next few weeks the two officers commanded the bloodless occupation of northern California, while the Mexican General José Castro, knowing his cause was lost, fled southward.

The conquest of southern California proved almost as easy. Frémont and his "California company of mounted riflemen" were sent to San Diego by sea to cut off the retreating remnants of the Mexican army while Stockton followed more slowly along the coast. General Castro, caught between the two forces, elected to fight just south of Los Angeles. There he met a "gallant sailor army" which was landed by Commodore Stockton at San Pedro and marched overland to the enemy's position. Before the Americans reached the battle ground the ill-trained Mexicans broke ranks to retreat pellmell toward the border. On August 13, 1846, Frémont and Stockton entered Los Angeles where, four days later, the commodore formally annexed California to the United States with Frémont as its military governor.

The province proved easier to take than to hold. No sooner had the two commanders started north than Californians at Los Angeles rose in rebellion against the harsh military rule of subordinates left to control the city. By September, 1846, all southern California was in the hands of the rebels, who could field an army of two hundred ill-equipped troops. Once more Stockton and Frémont hurried south, with Stockton going first and Frémont following more slowly by land. The naval force which landed at San Diego found itself so outclassed by the insurgents that only the timely arrival of Colonel Kearny from New Mexico saved the day. After fighting his way into San Diego by defeating the revolutionists at nearby San Pasqual, Kearny joined Stockton in a successful attack on Los Angeles where they waited the coming of Frémont. The rebels were waiting too, but with less heart, for their ammunition was nearly exhausted and their antiquated firearms beyond repair. When the blustering army officer appeared with an unruly following of four hundred Bear Flaggers, Mountain Men, and Indians they decided surrender was safer than battle. By mid-January, 1847, the counter-rebellion was over. A month later orders from Washington installed Kearny as governor of the new territory.

The conquest of California and New Mexico gave the United States Mexico's northern provinces only six months after war was declared. There remained the task of "conquering the peace" by inflicting such a decisive defeat that possession could be permanent. The task fell to General Zachary Taylor, whose army was poised on the banks of the Rio Grande ready to begin the decisive march on Mexico City. After spending several months whipping his raw recruits into shape, Taylor launched the invasion on August 19, 1846, with the city of Monterrey as his first objective. The town of Matamoros, just south of the river, fell without serious resistance, and Monterrey followed after three days of desperate fighting (September 21-23, 1846). There the Americans paused for eight weeks before advancing to Buena Vista where they were joined by a smaller force of Texas volunteers under General John E. Wool who had captured Monclova and Parras as they marched south. The combined armies settled down to wait the arrival of the 15,000 Mexicans General Santa Anna was leading northward. The expected attack came on February 22, 1847, when the Mexican force was hurled against the strong American position. For two days the battle raged before Santa Anna, despairing of dislodging the invaders from their mountain ravines, ordered a retreat.

This Battle of Buena Vista left the road to Mexico City open, but General Taylor was denied the glory of capitalizing on his triumph. By that time President Polk was growing alarmed at the mounting popularity of "Old Rough and Ready;" if Taylor was allowed to capture Mexico City the Whigs would be supplied with a military hero for the election of 1848.

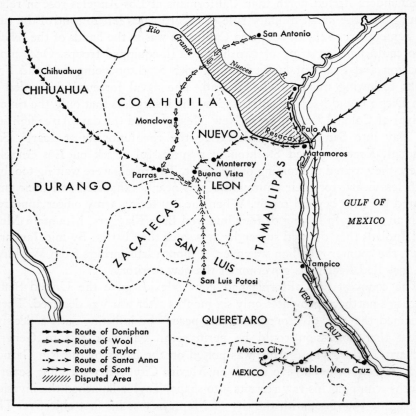

The Mexican Campaigns, 1846-1847

Hence the invasion plans were changed. The enemy capital would be taken, the President decided, not from the north but by an amphibious operation under General Winfield Scott, a pompous Whig with no popular appeal.

Sailing from New Orleans, General Scott's force landed just south of Vera Cruz on March 9, 1847. Guns were dragged ashore to begin an eighteen-day siege which ended when the strongly defended city capitulated.

The road to Mexico City which lay ahead was a tortuous one, running steeply upward through mountain passes where Santa Anna with his defenders were prepared to resist every step. When General Scott reached the first canyon, the Cerro Gordo, he recognized the impossibility of a frontal attack and sent a subordinate, Captain Robert E. Lee, to seek an alternate route. When Lee returned with news of a rough woodland path around the Cerro Gordo, the main force was sent ahead at once, while a small party stayed behind to distract the Mexicans. Santa Anna learned of the maneuver in time to withdraw before being surrounded, but the pass was won.

Fighting constant small engagements, the invading army reached the large city of Puebla on May 15, 1847. There Scott, knowing the impossibility of keeping his supply lines open in a mountainous country where guerrilla bands operated freely, cut himself off from the coast and moved boldly ahead with 10,000 men, living off the country. Fighting upward over the rim of towering peaks that surrounded the Mexican plateau, the Americans burst at last into the lake-studded Valley of Mexico which sheltered their objective. By the end of August, 1847, they were at the gates of Mexico City.

The long-sought prize was far from won. The Mexican capital stood in the midst of an extensive marsh which could be crossed only on stone causeways. Dominating the approach to two passageways was the towering hill of Chapultepec, whose precipitous walls bristled with soldiers. On September 13, 1847, the yelling Americans stormed over this barrier, then out upon the causeways, where pillars supporting aqueducts afforded some protection. Leaping from post to post in a manner reminiscent of Indian warfare, they reached the fortified city, burrowed under its stone walls, and on the evening of September 13 swept into its narrow streets. For three more days the defenders held out, contesting each foot in bitter hand-to-hand fighting, before Santa Anna ran up a white flag on September 17, 1847. The Mexican War was over; there remained the task of dictating the peace to a conquered people.

President Polk had anticipated the necessity. When General Scott invaded Vera Cruz he was accompanied by the chief clerk of the state department, Nicholas P. Trist, whose instructions authorized an immediate peace when Mexico City was taken. From the first Trist and Scott were at sword's point; the general resented the appointment of a "clerk" to carry on negotiations which he felt were within his own realm, while Trist's arrogant nature and blundering conduct did not ease the situation. For several weeks they kept up an angry correspondence—enlivened by one thirty-page note from Trist—and besieged their Washington superiors with such abusive messages the President was finally forced to intercede. After one letter from Trist which was "arrogant, impudent, and very insulting to the government, and even personally offensive," Polk on October 6, 1847, ordered the recall of his representative.

By the time news of the dismissal reached Mexico the situation was changed. Trist and Scott, having patched up their differences, were bosom companions. Moreover Mexico City was in American hands, General Santa Anna had abdicated as president, and all was in confusion. Scott in particular feared that unless peace were concluded at once Mexico would be plunged into such anarchy that more fighting would be required. His arguments caused Trist to violate instructions and proceed with the peace treaty. Meeting with representatives of a provisional government at the nearby city of Guadalupe Hidalgo, the American negotiator laid down his terms as an ultimatum: the United States wanted the Rio Grande boundary for Texas, and all New Mexico and California; in return it would pay Mexico $15,000,000 and assume claims against the government amounting to $3,250,000. Those were the provisions embodied in the Treaty of Guadalupe Hidalgo which was signed on February 2, 1848.

Mexico's one stroke of good fortune during the whole exploitive war was Trist's refusal to resign. The terms he dictated were those acceptable to the United States at the beginning of the contest; in the year and a half that followed opinion in the United States changed radically. The ease with which American armies won victories apparently demonstrated something long suspected: the Mexicans were a misgoverned, misdirected people entirely unfit to develop the rich country where they lived. Hence the manifest destiny of the United States was clearly to annex all Mexico, that its downtrodden peons might have the advantage of democracy and enlightened rule! The demand gained weight with each passing month of the war. The New York *Evening Post* spoke for multitudes when it insisted Polk should never "resign this beautiful country to the custody of the ignorant cowards and profligate ruffians who have ruled it for the last twenty-five years." So did the Washington *Union* when it suddenly discovered Mexico was "a paradise blessed with every variety of climate, every capacity of soil, and almost every species of fruit and flower on the face of the earth."

As popular sentiment for the acquisition of all Mexico gained strength, politicians leaped upon the band wagon. One New York senator toasted an American Union "embracing the whole of the North American continent," and at least two of Polk's cabinet members—Robert J. Walker of Mississippi and James Buchanan of Pennsylvania—openly favored taking all Mexico. Their influence on the President was such that had Trist withdrawn gracefully the new commissioner would probably have insisted on complete annexation. Once the treaty was drafted, however, Polk did not dare repudiate his agent. Reluctantly, he submitted the document to the Senate for ratification, despite the "exceptional conduct of Mr. Trist." After a few minor amendments the peace party carried the day over the total-annexationists; on March 10, 1848, the treaty was accepted by a vote of thirty-eight to fourteen. Thus was the peace confirmed which had been "negotiated by an unauthorized agent, with an unacknowledged government, submitted by an accidental President to a dissatisfied Senate."

The expansionists who professed disappointment at the failure to take all Mexico could take solace as they surveyed the history of the years between 1845 and 1848. The territorial gains of that brief period were enough to satisfy all but the most rabid advocates of manifest destiny. The United States, by acquiring Texas, Oregon, the Southwest, and California, added 1,200,000 square miles to its domains, virtually doubled its territory, and extended its boundaries to the Pacific. Only one more step was needed to complete the nation's expansion. The southern border established by the Mexican Treaty—along the Gila and Colorado rivers—was found unsatisfactory when transcontinental railroad routes were surveyed during the 1850's. To provide a right-of-way south of the Gila, the United States minister at Mexico City, James Gadsden, in December, 1853, arranged to buy an additional triangle of land for $10,000,000. The Gadsden Purchase gave the nation the continental boundaries of today.

The expansionist spree was not to pass without a sobering aftermath. For two decades before the Mexican War the spectre of sectional conflict increasingly haunted the United States as North and South drifted apart over the slavery issue; now the Treaty of Guadalupe Hidalgo brought the American people face to face with the whole terrifying question. What should happen to the lands acquired from Mexico? Should they be thrown open to slavery, or should Congress ban the southern institution there? Should they be divided into slave states to bolster the waning political strength of the South, or made into free states to increase the North's congressional supremacy? Four years of bitter debate, four years of frayed nerves and flaring tempers that brought the nation close to war, were needed before those pressing queries were temporarily answered.

The controversy was touched off by David Wilmot, a Pennsylvania Democrat who sat in the House of Representatives. Casting about for some means to regain local popularity lost by supporting his party's low tariff measures, Wilmot decided an appeal to his constituents' antislavery sentiments would be most effective. An appropriation bill before the House soon after war began gave him his opportunity. Rising to the occasion in

August, 1846, he moved a proviso that slavery be forever barred from all lands obtained from Mexico. The Wilmot Proviso ended one era in the history of the United States. Gone was the day when cautious politicians could keep the slavery issue below the surface in their anxiety to preserve the Union and national parties. Southern Whigs and Democrats combined to denounce the Proviso as a gross invasion of sacred rights, while northerners of both parties united in its praise. From Congress the argument spread to the state legislatures, to street corners where angry men shouted insults or exchanged blows, to country stores where cracker-barrel antagonists pleaded for their sections, to farm gatherings, and to the teeming streets of cities. Everywhere men argued the merits of slavery with a conviction that boded ill for continued national harmony.

From the welter of words emerged a half-dozen solutions to the problem propounded by Wilmot's proviso. Extreme northerners insisted Congress could and should bar slavery from the western territories. They maintained the legislature's constitutional power was adequate, for the Constitution authorized it to "make all needful rules and regulations respecting the territory or other property belonging to the United States." Moreover, they said, Congress was prohibited from placing more Negroes in bondage —and this would be the result of opening more land to slavery—by the Fifth Amendment forbidding the United States to deprive any person of his liberty without due process of law. Southern fire-eaters, on the other hand, held the government had no power to ban slavery in the West. The territories, they insisted, belonged not to the United States but to the states united; Congress simply administered each territory for its real owners— the states—as an attorney might administer property for a group of partners. Hence the final decision on the use of any territory rested with the states. If Mississippi decided its citizens could take their slave property into New Mexico, Congress had no legal right to interfere. Those were the extreme parties in the sectional debate, one demanding congressional action, the other insisting the legislature had no right to act.

Moderates on both sides of Mason and Dixon's line, seeking a solution that would avoid the dangerous constitutional issue, evolved other answers. Southerners of this ilk favored extending the Missouri Compromise line of 36°30′ to the Pacific, realizing this would give them most of the plundered Mexican lands for slavery. Northerners countered by insisting international law settle the issue; under accepted doctrine the region secured from Mexico, having been free under its former owner, would remain free until Congress acted specifically to allow slavery there. Other sincere compromisers, North and South, proposed throwing the whole question into the lap of the Supreme Court with the nation pledged to accept any decision, or favored "squatter sovereignty" to decide whether slaves could be taken into New Mexico and California. Proponents of the latter view came largely from the western border states, for that method—allowing settlers in each territory to decide whether they wanted slavery or freedom—appealed to the democratic instincts of the frontier.

The sharp division of opinion fed the flames of controversy but precluded any settlement before the election of 1848 offered an opportunity to test popular opinion. As usual in such a period of crisis, however, the people were not given a chance to express themselves; leaders of both parties were so anxious to keep northern and southern wings united they declined to meet the issue squarely. The Whigs, whose principal strength was in the North, nominated General Zachary Taylor, a Louisiana slaveholder, and went before the country without a platform. The Democrats, who looked to the South for support, chose a colorless northerner from Michigan, Lewis Cass, and in their platform avoided all mention of the one problem absorbing national attention. Only a minor party, the Free-Soil Party, took a definite stand in the election. Its members—abolitionists, northern Whigs, and Barnburning Democrats (so-called by enemies who accused them of being as anxious for reform as the Dutch farmer who burned down his barn to rid it of rats)—nominated Martin Van Buren and went before the nation with a platform pledge of "Free soil, free speech, free labor and free men" designed to appeal especially to the homestead-loving, slavery-hating West. Van Buren failed to win any electoral votes, but his Democratic followers in New York supported him so enthusiastically the state went Whig, and with it the nation. The result was no mandate on slavery; Cass carried eight free and seven slave states, Taylor seven free states and eight slave.

Zachary Taylor entered the White House in the spring of 1849 with few commitments and fewer ideas. He was a simple soldier, distrustful of politicians and inclined to view the slavery controversy as a teapot tempest that could best be quieted by compromise. If Congress had been able to pass any middle-of-the-road measure he would gladly have affixed his signature, but Congress wrangled instead, and while the argument went on the situation changed abruptly. Overnight the question of slavery in the Southwest was lifted from the realm of the academic to the point where a solution was imperative.

Workmen who discovered flakes of dull yellow metal in a mill race they were constructing on the lands of John A. Sutter were responsible. By mid-March of 1848 the exciting news was out, despite Sutter's efforts to keep the find a secret, and by mid-May San Francisco was deserted as the nation's greatest gold rush began. The East learned of the discovery in September,

1848, when alarmed reports arrived from Thomas O. Larkin, the consul at Monterey, accompanied by a little box of dust and nuggets from the territorial governor. The dispatches told an exciting story—of neglected shops and abandoned farms throughout California, of shiftless loafers washing out $50 worth of gold a day with nothing but a shovel and dishpan, of fabulous strike following fabulous strike, of the fortunes awaiting all who cared to pan the American River or the other streams that flowed westward from the Sierra Nevadas into the Sacramento Valley. When President Polk incorporated the reports in his December, 1848, message to Congress the whole country—the whole world—went mad. The rush to California was on.

Within a month sixty-one crowded ships were on their way around South America, many of them leaky tubs rescued from well-earned retirement to exact the scandalous fees fortune seekers willingly paid for passage to the "diggings." Those who could not afford the outrageous rates spent the winter gathering equipment for the overland journey. By the middle of May, 1849, 5,000 wagons were plodding westward along the California Trail; two weeks later an observer reported that 12,000 wagons had crossed the Missouri River and that 40,000 men were bound for the distant El Dorado. Others made their way to Santa Fe, using the old trail or following the Arkansas River west from Ft. Smith, then struck out along Colonel Kearny's Gila River route or the Old Spanish Trail to the coast. Over those tortuous paths gold hunters poured by the tens of thousand that summer, as all America chanted:

> Oh Susanna, don't you cry for me,
> I'm off to California with my washbowl on my knee.

Suffering was intense among the ill-trained emigrants who knew nothing of plains travel save the little they learned from equally ignorant guidebook writers or newspaper editors. On the heavily traveled trails across the Plains the cholera that lurked in every muddy waterhole took a toll of 5,000 lives; those who wandered from the popular paths frequently succumbed to starvation or Indian attack. In the Rocky Mountains more fell prey to dysentery or mountain fever as they struggled upward over steep trails with worn draft animals and overloaded wagons. Beyond South Pass lay the dust and heat of alkali deserts, where the infrequent water holes were often poisonous and the rare clumps of pasturage usually exhausted within a few weeks. By the autumn of 1849 skeletons of dead horses and cattle lined the side of the road for hundreds of miles, while unmarked graves of humans were appallingly numerous. Yet the worst trials lay ahead where the steep, barren slopes of the Sierra Nevadas reared skyward across the path of the Forty-Niners. Weary immigrants often abandoned their wagons or ate their starving pack animals, as they sought strength to surmount the barrier. Others died like flies in snow-choked passes or, if they sought a route around the southern tip of the mountains, wandered into the dread Death Valley—a region of "dreadful sands and shadows . . . salt columns, bitter lakes, and wild, dready, sunken desolation." Those who survived to reach the gold fields were indeed well tested.

They needed their stamina in the roaring frontier communities that sprang up around the "diggings." In those ramshackle mining camps—appropriately labeled Poker Flat, Hangtown, Whiskey Bar, Placerville, Hell's Delight, Git-up-and-git, Skunk Gulch, Dry Diggings, Red Dog, Grub Gulch, and the like—where rooms rented for $1,000 a month and eggs cost $10 a dozen, were assembled the most colorful desperadoes ever gathered in one spot. Mingling together were Missouri farmers, Yankee sailors, Georgia crackers, English shopkeepers, French peasants, Australian sheepherders, Mexican peons, "heathen Chinee," and a liberal sprinkling of "assassins manufactured in Hell," all drawn to California by the magnet of gold. There fortunes were made in a day of grubbing and lost in a night of faro or red dog; there outlaws and women of easy virtue rubbed shoulders with ministers and sober farmers. A hundred thousand people lived in California by the end of 1849, most of them respectable souls who wanted a better means of keeping order than the vigilance committees they set up themselves.

That was the situation which forced Congress to end its academic debate over slavery and come to grips with the problem. Some government must be provided before complete chaos reigned in California. President Zachary Taylor, gruff old militarist that he was, saw this and decided to act. His solution was to urge Californians to draw up a constitution and apply for admission as a state directly, thus dodging the question of congressional power over territories. A hint was all they needed; on August 1, 1849, a popular election named members of a constitutional convention which met in a Monterey schoolhouse in September, worked for six weeks, and emerged with an acceptable frame of government. A controversial clause barring slavery from the state was accepted unanimously and without debate. The document was overwhelmingly ratified by the people in mid-November, a governor and legislature chosen, and California was a state in everything but name. Congress must decide whether to accept the new commonwealth or face the wrath of Californians.

The question was placed squarely before the session which assembled in December, 1849, when a blunt message from President Taylor recommended that the new state be admitted and that New Mexico and Utah be organized as territories without reference to slavery. Congressional nerves were too frayed by years of argument to accept the proposals docilely. Southerners, horrified at the prospect of a free California upsetting the Senate balance between slave and free states, rose as a man to denounce Taylor's solution. John C. Calhoun, the grand old statesman of the section, led the attack; "I trust," he told his colleagues, "we shall persist in our resistance until the restoration of all our rights, or disunion, one or the other, is the consequence. We have borne the wrongs and insults of the North long enough." As northern extremists answered in equally fiery words, disunion seemed near. Never had the nation faced such grave peril.

Fortunately there were those in Congress who placed national interest above section passion. They knew the heated debate was useless; California was already free and no amount of argument could make the high plateaus or sandy deserts of New Mexico and Utah suitable to slavery. Surely there must be some basis for compromise among the many problems revolving around slavery then plaguing the nation. That was the hope of two men in particular, Henry Clay of Kentucky and Stephen A. Douglas of Illinois, both senators from border states that would suffer greatly in any civil conflict. Together the strangely assorted pair—one a venerable Whig, the other a young Democrat—pieced together a legislative program designed to preserve the Union they both loved. California, they proposed, should be admitted as a free state. The remaining Mexican lands would be divided into the territories of New Mexico and Utah without mention of slavery, but with the understanding that the Supreme Court settle any disputes over the question during the territorial period and that the settlers themselves decide whether they should become slave or free states. The slave trade, they suggested, should be abolished in the District of Columbia but slavery be continued there. The Fugitive Slave Act should be strengthened. Texas must surrender its claim to a western boundary at the Rio Grande in favor of New Mexico, but in return the United States would assume the $10,000,000 debt acquired during the period of Texan independence.

The introduction of those proposals by Clay and Douglas launched the most superb debate in the Senate's history. Clay opened the contest on February 5, 1850, with a brilliant two-day speech that recalled "Young Harry of the West" to his enthralled listeners. From the North he asked acceptance of the substance of the Wilmot Proviso without demanding the principle; "You have got what is worth more than a thousand Wilmot Provisos," he told his northern colleagues. "You have nature on your side —facts upon your side—and this truth staring you in the face that there is no slavery in those territories." From the South he sought a promise of peace, reminding southerners of the benefits derived from the Union and warning them peaceful secession was impossible. His stirring words were echoed by Douglas and other moderates who saw compromise as the only means of avoiding a costly war.

The extremists refused to listen. John C. Calhoun, so old and weak his speech was read for him, warned that the South would accept nothing less than all the Mexican territories and a constitutional amendment protecting its institutions from the aggressions of the majority North. William H. Seward and Salmon P. Chase, speaking for extreme northerners, denounced Clay's program in equally harsh terms as "radically wrong and essentially vicious." Congress, Seward said, might be willing to open the territories to slavery, "but there is a higher law than the Constitution," the law of God, which was broken by "all measures which fortify slavery or extend it." To those men, as to Calhoun, there could be no compromise.

Theirs was not the final word. This was spoken by a moderate northerner, Daniel Webster of Massachusetts, whose magnificent "Seventh of March" speech did much to shape congressional sentiment. "I speak to-day for the preservation of the Union," were his impressive opening words. "Hear me for my cause." They listened spellbound, the hundreds who crowded the benches and galleries of the Senate chamber, as his tired voice gained the strength of conviction. Northerners, he pleaded, should not attempt "to reaffirm an ordinance of nature, nor to reenact the will of God" by forbidding slaves in a region where none could exist; southerners should give up the dream of peaceful secession and escape from the "caverns of darkness" into the "fresh air of liberty and union." His stirring words, resounding throughout the nation, stirred up a ground swell of sentiment for compromise. "Union Meetings" were held in northern city after northern city, while in the South a convention that assembled at Nashville to talk secession adjourned after passing a few harmless resolutions. Clearly the majority preferred Clay's compromise to civil war.

This sentiment gained a champion in the White House when the death of President Taylor on July 9, 1850, elevated Millard Fillmore to the presidency. Taylor was a blunt old soldier whose bull-headed opposition to Clay's measures reflected the attitude of Seward whom he followed; Fillmore was a weak-kneed second-rater to whom compromise was second nature. His pressure upon congressmen, coinciding with growing popular support, convinced Clay and Douglas the time was ripe for a vote. One by one the bills were taken up and passed during the early weeks of September, to form the Compromise of 1850. California entered the Union as a free state, Utah and New Mexico were organized as territories with the understanding they become states with or without slavery as their constitutions dictated, the Texan boundary was placed at the 103rd meridian and the state's debt assumed by the United States, slavery was continued in the District of Columbia but the slave trade was abolished there, and a more stringent fugitive slave law was placed on the statute books.

When Millard Fillmore fixed his signature to the Compromise of 1850 he rolled back the clouds of war. Frantic efforts by Union-loving statesmen such as Clay and Webster temporarily dissolved the crisis created by manifest destiny. But the day of compromise was drawing to a close as an older generation passed from the scene and younger fire-eaters, bred in an atmosphere of conflict, assumed control of Congress. Those were the men who must meet the new crises created by the advancing frontier, and their failure led the nation straight along the road to civil conflict.

# CHAPTER XXIX

# The West and Slavery

## 1850-1860

The decade of the 1850's brought the slavery controversy to the bloody climax of civil war. Every step taken during that fateful ten-year period—every political contest, every election, every congressional debate, every economic gain—carried the nation closer to the irrepressible conflict. For no compromise, such as the crazy-quilt fabric pieced together by Clay and Douglas in 1850, could do more than delay the separation of North and South. The economic and emotional gulf between the sections was so great that every minor irritant was magnified into a major difference by inflamed partisans on both sides of Mason and Dixon's line. So long as disputes arose the sections could know no peace, and so long as the frontier moved westward disputes must arise. Each advance of settlement reopened the sore question of slavery's status in the territories, until the nation's nerves were so frayed that war seemed a necessary balm.

A casual observer during the years just after the Compromise of 1850 was adopted would have noticed few surface indications of the widening sectional breach. Some southerners grumbled over the loss of California to free staters, some northerners harangued against the inhumanity of the fugitive slave act, but the majority accepted the compromise as a heaven-sent blessing which would settle the slavery issue for all time. National satisfaction was strengthened by the industrial boom launched by California's gold; the prosperous people wanted nothing to interfere with the pleasant task of money-making. In most southern elections held during 1851, union candidates triumphed decisively over secession-minded radicals, although in South Carolina and Mississippi the contest was close. In the North, too, abolitionists lost popularity. Throughout the country a grateful people, worn by four years of controversy, returned thankfully to normal pursuits.

Beneath the surface calm, however, were indications of the brewing storm. The presidential election of 1852 provided the first warnings for those wise enough to see. Apparently both major parties followed their usual practices; the Democrats nominated a mediocre northerner, Franklin Pierce of New Hampshire, whose principal political virtues were a handsome face, a winning smile, and a well-publicized letter unequivocally endorsing the Compromise of 1850; the Whigs selected another military hero, General Winfield Scott of Mexican War fame, whose views of public issues were as obscure as his mental processes. The uninspired candidates devoted a spiritless campaign to praising the Compromise and swearing undying enmity to sectional discord. Only the Free-Soilers recognized that the slavery issue was dormant rather than dead, but their demands for congressional exclusion of bonded labor from the territories aroused little interest among a people who believed the western problem solved for all time.

To those who viewed the lackadaisical campaign as a sign of harmony the results came as a shock. The Democrats won a sweeping victory for their latest nonentity, losing only Massachusetts, Vermont, Kentucky, and Tennessee. The impressive triumph was made possible by two significant shifts within the ranks of the opposing parties. One was such a wholesale exodus of Barnburning Democrats from the Free-Soilers that the party's popular vote fell off by half as compared to 1848—an encouraging sign to those seeking sectional peace. The other and more important development was a movement of southern planters out of the Whig and into the Democratic Party. Wealthy cotton kings took that step partly because they could not reconcile their states' rights views with General Scott's military nationalism, partly because the growing conservatism of the Democrats appealed to them as men of property. The deflection of its whole southern wing seriously weakened the Whig Party at a time when national organizations were needed to bind the country together.

Before the year was out the Whigs suffered another telling blow in the deaths of Henry Clay and Daniel Webster. Those two grand old statesmen had held the party together through their personal influence; now younger leaders whose traditions were sectional rather than national assumed control. The result was complete disintegration. Some northern Whigs who had long seethed against a political alliance with slaveholders, began calling themselves "Conscience Whigs" and talking much as the Free-Soilers talked in 1848. Their leaders were men of the stamp of Charles Sumner of Massachusetts, William H. Seward of New York, and Abraham Lincoln of Illinois. Others in the North, organized as "Cotton Whigs," tried to carry on the tradition of compromise laid down by Clay and Webster. The remnants of the party in the South, the "Southern Whigs," had nothing to do with either faction. One political link was irreparably broken.

Although the shifting political allegiances apparently benefited the Democrats, the party was actually left weaker in everything but numerical strength. Its members had for some time been divided into northern and southern wings which were so evenly balanced that neither could dominate the other. With the migration of great planters into Democratic ranks, the southern faction gained enough strength to dictate the party's national strategy in the interests of the South. This was dangerous. For a time southerners might register some gains, but if they pressed their cause too vigorously northern Democrats would surely reach a point of rebellion. Then the last political bond uniting the sections would be severed. The history of the next half-dozen years amply demonstrated the reality of the peril, for the continued demands of southern Democrats finally led the nation into war.

The one thing the South wanted above all else was more land for slavery. Some they hoped to obtain beyond the borders of the United States; their attempts to secure Cuba, Nicaragua, and other bordering territories black ened the pages of American diplomacy during the periods of Democratic control in the 1850's. More would have to be secured within the country, and the Democrats' drive to obtain this touched off the sectional conflict. Northerners believed the status of slavery in the West settled for all time. The Missouri Compromise decreed that all lands east of the Rockies and north of the line of 36° 30' should become free territories, all south of the line slave. The Compromise of 1850 cared for the matter in the domains taken from Mexico. That division, which satisfied all but the most extreme northerners, was far from acceptable to the South. Slavery was a dynamic institution which must expand to endure. This realization kept southern Democrats constantly alert for a chance to open more territory to their peculiar institution. Their opportunity came in January, 1854, when the Kansas-Nebraska Bill was laid before Congress.

The act's sponsor was the idol of the northern Democrats, Senator Stephen A. Douglas of Illinois, whose faithful followers fondly dubbed him the "Little Giant" or the "Steam Engine in Britches." He proposed that the unorganized area of the Great Plains be divided into the two terri- tories of Kansas and Nebraska, the boundaries of Kansas to be those of today extended to the Rockies, those of Nebraska to include all the region north to the 49th parallel. Both would be opened to slavery during the early territorial stages, but eventually the people of each would decide by popular vote whether they wanted the institution—a device Douglas called "Popular Sovereignty." He recognized that slavery could not legally exist in the area north of 36° 30′ so long as the Missouri Compromise remained on the statute books; hence the Kansas-Nebraska Act formally repealed the venerable ordinance, declaring instead that the true intent of Congress was "not to legislate slavery into any Territory or State, nor to exclude it therefrom, but to leave the people thereof perfectly free to . . . regulate their domestic institutions in their own way." That was the measure pushed through Congress on May 25, 1854, by a smoothly functioning Democratic machine.

Why did Douglas, a northerner, sponsor such a harmony-shattering bill? A political squabble among the Democrats of Missouri first suggested the idea to him. There Senator Thomas Hart Benton and his fellow moderates had for several years been locked in conflict with a group of violently pro-southern Democrats led by the other Missouri senator, David R. Atchison. The struggle cost Benton his senate seat in 1851 when he was defeated by a coalition of Atchison Democrats and rebelling Whigs, but the old statesman was not ready to give up. He knew Atchison would be up for re-election in 1854, and that a sufficiently attractive issue would not only allow him to win revenge but to oust his opponent from the Senate. Casting about for such a cause, Benton hit upon the idea of appealing to Missouri frontiersmen by promising, if elected, to open the region west of Missouri to settlement. The alarmed Atchison realized his opponent would probably triumph unless an even more attractive program was laid before Missourians. By the autumn of 1853 he had the answer; he would, he told his constituents, not only press for organization of the western territories but insist they be opened to slavery on the basis of popular sovereignty. To demonstrate his good faith, Atchison in November, 1853, suggested that his good friend, Stephen A. Douglas, introduce such a bill in his capacity as chairman of the Territorial Committee of the Senate.

Douglas was delighted to do so, as the organization of the region west of Missouri and Iowa fitted in well with his own ambitions. He was deeply involved in a controversy over the route for a transcontinental railroad. Army surveys completed in 1853 indicated that two possible routes might be employed, one through South Pass to connect San Francisco with either Chicago or St. Louis, the other uniting New Orleans and Los Angeles by a line across Texas and the Gila Valley. As everyone agreed one road would suffice for all time, southerners were determined the latter route should be selected, thus securing for their section the perpetual commercial benefits of the California trade. They argued that the southern road would run through organized territory, that local traffic from settled areas along the way would reduce through transportation costs, and that easy contours would facilitate construction. Douglas, together with other northerners, was equally set on a railroad with an eastern terminus at Chicago. If he could persuade Congress to select the central route he would win the eternal gratitude of northerners and his own Illinois constituents, as well as improving himself financially by advancing the price of his extensive Chicago real estate holdings. The line could never be built, however, so long as the Louisiana Purchase was unorganized. Senator Atchison's proposed territory beyond Missouri and Iowa would answer the principal southern argument against the central route.

As Douglas mulled over the suggestion, however, he realized a bill to erect one territory there would never do. The first pioneers into the region would come from Missouri and Arkansas rather than thinly settled Iowa or distant Illinois, and would locate the territorial capital in the southern portion. A Pacific railroad through that city would emerge at St. Louis rather than Chicago, doing nothing for Douglas' political ambitions or financial hopes. The only answer was two territories rather than one, allowing the road to pass through the capital of the northern territory directly west of Chicago. That was in Douglas' mind when he recommended the organization of both Kansas and Nebraska on the basis of popular sovereignty.

No sooner was the bill framed than the Illinois senator realized he had arranged a masterful political *coup*. Kansas, he saw, would doubtless be won for slavery by immigrants from adjacent Missouri, while Nebraska, lying west of Iowa, would become a free territory. Thus both North and South would gain. The South would secure a new slave state and repeal of the Missouri Compromise. In return the section would give up hopes of a southern railroad, awarding the North that coveted concession together with an additional free state. Douglas believed a grateful people would hail him as the hero who solved the problem of sectionalism, saved the Union, and provided an orderly means of settling the slavery controversy for all time to come. The presidency, surely, would be the only fitting reward for such a service.

His error—natural in a practical politician—was the failure to understand the deep emotional conviction motivating both sections. To a majority of Americans the real issue was not a Pacific railroad or a territory of Kansas, but "Southern Rights" versus "Northern Freedom." That alone accounted for the national reaction when news of the Kansas-Nebraska Act was flashed through the land. The South was overjoyed; Democratic politicians had won the thing southerners most wanted: more land for slavery. But the southern joy was more than matched by northern anger.

The Missouri Compromise—a measure as inviolate as the Constitution—had been repealed by the hated slaveholders! "A violation of a sacred pledge," "a criminal betrayal of precious rights," "an enormous crime"—those were the epithets hurled by outraged northerners. Douglas, who had expected the worshipful thanks of his countrymen, found himself so unpopular in the North that he could, as he expressed it, travel from Boston to Chicago by the light of his burning effigies. Once more emotionalism ruled the United States, and this time there was no Henry Clay to lead the nation back to sanity.

The first result was a new shifting of party lines. The Democrats suffered least, despite the loss of some northerners who angrily withdrew from the party to take the name of Anti-Nebraska Democrats. The majority, however, even in the North, clung to the hope the Kansas-Nebraska Act would, as Douglas prophesied, reduce slavery from a national issue to a local problem. So long as they could follow Douglas and convince themselves they were pursuing a compromising course they were willing to stay in the party. The Whigs, who had been vainly trying to patch up their differences since 1852, were less fortunate. Southern Whigs, convinced the Democrats truly represented southern interests, abandoned their dying organization in droves, while Northern Whigs, left without a party, drifted into one or the other of the two new parties the Kansas-Nebraska Act helped create.

One, the American Party, had been gaining strength for some years before Douglas' measure brought an unexpected influx of members. Its objectives—to drive Papists and foreigners from the land—were no more truly American than the elaborate secret ritual which pledged its adherents to vote only for native-born Protestants. Yet the Know-Nothings (so named because they parried all queries about their order by saying "I know nothing about it") increased in power rapidly after 1850 when the Compromise, by apparently settling the slavery issue, allowed bigots to turn their invective against Popery and the foreign-born. The parade into the party's ranks assumed mass proportions after passage of the Kansas-Nebraska Act, for the order's stress on unity and nationalism indicated that it would rise above any sectional strife. The American Party carried six states in 1854 and 1855, and almost captured seven more, largely in New England and the border states. Fortunately its members split over slavery before the election of 1856, or the United States might have enthroned intolerance in the White House.

The second party to emerge from the political chaos created by the Kansas-Nebraska Act originated in the Middle West where indignation was particularly high. At a dozen places in the upper Mississippi Valley grumbling farmers met simultaneously to talk of the need for a new antislavery party that could combat the latest aggression of the slavocracy. One of the gatherings, held at Jackson, Michigan, on July 6, 1854, hit upon the happy device of reviving the name of Jefferson's old party and suggested they call themselves Republicans. The idea took hold at once; in community after community former Free-Soilers, Anti-Nebraska Democrats, and Conscience Whigs flocked together to form local units of the Republican Party, all of them pledged to prevent the extension of slavery into the territories. By the fall of 1854 the lusty new organization was firmly planted in the Old Northwest, although its strength elsewhere remained slight. Some emotional stimulus was needed before the young party could win northeastern conservatives.

This was provided by the disgraceful events taking place in Kansas. The Kansas-Nebraska Act brought no more peace to that unfortunate territory than to the nation. Perhaps popular sovereignty would have operated well applied to a well-settled region, but when inflicted on a newly opened territory it invited trouble. Northern abolitionists, angry at what seemed a deliberate southern attempt to rob them of Kansas, struck the first blow. Why not, they argued, frustrate the evil design by sending enough free-soilers into the territory to outvote the slaveholders who moved there? As the possibility dawned on abolitionists they hurriedly formed societies to collect funds, equip immigrants, and send them wholesale into the disputed region. Most prominent was the New England Emigrant Aid Society, chartered in April, 1854, by Eli Thayer, a Massachusetts free-soiler. By midsummer Thayer, enriched by contributions from a host of New England financiers, could boast that his society would have a thousand settlers in Kansas by the end of August and 20,000 by the first of the year.

Those extravagant claims had no basis in fact. During the critical years when the fate of Kansas hung in the balance only 4,208 pioneers moved there from New England, the center of abolitionism, and of those only 1,240 were aided by the Emigrant Aid Society. New Englanders were migrating during the 1850's, but to regions where life and property were secure; 90,000 settled in the free states of the Old Northwest and 5,799 in slave Missouri. This was also true of the other northeastern states. New York contributed 6,331 settlers to doubtful Kansas while sending 220,000 to the upper Mississippi Valley. Nor did southerners show any greater inclination to move there. The southeastern states sent only a handful of frontiersmen to Kansas, despite the efforts of one Jefferson Buford, a rabid proslavery man, who led one band of ruffians westward to offset the work of the Emigrant Aid Societies. Instead Kansas was peopled by pioneers from adjacent states. Ohio, Indiana, and Illinois sent 30,929 northern immigrants, while the southwestern states of Missouri, Kentucky, and Tennessee contributed 20,481. Obviously the forces which had led to the peopling of every frontier—proximity, overcrowding at home, the hope of gain—were responsible for the peopling of Kansas rather than any idealistic hope of saving the world. In all probability the threat of trouble over slavery kept settlers out rather than luring them in, particularly slaveholders who dared not risk their heavy property investment.

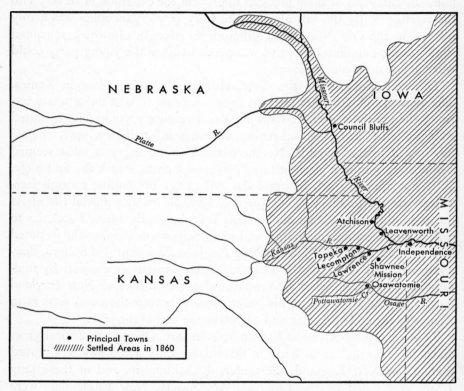

The Settlement of Kansas and Nebraska, 1854-1860

Despite the failure of the Emigrant Aid Societies, several thousand farmers lived in Kansas by the spring of 1855 when the territorial governor, Andrew H. Reeder, a proslavery Pennsylvania Democrat, set the date for an election to choose a legislature. Southerners, who had drifted across from Missouri to settle along the Missouri Valley, were in a majority at the time, but Missourians were unwilling to leave anything to chance. On the day of the election 5,000 "Border Ruffians," all armed to the teeth, swarmed into Kansas, took control of the voting booths, and cast four times as many ballots as there were registered voters in the territory. Governor

Reeder, southern sympathizer though he was, protested in vain. Democratic officials in Washington turned a deaf ear as the solidly proslave legislature met at the town of Shawnee Mission to pass laws which limited office holding to believers in slavery, provided for the imprisonment of anyone declaring the institution did not legally exist in the territory, and inflicted punishment on all speaking or writing against slaveholding. When Governor Reeder objected again he was dismissed from office.

Free-staters, realizing the harsh measures would send half their members to jail, countered by holding an election of their own, this time to choose members of a constitutional convention which could seek admission for Kansas as a free state. Delegates selected in the one-sided contest met at Topeka in October, 1855, drafted a frame of government forbidding slavery, and authorized the election of state officials. Two months later the constitution was overwhelmingly ratified (as southerners abstained from voting) and a northern government set up. Kansas now had two separate communities, each with its own legislature, governor, and delegate to Congress. The proslave men were grouped around Leavenworth and Atchison in the Missouri Valley, the free staters about Topeka and Lawrence on the Kansas River. Both contained an unhealthy sprinkling of cutthroats attracted by the promise of trouble, while southerners could count on support from Missouri "Border Ruffians" who were always spoiling to "clean out the abolition crowd." Civil conflict was inevitable.

It began in the spring of 1856 when a proslave sheriff visiting Lawrence was shot in the back by an unknown assassin. Although the cowardly act was disavowed by free-soilers, a southern grand jury handed down indictments for treason against half the leading citizens of Lawrence. The federal marshal appointed to deliver the warrants, correctly anticipating resistance, led eight hundred heavily armed bushwhackers and Border Ruffians into the free-state town in May, 1856. While northerners stood angrily aside the gang of ruffians destroyed the printing press of the local paper, tore down a hotel, burned the home of several suspected abolitionists, and ransacked the town.

This wanton act profoundly impressed both North and South. Moderation vanished; Kansas overnight became a testing ground for the forces of slavery and freedom. Southern editors pictured the "Border Ruffians" as proud knights battling for a holy cause and demanded legislative appropriations to send armed bands into Kansas; northerners glorified the free-state bushwhackers as crusaders for freedom and requested renewed support for the Emigrant Aid Societies. The tense state of the nation's nerves was indicated by a meeting at a New Haven church to raise money for seventy Kansas-bound immigrants. The Reverend Henry Ward Beecher, in addressing the gathering, urged the settlers to go armed and boldly proclaimed that the dread Sharpe's rifle was a greater moral force for Kansas than the Bible. From that time on easterners entering the disputed territory carried "Beecher's Bibles," as the rifles were dubbed, and went prepared to fight for their rights. Open civil war was near.

Fighting began not long after the Lawrence raid. Old John Brown, a half-crazed religious fanatic whose Old Testament God demanded the spilling of blood for blood, touched off the conflict. Brooding over the sack of Lawrence, he convinced himself that he was divinely appointed to right the wrongs done by southerners. With his four sons and a few other deluded free-staters, John Brown slipped out of the frontier town of Osawatomie on the night of May 24, 1856, stole quietly upon the neighboring southern hamlet of Pottawatomie Creek, and hacked five southerners to death in cold blood. The "Pottawatomie Massacre" precipitated war in Kansas. For three months crops were neglected as bands of "Border Ruffians" or northern bushwhackers roamed the territory, burning, pillaging, and murdering, until the sky over the war-torn region was alight from flaming dwellings. Some $2,000,000 worth of property and two hundred lives were sacrificed as "Bleeding Kansas" earned its name.

Just how much of the bloodshed was due to conflicts over slavery and how much to the turbulence normal in a frontier community can never be known. In all probability disputed land titles cost as many lives as the slave issue. Those stemmed from the negligence of government surveyors; not until the summer of 1856 were enough lands plotted to allow the first public sales. In the meantime thousands of pioneers squatted on farms and formed claims clubs to protect their holdings. Doubtless many of the battles were fought between squatters and later-comers who had purchased previously occupied land; that was indicated by the fact the conflict reached a crisis in every region where surveys were just completed. Other minor wars were probably engineered by rival speculators in townsites, for overlapping grants to those prized spots were often made. Each clash was magnified by the nation's press into a struggle between the forces of slavery and freedom. The rampaging frontier was made to appear as a testing ground for a sectional conflict.

The effect was startling. "Bleeding Kansas" divided the nation as no other issue during the crucial decade. Southerners, reading distorted accounts of outrages committed upon their fellow countrymen, came to believe all free staters were fanatical ruffians who would be satisfied by nothing less than the annihilation of every slaveholder. Northerners, learning from their papers of "bar-room rowdies . . . parading the country chopping single persons . . . to pieces, and frightening women and children," accepted rough-necked "Border Ruffians" as typical of all southerners. To men who believed in that way the day of compromise was past. The North, which had docilely accepted southern presidents, laws, and economic control for a generation, saw that the time had come to draw the line. From now on, grim free-staters told themselves, they would force their will on the minority South. A section which condoned the sack of Lawrence and the rape of Kansas deserved no compassion.

The spread of that sentiment among northerners proved a godsend to the Republican Party. Its principles were those gaining credence; the majority North, Republicans believed, should control the nation in its own interest without paying heed to the minority South. In the past sober men had refused to support an organization which proposed to substitute force for compromise, knowing the dangerous doctrine would breed disunion. Now caution was forgotten with each dispatch from "Bleeding Kansas"; through 1855 and 1856 thousands upon thousands of northerners flocked into Republican ranks. By the fall of 1856 the party could enter the presidential lists, with John C. Frémont as its candidate and the demand for free territories as its platform. Although the Democrats triumphed with their proslavery Pennsylvanian, James Buchanan, Frémont came closer to uniting North and West against the South than had any previous presidential aspirant. He carried every state north of Mason and Dixon's line save Indiana, Illinois, Pennsylvania, New Jersey, and California, to win 114 electorial votes. Sectional lines were drawing tighter and the end of the Union was in sight, for if ever the Republican principle of majority rule was accepted by the nation the South would certainly secede.

The event which swung northern opinion to that point occurred only two days after James Buchanan entered the White House: the Supreme Court's decision in the case of *Dred Scott vs. Sanford*. The years of litigation that culminated in the momentous opinion began when Dred Scott, a Negro slave owned by an army surgeon named Dr. John Emerson, was taken from his Missouri home for brief residences at Ft. Armstrong in Illinois and Ft. Snelling in the unorganized territory later to become Minnesota. In 1838 master and slave returned to Missouri where, eight years later, Dr. Emerson died, leaving Dred Scott to his widow. Anxious to be rid of the shiftless Scott but unable to free him under state law, Mrs. Emerson arranged for him to sue for his freedom in the Missouri courts, knowing that they had repeatedly held that residence in a free state or territory automatically freed a slave. To her disgust, the state supreme court reversed past precedents, largely because its pro-Atchison members were anxious to embarrass Thomas Hart Benton, and ruled that Scott's status must be determined by Missouri law since he voluntarily returned there.

Mrs. Emerson, whose natural desire to free her troublesome servant had been bolstered by remarriage to a Massachusetts abolitionist, Dr. C. C. Chaffee, was unwilling to accept defeat. If, however, she appealed to the federal courts the problem of jurisdiction intervened, for their authority did not extend to suits arising between citizens of one state. That obstacle was overcome by the fictitous sale of Dred Scott to Mrs. Emerson's brother, J. F. A. Sanford of New York, and the case reopened in the United States Circuit Court of Missouri which held as had the state court. Appeal was then carried to the Supreme Court, where the suit was argued in February, 1856, and again in January, 1857. After listening to counsels' pleas the judges, in their mid-February conference, decided to brush aside the question of jurisdiction and decide the case against Scott on the grounds that the state supreme court's interpretation of Missouri law kept him in slavery.

At that point two northern members of the bench let it be known they intended to write dissenting opinions upholding the constitutionality of the Missouri Compromise—the statute under which Minnesota was free—using as an excuse Scott's brief residence there. Their motives were hardly laudable; Justice Benjamin R. Curtis of Massachusetts wished to popularize himself in Boston before retiring from the Court to resume private practice, and Justice John McLean of Ohio hoped to attract such favorable attention from Republicans that he could win the party's presidential nomination in 1860. Their selfish ambitions did the justices little good and the nation great harm, for the remaining judges—seven of whom were Democrats and five from the South—were unwilling to allow them to defend congressional exclusion of slavery from the territories without rebuttal. Abandoning their intention to dismiss the Dred Scott case on local grounds, the majority instructed the chief justice, Roger B. Taney of Maryland, to write an opinion denying Congress the power to ban slavery from federal territories.

The ingenious argument penned by Taney ran something like this: The Supreme Court, he wrote, could accept jurisdiction only in disputes arising between citizens of different states. Dred Scott was not entitled to become a litigant because he was not a citizen. He was not a citizen because he was a Negro, and at that point Judge Taney examined post-Revolutionary state laws to show that framers of the Constitution did not consider colored persons capable of citizenship. Moreover, the Chief Justice went on, Scott was not a citizen because he was still a slave. He had not been made free by his residence in Illinois; as a resident of Missouri the laws of any state in which he visited did not affect his status. Nor was he made free by his years in Minnesota Territory, for Minnesota was not legally free. Slaves,

Taney held, were specifically protected from federal interference by the Fifth Amendment to the Constitution which prohibited Congress from depriving any person of his property without due process of law. To restrict the use of a man's property was to deprive that man of property. Therefore Congress could not legally bar slavery from the territories, and the Missouri Compromise was unconstitutional. Taney concluded the national legislature's only power over slavery "was the power coupled with the duty of guarding and protecting the owner in his rights."

The Dred Scott case was the most serious blow yet dealt to the ambitions of the North and the Republican Party. It was denounced in vitriolic language everywhere—"a wicked and false judgment," "willful perversion," "a new and atrocious doctrine," "the deadliest blow which has been aimed at the liberties of America since the days of Benedict Arnold," "entitled to just as much moral weight as would be the judgment of a majority of those congregated in any Washington bar-room"—those were some of the milder phrases hurled by indignant editors. Yet no amount of name-calling could disguise the fact that the judgment stood, and that a Democratic president was ready to enforce it. The sole Republican hope was to win control of the national government, pack the Supreme Court, and secure a reversal. Unless that was done the party was doomed, for it could no longer promise to ban slavery from the territories when the Supreme Court ruled Congress lacked power. Disgruntled Republicans found solace only in the outraged state of northern opinion. Even moderates believed themselves victims of a southern conspiracy to open territory after territory to slavery until bonded labor engulfed the nation. Fear for their own security, coupled with sympathy for the slaves, drove them into Republican ranks as never before. Each election through 1857 and 1858 showed the party's growing strength.

The Democrats, on the other hand, were grievously weakened by the Dred Scott decision. So long as the party advocated popular sovereignty it could retain a national organization, attracting to its fold southerners hoping to secure Kansas for slavery, westerners won over by the doctrine's democratic features, and easterners willing to embrace any compromise allowing them to continue business relations with the South. Now southern members renounced popular sovereignty in favor of the Dred Scott doctrine which promised all the West to slaveholders. Northern Democrats, unwilling to go that far, still hesitated to desert their party, knowing they must align themselves with the violently pronorthern Republicans. For a time they waited, still hoping for some middle-of-the-road solution which would save their southern trade and their beloved nation. In this crisis they turned naturally to their leader, Stephen A. Douglas. Could he find some way out of the dilemma? Upon the broad shoulders of the Little Giant rested the fate of the Democratic Party and the Union.

Douglas, realizing the importance of his decision, hesitated as long as possible before taking a stand, but was finally forced to declare himself when his Republican opponent in the Illinois senatorial election of 1858, Abraham Lincoln, pinned him down with a direct question: "Can the people of a United States territory in any lawful way exclude slavery from its limits prior to the formation of a State Constitution?" The Democratic leader had to decide between two unpleasant possibilities; if he answered "yes" he would please northern members of his party but offend the South, if he answered "no" he would satisfy southerners but lose his northern following. Douglas did not go back on his principles. His answer was known from the town in which it was delivered as the Freeport Doctrine. If the people of any territory wanted slavery, he said, they could choose a legislature pledged to enact laws necessary to protect the institution; if they were opposed they could elect free-state delegates who could by "unfriendly legislation" exclude it entirely. Popular sovereignty still existed, despite the Dred Scott decision!

The Freeport Doctrine re-elected Douglas to the Senate but split the Democratic Party in two. Southerners were horrified. Their former champion had threatened slavery by advising territorial legislatures not to enact "black codes"; he had defied the law of the land by urging citizens to violate the clear injunction of the Supreme Court. Every Democrat south of Mason and Dixon's line turned as a man from this Judas, leaving Douglas with only his northern supporters. The last political link binding the nation was severed.

Nor did events during the next two years strengthen Douglas' position in his own section. That rested on the success of popular sovereignty and every post from Kansas demonstrated the continued failure of the doctrine as a means of settling the slavery question. The aggressors in the troubled territory now were proslavery men who saw that drastic action was needed before continued migration from the more populous free states robbed them of their last chance to make Kansas slave. Taking advantage of the fact that a sympathetic Democratic government sat in Washington, they called a constitutional convention together at Lecompton in the fall of 1857, drafted a violently proslavery frame of government, arranged a ratification election which gave the people no chance to express themselves (they could only vote for the constitution with or without a provision to admit more slaves), and in the spring of 1858 asked that Kansas be admitted as a state. President Buchanan blindly submitted the Lecompton

Constitution to Congress with the recommendation that it be accepted "to restore peace and quiet to the whole country."

The Republicans were solidly opposed; so was Douglas who courageously denounced the measure as not representative of majority will in Kansas, even though his words cost him the last hope of southern support. Democratic leaders, realizing the Lecompton Constitution was doomed to defeat, made a last desperate effort. Once more the people of the territory were asked to vote on the measure, this time with the promise of a sizeable land grant (of the sort usually given new states) if the constitution was accepted. When they marched to the polls in August, 1858, they overwhelmingly rejected the tempting offer rather than accept slavery. Kansas had to wait until 1861 for statehood, but its struggle for admission had hopelessly divided the Democrats.

The depth of the gulf was shown when party delegates met at Charleston to name the Democratic candidate for the election of 1860. The platform committee submitted two planks, one calling upon the federal government to protect slavery in the territories, the other upholding the right of the people to decide on their own institutions, subject to the decisions of the Supreme Court. When the latter was adopted by northern representatives the southern delegates stalked from the convention hall in open rebellion. Adjourning to Baltimore, they named John C. Breckinridge of Kentucky as their standard bearer. In the meantime the northern Democrats selected Stephen A. Douglas as their candidate. The Democratic split was a reality.

This was a golden opportunity for the Republicans who met in a specially built "wigwam" in Chicago amidst an atmosphere of wild excitement. Yet the prospect of victory over a divided opposition did not stampede party leaders into any foolish moves. They realized northern moderates must be won over to insure a triumph, and that this could only be accomplished by nominating a middle-of-the-roader for the presidency and by drafting a platform with a wide popular appeal. Hence they passed over William H. Seward, whose outspoken references to a "higher law" and an "irrepressible conflict" made him inacceptable to all but radical free-staters, in favor of Abraham Lincoln of Illinois, who was known as a sincere lover of union. The platform was equally appealing; in place of the simple pledge to exclude slavery from the territories used in 1856, the document of 1860 promised homestead legislation to please the westerners, protective tariffs to win over eastern manufacturers, and an extensive program of government-supported internal improvements and railroads to attract business interests in both sections.

There remained in the United States a group of men satisfied with neither the Douglas Democrats, the Breckinridge Democrats, nor the Lincoln Republicans. Most were elderly individuals, bred in a tradition of union and compromise, who deplored without thoroughly understanding the sectional strife over slavery; others were former Know-Nothings who placed nationalism above all else. Their representatives met at Baltimore during the summer of 1860, organized themselves into a Constitutional Union Party, and selected a dull old antiquarian, John Bell of Tennessee, as their presidential candidate. The platform ignored slavery and urged the people to uphold the Constitution, the laws of the nation, and the Union.

The campaign between the four parties was one of the bitterest in the country's history, but the outcome was predestined. The South divided its vote between Breckinridge and Bell, the latter receiving his principal support in the rich-soil regions where wealthy planters shied from a sectional candidate who threatened secession. The border states cast their ballots for Bell and Douglas, for there too compromise seemed more expedient than civil war. The Northeast voted almost solidly for Lincoln, with a sprinkling of Douglas supporters among business men whose trade connections lay south of Mason and Dixon's line. If the final decision had rested among those three sections no one candidate could have secured a majority; the election would have been thrown into the House of Representatives where Democratic strength would probably have placed Breckinridge in the presidency. The outcome of the crucial contest hung on the vote of the Northwest.

A decade earlier that section would have voted for compromise, hanging as it did in the balance between North and South. Its strong union sentiment in 1850 had stemmed partly from a population drawn equally from southern and northeastern states, partly from a traditional legislative alliance with the agricultural cotton belt, and partly from trade connections maintained with both the other sections. So long as the upper Mississippi Valley divided its allegiance and commerce there could be no decision on the slavery question, for neither of the two major antagonists dared act while the unstable section balanced between them. As late as 1856 the Democratic Party registered thumping victories there; if those had been repeated in 1860 Lincoln would have been defeated and the Civil War postponed. Yet Lincoln carried the Northwest. The swing of that section from the Democratic to the Republican column—from divided allegiance to an open alliance with the North—made the irrepressible conflict inevitable. The shift in northwestern opinion between 1850 and 1860 was due to an influx of freedom-loving settlers, to growing realization that the section's legislative needs could best be secured by co-operating with the Northeast, and to a revolution in trade routes.

The new settlers who helped revise northwestern sentiment came partly from the Northeast, bearing with them strong antislavery concepts. More than 300,000 pioneers from New England and New York reached the upper Mississippi Valley during the 1850's. The South contributed few newcomers, for feeling over slavery was then so strong southerners hesitated to migrate to free states. More important than internal migration in explaining growing Republican strength in the Northwest was immigration from abroad. During the decade, over 1,000,000 Germans had landed on American shores, three-quarters of whom settled in the upper Mississippi Valley. They brought with them a hatred of slavery and a love of freedom inspired by the ill-fated liberal revolutions of 1848 in Germany. At first they joined the Democratic Party, whose name and traditions seemed to promise the democracy they sought, but in 1860 they realized their error and deserted wholesale into Republican ranks. Germans in the seven northwestern states cast 283,748 ballots for Lincoln, a figure gaining significance from the fact Lincoln's majority over Douglas there was only 149,807. Without the votes of northeasterners and immigrants, the Northwest would have been in the Democratic column when results were tabulated.

Equally important in explaining the section's swing was the growth of a Northeast-Northwest legislative alliance on all important national issues. Their traditional agreement on one public question—the tariff—was emphasized again in 1857 when a new Democratic-sponsored bill lowered customs duties even beyond the point reached in the Walker Tariff of 1846. The cry of anger from western and eastern newspapers indicated their common hatred of a cotton south which was attempting to strangle their economy for its own ends. They united, too, in denouncing the southern attack on federally supported internal improvements. Under the Democratic presidents who controlled the nation after 1852, appropriations for river and harbor bills were reduced to the vanishing point, to the disgust of both western farmers seeking outlets for their goods and eastern manufacturers looking for national markets.

The legislative issue which gave Northeast and Northwest the best chance to realize their common interests was Homestead. In the past they had sharply disagreed on land policy; the westerners favoring liberal laws, the easterners distrustful of measures which would drain laborers from factories. That division was forgotten as all classes in both sections united behind a measure to give settlers 160 acres of the public domain. Western support was consistent with its past policy, but eastern enthusiasm represented a break with precedent. This was due to the flood of Irish immigration that swept over the Northeast after 1845, creating an inexhaustible labor pool which convinced industrialists no amount of free land could deplete their supply of workers. No longer plagued by this fear, they looked upon Homestead as a device to build western markets for their manufactured goods. The South, on the other hand, was unalterably opposed, partly because land would be given in small units unsuited to slavery, partly because a free public domain would attract freedom-loving immigrants to the frontier. The clear sectional alignment on the issue was demonstrated in 1852, 1858, and 1859 when Homestead bills passed the northern-dominated House of Representatives, only to meet defeat in the Senate where the South's strength was greater. A measure squeezed through both houses in 1860 was vetoed by a Democratic president. On that issue, as on all others, North and West stood as one against a common enemy.

Even more important in explaining the swing of the Northwest were the section's shifting trade routes. Before 1850 its agricultural surpluses were exported southward along the Mississippi artery and to the East over the New York or Pennsylvania canal systems, with the bulk of the heavy goods reaching markets via New Orleans. The commercial alliance between South and West was broken during the 1850's by the railroad. For the first time the Appalachian Mountain barrier was bridged and the rich markets of the Atlantic seaboard opened to westerners. The steel network binding the North together in 1860 symbolized the section's new unity and provided an economic basis for the sectional realignment which found expression in war.

The race of eastern railroad promoters to tap markets in the Northwest began during the 1840's when roads were started westward from New York, Philadelphia, and Baltimore. Baltimore's venture, the Baltimore and Ohio Railroad, bogged down under financial difficulties in 1842 but was revived six years later and in 1853 emerged at Wheeling on the Ohio River. Philadelphia's western connection, the Pennsylvania Railroad, was opened as far as Pittsburgh a year later when the last difficult strip of mountain terrain was surmounted. From New York two lines were completed to Lake Erie during the decade. One was the result of a stock exchange among the numerous end-to-end roads which crossed the state from Albany to Buffalo; in 1853 they were brought together as the New York Central Railroad, with connections at Albany to New York City and Boston. The other was the New York and Erie Railroad, which was opened between New York City and Dunkirk on Lake Erie in 1852. By the middle 1850's four trunk lines were in operation between the principal coastal ports of the North Atlantic and the waterways of the Northwest. In addition two roads, the Grand Trunk and the Great Western, connected the Great Lakes with eastern Canada.

The railroads would have had little effect on western trade had not

their construction been paralleled by a burst of road building in the upper
Mississippi Valley states. During the decade nearly 10,000 miles of track

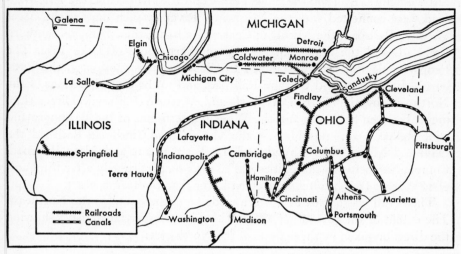

Transportation Routes in the Northwest, 1850

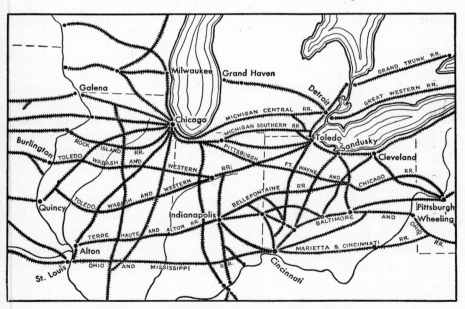

Transportation Routes in the Northwest, 1860

were laid in that section. Many of the new lines were of only local importance, but more were built with an eye to extending eastern trunk lines
and played an important role in developing trade with the seaboard. That

was especially the case after 1857 when a depression forced many small roads into such financial difficulties that they were absorbed by the main east-west lines. By 1860 the New York Central Railroad and the Erie Railroad were connected with the Mississippi River by such lines as the Great Western Railroad, the Michigan Central Railroad, the Michigan Southern Railroad, and the roads skirting the southern shore of Lake Erie. The Pennsylvania Railroad was joined to Chicago by its subsidiary, the Pittsburgh, Ft. Wayne and Chicago Railroad, and to the central sections of the Northwest by the Toledo, Wabash and Western Railroad. Direct shipments between St. Louis and the Wheeling terminus of the Baltimore and Ohio Railroad were possible over the Marietta and Cincinnati Railroad, the Ohio and Mississippi Railroad, and the Terre Haute and Alton Railroad. Competition between those lines was so intense, particularly after the Panic of 1857, that freight rates were often lower than by steamboat.

The result was a shift in western trade from the South to the Northeast. The extent of the revolution was revealed by commercial statistics showing the direction taken by the exports of the Northwest:

|  |  | TO THE EAST |  | TO THE SOUTH |  |
|---|---|---|---|---|---|
| CORN | 1850 | 3,600,000 | bushels | 2,400,000 | bushels |
|  | 1860 | 19,200,000 | bushels | 4,800,000 | bushels |
| PORK | 1850 | 300,000 | barrels | 1,200,000 | barrels |
|  | 1860 | 930,000 | barrels | 570,000 | barrels |
| WHISKEY | 1850 | 66,000 | barrels | 134,000 | barrels |
|  | 1860 | 310,000 | barrels | 190,000 | barrels |
| WHEAT | 1850 | 5,000,000 | bushels | 500,000 | bushels |
|  | 1860 | 28,420,000 | bushels | 580,000 | bushels |
| FLOUR | 1850 | 2,070,000 | barrels | 930,000 | barrels |
|  | 1860 | 4,345,000 | barrels | 1,155,000 | barrels |

The swing of the Northwest into the northern camp, brought about by the growth of a freedom-loving population, a fight for a common legislative program, and the cementing of commercial ties, proved decisive in the election of 1860. Had the section voted as it had a decade before Lincoln would have been defeated, for his margin of victory was small. His 190 electoral votes gave him a majority in the electoral college, yet his popular vote was only 40 per cent of the total cast and 1,000,000 less than that of his combined opponents. Lincoln owed his triumph to his impressive following in the Northeast and to a narrow victory over Douglas in each of the northwestern states. Shifting opinion in that crucial section placed a Republican in the White House.

The secession of the southern states was inevitable. South Carolina, where the tradition of rebellion was strong, led the way as soon as the election results were known. A Charleston convention in December, 1860, unanimously declared "the union now subsisting between South Carolina and the other states" forever at an end. One by one the other slave states of the lower South followed South Carolina into their newly formed Confederate States of America. Only Lincoln's decision not to let the "erring sisters depart in peace" was needed to touch off the Civil War.

That titanic four-year struggle touched the trans-Mississippi West only lightly. The states there cast their lot with one side or the other; Louisiana, Arkansas, and Texas with the Confederacy, Missouri and Iowa with the federal government. Most territories found the decision equally easy; Kansas and Nebraska were so strongly pro-Union they were rewarded with statehood during or just after the war, and although Utah had little liking for the United States, it too remained loyal. Only in New Mexico was there any question.

That thinly settled region was peopled by proslavery southerners who would doubtless have joined the Confederacy at once except for the garrison of 1,200 federal troops standing guard over them when war broke out. Their bias was expressed in March, 1861, when frontiersmen in the western portions of the territory met at Mesilla and after repudiating the government of both New Mexico and the United States, declared "the people of Arizona" a part of the Confederate States of America. Their action suggested a bold scheme to Confederate leaders. Why not send an army into the Southwest? The loyal southerners there would rise as a man to support such an expedition, making possible the conquest of the area between Texas and southern California. This would give the South an outlet in the Pacific, room for slavery expansion, and power needed for a place in the congress of nations. The Confederate attempt to carry out that plan accounted for the only military activity in the trans-Mississippi West.

The southerners dispatched a flying squad of mounted riflemen to the Arizona country before federal troops could put down the rebellion there. Those frontiersmen, after a dash across the Plains from Texas, reached Mesilla in late July, 1861, and quickly overwhelmed the few Union troops stationed there. In the meantime a larger Confederate force, led by Brigadier-General George H. Sibley and made up of 1,750 men, started west to drive federal forces from the forts guarding eastern New Mexico. They reached Ft. Craig, the principal Union stronghold, in February, 1862, only to find the thousand soldiers there so strongly fortified that a long siege would be required. Rather than risk prolonged operations in an arid region where supplies were difficult to obtain, General Sibley by-passed Ft. Craig, moving on to Albuquerque and Santa Fe which were occupied without resistance. Starting northward toward Ft. Union where large quantities of goods were stored, he met his first serious opposition—a ragged army of grizzled Mountain Men and prospectors who had hurried south on their own initiative upon learning of the Confederate advance. The two forces met in a pitched fight near Santa Fe. Although the southerners won the battle they lost so many supplies that General Sibley dared not risk another attack. He retreated to Texas, losing about half his men to desert heat and Union guerrilla bands on the way. At the same time a federal force from California freed Arizona of its Confederate invaders. Those skirmishes ended fighting in the Far West, which remained securely in Union hands until northern victory ended the four-year-long conflict.

# CHAPTER XXX

# The Miners' Frontier

## 1858-1875

During the three decades following the Civil War wave after wave of pioneers swept over the trans-Mississippi West—miners, expressmen, Indian fighters, cowmen, pioneer farmers, and equipped farmers—all bent on stripping away wealth hidden in mountain canyons or spread temptingly in the form of lush green pasture lands and fertile prairies. The miners were first on the scene. Between 1858 and 1875 they carried their rough brand of civilization into the mountainous regions of Colorado and Nevada, across the deserts of Arizona, over the inland empire of Oregon, Washington and Idaho, and through the wilds of Montana to the domed Black Hills of South Dakota. They found a fortune in gold and silver, and left behind a partly settled country.

To the westerner there was nothing remarkable in the fact that the mining frontier advanced rapidly while the United States was fighting a war for existence. That he should travel east to lend his weight to Union or Confederacy never entered his head or, if it did, was dismissed as a fantastic notion. He was, like all frontiersmen, concerned not with distant events but with affairs transpiring under his nose. His provincialism rested partially on the isolation of pioneer settlements, but was due primarily to the limitless economic opportunities offered by the frontier; why bother with the outside world when a fortune lay on your own doorstep? Whenever chances for economic betterment were greatest, preoccupation with local affairs mounted. That certainly was the case during the Civil War. What mattered that eastern streams ran red with blood when western streams concealed pockets of yellow gold? Westerners suffered no pangs of conscience as they ignored the war raging beyond the Mississippi to search for precious metals.

Although this attitude was typical, the miners differed from usual American frontiersmen. They occupied not fertile valleys or rich farm lands but the most unattractive portions of the Far West—steep mountain sides where roaring creeks covered deposits of precious metal, parched deserts where shifting sands hid beds of ore, arid highlands where jagged rock outcroppings shielded mineral-bearing lodes. The miners peopled thousands of square miles of mountain and desert that would have been avoided had farmers been the only pioneers. They were unusual, moreover, in that they moved not from east to west in the usual frontier pattern, but from west to east. For prospectors in most gold fields came from California rather than the settled areas of the Mississippi Valley.

Conditions within the far western state drove them out. They had gone there in the gold rush of 1849, at a time when gold nuggets or "dust" were relatively easy to obtain. Small quantities of the metal were present in rivers flowing westward into the Sacramento and San Joaquin valleys from the Sierra Nevadas, resting in pockets at the bottom of the streams. The particles were obtainable by a simple process called placer mining. A prospector needed only to throw a few shovelfuls of dirt into a "washing pan," twirl them about with water to wash gravel and stone away, and scrape away the grains of heavy gold left at the bottom. Where "pay dirt" was not rich enough to make that method profitable, other devices were used. One was a "cradle," a crude contraption which the miner rocked with one hand while dipping in gravel and water with the other; the sand was washed away to leave particles of gold trapped against wooden cleats. Another was the "sluice box" or "long tom," a long wooden box fitted with cleats at its lower end, into which a stream was diverted while miners shoveled in pay dirt. The rushing water carried away the dirt, while the cleats captured the dust and nuggets. All those methods could be used by individuals or small groups, for they required neither capital nor experience. They were employed by the '49ers in the first exploitation of California's wealth.

By the middle 1850's, however, the day of the individual prospector was drawing to an end. Most rich "diggings" were already appropriated, and the region had been so thoroughly prospected there was no chance of finding more. Gold remained, but it was locked in lodes of quartz or buried deep beneath debris laid down by the passing centuries. To extract the precious metal crushing mills must be built, the stubborn quartz crumbled to the point where the gold could be dissolved in mercury, and the quicksilver evaporated in large retorts. Or shafts must be sunk to reach beds of ore fifty or one hundred feet below the surface. Both mills and tunnels were beyond the financial means of the average miner. Gold continued to be mined in California, but eastern capitalists provided the funds while machines did the work. Thousands upon thousands of prospectors were left without any hope of making the "strike" that meant prosperity.

Any other form of life was unthinkable to most of them. They were inoculated with the feverish restlessness peculiar to the miner; in their eyes every rock outcropping, every cascading stream, might conceal a pocket of dull yellow metal worth a king's ransom. Nothing would satisfy them but a continuous quest for illusive fortune. Their needs were simple: a grub stake, a washing pan, a pack mule, endless hope. Their hunting ground was all the West, from the Pacific to the Rockies and from the mountains of British Columbia to the sun-dried valley of the Gila River. Throughout the late 1850's and 1860's they tramped over that domain, panning each likely stream and scanning each vein of rock for the telltale glint of yellow metal. Most failed to find enough gold to pay for their grub stakes, but a fortunate few stumbled upon rich pockets. Whenever such a strike was made a rush followed, with "yonder-siders" from California, "greenhorns" from the East, and grizzled prospectors from all the West, racing pellmell to the spot. Those not drawn away by later rushes stayed to build the first permanent settlements in the Rocky Mountain country and much of the Great Basin.

The process began in 1858 with discoveries in Colorado, Nevada, and British Columbia. The Colorado strike was most exciting. Rumors of gold in the mountainous country below South Pass had persisted for years—kept alive by tales of trappers who emerged with handfuls of nuggets, or Indians who shot bullets of yellow metal—before a party of California-bound '49ers first investigated the region. The slight signs of "color" in their washing pans were not enough to detain them long, but when they returned to the East without any of California's riches, they fell to thinking of Colorado's possibilities. Two of the group, Captain John Beck of the Oklahoma country and W. Green Russell of Georgia, decided to return, readily persuading about a hundred Indians and frontiersmen to accompany them. They started west along the Arkansas River in the spring of 1858, descended Cherry Creek to the headwaters of the South Platte, and there began panning streams. Ten days later they were joined by a party of prospectors from eastern Kansas who directed their search to the region about Pike's Peak. Findings were so few many drifted back East before late July when a member of the Beck-Russell party struck "pay dirt" near present-day Denver. Both groups then concentrated on that proven region, making a number of small strikes during the summer.

News of the discoveries, carried to the Mississippi Valley by travelers, found its way into Missouri newspapers in exaggerated form, for understatement was never a weakness of frontier editors. Moreover the Panic of 1857 was depressing business, and a gold rush would restore prosperity to pioneer towns where miners bought supplies. So writers filled their

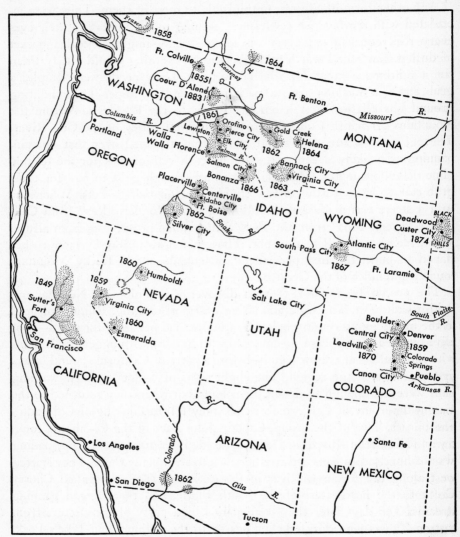

The Miners' Frontier, 1858-1875

columns with feverish stories of prospectors whose daily take with a shovel and washing pan was $20, of an overland immigrant who used a hatchet and frying pan to wash three ounces of dust from Cherry Creek in an hour, of riches dwarfing those of California in the new El Dorado. Those tall tales were eagerly scanned by poverty-ridden frontiersmen; within a month the whole frontier flamed with excitement as farmers traded their goods for mining equipment and covered wagons. Throughout September and October they streamed west by the hundreds, to spread over the hills of the Pike's Peak country (as the whole region was called for want of a better name) in search of gold. So little was found that most of the newcomers returned that fall, although a few remained, convinced that the meagre findings indicated an undiscovered pocket nearby. Most of those who spent the cold winter of 1858-59 in the West lived in a mining camp at the junction of Cherry Creek and the South Platte called Denver.

A few defeated prospectors who retreated east were honest enough to tell the truth—that almost no gold had been found in the Pike's Peak country—but more preferred to spin fantastic tales of the region's remarkable riches. Their stories touched off one of the wildest rushes in the nation's history. All that winter western Missouri towns bustled with activity as storekeepers crammed shelves with sides of bacon, sacks of flour, cases of canned beans, and bundles of the shovels and pans needed by gold seekers. Horses and oxen were in such demand that prices soared. Wagonmakers labored long hours on every type of vehicle from roomy covered wagons to flimsy handcarts that could be pushed across the Plains. And there was scarcely a Mississippi Valley barroom from Iowa to Arkansas not jammed with knots of men eagerly poring over the *Pike's Peak Guide* which an enterprising printer had hurried from the presses. Those who knew the signs agreed all was in readiness for a rush rivaling that of 1849.

The first breath of spring started the hordes westward. Steamboats crowded to the rails poured throngs of immigrants ashore at every Missouri River town. "The streets," wrote one resident, "are full of people buying flour, bacon, and groceries, with wagons and outfits, and all around the town are little camps preparing to go west." All through April, May, and June they left the jumping-off places in a regular parade of Conestoga wagons, hand carts, men on horseback, men on foot—each with "Pike's Peak or Bust" crudely printed on their packs or wagon canvas. Most used the well-marked trail along the Platte and South Platte, others followed the Arkansas, or Kansas, or Smoky Hill rivers. By the end of June more than 100,000 "fifty-niners" were in the Pike's Peak country.

Their reception was disheartening. They spread out over the eastern Rockies, laying out mining camps as they went—Pueblo, Canon City, Boulder, and a host of others. They panned every stream, chipped every promising rock outcropping, and found nothing. This was not what the guide books led them to expect; the land was supposed to be yellow with gold. Disappointment spread among them. They had, in the phrase of the day, been "humbugged." In disgust they started east again, the hopeful slogan of "Pike's Peak or Bust" scratched from their wagons and the truthful "Busted, by God," scrawled in its place. By midsummer half of the 50,000 miners who actually reached Colorado were back in their eastern homes. The Pike's Peak gold rush of 1859 was one of the greatest fiascos in the history of the frontier.

Perseverance rewarded the several thousand miners who stayed on at Denver. In May, 1859, a wandering prospector, John H. Gregory, "struck it rich" on the north fork of Clear Creek. News of pay dirt yielding $2 a pan, proclaimed to the world by a frenzied extra of the newly started *Rocky Mountain News,* brought the usual rush of gold seekers from the whole Pike's Peak region converging on Gregory Gulch to stake out claims. By the middle of June 5,000 people lived there, most of them in a mining camp called Central City, and twenty sluice boxes were in operation. Disappointment soon replaced hope for the majority as the good claims were snapped up by the fortunate few, leaving the luckless many to wander on in their weary search. Their redoubled efforts, now they knew Colorado contained gold, led to a number of smaller strikes along the eastern front of the mountains. At each a mining camp sprang up, complete with an assortment of shacks made from flour sacks or old shirts, a dance hall, gambling dens, bawdy houses, and enough saloons to satisfy the insatiable thirst of hardworking miners.

Life in the mining camps—whether in California, the Pike's Peak country, or later communities—followed a unique pattern. Within their straggling borders the distinctive features of frontier existence were present in exaggerated form. On all frontiers men outnumbered women; in mining camps respectable ladies were so rare that men often gathered to gape admiringly at a woman's dress hung on a line. All western communities were cosmopolitan; at the diggings college graduates rubbed elbows with illiterates, ministers and rogues worked side by side over sluice boxes, southern planters swung their picks beside Yankee abolitionists, drunken jailbirds mingled with pious deacons. Every frontier attracted lawless outcasts; in the gold fields the promise of easy money lured an unusually large number of desperadoes, gamblers, and harpies to prey on the physical or moral weakness of prospectors. Many frontiersmen squatted on government land; at the mines all were illegal trespassers on territory belonging to Indian tribes and the United States. Through the history of American expansion westerners had attempted to solve problems stemming from their unique environment by developing democratic institutions, casting off eastern control, and administering their own peculiar brand of justice. In the mining camps, frontier democracy, provincialism, and rough-and-ready legal practices were developed to the unusual degree required by unusual conditions.

The first miners in each new gold field were usually orderly men who were content to prospect without any social organization. With the initial strike and the rush of newcomers, some government was needed to protect the claims of those already there and provide for an equitable division of the remaining lands. As soon as the need became apparent a few leading miners issued a call for a mass meeting. This assembled in the camp's main street, a chairman was elected by voice vote, and laws were passed—regulating the size of the claim each prospector could stake out, outlining the procedure necessary to hold a claim, prescribing means for settling disputes and punishing crimes. Usually a committee of three or four "judges" to enforce the rough codes was named, but ultimate responsibility for their execution remained in the mass meeting, which might be summoned whenever an emergency arose. The simple democracy of the mining camps was typical of the frontier; from the days of the Mayflower Compact and the Watauga Association westerners had set up their own governments whenever they found themselves beyond the pale of the law.

The mass meeting, effective as it was in dealing with most problems rising in mining camps, failed to provide a satisfactory law-enforcement machinery. The miners were partly responsible, for they were hardened individualists who paid little attention to community affairs unless their own interests were threatened. Even more to blame were the roaring reprobates attracted to the diggings by the promise of easy money. They came by the score—shifty-eyed saloon keepers from the dives of New York, smooth-tongued gamblers from the East, painted harlots from the streets of Paris, Mexican outlaws from Sonora, "Sydney coves" from the penal colonies of Australia, gunmen and desperadoes from the wide-open towns of the Mississippi Valley—all lured by the prospect of helping themselves to dust and nuggets grubbed out by the miners. They flocked into each new mining camp in such numbers they eventually "took over" the town; then began a period of debauchery, murder, and claim jumping that the peace officers appointed by the mass meeting were powerless to stop.

Whenever that occurred the law-abiding majority moved into action. A few citizens led the way; meeting secretly they organized a vigilance committee, complete with a written constitution pledging members to co-operate until order was restored. Others were quietly added until the committee was large enough to challenge the outlaws, then a few ringleaders among the desperadoes were selected for punishment, hunted down by the vigilantes, and after a brief trial, sentenced to "stretch hemp." Executions were carried out on the spot, usually from a limb of the nearest tree. Only a few hangings were needed to send the camp's rogues scurrying to safety, nor were they likely to return, for once a vigilance committee established its authority a simple warning was enough to drive out the most hardened criminal. Organizations of that sort were formed in all the Colorado camps, as they had been in every gold field since 1851 when the first was set up at San Francisco.

Both vigilantes and mass meeting were looked upon as temporary stop-gaps, to be disbanded as soon as governmental machinery was provided by the United States. Two things were necessary: laws regulating the use of the public domain by miners, and a stable government. The first could be provided only by Congress, which proved distressingly lax in dealing with the problem. As early as December, 1848, when the first reports of gold discoveries in California reached the East, President Polk recommended a law governing the disposal of gold-bearing lands which would "bring a large return of money to the treasury and at the same time . . . lead to the development of their wealth by individual proprietors and purchasers." His sensible proposal was completely ignored; not until 1853 was any measure passed and that only excluded mineral lands from pre-emption. Belatedly, in 1866, Congress ruled that mining territory was open to all citizens, "subject to such regulations as may be prescribed by law, and subject also to local customs or rules of miners in the several mining districts." This unusual measure, which simply recognized the right of miners to make their own laws, was one of the few congressional statutes in the history of the frontier that did not try to inflict eastern institutions on the West.

The orderly government desired by miners was easier to obtain, for their pressure could prod indifferent Washington officials into action. The demand was usually voiced by the first prospectors on each new mining frontier; in the Pike's Peak country the few hardy souls who spent the winter of 1858-59 in Denver initiated the movement. Their thoughts turned to politics when an early snow in November, 1858, stopped all prospecting. An election late that month named delegates to visit Washington with a demand for organization as the Territory of Jefferson, a step which aroused a foreign traveler who happened to be present to write: "Making governments and building towns are the natural employments of the migratory Yankee. He takes to them as instinctively as a young duck to water. Congregate a hundred Americans anywhere beyond the settlements and they immediately lay out a city, frame a state constitution and apply for admission into the Union, while twenty-five of them became candidates for the United States Senate."

When Congress refused their request the miners took matters into their own hands. A meeting of delegates from six camps, held at Denver on April 15, 1859, put the issue squarely before the people: "Shall it be a government of the knife and revolver or shall we unite in forming here in our golden country, among the ravines and gulches of the Rocky Mountains, and the fertile valleys of the Arkansas and Plattes, a new and independent state?" Their answer was a call for a convention to draft a constitution for the state of Jefferson. By the time this assembled in June, 1859, the rush of '59ers was over and the prospects of maintaining a permanent population so uncertain that the delegates agreed to postpone action until autumn. They met again in October, after a popular referendum showed a majority favored immediate statehood, this time to draw up a frame of government for the proposed state. When this was ratified two weeks later a governor and legislature were chosen to govern the territory until Congress acted. That the interim government lacked any legal basis for existence did not bother the frontiersmen. "We claim," wrote the editor of the *Rocky Mountain News*, "that any body, or community of American citizens, which from any cause or any circumstance is cut off from, or from isolation is situated as not to be under, any active and protecting branch of the central government, have a right, if on American soil, to frame a government, and enact such laws and regulations as may be necessary for their own safety, protection and happiness."

Despite those bold words the temporary government did not work satisfactorily; its decrees were ignored by miners whose governmental needs were satisfied by local mass meetings and its officials soon tired of serving without pay. Only congressional action would save the situation, but Congress was in no mood to act. Each petition from the Territory of Jefferson was either brushed aside or hopelessly entangled in the raging slavery controversy; not until the southern states left the Union did Colorado achieve territorial organization with boundaries those of today. From that time on the region developed steadily. During the early 1860's shafts were sunk to the rich mother lodes near Boulder and Denver, machinery hauled in, labor and capital imported from the East, and precious metal extracted in fabulous quantities. Farmers drifted in, lured by high prices, attractive markets, and fertile mountain valleys. New mines were opened as prospectors uncovered beds of silver ore near Leadville in the 1870's and deposits of gold on Cripple Creek a few years later. Colorado entered the Union as a state in 1876, already well beyond the frontier stage.

While the Pike's Peak country was undergoing this transformation, other miners found fame and fortune in the Mountains surrounding the Carson River Valley of Nevada. Prospectors turned their attention to that region during the middle 1850's, acting under the sensible belief that if gold was found on the western slopes of the Sierra Nevadas it might also exist in the eastern foothills. Much activity was centered in two promising canyons that ran down the side of Davidson Mountain in the eastern Sierras: Gold Canyon and Six Mile Canyon. The little band of prospectors who worked their way up those gulches found enough pay dirt to justify building sluice boxes on Gold Hill in Gold Canyon during the autumn of 1858. The following spring brought new problems, for as the winter snow melted water needed to work the "placers" became scarce. Some miners tried to remedy the situation by digging a reservoir for spring water at the head of Six Mile Canyon. Not far below the surface they uncovered a vein of bluish rock, thickly flecked with gold. News of their discovery soon reached the ears of a shiftless old prospector, Henry Comstock, who not only rushed to the spot in time to stake a claim for himself, but gave the find his name. The lucky miners had stumbled upon the fabulous Comstock Lode!

The fortunate few who obtained "feet" began operations at once, digging out the rock, separating the chunks of gold from a troublesome black substance which encased the precious metal, and shipping out from $500 to $1,000 worth a day. That went on for some weeks before one of the diggers decided to have the "black stuff" they were throwing aside assayed. The word sent back from California where the analysis was made electrified the West. That "base metal" was worth $1,595 in gold and $4,791 in silver a ton. Overnight the western world learned of the unbelievable riches in the Washoe District—so named for the Indians who lived there—and the stampede was on. Four thousand prospectors from California reached Nevada before autumn snows clogged the mountain passes, 10,000 more came in 1860. They blanketed the district with their claims and camps, although most stayed close to Davidson Mountain where the Comstock Lode was located. There the leading mining camp was Virginia City, named for a bibulous character, "Old Virginny," who, stumbling from his tent one night when roaring drunk, broke a bottle of whiskey, and rising to his knees shouted, "I baptize this town Virginia Town." The cluster of smoky caves, leaky tents, and ramshackle saloons was the center of the Washoe mines.

They lived in a fantastic world, the prospectors who reached Nevada during 1859 and 1860. Few of them could mine, for the gold was locked in quartz veins that could only be crushed with expensive machinery. So they spent their days staking out claims, their nights peddling shares in imaginary mines. Everyone was feverishly happy in that land of penniless millionaires. No one had enough money to pay his grocery bill, but everyone owned 30,000 or 40,000 "feet" in a dozen claims—the "Branch Mint," the "Root-Hog-or-Die," the "Let-Her-Rip," the "Treasure Trove," the "Grand Mogul"—that would soon be worth fortunes.

Gradually order replaced chaos as capital flowed in. Quartz mills were built at Gold Hill and Virginia City, lumber hauled in for homes, roads laid out across the mountains to California, express companies formed to carry out gold and bring in supplies needed by 15,000 people. The improvements helped translate the wild dreams of the miners into equally wild actuality. Fortune nodded to only a few—less than a dozen of the 3,000 mines staked out ever proved profitable—but their profits were unbelievable as each lode was followed deep into the earth. More than $15,000,000 worth of precious metal was taken from Davidson Mountain in the next four years; wealth then transformed Virginia City into a metropolis complete with five newspapers and a stock exchange; wealth that allowed rough miners who had lived on bacon and beans for years to revel in a diet of oysters, strawberries, squab, and champagne.

Prospectors who failed to strike it rich in the Washoe District sought a new Comstock Lode in other mountainous areas of western Nevada. By the end of 1860 news of strike after strike was sending Virginia City's miners off in a series of rushes that often emptied the city. One group of mines was opened in the Esmeralda Mountains southwest of Walker Lake, another in the Humboldt Mountains northeast of Washoe. Although neither proved as rich as the Davidson Mountain country every new discovery launched a period of wild trading in "feet" similar to that in Virginia City.

Expansion strengthened a demand for territorial organization which forced Congress to set aside western Utah as Nevada Territory in 1861. Governor James W. Nye, a New York politician, unwittingly brought himself undying fame by selecting as his secretary a young Missourian, Orin Clemens, who took west with him his younger brother, Samuel. Mark Twain's experiences in the mines of Washoe, Humboldt, and Esmeralda gave him material for *Roughing It*, a classic description of life in the Far West. Even that notable contribution failed to satisfy the Nevadians, who soon clamored for statehood. Under ordinary circumstances Congress would have brushed aside a request from a territory whose population of 20,000 was far below the standard, but in 1863 Republican leaders were willing to welcome any region which would assure Abraham Lincoln more electoral votes in 1864 and help ratify the Thirteenth Amendment. Although Democrats protested vehemently, Lincoln's support and the argument that any state with mines producing $24,000,000 yearly would soon attract a larger number of people, carried the day. On October 31, 1864, Nevada became a state; eight days later its voters rewarded Republicans by returning a thumping majority for the President's re-election.

The new state's palmiest days lay just ahead. During the next decade mine after mine was opened, as the Comstock Lode or similar veins were tapped at different subterranean spots by small companies. The greatest discovery came in 1873 when four miners, organized as the Consolidated Virginia, decided to test the theory that the Comstock grew wider deep within the bowels of the earth. Scraping together needed cash and equipment, they began the back-breaking task of boring through the flinty rock of Davidson Mountain. At 1,167 feet they struck the Big Bonanza; the lode at that point was fifty-four feet wide and filled with gold and silver. This richest find in the history of mining not only brought the prospectors a fortune of $200,000,000 but sent other miners to tunneling in the hope of striking similar hidden wealth. For the next years the air about Virginia City rang with the clank of metal drills and the boom of blasting powder as new mines were opened. Most proved fruitless but a few elevated their owners from paupers to millionaire "Kings of the Comstock" with ugly mansions on Virginia City's twisted streets or San Francisco's Nob Hill. For another ten years boring went on, until deepening shafts raised costs beyond the point where profits could be made. By 1890 the boom was over. Nevada sank into sleepy lethargy until its people discovered that gold was as plentiful in the pockets of tourists and divorce-seekers as in the pockets of streams or lodes.

While rich Washoe went through its evolution, prospectors carried the mining frontier into the Southwest. The first rush occurred in 1858 when dust was discovered along the lower Gila River. The find proved disappointing; but a new strike on the Colorado in 1862 led to a stampede from California, this time with permanent results. Tucson, the leading town, developed overnight into the "Sodom and Gomorrah" of the West, with such a colorful collection of cutthroats that sober citizens believed the influx due more to the San Francisco vigilance committee than to the attractiveness of the mines. Their demand for an orderly government forced Congress to create the Territory of Arizona in February, 1863. A year later the first crushing mills began the district's transformation into a staple mining region.

More important than the expansion of the miners' frontier into the South was its parallel movement northward into Washington, Canada, Idaho, and Montana. The first strikes were made in the "Inland Empire" of the Columbia Plateau where the Snake and Columbia rivers twisted their way to the sea through deep lava beds. Gold was discovered in 1855 near Ft. Colville, a former Hudson's Bay Company post on the upper Columbia, and although the find proved disappointing, prospectors were encouraged to wander over the region in the hopes of richer deposits. Some, pushing northward into the wilds of British Columbia with their washing pans, found "color" in the Fraser River during the fall of 1857. By the following spring all the West knew a new El Dorado waited exploitation, where Indians were friendly and miners could pan out from $10 to $50 worth of dust daily. The rush from California that followed dwarfed even the stampede to Washoe going on at the same time; roads to Stockton and Sacramento were jammed with prospectors making their way to the coast where they fought to board steamboats for the journey north. Thirty-five thousand people left the state for the Fraser River in 1858, most of them soon to return with the disappointing news that the gold-bearing sand bars of the river were so flooded mining was impossible.

Those who stayed fanned out in two directions in their continuous hunt for the illusive yellow metal. Some prospected northward along the Fraser to Cariboo Lake where they found enough gold to attract 1,500 miners during 1860 and 1861. More drifted southward into the Snake River Valley where their spectacular strikes during the next four years lured the first permanent settlers to Idaho. The first was made by a party of a dozen miners under Captain E. D. Pierce who in August, 1860, found pockets of gold about twenty-five miles from the mouth of the Clearwater River. Exaggerated stories of their success inspired such a stampede during the spring of 1861 that several thousand miners occupied the district by the end of June, living in such camps as Orofino and Pierce City, and supplied from the nearby city of Lewiston which was founded by opportunistic merchants as an outfitting point. Although the Clearwater mines sent out $100,000 worth of dust monthly, most newcomers failed to find good sites not already pre-empted. After satisfying themselves the unworked streams nearby contained no hidden wealth they struck out southward once more, some to the South Fork of the Clearwater where the camp of Elk City was laid out, others to the Salmon River Valley where the town of Florence was established. The pockets there were fabulously rich; one miner panned out $6,000 worth of dust in one day while another found shining scales worth $500 in the bottom of one pan.

Finds such as those brought a rush of population to the upper Snake River Valley during 1862; all through the spring every steamer dumped hordes of "yonder-siders" from California on the Portland docks, every wagon train from the East brought throngs of "greenhorns" from the Missouri Valley or seasoned prospectors from the Pike's Peak country. Twenty thousand miners were at work in the Clearwater and Salmon River gold fields by the close of the year. Some who failed to find likely spots moved south, panning the tributaries of the Snake as they went. One found pay dirt on the Boise River during the autumn; during 1863 the stampede to that region scattered mines and camps—Placerville, Centerville and Idaho City—along the valley. Another struck it rich on the Owyhee River; 2,500 miners followed him there to set up placers and sluice boxes around their camp at Silver City. The rushes to a region still held by Indians forced the government to build Ft. Boise as protection from the justly outraged red men.

On the heels of the prospectors, there as everywhere on the mining frontier, came permanent settlers. Mining camps attracted not only faro dealers, bawdy house operators, and dance hall girls, but merchants, lawyers, and editors willing to endure slovenly life for the high prices their services could command. Settling first in the remote diggings, they gradually drifted to strategically located spots which became the commercial centers of every region. In the Inland Empire, Walla Walla rapidly developed pre-eminence, serving as an emporium for the Snake River mines and the gold fields opened along the Kootenay River of Canada in 1864. Lewiston, at the junction of the Snake and Clearwater rivers, was a lesser center, while in the southern Snake Valley, Idaho City forged ahead of competitors. In 1863 it boasted a population of 6,000 people, "elegant dance halls," roaring saloons, thriving faro parlors, a hospital, a theater, churches, a fire department, and three newspapers. The high prices asked in mining towns lured farmers to the neighboring countryside, for there were few places in the United States where flour sold for $28 a hundred, corn meal at $19, chickens at $5 apiece, butter at $1.20 a pound, and potatoes at twenty cents a pound. Gradually the region about Walla Walla filled up with industrious husbandmen.

Farmers, merchants, and miners united in demanding an orderly government, pointing out that the Idaho country could never be satisfactorily governed so long as it remained a part of Washington Territory. Petitions for separate organization were circulated in the mining camps as early as 1860, but Congress paid no heed until 1863 when the growing agricultural population and the introduction of mining machinery indicated the settlements were permanent. The Territory of Idaho, established in March of that year, included all of Montana and most of Wyoming.

Even as Congress acted, miners were stampeding into the eastern sections of the new territory. The pioneers on that frontier were two brothers, James and Granville Stuart, who in 1862 began prospecting the wild country near the headwaters of the Missouri River. On Gold Creek, a mountainous fork of the Clark's Fork River, they found enough pay dirt to justify building sluice boxes. News of their moderate success fell on the ears of a party of disappointed '59ers from Pike's Peak making their way overland to the Salmon River gold fields. Abruptly changing their plans, they started north from the Oregon Trail, panning streams as they went in true prospector style. On Beaverhead River, a tributary of the Jefferson River, they found a large pocket of gold. Others followed them in, until by the autumn of 1862 four hundred miners were in the district, all building sluice boxes or throwing up the crude shacks of their camp, Bannack City.

Those pioneering achievements paved the way for the great Montana gold rush of 1863. The time was ripe for a new stampede. Favorable spots along the Snake River were already appropriated, releasing hundreds of prospectors who were ready to race to any new field. They could reach the Montana mines easily over a military highway, the Mullan Road, which was opened in early 1863 between Walla Walla and Ft. Benton, at the head of steamboat navigation on the Missouri. The combination of available population and easy transportation started the tide rolling as soon as snow melted that spring. Hundreds swarmed in to stake claims about Bannack City; others struck out over the neighboring mountain country in pursuit of wealth. The most fortunate stumbled upon gold in Alder Gulch, a tributary of the Gallatin River. Their attempt to keep the find a secret failed when one miner from the Gulch visited Bannack for supplies; he was followed back by two hundred prospectors and the rush began. Virginia City, the camp established by the newcomers, within a year boasted a population of 4,000 men who amused themselves in eight billiard halls, five gambling establishments, three hurdy-gurdies, several bawdy houses, innumerable saloons, and two churches. Thirty million dollars worth of dust and nuggets were taken out of Alder Gulch during the next three years.

Even those riches were rivaled by those of the last great strike in the upper Missouri country. The fortunate miner responsible was a venerable Georgian, John Cowan, who worked his way down the Missouri during the spring of 1864 without detecting a trace of pay dirt. With supplies exhausted and on the point of turning back, he decided to test one last spot, which he called Last Chance Gulch. The pans of yellow nuggets that he found there attracted a rush of miners; Helena was laid out as a mining camp, sluice boxes built, new mines opened in a dozen gulches nearby, and the process begun of extracting the $16,000,000 worth of gold concealed in the region. Helena, conveniently situated on the trade route between Ft. Benton and Bannack and Virginia Cities, rapidly developed into one of the leading commercial emporiums of the mountain country.

The influx of merchants and farmers into fertile mountain valleys nearby, together with the discovery of mineral-bearing lodes which promised rich yields when quartz-crushing machinery could be brought in, testified to the permanence of the fields and accentuated the demand for a stable government. Petitions circulated among the mining camps were sympathetically received by Congress, which in May, 1864, created Montana Territory. The legislature, meeting in Bannack City in December, chose Virginia City as the territorial capital and adopted a seal depicting a miner's pick and shovel and a farmer's plow against a mountain background.

Despite those symbols of permanence, new gold rushes continued to thrill the prospectors of Idaho and Montana. One occurred in 1866 when pay dirt was found on the upper Salmon River; 5,000 miners stampeded to the spot during the summer, to lay out such camps as Salmon City and Bonanza. One famous spot there, the Charles Dickens Mine, yielded $1,000 a day in dust until the surface wealth was skimmed off. Another exciting strike was made a year later along the Sweetwater River of the Wyoming country; South Pass City and Atlantic City sprang up to hold the hordes who raced to the newest El Dorado. The pockets proved shallow, however, and by 1870 the Sweetwater boom was over, leaving behind no residue of farmers and merchants as a permanent population. The next rush was to the Coeur d'Alene Mountains of northern Idaho where pockets of gold were found in 1883. Those also proved so disappointing that by 1886 the prospectors were drifting away, leaving scarred hills, slashed gullies, and deserted ghost towns behind them.

The subsequent development of the northern Rocky Mountain mining country paralleled that of Nevada or Colorado. There as elsewhere early miners only captured a small portion of the surface wealth in their placers; the real riches lay far below the surface, encased in veins of quartz. During the 1870's and 1880's eastern capital moved into Idaho to extract the hidden fortunes; shafts were sunk, crushing mills built, and mine after mine opened. The most famous was the Bunker Hill and Sullivan Mine, discovered in 1885 by a wandering prospector who, pausing to rest on a pile of rock while chasing a runaway mule, found the stones streaked with lead and silver. Investigation disclosed his impromptu resting place to be part of a great dike of precious metals which eventually yielded $250,000,000 worth of silver and lead. Workers brought in to extract such wealth provided Montana and Idaho with permanent populations.

One region remained to be exploited by the drifting prospectors who were always on the fringes of the mining frontier—the Black Hills of Dakota. Rumors that those domed mountains cradled pockets of gold persisted among the mining camps. For years the West heard stories of Indians who appeared at Ft. Laramie with bags full of nuggets, of military commanders who found such wealth they kept their discoveries secret lest their men desert, of occasional prospectors who found pay dirt rivaling that about Sutter's Fort. The tales were not tested so long as gold fields farther west remained to be exploited, for the Black Hills country was occupied by warlike Sioux Indians and guarded by federal troops pledged to keep out all intruders. By 1874, however, the western mines were passing into the hands of eastern capitalists. Thousands of prospectors turned toward the Black Hills, certain that the forest-clad slopes concealed the riches fickle fate had denied them elsewhere. From Massachusetts to California expeditions were formed that spring to force their way past the soldiers ringing the promised land. Observers agreed that if they succeeded the stampede would dwarf the rush to Pike's Peak or the Washoe District.

The military authorities, aware the best way to stop the invasion was to disprove the rumors of Black Hills gold, decided upon an official investigation. The expedition fitted out for the purpose—1,200 soldiers and scientists under General George A. Custer—returned in August with upsetting news; gold was present in payable quantities all through the district! The fat was in the fire. A proclamation from abashed army officials barring settlers from the territory did no good; from the entire west miners gathered, ready to defy the troops who barred their path. They concentrated especially at Sioux City, Iowa, where the editor of the Sioux City *Times* turned his paper into a screaming advertisement for the Black Hills' gold fields. Through the winter of 1874–75 they jammed the town's hotels and filled two large tents erected in the main street, ready to leave whenever the soldiers relaxed their vigilance. One party of twenty-eight frontiersmen broke through the cordon in December, made their way to the mines through the Dakota badlands, and pitched camp on French Creek where they panned gold until troops ejected them.

Their tales of Dakota wealth, magnified by every teller, ruined the government's last chance to hold the Black Hills for the Indians. Throughout the summer bands of miners filtered through the ring of guardians to pan gold furiously for a time before being driven out. In August, 1875, six hundred miners were ousted, only to return again. As the game of hide-and-seek went on, military leaders realized no amount of force could hold back the miners indefinitely; the only solution was to extinguish the Indian title. When a nine-day conference with the Sioux in September failed to wring any concessions from the red men, disgusted federal agents decided to let the miners take their own chances. In October the Black Hills were thrown open to all comers who dared risk attack.

The rush began at once. From Iowa and the gold fields of the West prospectors came in droves, to swarm over the region with wash pans in hand, ready to set up placers at the first hint of yellow metal. Most of the 15,000 who entered that fall concentrated on the French Creek region where a town named Custer City was built, a mining district laid out, and laws governing the location of claims adopted. During the winter new discoveries in Deadwood Gulch sent a rush to that northerly valley. In April, 1876, Deadwood was founded, a ramshackle town of one saloon-filled street that twisted through the gulch, catering to the wide-open tastes of 7,000 miners "who had no Puritan prejudices to overcome." Custer City and

Deadwood remained the leading cities during the mushroom stages of the rush, although camps were established at Lead City and Spearfish during 1876.

The Wild West made its last glorious stand in the Black Hills mining camps. Deadwood was the rip-roaring center of frontier lawlessness. There the faro games were wilder, the hurdy-gurdy dance halls noisier, the street brawls more common, than in any other western town. There congregated road agents, gunmen, murderers, bawds, and gamblers driven from more orderly communities by vigilantes—Wild Bill Hickok, California Jack, Bed Rock Tom, Poker Alice, Calamity Jane. There stagecoaches were robbed with such montonous regularity the local paper dismissed one such incident with: "We have again to repeat the hackneyed phrase, 'the stage has been robbed!'" There desperadoes from the hills regularly roared in to "take over the town," while storekeepers boarded up their doors, shut out their lights, and unashamedly hid until danger was past. There the vigilance committee "stretched hemp" over the necks of more unregenerate cutthroats than in all the gold fields from Pike's Peak to Sutter's Fort. Deadwood's place in the criminal sun was brief, but during those hectic years no other spot in the nation could boast such unrestrained lawlessness as that famous mining camp.

The eastward advance of the mining frontier ended with the Black Hills rush. Much gold and silver remained locked in the hills of the Far West after 1875, waiting to be extracted by trained engineers or unromantic wage earners. The day of prospector and placer miner was at an end, but they left in their wake a sprinkling of busy towns and prosperous farming communities over half the trans-Mississippi country.

# CHAPTER XXXI

# The Transportation Frontier

## 1858-1884

The rapidity of the mining frontier's advance greatly alarmed both East and West. In the past, easterners knew, pioneer communities were so near settled regions their economic and spiritual needs could be supplied by the older society. Now miners lived in isolated islands of settlement, scattered far and wide over the mountainous West, where they were distant from the civilization of the East. If left to themselves they might drift into lawless or pagan practices detrimental to the nation. Their salvation and the country's fate depended on the rapid development of transportation lines with the States. Frontiersmen of the Far West were equally insistent on better communications, knowing that roads would mean lower commodity prices for mining camps and more frequent news of happenings in the East. Both easterners and westerners agreed the improvements would require government support. Their pressure on Washington forced Congress to grant a series of subsidies between the middle 1850's and 1871 to express companies, stagecoach lines, telegraph corporations, and railroads. Federal aid not only gave the West needed economic outlets but opened vast portions of the continent to settlement.

The government's first attempts to provide communication facilities for westerners were hardly successful. In 1848 contracts were awarded for semi-monthly mail service between New York and San Francisco by sea; under the arrangement letters were carried to Panama by the United States Steamship Company, carted across the isthmus, and sent northward on vessels of the Pacific Mail Steamship Company. The high costs (twelve to eighty cents an ounce) and the thirty days required for the roundabout journey only stimulated California's demand for overland service. Nothing would satisfy the miners but a direct route across the continent, with frequent way stations where horses could be changed often enough to assure the constant movement of the mails. Through the early 1850's western pressure on the government mounted, reaching a climax in 1856 when a giant petition, signed by 75,000 Californians, was laid before Congress. Daily mails over a road through South Pass, the signers agreed, were needed to quench the westerners' thirst for news.

No sooner was debate on the request begun than the sectional issue intruded. Southerners denounced the South Pass route, knowing that its eastern terminus at St. Louis or Chicago would not only benefit the North economically but presage a transcontinental railroad along the path pioneered by stagecoaches. This the South was bound to resist, so effectually that a congressional decision on the issue was impossible. Instead the legislators in 1857 dodged the sectional question by appropriating money to survey and improve two roads, one from Ft. Kearney through South Pass to California, the other from El Paso to Ft. Yuma on the southern border of the state. Although unable to follow the same expedient in granting subsidies, congressmen hit upon an equally compromising device. The Post Office Appropriation Act of 1857 authorized the postmaster general to call for bids on a semi-weekly or weekly mail service from "such point on the Mississippi River as the contractors may select, to San Francisco." The company chosen must, according to the bill, guarantee delivery within twenty-five days in return for an annual subsidy of $600,000.

Southern congressmen supported the measure, which seemingly favored the short South Pass route over the longer roads across the Southwest, only because they knew their interests would be protected by the postmaster general, Aaron V. Brown of Tennessee. They were not disappointed. Brown, an ardent southerner, after throwing out all bids from northern companies, selected the offer of a firm headed by two seasoned expressmen, John Butterfield and William G. Fargo of New York, largely because they proposed to use a road from St. Louis or Memphis through Ft. Smith, El Paso, and Ft. Yuma to San Francisco. Objections to the roundabout "oxbow" route, as northerners derisively labeled it, were brushed aside with the assertion that the plentiful grasslands and healthy climate of the Southwest justified the greater distance!

A year of preparation was needed before the Butterfield Overland Express started its first stagecoaches across the continent. First a trail was marked out over the 2,795 miles between St. Louis and San Francisco. Along this crude "stations" of wood or adobe were scattered at ten-mile intervals, where horses and mules could be sheltered, fodder stored, and food provided for passengers whose stomachs were strong enough to face the Plains fare of bacon, beans, bread, and what passed in the West for coffee. Each of the lonely outposts was placed under an "agent" who was usually a profane cutthroat wanted by half a dozen vigilance committees, and every two hundred miles of road was entrusted to a "district agent" who differed from his unruly subordinates only in being quicker on the draw. Drivers, most of them swaggering bullies, were hired to handle the thousand mules and five hundred horses purchased by the company.

The coaches introduced by the Butterfield Overland Express revolutionized western travel. Known as Concord Coaches for their manufacturer —the Abbott-Downing Company of Concord, New Hampshire—they were far better suited to journeys across plains and deserts than any earlier

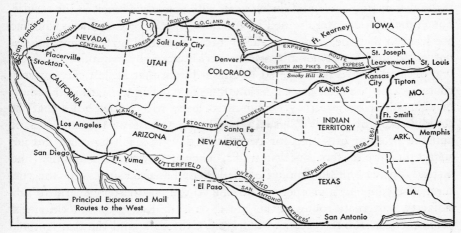

Overland Transportation, 1858-1875

vehicle. The wheels were heavy, with broad iron tires that would not sink in soft sand, and were set wide apart to keep the stage from tipping. The iron-reinforced wooden body was swung on leather thoroughbraces which absorbed some of the worst shocks, and was provided with leather curtains to protect the nine passengers from rain or cold. The driver and conductor, and sometimes a passenger or two, rode high up on the boxlike structure, while to the rear was a triangular "boot" which held mail sacks and luggage. The gaudily painted red or green vehicles were pulled by four galloping horses or half a dozen scampering mules.

They were used first on a large scale on September 15, 1858, when preparations for overland service were completed. That morning two coaches started on their lonely journey, one from the railroad terminus at Tipton, Missouri, the other from San Francisco. For three weeks they careened across the prairies, one racing east and the other west, as road-building crews stopped to cheer and frontiersmen gathered from miles around to gape at the latest evidence of civilization. Hardships were many on the first run, but on the morning of October 10 one dust-stained coach swept into San Francisco, twenty-four days out of Missouri. "Had I not just come out over the route," wrote a tired correspondent who made the journey, "I would be perfectly willing to go back by it." In the meantime the east-bound coach reached St. Louis in a little less than twenty-one days. "I congratulate you on the result," President Buchanan wired Butterfield. "It is a glorious triumph for civilization and the Union."

For the next three years Butterfield Overland Express coaches raced over the trails blazed by those pioneers, two each week in each direction, through rain and snow and desert heat, with scarcely a break in the service. Sometimes stations were raided by bands of Apache or Comanche who had not learned that the condemned army bacon provided by the company was not worth stealing. Sometimes coaches were attacked by marauding savages; one overland driver complained to Mark Twain that he left the southern route because "he came as near as anything to starving to death in the midst of abundance, because they kept him so leaky with bullet holes that 'he couldn't hold his vittels'." Usually passengers were few; the fare of $200 and the prospect of sitting for twenty-two days in a jolting coach did not attract pleasure seekers. But way traffic, generous government subsidies, and a steady increase in the amount of mail carried assured success for the venture. The company's prosperity encouraged the postmaster general to subsidize two alternate routes in the late 1850's, the Kansas and Stockton Express between Kansas City and Stockton, California, and the San Antonio Express connecting Texas with San Diego.

The support given southwestern routes by the Democratic officials who dominated national affairs under President Buchanan meant the early development of the central road across the continent would be left to private initiative. Interest in the possibility mounted during the middle 1850's as individual freighters, realizing that profits could be obtained by supplying Mormons and California miners with eastern goods, began plying the Platte River route with small wagon trains. Scarcely had trade begun when one freighter, an experienced Missourian named Alexander Majors, decided to monopolize the business. In 1855 he formed a partnership with two other plainsmen, William H. Russell and W. B. Waddell. The firm of Russell, Majors and Waddell, starting operations with three hundred wagons, grew so rapidly that by 1858 it operated 3,500 covered vehicles, employed 4,000 men, and owned 40,000 draft oxen. For the next few years it dominated freighting on the central Plains, carrying food and industrial produce to army camps or mining fields, and bringing out hides and precious metals.

Russell, Majors and Waddell prospered because they devised efficient methods for overland travel. Every wagon train they sent out from Missouri contained twenty-five covered wagons, each carrying three tons of goods and pulled by twelve oxen. A "bullwhacker" walked beside each wagon, controlling the animals with a twelve-foot bullwhip which cracked like a rifle when flicked against the oxen. Most drivers were rough-and-tumble desperadoes whose sulphurous profanity and fondness for drunken brawling made them known and feared along the whole frontier, although Alexander Majors, a pious man, tried to attract more orderly employees by promising each a Bible and hymn book. Probably those inducements did less to keep bullwhackers in check than the wagonmaster who accompanied each train on its lonely march across the prairies. Those officials and their men, plodding along at the rate of fifteen miles each day, sleeping under the stars at night, supplied the isolated settlements of the Far West with necessities for almost a decade.

Profits from freighting encouraged Russell, Majors and Waddell to launch two other experiments in transportation—the Pony Express, and the Leavenworth and Pike's Peak Express. The romantic plan for the first was hatched in the fertile mind of William H. Russell, a loyal northerner who felt any financial sacrifice justified to prove the superiority of the South Pass route over the southern trail followed by the Butterfield Overland Express. That could be done, he decided after conversations with friends in Washington during the winter of 1859-60, by setting up a faster mail service between San Francisco and Missouri. His partners, although less enthusiastic, decided to risk the venture without government subsidies. During the early spring 190 way stations were built at ten-mile intervals between St. Joseph, Missouri, the western terminus of the railroads, and San Francisco, each equipped with an agent and well-trained hostlers. Five hundred horses, carefully selected for speed and endurance, were distributed along the route. Riders were chosen with equal care, all of them light young men or boys with courage and stamina needed for long hours in the saddle. Special equipment was purchased—close-fitting clothes for the riders, thin racing saddles, flat mail pouches that offered no wind resistance.

Service began on April 3, 1860, when crowds at St. Joseph and San Francisco cheered away the first two riders. Each drove his horse at full gallop for ten miles, then came crashing into a station where another mount was held, saddled and ready to be away. In a twinkling the mail pouches were flung across the new saddle, the rider leaped upon them and was off. Each rider rode seventy-five miles at that breakneck pace, then turned his pouches over to another and rested for the return trip. Ten and one-half days were required for the first trip, ten less than were needed by the fastest stagecoach. Here was something to catch the imagination of the nation. Eighty riders constantly in the saddle, forty of them flying east, forty of them west, over rolling prairie or tortuous mountain trails, with never a halt for snow or sleet or even Indian attack. Little wonder that one youngster who first saw the West as a pony express rider, "Buffalo Bill" Cody, came to typify the wild-western frontier to generations of Americans.

The pony express was richer in romance than profits. The rates were high enough—from $2 to $10 an ounce—and the number of letters carried increased from 41 on the first trip to 350 a year later, but no amount of business could carry the tremendous expenses without a government subsidy. Money from the vast resources of Russell, Majors and Waddell kept the pony express alive until October, 1861, when it was driven from existence by an exciting new competitor, the electric telegraph. Federal funds were behind that novel means of transmitting intelligence; a congressional promise of $40,000 yearly to any company completing a line to the Pacific brought two concerns into the field. One, the Pacific Telegraph Company, began building westward from Kansas City in the spring of 1860, racing across the Plains in the hope of entering Salt Lake City before the lines of its eastward-building rival, the California State Telegraph Company, reached that strategic point. When wires of the two companies were joined on October 22, 1861, the time between the coasts was reduced from days to a fraction of a second and the day of the pony express was over.

The second venture of Russell, Majors and Waddell—an overland express service over the central route—proved even more disastrous financially. Once more William H. Russell was responsible. Northern patriot that he was, he allowed himself to be convinced that stagecoaches could operate between Missouri and Denver without government subsidies. Heavy traffic from the Colorado gold fields, Russell believed, would support the venture. With his reluctant partners, Russell in 1859 chartered the Leavenworth and Pike's Peak Express, authorized to inaugurate daily service between eastern Kansas and Denver. Stations were laid out, fifty Concord coaches purchased, and drivers and agents hired. Expected profits did not materialize, largely because the Colorado mines failed to produce the wealth anticipated. In desperation the partners attempted to save their investment by plunging more deeply; late in 1859 they purchased a small company which had been running occasional stages between St. Joseph, Missouri, and Salt Lake City, as a means of entering the Mormon capital where the California Stage Company provided connections with San Francisco. Their reorganized concern, the Central Overland, California and Pike's Peak Express Company, tried to maintain daily service over both the Platte River and Smoky Hill River routes, but lost money so steadily critics soon applied its well-known initials to the slogan, "Clean Out of Cash and Poor Pay."

The outbreak of civil war brought a glimmer of hope to the harassed partners; Congress might be willing to award them the subsidy earlier diverted to the Ft. Yuma route. Even that dream went glimmering in March, 1861, when the coveted grant went instead to the Butterfield Overland Express, with the understanding its equipment be moved north to provide daily service between St. Joseph and Placerville, California. The struggling Central Overland, California and Pike's Peak Express Company managed to secure a share of the $1,000,000 annual subsidy when Russell Majors and Waddell arranged with the Butterfield interests to carry the mails as far west as Salt Lake City, while the southern company cared for service from that point to California. Even that was not enough to straighten the partners' tangled finances; after a year of combatting hostile Indians and adverse weather the Central Overland, California and Pike's Peak Express Company went into bankruptcy. On March 22, 1862, its meagre assets were purchased at public auction by the man who dominated western transportation for the next five years: Ben Holladay.

Holladay was a coarse illiterate, endowed by nature with shrewd cunning and an uncanny executive skill. Within a few months his smooth-running coaches were operating on schedule, attracting more passengers, and paying handsome dividends. Some of the revenue was used to buy improved Concord coaches, hire better drivers, and erect handsome stations where travelers could expect something better than the mouldy bread and spoiled pork inflicted on them in the past. More money went into lines to mining camps in Idaho, Montana, and Colorado, until Holladay controlled 5,000 miles of stage routes and was truly the "Napoleon of the Plains." Over this empire he ruled with an iron hand, riding constantly over his lines, goading his men on, and overawing the cutthroats who manned his stations, until he became a legendary figure in the West. Mark Twain caught the spirit of that frontier adulation in *Roughing It* when he recorded a conversation between an elderly pilgrim to the Holy Land and an impetuous young man who had once traveled in one of Holladay's coaches:

> "Jack, do you see that range of mountains over yonder that bounds the Jordan Valley? The mountains of Moab, Jack! Think of it, my boy—the actual mountains of Moab—renowned in Scripture history! We are actually standing face to face with those illustrious crags and peaks—and for all we know (dropping his voice impressively), *our eye may be resting at this very moment upon the spot* WHERE LIES THE MYSTERIOUS GRAVE OF MOSES! THINK OF IT, JACK!"

"Moses *who?*" (falling inflection).

"Moses *who!* Jack, you ought to be ashamed of yourself—you ought
to be ashamed of such criminal ignorance. Why, Moses, the great
guide, soldier, poet, lawgiver of ancient Israel! Jack, from this spot
where we stand, to Egypt, stretches a fearful desert three hundred
miles in extent—and across that desert that wonderful man brought
the children of Israel!—guiding them with unfailing sagacity for
forty years over the sandy desolation and among the obstructing rocks
and hills, and landed them at last, safe and sound, within sight of this
very spot; and where we now stand they entered the Promised Land
with anthems of rejoicing! It was a wonderful, wonderful thing to
do, Jack! Think of it!"

"*Forty years? Only three hundred miles?* Humph! Ben Holladay
would have fetched them through in thirty-six hours."[1]

More than Holladay's genius was needed to keep western coaching
alive, for by the middle of the 1860's the inevitability of progress placed
the stamp of doom on his giant enterprises. He was wise enough to see the
handwriting on the wall and sell out in 1866 to Wells Fargo and Company, a New York concern which had previously purchased Butterfield's
interests west of the Rockies. Holladay acted none too soon. Within three
years overland staging was relegated to a secondary place in frontier life
by the coming of the railroad.

During the decade when stage coaching was at its heyday in the Far
West, railways advanced slowly into the trans-Mississippi country. Construction was centered first in the humid regions adjacent to the Father of
Waters, where thickening settlement and heavy agricultural yields promised adequate way traffic. During the 1850's the object of most promoters
was to reach the Missouri River. First to be chartered were two Missouri
roads, the Missouri Pacific Railroad which connected St. Louis and Kansas
City (1851–1865), and the Hannibal and St. Joe Railroad between Hannibal and St. Joseph (1851–1859), but by the close of the decade activity
shifted to Iowa continuations or railroads from Chicago. The pioneering
line in that state was the Chicago and Northwestern Railroad; in 1855
its tracks reached the Mississippi opposite Clinton, Iowa, and during the
next decade it pushed construction on to Council Bluffs on the Missouri.
Close behind was the Rock Island Railroad which not only reached the
Mississippi in 1854 but a year later opened the first bridge across the river,
to the delight of awe-struck westerners. Its tracks entered Council Bluffs
in 1869. The Chicago, Burlington and Quincy Railroad, building westward

[1] Samuel L. Clemens, *Roughing It* (New
York, 1871), I, 58. Reprinted by special        permission of the publishers, Harper and
Brothers.

from Burlington through the Civil War decade, reached Council Bluffs in 1869 and Ft. Kearney, Nebraska, by 1873 when a depression stopped work. Northern Iowa was crossed by the Illinois Central Railroad, which completed its line from Dubuque to Sioux City in 1870.

Other railroad magnates turned their attention to the Minnesota country. A leading role there was played by the Chicago, Milwaukee and St. Paul Railroad, which by 1873 not only connected Chicago with Minneapolis and St. Paul, but operated a branch line half way across northern Iowa. Equally active was the Chicago and Northwestern Railroad which entered the territory in 1867 with the purchase of a defunct road that had attempted to build westward from Winona. When the Panic of 1873 ended construction, track extended across Minnesota and a short distance into Dakota Territory. Smaller lines, in the meanwhile, built northward from the Twin Cities; one, the Lake Superior and Mississippi Railroad, entered Duluth before 1873. By that time the northern tier of Mississippi states were crisscrossed by a number of east-west roads providing adequate transportation.

Less important in the development of the trans-Mississippi transportation network were the north-south lines begun just after the Civil War to connect points in Missouri or Kansas with the Gulf of Mexico. One, the Missouri, Kansas and Texas Railroad, building south from Topeka, reached the Kansas border in 1870 after a race with a rival concern that was pushing its tracks out from Kansas City. Its reward was a generous land grant and a right of way across the Indian Territory; an inducement which speeded construction until the "Katy's" tracks crossed the Red River in 1872, to join with those of the Houston and Texas Central Railroad. Its only rival in the Gulf trade was the St. Louis, Iron Mountain and Southern Railroad. That line reached Texarkana in 1873 where it met the already completed International and Great Northern Railroad.

The imposing railway network laid down in the tier of states bordering the Mississippi was made possible by financial aid from hamlets through which the roads passed, the state in which they lay, and the federal government. The last source was most bountiful; from 1850 to 1871 Congress granted the public domain freely to western states with the understanding they pass the awards on to railroads in the form of land bounties. Every trans-Mississippi state but Texas (which controlled its own domain) shared in this largess, and each in turn doled out millions of acres in alternate sections which were sold by roads to meet construction costs. When promoters turned to railroad building in the Plains region west of the first tier of trans-Mississippi states, they faced a different situation. That giant grassland supported no settlers to provide roads with way traffic, no towns to offer aid, no states to pledge credit, no pioneers to purchase land grants.

Building there was a task to try the skill of America's engineers and financiers.

That a transcontinental railroad must be built was acknowledged by all after the middle 1850's. The nation first began to visualize a Pacific road in January, 1845, when a New York business man and China trader, Asa Whitney, proposed to Congress that the government grant a sixty-mile strip between Lake Superior and the Oregon country to any company willing to risk construction. After this visionary plan was pigeonholed, Whitney launched a propaganda campaign to convince both congressmen and people the project was feasible; for the next decade he spoke and wrote constantly in behalf of a Pacific railroad, showering Congress with petitions as he did so. Gradually public opinion was won to his side, partly by his arguments, but more by the realization that heavily populated California could be kept satisfied only with better transportation. By 1853 the most hardheaded realists agreed a transcontinental road was necessary and the most rugged individualists admitted government aid must be forthcoming for the project.

Unfortunately the conversion of public opinion coincided with the rise of sectional antagonism; by the time Congress admitted a railroad should be built no one could agree upon the route. Feeling was especially bitter because all believed one road to the Pacific would suffice forever, giving the section securing its eastern terminus a perpetual economic advantage. Southerners insisted the government support a line along the Butterfield Overland Express route or one following the Canadian or Red rivers; northerners demanded a railway through South Pass. As Congress debated through the early years of the pre-Civil War decade, one group of realists concluded the problem might be settled by nature; perhaps one route was sufficiently superior to be used regardless of sectional feeling. To test that theory, Congress, in the spring of 1853, authorized the army to survey all feasible routes between the Mississippi Valley and the Pacific.

The findings, presented in ten bulky volumes in 1855, failed to still sectional clamor, for the surveys showed that four routes were practical: one between Lake Superior and Portland, another through South Pass to San Francisco, a third along the Red River to southern California, and a fourth across southern Texas and the Gila Valley. Two northern and two southern possibilities did little to make a decision easier, but the great compromiser, Stephen A. Douglas, tried to find a solution. After preparing the way for his favored South Pass route by organizing the western territories in the Kansas-Nebraska Act, he proposed that Congress aid three railroads: a Northern Pacific Railroad from Wisconsin to Puget Sound, a Central Pacific Railroad from Missouri or Iowa to San Francisco, and a Southern

Pacific Railroad from Texas to southern California. His catchall proposal might have satisfied the warring sections, but the expenses involved were too staggering to be considered. So long as sectionalism plagued the nation, no road could be built. The long debate, however, taught Congress that land grants and direct loans would be needed before private capitalists could be persuaded to undertake the project.

The opportunity to apply those lessons came with the secession of the Confederate states. Congress, controlled after 1861 by northerners who agreed on the central route, only needed prodding to act. That came from California in the person of Theodore D. Judah. Judah was a gifted engineer, chock-full of vision and energy, who had joined with four other promoters from his home state—Leland Stanford, Collis P. Huntington, Mark Hopkins and Charles Crocker—to charter the Central Pacific Railroad of California. They proposed building eastward from San Francisco to the state border, and wanted both federal support and the promise of a line to connect their road with the Mississippi Valley. That was what Judah was after when he descended on Washington late in 1861, his valise jammed with plans and his head with grandiose schemes. His persistent lobbying was rewarded on July 1, 1862, when Congress passed a law launching the first Pacific railroad.

Two companies, the measure decreed, would build the road. The Central Pacific Railroad was assigned the difficult task of bridging the Sierra Nevadas in California. The other, incorporated by Congress as the Union Pacific Railroad, was authorized to build westward from the 100th meridian, climb the Rockies near South Pass, and meet the Central Pacific at the California-Nevada line. East of the 100th meridian five branches were to radiate out to Kansas City, Leavenworth, St. Joseph, Sioux City, and Omaha—a device used to forestall local jealousies. Each road was granted a four-hundred-foot right-of-way, together with ten alternate sections of land for each mile of track laid. In addition the government agreed to loan the companies on a first mortgage basis $16,000 for each mile built in level country, $32,000 a mile in the foothills, and $48,000 in the mountains. Generous as the terms were—one critic complained that "while fighting to retain eleven refractory states the nation permits itself to be cozened out of territory sufficient to form twelve new republics"—they failed to attract private capital needed by the Union Pacific. After two years of stalemate Congress came to the company's aid in July, 1864, by doubling the land grant, reducing the government loan to the status of a second mortgage, and increasing the number of $100 shares it was authorized to sell from 100,000 to 1,000,000. Money poured in then, and construction began.

The Central Pacific was off first in the race across the continent, spurred on by a loan of $1,659,000 from California, and President Lincoln's geographical legerdemain in shifting the Sierra Nevadas westward into the Sacramento Valley to allow the company to borrow $48,000 a mile when building across level country. The first track was laid in 1863 and inched forward slowly during the next years—twenty miles in 1864, twenty more in 1865, thirty in 1866, forty-six in 1867. The construction gangs were in the mountains then, battering their way over steep grades and around precipices of living rock, but the promoters had solved their worst problem —how to obtain labor in a frontier community—by importing gangs of Chinese coolies. Seven thousand pig-tailed workers hacked out the right-of-way, their broad straw hats and flapping trousers forming a picturesque sight as they trundled wheelbarrows of dirt or scampered away from charges of blasting powder. In the summer of 1867 the crest of the Sierras was crossed and only easier downgrades lay ahead. Anticipating that happy moment, the Central Pacific in 1866 wrung from Congress the right to lay its tracks on across the Nevada deserts "until they shall meet and connect with the Union Pacific Railroad."

By that time work on the Union Pacific was well under way. Construction was slow at first, as the company struggled to obtain workers and material from a war-burdened nation; only forty miles of track stretched west from Omaha at the close of 1865. During the next two years conditions improved rapidly. Gangs of Irish laborers drifted westward with the close of the war, seeking jobs on the construction crews. In 1867 the Chicago and Northwestern Railroad reached Council Bluffs, ending expensive steamboat transportation of rails and materials. Yet plentiful labor, adequate supplies, and an easy roadbed across the Plains did not solve the Union Pacific's construction problems. Everything needed had to be brought into that barren country; ties from the forests of Minnesota, stone from the quarries of Wisconsin, rails from the steel mills of Pennsylvania. Moreover the Indians were on the warpath, necessitating frequent halts while workers snatched rifles from "track trains" to beat off attacks.

Still the work went on. A hundred mile stretch would be surveyed, graded, bridges built. Then came the track layers. "A light car, drawn by a single horse, gallops up to the front with its load of rails. Two men seize the end of a rail and start forward, the rest of the gang taking hold by twos until it is clear of the car. They come forward at a run. At the word of command, the rail is dropped in its place, right side up, with care, while the same process goes on on the other side of the car. Less than thirty seconds to a rail for each gang, and so four rails go down to the minute. . . . The moment the car is empty it is tipped over on the side of the track to let the next loaded car pass it, and then it is tipped back again; it is a sight to see it go flying back for another load, propelled by a horse at full gallop at the end of 60 or 80 feet of rope, ridden by a young Jehu, who drives furiously. Close behind the first gang come the gaugers, spikers and bolters, and a lively time they make of it. It is a grand Anvil Chorus that these sturdy sledges are playing across the plains." So they swept across the continent in a mighty symphony of motion. Two hundred and sixty-six miles of track went down in 1866, 240 in 1867. In November of that year the gleaming rails reached Cheyenne and started their climb upward toward the pass that would span the Rockies.

Behind them they left a chain of ramshackle towns, sixty or seventy miles apart, that marked the temporary halting places of construction crews. Julesburg, Cheyenne, Laramie City—those are today the ghosts of that migrating "Hell on Wheels" which followed the Union Pacific across the continent. For a few months, or perhaps a whole winter, the gangs of workers would live in one of the outposts, going out to work each day on the "track trains." Then, when the track had nosed out far ahead, the signal to move was given. All fell to work; in a few hours the town was dismantled, piled aboard flatcars, and on its way west, with inhabitants riding atop their dismantled homes. Sixty miles up the road they halted. Willing hands raised the "Big Tent," a floored canvas structure a hundred feet long and forty wide, which held a sumptuous bar, a dance floor, and elaborate gambling paraphernalia. Around it they threw up the ramshackle shacks or tents which held twenty-two more saloons, five dance halls, living quarters for the workers, and homes for the "girls" who were always ready to take away any portion of the workers' wages left by the faro dealers. Some 3,000 people drifted westward with that peripatetic Gomorrah— workers, bartenders, prostitutes, gamblers, speculators, outlaws, renegades, road agents, outcasts. "Hell," one journalist observed, "would appear to have been raked to furnish them."

Nightly dissipation did not slow down the workers who, by the spring of 1868, realized they were not mere laborers on a railroad but participants in the greatest race in history. The Central Pacific was winging across the level deserts of Nevada. The Union Pacific was battling through South Pass. Between them lay the plains of Utah, which an amiable government defined as mountain country, entitling builders to loans of $48,000 a mile as well as lucrative land grants. Each company spurred its men relentlessly in hope of grabbing off a major share of that prize. Five miles, seven miles, finally ten miles of track a day were laid by hustling crews, while far ahead graders worked feverishly to add government land and dollars to their companies' treasuries. The Central Pacific built 360 miles of road in 1868, the Union Pacific 425. For a time, so great was the competition, they seemed destined never to meet; Congress had set no junction point and when the grading crews met they passed each other, laying out parallel roads a short distance apart. The farce only ended when Washington officials ruled the two roads must join at Promontory, Utah, a short distance from Ogden, Utah.

There, in mid-May, 1869, a little knot of workers and officials watched the placing of the last silver-bound laurel tie, the fixing of the last steel rail, the presentation of the golden spike which would bind the two roads together. "Hats off!" signaled a telegraph operator to all the listening nation. "Prayer is being offered." Thirteen minutes later, and with a sense of relief at getting down to business at last: "We have got done praying. The spike is about to be presented." A few well-aimed blows (after Leland Stanford missed with the first swing of his sledge), the tracks were joined, and two locomotives steamed forward until their pilots touched—

"Facing on a single track,
Half a world behind each back."

The United States celebrated that night; "Chicago made a procession seven miles long; New York hung out bunting, fired a hundred guns, and held thanksgiving services in Trinity; Philadelphia rang the old Liberty Bell; Buffalo sang the 'Star-Spangled Banner.'" Well might a war-torn people cheer the forging of a new bond of union.

Nor did they have long to wait before celebrating again. Long before the last golden spike sank into the laurel tie at Promontory Point the nation, realizing one transcontinental railroad would never suffice, gave its blessing to half a dozen other projects designed to connect the two oceans. First to start westward was the Kansas Pacific Railroad, which was originally chartered to connect the Union Pacific with Kansas City. Its plans were changed in 1866 when financial difficulties beset the road; a revised charter authorized a direct line between Kansas City and Denver, with a branch extending on to the Union Pacific at Cheyenne. The prospect of securing both a generous land grant and the trade of the Colorado mines brought such a flood of support from investors that the Kansas Pacific was operating by the fall of 1870.

More important was the first of the southern lines, the Atchison, Topeka and Santa Fe Railroad. When the road was chartered in 1859 its president, Cyrus K. Holliday, hoped only to connect Atchison with the Kansas capital at Topeka, but a bountiful federal land grant in 1863 encouraged him to extend track on to Santa Fe. Five years were needed to find a construction company willing to undertake the task, then building progressed rapidly until 1873 when the Santa Fe reached LaJunta, Colorado. From that point

Holliday decided to extend his line in two directions, one west through Pueblo and the Royal Gorge of the Arkansas River to the mining region about Leadville, the other south through Raton Pass to Santa Fe. Before either could be built he found he must displace a formidable rival.

The Santa Fe's competitor was the Denver and Rio Grande Railroad, which had been incorporated in 1870 by Denver business men. Their motives were understandable. The Kansas Pacific Railroad, they believed, would drain the trade of the entire Rocky Mountain country eastward through their city. The coming of the Santa Fe threatened to upset their

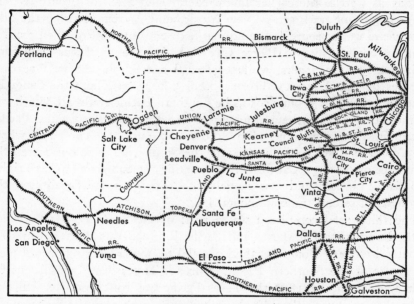

Principal Pacific Railroads in 1883

plans, for southern Colorado would prefer to ship goods out by rail directly, rather than via Denver. Their answer was to challenge the interloper by building the Denver and Rio Grande which would not only tap the trade of southern Colorado but compete for New Mexico's commerce. Track was laid from Denver to Pueblo when the Panic of 1873 stopped construction for three years. That delay was fortunate for the Santa Fe. Speed was vital in reaching both Leadville and New Mexico, for both could be entered only through narrow passes holding only one line of track. While work on the Denver and Rio Grande was at a standstill, the better-financed eastern road usurped one of the routes, the Raton Pass into Santa Fe, by pushing its track southward to the New Mexican City in 1879. Its defeated rival, after a series of law suits and near-battles between construction crews, captured control of the other; its right-of-way through the Royal Gorge of the Arkansas River prevented the Santa Fe from extending westward beyond Pueblo.

The end of the "Rio Grande War" left the Santa Fe's managers free to concentrate on newly aroused transcontinental ambitions. That was in their minds when, in 1880, they bought control of a defunct line, the Atlantic and Pacific Railroad, which had progressed no farther than the town of Vinita, Indian Territory, in its efforts to connect St. Louis with southern California. The purchase gave the Santa Fe a chance to enter St. Louis directly as well as the earlier line's federal land grant of twenty sections for each mile of track across New Mexico and Arizona. During the next three years work progressed rapidly at both ends of the expanded road. A branch from Wichita to Pierce City provided the St. Louis connection desired by the managers, while construction crews in the west reached Needles on the Arizona-California border, in 1883. There the Santa Fe joined another newly built road, the Southern Pacific Railroad, which was operated by the same group of financiers who controlled the Central Pacific. Extending from San Francisco to Needles and Yuma, the two points where the Colorado River could be crossed, the Southern Pacific dominated the commerce of southern California. By granting the Santa Fe trackage rights into San Francisco and Los Angeles, the Southern Pacific allowed the forging of a second transcontinental link.

The third road completed was a rival of the Santa Fe for the trade of the Southwest. The Texas and Pacific Railroad was chartered in 1871 to build westward along the 32nd parallel to Yuma where it would meet the tracks of the Southern Pacific Railroad. Times were inauspicious for such a program; by 1877 the Texas Pacific was bankrupt after building no farther westward than Ft. Worth, Texas. The alarmed managers of the Southern Pacific realized that their expensive line, which was completed to Yuma that year, would pay no dividends without an eastern connection. After vainly pleading with Congress for the right to take over the land grant of the Texas and Pacific Railroad they decided to go ahead without congressional aid. Charters obtained from the Arizona and New Mexico territorial governments allowed construction to proceed rapidly eastward. In 1881 the directors of the Texas and Pacific, realizing they had lost the chance to build beyond Texas, transferred their western land grants to the Southern Pacific in return for an agreement that the two lines should meet in El Paso. Although Congress refused to sanction the transfer, the roads did join in 1882, completing another route across the continent. A year later the Southern Pacific secured its own line across Texas by purchasing the Galveston, Harrisburg and San Antonio Railroad.

While southern and central railroads were forging bonds between

California and the Mississippi Valley, a fourth transcontinental line was pushing slowly across the northern plains and mountains. The Northern Pacific Railroad was chartered by the United States in 1864 to build from Lake Superior to Portland, Oregon. Although a generous land grant was provided—twenty sections to the mile in the states and forty in the territories—the failure of Congress to authorize mileage loans plunged the road into financial difficulties from the beginning. In 1869, with not a mile of track laid, the directors turned from the experienced railroaders who had managed the enterprise to seek the support of the nation's leading financial house, Jay Cooke and Company. After a thorough investigation Cooke, who was personally interested through his heavy investments in Minnesota land, agreed to act as the company's financial agent.

Money flowed in then. Construction began in 1870 and proceeded rapidly across Minnesota and Dakota to the Missouri River where the town of Bismarck was laid out; at the same time lines to Minneapolis and Duluth were added to the Northern Pacific's growing empire. Progress was short-lived, however, for the financial structure reared by Cooke was unsound. The heavy bonuses paid his banking house by the railroad, the large percentage exacted for selling bonds, and the generous blocks of stock distributed among influential politicians, left so little actual cash that construction could continue only as long as investors continued to buy stock. When rumors of mismanagement, extravagence, and corruption slowed down sales in the spring of 1873 Jay Cooke realized the cause was hopeless. On September 18, 1873, his banking house closed its doors, plunging the nation into a prolonged panic. For two years more the Northern Pacific struggled along, vainly seeking funds in a depression-ridden land, but in 1875 it too passed into bankruptcy.

Meanwhile, in Oregon developments were taking place which were to have a profound influence on the future of the Northern Pacific. One of the early railroads there was the Oregon and California, projected from Portland to the California boundary. Its bonds had been bought extensively by German investors. When the road became involved in financial difficulties in the 1870's, the German bondholders sent an agent to Oregon to investigate and report to them. This agent was Henry Villard, an immigrant from Germany who had made a reputation as a newspaper correspondent in his adopted country. Impressed by what he saw on his initial visit to Oregon in behalf of the bondholders, Villard decided to identify himself with transportation developments in the Pacific Northwest. In 1879 he acquired control of the Oregon Steam Navigation Company, a Portland enterprise which had dominated traffic on the Columbia between that city and the Inland Empire. He thereupon organized a new corporation, the Oregon Railway and Navigation Company, for the purpose of building a rail line along the water-level route on the south bank of the Columbia. This road would not only control rail traffic along the Columbia, but it would also serve as the outlet to tidewater for any transcontinental railway which might be built from the East to the Northwest Coast. In this way he would make Portland the commercial center of the Pacific Northwest.

Just as Villard was getting his plans under way the Northern Pacific was undergoing a financial renaissance after its bankruptcy of the middle seventies. In 1879 it began to push its rails west from Bismarck in Dakota Territory. Its objective was Tacoma, a terminal city which it planned to build on Puget Sound. Villard, as well as Portland interests generally, was well aware that Portland was handicapped by the obstructions to the navigation of the lower Columbia River. He knew it would be difficult for her to hold her own commercially with a rail terminus on Puget Sound, with its fine harbor facilities. Fearing the completion of the Northern Pacific to Tacoma would ruin his own interests centered at Portland, Villard sought to dissuade the Northern Pacific from building along the north bank of the Columbia, or directly across the Cascade Mountains to Tacoma. He offered that company the use of his Oregon Railway and Navigation tracks leading along the south bank of the Columbia to Portland. When this offer was spurned by the Northern Pacific, Villard, to protect his Portland interests, resolved to obtain financial control of the Northern Pacific. This he achieved through his famous "Blind Pool" in the spring of 1881.

He then assumed the presidency of the Northern Pacific, organized the Oregon and Transcontinental Company to unify his various interests, and completed the Northern Pacific in the autumn of 1883. Its western terminus was Portland. When financial reverses forced his resignation early in the next year, however, control of the Northern Pacific reverted to the group whose objective it had been to build to Puget Sound. These men soon revived their original plan. By 1887 they had built a line from the point of confluence of the Snake and Columbia rivers through the Yakima country, across the Cascade Range to Tacoma. The Northern Pacific had finally been completed from Lake Superior to Puget Sound.

The period of competitive railroad building which ended in 1883 with the completion of the Northern Pacific and the Santa Fe left the United States spanned by four transcontinental roads, rather than the one envisaged by Asa Whitney and his fellow-dreamers of the pre-Civil War years. East and West were united, firmly bound by economic ties. But more important was the effect of the roads on the country they crossed in their long journey between the Mississippi and the Pacific. That vast domain—the Great Plains—was for the first time accessible to settlers, its isolation a thing of the past. The way was open for the migration of cattle-men and farmers into America's last unsettled frontier.

# CHAPTER XXXII

# The Indian Barrier

## 1860-1887

The advance of the mining frontier and spread of a transportation network across the Great Plains brought the United States face to face with the recurrent Indian problem once more. What should be done with the red men who roamed prairies and hunted in mountain valleys coveted by whites? The blundering attempts of heartless federal officials to answer that question plunged the West into a period of warfare which only ended when the beaten natives, their power and spirit broken, were crowded onto reservations where they no longer blocked the westward march of settlers. The Indian barrier was shattered in the post-Civil War years, but only at a cost of blood, wealth, and human decency which will forever stain the annals of the American frontier.

Geographical conditions divided the problem into two parts. The first—how to subdue red men occupying the mountainous lands invaded by miners—proved easy to solve. The pattern followed everywhere on the mining frontier was established by the '49ers. The 150,000 "Digger" Indians who occupied California were a peaceful, pastoral people, subsisting upon grubs and roots, and living in small units which failed to give them the strength of numbers. The miners fell upon them with savage fury, driving them from their homes, murdering their warriors, and using every feeble attempt at retaliation as an excuse to exterminate whole tribes. When the federal government belatedly intervened, only a handful of "Diggers" remained to be herded into reservations. A similar fate awaited the Snake and Bannock of the Oregon country and southern Idaho, and the Ute who occupied much of Utah and Nevada; all primitive tribesmen with neither inclination nor strength to resist the miners' assault on their homelands. Intermittent warfare between them and the whites went on between 1850 and 1855 when bribes and repeated defeats forced them to throw themselves on the mercy of the Americans. Six years later the Ute ceded most of their Utah lands to the United States in return for a small reservation northeast of Great Salt Lake.

The natives of the southwestern mountain country proved more troublesome, for that was the land of the savage Apache and Navaho tribes. Their warlike reputation was sufficiently awe-inspiring to keep prospectors away until the 1850's when a number of federal forts, garrisoned by 1,500 troops, were scattered through the region. Military invasion only inspired attack; haphazard fighting that began in 1851 reached a climax in 1860 when serious warfare broke out. For the next four years bands of Apache and Navaho, mounted on swift ponies and thoroughly at home in that wild country of canyons and deserts, fought so savagely that victory seemed near, but in the end government strength triumphed. During the campaigns of 1863-64, 664 Indians were killed and 8,793 captured—most of them by Colonel Kit Carson who pinned 7,000 in a canyon at one time—in a series of 143 battles which sapped native strength to the breaking point. By 1865 they were ready to submit to the fate awaiting them: crowding upon small reservations. The Navaho went first, to a reserve surrounding Ft. Sumner on the Pecos River; the Apache followed between 1871 and 1873 when they were assigned a number of small areas in New Mexico and Arizona. Many warriors, refusing to give up their nomadic ways, broke away to raid travelers and settlers for another decade.

Troublesome as were the mountain Indians, they were easier to handle than the second group challenging American authority during those years: the tribesmen of the Great Plains. All—from the Sioux and Crows in the north to the Kiowa and Comanche of the Southwest—were skilled horsemen, able to sweep swiftly across the Plains, fall suddenly on their prey, and disappear with the speed of the wind. All fought with uncanny ability, dropping their bodies behind their galloping ponies, then rising unexpectedly to launch their weapons. All were equipped with stout ash bows, three feet or less long, so effective that a warrior could drive deadly barbed arrows clear through a buffalo while racing along at top speed. For Plains warfare their weapons were more effective than the muzzle-loading rifles issued to federal troops; a Comanche could send twenty arrows at a foe during the minute required to reload one of the cumbersome guns. Even the introduction of famed Colt "six-shooters" during the 1850's did not entirely offset the natives' advantage. The Indians of the Great Plains were dangerous antagonists in any war.

A conflict seemed remote when the invasion of the West by '49ers began. Everyone knew the central grassland was a Great American Desert, usable only by the primitive red men—both native and intruded eastern Indians—who lived there. So long as the United States held to the concept of "One Big Reservation" the two races could live in peace, but any attempt to oust the tribesmen from their hunting grounds was sure to mean trouble. The advance of the mining and transportation frontiers launched the conflict. The mass migrations across the Plains, the development of freighting and express lines, the plans for transcontinental railroads, all demonstrated during the early 1850's that the policy of "One Big Reservation" was destined to speedy extinction. Gradually the demand grew for opening the central portion of the Indian country—the lands of Kansas and Nebraska where most transportation routes were concentrated—by pushing natives northward to unwanted lands beyond Nebraska, or south of the Kansas border. Frontier pressure for that highway forced the United States to abandon its policy of "One Big Reservation" for a system of "Concentration" which led directly to war.

The first step in applying the new policy was taken in 1851 when chiefs of the principal Plains tribes were assembled at Ft. Laramie by Thomas Fitzpatrick, the agent controlling that Platte River outpost. In return for gifts, annuities, and bounties, the Indians agreed to accept definite tribal limitations. These were carefully marked out for the visiting warriors. The Sioux were assured the Dakota country north of the Platte River, the Mandan and Grosventres a triangle just east of the Yellowstone, the Assiniboin the region west of that stream, the Crows a large area west of the Powder River, the Blackfeet the mountainous country about the headwaters of the Missouri, the Cheyenne and Arapaho the foothills of Colorado between the North Platte and Arkansas rivers. There, they were told, they could live unmolested for all time, each tribe secure in the knowledge its lands were clearly defined. Little did the innocent chiefs realize they were victims of a device often used by the United States. Once their tribal territories were marked out, any one group could be forced to cede its holdings to the United States without arousing the others.

Only the Indians' failure to see the handwriting on the wall kept the frontier at peace for another decade. During those years the attention of the Indian Office was focused on intruded eastern tribes whose reservations bordered the western boundaries of Iowa and Missouri. With the organization of Kansas and Nebraska territories in 1854 their removal became necessary. Between 1854 and 1859 they were forced to give up their reserves in return for smaller reservations or the doubtful privilege of moving west to mingle with the Plains Indians. By 1860 most of Kansas and Nebraska and a corner of the Dakota country were freed of their native occupants. "By alternate persuasion and force," wrote a heart-sick agent, "some of these tribes have been removed, step by step, from mountain to valley, and from river to plain, until they have been pushed half-way across the continent. They can go no further: on the ground they now occupy the crisis must be met, and their future determined."

The crisis was not long in coming. The discovery of gold in the Pike's

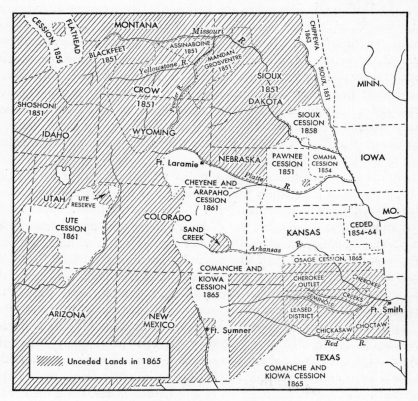

Indian Land Cessions, 1850-1865

Peak country touched off the inevitable conflict. A hundred thousand miners crossed the Plains in 1859, elbowed their way into Cheyenne and Arapaho lands, and drove the Indians from their homes. Resentment bred of those outrages was infectious. The northern tribes were already restless; surveyors were among them with tales of iron horses soon to bring thousands of settlers into the West; prospectors were searching for precious metals in the beaver streams of the Rockies. Moreover a few farseeing chiefs realized they were caught in a vise between the mining frontier, advancing steadily from the west, and the agricultural frontier, pressing relentlessly from the east. They must resist or be exterminated. War talk was common among the Plains Indians by 1860.

Fighting began in the Colorado country. There federal agents, sensing trouble in the growing sullenness of the Cheyenne and Arapaho, decided to forestall an attack by removing the natives from contact with the whites. Calling the chiefs of the two tribes into conference at Ft. Lyon on February 18, 1861, government officials forced them to abandon all claims to the area guaranteed them at Ft. Laramie in return for a small reservation between the Arkansas River and Sand Creek in eastern Colorado. That was going too far. Many warriors, refusing to abandon their nomadic ways, renounced the chiefs responsible for the treaty and took to the war path. For three years they raided mining camps and mail coaches while Colorado's territorial governor pleaded in vain for federal protection. When none was forthcoming from the war-rent East he took matters into his own hands. On June 24, 1864, all warring bands were ordered to proceed at once to Ft. Lyon; those refusing to obey were threatened with extermination. The harsh ruling only goaded the Indians into fiercer resistance. During the next few months they spread a path of desolation from the North Platte to the Arkansas, murdering settlers, burning homes, destroying overland mail stations, and pillaging travelers. By the autumn of 1864 all the Colorado countryside was in ruins and Denver isolated.

Fall, however, turned the Indians' thoughts toward peace, for tribal tradition dictated that fighting cease during cold winter months. Chief Black Kettle, their leader, had that in mind when he sought out the federal commander at Ft. Lyon in late August, 1864, only to be told the official possessed no authority to end the war. The Colorado governor, Black Kettle was informed, must accept their surrender. A conference with that belligerent leader proved equally fruitless. After listening to the chieftain's plea for peace, Governor John Evans gruffly told him the war would go on; the white men, he said, were about to stop fighting among themselves "and the Great Father will not know what to do with his soldiers, except to send them after the Indians on the plains." His dire warning was echoed by the commander of the Colorado militia, Colonel J. M. Chivington, who glumly watched the Indians during the meeting. "My rule for fighting white men or Indians," he told Black Kettle bluntly, "is to fight them until they lay down their arms and submit."

Those threatening words should have convinced the chiefs that only more war would satisfy the Americans' lust for revenge, yet the yearning for peace was strong and they turned again to Ft. Lyon, hoping a new commander just appointed there would accept their surrender. That inexperienced leader was uncertain of his authority; at first he promised the Indians protection, then reversed himself and ordered them to leave the fort. Black Kettle, believing the war was over, led his seven hundred followers to a camp on Sand Creek, confident that federal troops would protect them from the Colorado militia. Scarcely had they departed when a regiment of a thousand territorial volunteers under Colonel Chivington entered Ft. Lyon,

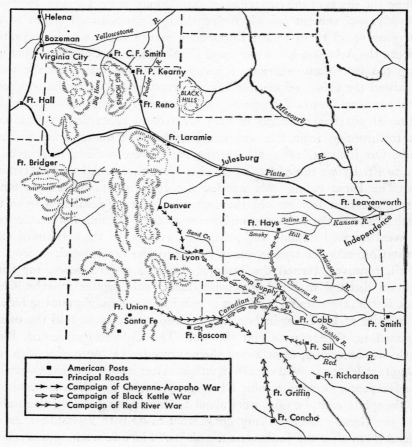

Indian Wars, 1860-1875

hot on the trail of the retreating tribe. The vacillating commander assured the militiamen he had not guaranteed the Indians protection and encouraged them to attack at once. The stage was set for one of the bloodiest events in the annals of Indian warfare.

Colonel Chivington and his men left Ft. Lyon after sundown on the night of November 28, 1864. By daybreak of the next day they surrounded the camp where five hundred unsuspecting natives slept peacefully. With the first streak of light across the Plains the militia charged, rushing pell-mell upon the confused red men, firing and tomahawking as they went. In vain did Black Kettle raise first an American flag, then a white flag. The disordered natives were driven across the camp, down into the dry bed of Sand Creek, back against the high banks on the other side. Even women and children who sought refuge in caves were dragged out to be shot or knifed. "They were scalped," a watching trader later testified, "their brains knocked out; the men used their knives, ripped open women, clubbed little children, knocked them in the head with their guns, beat their brains out, mutilated their bodies in every sense of the word." Within a few hours the battered corpses of 450 Indians covered the battleground, although Black Kettle and a few younger warriors managed to escape.

The Chivington Massacre accomplished little. Word of the American brutality, carried across the Plains by survivors, inspired the remaining Cheyenne and Arapaho to greater savagery. Through the winter of 1864-65 raiding parties ranged the Platte Valley, sacking ranches, ripping down telegraph wires, raiding overland mail stations at Julesburg and other spots, and fighting pitched battles with troops sent against them. Yet the threat of another massacre could not be forgotten, and when peace commissioners arrived in October, 1865, the Indians were ready to lay down their arms. In conferences that followed the Cheyenne and Arapaho agreed to surrender unconditionally and to give up their Sand Creek reservation in return for lands to be assigned them elsewhere. At the same time representatives of the Kiowa and Comanche tribes were forced to abandon all claims to central Texas, western Kansas, and eastern New Mexico, accepting instead a restricted hunting ground in the Panhandle country. With the end of Cheyenne-Arapaho War peace descended on the Southwest.

Scarcely was the ink upon the treaty dry, however, before a new conflict broke out in the North—the Sioux War of 1865-67. The forces compelling the 16,000 tribesmen of the powerful confederation to take up the scalping knife were many. Some young braves were inflamed by tales of Indian gallantry carried northward from the scene of the Cheyenne-Arapaho War, or were angered by the Chivington Massacre. Others were aroused by news from the East; the Minnesota Sioux had gone on the warpath in 1862-63 and after their defeat had scattered among the Plains Indians urging revenge. Still more were alarmed by the American advance into Montana Territory; by 1865 Virginia City, Bozeman, and Helena were thriving mining communities. The final straw was a federal effort to connect Montana with the East by road. The inaccessibility of the region had long annoyed miners; their supplies had to be carted in by a roundabout trail through South Pass to Ft. Hall and Virginia City, or brought to Ft. Benton by steamboat for transportation overland along the Mullan Road. Neither route was satisfactory, for steamboats could reach Ft. Benton only during the few months when water was high on the Missouri, and the Ft. Hall road was circuitous and expensive. Their demand for a better outlet forced the United States to survey a new road during the summer of 1865, one that branched northward from Ft. Laramie, crossed the Powder River, skirted the foothills of the Big Horn Mountains, and emerged at Bozeman, Montana.

News that the United States planned to build the "Powder River Road" or "Bozeman Trail" goaded the Sioux into action. The proposed highway would ruin one of their favorite hunting grounds: the rolling foothills of the Big Horns, where every slope was "covered with a fine growth of grass, and in every valley there is either a rushing stream or some quiet babbling brook of pure, clear snow-water filled with trout, the banks lined with trees —wild cherry, quaking asp, some birch, willow, and cottonwood." The Sioux loved to pitch their tepees beneath the sheltering mountains in that idyllic spot while replenishing their larders from nature's abundance; bear, deer, buffalo, elk, antelope, rabbits, and sage hens were so plentiful hunting was easy. They would never stand aside while white men usurped their treasured Utopia.

Their chief, Red Cloud, first protested, then warned that any attempt to build the Powder River Road would be resisted. His threat was met during the summer of 1865 when a column of troops marched through the Big Horn country, accomplishing little, but letting the Sioux know war was under way. A year later soldiers were again in the disputed region, with orders to secure the proposed road by building forts along the route. Three outposts were started—Ft. Reno on the Powder River, Ft. Philip Kearny somewhat northward, and Ft. C. F. Smith at the junction of the Big Horn and the Powder River Road. Through the summer of 1866 troops working on the fortifications were under almost constant attack; every straggler was cut down, every wagon train bringing in supplies raided, every wood-cutting party attacked. Skirmishing reached a climax in December when a wood train near Ft. Philip Kearny was assaulted. The relief party under Captain W. J. Fetterman foolishly pursued the Indians deep into the wilderness, was ambushed, and all eighty-two of its members slaughtered.

The Fetterman Massacre greatly affected both antagonists. The Sioux were overjoyed; the warriors carried on the attack so furiously that by the spring of 1867 the soldiers along the Powder River Road were virtually besieged in their forts. The Americans, on the other hand, were plunged into a period of gloomy soul-searching. Such slaughter, critics pointed out, called for a thorough investigation of the entire Indian administration. "Our whole Indian policy," proclaimed the *Nation*, "is a system of mismanagement, and in many parts one of gigantic abuse." Humanitarians agreed the causes were twofold. Partially to blame was the division of authority between the Department of the Interior and the War Department. The former, through its Indian office, attempted to placate the tribes with gifts, reservations, and annuities; the latter punished the red men savagely for every infraction of rules. Equally responsible for the difficulties, eastern critics insisted, was the constant encroachment of whites on lands guaranteed natives, often with federal protection. They maintained war would cease only when the tribes were treated with justice and the "fire and sword" policy of the military brought to an end. Both criticisms pointed to one solution: let peace advocates settle the Indian problem in their own way without any War Department meddling.

That viewpoint was brought home to Congress in March, 1867, by the report of a committee which used the Chivington Massacre as the basis for an attack on the army's role in the West. A bill "for establishing peace with certain Indian tribes now at war with the United States," was promptly introduced and as promptly passed. A Peace Commission of four civilians and three generals, the measure provided, should first bring the Sioux War to a close, then assure peace between the races by removing the causes for Indian wars. That could be done, Congress felt, by persuading the red men to abandon their nomadic ways for protected lives on out-of-the-way reservations. Armed with those instructions, commissioners set out for the West in August, 1867.

Their coming heralded a new day in the dreary history of federal Indian policy. In past years the system of "One Big Reservation" had given way to "Concentration"; now "Concentration" was doomed to succumb to the device of "Small Reservations." That, members of the Peace Commission agreed, was the only workable solution to the West's racial problem. Red men must be segregated at isolated points where, as wards of the government, they could be taught to live in fixed homes, till the soil, and begin a transition to civilized ways which would culminate when they could be assimilated as ordinary citizens. Both expansionist westerners and humanitarian easterners would certainly approve. Frontiersmen would be satisfied because sedentary tribesmen required less space than hunters, releasing thousands of acres for settlement. Friends of the Indians would be pleased because isolation would separate Indians from sinful white men, protect their territory from avaricious land grabbers, and assure them a chance to develop into assimilable citizens.

The Peace Commissioners in a preliminary conference at St. Louis agreed that two reservations would hold all the Plains Indians. One would be in the Black Hills country of Dakota Territory; there they planned to concentrate the 54,000 tribesmen who roamed the northern grasslands. The 86,000 southern Indians they hoped to crowd into present-day Oklahoma. Each tribe, they decided, would be assigned definite lands where the natives could be supervised and instructed by agents of the Indian Office. Both districts would be provided with territorial governors "of unquestioned integrity and purity of character" who would plan a broad program of progressive civilization for their charges.

The sites selected for the reservations seemed ideal to the commissioners. The Black Hills country was far from the transcontinental transportation routes, and so hilly it would attract no settlers. The Oklahoma country was even better. The region had, in the 1830's, been divided among the Five Civilized tribes of the Southeast. The natural sympathy of the southern Indians for the Confederate cause during the Civil War allowed the United States to trump up false charges of treason as an excuse to strip away some of their lands. Federal agents, meeting with the chiefs in the spring of 1866, forced them to surrender most of western Oklahoma; the Creeks sold half their lands for thirty cents an acre, the Seminole turned their property in at fifteen cents an acre and were required to buy a smaller reservation at fifty cents an acre, the Chickasaw and Choctaw gave up their claims to a "leased district" west of their reserves, and the Cherokee abandoned rights to the "Cherokee Outlet" beyond the 96th meridian. With the five tribes crowded into the eastern half of the district, the western was freed to receive the southern Plains Indians the Peace Commissioners hoped to place there. In both North and South the way was cleared for the inauguration of the "Small Reservation" system.

The commissioners met representatives of the southwestern tribes first at a great council on Medicine Lodge Creek. The Kiowa and Comanche were dealt with on October 21, 1867; after feasting, threats, and bribery they consented to accept a 3,000,000 acre reservation between the Red and Washita rivers in western Indian Territory where they would be fed and clothed until they learned how "to walk on the white man's road." A week later the Cheyenne and Arapaho succumbed to similar lures and accepted a barren reserve fringed by the Cimarron and Arkansas rivers. Even that sandy waste, where streams ran dry in summer and icy blasts whistled in winter, seemed a welcome haven to tribesmen who had drifted without homes since the Sand Creek Reservation had been taken from them in 1865. At the same time other federal agents were busy with the peaceful tribes of the eastern Plains country, assigning lands taken from the Five Civilized tribes to the Osage, Pawnee, Oto, and Kansa tribes, and to eastern Indians ousted from Kansas or Nebraska.

Their principal task in the South accomplished, the Peace Commissioners turned to ending the Sioux War. They were wise enough to see the Indians would never cease fighting so long as the government insisted on the Powder River Road; by the time they reached the Ft. Laramie conference ground in the spring of 1868 they had decided to surrender on that point. Chief Red Cloud and his fellow warriors were so pleased that negotiations moved smoothly. In a treaty signed on April 29, 1868, the Sioux agreed to cease fighting and accept a permanent reservation in Dakota Territory west of the Missouri River. They were allowed to use their old hunting grounds until the lands were wanted by the United States, while the country just east of the Big Horns was recognized as unceded Indian territory. The government, in turn, stopped work on the Powder River Road and abandoned the three forts guarding the highway.

The Ft. Laramie and Medicine Lodge treaties cleared the central Plains of red men but the Rocky Mountain country was still in Indian hands. Federal agents turned to the task of extending the "Small Reservation" policy there during the summer and fall of 1868. The Colorado Ute bowed before their demands first, accepting a large reserve in the western quarter of the territory. A few weeks later the Shoshoni and Bannock tribes ceded their lands in Wyoming and Idaho in return for annuities and two small reservations, one on the Wind River and the other near Ft. Hall. The Navaho and Apache of Arizona and New Mexico also agreed to settle down on small reservations scattered through those territories. "We have now selected and provided reservations for all, off the great road," wrote the western military commander in September, 1868. "All who cling to their old hunting-grounds are hostile and will remain so till killed off."

That estimate of the situation, grim as it was, was overoptimistic. Assigning Indians to reservations was one thing, but forcing them to live within narrow limits was quite another. A few old chiefs who were dulled by feasting and corrupted by bribes into signing away millions of acres of tribal lands could not force 100,000 red men to change their whole way of life. Rather than trooping docilely to their new homes, most younger warriors and many minor chiefs refused to abide by the treaties, denounced the leaders who signed them, and prepared to fight before surrendering their nomadic habits. By the fall of 1868 warfare along the borderland was in full swing, and this time a full decade of terrorism was required before the last beaten brave sullenly accepted the manner of living decreed by his white masters.

The struggle began in August, 1868, when bands of Cheyenne, Arapaho, Kiowa, and Comanche wrung an issue of new guns from a soft-hearted federal agent. Well armed, and led by Chief Black Kettle who still smarted under his defeat at the Chivington Massacre, they started north at once, to murder and pillage along the Smoky Hill and Saline valleys of Kansas. Black Kettle's raid inspired a general uprising in the Southwest; by early fall the countryside from Kansas to Texas was filled with 2,000 roving Cheyenne, Arapaho, Comanche, Kiowa, and Apache warriors.

General Philip H. Sheridan, who commanded the American army in the West, realized his 2,600 troops could never track down the widely roaming

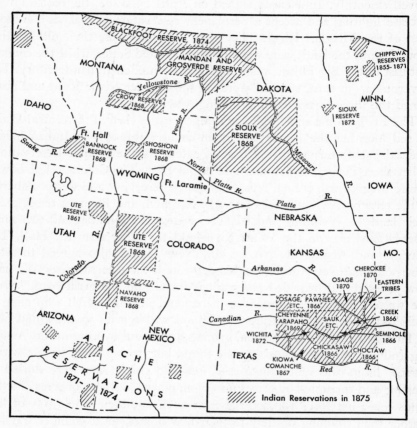

The Indian Frontier, 1866-1875

raiders and spent the next few months training his men for a winter campaign. He planned three expeditions. Two would move eastward from Ft. Lyon, Colorado, and Ft. Bascom, New Mexico, driving the Indians into the Washita River Valley where they would be crushed by the main army from Ft. Hays, Kansas. By mid-November all was in readiness. The two columns from the western forts set out at that time, while the principal force, commanded by Colonel George A. Custer, drove southward to Camp

Supply on the North Fork of the Canadian. There they were joined by a regiment of Kansas frontiersmen under the governor of the state who had resigned his post for a chance to "whup the redskins." The enlarged army, advancing slowly through hostile territory, soon stumbled across a fresh Indian trail in the foot-deep snow. Colonel Custer, throwing orders to the winds, took up the pursuit at once and on November 26, 1868, reached the native camp in the Washita Valley.

His scouts reported that he had flushed important game; Chief Black Kettle and several hundred Cheyenne and Arapaho warriors were in the encampment. Custer arranged his attack carefully. That night four columns of soldiers slipped cautiously through trees fringing the river bank to surround the Indian position. At daybreak they rushed upon the red men, who had not expected a winter campaign and were taken completely by surprise. For a few hours furious hand-to-hand fighting raged along the banks of the Washita, but when the battle ended the bodies of 103 natives —including Chief Black Kettle—were strewn over the camp ground. Custer hurriedly slipped back to Camp Supply before braves from other camps along the valley could rally. His decisive victory broke native resistance; when Custer's force returned two months later the surviving chiefs were escorted to Ft. Cobb, a federal outpost on the Washita, where they signed agreements accepting reservations. The Kiowa and Comanche were hurried away to lands assigned them in the Medicine Lodge Treaties, the Cheyenne and Arapaho to a reserve along the upper Washita River. In March, 1869, General Sheridan reported all southwestern tribes safely in the Indian Territory.

His estimate was also overoptimistic. Federal officials, who had discovered that settling Indians on reservations was more difficult than assigning them lands, soon learned that keeping the red men within the narrow confines of reserves was equally impossible. Within two years bands of braves roamed the Texas Panhandle, stealing cattle, raiding isolated homesteads, and attacking overland freighters, until all the southwestern frontier clamored for relief. The volume of protest was so great by 1871 that General William Tecumseh Sherman, who had replaced Sheridan as commander of the western armies, felt called upon to investigate. Traveling northward from San Antonio to Ft. Richardson he found evidence of Indian depredation on every hand, here a ruined home, there a scarred barn, everywhere the fresh graves of slaughtered victims. When he reached Ft. Richardson word waited him that set his blood boiling; a wagon train bound for the fort had just been ambushed and seven drivers killed. Savages who carried the attack to his doorstep, he vowed, must be punished.

While Sherman was still in that mood one of the raiders, Chief Satanta.

boldly visited the fort to collect his annuities. He was arrested, and with two confederates sent to neighboring Jacksboro to stand trial for murder before a Texas civil court. One Indian was shot while trying to escape, but the other two were sentenced to be hanged after a dramatic trial which aroused national interest. General Sherman was greatly pleased; he believed he had discovered a more effective means of dealing with frontier marauders than turning them over to soft-hearted agents for a meaningless reprimand. His self-congratulations came too soon, for the clamor of eastern humanitarians forced the Texas governor to commute the sentences of the two chiefs to life imprisonment and finally to pardon them altogether. Sherman was outraged. "I believe Satanta and Big Tree will have their revenge," he wrote the governor, ". . . and if they are to have scalps, that yours is the first that should be taken."

Satanta and Big Tree did have their revenge. Their return to freedom encouraged Indian attacks that cost sixty Texans their lives in 1874 and plunged the Southwest into its last major conflict—the Red River War. This time the federal officials decided the natives must be so thoroughly crushed they would never again risk the wrath of their overlords. Three thousand troops were distributed among the forts surrounding the upper Red River Valley—Ft. Union, Camp Supply, Ft. Sill, Ft. Griffin, and Ft. Concho. At an appointed time five formidable columns advanced upon the Indian stronghold. The natives struck back—fourteen pitched battles were fought—but by mid-November, 1874, the Americans were so successful General Sherman cautioned his men to "ease down on the parties hostile at present." All winter the Red River War went on, until June when resistance ended. Discouraged and worn, the half-starved red men straggled back to their reservations, convinced at last they must accept the fate meted out by white masters.

One more war was needed to teach the northern plainsmen that lesson. The Sioux were the aggressors, although Americans really goaded them into war. Some natives were aroused by corruption in the Interior Department; they complained that supplies promised the Black Hills reservation were too few and consisted of mouldy flour, spoiled beef, and moth-eaten blankets. Others were alarmed by the steady advance of the Northern Pacific Railroad toward their territory. More were driven to rebellion by the Black Hills gold rush. By the summer of 1875 a thousand prospectors were tramping over their reservation while Indian Office officials sought in vain to buy the Sioux lands. When negotiations broke down in the autumn the United States washed its hands of the matter, opening the Indian lands to any miners who dared risk native wrath. They poured in by the tens of thousands that winter, all intent on staking claims without reference to the rights of the true owners. Little wonder the red men were ready to rebel by the spring of 1876.

The conflict was touched off by the authorities. They knew that many younger braves were slipping away from the reservation to join bands of "non-treaty" Indians in the country east of the Big Horn. Fearing trouble, they ordered all Sioux, regardless of treaty guarantees which allowed them to hunt on the northern Plains, to return to the reserve by February 1, 1876. Two leaders of the Teton Dakota, Sitting Bull and Crazy Horse, not only refused but started collecting supplies on the Little Big Horn River

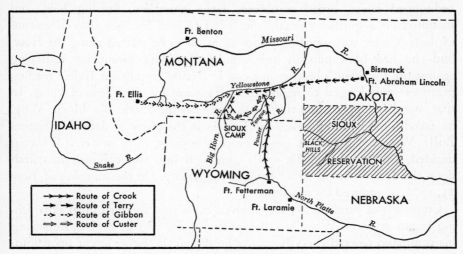

The Sioux War of 1875-1876

with every indication that they meant to fight. When futile gestures by the Indian Office failed to win over the rebellious warriors, the problem was dumped on the army in March, 1876. A new Indian war was under way.

Once more the military experts sent three columns of converging troops against the enemy's headquarters in the Big Horn country; one under General George Crook moved northward from newly built Ft. Fetterman on the upper North Platte, a second commanded by General Alfred H. Terry started westward from Ft. Abraham Lincoln in Dakota Territory, and a third led by Colonel John Gibbon advanced eastward from Ft. Ellis in Montana. In mid-June Terry reached the junction of the Rosebud and Yellowstone without having sighted any Sioux. Scouts, however, reported that a large band of Indians had crossed the Rosebud on its way to Sitting Bull's headquarters on the Little Big Horn. General Terry, commander of the united force, devised a sensible campaign at once. One of his young subordinates, Colonel George A. Custer of southern Plains fame, was sent south along the Rosebud to track the Indians to their camp site, then swing his command around them so they could not retreat into the Big Horn Mountains. General Terry led the main army across country to the Big Horn River, planning to ascend that stream to the red men's camp. His strategy would have succeeded but for one unpredictable factor: the recklessness of Colonel Custer.

That dashing young officer was a vain and foolhardy leader. "Clad in buckskin trousers from the seams of which a large fringe was fluttering, red-topped boots, broad sombrero, large gauntlets, flowing hair, and mounted on a spirited animal," he loved to lead his men into dangerous exploits. Custer was smarting under an insult as he started along the Rosebud—he had been publicly rebuked by President Grant for testifying against the President's brother in a case involving fraudulent Indian trading practices—and longed to regain his self-esteem by some feat of valor. In that mood he approached the Sioux camp on the Little Big Horn. Why, he asked himself, should General Terry win the glory of defeating Sitting Bull? Why not attack at once before the main force arrived? Having decided, Custer divided his small command into two columns to march upon the Indians along either bank of the stream. On the morning of June 25, 1876, he ordered the advance.

Custer's own band of 265 men moved cautiously forward until skirmishing began at noon. When scouts reported many natives fleeing, he swung his command toward the village. As he did so the Sioux swept upon him. Instead of surprising a small Indian camp he had stumbled upon native headquarters where 2,500 warriors lay in wait! Quickly they surrounded his little force, pouring in a deadly fire as they surged around the thinning cluster of soldiers. Within a few hours all was over; Custer and his entire army lay dead on the battlefield. A similar fate for the column on the left bank of the stream was averted by the timely arrival of General Terry with the main army. The Battle of the Little Big Horn—"Custer's Last Stand" in the phrase of the day—was one of the most decisive defeats in the history of Indian warfare.

The victory did the Sioux little good. They were driven slowly eastward during the summer, into the Tongue River Valley, where they made the mistake of disclosing their position by attacking a wagon train bound for General Terry's forces. The troops closed in at once, catching 3,000 natives in a trap. On October 31, 1876, the Indians surrendered. Scattered bands still roamed the hills, but the decisive American victory and the approach of winter took the heart out of their attacks. Gradually they drifted back to the reservation, prepared to accept their fate. Only Chief Sitting Bull and a few die-hards refused to give up; they fled to Canada where they remained until 1881 when starvation forced them to plead for peace.

Although the Sioux War ended major Indian fighting in the West, sporadic outbreaks occurred for some years as fragments of tribes broke from their reservations for brief raids before being run down by troops. In 1877 the Nez Percé tribe of the Grand Ronde country of Oregon, led by Chief Joseph, ravaged the frontier for almost a year before admitting defeat. Instead of being sent back to their old reserves, they were assigned barren lands in the Indian Territory where they rapidly succumbed to malaria and other diseases. The Apache of New Mexico also caused intermittent trouble between 1871 and 1882 when the last defeated warrior was chased upon a reservation.

A final incident took place in 1890 when the Teton Sioux of South Dakota, poorly fed by corrupt government agents, facing the results of a serious drought, and with their reservations cut in half by a new treaty, became restless. While in this dissatisfied state, news reached them of a Paiute messiah, Wovoka, who promised all Indians that the performance of certain dances and rites would lead to the return of their lands and the disappearance of the whites. A large number of the despairing Sioux forsook all else to practice the "Ghost Dances," as the Americans disparagingly labeled the Wovoka ceremonies. This unusual activity alarmed whites into calling for troops, whose arrival only accentuated native fear of aggression. When military leaders tried to stop the dancing "craze," Indian resistance led to the death of a number of warriors including Sitting Bull, while a bungling army attempt to disarm another band of Sioux resulted in the massacre of two hundred Dakota warriors, women, and children at the "Battle" of Wounded Knee. This ended the uprising, for the Indians realized they were helpless before the rapid-fire Hotchkiss guns of the soldiers.

In the long run the collapse of native resistance was due neither to improved armament nor superior strategy, but to a factor over which neither antagonist had any control: the extermination of the buffalo. Those shaggy beasts were food and shelter for Plains Indians; so long as giant herds roamed the West the red man could continue his nomadic ways, drifting across the grasslands in their wake. Once the buffalo vanished the Indian's livelihood was gone and he had no choice but to accept federal bounty. The slaughter of the two giant herds that grazed the plains—one north and the other south of the central overland route—began when the Union Pacific was built in 1867 and lasted until 1883 when the bison were virtually exterminated.

Probably 13,000,000 buffalo lived in the West when the first hunters arrived with their powerful, long-range rifles. They fell mercilessly upon the stupid beasts, shooting them from train windows, pursuing them on horseback, and butchering them as they forded streams. Thousands of "sportsmen" took advantage of the opportunity to kill indiscriminately between 1867 and 1872, with no other reward than the sight of dying animals. The herds might have survived that onslaught, but their fate was sealed when a Pennsylvania tannery discovered in 1871 that buffalo hides could be used for commercial leather. With every bison worth from $1 to $3, professional hunters swarmed over the Plains to exploit the new source of wealth. Between 1872 and 1874 3,000,000 beasts were killed yearly; after that the rate of slaughter increased as companies sent bands of hired hunters into the field. Groups of eight or nine plainsmen, armed with long-range rifles and accompanied by wagons to carry out the hides, could kill and skin fifty or more bison daily. By 1878 the southern herd was exterminated; in 1883 the buffalo vanished from the northern Plains. A museum expedition seeking specimens that year found less than two hundred in all the West, while by 1903 the number had dwindled to thirty-four. Little wonder that the Indians, their staff of life gone, were forced to accept a servile fate as wards of the government.

But the problem of dealing with the redskinned Americans was not settled when they abandoned their nomadic ways. A policy that would allow the two races to live together was needed. The old system failed, all agreed, because it emphasized tribal units; since the beginning of settlement tribes had been treated as sovereign nations capable of enforcing treaty obligations, when actually they were dependent social groups without national rights. Treaties between Indians and the United States bound only the red men, yet whenever the federal government broke a covenant war resulted. The solution, reformers conceded, was to treat natives as individuals while training them to assume the responsibilities of citizenship.

Congress inaugurated the new policy in 1871 when it decreed that no Indian tribe "shall be acknowledged or recognized as an independent nation, tribe or power, with whom the United States may contract by treaty." This encouraged the Indian Office to weaken tribal organization by breaking down the power of chiefs. Agents were told to help their wards establish councils to usurp governmental powers formerly exercised by leaders; such units were formed among the Apache in the early 1880's and copied elsewhere. An Indian Office order of 1883 went a step farther by setting up court systems to relieve chiefs of judicial functions. Two years later a congressional decree extended the jurisdiction of federal courts over Indians on reserves. Step by step the tribal organization disintegrated until the red men were treated as individuals.

At the same time natives were trained to assume new responsibilities. Higher education began in 1879 when the Carlisle Indian School of Carlisle, Pennsylvania, threw open its doors to fifty Pawnee, Kiowa, and Cheyenne brought east for the experiment. Their success convinced Congress the red men were capable of improvement and encouraged the first sizable appropriations for Indian schools during the early 1880's. From that time on sums annually set aside for the purpose increased, some for eastern boarding schools such as Carlisle, but more for day schools on the western reservations. Emphasis was placed on mechanical and agricultural subjects which would fit red men for the white men's way of life, as well as on courses designed to train Indians for citizenship.

The final step in formulating the new policy was to carry the principle of individualism into land ownership by giving each native a farm. Agitation for division of tribal lands developed rapidly during the 1880's, with support from two strangely divergent groups. One was made up of land-hungry frontiersmen who recognized that any splitting of the reservations would release thousands of acres for white settlers. The other was composed of eastern humanitarians—the "Lo! the Poor Indian" reformers as westerners dubbed them—who sincerely believed assimilation the only answer to the West's racial problem and sought to hasten the mingling by turning natives from the chase to agriculture. Organized in such societies as the Indian Rights Association, and aided by such publications as the magazine *Council Fire* (1878), they were in a position to propagandize both the government and the people. Their campaign was effective; thousands of Americans were won to the cause of reform by Helen Hunt Jackson's *A Century of Dishonor* (1881) and other sentimental distortions sponsored by humanitarians. By the middle 1880's reforming pressure on Congress was too strong to resist.

Within that body the Indians were championed by Henry L. Dawes, Senator from Massachusetts and chairman of the Senate Indian Committee. Long a friend of the red men, and convinced by 1885 that severalty would solve the racial problem, he threw himself into the contest with the vigor of a reformer. His reward came on February 8, 1887, when he watched President Grover Cleveland sign the Dawes Severalty Act. That important measure authorized the President to divide the lands of any tribe, giving each head of a family 160 acres, with lesser amounts to bachelors, women, and children. The plots, rather than going directly to the Indians, were to be held in trust by the government for twenty-five years, a device deemed necessary to prevent untrained natives from disposing of their holdings immediately. All those receiving grants were to be made citizens of the United States. Reservation lands remaining after the division were to be sold by the government, with profits deposited in a trust fund for educational purposes.

The Dawes Act was not the panacea envisaged by its backers; later congresses altered its provisions and in the twentieth century overthrew its basic premise by returning to a policy which respected Indians' cultural traditions rather than attempting to recast them in the white men's mold. But frontiersmen and humanitarians of the post-Civil War era, confident their solution was final, were satisfied. The last page was written on the saga of western warfare; the two races would live forever in peace. At last the restless pioneer could advance unmolested across the Great Plains where shaggy buffalo and tawny red men had long held sway.

# CHAPTER XXXIII

# The Cattlemen's Frontier

# 1865-1887

Indian removal paved the way for the conquest of America's last frontier—the Great Plains province. That gargantuan grassland had halted the westward march of farmers, who found its arid climate, sparse vegetation, and unfamiliar soils unsuited to pioneering techniques acquired in the humid East. Their reluctance to assault the unfamiliar plains environment provided an opportunity for another group of westerners—the cattlemen. In the two decades after the Civil War great herds of bellowing longhorns, guarded by colorfully garbed cowboys on spirited ponies, spread over the whole pastureland, bringing fortunes to their owners and romance to the annals of the frontier. That was the day of the cattleman, the day when the longhorn steer was King of the West.

The giant industry had its beginnings in southern Texas. Cattle introduced there by Spaniards in the eighteenth century—scrawny, tough beasts bred by Moorish herdsmen—multiplied rapidly, especially in the triangle formed by the junction of the Rio Grande and the Gulf of Mexico. Conditions were ideal in that spot; the climate warm, the grass green all year, water plentiful from tributaries of the Nueces, the range so open that cattle drifted from feeding ground to feeding ground without encountering trees. Moreover few Indian raiders ventured south of San Antonio. In that ideal setting Mexican ranchers learned how to care for cattle on the open range. They learned to herd on horseback, to identify their own beasts by brands, to use a "roundup" to mark new-born calves. By the time Americans invaded Texas the Nueces Valley was a great cattle range, where thousands of steers roamed freely over the unfenced grassland under the watchful eye of mounted cowboys.

The intruders from the United States were farmers rather than ranchers, but they contributed to the growth of the infant Texan cattle industry nevertheless. Their eastern milch cows, breeding with the Mexican herds, produced a variety of strains more suitable to the American market than the original Moorish type. One clearly distinguished breed was the "Texas-Mexican," tall and gaunt, splashed with patches of white, and with enormous horns twisting back toward the body. Another was the "Spanish," which resembled the crossbreed but was somewhat smaller with shorter horns and gentler spirit. A third, the "Long-haired Texans," were round, well-formed beasts with long legs, heavy body, medium horns, and a heavy coat of brownish color. The "Wild Cattle" of western Texas were thin, blue-horned, mealy-nosed, and brown in color. All were tough and wiry, able to care for themselves on parched summer prairies or during winter blizzards.

The Americans who controlled Texas after its independence paid little attention to the increasing herds, largely because no market for beef was near enough to make sales profitable. A few were driven to Austin or Galveston, a few more to New Orleans, some even to the Ohio Valley where an adventurous herdsman sold a thousand head in 1846. Others were marketed in the gold fields of Colorado, Arizona, and California during the late 1850's, but in each case the expenses of the drive and the difficulties of overland herding discouraged any large-scale attempts. For the most part the cattle were allowed to roam wild over the lush grasslands, drifting northward in search of new feeding grounds as they increased in numbers until they blanketed western Texas between the Rio Grande and the upper Panhandle. They multiplied especially during the Civil War years when drives to market were stopped by Union control of the Mississippi, until by the close of the war some 5,000,000 longhorns roamed Texas. Most were "mavericks" that could be claimed by anyone bothering to affix a brand, although a few were held on ranches in the belt of open country east of the Cross Timbers.

By 1865 a few astute Texans recognized that the millions of cattle might be turned into tidy profits. They knew good steers could be had for the asking in their own state, or could be purchased for $3 or $4 a head from ranchers. They learned that the upper Mississippi Valley, its livestock supplies depleted by war, was willing to pay up to $40 a head for marketable beasts. Only a little arithmetic was required to demonstrate the fortunes to be made from that price differential. If a cattleman could get a herd of 3,000 longhorns to the northern markets his profits would amount to $100,000; if all 5,000,000 Texas cattle could be driven north the state would be enriched to the extent of $180,000,000! Nor was this simply a fantastic dream. Texans were aware that the hardy animals could be driven overland without difficulty so long as the journey lay through open prairie. They knew, too, that railroads were jutting westward into the northern Plains; the Missouri Pacific Railroad reached Sedalia, Missouri, in 1865 and could be used as a shipping point to eastern markets. Why not capitalize upon the happy combination of circumstances to amass King Midas' own wealth for themselves?

The "Long Drive" was the result. During the winter of 1865-66 a number of Texans and a few business men from Iowa and Kansas quietly rounded up herds, laid in camp equipment, and hired cowboys. In late March, when the grass on the northern Plains began to green, they started. Each band of a thousand or more cattle was driven by half a dozen cowboys, all adept in the use of the lasso and six-shooter, and paid $25 to $40 a month. A chuck wagon carrying food and equipment, with the cook at the reins, broke trail, followed by the horse wrangler and his horses; then came the longhorns, strung out over a mile of prairie. At the "point" or head of the column two riders kept the cattle on their course, others guarded the flank, and two more rode at "drag" in the rear to spur on halting beasts. The whole "outfit" was commanded by a trail boss who received a salary of $125 a month.

Experience soon taught the bosses to drive the cattle slowly at first and to watch them carefully at night, but within a week the steers were "road broken" enough to move ahead more rapidly. After that the larger herds were guarded by only two hands at night, then drifted slowly away from the bedding ground at daybreak, grazing as they went. After an hour or so the pace was speeded up until noon when a halt was made at some stream where the cook, who had galloped ahead in the chuck wagon, had dinner waiting. The cattle grazed for a few hours while the men ate, then were driven rapidly on until nightfall. That was the pattern followed by the dozens of herds that left Texas in the spring of 1866; in all some 260,000 head started for the Missouri Pacific railhead at Sedalia.

Nevertheless the Long Drive was far from successful. Bad luck plagued drovers from the beginning. Heavy rains in Texas muddied trails, swelled streams, and made life so unpleasant that many cowboys deserted their jobs. Beyond the Red River where the Sedalia Trail crossed a corner of the Indian Territory herds were frequently stampeded by red men who then demanded a reward for returning the beasts to their owners. Still farther north the wooded hills of the Ozark Plateau terrified the cattle; longhorns accustomed to the open range bolted rather than enter forested regions. When that obstacle was passed another was encountered in the irate farmers of Missouri, who were out in force to repel herds which

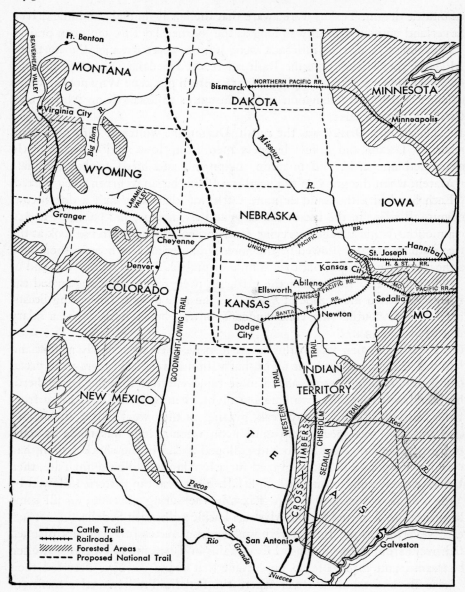

The Cattlemen's Frontier

might infect their own cows with the dread Texas Fever. At every county
line armed bands of backwoodsmen halted drovers, shot cattle, or fought it
out with cowboys. The successive barriers kept all but a few steers from
reaching Sedalia, but the $35 a head received for those convinced Texan

cattlemen the Long Drive would be successful if they could find a less hazardous route to market.

The honor of laying out a better trail went not to a drover but to Joseph M. McCoy, an Illinois meat dealer, who realized a fortune awaited anyone controlling the spot where southern sellers and northern buyers could meet most advantageously. That point, he reasoned, must lie on the Kansas Pacific Railroad, then building westward from Kansas City; this would allow herders to avoid wooded areas and settlements while driving cattle northward. Officials of the line proved so enthusiastic McCoy was able to exact promises of low freight rates from them, but the president of the road connecting Kansas City with St. Louis and the markets of the East, the Missouri Pacific Railroad, thought the plan fantastic and refused to cooperate. Undaunted, McCoy turned to a second railroad having eastern connections from Kansas City, the Hannibal and St. Joe Railroad. Before the winter of 1866-67 was over he signed a contract assuring him favorable shipping terms for cattle between the Plains and Chicago.

McCoy's next task was to select the point on the Kansas Pacific tracks where the Long Drive would end. After careful study he chose the little hamlet of Abilene, Kansas, because, as he wrote, "the country was entirely unsettled, well watered, excellent grass, and nearly the entire area of country was adapted to holding cattle." Abilene—a drowsy little village with a handful of settlers and so little business the one saloon keeper spent part of his time raising prairie dogs for tourists—was transformed overnight by his decision. During the spring of 1867 McCoy imported lumber for stockyards, pens, loading chutes, barns, a livery stable, and a hotel to house the cowhands. All was bustle and confusion as the building program was rushed to completion; by July McCoy was able to send riders southward to intercept Sedalia-bound herds with welcome news of a new market at Abilene. Unfortunately most of the drovers had gone too far to be turned back, but 35,000 Texas steers passed through McCoy's loading chutes that fall. The banquet held on September 5, 1867, to celebrate the first shipment of cattle east was a gala affair, where southern drovers and northern dealers toasted the wedding of their sections and talked joyfully of the profits that would be theirs in the future.

Abilene assured success for the Long Drive. Cattlemen who reached there in 1868 with 75,000 head were enthusiastic over the trail northward— the Chisholm Trail, they called it—and carried word to Texas of the ease with which steers could be driven where there were no settlements, hills, or wooded areas. Their advertising started the tide rolling; between 1868 and 1871 nearly 1,500,000 Texan beeves were loaded in the Abilene yards. By that time the advance of settlement in eastern Kansas and the march of railroads across the Plains conspired to shift the cattle trail farther westward. Ellsworth, lying sixty miles west of Abilene on the Kansas Pacific Railroad, and Newton on the newly built Atchison, Topeka and Santa Fe Railroad, were the terminal points for the Long Drive between 1872 and 1875, receiving about 1,500,000 head. After 1875 the center was Dodge City, Kansas, which shipped 1,000,000 Texas beeves eastward in the next four years. In all 4,000,000 cattle reached the Kansas railroads during the years when the Long Drive was a feature of the cattlemen's frontier.

That was the time when the "cow towns"—Abilene, Newton, Ellsworth, Dodge City—were catapulted into the national limelight as models of unbridled corruption. They were drab hamlets most of the time, their dusty streets lined with ramshackle saloons, gaudy dance halls, gambling dens, hurdy-gurdy palaces, and red-light houses, but when each new band of cowboys "hit town" at the end of the Long Drive they blossomed into tinseled paradises where the most discriminating tastes in debauchery could be satisfied. Mobs of mounted cowboys "took over" by day, their six-shooters roaring while respectable citizens cowered behind locked doors. Faro dealers and dance hall girls reigned at night, reaping a financial harvest that justified the dreary months of waiting between drives. Seldom did a group of drovers leave without contributing to the population of "boot hill"—the cemetery reserved for those who died with their boots on—for barroom brawls, drunken duels, and chance shootings were so common that no one bothered to punish the murderers. In the "cow towns," as in the mining camps, the combination of easy money, rugged life, and inadequate restraints created an atmosphere which to easterners typified the whole "Wild West."

Romantic as it was, the Long Drive was economically unsound. The difficulties which beset drovers were many. Their cattle lost so much weight in the 1,500 mile journey northward that few could be sold to eastern stockyards at good prices; most went as "feeders" to some Nebraska or Iowa farmer for fattening on corn. Their expenses increased steadily, especially after 1867 when natives in the Indian Territory discovered that an ancient congressional statute forbade traffic across their lands without special permission. First the Cherokee, then the tribes farther west, capitalized on the situation by charging ten cents a head for all steers driven through their reservations. Far worse, from the cattlemen's point of view, was the hostility of Kansans. Irate farmers, knowing Texas Fever was carried by disease-transmitting ticks which infected Texas cattle, were always out in force to repel northward-bound herds. At first they resorted to shooting, but that was outmoded when their control of state legislatures allowed them to erect legal barriers. Both Missouri and Kansas passed quarantine laws in

1867, forbidding the entrance of cattle during the summer and fall when ticks were most active, and Kansas in 1884 ruled that no Texas steers could be driven into the state except in December, January, and February. Drovers evaded the laws at first, but as the growing agricultural population demanded and secured enforcement, the Long Drive came to an end. Congress, after listlessly debating a "National Cattle Trail" immune to state interference, refused to aid the Texans. The only solution was to grow cattle near the railroads. That would not only allow cattlemen to evade barriers erected by farmers and Indians, but place them in a better position to bargain with buyers who dictated prices in the Kansas "cow towns."

In Texas railroads came to the cattle country. During the 1870's the Missouri, Kansas and Texas Railroad, the Texas and Pacific Railroad, and numerous other lines opened communication with St. Louis, New Orleans, and Memphis. The possibility of direct marketing encouraged dozens of ranchers to stake out claims on the grassland between the Cross Timbers and the Pecos Valley where nutritive bunch grass, mesquite, and grama grass provided adequate fodder. Within a decade the whole Panhandle was carved into enormous ranches, some of them so large that cowboys rode a hundred miles from their homes to reach their front gates.

The problem of growing cattle near the northern railroads was just as easily solved. The climate was harsh, with roaring winter gales and occasional ice storms, but cattle could weather the worst blizzards so long as they drifted before the wind with their rumps to the tempest. Only when ice blanketed the ground was there any real danger, and that happened infrequently. During most of the year steers could feast on short prairie grass or scrape away snow to munch winter-cured fodder. The longhorns' ability to thrive on the northern Plains was demonstrated long before the close of the Civil War by traders who bartered sleek oxen for worn-out livestock along the immigrant trails, and by small ranchers who supplied the Montana gold fields with fresh beef. By 1868 herds dotted the High Plains country from the Rio Grande Valley to the Big Horn Basin, amply demonstrating that cattle could be grown anywhere. Only two things were needed to transform the local industry into a mammoth enterprise: adequate markets and improved steers to satisfy the discriminating taste of eastern consumers.

Both were provided during the 1870's. Railroads pushed steadily across the northern Plains during the decade: the Union Pacific, the Kansas Pacific, the Santa Fe, the Northern Pacific, the Burlington, and other smaller lines. At the same time mechanical improvements in meat handling and slaughtering—modern killing methods, refrigerator cars, and cold storage—widened the market for western beef. From the open range to the kitchen range was an easy step, and the demand for American meat mounted until all the East and much of Europe was fed by Plains ranchers. The quality of western beef was improved at the same time. As tough Texas cows were brought north, they were bred with heavier Hereford and Angus bulls to produce round-bellied, white-faced cattle which combined the stamina of longhorns with the weight and tenderness of eastern breeds. Able to survive cold winters and fetch an excellent price at the Chicago stockyards, the hybrids proved an ideal stock for the northern range.

The distinctive breed was developed in Kansas, for there Texas longhorns and eastern cattle first met. From the beginning of the Long Drive enterprising ranchers were on hand to purchase cows that were too scrawny or sickly to be sold; they were then fattened on prairie grass, bred with Hereford bulls, and used to build up herds of healthy cattle that showed little trace of their rangy Texas ancestors. As the ventures proved profitable, more and more cattle were diverted from the "cow towns" to stock the northern range, while the brisk demand for Hereford bulls drove their price up to $1,000. By the end of the 1860's ranches covered most of Kansas and Nebraska as well as portions of the Indian Territory where land was leased from the natives. Many drovers from Texas, finding they must compete with sleek steers from the nearby range when selling their herds, moved to Kansas themselves or laid out ranches there where they could fatten and hybridize their stock before sale.

From Kansas ranching spread into Colorado as soon as the Kansas Pacific and Union Pacific railroads joined that area to the outside world. Most of the cows needed to stock the range came from Texas, driven northward over the Goodnight-Loving Trail after that route was laid out in 1866. By 1869 1,000,000 longhorns grazed within the borders of Colorado Territory, and the herds were improving so rapidly that stockmen clamored for laws against further Texas importations lest stray bulls corrupt their Hereford-crossed strains. Statutes authorizing ranchers to shoot any loose Texan bull on sight testified to the regard with which they held their herds.

The advance of the cattle frontier into Wyoming began in 1868 when a Colorado rancher, J. W. Iliff, drove one of his herds to the plains near Cheyenne. His exorbitant profits from sales of beef to construction crews on the Union Pacific Railroad and miners prospecting the South Pass country, called attention to the richness of the range; others followed until by 1871 100,000 cattle pastured there, most of them under the watchful eye of small cowmen who owned only a few hundred head. The number increased rapidly after 1873 when the panic hurried the stocking of the northern range by lowering the price of Texan cattle. The center of the industry in Wyoming was the Laramie Valley, a region of rolling bench lands where grass and water abounded, and in the plateau country just west of the Laramie Mountains. After those regions filled ranchers spread their herds over most of the territory.

Extensive cattle raising in Montana began in 1871 when eight hundred Texas longhorns were driven into the Beaverhead River Valley by an enterprising herder with an eye on the lush market in nearby mining camps. Plentiful grass in that mountainous upland and the failure of Montana's mining population to increase as rapidly as expected allowed the herds to multiply rapidly; by 1874 the surplus above local needs reached 17,000 head and good beef steers sold for as low as $10. Those depressed prices transformed Montana ranching from a local to a national enterprise; eastern buyers, hearing sleek beeves could be purchased for a low sum, flocked in during the autumn, ready to pay up to $18 a head. The herds were driven south to the Union Pacific tracks at Granger, Wyoming —a difficult route through sparsely grassed country—but profits were great enough to convince Montana ranchers they must look to the East rather than to mining camps for future markets.

With plentiful sales promised, the cattle frontier could move out of the mountain valleys into the broad plains of eastern Montana where rich grass, plentiful streams, and protecting hills offered ideal pasturage. For a few years the advance was slow; Sitting Bull was on the warpath and neither man nor beast was safe until after 1878 when the last band of Sioux was driven onto a reservation. Then great herds were driven north from Colorado or Wyoming to stock the promising grassland. "Eastern Montana has suddenly awakened," wrote an editor. ". . . Stock is pouring in from every hand." Marketing remained difficult—cattle must be driven south to the Union Pacific Railroad or east to the Northern Pacific tracks at Bismarck—but no amount of isolation could discourage a stock raiser in that day of expansion. Ranches filled Montana, then spilled over into Dakota territory during the 1870's.

By 1880 the cattle industry was firmly planted throughout the Great Plains. A traveler riding northward from lower Texas would seldom be out of sight of herds of white-faced longhorns, grazing under the watchful eye of bronzed cowboys; he would find them in the Panhandle country, along the Pecos Valley of New Mexico, on the sun-baked plains of the Indian Territory, among the rolling prairies of western Kansas and Nebraska, scattered through the high grasslands of eastern Colorado and Wyoming, and dotting the wind-swept plains of Montana and Dakota. Prosaic census figures described the expansion of the cattle frontier:

|  | CATTLE IN 1860 | CATTLE IN 1880 |
|---|---|---|
| KANSAS | 93,455 | 1,533,133 |
| NEBRASKA | 37,197 | 1,113,247 |
| COLORADO | none | 791,492 |
| WYOMING | none | 521,213 |
| MONTANA | none | 428,279 |
| DAKOTA | none | 140,815 |

Texas longhorns, Kansas Herefords, and adventurous cattlemen from all the West had created a new empire—the Cattle Kingdom. "Cotton was once crowned king," wrote an exuberant editor, "but grass is now."

Underlying the breath-taking expansion which engulfed an area half the size of Europe within a span of fifteen years was the age-old hope for sudden wealth. Conditions on the Great Plains seemed to promise cattlemen fabulous profits. The land was free—millions of acres of it—all carpeted with rich grass and safe from meddlesome government agents. Cattle to stock the range were cheap; longhorns could be purchased in Texas at $7 or $8 a head, driven north to a likely spot, crossed with an imported eastern bull, and allowed to multiply as nature dictated. The rancher had only to sit back and watch his wealth increase, knowing every healthy steer would fetch from $50 to $60 at the nearest railroad. A few years of frugal living, while profits were turned back into the herd, would allow any pioneer to pyramid a modest investment into a handsome fortune.

There was no lack of adventurers to people the cattlemen's frontier. Most were young men who had scraped necessary capital together, bought their herds, and started out alone in search of a likely grazing spot. Because grass and water were necessary, a site was always selected on the bank of a stream. There the prospective rancher either homesteaded 160 acres or simply appropriated the land he needed. If a few straggly trees grew nearby he built a log cabin; if not he scooped a dugout from the bank of the river or threw together a tent of buffalo skins. With that simple equipment, a supply of beans, bacon, and coffee, and a horse or two, he was ready to watch his cattle graze, watch them fatten, watch them multiply. When beef animals were cut away to be sold he used the proceeds to buy more stock, build a ranch house, and erect corrals for his horses. Three or four good years were enough to put the business on a paying basis, with herds so large cowboys were hired to watch them.

By that time other ranchers were moving in nearby, along the same stream or across the divide on the banks of the next waterway. They were not near neighbors in the eastern sense of the words—they might be fifteen or twenty miles away—but they were close enough to cause trouble unless a system of frontier law was devised. How could each rancher keep his cattle separate from those of his neighbor? How could he sustain his claim to a portion of the public domain? How could he keep newcomers from overcrowding the range? Distant legislatures could not solve those problems; like frontiersmen throughout America's history cattlemen must make their own laws. The body of custom and rule they worked out allowed expansion to go on with a minimum of disorder.

Basic to the system was the sensible concept that control of a stream included control of adjacent lands. Thus a rancher staking out a claim to one bank of a creek secured a "range right" to as much of the river as he pre-empted and all the land running back to the "divide," or highland separating his stream from the one lying beyond. This was his land, even though he did not own a foot of it legally; public opinion, backed by the effective argument contained in six-shooters, gave him a right to use it without fear of intrusion. The usual ranches in the Great Plains contained thirty or forty square miles.

The imaginary "range lines" between holdings were respected by humans, but cattle drifted from ranch to ranch in their search for better pasturage until herds of several owners were frequently hopelessly intermingled. Ranchers' attempts to keep their steers separate from those of their neighbors gave prominence to two customs—"line-riding" and the "roundup." In line-riding, cowboys were stationed along the borders of each ranch, usually in groups of twos, ten or twenty miles apart, with a dugout to protect them in winter and the open sky as their canopy in summer. Each morning they set out from their lonely posts, riding in opposite directions until they met the cowboy from the nearest camp on either side. Herds belonging to their employer were driven back from the border; those of neighbors were "drifted" in the direction of their own ranch.

Vigilant as line-riders might be, animals did intermingle. Twice each year, in the spring and fall, "roundups" were held to separate mixed herds and identify new-born calves. At the time agreed upon, each rancher sent a chuck wagon and "outfit" to a designated spot. Then the cowboys fanned out over the range, driving all cattle in the vicinity toward camp, until a herd of several thousand was assembled. While the milling mass of animals was held together, riders of the ranch where the roundup was held made the first "cut," riding skillfully through the herd to single out animals bearing their employer's brand. Those brands—distinctive marks burned into the flanks with red-hot branding irons—were registered to avoid confusion; some symbols of better-known ranches became as famous as baronial symbols of feudal days. As calves always followed the mothers, they could now be lassoed, thrown, and marked with the iron.

After the first division, cowboys from other ranches cut out their own cattle; a process repeated until the last cow was branded. Then the owner of the ranch where the roundup took place held back his herd while the rest were driven to the next ranch, where the procedure was duplicated. That went on until the last range was visited and the cattle of the whole region branded and returned to their owners. The work was hard—cowboys spent eighteen or twenty hours a day in the saddle for weeks at a time—but the roundup was one of the most colorful institutions in the history of the frontier. The thousands of bellowing cattle, blazing branding fires, scores of mounted cowboys, and scattered chuck wagons, all hazy with dust and drenched by a brilliant sun, caught the imagination of easterners as did nothing else in the Far West.

The color of the roundup owed much of its sharpness to the central figure of the Cattle Kingdom—the cowboy. That legendary figure was, like all frontiersmen, a product of the environment which sired his unusual profession; if he seemed strange to men of the East who later glorified him in song and cinema he differed only because he adjusted his life to his unique means of earning a living. His legs were bowed from long hours in the saddle, his eyes permanently squinted from gazing into the glaring sunlight, his skin weather-beaten and tanned from days in the open. He was courageous, as men had to be in a land where law was carried on the hip rather than in books, and he shared a high degree of resourcefulness with generations of frontiersmen whose isolation made self-reliance a necessity. Even his picturesque garb was entirely functional: chaps of leather to ease the strain of days in the saddle, boots to fit into stirrups, a "ten-gallon" hat to shade his eyes, jingling spurs to guide his horse when hands were busy with the lasso, gloves to protect his hands from the reins, handkerchief knotted about his neck to be pulled over the face during dust storms. Everything that he wore, everything that he did, was adjusted to the job he had to do.

Practical as he was, the cowboy was destined to only a brief career, for he was the symbol of the open range and by 1880 the days of the open range were numbered. Overstocking was responsible. During the early 1880's the whole western world awakened to the possibilities of the Cattle Kingdom. Markets were expanding as railroads pushed into the Great Plains and steamships brought European consumers closer to the United States. Soon the entire world would be willing to pay handsomely for western beef! Any doubting scoffer could be convinced by the steady price rise at the Chicago stock yards, an advance that carried choice steers to a high of eight or nine cents a pound. Anyone could reap a fortune by doing nothing more than watch his animals multiply on free government land.

Even the unvarnished truth would have started a rush to the Plains, but that was not the literary diet fed Americans by magazines and newspapers. Western editors, never notable for understatement, filled their columns with statistics proving that anyone investing $25,000 in cattle could run his fortune to $80,000 in five years, or stated authoritatively that profits of 40 and 50 per cent annually were the rule rather than the exception. Those tall tales were spread wholesale through the eastern farm journals. Typical was an item in the *Breeder's Gazette:*

> A good sized steer when it is fit for the butcher market will bring from $45.00 to $60.00. The same animal at its birth was worth but $5.00. He has run on the plains and cropped the grass from the public domain for four or five years, and now, with scarcely any expense to its owner, is worth forty dollars more than when he started on his pilgrimage. A thousand of these animals are kept nearly as cheaply as a single one, so with a thousand as a starter and an investment of but $5,000 in the start, in four years the stock raiser has made from $40,000 to $45,000. Allow $5,000 for his current expenses which he has been going on and he still has $35,000 and even $45,000 for a net profit. That is all there is to the problem and that is why our cattlemen grow rich.

Struggling farmers in the East, reading those statements, developed such a feverish state of mind that many accepted as true the sly tale given wide circulation by Bill Nye, the Laramie *Boomerang* humorist: "Three years ago a guileless tenderfoot came into Wyoming, leading a single Texas steer and carrying a branding iron; now he is the opulent possessor of six hundred head of fine cattle—the ostensible progeny of that one steer."

Propaganda such as that could have only one effect; by the summer of 1880 the rush to the new El Dorado was on. Trains were jam-packed with youngsters from eastern farms and factories, some with savings strapped about their waists, others ready to borrow at interest rates which varied from 2 per cent a month to 1 per cent a day. What did those fantastic charges matter when beef sold at the Chicago yards for $9.35 a hundred! Their frantic bidding on cattle to stock the range sent prices skyrocketing; ordinary stock that sold for $8 a head in 1879 brought $35 in Texas by 1882 and were resold in Wyoming at $60. So great was the demand that between 1882 and 1884 the eastern cattle shipped westward as range stock balanced the number sent east to market! While the boom lasted, between 1880 and 1885, the whole Plains country was inundated with thousands of ranchers and millions of cattle without stamina or experience to survive there.

More disastrous than the rush of men was the flow of capital from the East and Europe. Investors caught the fever in 1882 when they read in financial journals of the Prairie Cattle Company's 42 per cent dividend or the 40 per cent profits of Montana ranchers. Before the year was out business men, bankers, lawyers, and politicians were forming companies to share in those fortunes. Their recipe for prosperity was simple; they put up capital, a few ranchers were taken in to furnish experience, and the government provided land. During 1883 twenty stock-raising corporations, capitalized at $12,000,000, were formed in Wyoming alone. Some staked out range rights, but more consolidated smaller ranches already in existence; typical was the Swan Land and Cattle Company which used $3,750,000 raised by stock sales in the East to combine three eastern Wyoming ranches into a hundred-mile estate containing 100,000 head of cattle. All over the West grizzled cow hands who had "ridden the line" for years found themselves seated about directors' tables where eastern bankers listened respectfully to their opinions.

From the East the mania spread to Europe. English capitalists became interested when a parliamentary committee soberly reported in 1880 that profits of 33⅓ per cent could be expected in American ranching; an estimate which appeared less fantastic after an Edinburgh corporation, the Prairie Cattle Company, declared a dividend of 28 per cent in 1881. For the next four years English and Scottish investors, with the vision of 40 per cent profits before them, poured their money into corporations to compete with American companies for range rights and cattle. All over London "drawing rooms buzzed with stories of this last of bonanzas; staid old gentlemen, who scarcely knew the difference between a steer and a heifer, discussed it over their port and nuts." The flow of wealth from across the Atlantic hurried overstocking and brought the day of reckoning nearer.

Experienced cattlemen were thoroughly alarmed by 1885. They knew the arid plains could support the thousands of steers pastured there only when weather conditions were exceptionally favorable. They realized pasturage was wearing thinner each year, and that herds could no longer be driven to green feeding grounds when grass gave out, for all the Plains were pre-empted. In their panic they sought to insure themselves against the hard times ahead. Some fenced the range to protect their own pastures from intruding cattle; by the end of 1885 the Plains country was entangled in a barbed-wire network of its own making. One Colorado company had 1,000,000 acres enclosed, while a group of Texas Panhandle ranchers stretched a steel barrier from the Indian Territory to the Rio Grande to keep Kansas cattle from their feeding grounds. Few bothered to purchase the land they fenced; most simply enclosed part of the public domain, then stood ready to protect their holdings by "gun law."

Equally indicative of the fears besetting experienced ranchers during the cattle boom was the way in which they rushed into stock-breeders associations. Those co-operative enterprises offered many advantages; they kept intruders out of full-stocked ranges, supervised roundups, ran down "rustlers," fought prairie fires, offered bounties for wolves, and protected the brands of members. Usually they began as local groups, formed when stockmen of one region met, drew up articles of agreement to protect the range, and in typical frontier fashion agreed to abide by the will of the majority. As they multiplied several combined to form territorial associations which prescribed the roundup districts for a whole territory, formulated rules for branding and drives, restricted the number of cattle allowed on the range, and even set up courts to settle disputes between members. Live-Stock Associations blanketed the Great Plains by 1885, typifying both the frontiersmen's tendency toward self-government and the cattlemen's fear of range overstocking.

More than fencing and organization were needed to keep the cattle boom alive. By the summer of 1885 hundreds of ranchers felt the squeeze of mounting costs and falling prices. Each year more profits went into fencing, dues to Live-Stock Associations, and increasingly expensive cattle; each year after 1882 sums paid them at the Chicago stock yards diminished as overproduction drove beef prices downward. The experienced among them realized the downward spiral had begun; some sold their herds rather than risk wintering cattle insufficiently fattened on the overcrowded range, further depressing prices. To make matters worse a presidential order in August, 1885, forced stockmen who had leased lands in the Indian Territory to leave that region. Some 200,000 beeves were driven into the crowded ranges of Colorado, Kansas, and Texas that fall. Only a cycle of bad years was needed to prick the inflationary bubble and send the whole Cattle Kingdom toppling.

That began during the winter of 1885-86, a cold blustery winter which took a frightful toll on the northern Plains. The summer of 1886 was hot and dry, withering grass and drying up streams. Stockmen, noting the weakened condition of their herds, became panicky as fall approached. Some cattle were driven into Canada or onto leased lands on the Crow Reservation in Montana; others were sent east to be boarded by farmers along the agricultural frontier. Still more were dumped on the market. Prices tumbled amidst the selling spree, until steers worth $30 a year before went begging at $8 or $10 each. "Beef is low, very low, and prices are tending downward, while the market continues to grow weaker every day," complained the *Rocky Mountain Husbandmen*. "But for all that, it would be better to sell at a low figure, than to endanger the whole herd by having the range overstocked."

Those who sold, even at low prices, were wise. The winter of 1886 87 was long famous in western annals. Snow blanketed the northern Plains in November, so deep that starving animals could not paw down to grass. In early January a warm "chinook" wind brought some relief, but late in the month the worst blizzard ever experienced by ranchers howled across the West from Dakota to Texas. In the past cattle had withstood tempests by drifting before them; now they piled up against fences to die by the thousands. On the heels of the storm came a numbing cold which drove temperatures to sixty-eight degrees below zero. Ranchers, huddled about their stoves, did not dare think of what was happening on the range—of helpless cattle pawing at frozen snow in search of a little food or fighting to strip bark from willows and aspens along streams, "dogies" and unseasoned eastern cattle floundering in drifts, whole herds jammed together in ravines to escape the frosty blast and dying by the thousands. When spring finally came cattlemen saw a sight they spent the rest of their lives trying to forget. Carcass piled upon carcass in every ravine, gaunt skeletons staggering about on frozen feet, heaps of dead bodies along the fences, trees stripped bare of their bark—those were left as monuments to the thoughtless greed of ranchers.

The cold winter of 1886-87 ended the "open range" phase of the cattle industry. A few small ranchers struggled on, encouraged by excellent grazing conditions during the summer of 1887, but the great livestock corporations were unable to stand the strain. With creditors clamoring at their doorsteps they dumped steers on the market so rapidly the Chicago price for grass-fed beef tumbled from $2.40 a hundred in the spring of 1887 to $1.90 in the fall. Nor did conditions improve during the next half-dozen years as Texas growers unloaded stock no longer needed on the northern Plains, and farmers depressed the market by selling heavily during a cycle of dry years which depleted supplies of feed corn. Under those conditions company after company slid over the line into bankruptcy; the giant Swan Land and Cattle Company of Wyoming succumbed in May, 1887, and the Niobrara Cattle Company of Nebraska soon followed. The few that persisted faced constant criticism from those who remembered the suffering of 1886-87. "A man who turns out a lot of cattle on a barren plain without making provision for feeding them," wrote one western editor, "will not only suffer a financial loss but also the loss of the respect of the community in which he lives." In Wyoming alone the number of cattle declined from 9,000,000 head in 1886 to 3,000,000 nine years later.

Hostile public opinion and financial necessity both dictated that in the future cattle and grass be kept in even balance. That could not be done on the open range; the only solution was for each rancher to fence his lands, restrict his herds to a reasonable size, and insure adequate winter food by growing hay. Fencing went on rapidly in the High Plains country through the later 1880's—with cattlemen buying some land, leasing more, and enclosing all they dared in addition—until mowing machines and hay rakes were as common a sight in the West as chuck wagons in former days. And the cowboy, that romantic knight of the saddle, spent his days digging post holes, jacking up wagon wheels as fence tighteners, and haying. "I remember," reminisced one sadly, "when we sat around the fire the winter through and didn't do a lick of work for five or six months of the year, except to chop a little wood to build a fire to keep warm by. Now we go on the general roundup, then the calf roundup, then comes haying—something that the old-time cowboy never dreamed of—then the beef roundup and the fall calf roundup and gathering bulls and weak cows, and after all this a winter of feeding hay. I tell you times have changed." The day of the open range was gone; the West was becoming a land of big pastures, stocked with carefully bred, carefully sheltered beeves.

Oldtimers who sorrowed at those changes had another cause for alarm, for during the 1880's two dangerous invaders pressed upon the borders of the Cattle Kingdom. From the west came the sheepherders. Those unromantic individuals moved into the trans-Mississippi country during the 1870's, driven from their Ohio Valley pasturages by low prices for wool and high prices for feed. Seeking new grazing grounds where fodder was less expensive, they went first to California, New Mexico, and the mountain parks of the southern Rocky Mountains, then during the 1880's invaded the Plains country. Ranchers scoffed at first, but when they learned sheep could be raised with half the effort and twice the profit of steers, many made the transition. Others fought back. They claimed sheep ruined the grass by close cropping, and were ready to back their argument with "shooting irons." Open warfare between drovers and cowboys raged along the western border of the cow country for years, accounting for twenty deaths, a hundred injuries, and 600,000 sheep destroyed (most of them driven over cliffs) on the Wyoming-Colorado range alone. Yet no force could hold back such a profitable enterprise, and herds of bleating "woolies" encroached steadily on the cattlemen's domain.

More dangerous were the invaders pressing upon the eastern fringes of the Cattle Kingdom—the pioneer farmers. Their advance onto the Great Plains began just as ranchers staked out their empire, and for the next years they pressed westward, despite the bitter hostility of cowmen. The stubborn advance of homesteaders against gun-toting cowboys, sullen sheepherders, and the terrifying obstacles of nature wrote the last epic chapter in the history of the American frontier.

# CHAPTER XXXIV

# Opening the Great Plains

## 1870-1890

The unfamiliar environment of the Great Plains province could be utilized by American frontiersmen in two different ways. One was to devise an economic enterprise adapted to the section's unusual features; the cattlemen did that by perfecting grazing methods suited to an unfenced range. The other was to conquer nature's obstacles by man-made devices. The Plains were opened to pioneers during the 1870's not by adventurous trailblazers but by inventors toiling over drafting boards, laborers sweating over whirring machines, and production managers struggling with the complexities of assembly lines, for those were the men who applied the techniques of the industrial revolution to the unique problems of America's last frontier. Their success made expansion possible.

The task facing them—and the farmers who depended on their skill— was formidable. The Plains country was a vast grassland which stretched away to lonely horizons, unbroken except where straggling trees followed the course of some meandering stream. Nowhere could pioneers find materials and living conditions with which they were familiar. There was no lumber for homes, barns, or split-rail fences. There was no water save the muddy gruel in occasional rivers. There were no belts of trees to shelter them from the baking sun of summer or raging winter blizzards. And worst of all there was in all the province seldom enough rainfall; annual precipitation west of the 98th meridian was normally below the twenty inches required for agriculture. The frontiersman, to succeed in that subhumid region, must devise new farming methods or be provided with farm machinery which would allow him to cultivate a tract large enough to offset the low yield per acre. Those were the needs that must be filled by prophets of the industrial revolution.

Farmers did not have long to wait. The United States in the postwar years was entering upon its machine age; everywhere in the East smoke-belching factories multiplied as the nation, awakening to the possibilities of mechanization, enshrined mechanical efficiency as its new god. The atmosphere was conducive to rapid development in any industrial field which promised profits; let it be known a new gadget was needed and a dozen manufacturers set to work to satisfy the demand. Few fields promised better financial rewards than supplying western farmers. Thousands of pioneers were ready to advance into the Great Plains when provided with the mechanical means for doing so; the lucky artisan producing something they could use would reap a fortune. That was the incentive which set the wheels of industry turning; in a brief decade inventors perfected the wire fences, well-drilling machinery, and farm implements that allowed the Plains to be subdued.

Efficient fencing material was required first of all. Farmers realized that when the agricultural frontier touched the eastern fringes of the Cattle Kingdom in Kansas and Nebraska. Struggling to keep milling steers from trampling new-planted corn, they demanded that cattlemen fence the range; ranchers answered with equal venom that farmers should protect their own fields. Western newspapers bristled with letters arguing the question during the early 1870's, but no solution was possible until a good fencing material was devised. Wood, carted in from distant Wisconsin forests, was pro-hibitively priced. A Department of Agriculture report in 1871 estimated a 160 acre homestead which cost its owner $20 in land-office fees would require $1,000 worth of wooden fence "for protection against a single stock-grower, rich in cattle, and becoming richer by feeding them without cost on the unpurchased prairie." Sums such as that were unknown among pioneer farmers, let alone the additional amounts needed for repairs. The nation was sobered when the secretary of agriculture revealed in 1871 that its fences cost $2,000,000,000 and that the annual interest and upkeep cost was $2,000,000. The market for any manufacturer producing cheap fencing was unlimited.

That inventors rose to the challenge was shown by Patent Office records; while only one or two patents for new types of fences were issued yearly before the Civil War, in the decade afterward the number leaped to 122 annually. The fortunate individual who hit upon the best solution was Joseph F. Glidden, a farmer of De Kalb, Illinois. Faced with the problem of enclosing his own six-hundred-acre prairie farm, Glidden devised a practi-cal fence by twisting together two strands of wire in such a way they would hold pointed wire barbs at short intervals. After convincing himself the "barbed wire" fence could be produced cheaply, he patented his invention on November 24, 1874, rented a small factory in De Kalb, hired a crew of boys to string the barbs on the twisted strands, and began manufacturing his product as the Barb Fence Company. Within a few months Glidden's fencing was selling so well steam machinery was installed and production stepped up to five tons a day. Eager buyers took all he manufactured at eighteen cents a pound.

Eastern capitalists soon became interested. The nation's leading producer of ordinary wire, the Washburn and Moen Manufacturing Company of Worcester, Massachusetts, noticed the unusually large orders for its product arriving from De Kalb. An agent sent west to investigate during the summer of 1875 returned with samples which were turned over to a machine designer, with orders to develop a mechanical method for producing barbed wire. When that was perfected early the following year, representatives of the Worcester firm approached Glidden with an offer to buy out his patent. He consented to sell a half interest to Washburn and Moen for $60,000 and a royalty of twenty-five cents on every hundred pounds manufactured. The way was cleared for the large-scale production of the first practical fencing the world had known.

Work began in April, 1876, when a power machine was set up in De Kalb, and so brisk was demand that by the end of the year fifteen more were operating. Nearly 3,000,000 pounds of barbed wire fence were sold in 1876, 12,000,000 in 1877, 50,000,000 in 1879 and 80,000,000 in 1880. Three years later the Glidden factory was a giant two-story structure where 202 automatic machines transformed 1,400 miles of plain wire into 600 miles of fencing every ten hours. Mass production methods lowered the price steadily, from $20 a hundred pounds in 1870 to $10 in 1880 and less than $4 in 1890. The decline brought decent fences within the reach of all, and after the first skepticism was surmounted, its use spread like wildfire. Cattlemen and farmers both bought extravagantly, but barbed wire was primarily a farmers' weapon against trespassers.

As essential to Plains agriculture as good fencing was adequate water. Nature failed to provide enough except in eastern Texas, Kansas, and Nebraska. Over the Great Plains, moreover, the constant glare of the sun, the rapid runoff of sporadic rains on hard-packed soil, and ever-blowing winds which sucked up surface moisture, contributed to the sections' aridity. Before the province could be utilized means must be found to bring water to the land, or farming techniques suitable to a subhumid environment devised.

The first task proved difficult. Water could be brought to the soil by tapping surface accumulations through irrigation, or by elevating subsurface deposits through wells. Irrigation was feasible only along the western fringes of the Great Plains where streams gushing from the Rocky Mountains could be utilized. Projects of that sort, usually of a co-operative nature, were attempted in Colorado during the 1870's and in Wyoming a decade later, but the number of usable rivers was few and the amount of land brought under cultivation negligible. Elsewhere on the Plains irrigation experiments failed; even where storage facilities were provided by damming rivers the infrequent rains failed to keep pools filled and dams silted up so rapidly they proved useless. The sole results of numerous attempts were flattened pocket books and broken spirits.

Efforts to utilize the "ground water" which underlay the Great Plains proved almost as disheartening. Subterranean pools could be tapped only when conditions were favorable; the "water plane" which caught surface moisture as it seeped downward had to be near enough to make well drilling practicable, and soil texture sufficiently porous to allow pipe to penetrate. That was possible only where an impervious rock layer collected water in beds of gravel, and such spots were rare on the Plains. In some places eastward-flowing rivers cut so deeply that their beds lay below the water plane and drained away the deposits; in others loose-textured soils were lacking. Even where ground water existed the subsurface pools were too small and the rate of replacement too slow for extensive irrigation. How to secure water needed for farming was the most pressing problem in the Plains region.

The early pioneers, unaware of the difficulties awaiting them, turned first to methods used in the East; they tried to dig open wells from which water could be raised with the traditional oaken bucket and well sweep. The impossibility of sinking shafts in heavy prairie soil and the great depth of the water plane soon turned them to well-drilling machines which hammered pipes into the ground, but those too proved unsatisfactory. To reach the deposits was one thing; to raise water to the surface was another. Old-fashioned hand methods were outmoded in a region where wells must be several hundred feet deep to tap subterranean pools. Some mechanical device must be substituted.

Windmills promised to provide the solution. Constantly blowing winds swept the level surface of the Great Plains; the average wind velocity ranged from twelve to fourteen miles an hour in contrast with the eight or ten mile average in the eastern half of the United States. Why not use the free power to pump the subsurface water needed by the pioneers? That possibility occurred to several windmill manufacturers who moved their plants to Illinois and Wisconsin during the late 1860's. There they developed an instrument suited to western conditions; fragile blades used in the East were reduced in size, the complex mechanism employed to keep the mill headed into the wind replaced by a simple vertical fin, and a governor added to reduce the pitch of the blades when high winds revolved them too rapidly. By 1873 when the improvements were perfected a number of small plants were located along the eastern fringes of the prairie country, ready to meet the expected demand.

That this did not develop was due to the manufacturers' failure to solve one problem: how to lower the price to a level within the reach of the small farmer. Well drillers charged from $1.25 to $2 a foot for wells which in the Plains country ranged between fifty and five hundred feet deep. When a $100 windmill was added, the cost was more than $1,000, an impossible sum. Industrialists found a ready market for their products—in 1879 sixty-nine small plants produced $1,000,000 worth of windmills yearly—but most of the buyers were railroads, towns, and ranchers. Not until the 1890's did mounting farm incomes and reduced production costs allow small farmers to enjoy the luxury of a mechanical water supply.

With irrigation impossible and wells expensive, the only alternative was a method of tillage which would preserve the scant supplies of moisture in the ground. Once more farmers called upon scientists for help. The problem, the experts saw, was to devise a manner of cultivation which would bring subsurface water to plant roots by capillary action, then hold it in the ground by checking evaporation. Their answer was "dry farming." Farmers were advised to plow furrows twelve to fourteen inches deep, thus loosening the soil and allowing water to move upward as the principle of capillarity operated. They were told to harrow their fields after each rainfall, creating a dust mulch of fine soil particles that would stop the evaporation common in crusted earth where water escaped through tiny pores. In that way every drop of the precious liquid was stored near the plant roots. Dry farming was no panacea—the results were often uncertain and the method failed altogether in unusually dry years—but it did open sections of the West normally closed to agriculture.

Neither dry farming nor normal agriculture could have succeeded on the Great Plains without a further contribution from eastern inventors. Farm machinery, on a scale undreamed of in the humid East, was essential in the semiarid West. The dry farmer, faced with the necessity of harrowing his fields within forty-eight hours after each rainfall, needed mechanical help. The ordinary farmer was equally dependent on machinery in a land where large holdings were required to assure an adequate income. The subnormal rainfall was responsible; in the East 80 acres of properly drenched land provided a family with a comfortable living, but in the parched West 360 acres or more were needed to produce the same capital return. Large scale methods were essential, based on the substitution of machines for men. Before the conquest of the Plains could proceed the industrial revolution must provide pioneers with farm machinery.

All the machines needed in the West—chilled-iron and steel plows, grain drills, reapers, disk harrows, straddle-row cultivators, and threshing machines—were in use before the Civil War. The slight demand for labor savers on eastern farms kept prices high and improvements low; a greater demand was needed to encourage the development of cheap, durable farm implements. That developed in the upper Mississippi Valley during the war years; most men were drained away by enlistments, leaving only a few workers to produce grain needed for eastern laborers, warring armies, and a Europe beset by crop failures. They could meet the responsibility —and take advantage of skyrocketing prices—only by mechanizing production; the number of mowing machines in use increased fourfold between 1861 and 1865 and the manufacture of other farm machinery increased in proportion. After the war national prosperity and good markets abroad kept food prices so high farmers were encouraged to increase their output by investing in mechanical devices.

Their demand encouraged improvements in farm machinery that made the conquest of the Great Plains possible. The plow was one instrument that evolved rapidly. James Oliver of Indiana began the process in 1868 when he built a chilled-iron plow equipped with a smooth-surfaced moldboard that slipped through humus prairie soils without clogging; other inventors improved his basic implement by covering wearing surfaces with steel. By 1877 thoroughly modern plows were in use. The next step was to lift the farmer from the furrow to a seat on the machine, vastly speeding plowing. Patents for a sulky plow were taken out as early as 1844 but not until agriculture invaded the Plains was the need great enough to inspire improvements. These followed so rapidly that sixteen practical plows were manufactured by 1873. Other manufacturers, conscious of the need for speed on extensive western farms, provided the sulkies with additional shares, allowing a farmer to turn over two or three furrows at once.

Similar improvements speeded planting. The spring-tooth harrow, perfected by a Michigan mechanic in 1869, proved more usable on prairie soils than disk and spike-tooth implements, for its flexible teeth bounced over obstacles and automatically dislodged debris. When a farmer had prepared the ground, he could plant his grain with end-gate seeders, introduced in the early 1870's to scatter seed from the end of a wagon. By 1874 they were displaced by grain drills—machines equipped with small disks to open seed furrows in the soil and a battery of pipes which fed the grain from a large box into the ground. Scientific corn planting was made possible by the checkrower—an implement that spaced the corn in equidistant hills and made possible alternate cultivation horizontally and transversely across a field. One was patented by two Illinois inventors in 1864 and was in general use ten years later. Even more useful in the West was the lister (1880), a double-moldboard planting-plow which dug a deep furrow by casting the earth up on either side, planted corn at the bottom, and covered the seed, all in one operation. This allowed the deep planting needed in semiarid regions; as plants grew the ridges of earth between the rows were dragged back until a level field awaited the harvest.

The handling of hay, an essential crop on all western farms, was speeded by a number of inventions. The mowing machine was in use before the Civil War but the tripping, spring-tooth rake was a product of the 1860's, the harpoon fork which carried hay into barns along carrier tracks fitted to the ridge pole was perfected in 1864, and the hay loader was patented in 1876. The first practical baling press, with power provided by horses attached to a rotating sweep, was built by an Illinois mechanic in 1866.

Harvesting machinery was even more essential in a region where the crop might suffer from storms or heat if not gathered at just the moment of maturity. Reapers used in the past would not do; they simply cut wheat or oats and deposited the stalks on a platform where men riding there could tie them into bundles. The grain was then shocked to wait pickup wagons. This method not only caused constant grumbling among hired hands who were forced to tie furiously to keep up with the machine, but required a larger number of workers than could be obtained on the usual farm. Only a "binder," which would both cut and tie bundles of grain, would satisfy the Plains farmers. Ingenious automatic wire binders were developed by several inventors during the 1870's but proved unsatisfactory; the stiff wires had to be cut by hand before grain could be threshed or fed to cattle. Not until 1878 was the first successful cord binder perfected. That laborsaving machine, which allowed two men and a team of horses to harvest twenty acres of wheat a day, was in general use by 1880.

Even that was not fast enough to satisfy owners of the West's vast grain fields. Their demand for more efficient harvesters led to the development of the header during the 1880's. This large machine, which was pushed by a team of four horses, cut heads from stalks in a swath twice as wide as that left by a binder, then carried them over an endless belt to a specially built wagon driven alongside, its far side built high to catch the heads as they tumbled in. They were then stacked to wait the thresher, while the standing straw was either used for pasturage or plowed under. The combine, which cut and threshed grain in one operation, was introduced in the great grain fields of California in the 1880's but did not come into general use on the Plains until a decade or more later.

The evolution of the thresher was equally rapid. Two models were in use in 1870, one a cumbersome affair which drew its power from ten horses, employed nine men, and threshed 300 bushels daily, the other using only two horses and capable of separating 135 bushels each day. The first important improvement was made in 1882 when a blower was added to stack the straw; during the next few years inventors developed self-feeders, band-cutters, and automatic weighers. Steam power gradually replaced horse power. With the improved machines a smaller crew could handle twice or three times the amount of grain threshed at the close of the Civil War. Efficient corn harvesting implements were harder to perfect; the first practical cornhusker was not patented until 1890 and the first workable corn binder not until 1892. The silo, a barrel-like structure for storing feed corn, was invented in 1875 by a University of Illinois scientist and was soon in general use throughout the northern Plains.

The United States commissioner of labor, surveying improvements in farm machinery in the 1890's reduced the story of time and money saved in the production of each acre of produce to simple tabular form:

| CROP | TIME WORKED | | LABOR COST | |
|------|------|------|------|------|
| | HAND | MACHINE | HAND | MACHINE |
| WHEAT | 61 hours | 3 hours | $3.55 | $0.66 |
| CORN | 39 hours | 15 hours | 3.62 | 1.51 |
| OATS | 66 hours | 7 hours | 3.73 | 1.07 |
| LOOSE HAY | 21 hours | 4 hours | 1.75 | 0.42 |
| BALED HAY | 35 hours | 12 hours | 3.06 | 1.29 |

Those figures told a dramatic story. The industrial revolution freed American farmers from time shackles which had bound them since land was first tilled. They no longer needed to limit planting to the amount they could reap by hand in the ten-day period when grain was prime. A single farmer in the past knew he could plant no more than 7½ acres of wheat, for that was all he could cut during the limited harvesting season. The same farmer in 1890 could devote 135 acres to wheat, knowing his efficient binder could care for that amount without danger of spoilage. Farm machinery gave him tools needed for extensive agriculture.

Yet the pioneer farmer, indebted as he was to the industrial revolution, lost as much as he gained from the forces that ushered America into its machine age. For he needed not only fences and steel plows; he needed land as well. That must come from the government. In former years farmers were sufficiently powerful to win congressional support for a succession of laws liberalizing the land system, first by reducing the acreage obtainable, then by lowering the price, and finally by recognizing pre-emption and homestead. With the machine age control of the government slipped from the hands of farmers into those of eastern industrialists. The "robber barons," concerned less with expansion than exploitation, not only frustrated every western effort to erect a satisfactory land system but plundered the public domain so ruthlessly the frontier advance was seriously retarded.

When settlement of the Great Plains began, the Homestead Act of 1862 governed the disposal of land. That measure, passed with the best of intentions after a generation of agitation by eastern workers and western pioneers, seemed foolproof. Any adult citizen or any alien who had filed his first papers could, for a $10 fee, claim 160 acres of the public domain. After he had "resided upon or cultivated the same for a term of five years immediately succeeding the time of filing" and paid a few fees, he secured final title. The law apparently assured every underpaid laborer, every expansionistic westerner, a chance to secure a free farm.

In practice, however, the farmer benefited only slightly from the Homestead Act, and the laborer not at all. The latter, whose annual wages frequently did not exceed $250, had neither the entry fees to file a claim, the considerable sum necessary to move his family to the frontier, nor the money to buy expensive tools and farm equipment. Even in rare cases where a worker scraped enough together he lacked the experience needed to homestead virgin territory and the resources to support himself for two or three years before his farm became self-supporting. Possibly the Homestead Act could have served as a "safety valve" for laborers if the government provided free transportation and machinery as well as free land, although even that beneficence would not have endowed city dwellers with the desire to change their mode of life. Actually most pioneers who invaded the interior grasslands came from adjacent states and were drafted from the ranks of men already skilled in agriculture.

That the Homestead Act failed to benefit western farmers was due partly to deficiencies in the law and partly to successful efforts of speculators to circumvent the will of its authors. The inadequacies of the original law were accidental; its framers, whose experience was gathered in the humid East, drafted a measure that was unworkable in the semiarid West. In the Mississippi Valley a unit of 160 acres was generous; few frontiersmen bought more than eighty acres and a free grant of twice that amount seemed certain to satisfy the most avaricious. A farmer on the Great Plains needed far more or much less—2,000 to 50,000 acres if he was a rancher, 360 to 640 acres if he practiced extensive agriculture, 40 to 60 acres if he used irrigation. Nowhere west of the 98th meridian was 160 acres a workable agricultural unit. The Homestead Act prevented pioneers from acquiring the best amount of land for their needs.

Bad as it was, the measure was made worse as amendments were adopted by Congress, often under pressure of speculators seeking means of engrossing the West's resources. The first, the Timber Culture Act of March 13, 1873, was a sincere attempt to adjust the Homestead Act to western conditions. It allowed any homesteader to apply for an additional 160 acres, which would become his if he planted at least one-fourth to trees within four years. During the fifteen years the law was on the statute books, 65,292 individuals patented 10,000,000 acres. Few were speculators; the expense of planting trees and the long wait before final ownership did not appeal to those seeking a quick turnover. The Timber Culture Act not only encouraged needed reforestation but allowed thousands of homesteaders to expand their holdings to a workable size.

A second amendment, the Desert Land Act of March 3, 1877, although ostensibly designed to benefit the pioneer, was actually lobbied through Congress by cattlemen. Those wealthy individuals, sensing the end of the open range, were constantly seeking some means of purchasing government land at the minimum price. Under existing laws that was impossible; a rancher could homestead 160 acres, add another 160 under the Timber Culture Act, and buy an additional quarter section under the Pre-emption Act of 1841. Even if all his cowhands served as dummy entrymen he was unable to build up a sufficient acreage for extensive grazing. Ranchers, seeking a means of securing more, were largely responsible for the Desert Land Act. The measure provided that anyone could secure tentative title to 640 acres in the Great Plains or Southwest by an initial payment of twenty-five cents an acre. After three years, if he could prove he had irrigated a portion of the land and was willing to pay an additional dollar an acre, the tract became his. In the interim he could transfer the claim if he wished.

The act was an open invitation to fraud. Cattlemen could take out a claim, round up a few witnesses to swear they "had seen water on the claim" (which usually meant a bucket of water dumped on the ground), and secure title by paying $1.25 an acre. Cowboys could be hired to repeat the process, transferring their claims to employers after making the first entry. That the framers intended misuse of the law was clear in its terms, for no one could cultivate 640 acres of irrigated soil. Unfortunately not all frontiersmen saw through the subterfuge. Claims for 9,140,517 acres were filed under the Desert Land Act, but final patents were issued on only 2,674,695 acres. Three-quarters of the claimants gave up the struggle to irrigate worthless lands before the three year period expired; probably most of the remainder were ranchers.

The lumber interests, quick to learn a lesson from cattlemen, assured themselves a chance to raid natural resources with the Timber and Stone Act of June 3, 1878. That amazing measure, which applied only to lands "unfit for cultivation" and "valuable chiefly for timber" or stone in California, Nevada, Oregon, and Washington, allowed any citizen or first-paper alien to buy up to 160 acres at $2.50 an acre—about the price of one good log. It invited corruption; any timber magnate could use dummy entrymen to engross the nation's richest forest lands at trifling cost. Company agents rounded up gangs of alien seamen in waterfront boarding houses, marched them to the courthouse to file their first papers, then to the land office to claim their quarter section, then to a notary public to sign over their deeds to the corporation, and back to the boarding houses to be paid off. Fifty dollars was the usual fee, although the amount soon fell to $5 or $10 and eventually to the price of a glass of beer. By 1900 almost 3,600,000 acres of valuable forest land were alienated under the measure.

The homesteader, angered though he might be at the shameless exploitation of his nation's resources, reserved his greatest wrath for another representative of eastern capitalism—the speculator. That unpopular individual was as active in the West as he had been through the history of the frontier, gobbling up choice lands, engrossing town sites along streams and railroads, usurping river bottoms and irrigable areas, and piling up giant holdings to be held for high prices. The average small farmer, lured to the West by the hope of a free homestead, found he must accept an inferior farm far from transportation, or pay the exorbitant fees demanded by jobbers. The story of settlement under the Homestead Act was not one of downtrodden laborers rising to affluence through governmental beneficence, but a tale of fraud and monopoly which only ended with seven-eighths of the public domain in the hands of a favored few.

The methods used by speculators to acquire land were necessarily ingenious in a period when free farms were supposedly available to all. Some took advantage of deficiencies in federal laws. The Pre-emption Act of 1841 still remained on the statute books and after 1862 applied to unsurveyed lands, while the Homestead Act governed only surveyed lands. Astute jobbers, moving west in advance of surveying crews, pre-empted and purchased the best spots at $1.25 an acre. Others took advantage of the Homestead Act's failure to provide for cancellation of patent if the grant was sold or transferred. Dummy entrymen were used to secure quarter section after quarter section. The practice was encouraged by a "commutation clause" which allowed any homesteader not wishing to wait five years to purchase 160 acres for $1.25 an acre after six months' residence and certain rudimentary improvements. Jobbers employed gangs of hirelings to spend a summer on some favored spot, then bought the land at a price far below its actual worth.

Speculators were equally inventive in developing devices to circumvent the law's insistence on a suitable habitation. Some built miniature houses, then swore they had erected a "twelve by fourteen dwelling"—failing to specify they meant inches rather than feet. Others rented portable cabins which were wheeled from claim to claim for a $5 rental. Witnesses were hired to swear they had seen a dwelling on the property—omitting the fact the "dwelling" would be on a neighbor's homestead the next day. More threw up crude shacks that let in more climate than they kept out, or solemnly testified they lived in a shingled residence after precariously fastening two shingles to the sides of a tent. Land Office agents who should have detected those frauds could not; districts in the West were so large —some contained 20,000 square miles—that adequate inspection was impossible. Moreover poorly paid clerks who depended on fees for a living would not ferret out violations too scrupulously.

While thousands of acres passed into speculators' hands through fraudulent use of the Pre-emption and Homestead Acts, millions were engrossed by other means. By far the largest land jobbers in the West were the railroads, whose giant holdings did more than anything else to upset the homestead principle of "land for the landless." Those were secured between 1850 and 1871 when Congress freely awarded the public domain to induce construction; 181,000,000 acres were granted railroad corporations during those years, in addition to 3,000,000 acres given road and canal companies. Of the amount going to railroads 131,350,534 acres were given directly, largely to the transcontinental lines in the form of ten to forty alternate sections for each mile of track laid. The remaining 49,000,000 acres were granted through states or, in the case of Texas, by the state itself. In addition the roads were given 840,000 acres by local governments, towns, and individuals. Railroads were the nation's largest landowners when the settlement of the Great Plains began.

To make matters worse, from the settlers' point of view, the form in which grants were made withheld additional millions of acres from frontiersmen. Usually Congress gave each railroad a right-of-way together with alternate sections in a strip from twenty to eighty miles wide—twenty if the road was given ten sections to the mile, forty if the grant was for twenty sections, and eighty if forty sections were awarded. Usually the whole strip was withdrawn from settlement for several years while the road selected its right-of-way and decided which alternate sections to keep. Frequently even larger tracts were withheld; if lands within the grant were already occupied, the railroad could choose its acreage from nearby territory and the Land Office sometimes set aside strips 60 to 120 miles wide in which corporation officials could make their choice. Until they decided homesteaders were forced to stake their claims from thirty to sixty miles from transportation. Even when that was not done, alternate sections retained by the government near railroads were either sold at $2.50 an acre or limited to homesteads of eighty acres. Settlers wanting choice land adjacent to communication had to buy from railroads at a price which in 1880 averaged $4.76 an acre.

While large portions of the public domain went to railroads, equally vast amounts were given the states under the Morrill Land-Grant Act of 1862. That measure, which was designed to encourage agricultural education, granted each state 30,000 acres of western land for each of its senators and representatives in Congress, with the understanding the proceeds be used to endow colleges where young men could be trained in scientific farming. The older states, which benefited most because of their large population, were authorized to locate their acreage anywhere in the West. Thus New York selected forest lands in Wisconsin and prairie lands scattered through the western Mississippi Valley to utilize its 990,000 acre allotment. In all the states received 140,000,000 acres through the Morrill Act and similar measures. None was given to homesteaders; nearly all passed through the hands of speculators on its way to final users. Often jobbers purchased thousands of acres at fifty cents an acre, then resold to pioneers at prices ranging from $5 to $10.

Speculating companies also secured western territory by direct purchase. Although sales of that sort contradicted the spirit of the Homestead Act, Congress made no move to stop them and underpaid Land Office clerks could usually be persuaded to part with plots at $1.25 an acre. Lumbering and mineral interests were especially active in arranging sales; typical was the Higgins Land Company which obtained 11,000 acres of Minnesota iron land—some worth $50,000 an acre a few years later—for $14,000. Some of the best prairie land of Kansas, Nebraska, Dakota, and the Pacific states was sold to speculators in blocks of 10,000 to 600,000 acres before Congress ended the practice in 1889 by limiting purchases to 320 acres. Until that time more land was sold yearly after 1862 than before the Homestead Act was passed. Other jobbers secured western tracts by buying land warrants issued as bounties to veterans from the nation's many wars. Revolutionary scrip was still in circulation in the 1880's, as well as bounty warrants from all conflicts since that time, and could be bought for less than face value. Antique deeds and direct sales allowed speculators to secure about 100,000,000 acres between 1862 and the close of the century.

Another source of land for jobbers was the shrinking Indian reservations. As tribe after tribe surrendered its holdings during the period of concentration after the Civil War, the reserves were either sold by the Indians or disposed of by the government. In either case speculators benefited; natives were anxious to sell in large blocs and the United States, which was pledged to compensate tribes for confiscated lands, could not open the regions to homesteaders. Nearly all the plundered reservations were sold in giant tracts to speculators eager to purchase lands already improved by Indians. Not until 1887, when the Dawes Severalty Act stipulated that reservation land be sold to actual settlers in 160-acre units, was that source closed to jobbers, who in the meantime secured more than 100,000,000 acres of Indian territory.

Land Office officials, summing up the amounts given or sold to speculators and corporations, found the results impressive:

| | | |
|---|---|---|
| Grants to railroads | 181,000,000 | acres |
| Grants to states | 140,000,000 | acres |
| Direct sales by Land Office | 100,000,000 | acres |
| Indian lands sold | 100,000,000 | acres |
| Total | 521,000,000 | acres |

Half a billion acres were surrendered to monopolists in an era when orators boasted the United States was giving land free to its poverty-stricken masses! While the wealthy few engrossed those princely estates, only 600,000 patents to homesteads were issued, totaling 80,000,000 acres. If every homesteader was a bona fide farmer, only one acre out of every six was given away; actually many were dummy entrymen, cattlemen, and representatives of mining or lumbering companies. Probably not more than one acre in every nine went directly to small pioneers, the supposed beneficiaries of the Homestead Act!

The results of the incongruous land system were clear to every new settler who reached the West. He could, he found, either accept an isolated homestead on poor soil distant from transportation, or buy his farm from one of the speculators there before him. If the pioneer happened to arrive in Kansas between 1868 and 1872 he was confronted with a dozen advertisements for land that was "Better Than A Homestead"; the Union Pacific Railroad offered 1,200,000 acres at from $1 to $15 an acre, the Kansas Pacific Railroad 5,000,000 acres at $1 to $6, the Kansas and Neosho Valley Railroad 1,500,000 acres at $2 to $8, the Capital Land Agency 1,000,000 acres at comparable prices, the state of Kansas 500,000 acres of school and college lands at $3 to $5, the federal government 6,000 acres of Indian lands at the same rate, and smaller jobbers 350,000 acres at $3 to $10. That was typical of all the Great Plains country. Frontiersmen could get good land in the West, but they had to pay heavily for it.

Yet the Homestead Act, although failing to provide "free land for the homeless," did advertise the trans-Mississippi country. All the world knew that a bountiful government would award honest enterprise with priceless grants, and if hopeful homeseekers found only sordid speculation at the end of their rainbow, they nevertheless stayed on to break the plains. They had the tools needed for the conquest—fences, windmills, and farm machinery—and if they entered upon their task with bitterness in their hearts, they were still effective pioneers. The way was open for the advancing agriculture frontier.

# CHAPTER XXXV

# The Farmers' Frontier

## 1870-1890

The waning years of the nineteenth century witnessed the greatest movement of peoples in the history of the United States. Millions of farmers,
held back for a generation by the forbidding features of the Great Plains,
surged westward between 1870 and 1890. They filled Kansas and Nebraska,
engulfed the level grasslands of Dakota, occupied the rolling foothills of
Wyoming and Montana, and in a desperate bid for vanishing lands,
elbowed Indians from the last native sanctuary in Oklahoma. A larger domain was settled in the last three decades of the century than in all America's
past; 407,000,000 acres were occupied and 189,000,000 improved between
1607 and 1870; 430,000,000 acres peopled and 225,000,000 placed under
cultivation between 1870 and 1900. Surveying that breath-taking advance,
the director of the census announced in 1890 that the country's "unsettled
area has been so broken into by isolated bodies of settlement that there
can hardly be said to be a frontier line."

The forces which sent men westward through the nation's history operated during those years—dissatisfaction at home, alluring prospects ahead,
the hope for sudden wealth. Two groups felt their influence. One lived in
the Mississippi Valley states which, having followed the usual frontier
pattern by increasing their population for thirty years, were becoming so
overcrowded emigration was setting in. During the decade of the 1870's
every state bordering the Mississippi except Arkansas and Louisiana lost
population, and they remained static. Kansas gained 347,000 new settlers
during that ten-year period, while increases in Nebraska, Texas, and other
Plains states were proportional. The trend continued between 1880 and
1890 when Iowa, Missouri, and the states of the Old Northwest con-

tributed more than 1,000,000 pioneers to the advancing frontier. The greatest gains were registered in the area just west of the Minnesota-Louisiana tier, with Nebraska increasing its population by 240,000 people. The end of the westward movement was indicated during the next decade when Kansas, Nebraska, Iowa, Missouri, and Arkansas all lost settlers as hard times and the lure of the city turned men eastward once more.

The second group that helped people the Plains came from abroad. Some were Irish peasants who drifted westward as railroad laborers, then stayed to till the soil. Nebraska boasted six predominantly Irish colonies in 1890 (one named O'Neill), Minnesota had four, and Dakota Territory numbered 20,000 natives of Ireland among its inhabitants. Canada also contributed heavily in a period when the inflated American currency gave Canadian dollars twice their normal buying power. Still more came from northern Europe. Germans, already well established in the upper Mississippi Valley, continued to migrate by the thousands to Kansas, Nebraska, Dakota, Minnesota, and Texas. Peasants from the Scandinavian countries were even more numerous. The "America Fever" lured 10,000 immigrants from Norway, Sweden, and Denmark in 1865, and the number increased yearly until 1882 when 105,362 arrived. The rugged climate of Minnesota and Dakota appealed to those sturdy farmers; four hundred Minnesota towns bore Swedish names by 1890, while travelers in eastern Dakota reported that anyone speaking Norwegian could find companionship sooner than one whose sole language was English.

Both natives and foreigners who peopled the Great Plains were attracted by the most effective advertising campaign ever to influence world migrations. Steamship companies, anxious to reap a harvest of passenger fares, invested heavily in European newspaper space, marred the walls of half the Continent with their posters, and provided free transportation for immigrants wishing to revisit the old country providing they urged others to return. Western states maintained immigration bureaus in the East and Europe, where hired agents scattered propaganda and urged farmers to migrate to the land of plenty. Minnesota established its bureau in 1867, Iowa followed in 1870, and the other states fell into line during the next years. When compared with the Far West pictured by those expert boosters, even the Garden of Eden seemed unattractive.

Their efforts were surpassed by those of the West's principal colonizers—the land-grant railroads. They stood to benefit doubly from western settlement; newcomers would not only buy their land but create way traffic previously lacking in the sparsely settled region. Hence every western road set up both a Land Department, entrusted with selling the alternate sections granted by the government, and a Bureau of Immigration. The former

priced the land—usually at from $2 to $8 an acre—arranged credit terms
needed by immigrants, and supervised numerous devices to attract prospects: reduced round-trip tickets for possible buyers, land-viewing expeditions where purchasers were lavishly entertained, free transportation for
settlers' household effects, elaborate "reception houses" along the right of
way where buyers and land viewers were accommodated. Although the Burlington's boast that "better terms than these have never been offered to
purchasers of land and probably never will be," was exaggerated, Land
Departments did a yeoman's job of attracting settlers.

The Bureaus of Immigration were just as active. Their task was to advertise the Great Plains until all the rest of the world contributed a share
of its population to the area. If some who came settled on railroad lands
so much the better; those who did not were equally welcome as producers
of goods which the roads could carry. All railroads maintained agents in
eastern seaports to greet immigrants, arrange their transportation west, and
see to it that no rival company lured away prospective settlers. Agencies
were also set up in Europe; the Northern Pacific Railroad's pattern—a
central office in London with branches in Liverpool, Germany, Holland,
and the Scandinavian countries—was typical of most lines. Agents were
usually returned immigrants with outstanding persuasive powers, or the
leading personages in their communities. Ministers were often employed in
Scandinavian countries in the hope they could influence many to migrate
through personal appeal.

The agents' principal task was to let every European know the American
West was a land of milk and honey. Their brochures, newspaper advertisements, and posters were glossy examples of overstatement. The Northern
Pacific Railroad assured possible settlers the country it served was so healthy
every known malady was cured there, while the Platte Valley became, in
the language of a Union Pacific agent, "a flowery meadow of great fertility
clothed in nutritious grasses, and watered by numerous streams." Usually
the leaflets stressed profits awaiting settlers on the Great Plains; "many
fields of properly cultivated wheat," one Burlington advertisement declared, "have yielded *over thirty bushels of grain per acre, and many fields
of corn over seventy.*" Stories of personal success were often cited—of one
immigrant who reached the West in poverty seven years before and was
worth $10,000, of another whose $8,000 investment in Kansas lands yielded
$11,000 a year. Nor did such fortunes mean backbreaking toil; "settling on
the prairie which is ready for the plow," a Union Pacific writer pointed out,
"is different from plunging into a region covered with timber. Nature
seems to have provided protection for man and beast; all that is required
is diligent labor and economy to ensure an early reward." The women were

not forgotten. One Burlington brochure reminded them men so outnumbered ladies in the West that "when a daughter of the East is once beyond the Missouri she rarely recrosses it except on a bridal tour." Homes and wealth awaited everyone in the Shangri La pictured by the railroads!

The results of the advertising, and of promotional work carried on among veterans' organizations by company agents, cannot be assessed accurately. Occasionally agents could point to tangible examples—colonies of several hundred settlers from Germany or New England who moved west in a body—but most newcomers arrived as individuals. Undoubtedly thousands were influenced by the Bureaus of Immigration; propaganda campaigns on such a scale—both the Burlington and Union Pacific spent $1,000,000 on advertising—were certain to have some effect. No region in the history of the frontier benefited as did the Great Plains from induced colonization.

Effective as the appeals were, they succeeded only because western farming promised unusual profits. Every pioneer knew that steadily expanding markets awaited his produce. Native population increased rapidly in the prosperous postwar years, both by natural growth and the influx of 14,000,000 immigrants. More and more must be fed, for in that day of industrialization, non-food-producing city dwellers multiplied faster than the population as a whole. Americans were hearty eaters; two and one-half acres of farm and ten acres of pasture were required to provide the meat, eggs, poultry, and grain consumed by each yearly, in contrast to the quarter-acre needed in such a low-subsistence-level country as Japan. That meant a steady domestic market for everything the farmer grew, while any surpluses could be shipped abroad. England's consumption of American wheat increased yearly during the 1870's, reaching a high point in 1880 when 153,000,000 bushels were sold there for $191,000,000. Pioneers believed the demand would keep prices high forever. In proof they pointed to the fact that between 1866 and 1881 wheat seldom slumped below the dollar a bushel which meant prosperity for the producer. With profits virtually assured, a farm in western Kansas or Dakota seemed an absolutely safe investment.

Moreover scientists and industrialists were opening new markets for homesteaders. Their greatest contribution was an improved milling process which allowed the wheat frontier to extend into the Great Plains. That section, experiment showed, was ill suited to the soft winter wheat grown by eastern farmers; the cold winters of the northern Plains killed seed before it sprouted, while wide seasonable variations of heat and cold in Kansas or Nebraska destroyed the tender kernels. Only "hard" wheat could be grown there. Trial and error soon demonstrated that the hard spring variety grown in northern Europe thrived in the Minnesota-Dakota coun-try, while the Kansas-Nebraska region was ideally suited to hard-kerneled "Turkey Red" wheat imported from the Crimea. Neither could be grown commercially, however, until a satisfactory milling method was evolved. The older process—grinding between two grooved millstones set close together—would not do; the brittle husks splintered into such fine frag-ments they could not be sifted out, leaving the flour dirty and rancid. Moreover chunks of the glutinous kernel clung to the shattered husks and were lost. Hard wheat could never be marketed until those defects were overcome.

Minneapolis millers, anxious for profits that would be theirs if they found a means of milling spring wheat, solved the problem by developing the "New Process" method of making flour. This called for a series of successive grindings. First the hard kernels were cracked between two smooth grindstones, revolving slowly and set wide apart, which broke the berries into coarse particles without scorching them. The resulting mixture—half flour and half "middlings"—was then sifted through cloth to "bolt out" the flour, while the "middlings" passed to a "purifier" of moving sieves fanned by a strong air current that separated husks and bran from the white chunks of wheat kernel. Those were reground into a rich flour which, because of its higher gluten content, produced more bread per unit than ordinary starch flour. "New Process" flour was in such demand that the Washburn Mills of Minneapolis, the first to perfect the method in 1871, amassed profits of $650,000 in three years before competition lowered the price to a reasonable level. Within a short time the "gradual reduction" system was not only generally adopted but improved by substituting re-volving rollers for millstones, a device copied from Hungary where hard wheat was also grown. After experiments with metal and porcelain rollers, millers in 1879 perfected a corrugated, chilled-iron roller that was tough, long-lasting, and nonbreakable. When seven or eight were arranged in series, each grinding more finely than the last and with purifiers and sieves between, pure white flour was produced more rapidly and with one-third less power than with millstones. By 1881 the mills of Minneapolis, St. Louis, and Kansas City were ready to turn any quantities of hard wheat into "New Process" flour.

Improved methods for handling grain also broadened farmers' markets by reducing middlemen's fees. They were developed rapidly during the postwar years when national prosperity placed a premium on efficiency; in such an era older practices of moving bagged wheat by hand seemed out-moded. By the beginning of the 1870's a farmer could take his wagonload of wheat to an "elevator"—wood or concrete warehouses built along railroads—knowing that from then on it would be handled mechanically. Conveyor belts lifted the grain into a bin within the elevator, chutes carried it to waiting freight cars, locomotives pulled the loaded cars to lake ports where the golden kernels were cascaded directly into the holds of eastern-bound steamers, or to Minneapolis where moving belts unloaded the trains at the door of flour-mills. The thousands of bushels hourly handled by mechanical methods saved millions of dollars for farmers and consumers.

The vision of limitless markets conjured up in the minds of pioneers by these inventions was needed to hold them on the Great Plains when they learned the discrepancy between the promises of railroad advertisements and grim reality. Life was hard in a land where nature provided few comforts needed by man; every necessity must be painfully fashioned from inadequate materials by backbreaking toil. How to build a house where there was no timber, how to obtain water where there were no springs, how to keep warm where there was nothing to burn, how to battle the elements where there was no shelter—those were the problems faced by frontiersmen. Many failed to solve them and fled back east; those who stayed on conquered obstacles that would have defeated men of lesser stamina.

Adequate housing was the most pressing need. Pioneers usually built a dugout first, scooping a hole in the side of a hill, blocking the front with a wall of cut sod, and covering the top with a few poles which held up a layer of prairie grass and dirt. Although the flimsy dwellings were often washed away by rains and were always dirty, they housed whole families for months or even years before giving way to a more permanent structure—the sod house. That was made by turning over even furrows in a half-acre plot where turf was particularly thick. The long strips were then cut into three-foot sections, carted to the building site, and laid into walls, with joints broken as in brick laying and space provided for two windows and a door. If lumber was available the settler built a frame roof; if not he set a ridge pole on two forked sticks, laid more poles as rafters, and covered his house with a layer of prairie grass topped by another of thick sod. Ambitious farmers plastered their dwellings with a mixture of clay and ashes or smoothed the walls with a spade, but most left the rough sod where it was placed. A wooden door made from packing boxes, a cloth over the windows, a blanket hung down the center to make two rooms, a few chairs fashioned from such nail kegs and drygoods cases as were available, and the sod house was ready for occupancy.

The rough dwellings had some advantages—they were warm in winter and cool in summer, never blew down, and were safe from prairie fires—but life within their dank walls was thoroughly unpleasant. Even in dry weather dirt and straw which dropped from the ceiling was the despair of tidy eastern housewives. During rainy periods sod roofs became soggy quagmires that poured rivulets upon the homesteader, then dripped dismally for three days before drying. In those trying times the mud floors were too swampy to walk upon and wives could cook only with an umbrella held over the stove; after they were over every stitch of clothing must be hung out to dry. Little wonder that every family built a frame dwelling as soon as possible, or that a few years in a sod house convinced many a pioneer the Great Plains were no place for him.

The search for water was just as difficult. If the frontiersman lived near a stream he hauled the precious fluid to his home in barrels; if not he depended on rainwater collected in swampy buffalo wallows or in dug cisterns. Freezing in winter, hot and swarming with insects in summer, the ground water was a source of "prairie fever"—or typhoid—which ravaged Plains settlers. The only alternative was a hand-dug well. That difficult task was accomplished with the help of a wife or neighbor; while one dug, the other hauled the dirt to the surface in a bucket operated by a windlass until a hole several feet across reached down to water level. In lowlands near streams wells were only forty or fifty feet deep, but on higher table lands they extended downward two or three hundred feet before water was reached. The days of backbreaking work with pick and shovel that went into digging exemplified the difficulties of life on the Plains, yet not until the 1880's was well-drilling machinery sufficiently common to relieve pioneers of the task.

Fuel was as hard to get as water. Those who lived within forty or fifty miles of a stream gladly hauled wood that distance so long as the supply lasted; others depended on dried buffalo excrement which was gathered by the wagonload and piled in ricks for winter use. As the herds were eliminated even buffalo "chips" became so rare travelers usually carried a bag to salvage dung found along their way. Cow manure was also burned near the cattle trails; farmers encouraged drovers to bed down herds nearby, knowing several hundred pounds of fuel would be left behind. Those expedients were only temporary, and most plainsmen had to fall back on their own ingenuity to keep warm. Some grew sunflowers, cut the woody stalks while green, and seasoned them against the coming winter. More used hay, twisting the dried grass into "cats" so it would burn slowly, anl piling it about the door of their sod houses. Special stoves for hay burning were widely sold during the 1870's; one common type contained two long cylinders which were filled alternately, then fed into the firebox by a spring device until emptied. None of the ingenious contraptions worked well. They required constant refueling, filled sod houses with noxious gases, and constantly threatened to ignite the piles of inflammable hay nearby. Later farmers burned corncobs or dried cornstalks, but no satisfactory fuel was found until railroads brought coal into the Great Plains.

If the Plains environment made life difficult, the procession of the equinoxes made living intolerable. Every season brought new hardships for the pioneer. In the spring, floods often surged across the countryside as bank-level streams, swelled into torrents by the sudden runoff of winter snows, swept houses and livestock before them. Summer usually ushered in a searing wave of heat and drought that withered grass, cracked the parched soil, and burned young crops to a crisp. With the temperature hovering about the 110-degree mark for weeks at a time and south winds blowing across the baked countryside like blasts from hell, streams dried up, animals died, and men staggered through their tasks, their faces chalk-white with dried perspiration. Kansans might jest that sinners were always buried in overcoats to protect them from temperature changes, but in their hearts they knew the heat was no joking matter; one scorching summer sent 30,000 newcomers back to the more comfortable East.

During more temperate years a worse plague threatened plainsmen—a grasshopper invasion. They came without warning, those myriads of insects, flying before north winds in mile-wide clouds that blotted out the sun. When they settled they pelted the sides of houses like hailstones, covered trees so densely limbs broke, and buried the whole countryside under a living mass several inches deep. Chickens and hogs ate until they were sick; men with strings tied about their pant legs to keep pests from their clothing rushed to cover the well before the water was polluted. Nothing else could be saved. The hoppers ate everything: cornstalks, young grain, vegetables under the ground, leaves and bark from trees, sweaty wood from plow handles or pitchforks, weathered lumber on house walls, mosquito netting in the windows, and clothes within the cabins, leaving, as one settler put it, "nothing but the mortgage." There was no living in the desolation they left behind. Heartsick farmers slaughtered their livestock and headed east, with signs on their wagons proclaiming they came "From Kansas, where it rains grasshoppers, fire and destruction." Invasions did not come every year—the worst was in 1874 when the whole Great Plains country from Dakota to northern Texas was devastated—but no pioneer felt safe until autumn winds signaled the end of summer.

Then a new danger threatened. The tinder-dry grass, if ignited by a chance spark, would send prairie fires raging across miles of countryside. Few people lost their lives in conflagrations—farmers soon learned to keep a circle of land around their homes burned over as protection, and travelers carried matches to start backfires—yet property losses and discomfort were common. Even those were preferable to the hardships facing frontiersmen when autumn gave way to winter. Storms that swept the open grasslands during that season were awesome things; ice, dust, and snow particles were whipped before a raging wind with such force they sifted into the snuggest dwellings. Settlers, awakening after an all-night blizzard, found their furniture covered by inches of snow and their houses so cold food froze on the table, jars of preserves burst even near the stove, and bread was so frigid it could be sliced only after warming. Animals suffered more than humans. Ice covered cattle until their heads, as big as bushel baskets, had to be rested on the ground; smaller animals could only survive in settlers' houses. Often a pioneer family lived for days with horses, pigs, calves, and chickens cooped within a crowded sod house while the thermometer rested at twenty or thirty degrees below zero.

Although these intolerable conditions did not endure always, there was little in the environment of the Great Plains to attract pleasure seekers. But the frontiersmen who went west were after wealth rather than fun. What mattered a few discomforts when opportunity beckoned? Winter blizzards and summer droughts could be endured so long as the West held cheap lands, ready markets, and the thrill of pioneering. Every newcomer was sure nature would treat him kindly or that he was strong enough to battle the elements until prosperity smiled. That hope sent the farmers' frontier surging westward in the post-Civil War years.

When the movement began settlements planted during the prewar era fringed eastern Kansas and Nebraska. Atchison and Leavenworth on the Missouri, Topeka and Lawrence on the Kansas River, Omaha in Nebraska, and the dozen farming communities between, were all small, all nestled in river bottoms, and all in the primitive stage where new arrivals absorbed most local produce. With the close of the Civil War the influx began. Pioneers moved out along streams first of all, where rich alluvial soils and timber waited them, then after 1870 advanced onto the rolling plains. Every railroad building across Kansas or Nebraska drew settlers westward; along the tracks of the Kansas Pacific the frontier advanced a hundred miles between 1870 and 1872. "Settlements," wrote a passenger, "are springing up rapidly. Even the lapse of a few months makes a perceptible difference to the eye of the passing traveler." After 1875 when the Red River War cleared southwestern Kansas of Indians the tide swung in that direction, following the Santa Fe Railroad and scattering such towns as Wichita, Wellington, and Dodge City in its wake. Other settlers built their homes along the Union Pacific right-of-way in Nebraska. By 1880 both states were settled to the 98th meridian and adventurous farmers, misled by a cycle of unusually wet years, were pushing into semiarid regions beyond. Kansas boasted nearly 850,000 inhabitants that year and Nebraska more than 450,000. Every acre suitable to cultivation was under the plow.

Other frontiersmen turned northward to the Dakota country. The peopling of that region began in the late 1850's when settlers from Minnesota

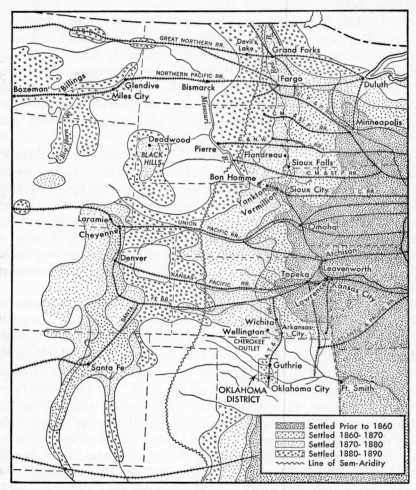

The Farmers' Frontier, 1870-1890

and Nebraska, lured by the advertising of two speculating concerns—the Western Town Company of Iowa and the Dakota Land Company of Minnesota—crossed the Missouri River to lay out the towns of Flandreau, Sioux Falls, Vermillion, Yankton, and Bon Homme. Although the thinly scattered pioneers were persistent enough to win organization for Dakota Territory in 1861, migration did not assume sizable proportions until

1868 when the Sioux Indians were driven to a reservation west of the Missouri River. The result was the first "Dakota Boom" between 1868 and 1873. Favorable weather and excellent crops contributed to the rush, but equally important were railroad connections that assured farmers decent markets. The Illinois Central Railroad brought southeastern Dakota within selling distance of Chicago when its tracks reached Sioux City in 1868, while branch lines to Yankton and Sioux Falls built during the next years made marketing even easier. Other roads opened the northeastern fringes of the territory at about the same time; the Chicago and Northwestern Railroad reached Watertown in 1873, the Northern Pacific Railroad extended to Bismarck, and the St. Paul and Pacific Railroad touched Wahpeton.

Each line attracted settlers. The region about Yankton and Vermillion received the first influx; by the end of 1868 10,000 pioneers were breaking sod there and others continued to come in such numbers land prices skyrocketed to $20 an acre. More moved northward along the Big Sioux River, or laid out such towns as Fargo and Grand Forks in the Red River Valley; the latter hamlet contained eight houses, a store, a hotel, and two saloons in 1872. More adventurous pioneers advanced across Dakota with the Northern Pacific Railroad, to found islands of settlement about Jamestown, Bismarck, and other outposts. Before the Panic of 1873 slowed the westward movement, Dakota boasted a population of more than 20,000.

Between 1873 and 1878, when the second "Dakota Boom" began, the territory grew slowly, but during those years the basis for a new rush was laid. Partially responsible was the Black Hills gold rush of 1875; the 10,000 prospectors who flocked to the mines created an unparalleled market for farm produce. Equally important was activity forced on the Northern Pacific Railroad by the Panic of 1873. Officials of that bankrupt line, realizing their road could never prosper until lands bordering its right of way were settled, decided on an experiment to demonstrate the area's fertility. An expert wheat grower from Minnesota, Oliver Dalrymple, was provided with eighteen sections of Red River Valley land and adequate capital for its development. Scorning traditional farming methods, Dalrymple hired gangs of workers, bought machinery by the carload, and launched a large-scale experiment that startled the whole West. The result was phenomenal: a yield of twenty-five bushels to the acre on a 4,500 acre plot that cost only $9.50 an acre to cultivate. With wheat selling at ninety cents a bushel profits were well over 100 per cent. Eastern capital, quick to sense opportunity, flowed in at once as syndicates bought up estates of from 5,000 to 100,000 acres along the Red River, a broad bottomland ideal for wheat growing. By 1878 "bonanza farms" covered the three-hundred-mile length of the valley.

The demonstrated success of these ventures, the chance of selling food to Black Hills miners, and the advertising of a territorial Bureau of Immigration established in 1875, all contributed to the "Dakota Boom" that set in after 1878, but more important was railroad activity in the northern Plains country. The westward-building lines from Iowa and Minnesota which stopped construction with the Panic of 1873 were fully revived by the end of the decade and ready to extend their tracks across Dakota Territory. Two, the Chicago, Milwaukee and St. Paul Railroad and the Chicago and Northwestern Railroad, reached the Missouri River in 1880, opening most of southeastern Dakota to settlement. The northern portions were served by the Northern Pacific Railroad which used the postdepression years to construct branches from its Bismarck line to La Moure and other pioneer towns. Both those roads were anxious to sell their federal land grants and build up way traffic; their advertising lured thousands of immigrants to the territory.

An even more energetic role was played by a newcomer among western lines, the Great Northern. The Great Northern Railroad was formed in 1879 by James J. Hill, a financial genius who recognized a profitable field for exploitation in the belt of Plains country lying north of the Northern Pacific tracks. After learning railroading as an employee of the St. Paul and Pacific Railroad, Hill used the Panic of 1873 to win control of the company that employed him, interested eastern capital, and by 1879 was ready to begin construction. Rails were laid northward to Fargo and Grand Forks, then the road turned west and built slowly across Dakota, reaching Devil's Lake in 1883 and Seattle in 1890. Its creeping progress was carefully planned by Hill. Realizing the Great Northern had no land grant and must depend on traffic for revenue, he made every effort to develop the country as construction went on; feeder lines were built, immigrants brought from Europe, model farms laid out, blooded cattle imported, money loaned to farmers, and free transportation offered homeseekers. The thousands of pioneers who broke the plains of northern Dakota were brought west by the road's colonization program.

With transportation provided and returning prosperity in the air, the way was open for the "Dakota Boom" of 1878–85. Settlers came by the thousands to the new El Dorado, from Europe and from the Mississippi Valley states. They filled the river bottoms, then pushed out across the Plains in the wake of railroads. "You may," wrote one observer, "stand ankle deep in the short grass of the uninhabited wilderness; next month a mixed train will glide over the waste and stop at some point where the railroad has decided to locate a town. Men, women and children will jump out of the cars, and their chattels will tumble out after them. From that

moment the building begins." All was bustle and excitement amidst such
scenes—streets jammed with homesteaders, railroad cars trundling westward at the rate of a thousand a week loaded with immigrants' goods,
crowds jamming land offices. Even the figures for homestead grants in the
territory reflected the feverish expansion:

| | | | |
|------|------------------|------|-------------------|
| 1877 | 213,000 acres    | 1883 | 7,317,000 acres   |
| 1878 | 1,377,000 acres  | 1884 | 11,083,000 acres  |
| 1879 | 1,657,000 acres  | 1886 | 3,075,000 acres   |
| 1882 | 4,360,000 acres  | 1888 | 1,881,000 acres   |

Nor did the grants include millions of acres sold by railroads or acquired
through other means than homesteading. So rapidly did land pass into
private hands that by 1885 all Dakota east of the Missouri River was
settled and the population was 550,000—a 400 per cent increase over 1880.
Crop failures during dry years at the close of the decade ended the boom
and drove some pioneers back east, but the census of 1890 showed 500,000
people still in the territory, occupying most of the lands suitable for
agriculture.

While Dakota boomed, the mountainous regions farther west gained
population more slowly. Wyoming's development began in early 1867
when speculators, anticipating the coming of the Union Pacific tracks, laid
out such towns as Cheyenne and Laramie along the right of way. Those
pioneer outposts grew so rapidly—Cheyenne contained a motley crew of
6,000 track layers, cattle rustlers, freighters, prospectors, trappers, ranchers,
gamblers, and dispensers of assorted vice by the end of the year—that
Wyoming won territorial organization in 1868. Farmers, however, avoided
the semiarid High Plains until the early 1880's when a few pioneers sought
homes along the eastern fringes of the Big Horn Mountains where streams
could be used for irrigation. Their success launched a mild rush to northern
Wyoming; 2,000,000 acres, irrigated by 5,000 miles of ditches, were placed
under cultivation during the decade. Yet only 62,255 people lived there
in 1890. Wyoming, with its vast stretches of arid or mountainous countryside, was destined to remain sparsely settled for many years.

That was also the fate of Montana. Farmers began drifting in during
the 1870's, attracted by the prospect of feeding the permanent mining
population in Butte and other mountain towns, but not until 1881 when
the Northern Pacific tracks entered the territory was there any sizable
influx. The newcomers followed the railroad westward, laying out such
towns as Glendive, Miles City, and Billings, and spread their farms across
the Yellowstone Valley. Montana gained 100,000 settlers during the dec-

ade, reaching a population of 132,000 in 1890, yet most of the territory was too arid or mountainous to attract farmers.

The "Dakota Boom" and the development of Wyoming and Montana during the 1880's created the usual demand for statehood. Throughout the decade petitions from the territories were ignored, largely because all three were predominantly Republican, and the Democrats, who controlled one or the other houses of Congress, refused to consider their admission. Not until 1888 when the election that placed Benjamin Harrison in the White House gave Republicans a slim majority in both House and Senate was action possible. The triumphant members of the party, after assuring themselves even greater strength by dividing Dakota Territory in two and heeding the pleas of rapidly growing Washington Territory, in February, 1889, authorized North Dakota, South Dakota, Montana, and Washington to frame constitutions. All were admitted in an "Omnibus Bill" adopted in November of that year. Wyoming and nearby Idaho, indignant at the slight, lost no time in drawing up their own frames of government and demanding statehood. Congress responded in 1890 by erecting the last of the northwest territories into states.

As the frontier swept across the northwestern Plains, another stream of pioneers moved into the Southwest. Texas was the mecca that lured many; during the 1870's the number of farms in the state increased from 61,125 to 174,184 and the line of settlement reached almost to the line of semi-aridity. The rapid advance, which paralleled the peopling of Kansas, set the stage for one of the most dramatic events in the history of American expansion. Ahead of the advancing arms of settlement were sterile lands unfit for farming; between them were millions of acres of good soil assigned to the twenty-two tribes that occupied the Indian Territory. Why, frontiersmen asked, should that rich domain be left in the hands of 75,000 primitive savages? Why should industrious Americans seek land in vain while each square mile of the West's finest garden spot was held by only one redskinned "varmint"? Why not open the Indian Territory to farmers who could make its treeless wastes blossom? That demand sent thousands of lawless intruders into the Indian Territory during the 1880's, forced the United States to recast its Indian policy, and culminated in the rush of "Oklahoma Boomers" onto the nation's last public domain.

The first interest in opening the Indian Territory was shown not by pioneers but by the railroads that crossed the region or planned to build there: the Atlantic and Pacific Railroad, the Missouri, Kansas and Texas Railroad, and the Atchison, Topeka and Santa Fe Railroad. Officials of those lines, aware that prosperity depended on developing way traffic, petitioned Congress to open some Indian lands as early as 1874, but a few years of halfhearted agitation convinced them Washington would never act until their pleas were backed by popular pressure. If that was needed, the railroads must produce it. They apparently found an instrument for their purpose in Elias C. Boudinot, a disgruntled Cherokee who had broken with his tribe and was working as a clerk in the national capital. Boudinot, after receiving several financial favors from the Missouri, Kansas and Texas Railroad, showed his gratitude by publishing a long article in the Chicago *Times* during the spring of 1879. The Indian country, he declared in his widely reprinted letter, contained 13,000,000 unsettled acres that belonged to no tribe and were really a part of the public domain. He told westerners the area could only be opened by public demand, and offered to supply all interested with maps and full instructions. Although proof is lacking, the expensive literature Boudinot sent out to questioners was probably supplied by railroads.

Like most effective propaganda, Boudinot's exaggerated statements contained a kernel of truth. Lying in the heart of the Indian Territory were 2,000,000 acres of good land which had been ceded to the United States by the Creeks and Seminole, and not yet assigned to any tribe. That was the mecca to which frontier eyes turned as railroad advertising centered western attention on the Indian country. All through the summer of 1879 camp fires of Kansas pioneers buzzed with talk of the "Oklahoma District" —its mild climate, its sparkling streams, its fertile soil. Editors in Missouri and Kansas, catching the fever, filled their columns with glowing descriptions, or apoplectically denounced the government for closing such a Garden of Eden to settlers. Excitable homeseekers, reading those tales, decided to take matters into their own hands. Little bands of them drifted into the Oklahoma District during the early summer, bent on staking out farms. Federal troops managed to check the invasion by barricading the Kansas border with six army camps, but no feeble barrier could keep frontiersmen from lands they wanted as their own.

That was demonstrated during 1880 when the "Boomers" found a leader. David L. Payne, who led the assault on the Oklahoma District for the next four years, was an Indian fighter, an unsuccessful homesteader, a congenital drifter, "a giant physically, tough as a pine knot, courageous as a lion, with a perfect ignorance of fear." He reached Kansas early in 1880, still smarting from his dismissal as assistant doorkeeper of the House of Representatives, and immediately led a party of eleven frontiersmen into the district. When they were discovered by troops and unceremoniously escorted back across the border, Payne was not discouraged; in June he started south again, this time with twenty followers. Once more soldiers found them, ushered them out of the Indian country, and fined them $1,000

—a sentence that meant nothing because neither Payne nor his ragged disciples owned any property. By October, 1880, he was in Kansas once more, organizing a force of several hundred homeseekers for a new invasion. Soldiers held them back by shooting their horses until an early autumn forced them to scatter, but Payne was undaunted. For the next two years he and his fellow "Boomers" played a game of hide-and-seek along the Kansas borderland; one indignant officer complained life there was reduced to chasing Payne into Oklahoma and driving him out again.

The preliminary invasions prepared the way for the first organized assault on the Indian Territory. David Payne fathered the attack. During the spring of 1883 he welded the Kansas homeseekers into a compact society—the Oklahoma Colony—with a set of officers (including Payne as president), dues of $2.50 a year, and an oath binding members to defy the government until Oklahoma District was theirs. Within a year the law-defying group boasted 40,000 members and a treasury balance of $100,000. The Oklahoma Colony gave Payne his last chance to open the Indian country by force. Gathering between five and six hundred heavily armed members at Hunnewell on the Kansas line, he led them south in the spring of 1884, publicly proclaiming his intention to shoot it out with any soldiers that tried to stop them. For a time the invaders clung to an outpost in the district, until pressure from troops whittled down their numbers to a point where Payne and a few followers could be arrested. Taken to Ft. Smith for trial, Payne was soon released to return to Kansas, where he was welcomed by a parade of "Boomers" carrying banners that proclaimed "On To Oklahoma," and "We Go This Time To Stay."

When Payne died in November his mantle descended to one of his lieutenants, W. L. Couch, who proved to be as aggressive as his predecessor. Bands of "Boomers" were sent into the territory through the winter of 1884–85, and while many were driven back, enough escaped the cordon of troops to build up a camp of four hundred men on Stillwater Creek. There they were discovered in January by a strong cavalry force. Couch refused to leave; he told the commander his followers were well armed and determined to fight for their land. Bloodshed was only avoided when the officers, wisely deciding against a frontal assault, threw a ring of soldiers around the "Boomer" camp. Unable to get supplies from Kansas, the four hundred invaders straggled back, muttering they would return.

With that fiasco, the scene of conflict shifted to Washington. Since the opening of the decade western congressmen, railroad lobbyists, and "Boomer" spokesmen had bombarded Congress with petitions, bills, and resolutions demanding the Indian Territory be opened. Their first victory came on March 3, 1885, when an appropriation act authorized the Indian Office to extinguish all native claims to the two unoccupied portions of the region—the Oklahoma District and the Cherokee Outlet. For the next three years Indian agents did nothing, knowing that any settlement would doom the whole reservation system. During that time Couch led party after party into Oklahoma whenever the border patrols turned their backs, while westerners in Washington urged the Indian Office to act. The pressure was too strong to be denied; in January, 1889, the Creeks and Seminole were forced to surrender their rights to the Oklahoma District in return for cash awards of $4,193,799. Two months later Congress officially opened the district to settlers under the Homestead Act, and authorized the chief executive to locate two land offices there. Acting under those instructions, President Harrison on March 23, 1889, announced the Oklahoma District would be thrown open at noon on April 22.

The month between March 23 and April 22, 1889, was one of feverish excitement along the borderland. From all the West the homeless, the speculators, the adventurers, flocked toward the still forbidden land. They jammed roads with their wagons, fought for space in towns, and scattered their rude shacks along the southern border of Kansas and the northern boundary of Texas. A few days before the opening all were allowed to surge across the Cherokee Outlet on the north and the Chickasaw reservation on the south to the borders of the promised land. There they waited, eager and impatient, for noon of April 22. On that sunny morning 100,000 persons surrounded the Oklahoma District, most of them strung along the northern border where for miles on end horsemen, wagons, hacks, carriages, bicycles, and a host of vehicles beggaring description stood wheel to wheel, awaiting the signal. At Arkansas City fifteen trains, so jammed with sweating humanity that platforms and roofs overflowed, were lined up, ready to steam forward along the Santa Fe tracks that crossed the district. Ahead were troops, stationed at regular intervals to hold back "Sooners" unwilling to wait the deadline.

Slowly the minutes ticked away toward the zero hour. Officers, their watches synchronized, waited with guns in air, ready to fire the shots that signaled the opening. At last the revolvers barked, and along the line pandemonium broke loose. Men whipped up their horses, wagons careened wildly forward, horses freed from overturned vehicles galloped madly about—all was hurrah and excitement. The Santa Fe trains, steaming slowly forward at a regulated pace which would not give their passengers an undue advantage, disgorged riders along the route as men leaped from roofs or platforms and rushed about in search of a claim. Noise and confusion reigned as the shouts of successful "Boomers," the crash of hammers on stakes, the clatter of wagons, the crash of overturned vehicles, and the curses of disappointed homeseekers mingled to create a bedlam unique in the annals of the nation.

Within a few hours the 1,920,000 acres of the Oklahoma District were settled. Everywhere homesteaders labored to erect shelters, while among them wandered the unsuccessful, still seeking some overlooked spot. Others marked out city lots; Oklahoma City had a population of 10,000 tent dwellers that night and Guthrie nearly 15,000. Within a few weeks the newborn cities were fully equipped with local governments—W. L. Couch was mayor of Oklahoma City—and the demand was mounting for territorial organization. Congress bowed to the pressure on May 2, 1890, when Oklahoma Territory was set up. Its population was increased during the next few years by a series of reservation "openings" as the Dawes Severalty Act was applied to tribe after tribe. The Sauk, Fox, and Potawatomi lands—900,000 acres in all—were thrown open in September, 1891; the 3,000,000 acres of the Cheyenne-Arapaho reservation in April, 1892. A more dramatic rush occurred at noon on September 16, 1893, when 100,000 homeseekers re-enacted the "Boomer" invasion of 1889 on the 6,000,000 acres of the Cherokee Outlet. Smaller openings during the next years gradually extended the settled areas, until by 1906 the Territory embraced the area covered by the state today and contained 500,000 inhabitants, in addition to scattered remnants of Indian tribes, now living on the 160 acre plots allotted them by the government. Oklahoma became a state in 1907.

The admission of Oklahoma left only the territories of New Mexico and Arizona outside the Union. Both were sparsely settled by ranchers, irrigation farmers, and townsmen who lived in villages fringing the Santa Fe and Southern Pacific Railroads' tracks; Arizona's population in 1900 was only 125,000 and New Mexico's 300,000. Yet the demand for statehood grew steadily during the early twentieth century. Congress tried to solve the problem in 1905 by admitting them as a single state, a suggestion which was indignantly rejected in both territories—Arizona because its small native population feared domination by mixed-blood Mexicans and Americans who controlled its neighbor, New Mexico because the move threatened its distinctive Spanish institutions. Not until 1912 did Washington back down and admit New Mexico and Arizona as separate states. Their constitutions, like those of the other western commonwealths, reflected the liberal political concepts of the frontier in clauses accepting initiative and referendum, direct primaries, short terms for elected officials, women's suffrage, limited executive power, and even—in the case of Arizona—the popular recall of judges.

With the entrance of those two states into the Union, the political organization of the West was completed. Forty-eight commonwealths stood as monuments to the frontiersmen who in three centuries carried the banner of civilization from the Atlantic to the Pacific. Yet the last chapters were still to be written in the epic of the advancing frontier. The economic and social problems created by the remarkable agricultural expansion of the post-Civil War years were destined to plague the nation for a half-century to come.

# CHAPTER XXXVI

# The Agrarian Revolt

# 1873-1896

The unprecedented expansion of the post-Civil War era had far-reaching repercussions. Never before had so many Americans faced the hardships of pioneer life; never before had such a sizable segment of the population shouldered the burdens of frontier debt. Earlier pioneers accepted deprivation and poverty meekly because isolation stifled protest; now farmers, united by improved communications and strengthened by numbers, rose to demand comforts and prosperity denied them by nature. From the 1870's to the 1890's their complaints resounded through the nation's legislative chambers, voiced by twangy westerners whose blunt speech and Lincolnesque garb alarmed orthodox easterners no less than their heretical economic doctrines. The agrarian revolt shattered political traditions, reshaped financial concepts, and laid the basis for social reforms that improved American society during the twentieth century.

The forces driving the western farmer into open rebellion were both social and economic. He knew his living conditions were miserable. The large-scale agriculture suited to the Plains doomed him to a lifetime of loneliness, separated from his nearest neighbor by half a mile of bleak prairie, and cut off entirely from the rest of the world in a day when automobiles, telephones, radios, and even rural mail deliveries were undreamed of. The work was drudgingly monotonous. For the housewife there were endless routine tasks: baking, sewing, cleaning, tending chickens and the garden plot, hauling water and fuel, helping out with the harvest, and bearing children amidst medieval conditions. For the farmer there was even less variety in a country where nature dictated specialization rather than diversification; he plowed his ground, planted his wheat or corn, cultivated his fields, harvested his crop, shivered through the winter, and started all over again. Day after day, year after year, the frontiersman plodded through that drudgery, seldom seeing a new face or hearing a new idea, and with nothing more to look forward to each night than the stuffy discomfort of a dirty sod house.

He had known hardship in the past, but then his lot was endurable because all men seemed just as unhappy. Now he contrasted his miserable existence with the joys of the city dweller. That was the era of the rise of the city when the nation buzzed with tales of newborn metropolitan splendors. Every magazine was studded with breathless articles describing the wonders of newfangled trolley cars and street lights, the gaiety of theaters and parties, the opportunities offered by museums, libraries, and schools. Even books designed to scare country youths from urban pitfalls— *The Spider and the Fly; or, Tricks, Traps, and Pitfalls of City Life by One Who Knows* (1873), *Metropolitan Life Unveiled; or the Mysteries and Miseries of America's Great Cities* (1882), and a host of others— painted sin in such glowing colors that farm living seemed less attractive. The city so dazzled America's imagination that the farmer, long the "bone and sinew of the nation," became a "hayseed" or a "rube" scorned by his urbane countrymen.

Gibes might have been endurable if profits had been high, but agricultural prices receded steadily between the Civil War and 1897 except for a brief boom during the early 1880's. The Department of Agriculture recorded the dismal story of the collapse in its annual record of amounts paid for major crops:

| YEAR | WHEAT | CORN | COTTON |
|---|---|---|---|
| 1870–1873 | 106.7 bushel | 43.1 bushel | 15.1 pound |
| 1874–1877 | 94.4 bushel | 40.9 bushel | 11.1 pound |
| 1878–1881 | 100.6 bushel | 43.1 bushel | 9.5 pound |
| 1882–1885 | 80.2 bushel | 39.8 bushel | 9.1 pound |
| 1886–1889 | 74.8 bushel | 35.9 bushel | 8.3 pound |
| 1890–1893 | 70.9 bushel | 41.7 bushel | 7.8 pound |
| 1894–1897 | 63.3 bushel | 29.7 bushel | 5.8 pound |

Even declining figures did not reveal the farmers' true plight; they were prices paid after carriers, handlers, and commission agents took their fees. What farmers received will never be known—they were poor bookkeepers —but the sum was small enough to convince them they were operating at a loss through most of the period. Wheat, they pointed out, cost sixty-five cents a bushel to grow and sold for forty-two cents; corn that cost them twenty cents a bushel went begging at ten cents. No economist was needed to tell them such returns did not justify the hardships of frontier life.

"There is," one of them concluded, "something radically wrong in our industrial system. There is a screw loose."

Eastern experts could tell them what was wrong. The trouble, according to those seers, was overproduction; the industrial revolution had opened grain and cotton producing areas in Canada, Australia, Argentina, Russia, India, and other underdeveloped countries as well as in the American West, flooding the world with more goods than could be consumed. Farmers were unimpressed by that explanation. The cause of their suffering, they insisted, was not overproduction but underconsumption. They pointed out that eastern workers starved because bread prices were too high, while western farmers burned their grain because wheat prices were too low. Why, they asked, should makers of clothes be underfed while makers of food were underclad? The answer was clear. Between producer and consumer were a number of "thieves in the night" who exacted too high a toll—railroads, grain elevator operators, bankers, and tax makers. If they could be eliminated, food prices would be so low easterners could buy according to their full capacity to consume and there would be no farm surpluses.

Railroads were the principal offenders in the farmers' eyes. Lines west of the Mississippi charged rates that seemed exorbitantly high to shippers, who were impressed by such figures as those illustrating ton-mile charges for typical years:

| Year | Pennsylvania RR east of Chicago | Burlington RR Chicago to Missouri River | Burlington RR west of Missouri River |
|------|------|------|------|
| 1873 | $1.26 | $1.61 | — |
| 1877 | .95 | 1.32 | $4.80 |
| 1881 | .86 | 1.16 | 3.20 |
| 1885 | .70 | .96 | 2.25 |
| 1889 | .69 | .87 | 1.59 |
| 1893 | .62 | .82 | 1.33 |
| 1897 | .56 | .78 | 1.28 |

The roads explained the discrepancies logically. Western railroads, they pointed out, ran through sparsely settled areas where way traffic was insignificant, hauls short, and traffic moved only in one direction; freight cars had to be "deadheaded" westward to carry out grain during the harvest season and eastward during the rest of the year when farmers had nothing to export. That cost money which shippers must pay.

None of the arguments impressed westerners. Railroads were unpopular anyway, as land monopolists and political dictators, and when wealthy directors tried to justify a system which forced shippers to pay the same amount to send a bushel of wheat from Fargo to Minneapolis as from Minneapolis to New York, farmers refused to listen. Their own explanations seemed more logical. Western railroads, they charged, were giant monopolies determined to charge all the traffic would bear. In proof they cited two damning practices. One was the manner in which lines paralleling the Great Lakes raised rates during the winter when water competition vanished; the other the device of "transit rates" adopted in the West to eliminate competitors. No road would accept produce for any point short of its easternmost terminal. Thus a Dakota farmer wishing to sell wheat in Minneapolis was forced to pay the full rate to Chicago before a railroad would take his load, then sell his unused transit rights between Minneapolis and Chicago at a heavy discount. Practices such as those convinced westerners the roads were deliberately robbing farmers for the benefit of overpaid officials and eastern stockholders.

Grain elevator operators were viewed with equal distrust. The elevators —great storage bins for grain that were scattered through the West by eastern corporations—were as monopolistic as the railroads; the roads refused to lay sidings for more than one in each community. As direct loading on freight cars was also forbidden by western lines, farmers could sell only to the local elevator operator, accepting any price he cared to pay. Most merchants were too wary to abuse their position openly, knowing their price must bear some relation to the Chicago quotations farmers read in their papers, but the system of "grading" universally employed offered chances for fraud that few could resist. Spring wheat which was "sound, plump and well-cleaned" and weighed at least fifty-eight pounds a bushel was to be graded No. 1, wheat that was "reasonably clean and of good milling quality" which tipped the scales at fifty-seven pounds No. 2, and "all inferior, shrunken, dirty" grain weighing between fifty-three and fifty-six pounds No. 3. Less ethical operators misgraded grain flagrantly, paying farmers for No. 2 when a load was of No. 1 quality; those with better-developed consciences resorted to "mixing." A wagon of No. 1 weighing fifty-nine pounds and a wagon of No. 2 weighing fifty-seven would be dumped together to form two loads of No. 1 at fifty-eight pounds. Grain growers, watching profits that should have been theirs vanish into the overstuffed pockets of elevator owners, were convinced the problem of underconsumption could not be solved as long as those middlemen stood between them and consumers.

Farmers believed monopolies raised the price of goods they bought as well as lowering the price of foods they sold. They knew that in the postwar industrial era the nation's manufacturing concerns were combining through trusts and pools into monopolistic giants capable of setting artificial

prices on any commodity; a 100 per cent increase in the cost of plows following one merger told them that. Why, they asked themselves, should they be
forced to pay unjust tribute to corporations producing the clothing they
wore, the machinery they used, the fertilizer for their fields, and the
furniture for their homes? Why not call upon the government to regulate
robber-baron industries in the public interest? If private enterprise would
not price goods fairly the people should step in!

Surveying the whole situation, the farmer in the early 1870's concluded
he was a badly abused individual, cheated by elevator owners, robbed by
railroads, and overcharged by manufacturers. His one chance to restore
prosperity was through political action; if he gained control of the government he could pass laws designed to dissolve monopolies, control prices,
and wipe out the barriers between him and eastern consumers. That was
the rallying cry which broke down the farmers' traditional dislike for
organization, and united them in a succession of crusading political parties.

First to emerge was a fraternal organization, the National Grange of the
Patrons of Husbandry, which was formed in 1867 by Oliver Hudson
Kelley, a Department of Agriculture clerk, to provide farmers with greater
social opportunities. Kelley believed that local branches, or Granges, would
help break the drudgery of farm life; members could meet monthly, listen
to talks on agriculture, partake of community pleasures, and enjoy the
ritualistic mumbojumbo with which he endowed his society. With that in
mind he forsook his government post to travel through the West organizing Granges. For a time he enjoyed indifferent success—members were few
in the nine states where branches were founded before 1870—but by the
close of 1871 the time for expansion was at hand. Prices were tobogganing
downward, debts mounting, resentment against monopolies growing. Farmers, looking about for some medium to express their discontent, turned to
the Patrons of Husbandry. Overnight the rivulet of new members swelled
to flood proportions; 1,105 lodges were formed in 1872, 8,400 more in the
panic year, and 4,700 in the first two months of 1874. By that time
1,500,000 farmers and their wives belonged to the Grange.

This was a political force to be reckoned with. Though the organization's
constitution forbad direct action, there was nothing to prevent members
from agreeing on candidates or issues as soon as a meeting adjourned.
Throughout the West and South Grangers placed representatives in office
during 1873 and 1874. Some were nominees of older parties willing to
embrace the farmers' platform, others the spokesmen for Reform or Anti-
Monopoly parties that sprang up in the emergency. Greatest success was
enjoyed in Illinois, Wisconsin, Iowa, and Minnesota, not because the
Grange was stronger there—Kansas and Nebraska had the highest propor-

tion of members—but because the Republican and Democratic parties were so evenly divided the embattled farmers held a balance of power. In those four upper Mississippi Valley states they were able to translate their discontent into a legislative attack on the two groups they most abhorred: greedy manufacturers, and selfish middlemen.

Co-operative buying and production were the Grangers' weapons against overcharging industrialists. "We propose," they declared in their 1874 national convention, "meeting together, talking together, working together, buying together, and in general acting together for our mutual protection and advancement." That was done by appointing state agents to negotiate with manufacturers, promising them large orders in return for low prices; when one willing to co-operate was found all Granges pooled their orders and bought directly. Farmers found they could affect amazing economies; reapers were purchased for $175 rather than $275, wagons for $90 instead of $150, sewing machines for half their usual cost of $100. Although some corporations refused to deal with the agents, others sprang up to capitalize on the vogue of direct selling. Notable was Montgomery Ward and Company which declared on opening its doors in 1872 that its purpose was to "meet the wants of the Patrons of Husbandry." Co-operative buying not only saved farmers thousands of dollars directly but forced local merchants to meet competition by lowering prices.

Encouraged by those successes, the Patrons of Husbandry entered the more hazardous field of production. In most western states local Granges purchased or founded grain elevators, packing plants, flour mills, banks, insurance companies, and other small businesses catering to the farmer; in Iowa alone thirty elevators were operated by the society. A more important experiment began in 1874 when the Iowa Grange began manufacturing reaping machines for sale at half the established price, later expanding to include three plow factories. Most experiments failed, partly because inexperienced management and inadequate capitalization handicapped production, but more because of the cutthroat competition of private manufacturers. Thoroughly alarmed by early Granger successes, corporations lowered prices to such impossible levels that the society's factories, which had sold at too low a cost to build up reserves, were forced into bankruptcy. The collapse of co-operative enterprises hastened the end of the Patrons of Husbandry, but not before they demonstrated that co-operation was an effective weapon against middlemen.

Their second objective—to curb monopolistic railroads and grain elevators—was harder to achieve. Competition was not the answer; any efficient transportation system in the thinly settled West must be monopolistic. The only solution was government regulation—state laws setting maximum rates railroads and elevators could charge for handling or storing grain. No other Granger demand aroused such a controversy, nor embodied such important national implications. The United States, a nation of rugged individualists who accepted a *laissez faire* philosophy as gospel, was asked to interfere in private business for the public good, even though men no longer completely controlled their own property. Little wonder the old order quaked with fear when irate farmers insisted upon such a fundamental change.

The demand for railroad and grain elevator regulation arose first in the four Upper Mississippi Valley states where the Grange was strongest politically. Crude laws, passed by farmer-controlled Illinois and Minnesota legislatures in 1871 proved ineffective, for astute corporation lawyers found them so full of legal defects that state courts declared them unconstitutional two years later. The adverse decision, coming in the middle of a panic year, touched off a rebellion through the Middle West. Angry farmers, newly organized by the Grange, met that summer in picnics and "sociables," listened to fiery speakers, and named Anti-Monopoly or Reform candidates for county and state offices. By autumn they were ready to march on the polls in such strength that agrarian spokesmen packed the legislatures of Illinois, Iowa, Wisconsin, and Minnesota—all pledged to curb monopolies.

The results were decisive. Illinois' farmer-controlled legislature led the way in the fall of 1873; its carefully framed law established a commission with authority to set maximum rates on both freight and passenger traffic. Railroads were allowed to seek increases when they could show any rate was discriminatory, but the measure expressly stated that the presence of competition at some points and not at others would not be considered justification for a charge of discrimination. Minnesota followed a year later when the legislature established uniform rates for the entire state. Wisconsin and Iowa set maximum rates, then named a commission to enforce the laws and collect information. In each state the issue of public welfare *versus* private enterprise was before the people by the close of 1874.

The faulty structure of the Granger Laws—any flat rate set by a legislature could readily be proven discriminatory—and the vicious campaign waged against them by the railroads through intentionally poor service and the malicious raising of all rates to the legal maximum, soon led to their repeal in Minnesota, Iowa, and Wisconsin. In Illinois, however, where the 1873 law was too well drawn to be attacked, the railroads sought to avoid regulation by appealing to the courts. The measure, they contended, violated the clause of the Fourteenth Amendment which forbad a state to deprive any person of life, liberty, or property without due process of law. Rate setting, by denying corporations the free use of their property, deprived them of property. That was the argument used by railroads and elevator owners to carry their case along the tortuous legal paths which finally ended in the United States Supreme Court in October, 1876.

Of the eight so-called "Granger Cases," the most significant was *Munn vs. Illinois*, which involved a statute setting rates for storing and handling grain. The Court, taking note of the fact that wheat from seven or eight states passed through only fourteen Chicago warehouses, propounded a vital question: should the nine corporations owning those elevators be allowed unrestrained control over the millions of farmers living in the Upper Mississippi Valley? The majority held they should not. Property, the justices agreed, ceased to be completely private whenever it was "affected with a public interest." This occurred when it was "used in a manner to make it of public consequence, and affect the community at large. When, therefore, one devotes his property to a use in which the public has an interest, he, in effect, grants to the public an interest in that use, and must submit to be controlled by the public for the common good, to the extent of the interest he has thus created." Grain elevators, railroads, gristmills, ferries, and other essential industries were defined by the Court as "clothed in a public interest" which justified state regulation without violating the Fourteenth Amendment.

The Granger Cases opened a new era in the relations of government and industry but the organization which gave them its name did not survive to enjoy its triumph. Farmers were losing interest by 1877. In some states, notably Wisconsin, railroads beat down their opponents by raising rates, curtailing service, and discriminating against Grange members until the people were convinced the transportation octopus was too powerful to be challenged. In others, such as Illinois, monopolies were frightened into such good behavior by the threat of further legislation that farmers believed the battle won and deserted the Grange. In still others, principally Iowa, the collapse of co-operatives embittered many who lost financially. After 1877 the Patrons of Husbandry reverted to their original status as a farmers' social club.

During the next few years agrarian discontent waned. An attempt was made to enlist westerners in the Greenback Party, an eastern organization which urged currency inflation by demanding the government continue greenbacks (unbacked paper currency issued during the Civil War) in circulation. Although Greenbackers polled 1,000,000 votes in the congressional elections of 1878—two-thirds of them from the Middle West—their political impotence was demonstrated a year later when the Resumption Act went into operation; this measure provided that after January 1, 1879, the number of greenbacks in circulation be reduced from $431,000,000 to $346,681,016 and that these be made redeemable at face value in gold. The act proved so popular in the increasingly conservative East that the Greenback Party was doomed when it entered the election of 1880. Despite the valiant campaign waged by its presidential candidate, James B. Weaver of Iowa, and despite a forward-looking platform which called for women's suffrage, a graduated income tax, congressional regulation of interstate commerce, and a more flexible currency, the party polled only 308,578 votes.

The Greenbackers failed to become a major medium for western malcontents only because times were inauspicious for a party promising currency inflation. Such a program appealed largely to debtors struggling to meet their obligations, while between 1880 and 1887 farmers were so pleasantly engrossed in acquiring debts that they gave no thought to repayment. The West was booming during those years. The weather was good; unprecedented rains turned semiarid lands of western Kansas and Nebraska into flowering gardens. The market was steady; the effects of the Panic of 1873 were forgotten as factories hired food-consuming workers to manufacture products demanded by a newly prosperous nation. Most important of all, money was plentiful, money for farm machinery, new lands, and better homes, that could be had almost for the asking.

Eastern investors were responsible. Where, capitalists asked themselves amidst the returning prosperity of the late 1870's, was the safest place for savings? Certainly not the banks and industries of the East; they were shown to be unsound during the panic. Western lands seemed the answer. Interest rates were high; farmers willingly paid from 6 to 8 per cent on mortgages and from 10 to 18 on chattels. The money was safe; prices were sure to increase steadily with free lands running out. No Gibraltar could be more secure than a juicy 8 per cent mortgage on a choice bit of Kansas property! So reasoned the nation's business men, and they rushed to capitalize before it was too late. Hundreds of mortgage companies were formed between 1875 and 1877, all with eastern headquarters, western branches, and agents scattered widely through the rural districts. For a small fee they would find western borrowers for eastern capital. Their task was not to raise money. Investors fought for that privilege; "my desk," wrote the leader of one company, "was piled high each morning with hundreds of letters, each enclosing a draft and asking me to send a farm mortgage from Kansas or Nebraska." Instead their principal energies went into convincing farmers to borrow money. Agents roamed the prairie states in horse and buggy, pleading with westerners to accept a loan. Never in the memory of pioneers was cash so plentiful.

Few farmers could resist the pressure. Newcomers to the West mortgaged their homesteads to buy farm machinery, mortgaged the farm machinery to provide money until the first crop was harvested, mortgaged the first crop to carry the family through the winter. Oldtimers, even though in no pressing need, succumbed to the blandishments of agents, reasoning that improved implements or an additional quarter-section of land would mean higher profits. New mortgage debts incurred in Kansas during 1885 were double—and in 1887 triple—those of 1880; in other western states the story was the same. By 1887 the per capita debt in the Plains country was the highest in the nation, despite the region's comparative poverty. In Kansas and North Dakota there was one mortgage for every two persons; in Nebraska, South Dakota, and Minnesota one for every three; in the five states as a whole at least one for each family.

As eastern capital flowed into the farm belt, land values skyrocketed. Kansas farms that cost $15 an acre a few years before changed hands at $270 an acre; open Colorado range which had been pastured free sold at $10 or $20 an acre. Speculation was especially rampant in western towns. Every tiny hamlet pictured itself as a future metropolis and planned accordingly, borrowing heavily from eastern capitalists to build courthouses, jails, schoolhouses, waterworks, electric light plants, and sewage systems. Fifteen Kansas towns installed streetcars during the boom, all with capital from the East. "Don't be afraid to go into debt," one exuberant editor counseled. "Spend money for the city's betterment as free as water. . . . Let the increase of population and wealth take care of taxes." Even that fantastic advice seemed reasonable. Wealth was increasing; town lots in Omaha, Wichita, Lincoln, Atchison, and dozens of other villages pyramided in price from $200 to $2,000 in a year, while forty-two sections of prairie adjoining Wichita were subdivided and sold during the spring of 1887 for $35,000,000! The West was in the midst of a speculative spree unrivaled since the 1830's.

Then came the day of reckoning. The weather was to blame. The cold winter of 1886-87 ruined cattlemen and closed one market for farm goods. The summer of 1887 was hot and dry. Day after day a blistering sun and searing south winds withered crops, then chinch bugs swarmed in to devour the few green stalks that survived. A few farmers gave up the struggle when they viewed their parched fields at harvest time, but most had enough faith in the future to stay on. But the next year was no better, nor the next. For ten dismal years rainfall in the Plains country failed to reach the twenty inches needed for agriculture. Every harvest season brought new disasters. Along the arid western fringes of the farming frontier homesteaders gave up the struggle and retreated east, their covered wagons proclaiming "In God We Trusted, in Kansas We Busted." Between 1888 and 1892 half the population of western Kansas moved out and 30,000 left South Dakota;

18,000 prairie schooners entered Iowa from Nebraska in 1891 alone. Just east of the deserted zone farmers, with a larger stake in lands and improvements, were unable to flee—only one in every eight moved east. They remained on overmortgaged farms, going deeper into debt each year, to form the group that expressed itself most violently during the agrarian revolt of the 1890's. Still farther east, along the Missouri River, was a belt where rainfall, although inadequate, was still sufficient for normal agriculture. The farmers there, although not as desperate as those farther west, were burdened with debts accumulated during the boom years.

All the frontier was ripe for revolt. The farmer realized his perpetual hard times were not, as he formerly believed, caused by railroads or elevator operators, but by the nation's financial structure. He had been encouraged to borrow money for expansion during the boom; now he needed cash desperately and none was forthcoming. Easterners closed their purses with the collapse of 1887, leaving him no alternative but to borrow from loan sharks who charged from 20 to 40 per cent interest, then took his entire crop as payment. Under those conditions he was unable to keep up interest payments on his mortgage and faced the threat of foreclosure. In Kansas alone 11,000 farm mortgages were foreclosed between 1889 and 1893. That meant an alarming increase in farm tenancy; by 1890 one-quarter of the farmers of Kansas were tenants or share-croppers, 17 per cent of those of Nebraska, 11 per cent of South Dakota, and 5 per cent of North Dakota. The West, it appeared, was becoming an area of landless peasants where loan sharks and corporations owned the soil. Even those who escaped were burdened with interest payments and staggering taxes inherited from the overambitious expansion of the boom period. One thing seemed clear. There was too little money in the nation. More was needed, to raise the tumbling prices of farm goods, to ease the weight of taxes, to lift the mortgage load from western shoulders. The currency supply of the United States, the westerner held, was both too inadequate and too inelastic to meet the needs of an expanding economy.

The inadequacy of the monetary system seemed obvious; the $2,000,000,000 in gold and greenbacks that served the nation in 1865 were still in circulation in 1890, caring for the needs of a doubled population and a tripled business activity. That meant a steady increase in the purchasing power of each dollar, or lowered prices. A dollar that had bought one bushel of wheat in 1865 paid for two bushels in 1890. Even that could have been endured if debts had declined proportionately, but the opposite was true. Every increase in the value of the dollar—each fall in the price level—made repayment more difficult. Supposing a farmer borrowed $1,000 in 1885 when No. 1 hard wheat sold at $1 a bushel, agreeing to pay the sum back in five years with 8 per cent interest. As far as he was concerned he had borrowed 1,000 bushels of wheat. But in 1890 when the loan was due, wheat sold at only fifty cents a bushel. He must pay back not 1,000 bushels but 2,000 bushels, plus interest which amounted not to $400 but to $500. Actually the dollar appreciation rate was so rapid during the 1880's that a loan contracted in 1880 increased 12 per cent in the next five years and another 12 per cent by 1890. The farmer saw no reason why he should be penalized for the sins of the nation; if the dollar was being overworked, currency should be increased proportionately with business activity so he could pay back his debts at a just figure.

The monetary system also suffered, westerners insisted, because of its inelasticity; money was never available at the time and place it was most needed. That not only hurt farmers whenever they marketed crops but threatened to keep them in economic thralldom for a generation. The immediate deficiencies were apparent with every harvest; when millions of dollars worth of produce were dumped on the nation's markets within a few weeks the static currency was so overburdened the value of the dollar shot upward, driving prices down. After the crop was disposed of dollars, no longer in such demand, declined in value, pushing prices upward just as farmers started buying. Those fluctuations, although not large, often made the difference between poverty and prosperity during bad years.

More serious were the long-term results of monetary inelasticity; the nation's money supply, instead of increasing when the need was greatest, actually declined. Three principal types of currency were in circulation: gold dollars which increased in volume slowly as bullion was mined, redeemable greenbacks to the set sum of $346,681,016, and National Bank Notes issued by federally chartered banks on the basis of their government bonds. The banknotes, although designed to make the currency system elastic, failed to do so, partly because the retirement of the national debt steadily reduced the number of bank-owned government bonds on which they were issued (the number decreased from $339,000,000 in 1873 to $168,000,000 in 1891) and partly because variations in the business cycle removed banknotes from circulation when they were needed most. That unhealthy situation was due to the tendency of nonbanker holders of government securities to sell heavily in periods of prosperity, driving the price down as they took their money into the stock market for speculation. The more conservative banks bought bonds heavily during such periods, thus increasing the supply of banknotes and speeding the inflationary trend. Then when a depression era began, former stock buyers hurried to purchase government bonds as a safer investment. That drove bond prices upward to a point where banks sold widely, reducing the number of banknotes in circulation and hurrying deflation. Farmers realized their country's inelastic currency made each depression more serious and each speculative splurge more dangerous.

The average westerner, although unfamiliar with the intricacies of monetary theory, was wise enough to see that the way to relieve a money shortage was to place more money in circulation. That would increase the consumptive power of eastern buyers, raise prices, and allow him to pay off his loans at a reasonable figure. In casting about for some safe medium which would bring a static currency and an expanding national economy into more equitable relationship without disastrous inflation, he hit upon silver dollars. Silver bullion, he knew, was pouring from western mines in large but controllable amounts. He realized, too, that through most of his nation's history, silver coins circulated freely along with gold coins, despite the difficulty of keeping the amount of precious metal in each balanced. That obstacle finally ended the system of bimetallism just before the West's need for additional currency became acute. The ratio of sixteen to one—sixteen times as much silver in silver dollars as gold in gold dollars —proved unsatisfactory after the '49 rush lowered the price of gold; so much was mined that it became less valuable, in relation to silver, than in the past. Silver dollars disappeared from the market as their owners, realizing the precious metal in them was worth more than its face value, melted them down for commercial sale. Congress simply recognized the situation in 1873 when it abolished the coinage of silver dollars, set up a limited legal-tender value for lesser silver coins, and placed the nation on a gold basis.

No sooner was the step taken than the situation changed. The large quantities of silver from the mines of Nevada, Arizona, and Colorado that poured into money markets during the 1870's drove down that metal's price in relation to gold; whereas the ratio in 1873 was 15.72 to 1 by 1878 the values stood at 17.72 to 1, and each year thereafter the discrepancy increased. Too late western farmers and silver miners wakened to the realization that the "Crime of 1873" deprived them of the cheaper currency they needed—a circulating medium which would bear a closer relationship to the price level than gold. Their protests, voiced largely by mining interests at first, gained them a slight concession in 1878 when Congress passed the Bland-Allison Act, authorizing the secretary of the treasury to buy not less than $2,000,000 nor more than $4,000,000 worth of silver bullion each month for coinage into silver dollars of full legal tender. The presidents who administered the measure during the next twelve years kept purchases at the legal minimum, buying $308,000,000 worth of bullion which was coined into $370,000,000—the $70,000,000 profit going to the government. That dribble of new currency scarcely replaced banknotes retired by debt payments. Something more drastic was needed to ease the financial burdens of the West. The "free and unlimited" coinage of silver at a ratio of 16 to 1 was the only answer!

The organization seized upon by embattled farmers to express this demand was the Farmers' Alliance, which through the late 1880's played the same role the Grange performed a decade earlier. Formed originally in 1874 by Texas cattlemen seeking a medium to combat horse thieves, the Alliance grew slowly in the Southwest until 1886 when it claimed 50,000 members. A division in the ranks that year opened the way to greater success; when a faction split away to protest the injection of political issues into the society's creed, its leaders decided to heal the breach by a program of expansion "so that the whole world of cotton raisers might be united for self-protection." The time was ripe for such a step. During 1887 two similar organizations in neighboring states—the Farmers' Union of Louisiana and the Agricultural Wheel of Arkansas—were merged with the older body under the name of the Farmers' and Laborers' Union of America. Within two years the Union reached into all southern states and boasted a membership of nearly 3,000,000. There, ready made, was an organization through which farmers of the Southwest could demand currency reform.

In the meantime a similar alliance took shape in the Northwest. Its patron saint was Milton George, editor of a Chicago farm journal called the *Western Rural*, and staunch opponent of railroads and monopolies. Casting about for some means of reviving agitation carried on by the Grange, George in 1880 conceived a Farmers' Alliance for his own section. The idea, well publicized by the *Western Rural*, took hold at once; by adopting a militant stand on political questions the Northwest Alliance won 100,000 members by the middle 1880's and was ready to capitalize on discontent that followed the collapse of the boom. Members came flocking in after 1886. "The people are aroused at last," wrote George in 1887. "Never in our history has there been such a union of action among farmers as now." The thousand new members a week who joined through 1890 allowed the secretary to boast, with pardonable enthusiasm, that the organization would soon number 2,000,000. Tailored to the needs of the Northwest as the Farmers' and Laborers' Union was to the Southwest, Milton George's creation gave farmers of the upper Plains a chance to carry their grievances into the political arena.

Their opportunity came in December, 1889, when leaders of the northern and southern alliances met at St. Louis in an effort to unite the two bodies. Although local jealousies prevented a merger, both seized the chance to draw up platforms which were found to be virtually identical; they favored a graduated income tax, government ownership of railroads, laws against excessive land holdings, strict government economy, the abolition of national banks, and the substitution of greenbacks for banknotes as currency, with the Southern Alliance asking also for free silver coinage at 16 to 1. Sectional lines had disappeared on fundamental issues; for all practical purposes western farmers were united in a powerful organization which, if employed politically, might move the mountains of eastern conservatism. That heady realization sent farmers into the elections of 1890 with the fervor bred of a generation of pent-up resentment against low prices, crushing debts, and burdensome taxes.

That they had no party through which to voice their grievances made no difference. In the Southwest they gained control of local Democratic machines; in the Northwest they held local conventions of Alliance delegates to form parties of their own—the People's Party, Independent Party, Industrial Party, and Alliance Party. The campaign they waged was not truly a campaign at all but, in the words of one observer, "a religious revival, a crusade, a pentecost of politics in which a tongue of flame sat upon every man, and each spake as the spirit gave him utterance." The people were wild with zeal as they rallied behind the holy cause. They drove for miles across the hot countryside to jam picnic grounds, churches, and opera houses; 1,600 teams converged on Hastings, Nebraska, in one day; crowds of 25,000 were reported in Kansas. They unfurled banners—"We Are Mortgaged, All But Our Votes," "Vested Rights Will Go Down Forever And Human Rights Will Prevail"—and they sang their songs:

> I was raised up in the kind of school,
>   Good-bye, my party, good-bye.
> That taught to bow to money rule,
>   Good-bye, my party, good-bye.
> And it made of me a "Kansas Fool,"
>   Good-bye, my party, good-bye.
> When they found I was a willing tool,
>   Good-bye, my party, good-bye.

But mostly they listened to orators.

The evangelists of the crusade were horny-handed sons and daughters of toil who needed no inspiration but fervent belief in their cause. Mary Elizabeth Lease was one, a thirty-seven-year-old veteran of life on a Kansas homestead who told her enthralled audiences: "What you farmers need to do is to raise less corn and more *Hell*." Jerry Simpson was another. Sailor, soldier, Kansas farmer, his rumpled clothes inspired a political opponent to remark that he probably wore no socks, winning him the nickname of "Sockless Jerry Simpson." Another was Ignatius Donnelly, a brilliant orator and inspired debater, whose impassioned pleas won thousands of Minnesota farmers. Still another was James B. Weaver, of Iowa, green-backer and politician, whose serenity in the midst of tumult proved as effective as the roaring enthusiasm of his contemporaries. But the real heroes were not spotlighted orators; they were the small farmers who spoke against monopoly and gold with an effectiveness born of conviction. "The farmers, the country merchants, the cattle-herders, they of the long chin-whiskers, and they of the broad-brimmed hats and heavy boots," wrote an observer, "had also heard the word and could preach the Gospel of Populism. The dragon's teeth were sprouting in every corner of the land. Women with skins tanned to parchment by the hot winds, with bony hands of toil and clad in faded calico, could talk in meeting, and could talk right straight to the point."

Throughout the West the people, swept along by evangelical zeal, marched grimly to the polls in the election of 1890. The results were impressive. Southern Alliance candidates won gubernatorial contests in four states, secured control of eight legislatures, and captured forty-four seats in the House of Representatives and three in the Senate. In the Northwest the victories, although less startling, were still decisive. Kansans gave Alliance nominees control of the lower house of the state legislature, placed five of them in the House of Representatives, and sent the bewhiskered William A. Peffer to the Senate. In Nebraska independents won both legislative houses and one of the State's three congressional seats. South Dakota elected an independent senator, and in other states Alliance candidates took so many votes from Republicans that an unusually large number of Democrats were placed in state and national offices. The embattled farmers, without even a political organization, seemed on the road to national success.

Alliance leaders, elated by victory and hopeful for the future, turned at once to the task of welding their followers into a united party. A meeting of 1,400 delegates from Southern and Northwestern Alliances held at Cincinnati in May, 1891, showed the time was not yet ripe; southerners were too hopeful of winning control of the Democratic Party to risk supporting a third party. When representatives met again on February 22, 1892, all doubts were dispelled; the continued conservatism of Democratic office-holders convinced even middle-of-the-road delegates from the South that independent action was needed to save the farmer. Realization that a new party was to be formed lent enthusiasm to the thousands of "grey-haired, sunburned and roughly clothed men" who gathered beneath fluttering flags in the St. Louis Exposition Music Hall on the anniversary of the first President's birth. A parade of speakers came first—Ignatius Donnelly, Mary Lease, "Sockless Jerry" Simpson, Terence Powderly of the Knights of

Labor. Then resolutions were adopted and a committee of fifteen named to set the time and place for a convention to nominate candidates for the 1892 election. Thus was born the People's Party. Nominations would be made, the fifteen committeemen decided, at Omaha on July 4, 1892.

The 1,300 delegates who assembled for that epoch-making meeting first drafted the new party's platform. After a ringing preamble based upon the proposition that "wealth belongs to him who creates it," the remarkable document listed the demands of the farmers: free and unlimited coinage of silver "at the present legal ratio of 16 to 1," a circulating medium of at least $50 a person, honesty and economy in government, a graduated income tax, postal savings banks, government ownership of railroads and telegraph lines, abolition of alien land holdings, and the reclamation of all lands held by "railroads and other corporations in excess of their actual needs." Other resolutions, not included in the platform but submitted at the same time, urged shorter working hours for labor, laws forbidding the admission of undesirable aliens, the direct election of senators, a single term for the President, and the general use of the initiative and referendum. When that forward-looking program was laid before the cheering delegates they roared their approval for forty minutes before enthusiam was stemmed. Well they might. The "Omaha Platform" promised to lift the West from its economic doldrums and usher in an era of justice, equality, and prosperity for common men throughout the nation.

Winning the election proved harder than formulating a progressive program. The People's Party nominee, James B. Weaver of Iowa, was a seasoned campaigner, but his long association with agrarian reform stamped him as a radical in the eyes of many moderates. Nor could the Populist workhorses—Mrs. Lease, Ignatius Donnelly and all the rest—arouse the same enthusiasm for shopworn issues they had two years before. The result became clear when ballots were counted. The Populists cast 1,000,000 votes —about 9 per cent of the total—and carried Kansas, Nevada, Colorado, and Idaho, as well as securing one electoral vote each from North Dakota and Oregon. The center of agrarian discontent was in the Plains states rather than the states bordering the Mississippi; in Minnesota the Populists, who had almost won in 1890, ran a poor third.

Far from discouraged, leaders of the People's Party looked eagerly toward the election of 1896, confident that the nation's unsound economy and the stupidity of the older parties would work in their favor during the four intervening years. They were not disappointed. Drought-withered crops, falling prices, and mounting debts continued to win converts, but even more effective were the blundering efforts of Republicans and Democrats to solve the West's problems. The former took the first step; in 1890 a Republican-dominated Congress, seeking to salve western wounds, passed the Sherman Silver Purchase Act, which authorized the Treasury Department to purchase 54,000,000 ounces of silver yearly—about double the amount prescribed by the Bland-Allison Act—for coinage into silver dollars, paying the miners in legal-tender certificates redeemable "in gold or silver." The carefully phrased measure not only preserved the gold standard by allowing the secretary of the treasury to redeem silver certificates in gold (a practice universally followed), but plunged the nation into a panic which brought agrarian discontent to a climax.

The causes underlying the Panic of 1893 were largely psychological. Locked in the treasury building at Washington was a reserve of gold bullion established in 1879 as backing for redeemable greenbacks in circulation. Popular fancy decided the reserve was the Gibraltar of American finance; so long as it remained large the currency system was safe, but should it fall below $100,000,000 (a meaningless figure fixed by the public as a safety line) money would be worthless. Until 1890 the fund was well over $200,000,000; then it began to decline as inept Republican tariffs cut down federal revenue and cautious financiers started hoarding gold. Year after year the reserve dwindled, until shortly after Grover Cleveland became president in the spring of 1893, it slipped below the $100,000,000 mark. Fear swept the nation. Industrialists cut pay rolls, merchants ended purchases, brokers dumped stocks, banks closed to escape runs, workers marched on Washington demanding relief. For the farmer, depression meant low prices would slide even lower; corn sank below fifteen cents a bushel, cotton sold for less than five cents a pound. Only one thing failed to decline during the summer of 1893—the debts.

The farmers knew how to restore prosperity. Throughout the West their anguished cry arose: stop deflation by restoring the free and unlimited coinage of silver! Everywhere prophets rose to drive the message home to the people. William H. Harvey was most prominent; his booklet, *Coin's Financial School,* argued for bimetallism in a language the ordinary person could understand. "Give the people back their favored primary money!" Harvey urged. "Give us two arms with which to transact business! Silver the right arm and gold the left arm! Silver the money of the people and gold the money of the rich!" But President Cleveland refused to listen. Fundamentally conservative, he believed the panic would end only when public confidence was restored by checking the drain on the government's gold reserve. Hence he called Congress into special session, used his patronage to secure support, and won repeal of the Sherman Silver Purchase Act. His futile gesture satisfied no one—continued redemption of greenbacks kept the bullion reserve below the $100,000,000 mark—while westerners were left apoplectic with rage. The Democrats, they believed, had sold out to the bankers; the Republicans were hopelessly reactionary. The common man's only hope was the People's Party.

The hue and cry for "free silver" which followed the Panic of 1893 did Populists an injustice. Until that time their platform was built on a broad foundation of reform in which monetary policy played a minor part; the delegates at the Omaha convention of 1892 cheered the railroad plank more than free silver and gave the land plank "a regular Baptist camp meeting chorus." Now other issues were forgotten as party leaders, sensing the popular demand for inflation, staked their hope for success on silver coinage. Their tactics not only pushed other reforms into the background and cost Populists the support of men who wanted railroad regulation or a democratized government structure, but allowed the older parties to steal some of their thunder. After 1893 the nation divided along sectional rather than political lines, with western Democrats and Republicans as rabid for free silver as Populists, and easterners of every complexion in favor of the gold standard. Yet inflationary sentiment was growing, and on that the People's Party pinned its hope for victory in 1896.

The party's leaders agreed upon an apparently foolproof strategy as the crucial contest drew near; they would delay their convention until after the older parties came out against free silver, then sweep up silverites and reformers who rebelled against such archaic conservatism. The wisdom of the course seemed justified when the Republicans met in June. Under the influence of their genial dictator, Marcus Hanna, they nominated the reactionary William McKinley of Ohio on a platform containing an unequivocal gold plank, whereupon thirty-four western delegates, led by Senator Henry M. Teller of Colorado, walked out in disgust. Delighted Populists, confident the rebels would bolster their own ranks, congratulated themselves on their tactics as they waited for Democrats to follow a similar course.

Unfortunately the Democratic Party refused to follow the expected pattern. When its convention assembled at Chicago, silverites from South and West shouted down the gold minority from the East and adopted a monetary plank demanding "the free and unlimited coinage of both gold and silver at the present legal ratio of sixteen to one." Then, still flushed with victory, Democratic inflationists sat spellbound as a thirty-six-year-old delegate from Nebraska, William Jennings Bryan, praised their action. They thrilled to his opening words as he proclaimed his intention to speak "in defense of a cause as holy as the cause of liberty—the cause of humanity;" they hung breathlessly on each syllable as he castigated Republicans in his magnificent conclusion: "If they dare to come out in the open field and defend the gold standard as a good thing, we will fight them to the uttermost. Having behind us the producing masses of the nation and the world, supported by the commercial interests, the laboring interests, and the toilers everywhere, we will answer their demand for a gold standard by saying to them: You shall not press down upon the brow of labor this crown of thorns, you shall not crucify mankind upon a cross of gold." Oratory carried the day; Democrats brushed aside preconvention favorites to make Bryan their presidential candidate.

Populists were in a quandary. Should they submerge their own party, cast their lot with the Democrats, and win free silver for the nation? Or should they retain their identity, split the silverite vote, and hand the United States over to gold-standard Republicans? For the indelible reformers who headed the People's Party, political suicide was preferable to national suicide; better to surrender hope of glory than burden the United States with "the cross of gold" for another four years. Fusionists dominated the convention which assembled at Chicago in late July 1896. Bryan was selected as the party's presidential candidate without serious opposition, but the Maine banker chosen by the Democrats for the vice-president's office, Arthur Sewall, was passed over in favor of Thomas Watson, a Georgia Populist. The platform advocated reform in transportation, the land system, and other matters dear to farmers, as well as free silver.

The "Battle of the Standards"—silver and gold—was one of the most bitterly contested elections in history. Bryan, instilled with some of the Populists' crusading zeal, staged a spectacular campaign in which he traveled 13,000 miles, visited two-thirds of the states, and gave four hundred empassioned speeches. Behind him were the common people; against him the forces of wealth and industry. "There are but two sides in the conflict that is being waged in this country today," declared a Populist Manifesto. "On the one side are the allied hosts of monopolies, the money power, great trusts and railroad corporations, who seek the enactment of laws to benefit them and impoverish the people. On the other are the farmers, laborers, merchants, and all other people who produce wealth and bear the burdens of taxation. . . . Between these two there is no middle ground." This was a class struggle, and the lower classes were on the march.

Despite their fervent belief in a just cause, Bryan and his cohorts faced insurmountable obstacles. Employers used wage cuts or layoffs to force workers into the Republican column; newspapers reflected the conservatism of their owners by solidly supporting McKinley. A worse handicap was confusion resulting from the separate vice-presidential candidates of Populists and Democrats. The result was a victory for McKinley, with a majority of 600,000 popular votes, and 271 electoral votes to 176 for Bryan. His strength lay north of the Ohio and east of the Mississippi where the Grange states of the Old Northwest were now in the Republican column; Bryan carried all the West except Minnesota, Iowa, North Dakota, California, and Oregon, and won most of the South. McKinley's victory—and a Gold Standard Act adopted in 1900—sounded the death knell of the People's Party. In 1900 they fused with the Democrats once more, even though Bryan subordinated free silverism to anti-imperialism, but in 1904 and 1908 their own candidates were in the field. The disheartening showing—only 29,000 votes in 1908—forced the party's dissolution.

Even in defeat the Populists triumphed, for their decline was hastened by a gradual realization of their demands. They wanted prosperity; after 1897 good times descended on the West in the wake of plentiful rains. They wanted inflation; gold discoveries in Alaska, Africa, and Australia poured such quantities of bullion into parched channels of trade that between 1897 and 1906 the money per capita increased from $22.92 to $32.77, and in 1920 passed the $50 mark set by farmers as their ideal. They wanted relief from debt; rising prices after 1897 allowed them to meet creditors' demands. They wanted progressive government reform; the conservative Theodore Roosevelt gave them railroad regulation, the reactionary William Howard Taft postal savings banks, and the liberal Woodrow Wilson a flexible currency through the medium of the Federal Reserve System. The initiative and referendum the Populists desired, and the recall they considered too radical to ask, were in general use by 1912. One by one the principles of the "Omaha Platform" were accepted, until farmers' demands that seemed radical in the 1890's appeared conservative in the 1940's.

The agrarians fought a brave fight, and cannot be blamed if they mistook temporary relief for permanent victory. When high prices in the early twentieth century convinced them, falsely, that their battle was won, they furled their banners with the relief all men feel when a conflict ends. They could not know the decade of the 1920's would find their sons facing the same grinding debts, the same starvation wages, the same ruthless exploitation by eastern interests. The plight of the farmer in a settled, industrialized continent was one of the most perplexing problems bequeathed to future generations by the passing of the frontier.

# CHAPTER XXXVII

# The Frontier Heritage

What was the frontier's bequest to the future? How did the continuous rebirth of civilization in successive geographic areas, which went on during the three centuries required to settle the continent, affect the characters and the institutions of the pioneers and their children? Are the traits that supposedly distinguish Americans from other peoples of today's world traceable to this unique experience in their history? And, if this is the case, how can the nation—a nation that has been expanding through most of its existence —adjust itself to the necessity of living within closed borders? Only an answer to these questions will demonstrate America's debt to the frontiersmen who blustered their way from Atlantic to Pacific, leaving behind a residue of national characteristics and unsolved problems which were the pioneers' most important bequest to later generations.

That the frontier should reshape the traits and institutions of those who came under its influence is easy to understand. For the frontier was something more than a migrating geographic area advancing westward across the forests and prairies of the continent; frontiering was a process through which imported European customs and habits were gradually "Americanized." This was made possible by the continuous re-evolution of social forms amidst primitive conditions; on each successive frontier society began anew, then struggled upward to the complexities of civilization once more. During each rebirth something of the old was cast aside, something of the new borrowed from the distinctive environment. Environmental factors were, of course, not the only ones that contributed to the uniqueness of the social orders that finally developed. The transformation occurred partly because men in the West had abandoned civilization and were starting life afresh, partly because they were adjusting to new physical conditions, partly because they lost much "cultural baggage" while migrating westward, and partly because they deliberately left behind features of the older society which they disliked. The frontier zones, as a result, were areas of rapid and effective Americanization; the new Wests were the most typical and influential portions of the United States. As they became Easts with the regression of the advancing frontier, traces of the pioneering experience remained. They still remain, to endow America with many of the unusual characteristics of its distinctive civilization.

Of the imported institutions that were modified by the frontier process, the agencies of government were most prominent. The West's role was to stimulate and accelerate the trend toward democracy long apparent in the western world. The pioneer environment fostered the democratic surge in at least three ways. In a new country freedom of economic opportunity tended to blur imported class lines; all men were either land owners or potential land owners whose stake in society entitled them to a voice in its management. In the East, on the other hand, the wealthy feared an unchecked democracy which might attack vested interests. Westerners, moreover, sincerely believing that they alone could solve their unique problems, were in constant rebellion against control from Europe or the East; their interest in self-government was not theoretical but based on a practical desire to get things done that they wanted done. And finally, the West, a region of poverty and discontent, embraced democratic concepts as have all such areas in modern history. Western belief in democracy was more practical than idealistic, but was no less sincere for that reason.

This did not mean that class distinctions and aristocratic concepts were absent everywhere in the West. Probably the first pioneers on every new frontier viewed their fellow men as completely equal—the primitive governmental associations in early farming communities or mining camps reflected such an attitude—but with the coming of wealthier farmers, merchants, and lawyers differences developed rapidly. These newcomers were driven to think of themselves as superior to the masses, partly because of their greater wealth, and partly because nearly all were speculators in farm lands or town sites. As speculators they were hated by the less fortunate who made up the bulk of the population; sensing this antipathy they tended to withdraw within their own class and grow increasingly conservative in both local and national politics. Pioneer Kentucky and Tennessee during the post-Revolutionary years contained a sizable group of well-to-do aristocrats who favored the Federal Constitution and. voted the Federalist ticket; the Old Northwest a half-century later cast a surprisingly large number of ballots for the conservative Whig Party; the trans-Mississippi regions which went wild for William Jennings Bryan and "free silver" in the waning years of the nineteenth century contained a plentiful sprinkling of standpat Republicans. The western environment was not so favorable to democracy that aristocratic beliefs could not take root there.

Nor did the frontier serve as a breeding ground for startling new democratic concepts. The European world was well along the road toward political equalitarianism when the settlement of the United States began; the American wilderness simply provided a congenial environment for the well-established movement toward democracy. This was shown by the governmental institutions adopted by westerners; in each new state frontiersmen showed themselves to be imitative rather than creative by adopting the most liberal features of constitutions already operating in the East. Nearly all vested unusual power in the legislature, which was considered more responsive to public opinion than the governor, and provided for a rapid rotation of legislators by limiting office holding to short terms. More significant was the western tendency to extend the elective process to a wider range of officials; governors, legislators, and even judges were usually chosen by the people. Later in the nineteenth century the newer states pioneered in bringing legislation under the public thumb by such devices as the initiative, referendum, and recall. Seldom did the westerners initiate these practices, but they consistently imitated the most liberal examples provided by the East.

The frontier environment also accelerated the democratic movement aimed at sweeping away property qualifications for the franchise. This was launched in the East during the Revolutionary period when six states liberalized their qualifications for voting, yet a frontier state, Vermont, was the first to adopt complete manhood suffrage. Ohio followed its example when it entered the Union in 1802, Indiana became a state in 1816 without any restrictions on the ballot box, and others that followed generally allowed all adult males to vote. Westerners also showed a more enlightened attitude than easterners by wiping out religious or property qualifications for office holding. In general the frontier fostered, if it did not innovate democratic practices.

Scarcely less important in reshaping the nation's institutions was the strong spirit of nationalism which permeated each western community. This sprang partly from the accident of migration—men drawn from many states felt less loyalty to their new homeland than to the nation—and partly from western dependence on the federal government for practical help. Only the United States could protect them from Indians, provide them with roads and canals, enact the protective tariffs which would provide home markets for their agricultural surpluses, and fashion a land system that would stimulate the filling in of the pioneer communities. The steady growth of national power at the expense of the state during the nineteenth century was due in part to western demands.

Not only did institutions, but the character of men and women, change through contact with the wilderness. This did not mean that the frontier moulded all under its influence into identical beings; inherited cultural traits were too strong to be sloughed off entirely. Yet the western environment did endow pioneers with unique characteristics which all shared. This was accomplished partly by the selective process which operated in all migrations; timid conformists were left behind, for only brash, ambitious, dissatisfied, materialistic, nonconformists were willing to risk the tribulations of wilderness existence. The attitudes of the selected groups which arrived in the West were further modified by the frontier environment. The geographic conditions under which they lived were partly responsible: pioneering in an area where an all-powerful nature destroyed most of civilization's gains, where dangers were plentiful and hardships common, where isolation cut them off from the stimulating thought currents of Europe or the East, frontiersmen tended to concentrate on immediate problems and grow indifferent to the society beyond their communities. The economic atmosphere surrounding them was equally important; in a region where land was cheap and labor scarce every individual with grit, strength, and brains was assured a golden future. Westerners lived in a narrow world geographically, but in a world of boundless horizons economically.

These conditions instilled into them numerous traits commonly associated with nineteenth-century America. The average frontiersman was a coarse materialist; he had too many physical tasks to accomplish to fritter away his time on aesthetic or intellectual subjects. Yet his economic ambitions made him culturally ambitious, if not for himself, at least for his children. Schools and colleges were common on the town frontier, while libraries often preceded distilleries into western communities. The frontiersman was an inventive genius with a jack-of-all-trades ability to meet his own needs; he had to be in a land where division of labor was unknown and importations expensive. He was prone to move at the slightest excuse; ancestral ties meant nothing when opportunity lay ahead. He was careless of nature's bounties, feeling that the nation's boundless resources were sufficient for all later generations; if they proved not to be he shrugged away responsibility for the future by asking what posterity had done for him. Even today Americans are known for their materialism, their inventiveness, their mobility, and their wastefulness. They are known also for their buoyant optimism and rugged individualism, and these too were characteristics accentuated by the frontier.

The typical frontiersman was an incurable optimist; he had to be to withstand the rigors of western life. Engaged in a continuous tussle with stubborn nature, living amidst squalor and poverty, threatened by the vagaries of climate, endangered by lurking savages, separated from the comforts of civilization, and pursued by memories of the unpleasant eastern experience that drove him west, he could find solace in the future alone. He lived in a world of dreams, dwelling constantly on that not-too-distant day when the approaching railroad would open new markets, the price of corn advance, or a wealthy newcomer pay a high price for that extra quarter-section he was holding for speculative resale. "The vastness of the wilderness," wrote Frederick Jackson Turner, "kindled his imagination. His vision saw beyond the dank swamp at the edge of the great lake to the lofty buildings and jostling multitudes of a mighty city; beyond the rank, grass-clad prairie to the seas of golden grain; behind the harsh life of the log hut and the sod house to the home of his children, where should dwell comfort and the higher things of life, though they might not be for him." The frontiersman had faith in his country and its democratic institutions, hope for the improvability of mankind, a boundless belief in the destiny of the United States, and a rambunctious confidence in his ability to make his dreams come true.

Individualism was another trait fostered by the frontier environment. This stemmed not from the necessities of isolated living—pioneers usually settled in groups for companionship, safety, and mutual aid—but from the limitless opportunity present in a region where land was abundant and men few. Hence western individualism was unique. In some ways the frontiersman was a slave to convention; he patterned his dress, his agricultural methods, and his living habits on those of his fellow men and had no interest in individual nonconformity. He relied on the immediate social group far more than easterners; on the most advanced frontiers pioneers often purchased draft animals or farm machinery in common; in more thickly settled regions they held community gatherings for house-raisings, logrollings, husking bees, apple parings, camp meetings, play parties, and a host of other activities; when threatened with outside interference they formed extra-legal squatters' associations, cattle raisers' associations, or miners' camps. Yet the frontiersman did cling to certain individualistic tenets: he resented any interference—by government or society—with his unrestrained exploitation of natural resources, he rebelled against social controls from the East, and he protested all personal limitations on his conduct, insisting that they were unnecessary in a land where men did not live elbow to elbow.

This far did frontier individualism go, and no farther. The westerner had no unwavering faith in individual freedom, no unreasoning abhorrence of governmental controls, no theoretical dislike of central authority. Instead he was willing to call upon the national or state government for aid whenever that seemed wise. Frontiersmen constantly besieged the United States with requests to build roads or canals, regulate land sales in the interests of settlers, improve rivers and harbors, create proper credit facilities, and punish industrial monopolies. At times they went beyond to demand government ownership of essential utilities, not because they believed in a socialist state, but because this seemed essential to secure needed services. In the 1830's the Ohio Valley solidly supported government construction of canals and railroads, knowing that private enterprise lacked the capital for such a building program; in the 1870's, when monopolistic railroads, grain elevators, and farm implement companies threatened western agriculture, the prairie states raised their voices in behalf of government ownership. Never a consistent theorist, the frontiersman vacillated in basic policy, choosing the path which at the moment seemed to promise greater immediate returns. Nevertheless his impatience with interference, his insistence on his right to exploit the nation's resources, and his determination to advance his own welfare at the expense of society or posterity have been since identified with American individualism.

The composite frontiersman who emerged from the frontier process defies accurate description, largely because his characteristics varied with time and place, and depended partially on the inherited traits that he carried to the West. In general, however, the distinctive western environment endowed him with certain typically American attitudes. He was materialistic, mobile, versatile, inventive, careless of natural resources, optimistic, and nationalistic. He believed in democracy, and when setting up governmental agencies usually patterned them after the most liberal examples provided by the East. He reshaped institutions to be workable, without regard to precedent or tradition. He was individualistic to the extent that he resented governmental interference which would check his own progress, but he did not reject beneficial external aid or rebel against community controls. Above all, the product of the frontier was a practical opportunist, little concerned with the past or with theory, whose institutions and characteristics were shaped by the opportunity for material gain present in a new country.

This attitude meant trouble when the frontier passed from the American scene. For the three centuries needed to settle the continent, generation after generation had looked to the receding area of free land in the West as a region of potential opportunity. Actually few easterners could go there; most lacked the skills or wealth or spirit of adventure needed to grapple with a primitive wilderness. Yet all solaced themselves with the belief that in time of stress that secure harbor awaited them or their neighbors. All thought too that the United States was great because newly tapped resources turned the wheels of industry, prosperous because the continuous westward drain of surplus manpower kept wages up and the living standard high. Whether true or false, these concepts were so often voiced by orators, writers, and politicians that they were accepted by a majority of nineteenth-century Americans. Belief in the frontier as a source of opportunity, strength, and wealth was rooted in the national tradition.

To make matters even worse, most Americans were confident that the area of free land would last forever. Every school book provided them with staggering statistics concerning the public domain: the United States, they knew, acquired 1,465,000,000 acres of land between 1783 and 1860; enough, when made into 160 acre farms, to provide homes for 9,000,000 families. Not even the most feverish imagination could picture such a supply being exhausted in a mere half-century; surely the secretary of war had been right in 1827 when he confidently reported that five hundred years would be required to fill the West. Lulled by such prospects, and unaware as were western "boomers" that most of the lands beyond the Mississippi were unsuitable for habitation, the great mass of the people in the 1880's still looked to a rosy future of continuous expansion. To them the announcement of the Superintendent of the Census in 1890 that the country's "unsettled area has been so broken into by isolated bodies of settlement that there can hardly be said to be a frontier line" remaining, came as a distinct shock. Since that time they have been adjusting themselves—economically, psychologically, and politically—to life in a nonexpanding land.

The economic impact of the passing of the frontier was comparatively slight, largely because the westward movement continued after 1890 as before. Good land still waited newcomers in the West, for despite the pronouncement of the Census Bureau, only a thin film of population covered that vast territory. All the Far West, with the exception of California, contained fewer farms in 1890 than the single state of Mississippi, and only half as many as Ohio. Even the tiny state of Delaware which, as one of its citizens once remarked, had three counties at low tide and two at high, boasted more farms than Idaho or Montana, three times as many as Wyoming, and seven times as many as Arizona or Montana. Nor was this discrepancy due entirely to the larger farms of the semiarid trans-Mississippi country; in the entire area, again omitting California, only twice as many acres were under cultivation as in the single state of Ohio. Seekers after economic betterment could still follow Horace Greeley's advice in the first years of the twentieth century as they had in the nineteenth.

They did so. Through the history of man's migrations population has tended to flow away from regions of excessive competition and declining opportunity to newer areas where lands are cheaper, competitors fewer, and the chances for speculative gain greater. To thousands of Americans, reacting in this normal way, the West was still the land of promise. They continued to move there; some to fill the gaps between widely scattered farms in previously settled lands; others to new frontiers in Montana and Idaho where thousands of acres of open range were placed under the plow. The lands were not the best in the West—those had been usurped by the first comers—but that did not deter homeseekers in a day when such scientific improvements as irrigation and dry farming promised to transform deserts into fertile fields. The persistence of the westward movement during the first years of the twentieth century was shown by the continuing demand for government land; four times as many acres were homesteaded after 1890 as before, and twice as many since 1910 as in the prior fifty years. The continued drift westward was also demonstrated by the steady movement of the nation's center of population; in 1890 this median point was in central Indiana, in 1920 it lay sixty-two miles farther westward, and in 1940 was near Carlisle, Indiana, thirty-five miles beyond. The West was still draining excesses from the East as it had through the country's adolescent years, although at a less feverish pace.

Nor was the trans-Mississippi area the only frontier attracting Americans during the opening decades of the twentieth century. Pioneers, never respecters of international boundaries, found a new land of opportunity in the Prairie Provinces of Canada. Attention turned to that fertile country as soon as cheap lands vanished in the United States; between 1900 and 1920 almost 1,250,000 Americans made their way northward to homestead in Manitoba, Alberta, or Saskatchewan. So great was the rush that the scenes were reminiscent of some of the earlier migrations to the western frontier: thousands crowded on trains of the "Soo Line" from St. Paul to Portal, thousands of others moved north in caravans of covered wagons. The lure was cheap land, accentuated as always by the speculative profits waiting immigrants. A farmer who could sell his 320-acre Dakota farm in 1910 for $50 an acre, then purchase a similar homestead in Saskatchewan for $2 an acre, could count on a profit of some $14,000 even after deducting his moving expenses. Moreover he was sure that his new farm would yield equally large speculative returns. "There is," one explained, "no way people can pick up $3,000 easier than to come up and homestead here for three years. There will be 160 acres for nothing, and if the land is any good, at the end of three years you can sell it for $20 an acre." Those were the prospects that lured more than a million opportunity-seekers to the "last best West."

Continued expansion into the Canadian Northwest and the submarginal lands of the American Far West softened the impact of the frontier's closing on the nation's economy but had little influence on the popular mind. The psychological effects of the dramatic Census Bureau announcement of 1890 far outweighed the material. Suddenly, unexpectedly, the nation realized that its age of expansion was over, its age of adjustment to closed boundaries at hand. To thousands of thinking citizens the implications seemed staggering. Overnight they must answer a dozen difficult questions. Could the farmer, who had traditionally produced cash crops with little capital expenditure on permanent improvements, adjust himself to the European habits of soil conservation and stability? Could the worker, who (in popular belief at least) had been able to escape economic storms by fleeing westward, maintain the high wages on which the nation's living standard was based? Could the government, which (it was fondly believed) had been kept on an even keel by the escape of discontented elements through a frontier "safety valve," prevent "radicals" from gaining control? Could the national economy, which had been geared for three centuries to continuous expansion, survive without new natural resources to exploit? Little wonder that the American people, asking themselves these questions and others like them, succumbed to a panicky fear that helped transform their rural economy, their foreign policy, and their theories of government.

Their hysteria was no better shown than in the skyrocketing prices for farm lands and commodities during the first two decades of the twentieth century. To the farmer this was a delightful—and unaccountable—phenomenon. Since the Panic of 1873 he had watched the cash return from his crops sink lower and lower, as debts mounted and political discontent grew in proportion. Then, suddenly, in 1897 the tide turned. Buyers offered decent prices for wheat, corn that had not been worth marketing began to flow eastward once more, and likestock was in steady demand. For the next years prices moved rapidly upward. Taking the year 1899 as a standard with commodity values at 100, the price index during the following decade was: 1900, 106.4; 1905, 133; 1910, 189.2. The upward spiral was arrested somewhat after 1910, only to climb again with the outbreak of World War I and the mounting demand for American foodstuffs in warring Europe. During all those years, and until 1920, the farmer experienced a prosperity that he had almost forgotten how to enjoy.

The reasons for this inflationary trend in agricultural prices were many. Partly responsible was the general upward swing of the price index as new gold discoveries in Alaska, Africa, and Australia increased the world's supply of money. Partly to blame, too, was the working of the law of supply and demand; lagging farm production during the drought and low-price years between 1887 and 1896 had failed to keep pace with the needs of the growing population. New industrial uses for corn and other farm produce also increased demand just at a time when the supply was short. Those were the real reasons for agricultural prosperity in the early twentieth century, but to the average American another seemed even more important.

The connection between mounting prices and the close of the frontier was inescapable. American lands were running out!

Popular reaction to this grim realization was expressed in several ways. Scholars wrote warnings to future generations in which the term, "law of diminishing returns," frequently figured. Beyond a certain limit of productiveness, they pointed out, an increased application of labor and capital to natural resources would not result in a proportionate increase in yield. The United States had reached that point with the end of the frontier; the virgin fertility of the soil was skimmed off and production in the future would be more halting and expensive. Hence, the prophets insisted, the era of cheap food had passed forever; no longer would American grains allow the world's population to increase as it had in the nineteenth century; no longer could people concentrate in cities and be assured a cheap living. Ahead lay a period of mounting prices, growing scarcity, and a declining standard of living. In the future natural resources must not be squandered; salvation depended on saving and conservation.

Other less responsible seers were even more calamitous as they viewed the end of the era of free land. "With our increasing population," wrote Theodore Roosevelt, "the time is not far distant when the problem of supplying our people with food will become pressing." Said another public leader: "We must increase production per acre by more intelligent methods, or we must face the relentless certain day when we shall not produce enough to supply our own necessities." Even James J. Hill, president of the Great Northern Railroad and thorough student of western conditions, reflected the general alarm: "in twenty-five years," he wrote, "we shall have a nation-wide famine." Amidst such forebodings the nation hurried to preserve its dwindling food supplies against the day of scarcity; exports of wheat to Europe fell off 100,000,000 bushels in the first decade of the twentieth century.

When prophets and public spokesmen voiced such alarming sentiments, little wonder that the ordinary people succumbed to hysterical fear. This was best shown in the skyrocketing of land prices between 1900 and 1920. Everyone wanted farm land, to hold against the day when real famine would send values to even more stratospheric levels. So they rushed to buy; retired farmers bought farm after farm with assurance that their savings were safer than in a bank; eastern capitalists shipped their money westward to share in the virtually guaranteed profits; owners of small farms mortgaged their paid-for acres to buy still more. With demand unlimited and the supply restricted the resulting price rise was inevitable. Lands six miles from a railroad that had sold for $3 an acre in the 1870's went freely in 1910 at $150 an acre. Between 1900 and 1910 prices for farm lands throughout the United States increased 118.1 per cent; in Nebraska the increase was 231.8 per cent, in North Dakota 321.3 per cent, in Idaho 353 per cent, in South Dakota 377.1 per cent. During the next decade prices continued to rise, but at a less rapid pace.

This upward spiraling of land values inevitably affected the farmer. His immediate reaction was one of delighted approval. Never had he known such prosperity; not only did high commodity prices assure him a comfortable living, but the rapid increase in the value of his property transformed him into a wealthy man through no effort of his own. Had he but known, however, those high land prices forecast a troubled future. They meant, for one thing, that he would have to resort to crop specialization to secure an adequate return on his invested capital. By 1920 the one-crop system was as firmly planted in the West as in the South, with hard spring wheat grown almost exclusively in the northern Plains country, hard winter wheat between northern Texas and southern Nebraska, corn in the area about Iowa, and dairy products in the urbanized regions of Illinois, Wisconsin, eastern Iowa, and southern Minnesota. Farmers whose future was mortgaged to one crop were less well equipped to withstand periods of drought or low prices than those practicing diversified agriculture. Even more dangerous was the increase in farm tenancy as eastern investors or western syndicates rushed to secure land in that day of rising prices. By 1920, forty per cent of the farms of Iowa and fifty per cent of the farms of Illinois were owned by absentee landlords. Although tenancy was as low as twenty per cent in some of the newer regions of the West, the trend was clearly toward a system of absentee ownership, share cropping, and the development of a peasant class.

American agriculture could have withstood the disadvantages of specialization and tenancy if the demand for produce had continued high, and if no new competitors had appeared. Unfortunately for the farmer, fate decreed that neither should be the case. Demand steadily declined as the population, which had been growing rapidly in Europe and America during the nineteenth century, leveled off in the twentieth, a victim of modern warfare and a lowered birth rate. Moreover the restrictive immigration laws of the 1920's further restricted the farmers' markets by cutting down the number of food-consuming aliens reaching the East. Equally damaging was the intrusion of new competitors into the world's markets. New hitherto-undeveloped lands brought under cultivation during the prosperous years of the early twentieth century—in Canada, Australia, South America, and Russia especially—were by the 1920's pouring their cheap produce into the food baskets of the western world. Now the American farmer must compete with them, as well as with the improved yields of his own neighbors, made possible by technical improvements and increased care in cultivation.

The result was far from that envisaged by the seers of the early twentieth century. Instead of having too little food, the nation found itself with too much. The artificial demand created by World War I kept prices up until 1920, then the break came. The total farm income of the United States, which had touched a high point of $17,600,000,000 in 1919, slumped to only $10,260,000,000 that year. Six years later it had crept up to $12,985,000,000, but with the industrial depression of 1929 it started down again, reaching $6,900,000,000 in 1931. During the next decade, and until a second world war provided temporary relief, the American farmer existed only through federal bounty. Such were the results of over-expansion in land and prices that followed the closing of the frontier.

The end of the era of westward expansion, although most notable in its effect on the farmer, was not without influence on other aspects of American life. One immediate result was to strengthen popular support for the nation's newly launched imperialistic foreign policy. To say that the vanishing frontier was alone responsible for the jingoism of the 1890's would be a gross exaggeration; improved transportation facilities, the demand of industrialists for markets, the export of surplus capital abroad, and the example set by European nations were all equally important. Yet, for the man on the street, there was a direct connection between the Census Bureau's announcement of 1890 and the need for overseas possessions. With opportunity drawing to a close within the nation's borders, he reasoned, the government's duty was to provide areas for exploitation elsewhere. Hence he gave enthusiastic approval as his leaders grabbed Puerto Rico and the Philippines from Spain in 1898, added the Hawaiian Islands and other Pacific possessions during the next years, muscled Panama from Colombia in 1903, and extended American rule over the Caribbean during the next decade. To many Americans these lands were new frontiers, waiting development by a new type of pioneer from the United States.

More thoughtful men, realizing that no amount of external expansion could replace the vanishing lands of the West, recognized that the nation must learn to live within its fixed borders. This, they saw, would require a new and more positive role for the federal government. In the past the limitless opportunity awaiting everyone in the expanding United States minimized the need for governmental interference in the affairs of individuals. Men could look after themselves; Congress could stand aside while the citizens worked out their own economic destiny amidst the plentiful natural resources available in the nineteenth century. In the future chances for individual success would lessen as free lands vanished. Instead competition for the limited resources remaining would inevitably increase as the continent filled in. Only positive government action would prevent the development of a dog-eat-dog social order in which the few would gain at the expense of the many.

This realization has shaped the political philosophy of progressive American statesmen virtually since the beginning of the twentieth century. It underlay the conservation policies and "trust busting" of Theodore Roosevelt, who realized that the nation's dwindling resources must not only be preserved but kept from falling into the hands of the "interests" if society was to endure. It was basic to the "New Freedom" of Woodrow Wilson, who sought to insure the individual continuing economic opportunity in a frontierless land by checking the trend toward monopoly that was so prevalent in industry. And it was carried to a logical conclusion by Franklin D. Roosevelt, whose "New Deal" was based upon the premise that men must learn to live with each other when flight to the West was impossible. "Today," President Roosevelt declared in a radio address in 1935, "we can no longer escape into virgin territory: we must master our environment. . . . We have been compelled by stark necessity to unlearn the too comfortable superstition that the American soil was mystically blessed with every kind of immunity to grave economic maladjustments, and that the American spirit of individualism—all alone and unhelped by the cooperative efforts of government—could withstand and repel every form of economic disarrangement or crisis."

Acting upon this premise, these and other statesmen of the twentieth century worked diligently to awaken a reluctant American people to the necessities of a closed-space existence. They sought to curb industrial monopolies, made suddenly more dangerous in a land where opportunity for competition in new areas had diminished. They tried to regulate the country's distribution facilities, lest excessive profits for middlemen lower the standard of living. They encouraged workers and farmers to act co-operatively in an effort to wring a more equitable share of the nation's wealth from industry. They set up social security systems to provide old-age pensions, unemployment relief, and disability payments for those temporarily or permanently unable to cope with the problems of society. They attempted, in other words, to secure for individuals through positive governmental action the social welfare and economic opportunity that was once provided by free land.

That the West itself opposed rather than aided this adjustment is not surprising. There the frontier traditions of individualism, surface-skimming waste, brash over-confidence, and reckless speculation were best perpetuated; the pioneer had always been too absorbed in his own pursuit of wealth to pay much attention to the needs of society. Moreover the West had, throughout its history, been a stronghold of political conservatism, despite outraged cries of easterners against western "radicalism." Its periodic protests were really leveled against change, and its fundamental desire was to maintain the democratic, agrarian, social order of the eighteenth century, in the increasingly industrialized world of the nineteenth and twentieth centuries. This was the purpose of the wild "men of the western waters" who in Jackson's day lifted their voices against the financial policies of New England manufacturers. This was the ambition of the Grangers who in the 1870's urged an end to monopolies and a return to free competition. This was the hope of the Populists, who in the 1890's pleaded for the easier money supply that the nation had known before a capitalistic creditor class took over the reins of government. And this was the dream of the farmers who in the 1930's shifted the center of conservative Republicanism to the upper plains states in their vain effort to check a "New Deal" which promised to adjust the entire nation to the needs of a modern industrial world.

Thus the passing of the frontier has important political implications for the future. As western agrarian influence declines in American politics, with the corresponding shift in power to the industrial centers of the East, the way will be opened for the triumph of those newer forces that are today equipping the United States to face the problems of the twentieth century. The hardy, self-reliant men and women who through three centuries conquered the continent have played their role in the drama of American development; as they pass from the scene a new generation, freed from the prejudices of an outworn past where the needs of individuals transcended the needs of society, will blaze the trails into the newer world of co-operative democracy that is America's future.

# Bibliographical Note

The following bibliography is highly selective. Only the most recent works on each subject, those considered best by the authors, and those bearing particularly on topics discussed in the text are included. Space limitations exclude many valuable monographs which, because of their specialized nature, would be of little value to students. The works listed are intended to serve as a guide to further reading for interested inquirers rather than as a definitive bibliography of frontier history. Because so much valuable material is contained in historical journals, many of which are referred to repeatedly, the titles have been abbreviated. The following key lists the abbreviations used:

*A.A.A.G.*   Annals of the Association of American Geographers
*A.A.A.P.S.S.*   Annals of the American Academy of Political and Social Science
A.A.S., *Proceedings*   American Antiquarian Society, Proceedings
*A.B.E.*   American Bureau of Ethnology
*A.E.R.*   American Economic Review
*A.H.*   Agricultural History
A.H.A., *Annual Report*   American Historical Association, Annual Report
*A.H.R.*   American Historical Review
A.H.S., *Transactions*   Alabama Historical Society, Transactions
*A. of I.*   Annals of Iowa
*A. of W.*   Annals of Wyoming
*A.P.S.R.*   American Political Science Review
*Ariz. H.R.*   Arizona Historical Review
*B.A.G.S.*   Bulletin of the American Geographical Society
B.H.S., *Publications*   Buffalo Historical Society, Publications
*Ca.H.R.*   Catholic Historical Review
C.H.A., *Report*   Canadian Historical Association, Report
*C.H.R.*   Canadian Historical Review
C.H.S., *Collections*   Chicago Historical Society, Collections
*C.H.S.Q.*   California Historical Society Quarterly
*C.M.*   Colorado Magazine
*C.O.*   Chronicles of Oklahoma
C.S.M., *Publications*   Colonial Society of Massachusetts, Publications
*E.H.R.*   English Historical Review
E.T.H.S., *Publications*   East Tennessee Historical Society, Publications
*F.C.H.Q.*   Filson Club History Quarterly
*F.H.Q.*   Florida Historical Quarterly
*G.H.Q.*   Georgia Historical Quarterly

*G.R.*    Geographical Review
*H.A.H.R.*    Hispanic American Historical Review
*H.O.*    Historical Outlook
*H.Q.*    History Quarterly
*I.H.B.*    Indiana Historical Bulletin
I.H.S., *Publications*    Indiana Historical Society, Publications
*I.J.H.P.*    Iowa Journal of History and Politics
*I.M.H.*    Indiana Magazine of History
I.S.H.S., *Transactions*    Illinois State Historical Society, Transactions
*J.E.B.H.*    Journal of Economic and Business History
*J.I.S.H.S.*    Journal of the Illinois State Historical Society
*J.L.P.U.E.*    Journal of Land and Public Utility Economics
*J.M.H.*    Journal of Modern History
*J.Miss.H.*    Journal of Mississippi History
*J.P.E.*    Journal of Political Economy
*J.S.H.*    Journal of Southern History
*K.H.Q.*    Kansas Historical Quarterly
K.S.H.S., *Collections*    Kansas State Historical Society, Collections
*K.S.H.S.R.*    Kentucky State Historical Society Register
*L.H.Q.*    Louisiana Historical Quarterly
*M.A.*    Mid-America
*Ma.H.M.*    Maryland Historical Magazine
*M.H.*    Minnesota History
*M.H.B.*    Minnesota History Bulletin
*M.H.M.*    Michigan History Magazine
*M.H.R.*    Missouri Historical Review
M.H.S., *Collections*    Minnesota Historical Society, Collections
M.H.S., *Publications*    Mississippi Historical Society, Publications
M.P.H.S., *Collections*    Michigan Pioneer and Historical Society, Collections
M.V.H.A., *Proceedings*    Mississippi Valley Historical Association, Proceedings
*M.V.H.R.*    Mississippi Valley Historical Review
N.    The Nation
*N.C.H.R.*    North Carolina Historical Review
*N.D.H.Q.*    North Dakota Historical Quarterly
*N.R.*    New Republic
*N.Y.H.*    New York History
N.Y.S.H.A., *Proceedings*    New York State Historical Association, Proceedings
*N.E.Q.*    New England Quarterly
*N.H.*    Nebraska History
*N.H.B.*    Nebraska History Bulletin
*N.L.B.*    Nebraska Law Bulletin
*N.M.H.R.*    New Mexico Historical Review
*O.A.H.Q.*    Ohio Archaeological and Historical Quarterly

*O.H.Q.* · Oregon Historical Quarterly
O.V.H.A.,*Proceedings* Ohio Valley Historical Association, Proceedings
*P.* Palimpsest
*P.H.* Pennsylvania History
*P.H.R.* Pacific Historical Review
*P.M.H.B.* Pennsylvania Magazine of History and Biography
*P.N.Q.* Pacific Northwest Quarterly
*P.S.Q.* Political Science Quarterly
*Q.J.U.N.D.* Quarterly Journal of the University of North Dakota
*Q.J.N.Y.S.H.A.* Quarterly Journal of the New York State Historical Association
*R.E.S.* Review of Economic Statistics
*S.A.Q.* South Atlantic Quarterly
*S.D.H.C.* South Dakota Historical Collections
*S.E.J.* Southern Economic Journal
*S.H.Q.* Southwestern Historical Quarterly
S.H.S.N.D., *Collections* State Historical Society of North Dakota, Collections
S.H.S.W., *Proceedings* State Historical Society of Wisconsin, Proceedings
*S.R.L.* Saturday Review of Literature
*S.S.* Social Studies
*T.H.M.* Tennessee Historical Magazine
*T.S.H.A.Q.* Texas State Historical Association Quarterly
*U.H.Q.* Utah Historical Quarterly
U. of K., *Bulletin* University of Kansas, Bulletin
*V.M.H.B.* Virginia Magazine of History and Biography
W.A.S.A.L.,*Transactions* Wisconsin Academy of Science, Arts and Letters, Transactions
*W.H.Q.* Washington Historical Quarterly
W.H.S., *Proceedings* Wisconsin Historical Society, Proceedings
*W.M.C.Q.* William and Mary College Quarterly
*W.M.H.* Wisconsin Magazine of History
*W.P.H.M.* Western Pennsylvania Historical Magazine
W.R.H.S., *Report* Western Reserve Historical Society, Report
*W.V.H.* West Virginia History
*Y.R.* Yale Review

# I THE FRONTIER HYPOTHESIS

The Turnerian Thesis. Any study of the American frontier should begin with the stimulating essay by Frederick Jackson Turner, "The Significance of the Frontier in American History," in the same author's *The Frontier in American History* (New York, 1920). The same volume contains numerous other studies dealing with aspects of the problem. Scarcely less significant are Turner's additional essays in *The Significance of Sections in American History* (New York, 1932), which deal more specifically with the problem of sectionalism as an aftermath of the frontier's advance. Essays not printed in these two volumes have been collected by Fulmer Mood, ed., *The Early Writings of Frederick Jackson Turner* (Madison, 1938).

Turner's place in the field of American historiography has been examined by numerous writers, many of whose findings are listed in the helpful bibliography by Everett E. Edwards, "References on the Significance of the Frontier in American History," United States Department of Agriculture, *Bibliographic Contributions*, No. 25 (Washington, 1935). Students who suggested the frontier hypothesis before Turner are discussed in Herman C. Nixon, "The Precursors of Turner in the Interpretation of the American Frontier," *S.A.Q.*, XXVIII (January, 1929), and more fully in Fulmer Mood, "The Concept of the Frontier, 1871–1898: Comments on a Select List of Source Documents," *A.H.* XIX (January, 1945). Fulmer Mood, "The Development of Frederick Jackson Turner as a Historical Thinker," C.S.M., *Transactions*, XXXIV (Boston, 1943), surveys Turner's early life and education for sources of his ideas, while the same author in "The Historiographic Setting of Turner's Frontier Essay," *A.H.*, XVII (July, 1943), describes the state of historical writing when the first essay was produced. The same subject is canvassed less thoroughly in Joseph Schafer, "Turner's America," *W.M.H.*, XVII (June, 1934), while Rudolph Freund, "Turner's Theory

of Social Evolution," *A.H.*, XIX (April, 1945), examines the concept of social evolution with which Turner was familiar.

A sympathetic interpretation of Turner's thesis by Avery Craven is in William T. Hutchinson, ed., *The Marcus W. Jernegan Essays in American Historiography* (Chicago, 1937), and a less penetrating evaluation by Carl Becker in Howard W. Odum, ed., *American Masters of Social Science* (New York, 1927). Merle Curti, "The Section and the Frontier in American History: The Methodological Concepts of Frederick Jackson Turner," in Stuart A. Rice, ed., *Methods in Social Science* (Chicago, 1931), is a stimulating appraisal of Turner's methodology and influence on history. A colorful interpretation of the frontier process, showing the Turner influence strongly, is John C. Parish, *The Persistence of the Westward Movement and Other Essays* (Berkeley, 1943), while Avery Craven, "The 'Turner Theories' and the South," *J.S.H.*, V (August, 1939), sympathetically applies the hypotheses to one section. Bayrd Still, "Patterns of Mid-Nineteenth Century Urbanization in the Middle West," *M.V.H.R.*, XXVIII (September, 1941), shows the influence of the urban frontier in the Northwest during the first half of the nineteenth century.

Criticisms of the Hypothesis. A convenient summary of early criticism is in R. L. Lokken, "The Turner Thesis: Criticisms and Defense," *S.S.*, XXXII (December, 1941). These began in the 1920's with John C. Almack, "The Shibboleth of the Frontier," *H.O.*, XVI (May, 1925), a rambling attack from a mildly Marxian point of view. Charles A. Beard, "Culture and Agriculture," *S.R.L.*, V (October, 1928), continued the assault by charging that the frontier thesis explained American development less accurately than such economic forces as capitalism, the slave system, or the labor conflict. This theme was expanded by Louis M. Hacker in two articles: "Sections—or Classes," *N.*, CXXXVII (July, 1933), and "Frederick Jackson Turner;

Non-Economic Historian," *N.R.*, LXXXIII (June 5, 1935), both of which condemned Turner for ignoring the influence of the class struggle in America's past. Frederic L. Paxson, "Generation of Frontier Hypotheses," *P.H.R.*, II (March, 1933), summed up the early criticisms, although he generally accepted the frontier hypothesis. Nevertheless he was answered by Turner's staunchest defender, Joseph Schafer, "Turner's Frontier Philosophy," *W.M.H.*, XVI (June, 1933).

More serious than the early assaults were those that began in the 1930's directed against specific aspects of the frontier thesis. One statement of Turner, that democracy sprang from the American forest, was disputed by Benjamin F. Wright, Jr., in two essays: "American Democracy and the Frontier," *Y.R.*, XX (December, 1930), and "Political Institutions and the Frontier," in Dixon R. Fox., ed., *Sources of Culture in the Middle West* (New York, 1934). Both emphasized the world trend toward democracy and pointed out the imitative nature of western political institutions.

Turner's assertion that the frontier acted as a "safety valve" for oppressed eastern workers was first seriously challenged in two independently prepared articles: Carter Goodrich and Sol Davison, "The Wage Earner and the Western Movement," *P.S.Q.*, L (June, 1935), and LI (March, 1936), and Murray Kane, "Some Considerations on the Safety Valve Doctrine," *M.V.H.R.*, XXIII (September, 1936). They were answered by Joseph Schafer in three articles: "Some Facts Bearing on the Safety-Valve Theory," *W.M.H.*, XX (December, 1936), "Concerning the Frontier as Safety Valve," *P.S.Q.*, LII (September, 1937), and "Was the West a Safety Valve for Labor," *M.V.H.R.*, XXIV (December, 1937). The meager statistics advanced by Schafer to prove the frontier was a safety valve were questioned by Carter Goodrich and Sol Davison, "The Frontier as Safety Valve: A Rejoinder," *P.S.Q.*, LIII (June, 1938). The failure of the Homestead Act to attract

eastern workers was demonstrated in Fred A. Shannon, "The Homestead Act and the Labor Surplus," *A.H.R.*, XLI (July, 1936), while Rufus 'S. Tucker, "The Frontier as an Outlet for Surplus Labor," *S.E.J.*, VII (October, 1940), analyzed population trends to reach the same conclusion. A practical demonstration of the impossibility of the West serving as a safety valve is in Clarence H. Danhof, "Farm-Making Costs and the 'Safety Valve': 1850–60," *J.P.E.*, XLIX (June, 1941). A final word on the subject was voiced by Fred A. Shannon, "A Post Mortem on the Labor-Safety-Valve Theory," *A.H.*, XIX (January, 1945), which argued that the frontier after the 1840's was not even an outlet for potential wage earners.

During the 1940's the attacks on the frontier hypothesis broadened to include other features. Murray Kane, "Some Considerations on the Frontier Concept of Frederick Jackson Turner," *M.V.H.R.*, XXVII (December, 1940), contended that Turner was at fault in explaining migration solely in geographic terms, rather than as a complex social phenomenon. James C. Malin, *Essays in Historiography* (Lawrence, 1946), similarly deplored Turner's emphasis on a "space concept" to the exclusion of other forces. More devastating were two articles by George W. Pierson, "The Frontier and Frontiersmen of Turner's Essays," *P.M.H.B.*, LXIV (October, 1940), and "The Frontier and Our Institutions," *N.E.Q.*, XV (June, 1942), the first questioning the concept that American traits stemmed largely from the frontier, the second that the country's institutions derived from the western environment. Less critical of Turner was Gilbert J. Garraghan, "Non-Economic Factors in the Frontier Movement," *M.A.*, XXIII (October, 1941), which pointed out that religious forces were as important as economic in sending men west.

The Physiographic Basis of Sectionalism. A useful description of the physiographic provinces making up the United States is in Wallace W. Atwood, *The Physiographic*

*Provinces of North America* (Boston, 1940).
J. W. Powell, "Physiographic Regions of
the United States," in National Geographic
Society, *The Physiography of the United
States* (New York, 1896), is brief but help-
ful. General accounts are in J. Russell Smith,
*North America* (New York, 1925), C.
Langdon White and Edwin J. Foscue, *Re-
gional Geography of North America* (New
York, 1943), and especially Ralph H.
Brown, *Historical Geography of the United
States* (New York, 1948).

## II EUROPE'S FIRST FRONTIER

Spain in America. Curtis P. Nettels, *Roots
of American Civilization* (New York,
1938), and Max Savelle, *Foundations of
American Civilization* (New York, 1942),
contain brief accounts. Silvio Zavala, *New
Viewpoints on the Spanish Colonization of
America* (Philadelphia, 1943), describes
Spanish colonizing methods in the light of
modern scholarship.

The narratives of the principal explorers
are in Frederick W. Hodge and Theodore H.
Lewis, *Spanish Explorers in the Eastern
United States, 1528–1543 (Original Narratives of Early American History*, New York,
1907). Cleue Hallenbeck, *Álvar Núñez
Cabeza de Vaca* (Glendale, 1940) repro-
duces documents dealing with de Vaca's
journey, while de Soto's wanderings are described by contemporaries in Edward G.
Bourne, ed., *Career of Hernando de Soto*
(New York, 1904), and James A. Robertson, ed., *True Relation of the Hardships
Suffered by Governor Fernando de Soto*,
2 v. (Deland, 1923). The chronicles of
Don Tristán de Luna Y Arellano's ill-
fated attempt to settle Florida are in Herbert I. Priestly, ed., *The Luna Papers*, 2 v.
(Deland, 1928). Herbert E. Bolton, ed.,
*Arredondo's Historical Proof of Spain's
Title to Georgia* (Berkeley, 1925), prints
documents on the origins of the mission
system.

Early Spanish exploration and attempts
at settlement are described in two books by
Woodbury Lowery, *Spanish Settlements*
*within the Present Limits of the United
States, 1513–1561* (New York, 1901) and
*Spanish Settlements within the Present Lim-
its of the United States. Florida, 1562–1574*
(New York, 1905). Herbert E. Bolton, *The
Spanish Borderlands (Chronicles of America
Series*, New York, 1921), covers the same
material in briefer form, while John B.
Brebner, *Explorers of North America, 1492–
1806* (New York, 1933), deals with the
principal explorations. Edward W. Lawson, *The Discovery of Florida and its Discoverer Juan Ponce De Leon* (St. Augustine, 1946) deals with the early period.
The de Soto expedition is thoroughly studied in T. Maynard, *De Soto and the Conquistadores* (New York, 1930). F. A. Kirk-
patrick, *The Spanish Conquistadores* (New
York, 1934), treats the early phases of the
Spanish conquest exhaustively.

Spain's attempts to occupy the Georgia
coast are described in several articles. J. G.
Johnson, "A Spanish Settlement in Carolina,
1526," *G.H.Q.* VII (December, 1923),
deals with the Aylön expedition to San
Miguel de Guadalupe; J. G. Johnson, "The
Spaniards in Northern Georgia during the
Sixteenth Century," *G.H.Q.*, IX (June,
1925), describes Menéndez's attempts to
found interior forts; and Mary Ross, "The
Spanish Settlement of Santa Elena," *G.H.Q.*,
IX (December, 1925), treats the beginnings
of Port Royal. Any study of the Spanish
mission frontier should begin with Herbert
E. Bolton, "The Mission as a Frontier
Institution in the Spanish-American Colo-
nies," *A.H.R.*, XXIII (October, 1917). The
two standard works on the missions in eastern North America are Herbert E. Bolton
and Mary Ross, *The Debatable Land*
(Berkeley, 1925), and John T. Lanning,
*The Spanish Missions of Georgia* (Chapel
Hill, 1935).

Spain's efforts to hold her North American
empire are described in Verne E. Chatelain,
*The Defenses of Spanish Florida, 1565–
1763* (Washington, 1941), Mary Ross,
"French Intrusions and Indian Uprisings in
Georgia and South Carolina, 1577–1580,"

*G.H.Q.*, VII (September, 1923), J. G. Johnson, "The Yamassee Revolt of 1597 and the Destruction of the Georgia Missions," *G.H.Q.*, VII (March, 1923), and Mary Ross, "The Restoration of the Spanish Missions in Georgia, 1598–1606," *G.H.Q.*, X (September, 1926).

France in America. Collected documents on the Cartier voyages are in Henry S. Burrage, ed., *Early English and French Voyages, 1534–1608 (Original Narratives of Early American History*, New York, 1906), and three volumes edited by H. P. Biggar:*The Precursors of Jacques Cartier* (Ottawa, 1911), *The Voyages of Jacques Cartier* (Ottawa, 1924), and *A Collection of Documents Relating to Jacques Cartier and the Sieur de Roberval* (Ottawa, 1930). The Champlain narratives have been collected in six volumes edited by H. P. Biggar and others, *The Works of Samuel de Champlain* (Toronto, 1922–1936). Also useful are W. L. Grant, ed., *Voyages of Samuel de Champlain, 1604–1618 (Original Narratives of Early American History*, New York, 1907), and Edward G. Bourne, *The Voyages and Explorations of Samuel de Champlain*, 2 v. (Toronto, 1911).

Among the secondary works dealing with French expansion in the St. Lawrence Valley, Francis Parkman, *Pioneers of France in the New World* (Boston, 1885), still holds top rank. William B. Munro, *Crusaders of New France (Chronicles of America Series*, New Haven, 1918), and Reuben G. Thwaites, *France in America, 1497–1763 (The American Nation: A History*, New York, 1905), deal with the same period. A fuller account is in George M. Wrong, *The Rise and Fall of New France*, 2 v. (New York, 1928). The careers of Cartier and Champlain are described in two volumes of *The Chronicles of Canada*, 32 v. (Toronto, 1914–1916): Stephen Leacock, *Mariner of St. Malo*, and Charles W. Colby, *Founder of New France*.

Early French exploration is discussed in Lawrence J. Burpee, *The Discovery of Canada* (New York, 1926), and John B. Brebner, *Explorers of North America, 1492–1806* (New York, 1933). H. P. Biggar, *The Early Trading Companies of New France* (Toronto, 1901), first demonstrated the relationship between the fisheries and the fur trade. The influence of trade on French expansion is described in H. A. Innis, *The Fur Trade in Canada* (New Haven, 1930), and Clarence Vandiveer, *The Fur-Trade and Early Western Exploration* (Cleveland, 1929).

## III ENGLISHMEN ON THE TIDEWATER

English Exploration and Settlement. The English voyages of discovery are described in James A. Williamson, *A Short History of British Expansion* (London, 1922), J. Holland Rose, ed., *The Cambridge History of the British Empire. The Old Empire* (New York, 1929), and more fully in James A. Williamson, *The Voyages of the Cabots and the English Discovery of North America under Henry VII and Henry VIII* (London, 1929). Colony founding and institutional development in English America are the themes of Charles M. Andrews, *The Colonial Period of American History. The Settlements*, 3 v. (New Haven, 1934–37), and Herbert L. Osgood, *The American Colonies in the Seventeenth Century*, 3 v. (New York, 1904–07). The latter contains chapters on the land system, defense, and Indian relations. Works concerned more specifically with the southern colonies include, Mary Johnson, *Pioneers of the Old South (Chronicles of America Series*, New Haven, 1918), William E. Dodd, *The Old South. Struggles for Democracy* (New York, 1937), and Thomas J. Wertenbaker, *The Old South: The Founding of American Civilization* (New York, 1942). Thomas J. Wertenbaker, *The First Americans, 1607–1690 (History of American Life Series*, New York, 1927), and Louis B. Wright, *The Atlantic Frontier* (New York, 1947), deal with social and economic conditions in the English colonies, while C. Wissler, ed., *Adventures in the Wilderness (The Pageant of*

*America,* New York, 1925), is a pictorial representation.

Geographic conditions in the Tidewater are described in Ralph H. Brown, *Historical Geography of the United States* (New York, 1948), Ellen C. Semple, *American History and Its Geographic Conditions* (Boston, 1933), and George T. Surface, *Studies on the Geography of Virginia* (Philadelphia, 1907).

Virginia and Maryland. Documentary materials dealing with settlement and expansion are in Alexander Brown, ed., *The Genesis of the United States,* 2 v. (Boston, 1890), Lyon G. Tyler, ed., *Narratives of Early Virginia, 1606–1625 (Original Narratives of Early American History,* (New York, 1907), and Clayton C. Hall, ed., *Narratives of Early Maryland, 1633–1684 (Original Narratives of Early American History,* New York, 1910). C. M. Andrews, ed., *Narratives of the Insurrections, 1675–1690 (Original Narratives of Early American History,* New York, 1915), contains the records of Bacon's Rebellion.

Secondary works concerned largely with seventeenth-century Virginia include Thomas J. Wertenbaker, *Virginia Under the Stuarts, 1607–1688* (Princeton, 1914), and the same author's *The Planters of Colonial Virginia* (Princeton, 1922), which emphasizes the effect of agriculture on the colony's institutions. Mathew P. Andrews, *The Soul of a Nation: The Founding of Virginia* (New York, 1943), deals in detail with the first twenty years of Virginia history. Two volumes by Philip A. Bruce, *Economic History of Virginia in the Seventeenth Century,* 2 v. (New York, 1896), and *Institutional History of Virginia in the Seventeenth Century,* 2 v. (New York, 1910), contain accounts of agricultural development, Indian defense, and the land system.

On early Maryland history the student may consult Newton D. Mereness, *Maryland as a Proprietary Province* (New York, 1901), Bernard C. Steiner, *Beginnings of Maryland* (Baltimore, 1903), or Mathew P. Andrews, *The Founding of Maryland* (Baltimore, 1933).

The history of agricultural expansion in the Tidewater remains to be written, although the possibilities of such a study are suggested in the first essay in Thomas P. Abernethy, *Three Virginia Frontiers* (University, Louisiana, 1941). Scattered information is in L. C. Gray, *History of Agriculture in the Southern United States to 1860,* 2 v. (Washington, 1933), Lyman Carrier, *The Beginnings of American Agriculture* (New York, 1923), and Meyer Jacobstein, *The Tobacco Industry in the United States* (New York, 1907). One important expelling force is studied in A. O. Craven, *Soil Exhaustion as a Factor in the Agricultural History of Virginia and Maryland* (Urbana, 1925), while Vertrees J. Wyckoff, *Tobacco Regulation in Colonial Maryland* (Baltimore, 1936), explores another aspect of the same problem.

The effect of the land system on southern expansion still waits study. Amelia C. Ford, *Colonial Precedents of Our National Land System* (Madison, 1910), contains some scattered information but is far from adequate. A few students have more recently demonstrated the rich returns awaiting scholars who delve into the land office records of Virginia and Maryland: Abbot E. Smith, "The Indentured Servant and Land Speculation in Seventeenth Century Maryland," *A.H.R.,* XL (April, 1935), V. J. Wyckoff, "The Size of Plantations in Seventeenth-Century Maryland," *Ma.H.M.* XXXII (December, 1937), and V. J. Wyckoff, "Land Prices in Seventeenth-Century Maryland," *A.E.R.,* XXVII (March, 1938). More important is the careful study of the land system in one part of Virginia, Susie M. Ames, *Studies of the Virginia Eastern Shore in the Seventeenth Century* (Richmond, 1940), David W. Eaton, *Historical Atlas of Westmoreland County, Virginia* (Richmond, 1942), also contains some information. For the effect of labor conditions on expansion the student may consult Marcus W. Jernegan, *Laboring and Dependent Classes in Colonial America* (Chicago, 1931), and Ulrich B. Phillips, *American Negro Slavery* (New York, 1918).

The story of the Virginia fur trade and Indian relations remains to be told. A. J. Morrison, "The Virginia Indian Trade to 1673," *W.M.C.Q.*, I (October, 1921), is brief. One phase of the defense problem is discussed in John S. Bassett's introduction to *The Writings of Colonel William Byrd* (New York, 1901). The standard account of Bacon's Rebellion is Thomas J. Wertenbaker, *Torchbearer of the Revolution* (Princeton, 1940).

The Carolina Frontier. Documents on early Carolina history are in Alexander S. Salley, *Narratives of Early Carolina, 1650–1708* (*Original Narratives of Early American History*, New York, 1911), while two standard secondary accounts of South Carolina are Edward McCrady, *The History of South Carolina under the Proprietary Government, 1670–1719* (New York, 1897), and David D. Wallace, *The History of South Carolina*, 4 v. (New York, 1934–35). The agricultural advance is considered in W. A. Schaper, "Sectionalism and Representation in South Carolina," A.H.A., *Annual Report for 1900* (Washington, 1901), and St. Julian R. Childs, *Malaria and Colonization in the Carolina Low Country, 1526–1692* (Baltimore, 1940).

The most important work on the Carolina fur trade and the conflicts with New Spain is Verner W. Crane, *The Southern Frontier, 1670–1732* (Durham, 1928). Other aspects of the international struggle on the southern borderland are considered in Herbert E. Bolton, "Spanish Resistance to the Carolina Traders in Western Georgia (1680–1704)," *G.H.Q.*, IX (June, 1925), Herbert E. Bolton and Mary Ross, *The Debatable Land* (Berkeley, 1925), and J. G. Johnson, "The Spanish Period of Georgia and South Carolina History, 1566–1702," *University of Georgia Bulletin*, XXIII (May, 1923). John R. Swanton, *The Early History of the Creek Indians and their Neighbors* (Washington, 1922), is also informative.

## IV THE NEW ENGLAND FRONTIER

General Works. The comprehensive works by Andrews and Osgood cited in the previous chapter are essential to understanding the settlement of New England, as is Percy W. Bidwell and John I. Falconer, *History of Agriculture in the Northern United States, 1620–1860* (Washington, 1925). Charles M. Andrews, *The Fathers of New England* (*Chronicles of America Series*, New Haven, 1919), and James T. Adams, *The Founding of New England* (Boston, 1921), are also valuable, although the latter's contention that economic factors motivated the Puritan migration is challenged by Nellis M. Crouse, "Causes of the Great Migration, 1630–1640," *N.E.Q.*, V (January, 1932). Of particular importance to students of the frontier is Lois K. Mathews, *The Expansion of New England* (Boston, 1909). R. A. East, "Puritanism and New Settlement." *N.E.Q.*, XVII (June, 1944), deals with the expelling effect of religious conflicts.

Studies of Specific Colonies. The classic account of Plymouth settlement, written by a contemporary, is William Bradford, *History of Plymouth Plantation* (*Original Narratives of Early American History*, New York, 1908). More recent accounts include Ronald G. Usher, *The Pilgrims and Their History* (New York, 1918), Arthur Lord, *Plymouth and the Pilgrims* (Boston, 1920), and George F. Willison, *Saints and Strangers* (New York, 1945). The Mayflower Compact as a frontier document is considered in Lois K. Mathews, "The Mayflower Compact and Its Descendants," M.V.H.A., *Proceedings*, VI (1912–13).

Among the many books on the early development of Massachusetts are Frances Rose-Troup, *The Massachusetts-Bay Company and Its Predecessors* (New York, 1930), and Charles E. Banks, *The Planters of the Commonwealth* (Boston, 1930). Useful biographies include: Samuel E. Morison, *Builders of the Bay Colony* (Boston, 1930), Lawrence S. Mayo, *John Endecott: A Biography* (Cambridge, 1936), and Frances Rose-Troup, *John White* (New York, 1930). John Winthrop's account is edited by James K. Hosmer, *Winthrop's Journal "History of New England," 1630–1649*, 2 v. (*Original Narratives of Early American History*, New York, 1908).

The westward movement into the Connecticut Valley can be studied in scholarly pamphlets sponsored by the Connecticut Tercentenary Commission: Dorothy Deming, *The Settlement of the Connecticut Towns* (New Haven, 1933), Charles M. Andrews, *The Beginnings of Connecticut, 1632–1662* (New Haven, 1934), and Lois K. Mathews Rosenberry, *Migrations from Connecticut Prior to 1800* (New Haven, 1934). No adequate life of Thomas Hooker exists, although light on his frontier career is thrown by Perry G. Miller, "Hooker and Connecticut Democracy," *N.E.Q.*, IV (October, 1931). Harral Ayres, *The Great Trail of New England* (Boston, 1940), traces the routes used in migrations to the Connecticut Valley. The standard work on the New Haven Colony is Isabel M. Calder, *The New Haven Colony* (New Haven, 1934).

Rhode Island's history is told in Irving B. Richman, *Rhode Island, Its Making and Its Meaning*, 2 v. (New York, 1902), but Samuel H. Brockunier, *The Irrepressible Democrat. Roger Williams* (New York, 1940), is essential to any understanding of the colony's early years. The wanderings of another Rhode Island founder are traced by Kenneth W. Porter, "Samuell Gorton. New England Firebrand," *N.E.Q.*, VII (March, 1934). A special section of Rhode Island is studied in Edward Channing, *The Narragansett Planters* (Baltimore, 1886).

General works on the Middle Colonies include Maud W. Goodwin, *Dutch and English on the Hudson* (*Chronicles of America Series*, New Haven, 1919), Sidney G. Fisher, *The Quaker Colonies* (*Chronicles of America Series*, New Haven, 1919), and

Thomas J. Wertenbaker, *The Founding of American Civilization. The Middle Colonies* (New York, 1938). Particularly useful for New York is the co-operative work edited by A. C. Flick, *History of the State of New York*, 10 v. (New York, 1932–37), and S. G. Nissenson, *The Patroon's Domain* (New York, 1937), a legalistic study of the land system. The Swedish settlements on the Delaware are described in Amandus Johnson, *The Swedish Settlements on the Delaware, 1638–1664.* 2 v. (New York, 1911), and more readably in Christopher Ward, *The Dutch and Swedes on the Delaware, 1609–64* (Philadelphia, 1930).

The New England Land System. The origin of the town system of settlement is explained in John F. Sly, *Town Government in Massachusetts (1620–1930)* (Cambridge, 1930), while the development of several selective towns is traced in Anne B. MacLear, *Early New England Towns* (New York, 1908). Two important studies that throw light on the land system developed within the towns are Roy H. Akagi, *The Town Proprietors of the New England Colonies* (Philadelphia, 1924), and Florence M. Woodard, *The Town Proprietors in Vermont* (New York, 1936). The growth of speculative enterprise in Maine, Rhode Island, and the Middle Colonies still awaits study.

Indians and the Fur Trade. No subjects in colonial history deserve investigation more than the fur trade, Indian relations, and defense. Francis X. Moloney, *The Fur Trade in New England, 1620–1676* (Cambridge, 1931), is thoughtful, but limited in scope; Arthur H. Buffinton, "New England and the Western Fur-Trade, 1629–1675," *C.S.M.*, *Publications*, XVIII (Boston, 1917), deals only with international conflicts arising from trade; and Charles H. McIlwain, ed., *An Abridgment of the Indian Affairs . . . by Peter Wraxall* (Cambridge, 1915), serves as a guide to further study rather than a final treatment. A comprehensive work is badly needed, as well as special studies of phases and leaders. Daniel S. Updike, *Richard Smith: First English Set-*

*tler of the Narragansett Country, Rhode Island* (Boston, 1937), shows the possibility of the latter type of work. No study of Indian-white relations has appeared, although Lloyd C. M. Hare, *Thomas Mayhew, Patriarch to the Indians* (New York, 1932), sheds light on Puritan efforts to christianize the red men. The only investigation of the defense problem is the brief essay by Frederick J. Turner, "The First Official Frontier of the Massachusetts Bay," *The Frontier in American History* (New York, 1920). Books on the militia system and on defense are needed.

More attention has been paid to the Indian wars. Documents are in Charles H. Lincoln, ed., *Narratives of the Indian Wars, 1675–1699* (Original Narratives of Early American History, New York, 1913), and Charles Orr, *History of the Pequot War* (Cleveland, 1897). Herbert M. Sylvester, *Indian Wars of New England*, 3 v. (Boston, 1910), is voluminous but uncritical. A brief account of the Pequot War is Howard Bradstreet, *The Story of the War with the Pequots, Re-Told* (New Haven, 1933), while George W. Ellis and John E. Morris, *King Philip's War* (New York, 1906), deals with that conflict.

## V THE OLD WEST

General Works. Frederick Jackson Turner, "The Old West," *The Frontier in American History* (New York, 1920), is the best comprehensive account, although fuller information on the land system, fur trade, Indian defense, and colonial wars is in Herbert L. Osgood, *American Colonies in the Eighteenth Century*, 4 v. (New York, 1924–25).

Exploration and Settlement of the Piedmont. The standard work on exploration is Clarence W. Alvord and Lee Bidgood, *The First Explorations of the Trans-Allegheny Region by the Virginians, 1650–1674* (Cleveland, 1912). This should be supplemented with Fairfax Harrison, "Western Explorations in Virginia between Lederer and Spotswood," *V.M.H.B.*, XXX (October,

1922), and Lyman Carrier, "The Veracity of John Lederer," *W.M.C.Q.*, XIX (October, 1939). A brief but helpful introduction to the story of expansion into the Piedmont and Great Valley is in Thomas P. Abernethy, *Three Virginia Frontiers* (University, Louisiana, 1941). F. B. Kegley, *Kegley's Virginia Frontier* (Roanoke, 1938), contains a mass of ill-digested information on the Great Valley Settlements, while Leonidas Dodson, *Alexander Spotswood, Governor of Colonial Virginia, 1710–1722* (Philadelphia, 1932), explores the career of a leading advocate of expansion. Material on the westward movement in North Carolina may be gleaned from Archibald Henderson, *North Carolina: the Old North State and the New*, 2 v. (Chicago, 1941). David D. Wallace, *The History of South Carolina*, 4 v. (New York, 1934–35) contains much information, although Robert I. Meriwether, *The Expansion of South Carolina, 1729–1765* (Kingsport, Tennesseee, 1941), is more valuable. The latter, although overdetailed, represents the type of careful regional study necessary before the final history of the settlement of the Old West can be written.

The Middle Colonies. Necessary to an understanding of the New York frontier is Ruth L. Higgins, *Expansion in New York with Especial Reference to the Eighteenth Century* (Columbus, 1931). A special account of the land system is Charles W. Spencer, "The Land System of Colonial New York," *N.Y.S.H.A.*, Proceedings, XVI (1917).

The frontier movement in Pennsylvania is touched upon in the general histories of the colony, of which the most recent is Wayland F. Dunway, *A History of Pennsylvania* (New York, 1935). Documents are in Sylvester K. Stevens and Donald H. Kent, eds., *Wilderness Chronicles of Northwestern Pennsylvania* (Harrisburg, 1941), while Charles A. Hanna, *The Wilderness Trail*, 2 v. (New York, 1911), contains a mass of ill-digested but valuable information on the movement into the Susquehanna Valley. The

career of a leading frontiersman is studied in
Irma J. Cooper, *The Life and Public Services of James Logan* (New York, 1921).
Good studies of the Pennsylvania land system, and of the westward penetration of
traders and farmers, are needed.

The best work on early German migration
to the Middle Colonies is Walter A. Knittle,
*Early Eighteenth Century Palatine Emigra-
tion* (Philadelphia, 1937), which deals with
immigration to New York, 1708–10. Later
migrations are studied less thoroughly in
Albert B. Faust, *The German Element in the
United States*, 2 v. (Boston, 1909). The
history of the Palatines in Pennsylvania is
treated in Jesse L. Rosenberger, *The Pennsylvania Germans* (Chicago, 1923), and
their social development in Ralph Wood,
ed., *The Pennsylvania Germans* (Princeton,
1942). The German advance into the Great
Valley is the theme of John W. Wayland,
*The German Element of the Shenandoah
Valley of Virginia* (Charlottesville, 1907).

On the Scotch-Irish settlements, Henry J.
Ford, *The Scotch-Irish in America* (Princeton, 1915), is adequate although far from
complete. A later work, Maude Glasgow,
*The Scotch-Irish in Northern Ireland and
in the American Colonies* (New York,
1936), adds little, while Charles A. Hanna,
*The Scotch Irish*, 2 v. (New York, 1902),
and Charles K. Bolton, *Scotch-Irish Pioneers
in Ulster and America* (Boston, 1910), contain a mass of undigested information. The
religious practices of the group are studied
in Guy S. Klett, *Presbyterians in Colonial
Pennsylvania* (Philadelphia, 1937).

Settlement of the New England Back
Country. In addition to the works cited in
Chapter IV, James T. Adams, *Revolutionary
New England, 1691–1776* (Boston, 1923),
is helpful. The works of Akagi and Wood-
ard on the land system deal also with the
eighteenth century. Expansion into western
Connecticut is studied in Albert L. Olson,
*Agricultural Economy and Population in
Eighteenth-Century Connecticut* (New Ha-
ven, 1935), and into Vermont in Matt B.
Jones, *Vermont in the Making, 1750–1777*

(Cambridge, 1939), Frederic F. Van de
Water, *The Reluctant Republic, Vermont,
1724–1791* (New York, 1941), and Charles
M. Thompson, *Independent Vermont* (Boston, 1942). The impact of the Massachusetts and New York frontiers is described in
Oscar Handlin, "The Eastern Frontier of
New York," *N.Y.H.*, XVIII (January,
1937). Julian P. Boyd's introduction to *The
Susquehannah Company Papers*, 3 v.
(Wilkes-Barre, 1930–31), treats the westward movement into Pennsylvania, a subject explored more briefly in the same
author's *The Susquehannah Company: Connecticut's Experiment in Expansion* (New
Haven, 1935).

Significance of the Old West. Theodore
Roosevelt, *The Winning of the West*, 6 v.
(New York, 1889), is a classic description
of social life, while Thomas J. Wertenbaker, *The Founding of American Civilization. The Middle Colonies* (New York,
1938), stresses foreign contributions. Joseph Doddridge, *Notes on the Settlement and
Indian Wars of the Western Parts of Virginia and Pennsylvania* (Pittsburgh, 1912),
is a delightful contemporary description. A
modern account of life in the back country
is D. Huger Bacot, "The South Carolina Up
Country at the End of the Eighteenth Century," *A.H.R.*, XXVIII (July, 1923). The
evolution of a distinctive frontier architec-
ture is traced in Harold R. Shurtleff, *The
Log Cabin Myth* (Cambridge, 1939), and
of the frontier's chief weapon in John G.
Dillin, *The Kentucky Rifle* (Washington,
1924), and Felix Reichmann, "The Pennsylvania Rifle: A Social Interpretation of
Changing Military Techniques," *P.M.H.B.*,
XLIX (January, 1945).

No single work deals with the sectional
conflicts of the eighteenth century. Specialized studies for individual colonies include:
Charles H. Lincoln, *The Revolutionary
Movement in Pennsylvania* (Philadelphia,
1901), Irving Mark, *Agrarian Conflicts in
Colonial New York, 1711–1775* (New
York, 1940), Charles H. Ambler, *Sectionalism in Virginia from 1776 to 1861* (Chi-

cago, 1910), John S. Bassett, "The Regulators of North Carolina," A.H.A., *Annual Report for 1894* (Washington, 1895), Archibald Henderson, "The Origin of Regulation in North Carolina," *A.H.R.*, XXI (January, 1916), Marshall DeL. Haywood, *Governor William Tryon* (Raleigh, 1903), and William A. Schaper, "Sectionalism and Representation in South Carolina," A.H.A., *Annual Report for 1900* (Washington, 1901). A valuable interpretation is Max Farrand, "The West and the Principles of the Revolution," *Y.R.*, XVII (May, 1908).

## VI THE FRENCH BARRIER

General Works. Among the general histories which deal extensively with French Canada are: George M. Wrong, *The Rise and Fall of New France*, 2 v. (New York, 1928), Herbert I. Priestley, *France Overseas through the Old Régime* (New York, 1939), Morden H. Long, *A History of the Canadian People* (New York, 1942), and Donald G. Creighton, *Dominion of the North: A History of Canada* (Boston, 1944). More detailed information is in the collaborative work edited by Adam Shortt and Arthur G. Doughty, *Canada and Its Provinces*, 23 v. (Toronto, 1914–17). An interpretive article dealing with French expansion is Louise P. Kellogg, "France and the Mississippi Valley: A Résumé," *M.V.H.R.*, XVIII (June, 1931). The influence of the fur trade on expansion is the theme of Harold A. Innis, *The Fur Trade in Canada* (New Haven, 1930), and Clarence A. Vandiveer, *The Fur-Trade and Early Western Exploration* (Cleveland, 1929).

Early Explorers and Missionaries. John B. Brebner, *The Explorers of North America* (New York, 1933), is brief and convenient, but may be supplemented with Paul L. Haworth, *Trailmakers of the Northwest* (New York, 1921), which deals specifically with French explorers. Documents on exploration are in Louise P. Kellogg, ed., *Early Narratives of the Northwest, 1634–1699 (Original Narratives of Early American History*, New York 1917), and more

fully in Pierre Margry, *Découvertes et Établissements des Français*, 6 v. (Paris, 1879–88). The standard work on Jolliet and and Marquette is Francis B. Steck, *The Jolliet-Marquette Expedition, 1673* (Washington, 1927), and on the adventures of Radisson and Groseilliers, Grace L. Nute, *Caesars of the Wilderness* (New York, 1943). Narratives of the latter's voyages have been edited by Gideon D. Scull, *Radisson's Voyages* (Boston, 1885).

Documents dealing with French missionary activity are in Reuben G. Thwaites, ed., *The Jesuit Relations, 1610–1791*, 73 v. (Cleveland, 1896–1901). A journal of an early missionary party, edited by George M. Wrong, is Father Gabriel Sagard, *The Long Journey to the Country of the Hurons* (Toronto, 1939). Secondary accounts of missionary activity include: Francis Parkman, *The Jesuits in North America* (Boston, 1898), Thomas G. Marquis, *The Jesuit Missions (Chronicles of Canada Series*, Toronto, 1916), and Sister Mary D. Mulvey, *French Catholic Missionaries in the Present United States (1604–1791)* (Washington, 1936). Sister Mary G. Leger, *The Catholic Indian Missions in Maine (1611–1820)* (Washington, 1929), deals with the Jesuits on that borderland, Frank H. Severance, *Old Trails on the Niagara Frontier* (Cleveland, 1903) studies their activities south of Lake Ontario, George Paré "The St. Joseph Mission," *M.V.H.R.*, XVII (June, 1930), considers their expansion into Michigan, and Sister Mary B. Palm, *The Jesuit Missions of the Illinois Country, 1673–1763* (St. Louis, 1931), treats their occupation of Illinois.

The Period of Expansion, 1670-1690. Louise P. Kellogg, *The French Régime in Wisconsin and the Northwest* (Madison, 1925), and Clarence W. Alvord, *The Illinois Country, 1673–1818 (Centennial History of Illinois*, Springfield, 1920), describe the French occupation of the Northwest. The same story is more popularly told in the classic volumes of Francis Parkman: *La Salle and the Discovery of the Great West, The Old Régime in Canada under Louis XIV*, and *Count Frontenac and New France under Louis XIV* (Boston, 1898). Thomas Chapis, *The Great Intendant* (*Chronicles of Canada Series*, Toronto, 1914), deals with Talon, while biographies of Frontenac include: Charles W. Colby, *The Fighting Governor* (*Chronicles of Canada Series*, Toronto, 1915), William D. Le Sueur, *Count Frontenac* (*Makers of Canada Series*, New York, 1926), and Jean Delanglez, *Frontenac and the Jesuits* (Chicago, 1939).

The narratives of La Salle's expeditions are in Isaac J. Cox, ed., *The Journeys of La Salle*, 2 v. (New York, 1905), while the story of his explorations is told in Marc de Villiers, *L'expédition de Cavelier de la Salle dans le Gulfe du Mexique* (Paris, 1931). Daniel C. Draper, "La Salle and the Ohio River," *W.V.H.*, II (January, 1941), concludes La Salle's early explorations carried him to the Mahoning River. Father Hennepin's exaggerated account of his exploits is in Reuben G. Thwaites, ed., *Louis Hennepin*, 2 v. (Chicago, 1903), and Grace L. Nute, ed., *Father Louis Hennepin's Description of Louisiana* (Minneapolis, 1938).

Documents on the French occupation of the Northwest are in Theodore C. Pease and Raymond C. Werner, eds., *The French Foundations, 1680–1693* (Springfield, Illinois, 1934). Local studies touching on the expansion include: Milo M. Quaife, *Chicago and the Old Northwest* (Chicago, 1913), Peter L. Scanlan, *Prairie du Chien: French, British, American* (Prairie du Chien, 1937), and Grace L. Nute, *The Voyageur's Highway: Minnesota's Border Lake Land* (St. Paul, 1941). Indian warfare in the Northwest is admirably described in George T. Hunt, *The Wars of the Iroquois* (Madison, 1940), while documents on the subject are in Emma H. Blair, ed., *Indian Tribes of the Upper Mississippi and the Great Lakes Region*, 2 v. (Cleveland, 1912). The early history of the Hudson's Bay Company is summarized in Douglas Mackay, *The Honourable Company* (London, 1937).

Conflict on the Northern Borderland, 1690–1715. No single historian has de-

scribed either the French-English wars for North America or any one of the contests. Francis Parkman, *A Half Century of Conflict*, 2 v. (Boston, 1898), provides the only connected account, although a briefer story is in George M. Wrong, *The Conquest of New France* (*Chronicles of America Series*, New Haven, 1918), and a pictorial version in William Wood and Ralph H. Gabriel, *The Winning of Freedom* (*The Pageant of America*, New Haven, 1927).

The influence of New York fur traders on the beginning of conflict deserves a full-length study along lines laid down in the introduction to Charles H. McIlwain, *An Abridgement of the Indian Affairs . . . by Peter Wraxall* (Cambridge, 1915). Several articles deal with aspects of the problem: Arthur H. Buffinton, "The Policy of Albany and English Westward Expansion," *M.V.H.R.*, VIII (March, 1922), Helen Broshar, "The First Push Westward of the Albany Traders," *M.V.H.R.*, VII (December, 1920), and William T. Morgan, "The Five Nations and Queen Anne," *M.V.H.R.*, XIII (September, 1926). Ruth L. Higgins, *Expansion in New York with Especial Reference to the Eighteenth Century* (Columbus, 1931), is valuable for New York warfare, while James T. Adams, *Revolutionary New England, 1691–1776* (Boston, 1923), describes the conflict on the New England borderland. The latter should be supplemented by Ronald O. MacFarlane, "The Massachusetts Bay Truck-Houses in Diplomacy with the Indians," *N.E.Q.*, XI (March, 1938), and Arthur H. Buffinton, "The Isolationist Policy of Colonial Massachusetts," *N.E.Q.*, I (April, 1928).

Conflict on the Southern Borderland, 1690–1715. The French-Spanish-English conflicts are described in Verner W. Crane, *The Southern Frontier, 1670–1732* (Durham, 1928), and Herbert E. Bolton and Mary Ross, *The Debatable Land* (Berkeley, 1925). Efforts of the warring nations to secure Indian allies are recounted in John R. Swanson, *Early History of the Creek Indians and Their Neighbors* (Washington,

1922), and John R. Swanton, *Indian Tribes of the Lower Mississippi Valley and Adjacent Coast to the Gulf of Mexico* (Washington, 1911). The expansion of the English trading frontier is the theme of Mary Rothrock, "Carolina Traders among the Overhill Cherokees, 1690–1760," E.T.H.S., *Publications* I (1929), and W. Neil Franklin, "Virgina and the Cherokee Indian Trade, 1673–1752," E.T.H.S., *Publications*, IV (1932).

The conflict over the founding of Louisiana is treated in Frank E. Melvin, "Dr. Daniel Coxe and Carolana," *M.V.H.R.*, I (September, 1914), and William E. Dunn, "French and Spanish Rivalry in the Gulf Region of the United States, 1678–1702," University of Texas, *Bulletin* (Austin, 1917). The latest biography of the successful contestant is Grace King, *Jean Baptiste le Moyne Sieur de Bienville* (New York, 1892), while the fullest local account is Peter J. Hamilton, *Colonial Mobile* (Boston, 1910). Charles Gayarré, *History of Louisiana*, 4 v. (New Orleans, 1903), is the standard history of the colony. Later conflicts are described in Stanley Faye, "The Contest for Pensacola Bay and Other Gulf Ports, 1698–1722," *F.H.Q.*, XXIV (January, 1946). The early development of Louisiana is described in N. M. Miller Surrey, *The Commerce of Louisiana during the French Régime, 1699–1763* (New York, 1916), and N. M. Miller Surrey, "The Development of Industries in Louisiana during the French Regime, 1673–1763," *M.V.H.R.*, IX (December, 1922).

The Southern Frontier, 1715–1740. The Franco-Spanish conflicts on the western borders of Louisiana are described in Isaac J. Cox, "The Significance of the Louisiana-Texas Frontier," M.V.H.A., *Proceedings*, III (1909–10), and William E. Dunn, "Spanish Reaction against the French Advance toward New Mexico, 1717–1727," *M.V.H.R.*, II (December, 1915). The founding of Georgia is treated in Amos A. Ettinger, *James Edward Oglethorpe, Imperial Idealist* (Oxford, 1935), E. Merton

Coulter, *A Short History of Georgia* (Chapel Hill, 1933), E. Merton Coulter, *Georgia: A Short History* (Chapel Hill, 1947), and Verner W. Crane, "Projects for Colonization in the South, 1684–1732," *M.V.H.R.*, XII (June, 1925). Verner W. Crane, *The Southern Frontier, 1670–1732* (Durham, 1928), is the best account of the conflict in the Southeast to 1732, while the story is continued in less satisfactory form in John P. Corry, *Indian Affairs in Georgia, 1732–1756* (Philadelphia, 1936), and James G. Johnson, *The Colonial Southeast, 1732–1763; An International Contest for Territorial and Economic Control* (Boulder, 1932). Georgia-Creek relations are considered in E. Merton Coulter, "Mary Musgrove, 'Queen of the Creeks': A Chapter of Early Georgia Troubles," *G.H.Q.*, XI (March, 1927), while an important episode in the conflict is treated in John T. Lanning, *The Diplomatic History of Georgia: A Study of the Epoch of Jenkin's Ear* (Chapel Hill, 1936).

The Northwestern Frontier, 1715–1740. In addition to the standard volumes by Kellogg and Alvord cited above, information is contained in Ida A. Johnson, *The Michigan Fur Trade* (Lansing, 1919), and Murray G. Lawson, *Fur: A Study in English Mercantilism, 1700–1775* (Toronto, 1943). The Fox Wars are fully described in Louise Kellogg, "The Fox Indian Wars during the French Régime," S.H.S.W., *Proceedings* (1907). The narratives of La Vérendrye are in Lawrence J. Burpee, ed., *Journals and Letters of La Vérendrye and His Sons* (Toronto, 1927), while the career of that explorer is recounted in Lawrence J. Burpee, *Pathfinders of the Plains* (*Chronicles of Canada Series*, Toronto, 1915), and Arthur S. Morton, "La Vérendrye," *C.H.R.*, IX (March, 1929). Solon J. Buck, "The Story of the Grand Portage," *M.H.B.*, V (February, 1923), deals with expansion west of Lake Superior.

The Northern Frontier, 1715–1740. In addition to the works listed above on the New York-New England region, informa-

tion may be found in two studies by Frank
H. Severance: "The Story of Joncaire,"
B.H.S., *Publications*, IX (1906), and *An
Old Frontier of France; the Niagara Region
and Adjacent Lakes Under French Control*,
2 v. (New York, 1917). Sir William Johnson still waits an adequate biography, although Arthur Pound, *Johnson of the Mohawks* (New York, 1930), is useful. Johnson's papers have been edited by James Sullivan and Alexander C. Flick, *The Papers of
Sir William Johnson*, 9 v. (Albany, 1921–
39). An account of relations between New
York and the Iroquois, based on papers of
the Society for the Propagation of the Gospel, is John W. Lydekker, *The Faithful Mohawks* (New York, 1938). Books previously
cited on New England's northern frontier,
may be supplemented by a valuable re-
interpretation of Lovewell's War: Fannie H.
Eckstorm, "The Attack on Norridgewock:
1724," *N.E.Q.*, VII (September, 1934). New
England's role in the warfare of the 1740's
is recounted in Louis E. de Forest, ed.,
*Louisbourg Journals, 1745* (New York,
1932), and Arthur H. Buffinton, "The
Canada Expedition of 1746," *A.H.R.*, XLV
(April, 1940).

The Ohio Valley Frontier, 1720–1754.
The westward movement of the Pennsyl-
vania trading frontier is studied in Wayland
F. Dunaway, *A History of Pennsylvania*
(New York, 1935), Beverley Bond, Jr., *The
Foundations of Ohio* (*The History of Ohio*,
Columbus, 1941), George A. Cribbs, *The
Frontier Policy of Pennsylvania* (Pitts-
burgh, 1919), and C. Hale Sipe, *Indian
Wars of Western Pennsylvania* (Harrisburg,
1929). The contest of the Virginia and
Pennsylvania traders for the commerce of
the region is described in W. Neil Franklin,
"Pennsylvania-Virginia Rivalry for the In-
dian Trade of the Ohio Valley," *M.V.H.R.*,
XX (March, 1934). Thorough biographies
of the leading Pennsylvania expansionists
are: Paul A. W. Wallace, *Conrad Weiser,
1696–1760* (Philadelphia, 1945), Arthur
D. Graeff, *Conrad Weiser, Pennsylvania
Peacemaker* (Fogelsville, Pennsylvania,

1946), and Albert T. Volwiler, *George
Croghan and the Westward Movement,
1741–1782* (Cleveland, 1926). French ac-
tivities in the region are the theme of George
A. Wood, "Céloron de Blainville and French
Expansion in the Ohio Valley," *M.V.H.R.*,
IX (March, 1923), Charles W. Dahlinger,
*The Marquis Duquesne, Sieur de Menne-
ville* (Pittsburgh, 1932), and Norman W.
Caldwell, *The French in the Mississippi
Valley, 1740–1750* (Urbana, 1941). Calvin
Goodrich, *The First Michigan Frontier*
(Ann Arbor, 1940), deals with the upper
lakes region.

The Seven Years' War. Among the dozens of general accounts of the war, which
range from Francis Parkman's vivid *Montcalm and Wolfe*, 2 v. (Boston, 1898), to
laborious monographs, the most useful recent
books are: Lawrence H. Gipson, *The British
Empire Before the American Revolution*,
Vols. V (*Zones of International Friction,
1748–1754*), and VI (*The Great War for
the Empire; 1754–1757*) (New York, 1942–
46), Walter L. Dorn, *Competition for Empire, 1740–1763* (New York, 1940), Sig-
mund Samuel, *The Seven Years War in
Canada* (Toronto, 1934), and Julian S.
Corbett, *England in the Seven Years' War*,
2 v. (London, 1907). Recent biographies of
leaders include: J. C. Long, *Mr. Pitt and
America's Birthright* (New York, 1940),
F. E. Whitton, *Wolfe and North America*
(Boston, 1929), W. T. Waugh, *James
Wolfe* (Montreal, 1928), J. C. Long, *Lord
Jeffery Amherst* (New York, 1933), and
Stanley M. Pargellis, *Lord Loudoun in
North America* (New Haven, 1933).

The part played by the Ohio Company
in opening the struggle is traced in Kenneth
P. Bailey, *The Ohio Company of Virginia
and the Westward Movement, 1748–1792*
(Glendale, 1939). The journals of the company's leading explorer are in William M.
Darlington, ed., *Christopher Gists's Journals* (Louisville, 1898). The career of another pioneer active in the West is the theme
of Lilly L. Nixon, *James Burd, Frontier Defender* (Philadelphia, 1941). Virginia's role

in precipitating conflict is traced in the standard biography of the colonial governor, Louis K. Koontz, *Robert Dinwiddie* (Glendale, 1940), while Washington's expeditions of 1753 and 1754 are described in Charles H. Ambler, *George Washington and the West* (Chapel Hill, 1936). Washington's account of his journeys is in J. M. Toner, ed., *Journal of Colonel George Washington . . . Across the Allegheny Mountains in 1754* (Albany, 1893). An overall picture of the controversies leading the two countries into war is Max Savelle, *The Diplomatic History of the Canadian Boundary, 1749-1763* (New Haven, 1940).

Recent conclusions concerning Braddock's expedition are embodied in Thad W. Riker, "The Politics Behind Braddock's Expedition," *A.H.R.*, XIII (July, 1908), and Stanley Pargellis, "Braddock's Defeat," *A.H.R.*, XLI (January, 1936). John B. Brebner, *New England's Outpost. Acadia before the Conquest of Canada* (New York, 1927), describes the Acadian campaigns, although the same material is covered more thoroughly in J. Clarence Webster, *The Forts of Chignecto; A Study of the Eighteenth Century Conflict between France and Great Britain in Acadia* (St. John, New Brunswick, 1930).

The defenses of the Middle Colonies, made necessary by Braddock's defeat, are described in such works as: G. D. Albert, *Frontier Forts of Western Pennsylvania* (Harrisburg, 1900), C. Hale Sipe, *Fort Ligonier and Its Times* (Harrisburg, 1932), J. M. King, "Colonel John Armstrong," *W.P.H.M.*, X (July, 1927), John S. Fisher, "Colonel Armstrong's Expedition against Kittanning," *P.M.H.B.*, LI (January, 1927), and Mary C. Darlington, *History of Colonel Henry Bouquet and the Western Frontiers of Pennsylvania, 1747-1764* (n.p., 1920). The Forbes' expedition can be studied in Alfred P. James, ed., *Writings of General John Forbes Relating to His Service in North America* (Pittsburgh, 1938). Virginia's role in the war is treated in Hayes Baker-Crothers, *Virginia and the French and*

*Indian War* (Chicago, 1928), Louis K. Koontz, *The Virginia Frontier, 1754-1763* (Baltimore, 1925), and Roy B. Cook, "Virginia Frontier Defenses, 1719-1795," *W.V.H.*, I (January, 1940).

The story of the Cherokee War is contained in scattered articles: W. Neil Hamilton, "Virginia and the Cherokee Indian Trade, 1753-1775," *E.T.H.S., Publications*, V (1933), Philip M. Hamer, "Anglo-French Rivalry in the Cherokee Country, 1754-1757," *N.C.H.R.*, II (July, 1925), Philip M. Hamer, "Fort Loudoun in the Cherokee War, 1758-1761," *N.C.H.R.*, II (October, 1925), and Samuel C. Williams, "Fort Robinson on the Holston," *E.T.H.S., Publications*, IV (1932).

The French exodus from the interior after defeat is described in Louise P. Kellogg, "La Chapelle's Remarkable Retreat Through the Mississippi Valley, 1760-1761," *M.V.H.R.*, XXII (June, 1935). Documents on the diplomacy of the peace are in Theodore C. Pease, ed., *Anglo-French Boundary Disputes in the West, 1749-1763* (Springfield, Illinois, 1936). The establishment of the western boundary is considered in Theodore C. Pease, "The Mississippi Boundary of 1763: a Reappraisal of Responsibility," *A.H.R.*, XL (January, 1935), and Arthur S. Aiton, "The Diplomacy of the Louisiana Cession," *A.H.R.*, XXXVI (July, 1931). British occupation of one conquered territory is described in C. N. Howard, "The Military Occupation of British West Florida, 1763," *F.H.Q.*, XVII (January, 1939).

## VII BRITISH WESTERN POLICY

General Works. The most thorough study of British western policy between 1763 and 1775 is Clarence W. Alvord, *The Mississippi Valley in British Politics*, 2 v. (Cleveland, 1917), although the author's over-enthusiastic appraisal of Lord Shelburne should be tempered by a reading of R. A. Humphreys, "Lord Shelburne and the Proclamation of 1763," *E.H.R.*, XLIX (April, 1934), and R. A. Humphreys, "Lord Shelburne and British Colonial Policy, 1766–1768," *E.H.R.*, L (April, 1935). Alvord's judgments are based on the sound but laudatory biography by Lord Edmund Fitzmaurice, *Life of William, Earl of Shelburne*, 3 v. (London, 1912).

Arthur Pound, *Johnson of the Mohawks* (New York, 1930), is inadequate in its treatment of Sir William Johnson's superintendency, although the deficiency is partially remedied by the thorough study of his lieutenant by Albert T. Volwiler, *George Croghan and the Westward Movement, 1741–1782* (Cleveland, 1926). Equally essential to an understanding of the period is the scholarly biography of Colonel John Stuart, John R. Alden, *John Stuart and the Southern Colonial Frontier* (Ann Arbor, 1944). Additional light is thrown on Indian relations along the southern frontier by Clarence E. Carter, "British Policy towards the American Indians in the South, 1763–1768," *E.H.R.*, XXXIII (January, 1918), Helen L. Shaw, *British Administration of the Southern Indians, 1756–1783* (Lancaster, Pennsylvania, 1931), and Merritt B. Pound, "Colonel Benjamin Hawkins—North Carolinian—Benefactor of the Southern Indians," *N.C.H.R.*, XIX (January, 1942, and April, 1942). The superintendents' activity in redrawing the Proclamation Line is described in Max Farrand, "The Indian Boundary Line," *A.H.R.*, X (July, 1905), and Ray A. Billington, "The Ft. Stanwix Treaty of 1768," *N.Y.H.*, XXV (April, 1944).

Land Speculation. The principal study of speculation in the pre-Revolutionary years, Thomas P. Abernethy, *Western Lands and the American Revolution* (New York, 1937), is as essential to an understanding of the period as Alvord's work. In addition several monographs deal more fully with specific speculating concerns: Kenneth P. Bailey, *The Ohio Company of Virginia and the Westward Movement, 1748–1792* (Glendale, 1939), George E. Lewis, *The Indiana Company, 1768–1798* (Glendale, 1941), Archer B. Hulbert, "Washington's 'Tour of the Ohio' and Articles of 'The Mississippi Company'," *O.A.H.Q.*, XVII (October,

1908), Archibald Henderson, "Dr. Thomas Walker and the Loyal Land Company of Virginia," *A.A.S.*, *Proceedings*, n.s., XLI (1931), and Clarence W. Alvord, ed., *The Illinois-Wabash Company* (Chicago, 1915). Washington's many speculative enterprises are considered in Charles H. Ambler, *George Washington and the West* (Chapel Hill, 1936), and Roy B. Cook, *Washington's Western Lands* (Strasburg, Virginia, 1930). General accounts that touch on speculation are Shaw Livermore, *Early American Land Companies* (New York, 1939), and Temple Bodley, *Our First Great West* (Louisville, 1938).

Pontiac's Rebellion. Francis Parkman, *Conspiracy of Pontiac*, 2 v. (Boston, 1910), although half a century old, is still sound, although Howard H. Peckham, *Pontiac and the Indian Uprising* (Princeton, 1947) is more scholarly. Briefer accounts are in Frederic A. Ogg, *The Old Northwest* (*Chronicles of America Series*, New Haven, 1921), and Thomas G. Marquis, *The War Chief of the Ottawas* (*Chronicles of Canada Series*, Toronto, 1915). Studies of the principal military leader include E. Douglas Branch, "Henry Bouquet: Professional Soldier," *P.M.H.B.*, LVII (January, 1938), Mary C. Darlington, *History of Colonel Henry Bouquet and the Western Frontiers of Pennsylvania, 1747–1764* (n.p., 1920), and Pennsylvania Historical Commission, *The Papers of Colonel Henry Bouquet* (Harrisburg, 1940— in progress).

British Occupation of the Illinois Country and the Northwest. Three volumes edited by Clarence W. Alvord and Clarence E. Carter contain the essential documents: *The Critical Period, 1763–1765* (Springfield, Illinois, 1915), *The New Regime, 1765–1767* (Springfield, 1916), and *Trade and Politics, 1767–1769* (Springfield, 1921). The standard secondary work on the Illinois country is Clarence E. Carter, *Great Britain and the Illinois Country, 1763–1774* (Washington, 1910), although Clarence W. Alvord, *The Illinois Country, 1763–1818* (*Centennial History of Illinois*, Springfield, 1920), contains a brief account. These books should be supplemented by two studies of trading activity in Illinois: Max Savelle, *George Morgan, Colony Builder* (New York, 1932), and William V. Byars, *B. and M. Gratz, Merchants in Philadelphia, 1754–1798* (Jefferson City, Missouri, 1916). Reasons for the failure of Morgan's concern are discussed in Charles M. Thomas, "Successful and Unsuccessful Merchants in the Illinois Country," *J.I.S.H.S.*, XXX (January, 1938).

The standard works on the British occupation of the Northwest are Louise P. Kellogg, *The British Régime in Wisconsin and the Northwest* (Madison, 1935), and Nelson V. Russell, *The British Régime in Michigan and the Old Northwest* (Northfield, Minnesota, 1939). Wayne E. Stevens, *The Northwest Fur Trade, 1763–1800* (Urbana, 1928), deals with that important subject, while the effect of the trade on British western policy is considered in Marjorie G. Reid, "The Quebec Fur-Traders and Western Policy," *C.H.R.*, VI (March, 1925).

British Occupation of Florida. Two articles by Clarence E. Carter, "The Beginnings of British West Florida," *M.V.H.R.*, IV (December, 1917), and "Some Aspects of British Administration in West Florida," *M.V.H.R.*, I (December, 1914), are useful, although the fullest study is Cecil Johnson, *British West Florida, 1763–1783* (New Haven, 1943). On East Florida the student may consult Wilbur H. Siebert, "The Departure of the Spaniards and Other Groups from East Florida, 1763–1764," *F.H.Q.*, XIX (October, 1940), and Charles L. Mowat, "The Land Policy in British East Florida," *A.H.*, XIV (April, 1940).

The Quebec Act. The two latest works on the measure are Reginald Coupland, *The Quebec Act* (Oxford, 1925), and Charles H. Metzger, *The Quebec Act, a Primary Cause of the American Revolution* (New York, 1936). The administration of the act is considered in Hilda M. Neatby, *The Administration of Justice under the Quebec Act* (Minneapolis, 1937).

## VIII SETTLEMENT CROSSES THE MOUNTAINS

General Works. No single book traces the history of the trans-Appalachian frontier. Theodore Roosevelt, *The Winning of the West*, 6 v. (New York, 1889–1896), first called attention to the importance of the region in the history of American expansion. Many aspects of settlement are considered in Thomas P. Abernethy, *Western Lands and the American Revolution* (New York, 1937), and in Constance L. Skinner, *Pioneers of the Old Southwest (Chronicles of America Series*, New Haven, 1919).

Expansion of the Northern Frontier. An early study of the advance of settlement into western Pennsylvania, Alfred P. James, "The First English-Speaking Trans-Appalachian Frontier," *M.V.H.R.*, XVII (June, 1930), although still useful, has been supplanted by Solon J. Buck and Elizabeth H. Buck, *The Planting of Civilization in Western Pennsylvania* (Pittsburgh, 1939). Other accounts of the occupation of the region are: C. M. Bomberger, *A Short History of Westmoreland County* (Jeanette, Pennsylvania, 1942), Kenneth P. Bailey, *Thomas Cresap, Maryland Frontiersman* (Boston, 1944), and Kenneth P. Bailey, "Christopher Gist and the Trans-Allegheny Frontier," *P.H.R.*, XIV (March, 1945). Social conditions are described in J. E. Wright and Doris S. Corbett, *Pioneer Life in Western Pennsylvania* (Pittsburgh, 1940), while sources are collected in Sylvester K. Stevens and Donald H. Kent, eds., *Wilderness Chronicles of Northwestern Pennsylvania* (Harrisburg, 1941).

The West Virginia frontier is considered in Ruth W. Dayton, *Pioneers and Their Homes on the Upper Kanawha* (Charleston, W.Va., 1948), Lewis P. Summers, *History of Southwest Virginia, 1746–1786* (Richmond, 1903), Lucullus McWhorter, *The Border Settlers of Northwest Virginia from 1767 to 1795* (Hamilton, Ohio, 1915), Charles H. Ambler, *A History of West Virginia* (New York, 1933), and Charles H. Ambler, *West Virginia: The Mountain State* (New York, 1940).

The Holston and Watauga Frontiers. A thorough account is Samuel C. Williams, *Dawn of Tennessee Valley and Tennessee History* (Johnson City, Tennessee, 1937), and a briefer study is Thomas P. Abernethy, *From Frontier to Plantation in Tennessee* (Chapel Hill, 1932). Information will also be found in Philip H. Hamer, ed., *Tennessee, a History, 1673–1932*, 4 v. (New York, 1933), and John P. Arthur, *Western North Carolina* (Raleigh, 1914). One important settlement is described in William A. Pusey, "The Location of Martin's Station, Virginia," *M.V.H.R.*, XV (December, 1928). Frederick J. Turner, "Western State-Making in the Revolutionary Era," *A.H.R.*, I (October, 1895, and January, 1896), first placed the Watauga Association in its true place in frontier history. The standard biography of a leader of the settlement is Carl S. Driver, *John Sevier, Pioneer of the Old Southwest* (Chapel Hill, 1932).

Lord Dunmore's War. The history of the war may be traced in the introductions and documents in Reuben G. Thwaites and Louise P. Kellogg, *Documentary History of Lord Dunmore's War* (Madison, 1905), although the causes of the struggle cannot be understood without consulting Randolph C. Downes, "Dunmore's War: An Interpretation," *M.V.H.R.*, XXI (December, 1934), and Percy B. Caley, "Lord Dunmore and the Pennsylvania-Virginia Boundary Dispute," *W.P.H.M.*, XXII (June, 1939). The principal battle has been described in Virgil A. Lewis, *History of the Battle of Point Pleasant* (Charleston, 1909).

The Kentucky Frontier. Much information can be gleaned from the histories of Kentucky, of which the most recent are Temple Bodley, *History of Kentucky before the Louisiana Purchase in 1803* (Chicago, 1928), and Thomas D. Clark, *A History of Kentucky* (New York, 1937). A fuller account is Robert S. Cotterill, *History of Pioneer Kentucky* (Cincinnati, 1917), while a valuable interpretative essay is in Thomas P. Abernethy, *Three Virginia Frontiers* (University, Louisiana, 1941). Willard R.

Jillson, *Pioneer Kentucky* (Frankfort, 1934), contains some scattered information of importance.

The career of Dr. Thomas Walker is described in Ann W. Burns, *Daniel Boone's Predecessor in Kentucky* (Frankfort, 1930), while Lucien Beckner, "John Findley: The First Pathfinder of Kentucky," *H.Q.*, I (April, 1927), deals with another pioneer. Of the more than fifty biographies of Daniel Boone, the most complete is John Bakeless, *Daniel Boone* (New York, 1939). Boone's Wilderness Road is also described in numerous works, of which the most recent are William A. Pusey, *The Wilderness Road to Kentucky* (New York, 1921), and Robert L. Kincaid, *The Wilderness Road* (Indianapolis, 1947).

The first historian to demonstrate the importance of the Transylvania Company in the settlement of Kentucky was Archibald Henderson, *The Conquest of the Old Southwest* (New York, 1920). Professor Henderson's distant relationship to Judge Richard Henderson so blinded him to his ancestor's faults that he lauded the pioneer beyond reason, going so far as to uphold the legality of the Treaty of Sycamore Shoals and the Camden-Yorke decision. Hence his study has been supplanted by William S. Lester, *The Transylvania Company* (Spencer, Indiana, 1935). A little-known activity of the company is the theme of Samuel C. Williams, "Henderson and Company's Purchase Within the Limits of Tennessee," *T.H.M.*, V (April, 1919).

Among the best of the many histories of pioneer settlements in Kentucky are: George W. Ranck, *Boonesborough* (Louisville, 1901), Willard R. Jillson, *Harrod's Old Fort* (Frankfort, 1929), and Calvin M. Fackler, *Early Days of Danville* (Danville, 1941). Readable contemporary accounts of the settlements include Lewis H. Kilpatrick, ed., "Journal of William Calk," *M.V.H.R.*, VII (March, 1921), and Louise P. Kellogg, "A Kentucky Pioneer Tells Her Story of Early Boonesborough and Harrodsburg," *F.C.H.Q.*, III (October, 1929).

## IX THE WEST IN THE AMERICAN REVOLUTION

General Accounts. No history of the West in the Revolutionary War has been written. A history of the war, with chapters on the frontier, is Claude H. VanTyne, *The American Revolution* (*The American Nation: A History*, New York, 1905), while Thomas P. Abernethy, *Western Lands and the American Revolution* (New York, 1937), also contains useful material. Theodore Roosevelt, *The Winning of the West*, 6 v. (New York, 1889–1896), although voluminous, is notable more for its vivid style than for its accuracy. Temple Bodley, *Our First Great West: In Revolutionary War, Diplomacy and Politics* (Louisville, 1938) is unbalanced and antiquarian in tone.

The War in the South. Brief general accounts are in Thomas P. Abernethy, *From Frontier to Plantation in Tennessee* (Chapel Hill, 1932), and Archibald Henderson, *Conquest of the Old Southwest* (New York, 1920), but the modern story of the early phases of the war in the Southwest must be pieced together from monographs: Philip M. Hamer, "John Stuart's Indian Policy During the Early Months of the Revolution," *M.V.H.R.*, XVII (December, 1930), Philip M. Hamer, "The Wataugans and the Cherokee Indians in 1776," E.T.H.S., *Publications*, III (1931), Randolph C. Downes, "Cherokee-American Relations in the Upper Tennessee Valley, 1776–1791," E.T.H.S., *Publications*, VIII (1936), and Robert S. Cotterill, "The Virginia-Chickasaw Treaty of 1783," *J.S.H.*, VIII (November, 1942). Documents dealing with an important treaty have been collected by Archibald Henderson, ed., "The Treaty of Long Island on the Holston, July, 1777," *N.C.H.R.*, VIII (January, 1931). Charles C. Royce, *The Cherokee Nation of Indians* (Washington, 1887) is a standard history of the tribe.

A thorough work on the Virginia frontier is Freeman H. Hart, *The Valley of Virginia in the American Revolution, 1763–1789* (Chapel Hill, 1942), while Tennessee dur-

ing the period is studied in Samuel C. Williams, *Tennessee During the Revolutionary War* (Nashville, 1944). The latter book's description of the founding of Nashville may be supplemented by William H. McRaven, *Life and Times of Edward Swanson* (Nashville, 1937), and Archibald Henderson, "Richard Henderson: The Authorship of the Cumberland Compact and the Founding of Nashville," *T.H.M.*, II (September, 1916). A biography of James Robertson is needed.

The War in the Northwest. Particularly useful for the war in Kentucky are John Bakeless, *Daniel Boone* (New York, 1939), William S. Lester, *The Transylvania Company* (Spencer, Indiana, 1935), and Robert S. Cotterill, *History of Pioneer Kentucky* (Cincinnati, 1917). The siege of Boonesborough is described in George W. Ranck, *Boonesborough* (Louisville, 1901).

George Rogers Clark has inspired as much authorship as Daniel Boone. Documents dealing with his career have been edited by James A. James, *George Rogers Clark Papers, 1771–1784*, 2 v. (Springfield, Illinois, 1912–26), and Milo M. Quaife, *The Capture of Old Vincennes* (Indianapolis, 1927). The most useful biography, which is also the best history of the war in the Northwest, is James A. James, *The Life of George Rogers Clark* (Chicago, 1928), although Temple Bodley, *George Rogers Clark* (Boston, 1926), is of some use. A brief summary of his career is in Theodore C. Pease and Marguerite J. Pease, *George Rogers Clark and the Revolution in Illinois, 1763–1787* (Springfield, Illinois, 1929). Clarence W. Alvord, ed., *The Illinois-Wabash Land Company* (Chicago, 1915), suggests that land speculation was one factor encouraging Clark to undertake his Illinois campaigns.

A controversial literature has developed over the influence of Clark's campaigns on the peace commissioners who awarded the Northwest to the United States. James A. James insists that Clark won the Northwest, in his book and in two articles: "To What Extent Was George Rogers Clark in Military Control of the Northwest at the Close of the American Revolution?" A.H.A., *Annual Report for 1917* (Washington, 1920), and "The Northwest: Gift or Conquest?" *I.M.H.*, XXX (March, 1934). The opposite point of view, that Clark no longer controlled the West in 1783, is defended by Clarence W. Alvord, "Virginia and the West; An Interpretation," *M.V.H.R.*, III (June, 1916). That the American peace commissioners knew of Clark's conquest is shown in a letter edited by Lewis J. Carey, "Franklin is Informed of Clark's Activities in the Old Northwest," *M.V.H.R.*, XXI (December, 1934).

The history of the Illinois country after Clark's conquest may be traced in the two volumes of documents edited by Clarence W. Alvord: *Cahokia Records, 1778–1790* (Springfield, Illinois, 1907), and *Kaskaskia Records, 1778–1790* (Springfield, 1909). Secondary accounts dealing with the period are Clarence W. Alvord, *The Illinois Country, 1673–1818 (Centennial History of Illinois,* Springfield, 1920), Robert L. Schuyler, *The Transition in Illinois from the British to American Government* (New York, 1909), and Carl E. Boyd, "The County of Illinois," *A.H.R.*, IV (July, 1899).

The Revolution in the upper Northwest is described in Louise P. Kellogg, *The British Régime in Wisconsin and the Northwest* (Madison, 1935), and Nelson V. Russell, *The British Régime in Michigan and the Old Northwest* (Northfield, Minnesota, 1939). Indian diplomacy in the region is the theme of Louise P. Kellogg, "Indian Diplomacy During the Revolution in the West," I.S.H.S., *Transactions*, XXXVI (1929), while Nelson V. Russell, "The Indian Policy of Henry Hamilton, a Revaluation," *C.H.R.*, XI (March, 1930), exonerates the Detroit commander of the charge of being a "hair buyer." The career of one of the Detroit Tory leaders is traced in Thomas Boyd, *Simon Girty, The White Savage* (New York, 1928).

Documents on the contest for the upper Ohio Valley have been edited by Reuben G. Thwaites and Louise P. Kellogg: *The Revolution on the Upper Ohio, 1775–1777* (Madison, 1908), *Frontier Defense on the Upper Ohio, 1777–1778* (Madison, 1912), *Frontier Advance on the Upper Ohio, 1778–1779* (Madison, 1916), and *Frontier Retreat on the Upper Ohio, 1779–1781* (Madison, 1917). The story of warfare there is told in a series of monographs. Max Savelle, *George Morgan, Colony Builder* (New York, 1932), and Randolph C. Downes, "George Morgan, Indian Agent Extraordinary, 1776–1779," *P.H.*, I (October, 1934), deal with the early years, as does Percy B. Caley, "The Life-Adventures of Lieutenant-Colonel John Connolly," *W.P.H.M.*, XI (January, 1928), and following issues. The later period is studied in Randolph C. Downes, "Indian War on the Upper Ohio, 1779–1782," *W.P.H.M.*, XVII (June, 1934), which concludes that the American hold on the region gradually declined. Other accounts of important events in the area are: Milo M. Quaife, "The Ohio Campaigns of 1782," *M.V.H.R.*, XVII (March, 1931), Louis E. Graham, "Fort McIntosh," *W.P.H.M.*, XV (May, 1932), and Marie J. Kohnova, "The Moravians and Their Missionaries. A Problem in Americanization," *M.V.H.R.*, XIX (December, 1932). Warfare in Pennsylvania is described in Lewis S. Shimmell, *Border Warfare in Pennsylvania during the Revolution* (Harrisburg, 1901).

The New York Frontier During the Revolution. A thorough account of the war in western New York is Francis W. Halsey, *The Old New York Frontier* (New York, 1901), although the story is told more briefly in Alexander C. Flick, *History of the State of New York,* 10 v. (New York, 1932–37). Another scholarly treatment is Howard Swiggett, *War Out of Niagara* (New York, 1933). The careers of Tory raiders who ravaged the frontier are traced in Ernest A. Cruikshank, *The Story of Butler's Rangers and the Settlement of Niagara* (Welland, Ontario, 1894), William L.

Stone, *Life of Joseph Brant* (New York, 1838), and Mabel G. Walker, "Sir John Johnson, Loyalist," *M.V.H.R.*, III (December, 1916). A thorough history of the most important campaign is Alexander C. Flick, *The Sullivan-Clinton Campaign in 1779* (Albany, 1929).

The War on the Mississippi River. The best account of the struggle for the lower Mississippi is John W. Caughey, *Bernardo de Gálvez in Louisiana, 1776–1783* (Berkeley, 1934), which may be supplemented by Elizabeth H. West, "The Indian Policy of Bernardo de Gálvez," M.V.H.A., *Proceedings*, VIII (1915). Other important studies are: John W. Caughey, "Willing's Expedition Down the Mississippi," *L.H.Q.*, XV (January, 1932), Kathryn Abbey, "Peter Chester's Defense of the Mississippi After the Willing Raid," *M.V.H.R.*, XXII (June, 1935), and D. C. Corbitt, "James Colbert and the Spanish Claims to the East Bank of the Mississippi," *M.V.H.R.*, XXIV (March, 1938). The activities of the leading American in the region are described in James A. James, *Oliver Pollock: The Life and Times of an Unknown Patriot* (New York, 1937).

Studies of the relations between Spain, England, and the United States on the upper Mississippi include: Abraham P. Nasatir, "The Anglo-Spanish Frontier in the Illinois Country during the American Revolution, 1778–1783," *J.I.S.H.S.*, XXI (October, 1928), James A. James, "Spanish Influence in the West during the American Revolution," *M.V.H.R.*, IV (September, 1917), and James A. James, "The Significance of the Attack on St. Louis, 1780," M.V.H.A., *Proceedings*, II (1908-09). The motives behind the Spanish attack on St. Joseph are discussed in Lawrence Kinnaird, "The Spanish Expedition Against Fort St. Joseph in 1781, A New Interpretation," *M.V.H.R.*, XIX (September, 1932), while the expedition is described in Frederick Teggart, "The Capture of St. Joseph, Michigan, by the Spaniards in 1781," *M.H.R.*, V (July, 1911).

Revolutionary Diplomacy and the Peace.

A thorough treatment is Paul C. Phillips, *The West in the Diplomacy of the American Revolution* (Urbana, 1913), and a briefer account is Samuel F. Bemis, *The Diplomacy of the American Revolution* (New York, 1935). The same author's *Pinckney's Treaty* (Baltimore, 1926), devotes considerable space to the diplomacy of the peace settlement. Paul C. Phillips studies the attitudes of the various states toward cession of the West to Spain or England in "American Opinion Regarding the West, 1778–1783," M.V.H.A., *Proceedings*, VII (1913-14). The effect of the fur trade on the peace conference needs further study, although the subject is touched on in Wayne E. Stevens, *The Northwest Fur Trade, 1783–1800* (Urbana, 1928).

## X THE WESTERN PROBLEM

General Works. The new nation's attempt to develop a western policy is treated in no one book, although the scattered chapters in Andrew C. McLaughlin, *Confederation and Constitution* (*The American Nation: A History*, New York, 1905), Frederick A. Ogg, *The Old Northwest* (*Chronicles of America Series*, New Haven, 1921), and Thomas P. Abernethy, *Western Lands and the American Revolution* (New York, 1937), are helpful. Theodore Roosevelt, *The Winning of the West*, 6 v. (New York, 1889–1896), is colorful but spotty, while A. B. Hinsdale, *The Old Northwest* (New York, 1888) deals largely with legalistic aspects.

Land Cessions. A thorough study of the land cessions is needed. The older standard account, Herbert B. Adams, *Maryland's Influence upon Land Cessions to the United States* (Baltimore, 1885), has been challenged by the studies of Merrill Jensen: "The Cession of the Old Northwest," *M.V.H.R.*, XXIII (June, 1936), "The Creation of the National Domain, 1781–1784," *M.V.H.R.*, XXVI (December, 1939), and *The Articles of Confederation* (Madison, 1940), which emphasize the influence of land speculators. The same theme is stressed in St. George L. Sioussat, "The Chevalier De La Luzerne and the Ratification of the Articles of Confederation in Maryland, 1780–1781," *P.M.H.B.*, LX (October, 1936).

The standard history of the South Carolina cession is R. S. Cotterill, "The South Carolina Land Cession," *M.V.H.R.*, XII (December, 1925). Works on the Georgia cession, which was not completed until 1802, are listed in Chapter XI.

North Carolina's Cession and the State of Franklin. The fullest history is Samuel C. Williams, *History of the Lost State of Franklin* (New York, 1933), but a more interpretative account is in Thomas P. Abernethy, *From Frontier to Plantation in Tennessee* (Chapel Hill, 1932). Also valuable are chapters in Carl S. Driver, *John Sevier* (Chapel Hill, 1932), and the study of the national implications of the cession by St. George L. Sioussat, "The North Carolina Cession of 1784 in its Federal Aspects," *M.V.H.A.*, *Proceedings*, II (1908–09). Indian problems of the Franklin leaders are described in Randolph C. Downes, "Cherokee-American Relations in the Upper Tennessee Valley, 1776–1791," *E.T.H.S.*, *Publications*, VIII (1936), and Charles C. Royce, "The Cherokee Nation of Indians," *A.B.E.*, *Fifth Annual Report* (1883–84). Excellent maps of Indian land cessions are in the same author's "Indian Land Cessions in the United States," *A.B.E.*, *Eighteenth Annual Report* (1896–97). Some information is in George D. Harmon, *Sixty Years of Indian Affairs, 1789–1850* (Chapel Hill, 1941).

Organization of the Land System. The most thorough account is Payson J. Treat, *The National Land System, 1785–1820* (New York, 1910), while briefer summaries are in Benjamin H. Hibbard, *A History of the Public Land Policies* (New York, 1924), and Roy M. Robbins, *Our Landed Heritage* (Princeton, 1942). Rudolf Freund, "Military Bounty Lands and the Origins of the Public Domain," *A.H.*, XX (January, 1946), shows the effect of the

war veterans' pressure in shaping policies. Useful also is Henry Tatter, "State and Federal Land Policy during the Confederation," *A.H.*, IX (October, 1935). Documents are conveniently collected in Thomas Donaldson, ed., *The Public Domain. Its History* (Washington, 1884).

The Northwest, 1783–87. A brief history of Indian relations and settlement in the Northwest is in Beverley W. Bond, Jr., *The Foundations of Ohio* (*The History of Ohio*, Columbus, 1941), while the opening chapters of Randolph C. Downes, *Frontier Ohio, 1788–1803* (Columbus, 1935), touch on the same period. Also essential is James A. James, *Life of George Rogers Clark* (Chicago, 1928), which describes Indian and military affairs thoroughly. More light is thrown on an important Indian treaty by Henry S. Manley, *The Treaty of Fort Stanwix, 1784* (Rome, New York, 1932), and on the Treaty of Ft. McIntosh by Louis E. Graham, "Fort McIntosh," *W.P.H.M.*, XV (May, 1932). The leading military expedition is exhaustively studied in Leonard C. Helderman, "The Northwest Expedition of George Rogers Clark, 1786-1787," *M.V.H.R.*, XXV (December, 1938).

Events in regions adjacent to the Ohio country may be traced in: Solon J. Buck and Elizabeth H. Buck, *The Planting of Civilization in Western Pennsylvania* (Pittsburgh, 1939), Louise P. Kellogg, *The British Régime in Wisconsin and the Northwest* (Madison, 1935), Nelson V. Russell, *The British Régime in Michigan and the Old Northwest* (Northfield, Minnesota, 1939), and Clarence W. Alvord, *The Illinois Country, 1673–1818* (*Centennial History of Illinois*, Springfield, 1920).

The relation of the fur trade to Indian diplomacy in the Northwest is thoroughly studied in Wayne E. Stevens, *The Northwest Fur Trade, 1763–1800* (Urbana, 1928). The latest book on the Montreal firm active at this time is Gordon R. Davidson, *The North West Company* (Berkeley, 1918). Indian relations are also considered in Walter H. Mohr, *Federal Indian Relations, 1774–1788* (Philadelphia, 1933), while maps of treaties made during the period are in C. E. Sherman, "Original Land Subdivisions," *Ohio Cooperative Topographical Survey*, III (1925).

The Ohio Company. An excellent history of the company is in the introduction to Archer B. Hulbert, ed. *The Records of the Original Proceedings of the Ohio Company*, 2 v. (Marietta, Ohio, 1917). Business and legalistic aspects are treated in Shaw Livermore, *Early American Land Companies* (New York, 1939). Biographies of the leaders include: Charles S. Hall, *Life and Letters of General Samuel Holden Parsons* (Binghamton, New York, 1905), Mary Cone, *Life of Rufus Putnam* (Cleveland, 1886), and W. P. and J. P. Cutler, *The Life, Journals and Correspondence of Rev. Manasseh Cutler*, 2 v. (Cincinnati, 1888). All deserve more modern treatment.

The Ordinance of 1787. The only history of the ordinance is Jay A. Barrett, *Evolution of the Ordinance of 1787* (New York, 1901), which is hopelessly out of date, as is George H. Alden, "Evolution of the American System of Framing and Admitting New States into the Union," *A.A.A.P.S.S.*, XVIII (November, 1901). Neither takes into account the important western influences leading to the Ordinance. These were first demonstrated in Frederick J. Turner, "Western State-Making in the Revolutionary Era," *A.H.R.*, I (October, 1895, and January, 1896). The subject is considered in less satisfactory form in George H. Alden, *New Governments West of the Alleghenies before 1780* (Madison, 1897), while an example of the separatist tendency is described in Randolph C. Downes, "Ohio's Squatter Governor: William Hogland of Hoglandstown," *O.A.H.Q.*, XLIII (April, 1934). The results of these researches are embodied in a brief interpretative account of the Ordinance by Theodore C. Pease, "The Ordinance of 1787," *M.V.H.R.*, XXV (September, 1938), but a full-length study is needed.

Land Speculation in the Ohio Country, 1787–90. A thorough history of the Symmes Purchase is in the introduction to Beverley W. Bond, Jr., *The Correspondence of John Cleves Symmes, Founder of the Miami Purchase* (New York, 1926). The Scioto speculation is studied in Archer B. Hulbert, "The Methods and Operations of the Scioto Group of Speculators," *M.V.H.R.*, I (March, 1915), and II (June, 1915), and in Joseph S. Davis, *Essays in the Earlier History of American Corporations* (Cambridge, 1917). The story of settlement on the company lands is told in Theodore T. Belote, *The Scioto Speculation and the French Settlement at Gallipolis* (Cincinnati, 1907). The careers of two men who figured prominently in the speculation are described in Archer B. Hulbert, "Andrew Craigie and the Scioto Associates," A.A.S., *Proceedings*, n.s. XXIII (1913), and Charles B. Todd, *Life and Letters of Joel Barlow* (New York, 1886).

Early Settlement and Government in the Ohio Country. Establishment of the first government in Ohio is described in Beverley W. Bond, Jr., "An American Experiment in Colonial Government," *M.V.H.R.*, XV (September, 1928), and Elbert J. Benton, "Establishing the American Colonial System in the Old Northwest," I.S.H.S., *Transactions*, XXIV (1918). Documents dealing with the subject are in the second and third volumes of Clarence E. Carter, ed., *The Territorial Papers of the United States* (Washington, 1934—in progress), and in Archer B. Hulbert, ed., *Ohio in the Time of the Confederation* (Marietta, Ohio, 1918). Reports of the first governor are in W. H. Smith, ed., *The St. Clair Papers: The Life and Public Services of Arthur St. Clair*, 2 v. (Cincinnati, 1882).

## XI THE WEST IN AMERICAN DIPLOMACY, 1783-1790

Diplomatic Problems in the Northwest. Excellent brief accounts are in Randolph C. Downes, *Council Fires on the Upper Ohio* (Pittsburgh, 1940), Randolph C. Downes,

*Frontier Ohio, 1788–1803* (Columbus, 1935), A. L. Burt, *The United States, Great Britain, and British North America, 1783–1815* (New Haven, 1940), and Arthur P. Darling, *Our Rising Empire, 1763–1803* (New Haven, 1940).

The problem of the Northwest Posts was first presented in true historical perspective by Andrew C. McLaughlin, "The Western Posts and British Debts," A.H.A., *Annual Report for 1894* (Washington, 1895). The view that England retained the posts to prevent an Indian uprising is ably argued by A. L. Burt, "A New Approach to the Problem of the Western Posts," C.H.A., *Report for 1931* (Ottawa, 1932), while C. S. Graham, "The Indian Menace and the Retention of the Western Posts," *C.H.R.*, XV (March, 1934), presents documentary evidence to support this view. Early efforts to evict the British are described in Frank H. Severance, "The Peace Mission to Niagara of Ephriam Douglass," B.H.S., *Publications*, XVIII (1914). The influence of the fur traders on British policy is discussed in Wayne E. Stevens, *The Northwest Fur Trade, 1763–1800* (Urbana, 1928) and Ida Johnson, *The Michigan Fur Trade* (Lansing, 1919).

British relations with the Indians of the Northwest are treated in: Louise P. Kellogg, *British Régime in Wisconsin and the Northwest* (Madison, 1935), Nelson V. Russell, *British Régime in Michigan and the Old Northwest* (Northfield, Minnesota, 1939), George D. Harmon, *Sixty Years of Indian Affairs, 1789–1850* (Chapel Hill, 1941), Orpha E. Leavitt, "British Policy on the Canadian Frontier," W.H.S., *Proceedings for 1915* (Madison, 1916), and Philip M. Hamer, "The British in Canada and the Southern Indians, 1790–1794," E.T.H.S., *Publications*, II (1930). Documents are in Ernest A. Cruikshank, ed., *The Correspondence of Lieutenant Governor John Graves Simcoe* (Toronto, 1931).

A full account of Indian warfare in the Ohio country is in the two most recent biographies of Wayne: Thomas A. Boyd,

*Mad Anthony Wayne* (New York, 1929), and Harry E. Wildes, *Anthony Wayne: Trouble Shooter of the American Revolution* (New York, 1941). Interesting documents on the Wayne expeditions are Milo M. Quaife, ed., "General James Wilkinson's Narrative of the Fallen Timbers Campaign," *M.V.H.R.*, XVI (June, 1921), and William Clark, "William Clark's Journal of General Wayne's Campaign," *M.V.H.R.*, I (December, 1914). The efforts of the agent who kept the Iroquois from joining the Ohio Indians against Wayne are described in Joseph D. Ibbotson, "Samuel Kirkland, the Treaty of 1792, and the Indian Barrier State," *N.Y.H.*, XIX (October, 1938).

The standard work on Jay's Treaty is Samuel F. Bemis, *Jay's Treaty* (New York, 1924), while the best biography is Frank Monaghan, *John Jay* (New York, 1935). The Treaty of Greenville is considered in Frazer E. Wilson, *The Peace of Mad Anthony* (Greenville, 1909), and Preston Slosson, "The Significance of the Treaty of Greene Ville," *O.A.H.Q.*, LV (January–March, 1946).

Diplomacy in the Southwest. The standard work which covers the period thoroughly is Arthur P. Whitaker, *The Spanish-American Frontier: 1783–1795* (Boston, 1927). E. W. Lyon, *Louisiana in French Diplomacy, 1759–1804* (Norman, 1934), describes the role of France in the complex negotiations, while the opening chapters of Samuel F. Bemis, *Pinckney's Treaty* (Baltimore, 1926), stress diplomatic aspects. A briefer pioneering study is Isaac J. Cox, "The New Invasion of the Goths and Vandals," M.V.H.A., *Proceedings*, VIII (1914–15). The best biography of the Spanish governor during the period is Caroline M. Burson, *The Stewardship of Don Esteban Miró, 1782–1792* (New Orleans, 1924). Special aspects of the Anglo-Spanish dispute are discussed in Abraham P. Nasatir, "The Anglo-Spanish Frontier on the Upper Mississippi, 1786–1796," *I.J.H.P.*, XXIX (April, 1931), and Lawrence Kinnaird, *New Spain and the Anglo-American West*, 2 v.

(Los Angeles, 1932). Documents are in J. A. Robertson, ed., *Louisiana Under the Rule of Spain, France, and the United States, 1785–1807*, 2 v. (Cleveland, 1911).

The efforts of both Spanish and American antagonists to secure Indian allies in the Southwest are described in: Randolph C. Downes, "Creek-American Relations, 1782–1790," *G.H.Q.*, XXI (June, 1937), Lawrence Kinnaird, "International Rivalry in the Creek Country," *F.H.Q.*, X (October, 1931), Jane M. Berry, "The Indian Policy of Spain in the Southwest, 1783–1795," *M.V.H.R.*, III (March, 1917), and Arthur P. Whitaker, "Spain and the Cherokee Indians, 1783–98," *N.C.H.R.*, IV (July, 1927). Two careful studies of the principal Creek chief are Arthur P. Whitaker, "Alexander McGillivray," *N.C.H.R.*, V (April, 1928), and John W. Caughey, *McGillivray of the Creeks* (Norman, 1938). The Loyalist firm which supplied McGillivray with ammunition is studied in Marie T. Greenslade, "William Panton," *F.H.Q.*, XIV (October, 1935), and Robert S. Cotterill, "A Chapter of Panton, Leslie and Company," *J.S.H.*, X (August, 1944). Documents are in Arthur P. Whitaker, *Documents Relating to the Commercial Policy of Spain in the Floridas* (Deland, Florida, 1931), and D. C. Corbitt, "Papers Relating to the Georgia-Florida Frontier, 1784–1800," *G.H.Q.*, XX (December, 1936), and later numbers.

The Spanish Conspiracy. The first modern account of the conspiracy in Kentucky was William R. Shepherd, "Wilkinson and the Beginnings of the Spanish Conspiracy," *A.H.R.*, IX (April, 1904), which demonstrated that the intrigue originated with Wilkinson rather than the Spaniards. Other scholars have added much to the original story: Isaac J. Cox, "Wilkinson's First Break with the Spaniards," *O.V.H.A.*, *Proceedings*, VIII (1914), Isaac J. Cox, "General Wilkinson and His Later Intrigues with the Spaniards," *A.H.R.*, XIX (July, 1914), Arthur P. Whitaker, "James Wilkinson's First Descent to New Orleans in

1787," *H.A.H.R.*, VIII (February, 1928), and Thomas R. Hay, "Some Reflections on the Career of General James Wilkinson," *M.V.H.R.*, XXI (March, 1935). The latter argues that Wilkinson was never serious in his intrigues with Spain. Two recent biographies tell the story of the Kentucky conspiracy in detail: James R. Jacobs, *Tarnished Warrior: Major-General James Wilkinson* (New York, 1938), and Thomas R. Hay and M. R. Werner, *The Admirable Trumpeter: A Biography of General James Wilkinson* (New York, 1941).

The Spanish Conspiracy in Tennessee is described in Arthur P. Whitaker, "Spanish Intrigue in the Old Southwest: An Episode, 1788–89," *M.V.H.R.*, XII (September, 1925). The same author shows the connection between the intrigue and land speculation in "The Muscle Shoals Speculation, 1783–1789," *M.V.H.R.*, XIII (December, 1926), a thesis carried farther by Thomas P. Abernethy, *From Frontier to Plantation in Tennessee* (Chapel Hill, 1932). Sevier's role is examined in Carl S. Driver, *John Sevier* (Chapel Hill, 1932). Other treatments of the subject are: Archibald Henderson, "The Spanish Conspiracy in Tennessee," *T.H.M.*, III (December, 1917), and Albert V. Goodpasture, "Dr. James White," *T.H.M.*, I (December, 1915). One aspect of Spanish immigration policy is explored in Max Savelle, "The Founding of New Madrid," *M.V.H.R.*, XIX (June, 1932).

International Conflict and the Genet Mission. The effect of the Nootka Sound Controversy on diplomacy in the Southwest is described in William R. Manning, "The Nootka Controversy," A.H.A., *Annual Report for 1904* (Washington, 1905), and Frederick J. Turner, "English Policy Toward America in 1790–1791," *A.H.R.*, VII (July, 1902).

The Genet mission is studied in two articles by Frederick J. Turner: "The Origin of Genet's Projected Attack on Louisiana and the Floridas," *A.H.R.*, III (July, 1898), and "The Policy of France

Toward the Mississippi Valley in the Period of Washington and Adams," *A.H.R.*, X (January, 1905). Both are reprinted in the author's *The Significance of Sections in American History* (New York, 1932). Special aspects of the Genet mission are studied in: E. Merton Coulter, "The Efforts of the Democratic Societies of the West to Open the Navigation of the Mississippi," *M.V.H.R.*, XI (December, 1924), Archibald Henderson, "Isaac Shelby and the Genet Mission," *M.V.H.R.*, VI (March, 1920), and E. Merton Coulter, "Elijah Clarke's Foreign Intrigue and the 'Trans-Oconee Republic,'" *M.V.H.A.*, *Proceedings*, X (1919–20).

Spanish intrigue in Kentucky after the Genet mission is treated in the biographies of Wilkinson and in Arthur P. Whitaker, "Harry Innes and the Spanish Intrigue: 1794–1795," *M.V.H.R.*, XV (September, 1928).

The Yazoo Land Companies. The attempt of Georgia speculators to expand westward is considered in Edmund C. Burnett, ed., "Papers Relating to Bourbon County, Georgia," *A.H.R.*, XV (October, 1909, and January, 1910), Samuel B. Adams, "The Yazoo Fraud," *G.H.Q.*, VII (June, 1923), and Arthur P. Whitaker, ed., "The South Carolina Yazoo Company," *M.V.H.R.*, XVI (December, 1929). The career of the South Carolina Yazoo Company's agent is traced in John C. Parrish, "The Intrigues of Dr. James O'Fallon," *M.V.H.R.*, XVII (September, 1930). Indian problems arising from the attempted expansion are considered in Randolph C. Downes, "Creek-American Relations, 1790–1795," *J.S.H.*, VIII (August, 1942), D. L. McMurry, "The Indian Policy of the Federal Government and the Economic Development of the Southwest, 1789–1801," *T.H.M.*, I (March, 1915, and June, 1915), and George D. Harmon, *Sixty Years of Indian Affairs, 1789–1850* (Chapel Hill, 1941).

The Treaty of San Lorenzo. The standard works are Arthur P. Whitaker, *The Mis-*

*sissippi Question, 1795–1803* (New York, 1934), and Samuel F. Bemis, *Pinckney's Treaty* (Baltimore, 1926). Bemis maintains that Godoy had no knowledge of the terms of Jay's Treaty when he ended negotiations with Pinckney and acquiesced in American demands to win American friendship in face of a threatening Anglo-American alliance. Whitaker argues that Godoy had a copy of Jay's Treaty during the latter stages of his conferences with Pinckney. He explains the Spanish surrender in terms of the failure of the nation's frontier policy and the critical European situation. Whitaker demonstrates the correctness of his stand in two articles: "New Light on the Treaty of San Lorenzo: An Essay in Historical Criticism," *M.V.H.R.*, XV (March, 1929), and "Godoy's Knowledge of the Terms of Jay's Treaty," *A.H.R.*, XXXV (July, 1930).

Spanish-American Conflicts after Pinckney's Treaty. The period is thoroughly covered in Whitaker, *The Mississippi Question*. Isaac J. Cox, *The West Florida Controversy* (Baltimore, 1918) also surveys the situation in its opening chapters. Efforts of the United States to win over the southwestern Indians are the theme of Royal B. Way, "The United States Factory System for Trading with the Indians, 1796–1822," *M.V.H.R.*, VI (September, 1919). The Blount Conspiracy is described in Isabel Thompson, "The Blount Conspiracy," *E.T.H.S.*, *Publications*, II (1930).

The Louisiana Purchase. Excellent accounts are in Whitaker, *The Mississippi Question*, and E. Wilson Lyon, *Louisiana in French Diplomacy, 1759–1804* (Norman, 1934). The same author has produced a sound biography of Francois Barbe-Marbois, *The Man Who Sold Louisiana* (Norman, 1942). The efforts of France to secure Louisiana from Spain are described in Mildred S. Fletcher, "Louisiana as a Factor in French Diplomacy from 1763 to 1800," *M.V.H.R.*, XVII (December, 1930). An explanation of Spain's retention of Louisiana in 1795 is in Arthur P. Whitaker,

"Louisiana in the Treaty of Basel," *J.M.H.*, VIII (March, 1936). André LaFargue, "The Louisiana Purchase: The French Viewpoint," *L.H.Q.*, XXIII (January, 1940), argues that the cession of the province to the United States benefited France.

The closing of deposit at New Orleans in 1802 is studied in E. Wilson Lyon, "The Closing of the Port of New Orleans," *A.H.R.*, XXXVII (January, 1932), and Arthur P. Whitaker, "France and the American Deposit at New Orleans," *H.A.H.R.*, XI (November, 1931).

The growth of American interest in Louisiana is traced in James A. James, "Louisiana as a Factor in American Diplomacy, 1795–1800," *M.V.H.R.*, I (June, 1914), Louis Pelzer, "Economic Factors in the Acquisition of Louisiana," M.V.H.A., *Proceedings*, VI (1912–13), and W. Edwin Hemphill, "The Jeffersonian Background of the Louisiana Purchase," *M.V.H.R.*, XXII (September, 1935). The early years of the new American province are viewed in Philip C. Brooks, "Spain's Farewell to Louisiana, 1803–1821," *M.V.H.R.*, XXVII (June, 1940), and Lauro A. de Rojas, "A Consequence of the Louisiana Purchase," *L.H.Q.*, XX (April, 1938).

## XII SETTLING THE APPALACHIAN PLATEAU

Sources and Routes of Westward Migration. The only satisfactory study of the expelling forces driving easterners westward during the period is Lewis D. Stilwell, *Migration from Vermont (1776–1860)* (Montpelier, 1937), although the problem is touched upon in Harold F. Wilson, *The Hill Country of Northern New England* (New York, 1936), Richard J. Purcell, *Connecticut in Transition, 1775–1818* (Washington, 1918), Avery O. Craven, *Soil Exhaustion as a Factor in the Agricultural History of Virginia and Maryland, 1606–1860* (Urbana, 1925), and John D. Barnhart, "Sources of Southern Migration into the Old Northwest," *M.V.H.R.*, XXII

(June, 1935). Studies similar to Stilwell's for other regions would be welcomed.

Equally neglected is the subject of road building between East and West. Works dealing with transportation in general scarcely touch upon the subject: Balthasar H. Meyer, ed., *History of Transportation in the United States before 1860* (Washington, 1917), Seymour Dunbar, *History of Travel in America*, 4 v. (Indianapolis, 1915), and Malcolm Keir, *The March of Commerce* (*The Pageant of America*, New Haven, 1927). Scattered information is also in Archer B. Hulbert, *Historic Highways of America*, 16 v. (Cleveland, 1902–05). A thorough study of travel routes would help explain the nature of western settlement. An able work for a nearby region is William J. Wilgus, *The Role of Transportation in the Development of Vermont* (Montpelier, 1945).

Growth of Settlement in Kentucky and Tennessee. The works cited in Chapter VIII contain information, especially Thomas P. Abernethy, *From Frontier to Plantation in Tennessee* (Chapel Hill, 1932), and Robert S. Cotterill, *History of Pioneer Kentucky* (Cincinnati, 1917). An interpretative essay is William B. Hamilton, "The Southwestern Frontier, 1795–1817: An Essay in Social History," *J.S.H.*, X (November, 1944). Special aspects are considered in Stanley J. Folmsbee and Lucile Deaderick, "The Founding of Knoxville," E.T.H.S., *Publications*, XIII (1941), and Samuel C. Williams, "The Admission of Tennessee into the Union," *T.H.M.*, IV (December, 1945).

The Occupation of Central and Western New York. General works touching on the subject are Alexander C. Flick, ed., *History of the State of New York*, 10 v. (New York, 1932–37), Ruth L. Higgins, *Expansion in New York with Especial Reference to the Eighteenth Century* (Columbus, 1931), Dixon R. Fox, *Yankees and Yorkers* (New York, 1940), and Lois K. Mathews, *The Expansion of New England* (Boston, 1909). The settlement of the Massachusetts boundary dispute and removal of the Indians is described in Thomas C. Cochran, *New York in the Confederation* (Philadelphia, 1932), while the occupation of the Susquehanna region is considered in Francis W. Halsey, *The Old New York Frontier* (New York, 1901). Factors encouraging land speculation are assessed in Dixon R. Fox, *Decline of Aristocracy in the Politics of New York* (New York, 1918) and less satisfactorily in Aaron M. Sakolski, *The Great American Land Bubble* (New York, 1932).

The occupation of the region east of the Genesee River is treated in Orsamus Turner, *History of the Pioneer Settlement of Phelps and Gorham's Purchase, and Morris' Reserve* (Rochester, 1851), which is still valuable despite its age. Two leading speculators are studied in George H. Humphrey, *Nathaniel Gorham* (Rochester, 1927), and Ellis P. Oberholtzer, *Robert Morris, Patriot and Financier* (New York, 1903) which, if playing no other part, demonstrate the need for investigations of these important figures.

The standard work on the Pulteney Estates is Paul D. Evans, "The Pulteney Purchase," *Q.J.N.Y.S.H.A.*, III (April, 1922), although additional material is in Helen I. Cowan, *Charles Williamson: Genesee Promoter* (Rochester, 1941), and John G. Van Deusen, "Robert Troup: Agent of the Pulteney Estates" *N.Y.H.*, XXIII (April, 1942). Equally valuable is Jeannette B. Sherwood, "The Military Tract," *Q.J.N.Y.S.H.A.*, VII (July, 1926). A biography of an early settler is Herbert B. Howe, *Jedediah Barber, 1787–1876: A Footnote to the History of the Military Tract of Central New York* (New York, 1939). An attempted land speculation in the region is described in Albert C. Bates, "The Connecticut Gore Land Company," *A.H.A., Report for 1898* (Washington, 1899).

A thorough study of the settlement of western New York is in Paul D. Evans, *The Holland Land Company* (Buffalo,

1924). Orsamus Turner, *Pioneer History of the Holland Purchase of Western New York* (Buffalo, 1849) is antiquarian but interesting. Leaders of the company are described in Catherine Mathews, *Andrew Ellicott, His Life and Letters* (New York, 1908), Helen L. Fairchild, ed., *Francis Adrian Van Der Kemp, 1752–1829* (New York, 1903), and G. H. Bartlett, "Andrew and Joseph Ellicott," B.H.S., *Publications*, XXVI (1922). The conflict between the Holland Land Company and the New York Genesee Company is described in Julian P. Boyd, "Attempts to Form New States in New York and Pennsylvania in 1786–1796," *Q.J.N.Y.S.H.A.*, XXIX (July, 1931). The early history of a leading city is told in Blake McKelvey, *Rochester: The Water Power City, 1812–1854* (Cambridge, 1945).

The Occupation of Northern New York and Western Pennsylvania. In addition to works cited above, several studies deal with northern New York; Dorothy K. Cleaveland, "Trade and Trade Routes of Northern New York from the Beginning of Settlement to the Coming of the Railroad," N.Y.S.H.A., *Proceedings*, XXI (1923), Charles H. Leete, "The Saint Lawrence Ten Towns," *Q.J.N.Y.S.H.A.*, X (October, 1929), and Alta M. Ralph, "The Chassanis or Castorland Settlement," *Q.J.N.Y.S.H.A.*, X (October, 1929).

The occupation of western Pennsylvania is described in Solon J. Buck and Elizabeth H. Buck, *The Planting of Civilization in Western Pennsylvania* (Pittsburgh, 1939). John E. Winner, "The Depreciation and Donation Lands of Pennsylvania," *W.P.H.M.*, VIII (January, 1925), deals with the settlement of the military reserves, while conflicts between the state and speculating concerns are summarized in: Walter J. McClintock, "Title Differences of the Holland Land Company in Northwestern Pennsylvania," *W.P.H.M.*, XXI (June, 1938), and Elizabeth K. Henderson, "The Northwestern Lands of Pennsylvania, 1790–1812," *P.M.H.B.*, LX (April, 1936). A history of the Pennsylvania Population Company is needed.

Extension of Settlement in the Northwest. Two books that describe the occupation of the Ohio country are Beverley W. Bond, Jr., *The Civilization of the Old Northwest* (New York, 1934), and Randolph C. Downes, *Frontier Ohio, 1788–1803* (Columbus, 1935). Briefer are Eugene H. Roseboom and Francis P. Weisenburger, *A History of Ohio* (New York, 1934), Beverley W. Bond, Jr., *The Foundations of Ohio* (*The History of Ohio*, Columbus, 1941), and Ralph H. Gabriel, *The Lure of the Frontier* (*The Pageant of America*, New Haven, 1929). Biographies of leaders include Julia P. Cutler, *Life and Times of Ephraim Cutler* (Cincinnati, 1890), David M. Massie, *Nathaniel Massie, A Pioneer of Ohio* (Cincinnati, 1896), and Freeman Cleaves, *Old Tippecanoe, William Henry Harrison and His Times* (New York, 1939). Essential documents are in Clarence E. Carter, ed., *The Territorial Papers of the United States* (Washington, 1934—in progress), and valuable descriptions in Reuben G. Thwaites, ed., *Early Western Travels, 1748–1846*, 32 v. (Cleveland, 1904–07). Payson J. Treat, *The National Land System, 1785–1820* (New York, 1920), describes the Land Act of 1800, although a study of the actual operation of the land system in the Northwest is needed.

A thorough account of the Connecticut Land Company is in Claude L. Shepard, "The Connecticut Land Company and Accompanying Papers," *W.R.H.S., Annual Report*, XCVI (1916), while the settlement of the western portion of the Western Reserve is considered in Helen M. Carpenter, "The Origin and Location of the Fire Lands of the Western Reserve," *O.A.H.Q.*, XLIV (1935), Alfred Mathews, *Ohio and Her Western Reserve* (New York, 1902), and Karl F. Geiser, "New England and the Western Reserve," *M.V.H.A., Proceedings*, VI (1912–13).

Most of the books cited on Ohio contain material on the evolution of a government system. They should be supplemented with: Randolph C. Downes, "The Statehood Contest in Ohio," *M.V.H.R.*, XVIII (September, 1931), William Utter, "Saint Tammany in Ohio: A Study in Frontier Politics," *M.V.H.R.*, XV (December, 1928), John D. Barnhart, "The Southern Influence in the Formation of Ohio," *J.S.H.*, III (February, 1937), and John D. Barnhart, "The Southern Element in the Leadership of the Old Northwest," *J.S.H.*, I (May, 1935).

Economic developments in the Northwest during the period are surveyed in William F. Gephart, *Transportation and Industrial Development in the Middle West* (New York, 1909), Charles H. Ambler, *A History of Transportation in the Ohio Valley* (Glendale, 1932), and the interpretative article by Randolph C. Downes, "Trade in Frontier Ohio," *M.V.H.R.*, XVI (March, 1930). Water transportation is considered in W. Wallace Carson, "Transportation and Traffic on the Ohio and Mississippi Before the Steamboat," *M.V.H.R.*, VII (June, 1920), Archer B. Hulbert, "Western Ship-Building," *A.H.R.*, XXI (July, 1916), and especially Leland D. Baldwin, *The Keelboat Age on Western Waters* (Pittsburgh, 1941). No satisfactory history of land travel exists, although Clement L. Martzolff, "Zane's Trace," *O.A.H.Q.*, XIII (1904), contains some information.

Cultural progress among the pioneers is the theme of Beverley W. Bond, Jr., *The Civilization of the Old Northwest* (New York, 1934), and James M. Miller, *The Genesis of Western Culture: The Upper Ohio Valley, 1800–1825* (Columbus, 1938). A good interpretative essay by Avery Craven is in Dixon R. Fox, ed., *Sources of Culture in the Middle West* (New York, 1934), while Joseph Schafer, "Beginnings of Civilization in the Old Northwest," *W.M.H.*, XXI (December, 1937), and Logan Esarey, "The Literary Spirit Among the Early Ohio Valley Settlers," *M.V.H.R.*, V (September, 1918), touch on early literature.

XIII THE WEST IN THE WAR
     OF 1812

General Works. Henry Adams, *History of the United States during the Administrations of Jefferson and Madison*, 9 v. (New York, 1889–91), is still standard despite its age. Less colorful, but utilizing the findings of modern scholarship, is A. L. Burt, *The United States, Great Britain and British North America, 1783–1815* (New Haven, 1940). Other works that deal largely or entirely with the war are: William Wood, *The War with the United States* (*Chronicles of Canada Series*, Toronto, 1915), Frederic A. Ogg, *The Old Northwest* (*Chronicles of America Series*, New Haven, 1921), and Kendric B. Babcock, *The Rise of American Nationality, 1811–1819* (*The American Nation: A History*, New York, 1906).

Causes of the War. A good introduction to the problem is Warren H. Goodman, "The Origins of the War of 1812: A Survey of Changing Interpretations," *M.V.H.R.*, XXVIII (September, 1941). A number of explanations have been advanced by monograph writers. George R. Taylor, "Agrarian Discontent in the Mississippi Valley Preceding the War of 1812," *J.P.E.*, XXXIX (August, 1931), and "Prices in the Mississippi Valley Preceding the War of 1812," *J.E.B.H.*, III (November, 1930), shows the effect of hard times on western war demands. His findings are bolstered by Thomas S. Berry, *Western Prices Before 1861* (Cambridge, 1943). Julius W. Pratt, *Expansionists of 1812* (New York, 1925), holds that a desire for expansion into Canada and the Floridas drove the West to war, a point of view anticipated by Christopher B. Coleman, "The Ohio Valley in the Preliminaries of the War of 1812," *M.V.H.R.*, VII (June, 1920). The expansionist argument is carried a step farther by Louis M. Hacker, "Western Land Hunger and the War of 1812: A Conjecture," *M.V.H.R.*, X (March, 1924), who argues that the need for more land as settlement approached the prairies underlay the western desire for Canada. This is re-

futed by Julius W. Pratt, "Western Aims in the War of 1812," *M.V.H.R.*, XII (June, 1925), which emphasises the Indian menace as a motive leading to a desire for Canada.

The expansion southward which preceded the outbreak of the war is studied in Isaac J. Cox, *The West Florida Controversy, 1798–1813* (Baltimore, 1918). The history of East Florida is told in Herbert B. Fuller, *The Purchase of Florida: Its History and Diplomacy* (Cleveland, 1906).

The Outbreak of Indian Warfare. American relations with the Indians are described in: George D. Harmon, *Sixty Years of Indian Affairs, 1789–1850* (Chapel Hill, 1941), and Annie H. Abel, "A History of Events Resulting in Indian Consolidation West of the Mississippi," A.H.A., *Annual Report for 1906*, I (Washington, 1908). Harrison's treaty-making activities which drove the Indians to the warpath are discussed fully in Freeman Cleaves, *Old Tippecanoe: William Henry Harrison and His Times* (New York, 1939). Other biographies include Dorothy B. Goebel, *William Henry Harrison* (Indianapolis, 1926), M. Dawson, *William Henry Harrison* (Cincinnati, 1924), and James A. Green, *William Henry Harrison: His Life and Times* (Richmond, 1941). The same story is more briefly told in Beverley W. Bond, Jr., *The Civilization of the Old Northwest* (New York, 1934). Special phases of Harrison's activity are considered in Elmore Barce, "Governor Harrison and the Treaty of Fort Wayne, 1909," *I.M.H.*, XI (December, 1915), and Alfred Pirtle, *The Battle of Tippecanoe* (Louisville, 1900). Maps of the Indian cessions are in Charles C. Royce, "Indian Land Cessions in the United States," B.A.E., *Eighteenth Annual Report* (Washington, 1899).

John M. Oskison, *Tecumseh and His Times: The Story of a Great Indian* (New York, 1938) is prejudiced in favor of Tecumseh. Ethel T. Raymond, *Tecumseh* (*Chronicles of Canada Series*, Toronto, 1915), maintains a better balance.

The clash of fur trading interests which

helped precipitate war has not been adequately studied. Kenneth W. Porter, *John Jacob Astor, Business Man*, 2 v. (Cambridge, 1931) deals with the leading American trader. This may be supplemented by the discussion of the interrelationship of Canadian and American companies in Wayne E. Stevens, "Fur Trading Companies in the Northwest, 1760–1816," M.V.H.A., *Proceedings*, IX (1916–17). American efforts to win Indian allegiance through trade are the theme of Royal B. Way, "The United States Factory System for Trading with the Indians, 1792–1822," *M.V.H.R.*, VI (September, 1919), and Edgar B. Wesley, "The Government Factory System Among the Indians," *J.E.B.H.*, IV (May, 1932).

The Military Phase of the War. The course of the war in the Ohio country may be traced in the biographies of Harrison cited above or in William T. Utter, *The Frontier State, 1803–1825* (*The History of Ohio*, Columbus, 1942). Works on General Hull include: Ernest A. Cruikshank, ed., *Documents Relating to the Invasion of Canada and the Surrender of Detroit, 1812* (Ottawa, 1913), and Milo M. Quaife, "General William Hull and His Critics," *O.A.H.Q.*, XLVII (April, 1938), the last a vigorous defense. Also important is Louise P. Kellogg, "The Capture of Mackinac," W.H.S., *Proceedings* (1912). Harrison's successful campaign is described in Beverley W. Bond, Jr., "William Henry Harrison in the War of 1812," *M.V.H.R.*, XIII (March, 1927), and Bennett H. Young, *The Battle of the Thames* (Louisville, 1903), while the Battle of Lake Erie is considered in Theodore Roosevelt, *The Naval War of 1812* (New York, 1882), Paul L. Haworth, "The Battle of Lake Erie," M.V.H.A., *Proceedings*, V (1911–12), and the biographies of Perry, of which the most recent is Charles J. Dutton, *Oliver Hazard Perry* (New York, 1935). Documents dealing with the Great Lakes country as well as the Niagara frontier are in William Wood, ed., *Select British Documents*

*of the Canadian War of 1812*, 4 v. (Toronto, 1920–28).

The war in the Wisconsin country is described in Louise P. Kellogg, *The British Régime in Wisconsin and the Northwest* (Madison, 1935); and Julius W. Pratt, "The Fur Trade Strategy and the American Left Flank in the War of 1812," *A.H.R.*, XL (January, 1935). Milo M. Quaife, *Chicago and the Old Northwest* (Chicago, 1913), contains an account of the Ft. Dearborn massacre, while the career of the leading British agent in the region is recounted in Louis A. Tohill, "Robert Dickson, British Fur Trader on the Upper Mississippi," *N.D.H.Q.*, III (October, 1928–April, 1929).

A detailed history of the war on the Niagara frontier is L. L. Babcock, "The War of 1812 on the Niagara Frontier," B.H.S., *Publications*, XXIX (Buffalo, 1927), while documents are in Ernest A. Cruikshank, *Documentary History of the Campaign upon the Niagara Frontier in the Years 1812, 1813, 1814*, 7 v. (Welland, 1899–1905). Jackson's campaigns in the Southwest are described in his biographies, of which the two most recent are John S. Bassett, *Life of Andrew Jackson*, 2 v. (New York, 1911), and Marquis James, *Andrew Jackson The Border Captain* (Indianapolis, 1933). More detailed studies are H. S. Hablert and T. H. Ball, *The Creek War of 1813 and 1814* (Chicago, 1895), and D. Rowland, *Andrew Jackson's Campaign Against the British* (New York, 1926).

The West in the Peace Negotiations. A special study is Frank A. Updyke, *The Diplomacy of the War of 1812* (Baltimore, 1915). Useful also is the article on James Monroe by Julius W. Pratt in Samuel F. Bemis, ed., *American Secretaries of State and Their Diplomacy*, III (New York, 1927), and Charles M. Gates, "The West in American Diplomacy, 1812–1815," *M.V.H.R.*, XXVI (March, 1940).

# XIV SETTLING THE LAKE PLAINS

General Works. Excellent interpretative

chapters are in Frederick J. Turner, *The United States, 1830–1850* (New York, 1935), while the same author's *Rise of the New West* (*The American Nation: A History,* New York, 1906), is also useful. Henry B. Hubbart, *The Older Middle West, 1840–1880* (New York, 1936), although dealing largely with problems arising after settlement, contains helpful background material. Lois K. Mathews, *The Expansion of New England* (Boston, 1909), traces the migration of the leading population group, while Joseph Schafer, "Peopling the Middle West," *W.M.H.*, XXI (September, 1937), is a statistical interpretation.

Removal of the Indians. George D. Harmon, *Sixty Years of Indian Affairs* (Chapel Hill, 1941), does little more than list treaties. More helpful is the discussion of an important conference, Robert L. Fisher, "The Treaties of Portage des Sioux," *M.V.H.R.*, XIX (March, 1933), and the account of a leading agent by Harlow Lindlay, "William Clark, the Indian Agent," *M.V.H.A., Proceedings,* II (1908–09). Frontier defense is the theme of Edgar B. Wesley, *Guarding the Frontier: A Study of Frontier Defense from 1815 to 1825* (Minneapolis, 1935), and Henry P. Beers, *The Western Military Frontier, 1815–1846* (Philadelphia, 1935). The leading forts have been described in Louise P. Kellogg, "Old Fort Howard," *W.M.H.*, XVIII (December, 1934), Bruce E. Mahan, *Old Fort Crawford and the Frontier* (Iowa City, 1926), Andrew J. Turner, "History of Fort Winnebago," W.H.S., *Collections,* XIV (Madison, 1908), and Marcus L. Hansen, *Old Fort Snelling, 1819–1858* (Iowa City, 1918).

The latest accounts of the Black Hawk War include Cyrenus Cole, *I Am A Man —The Indian Black Hawk* (Iowa City, 1938), and Joseph I. Lambert, "The Black Hawk War: A Military Analysis," *J.I.S.H.S.*, XXXII (December, 1939). Black Hawk's own story is in Milo M. Quaife, ed., *Life of Black Hawk* (Chicago,

1916), while the career of one of his principal opponents is considered in Louis Pelzer, *Henry Dodge* (Iowa City, 1911). The removal of the defeated Indians is described in Grant Foreman, *The Last Trek of the Indians* (Chicago, 1946).

Sources and Routes of Westward Migration. General histories of transportation, such as B. H. Meyer, ed., *History of Transportation in the United States before 1860* (Washington, 1917), have only scattered information on the turnpikes of this period. More useful for limited areas are Frederic J. Wood, *The Turnpikes of New England* (Boston, 1919), Joseph A. Durrenberger, *Turnpikes; A Study of the Toll Road Movement in the Middle Atlantic States and Maryland* (Valdosta, Georgia, 1931), and Wilbur C. Plummer, *The Road Policy of Pennsylvania* (Philadelphia, 1925). The story of the Old National Road is told in Archer B. Hulbert, *The Cumberland Road* (*Historic Highways of America,* Cleveland, 1904), and Philip D. Jordan, *The National Road* (New York, 1948), while transportation on the Great Lakes is the theme of Walter Havighurst, *The Long Ships Passing: The Story of the Great Lakes* (New York, 1942).

The expelling factors driving immigrants from New England are discussed in Lewis D. Stilwell, *Migration from Vermont (1776–1860)* (Montpelier, 1937), and Percy W. Bidwell, "The Agricultural Revolution in New England," *A.H.R.*, XXVI (July, 1921). The effect of the decline in wool growing on migration is shown in Harold F. Wilson, "The Rise and Decline of the Sheep Industry in Northern New England," *A.H.*, IX (January, 1935). Additional studies of factors influencing emigration are needed.

No thorough study has been made of the relation between geographic factors and settlement in the Old Northwest. Helpful, although limited in scope, are: George J. Miller, "Some Geographic Influences in the Settlement of Michigan," *B.A.G.S.*, XLV

(1913), and William J. Peterson. "The Geography of Wisconsin Territory," *P.*, XIX (January, 1938).

The Settlement of Indiana. A helpful history of the state is Logan Esarey, *A History of Indiana from Its Exploration to 1850* (Indianapolis, 1915). This should be supplemented with two articles explaining the lag in settlement: Richard Power, "Wet Lands and the Hoosier Stereotype," *M.V.H.R.*, XXII (June, 1935), and Paul W. Gates, "Land Policy and Tenancy in the Prairie Counties of Indiana," *I.M.H.*, XXXV (March, 1939), which discuss the poor advertising received by early Indiana and land speculation there.

The Settlement of Illinois. The most usable history of the state is Theodore C. Pease, *The Frontier State, 1818–1848* (*Centennial History of Illinois*, Springfield, 1918). The situation in Illinois when statehood was secured is described by Solon J. Buck, *Illinois in 1818* (*Centennial History of Illinois*, Springfield, 1917). Also helpful for the occupation of the region about Chicago are Milo M. Quaife, *Chicago and the Old Northwest* (Chicago, 1913), and Bessie L. Pierce, *A History of Chicago, The Beginning of A City, 1673–1848* (New York, 1937). Dealing more specifically with the settlement process are Arthur C. Boggess, *The Settlement of Illinois, 1778–1830* (Chicago, 1908), and William V. Pooley, *The Settlement of Illinois from 1830 to 1850* (Madison, 1908). The omission of any discussion of land speculation in these two books is partially offset by Paul W. Gates, "Disposal of the Public Domain in Illinois, 1848–1856," *J.E.B.H.*, III (February, 1931). The development of agricultural techniques necessary for prairie farming are described in Percy W. Bidwell and John I. Falconer, *History of Agriculture in the Northern United States, 1620–1860* (Washington, 1925).

The development of the Galena lead mining district is described in several monographs: Reuben G. Thwaites, "Early Lead Mining in Illinois and Wisconsin," A.H.A., *Annual Report for 1893* (Washington, 1894), B. H. Schockel, "Settlement and Development of the Lead and Zinc Mining Region with Special Emphasis upon Jo Daviess County, Illinois," *M.V.H.R.*, IV (September, 1917), John A. Wilgus, "The Century Old Lead Region in Early Wisconsin History," *W.M.H.*, X (June, 1927), and William J. Peterson, "The Lead Traffic on the Upper Mississippi, 1823–1848," *M.V.H.R.*, XVII (June, 1930).

The Settlement of Michigan. The standard account is George N. Fuller, *Economic and Social Beginnings of Michigan* (Lansing, 1916). Additional information is in George Catlin, *The Story of Detroit* (Detroit, 1923), and Milo M. Quaife and Sidney Glazer, *Michigan* (New York, 1948).

The Settlement of Wisconsin. The most recent history of the state is William F. Raney, *Wisconsin: A Story of Progress* (New York, 1940). This should be supplemented by the careful accounts of regional settlement prepared by Joseph Schafer under the general title of the *Wisconsin Domesday Book: Town Studies* (Madison, 1924), *Four Wisconsin Counties* (Madison, 1927), *The Wisconsin Lead Region* (Madison, 1932), and *The Winnebago-Horicon Basin* (Madison, 1937). Useful also is W. C. McKern, "The First Settlers of Wisconsin," *W.M.H.*, XXVI (December, 1942).

The Foreign-born in the Northwest. General accounts are in the standard histories of immigration: Carl Wittke, *We Who Built America* (New York, 1939), George M. Stephenson, *A History of American Immigration* (Boston, 1926), and Marcus L. Hansen, *The Atlantic Migration* (Cambridge, 1940). More detailed studies of the Scandinavians who played such a prominent role in the Northwest are: Kendric C. Babcock, *The Scandinavian Element in the United States* (Urbana, 1914), Theodore C. Blegen, *Norwegian Migration to America, 1825–1860* (Northfield, Minnesota, 1931), and Lawrence M. Larson, "The

Norwegian Element in the Northwest," *A.H.R.*, XL (October, 1934).

Political Conflicts in the Old Northwest. The antagonisms that developed when northerners, southerners, and the foreign born tried to frame political institutions are touched upon in: Solon J. Buck, "The New England Element in Illinois Politics before 1833," M.V.H.A., *Proceedings*, VI (1912–13), John D. Barnhart, "The Southern Influence in the Formation of Illinois," *J.I.S.H.S.*, XXXII (September, 1939), John D. Barnhart, "Southern Influence in the Formation of Indiana," *I.M.H.*, XXXIII (September, 1937), Bayrd Still, "State Making in Wisconsin, 1846–48," *W.M.H.*, XX (September, 1936), and Frederic L. Paxson, "A Constitution of Democracy— Wisconsin, 1847," *M.V.H.R.*, II (June, 1915). Documents relating to the Wisconsin constitution have been edited by Milo M. Quaife: *The Movement for Statehood* (Madison, 1918), *The Convention of 1846* (Madison, 1919), *The Struggle over Ratification* (Madison, 1920), and *The Attainment of Statehood* (Madison, 1928).

## XV SETTLING THE GULF PLAINS

General Works. No history of southern migration into the Gulf Plains has been written. Scattered information is in: R. S. Cotterill, *The Old South* (Glendale, 1939), William B. Hesseltine, *History of the South* (New York, 1936), Frederick J. Turner, *Rise of the New West 1819–1828* (*The American Nation: A History*, New York, 1906), and especially Frederick J. Turner, *The United States, 1830–1850* (New York, 1935). Ulrich B. Phillips, *American Negro Slavery* (New York, 1918) is wider in scope than the title indicates, while the same author's *Life and Labor in the Old South* (Boston, 1929), is a delightful account of social and economic development. Everett Dick, *The Dixie Frontier* (New York, 1948), also deals with social aspects. William E. Dodd, *The Cotton Kingdom* (*Chronicles of America Series*, New Haven, 1921), is another thoughtful

interpretation of southern life. Ulrich B. Phillips, "The Origin and Growth of the Southern Black Belts," *A.H.R.*, XI (July, 1906), presents statistics illustrating the spread of the plantation system westward, while two interpretative essays on the same theme are: Frank L. Owsley, "The Pattern of Migration and Settlement on the Southern Frontier," *J.S.H.*, XI (May, 1945), and William O. Lynch, "The Westward Flow of Southern Colonists before 1861," *J.S.H.*, IX (August, 1943).

Additional information on the southern frontier can be gleaned from histories of agriculture, of which the most useful for the region is Lewis C. Gray, *History of Agriculture in the Southern United States to 1860*, 2 v. (Washington, 1933). Harry B. Brown, *Cotton* (New York, 1927), is also helpful.

Among documentary collections the most important are Clarence E. Carter, ed., *The Territorial Papers of the United States* (Washington, 1934—in progress). Documents on social and economy conditions, edited by Ulrich B. Phillips, are in the *Documentary History of American Industrial Society*, 11 v. (Cleveland, 1909–11).

Indian Removal. A series of scholarly volumes by Grant Foreman tell the story of Indian removal: *Indians and Pioneers* (New Haven, 1930), *Indian Removal: The Emigration of the Five Civilized Tribes of Indians* (Norman, 1932), *Advancing the Frontier* (Norman, 1933), and *The Five Civilized Tribes* (Norman, 1934). Briefer accounts are in George D. Harmon, *Sixty Years of Indian Affairs* (Chapel Hill, 1941), Annie H. Abel, "The History of Events Resulting in Indian Consolidation West of the Mississippi,'" A.H.A., *Annual Report for 1906* (Washington, 1908), J. P. Kinney, *A Continent Lost—A Civilization Won. Indian Land Tenure in America* (Baltimore, 1937), and William C. MacLeod, *The American Indian Frontier* (New York, 1928). Maps of the cessions are in Charles C. Royce, "Indian Land Cessions in the United States," B.A.E., *Eighteenth Annual Report* (Washington, 1899).

Several special studies deal with individual regions or tribes. Ulrich B. Phillips, "Georgia and State Rights," A.H.A., *Annual Report for 1901* (Washington, 1902), describes removals from that state. On the Cherokee the student should consult Wilson Lumpkin, *The Removal of the Cherokee Indians*, 2 v. (New York, 1908), Marion L. Starkey, *The Cherokee Nation* (New York, 1946), Rachel C. Eaton, *John Ross and the Cherokee Indians* (Chicago, 1921), and Ralph H. Gabriel, *Elias Boudinot, Cherokee, and His America* (Norman, 1941). Legal aspects of Cherokee removal are summarized in the standard biographies of Chief Justice Marshall: Albert J. Beveridge, *The Life of John Marshall*, 4 v. (Boston, 1916–19), and Edward S. Corwin, *John Marshall and the Constitution* (*Chronicles of America Series*, New Haven, 1919). Diaries of migrating Indians are available in: Grant Foreman, ed., "Journey of a Party of Cherokee Emigrants," *M.V.H.R.*, XVIII (September, 1931), and Gaston Litton, ed., "The Journal of a Party of Emigrating Creek Indians, 1835–1836," *J.S.H.*, VII (May, 1941). Removal of the other southern tribes may be studied in J. H. Malone, *The Chickasaw Nation* (Louisville, 1923), J. W. Wade, "The Removal of the Mississippi Choctaws," *M.H.S.*, *Publications*, VIII (1904), and C. MacCauley, "The Seminole Indians of Florida," B.A.E., *Fifth Annual Report* (Washington, 1884). An unpleasant aftermath of removal is considered in James W. Silver, "Land Speculation Profits in the Chickasaw Cession," *J.S.H.*, X (February, 1944).

Causes of the Migration. The decaying agriculture of the Southeast which drove settlers westward is studied in Avery O. Craven, *Soil Exhaustion as a Factor in the Agricultural History of Virginia and Maryland, 1606–1860* (Urbana, 1926). The part played by the plantation system in causing soil exhaustion has been disputed

among historians. W. H. Yarbrough, *Economic Aspects of Slavery in Relation to Southern and Southwestern Migration* (Nashville, 1932), holds wasteful slave labor largely responsible, while Ulrich B. Phillips, "Plantations with Slave Labor and Free," *A.H.R.*, XXX (July, 1925), contends that free labor exhausted the soil as rapidly as slave. Phillip's point is examined in two articles by Robert R. Russel, "General Effects of Slavery upon Southern Economic Progress," *J.S.H.*, IV (February, 1938), and "The Effects of Slavery upon Nonslaveholders in the Ante Bellum South," *A.H.*, XV (April, 1941). William C. Bagley, *Soil Exhaustion and the Civil War* (Washington, 1942), argues that the South was driven into war by its exhausted lands.

Development of Transportation Routes. General books on transportation, such as Balthasar H. Meyer, ed., *History of Transportation in the United States before 1860* (Washington, 1917), and Thomas H. Mac-Donald, *History and Development of Road Building in the United States* (Washington, 1926), contain only scattered information on roads between Southeast and Southwest. Ulrich B. Phillips, *History of Transportation in the Eastern Cotton Belt to 1860* (New York, 1908), and Randle B. Truett, *Trade and Travel Around the Southern Appalachians before 1830* (Chapel Hill, 1935), have only sketchy accounts of road travel. The scant information unearthed by scholars is contained in specialized articles: Julian P. Bretz, "Early Land Communications with the Lower Mississippi Valley," *M.V.H.R.*, XIII (June, 1926), Peter J. Hamilton, "Early Roads in Alabama," A.H.S., *Transactions*, II (1897–98), William A. Love, "General Jackson's Military Road," *M.H.S.*, *Publications*, XI (1910), and R. S. Cotterill, "The Natchez Trace," *T.H.M.*, VII (April, 1921). A thorough study of the subject is needed.

The Geography of the Gulf Plains. Soil maps are in the Department of Agriculture, *Atlas of American Agriculture* (Washington, 1936). The subject is discussed in Hugh H. Bennett, *The Soils and Agriculture of the Southern States* (New York, 1921), Rupert B. Vance, *Human Geography of the South* (Chapel Hill, 1932), and A. E. Parkins, "The Antebellum South: A Geographer's Interpretation," *A.A.A.G.,* XXI (March, 1931). Special studies of Alabama conditions are Herdman F. Cleland, "The Black Belt of Alabama," *G.R.,* X (December, 1920), and Roland Harper, "Some Relations of Soil, Climate, and Civilization in the Southern Red Hills of Alabama," *S.A.Q.,* XIX (July, 1920).

The Course of Settlement. The movement of population into western Georgia is briefly described in E. Merton Coulter, *Georgia: A Short History* (Chapel Hill, 1947), and Ralph B. Flanders, *Plantation Slavery in Georgia* (Chapel Hill, 1933). The effect of the state's land system on migration is touched upon in Enoch M. Banks, *The Economics of Land Tenure in Georgia* (New York, 1905).

The only adequate study of migration into any portion of the Southwest is Thomas P. Abernethy, *The Formative Period in Alabama, 1815–1828* (Montgomery, 1922). For the period not covered in this work reliance must be placed on the scattered references in Albert B. Moore, *History of Alabama* (Tuscaloosa, 1935), and Charles S. Davis, *The Cotton Kingdom in Alabama* (Montgomery, 1939). Materials on Mississippi are even more unattainable. Some information is in the histories of the state, of which the most recent is Roland Dunbar, *History of Mississippi*, 2 v. (Chicago, 1925), and in the introductory chapters of Percy L. Rainwater, *Mississippi: Storm Center of Secession, 1856–1861* (Baton Rouge, 1938). Expansion into western Tennessee is considered in Samuel C. Williams, *Beginnings of West Tennessee, in the Land of the Chickasaws, 1541–1841* (Johnson City, Tennessee, 1930), and into Florida in Sidney W. Martin, *Florida During the Territorial Days* (Athens, Georgia, 1944), and Kathryn T. Abbey, *Florida,*

*Land of Change* (Chapel Hill, 1941). A thorough treatment of the frontier movement in the Gulf States is needed.

Social Conditions in the Southwest. In addition to such works as Phillips, *Life and Labor in the Old South*, and Dodd, *The Cotton Kingdom*, the student may consult two thoughtful essays: Thomas P. Abernethy, "Social Relations and Political Control in the Old Southwest," *M.V.H.R.,* XVI (March, 1930), and Paul H. Buck, "The Poor Whites of the Ante-Bellum South," *A.H.R.,* XXXI (October, 1925). A thorough study for one region is Blanche H. Clark, *The Tennessee Yeoman, 1840–1860* (Nashville, 1942).

# XVI THE ECONOMICS OF SECTIONALISM

Development of Western Agriculture. Useful are the general histories of agriculture: Percy W. Bidwell and J. I. Falconer, *History of Agriculture in the Northern United States, 1620–1860* (Washington, 1925), Lyman Carrier, *Beginnings of Agriculture in America* (New York, 1923), and Joseph Schafer, *The Social History of American Agriculture* (New York, 1936). The westward migration of wheat growing may be traced in Louis B. Schmidt, "The Westward Movement of the Wheat Growing Industry in the United States," *I.J.H.P.,* XVIII (July, 1920), and of corn growing in Eugene C. Brooks, *The Story of Corn and the Westward Migration* (Chicago, 1916) and Louis B. Schmidt, "The Westward Movement of the Corn Growing Industry in the United States," *I.J.H.P.,* XXI (January, 1923). A general history of livestock raising is James W. Thompson, *A History of Livestock Raising in the United States, 1607–1860* (Washington, 1942), while conditions in the Northwest are described in Charles R. Leavitt, "Transportation and the Livestock Industry in the Middle West to 1860," *A.H.,* VIII (January, 1934).

Special studies of agriculture in the western states include: W. A. Lloyd, J. I. Falconer, and C. E. Thorne, *Agriculture of Ohio* (Wooster, 1918), William C. Latta, *Outline History of Indiana Agriculture* (Lafayette, 1938), W. C. Flagg, *Agriculture of Illinois* (Springfield, 1875) and Joseph Schafer, *History of Agriculture in Wisconsin* (Madison, 1922).

General Works on Transportation. Most useful is Balthasar H. Meyer, ed., *History of Transportation in the United States before 1860* (Washington, 1917), although Seymour Dunbar, *History of Travel in America*, 4 v. (Indianapolis, 1915), contains colorful material. Archer B. Hulbert, *Paths of Inland Commerce* (*Chronicles of America Series*, New Haven, 1920), and Malcolm Keir, *The March of Commerce* (*The Pageant of America*, New Haven, 1927), are brief and general. A thorough study of American transportation is needed, but much specialized research is necessary before one can be written.

The Steamboat Era. The forthcoming volume by Louis Hunter, *Steamboats on the Western Rivers* is thorough and scholarly. Steamboating on the Great Lakes is popularly treated in Walter Havighurst, *The Long Ships Passing* (New York, 1942). Special studies of transportation on western rivers include: for the upper Mississippi, Mildred L. Hartsough, *From Canoe to Steel Barge* (Minneapolis, 1934), for the Ohio River, Archer B. Hulbert, *Waterways of Western Expansion* (*Historic Highways of America*, Cleveland, 1903), and Charles H. Ambler, *History of Transportation in the Ohio Valley* (Glendale, 1932), and for the Tennessee River, Tennessee Valley Authority, *History of Navigation on the Tennessee River System* (Washington, 1937). The canal around the Falls of the Ohio is described in Heber P. Walker, "Louisville and Portland Canal," *I.M.H.*, XXVIII (March, 1932), while Louis Hunter, "Studies in the Economic History of the Ohio Valley," *Smith College Studies in History*, XIX (1933–34), discusses the effect of weather on navigation.

The Canal Era. Two general works on canal building are Alvin F. Harlow, *Old Towpaths* (New York, 1928), and Archer B. Hulbert, *The Great American Canals* (*Historic Highways of America*, Cleveland, 1904). A brief account of the Erie Canal is in Alexander C. Flick, *History of the State of New York*, 10 v. (New York, 1932–37), while the full story is told in Noble E. Whitford, *History of the Canal System of the State of New York* (Albany, 1906). James W. Livingood, *The Pennsylvania-Baltimore Trade Rivalry, 1780–1860* (Harrisburg, 1947), is an important study. The Pennsylvania system is discussed in Theodore B. Klein, *The Canals of Pennsylvania and the System of Internal Improvements* (Harrisburg, 1900), and the Maryland system in George W. Ward, *The Early Development of the Chesapeake and Ohio Canal Project* (Baltimore, 1899), Walter S. Sanderlin, *The Great National Project* (Baltimore, 1947), and the opening chapters of Edward Hungerford, *The Story of the Baltimore and Ohio Railroad, 1827–1927*, 2 v. (New York, 1928).

The Southern Railroad System. The attempts of Charleston and Savannah to reach the West are recounted in Ulrich B. Phillips, *A History of Transportation in the Eastern Cotton Belt to 1860* (New York, 1908), while a more detailed study of one Georgia road is James H. Johnston, *The Western and Atlantic Railroad of Georgia* (Atlanta, 1931). Equally valuable for Tennessee is Stanley J. Folmsbee, *Sectionalism and Internal Improvements in Tennessee, 1796–1845* (Philadelphia, 1939). The remainder of the history of railroad building in the South must be pieced together from scattered articles. These include, for Tennessee, St. George L. Sioussat, "Memphis as a Gateway to the West," *T.H.M.*, III (March, 1917, and June, 1917), T. D. Clark, "The Building of the Memphis and Charleston Railroad," *E.T.H.S.*, *Publications*, VIII (1936), and Addie L. Brooks, "Early Plans for Railroads in West Tennessee, 1830–1845," *T.H.M.*, III (October, 1932).

Materials on other southern states are

less plentiful. R. S. Cotterill, "The Beginnings of Railroads in the Southwest," *M.V.H.R.*, VIII (March, 1922), deals partially with Alabama. Another road in that state is the theme of T. D. Clark, "The Montgomery and West Point Railroad Company," *G.H.Q.*, XVII (December, 1933). The one work on Mississippi Railroads, Charles R. Johnson, "Railroad Legislation and Building in Mississippi, 1830–1840," *J.M.H.*, IV (October, 1942), is little more than a listing of charters. Kentucky's one railroad of the period is studied in T. D. Clark, "The Lexington and Ohio Railroad —A Pioneer Venture," *K.S.H.S.R.*, XXXI (January, 1933). Early Florida building is described in T. Frederick Davis, "Pioneer Florida: The First Railroads," *F.H.Q.*, (January, 1945).

Internal improvements in the Northwest. A brief account of Ohio canal building is in Francis P. Weisenburger, *The Passing of the Frontier* (*The History of Ohio*, Columbus, 1941), and the full story in C. C. Huntington and C. P. McClelland, *Ohio Canals, Their Construction, Cost, Use and Partial Abandonment* (Columbus, 1905). Chester E. Finn, "The Ohio Canals; Public Enterprise on the Frontier," *O.A.H.Q.*, LI (January, 1942, and March, 1942), is a sound interpretation, while financial aspects are considered in Ernest L. Bogart, *Internal Improvements and State Debt in Ohio* (New York, 1924). Construction of the two leading canals is described in Arthur H. Hirsch, "The Construction of the Miami and Erie Canal," M.V.H.A., *Proceedings*, X (1919-20), and John J. George, "The Miami Canal," *O.A.H.Q.*, XXXVI (January, 1927).

Indiana's canal system is treated in Logan Esarey, "Internal Improvements in Early Indiana," I.H.S., *Publications*, V (1912), while Elbert J. Benton, *The Wabash Trade Route in the Development of the Old Northwest* (Baltimore, 1903), shows the relationship between the improvements and subsequent economic development. Lee New-comer, "Construction of the Wabash and Erie Canal," *O.A.H.Q.*, XLVI (April, 1937), tells of the story of the principal canal, while the same author discusses financial aspects in "A History of the Indiana Internal Improvement Bonds," *I.M.H.*, XXXII (June, 1936).

A compact history of the Illinois system is in Theodore C. Pease, *The Frontier State, 1818–1848* (*Centennial History of Illinois*, Chicago 1919), and the full story in James W. Putnam, "An Economic History of the Illinois and Michigan Canal," *J.P.E.*, XVII (May, June, and July, 1909), and the same author's "The Illinois and Michigan Canal. A Study in Economic History," C.H.S., *Collections*, X (1917). The one railroad built at the time is described in H. J. Stratton, "The Northern Cross Railroad," *J.I.S.H.S.*, XXVIII (July, 1935).

The only works on Michigan internal improvements are: Lew A. Chase, "Michigan's Share in the Establishment of Improved Transportation between the East and the West," M.P.H.S., *Collections*, XXXVIII (1912), and Leo Van Meer, "Clinton-Kalamazoo Canal," *M.H.M.*, XVI (Spring, 1932).

The Effect of Internal Improvements on Trade Routes. The standard account is A. L. Kohlmeier, *The Old Northwest as the Keystone of the Arch of American Federal Union: A Study in Commerce and Politics* (Bloomington, Indiana, 1938). R. B. Way, "The Commerce of the Lower Mississippi Valley in the Period 1830–1860," M.V.H.A., *Proceedings*, X (1918-19), is concerned with trade over one of the Northwest's outlets.

## XVII THE EMERGENCE OF A SECTIONAL PATTERN

General Works. An important interpretation is in Frederick J. Turner, "The Significance of the Section in American History," *The Significance of Sections in American History* (New York, 1932), while the best general survey is the same author's *The United States, 1830–1850* (New York, 1935). Useful for political background are Hugh R. Fraser, *Democracy in the Making: The Jackson-Tyler Era* (Indianapolis, 1938), William MacDonald, *Jacksonian Democracy (The American Nation: A History*, New York, 1906), and Frederic A. Ogg, *The Reign of Andrew Jackson (Chronicles of America Series*, New Haven, 1919). Arthur M. Schlesinger, Jr., *The Age of Jackson* (Boston, 1945), is a brilliant interpretation of the whole era.

Biographies of the leading political figures of the day also contain much information on the sectional controversies. The most recent studies of Jackson are: John S. Bassett, *Life of Andrew Jackson*, 2 v. (New York, 1911), and Marquis James, *Andrew Jackson, Portrait of a President* (Indianapolis, 1937). Thomas P. Abernethy, "Andrew Jackson and the Rise of Southwestern Democracy," *A.H.R.*, XXXIII (October, 1927), is essential to an understanding of Jackson's background. Henry Clay's career is surveyed in Glyndon G. Van Deusen, *The Life of Henry Clay* (Boston, 1937), and Bernard Mayo, *Henry Clay* (Boston, 1937—in progress). The standard work on Daniel Webster is Claude M. Fuess, *Daniel Webster*, 2 v. (Boston, 1930). On Calhoun consult Charles M. Wiltse, *John C. Calhoun, Nationalist, 1782–1828* (Indianapolis, 1944), and W. M. Meigs, *The Life of John Caldwell Calhoun*, 2 v. (New York, 1917). Two recent biographies of Van Buren are D. T. Lynch, *Martin Van Buren* (New York, 1929), and Alexander Holmes, *The American Talleyrand* (New York, 1935).

Growth of Western Nationalism. An excellent introduction is Homer C. Hockett, *Western Influences on Political Parties to 1825* (Columbus, 1917). The effects of the Panic of 1819 are described in Samuel Rezneck, "The Depression of 1819–1822, A Social History," *A.H.R.*, XXXIX (October, 1933), while the ambitions of the West for new trade outlets are the theme of

Curtis Nettels, "The Mississippi Valley and the Constitution, 1815–29," *M.V.H.R.*, XI (December, 1924), and R. B. Way, "The Mississippi Valley and Internal Improvements," M.V.H.A., *Proceedings*, IV (1910–11). The same subject is treated in Emory R. Johnson, *History of Domestic and Foreign Commerce of the United States*, 2 v. (Washington, 1915).

Growth of Southern Nationalism. General treatments are in Emory Q. Hawk, *Economic History of the South* (New York, 1934), and Robert S. Cotterill, *The Old South* (Glendale, 1939), but the subject is considered most fully in Jesse T. Carpenter, *The South as a Conscious Minority, 1789–1861* (New York, 1930). The Missouri Compromise is discussed in Frank H. Hodder, "Side Lights on the Missouri Compromise," A.H.A., *Annual Report for 1909* (Washington, 1911), and especially in Everett S. Brown, *The Missouri Compromise and Presidential Politics* (St. Louis, 1926).

The Tariff and Public Lands. Detailed summaries of tariffs are in Edward Stanwood, *American Tariff Controversies in the Nineteenth Century*, 2 v. (Boston, 1903). M. R. Eiselen, *The Rise of Pennsylvania Protectionism* (Philadelphia, 1932), traces the growth of protariff sentiment in an important eastern state. A similar study of the Northwest is needed.

General histories of the land question include Roy M. Robbins, *Our Landed Heritage* (Princeton, 1942), and Benjamin H. Hibbard, *A History of Public Land Policies* (New York, 1924). More important for this period is Raynor G. Wellington, *Political and Sectional Influence of the Public Lands, 1828–1842* (n.p., 1914), which is a detailed study of the relationship of land, tariff, and financial questions. St. George L. Sioussat, "Some Phases of Tennessee Politics in the Jackson Period," *A.H.R.*, XIV (October, 1908), deals with a local phase.

The influence of speculators on land sales during the 1830's still awaits a historian.

Aaron M. Sakolski, *The Great American Land Bubble* (New York, 1932), is general and popular. Three articles by Paul W. Gates show the importance of the subject: "The Role of the Land Spectacular in Western Development," *P.M.H.B.*, LXVI (July, 1942), "Southern Investments in Northern Lands Before the Civil War," *J.S.H.*, V (May, 1939), and "Frontier Landlords and Pioneer Tenants," *J.I.S.H.S.*, XXXVIII (June, 1945). Arthur H. Cole, "Cyclical and Sectional Variations in the Sale of Public Lands, 1816–60," *R.E.S.*, IX (January, 1927), demonstrates that land sales varied with commodity prices and were largely speculative.

The Nullification Controversy. The standard work is Chauncey S. Boucher, *The Nullification Controversy in South Carolina* (Chicago, 1916), although useful material is also in W. A. Schaper, "Sectionalism and Representation in South Carolina," *A.H.A.*, *Annual Report for 1900* (Washington, 1901), and F. Bancroft, *Calhoun and the South Carolina Nullification Movement* (Baltimore, 1928).

The Bank War and Party Politics. The standard work on the bank is Ralph C. H. Catterall, *The Second Bank of the United States* (Chicago, 1903), but more modern interpretations of the controversy are in two recent biographies of Taney: Bernard C. Steiner, *Life of Roger Brooke Taney* (Baltimore, 1922), and Carl B. Swisher, *Roger B. Taney* (New York, 1935), The effect of the bank war on the election of 1832 is considered in Samuel R. Gammon, *The Presidential Campaign of 1832* (Baltimore, 1922).

Two thorough works on the origin of the Whig Party are E. Malcolm Carroll, *Origins of the Whig Party* (Durham, 1925), and George R. Poage, *Henry Clay and the Whig Party* (Chapel Hill, 1936). Local histories of the Whig Party include: Arthur C. Cole, *The Whig Party in the South* (Washington, 1913), Henry R. Mueller, *The Whig Party in Pennsylvania* (New York, 1922), Henry H. Simms, *The Rise of the Whigs in Virginia, 1824–1840* (Richmond, 1929), and Thomas P. Abernethy, "The Origin of the Whig Party in Tennessee," *M.V.H.R.*, XII (March, 1926).

Wildcat Banking in the Middle 1830's. Two general works providing background material are Davis R. Dewey, *Financial History of the United States* (10th edn., New York, 1928), and William J. Shultz and M. R. Caine, *Financial Development of the United States* (New York, 1937). More detailed, but essential to an understanding of the banking situation, is Sr. M. Grace Madeleine, *Monetary and Banking Theories of Jacksonian Democracy* (Philadelphia, 1943). The flow of British capital which stimulated bank expansion is described in Leland H. Jenks, *The Migration of British Capital to 1875* (New York, 1927), and Reginald C. McCrane, *Foreign Bondholders and American State Debts* (New York, 1935).

No history of state banking during the period exists. The best summaries are Leonard C. Helderman, *National and State Banks* (Boston, 1931), which is concerned with precedents for later banking practices, and Davis R. Dewey, *States Banking before the Civil War* (Washington, 1910), which describes methods rather than history. Instead the story of state banking must be pieced together from the plentiful local accounts.

For the Northwest these include: Ernest L. Bogart, *Financial History of Ohio* (Urbana, 1912), George W. Dowrie, *The Development of Banking in Illinois, 1817–1863* (Urbana, 1913), Logan Esarey, *State Banking in Indiana* (Bloomington, 1912), James E. Hagerty, "Early Financial History of Indiana, 1816–1872," *I.H.B.*, XIV (October, 1937), T. H. Hinchman, *Banks and Banking in Michigan* (Detroit, 1887), W. O. Hedrick, "The Financial and Tax History of Michigan," *M.H.M.*, XXII (Winter, 1938), and John R. Cable, *The Missouri State Bank* (New York, 1923).

Among the histories of banking in southern states are: Alfred C. Bryan, *History of State Banking in Maryland* (Baltimore,

1899), Kathryn T. Abbey, "The Union Bank of Tallahassee: An Experiment in Territorial Finance," *F.H.Q.*, XV (October, 1937), Thomas P. Govan, "Banking and the Credit System in Georgia, 1810–1860," *J.S.H.*, IV (May, 1938), Claude A. Campbell, *The Development of Banking in Tennessee* (Nashville, 1932), Elmer C. Griffith, "Early Banking in Kentucky," M.V.H.A., *Proceedings*, II (1910), Charles H. Brough, "The History of Banking in Mississippi," M.H.S., *Publications*, III (1904), Stephen A. Caldwell, *A Banking History of Louisiana* (Baton Rouge, 1935), and W. B. Worthen, *Early Banking in Arkansas* (Little Rock, 1906).

## XVIII THE SHIFTING SECTIONAL PATTERN

General Works. Frederick J. Turner, *The United States, 1830–1850* (New York, 1935), is invaluable for this period. In addition to the biographies cited in the previous chapter, the following deal with leaders who gained ascendancy after 1837: Freeman Cleaves, *Old Tippecanoe: William Henry Harrison and His Times* (New York, 1939), Oliver P. Chitwood, *John Tyler* (New York, 1939), Eugene I. McCormac, *James K. Polk: A Political Biography* (Berkeley, 1922), Andrew C. McLaughlin, *Lewis Cass* (Boston, 1891), Holman Hamilton, *Zachary Taylor: Soldier of the Republic* (Indianapolis, 1941), and Brainerd Dyer, *Zachary Taylor* (Baton Rouge, 1946) Polk's fascinating diary has been edited by Milo M. Quaife, *The Diary of James K. Polk during His Presidency*, 4 v. (Chicago, 1910). A detailed study of politics during Tyler's administration is Oscar D. Lambert, *Presidential Politics in the United States: 1841–1844* (Durham, 1936).

Origins of Abolitionism. No satisfactory history of the abolition movement has been written, although the compact volume by Dwight L. Dumond, *Antislavery Origins of the Civil War in the United States* (Ann Arbor, 1939), illustrates the importance of his forthcoming work on the subject. Earlier

histories such as Jesse Macy, *The Anti-Slavery Crusade* (*Chronicles of America Series*, New Haven, 1919), and Albert B. Hart, *Slavery and Abolition, 1831–1841* (*The American Nation: A History*, New York, 1906) are out of date. Helpful general chapters are in Avery Craven, *The Coming of the Civil War* (New York, 1942).

The early phases of the antislavery movement are described in Mary S. Locke, *Anti-Slavery in America* (*1619–1808*) (Boston, 1901), and Alice D. Adams, *The Neglected Period of Anti-Slavery in America, 1808–1831* (Boston, 1908). The latter should be supplemented with Early L. Fox, *The American Colonization Society* (Baltimore, 1919). On the important period of the 1830's the best study is Gilbert H. Barnes, *The Anti-Slavery Impulse, 1830–1844* (New York, 1933), which first called attention to T. D. Weld and the role of the West in abolitionism. Documents on this phase of the movement are in Gilbert H. Barnes and Dwight L. Dumond, eds., *Letters of Theodore Dwight Weld, Angelina Grimké Weld and Sarah Grimké, 1822–1844*, 2 v. (New York, 1934).

Biographies of other abolition leaders include: Wendell P. Garrison and F. J. Garrison, *William Lloyd Garrison, 1805–1879*, 4 v. (Boston, 1885–89), William Birney, *James G. Birney and His Times* (New York, 1890), Dwight L. Dumond, ed., *Letters of James Gillespie Birney*, 2 v. (New York, 1938), and Ralph V. Harlow, *Gerrit Smith*, (New York, 1939).

Early political activities of the abolitionists are studied in Theodore C. Smith, *The Liberty and Free Soil Parties in the Northwest* (New York, 1897), and Julian P. Bretz, "The Economic Background of the Liberty Party," *A.H.R.*, XXXIV (January, 1929).

Southern reaction to the abolitionist attack is thoroughly considered in Jesse T. Carpenter, *The South as a Conscious Minority, 1789–1861* (New York, 1930). Attempts of the South to develop its own manufacturing and trade are described in Robert R. Russel, *Economic Aspects of Southern Sectionalism, 1840–1861* (Urbana, 1923), while Arthur Y. Lloyd, *The Slavery Controversy, 1830–1860* (Chapel Hill, 1939), deals largely with southern answers to northern propaganda. The careers of two prominent southern nationalists are traced in Laura A. White, *Robert Barnwell Rhett: Father of Secession* (New York, 1931), and James B. Ranck, *Albert Gallatin Brown: Radical Southern Nationalist* (New York, 1937).

The Panic of 1837. The standard work is Reginald C. McCrane, *The Panic of 1837* (Chicago, 1924), while the social effects of the panic are treated in Samuel Rezneck, "The Social History of an American Depression, 1837–1843," *A.H.R.*, XL (July, 1935). The problem of the surplus revenue is considered in Edward G. Bourne, *The History of the Surplus Revenue of 1837* (New York, 1885).

The Depression and Financial Problems. The story of Van Buren's struggle for the Subtreasury Plan is told in David Kinley, *The Independent Treasury of the United States* (New York, 1893). Debt repudiation is treated in William A. Scott, *The Repudiation of State Debts* (New York, 1893). The histories of state banks listed in the last chapter deal with the financial collapse during the depression and the growth of "No-Bank" feeling in the West, but should be supplemented with: W. W. Wright, "Early Legislation Concerning Wisconsin Banks," *W.H.S.*, *Proceedings for 1895* (Madison, 1896), Leonard B. Krueger, *History of Commercial Banking in Wisconsin* (Madison, 1933), and Howard H. Preston, *History of Banking in Iowa* (Iowa City, 1922).

Land Policy and Sectionalism. The histories of land policy cited in the last chapter, and especially that by Wellington, are equally important for this period. Specialized works dealing with aspects of the problem after 1837 are: Roy M. Robbins, "Preemption—A Frontier Triumph," *M.V.H.R.*, XVIII (December, 1931), and Benjamin F. Shambaugh, "Frontier Land Clubs or Claims Associations," A.H.A. *Annual Report for 1900* (Washington, 1901). Southern reaction to the land and tariff legislation of the period is the theme of James E. Winston, "The Mississippi Whigs and the Tariff, 1834–1844," *M.V.H.R.*, XXII (March, 1936).

The history of the Homestead Law is told in George M. Stephenson, *The Political History of the Public Lands from 1840 to 1862* (Boston, 1917). Three studies of growing sentiment for Homestead among eastern workers are: Helen S. Zahler, *Eastern Workingmen and National Land Policy, 1829–1862* (New York, 1941), Roy M. Robbins, "Horace Greeley: Land Reform and Unemployment, 1837–1862," *A.H.*, VII (January, 1933), and William Trimble, "Diverging Tendencies in New York Democracy in the Period of the Locofocos," *A.H.R.*, XXIV (April, 1919). The early legislative history of Homestead measures is treated in John S. Sanborn, "Some Political Aspects of Homestead Legislation," *A.H.R.*, VI (October, 1900), and St. George L. Sioussat, "Andrew Johnson and the Early Phases of the Homestead Bill," *M.V.H.R.*, V (December, 1918). Forces leading toward a South-West alliance in the 1840's are described in Henry C. Hubbart, "Pro-Southern Influences in the Free West, 1840–1865," *M.V.H.R.*, XX (June, 1933).

## XIX RAILROADS AND SECTIONALISM

General Works on Railroads. The histories of transportation cited in Chapter XVI contain some material. No satisfactory story of railroad building has been told, although the following are helpful: Lewis H. Haney, *A Congressional History of Railways in the United States to 1850* (Madison, 1908), John Moody, *The Railroad Builders* (*Chronicles of America Series*, New Haven, 1919), John W. Starr, *One Hundred Years of Railroading* (New York, 1928), Slason Thompson, *A Short History of American Railways* (New York, 1925), and Charles

F. Carter, *When Railroads Were New* (New York, 1926). Thorough studies of local aspects of railroad building are needed before the final history of the subject can be written.

The East-West Railroads. The standard work on the Baltimore and Ohio Railroad is Edward Hungerford, *The Story of the Baltimore and Ohio Railroad, 1827–1927*, 2 v. (New York, 1928). The history of the New York lines later consolidated into the New York Central system is told in Frank W. Stevens, *The Beginnings of the New York Central, 1826–1853* (New York, 1926), Edward Hungerford, *Men and Iron; The History of the New York Central* (New York, 1938), and Alvin F. Harlow, *The Road of the Century* (New York, 1947). A briefer account, written by Edward Hungerford, is in Alexander C. Flick, ed., *History of the State of New York*, 10 v. (New York, 1932–37). Edward Hungerford, *Men of Erie* (New York, 1946), describes that road. A thorough description of the Pennsylvania system is in H. W. Schotter, *The Growth and Development of the Pennsylvania Railroad Company* (Philadelphia, 1927). No history of Boston's attempt to tap western trade has been written.

Railroads in the Northwest. Year-by-year maps of construction are in Frederic L. Paxson, "The Railroads of the 'Old Northwest' before the Civil War," W.A.S.A.L., *Transactions*, XVII (October, 1912). Only a few scattered studies of railroad building in the Northwest exist: Frank F. Hargrave, *A Pioneer Indiana Railroad; the Origin and Development of the Monon* (Indianapolis, 1932), William F. Raney, "The Building of the Wisconsin Railroads," *W.M.H.*, XIX (June, 1936), William K. Akerman, *Early Illinois Railroads* (Chicago, 1884), and August Derleth, *The Milwaukee Road* (New York, 1948). The possibility of thorough studies is demonstrated by Paul W. Gates, *The Illinois Central Railroad and its Colonization Work* (Cambridge, 1934). which stands as a model for future historians of individual lines. A factual history

of the land grant policy which resulted in the Illinois Central grant is in John B. Sanborn, *Congressional Grants of Land in Aid of Railways* (Madison, 1899).

The Southern Railroads. Many of the works cited in Chapter XVI have material on this period, especially Ulrich B. Phillips, *History of Transportation in the Eastern Cotton Belt to 1860* (New York, 1908). The Memphis Convention and its effect on railroad building are described in Herbert Wender, *Southern Commercial Conventions* (Baltimore, 1930). The best account of southern construction after 1837 is in two articles by R. S. Cotterill, "Southern Railroads and Western Trade, 1840–1850," *M.V.H.R.*, III (March, 1917), and "Southern Railroads, 1850–1860," *M.V.H.R.*, X (March, 1924). North Carolina's attempt to reach the West is treated in Cecil K. Brown, *A State Movement in Railroad Development* (Chapel Hill, 1928). Materials on Tennessee railways include: Stanley J. Folmsbee, *Sectionalism and Internal Improvements in Tennessee, 1796–1845* (Philadelphia, 1939), T. D. Clark, "The Development of the Nashville and Chattanooga Railroad," *T.H.M.*, III (April, 1935), J. W. Holland, "The East Tennessee and Georgia Railroad, 1836–1860," E.T.H.S., *Publications*, III (1931), and J. W. Holland, "The Building of the East Tennessee and Virginia Railroad," E.T.H.S., *Publications*, IV (1932). Similar studies are needed for railroads south of Tennessee. The only line adequately treated is the Mobile and Ohio Railroad in Thomas D. Clark, *A Pioneer Southern Railroad from New Orleans to Cairo* (Chapel Hill, 1936). The same author deals with the Louisville and Nashville Railroad in *The Beginning of the L. and N.* (Louisville, 1933).

Western Trade. Louis B. Schmidt, "The Internal Grain Trade of the United States, 1850–1860," *I.J.H.P.*, XVIII (January, 1920), studies the production and consumption of food in each section during the pre-Civil War decade. Two brief treatments of the foreign grain trade are: Herbert J. Wunderlich, "Foreign Grain Trade of the

United States, 1835–1860," *I.J.H.P.*, XXXIII (January, 1935), and Thomas P. Martin, "Cotton and Wheat in Anglo-American Trade and Politics, 1846–1852," *J.S.H.*, I (August, 1935). Neither covers the subject thoroughly; the history of the western grain trade, both foreign and domestic, needs further study. Fred M. Jones, *Middlemen in the Domestic Trade of the United States, 1800–1860* (Urbana, 1935), explores one local aspect.

The standard work on the export and import trade of the Northwest is A. L. Kohlmeier, *The Old Northwest as the Keystone of the Arch of American Federal Union: A Study in Commerce and Politics* (Bloomington, Indiana, 1938). The author's meticulous research has been utilized in preparing the tables in this chapter. Additional interpretative material is in Henry C. Hubbart, *The Older Middle West, 1840–1880* (New York, 1936), and R. R. Russel, "A Revaluation of the Period before the Civil War: Railroads," *M.V.H.R.*, XV (December, 1928).

## XX THE NATURAL SETTING

Geographic Conditions in the Far West. A helpful discussion of physiographic regions in the United States is, Nevin M. Fenneman, "Physiographic Divisions of the United States," *A.A.A.G.*, XVIII (1928). The most thorough account of western geographic conditions is the same author's *Physiography of Western United States* (New York, 1931). Brief special studies include: William J. Peterson, "Geography of Iowa Territory," *P.*, XIX (July, 1938), and Chessley L. Posey, "Influence of Geographic Factors in the Development of Minnesota," *M.H.*, II (August, 1918).

General Works on the American Indian. A helpful bibliography to a vast literature is George P. Murdock, *Ethnographic Bibliography of North America* (New Haven, 1941). Frederick W. Hodge, ed., *Handbook of American Indians North of Mexico*, 2 v. (Washington, 1912), is an invaluable encyclopaedia for general reference. A survey

of the archaeology of North America by cultural areas is in *Essays in Honor of J. R. Swanton* (Washington, 1940), while Alfred L. Kroeber, *Cultural and Natural Areas of Native North America* (Berkeley, 1939), is a detailed study of the relationship of areas and culture.

A useful survey is Clark Wissler, *The American Indian* (New York, 1922), while the same author's *Indians of the United States* (New York, 1940) is a popular treatment of cultural areas by linguistic families. Rose Palmer, *The North American Indians* (Washington, 1929), contains much on everyday life, and E. R. Embree, *Indians of the Americas* (Boston, 1939), is a general treatment.

Numerous works deal with specific cultural areas or linguistic stocks. Clark Wissler, *North American Indians of the Plains* (New York, 1927), is a standard work for that area, while Pliny E. Goddard, *Indians of the Southwest* (American Museum of Natural History, *Handbook Series*, No. 2, New York, 1931) deals with the southern Plains country. For the Intermontane Province, Julian H. Steward, *Basin-Plateau Sociopolitical Groups* (Washington, 1938), is a study of all groups on an ecological basis. A. L. Kroeber, *Handbook of the Indians of California* (Washington, 1925), is an encylopedic approach to that area. Pliny E. Goddard, *Indians of the Northwest Coast* (New York, 1934), treats the native groups of the Pacific Northwest.

Brief accounts of individual tribes include: George E. Hyde, *Red Cloud's Folk: A History of the Oglaga Sioux* (Norman, 1937), W. J. McGee, "The Siouan Indians," B.A.E., *Fifteenth Annual Report* (Washington, 1897), R. N. Richardson, *The Comanche Barrier to South Plains Settlement* (Glendale, 1933), James Mooney, "Calendar History of the Kiowa Indians," B.A.E., *Seventeenth Annual Report* (Washington, 1898), Clyde Kluckhohn and D. C. Leighton, *The Navaho* (Cambridge, 1946), and George B. Grinnell, *The Cheyenne Indians*, 2 v. (New Haven, 1923). George P.

Murdock, *Our Primitive Contemporaries* (New York, 1931), has chapters on the Crow and Hopi, while C. Daryll Forde, *Habitat, Economy and Society* (London, 1942), contains information on the Paiute, Blackfoot, Hopi, and Yuma tribes. Ralph Linton, ed., *Acculturation in Seven American Indian Tribes* (New York, 1940), discusses changes among western Indians since their first contact with whites.

## XXI THE SPANISH BARRIER

General Works. The story of the expansion of the Mexican frontier northward can be pieced together from the mosaic of scholarly studies inspired by Herbert E. Bolton. Professor Bolton has contributed one popular account, *The Spanish Borderlands (Chronicles of America Series*, New Haven, 1921), and has edited narratives of some explorers in *Spanish Exploration in the Southwest, 1542–1706 (Original Narratives of Early American History*, New York, 1916). His point of view is reflected in Rupert N. Richardson and C. C. Rister, *The Greater Southwest* (Glendale, 1934), which devotes two chapters to Spanish expansion, and Herbert I. Priestley, *The Coming of the White Man (History of American Life Series*, New York, 1930), which describes social and economic conditions on the southwestern frontier.

Early Mexican Exploration. No satisfactory history of Mexico has been written, although Herbert I. Priestley, *The Mexican Nation: A History* (New York, 1923), contains a mass of information. The two most recent biographies of Cortés are Salvador de Madariaga, *Hernán Cortés, Conqueror of Mexico* (New York, 1941), and Henry Wagner, *The Rise of Fernando Cortés* (Los Angeles, 1944). The standard biography of the first viceroy is Arthur S. Aiton, *Antonio de Mendoza, First Viceroy of New Spain* (Durham, 1927).

Brief accounts of Spanish exploration are in John B. Brebner, *The Explorers of North America, 1492–1806* (New York, 1933). Carl Sauer, *The Road to Cibola* (Berkeley,

1932), traces in detail the land route northward used by the expeditions. The most recent collection of narratives of the Coronado expedition is by George P. Hammond and Agapito Rey, eds., *Narratives of the Coronado Expedition, 1540–1542*, 2 v. (Albuquerque, 1940), although early documents edited by George P. Winship, *The Coronado Expedition, 1540–1542* (Washington, 1896) and *The Journey of Francisco Vásquez de Coronado, 1540–1542* (San Francisco, 1933), are still useful. The standard secondary account is A. Grove Day, *Coronado's Quest* (Berkeley, 1940). Two minor explorers connected with the Coronado expedition are described in: Mabel Farnhum, *The Seven Golden Cities* (Milwaukee, 1943), which deals with Fray Marcos de Niza, and Ronald L. Ives, "Melchoir Diaz—the Forgotten Explorer," *H.I.H.R.*, XVI (February, 1936). Arthur S. Aiton, "Coronado's Muster Role," *A.H.R.*, XLIV (April, 1939), shows the explorer's equipment was less elaborate than usually pictured.

Early Advance of the Mexican Frontier. The movement of population northward across Mexico still awaits study. The subject is touched upon in Hubert H. Bancroft, *History of the North Mexican States and Texas*, 2 v. (San Francisco, 1884–89), and in the introductions to Charles W. Hackett, ed., *Historical Documents Relating to New Mexico, Nueva Vizcaya, and Approaches Thereto*, 3 v. (Washington, 1923–37). An account of the frontier thrust into one northern Mexican province is J. Lloyd Mecham, *Francisco de Ibarra and Nueva Vizcaya* (Durham, 1927).

The effect of Drake's voyage on Spanish interest in the northern provinces is assessed in Henry R. Wagner, *Sir Francis Drake's Voyage around the World, Its Aims and Achievements* (San Francisco, 1926), while the same author describes the resulting activity along the California coast in *Spanish Voyages to the North-West Coast of America in the Sixteenth Century* (San Francisco, 1929). Two articles by Charles E. Chapman also deal with voyages of the period: "Gali and Rodriguez Cermenho: Exploration of California," *S.H.Q.*, XXIII (January, 1920), and "Sebastian Vizcaino: Exploration of California," *S.H.Q.*, XXIII (April, 1920).

The Founding of New Mexico. The early history of the region is described in F. W. Hodge, "The Six Cities of Cibola, 1581–1680," *N.M.H.R.*, I (October, 1926), and George P. Hammond and Agapito Rey, eds., *Expedition into New Mexico made by Antonio de Espejo, 1582–1583* (Los Angeles, 1929). The standard account of Spanish settlement there is George P. Hammond, *Don Juan de Oñate and the Founding of New Mexico* (Santa Fe, 1926). Additional material will be found in histories of New Mexico: Hubert H. Bancroft, *History of Arizona and New Mexico, 1530–1888* (San Francisco, 1889), and Ralph E. Twitchell, *The Leading Facts of New Mexican History*, 2 v. (Cedar Rapids, Iowa, 1914).

The Advance of the Mexican Frontier in the Eighteenth Century. The advance of the Jesuit mission frontier up the west coast of Mexico has attracted the attention of several scholars. Herbert E. Bolton first called attention to the mission station as a frontier institution in "The Mission as a Frontier Institution in the Spanish-American Colonies," *A.H.R.*, XXIII (October, 1917). A later article by the same author, "The Black Robes of New Spain," *Ca. H. R.*, XXI (October, 1935), surveys their Mexican advance in general terms. More detailed treatments are in the following works: William E. Shiels, *Gonzalo de Tapia (1561–1594)* (New York, 1934), Peter M. Dunne, *Pioneer Black Robes on the West Coast* (Berkeley, 1940), which tells of the mission advance along the west coast between 1591 and 1632, and Peter M. Dunne, *Pioneer Jesuits in Northern Mexico* (Berkeley, 1944), which deals with expansion in the Sierra Madres country during the same period. Similar studies for northern Mexico, and for the Franciscans and Dominicans in central and eastern Mexico, are needed.

The advance of one arm of settlement toward Texas is described in Anne E. Hughes, *The Beginning of Spanish Settlement in the El Paso District* (Berkeley, 1914). The retreat of the New Mexican frontier to El Paso after the Pueblo Revolt of 1680 is the theme of Charles W. Hackett, "The Revolt of the Pueblo Indians of New Mexico in 1680," *T.S.H.A.Q.*, XV (October, 1911), and the same author's documentary collection, *Revolt of the Pueblo Indians of New Mexico and Otermin's Attempted Reconquest, 1680–1682* (Albuquerque, 1942). The standard account of the reconquest is J. Manuel Espinosa, *Crusaders of the Rio Grande* (Chicago, 1942).

Herbert E. Bolton, *Rim of Christendom* (New York, 1936), is the final word on the occupation of the Arizona country. He has also edited *Kino's Historical Memoir of Pimería Alta, 1683–1711*, 2 v. (Cleveland, 1919), and written a brief life of Kino: *The Padre on Horseback* (San Francisco, 1932). Additional information on the region is in Frank C. Lockwood, *Pioneer Days in Arizona from the Spanish Occupation to Statehood* (New York, 1932), and Calvin Ross, *River of the Sun. Stories of the Storied Gila* (Albuquerque, 1946).

The Occupation of Texas. A useful brief history is Rupert H. Richardson, *Texas, the Lone Star State* (New York, 1943). Fuller accounts are in Robert C. Clark, *The Beginnings of Texas, 1684–1718* (Austin, 1907), Herbert E. Bolton, "The Spanish Occupation of Texas, 1519–1690," *S.H.Q.*, XVI (July, 1912), and especially Carlos E. Castañeda, *Our Catholic Heritage in Texas*, 4 v. (Austin, 1936–39), which describes missionary activity between 1519 and 1782. LaSalle's intrusion is described in William E. Dunne, *Spanish and French Rivalry in the Gulf Region of the United States, 1678–1702* (Austin, 1917), and documents are in Charles W. Hackett, ed., *Pichardo's Treatise on the Limits of Louisiana and Texas* (Austin, 1931).

The Spanish recovery of Texas is discussed in Charmion C. Shelby, "St. Denis's

Second Expedition to the Rio Grande, 1716–1719," *S.H.Q.*, XXVII (January, 1924), and Charles W. Hackett, "The Marquis of San Miguel de Aguayo and His Recovery of Texas from the French, 1719–1723," *S.H.Q.*, XLIX (October, 1945). An important document is Fritz L. Hoffman, ed., *Fray Francisco Céliz, Diary of the Alarcón Expedition into Texas, 1718–1719* (Los Angeles, 1935).

Conflict on the French-Spanish Borderland. Two interpretative essays on the conflict are Isaac J. Cox, "The Louisiana-Texas Frontier," *S.H.Q.*, XVII (July, 1913, and October, 1913), and "The Significance of the Louisiana-Texas Frontier," *M.V.H.A., Proceedings*, III (1909-10). The French trader invasion is described in Frederick W. Hodge, "French Intrusion toward New Mexico in 1695," *N.M.H.R.*, IV (January, 1929), Charmion C. Shelby, ed., "Projected French Attacks upon the Northeastern Frontier of New Spain, 1719–1721," *H.A.H.R.*, XIII (November, 1933), and Gilbert J. Garraghan, *Chapters in Frontier History* (Milwaukee, 1934). Spanish attempts to repel the invaders are the theme of William E. Dunn, "Spanish Reaction Against the French Advance toward New Mexico, 1717–1727," *M.V.H.R.*, II (December, 1915), and Charles W. Hackett, "Policy of the Spanish Crown Regarding French Encroachments from Louisiana, 1721–1762," *New Spain and the Anglo-American West* (Los Angeles, 1932). The defeat of one Spanish expedition is discussed in Alfred B. Thomas, "Massacre of the Villasur Expedition," *N.H.*, VII (July, 1924, and September, 1924). French trade with Santa Fe is described in Herbert E. Bolton, "French Intrusions into New Mexico, 1749–1752," *The Pacific Ocean in History* (New York, 1917).

Herbert E. Bolton, *Texas in the Middle Eighteenth Century* (Berkeley, 1915), contains the classic account of Spanish activity following the French threats. A more detailed story of the occupation of the coast is in Lawrence F. Hill, *José de Escandón and the Founding of Nuevo Santander* (Columbus, 1926), while expansion northward into the Apache country is considered in two articles by William E. Dunn: "Missionary Activities Among the Eastern Apaches," *T.S.H.A.Q.*, XV (January, 1912), and "The Apache Mission on the San Sabá River," *S.H.Q.*, XVII (April, 1914). Defensive measures and the expansion of New Mexico's trading frontier are treated in Alfred B. Thomas, *After Coronado* (Norman, 1935), Joseph J. Hill, "Spanish and Mexican Exploration and Trade Northwest from New Mexico into the Great Basin, 1765–1853," *U.H.Q.*, III (January, 1930), and Alfred B. Thomas, "Spanish Expeditions into Colorado," *C.M.*, I (November, 1924). Documents are in Alfred B. Thomas, ed., *The Plains Indians and New Mexico, 1751–1778* (Albuquerque, 1940).

The Occupation of California. Two recent brief histories are Robert G. Cleland, *From Wilderness to Empire* (New York, 1944), and John W. Caughey, *California* (New York, 1940). Charles E. Chapman, *The Founding of Spanish California, 1687–1783* (New York, 1916), and *A History of California: The Spanish Period* (New York, 1921), are fuller. John W. Caughey, *History of the Pacific Coast* (Los Angeles, 1933), gives a rounded picture.

The Russian threat is summarized in Raymond H. Fisher, *The Russian Fur Trade, 1550–1700* (Berkeley, 1943), while the Spanish agent who capitalized on fears of Russia is discussed by Herbert I. Priestley, *José de Gálvez, Visitor-General of New Spain* (Berkeley, 1916). Narratives of the Portolá and Serra expedition have been edited by Herbert E. Bolton, *Fray Francisco Palóu's Historical Memoirs of New California*, 4 v. (Berkeley, 1926), and Douglas S. Watson, *The Spanish Occupation of California* (San Francisco, 1934). The standard biography of Portolá's chronicler is Herbert E. Bolton, *Fray Juan Crespi, Missionary Explorer of the Pacific Coast, 1769–1774* (Berkeley, 1927). Father Zephyrin Engelhardt, *The Missions and Missionaries of California*, 4 v. (San Francisco, 1908–15), is a standard account of Franciscan activity, although John A. Berger, *The Franciscan Missions of California* (New York, 1941), is more readable. Herbert I. Priestley, *Franciscan Explorations in California* (Glendale, 1947), deals with a special phase.

The chronicles dealing with Garcés are collected in Elliott Coues, ed., *On the Trail of a Spanish Explorer, the Diary and Itineracy of Francisco Garcés*, 2 v. (New York, 1900), and with Anza in Herbert E. Bolton, ed., *Anza's California Expeditions*, 5 v. (Berkeley, 1930). The first volume of the latter set is a scholarly introduction by Bolton. The narrative of Anza's second expedition has been edited by Herbert E. Bolton, *Font's Complete Diary, A Chronicle of the Founding of San Francisco* (Berkeley, 1933). The standard secondary account of this expedition, Herbert E. Bolton, *Outpost of Empire* (New York, 1931), is a scholarly history of the founding of San Francisco.

## XXII THE TRADERS' FRONTIER

The Extension of the Spanish Trading Frontier. Louis Houck, *The Spanish Regime in Missouri*, 2 v. (Chicago, 1909), contains useful documents, while the story of Spanish expansion northward along the Missouri is told in a series of articles by Abraham P. Nasatir: "Jacques D'Eglise on the Upper Missouri, 1791-1795," *M.V.H.R.*, XIV (June, 1927), "Anglo-Spanish Rivalry on the Upper Missouri," *M.VH.R.*, XVI (December, 1929, and March, 1930), "Spanish Exploration of the Upper Missouri," *M.V.H.R.*, XIV (June, 1927), "Anglo-Spanish Rivalry in the Iowa Country, 1797-1798," *I.J.H.P.*, XXVIII (July, 1930), and "The Formation of the Missouri Company," *M.H.R.*, XXV (October, 1930). Annie H. Abel, ed., *Tabeau's Narrative of Loisel's Expedition to the Upper Missouri* (Norman, 1939), is a chronicle of one of the traders. Early American penetration into Louisiana is described in Lawrence Kinnaird, "American Penetration into Spanish Louisiana," *New Spain and the Anglo-American West*, 2 v. (Los Angeles, 1932).

American Exploration of the Far West. No single volume deals with the explorers, but brief accounts are in: Cardinal Goodwin, *The Trans-Mississippi West* (New York, 1922), Katherine Coman, *Economic Beginnings of the Far West*, 2 v. (New York, 1912), W. J. Ghent, *The Early Far West* (New York, 1931), LeRoy R. Hafen and Carl C. Rister, *Western America* (New York, 1941), Walter F. McCaleb, *The Conquest of the West* (New York, 1947), and J. Bartlet Brebner, *The Explorers of North America, 1492-1806* (New York, 1933). E. W. Gilbert, *The Exploration of Western America, 1800-1850* (Cambridge, England, 1933), is a fuller treatment by a geographer. Reuben G. Thwaites, *A Brief History of Rocky Mountain Explorations* (New York, 1914) is useful for a limited area.

The narratives of the Lewis and Clark expedition are in Reuben G. Thwaites, ed., *Original Journals of the Lewis and Clark Expedition, 1804-1806*, 8 v. (New York, 1904-05). Among the many secondary accounts of the expedition, Olin D. Wheeler, *The Trail of Lewis and Clark*, 2 v. (New York, 1904), is complete, although additional light is shed in a biography of one of the leaders: C. M. Wilson, *Meriwether Lewis of Lewis and Clark* (New York, 1934). John Bakeless, *Lewis and Clark* (New York, 1947), is readable and sound. Jefferson's reasons for sending the explorers across the continent are assessed in Ralph B. Guinness, "The Purpose of the Lewis and Clark Expedition," *M.V.H.R.*, XX (June, 1933).

Isaac J. Cox, "Explorations of the Louisiana Frontier, 1803-1806," *A.H.A., Annual Report for 1904* (Washington, 1905), deals with the Dunbar-Hunter and Freeman expeditions. Documents on Pike's explorations are in Elliott Coues, ed., *The Expeditions of Zebulon Montgomery Pike to Headwaters of the Mississippi River*, 3 v. (New York, 1895), and Archer B. Hulbert, ed., *Zebulon Pike's Arkansaw Journal* (*Overland to the Pacific Series*, Denver, 1932). Exploration of the upper Mississippi after the War of 1812 is discussed in Marcus L. Hansen, *Old Fort Snelling, 1819–1858* (Iowa City, 1918). The standard narrative of Long's explorations is Edwin James, *An Account of an Expedition from Pittsburgh to the Rocky Mountains,* in Reuben G. Thwaites, ed., *Early Western Travels, 1748– 1846,* 32 v. (Cleveland, 1904–06). The connection between the explorations of the period is considered in Cardinal Goodwin, "A Larger View of the Yellowstone Expedition," *M.V.H.R.,* IV (December, 1917).

General Works on the Fur Trade. The most useful single work is Hiram M. Chittenden, *The American Fur Trade of the Far West,* 3 v. (rev. edn., New York, 1935), although Clarence A. Vandiveer, *The Fur Trade and Early Western Exploration* (Cleveland, 1929), is also usable. Isaac Lippincott, *A Century and a Half of Fur Trade at St. Louis* (St. Louis, 1916), stresses commercial aspects, while the effect of the trade on settlement is the theme of Willoughby M. Babcock, "The Fur Trade as an Aid to Settlement," *N.D.H.Q.,* VII (January, 1933). Everett Dick, *Vanguards of the Frontier* (New York, 1941), has chapters on the Rocky Mountain trade.

The Fur Trade in the Northern Rockies. The activities of Manuel Lisa are described in George F. Robeson, "Manuel Lisa," *P.,* VI (1925), and Charles A. Gianini, "Manuel Lisa," *N.M.H.R.,* II (1927). Stallo Vinton, *John Colter, Discoverer of Yellowstone Park* (New York, 1926), is a helpful biography of a leading trader under Lisa.

The American Fur Company still awaits a historian, although the biography of its founder by Kenneth W. Porter, *John Jacob Astor, Business Man,* 2 v. (Cambridge, 1931), devotes several chapters to its activities. The Astoria enterprise is described in classic and reasonably accurate form in Washington Irving, *Astoria* (New York, 1846). The diary of one of the trader-founders, Alexander Ross, is in Reuben G. Thwaites, *Early Western Travels,* 32 v. (New York, 1904–06). Lisa's dramatic efforts to overtake the Overland Astorians are described by a member of the party, John C. Luttig, *Journal of a Fur-trading Expedition on the Upper Missouri, 1812–1813* (St. Louis, 1920).

A brief history of the Hudson's Bay Company's expansion into the northern Rockies is in Douglas MacKay, *The Honourable Company* (London, 1936), but a fuller and more satisfactory account is in the introduction to Frederick Merk, *Fur Trade and Empire, George Simpson's Journal (Cambridge,* 1931). R. G. Montgomery, *The White-headed Eagle: John McLoughlin, Builder of an Empire* (New York, 1934), is a biography of the company's factor in the Northwest. The efforts of the company to expand into the northern Rockies are described in W. T. Atkin, "Snake River Fur Trade, 1816–1824," *O.H.Q.,* XXXV (December, 1934) and especially in Frederick Merk, "Snake Country Expedition, 1824–25: An Episode of Fur Trade and Empire," *M.V.H.R.,* XXI (June, 1934).

The Fur Trade in the Central Rockies. The standard work on the pioneering journeys of Ashley and Jedediah Smith is Harrison C. Dale, *The Ashley-Smith Explorations and the Discovery of a Central Route to the Pacific, 1822–1829* (Cleveland, 1918). Additional documents are in Maurice Sullivan, ed., *Travels of Jedediah Smith* (Santa Ana, California, 1934), while interpretative comments are made by Donald M. Frost, *Notes on General Ashley, the Overland Trail, and South Pass* (Worcester, 1945).

Among the more authentic biographies of Mountain Men, the following are typical: Stanley Vestal, *Mountain Men* (Cambridge, 1937), LeRoy R. Hafen and W. J. Ghent, *Broken Hand, the Life Story of Thomas Fitzpatrick* (Denver, 1931), Charles Kelly and M. L. Howe, *Miles Goodyear, First Citizen of Utah* (Salt Lake City, 1937), Charles L. Camp, *James Clyman, American Frontiersman, 1792–1881* (San Francisco, 1928), J. Cecil Atler, *James Bridger, Trapper, Frontiersman, Scout and Guide* (Salt

Lake City, 1925), Alpheus H. Favour, *Old Bill Williams, Mountain Man* (Chapel Hill, 1936), Charles Kelly, *Old Greenwood* (Salt Lake City, 1936), W. H. Ellison, *The Life and Adventures of George Nidever, 1802–1883* (Berkeley, 1937), and Stanley Vestal, *Jim Bridger: Mountain Man* (New York, 1946).

Material on the trading posts established in the West will be found in: LeRoy R. Hafen and Francis M. Young, *Fort Laramie and the Pageant of the West, 1834–1890* (Glendale, 1938), LeRoy R. Hafen, "The Early Fur Trade Posts on the South Platte," *M.V.H.R.*, XII (December, 1925), and LeRoy R. Hafen, "Fort Jackson and the Early Fur Trade on the South Platte," *C.M.*, V (February, 1928).

The Santa Fe Trade. Among more recent popular histories are R. L. Duffus, *The Santa Fe Trail* (New York, 1930), and Stanley Vestal, *The Old Santa Fe Trail* (Boston, 1939). Hiram M. Chittenden, *The American Fur Trade of the Far West*, 3 v. (rev. edn. New York, 1935) has a briefer account. Early attempts to open the trade are described in Alfred B. Thomas, "The First Santa Fe Expedition, 1792–1793," *C.O.* IX (June, 1931), Joseph J. Hill, "An Unknown Expedition to Santa Fe in 1807," *M.V.H.R.*, VI (March, 1920), and Isaac J. Cox, "Opening the Santa Fe Trail," *M.H.R.*, XXV (October, 1930). Narratives of the three expeditions of 1821 are: Walter B. Douglas, ed., *Three Years Among the Indians and Mexicans by Thomas James* (St. Louis, 1916), Elliott Coues, ed., *The Journal of Jacob Fowler* (New York, 1898), and Archer B. Hulbert, ed., *Southwest on the Turquoise Trail; the First Diaries on the Road to Santa Fe* (*Overland to the Pacific Series*, Denver, 1933). The classic description of the trade by a trader is Josiah Gregg, "Commerce of the Prairies," in Reuben G. Thwaites, ed., *Early Western Travels*, 32 v. (Cleveland, 1904–06). Doubts on Gregg's authorship are cast by John T. Lee, "The Authorship of Gregg's 'Com-

merce of the Prairies'," *M.V.H.R.*, XVI (March, 1930).

Other accounts of travel over the trail include: James J. Webb, *Adventures in the Santa Fé Trade, 1844–1847* (*Southwest Historical Series*, Glendale, 1931), and the following journals in the *M.H.R.;* "Journals of Captain Thomas Becknell," IV (January, 1910), "M.M. Marmaduke's Journal," VI (October, 1911), and "Major Alphonse Wetmore's Diary of a Journey to Santa Fe," VIII (July, 1914).

Special aspects of the Santa Fe trade are considered in William R. Manning, "Diplomacy Concerning the Santa Fe Road," *M.V.H.R.*, I (March, 1915), and Henry P. Beers, "Military Protection of the Santa Fe Trail to 1843," *N.M.H.R.*, XII (April, 1937). F. F. Stephen, "Missouri and the Santa Fe Trade," *M.H.R.*, X (July, 1916), deals with the impact of the trade on the state's economy.

Fur Trade in the Southwest. A helpful general work is Grant Foreman, *Pioneer Days in the Old Southwest* (Cleveland, 1926), which describes trade in the Southwest between 1800 and 1840. Thomas M. Marshall, "St. Vrain's Expedition to the Gila in 1826," *The Pacific Ocean in History* (New York, 1917), deals with the first American trading expedition into the region, while George B. Grinnell, "Bent's Old Fort and Its Builders," *K.S.H.S.*, *Collections*, XV (1919–22), discusses the origins of that famous outpost. Travelers' impressions are recorded in: John F. McDermott, ed., *The Western Journals of Washington Irving* (Norman, 1944), John F. McDermott, ed., *Tixier's Travels on the Osage Prairies* (Norman, 1940), and Lewis H. Garrard, *Wahto-yah and the Taos Trail* (*Southwest Historical Series*, Glendale, 1938).

## XXIII THE MISSISSIPPI VALLEY FRONTIER

General Works. Chapters on the settlement of the Mississippi Valley are in Cardinal Goodwin, *Trans-Mississippi West* (New

York, 1922), Frederic L. Paxson, *Last American Frontier* (New York, 1910), and LeRoy R. Hafen and Carl C. Rister, *Western America* (New York, 1941).

Peopling the Lower Mississippi Valley. Charles E. Gayarré, *History of Louisiana*, 4 v. (New Orleans, 1903), and Alcée Fortier, *History of Louisiana*, 4 v. (New York, 1904), have material on that state. John G. Fletcher, *Arkansas* (Chapel Hill, 1947), is popular. A useful short history of Missouri is Eugene M. Violette, *A History of Missouri* (New York, 1918), although Louis Houck, *A History of Missouri*, 3 v. (Chicago, 1908), is more thorough. The story of the settlement of the state is told in James F. Ellis, *The Influence of Environment on the Settlement of Missouri* (St. Louis, 1929), and in three articles: Hattie M. Anderson, "Missouri, 1804–1828: Peopling a Frontier State," *M.H.R.*, XXXI (January, 1937), Jonas Viles, "Population and Extent of Settlement in Missouri before 1804," *M.H.R.*, V (July, 1911), and Eugene M. Violette, "Early Settlements in Missouri," *M.H.R.*, I (October, 1906). Garland C. Broadhead, "Early Missouri Roads," *M.H.R.*, VIII (January, 1914), studies the effect of transportation routes on settlement.

Establishing a Permanent Indian Frontier. An illuminating article, Ralph C. Morris, "The Notion of a Great American Desert East of the Rockies," *M.V.H.R.*, XIII (September, 1926), traces the growth of the desert concept. The early work on Indian removal by Annie H. Abel, "History of Events Resulting in Indian Consolidation West of the Mississippi," A.H.A., *Annual Report for 1906* (Washington, 1908), should be supplemented by Grant Foreman, *The Last Trek of the Indians* (Chicago, 1946), which deals with the movement of Indians from the Old Northwest into Kansas and Nebraska. Bruce E. Mahan, *Old Fort Crawford and the Frontier* (Iowa City, 1926), also touches on the planting of the northern tribes. The development of an Indian policy for the transplanted natives of the Northwest is the theme of James C. Malin, "Indian Policy and Western Expansion," U. of K., *Bulletin*, II (1921).

The standard works on the southeastern tribes which were moved to the Indian Territory are by Grant Foreman: *Indians and Pioneers* (Norman, 1936), traces the history of the Oklahoma country to 1830; *Indian Removal* (Norman, 1932), deals with the transfer of the Indians to the region; and *Advancing the Frontier* (Norman, 1933), continues their story to 1860. A brief history of an important fort in the Southwest is also by Grant Foreman, *Fort Gibson* (Norman, 1936), while relationships between troops and Indians are considered in William B. Morrison, *Military Posts and Camps in Oklahoma* (Oklahoma City, 1936).

The reaction of the Plains Indians to the intrusion of eastern tribes is considered in Rupert N. Richardson, *The Comanche Barrier to South Plains Settlement* (Glendale, 1933), and in the histories of tribes cited in Chapter XX. Lucy E. Textor, *Official Relations between the United States and the Sioux Indians* (Palo Alto, 1896), touches upon the same subject in the Northwest.

The Settlement of Iowa. Brief histories of Iowa include Cyrenus Cole, *A History of the People of Iowa* (Cedar Rapids, 1921), and I. B. Richman, *Ioway to Iowa* (Iowa City, 1931). The story of the capital city is told in Benjamin F. Shambough, *The Old Stone Capital Remembers* (Iowa City, 1939), while the same author has edited *Documentary Material Relating to the History of Iowa*, 3 v. (Iowa City, 1897–1901).

Works dealing specifically with settlement are: Cardinal Goodwin, "The American Occupation of Iowa, 1833–1860," *I.J.H.P.*, XVII (January, 1919), and J. A. Swisher, "The First Land Sales," *P.*, XIX (November, 1938). Among the useful biographies of early settlers are: Louis Pelzer, *Henry Dodge* (Iowa City, 1911), J. A. Swisher, *Leonard Fletcher Parker* (Iowa City, 1927), and John C. Parish, *Robert Lucas* (Iowa

City, 1927). The importance of alien groups in the occupation of the region is considered in Melvin Gengerich, *Menonites in Iowa* (Iowa City, 1939), Jacob Van der Zee, *The Hollanders of Iowa* (Iowa City, 1912), and Jacob Van der Zee, *The British in Iowa* (Iowa City, 1922).

The beginnings of government in Iowa may be traced in: Kenneth E. Colton, "Iowa's Struggle for a Territorial Government," *A. of I.*, XXI (April, 1938), and James A. James, *Constitution and Admission of Iowa into the Union* (Baltimore, 1900).

The Settlement of Minnesota. Theodore C. Blegen, *Building Minnesota* (Boston, 1938), is the standard brief history. Indian relations at the beginning of settlement are traced in Willoughby M. Babcock, Jr., "Major Lawrence Talioferro, Indian Agent," *M.V.H.R.*, XI (December, 1924), and Marcus L. Hansen, *Old Fort Snelling, 1819–1858* (Iowa City, 1918). No adequate history of the lumbering industry has been written, but scattered information is in: William H. C. Folsom, "History of Lumbering in the St. Croix Valley," M.H.S., *Collections*, IX (1901), and Daniel Stanchfield, "History of Pioneer Lumbering on the Upper Mississippi and Its Tributaries," M.H.S., *Collections*, IX (1901).

The advance of the farm frontier is treated in Cardinal Goodwin, "The Movement of American Settlers into Wisconsin and Minnesota," *I.J.H.P.*, XVII (July, 1919), Dan E. Clark, "The Westward Movement in the Upper Mississippi Valley During the Fifties," M.V.H.A., *Proceedings*, VII (1913–14), and Livia Appel and T. C. Blegen, "Official Encouragement of Immigration to Minnesota during the Territorial Period," *M.H.*, V (August, 1923). The early settlement of the Red River Valley is considered in John P. Pritchett, *The Red River Valley, 1811–1849* (New Haven, 1942). Biographies of early settlers include: Solon J. Buck, *William Watts Folwell* (Minneapolis, 1933), Frank A. Day and T. M. Knappen, *Life of John Albert John-*

son (Chicago, 1910), George M. Stephenson, *John Lind of Minnesota* (Minneapolis, 1935), Theodore G. Blegen, ed., *The Unfinished Autobiography of Henry Hastings Sibley* (Minneapolis, 1932), and Rodney C. Loehr, ed., *Minnesota Farm Diaries* (St. Paul, 1939).

The governmental beginnings in Minnesota are treated in William Anderson and A. J. Lobb, *History of the Constitution of Minnesota* (Minneapolis, 1921).

## XXIV THE ANNEXATION OF TEXAS, 1825-1845

General Works. Good brief accounts of the American penetration of Texas may be found in G. P. Garrison, *Westward Extension, 1841–1850* (New York, 1906); in Katharine Coman, *Economic Beginnings of the Far West*, 2 v. (New York, 1912); and in Nathaniel W. Stephenson, *Texas and the Mexican War* (New Haven, 1921). Of the general histories of Texas, several of the older ones are still of value. The most satisfactory comprehensive account is H. H. Bancroft, *History of the North Mexican States and Texas*, 2 v. (San Francisco, 1884–89), which is important alike for critical treatment and bibliographical data. William Kennedy, *Texas: The Rise, Progress and Prospects of the Republic of Texas*, 2 v. (London, 1841), although written to stimulate British interest in Texas, is sound and objective. Henderson Yoakum, *History of Texas from its first settlement in 1685 to its Annexation to the United States in 1846*, 2 v. (New York, 1856), is of permanent value by virtue of the fact that it is based in part on materials which have since disappeared. Later works are G. P. Garrison, *Texas: A Contest of Civilizations* (Boston, 1903), a brief account based on thorough knowledge of the sources; Rupert N. Richardson, *Texas, The Lone Star State* (New York, 1943), a one volume synthesis of the latest researches on the subject; and Louis J. Wortham, *A History of Texas: from Wilderness to Commonwealth*, 5 v. (Fort Worth, 1924), journalistic in character but embodying the results of much recent research.

The leading authority on the American colonization of Texas is Eugene C. Barker, whose *Life of Stephen F. Austin* (Nashville and Dallas, 1925), is the standard work on the subject. Barker has also edited *The Austin Papers*, A.H.A., *Annual Report for 1919*, II (Washington, 1924) and A.H.A. *Annual Report for 1922*, II (Washington, 1928). A third volume bears the title *The Austin Papers, October, 1834—January 1837* (Austin, 1926). With Amelia W. Williams, Barker has also edited *The Writings of Sam Houston, 1813–1863*, 8 v. (Austin, 1938–43). Eugene C. Barker, "The Government of Austin's Colony, 1821–1831," *S.H.Q.*, XXI (January, 1918) is the definitive treatment of this subject. Ethel Z. Rather, "DeWitt's Colony," *T.S.H.A.Q.*, VII (October, 1904) is an excellent discussion of the American colony which was second only to that of Austin.

On the Texas Revolution there are four articles by Eugene C. Barker: "Land Speculation as a Cause of the Texas Revolution," *T.S.H.A.Q.*, XVIII (July, 1914); "The San Jacinto Campaign," *T.S.H.A.Q.*, IV (April, 1901); "President Jackson and the Texas Revolution," *A.H.R.*, XII (July, 1907); "The Finances of the Texas Revolution," *P.S.Q.*, XIX (December, 1904). An interesting study of public opinion in a northern state with respect to the Texas Revolution is James E. Winston, "New York and the Independence of Texas," *S.H.Q.*, XVIII (April, 1915).

Important for the independent Republic of Texas are Marquis James, *The Raven; a Biography of Sam Houston* (Indianapolis, 1929); G. P. Garrison, ed., *Texan Diplomatic Correspondence*, A.H.A. *Annual Report for 1907 and 1908* 3 v. (Washington, 1908–11); William C. Binkley (ed.) *The Official Correspondence of the Texas Revolution* (2 vols., New York, 1936), William R. Hogan, *The Texas Republic* (Norman, 1946), and Herbert Gambrell, *Anson Jones: The Last President of Texas* (New York, 1948).

British interest in Texas can best be studied in E. D. Adams, *British Interests in Texas* (Baltimore, 1910) and in E. D. Adams, ed., "British Correspondence Concerning Texas," *S.H.Q.*, XVIII-XXI (July, 1914–July, 1917).

Several works dealing with American diplomacy of the period contain valuable material on the foreign relations of Texas. Among them are: George L. Rives, *The United States and Mexico, 1821–1842* 2 v. (New York, 1913); and J. S. Reeves, *American Diplomacy under Tyler and Polk* (Baltimore, 1907).

On annexation the standard work is Justin Smith, *Annexation of Texas* (New York, 1911). Useful also are G. P. Garrison, "The First Stages of the Movement for the Annexation of Texas," *A.H.R.*, X (October, 1904); Elizabeth H. West, "Southern Opposition to the Annexation of Texas," *S.H.Q.*, XVIII (July, 1914); and St. George L. Sioussat, "John Caldwell Calhoun," *The American Secretaries of State and their Diplomacy*, V (New York, 1928).

## XXV THE OCCUPATION OF OREGON, 1825-1846

General Works. Older treatments are H. H. Bancroft, *History of Oregon* 2 v. (San Francisco, 1886–88); Hall Jackson Kelley, *History of the Settlement of Oregon and the Interior of Upper California* (Springfield, Mass., 1868); W. H. Gray, *History of Oregon, 1792–1849* (Portland, 1870); and S. A. Clarke, *Pioneer Days of Oregon Territory* 2 v. (Portland, 1905). Of more recent accounts Joseph Schafer, *History of the Pacific Northwest* (New York, 1918) is excellent, as are the more detailed volumes by George W. Fuller, *A History of the Pacific Northwest* (New York, 1931), and Oscar O. Winther, *The Great Northwest* (New York, 1947).

A valuable collection of documentary material pertaining to developments discussed in this chapter is to be found in Archer Butler Hulbert and Dorothy Printup Hulbert, eds., *Overland to the Pacific*, III-VIII (Denver, 1933–41).

Important material on the Hudson's Bay Company is found in Frederick Merk, ed., *Fur Trade and Empire: George Simpson's Journal, 1824–1825* (Cambridge, 1931) and F. V. Holman, *Dr. John McLoughlin, The Father of Oregon* (Cleveland, 1907).

The role of John Floyd in Oregon history is discussed in C. H. Ambler, *Life and Diary of John Floyd* (Richmond, 1918) and in the same author's "The Oregon Country, 1810–1830; A Chapter in Territorial Expansion," *M.V.H.R.*, XXX (June, 1943). The Report of Floyd's Committee of 1821 with respect to the Oregon Country has been reprinted in the *O.H.Q.*, VIII (March, 1907). Another study of Floyd's efforts is Verne Blue, "Oregon Question, 1818–1828," *O.H.Q.*, XXIII (September, 1922).

The most satisfactory study of Kelley's influence is Fred Wilbur Powell, *Hall Jackson Kelley, Prophet of Oregon* (Portland, 1917), reprinted from the *O.H.Q.*, XVIII (1917). Wyeth's connection with Oregon is illumined in F. G. Young, ed., *Correspondence and Journals of Nathaniel J. Wyeth, 1831–1836*, in *Sources of the History of Oregon*, I (Eugene, 1899).

The coming of the missionaries is discussed in Cornelius J. Brosnan, *Jason Lee, Prophet of the New Oregon* (New York, 1932); in D. Lee and J. H. Frost, *Ten Years in Oregon* (New York, 1844); in W. I. Marshall, *Acquisition of Oregon and the Long Suppressed Evidence about Marcus Whitman* (Seattle, 1911), in which the Whitman legend is exploded in detail; in Edward G. Bourne, "Aspects of Oregon History before 1840," *O.H.Q.*, VI (September, 1905); in the same author's *Essays in Historical Criticism* (New York, 1901), in which the Whitman legend is exposed; and in W. J. Ghent, *The Road to Oregon* (New York, 1929). Much documentary material on the missionaries is in Hulbert, ed., *Overland to the Pacific*, V-VIII, mentioned above.

On the overland migrations to Oregon the most complete single account is J. C. Bell, *Opening a Highway to the Pacific, 1838–1846* (New York, 1921). W. J. Ghent, *The Road to Oregon* (New York, 1929), and Jay Monaghan, *The Overland Trail* (Indianapolis, 1947), are also good general accounts. More specialized studies of the migrations are F. G. Young, "Oregon Trail," *O.H.Q.*, I (December, 1900), and H. C. Dale, "Organization of the Oregon Emigrating Societies," *O.H.Q.*, XVI (September, 1915). A classic account of the great migration of 1843 by one who participated in it is Jesse Applegate "A Day with the Cow Column," *O.H.Q.*, I (December, 1900).

For the evolution of the provisional government in Oregon see F. G. Young, "Ewing Young and his Estate," *O.H.Q.*, XXI (September, 1920); J. R. Robertson, "Genesis of Political Authority and of a Commonwealth Government in Oregon," *O.H.Q.*, I (March, 1900); and R. C. Clark, "How British and American Subjects Unite in a Common Government for Oregon Territory in 1844," *O.H.Q.* (September, 1920).

General accounts of the diplomacy of the Oregon question are J. S. Reeves, *American Diplomacy under Tyler and Polk* (Baltimore, 1907) and Eugene I. McCormac, *James K. Polk: A Political Biography* (Berkeley, 1922). This subject is also discussed by St. George L. Sioussat in his sketches of "John Caldwell Calhoun" and "James Buchanan," in *The American Secretaries of State and Their Diplomacy*, V (New York, 1928).

More specialized studies of Oregon diplomacy are Joseph Schafer, "The British Attitude toward the Oregon Question, 1815–1846," *A.H.R.*, XVI (January, 1911); Frederick Merk, "Oregon Pioneers and the Boundary Settlement," *A.H.R.*, XXIX (July, 1924), which places the role of the pioneers in a new and significant perspective; Frederick Merk, "British Government Propaganda and the Oregon Treaty," *A.H.R.*, XL (October, 1934); and Frederick Merk,

"British Party Politics and the Oregon Treaty," *A.H.R.*, XXXVII (July, 1932).

## XXVI THE GREAT BASIN FRONTIER

General Works. The literature on Mormonism is voluminous and usually unreliable. Two strongly anti-Mormon histories of the church are William A. Linn, *The Story of the Mormons* (New York, 1902), and Harry M. Beardsley, *Joseph Smith and His Mormon Empire* (Boston, 1931), but a better-balanced treatment of the sect's early years is in Fawn M. Brodie, *No Man Knows My History. The Life of Joseph Smith* (New York, 1945). Equally prejudiced are the official histories of the church, of which the most important is Brigham H. Roberts, *A Comprehensive History of the Church of Jesus Christ of Latter-Day Saints*, 6 v. (Salt Lake City, 1930). The most recent biographies of Brigham Young are Morris R. Werner, *Brigham Young* (New York, 1925), and Susa Y. Gates and L. B. Widstoe, *The Life Story of Brigham Young* (New York, 1930).

The Mormon Migration Westward. Mormon persecution in the East is discussed in Herman C. Smith, "Mormon Troubles in Missouri," *M.H.R.*, IV (July, 1910), and Rollin J. Britton "Early Days on Grand River and the Mormon War," *M.H.R.*, XIII (January, 1919)–XIV (April-July, 1920). D. C. Bloomer, "The Mormons in Iowa," *A. of I.*, II (1895–97), and R. E. Harvey, "The Mormon Trek Across Iowa Territory," *A. of I.*, XXVIII (July, 1946), trace the first stages of the Mormon journey westward. A journal of one of the immigrants has been printed: William Clayton's *Journal* (Salt Lake City, 1921). The adventures of the band of Mormons who reached Utah by sea are chronicled in the biography of their leader, James A. B. Scherer, *The First Forty-Niner* (New York, 1925).

A thorough consideration of the first settlement of Utah is in Andrew I. Neff, *History of Utah, 1847–1869* (Salt Lake City, 1940), although Hubert H. Bancroft,

*History of Utah, 1540–1886* (San Francisco, 1889), is still of some use. C. D. Harris, *Salt Lake City, a Regional Capital* (Chicago, 1940), recounts the history of the capital city.

The Expansion of Mormon Settlements. A thorough study is Nels Anderson, *Desert Saints: The Mormon Frontier in Utah* (Chicago, 1942), while Milton R. Hunter, *Brigham Young the Colonizer* (Salt Lake City, 1943), contains an enlightening account of expansion, industrial development, and the land system. The latter work is briefly summarized by its author in "Brigham Young, Colonizer," *P.H.R.*, VI (December, 1937). Equally important is the study of relations between the Mormons and the United States in Leland H. Creer, *Utah and the Nation* (Seattle, 1929). An adequate but laudatory biography of one of the leading Utah frontiersmen is John H. Evans, *Charles Coulson Rich: Pioneer Builder of the West* (New York, 1936). Andrew Jenson, *History of the Scandinavian Mission* (Salt Lake City, 1927), recounts Mormon efforts to attract immigrants from northern Europe.

The emphasis of the Mormons on group activity have been assessed in Ephraim E. Ericksen, *The Psychological and Ethical Aspects of Mormon Group Life* (Chicago, 1923), and described in William J. McNiff, *Heaven on Earth: A Planned Mormon Society* (Oxford, Ohio, 1940). Edward J. Allen, *The Second United Order Among the Mormons* (New York, 1936), although dealing with a communistic experiment undertaken between 1874 and 1885, is valuable in explaining earlier trends.

No separate study of the Mormon War of 1857–58 has been written, but information may be gleaned from: O. G. Hammond, ed., *The Utah Expedition, 1857–1858; Letters of Captain Jesse A. Gove* (Concord, New Hampshire, 1928), and Charles W. Penrose, *The Mountain Meadows Massacre* (Salt Lake City, 1884). The career of the mediator who ended the conflict is traced in Oscar O. Winther, ed., *The*

*Private Papers and Diary of Thomas Lieper Kane, A Friend of the Mormons* (San Francisco, 1937).

## XXVII THE CONQUEST OF CALIFORNIA, 1830-1846

General Works. The most voluminous single work on California is H. H. Bancroft, *History of California*, 7 v. (San Francisco, 1884–90), which has been the foundation for a large part of the subsequent work on the subject. Other valuable general accounts are Theodore H. Hittell, *History of California* 4 v. (San Francisco, 1885–97) and Zoeth S. Eldredge, *History of California*, 5 v. (New York, 1915). Of one volume histories of California the most important for the period of this chapter are Robert G. Cleland, *A History of California: The American Period* (New York, 1922), which was extensively used in the preparation of this chapter; Robert G. Cleland, *From Wilderness to Empire: A History of California* (New York, 1944), a more popular, but no less careful account; John W. Caughey, *California* (New York, 1940), which is a scholarly synthesis of a wide range of materials; and Irving B. Richman, *California Under Spain and Mexico, 1535–1847* (Boston, 1911).

On the sea otter trade the only complete account is Adele Ogden, *The California Sea Otter Trade, 1784–1848* (Berkeley, 1941). A contemporary narrative growing out of this trade is William Shaler, *Journal of a Voyage from China to the Northwestern Coast of America Made in 1804*, originally published in the *American Register*, III (1808).

The hide and tallow trade provides the inspiration for two notable contemporary books: Richard H. Dana, Jr., *Two Years Before the Mast* (New York, 1840), "probably the most widely read book relating to California"; and Alfred Robinson, *Life in California* (New York, 1846). Recent studies of the trade are two articles by Adele Ogden: "Hides and Tallow: McCulloch, Hartnell and Company, 1822–1828,"

*C.H.S.Q.*, VI (September, 1927); and "Boston Hide Droghers along the California Shores," *C.H.S.Q.*, VIII (December, 1929).

Early trade between Santa Fe and Southern California is treated in Eleanor Lawrence, "Mexican Trade between Santa Fe and Los Angeles, 1830–1848," *C.H.S.Q.*, X (March, 1931); and in J. J. Hill, "The Old Spanish Trail," *H.A.H.R.*, IV (August, 1921).

For the overland fur traders the standard general work is Hiram M. Chittenden, *The American Fur Trade in the Far West*, 3 v. (New York, 1902). A popular general account is Stanley Vestal, *Mountain Men* (Boston, 1937). A classic contemporary account is James Ohio Pattie, *The Personal Narrative of James Ohio Pattie* (Cincinnati, 1831), reprinted (Cleveland, 1925). The explorations of Jedediah Smith receive thorough treatment in H. C. Dale, *The Ashley-Smith Explorations and the Discovery of the Central Route to the Pacific, 1822–1829* (Cleveland, 1918). Smith has also been the subject of two studies by Maurice S. Sullivan: *The Travels of Jedediah Smith* (Santa Ana, 1934); and *The Life of Jedediah Smith* (New York, 1937). Among other studies of individual Mountain Men are: Edwin L. Sabin, *Kit Carson Days, 1809–1868*, 2 v. (New York, 1914); Stanley Vestal, *Kit Carson: The Happy Warrior of the Old West* (Boston, 1928); and Douglas S. Watson, *West Wind: The Life Story of Joseph Reddeford Walker, Knight of the Golden Horseshoe* (Los Angeles, 1934).

Material concerning some of the permanent settlers in California before 1841 is to be found in: George D. Lyman, *Dr. John Marsh Pioneer* (New York, 1930), a definitive study of the Harvard graduate and physician who became a prominent figure in the province; Reuben L. Underhill, *From Cowhide to Golden Fleece* (Stanford University, 1939), the most satisfactory study of Thomas O. Larkin, merchant, American consul in California, and later confidential agent of the Polk administration there; and William H. Davis, *Sixty Years in California* (San Francisco, 1889), enlarged and republished as *Seventy-five Years in California* (San Francisco, 1929), the memoirs of one who was prominent in California from the early days of the Mexican period. Two recent biographies of Sutter are Julian Dana, *Sutter of California: A Biography* (New York, 1936) and James Peter Zollenger, *Sutter: The Man and His Empire* (New York, 1939).

The overland migrations are treated in Rockwell D. Hunt, *John Bidwell, A Prince of California Pioneers* (Caldwell, Idaho, 1942); C. F. McGlashan, *The History of the Donner Party* (Truckee, California, 1879); and George R. Stewart, Jr., *Ordeal by Hunger: The Story of the Donner Party* (New York, 1936).

On the American acquisition of California must be included the contemporary work of Alexander Forbes, *California: A History of Upper and Lower California* (London, 1839). This was the first work in English dealing wholly with California. Written with the purpose of encouraging British occupation of California, it had an important influence in arousing American interest in the province. Another contemporary account which influenced American sentiment was Thomas Jefferson Farnham, *Travels in the Californias and Scenes in the Pacific Ocean* (New York, 1844). The standard work on annexationist sentiment in the United States is Robert G. Cleland, "The Early Sentiment for the Annexation of California: An Account of American Interest in California, 1835–1846," *S.H.Q.*, XVIII (July, 1914 to January, 1915). E. D. Adams, "English Interest in the Annexation of California," *A.H.R.*, XIV (July, 1909), shows that American fears of official British designs upon California were groundless. Standard accounts of the diplomatic history of the acquisition of California are J. S. Reeves, *American Diplomacy under Tyler and Polk* (Baltimore, 1907); Eugene I. McCormac, *James K. Polk: A Political Biography* (Berkeley, 1922); and St.

George L. Sioussat, "James Buchanan," in *The American Secretaries of State and Their Diplomacy*, V (New York, 1928).

## XXVIII THE MEXICAN WAR

General Works. The most thorough study of relations between the United States and Mexico preceding the outbreak of the war is George L. Rives, *The United States and Mexico, 1821–1848*, 2 v. (New York, 1913). Briefer accounts are in J. Fred Rippy, *The United States and Mexico* (New York, 1931), and Nathaniel W. Stephenson, *Texas and the Mexican War* (*Chronicles of America Series*, New Haven, 1921). The standard biography of the American President is Eugene I. McCormac, *James K. Polk: A Political Biography* (Berkeley, 1922). Milo M. Quaife, ed., *The Diary of James K. Polk during His Presidency*, 4 v. (Chicago, 1910), give an intimate picture of American politics.

Causes of the Mexican War. The older historical point of view, that the war was caused by aggressive slaveholders seeking more land, was first successfully challenged by Justin H. Smith, *The War with Mexico*, 2 v. (New York, 1919), which remains the standard account of the struggle. Smith's thesis, that Mexican inefficiency justified war on the part of the United States, has been modified by later scholars studying specific phases of the problem. H. Donaldson Jordan, "A Politician of Expansion: Robert J. Walker," *M.V.H.R.*, XIX (December, 1932), holds Polk and his cabinet at least as responsible as Mexico, a view anticipated in William E. Dodd, *Robert J. Walker, Imperialist* (Chicago, 1914). Richard R. Stenberg, "The Failure of Polk's Mexican War Intrigue of 1845," *P.H.R.*, IV (March, 1935), goes beyond by charging that Polk tried to precipitate war in 1845.

Modern scholars recognize that western expansionism was at least as influential in inclining the United States toward war as southern imperialism. This view was advanced in William E. Dodd, "The West and the War with Mexico," *J.I.S.H.S.*, V

(July, 1912). Charles S. Boucher, "In *Re* that Aggressive Slavocracy," *M.V.H.R.*, VIII (June-September, 1921), shows that most influential slaveholders opposed the war. This thesis is developed in Clayton S. Ellsworth, "The American Churches and the Mexican War," *A.H.R.*, XLV (January, 1940), which demonstrates that churches in the West favored American entrance while those in the East were opposed. A complete restudy of the causes of the war would be welcomed.

California and the Bear Flag Revolt. All histories of California deal extensively with the Bear Flag Revolt and annexation. The fullest treatment is in Robert G. Cleland, *A History of California: The American Period* (New York, 1922), but thorough accounts are also in John W. Caughey, *California* (New York, 1940), and Robert G. Cleland, *From Wilderness to Empire* (New York, 1944).

Fremont's controversial role in the Bear Flag Revolt is discussed by his biographers, Allan Nevins, *Fremont: Pathmarker of the West* (New York, 1939), and Cardinal Goodwin, *John Charles Frémont* (Palo Alto, 1930). The explorer's own story is told in *Memoirs of My Life* (New York, 1887). Two recent articles illustrate the lack of agreement among historians on Fremont's part in the revolt. Richard R. Stenberg, "Polk and Frémont, 1845–1846," *P.H.R.*, VII (September, 1938), holds that Polk encouraged Frémont to help free California, while George Tays, "Frémont Had No Secret Instructions," *P.H.R.*, IX (June, 1940), argues from the same evidence that the explorer acted on his own initiative. Lieutenant Gillespie's mysterious role in the drama is surveyed in George W. Ames, ed., "Gillespie and the Conquest of California," *C.H.S.Q.*, XVII (June-September, 1938). Reuben L. Underhill, *From Cowhide to Golden Fleece* (Stanford, 1939), is the standard biography of Thomas O. Larkin. A victim of the revolt is described in a laudatory biography by Myrtle M. McKittrick, *Vallejo, Son of California* (Portland, 1944).

The Military Phase. A thorough history of the campaigns is in Justin H. Smith, *The War With Mexico*, 2 v. (New York, 1919). Biographies of the competing generals contain additional material. Recent studies of the Mexican commander include: Wilfrid H. Callcott, *Santa Anna. The Story of an Enigma Who Once Was Mexico* (Norman, 1936), and Frank C. Hanighen, *Santa Anna, The Napoleon of the West* (New York, 1934). For the two American leaders the student may consult: Holman Hamilton, *Zachary Taylor* (New York, 1942), Silas B. McKinley and Silas Bent, *Old Rough and Ready: The Life and Times of Zachary Taylor* (New York, 1946), Brainerd Dyer, *Zachary Taylor* (Baton Rouge, 1946), Arthur D. H. Smith, *Old Fuss and Feathers: The Life and Exploits of Lt.-General Winfield Scott* (New York, 1937), and Charles W. Elliott, *Winfield Scott: The Soldier and the Man* (New York, 1937).

Soldiers' memoirs, which deal largely with the romantic Doniphan and Kearny expeditions, include: Ralph P. Bieber, ed., *Journal of a Soldier under Kearny and Doniphan, 1846–1847* (Southwest Historical Series, Glendale, 1935), Ralph P. Bieber, ed., *Marching With the Army of the West, 1846–1848* (Southwest Historical Series, Glendale, 1936), and Stella M. Drumm, ed., *Down the Santa Fé Trail and Into Mexico: the Diary of Susan Shelby Magoffin, 1846–1847* (New Haven, 1926). The journal of one of General Scott's aids is printed in William S. Myers, ed., *The Mexican War Diary of George B. McClellan* (Princeton, 1917).

The Diplomacy of the War and Peace. The standard account is Jesse S. Reeves, *American Diplomacy under Tyler and Polk* (Baltimore, 1907) but brief summaries are in James M. Callahan, *American Foreign Policy in Mexican Relations* (New York, 1932), Samuel F. Bemis, ed., *The American Secretaries of State and Their Diplomacy*, 10 v. (New York, 1927–29), and histories of American foreign policy, of which the two most recent are Thomas A.

Bailey, *A Diplomatic History of the American People* (New York, 1942), and Samuel F. Bemis, *A Diplomatic History of the United States* (New York, 1942),

Louis M. Sears, "Nicholas P. Trist, A Diplomat with Ideals," *M.V.H.R.*, XI (June, 1924), describes the American negotiator, while the treaty of peace is considered in Julius Klein, *The Making of the Treaty of Guadaloupe Hidalgo on February 2, 1848* (Berkeley, 1905). The standard work on changing American sentiment toward Mexico during the war is John D. P. Fuller, *The Movement for the Acquisition of All Mexico, 1846–1848* (Baltimore, 1938).

The thorough study of the Gadsden Purchase by Paul N. Garber, *The Gadsden Treaty* (Philadelphia, 1923), may be supplemented with three articles by J. Fred Rippy: "The Boundary of New Mexico and the Gadsden Treaty," *H.A.H.R.*, IV (November, 1921), "Anglo-American Filibusters and the Gadsden Treaty," *H.A.H.R.*, V. (May, 1922), and "The Negotiation of the Gadsden Treaty," *S.H.Q.*, XXVII (July, 1923).

The Origins of the Controversy over Slavery in the Territories. The origins of the Wilmot Proviso are considered in Charles B. Going, *David Wilmot, Free Soiler* (New York, 1924), while Richard R. Stenberg, "The Motivation of the Wilmot Proviso," *M.V.H.R.*, XVIII (March, 1932), argues that Wilmot's political ambitions led him to introduce the measure. Constitutional arguments advanced in the debate that followed are weighed in Jesse T. Carpenter, *The South as a Conscious Minority, 1789–1861* (New York, 1930), and Milo M. Quaife, *The Doctrine of Non-Intervention with Slavery in the Territories* (Chicago, 1910). The part of the Free Soil Party in the elections of 1848 is treated in Theodore C. Smith, *The Liberty and Free Soil Parties in the Northwest* (Cambridge, 1897).

The role of Stephen A. Douglas in drafting the Compromise of 1850 is explained in George D. Harmon, "Douglas and the Compromise of 1850," *J.I.S.H.S.*, XXI (January, 1929), and Frank H. Hodder, "The Authorship of the Compromise of 1850," *M.V.H.R.*, XXII (March, 1936). Full accounts are also in the biographies of Clay, and especially George R. Poage, *Henry Clay and the Whig Party* (Chapel Hill, 1936). The southern reaction to the measure is considered in Richard H. Shryock, *Georgia and the Union in 1850* (Philadelphia, 1926), Arthur C. Cole, "The South and the Right of Secession in the Early Fifties," *M.V.H.R.*, I (December, 1914), and Robert P. Brooks, "Howell Cobb and the Crisis of 1850," *M.V.H.R.*, IV (December, 1917).

The California Gold Rush. Good brief descriptions will be found in the histories of California cited earlier in this chapter, but the best account is Rodman W. Paul, *California Gold* (Cambridge, 1947). The discovery of gold is recounted in the standard biography of John Sutter: James P. Zollinger, *Sutter, the Man and His Empire* (New York, 1939). Numerous popular writers have described the rush and life in the mining camps; among the most useful are: Owen C. Coy, *Gold Days* (Los Angeles, 1929), Valeska Bari, *The Course of Empire* (New York, 1931), Glenn C. Quiett, *Pay Dirt* (New York, 1934), Joseph H. Jackson, *Anybody's Gold* (New York, 1941), and Stewart E. White, *The Forty-Niners* (*Chronicles of America Series*, New Haven, 1918). Routes to California are described in Ralph P. Bieber, "The Northwestern Trails to California in 1849," *M.V.H.R.*, XII (December, 1925), and John W. Caughey, "Southwest from Salt Lake in 1849," *P.H.R.*, VI (June, 1937).

Virtually every literate miner who started for California kept a journal. Scores of these have been published. One of the best is a synthetic diary by Archer B. Hulbert, *Forty-Niners* (Boston, 1931). Others are collected in Ralph P. Bieber, *Southern Trails to California in 1849* (*Southwest Historical Series*, Glendale, 1937). Typical of dozens of individual journals are: John Steele, *Across the Plains in 1850* (Chicago, 1930), G. W. Read, *A Pioneer of 1850* (Boston, 1927), Douglas S. Watson, ed., *The Santa Fe Trail to California, 1849–1852: The Journal of H. M. T. Powell* (San Francisco, 1933), William C. Manly, *Death Valley in '49* (Santa Barbara, 1924), Grant Foreman, ed., *Marcy and the Gold Seekers* (Norman, 1939), Octavius T. Howe, ed., *Argonauts of '49* (Cambridge, 1923), Carolyn H. Ross, ed., *The Log of a Forty-Niner* (Boston, 1923). David M. Potter, ed. *Trail to California* (New Haven, 1945), and George W. B. Evans, *Mexican Gold Trail: The Journal of a Forty-Niner* (San Marino, 1945). A guide used by immigrants has been made available in Joseph E. Ware, *The Emigrants' Guide to California* (John W. Caughey, ed., Princeton, 1932).

## XXIX THE WEST AND SLAVERY

General Works. The standard longer work is James F. Rhodes, *History of the United States from the Compromise of 1850*, 7 v. (New York, 1893–1906), but a convenient summary of the findings of more recent scholars is in Henry H. Simms, *A Decade of Sectional Controversy, 1851–1861* (Chapel Hill, 1942). Avery Craven, *The Coming of the Civil War* (New York, 1942), is another modern account. A brief history of the period is in the opening chapters of J. G. Randall, *The Civil War and Reconstruction* (Boston, 1937), while social aspects are the theme of Arthur C. Cole, *The Irrepressible Conflict, 1850–1865* (*History of American Life Series*, New York, 1934).

The Period of Calm, 1850–1854. The standard account is Roy F. Nichols, *Franklin Pierce: Young Hickory of the Granite Hills* (Philadelphia, 1931), which like all good biographies is a history of a period as well as a man. The same author studies the politics of the era in *The Democratic Machine, 1850–1854* (New York, 1923). Undercurrents in the South that doomed the era of peace are the theme of Laura A. White, *Robert Barnwell Rhett, Father of*

*Secession* (New York, 1931), and Henry H. Simms, *Life of Robert M. T. Hunter: a Study in Sectionalism and Secession* (Richmond, 1935). The basis for growing secession sentiment is considered in P. L. Rainwater, "Economic Benefits of Secession: Opinions in Mississippi in the 1850's," *J.S.H.*, I (November, 1935).

The Kansas-Nebraska Act. Douglas' reasons for introducing the unpopular measure have long been disputed by historians. The older view, that he was seeking southern votes for the presidency, was challenged by P. Orman Ray, *The Repeal of the Missouri Compromise* (Cleveland, 1909), which advanced the thesis that Senator Atchison of Missouri originated the bill for his own political purposes. This interpretation was challenged by Frank H. Hodder in two articles: "The Genesis of the Kansas-Nebraska Act," *S.H.S.W.*, *Proceedings for 1912* (Madison, 1912), and "The Railroad Background of the Kansas-Nebraska Act," *M.V.H.R.*, XII (June, 1925), in which he held that Douglas devised the measure to secure a Pacific railroad terminus at Chicago. Although Ray argued against Hodder's interpretation in "The Genesis of the Kansas-Nebraska Act," *A.H.A.*, *Annual Report for 1914* (Washington, 1916), most students agree that Douglas' railroad ambitions were primarily responsible for his sponsorship of the act.

Various other aspects of the Kansas-Nebraska Act have been explored by historians. Its relation to Indian policy is considered in Roy Gittinger, "The Separation of Nebraska and Kansas from the Indian Territory," *M.V.H.R.*, III (March, 1917). Henry B. Learned, "The Relation of Philip Phillips to the Repeal of the Missouri Compromise in 1854," *M.V.H.R.*, VIII (March, 1922), shows that this Alabama representative suggested to Douglas that the act specifically repeal the Missouri Compromise. Two sound biographies of Douglas throw additional light on the measure: Allen Johnson, *Stephen A. Douglas: A Study in American Politics* (New York, 1908) and George F.

Milton, *The Eve of Conflict. Stephen A. Douglas and the Needless War* (Boston, 1934).

The political results of the Kansas Nebraska Act are considered in Ray A. Billington, *The Protestant Crusade, 1800–1860* (New York, 1938), which deals with the Know-Nothings, and Andrew W. Crandall, *The Early History of the Republican Party, 1854–1856* (Boston, 1930). The Republican role in the election of 1856 is described in Ruhl J. Bartlett, *John C. Frémont and the Republican Party* (Columbus, 1930), and in the various biographies of Frémont, of which the latest is Allan Nevins, *Frémont, Pathmarker of the West* (New York, 1939).

Bleeding Kansas, 1854–1857. The view originally held by historians, that the New England Emigrant Aid Society saved Kansas for freedom, was set forth in Eli Thayer, *A History of the Kansas Crusade* (New York, 1889). This interpretation was first challenged by William O. Lynch, "Popular Sovereignty and the Colonization of Kansas from 1854 to 1860," M.V.H.A., *Proceedings*, IX (1917–18), which used census statistics to prove that few New Englanders reached Kansas during the decade. Additional proof of this view, gleaned from the papers of the company itself, is presented in Ralph V. Harlow, "The Rise and Fall of the Kansas Aid Movement," *A.H.R.*, XLI (October, 1935). A thorough study of the company is in Samuel A. Johnson, "The Genesis of the New England Emigrant Aid Society," *N.E.Q.*, III (January, 1930), while Robert E. Moody, "The First Year of the Emigrant Aid Company," *N.E.Q.*, IV (January, 1931), adds additional information. Efforts of the company to bring settlers from England are assessed in Percy W. Bidwell, "The New England Emigrant Aid Company and English Cotton Supply Associations," *A.H.R.*, XXIII (October, 1917).

Traditional northern views of the Kansas warfare have been challenged by James C. Malin, "The Proslavery Background of the Kansas Struggle," *M.V.H.R.*, X (December, 1923), and the same author's *John Brown and the Legend of Fifty-Six* (Philadelphia, 1942). These studies suggest that land conflicts and frontier skirmishing were responsible for much of the warfare, and indicate that a thorough restudy of the whole episode is needed. Additional information on the South's efforts to secure Kansas are in Walter L. Fleming, "The Buford Expedition to Kansas," *A.H.R.*, IV (October, 1900), Mary J. Klem, "Missouri in the Kansas Struggle," M.V.H.A., *Proceedings*, IX (1917–18), and Elmer L. Craik, "Southern Interest in Territorial Kansas, 1854–1858," K.S.H.S., *Collections*, XV (1919–22). The career of the North's leading agitator is studied in the biography by Malin listed above, and more briefly in Robert P. Warren, *John Brown. The Making of a Martyr* (New York, 1929). W. H. Isely, "The Sharps Rifle Episode in Kansas History," *A.H.R.*, XII (April, 1907), deals with efforts of the Emigrant Aid Companies to arm settlers.

The Dred Scott Case, 1857. Brief discussions are in the constitutional histories of the United States: Andrew C. McLaughlin, *Constitutional History of the United States* (New York, 1935), Homer C. Hockett, *Constitutional History of the United States, 1827–1876*, 2 v. (New York, 1939), and Carl B. Swisher, *American Constitutional Development* (Boston, 1943), as well as in biographies of Justice Taney: Carl B. Swisher, *Roger B. Taney* (New York, 1935), and Charles W. Smith, *Roger B. Taney, Jacksonian Jurist* (Chapel Hill, 1936). The case is placed in its historical setting by Charles Warren, *The Supreme Court in United States History*, 2 v. (Boston, 1926).

The modern interpretation of the decision began with an article by Frank H. Hodder, "Some Phases of the Dred Scott Case," *M.V.H.R.*, XVI (June, 1929), which demonstrates that the majority opinion was forced on the Democratic judges by the ambitions of the two Republican justices on the bench. The political aspirations of one of these northerners are surveyed in Francis P. Weisenburger, *The Life of John Mc-Lean* (Columbus, 1937). E. I. McCormac, "Justice Campbell and the Dred Scott Case," *M.V.H.R.*, XIX (March, 1933), shows that one of the southern justices reversed a former opinion to agree with his colleagues.

Two studies of the case in the Missouri courts show the impact of the slavery controversy on changing legal opinion. Helen T. Catterall, "Some Antecedents of the Dred Scott Case," *A.H.R.*, XXX (October, 1924), demonstrates that in eight previous cases the Missouri Supreme Court held a slave was freed by residence in a free state. That the state court's changed opinion in the Dred Scott Case was due to a desire to embarrass the Benton faction politically is argued by Richard R. Stenberg, "Some Political Aspects of the Dred Scott Case," *M.V.H.R.*, XIX (March, 1933).

The Triumph of Sectionalism, 1857–1861. The Lincoln-Douglas debates are described in the biographies of Douglas listed above, and in the multitudinous lives of Lincoln, of which the most useful for this period is Albert J. Beveridge, *Abraham Lincoln, 1809–1858*, 2 v. (Boston, 1928). Arthur C. Cole, *The Era of the Civil War* (*Centennial History of Illinois*, Springfield, 1919), gives the local background. Political events following the debates are the theme of Philip Auchampaugh, *James Buchanan and His Cabinet* (Duluth, 1926), and Roy F. Nichols, *The Disruption of American Democracy* (New York, 1948). Frank H. Hodder, "Some Aspects of the English Bill for the Admission of Kansas," *A.H.A.*, *Annual Report for 1906* (Washington, 1908), shows the "land bribe" offered Kansas was only the usual land grant to a new state.

The standard account of the election of 1860 is still Emerson D. Fite, *The Presidential Election of 1860* (New York, 1911), which fails to analyze sectional aspects of the contest. The forces drawing West and Northeast together are described in William E. Dodd, "The Fight for the Northwest, 1860," *A.H.R.*, XVI (July, 1911), and more fully in the thoughtful study by Henry C. Hubbart, *The Older Middle West, 1840–1860* (New York, 1936). Intellectual forces tending to unite these two sections are touched upon in Philip D. Jordan, ed., *Letters of Eliab Mackintire of Boston* (New York, 1936), but deserve further study. George M. Stephenson, *The Political History of Public Lands from 1840 to 1862* (Boston, 1917) deals with the legislative alliance on the land question. A similar study of the internal improvements question is needed. The problem is briefly treated in Hubbart, *Older Middle West*, cited above.

The sectional aspect of railroad building during the decade of the 1850's is the theme of Robert R. Russel, "A Revaluation of the Period before the Civil War: Railroads," *M.V.H.R.*, XV (December, 1928), while construction is described in the works cited in Chapter XIX. The shifting trading allegiances of the West are discussed in A. L. Kohlmeier, *The Old Northwest as the Keystone of the Arch of American Federal Union: A Study in Commerce and Politics* (Bloomington, Indiana, 1938). Donald V. Smith, "The Influence of the Foreign Born of the Northwest in the Election of 1860," *M.V.H.R.*, XIX (September, 1932), deals with that important subject.

The West in the Civil War. The struggle between northern and southern partisans for control of California is pictured in Joseph Ellison, *California and the Nation, 1850–1869* (Berkeley, 1927). No similar studies of the secession contest in other western states have been made. An important aspect of the problem is treated in Charles W. Ramsdell, "The Frontier and Secession," *Studies in Southern History and Politics; Inscribed to William Archibald Dunning* (New York, 1914), which shows the frontier counties of Texas most strongly inclined to rebellion, due to the government's failure to provide adequate defense.

The history of warfare and border skirmishing in the Far West is still to be written. The wartime activities of one group of Indians, the Five Civilized Tribes of Oklahoma, are described in Annie H. Abel, "The Indians in the Civil War," *A.H.R.*, XV (March, 1910), while Samuel J. Crawford, *Kansas in the Sixties* (Chicago, 1911), touches upon the activities of the Kansas Indians. The aid given federal troops by Colorado miners is discussed in William C. Whitford, *Colorado Volunteers in the Civil War* (Denver, 1906).

## XXX THE MINERS' FRONTIER

General Works. No single book tells the story of the advancing mining frontier. Thomas A. Rickard, *A History of American Mining* (New York, 1932), is technical, and Glenn C. Quiett, *Pay Dirt* (New York, 1936), popular. A brief general account of mining in the Southwest is in Rupert N. Richardson and C. C. Rister, *The Greater Southwest* (Glendale, 1935), and in the Northwest in Harold E. Briggs, *Frontiers of the Northwest* (New York, 1940).

The Mining Frontier in Colorado. Of the histories of the state which contain full accounts, the two most recent are LeRoy R. Hafen, *Colorado, the Story of a Western Commonwealth* (Denver, 1933), and Percy S. Fritz, *Colorado, the Centennial State* (New York, 1941). Popular histories of Colorado mining are numerous, the most modern being G. F. Willison, *Here They Dug the Gold* (New York, 1931). Two of the leading miners are described in Frank Waters, *Midas of the Rockies. The Story of Stratton and Cripple Creek* (New York, 1937), and Lewis C. Gandy, *The Tabors, a Footnote of Western History* (New York, 1932). LeRoy R. Hafen, "Cherokee Goldseekers in Colorado," *C.M.*, XV (May, 1938), deals with the first discoveries. Governmental beginnings are the theme of Frederic L. Paxson, "The Territory of Colorado," *A.H.R.*, XII (October, 1906). Contemporary accounts of the Pike's Peak

rush have been edited by LeRoy R. Hafen in three volumes of the *Southwest Historical Series: Pike's Peak Gold Rush Guide Books of 1859* (Glendale, 1941), *Overland Routes to the Gold Fields, 1859, from Contemporary Diaries* (Glendale, 1942), and *Colorado Gold Rush; Contemporary Letters and Reports, 1858–1859* (Glendale, 1941). Another contemporary description by a competent observer, also edited by LeRoy R. Hafen, is Henry Villard, *The Past and Present of the Pike's Peak Gold Regions* (Princeton, 1932).

The Mining Frontier in Nevada. Grant H. Smith, *History of the Comstock Lode* (Reno, 1943), is standard. A thorough account is in the most recent history of the state, Effie M. Mack, *Nevada, a History of the State from the Earliest Times through the Civil War* (Glendale, 1936), but the older chronicle by Hubert H. Bancroft, *History of Nevada, Colorado and Wyoming, 1540–1888* (San Francisco, 1890), is still of some use. Popular histories of mining in the state include: William Wright, *History of the Big Bonanza* (Indianapolis, 1931), C. B. Glasscock, *Gold in Them Hills* (Indianapolis, 1932), Miriam Michelson, *The Wonderlode of Silver and Gold* (Boston, 1934), G. D. Lyman, *The Saga of the Comstock Lode* (New York, 1934), and G. D. Lyman, *Ralston's Ring; California Plunders the Comstock Lode* (New York, 1937). Dan De Quille, *The Big Bonanza* (New York, 1947), is a reprint of a fine contemporary account.

The Mining Frontier in Arizona. No adequate history of the Arizona mines exists, nor does the older history of the state by Thomas E. Farish, *History of Arizona*, 4 v. (Phoenix, 1915–16), tell the full story. More colorful is the account of mining in Francis C. Lockwood, *Pioneer Days in Arizona* (New York, 1932). Life during the rush is vividly described in a contemporary diary edited by Clement Eaton, "Frontier Life in Southern Arizona, 1858–1861" *S.H.Q.*, XXXVI (January, 1933).

The Mining Frontier in the Northwest. The standard account is William J. Trimble, *The Mining Advance into the Inland Empire* (Madison, 1914). Detailed descriptions of the Washington rushes are in John W. Caughey, *History of the Pacific Coast* (New York, 1938), George W. Fuller, *A History of the Pacific Northwest* (New York, 1931), and George W. Fuller, *The Inland Empire of the Pacific Northwest*, 3 v. (Spokane, 1928). Edmond S. Meany, *History of the State of Washington* (New York, 1909), is still useful, as is Hubert H. Bancroft, *History of Washington, Idaho and Montana, 1845–1889* (San Francisco, 1890). Routes to the Washington gold fields are described in Oscar O. Winther, "Inland Transportation and Communication in Washington, 1844–1859," *P.N.Q.*, XXX (October, 1939). The Fraser River rush is described in Raymond E. Lindgren, "John Damon and the Fraser River Rush," *P.H.R.*, XIV (June, 1945).

The Mining Frontier in Idaho. A thorough account is in the work by Trimble cited above. The same author, in "A Reconsideration of the Gold Discoveries in the Northwest," *M.V.H.R.*, V (June, 1918), deals more fully with the first strikes. Later phases of Idaho mining are popularly treated in W. T. Stoll and H. W. Whicker, *Silver Strike: The True Story of Silver Mining in the Couer d'Alenes* (Boston, 1932), and Angus Murdock, *Boom Cooper* (New York, 1943).

The Mining Frontier in Montana. The account in Trimble may be supplemented by the thorough study of Merrill G. Burlingame, *The Montana Frontier* (Helena, 1942). Popular but informative histories of the state which touch on the mining frontier are C. P. Connolly, *The Devil Learns to Vote; the Story of Montana* (New York, 1938), and Joseph K. Howard, *Montana, High, Wide and Handsome* (New Haven, 1943). Reminiscences of the Stuart brothers who made the first strikes are in Paul C. Phillips, ed. *Forty Years on the Frontier as Seen in the Journals and Reminiscenses of Granville Stuart*, 2 v. (Cleveland, 1925).

Specific studies of the Montana fields include a careful analysis of the food supply problem: H. A. Texler, *Flour and Wheat in the Montana Gold Camps, 1862–1870* (Missoula, 1918). Works on road building are: H. A. Texler, "Missouri-Montana Highways," *M.H.R.*, XII (January, 1918, and April, 1918), Henry L. Talkington, "Mullan Road," *W.H.Q.*, VII (October, 1916), W. M. Underhill, "The Northern Overland Route to Montana," *W.H.Q.*, XXIII (July, 1932), and Oscar O. Winther, "Early Commercial Importance of the Mullan Road," *O.H.Q.*, XLVI (March, 1945). Robert L. Housman, "The First Territorial Legislature in Montana," *P.H.R.*, IV (December, 1935), deals with governmental beginnings.

The Mining Frontier in the Dakotas. A full description is in Harold E. Briggs, "The Black Hills Gold Rush," *N.D.H.Q.*, V (January, 1931). Popular accounts include G. W. Stokes and Howard Driggs, *Deadwood Gold* (New York, 1926), and Estelline Bennett, *Old Deadwood Days* (New York, 1935). Among the histories of Dakota Territory, the fullest is George W. Kingsbury, *The History of Dakota Territory* (Chicago, 1915). Edna L. Waldo, *Dakota* (Caldwell, 1936), is an informal history that includes a colorful chapter on the Black Hills rush.

The Mining Camps. Jim D. Hill, "The Early Mining Camp in American Life," *P.H.R.*, I (September, 1932), deals with the governmental organizations which sprang up in the camps, while laws passed by these primitive organizations are described in Thomas M. Marshall, "The Miners' Laws of Colorado," *A.H.R.*, XXV (April, 1920). Charles H. Shinn, *Land Laws of Mining Districts* (Baltimore, 1885. Reprinted, New York, 1948), is a pioneering study of the same problem. Efforts of Congress to enact a workable mining law are considered in Joseph Ellison, "The Mineral Land Question in California, 1848–

1866," *S.H.Q.*, XXX (July, 1926).

A good introduction to vigilante justice is Hubert H. Bancroft, *Popular Tribunals*, 2 v. (San Francisco, 1887), which faithfully records virtually every instance of frontier justice. The origin of vigilance committees in the California fields is authoratively treated in Mary F. Williams, *History of the San Francisco Committee of Vigilance of 1851* (Berkeley, 1921), while records of the committee are edited by the same author in *Papers of the San Francisco Committee of Vigilance of 1851* (Berkeley, 1919). A popular history of the San Francisco committee of 1856, which violently defends its work, is Stanton A. Coblentz, *Villains and Vigilantes* (New York, 1936).

## XXXI THE TRANSPORTATION FRONTIER

General Works. No single history of western transportation has been written. Brief accounts are in such works as Frederic L. Paxson, *Last American Frontier* (New York, 1910), and Rupert N. Richardson and C. C. Rister, *The Greater Southwest* (Glendale, 1935). Seymour Dunbar, *A History of Travel in America*, 4 v. (Indianapolis, 1915), contains some colorful material.

Establishing a Mail Service. Water communication between the East and California is described in a series of articles by John H. Kemble: "Pacific Mail Service between Panama and San Francisco, 1849–1851," *P.H.R.*, II (December, 1933), "The Genesis of the Pacific Mail Steamship Company," *C.H.S.Q.*, XIII (September, 1934), and "The Panama Route to the Pacific Coast, 1848–1869," *P.H.R.*, VII (March, 1938).

The sectional struggle over subsidies for an overland mail service is considered in Curtis Nettels, "The Overland Mail Issue in the Fifties," *M.H.R.*, XVIII (July, 1924). LeRoy R. Hafen, *The Overland Mail, 1849–1869* (Cleveland, 1926), is a scholarly work on the whole subject of western mail routes. The Butterfield Mail is

authoritatively treated in Roscoe Conkling and Margaret B. Conkling, *The Butterfield Overland Mail, 1858–1869* (Glendale, 1946), and Rupert N. Richardson, "Some Details of the Southern Overland Mail," *S.H.Q.*, XXIX (July, 1925).

Freighting on the Plains. A study of Plains freighting is badly needed. The leading freighter describes his own experiences in Alexander Majors, *Seventy Years on the Frontier* (Chicago, 1893), while additional information is in W. F. Hooker, *The Bullwhacker. Adventures of a Frontier Freighter* (Yonkers-on-Hudson, 1925). A local study is Harold E. Briggs, "Early Freight and Stage Lines in Dakota," *N.D.H.Q.*, III (July, 1929).

Overland Expressing. A sound survey of the subject is Oscar O. Winther, *Via Western Express & Stagecoach* (Stanford, 1945), and a less thorough study: Alvin F. Harlow, *Old Waybills: The Romance of the Express Companies* (New York, 1934). Oscar O. Winther, *Express and Stagecoach Days in California* (Stanford, 1936), is the standard work for that area, while Chester L. White "Surmounting the Sierras," *C.H.S.Q.*, VII (March, 1928), deals with the extension of service eastward. The history of one of the leading California companies is recounted in Neill C. Wilson, *Treasure Express: Epic Days of Wells Fargo* (New York, 1936).

The beginnings of stagecoach service on the central route are described in LeRoy R. Hafen, "Early Mail Service to Colorado," *C.M.*, II (January, 1925), Margaret Long, "The Route of the Leavenworth and Pike's Peak Express," *C.M.*, XII (September, 1935), George A. Root and R. K. Hickman, "Pike's Peak Express Companies: Solomon and Republican Route," *K.H.Q.*, XIV (August, 1944), and George A. Root and R. K. Hickman, "Pike's Peak Express Companies: The Platte Route," *K.H.Q.*, XV (November, 1945). The standard work on expressing in the 1860's is J. V. Frederick, *Ben Holladay* (Glendale, 1940).

A thorough description of the Pony Express is in Hafen, *The Overland Mail*, cited above. Recent popular accounts include: L. P. Houck, *The Youngest Rider* (Boston, 1927), Arthur Chapman, *The Pony Express; the Record of a Romantic Adventure in Business* (New York, 1932), and Howard R. Driggs, *The Pony Express Goes Through* (New York, 1935). Robert L. Thompson, *Wiring a Continent* (Princeton, 1947), tells the story of telegraph construction.

Building the Railroads. The general histories of railroad building cited in Chapter XIX may be supplemented by special studies of the western lines. Of these the most thorough is Robert E. Riegel, *The Story of the Western Railroads* (New York, 1926). A popular account is Glenn C. Quiett, *They Built the West. An Epic of Rails and Cities* (New York, 1934), while Frederic L. Paxson, *Last American Frontier* (New York, 1910), contains a brief history.

Railroad construction in the tier of states of the Mississippi is well-described in Riegel, *Story of the Western Railroads*, and in the same author's "Trans-Mississippi Railroads During the Fifties," *M.V.H.R.*, X (September, 1923). Two of the important lines are studied in Robert E. Riegel, "The Missouri Pacific Railroad to 1879," *M.H.R.*, XVIII (October, 1923), and Richard C. Overton, *Burlington West* (Cambridge, 1941), a history of the Chicago, Burlington and Quincy Railroad. Unfortunately other roads have not been so kindly treated by historians. The only history of the Chicago, Milwaukee and St. Paul Railroad is the antiquated work by I. W. Cary, *The Organization and History of the Chicago, Milwaukee and St. Paul* (Milwaukee, 1893), and of the Chicago and Northwestern Railroad the equally dated study by William H. Stennett, *Yesterday and Today* (Chicago, 1910). Thorough investigations of these and similar roads are needed. Southern railroad building is described in S. G. Reed, *A History of Texas Railroads* (Houston, 1941).

Early agitation for a Pacific Railroad is considered in: Robert S. Cotterill, "The National Railroad Convention in St. Louis, 1849," *M.H.R.*, XII (July, 1918), Robert S. Cotterill, "Early Agitation for a Pacific Railroad, 1845–1850," *M.V.H.R.*, V (March, 1919), and Margaret L. Brown, "Asa Whitney and His Pacific Railroad Publicity Campaign," *M.V.H.R.*, XX (September, 1933). Congressional debates on the issue are analyzed in Robert R. Russel, "The Pacific Railway Issue in Politics Prior to the Civil War," *M.V.H.R.*, XII (September, 1925), while the surveys of routes inspired by the controversy are described in George L. Albright, *Official Exploration for the Pacific Railroads, 1853–1855* (Berkeley, 1921).

A standard history of the Union Pacific is Nelson Trottman, *History of the Union Pacific* (New York, 1923), which stresses financial aspects. Edwin L. Sabin, *Building the Pacific Railway* (Philadelphia, 1919), is an earlier popular account. Construction problems are considered in the biography of the chief engineer: Jacob R. Perkins, *Trails, Rails and War; the Life of General G. M. Dodge* (Indianapolis, 1929). A thorough study of the Central Pacific is in the biography of one of its founders, George T. Clark, *Leland Stanford* (Palo Alto, 1931), and a more popular account in Oscar Lewis, *The Big Four: the Story of Huntington, Stanford, Hopkins, and Crocker, and of the Building of the Central Pacific* (New York, 1938). Harry J. Carman and Charles H. Mueller, "The Contract and Finance Company of the Central Pacific Railroad," *M.V.H.R.*, XIV (December, 1927), deals with the financing and building of the road.

The only histories of the Santa Fe are two popular accounts: Glenn D. Bradley, *The Story of the Santa Fe* (Boston, 1920), and James Marshall, *Santa Fe* (New York, 1946). Stuart Daggett, *Chapters on the History of the Southern Pacific* (New York, 1922), describes that line. The struggle between the Texas and Pacific Railroad and the Southern Pacific is surveyed in Lewis B. Lesley, "A Southern Transcontinental Railroad into California: Texas and Pacific versus Southern Pacific, 1865–1885," *P.H.R.*, V (March, 1936). The standard work on the Northern Pacific under Villard's control is James B. Hedges, *Henry Villard and the Railways of the Northwest* (New Haven, 1930). Villard's own story is told in his *Memoirs*, 2 v. (Boston, 1904), and in an account of his activities edited by his son, Oswald G. Villard, ed., *The Early History of Transportation in Oregon* (Eugene, 1944). Information on the early history of the Northern Pacific is in the biographies of its financier: Ellis P. Oberholtzer, *Jay Cooke, Financier of the Civil War*, 2 v. (Philadelphia, 1907), and Henrietta M. Larson, *Jay Cooke, Private Banker* (Cambridge, 1936). Harold A. Innis, *A History of the Canadian Pacific Railway* (London, 1923), deals with a rival of the Northern Pacific.

## XXXII THE INDIAN BARRIER

General Works. No satisfactory history of Indian relations in the Far West has been written. William C. Macleod, *The American Indian Frontier* (New York, 1928), contains a brief, biased account, while Frederic L. Paxson, *Last American Frontier* (New York, 1910), devotes several chapters to the Plains warfare. Frederick W. Hodge, ed., *Handbook of the American Indians North of Mexico* (Washington, 1912), contains a mine of information on forts, treaties, and other matters. Maps of the Indian land cessions are in Charles C. Royce, "Indian Land Cessions in the United States," B.A.E., *Eighteenth Annual Report* (Washington, 1899).

Early Indian Policy in the Far West. The development of Indian policy between 1830 and 1854 is clearly described in James C. Malin, "Indian Policy and Westward Expansion," U. of K., *Bulletin*, II (1921). The Ft. Laramie Treaties of 1851 are considered in LeRoy R. Hafen and F. M. Young, *Fort Laramie and the Pageant of*

*the West* (Glendale, 1938), LeRoy R. Hafen and W. J. Ghent, *Broken Hand, the Life Story of Thomas Fitzpatrick* (Denver, 1931), and LeRoy R. Hafen, "Thomas Fitzpatrick and the First Indian Agency of the Upper Platte and Arkansas," *M.V.H.R.*, XV (December, 1928). The career of the agent who took Fitzpatrick's place after 1854 is considered in Alban W. Hoopes, "Thomas S. Twiss, Indian Agent on the Upper Platte, 1855–1861," *M.V.H.R.*, XX (December, 1933).

Early Warfare in the Mountain Country. The Apache wars in the Southwest are briefly described in Bertha Blount, "The Apache in the Southwest, 1846–1886," *S.H.Q.*, XXIII (July, 1919), and more fully in Frank C. Lockwood, *Apache Indians* (New York, 1938). Paul I. Wellman, *Death on the Desert* (New York, 1913), is a popular account of the Apache and Navaho wars. Kit Carson's participation in the conflicts is described in Edwin L. Sabin, *Kit Carson Days*, 2 v. (New York, 1935).

Warfare on the Plains. Paul I. Wellman, *Death on the Prairie* (New York, 1934), is a popular history of Plains warfare. An earlier account that is still usable is Jacob P. Dunn, *Massacre of the Mountains. A History of the Indian Wars of the Far West* (New York, 1886). The two leading military commanders have published their reminiscences: William T. Sherman, *Personal Memoirs*, 2 v. (New York, 1890), and Philip H. Sheridan, *Personal Memoirs*, 2 v. (New York, 1888). Memoirs of other soldiers include: James H. Cook, *Fifty Years on the Old Frontier* (New Haven, 1923), Charles J. Crane, *Experiences of a Colonel of Infantry* (New York, 1923), Robert G. Carter, *The Old Sergeant's Story* (New York, 1926), George A. Forsythe, *The Story of the Soldier* (New York, 1909), William F. Drannan, *Thirty-one Years on the Plains and in the Mountains* (Chicago, 1909), and William S. Hancock, *Reminiscences of William Scott Hancock* (New York, 1887).

The extermination of the buffalo herds which so affected the Plains Indians is described in: M. D. Garretson, *The American Bison* (New York, 1938), Homer C. Wheeler, *Buffalo Days* (Indianapolis, 1925), E. Douglas Branch, *Hunting the Buffalo* (New York, 1929), and Paul I. Wellman, *The Trampling Herd* (New York, 1939). Carl C. Rister, "The Significance of the Destruction of the Buffalo," *S.H.Q.*, XXXIII (July, 1929), deals with the southern herd, while the slaughter of the northern herd is considered in H. A. Trexler, "The Buffalo Range of the Northwest," *M.V.H.R.*, VII (March, 1921), and Harold E. Briggs, *Frontiers of the Northwest* (New York, 1940). John R. Cook, *The Border and the Buffalo* (Topeka, 1907), is a memoir of a buffalo hunter.

Warfare on the Southern Plains. A thorough survey is in two books by Carl C. Rister, *The Southwestern Frontier, 1865–1881* (Cleveland, 1928), and *Border Command. General Phil Sheridan in the West* (Norman, 1944). Rupert N. Richardson and C. C. Rister, *The Greater Southwest* (Glendale, 1935), contains a briefer account.

The story of the Cheyenne-Arapaho War is told in George B. Grinnell, *The Fighting Cheyennes* (New York, 1915), and the same author's *The Cheyenne Indians*, 2 v. (New Haven, 1923). The concentration of the Five Civilized tribes to make room for the intruded Plains Indians is described in Roy Gittinger, *The Formation of the State of Oklahoma* (Berkeley, 1917), and in the works of Grant Foreman cited in Chapter XXIII.

The standard study of Comanche warfare is Rupert N. Richardson, *The Comanche Barrier to South Plains Settlement* (Glendale, 1933), while the Kiowa wars are treated in James Mooney, "Calendar History of the Kiowa Indians," B.A.E., *Seventeenth Annual Report* (Washington, 1898). A colorful but sound history of the Comanche-Kiowa wars is in W. S. Nye, *Carbine and Lance, the Story of Old Fort Sill* (Norman, 1937). Special studies of one important battle include Paul Nesbitt, "Battle of the Washita," *C.O.*, III (April, 1925), and the colorful account written by a newspaper correspondent who accompanied the troops, De B. Randolph Keim, *Sheridan's Troopers on the Borders* (Philadelphia, 1885). Carl C. Rister. "Significance of the Jacksboro Indian Affair of 1871," *S.H.Q.*, XXIX (January, 1926), deals with that important episode. The reminiscences of a plainsman who participated in the wars are in Carl L. Cannon, ed., *Scout and Ranger, Being the Personal Adventures. of James Pike* (Princeton, 1932).

Warfare on the Northern Plains. A general account of the Sioux wars is in L. E. Textor, *Official Relations between the United States and the Sioux Indians* (Palo Alto, 1896). The Powder River Road controversy which touch off the conflict is studied in Grace R. Hebard and A. R. Brininstool, *The Bozeman Trail*, 2 v. (Cleveland, 1922). The wars from the Indian point of view are described in George E. Hyde, *Red Cloud's Folk, A History of the Ogalala Sioux Indians* (Norman, 1937), and Stanley Vestal, *Sitting Bull, Champion of the Sioux* (Boston, 1932), and from the point of view of the Americans in Frederick F. Van de Water, *Glory Hunter: A Life of General Custer* (Indianapolis, 1934). The story of the steamboat captain who supplied the American armies is told in Joseph M. Hanson, *The Conquest of the Missouri* (New York, 1946), while a newspaper correspondent who observed the campaigns describes his experiences in John F. Finerty, *War-Path and Bivouac, or the Conquest of the Sioux* (Chicago, 1890).

The Last Indian Wars. The Nez Percé War is described in a sympathetic biography of the Indian leader: Chester A. Fee, *Chief Joseph* (New York, 1936). For the Bannock War see George F. Brimlow, *The Bannock War of 1878* (Caldwell, 1938), and for the Dull Knife Raid, Dennis Collins, *The Indian's Last Fight, or the Dull*

*Knife Raid* (Girard. Kansas, n.d.). The Apache War of the 1880's is described by participants in: George Crook, *Résumé of Operations Against the Apache Indians from 1882 to 1866* (Washington, 1886), George Crook, *General George Crook: His Autobiography* (Norman, 1946), and Nelson A. Miles, *Personal Recollections of Nelson A. Miles* (Chicago, 1896). The war from the Apache point of view is considered in Woodworth Clum, *Apache Agent: the Story of John P. Clum* (Boston, 1936). The Geronimo warfare is the theme of Britton Davis, *The Truth About Geronimo* (New Haven, 1929), and the Ghost Dance Wars in Elaine G. Eastman, "The Ghost Dance War and Wounded Knee Massacre of 1890–1891," *N.H.*, XXVI (January, 1945, and March, 1945), and James Mooney, "The Ghost-Dance Religion and the Sioux Outbreak of 1890," *B.A.E.*, *Fourteenth Annual Report* (Washington, 1896).

Developing an Indian Policy. The standard work is Loring B. Priest, *Uncle Sam's Stepchildren: The Reformation of United States Indian Policy, 1865–1887* (New Brunswick, 1942). Another recent work traces the application of the policy: Flora W. Seymour, *Indian Agents of the Old Frontier* (New York, 1941). Criticisms from the viewpoint of the military are voiced in Alice B. Baldwin, ed., *Memoirs of the Late Frank D. Baldwin* (Los Angeles, 1929), and James B. Fry, *Army Sacrifices; or Briefs from Official Pigeon-Holes* (New York, 1879). Works of peace advocates defending the policy include: Francis A. Walker, *The Indian Question* (Boston, 1874), and George W. Mannypenny, *Our Indian Wards* (Cincinnati, 1880). The most effective argument for reform was voiced by Helen H. Jackson, *A Century of Dishonor* (New York, 1881).

## XXXIII THE CATTLEMEN'S FRONTIER

Three standard books tell the story thoroughly: Ernest S. Osgood, *The Day of the Cattleman* (Minneapolis, 1929), Edward E. Dale, *The Range Cattle Industry* (Norman, 1930), and Louis Pelzer, *The Cattlemen's Frontier* (Glendale, 1936). Edward E. Dale, *Cow Country* (Norman, 1942), is a popular treatment based on the author's earlier scholarly work. Chapters in Walter P. Webb, *The Great Plains* (Boston, 1931), and Fred A. Shannon, *The Farmer's Last Frontier* (*The Economic History of the United States*, New York, 1945) are also essential to understanding the spread of the range cattle industry, while Frederic L. Paxson, "The Cow Country," *A.H.R.*, XXII (October, 1916), is still useful.

The Origins of Texas Ranching. A thorough study is Clara M. Love, "History of the Cattle Industry in the Southwest," *S.H.Q.*, XIX (April, 1916), and XX (July, 1916), but good brief accounts are in Rupert N. Richardson, *The Greater Southwest* (Glendale, 1935), Carl C. Rister, *The Southwestern Frontier, 1865–1881* (Cleveland, 1928), and Rupert N. Richardson, *Texas* (New York, 1943). J. Frank Dobie, *A Vaquero of the Brush Country* (Dallas, 1929), colorfully describes wild cattle roundups along the Rio Grande.

The Long Drive. A special account is H. S. Tennant, "The Two Cattle Trails," *C.O.*, XIII (March, 1936), while life along the Chisholm Trail has been described by early cattlemen in Sam P. Ridings, *The Chisholm Trail* (Guthrie, 1936), and John Rossel, "The Chisholm Trail," *K.H.Q.*, V (February, 1936). Reminiscences and diaries of herders who traveled the trails are collected in J. Marvin Hunter, ed., *Trail Drivers of Texas* (Nashville, 1925), E. S. Ricker, "The Texas Trail," *N.H.*, XVI (October, 1935), and George C. Duffield, "Driving Cattle from Texas to Iowa, 1866," *A. of I.*, XIV (April, 1924). The cow towns of Kansas are described in F. B. Streeter, *Prairie Trails and Cow Towns* (Boston, 1936), Henry Stuart, *Conquering Our Great American Plains* (New York, 1930), and Robert M. Wright, *Dodge City, the Cowboy Capital* (Topeka, 1913). Carl C. Rister, "Outlaws and Vigilantes of the

Southern Plains," *M.V.H.R.*, XIX (March, 1933), touches upon lawnessness in the cow towns. The cross breeding of Texas long-horns with eastern strains is considered in John M. Hazelton, *History and Handling of Hereford Cattle* (Kansas City, 1925).

Development of the Northern Range. In addition to the general works cited above, the extension of the cattle frontier over the Northwest is described in two works by Harold E. Briggs, *Frontiers of the North-west* (New York, 1940), and "The Development and Decline of Open Range Ranching in the Northwest," *M.V.H.R.*, XX (March, 1934). The Colorado industry is thoroughly treated in O. B. Peake, *The Colorado Range Cattle Industry* (Glendale, 1939), and Wyoming ranching in W. E. Guthrie, "The Open Range Cattle Business in Wyoming," *A. of W.*, V (July, 1927), Dan W. Greenburg, *Sixty Years, . . . The Cattle Industry in Wyoming* (Cheyenne, 1932), and C. G. Coutant, *History of Wyoming* (Laramie, 1899). Louis Pelzer, "The Cattleman's Commonwealth on the Western Range," *M.V.H.R.*, XIII (June, 1926), tells the story of the Wyoming Stock Growers Association. For the Montana phase of the industry consult Merrill G. Burlingame, *The Montana Frontier* (Helena, 1942), and J. Orin Oliphant, "The Cattle Trade from the Far Northwest to Montana," *A.H.*, XI (April, 1932). Ranching in Dakota is described in Harold E. Briggs, "Ranching and Stock Raising in the Territory of Dakota," *S.D.H.C.*, XIV (1928).

The Invasion of the Indian Territory. Several articles by Edward E. Dale canvas the subject thoroughly: "The Ranchman's Last Frontier," *M.V.H.R.*, X (June, 1923), "The History of the Ranch Cattle Industry in Oklahoma," A.H.A., *Annual Report for 1920* (Washington, 1925), and "Ranching on the Cheyenne-Arapaho Reservation," *C.O.*, VI (March, 1928).

Ranchers and Cowboys. The literature on the cowboy is voluminous and unreliable. Andy Adams, *The Log of a Cowboy* (Boston, 1903), is one of the few trustworthy

volumes of reminiscences, while good descriptions of cowboy life are in Philip A. Rollins, *The Cowboy* (New York, 1922), and E. Douglas Branch, *The Cowboy and His Interpreters* (New York, 1926). Carl C. Rister, *Southern Plainsmen* (Norman, 1938), has a colorful chapter on the cowboys.

Histories of some of the famous western ranches include: Harley T. Burton, "History of the JA Ranch," *S.H.Q.*, XXXI (October, 1927)-XXXII (July, 1928), Bertha M. Kuhn, "The W-B Ranch on the Missouri Slope," S.H.S.N.D., *Collections* V (1923), William C. Holden, *The Spur Ranch* (Boston, 1934), J. Evetts Haley, *The XIT Ranch* (Chicago, 1929), and Ellsworth Collings, *The 101 Ranch* (Norman, 1937). Helpful biographies of leading ranchers are: J. Evetts Haley, *Charles Goodnight, Cowman and Plainsman* (Boston, 1936), A. B. Wood, "The Coad Brothers; Panhandle Cattle Kings," *N.H.*, XIX (January, 1938), and Lincoln Lang, *Ranching with Roosevelt* (Philadelphia, 1926). Memoirs of former ranchers include Frank S. Hastings, *A Ranchman's Recollections* (Chicago, 1921), and John Clay, *My Life on the Range* (Chicago, 1924), while the reminiscences of the meat dealer responsible for helping shape the cattle kingdom are recorded in Joseph G. McCoy, *Historic Sketch of the Cattle Trade of the West and South-west* (Washington, 1932).

The Decline of Open Range Ranching. The cattlemen's financial struggles during the 1880's are described in Louis Pelzer, "Financial Management of the Cattle Ranges," *J.E.B.H.*, II (August, 1930), and Charles I. Bray, *Financing the Western Cattlemen* (Ft. Collins, Colorado, 1928). Troy J. Cauley, "Early Business Methods in the Texas Cattle Industry," *J.E.B.H.*, IV (May, 1932), discusses business methods used in the long drives. One of the principal hazards leading to the end of the open range, the grass fire, is the theme of J. A. Rickard, "Hazards of Ranching on the South Plains," *S.H.Q.*, XXXVII (April, 1934), while the disastrous winter which doomed the northern open range industry is pictured in Robert S. Fletcher, "That Hard Winter in Montana, 1886–1887," *A.H.*, IV (October, 1930). The transition to "big pasture" ranching is described in Robert S. Fletcher, "The End of the Open Range in Eastern Montana," *M.V.H.R.*, XVI (September, 1929), and Edward E. Dale, "The Cow Country in Transition," *M.V.H.R.*, XXIV (June, 1937).

The Spread of the Sheep Range. The standard work is Charles W. Towne and Edward N. Wentworth, *Shepherd's Empire* (Norman, 1945), although L. G. Connor, "A Brief History of the Sheep Industry in the United States," A.H.A., *Annual Report for 1918* (Washington, 1921), is still useful. The coming of herds to the Northwest is discussed in Harold E. Briggs, "The Early Development of Sheep Ranching in the Northwest," *A.H.*, XI (July, 1937), while trails used by drovers are exhaustively described in Edward N. Wentworth, *America's Sheep Trails* (Ames, Iowa, 1948).

## XXXIV OPENING THE GREAT PLAINS

General Works. The concept of the Great Plains country as a region whose hostile environment could be conquered only after the industrial revolution reached maturity is developed in the stimulating book by Walter P. Webb, *The Great Plains* (Boston, 1931). The volume and its point of view are criticised in Fred A. Shannon, "An Appraisal of Walter Prescott Webb's The Great Plains: A Study in Institutions and Environment," *Critiques of Research in the Social Sciences* (New York, 1940), but Webb's book is nevertheless essential to an understanding of the Plains country. Fred A. Shannon, *The Farmer's Last Frontier* (*The Economic History of the United States*, New York, 1945), admirably considers the agricultural adjustments demanded by the conquest of the grasslands.

Development of Farm Machinery. Thorough accounts of the invention of barbed wire fencing are in Webb, *The Great Plains,* and Earl W. Hayter, "Barbed Wire Fencing—a Prairie Invention; Its Rise and Influence in the Western States," *A.H.*, XIII (October, 1939). Clarence H. Danhof, "The Fencing Problem in the Eighteen-Fifties," *A.H.*, XVIII (October, 1944), gives an interesting background.

Shannon, *The Farmer's Last Frontier,* briefly describes improvements in farm machinery, while Leo Rogin, *The Introduction of Farm Machinery in Its Relation to the Productivity of Labor* (Berkeley, 1931), demonstrates the effect of the inventions on frontier expansion. The story of the reaper is told in William T. Hutchinson, *Cyrus Hall McCormick,* 2 v. (New York, 1930–35). Neil M. Clark, *John Deere: He Gave to the World the Steel Plow* (Moline, Illinois, 1937), is a laudatory history of a leading plow manufacturer. The evolution of planting machinery is described in Russell H. Anderson, "Grain Drills Through Thirty-Nine Centuries," *A.H.*, X (October, 1936). Lynn W. Ellis and Edward A. Rumley, *Power and the Plow* (New York, 1911), deals with the early development of power machinery.

The Land System. The two standard histories of the land system, Benjamin H. Hibbard, *A History of Public Land Policies* (New York, 1924), and Roy M. Robbins, *Our Landed Heritage* (Princeton, 1942), provide background information, but any study of the public domain in the post-Civil War era should begin with Paul W. Gates, "The Homestead Act in an Incongruous Land System," *A.H.R.*, XLI (July, 1936), which demonstrates that the Homestead Act did not mean free land for all. Roy M. Robbins, "The Public Domain in the Era of Exploitation, 1862–1901," *A.H.*, XIII (April, 1939) explores other aspects of the problem. Shannon, *The Farmer's Last Frontier,* contains chapters summarizing recent studies of the subject. The failure of the Homestead Act to attract eastern workers is explained in Fred A. Shannon, "The Homestead Act and the Labor Surplus," *A.H.R.*, XLI (July, 1936).

The systematic exploitation of the public domain by corporations is treated in William F. Raney, "The Timber Culture Acts," M.V.H.A., *Proceedings*, X (1919–20), and John T. Ganoe, "The Desert Land Act in Operation, 1877–1891," *A.H.*, XI (April, 1937). Fremont P. Wirth, *The Discovery and Exploitation of the Minnesota Iron Lands* (Cedar Rapids, 1937), describes the engrossment of one type of land, while John Ise, *The United States Forest Policy* (New Haven, 1920), deals with timbered areas.

John B. Sanborn, *Congressional Grants of Land in Aid of Railways* (Madison, 1899), describes the legislative measures through which railroads acquired their western land holdings, but fails to show the effects of the grants on settlement. The struggle of the land office to end some of the worst abuses of the system is the theme of John B. Rae, "Commissioner Sparks and the Railroad Land Grants," *M.V.H.R.*, XXV (September, 1933), while the system is defended by a spokesman for the railroads in Robert S. Henry, "The Railroad Land Grant Legend in American History Texts," *M.V.H.R.*, XXXII (September, 1945). David M. Ellis, "The Forfeiture of Railroad Land Grants, 1867–1894," *M.V.H.R.*, XXXIII (June, 1946), deals with the return of lands to the government. The whole subject deserves additional study.

The disposal of Indian reservation lands also needs investigation. Paul W. Gates, "A Fragment of Kansas History; the Disposal of the Christian Indian Tract," *K.H.Q.*, VI (August, 1937), illustrates the possibility of the subject. The same author's *The Wisconsin Pine Lands of Cornell University: A Study in Land Policy and Absentee Ownership* (Ithaca, 1943), is a case history of one state's educational land grants.

The operation of the land system in various western states is considered in Addison E. Sheldon, *Land Systems and Land Policies in Nebraska* (Lincoln, 1936), Roy M. Robbins, "The Federal Land System in an Embryo State: Washington Territory, 1853–1890," *P.H.R.*, IV (December, 1935), and Charles L. Green, *The Administration of the Public Domain in South Dakota* (Pierre, 1940).

## XXXV THE FARMERS' FRONTIER

Forces Encouraging Migration. A thorough discussion is in Fred A. Shannon, *The Farmer's Last Frontier* (*The Economic History of the United States*, New York, 1945). A more extended study of population movements is in Charles W. Thornthwaite and Helen I. Slentz, *Internal Migration in the United States* (Philadelphia, 1934), and Carter L. Goodrich, *Migration and Economic Opportunity* (Philadelphia, 1936). Foreign immigration to the West is considered in the standard histories of immigration, of which the latest are George M. Stephenson, *A History of American Immigration* (Boston, 1926), and Carl F. Wittke, *We Who Built America: The Saga of the Immigrant* (New York, 1939). Norwegian immigration during the period is described in Carlton C. Qualey, *Norwegian Settlement in the United States* (Northfield, 1938), and Swedish in George M. Stephenson, "Background of the Beginnings of Swedish Immigration, 1850–1875," *A.H.R.*, XXXI (July, 1926), and K. C. Babcock, *The Scandinavian Element in the United States* (Urbana, 1914). The Mennonite migration from Russia is considered in Charles H. Smith, *The Coming of the Russian Mennonites* (Chicago, 1927).

The role of the railroads as colonizing agents was first explored in two articles by James B. Hedges, "Promotion of Immigration to the Pacific Northwest by the Railroads," *M.V.H.R.*, XV (September, 1928), and "The Colonizing Work of the Northern Pacific Railroad," *M.V.H.R.*, XIII (December, 1926). Harold F. Peterson, "Some Colonization Projects of the Northern Pacific Railroad," *M.H.*, X (June, 1929), deals with the same road. The part played by the Chicago, Burlington and Quincy Railroad is described in Richard C. Overton, *Burlington West* (Cambridge, 1941), and by the Southern Pacific in Edna M. Parker, "The Southern Pacific Railroad and the Settlement of Southern California," *P.H.R.*, VI (June, 1937). Similar studies of other western lines are needed. Herbert S. Schell, "Official Immigration Activities of Dakota Territory," *N.D.H.Q.*, VII (October, 1932), touches upon another little-explored aspect of history.

Henrietta M. Larson, *The Wheat Market and the Farmer in Minnesota* (New York, 1926), shows the effect of grain prices on settlement, while Louis B. Schmidt, "The Westward Movement of the Wheat Growing Industry in the United States," *I.J.H.P.*, XVIII (July, 1920), traces the migration. A thorough discussion of the new milling methods is in Charles B. Kuhlman, *The Development of the Flour-Milling Industry in the United States* (Boston, 1929). Improvements in handling grain are described in Guy A. Lee, "The Historical Significance of the Chicago Grain Elevator System," *A.H.*, XI (January, 1937).

The standard work on social conditions in the prairie country is Everett Dick, *The Sod-House Frontier, 1854–1890* (New York, 1937), which describes obstacles facing farmers as well as living conditions. James C. Malin, "Dust Storms," *K.H.Q.*, XIV (May, 1946), and later issues, deals with another menace to settlers.

The Kansas-Nebraska Frontier. The way in which farmers adapted to the Kansas environment is considered in James C. Malin, *Winter Wheat in the Golden Belt of Kansas* (Lawrence, 1944), and the same author's "The Adaptation of the Agricultural System to Sub-Humid Environment," *A.H.*, X (July, 1936). The settlement process is mentioned in the numerous histories of the two states, of which the latest are Adolph Roenigk, ed., *Pioneer History of Kansas* (Lincoln, 1933), Thomas A. McNeal, *When Kansas Was Young* (New York, 1922), Leola H. Blanchard, *Conquest of Southwest Kansas* (Wichita, 1931), and Addison E. Sheldon, *History of Nebraska* (Lincoln, 1913). Reminiscences of pioneers give

a realistic picture of life in early Kansas and Nebraska. John Ise, *Sod and Stubble; the Story of a Kansas Homestead* (New York, 1936), pieces together the memories of many pioneers to create a readable social history. The same author edits the letters of an early settler in Howard Ruede, *Sod-House Days. Letters from a Kansas Homesteader, 1877–1878* (New York, 1937). Another modern publication is Adela E. R. Orpen, *Memories of the Old Emigrant Days in Kansas, 1862–1865* (New York, 1928).

The Northwestern Frontier. Harold E. Briggs, *Frontiers of the Northwest* (New York, 1940), describes the settlement process thoroughly, while Edna L. Waldo, *Dakota: An Informal History of Territorial Days* (Caldwell, 1936), is popular. Other recent histories of North or South Dakota which devote some space to the territorial period include Lewis F. Crawford, *History of North Dakota* (New York, 1931), and W. M. Wemett, *The Story of the Flickertail State* (Valley City, 1923). The evolution of bonanza farms in the Red River Valley is considered in Harold E. Briggs, "Early Bonanza Farming in the Red River Valley of the North," *A.H.*, VI (January, 1932), and Alva H. Benton, "Large Land Holdings in North Dakota," *J.L.P.U.E.*, I (October, 1925). C. H. Grinling, *The History of the Great Northern Railway, 1845–1895* (London, 1898), and Joseph G. Pyle, *The Life of James J. Hill*, 2 v. (New York, 1917), throw light on railroad efforts to induce immigration. Information on settlement is also in Charles L. Green, *The Administration of the Public Domain in South Dakota* (Pierre, 1940).

The extension of the agricultural frontier into Wyoming, Montana, and Colorado is touched upon in Hubert H. Bancroft, *History of Nevada, Colorado and Wyoming, 1540–1888* (San Francisco, 1890), I. S. Bartlett, *History of Wyoming* (Chicago, 1918), Alvin T. Steinel, *History of Agriculture in Colorado, 1858–1926* (Denver, 1926), and Merrill G. Burlingame, *The Montana Frontier* (Helena, 1942). A valuable regional study is Charles Lindsay, *The Big Horn Basin* (Lincoln, 1932).

The statehood process in the Northwest is described in Frederic L. Paxson, "The Admission of the Omnibus States, 1889–90," W.H.S., *Proceedings for 1911* (Madison, 1912), John D. Hicks, "Six Constitutions of the Far Northwest," M.V.H.A., *Proceedings*, IX (1917–18), and more fully in John D. Hicks, *The Constitutions of the Northwest States* (Lincoln, 1923).

The Southwestern Frontier. A well-rounded history of Oklahoma is Grant Foreman, *A History of Oklahoma* (Norman, 1942), while a scholarly study of the settlement process is in Roy Gittinger, *The Formation of the State of Oklahoma* (Berkeley, 1917). A thorough account of Boomer activity is in Carl C. Rister, *Land Hunger: David L. Payne and the Oklahoma Boomers* (Norman, 1942). Town planting by the '89ers is described in Gerald Forbes, *Guthrie: Oklahoma's First Capital* (Norman, 1938), and John Alley, *City Beginnings in Oklahoma Territory* (Norman, 1939). Reminiscences of pioneers who participated in the early rushes include: Seth K. Humphrey, *Following the Prairie Frontier* (Minneapolis, 1931), and Irving Geffs, *The First Eight Months of Oklahoma City* (Norman, 1939).

The peopling of New Mexico and Arizona is treated in Hubert H. Bancroft, *History of Arizona and New Mexico* (San Francisco, 1889), Ralph E. Twitchell, *Leading Facts of New Mexico History*, 2 v. (Cedar Rapids, 1911), and Frank C. Lockwood, *Pioneer Days in Arizona* (New York, 1932), although the process deserves greater study. An account of Arizona's struggle for statehood is in H. A. Hubbard, "The Arizona Enabling Act and President Taft's Veto," *P.H.R.*, III (September, 1934).

## XXXVI THE AGRARIAN REVOLT

General Works. A brief survey of farmer's uprisings is in Solon J. Buck, *The Agrarian Crusade* (*Chronicles of America Series*, New Haven, 1921), but this should be supplemented with the stimulating chapters on the causes of agrarian unrest in John D. Hicks, *The Populist Revolt* (Minneapolis, 1931). Fred A. Shannon, *The Farmer's Last Frontier* (*The Economic History of the United States*, New York, 1945), also surveys the whole problem, as does the thoughtful interpretation by Chester M. Destler, *American Radicalism, 1865–1901* (New London, 1946). Arthur M. Schlesinger, *The Rise of the City* (*History of American Life Series*, New York, 1933), deals with social factors creating dissatisfaction in the West. The political story is told in Nathan Fine, *Labor and Farmer Parties in the United States, 1828–1928* (New York, 1928), and more fully in Fred E. Haynes, *Third Party Movements Since the Civil War* (Iowa City, 1916). Interpretive articles include: James A. Woodburn, "Western Radicalism in American Politics," *M.V.H.R.*, XIII (September, 1926), and John D. Hicks, "The Third Party Tradition in American Politics," *M.V.H.R.*, XX (June, 1933).

The Granger Movement. The standard work is Solon J. Buck, *The Granger Movement* (Cambridge, 1913). Arthur E. Paine, *The Granger Movement in Illinois* (Urbana, 1904), tells the story of an important state. The manner in which the Panic of 1873 aroused agrarian discontent is analyzed in O. V. Wells, "The Depression of 1873–1879," *A.H.*, XI (July, 1937), while resentment against the banking system is analysed in George L. Anderson, "Western Attitude towards National Banks, 1873–1874," *M.V.H.R.*, XXIII (September, 1936). A careful study which explains why farmers resented industrial monopolies is Earl W. Hayter, "Western Farmers and the Drivewell Patent Controversy," *A.H.*, XVI (January, 1942). Efforts of Grangers to protect themselves from monopolistic corporations are discussed in Arthur H. Hirsch, "Efforts of the Grange in the Middle West to Control the Price of Farm Machinery, 1870–1880," M.V.H.R., XV (March, 1929).

The Greenback Interlude. The only political study is Orin G. Libby, " A Study of the Greenback Movement, 1876–1884,"

W.A.S.A.L., *Transactions*, XII (Madison, 1898). This should be supplemented by more recent works on the party in western states: Ellis B. Usher, *The Greenback Movement of 1875–1884 and Wisconsin's Part In It* (Milwaukee, 1911), Clyde O. Ruggles, "The Economic Basis of the Greenback Movement in Iowa and Wisconsin," *M.V.H.A., Proceedings*, VI (1912–13), and Reginald C. McCrane, "Ohio and the Greenback Movement," *M.V.H.R.*, XI (March, 1925). The standard biography of the party's presidential candidate is Fred E. Haynes, *James Baird Weaver* (Iowa City, 1919).

The Farmers' Alliance. John D. Hicks describes the movement in *The Populist Revolt*, cited above, and more fully with John D. Barnhart, "The Farmers' Alliance," *N.C.H.R.*, VI (July, 1929). Local studies include: John D. Hicks, "The Origin and Early History of the Farmers' Alliance in Minnesota," *M.V.H.R.*, IX (December, 1922), Homer Clevenger, "The Farmers' Alliance in Missouri," *M.H.R.*, XXXVIII (October, 1944), and Ralph Smith, "The Farmers' Alliance in Texas, 1875–1900," *S.H.Q.*, XLVIII (January, 1945). Herman C. Nixon, "The Cleavage within the Farmers' Alliance Movement," *M.V.H.R.*, XV (June, 1928), deals with divisions among the members.

The Populist Party. John D. Hicks, *The Populist Revolt* (Minneapolis, 1931), is the standard account. Two underlying causes of discontent, the hard times following the boom of the early 1880's, and the monetary situation, have been explored. The boom period and its aftermath are described in Hallie Farmer, "The Economic Background of Frontier Populism," *M.V.H.R.*, X (March, 1924), Raymond C. Miller, "The Background of Populism in Kansas," *M.V.H.R.*, XI (March, 1925), and Herbert L. Glynn, "The Urban Real Estate Boom in Nebraska during the Eighties," *N.L.B.*, VI (May, 1928), and VII (November, 1928). Equally important is a careful study by John D. Barnhart, "Rainfall and the Populist Party in Nebraska," *A.P.S.R.*, XIX (Au-

gust, 1925), which shows the correlation between drought areas and the vote for independent candidates. Hallie Farmer, "The Railroads and Frontier Populism," *M.V.H.R.*, XIII (December, 1926), treats the farmers' dissatisfaction with railroads.

The monetary situation is briefly described in Davis R. Dewey, *Financial History of the United States* (New York, 1922). The conflict over the silver question within the older parties is the theme of Fred Wellborn, "The Influence of the Silver-Republican Senators, 1889–1891," *M.V.H.R.*, XIV (March, 1928), and James A. Barnes, "The Gold Standard Democrats and the Party Conflict," *M.V.H.R.*, XVII (December, 1930). W. Jett Lauck, *The Causes of the Panic of 1893* (Boston, 1907), deals with the financial background, while Jeanette P. Nichols, "The Politics and Personalities of Silver Repeal in the United States Senate," *A.H.R.*, XLI (October, 1935), describes the repeal of the Sherman Silver Purchase Act.

The early growth of the Populist Party is the theme of John D. Hicks, "The Birth of the Populist Party," *M.H.*, IX (September, 1928). J. Martin Klotsche, "The 'United Front' Populists," *W.M.H.*, XX (June, 1937), discusses the attempt of various reform groups to gain control of the party. The party's role in the election of 1892 is considered in George H. Knoles, *The Presidential Campaign and Election of 1892* (Stanford, 1942), and in the election of 1896 in William J. Bryan, *The First Battle* (Chicago, 1896).

Local studies of Populism in western states include: John D. Hicks, "The People's Party in Minnesota," *M.H.B.*, V (November, 1924), Paul R. Fossum, *The Agrarian Movement in North Dakota* (Baltimore, 1925), Herman C. Nixon, "The Economic Basis of the Populist Movement in Iowa," *I.J.H.P.*, XXI (July, 1923), Herman C. Nixon, "The Populist Movement in Iowa," *I.J.H.P.*, XXIV (January, 1926), Leon W. Fuller, "Colorado's Revolt Against Capitalism," *M.V.H.R.*, XXI (December, 1934), Chester M. Destler, "Consummation of a Labor-Populist Alliance in Illinois, 1894,"

*M.V.H.R.*, XXVII (March, 1941), Roscoe C. Martin, *The People's Party in Texas* (Austin, 1933), and Melvin J. White, "Populism in Louisiana During the Nineties," *M.V.H.R.*, V (June, 1918).

Colorful accounts of Populism are in such biographies as John D. Hicks, "The Political Career of Ignatius Donnelly," *M.V.H.R.*, VIII (June-September, 1921), C. Vann Woodward, *Tom Watson: Agrarian Rebel* (New York, 1938), Elmer Ellis, *Henry Moore Teller, Defender of the West* (Caldwell, 1941), and Francis B. Simkins, *Pitchfork Ben Tillman, South Carolinian* (Baton Rouge, 1944).

The economic recovery which spelled doom for the Populists is assessed in Gerald T. White, "Economic Recovery and the Wheat Crop of 1897," *A.H.*, XIII (June, 1939).

## XXXVII THE FRONTIER HERITAGE

General Works. Material on the impact of the frontier on American traits and institutions will be found in Frederick Jackson Turner's essays, in discussions of the frontier hypothesis, and in criticisms of Turner's works listed in the bibliography to Chapter I.

The Closing of the Frontier. No single study deals with the impact of the closing of the frontier on American life or thought. The subject deserves attention from historians. Frederick L. Paxson, *When the West Is Gone* (Boston, 1930), treats some aspects of the subject briefly, while D. W. Brogan, "The Rise and Decline of the American Agricultural Interest," *E.H.R.*, V (April, 1935), deals with agriculture in a nonexpanding land. A contemporary point of view, expressing the alarmist atmosphere of the early twentieth century, is in William C. Trimble, "Influence of the Passing of the Public Lands," *A.M.*, CXIII (June, 1914). Agricultural conditions during those years are admirably described in John D. Hicks, "The Western Middle West, 1900–1914," *A.H.*, XX (April, 1946), while the continued expansion into the Far West is the theme of the opening essay in John C. Parrish, *The Persistence of the Westward Movement and Other Essays* (Berkeley, 1943). The opening of the Prairie Province frontier is described in Paul F. Sharp, "The American Farmer and the 'Last Best West'," *A.H.*, XXI (April, 1947). The need of expanding governmental activity as a result of the frontier's passing is stressed in such works as Henry A. Wallace, *New Frontiers* (New York, 1934).

# Index

Territory, 273–4; leads attack on Ft.
Malden, 280.

Hunt, Wilson Price, leads Overland Astorians, 456.

Hunter, John, explores Red River country,
450.

Huntington, Collis P., promotes Pacific railroad, 643.

Huron Indians, as allies of French, 33–4;
French traders among, 103; in Iroquois
wars, 104, 107; in French-English wars,
123.

Hutchinson, Anne, banished from Massachusetts, 62.

Ibarra, Francisco de, as governor of Nueva
Vizcaya, 425.

Iberville, Pierre Le Moyne de, in King William's War, 111; founds Louisiana, 113.

Idaho, mining in, 627–8, 630; governmental
beginnings in, 628; admitted as state, 716;
People's Party victory in, 738.

Idaho City, Idaho, settled, 627; growth of,
628.

Iliff, J. W., begins ranching in Wyoming,
678.

Illinois, territory of created, 267; settlement
of, 294–7, 306–8; admitted as state, 309;
canal building in, 344–5; opposition to
banks in, 377; railroad building in, 393–
4; Mormons in, 535–7; migration from
to Kansas, 599; Lincoln-Douglas debates
in, 606; success of Patrons of Husbandry
in, 726–7; enacts Granger Laws, 728–9.
See Illinois Country.

Illinois Central Railroad, projected, 345;
built, 394; extended westward, 641; opens
Dakota Territory, 713.

Illinois Company, formed, 144.

Illinois Country, occupied by French, 112–3,
118; occupied by English, 139; trade in,
141–2; land speculation in, 152; captured
by George Rogers Clark, 181–3; in Revolution, 186–8; ceded to United States by
Indians, 273; conquered in War of 1812,
284.

Illinois Land Company, formed, 152; seeks
land cessions by states, 200–2.

Illinois and Michigan Canal, built, 344–5.

Illinois-Wabash Land Company, seeks land
cessions by states, 200–2.

Immigration Bureaus, established by states,
704; established by western railroads,
705–6.

Indentured Servants, on Tidewater frontier,
45; in Piedmont, 83.

Independence, Missouri, as terminus of Santa
Fe trail, 463; settled, 468; as terminus of
Oregon Trail, 524.

Independent Treasury System, advocated by
Van Buren, 373–4; adopted, 376; repealed
by Whigs, 380; restored, 382.

Indiana, created as territory, 267; settlement
of, 294–7, 301–6; constitution of, 309;
canals in, 343–4; railroads in, 392–3; migration from to Kansas, 599.

Indiana Company, organized, 144; at Ft.
Stanwix conference, 148–9; seeks grant in
West, 150–1; revived, 152; urges land
cessions by states, 200–2.

Indian Policy, on Tidewater frontier, 46;
development of by United States, 209–11;
on eve of War of 1812, 273–4; in the
Lake Plains region, 291–2; removal policy in Northwest, 297–8, 301; removal
policy in Gulf Plains, 312–7; on Great
Plains, 368–73, 468–73; criticism of,
658–9; changes in Far West, 659–60,
668–70.

Indian Reservations, on Tidewater frontier,
46; in early New England, 73; in Virginia Piedmont, 83; proposed on Great
American Desert, 468–71; in Southwest,
651–3; on Great Plains, 659–61; sale of
to speculators, 700–1; closing of, 717–20.

Indian Rights Association, agitates for
change in policy, 669.

Indians, as allies of French, 33–4; attack
Virginia settlers, 41, 45–6, 50; in Carolinas, 53–5; wars with in New England,
63–4, 73–9; in French-English conflicts,
103–30; in Revolution, 174–91; development of federal policy for, 209–11; removal of from New York, 251; treaties
with in Ohio Valley, 272–6; removal of
from Lake Plains country, 297–301; removal of from Gulf Plains, 312–7; of
Great Plains, 409–13; of Intermontane
Province, 416–19; of Pacific Coast,
420–1; established on Great Plains, 468–
73; driven from Great Plains, 651–70;
interfere with Long Drive, 676; driven
from Oklahoma, 717–20.

Indian Springs, Treaty of, 313.

Indian Territory, see Oklahoma.

Indian Wars, in Spanish Florida, 26–7;
French pioneers in, 34; in early Virginia,